Selected Descriptive Statistics	Application	Location
Joint probability	Likelihood of selecting an observation wherein two conditions are present	Chapter 8
Conditional probability	Likelihood that one event depends on another event occurring	Chapter 8
Marginal probability	Likelihood of an independent event's occurrence	Chapter 8
Confidence interval	Range of values wherein samples drawn from a population are apt to fall	Chapter 9
Single or one-sample t test	Determines whether observed sample mean represents a population	Chapter 10
Independent groups t test	Examines mean difference between sample means from two groups	Chapter 10
Effect size r	Magnitude of effect associated with an independent variable	Chapter 10
Estimated omega squared ($\hat{\omega}^2$)	Degree of association between an independent variable and a dependent measure	Chapters 10, 11, 12, 13
Correlated or dependent groups t test	Determines difference between two means drawn from the same sample at two different points in time	Chapter 10
One-way ANOVA	Determines differences between means of two or more levels of an independent variable	Chapter 11
Tukey's HSD test	Identifies any pairwise differences between more than two means	Chapters 11, 12, 13
Effect size $\mathbf{f}$	Magnitude of effect associated with an independent variable used in an ANOVA	Chapters 11, 12, 13
Two-way ANOVA	Identifies differences between means representing the independent effects and interaction of two variables	Chapter 12
One-factor repeated-measures ANOVA	Identifies mean differences among three or more sample means representing different levels of an independent variable	Chapter 13
Mixed design ANOVA	Examines mean differences and interactions caused by between- and within-group factors	Chapter 13

Nonparametric ("assumption free") Statistics	Application	Location
Chi-square "goodness-of-fit" test	Examines whether categorical data conform to proportions specified by a null hypothesis	Chapter 14
Chi-square test of independence	Determines whether frequencies associated with two nominal variables are independent	Chapter 14
Phi coefficient (ϕ)	Assesses association between two dichotomous variables	Chapter 14
Cramer's V	Assesses association between two dichotomous variables when one or both are more than two levels	Chapter 14
Mann-Whitney U test	Identifies differences between two independent samples of ordinal data	Chapter 14
Wilcoxon matched-pairs signed-ranks test	Identifies differences between two dependent samples of ordinal data	Chapter 14
Spearman rank-order correlation coefficient (r_S)	Assesses strength of association between ordinal data	Chapter 14

STATISTICS AND DATA ANALYSIS FOR THE BEHAVIORAL SCIENCES

STATISTICS AND DATA ANALYSIS FOR THE BEHAVIORAL SCIENCES

DANA S. DUNN

Moravian College

Boston   Burr Ridge, IL   Dubuque, IA   Madison, WI   New York   San Francisco   St. Louis
Bangkok   Bogotá   Caracas   Lisbon   London   Madrid
Mexico City   Milan   New Delhi   Seoul   Singapore   Sydney   Taipei   Toronto

McGraw-Hill Higher Education ✖

A Division of The **McGraw-Hill** *Companies*

STATISTICS AND DATA ANALYSIS FOR THE BEHAVIORAL SCIENCES

Published by McGraw-Hill, an imprint of The McGraw-Hill Companies, Inc., 1221 Avenue of the Americas, New York, NY 10020. Copyright © 2001 by The McGraw-Hill Companies, Inc. All rights reserved. No part of this publication may be reproduced or distributed in any form or by any means, or stored in a database or retrieval system, without the prior written consent of The McGraw-Hill Companies, Inc., including, but not limited to, in any network or other electronic storage or transmission, or broadcast for distance learning.

Some ancillaries, including electronic and print components, may not be available to customers outside the United States.

This book is printed on acid-free paper.

2 3 4 5 6 7 8 9 0 VNH/VNH 0 9 8 7 6 5 4 3 2 1

ISBN 0–07–234764–3

Vice president and editor-in-chief: *Thalia Dorwick*
Editorial director: *Jane E. Vaicunas*
Executive editor: *Joseph Terry*
Marketing manager: *Chris Hall*
Project manager: *Susan J. Brusch*
Senior media producer: *Sean Crowley*
Production supervisor: *Kara Kudronowicz*
Coordinator of freelance design: *David W. Hash*
Cover/interior designer: *Rebecca Lloyd Lemna*
Senior photo research coordinator: *Carrie K. Burger*
Senior supplement coordinator: *Jodi K. Banowetz*
Compositor: *York Graphic Services, Inc.*
Typeface: *10/12 Minion*
Printer: *Von Hoffmann Press, Inc.*

Photo credit
Figure 1.5; ©*Corbis/Bettmann*

The credits section for this book begins on page C–1 and is considered an extension of the copyright page.

Library of Congress Cataloging-in-Publication Data
Dunn, Dana.
    Statistics and data analysis for the behavioral sciences / Dana S. Dunn.—1st ed.
    p. cm.
    Includes bibliographical references and index.
    ISBN 0-07-234764-3
    1. Psychometrics. 2. Psychology—Research—Methodology. I. Title.

BF39 .D825   2001
150′ .1′5195—dc21
                          00-030546
                          CIP

www.mhhe.com

To the memory of my father and grandfather,
James L. Dunn and Foster E. Kennedy.

"WHAT'S PAST IS PROLOGUE" —*THE TEMPEST* (ACT II, SC. I)

ABOUT THE AUTHOR

DANA S. DUNN

Dana S. Dunn is currently an Associate Professor and the Chair of the Department of Psychology at Moravian College, a liberal arts and sciences college in Bethlehem, Pennsylvania. Dunn received his Ph.D. in experimental social psychology from the University of Virginia in 1987, having previously graduated with a BA in psychology from Carnegie Mellon University in 1982. He has taught statistics and data analysis for over 12 years. Dunn has published numerous articles and chapters in the areas of social cognition, rehabilitation psychology, the teaching of psychology, and liberal education. He is the author of a research methods book, *The Practical Researcher: A Student Guide to Conducting Psychological Research* (McGraw-Hill, 1999). Dunn lives in Bethlehem with his wife and two children.

CONTENTS IN BRIEF

CONTENTS

PREFACE

In my view statistics has no reason for existence except as a catalyst for learning and discovery.

—— GEORGE BOX

This quotation serves as the guiding rationale for this book and, I hope, provides an outlook for teaching and learning about statistics. From the main content to the pedagogical aids and end-of-the-chapter exercises, this textbook fosters learning and discovery. As students learn how to perform calculations and interpret the results, they will discover new ways to think about the world around them, uncover previously unrecognized relationships among disparate variables, and make better judgments about how and why people behave the way they do.

Statistics and Data Analysis for the Behavioral Sciences teaches the theory behind statistics and the analysis of data through a practical, hands-on approach. Students will learn the "how to" side of statistics: how to select an appropriate test, how to collect data for research, how to perform statistical calculations in a step-by-step manner, how to be intelligent consumers of statistical information, and how to write up analyses and results in American Psychological Association (APA) style. Linking theory with practice will help students retain what they learn for use in future behavioral science courses, research projects, graduate school, or any career where problem solving is used. Combining statistics with data analysis leads to a practical pedagogical goal—helping students to see that both are tools for intellectual discovery that examine the world and events in it in new ways.

To the Student

Two events spurred me to write this book, and I want you to know that I wrote it with students foremost in my mind. First, I have taught statistics for over 12 years. In that time, I've come to believe that some students struggle with statistics and quantitative material simply because it is not well presented by existing textbooks. Few authors, for example, adequately translate abstract ideas into concrete terms and examples that can be easily understood. Consequently, as I wrote this book, I consciously tried to make even the most complex material as accessible as possible. I also worked to develop applications and asides that bring the material to life, helping readers to make connections between abstract statistical ideas and their concrete application in daily life.

Second, the first statistics course that I took as an undergraduate was an unmitigated disaster, really, a nightmare—it was dull, difficult, and daunting. I literally had no idea what the professor was talking about, nor did I know how to use statistics for any purpose. I lost that battle but later won the war by consciously trying to think about how statistics and the properties of data reveal themselves in everyday life. I came to appreciate the utility and even—dare I say it—the beauty of statistics. In doing so, I also vowed that when I became a professor, no student of mine would suffer the pain and intellectual doubt that I did as a first-time statistics student. Thus, I wrote this book with my unfortunate "growing" experience in mind. I never want anyone in my classes or using my book to feel the anxiety that I did and, though it is a cliché, I think that the book is better because of my trying first experience.

How can you ensure that you will do well in your statistics class? Simple: Attend classes, do the reading, do the homework, and review what you learn regularly. Indeed, it is a very good idea to reserve some meaningful period of time *each day* for studying statistics and data analysis (yes, I am quite serious). When you do not understand something mentioned in this book or during class, ask the instructor for clarification *immediately,* not later, when your uncertainty has had time to blossom into full-blown confusion (remember my first experience in a statistics class—I know whereof I speak). Remember, too, the importance of reminding yourself that *statistics is for something*. You should be able to stop at any given point in the course of performing a statistical test in order to identify what you are doing, why, and what you hope to find out by using it. If you cannot do so, then you must backtrack to the point where you last understood what you were doing and why; to proceed without such understanding is not only a waste of time, it is perilous, even foolhardy, and will not help you to comprehend the material. By the way, if you feel that you need a review of basic mathematics, Appendix A provides one, including some helpful ideas on dealing with math anxiety.

Beyond these straightforward steps, you should also take advantage of the pedagogical tools I created for this book. They are reviewed in detail in the *To the Instructor* section, and I suggest you take a look at their descriptions below. I do, however, take the time to explain these tools and their use *as they appear* in the first few chapters of the book. I urge you to take these devices seriously, to see them as complementary to and not replacements for your usual study habits. I promise you that your diligence will have a favorable payoff in the end—actual understanding, reduced anxiety, and probably a higher grade than you expected when you first began the class.

To the Instructor

This book was written for use in a basic, first, non-calculus-based statistics course for undergraduate students in psychology, education, sociology, or one of the other behavioral sciences. I assume little mathematical sophistication, as any statistical procedure is presented conceptually first, followed by calculations demonstrated in a step-by-step manner. Indeed, it is important for both students and instructors to remember that statistics is *not* mathematics, nor is it a subfield of mathematics (Moore, 1992).

This book has a variety of pedagogical features designed to make it appeal to instructors of statistics (as well as students) including the following:

Decision Trees.   Appearing on the opening page of each chapter, these very simple flow charts identify the main characteristics of the descriptive or inferential procedures reviewed therein, guiding readers through what a given test *does* (e.g., mean comparison), *when* to use it (i.e., to what research designs does it apply), and *what* sort of data it analyzes (e.g., continuous). At the close of each chapter, readers are reminded to rely on the decision trees in a section called "Looking forward, then back." A special icon (⚏) prompts them to recall the features found in the decision tree(s) opening the chapters.

Key Terms and Concepts.   Key terms (e.g., mean, variance) and concepts (e.g., random sampling, central limit theorem) are highlighted throughout the text to gain readers' attention and to promote retention. An alphabetical list of key terms (including the page number where each is first cited) appears at the end of every chapter.

Marginal Notes.   The reader's attention will occasionally be drawn by marginal notes—key concepts, tips, suggestions, important points, and the like—appearing in the margins of the text. An icon ▽ drawn from the book's cover design identifies these brief marginal notes.

Straightforward Calculation of Descriptive and Inferential Statistics by Hand.   Statistical symbols and notation are explained early in the book (chapter 1). All of the descriptive and inferential statistics in the book are presented conceptually in the context of an example, and then explained in a step-by-step manner. Each step in any calculation is numbered for ease of reference (example: [2.2.3] refers to chapter 2, formula 2, step 3). Readers who have access to a basic calculator can do any statistical procedure presented in the book. Naturally, step-by-step advice also teaches students to read, understand, and use statistical notation as well as the statistical tables presented in Appendix B. Appendix A reviews basic mathematics and algebraic manipulation for those students who need a self-paced refresher course. The second half of Appendix A discusses math anxiety, providing suggestions and references to alleviate it.

Data Boxes.   Specific examples of published research or methodological issues using germane statistical procedures or concepts appear in Data Boxes throughout the text. By reading Data Boxes, students learn ways in which statistics and data analysis are tools to aid the problem solver. To quote Box, they are tools for "learning and discovery."

Focus on Interpretation of Results and Presenting Them in Written Form.   All statistical procedures conclude with a discussion of how to interpret what a result *actually* means. These discussions have two points: what the test literally concludes about some statistical relationship in the data and what it means descriptively—how did participants behave in a study, what did they do? The focus then turns to clearly communicating results in prose form. Students will learn how to put these results into words for inclusion in American Psychological Association (APA) style reports or draft articles. I used this approach successfully in a previous book (Dunn, 1999). Appendix C, which provides a brief overview of writing APA style reports, gives special emphasis to properly presenting research results and statistical information.

Statistical Power, Effect Size, and Planned and Post Hoc Comparisons.   Increasingly, consideration of statistical power and effect size estimates is becoming more commonplace in psychology textbooks as well as journals. I follow this good precedent by attaching discussion of the strength of association of independent to dependent variables along with specific inferential tests (e.g., estimated omega-squared—$\hat{\omega}^2$—is presented with the F ratio). In the same way, review of planned or post hoc comparisons of means are attached to discussions of particular tests. I focus on conceptually straightforward approaches for doing mean comparisons (e.g., Tukey's Honestly Significant Difference

[HSD] test), but I also discuss the important—but often neglected—perspectives provided by contrast analysis (e.g., Rosenthal & Rosnow, 1985).

Knowledge Base Concept Checks. Periodically, readers encounter digressions within each chapter called "Knowledge Bases," as in "students will add to their statistical knowledge base." Any Knowledge Base provides a quick concept check for students. In lieu of a diagnostic quiz, readers can think about and then answer a few questions dealing with the key points in the chapter section they just finished reading (these exercises will obviously help pace the students' reading of conceptually challenging material, as well). Completion of each Knowledge Base in the book will incrementally add to their knowledge base of statistical concepts and data analysis techniques. Answers to Knowledge Base questions are provided immediately after the questions.

Project Exercises.   Each chapter contains a "Project Exercise," an activity that applies or extends issues presented therein. Project Exercises are designed to give students the opportunity to think about how statistical concepts can actually be employed in research or to identify particular issues that can render data analysis useful for the design of experiments or the interpretation of behavior. On occasion, a chapter's Project Exercise might be linked to a Data Box.

End-of-Chapter Problems.   Each chapter in the text concludes with a series of problems. Most problems require traditional numerical answers, but many are designed to help students think coherently and write cogently about the properties of statistics and data. Answers to the odd-numbered problems are provided in the back of the textbook in Appendix E.

Special Appendixes.   Beyond the traditional appendixes devoted a review of basic math (with suggestions about combating math anxiety; Appendix A), statistical tables (Appendix B), and answers to odd-numbered end-of-chapter problems (Appendix E), I also include three more specialized offerings. Appendix C presents guidance on writing up research in APA style, highlighting specific ways to write and cogently present statistical results. Advice on organizing a research project using statistics and data analysis is presented in Appendix D. I emphasize the importance of being organized, how to manage time, and—most importantly—how to prepare raw data for analysis in this appendix. Finally, Appendix F introduces qualitative research approaches as emerging alternatives—not foils—for the statistical analysis of data. Though by no means commonplace, such approaches are gradually being accepted as new options—really, opportunities—for researchers.

Supplements

Statistics and Data Analysis for the Behavioral Sciences has several supplements designed to help both instructors and students. These supplements include:

***Elementary Data Analysis Using Microsoft Excel* by Mehan and Warner (2000).**   This easy to use workbook introduces students to Microsoft Excel speadsheets as a tool to be used in introductory statistics courses. By utilizing a familiar program such as Excel, students can concentrate more on statistical concepts and outcomes and less on the mechanics of software.

***Instructor's Manual* and Test Bank.**   The book has a detailed *Instructor's Manual* (IM) and Test Bank (TB). The IM includes syllabus outlines for one- or two-semester statistics courses, detailed chapter outlines, key terms, lecture suggestions, suggestions for classroom activities and discussions, film recommendations (where available and appropriate), and suggested readings for the instructor (i.e., articles and books containing teaching tips, exercises). The TB contains test items (i.e., multiple choice items, short essays, problems), and is also available on computer diskette for PC and Macintosh.

Dedicated Website.   The book has a dedicated website (www.mhhe.com.dunn) so that potential instructors can examine a synopsis of the book, its table of contents, descriptions of the available supplements, and ordering information. Links to other sites on the Web related to statistics, data analysis, and psychology (including links to other parts of the McGraw-Hill site) are available. In addition, portions of the *Instructor's Manual* and Test Bank appear on the website and are "password" accessible to instructors who have selected the text and their students. The website also has an online SPSS guide, which is an alternative to the expensive printed guides. Beginning with computing a correlation between two variables and a continuing with *t* tests, ANOVAs, and chi-square, this site will help your students understand the basics of the SPSS program.

Study Guide for Statistics and Data Analysis for the Behavioral Sciences.   Instructors (or students) can order a study guide to accompany *Statistics and Data Analysis for the Behavioral Sciences*. The *Study Guide* contains a review of key terms, concepts, and practice problems designed to highlight statistical issues. Answers to any problems will be provided in the back of the *Study Guide*.

ACKNOWLEDGMENTS

Writers of statistics books require willing, even charitable, readers of rough drafts. My colleagues and friends, Stacey Zaremba, Matthew Schulz, and Robert Brill, read and commented on most of the chapters in this book. Peter von Allmen and Jeanine S. Stewart provided valuable suggestions regarding specific issues and chapters. Dennis Glew and Clif Kussmaul improved the clarity of some examples. During spring 1999, several students in my Statistics and Research Methods class took the time to read initial drafts of the first half of the book, and their subsequent suggestions refined the material. The Reference Librarians and the Interlibrary Loan Department of Reeves Library helped me to track down sometimes obscure materials or references. Ever patient, Jackie Giaquinto shepherded the manuscript and me through our appropriate paces, and reminded me of my other responsibilities. Sarah Hoffman helped to pull bits and pieces of the manuscript together at the end of the revision process. I want to express my gratitude to the Moravian College Faculty Development and Research Committee for the summer grant that enabled me to finish the book on time. My friend, Steve Gordy, studiously avoided reading anything this time round, but his support was there, and welcome, nonetheless.

Beyond my campus, I am very grateful to the constructive comments and criticism offered by an excellent group of peer reviewers, including:

Charles Ansorge
University of Nebraska–Lincoln

Phillip J. Best
Miami University, Ohio

Thomas Billimeck
San Antonio College

Steven W. Brown
Rockhurst College

David L. DiLalla
Southern Illinois University–Carbondale

David Feigley
Rutgers University–New Brunswick Campus

K. Della Ferguson
Utica College

David Fitt
Temple University

O. Joseph Harm
University of South Carolina–Aiken

Rebecca Huselid
Hunter College

Arnold Hyman
University of New Haven

David Weissenburger
University of Central Texas

Elizabeth Krupinski
University of Arizona

Leonard Williams
Rowan University

Carrie Margolin
The Evergreen State College

Robert Woll
Siena College

and several anonymous reviewers. I followed many but not all of their recommendations, so any errors in omission, commission, inference, or good judgment are mine alone. Special thanks to Dennis Cogan, O. Joseph Harm, and Helen Kim for their assistance in providing accurate anwers to the problems and computations within this text.

This is the second book I have written with the McGraw-Hill College Division, and I remain convinced that the professionals who work there are rare and true. I hope our relationship is a long one. My editor and friend, Joe Terry, established the project's vision, and then developmental editor, Susan Kunchandy, helped to move it forward. Editorial director Jane Vaicunas continued to show confidence in my work. Barbara Santoro—a tireless and dedicated individual—answered all my queries, organized endless details, and provided help at every turn. Marketing manager Chris Hall provided sage advice about the book's development in its later stages. Project manager Susan Brusch steered the book (and me) skillfully through the production schedule. Wayne Harms created the book's elegant and clear design. I am grateful to copy editor, Pat Steele, for consistently improving my prose.

Finally, my family—past and present—enabled me to write this book. Daily, my wife, Sarah, and my children, Jake and Hannah, reminded me of the link between love and work. I am grateful for their patience and good humor. Dah K. Dunn's faith in my writing was as steadfast as ever. I dedicate this book to two fine men from my family.

READER RESPONSE

No book can satisfy every reader, but every author makes a genuine effort to try, anyway, and I am no different. I welcome your comments to this first edition of *Statistics and Data Analysis for the Behavioral Sciences*. I pledge to listen carefully to critical reactions as well as any compliments, using both to improve this book's pedagogy in the future. I encourage you to take a moment, log on to www.mhhe.com/dunn and complete the short questionnaire found on this website. Your questionnaire will be e-mailed to the publisher, who will share it with me. You may also contact me directly at the Department of Psychology, Moravian College, 1200 Main Street, Bethlehem, PA 18018-6650; via e-mail: dunn@moravian.edu. I sincerely look forward to hearing from you.

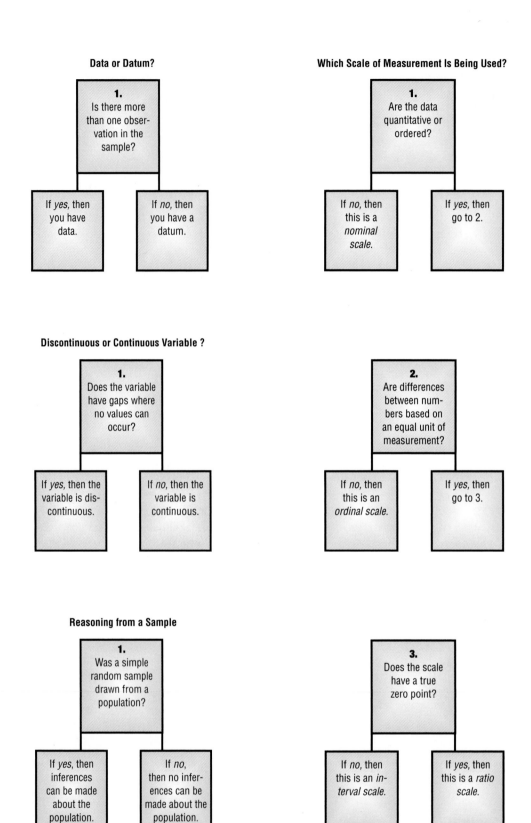

INTRODUCTION: STATISTICS AND DATA ANALYSIS AS TOOLS FOR RESEARCHERS

"In my view statistics has no reason for existence except as a catalyst for learning and discovery." This quotation from George Box serves as the guiding rationale for the book you are now reading. Here at the outset, it is essential for you to understand that statistics are aids to improving inference, guides that help us to make sense out of events in the world in particular ways. As an undergraduate student in psychology or a related behavioral science discipline, you should know that statistics and data analysis can help you to answer focused questions about cause and effect, to simplify complexity, to uncover heretofore unrecognized relationships among observations, and to make more precise judgments about how and why people behave the way they do. This book will teach you about some of the theory behind statistics and the analysis of data through a practical, hands-on approach. As you read, you will learn the "how to" side of statistics and data analysis, including:

■ How to select an appropriate statistical test
■ How to collect the right kinds of information for analysis
■ How to perform statistical calculations in a straightforward, step-by-step manner
■ How to accurately interpret and present statistical results
■ How to be an intelligent consumer of statistical information
■ How to write up analyses and results in American Psychological Association (APA) style

Linking theory with practice will help you to retain what you learn so that you can use it in future courses in psychology or the other behavioral sciences, research projects, graduate or professional school, or any career where problem solving, statistics, and data analysis are used.

But we are getting ahead of ourselves. First, we need to define some terms, terms that have been used as if you already understood them! What is a statistic, anyway? What is data analysis? Why are these terms important?

KEY TERM   A **statistic** is some piece of information that is presented in numerical form. For example, a nation's 5% unemployment rate is a statistic, and so is the average number of words per minute read by a group of second-graders or the reported high temperature on a July day in Juneau, Alaska.

The field of statistics—and the statisticians who work within it—focuses on appropriate ways to collect, codify, analyze, and interpret numerical information. The ways statisticians examine information are formalized into a set of rules and procedures commonly referred to as "statistics." Scholars, researchers, teachers, and students from many disciplines rely on these organized rules and procedures to answer questions and explore topics unique to their fields.

"Tonight, we're going to let the statistics speak for themselves."

Source: The Cartoon Bank: Ed Koren, *The New Yorker*.

KEY TERM   **Data analysis** refers to the systematic examination of a collection of observations. The examination can answer a question, search for a pattern, or otherwise make some sense out of the observations.

These observations are either numerical (i.e., quantitative) or not based on numbers (i.e., qualitative). If the observations are quantitative—for example, number of puzzles solved in an experiment—statistics are frequently used in the data analysis. What was the highest number solved? The lowest? In the case of qualitative information, some organizing principle—identifying the emotional content of words exchanged between husbands and wives, for instance—can draw meaning from the observations. Do women use words that establish relationships, whereas men rely on words that express their individuality?

Despite popular opinion, as terms, statistics and data analysis are neither synonymous nor redundant with one another. For our purposes, the first term emphasizes the importance of working through necessary calculations in order to identify or discover relationships within the quantitative results of research. The second term, however, acknowledges the interpretive, methodological, or analytic side of working with information—knowing, for instance, what information to collect and what to do with it once it is collected. Unlike the term statistics, data analysis also allows for the possibility that not

▽

Statistics and data analysis are complementary—not equivalent—terms.

all the information you encounter or are interested in will necessarily be quantitative in nature. As we will see later in this book (Appendix F), qualitative—that is, non-numerical, often descriptive or narrative—relationships within data can be equally revealing and, increasingly, social scientists are taking an active interest in them.

Key terms like these will be highlighted throughout the book. Whenever you come across a new term, plan to take a few minutes to study it and to make sure that you understand it thoroughly. Why? Because learning the vocabulary and conceptual background of statistics is akin to learning a foreign language; before you can have an actual conversation in, say, French or German, you need to know how to conjugate verbs, use pronouns, recognize nouns, and so on. Like learning the parts of speech in another language, it takes a bit of time and a little effort to learn the language of statistics. As you will see, it can be done—you *will* learn to use this new language, understand, and even benefit from it. One important point, though: the more you work with the statistical terms and their meanings, the more quickly they will become second nature to you—but you *must* make the effort starting here and now. Similar to studying a foreign language, statistical concepts build upon one another; learning the rudimentary parts of speech, as it were, is essential to participating in the more complex dialog that comes later.

Quantitative relationships are numerical. Qualitative relationships are based on descriptions or organizing themes, not numbers.

DATA BOX 1.A

What *Is* or *Are* Data?

Inexplicably, the word **data** has developed a certain cachet in contemporary society. Although it is usually associated with science, use of the word is now common in everyday speech. As a "buzz" word, it seems to lend an air of credibility to people's pronouncements on any number of topics. But what does the word data actually mean? "Data" refer to a body of information, usually a collection of facts, items, observations, or even statistics. The word is Latin in origin, meaning "a thing given." Thus, medical information from one patient, such as heart rate, blood pressure, and weight, constitute data, as does the same information from everyone admitted to a hospital in the course of a year. Conceptually, then, the term is flexible.

The grammatical usage of data, however, is proscribed. How so? The word "data" is plural—the word **datum,** which means a piece of information, is singular. So, all the medical entries on a patient's chart are data, whereas the patient's weight when admitted to the ward—say, 165 lb—is a datum. Why does this distinction matter? When writing about or describing data, you will want to be both correct and precise. Data are, datum is:

"These data are flawed." (correct)   "These data were helpful." (correct)
"This data is flawed." (incorrect)   "The data was helpful." (incorrect)
"The datum is flawed." (correct)   "The datum helped." (correct)

I urge you to listen carefully to how your friends, faculty, and family members use the term data—usually incorrectly, I'll wager—not to mention newscasters and some newspaper columnists, all professionals who should know better. Do your best to turn the tide by resolving to use the terms data and datum correctly from now on.

Tools for Inference: David L.'s Problem

Statistics and data analysis are tools that behavioral scientists use to understand the results of the research they conduct. As a tool, a statistical analysis is simply the means to accomplish some task—it is by no means as important as that task (Dunn, 1999). Students often see statistics as a hindrance, not a help, as something much more involved than the question they are trying to answer or the topic they are exploring. In fact, first-time statistics students can sometimes feel overwhelmed by the trappings of statistical analysis—the formulas, the math, the tables and graphs—so that they lose sight of what statistics are supposed to offer as a way of looking at things. Remember the message from George Box that appeared earlier—to paraphrase him, statistics are *for* something, they are supposed to enlighten us, to help us discover things. For most people, teachers like me and students like you, they are not ends in themselves.

Let's consider an example of how statistics can shed some light on a decision. Read the following "problem," as it deals with a situation you probably know firsthand. After you read the problem and think about it, take out a piece of paper and answer the question that appears below.

College Choice

David L. was a senior in high school on the East Coast who was planning to go to college. He had completed an excellent record in high school and had been admitted to his two top choices: a small liberal arts college and an Ivy League university. The two schools were about equal in prestige and were equally costly. Both were located in attractive East Coast cities, about equally distant from his home town. David had several older friends who were attending the liberal arts college and several who were attending the Ivy league university. They were all excellent students like himself and had interests that were similar to his. His friends at the liberal arts college all reported that they liked the place very much and that they found it very stimulating. The friends at the Ivy League university reported that they had many complaints on both personal and social grounds and on educational grounds. David thought that he would initially go to the liberal arts college. However, he decided to visit both schools for a day. He did not like what he saw at the private liberal arts college: Several people whom he met seemed cold and unpleasant; a professor he met with briefly seemed abrupt and uninterested in him; and he did not like the "feel" of the campus. He did like what he saw at the Ivy League university: Several of the people he met seemed like vital, enthusiastic, pleasant people; he met with two different professors who took a personal interest in him; and he came away with a very pleasant feeling about the campus.

> **Question.**   Which school should David L. choose, and why? Try to analyze the arguments on both sides, and explain which side is stronger. (Nisbett, Krantz, Jepson, & Fong, 1982, pp. 457–458)

College Choice: What Would (Did) You Do?

Where should David L. go to school? More than one waggish student has remarked that there is really no decision here: He should just go to the Ivy League university because his diploma will carry weight in the world four years hence! Other students compare the virtues of small versus large campuses—that is, intimate settings (i.e., you're noticed) are more desirable than sprawling ones (i.e., you're just a number). Let's try to approach the problem more critically—that is, statistically—and with fewer preconceptions about the two types of schools.

The situation faced by the fictional David L. is by no means unique: Many, perhaps most, college applicants must eventually select one school over another or possible others. As you may well know, such decisions are rarely easy to make, and any number of factors—what are typically called *variables*—can be influential.

KEY TERM   A **variable** is any factor that can be measured or have a different value. Such factors can vary from person to person, place to place, or experimental situation to experimental situation. Hair color can be a variable (i.e., blonde, brunette, redhead), as can a score on a personality test, the day of the week, or your weight.

As we will see later in the chapter, statistics usually rely on variables *X* and *Y* to represent numerical values in formulas or statistics about data.

Several variables stand out in the David L. problem. First and foremost, David's friends at the liberal arts institution were generally satisfied, as they told him they liked it and even found it to be a stimulating place. His pals at the Ivy League school, however, reported just the opposite, voicing complaints and qualifications on personal, social, and educational grounds. You will recall that David planned to go to the smaller school until visits at both places called his initial decision into question—he liked what he saw at the university but had an unpleasant time at the college. In short, his experiences were the opposite of his friends' experiences.

What else do we know? Well, a few factors appear to be what are called *constants,* not variables.

A **constant** is usually a number whose value does not change, such as π (pronounced "pie"), which equals 3.1416. A constant can also refer to a characteristic pertaining to a person or environment that does not change.

We know, for example, that David's friends attending both schools were strong students (like himself, apparently) and shared outlooks like his own. In other words, intellectual ability appears to be a constant, as David is not very different from his friends. Yet we know he had decidedly different experiences than they at the two schools. We also know that both schools are equally prestigious, cost about the same, are metropolitan, and are equidistant from his home. These normally important factors do not appear to be very influential in David's decision making because they, too, are constants and, in any case, he is more focused on his experiences at the schools than on money issues, location, or distance.

Variables take on different values, constants do not change.

Nonetheless, these constants *do* tell us something—and perhaps they should tell David something, as well. In a sense, his friends are constants and because they are so similar to him, he might do well to pay close attention to their experiences and to wonder rather critically why his experiences when he visited were so different from their own. What would a statistician say about this situation? In other words, could a rudimentary understanding of statistics and the properties of data help David choose between the small liberal arts college and the Ivy League university?

Approaching the problem from a statistical perspective would highlight two concepts relevant to David L.'s data—base rate and sampling. Base rate, in this case, refers to the common or shared reactions of his friends to their respective schools; that is, those attending the liberal arts college liked the place, while those at the Ivy League school did not. If we know that David L. is highly similar to his friends, shouldn't we assume that across time he will have reactions similar to theirs, that he will like the college but not the university? Thus, the base rate experiences of his friends could reasonably be weighed more heavily in the college choice deliberations than his own opinion.

Similarity of reaction leads to the second issue, that of sampling, which may explain why David's reactions were different from those of his peers. Put simply, is one day's exposure to *any* campus sufficient to really know what it is like? Probably not, especially when you consider that his friends have repeatedly sampled what the respective schools offer for at least a year, possibly longer. (Consider these thought questions: Did you know what your present school was *really* like before you started? What do you know *now* that you did not know *then*?) In other words, David really doesn't have enough information—enough data—to make a sound choice. His short visits to each campus were characterized by biased or distorted samples of information: he met few people and, on short visits, could not have learned all there was to know about either school. Sampling issues will be explored in greater detail shortly (but see Data Box 1.B later in the chapter for more detail on how people typically answer the David L. problem and factors that can influence such answers).

What did you do? That is, how did you select your present college or university? Were you unduly (or appropriately) influenced by the respective variables and constants found on your own campus? Did the weather matter—was a crisp, bright autumn day in October more pleasant (and influential) than a cold, rainy March visit? Were people cold and aloof or warm and friendly? What factors unique to you and your school helped you decide to enroll there? Finally, was David's situation similar to or dissimilar from your own?

Here is the important point: there is no *right* answer, rather, there are *possible* answers, the choice of which depends on the decision-maker's perspective and goal. An understanding of statistics and data analysis provides only one account—though admittedly a good one—of how one might decide between two similar scholastic alternatives. If David L. wanted to make a statistically sound inference, then he would assume his friends' experiences at the small liberal arts college or the Ivy League university were useful because they have repeatedly sampled what the respective institutions have to offer. He would also realize that his short-term experiences did not provide enough information to make a decisive choice.

On the other hand, he could avoid taking any statistical considerations into account and rely on his own opinion, which would be a different but acceptable way to proceed. Remember, statistics serve as inferential tools, as guidelines for a particular way to make a choice; the individual using them must interpret the result and decide how to proceed. The statistical analysis itself has no opinion, nor will it enroll at the college or university. As a data analyst, you must decide how to use the results and to determine what they mean for you. This interpretive choice is critical—and it is common to every statistical analysis you will do. *Statistics and data analyses are about thinking first, calculation second.*

▽

Statistics and data analysis highlight possible solutions or answers to questions, not absolute or definitive conclusions.

Statistics Is the Science of Data, *Not* Mathematics

Mathematics is an ancient discipline, but statistical reasoning did not really occur until late in the 17th century (Cowles, 1989), and the bulk of statistical advances took place in the 19th century (Moore, 1992). Mathematics and statistics are actually separate disciplines with very different agendas. Many students and more than a few behavioral scientists are surprised to learn that statistics is not a part of mathematics. Mathematics is the science of quantity and space and the analysis of relationships and patterns, whereas statistics is the science of data, data production, and inference (e.g., Moore, 1992). Both disciplines, however, rely on symbols to show relationships between quantities and differences among quantities.

▽

Statistics ≠ mathematics.

These definitions can seem to be similar, but let me illustrate the distinction between the two disciplines. If we take the simple average of the five numbers 80, 85, 90, 91, and 94, which is 88 (i.e., $80 + 85 + 90 + 91 + 94 = 440$, and $440/5 = 88$), we are performing a mathematical operation. If, however, those five numbers are test scores of gifted students in an advanced chemistry class, then the average becomes a statistical operation. This is particularly true if we try to determine why some students performed better than others, or if we compare the students' performance with those of another gifted group, and so on.

The field of statistics is concerned with making sense out of *empirical* data, particularly when those data contain some element of uncertainty so that we do not know the true state of affairs, how, say, a set of variables affect one another.

KEY TERM **Empirical** refers to anything derived from experience or experiment.

Empiricism is a philosophical stance arguing that all knowledge is developed from sensory experience. Indeed, one can verify what the world is like by experiencing it. I know the floor is solid because I am presently standing on it. If I had doubts about its structural integrity, I could do an experiment by testing how much weight it would support before buckling. The philosophical doctrine seen as the traditional foil to empiricism is called rationalism. Rationalism posits that reason is the source of all knowledge, and that such knowledge is completely independent of sensory experience, which is deemed faulty (Leahey, 1997).

Certainly it is the case that statistics relies on mathematical operations, but these operations are secondary to the process of reasoning behind statistics. In fact, I always tell students in my statistics classes that the meaning behind the data, the inferences we make about the data, are more important than the math. Please don't miss the subtle message here: Understanding how to do a mathematical procedure is very useful, as is getting the "right" answer, but these facts will not do you much good if you cannot interpret the statistical result. Thus, the ideal you should strive for is the ability to select an appropriate statistic, perform the calculation, *and* to know what the result means.

Some students who take a first statistics course are concerned about whether their math background is sufficient to do well in the class. Other students are actually fearful of taking statistics precisely because they believe that they will do poorly because of the math involved. If you fall into either group, let me offer some solace. First, I firmly believe that if you can balance your checkbook, then you will be able to follow the formulas and procedures presented in this book. Second, Appendix A contains a review of simple mathematics and algebraic manipulation of symbols if you feel that your math skills are a little rusty. If so, consult Appendix A after you finish reading this chapter. Third, you may actually be experiencing what is commonly called math anxiety. To help with the latter possibility, a discussion of this common—and readily curable—form of anxiety, as well as references, can also be found in Appendix A. Finally, a project exercise presented at the end of this chapter will help you to overcome the normal trepidation students feel when studying statistics for the first time.

Statistics, Data Analysis, and the Scientific Method

Researchers in the behavioral sciences use statistics to analyze data collected within the framework of the *scientific method*. There are numerous definitions for this method, but most of them entail similar elements.

KEY TERM The **scientific method** guides research by identifying a problem, formulating a hypothesis, and collecting empirical data to test the hypothesis.

The only new term here is *hypothesis,* and it may already be a familiar concept to you.

KEY TERM A **hypothesis** is a testable question or prediction, one usually designed to explain some phenomenon.

A developmental psychologist who is interested in how infants learn, for example, would rely on the scientific method to test her hypotheses. One perceptual hypothesis is that infants are most interested in information that is moderately novel. Infants like to look at objects that are not too familiar or that are not too novel; the former are boring and the latter can be confusing (McCall, Kennedy, & Appelbaum, 1977). By presenting a group of young children with different groupings of objects (e.g., blocks with patterns) representing different degrees of familiarity, the researcher could measure their interest—how long they look at each object, for instance. Different hypotheses examining the same issue are then combined to form what is called a *theory*.

KEY TERM   A **theory** is a collection of related facts, often derived from hypotheses and the scientific method, forming a coherent explanation for a larger phenomenon.

One theory is that infants' interests in novelty also reveal their innate preferences for learning. Some researchers have suggested that preferences for novelty, in turn, are linked with intelligence. Another theory suggests that intelligent infants are drawn to novel information more readily than less intelligent infants (e.g., Bornstein & Sigman, 1986). Note that these theories were developed by examining a variety of hypotheses and the results of many studies about how infants perceive the objects they encounter. A researcher using any theory would be aware of the existing data and would make certain to use the scientific method and careful reasoning before executing research aimed at testing any hypotheses consistent with it.

Inductive and Deductive Reasoning

What sort of reasoning underlies the scientific method? The scientific community uses two types of reasoning, inductive and deductive. Depending on what is already known about a research problem or theory, each form of reasoning serves a different function. The first, *inductive reasoning,* is also referred to as induction.

KEY TERM   Generalizing from one or more observations in the course of developing a more general explanation is called **inductive reasoning**. Observations are used to generate theories.

No doubt more than one developmental psychologist noticed that infants look for longer periods of time at moderately novel objects than with very familiar or completely unfamiliar displays. Once the psychologist noticed this modest behavioral discrepancy and then generated an explanation, which required induction—the data prompted the development of a theory. Such induction is ideal for developing preliminary hypotheses, which in turn can be refined into a coherent theory.

Induction: data lead to theory.

Formulating related concepts, generalizing from one instance to another, or making some prediction based on what is already known, are all examples of inductive reasoning (Holland, Holyoak, Nisbett, & Thagard, 1986). Induction is a powerful tool, but it can miss influential factors that could be responsible for whatever interesting phenomenon we are studying. It would be a mistake, for example, to assume that all the learning infants do is based on their abilities to visually discriminate the new from the old. How, after all, do children with visual impairments learn? The other sensory processes, especially hearing, must also play a prominent role in the acquisition of knowledge. Separate but complementary theories must be developed to explain auditory and other forms of learning, as well.

Psychology and the other behavioral sciences—economics, education, sociology, and anthropology—often rely on inductive reasoning, which is the hallmark of newer sciences. Why is inductive reasoning associated with these newer areas of empirical inquiry? In contrast to the natural sciences, the behavioral sciences usually lack unified theories and research methodologies. Psychology, for example, does not have a single, dominant approach that purports to explain the cognitive, emotional, physiological, and behavioral aspects of human behavior. Rather, there are many distinct approaches that seek to explain individual aspects of human behavior—just look at the table of contents of any introductory textbook in the field—suggesting that we are far from having a unified position that ties them all together (Kuhn, 1970, 1977; Watson, 1967).

Much older areas of science, especially physics, have unified theories that enable them to employ the second type of reasoning, which is called *deductive.*

KEY TERM

Deductive reasoning is characterized by the use of existing theories to develop conclusions, called deductions, about how some unexamined phenomenon is likely to operate. Theory is used to search for confirming observations.

Deduction promotes a particular type of prediction: whenever event *X* occurs, event *Y* usually follows. Deductive reasoning is essentially fact-based reasoning, so that what we already know points us in the direction of what we can also expect to be true. In physics, for example, Albert Einstein created the theory of relativity, which, among other things, posited that time was not absolute and that it depended on an object's state of motion. Initially, there was no experimental evidence to support his radical contentions, but across the 75 or so years since it first appeared, Einstein's theory has been overwhelmingly supported by experimental data. From theory, then, Einstein deduced how time and motion should behave.

As I am sure you recognize, our understanding of how infants learn is not as finely honed as what we know about time, motion, or the speed of light. Numerous theories in the behavioral sciences are still being developed, tested, revised, or discarded in accordance with empirical data and inductive reasoning. Until a generally accepted theory of human behavior based on facts arrives (if ever!), we will need to be content with inductive reasoning, and the statistical analyses which allow us to verify our induction.

Figure 1.1 illustrates the direction of inference inherent in inductive and deductive reasoning. As you can see, when observations lead a researcher to create a theory to explain some event, the process is inductive. Incidentally, the inferences David L. (and you) made about college choice were largely inductive. When an investigator relies on some existing theory to posit the existence of particular observations, the process is deductive. Let's turn now to consider how our ability to use these two types of reasoning can help us to determine when an observation is representative of the whole.

Deduction: theory leads to data.

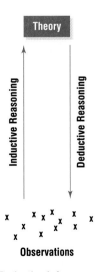

Figure 1.1 Direction of Inductive and Deductive Inferences

Populations and Samples

The idea of an adequate sample of data was informally introduced in the context of the David L. problem earlier in this chapter. In David's case, we were working with a more or less intuitive sense of what constitutes a good sample: How much of a campus do you have to see to know something about it? Are others' views useful as a sample of opinion about a campus, even when those views contradict your own experience? We now want to consider samples in a somewhat more formal, statistical sense.

Researchers usually talk about samples when they are trying to determine if some data properly characterize the *population* of interest.

KEY TERM   A **population** is a complete set of data possessing some observable characteristic, or a theoretical set of potential observations.

Perhaps because the word is commonly associated with groups of people—the population of a city or country, for instance—students are quick to assume that the term is exclusively demographic. Keep in mind that a population is *any* complete set of data, and these data can be animal, vegetable, or mineral. Test scores can comprise a population, as can birthrates of Monarch butterflies in Nebraska, sales figures for the East Coast fishing industry, or all the words printed in a given book like this one. Typically, of course, some numerical characteristic of the population will be used in statistical calculations.

When psychologists study people's behavior, they typically want to describe and understand the behavior of some population of people. The behavior studied can be an action, an attitude, or some other measurable response. Psychologists may talk about populations of people, but keep in mind that they are usually focused on a population of some characteristic *displayed* by the population of people. A developmental psychologist studying preschool social relations might work with a population of children who are 5 years of age or younger, observing the content of comments made by one peer to another. A gerontologist interested in memory decline and age could examine information processing speed and efficiency in recalling words among persons 80 years of age or older. Again, note that the term population does not literally mean "every person"; rather, it means the numerical responses for observations—here, comments or words—of every person within some identified group (e.g., children under age 5 years or persons 80 years or older).

When any psychologist examines the behavior of interest in a population, he or she cannot examine the responses of all members of that population. A given clinical psychologist who does therapy with people who have agoraphobia (i.e., fear of crowds or public spaces) does not literally work with *every person* who has the disorder. The group of people receiving research attention constitutes a *sample* from the population of people who have agoraphobia.

KEY TERM   A **sample** is a smaller unit or subset bearing the same characteristic or characteristics of the population of interest.

When researchers collect data from a sample, they hope to be able to demonstrate that the sample is representative of—is highly similar to—the population from which it was drawn. Why is it necessary to rely on a sample? Practically speaking, most populations are simply too large and unwieldy to allow a researcher to gauge every observation within them. Such undertakings would be too expensive, too time consuming, not feasible, and given good samples—the observations within them reflect the characteristics of their populations of origin—completely unnecessary anyway. Thus, the reactions of the group of agoraphobics to a new therapy are assumed to hold true in general for

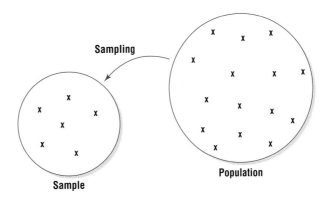

Figure 1.2 Samples Are Drawn from Some Population

Note: A sample is a subset of members of some larger population. Samples are used to learn what populations are like.

the population of all extant (or potential) agoraphobics. Similarly, a good sample of 80-year-old men and women should be sufficient to illustrate how aging affects processing speed and memory. In both cases, what we learn from a sample should enable us to accurately describe the population at large. Figure 1.2 illustrates this process: Samples are drawn from a population in order to discern what the population is like.

Wait a moment—what constitutes a good sample? How do we know if a sample approximates the characteristics of the population from which it was drawn? These and related questions are actually the foundation of statistics and data analysis, as all we will really do throughout this book is variations on this same theme: Does our sample of behavior accurately reflect its population of origin? Will an observed change in behavior in a sample reflect a similar change in behavior within the population? To answer these questions, researchers rely on statistics and what are called *population parameters*.

Adequate samples describe populations accurately.

KEY TERM A **population parameter** is a value that summarizes some important, measurable characteristic of a population. Although population parameters are estimated from statistics, they are constants.

Parameters are estimated but they do not change.

For all intents and purposes, we will probably never know the true parameters of any population unless it is reasonably small or extensive research funds are available. When you hear advertisers say, "four out of five dentists recommend" a mouthwash or toothpaste, for example, not all practicing dentists were asked to give an opinion! Generally, then, researchers must content themselves with estimating what the parameters are apt to be like. Many populations have parameters that could never be measured because their observations are constantly changing. Consider the number of people who are born and die in the United States each minute of every day—the American population is theoretically the same from moment to moment, but in practical terms it is ever changing. Despite this apparent change, we can still estimate the average height and weight of most Americans, as well as their projected life spans from sample statistics. That is, sample statistics enable us to approximate the population parameters.

When we discuss *sample statistics* and their relations to population parameters, the former term takes on added meaning.

KEY TERM A **sample statistic** is a summary value based upon some measurable characteristic of a sample. The values of sample statistics can vary from sample to sample.

That is, because different pieces of research rely on different samples, statistics based on sample data are *not* constants—the same variables collected in two different samples can take on different values. If a visual perception study reveals that people blink their eyes an average of 75 times a minute but another on the same topic finds that the average is closer to 77, is one study "right" and the other "wrong"? Of course not! The studies relied on different samples containing different people who were from the same population, and each sample probably differed in size (i.e., number of observations), when and where it was drawn, and so forth. It is quite common for one study to find sample statistics with values different from those found in other, similar pieces of research. Such subtle or not so subtle variations pose no problem because we are concerned with trying to *approximate* the characteristics of the larger population, which has unchanging values (i.e., parameters).

Thus, one very important conclusion can be drawn: *Although sample statistics are apt to change from sample to sample, a parameter, such as a population average, will not change.* This conclusion is shown in Figure 1.3. Different samples from a larger population can yield different sample statistics, but the parameters found in the relevant population are constant.

How, then, can we be sure that a given sample is actually representative of a population? We make use of another technique from the arsenal of statistics and data analysis—*simple random sampling.*

KEY TERM   **Simple random sampling** is a process whereby a subset is drawn from a population in such a way that each member of the population has the same opportunity of being selected for inclusion in the subset as all the others.

If no member of a group has a greater opportunity of being selected than any other, then there is no bias or undue influence affecting the sample's composition. If no individual or observation was more or less likely to be chosen than another, those actually selected should, therefore, be deemed representative of the population. A sample chosen in this way is called a *simple random sample.* All else being equal, a simple random sample enables a researcher to make inferences about the population and its

▽

Statistics are calculated from sample data, and they change from sample to sample.

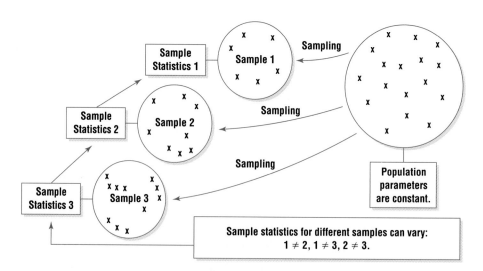

Figure 1.3   Different Samples Can Yield Different Sample Statistics

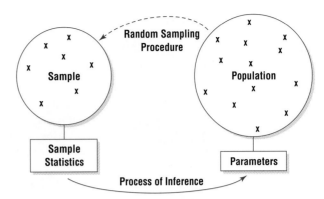

Figure 1.4 Random Sampling and the Process of Inference

parameters based on sample statistics. As shown in Figure 1.4, a sample drawn randomly from a population (see the arrow pointing from the right to the left at the top of the diagram) yields sample statistics, which are then used to infer the qualities of the population's parameters (note the arrow leading from the left to the right at the bottom of the diagram).

Let's consider the meaning of random samples in a practical, everyday example. When soliciting student opinion about a proposed tuition hike or a change in the policy regarding who can keep a car on campus, a college's administration would not just poll a few members of the senior class. On the contrary, administrators would be sure to ask members of the first-year, sophomore, and junior classes, as well. Further, there may be graduate or special students who lack a class label (e.g., second-year law students, part-time students, evening program students), but whose input would be desirable before any policy changes are implemented. The administrators involved in making new policies would want to know how the student community felt about any changes in advance, and a representative sample of student opinion is necessary to achieve that end.

Perhaps you are aware of the deleterious effects of nonrandom sampling in the history of American politics. Based on a mail poll conducted by the *Literary Digest* during the 1936 presidential election, Alfred Landon was predicted to defeat Franklin Delano Roosevelt by a wide margin—but FDR won handily in November. What happened? The pollsters' sample of registered voters was taken from car registration records, periodical subscription lists, and phone books, a procedure that worked well in determining the winner of several prior presidential contests (e.g., Shaughnessy & Zechmeister, 1994). What the pollsters failed to recognize was that the Great Depression encouraged less affluent voters to vote; although wealthier voters favored Landon, greater numbers of poorer voters wanted Roosevelt. These poorer voters were never polled, of course, because their names did not appear on the (unrepresentative) polling lists! At that time, poor Americans would be less likely to own cars or have phones, for example.

A similar situation occurred in the 1948 election. Polling results so strongly pointed to a winner that a famous headline—DEWEY DEFEATS TRUMAN—was determined in advance of the election results (e.g., Boyer, 1995; Donaldson, 1999). The surprise, though, was on the *Chicago Tribune:* Republican candidate Thomas Dewey did *not* defeat incumbent Democrat Harry S. Truman, as a combination of inadequate voter samples and swing votes (i.e., voters who changed from Dewey to Truman late in the election) carried the day. Having the last laugh on the paper and the pollsters, the triumphant Truman appeared in a now famous photograph holding up the offending headline (see Figure 1.5).

Figure 1.5   Sampling in the 1948 Election Went Awry, but Not in the Eyes of President-Elect Harry S. Truman

There is no substitute for an adequate—and random—sample.

The lesson here is a good one: Avoid overconfidence regarding research outcomes before the data are known to come from representative samples. These electoral incidents serve as strong reminders that there is no substitute for good, representative samples, and that wise researchers avoid counting the proverbial chickens (data) before they hatch (the results are in, analyzed, and interpreted). Though not perfect, sampling is now much more sophisticated and precise than earlier in the century, and there are appropriate techniques for random sampling that duly increase the chance of making correct inferences about data.

Descriptive and Inferential Statistics

When performing data analyses, researchers rely on both descriptive and inferential statistics. *Descriptive statistics* describe and summarize information collected from a sample, usually by reducing large amounts of numerical data into a more manageable form. When researchers collect data in a study, the data are typically a vast number of numbers, page after page of entries, or often today, a large computer spreadsheet of rows and columns of numbers. Even to the trained eye of the researcher who collected them, the data can seem incomprehensible. Descriptive statistics create order amid this numerical chaos by reducing large amounts of information into more meaningful—and more readily interpretable—forms.

KEY TERM   **Descriptive statistics** are statistical procedures that describe, organize, and summarize the main characteristics of sample data.

The usual information used to describe a sample includes number (e.g., How many people participated in the conference?), range (e.g., What was the length of the longest conference presentation? How long was the shortest talk?), frequency (e.g., How many men and women attended all the conference workshops?), and the most common index, the average (e.g., On average, how many days did people stay at the conference?).

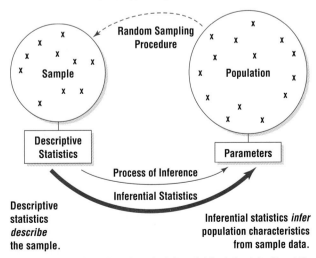

Even if a data set contains 200 observations (e.g., the grade point averages of all psychology majors at a college), a descriptive statistic like the average indicates what the academic performance of the typical major (e.g., 3.00 or B) is like. The main advantage associated with descriptive statistics, then, is simplicity—they tend to be concrete, easy to understand, and readily presentable to others (i.e., "The typical student in our program has a B average").

Inferential statistics extend the scope of descriptive statistics by examining the relationships within a set of data. In particular, inferential statistics enable the researcher to make inferences—that is, judgments—about a population based on the relationships within the sample data.

KEY TERM   **Inferential statistics** permit generalizations to be made about populations based on sample data drawn from them.

As you probably realize, inferential statistics are based on induction. That is, the observations constituting a sample are used to make generalizations about the population's characteristics—some data lead to a theory. Inferential statistics enable us to use what we know at one point in time to make assumptions about what we do not know, to reduce our uncertainty. As we will see later in this book, inferential statistics enable researchers to ask specific, testable questions about the sample data in order to draw tentative conclusions about the population.

Figure 1.6 summarizes the processes we have just reviewed. Descriptive statistics are calculated from the data collected in a random sample, and then inferential statistics are performed on the data to estimate the characteristics of the population. We assume that such inferences based on statistical evidence are true for the time being, and that any "truths" they disclose are suggestive and conditional—better samples, different data, a clearer sense of the population, or a revised theory can change the nature of what we know. Our clinician's treatment for agoraphobia might appear to help the members of his sample a great deal; however, it does not necessarily follow that the therapeutic intervention will help *all* persons affected by the disorder. Consider the real possibility that people with the most severe forms of the disorder never came to the clinic for treatment—they are literally afraid to leave the perceived security of their homes—and thus did not find themselves in this (or any) study. Future efforts could include more severe

Descriptive statistics *describe* samples.

Inferential statistics *infer* population characteristics.

Figure 1.6   Descriptive Statistics Describe a Sample. Inferential Statistics Infer Population Characteristics

DATA BOX 1.B

Reactions to the David L. Problem

Upon first blush, many respondents react to David L.'s dilemma (see p. 6) by relying on personal evidence (Nisbett, Krantz, Jepson, & Kinda, 1983), that is, his own opinion about his campus visits. To wit, "He's got to choose for himself, not his friends" (Nisbett et al., 1982, p. 458). Taking this course of action can be personally satisfying, if not statistically sound. Here is one statistically sound account, however, from a student who never had a course in statistics (from Nisbett et al., 1982, p. 458):

> I would say he should go to the liberal arts college. His negative experience there was a brief, very shallow contact with the school. His friends, all veritable clones of himself, have been there (presumably) for a while and know the place intimately, and like it, whereas the opposite statements are true of the Ivy League school. He would be justified, however, to go with his own feelings about the places. Often, this intuition is a higher perception that we can't analyze, and he may be right to go with it. I think, though, that the first choice I've mentioned is more reliable, for his experience is *too* limited with the two schools.

What prompts statistical versus nonstatistical answers? There are apparently situational factors that can cause people to respond differently to David's situation. Nisbett and his colleagues (1983) conducted a simple experiment where two groups of students received the same version of the David L. problem that you read. One of the groups, however, also received a cue highlighting sampling as a relevant issue that David himself chose to consider. Before learning the results of David's campus visits, the cued group read that:

> He proceeded systematically to draw up a long list, for both colleges, of all the classes which might interest him and all the places and the activities on campus that he wanted to see. From each list, he randomly selected several classes and activities to visit, and several spots to look at (by blindly dropping a pencil on each list of alternatives and seeing where the point landed). (Nisbett et al., 1983, p. 353)

Were readers' decisions influenced by the presence of the cue? Emphatically, yes. When the sampling cue was present, fewer participants (56%) recommended that David should attend the Ivy League university than when the cue was absent (76%). In other words, the cue encouraged them to think about the quality of David's visits—as representative samples—of the schools. Further, Nisbett et al. (1983) note that participants in the problem cue condition were more likely to refer to statistical concerns (recall the example shown above) regarding the adequacy of David's sample data. We will discuss experimentation in detail in chapter 2 and examine the utility of percentages for summarizing data in chapter 3.

Be certain to note, however, that in both of these groups, the majority of respondents *still* encouraged David to follow his heart when selecting a school rather than to use the statistically more valid opinions of his friends. You should think about why people are often apt to follow the personal and not the statistical, an issue we will come back to throughout the book in examples like this one.

---

cases of agoraphobia, thereby revealing the clinician's therapy to be less efficacious under some circumstances. No doubt you can imagine other occasions where the greater diversity present in a population could be masked within a given sample or samples.

Psychologists rely on inferential statistics to identify which variables cause predictable changes within experiments. How does X (e.g., an old familiar song) influence the occurrence of Y (e.g., retrieval of personal memories related to the time the song was popular)? Relationships like these will be presented in detail in chapter 2, but it is critical for you to appreciate this fact: *Inferential statistics do not prove any relationship among any variables definitively.* As noted earlier, our inductions can sometimes go awry, especially if some critical, influential variable goes unnoticed. This real possibility explains why researchers never assume that the results of any one study or experiment tell the whole story about a given topic. More data must be collected from different samples and new hypotheses must be tested to better understand some behavior. Note, however, that any such understanding is assumed to be temporary—as we will see in chapter 2 when we discuss the research loop of experimentation, new data and new understanding lead to theory revision and development.

Knowledge Base

Each chapter in this book contains one or more "Knowledge Bases." The idea is to increase your base of knowledge in statistics and data analysis, as well as to help you pace your reading of chapters. Take a few minutes and answer the following questions that review the first part of this chapter. Answers to the questions are provided below, so be sure to go back and review anything you miss.

1. True or False: As disciplines, statistics and mathematics study the same topics and answer the same questions.
2. Which of the following are variables, which are constants?
   a. Date of autumn's first frost
   b. Month of the year
   c. Your birth date
   d. π
   e. Score on a political science quiz
3. A developmental psychologist notices that children with older siblings tend to speak 2 to 3 months sooner than children with no siblings. The researcher concludes that sibling imitation is a key component in language acquisition. This is an example of (a) inductive or (b) deductive reasoning.
4. Determine which of the following statements are true and which are false:
   a. Samples try to characterize populations.
   b. Population parameters are always known.
   c. Different samples from the same population are not likely to have the same sample statistics.
   d. Random sampling insures that every member of a population has the same chance as all the others of being selected.
   e. Descriptive statistics allow researchers to determine if a sample adequately characterizes a population.

Answers

1. False
2. a. Variable
   b. Variable
   c. Constant
   d. Constant
   e. Variable
3. Inductive reasoning
4. a. True
   b. False
   c. True
   d. True
   e. False

Discontinuous and Continuous Variables

Now that we have a solid, conceptual background regarding the relationship between samples and populations, we need to refine our understanding of variables and the qualities they can possess. In behavioral science research, there are basically two types of variables—*discontinuous* and *continuous*—used in the design and analysis of experiments.

KEY TERM   A **discontinuous variable** is countable, and it has gaps between each number where no intermediate values can occur.

A discontinuous, sometimes called "discrete," variable is used to characterize data in terms of whole numbers (1, 2, 3, and so on) with no fractional counts occurring between them.

What does this definition mean in concrete terms? Imagine that you calculate the average number of siblings the members of your close circle of friends have, and it turns out to be 1.5 siblings. You know what this number means, that most people you know have one or two brothers or sisters, *not* literally 1 and 1/2 people. People constitute discontinuous data because real gaps occur between them. You may recall hearing about the archetypal American family with 2.5 children from decades past, as well, and you intuitively knew that meant an average of 2 or 3 children per household.

Although discontinuous data can take on the appearance of fractions when mathematical operations—addition, subtraction, multiplication, division—are performed upon them, they are really used to represent countable, whole numbers (e.g., 12 books, 27 cars, 3 professors). Within research projects, discontinuous data often denote categories of participant response (e.g., 1 = yes, 2 = no, 3 = no response), description (e.g., 1 = first year, 2 = sophomore, 3 = junior, 4 = senior, 5 = other), or actual counting of behavior (e.g., a pigeon in a Skinner box pecked a bar 35 times before receiving a food reward).

In contrast, a *continuous variable* fills the gaps between numbers with useable, useful information.

KEY TERM   A **continuous variable** can take on any numerical value on a scale, and there exists an infinite number of values between any two numbers on a scale.

We will be reviewing the types of scales most frequently used by behavioral scientists, most of which are continuous, shortly. For the present, think about some continuous variables you encounter with regularity, such as grade point average or time. If you have ever determined your grade point average (GPA) using the typical scale (i.e., A = 4.0, A− = 3.67, B+ = 3.33, etc.), then you know that it is entirely possible to achieve a GPA of 3.066 for one semester (i.e., the average of 5 course grades, such as B+, B−, A−, C+, and B+). The usual practice is to "round" a GPA like this to two places behind the decimal point, or 3.07 (see Data Box 1.C for guidelines on rounding numbers). As a continuous variable, however, there are an infinite number of fractional values that can occur between a solid A (4.00) and a solid B (3.00) average. In fact, there are an infinite number of possible values between the GPAs of 2.62 and 2.64!

Another continuous variable, time, can be parsed at any number of levels—hours, minutes, seconds, and milliseconds, for example, or as days, weeks, months, years, decades, and so on. Indeed, the only practical limitation on how any continuous variables are studied or reported is the precision of the measuring instruments involved. For most of us, noting that it is quarter past the hour, not 16 minutes and 32 seconds past, is sufficient to tell time, as is relying on a normal watch rather than an atomic clock in Greenwich to track time's passage.

In general, some particular unit of measurement tends to be identified with whatever continuous variable is under study, just as some whole counting unit is reserved for discontinuous variables. In the metric system, for example, the meter is the standard unit of measurement. In the United States, the Imperial system, which uses inches, feet, and yards as the standard units of measurement, has been preserved. Whether we assess the length of some distance using meters or feet, both can measure the same distance with equal accuracy—it is simply a matter of choosing which continuous form of measurement is desired by the user.

Given their fluid nature, continuous variables are often assigned to an interval of values along some scale. After all, if there is an infinite number of values between any two points, we have to assume that our measurement of a continuous variable could be in error; that is, the value identified today could be identified more precisely tomorrow. As a result, when we collect any data we are always approximating continuous variables, not isolating or pinpointing them. Statisticians advocate using what are called *true* or *real limits* to help locate continuous variables.

KEY TERM   **True limits** are a range of values within which a true value for some variable is contained. True limits are calculated by taking the value of a continuous variable and then adding and subtracting one half of the unit of measurement from it. True limits are sometimes called *real limits.*

▽

True limits delineate a range of values where a true value of some variable is presumably located.

Think about the last time you weighed yourself (never a pleasant task for most of us). Let's say that your bathroom scale indicated your weight was 158 pounds—is that your true and actual weight? Probably not. The presence or absence of clothing adds or subtracts weight, as does eating and drinking during the day, or exercising, running, walking, and so forth. Presumably, your weight changes subtly all the time, even before you start worrying about caloric intake. The true limits of your weight would be 157.5 and 158.5, respectively. The former value is called the **lower true limit** because it is one-half pound below the observed value of 158 and the latter is labeled the **upper true limit** because it falls one-half pound above the known value. By removing and adding one-half pound to the weight reported by your bathroom scale, an interval assumed to contain your true weight is created. The upper portion of Figure 1.7 diagrams these true limits around the observed weight.

It follows, of course, that a more precise measuring device would use a smaller unit of measurement. Your family doctor, for instance, might have a very well-calibrated scale, one putting your weight at 158.10 pounds. Is this your true weight? Again, no, but it may be closer to it, as the doctor's scale unit of measurement is 0.05 of a pound. As shown in the lower part of Figure 1.7, we would still need to identify an interval—here, between 158.05 and 158.15 pounds—around the observed value where the true value is

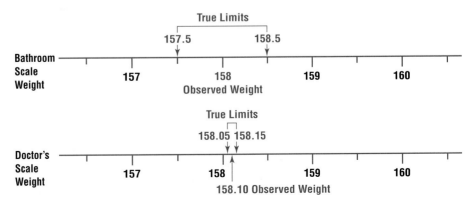

Figure 1.7 True Limits and Different Levels of Precision for Hypothetical Weight

DATA BOX 1.C

Rounding and Continuous Variables

Dividing one number by another is probably the most frequent mathematical operation done in statistical analyses. As you know from personal experience, the product of such division can sometimes be a number with seemingly innumerable places beyond the decimal point. When converted to its decimal form, for example, the simple fraction 1/6 is equal to 1.6666. The line across the top of the last 6 means that this series of numbers is without end. Some calculators, like mine for instance, round off the number stream; that is, the number is expressed to the nearest power of ten. My calculator reports that 1/6 is equal to 0.1667.

Where did that 7 come from? The fourth digit—originally a 6—was rounded up to 7 due to the fifth digit, also a 6 (note that this digit was implied but *not* displayed by the calculator). Whenever you round a number "up" or "down," you do so to what are called *significant digits*.

KEY TERM   **Significant digits** are the numbers beyond a decimal point that indicate the desired accuracy of measurement.

If a cognitive psychologist were reporting the average time it took for participants in an experiment to retrieve some fact from memory, the average could be reported to different significant digits (with corresponding true limits) depending on the desired level of accuracy. If the average retrieval time for a learned fact were 2.36453231 seconds, it could be reported to:

■ The nearest second: 2.4 seconds with true limits of 1.9 and 2.9 seconds (i.e., ± 0.5 of a second)

■ The nearest 1/10th of a second: 2.36 seconds with true limits of 2.41 and 2.31 seconds (i.e., ± 0.05 of a second)

■ The nearest 1/100th of a second: 2.364 with true limits of 2.3690 and 2.3590 (i.e., ± 0.005 of a second)

■ The nearest 1/1000th of a second: 2.3645 with true limits of 2.3650 and 2.3640 (i.e., ± 0.0005 of a second)

How far from the decimal point significant digits are reported is for the researcher to decide. The rules for rounding digits, however, are rather specific, and you should check the rounding performed on the reaction times to make sure you understand them:

1. Decide how many places beyond the decimal point a number should be reported. In general, I recommend that you round to two places beyond the decimal point. The American Psychological Association *Publication Manual* (APA, 1994) advocates that any reported statistic should be shown to two digits beyond what were shown in the raw (i.e., unanalyzed) data.

2. If you are rounding to two places beyond the decimal point, any remainder extending beyond the two places that is *less than* 5 should be dropped. Thus, 28.46455721 would be reported as 28.46.

3. If you are rounding to two places beyond the decimal point and the remainder extending beyond the two places is *greater than* 5, then 1 is added to the last number. Thus, 75.4582163 would be reported as 75.46.

4. If the remainder after the two places beyond the decimal is *exactly* 5, then (a) add 1 to the last digit if it is an *odd* number or (b) drop the remainder if the last digit is an *even* number. Thus, 1.235357 becomes 1.24 because the digit in the second place, a 3, is odd—and 418.72569143 becomes 418.72 because the digit in the second place, a 2, is an even number.

5. There is one final but *critical* rule about rounding: Do not do any rounding until the final calculation for a statistic is completed. *Rounding is reserved for answers or results that are reported.* If you round numbers early in a calculation, you will experience what is called *rounding error*—in your final calculation, your answer will either underestimate or overestimate the actual answer.

assumed to fall. Compare this finer measurement with the original weight shown in the upper portion of Figure 1.7. Both diagrams illustrate the same continuous variable but at different levels of precision; the basic relationships within the data, however, are the same.

True limits draw boundaries for identifying the probable location of any continuous variable. For the present, think about the message conveyed by true limits, that we never know the actual value of any continuous variable, and not the math involved. True limits will concern us again in chapter 3 when we learn to construct graphs.

Writing About Data: Overview and Agenda

When students take a course on statistics and the analysis of data, they sometimes become so involved in the calculation side of things that they lose sight of some other important activities. One of these activities, accurately interpreting the result of a statistical calculation, was discussed earlier. Another we have not discussed in any detail concerns the role writing plays in the calculation, interpretation, and presentation phases of any statistical analysis.

Writing in a statistics class?! Yes, writing. As a psychologist, teacher, and data analyst, I believe that nothing is as important as being able to share the results of your research efforts in writing. In fact, I am a fervent believer that writing should be the first and last consideration of all researchers (Dunn, 1999). I am sure that many readers are surprised to see a discussion of writing in a statistics book, but I hope to change that reaction to understanding and then agreement. In most research efforts (see chapter 2), statistical analyses take place after all the data have been collected. Once the results of the analyses are known, though, what happens next?

Writing is an integral part of the research process.

Researchers are under an obligation to share any new knowledge disclosed by their work with fellow investigators. The usual venues for sharing scholarly work are informal talks with colleagues at one's own college or university, classroom presentations to students, talks at professional conferences, or invited colloquia at other academic institutions. When a researcher prepares a speech for any one of these settings, you can be sure that some written summary of the research will be prepared—an outline will be generated, say, or a draft of the talk or speech will be sketched out. This preliminary writing is a necessary part of the analysis process because it brings clarity to the researcher's thinking, bolsters arguments, and places results in an interpretive framework.

Once the research results are presented to others, the next step is to write them up in the form of a professional publication. In the social sciences, research is usually shared in journal article form. Perhaps you have read a journal article or two in another class, such as research methods or one of psychology's subfields (e.g., social, cognitive, or developmental psychology). Most of the articles published in psychology journals adhere to what is commonly called "APA style," the standardized prose style encouraged by the American Psychological Association. Articles written in this style typically include a short Abstract; an introduction to the article's topic and relevant literature; a Method section detailing what was done; a Results section describing analyses and findings; a Discussion section, which puts the results into context; and a References section citing all works appearing in the article. In fact, Appendix D provides detailed guidance about writing in APA style, with special attention directed toward reporting statistical results (for greater detail on writing in APA style, see also APA, 1994; Dunn, 1999; Smyth, 1996). The main goal of this particular style of writing is a common standard, as well as the clear, coherent, and detailed explication of scientific results to any interested readers, lay or professional.

Although you are presumably enrolled in a statistics class, it is one that is likely to be geared toward the needs and interests of students enrolled in the behavioral sciences, most likely the field of psychology. As a result, you should be very interested in learning how writing can be linked to statistics and data analysis. You should want to know what to say about statistics and how to go about saying it. In most chapters in this book, I will provide concrete guidance about how to put statistical results into words that can be read and understood by others. These "asides" on writing will be highlighted and usually follow the presentation of a statistical test or data presentation. I urge you to give as much attention to how to write about the meaning of any given test statistic as you do its calculation. This extra effort will help you to learn and to retain the various statistical procedures better, and to present them in precise and accurate ways to others.

Scales of Measurement

When data are collected in a piece of research, they are usually based on some form of measurement. By measurement, we refer to the human proclivity to attach meaning to phenomena we do not yet understand. Whether we measure some aspect of nature in the physical world or people's beliefs in the social world, we try to categorize what we do not understand in light of what we do. Such measurement can involve attaching qualitative (descriptive) or quantitative (numerical) meaning to *stimuli*—observations, objects, places, events, ideas, or constructs—in some systematic way.

KEY TERM   **Stimuli** are aspects of the outside world that affect behavior or conscious experience. *Stimulus* is the singular form of stimuli.

Whatever system is used to organize the measurement of stimuli, it should be both valid and reliable, two methodological requirements we will review in detail in chapter 2.

Some forms of measurement readily lend themselves to statistical analysis but others do not, necessitating a different approach. When you completed various standardized intelligence tests during your elementary and secondary school years, some number—often an IQ score—was used to denote your measured intellectual ability. Such scores are organized in any number of ways, routinely reported in various ranges—high, average, and low, for example—and compared with one another on dimensions such as gender, family structure, and household income, to name but a few possibilities. Other numbers cannot be analyzed so easily (e.g., the number on a license plate, an individual's place in a line of people outside a theater, the number on a dormitory room door). Although these numbers identify, order, and locate, they lack deeper meanings or associations beyond a superficial level. Thus, it is important to recognize that forms of measurement provide greater or lesser degrees of information, and that they are more applicable to some tasks than to others.

Behavioral scientists rely on four scales of measurement in their research. These scales are usually called *nominal, ordinal, interval,* and *ratio.* Nominal and ordinal scales are qualitative in nature, where interval and ratio scales are exclusively quantitative. As you read about these scales and supporting examples, take careful note of their content, as well as when and how they can be used in research.

Symbols—letters or figures—designating a quantity or an operation are important to scales of measurement. Mathematical symbols will begin to appear more frequently in this and later chapters. Table 1.1 defines the basic mathematical symbols you will need to do the reading and the calculations in this book. You may not have used your math skills for quite some time, so a quick glance at Table 1.1 can serve as a good refresher (remember to consult Appendix A if you need additional help or greater detail). Statistical symbols will be introduced, defined, and explained one or two at a time later in this chapter and in subsequent chapters.

Table 1.1   Common Mathematical Symbols, Their Operations, and Supporting Examples

Mathematical Symbol	Operation	Example
$+$	addition	$5 + 3 = 8$
$-$	subtraction	$10 - 5 = 5$
$\times, (\ )$	multiplication	$5 \times 4 = 20, 8(7) = 56$
$\div, /$	division	$6 \div 2 = 3, 100/5 = 20$
$<$	less than	$2 < 3$
$>$	greater than	$7 > 5$
$\leq$	less than or equal to	$3.49 \leq 3.50$
$\geq$	greater than or equal to	$3.65 \geq 3.642$
$\neq$	not equal to	$34 \neq 18$
$\cong$	approximately equal to	$1.2123 \cong 1.21$

Nominal Scales

When an observation is simply given a name, a label, or otherwise classified, a nominal scale is being used. To be sure, nominal scales use numbers, but these numbers are not in any mathematical relationship with one another.

KEY TERM   A **nominal scale** uses numbers to identify qualitative differences among measurements. The measurements made by a nominal scale are names, labels, or categories, and no quantitative distinctions can be drawn among them.

Nominal scales are actually much more common to your experience than you realize. Can you recall the last time you purchased an appliance or a piece of stereo equipment? You probably filled out a warranty card and, while doing so, answered a variety of questions that superficially appeared to have little to do with the item. Typical questions concern gender ("Are you male or female?"), income ("Which of the following ranges best categorizes your household income?"), and hobbies ("Please check any of the below activities you do during your leisure time"). You probably checked a few boxes, dropped the card into the mail, and quickly forgot about it. The manufacturer, however, was deeply interested in these facts and quickly converted them into numerical equivalents: You could be a female (a 2 was checked) earning between $30,000.00 and $35,000.00 a year (a 4 was checked) who likes skiing (5), bodysurfing (12), and macramé (27). The information you provided, along with that of hundreds or thousands of other consumers, is summarized so that a profile of buyers can help the manufacturer target future advertising (i.e., toward who is or is not purchasing the product).

The point here is that nominal information can be easily coded (e.g., 1 = male, 2 = female), tallied (i.e., 4,000 women and 1,800 men bought the product in March last year), and interpreted (e.g., women buy the product more than men do). No information is lost in this process; rather, it is converted into numbers for a quick, summary review. These numbers can then be stored in computer files for examination, classification, and categorization.

Nominal scales dealing with individuals' characteristics are often used in psychological research. Gender is nominally scaled, as are race, ethnicity, religion, and many other variables. Indeed, nominal scaling can be performed on data that were collected using another scale. Imagine that we have a group of male and female college students answer a series of questions and complete a variety of psychological batteries dealing

Nominal scales name things.

Table 1.2   Nominal Scaling of Gender-Related Behavior

	Androgynous	Masculine	Feminine	Undifferentiated	Total
Participant gender					
Females	54	28	64	56	202
Males	64	68	16	50	198

Note: Each observation within a category represents one hypothetical respondent. The hypothetical sample has a total of 400 respondents.

with gender issues. Following research on androgyny, the combination of masculine and feminine psychological characteristics found in some individuals, we could categorize each of the respondents according to their gender-related responses to the measures (e.g., Bem, 1977; Spence & Helmreich, 1978). The standard classifications for gender-related behaviors are masculine, feminine, androgynous, and undifferentiated (i.e., individuals who do not think of themselves in gender-related ways).

Table 1.2 shows how the participants in this hypothetical project on gender could be categorized nominally. Notice that once a respondent is categorized, he or she can be placed in one and only one nominal category. Thus, for example, a given male participant could *not* be androgynous and masculine—he can appear in one category or the other. Not surprisingly, perhaps, there are more "masculine" males than females (i.e., 68 vs. 28) and more "feminine" females than males (i.e., 64 vs. 16). Interestingly, however, there are more androgynous males than females, but the reverse holds true for those students categorized as undifferentiated.

If pressed about a quantitative dimension for nominal scales, it is true that they possess an equivalence ($=$) or a nonequivalence ($\neq$) dimension. An observation is either equivalent to the others in a category, so that it is then counted as being part of that category, or not; if not, then it is included in another category. If one were studying smoking behavior among preadolescents, for example, a given participant could be categorized as "male smoker," "male nonsmoker," "female smoker," or "female nonsmoker." A 10-year-old female who smoked would be placed in the "female smoker" category—she is equivalent to the observation therein and not equivalent to any of the remaining three categories. Note also that $=$ and $\neq$ are effectively "all or nothing" for categorization purposes, so that a male smoker is $\neq$ to a female smoker. The male smoker is not "greater than" ($>$) or "less than" ($<$) the female smoker, however. Such ordering distinctions require an ordinal scale of measurement.

Ordinal Scales

When the measurement of an observation involves ranking or ordering based on an underlying dimension, an ordinal scale is being used.

KEY TERM   An **ordinal scale** ranks or orders observations based on whether they are greater than or less than one another. Ordinal scales do not provide information about how close or distant observations are from one another.

Ordinal scales rank or order things.

When we observe who graduated as valedictorian and salutatorian of a high school class, for example, we learn who had the highest and second highest GPA. We do not usually learn mathematically how far apart the GPAs of valedictorian and the salutatorian were from one another, or what common or disparate classes they took that contributed to their standings. We only know who had the highest and the next highest academic performance based on the underlying dimension of GPA.

Table 1.3   Ordinal Scaling—The Top Ten Films of All Time as Ranked by Two Friends

Top Ten Films	Friend 1's Rankings	Friend 2's Rankings
1. Citizen Kane	5	1
2. Casablanca	7	3
3. The Godfather	2	2
4. Gone with the Wind	6	9
5. Lawrence of Arabia	8	4
6. The Wizard of Oz	1	7
7. The Graduate	3	6
8. On the Waterfront	10	10
9. Schindler's List	4	5
10. Singin' in the Rain	9	8

Note: A rank of 1 refers to the most highly regarded film, a 2 the second most highly regarded film, and so on.

Source: American Film Institute (AFI)

Anytime we are presented with data pointing to who was fastest (or slowest) in a race, scored 12th highest on an exam, expressed the strongest reservations about a decision, won third place in a contest, or was least distressed by witnessing an accident, ordinal measurement is being used. The observations are compared to one another in terms of their greater or lesser magnitudes, so that the mathematical operations used for ordinal scaling are $>$ and $<$, respectively. These operations illustrate a modest improvement over nominal scaling because the observations are evaluated on one dimension as opposed to an either–or process of categorization.

Here is a different, but straightforward, example of a simple ordinal scale. Suppose you and a friend are discussing a recently published list of the top ten films of all time. It turns out you both have seen all ten, so you decide to determine your own rankings for the films; that is, which film did you like the most, second most, and so on. Table 1.3 illustrates (in order) the published list of the American Film Institute's (AFI) top 10 films of all time and the respective rankings of these same films by two friends. As you can see, the published ranking serves as the baseline data and the respective ordinal rankings of the two friends illustrate the deviations in liking from this list. The issue is not whose film taste is better or worse, rather that the same stimuli can be ordered differently by different people.

A modest irony associated with ordinal scaling is that we often assign the person (or stimulus) with the highest score or best performance on a given dimension a 1, which is actually the lowest score. In the earlier example concerning the valedictorian and the salutatorian, the two persons with the highest GPA (≤ 4.00, presumably) received a rank of 1 and 2, respectively. Does that "the highest score is first" irony matter? Not at all, just as long as the individuals performing the ranking use the system consistently. As casual observers, we are all quite familiar with the intent of most ordinal rankings, implicitly understand the irony involved, and take virtually no notice of it. Greater degrees of precision in measurement, however, are associated with interval and ratio scales.

Interval Scales

Interval scales are used when the distance between observations is measurable, equal, and ordinal, but a true zero point is unnecessary. What is a true zero point? A true zero point occurs when a scale cannot measure any observations or ratings at or below the scale's value of 0.

KEY TERM   An **interval scale** is quantitative, contains measurably equal distances between observations, but lacks a true zero point.

The basic mathematical operations of addition, subtraction, multiplication, and division can be performed on data collected from interval scales. When a zero point appears on an interval scale, however, its placement does not mean that information stops at that point. Think about it: If you have ever lived through a cold winter, you know that temperature does not stop being meaningful at 0° Fahrenheit. The recorded temperature can and often does fall below 0°, so that it becomes colder still. Indeed, "below zero" measurement entails the use of negative numbers (e.g., "With the wind chill, it was −5° below 0° last night").

▽

Interval scales are quantitative measures that lack a true zero.

The Fahrenheit scale found on most thermometers is an example of an interval scale you know well. Each degree entry on a thermometer is equally far apart from every other degree, a property that renders the relationships among temperatures meaningful. A temperature of 62° is objectively higher (and warmer) than 60°, and the same 2° differences exists between 53° and 55°—temperatures that are in turn cooler than the first pair.

Despite what appears to be a clear mathematical relationship in interval data, however, one cannot claim that one measure is twice or three times the magnitude of another. Though it is colder, a 20° winter day in Vermont is not 3 times colder than a 60° day in Georgia, for example. A person who receives a score of 50 on a scale that measures depressive symptoms is clearly at greater risk for depression than another person with a score of 25, but it would be incorrect to say that one is "twice as depressed as the other" (e.g., Radloff, 1977). The question becomes how much colder is one temperature than another or how much of a difference in risk for depression is illustrated by disparate scores on a standardized measure. Whether a meteorologist or a psychologist, a researcher must present interval scale results in ways that are true to the data—ordered mathematical relationships are fine, but they cannot be based on ratios.

Within behavioral science research, many personality scales, intelligence (IQ) measures, educational tests, and rating scales use an interval scale. Whether standardized or not, practically all the tests, quizzes, and exams that you have completed throughout your education are based on an interval scale of some type. Here is an important issue to think about: If an individual receives a score of 0 on a self-esteem scale or the equivalent score on a test of verbal skills, does such performance necessarily imply the complete absence of the relevant personality trait or verbal ability? Certainly not. Such performance simply indicates low—but not *no*—verbal ability, as well as very low levels of self-esteem. On an interval scale, then, a measure of 0 does not mean that the phenomenon being measured is absent. After all, the scale being used might not be sensitive enough to adequately measure the phenomenon of interest. A measurement of 0 does take on a precise meaning when appearing on a ratio scale, however.

Ratio Scales

The ratio scale incorporates all of the properties found in the previous three scales, as well as an absolute zero point.

KEY TERM   A **ratio scale** ranks observations, contains equal and meaningful intervals, and has a true zero point.

In the case of a ratio scale, a zero point is meaningful because it indicates a true absence of information. For instance, the zero measurement on a ruler means that there is no object being measured, just as a reading of 0 miles per hour (mph) on a speedometer indicates that the automobile is not in motion. The existence of a true zero point on a ratio scale enables users to describe measurements in terms of numerical ratios. Weight is a ratio scale, so that a 2-ton object is to a 1-ton object as a 4-ton object is to a 2-ton object (i.e., each is twice the weight of the other). Similarly, where height is concerned, a 6-ft person is twice as tall as a 3-ft person. The same relationship among ratios of length can be demonstrated on any standard yardstick or, for that matter, a more precise measuring device, such as a micrometer.

▽

Ratio scales are quantitative measures that have a true zero.

Most scales used by behavioral scientists and most used throughout this book turn out to be interval scales. Although nominal and ordinal scales are used in research, they lend themselves to a relatively small number of statistical tests (see chapter 14). Ratio scales are used less frequently in behavioral research than interval scales, but they are by no means rarities. Anytime a project involves the measurement of reaction time, the amplitude of sound or the intensity of light, or familiar measures such as height or weight or even the number of cigarettes smoked, a ratio scale is presumably being used.

Writing About Scales

Our review of the scales moved from the simplest variety to the most complex form of measurement. Table 1.4 summarizes the main points associated with the four scales of measurement. Nominal scales provide the least amount of information for researchers (see the arrow pointing up to the top left side of Table 1.4) and ratio scales provide the most (see the corresponding arrow pointing downward). As noted on the right side of Table 1.4, nominal and ordinal scales tend to identify qualitative relationships within data while interval and ratio scales focus on quantitative ones. The defining features of each scale, as well as representative examples, are presented in the center of Table 1.4.

I recommend that you refer back to Table 1.4 when preparing to describe a scale within a paper or a presentation, or even when solving a statistics problem. It is essential

Table 1.4   Comparing Qualities of Measurement Scales

	Scale Name	Defining Features	Examples	
	Nominal	Names, labels, categories Qualitative operations: =, ≠	Gender (1 = male, 2 = female) Ethnicity or religion of person Smoker vs. nonsmoker	More Qualitative

Provide Less Information	*Ordinal*	Observations ordered or ranked
		Qualitative operations: <, >
			Class rank (1st, 2nd, 3rd, 4th)
			Rank on personality measure
			    (high vs. low optimism)
			Self-esteem scale scores (10 = high
			    self-esteem, 1 = low self-esteem)	

	Interval	Order or ranking; equal intervals
		    between observations; no true zero
		    point
		Quantitative operations: +, −, ×, ÷
			Fahrenheit temperature
			Most standardized psychological tests
			    score on a measure of verbal ability
			IQ score	

Provide More Information	*Ratio*	Order or ranking; equal intervals
		    between observations; true zero
		    point
		Quantitative operations: +, −, ×, ÷
			Weight, height, reaction time,
			    number of bar presses, amplitude
			    of sound, intensity of light, speed
				More Quantitative

that you have a firm grasp of what sort of data a scale measures, as well as the operations that can be conducted on those data, before you write about them. Sometimes it is very clear which of the four scale types a given measure falls under, but other times a reader of the research literature or even an investigator will not be so certain.

Consider an example illustrating this uncertainty: When children are screened for special academic or remedial programs, various intelligence tests and achievement measures are used to assess their intellectual abilities. Most educators and administrators believe that such tests are interval scales but, oddly, they are often used as ordinal measures. Students with a measured IQ score of 130 are placed in the gifted program, for example, while those with an IQ of 85 or less end up in a remedial class. What happens to a child with an IQ of 129 or 86? Nothing, really; that is, the child remains in the regular classroom environment, receiving neither enrichment nor remediation. An observer might reasonably ask if a person with an IQ of 129 is *really* less gifted than the individual with an IQ of 130? Does it follow that a child with an IQ of 86 is at less risk educationally than children with 1 IQ point below her? Again, the key is knowing *what* a given scale is supposed to measure and *how* that measure is being used.

When writing about a scale, be sure to let the reader know if the scale was created previously for another purpose—it may be a standardized test or an existing personality measure—by providing a reference (see Appendix D). If the scale is unique to your piece of research, briefly describe how and why it was created. In either of these cases, readers will understand your research better if you provide detailed information about the scale you used. Be sure to note how many items appear on the scale, if some numerical rating or ranking was used (i.e., did respondents circle numbers? rank order preferences?), the range of scale scores (high to low), as well as the average given (if appropriate). Most of this information is germane to interval and ratio scales, of course. If you used a nominal or an ordinal scale, be sure to describe what was categorized or ranked, and how the procedure was performed on the data. If possible, create a table or a figure to summarize the relationships in the scale data (see chapter 3 for suggestions on pictorial representations).

One of the most helpful things you can do when writing about a particular scale is to share an item or two from it with readers. If items from the scale are shown, readers will gain a better sense of what it is designed to measure, as well as an appreciation of the respondents' point of view when completing it. Unless you are writing about a very familiar scale (e.g., the Scholastic Aptitude Test [SAT]), it is likely that most readers will not know the scale's characteristics. If there is nothing memorable to latch on to, lack of familiarity with a scale can quickly lead to reader disinterest or mild confusion. This problem is especially true in the psychological literature, where scales are routinely referred to by their acronyms (e.g., CES-D) instead of their actual names (e.g., The Center for Epidemiological Studies Depression Scale; Radloff, 1977). The shorthand of acronyms saves time and printed space, but their heuristic value as memory aids does little good for people who are unfamiliar with them.

Here is a description of the CES-D, an interval scale, excerpted from the Method section of an empirical article (Dunn, 1996, p. 290):

> **Depression.** Depressive symptomatology was assessed using the Center for Epidemiological Studies Depression Scale (CES-D; Radloff, 1977), a general measure of depressed affect or mood designed for use with cross-sectional samples in survey research. The CES-D's 20 items are scored on a 4-point scale (0 to 3) that measures the frequency of a symptom's occurrence during the previous week (e.g., "My sleep was restless"). Scores can range from 0 to 60 (present sample range was 0 to 41), and higher scores reflect a greater prevalence of depressive symptoms....

Strive to give readers sufficient detail about whatever measures you employ or analyze. Even a relatively brief description of a scale can give readers a coherent picture of who should complete the scale, how the scale is used and scored, and what a given item from it is like.

Shorter scales, those containing only an item or two, can be included in their entirety in any report. If interpersonal attraction were the topic of the study, the major question of interest might be: "Using the following rating scale, indicate the attractiveness of the person you just met." Such scales typically use a 1 ("not at all attractive") to 7 ("very attractive") rating scheme, where higher numbers on the scale correspond to higher levels of perceived attractiveness. Circling the number 4 on this scale would suggest a neutral level rating. Note that the same scale could use a rating system of -3 ("not at all attractive") to $+3$ ("very attractive"), where 0 would be the neutral midpoint. As you can see, the quantitative relationship among the numbers on the scale matters, but the particular numbers appearing on the scale do not—any numbers would do, as long as their meaning is clear to respondents (i.e., the numbers are ordered with equal intervals between them).

Knowledge Base

1. Indicate which of the following variables is discontinuous and which is continuous.
   a. Number of items selected from a menu
   b. Rated satisfaction with menu items
   c. Number of rats run in an experimental maze
   d. Volume gauge on a stereo system
   e. Car speedometer
2. Calculate the true limits for the following:
   a. 16 lb
   b. 27 minutes
3. Identify which scale of measurement best describes the following:
   a. Need for acceptance by others
   b. Democrat
   c. Second place in a pie eating contest
   d. Sensitivity to light

Answers

1. a. Discontinuous
   b. Continuous
   c. Discontinuous
   d. Continuous
   e. Continuous
2. a. 15.5 lb
   b. 16.5 lb, 26.5 minutes, 27.50 minutes
3. a. Interval
   b. Nominal
   c. Ordinal
   d. Ratio

Overview of Statistical Notation

Earlier in this chapter, learning statistics was described as being similar to learning a foreign language. We now need to learn the vernacular—the everyday, distinctive language—of statistics. This language relies on two elements that work in concert with one

Table 1.5   The Four Basic Statistical Symbols

Symbol	Meaning
X, Y	Variable X, variable Y
N	Total number of observations
Σ	To sum or the sum of

another: symbols and numbers. Numbers are familiar to you, but the symbols we will learn are probably new to you. Symbols are used in statistical formulas as directions or guidelines, nothing more. These symbols are usually shorthand for specific mathematical operations, the majority of which will be either familiar to you or very easy to learn. At other times, the symbols will serve as variables that can take on different values.

As you read this section of the chapter, make a concerted effort to learn what the symbols mean and how they are used. Again, your goal is to immerse yourself in the symbolic language of statistics so that it becomes second nature to you. Learning the rudiments of this language will enable you to broaden your vocabulary, so to speak, as you read and learn from subsequent chapters.

There are four basic symbols that appear throughout the various formulas presented in this book and they are highlighted in Table 1.5. In the future, refer back to this table when you need a quick summary. These symbols are the real "workhorses" of data analysis. As you study these symbols and the accompanying statistical notation, imagine that the numbers used to illustrate them are from interval or ratio scales.

Variables *X* and *Y*.   The first two symbols, X and Y, are used to represent variables, but usually indicate different types of information.

KEY TERM   *X* and *Y* are **variables** that take on the values of some set of observations or data.

Typically, these variables will be used to refer to the data collected in an experiment. Variable X could refer to friendly comments and Y could indicate the amount of time spent smiling in a study on peer friendships among adolescents. Variable X will be used more frequently than Y, as most formulas contain only one variable, but occasionally they will be used together in the same formula.

Notice that when they stand alone, X or Y refers to a set of data, not necessarily an individual observation. There is a particular notation for illustrating the scores or observations that comprise X. To indicate an observation within X, we use X_i, where the subscript i indicates a specific observed value for X. If there were five scores in X, say, 10, 14, 20, 21, and 36, these scores could be represented as X_1, X_2, X_3, X_4, and X_5. That is,

$$X_1 = 10, X_2 = 14, X_3 = 20, X_4 = 21, X_5 = 36.$$

In this case, X refers to the object being measured and the numbers 1 to 5 indicate the individual observations or participants comprising the data set of X. We can do the same with variable Y. Variable Y could indicate, say, a set of data with three observations:

$$Y_1 = 4, Y_2 = 7, Y_3 = 10.$$

In a large set of data collected for a study, there could be two different measures taken from each participant (i.e., X_i and Y_i). Data from the second participant in this study could then be referred to as X_2 and Y_2.

Please be aware that there is nothing magical about X or Y. Their use as variables is simply a convention (no doubt you remember using x in algebra). If you wished to do so, you could use letters like K and G in place of X and Y. You could even employ Z, the *de facto* variable of choice in those rare instances where a third variable is needed.

Total Observations Are Equal to N.　　The third basic symbol identifies the number of observations or participants available in a data set or for a particular analysis.

　　N signifies the total number of observations in a set of data.

In the data sets for X and Y we just examined, $N = 5$ and $N = 3$, respectively. That is, there were 5 scores for X and three scores for Y, or one from each participant in the two data sets. There might be 75 peers in the friendship study noted above, so $N = 75$. If there were 30 students enrolled in your statistics class, then $N = 30$, and so on. The symbol N always signifies the total number of observations within some data set.

Summation Rules.　　Unless you know the Greek alphabet, the fourth symbol will be new to you. In statistics, the symbol Σ (pronounced "sigma") means "to sum." In general, when you see the Σ before a string of numbers, you should add them together. If we use the observations for X from above, we can use Σ to sum them as follows:

$$\Sigma X = X_1 + X_2 + X_3 + X_4 + X_5.$$

This is the same as saying:

$$\Sigma X = 10 + 14 + 20 + 21 + 36.$$

If so, then,

$$\Sigma X = 101.$$

Take a moment and check your understanding of how Σ is used. Go back and perform the summation for the Y observations shown above (be sure to write out the individual observations with subscripts for Y, the actual scores for Y, and then the sum of Y):

$$\Sigma Y =$$

$$\Sigma Y =$$

$$\Sigma Y =$$

What was your answer? The sum of Y, or ΣY, is equal to 21. If you made an error, please go back and review the example for X, and then redo the summation for Y until you understand how to obtain the answer.

There is a slightly more formal way to express summation notation. The additional information actually makes the procedure for adding a string of numbers much easier to follow as long as you keep the basic process we covered in mind. It is also true that the additional notation will prove to be useful in more advanced calculations later on. For the present, imagine a new data set for X and that we want to sum all of the observations within it together. Another way to represent the summation would be:

$$X_1 + X_2 + X_3 + \cdots + X_N.$$

That is, all of the values of X—from the first value (X_1) to the last or Nth value (X_N)—must be added together, starting with $i = 1$. If there were six observations in X, they could be $X_1 = 5$, $X_2 = 9$, $X_3 = 11$, $X_4 = 9$, $X_5 = 6$, and $X_6 = 2$. The summation is written as

$$\sum_{i=1}^{N} X_i = 5 + 9 + 11 + 9 + 6 + 2 = 42.$$

Do you see the notations above and below the sigma? The $i = 1$ notation below the sigma means i adopts successive values from 1, 2, 3, 4, and so on up to N, the last observation in the data set, which appears at the top of the summation sign. In simple, descriptive terms, this summation means: "Add all the observations from $i = 1$ (X_1) through $i = N$ (X_N) together."

Of course, you will not always want to sum all the values within a data set. Many times, you will need to work with only a portion of the observations available. The statistical notation is flexible here, as well. Imagine that you were interested in summing only the first three numbers in the data set for X. This time, the summation notation would be written as

$$\sum_{i=1}^{3} X_i = X_1 + X_2 + X_3$$

Notice that now $i = 1$ (X_1) to $i = 3$ (X_3), not N. In turn, this means summing the first three observations in the data set, or

$$\sum_{i=1}^{3} X_i = 5 + 9 + 11 = 25.$$

What if the summation sign directs you to add only selected observations within the data set? Try solving this summation:

$$\sum_{i=3}^{4} X_i =$$

This time, you would start at $i = 3$ (X_3) and add it to $i = 4$ (X_4). Be sure that you understand how to read the notation, which is like a guidepost. You begin with the information under the summation sign ("start at $i = 3$") and add the observations until you reach the end point indicated above the sign ("include but stop at $i = 4$"). The answer to the above summation is 20. Was your sum correct? If not, please reread the section on summation before proceeding with the rest of the chapter.

What To Do When: Mathematical Rules of Priority

If you are like most people, you learned how to solve math equations—algebraic expressions containing numbers and symbols—once upon a time. It has probably been a while, however, and you may have forgotten what is variously called the "order of operations" or "mathematical rules of priority" for solving equations. "Order" and "priority" here mean that some actions must occur ahead of others when any statistical calculation is being performed. As you will see, some equations are simple and they contain very few operations. Other equations, however, have multiple operations—so many, in fact, that each must be done in a particular sequence.

The priority rules are actually straightforward and easy to follow, but please understand that they must be followed to the letter. In other words, some parts of an equation *must* be solved before others. If you fail to follow the priority guidelines by completing operations that should come later rather than sooner, your answer to the equation will be wrong. It is also the case that you will want to approach each equation you encounter in the same way; that is, you will want to identify which operation must be done first, which second, and so on. In truth, once you begin to view statistical equations in terms of the operations that comprise them, they will rarely seem complicated or threatening. You will know what to do because the rules of priority will guide you—and you will consistently solve the equation correctly. Thus, let me encourage you to "internalize" these rules as soon as possible, and to refer back to this section of the text whenever necessary.

In order to obtain a correct answer, some parts of an equation must be solved before others.

Always remember when solving an equation to:

1. Work from the left to the right.
2. Complete calculations that appear inside parentheses before those outside parentheses.

In addition, perform mathematical operations in this order:

1. Square a number, raise a number to another exponent, or take the square root of a number.
2. Change a number from positive to negative, or vice versa.
3. Multiply and/or divide a number. If multiplication and/or division must be done more than once in an equation, these operations should be done from the left to the right in the equation.
4. Add and/or subtract a number.

Before proceeding, please take a moment and read the rules a second time. Once you have done so, we can illustrate each rule using both symbols and numbers.

In general, you should do the calculations that begin on the left of an equation and work your way to the right. Please note that I wrote "in general," not "always." Further, we are usually solving for some variable. Consider this equation, where you would solve for X:

$$X = (2 + 6)^2 - 12 \times \frac{10}{5}.$$

You would begin at the left, which happens to contain an operation in parentheses. So, you would first perform the operation (here, addition) inside the parentheses,

$$X = (8)^2 - 12 \times \frac{10}{5}.$$

Then, you would square the value as indicated, recalling that any squares or exponents are next in priority,

$$X = 64 - 12 \times \frac{10}{5}.$$

In the next step, you would perform the multiplication and division. In this case, the division would take place first,

$$X = 64 - 12 \times 2,$$

then the multiplication,

$$X = 64 - 24.$$

Subtraction comes last, so you would take 24 from 64. The solution to the equation is the number 40, or $X = 40$.

Let's try another, one involving negative numbers and a square root. Here is the equation,

$$Y = \sqrt{4} - (-12 + 3).$$

Although we work from the left to the right, operations in parentheses still take precedence over the square root. A negative number is also present inside the parentheses, so you must remember that a larger negative number added to a smaller positive number results in a negative number, or

$$Y = \sqrt{4} - (-9).$$

In the next step, we can do the square root, which takes precedence over the negation,

$$Y = 2 - (-9).$$

The negation, the changing of two negative signs to a positive sign, follows,

$$Y = 2 + 9.$$

Finally, we finish the problem with addition for,

$$Y = 11.$$

If you had any difficulty with these mathematical operations—either understanding the priority of some operations over others or just doing the operations—take a few minutes and review the two sample equations. Before you do so, though, you might want to take a look at Table 1.6, which contains isolated examples of mathematical operations in order of their priority.

Up to this point, basic statistical notation, the priority rules, and some sample equations have been reviewed. One last step remains, which is to combine the statistical notation and priority rules into a few sample equations. Equations like these will recur throughout the text, but it is a good idea for you to begin to solve them now, so that their reintroduction in subsequent chapters will be familiar, not a surprise. I do *not* expect you to memorize what follows, rather I want you to *focus on understanding how the symbols and numbers work together to produce the answers.* Once you understand how these components work together in any given equation, you will be able to solve it with little or no difficulty.

Assume that you have two sets of data, X and Y, and each one contains four values.

$$X_1 = 5, \qquad Y_1 = 4,$$

$$X_2 = 3, \qquad Y_2 = 7,$$

$$X_3 = 6, \qquad Y_3 = 5,$$

$$X_4 = 9, \qquad Y_4 = 2.$$

Table 1.6   Review of Mathematical Operations in Order of Priority

Operation	Operator Format	Sample Operation
Squares, exponents, and square roots	X^2 Y^5 $\sqrt{X}$	$7^2 = 49$ $3^5 = 243$ $\sqrt{36} = 6$
Negation	$-Y$ $-(X)$ $(-X)(Y)$ $(-X)(-Y)$	-10 $-(5) = -5$ $(-4)(5) = -20$ $(-4)(-3) = 12$
Multiplication	$X \times Y$ $X(Y)$ $(X)(Y)$	$2 \times 8 = 16$ $8(7) = 56$ $(2)(15) = 30$
and		
Division	$X \div Y$ X/Y $(X + Y)/Z$	$8 \div 5 = 1.60$ $10/2 = 5$ $(10 + 8)/3 = 6$
Addition and Subtraction	$X + Y$ $X - Y$	$9 + 5 = 14$ $9 - 5 = 4$

Note: Entries are in order of priority, from higher to lower operations.

Although you already know the basic summation rule, we will repeat it here for both data sets,

$$\sum X = X_1 + X_2 + X_3 + X_4,$$

$$\sum X = 5 + 3 + 6 + 9,$$

$$\sum X = 23,$$

$$\sum Y = Y_1 + Y_2 + Y_3 + Y_4,$$

$$\sum Y = 4 + 7 + 5 + 2,$$

$$\sum Y = 18.$$

What if we squared each of the observations in a data set and then summed them? Here is what it would look like for X,

$$\sum X^2 = X_1^2 + X_2^2 + X_3^2 + X_4^2,$$

$$\sum X^2 = 5^2 + 3^2 + 6^2 + 9^2,$$

$$\sum X^2 = 25 + 9 + 36 + 81,$$

$$\sum X^2 = 151,$$

and for Y,

$$\sum Y^2 = Y_1^2 + Y_2^2 + Y_3^2 + Y_4^2,$$

$$\sum Y^2 = 4^2 + 7^2 + 5^2 + 2^2,$$

$$\sum Y^2 = 16 + 49 + 25 + 4,$$

$$\sum Y^2 = 94.$$

These are called "the sum of the squared values of X" and "the sum of the squared values of Y," respectively.

Another alternative is to sum the observations in the data sets and to then square the sum (recall that we previously determined the sums of X and Y). These products are the "sum of X squared" and "the sum of Y squared." For data set X it looks like,

$$(\sum X)^2 = (X_1 + X_2 + X_3 + X_4)^2,$$

$$(\sum X)^2 = (23)^2,$$

$$(\sum X)^2 = 529,$$

and for data set Y,

$$(\sum Y)^2 = (Y_1 + Y_2 + Y_3 + Y_4)^2,$$

$$(\sum Y)^2 = (18)^2,$$

$$(\sum Y)^2 = 324.$$

Please note that the sum of the squared values of X is *not* equal to the sum of X squared (nor, obviously, is the sum of the squared values of Y equal to the sum of Y squared). In the case of X, the rule is presented symbolically as:

$$\sum X^2 \neq (\sum X)^2.$$

In the data set for X we just reviewed, the product of the former is equal to 151, while the latter is 529. This is an important rule, one that we will revisit frequently in the course of learning statistical formulas. Learning it now will save you heartache, confusion, and redoing calculations later.

We can also perform what is called the "sum of the cross products," which uses multiplication.

$$\sum XY = X_1 Y_1 + X_2 Y_2 + X_3 Y_3 + X_4 Y_4,$$

$$\sum XY = 5(4) + 3(7) + 6(5) + 9(2),$$

$$\sum XY = 20 + 21 + 30 + 18,$$

$$\sum XY = 89.$$

Finally, we can produce what is called the "product of two sums" through multiplication.

$$(\sum X)(\sum Y) = (23)(18),$$

$$(\sum X)(\sum Y) = 414.$$

DATA BOX 1.D

The Size of Numbers Is Relative

Numbers are relative. The word myriad is related to the Greek words for both countless and 10,000. And the Egyptian hieroglyphic for a million was the god for air and space.

The Egyptian hieroglyph for one million.

MILLION (10^6)
1,000,000
BILLION (10^9)
1,000,000,000
TRILLION (10^{12})
1,000,000,000,000
DECILLION (10^{33})
1,000,000,000,000,000,000,000,000,000,000,000
GOOGOL (10^{100})
10,000,000,000,000,000,000,000,000,000,000,000-
000,000,000,000,000,000,000,000,000,000,000-
000,000,000,000,000,000,000,000,000,000,000
GOOGOLPLEX ($10^{(10^{100})}$)

The total number of elementary particles in the known universe is about 10^{100}, or less than a googol. How big is a googolplex? Write the numeral 1 followed by a letter-sized page of zeros. Continue writing zeros until you have a stack of paper that reaches the moon.

[Excerpted from "A Billion, A Trillion, Whatever" by Michael T. Kaufman. *The New York Times*, Sunday, October 18, 1998; Week in Review, Section 4, page 2.]

Mise En Place

When French chefs cook, they rely on a preparation technique known as **mise en place** (pronounced "meeze ehn plass"), which literally means "everything in its place." Before any recipe is executed, all the raw materials are gathered, chopped, diced, or otherwise readied, and then these ingredients are lined up in the order in which they will be used for cooking. In much the same way, you should have all of your statistical materials ready to go before you begin any data analyses. That is, the data should be collected and organized, appropriate formulas or procedures should be selected, and paper, sharp pencils, and a well-lighted working area set up.

The mise en place philosophy toward doing statistics also entails a regular rhythm, a standard routine, to your work. You should set out some time each day to study this book and to do your homework. I can guarantee you that you will learn more and perform better in your class if your reading, studying, and homework are done consistently. I can also assure you that you will experience difficulty if you do the work occasionally, haphazardly, or at the last minute. Again, your goal should be to understand and retain what you learn about statistics for the long term (i.e., future classes, research projects, career), not the short term (i.e., tomorrow's class, the quiz on Friday, next week's exam). Steady work on statistics will pay off, so before you start to "cook" with your statistics, repeat the mantra to yourself, "mise en place, mise en place."

About Calculators

Many years ago, I received a very expensive, programmable, scientific calculator as a gift. It has 34 buttons on it, each of which has 2 or 3 separate functions (or between 68 and 102 possible operations!). Its number display can go out to 10 places behind the decimal point, and it has 9 separate memories for number storage (I actually think there is still more memory, I just never learned to access it). In short, my calculator is a wonder in spite of the fact that by my estimate, I only know how to do about 5 or 10% of its functions.

Should you obtain one like mine to do the statistics presented in this book? Absolutely not. You should find a good calculator, but you will really only use the set of basic operations common to most calculators. The operations are addition, subtraction, multiplication, and division, of course, but also a key for taking square roots of numbers, and a squaring function or exponent key. Some memory storage capability, too, is desirable. In contrast to my calculator, though, less definitely *is* more.

Some calculators also have basic statistical procedures and tests programmed into them, which can be very useful for checking your answers to examples in the text or homework problems. You should *not* solve any statistics problems by using these programs, however, because one of the goals of this book is to teach you to work through the calculations by hand. Yes, hand calculations (supplemented by a calculator, of course) do take a bit more time, but they also help you to get a real feel for the data, a sense of where the numbers came from and how they are used to calculate a statistic.

I believe that you will retain more concepts from your class and the material in this book by doing the bulk of the work by hand. Calculators are necessary and very helpful tools, but they are only tools to augment, not replace, your understanding of mathematical and statistical operations. Whether you own, buy, or borrow one, make certain that it does what you need and that you avoid becoming distracted by functions you will not need for your course work. Just think of me and the 89 or so operations I have yet to figure out!

Knowledge Base

Examine these two data sets and then solve the expressions.

X	Y
7	1
5	3
10	5
2	5
6	6
3	2

1. $\sum X$

2. $\sum Y^2$

3. $(\sum X)^2$

4. $(\sum X)(\sum Y)$

5. $\sum XY$

Answers

1. 33
2. 100
3. 1,089
4. 726
5. 124

Project Exercise

AVOIDING STATISTICOPHOBIA

Each chapter in this book concludes with a project exercise, an activity that applies or extends some of that chapter's main points. These project exercises are designed to give you an opportunity to think about how statistical concepts can actually be employed in research or to identify particular issues that can render data analysis useful for the design of experiments or the interpretation of behavior. This first project exercise, however, has a different goal. It is meant to help you overcome some of the fears and prejudices you may unknowingly harbor toward statistics.

Take a few moments and answer the following questions:

1. When I think of learning about statistics, I feel _____.
2. When I look at this equation,

$$t = \frac{(\bar{X}_1 - \bar{X}_2) - (\mu_1 - \mu_2)}{s_{\bar{X}_1 - \bar{X}_2}}$$

I feel _____ .

Generally, students respond to both questions with a mixture of fear and trepidation. Dillon (1982) notes that students rarely respond with confident or interested comments. Instead, they express uncertainty or even fear by using words like "unsure," "nauseous," "panicky," "doomed," and "overwhelmed." When you answered the two questions, did words like these come to mind? If so, then you reacted like most students do the first time they encounter statistics.

Dillon (1982) labels this reaction "statisticophobia"—a fear of statistics. As I hope to prove to you, this condition is not terminal. Indeed, you can begin to overcome your statistical fears, if any, right now. First of all, you need to understand that the anxiety you feel toward learning statistics is shared anxiety—most students have it. I had it the first time I encountered the Σ! There is little doubt that most of the other students in your statistics class are "statisticophobes" as well, and that they had essentially the same reactions to this exercise.

Second, you need to recognize that it is not statistics per se that is the likely source of this anxiety. Instead, you should consider the possibility that your anxiety is more global, that it is probably associated with mathematics. Such math anxiety is a regrettable part of our cultural baggage, and it is something you should try to cope with or even overcome. Once again, I encourage you to consult Appendix A.

Third, mentally step back from the situation for a moment and consider this: Is it reasonable to express fear toward something you don't understand (yet)? In other words, why should you be bothered by something that you have not yet taken the time to learn? The equation shown in question 2 is the t test, a very useful test statistic that we will learn about in chapter 10. At this point, it *should* be unfamiliar to you—you *should not* understand it yet. Why bother wasting your time and energy on anticipatory fear early on? Give yourself and the course material a chance before you decide to give up on it. When the time comes, you will know how to perform the t test, as well as many other statistical tests. For the time being, try to keep an open mind and focus on learning the basic information presented in the beginning of this book. If you follow this advice, you will avoid statisticophobia and know exactly how to learn, interpret, and solve the statistical information that comes later. Heed the wisdom of a fortune cookie I received recently: "Don't be surprised by the emergence of undiscovered talents!"

LOOKING FORWARD THEN BACK

ike every chapter in this book, chapter 1 opened with some decision trees. These "trees" or, if you prefer, simple flow charts, are designed to help you *look forward* (i.e., aid in the planning of research or the analysis of data, or to anticipate the chapter's contents) or to *look back* (i.e., to review concepts after finishing reading a chapter or at some future when the need arises). Many of the decision trees in this book will be complex, whereas others will be simple, similar to the ones that open this chapter. Please rely on these decision trees to make the various decisions great and small that arise in the course of conducting research and analyzing data. I guarantee that following these flow charts will help you to be organized, planful, and certain about the choices you make when doing statistics and data analysis.

The first three decision trees that open the chapter are designed to prompt you, to prime your memory. These straightforward guides will help you to use the word "data" properly, label variables correctly, and think about the primary virtue of random sampling (i.e., it aids the process of inference from samples to populations).

The fourth decision tree is probably the most beneficial one here. Why? It will prevent you from forgetting the names and specific characteristics of the four scales of measurement. This particular decision tree will prove invaluable, especially when you must identify a scale in preparation for its analysis by some inferential statistical test (only certain types of scales can be analyzed by certain types of tests, a matter that will become increasingly apparent as you progress through this book).

Summary

1. The chapter opened by discussing the "how to" side of statistics, the focus of this book, as well as drawing a distinction between statistics and data analysis. A statistic is any information presented in numerical form, where data analysis is the systematic collection of observations. Both terms emphasize quantitative relationships, but because it is broader, data analysis also encompasses qualitative issues.

2. Statistics and data analysis are tools used to accomplish the task of interpreting human behavior—by themselves, they are not as important as that task.

3. Variables and constants were introduced in the context of the David L. problem, where they helped to guide college choice. Base rates—that is, a minimal consensus of opinion—and sampling issues were identified as essential ingredients in a statistically based college choice for David.

4. Although the disciplines of statistics and mathematics have different agendas, both share an appreciation for the scientific method, hypothesis testing, and theory development.

5. Inductive and deductive reasoning were presented as the dominant modes of reasoning in science. The behavioral sciences are largely inductive; that is, theories are created in order to search for confirming evidence.

6. Samples and simple random sampling were discussed as the only way to adequately characterize populations, or large, often theoretical sets of data. The parameters of populations are constants that cannot be known but are usefully approximated by sample statistics.

7. Descriptive statistics describe—that is, summarize the values in—samples, while inferential statistics allow researchers to determine if sample data are sufficient to characterize a population's parameters.

8. Discontinuous variables—those with real gaps where information does not occur—and continuous variables are commonly used in behavioral science research. These variables are related to the four scales of measurement: nominal, ordinal, interval, and ratio.

9. Researchers need to recognize that good writing and quality statistics and data analysis go hand in hand. Such writing is essential to the planning, interpretation, and dissemination of research results.

10. Basic statistical notation and the rules of mathematical priority were reviewed in detail. Readers were advised to adopt the "mise en place" philosophy, obtain a good but simple calculator, and avoid becoming "statisticophobes" by falling prey to math anxiety.

Key Terms

Constant *(p. 7)*
Continuous variable *(p. 20)*
Data *(p. 5)*
Data analysis *(p. 4)*
Datum *(p. 5)*
Deductive reasoning *(p. 11)*
Descriptive statistics *(p. 16)*
Discontinuous variable *(p. 20)*
Empirical *(p. 9)*
Hypothesis *(p. 9)*
Inductive reasoning *(p. 10)*

Inferential statistics *(p. 17)*
Interval scale *(p. 28)*
Lower true limit *(p. 21)*
Mise en place *(p. 39)*
N (p. 33)
Nominal scale *(p. 25)*
Ordinal scale *(p. 26)*
Population *(p. 12)*
Population parameter *(p. 13)*
Ratio scale *(p. 28)*
Sample *(p. 12)*

Sample statistic *(p. 13)*
Scientific method *(p. 9)*
Significant digits *(p. 22)*
Simple random sampling *(p. 14)*
Statistic *(p. 4)*
Stimuli *(p. 24)*
Theory *(p. 10)*
True limits *(p. 21)*
Upper true limit *(p. 21)*
Variable *(p. 6)*

Chapter Problems

1. What is a statistic? Can data analysis differ from statistical analysis? Why or why not?
2. Define the term *variable,* and then provide an example.
3. How do variables differ from constants? Give an example of each.
4. Explain how an appreciation for base rates and sampling issues could have helped David L. choose a college.
5. Why are mathematics and statistics different disciplines? What makes some mathematical operations statistical?
6. Use the terms *data, datum, stimulus,* and *stimuli* correctly in four different sentences.
7. What are empirical data?
8. Briefly describe the scientific method and the role hypotheses and theories play in it.

9. Define inductive and deductive reasoning, and then give an example of each process.
10. Explain the relationship between samples and populations, and sample statistics and population parameters. How does simple random sampling relate to these concepts?
11. Define simple random sampling.
12. Describe the difference(s) between descriptive and inferential statistics.
13. Can inferential statistics prove without any doubt that a given sample is from some particular population? Why or why not?
14. List three examples each of discontinuous and continuous variables.
15. Identify the upper and lower true limits for the following:
    a. 2,050 lb
    b. 58.30 minutes
    c. 3 inches
    d. a score of 70 on a 100-point test
16. Round the following numbers to two significant digits:
    a. 2178.762143
    b. 1.22222
    c. 3.41982
    d. 2.1
17. Why is writing relevant to statistics and data analysis? How can good, clear writing help investigators with their research?
18. A college entrance questionnaire asks first-year students to indicate their age, gender, hair color, height, weight, the number of books they read in the last 3 months, and their SAT scores.
    a. Indicate which of the variables is discontinuous or continuous.
    b. Identify which scale of measurement best describes each variable.
19. Name and define the four basic statistical symbols.
20. Briefly summarize the mathematical rules of priority.

21. Solve the following equations:
    a. $Y = (7 + 2)^2 - \sqrt{25}$
    b. $X = (10)^3 + (12 - 5) \times 4$
    c. $Y = \sqrt{10} - (-15 + 10)^2$
    d. $X = 8 \times 2 + (10 + 12)^2$
22. Using the following data, solve the expressions for:

    $X_1 = 12, X_2 = 2, X_3 = 15, X_4 = 10, X_5 = 7$

    $N =$

    $\sum_{i=1}^{N} X_i =$

    $\sum_{i=2}^{3} X_i =$

    $\sum_{i=4}^{N} X_i =$

23. Using the following data sets, solve the expressions:

X	Y	
4	7	$\sum X =$
2	2	$\sum Y =$
2	4	$\sum XY =$
3	4	$(\sum X)(\sum Y) =$
1	4	$\sum X^2 =$
5	1	$\sum Y^2 =$

24. Explain the "mise en place" philosophy in statistics and data analysis.
25. What is "statisticophobia"? How can it be overcome?

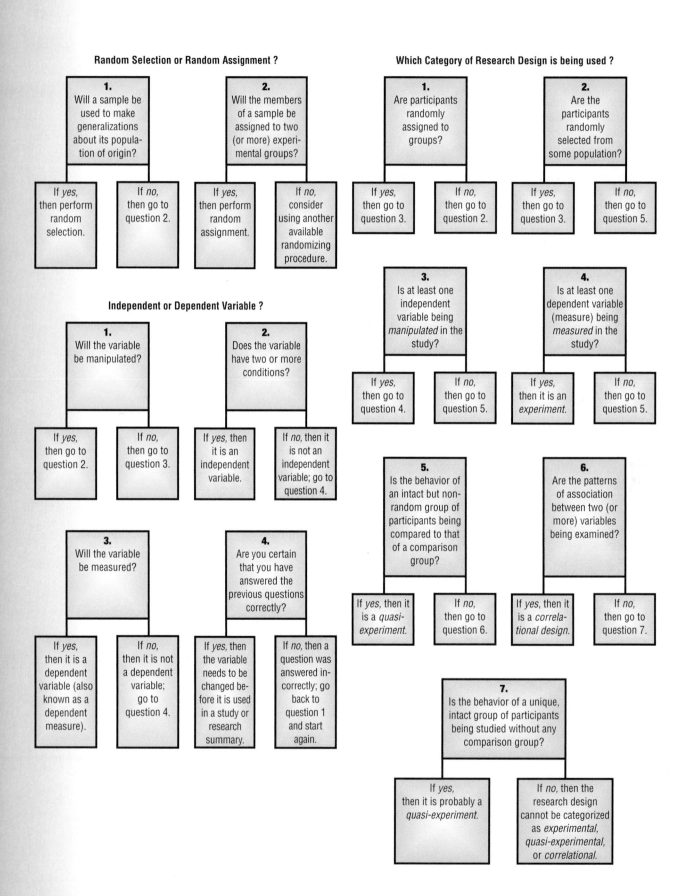

PROCESS OF RESEARCH
IN PSYCHOLOGY AND
RELATED FIELDS

ow is research in the behavioral sciences conducted? How do researchers go about designing experiments or other modes of inquiry that enable them to tease apart cause and effect relations in data? Is any particular approach to research superior to others? These and related questions will be answered in this chapter, which is devoted to explaining the theory and practice behind research ventures in psychology and related disciplines.

This second chapter is an interlude between chapter 1's overview of statistics and the emphasis on statistical concepts, formulas, and data analysis techniques to be found in subsequent chapters. This interlude is important because anyone who wants to learn to use statistics properly must have a context for their application to data. Knowledge cannot be acquired, understood, or meaningfully applied inside a vacuum. As you learned in the last chapter, statistics are *for* something—they are tools that mean very little unless they are used to answer a question or to discover heretofore unnoticed relationships among variables. In the behavioral sciences, notably psychology, statistics and data analysis are used to predict and to interpret human behavior in all its myriad forms. In this chapter, we will examine the fundamentals of basic experimentation and research design, the mechanics of the research enterprise. The message in this chapter is simple but important: Good research and quality research design are enhanced by rigorous and appropriate use of statistics and data analysis.

The Research Loop of Experimentation: An Overview of the Research Process

In chapter 1, we introduced the scientific method, the formalized procedures used to conduct research. The basic components of the scientific method include problem identification, formulation of a hypothesis, and collection of data to test the veracity of the

Step 1: **Collect observations or rely on existing theory**

Step 2: **Develop a testable hypothesis or hypotheses**

Step 3: **Conduct experiment(s) to test the hypothesis and to eliminate any alternative hypothesis(es)**

Step 4: **Analyze the data and interpret the results of the experiment(s)**

Step 5: **Begin the loop again: Go back to** step 1

Figure 2.1   The Research Loop of Experimentation

Adapted from Dunn (1999).

hypothesis. This account of the scientific method is both brief and idealized. We need to establish a better sense of how research actually gets done, and to do so we turn to the *research loop of experimentation* (Dunn, 1999; see also Platt, 1964).

The research loop of experimentation (Figure 2.1) is a series of steps that identify the work done at each stage of the research process. Although these steps appear to be discrete, numerous smaller activities occur between each one. Such smaller activities are practical matters that investigators routinely perform but rarely discuss with nonresearchers, what we might call the tacit or implicit side of conducting research. I mention this fact so that you will not make the mistake of viewing research as a cut-and-dried affair rather than a dynamic, detailed, and demanding enterprise.

In step 1 of the research loop (see Figure 2.1), an investigator observes some interesting relationship among some observations or decides to explore some as-yet-untested aspect of a theory. Thus, the impetus to initiate research can range from almost casual curiosity to theory extension, and a host of possible reasons for asking research question can fall between these extremes. Step 1 represents a scientific commitment, one that requires the investigator—whether student or professional—to think critically about the research topic before proceeding to the next step.

The second step entails the development of a research hypothesis or a testable question derived from the research topic (see Figure 2.1). In many investigations, the hypothesis identifies which variables will be manipulated and which will be measured to best answer questions of cause and effect. In others, the hypothesis is less specific and more oriented toward observing the relationships among variables in order to develop firmer speculations for future research.

As we will see later in chapter 9, any research project really has two hypotheses—one the investigator wants to put forth as a satisfactory account for some behavior, and the other, an alternative hypothesis that the investigator wants to invalidate. The latter usually offers an account of behavior opposite that of the research hypothesis. The idea here is to pit the research hypothesis against its alternate so that only one of them can be shown to offer superior explanatory power.

Step 3 is the data collection phase, which brings the theory and hypothesis together in some empirical fashion (see Figure 2.1). The empirical realization is usually (but not always) an *experiment*.

KEY TERM An **experiment** introduces intentional change into some situation so that reactions to it can be systematically observed, measured, and recorded.

In lieu of an experiment, step 3 could also involve a correlational investigation or what is called a quasi-experiment. Each of these research alternatives will be defined and discussed in detail below.

Step 3 also includes drawing a sample from some larger population and making certain that it was drawn randomly. If an experiment is conducted, some members of the sample are then given an experience that is consistent with the research hypothesis, while the others receive information fitting the alternative hypothesis.

In step 4, the results of the experiment are interpreted (see Figure 2.1). It is here that the bulk of the statistical analyses and accompanying scientific reasoning takes place. Descriptive statistics are calculated from the sample data, and inferential statistics are then employed to see how well the sample results fit the population parameters. In practical terms, the investigator tries to discern whether the manipulated variable(s) created the hypothesized change in the measured variable(s). If the hypothesized change took place, then there is evidence for the favored hypothesis and accompanying theory. The research hypothesis, then, is treated as a reasonable explanation for the cause and effect—the give and take—among the variables in the research. On the other hand, if unpredicted change or no change occurs, the investigator cannot be confident that the research hypothesis is tenable—instead, the opposing or alternative hypothesis is embraced for the time being.

The phrase "for the time being" is an apt one for the last step in the research loop of experimentation. In step 5, the process begins anew, and the researcher effectively goes back to step 1 where he or she had only some idea or bit of evidence about how and why some behavior occurs (see Figure 2.1). Even armed with the results of one experiment, the investigator is really starting over from scratch—the same process must be acted out again from start to finish to start again because research is really never finished! Variations of the original topic must be examined, cherished hypotheses must be revised or discarded, and new questions must be formulated. Some researchers spend their entire careers exploring subtle distinctions within the same topic, while others migrate from topic to topic as the spirit or scientific inspiration moves them.

The research loop of experimentation is recursive; that is, after completing four steps, a researcher loops back to step 1 to begin the process anew.

The research loop of experimentation should demonstrate to you that science is done in a somewhat cyclical way. The knowledge gained through this looping cycle advances gradually, even incrementally. Forward movement—the identification, classification, and application of scientific facts—is usually slow. The scientific community accepts results only after they are critically reviewed by peers or occasionally even debated. The results of related and disparate investigations are compared so that consistencies can be identified and inconsistencies can be explained or more thoroughly explored. The process of recursion inherent in the research loop of experimentation—that is, continually repeating the five main steps in order—advances knowledge by ensuring that established findings are continually examined in light of newer results, and that no data, no matter how persuasive, are seen as permanent.

Two other advantages are associated with the research loop of experimentation, the replication and extension of results. The term *replication* refers to repeating or redoing an investigation to verify that the results can be duplicated.

K E Y   T E R M

A **replication** study, which is usually an experiment, is performed to repeat or duplicate some scientific result.

Replication is a necessity in scientific research; indeed, many heralded findings are not accepted or "trusted" until they are independently confirmed by other investigators from different laboratories. To their credit, many researchers are loathe to share their results with the scientific community until they have verified them more than once. With its recursive design, the research loop of experimentation enables investigators to repeat the same study more than once.

What about extending known results? How does this process take place? Generally, extending known results occurs through what is called **conceptual replication.** A literal replication study is a relatively precise re-creation of what was done before, whereas a conceptual replication (sometimes called *systematic* replication; see Aronson, Ellsworth, Carlsmith, & Gonzales, 1990) keeps some aspects of the situation constant from the original work while allowing other parts to vary or be left uncontrolled. In other words, some part of the conceptual replication study *differs* from the original work. This research possibility is also covered by the research loop of experimentation. By changing the conditions from the original study somewhat in steps 1, 2, and 3 (see Figure 2.1), the investigator has the opportunity to see how well the observed result stands when change is introduced. If the result does not change, then the researcher knows that it is not unique to the way the original work was done. In this case, the result is strong and pronounced so that it is sometimes described as "robust." The result may change, of course, in which case the investigator must study the amount and direction of that change to learn if the "new" results point to unanticipated relationships with other variables or to a limit for the result. Such limits are often referred to as "boundary conditions" because the extent—the boundary—of the observed effect has been located.

Keep the research loop of experimentation in mind as you read the remainder of this chapter. As you will see, it serves as a useful guide—really, a guiding force—behind much of the work conducted in psychology and the other behavioral sciences.

Replication—literally repeating a procedure to find the same results to verify their accuracy—is a cornerstone of behavioral science research.

Populations and Samples Revisited: The Role of Randomness

Simple random sampling was introduced in chapter 1. As a means to reduce potential sources of bias so that samples can be deemed reasonably reflective of their parent populations, simple random sampling is an adequate technique. There are, however, other techniques to ensure that a sample is random, and some are better suited to the sorts of situations researchers actually encounter in their work. We will review a few of these techniques to prepare for the discussion of research design later in the chapter. But first, we must draw a distinction between random sampling, sometimes called random selection, and its more common cousin, *random assignment.*

Distinguishing Random Assignment from Random Sampling

In many ways, the ideal research situation is one where a sample of observations is drawn from a larger population in such a way that all members of that population have the same chance of being selected. Theoretically, when it is done correctly, this process of random sampling makes the sample a virtual copy of the population, albeit on a smaller scale. Simple random sampling poses a practical problem for most behavioral scientists, however: Most do not have access to adequate numbers of people to be able to draw a reasonably random sample.

How so? Consider the fact that the bulk of behavioral science research, especially in psychology, is conducted at colleges and universities. Would you consider a study that is comprised exclusively of 18- to 22-year-old males and females to be representative of the population at large? Before you answer, "Well, it depends," consider for a moment that the majority of published studies in psychology rely *almost exclusively* on 18- to 22-year old males and females (note, however, that most topics in psychology do *not* deal with topics related to postadolescence or early adulthood). As you can see, the restricted age range does pose some interpretive challenges—many interesting questions about human behavior are not germane to that particular 4-year span—that have not gone unnoticed (e.g., Dawes, 1991; Sears, 1986).

It is also the case that on any given college or university campus, only a relatively small percentage of the students are going to make themselves available to researchers. Such students are usually enrolled in introductory psychology courses where there is a research requirement. To wit, a student must complete some set number of hours (usually 3 or 4) in research participation across the semester. The restricted age range is now accompanied by a second bias, what is often called a problem of selection. Some students *choose* to take psychology courses, others do not, and so some students are available for research and others are not. Those available for research comprise a compromised group—mostly the same age, chose psychology as a college major, had to participate in research because of their course choice, and so on.

Finally, students are usually given the opportunity to choose those experiments they want to take part in and those they want to avoid. Traditionally, students go to the Psychology Department and sign up for a study whose brief description sounds interesting, but they can only sign up for some studies and not others because of time constraints, course schedules, and even the requirements of the experimenters (e.g., participants must be female, members of a fraternity or sorority, have 20:20 vision). These constraints pose yet another round of compromises that renders random sampling a virtual impossibility.

Most of the participants who end up taking part in research had to do so for educational reasons, or they just happened to be available and willing to take part in a research venture. In such situations, participants are often labeled a *convenience sample* because they were convenient for the experimenter to recruit. Another term used is *haphazard sample,* which has a slightly pejorative but honest ring to it in that the investigator relied on whoever happened to be around to participate in the research. Whatever we decide to call it, random sampling is precluded by the realities of the situation.

When random sampling is not a possibility in such circumstances, researchers often fall back on random assignment. That is, researchers work with the available pool of people by randomly placing them in one of the conditions of an experiment.

▽

Although it is desirable, random sampling is actually rare in behavioral science research— random assignment, however, is quite common.

KEY TERM **Random assignment** involves assigning participants randomly to the conditions or groups in an experiment.

Random assignment is used, then, when a researcher has a group of participants who need to be assigned to the unique conditions within an experiment. If an investigator has 40 participants (say, 20 males and 20 females) and two conditions in the experiment—one testing the research hypothesis and the other representing the alternative hypothesis—half of the men and women can be assigned randomly to each condition. As shown in Figure 2.2, the goal of this random assignment is to establish equivalent groups of participants *before* the experiment begins. If the groups are effectively the same at the start (i.e., every participant had the same chance of being assigned to one condition or the other), then any subsequent behavioral differences can be reasonably

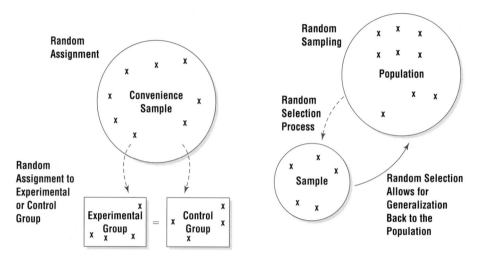

Figure 2.2   Random Assignment Is Not Random Sampling

attributed to the research hypothesis. Prior to random assignment, the participants do comprise a sample that is presumably from a larger population, but the researcher cannot assume that the sample is a representative one. Random assignment substantially reduces the possibility that any between-group differences exist at the outset of an experiment.

In defense of random assignment as a reasonable and useful research technique, take note that in most cases, simple random sampling is a very time consuming and expensive enterprise. Animal researchers, for example, depend on the animal subjects available in the vivarium or that happen to be sent by suppliers. These researchers are usually not concerned that the rats or pigeons they work with are going to have physical or behavioral characteristics that make them different from their respective, generic species. Furthermore, random assignment does such a reliable job at creating equivalent groups that even if it were feasible, random sampling would probably not add that much to the typical experiment. Thus, most research you read about or are apt to conduct yourself will rely on random assignment. In fact, it is actually rare to see random selection being used in published studies.

Some Other Randomizing Procedures

Random sampling and random assignment are the most basic techniques to ensure, respectively, that a sample characterizes a population or is free of bias at the outset of an experiment. We will review a few other sampling procedures that are variations on these basic approaches.

One common alternative to simple random sampling is called *systematic sampling*. In a systematic sample, a list of all members of the population is drawn up, and then every *n*th person is selected from it. For example, if you were interested in sampling the opinion of the members of a medium sized corporation (1,000 employees), you could obtain an alphabetized list of the workers and then sample every 10th name on it. You would then interview or survey the resulting 100 employees comprising the systematic sample. Although this is a good procedure, there are a few problems associated with it. The investigator must be certain that the list was drawn up without bias (i.e., all

Random assignment to condition is used to equalize groups at the outset of a study.

employees are included). Additionally, there may be some hidden biases embedded within the list. Even if the list is alphabetical, for example, some letters may be over-represented on it (many last names begin with "S") than others (few last names begin with "Q" or "Z"). For most situations, this alphabetization problem is probably minor, but the researcher must be aware of it nonetheless.

Some populations of people are made up of different sized groups or subpopulations. Consider a small college with an enrollment of 8,000 undergraduates. Is it the case that each class—first year through senior—has 2,000 students in it (i.e., 4 classes × 2,000 students in each = 8,000)? Probably not—why? Simply because the size of an entering class tends to shrink across a 4-year period, a phenomenon known in higher education as attrition. Some students drop out, leave for unknown reasons, transfer to another school, take time off, among a variety of other possibilities, across the standard 4 years of college (not to mention that some students take 5 years or longer to complete their degrees). A first-year class that began with 2,000 students might graduate with, say, 1,750 after 4 years. The important implication here is that the size of each of the four classes would differ within the college.

What does class size have to do with sampling? If you wanted to accurately assess student opinion in all four classes, you would need to know how many people were in each class. If one class has more students than another, you would not want to oversample the former (or undersample the latter). Further, you might also want to make sure that an appropriate representation of males and females within each class was collected (i.e., if a school has more men than women, are more men sampled than women?). To accurately represent various subgroups existing within a population, researchers often used a *stratified random sample*. A researcher will divide a population into "strata" or subgroups, and then randomly sample an appropriate number of observations from each one. Thus, relatively fewer first-year students than juniors or seniors would need to be sampled because there are relatively more of them available. Stratification turns out to be especially helpful when investigators are trying to ensure that minority groups are adequately represented in a sample.

A third technique is called *cluster sampling*. Sometimes it is too expensive or time consuming to sample an entire town or city, for example, and yet it is desirable to learn the opinion of its inhabitants. Cluster sampling involves identifying a few smaller units ("clusters") within the population and then sampling their opinion. Imagine you were running for city council and you wanted to get a sense of the impression your campaign was creating in the minds of voters. Instead of spending time and money to obtain a true random sample of voters, why not randomly select a few neighborhood blocks throughout the city? If there were 50 neighborhood blocks, you might randomly select five to visit. Each block would serve as a cluster within the larger population. You and your campaign workers could then go door to door within those five blocks to learn how your candidacy was faring. Cluster sampling is economical, quick to do, and enables researchers to study a few observations with some depth. It may lack the precision of a true random sample, but its practical orientation renders it a useful sampling tool for particular situations.

Convenience sampling was already identified as a nonrandom way to round up a group of people who are later randomly assigned to conditions in a study. One other nonrandom sampling technique will be mentioned here. *Quota sampling* entails selecting a number or "quota" of persons who fit some set of predetermined characteristics. If you were interested in the opinions of students involved in Greek life on your campus, you might decide to interview four members of each fraternity and sorority. A quota sample can be further refined along the lines of other demographic considerations (e.g., each of the four members from the fraternity and the sorority would

Table 2.1   A Sampling of Samples

Sampling Procedures with Randomization

Simple Random Sample—each member of a population has the same chance as every other member of being selected for inclusion in a sample.

Random Assignment—each member of a group is assigned at random to one condition within an experiment or study.

Systematic Sampling—a list of a population's members is created and then every *n*th member is included in the sample.

Stratified Random Sampling—a population is divided into subgroups (strata) and then a random sample of individuals is drawn from each subgroup.

Cluster Sampling—small units within a population (clusters) are identified at random and then each person in a unit is included in the sample.

Sampling Procedures without Randomization

Convenience or Haphazard Sample—a researcher recruits people who are accessible, available, and willing to take part in a piece of research. Individuals in the sample are meant to be more or less representative of the larger population.

Quota Sample—involves sampling a specified number of participants from a special interest group or groups within the larger population.

Census—a sample that includes each and every member (or score, unit, or observation) within a population.

---

hail from the first-year, sophomore, junior, or senior class). Quota samples are clearly biased, but they are biased toward involving special interest groups to obtain some information on the topic of interest.

Table 2.1 summarizes the sampling techniques we have discussed so far. You can refer back to this table when deciding what sort of sampling procedure would be appropriate for research you undertake, or when you read a study identifying a particular sampling procedure or that could be improved by better sampling.

Sampling Error

Our discussion of sampling here and in chapter 1 could lead readers to believe that proper use of randomization rules out most difficulties. This conclusion is largely true, but it neglects one important fact about sampling and populations—even very good samples are only relatively representative, not wholly representative, of a population. In other words, no sample is perfect nor can it completely portray a population's characteristics. Statisticians refer to the discrepancy between sample statistics and population parameters as *sampling error.*

KEY TERM   **Sampling error** is the difference existing between a sample statistic and its corresponding population parameter.

The word "error" in this context means that our measurement is not precise. A sample statistic is an estimate of some true score found in the population. Regardless of the quality of a study, there will always be some degree of sampling error. The error in measurement may be large or it may be small. Obviously, a researcher's goal is to minimize that error as much as possible.

Using a randomizing procedure is a good start, of course, and giving appropriate consideration to the size of a sample is another. Generally speaking, sampling error can be predicted by the size of a given sample. Here is a good rule of thumb: *Larger samples exhibit smaller amounts of sampling error than do smaller samples.* This rule makes good sense if you think about it for a moment. When trying to gauge public opinion, for example, is it wiser to ask a few people or a large number? As you well know from the countless opinion polls you have seen on television or read about in the paper, it is better to ask a fairly large number of people. Note that you need not ask everyone—a representative sample will do precisely because it will best approximate the public's opinion. By the way, if you were to poll everyone you would be performing a *census,* a sample that includes each and every member of a population (see Table 2.1).

We will not consider exactly *how many* people to include in a poll or an experiment at this point. For now, I would prefer that you remember that sampling error can be reduced substantially through randomization and by obtaining a reasonably large sample of observations. We will revisit the connection between size of a sample and error in a later chapter.

Larger samples characterize a population more accurately than smaller samples.

Knowledge Base

1. True or False: The repetitive nature of the research loop of experimentation ensures that knowledge advances incrementally and that established results are evaluated against new data.
2. True or False: A replication study maintains some aspects of the original study while varying others or leaving them uncontrolled.
3. True or False: The goal of random assignment is to create equivalent participant groups before an experiment begins.
4. Recruiting people who happen to be available or around is called a
   a. quota sample
   b. convenience sample
   c. random sample
   d. systematic sample
5. If you sample every 27th person in a large group, you are creating a
   a. quota sample
   b. convenience sample
   c. random sample
   d. systematic sample
6. Identifying and then sampling several smaller units within a larger population is called a
   a. quote sample
   b. haphazard sample
   c. cluster sample
   d. systematic sample
7. True or False: If a sample is carefully drawn, there can be no sampling error; that is, sample statistics will match corresponding population parameters.

Answers

1. True
2. False—the statement describes a conceptual replication.
3. True
4. b. Convenience sample
5. d. Systematic sample
6. c. Cluster sample
7. False—there will always be some degree of sampling error.

DATA BOX 2.A

Recognizing Randomness, Imposing Order

There is an irony in human behavior where randomness is concerned. We try to recognize randomness when it operates, but end up trying to impose order to make sense of it. The irony is that, by definition, random events have no order and make no "sense" in the way humans usually define it.

We persist, believing that even minor chaos cries out for order, which can sometimes get us into trouble where inference, accuracy, and understanding are concerned. Here are two prominent cases where we run into trouble—exerting control we do not have and relying too much on a judgment strategy called representativeness.

Illusory Control and Random Events. Life experiences teach us that skill and effort usually pay off, that we can be masters of our destinies. The problem is that we frequently assume control over events that are in actuality *not* controllable, and there is often a random element involved. Psychologist Ellen Langer coined the term *illusion of control* to explain what happens when people's expectations of personal success are inappropriately higher than the objective nature of their situation warrants. In general, this illusion operates when people insert skill-related behaviors into settings that have a random component. By skill-related behaviors, we refer to situations where control is a possibility, when we compete with others, have choice, exert effort, and the like.

In one famous study, choice was shown to elicit illusory control by encouraging people to overlook the role randomness played in the situation (Langer, 1975, study 2). Office workers were approached by a fellow worker and asked if they would like to take part in a lottery. Half of those approached were given the opportunity to choose a $1 lottery ticket (the tickets were cards with pictures of football players), while the remaining participants were assigned a card. All participants knew that the lottery winner would receive $50. The day before the lottery was to take place, all the office workers were asked *how much money* they would be willing to sell their lottery ticket to another person for (all the tickets were supposedly sold but a fellow employee still wanted to buy one).

Participants who *selected* their own ticket wanted an average of $8.67 to resell it, but those *assigned* a card only asked for an average of $1.96! Participants who had a choice were willing to resell it for over eight times the purchase price, which can be construed as indicative of their confidence of winning the lottery. Langer (1975; see also, Langer, 1983) concluded that the simple act of making a choice induced illusory control, enabling some participants to ignore the random information in the situation—only 1 ticket out of 50 could win and choosing (or not choosing) a ticket made absolutely no difference.

Can you think of any similar instances where you have subjectively tried to control something over which objective influence was not possible? What role, if any, did randomness play?

Independent and Dependent Variables

The review of the research loop of experimentation highlighted a role for theorizing and hypothesis development. That is, researchers typically work within some established research tradition or area of inquiry (see step 1 in Figure 2.1). Each investigator relies on an existing theory or develops a novel one to explain some behavior of interest. In turn, the investigator must define a question—the hypothesis—to pursue through the research (see step 2 in Figure 2.1). Once a question is formulated, particular variables must be identified for manipulation and measurement to see what effects they have on the behavior of interest. These variables—called *independent* and *dependent* variables—are the focus of this section of the chapter.

The Heuristic of Representativeness. A heuristic is a reliable shortcut, a rule of thumb that generally helps us make sound decisions. Sometimes, however, heuristics are overused or misapplied so that we misjudge the random elements at play. One prominent heuristic is called *representativeness*, or the degree to which an object's salient features are representative of—or similar to—features assumed to be characteristic of the category (Kahneman & Tversky, 1972, 1973).

Representativeness is ubiquitous, but we seem to misapply it when trying to understand base rates (recall the David L. problem from chapter 1) and how randomness can help (or hinder) our interpretation of them. Here is a brief personality description—read it, think about it, and then answer the question.

There is a group of 100 professionals, 70 of them are engineers and 30 are lawyers. One individual is selected at random from the group. His name is Dick. He is a 30-year-old man. He is married with no children. A man of high ability and high motivation, he promises to be quite successful in his field. He is well liked by his colleagues. Is Dick an engineer or a lawyer?

Did you pick engineer or lawyer? What led to your choice? If you look over the paragraph once more, you can see that no information that sheds light on Dick's actual profession was provided. Yet I have no doubt that many of you used the details provided (e.g., "married," "no children," "promises to be successful") to create a mental profile of Dick, which would in turn help you make the choice based on other information you have about engineers ("low social skills," "nerdy") or lawyers ("aggressive," "there are a lot of them out there").

The only information you need, though, is that (a) the choice was made randomly and (b) there are more engineers (i.e., 70) than lawyers (i.e., 30) in the sample. Given these considerations, Dick is apt to be an engineer. Kudos to you if you got it right, but I am guessing that some of you were mislead by the worthless evidence that made you downplay the role of randomness. If you had simply been told that the group of 100 was composed of 70 engineers and 30 lawyers, that 1 was selected, and you were then asked to indicate his profession, I have no doubt you would pipe up "engineer" in a heartbeat. Due to randomness, Dick *could be* a lawyer, but it is more likely he is an engineer—there are more engineers so it is more likely that an engineer was randomly selected. Tversky and Kahneman (1974) note that people get it right when no other evidence is shared, but they tend to be less confident or to make an error when worthless evidence draws their attention away from the role randomness plays.

How often does the representativeness heuristic lead you inferentially astray? When do you neglect base rates and randomness by focusing on extraneous details that trigger stereotypes? We will review other roles for randomness in this chapter and later in the book. Until then, the lesson is clear: When you recognize randomness is at work, avoid imposing order.

An experimenter manipulates independent variables, whereas dependent variables are measured by an experimenter.

Imagine that you are a cognitive psychologist who has applied interests in human memory. Cognitive psychologists often study the selection, perception, interpretation, storage, and retrieval of information from memory, as well as decision making and problem solving. Your general interest is how people search through memory to recall learned information, and your particular interest is improving search engines on the Internet so they become more compatible with human reasoning. When people sit down to search the Internet for information on some topic of interest, for example, how do they retrieve appropriate search terms from memory? Some people are more efficient at such searches than others; that is, they locate what they learned in memory with relative ease, while others seem to struggle a bit, gradually recalling useful search terms or helpful categories.

As a start to your research, you decide to examine how well people remember search terms on their own versus being given a cue to stimulate their recall. In the cognitive literature, this is a distinction between *free recall* and *recognition* in memory. Free recall is simply remembering whatever you can from some list of stimuli without regard to the order in which it was learned and without any prompting. In contrast, recognition involves being given a stimulus and then being asked if you saw it before, for example, or you could be asked to pick out previously encountered information from a list of alternatives.

Perhaps future Internet search engines, or "web browsers," should suggest related terms to users once a term is entered. These related terms would have to be intuitively related to the original search term, yet unique enough to access different material on the Internet. As each search occurs, the search engine would need to "learn" from a user's search style so that previously located terms would not repeated. In turn, the user would have to adapt to the search engine's style of responding to search terms with entries, websites, narrower or broader terms, and so on. Thus, computer hardware and software would need to complement human hardware and software.

To begin your research on human–computer compatibility with search terms, you decide to conduct a straightforward experiment illustrating memory differences between free recall and recognition for search terms one might use on the Internet to locate information on investing in the stock market. As a cognitive psychologist, you would be very familiar with the voluminous literature on human memory and related processes, as your theorizing about how people come up with search terms in memory would be based on it. The hypothesis you intend to test is derived from the available theory: Recognition searches of memory result in higher recall of search terms than do free-recall searches. You would then identify, define, and describe the variables that will be used in the experiment.

Generally, experimental research—indeed, almost any type of research—relies on the two types of variables mentioned earlier. The independent variable is the variable that is manipulated or allowed to vary in any experiment.

KEY TERM   An **independent variable** is the variable that is manipulated by a researcher. In experimental research, it must have two or more levels.

Laboratory experiments, for example, typically examine how the presence and absence of a given variable affects people's behavior. When a variable is sometimes present and other times absent within a study, the researcher is said to be "manipulating the independent variable."

An independent variable, then, must have at least two levels, usually an experimental treatment and a control treatment. Some study participants—usually half of those available—are exposed to the experimental treatment while the remainder experience the control treatment. The experimental treatment represents the hypothesis favored by the investigator.

Please be aware that an independent variable can have *more* than two levels. An independent variable can illustrate a range of values, for example, so it could have three levels—high, medium, and low. Alternatively, an independent variable could have four, five, six, or even more levels to it—the proverbial sky is the limit as long as the respective levels can reasonably be expected to elicit behavioral differences on the part of research participants. The researcher, too, must be sure that a more complicated independent variable, one with several levels, can be adequately manipulated in an experimental or other research context. Still, the best way to become familiar and comfortable with thinking about independent variables is to learn about their most basic form—one independent variable with two levels. Complexity in the form of several levels or even several independent variables will come later.

To continue our hypothetical cognitive example, the experimental treatment would be exposure to a recognition task subsequent to the learning phase. Half the participants could be given pairs of stock investment search terms to review, such that one member of each pair would be familiar (i.e., from the stimulus list used in the learning phase), such as "share," while the other would be novel, say, "security." The experimental treatment participants would simply indicate which term from each pair they recognized from the learning phase.

Participants receiving the control treatment, however, would not receive any recognition prompts—they would simply be asked to perform a free recall of whatever search terms they remembered. Notice that the control treatment really refers to the absence of any intervention at all, a condition that is used for comparison with the experimental treatment. Here is a key point: *The researcher compares the effects of both levels of the independent variable on some outcome variable to assess whether any observed difference can be attributed to the experimental treatment.*

What is an outcome variable? The outcome variable is otherwise known as the dependent variable or, as I prefer, the *dependent measure* (Dunn, 1999). The dependent measure is the variable that is *measured* in any experiment, and it *depends* on the independent variable; that is, the researcher assesses whether the manipulated variable created the predicted change in the variable that was measured as the experiment's outcome.

KEY TERM   A **dependent variable** or **measure** is the outcome variable, the one that is assessed to determine if the experimental treatment had any effect.

To continue our cognitive research example, the dependent measure would be the number of search terms recalled in the experimental group versus the control group. In line with the hypothesis, the predicted outcome would be that a relatively greater number of search terms would be recalled by participants in the experimental group (i.e., those who performed the recognition task) than the control group (i.e., those who performed the free-recall task). As the researcher, you would probably examine the average number of search terms recalled by participants in the two conditions, anticipating that a higher number in the experimental group than the control group.

Where are we in the research loop of experimentation? The identification and explication of independent variables and dependent measures occurs in step 2 (see Figure 2.1). Once the variable selection is accomplished, we then enter step 3 where the actual experiment is conducted (see Figure 2.1). This step entails recruiting participants and randomly assigning them to one of the two conditions in the experiment. As we discussed earlier, it is likely that you, the cognitive researcher, would also have to rely on a convenience sample. As you might imagine, step 3 is rather involved, as it involves staging your piece of research from start to finish. A review of the nuts-and-bolts of how to conduct an experiment is beyond the scope of this book but, if you are interested, you can consult any number of books for detailed advice (e.g., Dunn, 1999; Martin, 1996; Rosnow & Rosenthal, 1996; Shaughnessy & Zechmeister, 1997).

We now turn back to step 4 in the research loop of experimentation, which is concerned with interpreting the results from the memory experiment. The two averages—one representing the recognition group, the other the free recall group—would be compared with one another to see if the former was reliably larger than the latter. It is at this point in the research that statistical analysis comes into play, when the researcher tests the hypothesis by determining if the anticipated relationship is confirmed by the empirical data (i.e., a recognition task leads to higher levels of recall for search terms than no recognition task). Later in the text we will discuss the specific statistical tests that would be best suited to analyze the data collected in this hypothetical study. For now, concentrate on the fact that both the independent variable and the dependent measure have a role to play where statistical analyses are concerned. The independent variable is often used as what is called a "blocking" variable in the analyses, as here when the two discrete groups—recognition versus free recall—were presumed to exhibit different behavior. The dependent measure is important, too, because it serves as tangible behavioral evidence that *something* happened. Here, of course, the behavioral difference between the two groups suggests that recognition facilitates recall.

You should also focus on the fact that the statistical analyses occur after the data are collected, though the investigator would have determined the statistical test long before the first datum would be collected. That's right—statistical analyses are such an integral part of the research process that they must be planned well in advance of the actual research. If the analyses are not planned in advance, it is entirely possible to collect the wrong sort of data. In other words, one can inadvertently collect data that cannot be analyzed. The design of an experiment or a study, for instance, can necessitate the use of a particular statistical test or data analytic technique, but if the wrong type of data were collected, then no test can be performed on them. This problem is actually more common than you might guess, and we will discuss specific ways to avoid it by proper planning in chapter 15 (see also, Appendix D). In the mean time, we need to consider what sort of data can comprise a dependent measure.

Types of Dependent Measures

In chapter 1, we reviewed four scales of measurement—nominal, ordinal, interval, and ratio—that are typically used in behavioral research. We will now continue the discussion of measurement by reviewing four classes of dependent measures found in psychological research (that both happen to be four in number is coincidental, not by design). The scales of measurement can be thought of as complements to these classes of dependent measures; indeed, as you will see, the former can often be subsumed under the latter. The four classes of dependent measures are behavioral, self-report, physiological, and behavioroid measures.

A *behavioral measure* is one that can be seen or observed directly. Behavioral measures are usually physical, rather concrete, and easily coded (e.g., the number of times a person nods her head, the measured physical distance between two people, the duration of a smile). Practically any behavior a human or an animal performs can be used as a behavioral measure, so the only limit is the imagination and stamina of the researcher.

The one caveat associated with this endless behavioral variety, of course, is that any behavioral measure should conceptually correspond to the psychological process or construct it is meant to represent. In our hypothetical memory experiment, for example, the data—recognized or recalled search terms—comprise a behavioral measure because the research participants *did* something. That is, their behavior was either verbal (i.e., the participants said the terms they remembered aloud) or, as is common in memory experiments, they wrote down or circled words they remembered learning previously.

Self-report measures are almost as common as behavioral measures, and they are just what you would expect: people's verbal reactions to questions or some stimulus. Self-report measures come in a variety of forms. Some are open-ended questions that allow respondents to give detailed responses ("How did you feel about the story you just read?") while others are close-ended, requiring concise and direct answers ("How old are you?"). Surveys, standardized personality measures, essays, rating scales, attitude scales, mood instruments—almost anything that has a verbal component—can be labeled a self-report measure. The majority of self-report data are based on paper-and-pencil measures, where respondents write, circle, or check responses corresponding to their thoughts or feelings. Naturally, self-report data can also be drawn from videotapes, tape recordings, interviews, and even phone calls, though in psychological research the term most often refers to participants' own written comments.

There is a drawback to self-reports, however, in that it is very difficult, if not impossible, to verify their accuracy. If I ask someone why she acted a certain way, how will I know that she is telling me the truth? Moreover, how does she know what promoted her action? If you find these questions odd, then you will be surprised to learn that many psychologists are deeply concerned about linking what people say with what they actually do. Research evidence actually promotes the view that we often do not know why we act the way we do, rendering our self-reports and introspection suspect (e.g., Nisbett & Wilson, 1977; Wilson, 1994; Wilson, Dunn, Kraft, & Lisle, 1989; but see Ericsson & Simon, 1993). Although self-report measures are very useful, even integral to behavioral science research, a good research strategy is to bolster their effectiveness by simultaneously measuring related behavioral variables. What people say can then be compared to what they do.

Regarding the memory experiment, I hope that it is clear why search terms recalled or recognized do *not* constitute what is normally considered a self-report measure. The reason is that neither recall nor recognition of terms require participants to share any thoughts or feelings—the memory measure, then, represents a behavior rather than a response driven by attitude or opinion.

In contrast to the public nature of behavioral and self-report measures, *physiological measures* are markers of much more private, internal psychological states. Common physiological measures in psychological research include pupil dilation, blood pressure, heart rate, and galvanic skin response, an indicator of electrodermal activity. Please notice that each of these measures provide *indirect* evidence for an individual's psychological reactions. Why is the evidence indirect? Imagine that you were interested in studying how people can become physiologically aroused when they watch an exciting clip of film, say, a downhill ski run taken from the perspective of the skier. Instead of asking people how they felt about the film or watching their facial expressions—self-report and behavioral indicators, respectively—you could measure their heart rate, respiration levels, perspiration, and so on to study their arousal reactions.

The one problem with physiological measures is that they are often not easy to interpret; that is, despite their emotional differences, both fear and excitement tend to result in elevated heart rate, rapid breathing, and heightened perspiration. An investigator must develop a coherent, logical account of why particular physiological changes are caused by one stimulus and not another. Thus, physiological measures are still somewhat controversial, though they are becoming increasingly common in psychological research.

The fourth and final class of dependent measures is called *behavioroid measures*. Aronson and colleagues (1990), who wanted a way to describe situations where research participants provide future-oriented responses, coined the term behavioroid. In some studies, for example, participants are asked to volunteer to perform some activity in the future—devoting time to community service or visiting patients in a nursing home. The participants *never actually* perform the activities, of course, but their responses are treated in an "as if they did" manner. Researchers who use behavioroid measures are interested in studying participant commitment to some possible future event, not whether the event actually occurs. Really, anytime a

To examine the link (if any) between people's words and their deeds, self-report measures should be accompanied by behavioral measures.

Table 2.2 Four Classes of Dependent Measures with Supporting Examples

Class of Dependent Measure	Examples
Behavioral	Reaction time
	Body orientation or lean
	Proximity to or distance from others
	Number of pauses during speech
	Amount of wager in gambling task
	Number of flyers taken from a stack
	Time spent on the phone
	Number of eyeblinks per minute
	Recognition recall
	Free recall
Self-report	Responses to personality inventory
	Mood
	Rated liking for another person
	Endorsing self-descriptive adjectives
	Listing preferences (e.g., foods, activities)
	Rating emotions
	Attitudes (e.g., politics, gender roles)
Physiological	Heart rate (i.e., beats per minute)
	Blood pressure
	Pupil dilation
	EEG (electroencephalograph)
	EKG (electrocardiogram)
	MRI (magnetic resonance imaging)
	GSR (galvanic skin response)
Behavioroid	Volunteering to give blood
	Pledging to donate time, money, or service
	Reporting beliefs about future behavior

participant in a piece of research is asked to think about and react to some hypothetical event (e.g., "What is the first thing you would do if you won the lottery?"), a behavioroid measure is being used.

Table 2.2 summarizes the four classes of dependent measures found in psychological research. Be sure to examine the representative dependent measures listed within each class and try to remember some of them. As you learn statistical analyses in subsequent chapters, they will be easier to conceptualize if you recall dependent measures that can serve as examples.

Closing or Continuing the Research Loop?

The paradox of the research process is that when it works well, it asks more questions than it can answer— more research is therefore necessary, and the process begins again.

Where are we now in the research loop of experimentation? We completed the hypothetical experiment concerning memory for search terms on the Internet when we discussed the results and their interpretation (see step 4 in Figure 2.1). As can be seen back in Figure 2.1, the final step, step 5, involves looping back to step 1 and beginning the process again. In other words, the research does not end with one study—it might not end with 10 or even 20 studies. *Good research in psychology or any of the behavioral sciences generates more questions than it answers.* Other studies must be designed to clarify and extend (or limit, as the case may be) what is known. As a cognitive psychologist interested in applied memory research, the chances are very good that you would not be satisfied with the results of your one experiment. You would very likely want to look at those results in order to identify a question to pursue in the next experiment.

DATA BOX 2.B

Variable Distinctions: Simple, Sublime, and All Too Easily Forgotten

After years of teaching, I am convinced of one thing: One of the easiest concepts to forget is the distinction between independent variables and dependent measures. I am so convinced of this fact—particularly after having graded hundreds of exams and papers demonstrating the error—that I created this small Data Box to call your attention to the problem. You are probably not convinced of this fact, and I am guessing that more than a few readers believe they know the distinction cold. But why risk missing needless points on an exam or paper? Take a moment and review the distinction between these two critically important variable types one more time and ensure your future success.

Commit these facts to memory—I have tried to make them mnemonically meaningful:

■ *Independent variables **vary** in an experiment. Independent variables are manipulated, not measured.*

■ *Dependent measures are measured in an experiment; they **depend** on the independent variable for their values.*

Please understand that it is not necessary for the same researcher to continue a particular line of research using the research loop. Another investigator somewhere else may learn of the results and become interested in continuing the work or examining some empirical variation of it (recall the earlier discussion of replication and conceptual replication studies). Thus, step 5 is not an end but really only another beginning for researchers who use the research loop of experimentation.

The Importance of Determining Causality

Because this chapter was described as an interlude, we need to step back from our conceptual outline of the process and practice of research for a moment. In doing so, we should consider the overarching purpose behind careful sampling, randomization, the identification of independent variables and dependent measures, and the appropriate and rigorous use of statistics and data analysis. In pulling these and other research elements together, one single goal is involved: determining causality. By causality, we mean explaining how some observed cause led to some specific and observable effect.

Cause and effect are important—one should necessarily lead to the other—precisely because they allow investigators to explain both simple and complex relationships among variables in the world. The behavioral sciences seek to carve human behavior, as it were, at its joints by identifying what combination of present (or absent) variables elicits particular thoughts, feelings, or actions on the part of research participants. In turn, the identified variable combinations used in research are meant to stand in for the actual ebb and flow of variables in daily life, just as the participants are supposed to be representative of some local or more general population of people.

The gentle warning issued by various philosophers since the Enlightenment, notably those interested in establishing a philosophy of science, must be acknowledged and heeded: Science cannot prove any theory or other causal proposition. Rather, science can provide only a process whereby scientific theories become established through the gradual and systematic elimination of rival hypotheses (e.g., Cook & Campbell, 1979). Thus, psychological research like the hypothetical applied memory

Scientific truth is elusive, but careful, systematic research enables us to get ever closer to it.

DATA BOX 2.C

The "Hot Hand in Basketball" and the Misrepresentation of Randomness

Are you a basketball fan? Maybe you play the game?

Many basketball fans believe in streak shooting. So do players and coaches. Streak shooting—or having a "hot hand"—occurs when a player is assumed to have a better chance of making his next shot because he just made his last two or three shots. Essentially, players and observers alike believe that a player's chances of making a basket are *greater* following a hit than following a miss on a previous shot. Is streak shooting with a hot hand possible? Or, is it merely folklore?

According to psychologists Gilovich, Vallone, and Tversky (1985), there is no hot hand and that if not folklore, then it is certainly a cognitive illusion (c.f., Data Box 2.A). When we try to make random events "behave," we once again get into trouble by perceiving a particular pattern of events where there isn't one. Based on a detailed analysis of the shooting records of the Philadelphia 76ers, these researchers discovered that there is no positive association between the outcomes of successive shots. To support their argument, they also examined the free-throw records of the Boston Celtics and performed a controlled shooting experiment involving men and women players from Cornell University's varsity squads. None of the players on these three different teams had the hot hand because there were no shooting streaks.

What, then, is going on when we watch a game and *see* a shooting streak or, rather, what *appears* to be a shooting streak? When people witness a streak of shooting by a player, Gilovich et al. (1985) argue that fans and others are actually misperceiving chance—in this case, whether a made shot is followed by a hit or a miss. This misperception is fueled by the representativeness heuristic (see Data Box 2.A), which leads people to see chance shooting (i.e., a hit followed by a hit) to be streak shooting. The problem is that people assume that chance shooting has many more alterations (i.e., a hit followed by a miss, or vice versa) than it actually does. Thus, a streak of, say, four shots in a row (or four misses, for that matter) is perceived as a streak when it is in actuality not a departure from chance! In short, people want random sequences to be more balanced—that is, to have more alternations among hits and misses—than they actually are. In a statistical sense, each successive shot has nothing whatever to do with the previous shot; as statisticians put it, all shots are "independent" of one another.

Does this mean that basketball is more a game of chance than skill? Certainly not! Gilovich et al. (1985) are quick to point out that other variables such as player skill, distance to the basket, the play of the other team, and fan reaction matter a great deal where winning and losing are concerned—but there is no hot hand to save the day. These hot hand conclusions are controversial, as some researchers (Larkey, Smith, & Kadane, 1989) disagree with Gilovich and his colleagues (but see Tversky & Gilovich, 1989, for a riposte). Keep this research in mind the next time you watch a basketball game and try not to be seduced by the patterns of play the announcer or other fans perceive. It can be just as fun to predict the next play without relying on the hot hand.

experiment progresses forward only as rival hypotheses are tested against established wisdom; old data must sometimes yield to new.

To put it more bluntly still, we will never know the whole truth of human behavior, but each careful, systematic piece of research and its accompanying statistical analyses move us closer to it than we would otherwise be. We need to study how independent variable X caused a verifiable change in dependent measure Y—and to be sure, statistics and data analysis will help us do this—but we must also keep in mind that determining causal relations among variables is a process of successive approximation. By carefully and systematically eliminating rival accounts for human behavior, each study (or series of studies) gets us closer to an accurate portrayal of how psychological variables influence one another. Our portrayal, of course, will always be somewhat incomplete—actual behavior is dynamic and even the most sophisticated piece of research cannot capture it completely. Nonetheless, determining causality is the goal of research in psychology and the behavioral sciences, and the methodology, statistics, and data analysis techniques provide opportunity to approximate it.

Operational Definitions in Behavioral Research

When investigators conduct research, the variables they use must be defined in two ways. First, variables are presented within the context of the relevant theory and the hypothesis derived from it. To do so, researchers rely on *descriptive definitions*.

KEY TERM   A **descriptive definition** explains the relationship among variables in an abstract, conceptual manner.

In the hypothetical memory experiment on Internet search terms, for example, two abstract memory processes, recognition and recall, were descriptively defined as dependent measures. Recognition was descriptively defined as a memory process that enables individuals to differentiate information seen on a prior occasion from novel information. Although recall is a related process, it could be descriptively defined as the ability to produce some fact, word, or other stimulus from memory. Please note that these descriptive definitions are both general and conceptual, and that they could describe the event relevant to *any number* of memory experiments, not just one dealing with memory for Internet search terms.

Following any descriptive definition, a researcher must *operationally define* the variables that are being manipulated or measured. An operational definition takes a conceptual variable and converts it into a concrete, testable format, one usually consistent with the hypothesis.

KEY TERM   An **operational definition** renders hypothetical, often abstract variables into concrete operations that can be manipulated or measured empirically.

Operational definitions can be used to explicate independent variables as well as dependent measures; indeed, such definitions represent the empirical aspects, the literal "operations," of the variables being manipulated and measured. When the aforementioned recognition and recall processes were operationalized, recognition was defined as the ability to identify old from new search terms, while free recall was the ability to produce the search terms from memory in any order.

The goal of operational definitions is to make the concepts and terms used in research less subjective and less open to different—even competing—interpretations. If an operational definition is clear, then other researchers or interested readers of the scientific literature should agree that it is an understandable and acceptable choice for exploring some behavioral phenomenon. Although an operational definition can be understood and even agreed on by several investigators, be advised that there is no ideal or perfect description of any variable. Rather, there is a potentially endless list of competing operational definitions so that a researcher's job is to sort among the possibilities to find the one he or she believes is most appropriate for the current research. Some other investigator might use a different operational definition for the same variable, thereby developing an entirely different empirical realization. As an exercise, imagine for a moment how many different ways abstract ideas like happiness or helping could be operationalized—if you dipped into the relevant psychological

Table 2.3   Writing Descriptive and Operational Definitions

1. Write a brief description (three or four sentences) of the theory being used in the research.
2. Write a *descriptive definition* of the independent variable(s) from this theory. Do the same for any dependent measure(s) featured in the theory.
3. Write an *operational definition* for the independent variable(s) and the dependent measure(s) identified in step 2. Be certain to use concrete terms and familiar concepts in the *operational definitions.*
4. If you are using published research, what *operational definitions* have been used to examine these or similar independent variables and dependent measures? Write down these published *operational definitions* and then compare them to those generated in step 3.
5. Refine and finalize the *operational definitions* based on step 4. Write down the final *operational definitions.*

Source: Adapted from Dunn, 1999, Table 6.1, p. 175.

literature, you would be amazed by the variety of operational definitions and the ingenuity of the researchers in creating them.

Writing Operational Definitions

As you begin the process of linking statistics and data analysis to independent variables and dependent measures in research, it is important to clearly define variables. Table 2.3 provides some guidelines for writing operational definitions. This table will prove to be especially useful when you must describe any dependent measures that are used in statistical analyses. That is, before interested readers can understand the analysis you used and the results you obtained, they must first have a grasp of *what* the data were like that were analyzed. If you have a clear and firm grasp of the descriptive and operational nature of the variables used in any piece of research, you will be able to communicate your understanding in writing with confidence and certainty.

Knowledge Base

1. The_____is manipulated, whereas the_____is measured.
   a. dependent measure
   b. independent variable
2. An independent variable must have at least_____levels.
   a. 1
   b. 2
   c. 3 or more
   d. 6
3. Give one example of each of the four types of dependent measures: behavioral, self-report, physiological, and behavioroid.
4. You are a psychologist who is interested in aggression. Provide a descriptive definition and an operational definition for this concept.
5. Identify which of the following is likely to be an independent variable or a dependent measure.
   a. varied temperature
   b. ratings of personal attraction
   c. bright and dim lighting
   d. recognition test
   e. recall test
   f. hearing or reading a prepared speech.

6. True or False: Research in the behavioral sciences is a process of successive approximation to the true state of affairs in nature—we may not learn the truth, but research brings us ever closer to it.

Answers

1. b. independent variable; a dependent measure
2. b. 2
3. See Table 2.2 for examples
4. Examples: descriptive definition—aggression is the intent to harm another person. Operational definition—number of hostile comments made within an experiment.
5. Independent variable: a, c, f; dependent measure: b, d, e.
6. True

Reliability and Validity

The discussion of descriptive versus operational definitions reminds us that most research in the behavioral sciences examines what are often referred to as *hypothetical constructs*.

KEY TERM   A **hypothetical construct** is an image, an idea, or theory used to organize hypotheses and data. *Hypothetical constructs* enable researchers to speculate about the processes underlying, even causing, thought and behavior.

Hypothetical constructs cannot be seen, nor can you reach out and touch one. Their power is not physical but rhetorical—hypothetical constructs help researchers to create persuasive accounts of how variables appear to behave or influence one another.

You have lots of attitudes or opinions, for example, but you cannot show them to anyone. Rather, your thoughts, words, and deeds provide indirect evidence for your attitudes. If your political attitudes are liberal, then you probably vote for Democratic candidates, donate to left-wing causes, regularly read *The New York Times* in lieu of more conservative newspapers, and are unlikely to sport a "Rush is Right" bumpersticker on your car. You may also speak up about traditionally liberal causes, such as the environment, affirmative action, and the women's movement. Whether the example is behavioral or verbal, though, it is clearly the case that we are not "seeing" your actual liberal attitude—we are simply encountering aspects of what you say and do that *suggest* or *strongly imply* that you harbor liberal tendencies.

Do you see the subtle problem? Hypothetical constructs have no reality per se, but their presence is essential to theory development and the testing of hypotheses. If you want to predict which candidate is likely to be elected in a local or national election, for example, some knowledge of his or her political attitudes is critical—even if that attitude is only known imperfectly and indirectly. Similarly, I may believe that you have high self-esteem if you exude confidence, appear articulate, give a firm handshake, and look me in the eye when you speak to me. Can I actually see your high self-esteem? No, I only see traces of it via the (potential) effects it has on the way you present yourself. I could try to envision your self-esteem in a different way, however, by asking you to complete a standardized psychological instrument designed to measure self-esteem by reporting a score. Your score could then be compared to the known range of scores, as well as the average, so that I could determine if you do, indeed, have high self-esteem. Such test scores are proxy measures, close substitutes, for the actual but hypothetical level of an individual's self-esteem.

As you can no doubt appreciate, hypothetical constructs are integral to our theories and hypotheses—they are literally everywhere in the behavioral sciences—so that even if we have difficulty establishing their actual existence, we must try to verify their influence on behavior. Fortunately, psychologists and other behavioral scientists have focused on ways to carefully measure hypothetical constructs and to then provide supporting evidence for the measurements. Two main questions are relevant to the measurement of any psychological construct: Is the measurement of the construct (or variable thought to represent it) reliable? Is the construct's measure (or the variable serving as the surrogate) valid? We will review each question and its implications in detail.

Reliability

In everyday use, the word reliable corresponds to "trustworthy" or possibly "faithful" or even "true." In research terms, the word reliability has a more precise and circumscribed meaning: A reliable measure is one that is stable or consistent across time. That is, all else being equal, a reliable measure is anticipated to give the same measurement of the same phenomenon each and every time it is used.

KEY TERM   **Reliability** refers to a measure's stability or consistency across time. If used on the same stimulus, a *reliable* measure gives approximately the same result each time it is used.

An instrument—a survey, a personality questionnaire, a thermometer, a bathroom scale—is deemed reliable if it consistently gives the same answer, score, reading, weight, or result when the same person, object, or construct is measured on two or more occasions. Unless you have had an especially happy series of events in your life (or a number of crushing personal defeats), your score on a reliable self-esteem scale should not vary more than a few points from some original score each time you take it.

▽

Reliability = stability = consistency.

Given the earlier discussion of sampling error, though, we would not expect you to get the *exact* same score on the self-esteem measure each time. There is presumably a true score reflecting your self-esteem, but any given administration of a self-esteem measure—yielding what is called an *observed score*—will not necessarily capture it. If you took the same self-esteem measure, say, six times over a 3-year period, it is likely that the true score would fall somewhere among the six observed scores. If the self-esteem measure is a particularly reliable one, then the difference among the six scores is apt to be small (i.e., there is a low degree of measurement error). On the other hand, if the measure is not reliable (or you have recently experienced dramatic ups or downs in your life) then there is apt to be a relatively large amount of measurement error. Not only would the six observed scores vary greatly from one another, they would presumably differ rather substantially from the true (but unknown) score, as well. Let me reiterate the main point here one more time: Any measure is apt to demonstrate some measurement error or "drift" between true scores and observed scores—it is simply the case that a reliable measure shows less error or drift.

Thus far, our discussion of reliability has been conceptual. In actuality, reliability is very much a statistical matter. Countless standardized tests and personality inventories used in laboratories, clinics, classrooms, and courtrooms contain information regarding what are called **reliability coefficients.** A reliability coefficient is a numerical index of how stable or consistent the scores on a measure are across two or more administrations. Reliability coefficients are based on correlation, a method of measuring the association between two or more variables. Although we will introduce correlational research in this chapter, correlation is a basic and important statistical technique that we will need to spend sufficient time exploring later in this book. There are also several different types of reliability coefficients and we will discuss them, and the concept of correlation more broadly, in chapter 6. For the present, I recommend that you focus on the conceptual understanding of reliability as useful and desirable to any measure used in behavioral science research. We will also review the notion of reliability and its relation to sampling in chapter 9, when we discuss what are called sampling distributions.

We have examined why the measurement of a variable should be consistent or stable across time. We now turn to the necessity of demonstrating that a research measure is a valid one.

Validity

The intuitive meaning of the term *validity*—sound, just, or even well-founded—is close to its definition in research contexts: Does a measure actually measure what it is supposed to measure? The last phrase may seem like quite a mouthful, but this definition for validity gets right to the heart of the research enterprise.

KEY TERM   **Validity** is the degree to which an observation or a measurement corresponds to the construct that was supposed to be observed or measured.

A valid measure, then, actually measures or manipulates the construct of interest to an investigator.

Depending on the nature of the piece of research, validity can be discussed from several points of view. Although we will make note of some of these different kinds of validity, our primary concern will be *construct validity*.

KEY TERM   **Construct validity** examines how well a variable's operational definition reflects the actual nature and meaning of the theoretical variable.

Consider a research topic such as intelligence, which can be defined as the capacity to learn from experience and the ability to adapt to one's environment (e.g., Sternberg & Detterman, 1986). If a researcher were studying intelligence, then the intelligence test she chose to use would serve as the operational definition of intelligence. The test's construct validity can be determined by whether and how well it actually measures the theoretical construct commonly referred to as "intelligence."

Pause for a moment and think about exactly what sort of information you believe could reasonably be placed on a test designed to measure an individual's intelligence. I think you will agree that it is by no means easy to come up with indicators of intelligence that are fair, describe large numbers of people, differentiate among people's different levels of intelligence, and can be agreed on by psychologists and educators who concern themselves with the study of intelligence. In fact, defining intelligence descriptively and operationally, and then verifying its construct validity, is no small task, as it can involve verbal comprehension, math skills, pattern analysis, and memory (e.g., words, digits, objects). Besides performing the empirical side of research, then, investigators have their conceptual work cut out for themselves, as well.

Let's turn to reviewing the several different approaches to establishing the validity of a measure. The most basic form of validity is called **face validity.** When a measure is said to have face validity, it means that after a superficial analysis, it appears to be measuring what it set out to measure. To continue our intelligence example, any number of general knowledge tests would probably serve as reasonable evidence for a measure's face validity. Thus, a series of questions examining basic math and verbal skills would be appropriate, but more esoteric questions concerning the art of the high

▽

Validity is present when a hypothetical construct of interest is actually being observed or measured.

Renaissance or the poems of Octavio Paz might be out of place (i.e., too few people could answer them). Yet some people would associate esoteric knowledge as being more representative of "intelligence" than skill at answering more basic, even commonsensical, sorts of questions. As you can see, face validity is a start, but nothing prevents different researchers (or observers like us) from offering different claims about what is or is not a sign of intelligence.

Convergent validity reduces the difficulty posed by competing opinion or interpretation by focusing on comparing a measure with other related measures and variables. Responses to a novel measure for intelligence would be compared to people's responses on existing—previously validated—measures of intelligence. In other words, the new and existing measures would "converge" on the construct we refer to as intelligence. If the new measure really did tap into the construct, then the researcher would expect to find that it was at least moderately related to the existing measures of intelligence. To be safe, the researcher would probably also want to see how responses on the measures fared in comparison to responses on related constructs, such as problem solving and creativity. Note that problem solving and creativity are *related to* the construct of—but are *not* the same as—intelligence. In fact, the strength of the positive relationships among problem solving, creativity, and intelligence should be much lower than the patterns among the new and existing measures of the construct.

Most researchers also want to show that a new measure of a construct is *not* related to particular constructs or variables. In terms of theory and research practice, some measures should be specifically predicted to be unrelated to a new measure. This form of validity is called **discriminant validity** because a new measure should discriminate—differentiate or note differences—among a novel measure and other constructs or variables. After all, what use would a measure be if all other constructs were somehow related to it? Thus, our novel measure of intelligence would probably not be related to measures of aggression, sociability, risk-taking, or depression, and its level of association would presumably be low on a positive scale, close to zero, or perhaps even negative.

Finally, there are two types of validity that are particularly relevant to experimentation, though they do apply in varying degrees to any research effort. **Internal validity** is defined as the unambiguous effect of some independent variable on a dependent measure. That is, the causal relationship between what is manipulated in the experiment and its outcome is clear and free of competing interpretations. Internal validity addresses the "inside" of a piece of research while the second type, **external validity,** focuses on the "outside" implications of the research (Dunn, 1999). Specifically, external validity addresses the question of whether research results can generalize to other people, at other times, and in other places. This generalizability is of greatest concern for research that addresses "real-world" issues, such as the search for solutions to social problems, educational reform, and the psychological study of health and well-being. To be considered scientific and therefore useful for expanding knowledge, a study must have internal validity, but it need not possess much in the way of external validity (for more detail on this issue, see Mook, 1983).

A summary of these various approaches to validity can be found in Table 2.4. Similar to reliability, illustrating the presence or absence of validity within a piece of research relies on some statistical evidence. In general, this evidence entails demonstrating how a new measure is statistically associated (or not) with other measures—does it converge (i.e., associate highly and positively) or discriminate (i.e., have low or no association), for example. At this point, the conceptual background of validity is important for you to understand and use as you read the final section of this chapter, which deals with research designs. The statistical basis for validity will be visited later in the text in a variety of ways.

Table 2.4   A Guide to Various Approaches to Validity

Construct Validity	To what degree does the operational definition of a variable or measure correspond favorably to the actual but theoretical nature of the construct?
Face Validity	To what degree does a measure or variable appear to accurately represent a construct?
Convergent Validity	To what degree is a measure or variable related to other measures or variables in predictable ways? Is the association positive and moderate to strong?
Discriminant Validity	To what degree is a measure or variable *unrelated* to other measures and variables that it should not be related to? Is the association low on a positive scale, zero, or negative?
Internal Validity	Did the independent variable create a meaningful and verifiable change in the dependent measure? To what degree is the change measurable and unambiguous?
External Validity	To what degree do the results apply to other situations, other persons, and other times? Can the data be generalized beyond the original setting?

Knowledge Base

1. True or False: Although they are not real in any physical sense, hypothetical constructs allow researchers to build theories and test hypotheses.
2. You complete a personality measure once and then take it again 6 months later. The two scores are approximately equal to one another, indicating that the measure has a high degree of _____.
   a. Discriminant validity
   b. Reliability
   c. Convergent validity
   d. Internal validity
3. _____occurs when, as predicted, related measures are positively associated with a new measure or variable.
   a. Discriminant validity
   b. Reliability
   c. Convergent validity
   d. Internal validity.
4. In order to demonstrate_____, some variables should not be associated with a new measure or variable.
   a. Discriminant validity
   b. Reliability
   c. Face validity
   d. External validity
5. Although_____is desirable in an experiment,_____determines whether the results are viewed as scientifically worthy.
   a. Face validity
   b. Internal validity
   c. Reliability
   d. External validity

Answers

1. True
2. b. Reliability
3. c. Convergent validity
4. a. Discriminant validity
5. d. External validity; b. internal validity

🌙 Research Designs

The questions of interest to psychologists and other behavioral scientists are asked within the context of a *research design.*

KEY TERM   A **research design** is an organized collection of procedures used by researchers to collect behavioral data.

There are numerous research designs available, any one of which can be used for a distinct purpose or to answer a specific question about behavior. For the sake of clarity and to foster links between design and data analysis, we will define three main categories of research design. These three categories are correlational research, experiments, and quasi-experiments. These research designs are quantitative in nature; that is, they lend themselves to and make considerable use of statistical analyses. Qualitative designs tend not to rely on statistics, but they are very useful for examining behavioral phenomena that are not measurable in the traditional sense of the word (see Appendix F). Although we will discuss the basic features of each category of quantitative design, please be advised that by their very nature, research designs are tailored to the particular situation of interest to researchers—presenting them in a generic fashion does not do justice to their richness or applicability.

Correlational Research

Many research questions begin when an investigator is not sure how two or more variables relate to one another. Do they "go together" or, as psychologists and statisticians are wont to say, covary with one another? When variables covary with one another in some discernable pattern, they are described as "correlated." *Correlational designs* examine the pattern of association among variables, and such patterns are useful for planning future experiments or discovering unknown relations among variables.

KEY TERM   A **correlational design** is used to discover predictive relationships and the degree of association among variables.

The reason investigators study the covariation between (or among) variables is to establish predictive relationships. If grade point average (GPA) and debating skill were found to go together, then the admissions teams of law schools might be able to predict which applicants would make good lawyers. Thus, skilled speakers—those who interview well, for instance—would presumably have good grades, and applicants with high GPAs would presumably be able debaters.

This description of association between speaking skills and GPA is described as a **positive correlation.** A positive correlation occurs between two variables when as the value of one variable increases or decreases, the other variables behaves in a similar manner. In contrast, a **negative correlation** occurs when the value of one variable increases (e.g., GPA) as the other decreases (e.g., time spent socializing). Perhaps people

🔽

A correlation can be positive, negative, or zero, ranging in value from –1.00 to +1.00.

with higher grades socialize less than individuals with lower grades. No correlation, sometimes called a **zero correlation,** means that there is no clear pattern between two variables; speaking skills, socializing, and GPA do not covary—correlate—with one another in any discernable fashion.

Do you see any problems with the interpretations offered for these covarying variables? That is, are the positive or negative associations trustworthy or merely suggestive? To be sure, some skilled speakers do have high GPAs, but many do not, just as only some persons with high GPAs will be skilled speakers. Some sociable people, too, have very high grades despite the fact that they burn the candle at both ends (I'm guessing you know one or two people like this). The fundamental dictum regarding correlational research explains these counterexamples: *Correlation does not imply causation.* The reason that causality is not implicated in correlational research is because the variables involved are measured and the associations among them are identified, but no *manipulation* of some variables to test their affect on others occurs. Thus, variable X can cause a change in Y, Y can create change in X, or both X and Y can be affected by some unknown variable Z (see chapter 6). In fact, some unknown variables P, Q, and R could be the source of the relationship between X and Y! Correlation does not, cannot identify the causal relationships (if any) among some group of variables.

Figure 2.3 illustrates how two variables can be related to one another. A random or nonrandom (e.g., convenience) sample is drawn from some population. Sample participants react to variables—some independent, some dependent—some of which are correlated with one another. As you can see in Figure 2.3, the precise direction of association is unknown because the causal connections between (or among) the variables are not identified.

Where correlational research is concerned, then, researchers know association and not the causal ordering among the variables unless some are manipulated while others are measured. Learn the dictum now—correlation does not imply causation—so that it will serve you well in the future. If you follow it, you can be sure that you will not draw erroneous conclusions about behavior until you have causal, experimental evidence to support your speculations.

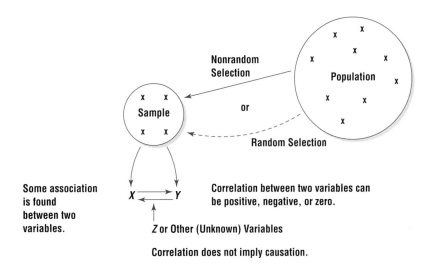

Figure 2.3   The Logic of Correlational Designs

Correlation implies association—not any causal relationship—between or among variables.

Correlational research is suggestive, as it points to potential causal variables but makes no firm conclusions about them. Indeed, alternative explanations for obtained results often abound. Correlational designs do not usually involve random assignment to condition, though they sometimes employ random selection (see Figure 2.3). As noted earlier, random assignment provides group equivalence before any measurement or intervention takes place. The absence of this form of randomization is the chief difference between correlational and experimental research designs.

Experiments

We discussed the basic framework of experimental designs earlier in the chapter. Some hypothesis derived from a theory is used to test the affects of manipulating two or more levels of an independent variable on some dependent measure. Participants are either randomly selected from a population before being placed in groups or they are randomly assigned to one of several experimental conditions (i.e., levels of the independent variable). The goal of experimentation is to specify a causal relationship based on intervening in some situation—Does the predicted change occur in the outcome (dependent) variable? You will recall that the hypothetical research on memory for Internet search terms illustrating these concepts in action.

One main methodological aspect of experimentation remains to be introduced, however. Even when all potentially influential variables are controlled, held constant, or selectively manipulated by a researcher, the experiment still may not represent a strong and clear test of the hypothesis. Why? Simply because one or more *confounded variables* may be present. The confounding of variables occurs when the influence of the independent variable becomes entangled with the effects of some other variable, one *not* under the control of the researcher. The dependent measure, in turn, is affected by this uncontrolled variable.

KEY TERM   A **confounded variable** is an uncontrolled variable that unknowingly but systematically varies with the independent variable, thereby preventing a clear interpretation of cause and effect between the independent variable and the dependent measure.

The chief concern about confounds is that they can systematically bias the results of any study. Of course, it is also true that it is impossible to think of or control for every possible variable that could affect the outcome and interpretation of a study. In fact, one of the reasons investigators run multiple studies to examine some behavioral phenomenon is to rule out potential confounds along the way. Such efforts are not only necessary where confounds are concerned, but they also enhance the reliability and validity of obtained results. Researchers, then, must do the best they can to identify and isolate the most probable confounds in their work.

Are there any confounded variables in the memory for Internet search terms experiment? Well, as the investigator, you might want to be concerned about the previous computer experiences of the research participants. Participants who have had a lot of computer experience, especially Internet experience, could systematically bias the results—their familiarity with Internet searching, for instance, gives them a distinct advantage over novice users. It is probably difficult to find many people who have not had some exposure to computers—the technology is now ubiquitous in homes, schools, and offices—but it may be possible to locate some individuals who have not had much experience searching the Internet. To avoid this confounded variable—prior computer experience—your primary concern should be to make certain that either all participants have little prior experience with the Internet or that those who have had considerable

Table 2.5 A Model of the Standard Experiment

	Treatment or Experimental Groups	
Sequence of Events	**Experimental**	**Control**
Random selection (if any) or recruitment	—	—
Random assignment (treatment or group)	—	—
Presentation of independent variable	Different	Different
Presentation of dependent measure	Identical	Identical
Statistical analysis of dependent measure to assess (treatment or group) difference	—	—

Source: Adapted from Dunn, 1999, Table 6.16 on p. 215.

experience are dropped from the study. In a future study, of course, you might want to specifically test whether such prior experience makes any difference in retaining search terms—but that is for another time.

Table 2.5 illustrates a model of the standard experiment. The sequence of events is presented on the left side of the table, and whether the experimental and control groups receive identical or different information is noted on the right. The discussion in this chapter, as well as Table 2.5, assumes a very basic experiment involving random assignment to one of two participant groups, manipulation of one independent variable, and measurement of one dependent measure. As you can see in Table 2.5, the participant groups receive different levels of the independent variable but the identical dependent measure so that any resulting differences can be assessed. Assessment of these differences (if any) relies on statistics and data analysis.

The basic model of the two-group experiment is graphically illustrated in Figure 2.4. Random assignment must be used to create two or more groups (prior

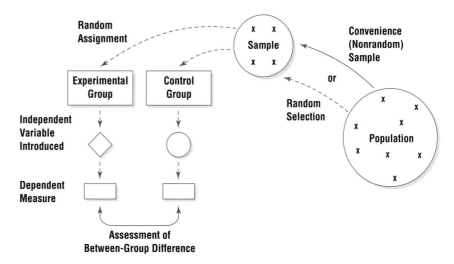

Figure 2.4 A Basic Two-Group Experiment Illustrated

random selection is optional), followed by the manipulation of the independent variable, the administration of the dependent measure, and the assessment of hypothesized differences.

As a mental exercise, review the sequence of events illustrated in Table 2.5 and Figure 2.4 with the hypothetical Internet search term study in mind. Can you "walk through it" in your mind and explain what happens at each stage in the sequence? Why is random assignment used? Why are the levels of the independent variable "different" and why are the dependent measures the "same"?

Naturally, many experiments are much more complex than this basic model, and there can be several participant groups and more than one manipulated or measured variable can appear in any one. Having two or three independent variables and dependent measures can be accommodated in an experiment, but the execution of the design and its logistics require careful planning and diligent organization. In a word, the researcher must be prepared to exercise a good deal of control when conducting an experiment. Exercising control is much easier to accomplish in the laboratory than in the real world, as will be shown by the discussion of quasi-experiments.

Quasi-experiments

Cook and Campbell (1979) coined the term "quasi-experiments" to apply to those research investigations that lacked one or more of the characteristics that denote a true experiment (e.g., randomization, manipulation of an independent variable, presence of a control group). Thus, a quasi-experiment is akin to an experiment, except for the fact that the actual causal dynamics underlying the research question remain somewhat obscure.

KEY TERM   A **quasi-experiment** is a research design resembling an experiment, but it lacks one or more key features heightening experimental control. *Quasi-experiments* enable investigators to approximate but not delineate causal effects.

Quasi-experiments are used to study those situations that do not lend themselves to experimentation. The most common reason a quasi-experiment is employed is due to the inability to randomly assign participants to some treatment condition or group corresponding to a level of an independent variable. Random assignment is not possible, for example, when a researcher wants to study the behavior of some intact group of persons who have experienced something unique. An investigator cannot randomly assign people to live along the San Andreas fault in California to assess their reactions to earthquakes, for example. Instead, investigators must be content with drawing conclusions about the experiences of those who choose to live there, even if that experience is "contaminated" by or confounded with many other influential variables (e.g., Pennebaker & Harber, 1993).

Use of a quasi-experimental design necessitates demonstrating that between-group differences are due to some treatment, a naturally occurring event (e.g., an earthquake), or something about the research participants themselves. Many times an adequate control or comparison group is not even available. For example, should you compare the responses of earthquake survivors with those of people who do not live in earthquake zones, or is it better to compare them with the survivors of other natural (e.g., floods, fires) or man-made (e.g., shipwrecks, plane crashes) disasters? Is it even necessary to have a control group (see Data Box 2.D)? Questions like these—and the concerns they raise—must be duly considered by researchers before any firm conclusions about the results of a quasi-experiment can be drawn.

DATA BOX 2.D

Quasi-experimentation in Action:
What to Do Without Random Assignment or
a Control Group

What recourse do researchers have when interesting behavioral phenomena occur in less than ideal research circumstances? They adapt by adopting one of many quasi-experimental approaches. We will briefly consider two excellent examples of quasi-experimental work that lacked random assignment and traditional control groups.

Baum, Gatchel, and Schaeffer (1983) studied stress reactions in the community surrounding Three Mile Island (TMI) after the nuclear accident that took place there back in the late 1970s. Clearly, this traumatic event had obvious societal implications for how people cope with sudden but unseen dangers—dangers with long-term consequences (e.g., cancer). A quasi-experimental approach was selected because few variables could be controlled, replication was neither desirable nor feasible, and the event could never be adequately simulated in a laboratory setting. For comparing stress reactions, the researchers used three **comparison groups** in lieu of a single control group. A comparison group is composed of individuals who *approximate* the characteristics found in the treatment group, but they are not usually randomly assigned nor can we be sure they were drawn from the same theoretical population.

Besides interviewing people living near TMI, Baum et al. (1983) also spoke to individuals dwelling near a functional nuclear power plant and a coal-powered energy facility, as well as a group who lived 20 miles from any power plant. The responses of the participants from the three comparison groups helped the investigators rule out alternative explanations for the stress reactions observed among the people living near the TMI facility. Over a year after the accident, TMI residents reported more physical symptoms, anxiety, depression, and social alienation than the members of the three comparison groups, who did not differ from one another on these psychosocial indicators.

In contrast to the work of Baum and his colleagues, the second study represents quasi-experimentation on a much smaller scale. Despite the lack of random assignment or any control (comparison) group, the psychosocial implications of this second study are as profound as the first. Pennebaker, Barger, and Tiebout (1989) conducted a quasi-experiment on the effects of disclosing long past traumatic experiences on health, predicting that higher levels of disclosure regarding the trauma would yield better health several months later. They filmed 33 Holocaust survivors who described their lives and fortunes during World War II, carefully monitoring various physiological measures as the survivors spoke on camera. Over a year later, Pennebaker and colleagues found that higher levels of disclosure were positively correlated with health indicators—sharing painful memories seemed to enhance health and well-being.

Strong conclusions about such correlational data are precluded, of course, but should we raise the lack of a control group as a concern? Probably not—what experience could rival the horror of the Holocaust, the murder of millions of European Jews at the hands of the Nazis in World War II? Of what use—scientific or otherwise—would there be in comparing the nightmare tales of survivors to the experiences of some arbitrary comparison group? Meaningful comparison groups sometimes elude us, and in this case, perhaps, we should be grateful. Many of Pennebaker et al.'s (1989) participants benefited from their testimonials, and the findings were consistent with other, more experimental evidence (e.g., Pennebaker, 1989). Lack of random assignment or control groups in quasi-experimental design, then, is often offset by the rich, humane quality these studies bring to the scientific enterprise.

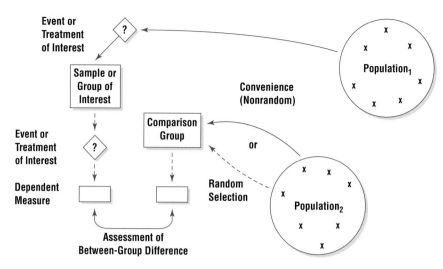

Figure 2.5   A Possible Quasi-Experimental Design Illustrated

The review of specific quasi-experimental designs is beyond the scope of this chapter (but see the two examples in Data Box 2.D). Figure 2.5 illustrates but one possible quasi-experimental design. As you can see, the intact group of interest was drawn (non-randomly) from one population and the comparison group from another. An event or treatment could occur to the group of interest either *before* or *after* recruitment (see Figure 2.5). Naturally, the comparison group has no similar experience; indeed, the only common experience the two groups share is the presentation of the dependent measure and the subsequent assessment of between group differences at the study's conclusion (see Figure 2.5).

Various other quasi-experimental designs exist and they can be found in any one of several references (e.g., Campbell, 1969; Campbell & Stanley, 1963; Cook & Campbell, 1979; Judd & Kenny, 1981). Keep in mind that the results from quasi-experiments are analyzed using the same statistical and data analytic techniques that are employed on experimental data. The difference, of course, is that investigators must spend more time and energy using statistical tools to rule out competing or alternative accounts for the results obtained in quasi-experiments.

Knowledge Base

1. A teacher observes a positive correlation between classroom seating and grades: Students who sit toward the front of the room have higher grades than those who sit in the back of the class do. Does it follow that seating leads to scholastic achievement? Why or why not?
2. Provide an example of (a) a positive correlation and (b) a negative correlation.
3. True or False: It is possible to identify and control for every confounded variable that could effect an experiment.
4. True or False: Research designs with more than one independent variable and dependent measure exist.
5. What makes a quasi-experiment different from an experiment?

Answers

1. No. Correlation does not imply causation.
2. Any two variable examples are fine. The positive correlation must indicate that as variable X increases (decreases), variable Y behaves similarly. The negative correlation must show that as variable X increases in value, variable Y decreases (and vice versa).
3. False: No piece of research can eliminate all potential confounded variables.
4. True
5. Quasi-experiments lack one or more defining experimental characteristics (e.g., control group, random assignment).

Project Exercise

USING A RANDOM NUMBERS TABLE

> The generation of random numbers is too important to be left to chance.
> — ROBERT R. COVEYOU (QUOTED IN GARDNER, 1975)

Randomness is a prominent theme in this chapter. We explored how random assignment is an extremely useful tool for establishing group equality when random selection is neither desirable nor in many cases possible. Random selection is most often used to determine whether a sample is representative of—can observations be generalized back to—its population of origin (recall Figure 2.2). We also reviewed the various guises randomization can be introduced into a piece of research through sampling (see Table 2.1). Discussion also focused on the natural, predictable ways humans selectively ignore randomness, try to tame it, or even characterize it in ways that ignore its fundamental nature (see Data Boxes 2.A and 2.C). The virtues of randomness outweigh its problems, however, and there is a clear advantage to understanding its use in research efforts (for a recent, extended discussion of randomness, see Bennett, 1998).

What we have *not* discussed about randomness is *how to use it* for purposes of random selection or random assignment within research contexts. As a teacher of statistics and an experimental social psychologist, I often worry that students never get a real feel for randomness or how to go about using it. Although we will encounter it many times in this book, notably when we discuss probability (chapter 8), I prefer that you begin to get a real sense of its applicability to research now. It is one thing to describe randomness conceptually—and you have learned how our penchant for order can get us into trouble on that front—but it is quite another to see it concretely and in action.

This chapter's project exercise was born out of a desire to give you a deeper understanding of randomness by having you make use of what is called a *random numbers table*.

KEY TERM A **random numbers table** contains numbers between 0 and 9 that were generated in an unbiased manner, so that each of the 10 numbers occurs equally often throughout the table in a patternless sequence.

A sample page from a random numbers table (Rand Corporation, 1955) is shown in Table 2.6. As you can see, the lines are numbered in the far right column (here, from rows 00001 to 00059). Take a moment and scan the remaining 10 columns of 5-digit number sequences. Because the table is comprised of randomly generated numbers, you can begin anywhere; you can read across a row, down a column of three-digit numbers, or up a sequence of single digits—it really does not matter. What does matter, of course, is using some population or sample to work with the random numbers table, and so we turn to an exercise for performing random selection and another for random assignment. Other randomization techniques can be found in Snedecor and Cochran (1980), and for interested readers, a work on the history of randomization is also available (Gigerenzer, Swijtink, Porter, Daston, Beatty, & Kruger, 1989).

Table 2.6   A Sample Random Numbers Table

Row number									
00000	10097	32533	76520	13586	34673	54876	80959	09117	39292	74945
00001	37542	04805	64894	74296	24805	24037	20636	10402	00822	91665
00002	08422	68953	19645	09303	23209	02560	15953	34764	35080	33606
00003	99019	02529	09376	70715	38311	31165	88676	74397	04436	27659
00004	12807	99970	80157	36147	64032	36653	98951	16877	12171	76833
00005	66065	74717	34072	76850	36697	36170	65813	39885	11199	29170
00006	31060	10805	45571	82406	35303	42614	86799	07439	23403	09732
00007	85269	77602	02051	65692	68665	74818	73053	85247	18623	88579
00008	63573	32135	05325	47048	90553	57548	28463	28709	83491	25624
00009	73796	45753	03529	64778	35808	34282	60935	20344	35273	88435
00010	98520	17767	14905	68607	22109	40558	60970	93433	50500	73998
00011	11805	05431	39808	27732	50725	68248	29405	24201	52775	67851
00012	83452	99634	06288	98033	13746	70078	18475	40610	68711	77817
00013	88685	40200	86507	58401	36766	67951	90364	76493	29609	11062
00014	99594	67348	87517	64969	91826	08928	93785	61368	23478	34113
00015	65481	17674	17468	50950	58047	76974	73039	57186	40218	16544
00016	80124	35635	17727	08015	45318	22374	21115	78253	14385	53763
00017	74350	99817	77402	77214	43236	00210	45521	64237	96286	02655
00018	69916	26803	66252	29148	36936	87203	76621	13990	94400	56418
00019	09893	20505	14225	68514	46427	56788	96297	78822	54382	14598
00020	91499	14523	68479	27686	46162	83554	94750	89923	37089	20048
00021	80336	94598	26940	36858	70297	34135	53140	33340	42050	82341
00022	44104	81949	85157	47954	32979	26575	57600	40881	22222	06413
00023	12550	73742	11100	02040	12860	74697	96644	89439	28707	25815
00024	63606	49329	16505	34484	40219	52563	43651	77082	07207	31790
00025	61196	90446	26457	47774	51924	33729	65394	59593	42582	60527
00026	15474	45266	95270	79953	59367	83848	82396	10118	33211	59466
00027	94557	28573	67897	54387	54622	44431	91190	42592	92927	45973
00028	42481	16213	97344	08721	16868	48767	03071	12059	25701	46670
00029	23523	78317	73208	89837	68935	91416	26252	29663	05522	82562
00030	04493	52494	75246	33824	45862	51025	61962	79335	65337	12472
00031	00549	97654	64051	88159	96119	63896	54692	82391	23287	29529
00032	35963	15307	26898	09354	33351	35462	77974	50024	90103	39333
00033	59808	08391	45427	26842	83609	49700	13021	24892	78565	20106
00034	46058	85236	01390	92286	77281	44077	93910	83647	70617	42941
00035	32179	00597	87379	25241	05567	07007	86743	17157	85394	11838
00036	69234	61406	20117	45204	15956	60000	18743	92423	97118	96338
00037	19565	41430	01758	75379	40419	21585	66674	36806	84962	85207
00038	45155	14938	19476	07246	43667	94543	59047	90033	20826	69541
00039	94864	31994	36168	10851	34888	81553	01540	35456	05014	51176
00040	98086	24826	45240	28404	44999	08896	39094	73407	35441	31880
00041	33185	16232	41941	50949	89435	48581	88695	41994	37548	73043
00042	80951	00406	96382	70774	20151	23387	25016	25298	94624	61171
00043	79752	49140	71961	28296	69861	02591	74852	20539	00387	59579

| **Table 2.6** | *(continued)* |

Row number									
00044	18633	32537	98145	06571	31010	24674	05455	61427	77938 91936
00045	74029	43902	77557	32270	97790	17119	52527	58021	80814 51748
00046	54178	45611	80993	37143	05335	12969	56127	19255	36040 90324
00047	11664	49883	52079	84827	59381	71539	09973	33440	88461 23356
00048	48324	77928	31249	64710	02295	36870	32307	57546	15020 09994
00049	69074	94138	87637	91976	35584	04401	10518	21615	01848 76938
00050	09188	20097	32825	39527	04220	86304	83389	87374	64278 58044
00051	90045	85497	51981	50654	94938	81997	91870	76150	68476 64659
00052	73189	50207	47677	26269	62290	64464	27124	67018	41361 82760
00053	75768	76490	20971	87749	90429	12272	95375	05871	93823 43178
00054	54016	44056	66281	31003	00682	27398	20714	53295	07706 17813
00055	08358	69910	78542	42785	13661	58873	04618	97553	31223 08420
00056	28306	03264	81333	10591	40510	07893	32604	60475	94119 01840
00057	53840	86233	81594	13628	51215	90290	28466	68795	77762 20791
00058	91757	53741	61613	62669	50263	90212	55781	76514	83483 47055
00059	89415	92694	00397	58391	12607	17646	48949	72306	94541 37408

PERFORMING RANDOM SELECTION

Perhaps you have a population of individuals—the members of a seminar class—and you want to draw a sample from it. Table 2.7 lists the 10 students (in alphabetical order) enrolled in the seminar. You elect to randomly select 5 individuals from the population of 10. (Please note that the procedure I am using here can be expanded for application to much larger populations—the logic is the same.)

Close your eyes and take your index finger (either hand) and place it anywhere on Table 2.6. When I did so, I landed on a number string in row 00038, column 2. The number string is 14938. If I read across and treat each digit in the string as corresponding to a one-digit numbered name in Table 2.7, then I have randomly selected Arletta, Doyle, Isaac, Carol, and Harriett to be the sample from the larger population (i.e., class).

Alternatively, I could have begun reading down the table from that first digit in row 00038, column 2 of Table 2.6. If so, then Areletta would still be in the sample, and she would be followed by (3) Carol and (2) Biff—I would then skip 1 because Arletta was

| **Table 2.7** | Population Comprised of 10 Students |

1. Arletta
2. Biff
3. Carol
4. Doyle
5. Ernest
6. Fran
7. Geoff
8. Harriet
9. Isaac
10. Jennie

already selected and 0 because it is not represented in the table—before moving on to pick (4) Doyle. I would then skip 3 and the series of three 4s (we already picked Carol and Doyle) before selecting the last two members of the sample, (7) Geoff and (9) Isaac. As you can see, we worked in a single column down from the first digit in row 00038, column 2—a 1—to the first digit in line 00049, column 2, which is a 9. That is all there is to it.

If the population had more than 10 members, say 50, then we could follow either of the same procedures outlined above with one exception. You would look at two-digit pairs of numbers in Table 2.6, so that the first string we saw (i.e., 14938) would be read as 14, 93, and instead of 8, we would link it to the next string to the right (i.e., 19476) for 81, 94, and 76. As you can see, some of these numbers do *not* appear between 1 and 50, so we would simply continuing reading across the table in two-digit pairs until we found the appropriate number of numbers (say, 10) between 01 and 50 to complete the random selection for the sample. Naturally, the same process could be used to read downward in the table (i.e., a 2-digit column, not 1). By the way, anytime you end a row or a column in the random numbers table, you move down to the next line (or up, as the case may be) and begin the process again.

Suggested Exercise: Add 10 names to Table 2.7 (i.e., there will now be 20) and then randomly select 10 names using one of the two random selection procedures presented above.

PERFORMING RANDOM ASSIGNMENT

As you might expect, the random selection exercise we just used can be adjusted to perform random assignment. Keep in mind that we use random selection when we have a clearly identified population to draw from, and that random assignment is typically employed when we have a convenience sample available. That is, we have a group of individuals who will be randomly assigned to experience one of two (or more) levels of an independent variable in an experiment. The following random assignment procedure is adapted from Salkind (1997) and Dunn (1999):

1. Recruit a convenience sample containing the number of participants you need. Imagine that the names in Table 2.7 comprise such a sample.
2. Assign numbers to each member in the sample (the names do not need to be in any special order). The names in Table 2.7 are already numbered 1 to 10.
3. Use a table of random numbers (see Table 2.6) to select the appropriate number to be placed in one condition (e.g., 5); remaining names will be assigned to the control condition.
4. You can start the random assignment procedure by closing your eyes and placing your finger anywhere on Table 2.6. Following essentially the same procedure outlined above for random selection, you can then begin to search for one-digit numbers from 1 to 10. The first five names selected are assigned to one group, the other five to the other group.

Suggested Exercise: Add 10 names to Table 2.7 (i.e., there will now be 20) and then randomly assign 10 names to one group—the remaining 10 will comprise the control group.

Thought Exercise: How could you use the random numbers table (Table 2.6) to assign members of some sample to three or four conditions in an experiment? Be creative but avoid making the procedure too cumbersome. Explain the logic of your strategy, and be sure that you do not violate randomness.

LOOKING FORWARD THEN BACK

The first decision tree opening this chapter highlights the difference between random selection and random assignment; the former emphasizes generalizability, whereas the latter is particularly practical, if not mandatory, when performing an experiment. Randomly selecting a sample and then randomly assigning members of that sample to independent groups would be ideal, of course, but most investigators are constrained by the limited availability of research participants—hence, random assignment is usually the preferred choice.

The second decision tree will enable you to verify whether a variable is dependent (it is going to be *measured*) or independent (it can be *manipulated*, such that some participants are exposed to one level while others encounter another). It is easy to forget which variable is which under what conditions, and this decision tree will always help you to remember.

Correctly categorizing a research design is the focus of the last decision tree. The simpler and better-defined research projects are usually quickly identified as experiments. Those lacking any random assignment are often classified as quasi-experiments, just as interest in how variables are associated with one another are apt to be correlational studies. This third decision tree can be used to categorize an experiment or other study you design, or to effectively identify the nature or characteristics of a study from the behavioral science literature.

Summary

1. The main message of this chapter was that good research and quality research designs are enhanced by the rigorous and appropriate use of statistics and data analysis.

2. The research loop of experimentation outlined five discrete steps that identify the work conducted at each stage of the research process, which is cyclical—research on any question never really ends. Activities known only to actual researchers occur between each of the steps in the research loop.

3. Experiments create influential changes into a setting so that participants' reactions can be observed, measured, and recorded. True experiments enable investigators to determine cause and effect relationships between variables.

4. In order to verify research results, duplicate or "replication" studies are frequently conducted. Some replications are literal, others are conceptual; that is, not all parts of the new study remain constant with the original.

5. Random assignment entails assigning participants from some sample—random or nonrandom—to one of the conditions or groups in an experiment. The goal of random assignment is to equalize groups prior to the manipulation and subsequent measurement of any variables.

6. Different types of random samples (e.g., stratified random sampling, quota sampling) were introduced, and each was shown to apply to particular research circumstances or to address certain needs.

7. Even the most meticulous research can have sampling error, the difference between a sample statistic's value and its corresponding population parameter. Generally speaking, large samples demonstrate lower sampling error than small samples.

8. To test hypotheses, researchers manipulate independent variables within experiments. Independent variables are under the researcher's control. An independent variable must have at least two different levels, one of which is the treatment of interest and the other traditionally represents a control condition.

9. A dependent measure is the outcome measure in an experiment or study. Its value depends on the effect of the independent variable. By assessing a dependent measure, a researcher can determine whether a treatment or intervention have any effect on behavior (i.e., did the predicted change occur?).

10. The four basic types of dependent measures were introduced: behavioral, self-report, physiological, and behavioroid.

11. Descriptive definitions explain theoretical relationships among variables, whereas operational definitions outline concrete operations of how these variables are actually measured or manipulated.

12. The measurement of any hypothetical construct should be both reliable and valid. That is, the measure should be stable, giving consistent readings across time. It should also be

demonstrated to be actually tapping into the theoretical construct it is supposed to measure.

13. Three classes of research designs—correlational, experimental, and quasi-experimental—were presented. Only experimental designs ensure that cause and effect relations among variables can be isolated. Correlated and quasi-experimental designs are suggestive but not definitive where causality is concerned.

14. Investigators must be careful to eliminate confounds, or uncontrolled variables that can systematically mask the effects, if any, among independent and dependent variables.

15. Random numbers tables contain sequences of numbers between 0 and 9 that were generated in an unbiased manner. Such tables have great utility when it comes to randomly assigning participants to groups or randomly selecting individuals to comprise a sample.

Key Terms

Comparison group *(p. 75 in Fig. 2.5)*
Conceptual replication *(p. 48)*
Confounded variable *(p. 72)*
Construct validity *(p. 67)*
Convergent validity *(p. 68)*
Correlational design *(p. 70)*
Dependent measure *(p. 57)*
Dependent variable *(p. 57)*
Descriptive definition *(p. 63)*
Discriminant validity *(p. 68)*

Experiment *(p. 47)*
External validity *(p. 68)*
Face validity *(p. 67)*
Hypothetical construct *(p. 65)*
Independent variable *(p. 56)*
Internal validity *(p. 68)*
Negative correlation *(p. 70)*
Operational definition *(p. 63)*
Positive correlation *(p. 70)*
Quasi-experiment *(p. 74)*

Random assignment *(p. 49)*
Random numbers table *(p. 77)*
Reliability *(p. 66)*
Reliability coefficient *(p. 66)*
Replication *(p. 48)*
Research design *(p. 70)*
Sampling error *(p. 52)*
Validity *(p. 67)*
Zero correlation *(p. 71)*

Chapter Problems

1. Describe the steps comprising the research loop of experimentation. Does it differ from the scientific method introduced in chapter 1? How does the research loop help investigators do research?

2. What is an experiment? What is the goal of experimentation? How does it differ from other forms of behavioral research?

3. What are replication studies and why are they scientifically useful? How does a conceptual (systematic) replication study differ from a standard replication?

4. What is random assignment? How and why is it useful in behavioral science research?

5. In terms of scientific utility and purpose, how does random assignment differ from random selection?

6. What is a convenience or haphazard sample?

7. Explain the difference between systematic random sampling and stratified random sampling. How are these sampling techniques used? Create a hypothetical example to illustrate each one.

8. Explain the difference between cluster sampling and quota sampling. How are these techniques used? Create a hypothetical example to illustrate each one.

9. Define sampling error? Why do researchers need to be concerned about it? Is sampling error common or rare in research? Why?

10. What can investigators do to reduce sampling error?

11. Define the term independent variable and provide a concrete example of one. How are independent variables used in research?

12. What is the minimum number of levels for an independent variable? Why? Is there a maximum number?

13. Define the term dependent measure (or variable) and provide a concrete example of one. How are dependent measures used in research?

14. How does the independent variable differ from a dependent measure?

15. Create a hypothetical experiment. Describe the randomizing procedure(s) you would use, as well as the hypothesis, the independent variable(s), and the dependent variable(s). What do you predict will happen in the experiment? Why?

16. Define the four types of dependent measures and then provide an example to represent each one.

17. Why does good research in the behavioral sciences generate more questions than it answers?

18. What is causality? Why is it important to research in the behavioral sciences? In what sort of research is causality illustrated?

19. What is a descriptive definition and how does it differ from an operational definition?

20. Create a descriptive definition for a variable of choice and then illustrate it using an operational definition.

21. Write operational definitions for each of the following variables: helping, fear, procrastination, tardiness, happiness, attraction, factual recall.

22. What are hypothetical constructs? Why are these constructs important to research efforts? Provide an example of one.

23. What is reliability and why is it important when measuring variables? Create an example to illustrate reliability.

24. In general, what does the term validity mean within behavioral science research? Provide a general example of validity.

25. What is construct validity? Why is it important? Provide a hypothetical example of construct validity.

26. What is face validity? Why is it used? Does it have any drawbacks?

27. Define convergent validity and discriminant validity. Are these concepts related? Illustrate using examples how these two types of validity are used in research.

28. What is internal validity? Why is it important to research?

29. What is external validity? Why is it important to research?

30. Describe a hypothetical experiment to illustrate the difference between internal and external validity.

31. What are the three categories of research design? Describe the strengths and weaknesses of each one.

32. Why are correlational research designs used? How do they differ from experiments or quasi-experiments?

33. Define the concept of correlation. Create hypothetical examples to illustrate a positive, a negative, and a zero correlation.

34. Does correlation imply causation? Why or why not?

35. What is a confounded variable in an experiment? Why does it prove to be problematic for understanding causality?

36. Why are quasi-experimental designs used in lieu of experimental designs? Do quasi-experimental research designs have an advantage over correlational designs? Why or why not?

37. What is a random numbers table? How would a researcher use one in her work?

38. Describe the procedure for using a random numbers table to perform random selection from some population.

39. Describe the procedure for using a random numbers table to perform random assignment for a basic two group experiment.

40. Why is randomization so important to research in the behavioral sciences?

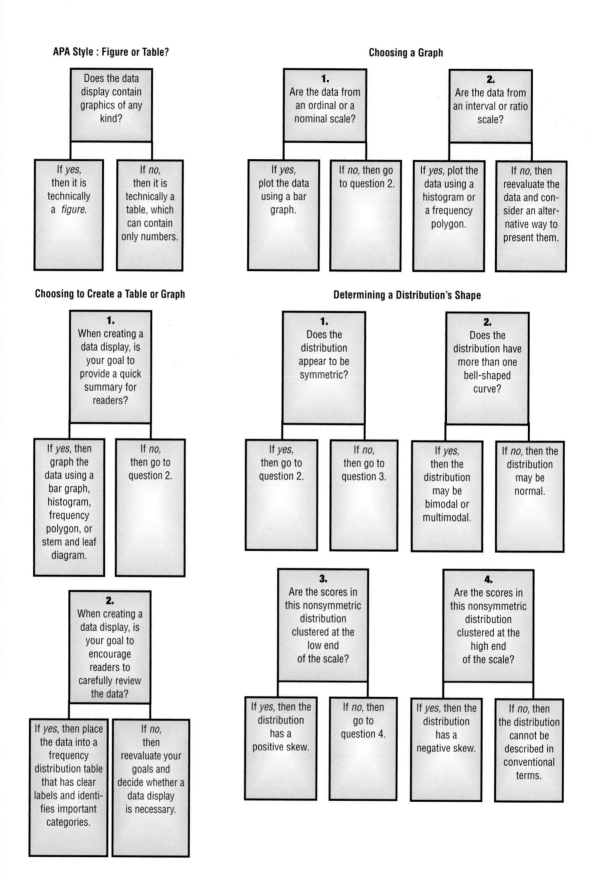

APA Style : Figure or Table?

Does the data display contain graphics of any kind?

If *yes*, then it is technically a *figure*.

If *no*, then it is technically a table, which can contain only numbers.

Choosing a Graph

1. Are the data from an ordinal or a nominal scale?

If *yes*, plot the data using a bar graph.

If *no*, then go to question 2.

2. Are the data from an interval or ratio scale?

If *yes*, plot the data using a histogram or a frequency polygon.

If *no*, then reevaluate the data and consider an alternative way to present them.

Choosing to Create a Table or Graph

1. When creating a data display, is your goal to provide a quick summary for readers?

If *yes*, then graph the data using a bar graph, histogram, frequency polygon, or stem and leaf diagram.

If *no*, then go to question 2.

2. When creating a data display, is your goal to encourage readers to carefully review the data?

If *yes*, then place the data into a frequency distribution table that has clear labels and identifies important categories.

If *no*, then reevaluate your goals and decide whether a data display is necessary.

Determining a Distribution's Shape

1. Does the distribution appear to be symmetric?

If *yes*, then go to question 2.

If *no*, then go to question 3.

2. Does the distribution have more than one bell-shaped curve?

If *yes*, then the distribution may be bimodal or multimodal.

If *no*, then the distribution may be normal.

3. Are the scores in this nonsymmetric distribution clustered at the low end of the scale?

If *yes*, then the distribution has a positive skew.

If *no*, then go to question 4.

4. Are the scores in this nonsymmetric distribution clustered at the high end of the scale?

If *yes*, then the distribution has a negative skew.

If *no*, then the distribution cannot be described in conventional terms.

CHAPTER 3

FREQUENCY DISTRIBUTIONS, GRAPHING, AND DATA DISPLAY

Patterns in a graph of data can be revealing. In the mid-19th century, a London physician plotted the location of residents who died in an on-going cholera epidemic (Gilbert, 1958; Tufte, 1983). Cholera is a dangerous bacterial infection of the small intestine marked by continuous watery diarrhea and severe dehydration. This deadly disease is most often transmitted through contaminated drinking water. Figure 3.1 shows Dr. John Snow's map of central London. The dots in Figure 3.1 represent deaths due to cholera, and the eleven Xs (×) mark water pumps in the downtown area. Snow concluded that the majority of the deaths occurred among people who lived close to and presumably drank from the Broad Street water pump (which is denoted by the × adjacent to the "D" in BROAD STREET in Figure 3.1). After examining the pattern of the dots on the map, he had the handle of the contaminated water pump removed and the cholera epidemic ended—after the loss of 500 souls living in the immediate neighborhood.

Although you will probably not draw maps or track diseases, you can still learn to organize information and identify relationships between variables, the real lessons of Snow's cholera map. Even the most interesting ideas or facts can be missed if they are not presented in ways that highlight their promise or meaning for interpreting behavior. Chapter 3 represents a return to the study of statistics and data analysis, as the material in this chapter is designed to help you develop basic skills for organizing, presenting, and explaining data. The research foundation interlude comprising chapter 2 provided essential background material, of course, as you needed a context for the descriptive statistical procedures that appear in this and the next chapter.

As you read this chapter, then, imagine that you have some set of data and that you are beginning to look for any underlying relationships or obvious patterns that might be in it. In this chapter, you will learn about frequency distributions, graphing, and data display. These three activities are related ways of summarizing data, and thus they fall

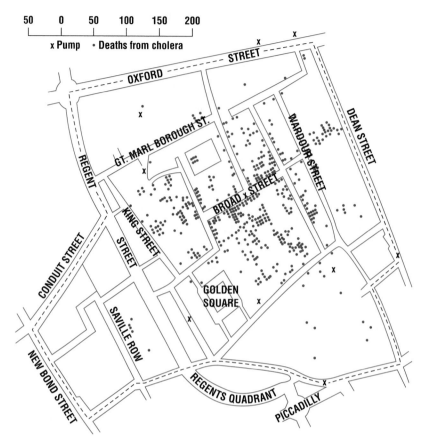

Figure 3.1   Dr. Snow's Central London Map of the 1854 Cholera Epidemic

Source: Tufte (1983), p. 24; Gilbert (1958).

under the heading of descriptive statistics, a rubric that was introduced in chapter 1. Why summarize data? There are two reasons for examining frequencies and graphing or displaying data. First, investigators examine their data to get a "feel" for it. What does the pattern of results look like? Do the data conform to any established patterns? Are participants' responses within anticipated boundaries or do some data fall at the extremes—the outer limits—of a scale? Thus, researchers summarize their data to fully understand it *before* they begin to ask questions about the hypothesis that was tested or whether any predictions were realized.

The second reason for investigators to summarize their data is for presentation to interested others. These "others" can include fellow researchers, students, or future readers of resulting publications. Summarizing data through plotting their frequency—how often they occur in a sample—or through some other means of display serves a public, educational function. Researchers want to share their work because science does not advance in a vacuum. By sharing any patterns in their data, investigators can begin to tell their research "story" to an audience. The initial audience may be a friend or two, or perhaps a colleague, but as clarity in the data emerges, a researcher's audience is apt to grow. Audiences, too, are not passive—they will ask questions of the researcher and the data—

Summaries—tables, figures, and graphs—educate and encourage viewers to think about relationships within data; sometimes, such summaries can spark controversies, leading to creative insights about behavior.

indeed, they will "demand" that any emerging facts or patterns be explained clearly and concisely. On occasion, members of a researcher's audience will challenge his or her conclusions, an event that is entirely acceptable within the framework provided by both the scientific method and the research loop of experimentation. What better way to anticipate or prepare for possible debate than to know your data set, as it were, inside and out? As you will see, the presentation of data in tabular or graphic form is both basic and critical to statistical analysis.

What is a Frequency Distribution?

Once the data from an experiment, correlational study, or quasi-experiment are collected and coded—converted to numbers for analysis—they must be organized before they can be examined or presented to others. The numbers comprising the data are usually drawn from a study's dependent measure, which in turn is based on one of the four scales of measurement (i.e., nominal, ordinal, interval, ratio) introduced in chapter 1. The best procedure for beginning the process of organizing and summarizing these numbers is to construct a *frequency distribution.*

KEY TERM   A **frequency distribution** is a table presenting the number of participant responses (e.g., scores, values) within the numerical categories of some scale of measurement.

Thus, frequency distributions display the *type* of responses made in a piece of research, as well as how many participants actually made each response (i.e., **frequency**).

Imagine you were interested in studying how transfer students adapt to a new campus environment. Personality factors certainly foster such adaptation, so you decide to measure the self-reported optimism-pessimism of new transfers to your institution. The data in Table 3.1 are scores on the Lift Orientation Test (LOT; Scheier & Carver, 1985). The LOT is an eight-item measure of dispositional optimism, a generalized expectation that future outcomes will be positive. Respondents with higher scores on the LOT can be described as optimistic, while those with lower scores tend toward pessimism. The LOT is comprised of favorable ("In uncertain times I usually expect the best") and unfavorable ("If something can go wrong for me, it will") statements. Respondents rate their agreement with each statement on a five-point interval scale (1 = strongly disagree to 5 = strongly agree). The ratings are then summed to create an optimism score for each respondent, and these scores can range from 8 to 40.

Table 3.1   Thirty Raw Scores on the Life Orientation Test

10	22	30	8	27
33	21	14	17	20
22	22	9	10	10
10	35	33	31	40
30	29	22	34	32
32	36	22	19	12

Note: Scores on the LOT can range from 8 to 40.

DATA BOX 3.A

Dispositional Optimism and Health: A Lot About the LOT

Michael F. Scheier (Carnegie Mellon University) and Charles S. Carver (University of Miami) created the Life Orientation Test (LOT) to assess people's generalized outcome expectancies—do people anticipate good or bad things to happen? The groundwork for development of the scale appeared in the researchers' theoretical work on attention, self-regulation, and cognition (e.g., Carver & Scheier, 1981). They theorize that people's expectancies for the future govern the sorts of actions they will take when faced with good or bad situations. Individuals will persist in efforts to overcome adverse circumstances as long as they believe their actions will matter. If they begin to doubt their abilities to deal with adversity, however, their goal persistence will be reduced. Optimism, then, leads to persistence where goals are concerned, whereas pessimism can lead to the alteration or even abandonment of particular goals.

How does maintaining the view that one's future will contain favorable outcomes affect health and psychological well-being? In their early work with the LOT, for example, Scheier and Carver (1985) used longitudinal results to show that optimists were less likely to report being bothered by common physical symptoms (e.g., dizziness, blurred vision, fatigue) across a 4-week period than were pessimists. A more recent study assessed the orientation of male patients about to undergo coronary artery bypass surgery. The results revealed that optimists experienced a quicker physical recovery and reported a better quality of life 6-months postsurgery than did pessimists (Scheier et al., 1989; see also Scheier et al., in press). The beneficial effects of an optimistic orientation for physical health and psychosocial well-being have been studied in disparate research samples (for a review see, Carver & Scheier, in press), including women undergoing in vitro fertilization (Litt, Tennen, Affleck, & Klock, 1992), persons adjusting to major life transitions (Aspinwall & Taylor, 1992), and males at risk for acquiring AIDS (Taylor et al., 1992).

There are now two versions of the LOT—the original and the LOT-R, a slight revision developed to address criticisms regarding the original scale (see Scheier, Carver, & Bridges, 1994). The LOT continues to be a widely used and cited instrument for social and health psychology. Scheier and Carver have used the scale in several large-scale studies of their own, and estimate that the dispositional optimism has been used in over 30 studies (M. F. Scheier, personal communication, December 18, 1998).

As you can see, the LOT scores are in their "raw"—that is, unorganized—form. It is difficult to look at the scores and draw any conclusions about them (or the sample they were drawn from) because they are not yet organized. Our "eye-balling" of the data tells us there are quite a few scores available, but there is no organizing scheme or framework to tell us much more than that. In fact, you would have to take more than a few moments to search through the data to identify the largest value, the smallest, the most or least frequently occurring score, and so on.

The structure imposed by a simple frequency distribution, however, enables a viewer to answer these and other questions with a glance. Indeed, a good frequency distribution enables viewers to get a sense of a piece of research in a few seconds. Besides learning how many respondents there were (the study's N), viewers should readily see how many responses were given in each of the available categories.

Table 3.2 shows the raw data from Table 3.1 placed into a simple frequency distribution. To construct this (or any) frequency distribution, scores are ranked from the highest to the lowest (see the column labeled X to the far left of Table 3.2). Thus, the highest score on the LOT is 40 ($X = 40$; see Table 3.2), and all other possible scores are

Frequency distributions simplify data for quick study. When they are constructed well, no valuable information is lost.

Table 3.2   Frequency Distribution for Life Orientation Test (LOT) Scores

X	f	fX	
40	1	40	(40 × 1 = 40)
39	0	0	(39 × 0 = 0)
38	0	0	(38 × 0 = 0)
37	0	0	(37 × 0 = 0)
36	1	36	(36 × 1 = 36)
35	1	35	(35 × 1 = 35)
34	1	34	(34 × 1 = 34)
33	2	66	(33 × 2 = 66)
32	1	32	(32 × 1 = 32)
31	1	31	(31 × 1 = 31)
30	2	60	(30 × 2 = 60)
29	1	29	(29 × 1 = 29)
28	0	0	(28 × 0 = 0)
27	1	27	(27 × 1 = 27)
26	0	0	(26 × 0 = 0)
25	1	25	(25 × 1 = 25)
24	0	0	(24 × 0 = 0)
23	0	0	(23 × 0 = 0)
22	5	110	(22 × 5 = 110)
21	1	21	(21 × 1 = 21)
20	1	20	(20 × 1 = 20)
19	1	19	(19 × 1 = 19)
18	0	0	(18 × 0 = 18)
17	1	17	(17 × 1 = 17)
16	0	0	(16 × 0 = 0)
15	0	0	(15 × 0 = 0)
14	1	14	(14 × 1 = 14)
13	0	0	(13 × 0 = 0)
12	1	12	(12 × 1 = 12)
11	0	0	(11 × 0 = 0)
10	4	40	(10 × 4 = 40)
9	1	9	(9 × 1 = 9)
8	1	8	(8 × 1 = 8)
	$\sum f = 30$	$\sum fX = 685$	

Note: The data in this table are the raw scores from Table 3.1.

noted beneath it until the lowest possible score (i.e., $X = 8$) is reached. Please note that the convention of ranking data from high to low is traditional but arbitrary—there would be nothing wrong with ranking them in a reverse order.

The next consideration is frequency, the number of times particular measurements appear in the data. Individuals giving the same response—here, having the same scores on the LOT—are grouped together (see the second column labeled f for "frequency" in Table 3.2). The sum of the frequencies ($\sum f$) is equal to N. As you can see at the bottom of the second column in Table 3.2, there are 30 transfer students in the sample (i.e., $N = 30$). As shown in Table 3.2, 5 transfer students scored a 22 on the LOT, and 4 others scored a 10. These are the most frequently occurring scores. The scores with the next highest frequency represent a tie—scores of 33 and 35 each had 2 respondents. The remaining scores in the distribution had either 1 or no respondents. Why bother indicating those scores lacking respondents? Well, 0 is a frequency and for reasons of consistency, clarity, and thoroughness, most frequency distributions routinely include those scores that lack corresponding respondents (e.g., no one in the sample scored a 37 on the LOT, so that the *f* for that score is 0). In fact, please note that 12 other individual scores had a frequency of 0, as well (see Table 3.2).

There are several virtues associated with any frequency distribution. First, a viewer can see the spread of scores—are they high or low, for example, or concentrated in one or several areas? Second, any given score can be considered in relation to all other scores. A score of 34 on the LOT can easily be seen as more frequent and higher than most other scores in the sample. Third, by looking at the base of the *f* column, the *N* of the respondents can be quickly known. Thus,

From this point forward in the book, all equations will be numbered. The numbering scheme will help you locate information you need quickly and easily. For example, 3.1.1 means "chapter 3, equation 1, step 1."

[3.1.1] $$\sum f = N,$$

[3.1.2] $$\sum f = 30.$$

Fourth, the data are organized and ready for use in additional analyses.

The sum of scores—that is, $\sum X$—is one quick calculation for other analyses that a researcher might want from data like those listed in Table 3.2. The sum of the scores cannot be determined simply by summing all the values of *X*, however. Why not? Because that summation ignores that fact that the different scores occur with different frequencies—the appropriate calculation must use both *X* and *f*. It is possible to add all the (raw) values appearing in Table 3.1 (i.e., $\sum X = 10 + 22 + 30 + \cdots + 12 = 685$), but that would be time consuming and defeat the purpose of creating a frequency distribution in the first place.

Instead, the quickest and easiest way to compute the $\sum X$ is to multiply each score of *X* by its corresponding frequency (*f*) and to then add the resulting products together. Symbolically, then,

[3.2.1] $$\sum X = \sum fX.$$

The third column in Table 3.2 shows the products for *fX* for each score. The $\sum fX$ is equal to 685, a sum shown at the bottom of the third column in the table. The fourth column in Table 3.2 shows the multiplication so that you can verify the numbers in the third (*fX*) column of the table. Please note that the fourth column of information is provided here for you to make certain you understand how $\sum fX$ was calculated in this example only. You need not add this fourth column to any frequency distribution you construct in the future (nor will it appear in later tables in the book).

Proportions and Percentages

Two other pieces of information—proportion and percentage—are often included in frequency distributions. As you will see, either one can be determined from the other.

A **proportion** is a number reflecting a given frequency's (*f*) relationship to the *N* of the available sample or group. Put another way, a proportion is a fractional value of the total group associated with each individual score. Let's consider an example using the data in Table 3.2. As shown in Table 3.2, 4 of the transfer respondents had a score of *X* = 10. The proportion would be 4 out of 30 respondents had *X* = 10, or 4/30 = .1333. The formula for determining a proportion, then, is

[3.3.1] $$proportion = p = f/N.$$

Proportions can be shown as fractions (i.e., 1/2) within text or a table, but they are usually presented in decimal form (i.e., 0.50). Table 3.3 repeats the information from

Table 3.3 Relative Frequency Distribution for Life Orientation Test (LOT) Scores

X	f	$p = f/N$	$p(100) = \%$
40	1	.0333	3.33
39	0	0	0
38	0	0	0
37	0	0	0
37	1	.0333	3.33
35	1	.0333	3.33
34	1	.0333	3.33
33	2	.0667	6.67
32	1	.0333	3.33
31	1	.0333	3.33
30	2	.0667	6.67
29	1	.0333	3.33
28	0	0	0
27	1	.0333	3.33
26	0	0	0
25	1	.0333	3.33
24	0	0	0
23	0	0	0
22	5	.1667	16.67
21	1	.0333	3.33
20	1	.0333	3.33
19	1	.0333	3.33
18	0	0	0
17	1	.0333	3.33
16	0	0	0
15	0	0	0
14	1	.0333	3.33
13	0	0	0
12	1	.0333	3.33
11	0	0	0
10	4	.1333	13.33
9	1	.0333	3.33
8	1	.0333	3.33
	$\sum f = 30$	1.00	100%

Note: The data in this table are the raw scores from Table 3.1.

Table 3.2 except that the new third column, which is labeled p, shows the proportions corresponding to each of the LOT scores. As noted at the bottom of column 3, all of the available proportions will sum to 1.00.

Although the two indexes are closely related, **percent** is a much more common index of relative position within data than is the proportion. A percent is a number that expresses the proportion of some score per hundred, and it is often used to simplify explaining a set of data or reporting relationships within it. Instead of reporting that 12 of the 30 transfer students came from a large state university, you could report that "40% came from large state universities, 50% came from liberal arts colleges, and the remaining 10% of the sample arrived from community colleges." Percents—or as they are interchangeably called, **percentages**—simplify numerical relationships by making the component parts sum to 100%.

When you know a proportion, its percentage equivalent is quickly and easily calculable (and vice versa).

Calculating percentages from proportional data is easy. Using the data from Table 3.2 once more, we can determine the percentage of transfer students who scored a 22 on the LOT. The percent formula entails multiplying a proportion by 100 or

[3.4.1] $$percent = (p) \times (100) = (f/N) \times (100),$$

[3.4.2] $$\left(\frac{5}{30}\right) \times (100) = (.1667) \times (100) = 16.67.$$

Thus, 16.67% of the transfer students had a score of 22 on the LOT.

A fourth column appears in Table 3.3 and it includes the percentage information for each of the scores of X on the LOT, which were calculated using formula 3.4.1. Please note that sum of any percentage information *must* be equal to 100% if all of the scores are accounted for in a table. If you add the percentage information appearing in column 4 of Table 3.3, it must—and does—add up to 100%.

Because both percentages and proportions illustrate the relationship of frequency (f) to the total number of scores or observations available, they are sometimes referred to as **relative frequencies.** These relative frequencies are then displayed within a *relative frequency distribution.*

KEY TERM   A **relative frequency distribution** indicates the percent or proportion of participants who received each of the raw scores of X.

Because it contains both proportions and percents, Table 3.3 is best described as a relative frequency distribution of scores on the LOT. Individual scores on the LOT can be examined in terms of their relative positions; that is, how they stand in relation to each other.

One final point: If you look carefully at Table 3.3, one thing should stand out— Although the original data from Table 3.1 are now organized, they have not *changed.* The data are merely being presented in different ways—they still contain the *same* information and disclose the *same* relationships. Whether you know that there were 4 people who had LOT scores of 10, or that the proportion of the sample with a score of 10 was .1333, or that 13.33% had a score of 10—you still know the same fact about the distribution—just in a slightly different way. Keep this flexible characteristic of summary statistics in mind as you continue reading this chapter.

Grouping Frequency Distributions

The organization found in both the standard and the relative frequency distribution is a considerable improvement over examining raw data scores. Yet, a review of Tables 3.2 and 3.3 reveals that there is still quite a bit of information to examine. The LOT scores presented in these tables run from a high of 40 to a low of 8, the actual range of possible scores on the scale. Despite organizing the data into a frequency distribution, there is still quite a bit of information to review at a glance. Are there ways to simplify the presentation of the LOT scores further? Many of the LOT scores have frequencies of 1 or even 0— perhaps the table would be easier and quicker to read if these low frequencies were combined together.

How can the data be combined or reduced without information loss? One way to compartmentalize data for summary purposes is to create a *grouped frequency distribution.*

KEY TERM   A **grouped frequency distribution** places raw scores into preset intervals of values.

Instead of examining one score or frequency at a time, a range of scores or frequencies falling inside an interval can be considered. These intervals represent groups of scores; hence the name grouped frequency distribution.

Grouped frequency distributions are not difficult to construct but there are a few guidelines that researchers typically follow. We will review these guidelines, demonstrating how the LOT scores can be grouped into intervals in the process. Please note that these are guidelines, not hard and fast rules—you may group a frequency distribution in any number of ways as long as it can be understood by you and interested others. Indeed, you need not follow these or any other guidelines as long as your data are grouped in a reasonably logical and consistent manner. I think, though, that the following guidelines will prove to be helpful to you.

1. Begin by calculating the difference between the highest and the lowest scores in a data set, and then add 1 to this difference. The resulting number represents the number of possible score values within a grouped frequency distribution. As shown by Table 3.2 or Table 3.3, the difference between the high (40) and low score (8) is 32. Adding 1 to this number indicates that there are 33 possible score values. Here is a formula illustrating the highest minus the lowest difference plus 1:

   [3.5.1]   number of possible scores $=$ (high score $-$ low score) $+$ 1,

   [3.5.2]   number of possible scores $= (40 - 8) + 1 = 32 + 1 = 33$.

2. How many classes do you want or need in a grouped frequency distribution? Some researchers advocate around 10 intervals in any grouped frequency distribution. Of course, a very small distribution with few observations could have far less than 10, just as a massive data set with hundreds and hundreds of entries might require 50 or 100 intervals. The best answer, then, is that "it depends." It depends on the use of the data, the number of scores available, the desires of the researcher, and the most important criterion of all—what will make the numbers most understandable for readers. As in so many things, experience is the best teacher.

   To proceed, select the number of intervals that you think will best present the information to others. To see how it will work within the data set I have, I arbitrarily decide to have eight intervals for the LOT scores. Divide the number of possible score values by this desired number of intervals (i.e., $33/8 = 4.125$). Depending on the product, you either round up or down to the nearest whole number. In the present example, I will round down because the nearest whole number is 4. The interval size for LOT scores, then, will be 4.

3. This third step entails arranging intervals in a table by starting from the lowest one and working to the highest point. The lowest score in the distribution is the *lower limit* of the first interval (i.e., the lowest possible LOT score is 8). Next, the *upper limit* of the interval must be determined using the following formula:

   [3.6.1]   upper limit $=$ lower limit $+$ (interval size $-$ 1),

   [3.6.2]   upper limit $= 8 + (4 - 1) = 8 + 3 = 11$.

   The first (lowest) interval of LOT scores will range between 8 (lower limit) and 11 (upper limit). You would then calculate the next interval by treating the next highest score as the lower limit of this second grouping (i.e., 12):

   [3.6.3]   upper limit $= 12 + (4 - 1) = 12 + 3 = 15$.

   Continue in this fashion until all the intervals are constructed and placed into a table.

   Table 3.4 shows the intervals for the grouped frequency distribution of the LOT scores. If you look carefully at Table 3.4, you will notice a few minor problems in the way the class intervals are constructed. First, there are nine class intervals rather than the eight I set out to create. Second, the top interval contains LOT scores from 40 to 44, but the highest possible score on the LOT is 40! What happened here? Standardized measures with fixed high and low scores often create minor problems like these,

Table 3.4   Intervals for Grouped Frequency Distribution for LOT Scores

Class Intervals of X
40–44
36–39
32–35
28–31
24–26
20–23
16–19
12–15
8–11

Note: The intervals in this table are based on the frequency distribution shown in Table 3.2, which in turn is based on the raw scores from Table 3.1.

Real data are rarely neat and tidy, and a good data analyst learns to be flexible by revising any data formulation or presentation as needed. Providing the clearest account of the information is always the goal.

and you will probably experience them again. That is, if you ever conduct independent or supervised research, you will probably rely on some published inventory, personality scale, or intelligence measure that has a fixed low and high score (most of the standardized tests you have taken all your life have these qualities, as well).

Thus, I purposefully selected this example so that you could experience real-life data problem that confronts many researchers. Sometimes, even the best laid plans—or easy to use guidelines—will not work for the data you possess. But, how do we present the LOT scores? When the dimensions of a measure are constrained by fixed upper and lower limits (i.e., scores), start constructing the intervals from the highest interval, not the lowest. To do so, you would *subtract* the interval size minus 1 number from the highest score and *work backward* to the lower limit of an interval. The first (highest interval) for the LOT data would be from 37 to 40, and it is calculated using:

[3.7.1]   lower limit = upper limit − (interval size − 1),

[3.7.2]   lower limit = 40 − (4 − 1) = 40 − 3 = 7.

A table can then be constructed in the same (albeit reverse) fashion as was discussed above. The revised grouped frequency distribution for the LOT data is shown in Table 3.5. As you can see, there is still a ninth interval—the lowest one—added to the original eight intervals envisioned in step 2. This addition is a small price to pay, as it were, so that the uppermost possible score is correct—and there is little difficulty posed by the fact that the lowest possible score on the LOT (i.e., 8) resides in the scoring interval 5–8 (see Table 3.5). A note about the range of fixed scores on any standardized measure is then added beneath the table.

4. Finally, we work with the actual data. Enter all of the raw scores into their appropriate scoring intervals and under a column labeled "frequency" or f (see Table 3.5).

5. I add this last step as an error check to avoid mistakes or misinterpretation: You should make certain that no errors have occurred in the construction of the grouped frequency distribution. To do so, check the following information in Table 3.5 and in any future tables you construct:

   ■ Are all the class intervals the same width? They should be the same width.
   ■ Do any class intervals overlap with one another? They should not.
   ■ Do all the data fit into the table? There should be no leftover scores.

Table 3.5   Revised Group Frequency Distribution for LOT Scores

Class Intervals of X	f
37–40	1
33–36	5
29–32	5
25–28	2
21–24	6
17–20	3
13–16	1
9–12	6
5– 8	1
	$\sum f = 30$

Note: The intervals in this table are based on the frequency distribution shown in Table 3.2, which in turn is based on the raw scores from Table 3.1.

By examining the grouped frequency distribution in Table 3.5, you can get a much clearer sense of the data. Most respondents scored above a 20 on the LOT, indicating that the majority of the sample could be described as optimistic. There was a pocket of pessimists who scored in the 9–12 interval, as well as two groups of five respondents scoring in the 29–32 and the 33–36 intervals, respectively. Finally, only 1 respondent fell into the highest (37–40) and the lowest (5–8) class intervals—most scored in the middle of the scale (21–24) or above. As you can see, a grouped frequency distribution like this one provides much more information more quickly than a standard or even a relative frequency distribution.

True Limits and Frequency Distributions

Continuous variables and true limits were both introduced in chapter 1. True limits were described as a range of values between which the value of a variable is apt to lie. They are calculated by adding and subtracting one half of a unit of measurement from the value of the known continuous variable. How do true limits apply to frequency distributions? Consider this example: If we know that a frequency (f) of five was associated with a score of 43 on some measure, does that mean that 5 respondents had a score of 43? No—not necessarily. Think back to the conceptual meaning of true limits and how it could apply here. What the f of 5 would really means is that five scores fall between the true limits of 42.5 and 43.5. In other words, each respondent is not assumed to actually have a score of 43 because of sampling error; however, the interval where their true scores should fall can be identified.

It follows, then, that the logic and utility of true limits can also be applied to interval values. Instead of adding or subtracting one half of a unit of measurement from a single number, these operations would be performed on the lower and upper limit of a given interval class. Let's return to the LOT data and Table 3.5. Thus, if we have an interval that falls between $X = 29$ and $X = 32$ (i.e., 29–32; see Table 3.5), we could instead expand the interval to fall between 28.5 (lower true limit) and 32.5 (upper true limit). The interval immediately below would become 24.5–28.5 and the one above would be 32.5–36.5. Here is the formula for calculating the upper and lower true limits for any interval:

[3.8.1]   interval true limit $= X \pm 0.5$ unit of measurement.

Table 3.6   Grouped Frequency Distribution of LOT Scores with True Limits and Class Intervals

Class Intervals of X	f
36.5–40.5	1
32.5–36.5	5
28.5–32.5	5
24.5–28.5	2
20.5–24.5	6
16.5–20.5	3
12.5–16.5	1
8.5–12.5	6
4.5– 8.5	1
	$\sum f = 30$

Note: The intervals in this table are based on the frequency distribution shown in Table 3.2, which in turn is based on the raw scores from Table 3.1.

Do you notice something interesting happening here with the interval values? The upper true limit of a given class is the same value as the lower true limit of the next class interval (or lower true limit of a given class is the upper true limit of the one below it). Table 3.6 illustrates these facts clearly. Why does this matter? No information is lost because no gaps appear in the LOT or whatever scale we choose to use. We may be partitioning a continuous variable to make sense out of it, but by using true limits with class intervals, we are making certain that nothing is being missed or overlooked.

The use of true limits within a grouped frequency distribution makes the display of data precise. As we will see shortly, it also prepares the data for ready use in graphs.

Knowledge Base

1. Construct a relative frequency distribution using the following data, and be sure to include a column for proportions and one for percentages.
   8, 9, 8, 8, 9, 10, 11, 14, 16, 8, 9, 12, 14, 13, 13, 11, 9, 10,
2. What is the $\sum f$ of the distribution in 1? What is the $\sum X$? What is the easiest way to calculate the $\sum X$ from a frequency distribution?
3. A group of scores ranges from 40 to 80. How many possible scores are there in the data set? What interval size is appropriate? How many intervals would you recommend?
4. You have an interval ranging from 58 to 62. What are its true limits?

Answers

1.

X	f	p	$\%$
16	1	.1111	11.11
15	0	0	0
14	2	.1111	11.11
13	2	.1111	11.11
12	1	.0556	5.56
11	2	.1111	11.11
10	2	.1111	11.11
9	4	.2222	22.22
8	4	.2222	22.22

2. $\sum f = 18; \sum X = 192;$ Using $\sum fX$ to calculate $\sum X$
3. Number of possible scores is 41 (i.e., [80–40] + 1); if 10 intervals are used, the interval size could be 4 (i.e., $41/10 = 4.1$, which rounds to 4).
4. The true limits are 57.5 to 62.5.

Graphing Frequency Distributions

Tables of numbers tell us quite a lot about what is happening within a data set. A well-constructed table of data invites a reader to review a study's results and to carefully consider what they mean. Many times, however, researchers want to convey information in a way that provides a summary and invites a quick perusal, not a labored review. (The distinction between tables and figures is discussed in detail in the project exercise appearing at the end of this chapter.) Quick reviews are possible when researchers present their data pictorially, that is, in the form of some type of *graph*.

KEY TERM   A **graph** is a diagram illustrating connections or relationships among two or more variables. *Graphs* are often made up of connecting lines or dots.

Graphs are different from figures, which in turn are different than tables. Learning the precise distinctions among them will enhance your understanding in the long run.

All graphs present data using a two-dimensional display composed of two perpendicular lines or axes. One axis—the **x axis**—is a horizontal line usually portrayed as running along the bottom of a graph (see Figure 3.2). The *x* axis is sometimes referred to as the *abscissa* and it is used to plot independent variables. The other axis, or **y axis,** is represented by a vertical line extending up and down the left side of the graph (see Figure 3.2). The alternate name for the *y* axis is the *ordinate*, and it traditionally plots dependent measures. Within most graphs, the two axes meet in the bottom-left corner at the value of 0. As one moves along the horizontal *x* axis from the lowest value (i.e., 0) to the right, the values for *x* increase. Similarly, the values for *y* begin at 0 and increase as you move up the vertical line to their highest point (see Figure 3.2). In general, the range of values is typically higher along the *x* axis than the *y* axis. This guideline creates graphics that are proportionally pleasing to the eye as well as accurate where data presentation is concerned.

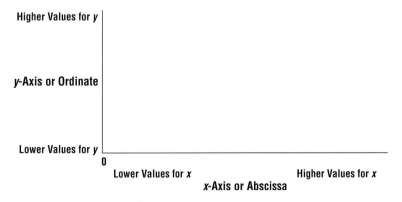

Figure 3.2   The Two Axes (*x* and *y*) Used for Graphing Data

Bar Graphs

The most basic graph is the **bar graph,** which consists of enclosed lines forming vertical bars rising along the *x* axis. Bar graphs are used to illustrate data from nominal or ordinal scales. Because of the discrete nature of these scale types, bar graphs always have space between each bar (i.e., no scale values exist between the bars). Another defining characteristic of bar graphs is that the *x* axis will not illustrate any quantitative measure or scale; instead, it will include labels referring to the nominal or ordinal categories being displayed. The *y* axis in a bar graph is quantitative, as it corresponds to the frequency of the nominal or ordinal data within each category.

Figure 3.3 shows a bar graph for a nominally scaled variable, the gender of respondents to an anonymous survey. The bar graph's virtue lies in the immediacy with which it conveys this (or any) information. You can tell with a glance at Figure 3.3 that more females than males completed and returned the survey—35 females versus 20 males. Remember that gender is discrete—a given individual is either categorized as a male or a female—so that the gap between the two bars indicates the absence of any meaningful information (see Figure 3.3). The relationship between the bars representing the number of males versus females is thus clear, obvious, and easy to follow. Researchers often use bar graphs when they wish to draw readers' attention to straightforward but still important information; indeed, if the information is not particularly noteworthy, then it should appear in the text, not a graph.

Naturally, bar graphs can be more complex than the example presented in Figure 3.3. If you were graphing the respective number of people from four (or more) different campus organizations, you would label each bar, plot its frequency, and make certain that none of the bars touched one another. On the other hand, I would caution you against making any bar graph too complicated by having too many bars to examine. How many is too many? The answer is probably more personal preference than analytic prowess, but I would say no more than 8 or 10 bars (though preferably fewer) to a single bar graph. Any more than that defeats the purpose of a bar graph's simplicity, while at the same time slowing viewers substantially.

Bar graphs are one of the most basic forms of data representation.

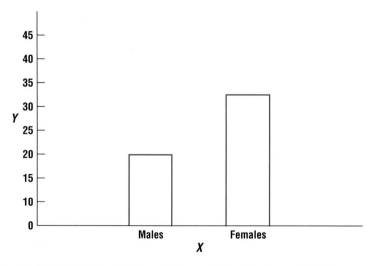

Figure 3.3 Bar Graph Indicating Number of Surveys Returned by Respondents' Gender

Histograms

Due to their quantitative nature, histograms are usually more complex than bar graphs.

Where slightly more complex or technical displays are concerned, a **histogram** is often a better choice than a traditional bar graph. This second level of graphing presents quantitative relationships from interval or ratio scales, and the data can be from either an ungrouped or a grouped frequency distribution. That is, frequencies can be plotted in a graph by individual scores or as they appear within ranges (i.e., class intervals) of scores. The main distinction between a bar graph and a histogram is that in the latter, the *x* axis displays a range of numerical values (see Figure 3.4). As noted in Figure 3.4, each of the bars has the same width and touches another, indicating that the scale of measurement for *x* is continuous and quantitative, not qualitative and discrete. Despite this additional quantitative information, a reader can still extract the main message of a given histogram. With a brief glance at title and contents of Figure 3.4, for example, readers can see the frequency of scores—high (5 scores of "8") as well as low (1 score of "3" and "10," respectively)—on a quiz.

Of course, the real advantage that histograms have over bar graphs is the way they portray class intervals with true limits. Indeed, there are two ways to indicate true limits of a grouped frequency distribution within a histogram. In the first place, the true limits could be *suggested* by showing the raw scores appearing at the upper and lower limit if each class interval, but then extending the width line of each bar one half a unit of measure. This method is shown in Figure 3.5 with a different set of hypothetical quiz scores. As you can see, the true limits are not labeled in the graph, but they are delimited by the placement of the columns (e.g., the vertical lines appearing halfway between 3 and 4, as well as 6 and 7, to indicate the upper and lower true limits of the class interval 4–6). For purposes of convenience and comparison, a table of the grouped frequency distribution data also appears in Figure 3.5.

The second method for displaying grouped frequency data actually includes the true limits along the *x* axis. Figure 3.6 presents the same data shown in Figure 3.5, but this time the true limits are clearly indicated. Thus, the same information can be conveyed in a slightly different way. In some situations, a researcher might want to draw

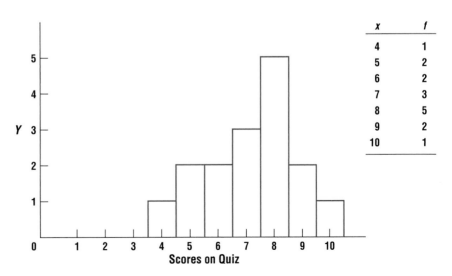

x	f
4	1
5	2
6	2
7	3
8	5
9	2
10	1

Figure 3.4 Frequency of Scores on a Hypothetical 10-point Quiz

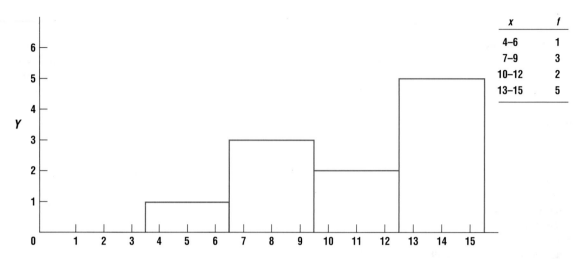

Figure 3.5   Histogram of Grouped Frequency Distribution of Quiz Scores

Note: This graph suggests the true limit of a grouped frequency distribution. The vertical lines associated with each bar appear half way above and below each of the inervals identified in the grouped frequency distribution shown in the above-right corner of the graph.

attention to the true limits of a grouped frequency distribution by actually placing them in a figure. Other times, it may be appropriate to simply suggest their presence. As a data analyst, you can determine which approach best fits your research needs.

Frequency Polygons

Data display is not limited to the boxlike presentation of bar graphs or histograms. A researcher can also display frequency data within a **frequency polygon.** As you may remember from geometry, a polygon is a multisided figure that has three or more sides, which are usually straight or flat. A frequency polygon illustrates data from grouped frequency distributions using a series of interconnected lines and is meant for graphing

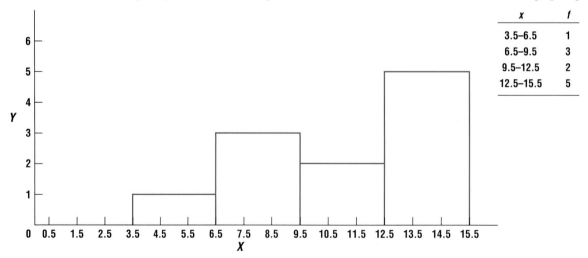

Figure 3.6   Histogram of Grouped Frequency Distribution of Quiz Scores with True Limits

Note: This histogram identifies the true limits of the grouped frequency distribution shown in the upper right corner of the graph. Please note that these data are the same as those shown in Figure 3.5.

data from interval or ratio scales. These lines are connected to form the frequency polygon, or "curve," as some researchers prefer to call it.

To create a basic frequency polygon, a single dot is placed above each number (e.g., score, category) along the x axis. The height or placement of the dot is determined by the frequency corresponding to the number. Once all the dots are placed in the space to the right of the y axis and above the x axis, a line is then drawn to connect them all together. It is traditional to begin drawing the line at the 0 point where the two axes join. The line forms the polygon, as the space between any two points creates a "side" of the figure.

Figure 3.7 shows a basic frequency polygon plotting the grouped frequency data from Figure 3.4 (i.e., refer especially to the small grouped frequency distribution shown in the upper right portion of Figure 3.4).

What if a researcher wants to show a frequency polygon that displays class intervals, even the true limits associated with class intervals? This desire can be accommodated with little effort, as only minor calculations are involved. The goal involved is placing the dot above the *midpoint* of a class interval. The minor calculation to locate this midpoint is determining the average of each of the class interval limits. If the class interval runs from 10 to 12, you would add the upper and lower limits together and then divide by 2 to find the midpoint. The formula would be:

[3.9.1] $$\frac{\text{upper limit} + \text{lower limit}}{2} = \text{midpoint of the interval, or}$$

[3.9.2] $$\frac{10 + 12}{2} = \frac{22}{2} = 11.$$

Naturally, the same procedure would be performed if true limits were being graphed. The true limits for the interval $10 - 12$ are 9.5 and 12.5, respectively, so:

[3.9.3] $$\frac{9.5 + 12.5}{2} = \frac{22}{2} = 11.$$

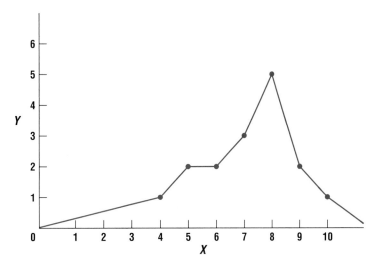

Figure 3.7 Frequency Polygon of Scores on a 10-point Quiz

Note: The data in this graph are from Figure 3.4.

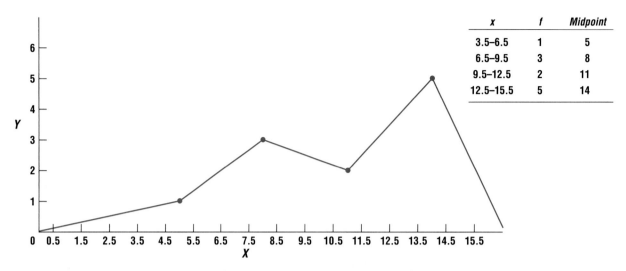

x	f	Midpoint
3.5–6.5	1	5
6.5–9.5	3	8
9.5–12.5	2	11
12.5–15.5	5	14

Figure 3.8 Frequency Polygon for Hypothetical Quiz Scores with True Limits

Note: The data in this graph were taken from Figure 3.5

Figure 3.8 is a frequency polygon based on the data from Figure 3.5. The polygon is formed by connecting the dots placed above the midpoint of the true limits of each class interval.

Misrepresenting Relationships: Biased or Misleading Graphs

Seek simplicity and distrust it.

—Alfred North Whitehead

We mentioned that some of the goals of graphing were the quick and clear presentation of information so interested observers can understand the relationships between two variables of interest. As a reader of books and periodicals in the behavioral sciences, however, you must be wary about how data are presented to you. Few graphs intentionally lie about actual relationships in data (but see Tufte, 1983), however, many graphs can be misleading about the magnitude of relationships between variables. You should learn to detect when you are (potentially) being misled by purported relationships between variables.

Besides being a consumer of graphic images, if you will, it is very likely that you will also be a creator of graphs and charts. Many readers, for example, will want to present data from some class project in a graph. Others will conduct independent or supervised research with a faculty member who will expect that they know how to summarize data relationships in concise but meaningful forms. Still other students are planning to attend graduate school or begin a career where quantitative skills (and information) abound. For these and many other reasons, it is likely that you will be pressed to create a histogram or frequency polygon at some point in the future. Why not plan ahead by learning to identify and avoid creating biased or otherwise misleading data presentation right now?

Edward R. Tufte (1983), the dean of graphic images, has published several books detailing how to properly present data in graphic form. He argues for what he calls graphical integrity. In other words, a graph should mean what it actually says, and it should not include any deceptive information. As Tufte put it, "Graphical excellence be-

"Data is power (sic)"

—Anonymous Researcher

gins with telling the truth about the data" (Tufte, 1983, p. 53). To help readers and producers of graphics develop acumen in this regard, Tufte listed several principles to keep in mind as you examine or develop any graphic display. Here are a few of them (from Tufte, 1983, p. 77)

- Emphasize how the data vary, not how the design presenting them can vary. Focus on the numbers, not fonts, colors, textures, or other stylistic additions that distract readers.
- To defeat distortion and ambiguity in a data presentation, clear and detailed labels should appear with any graph. Where necessary, explanations can be written on the actual graph, just as any important events in the data should be labeled.
- A good graphic should never quote data out of their proper context.

The last principle—presenting information in proper context—is a good one to use as an illustration of how factual relationships within a set of data can be properly used or easily abused. By "context," we refer to how some data or datum compares to other relevant information. Consider graph (a) in Figure 3.9, which shows traffic deaths in the state of Connecticut before (1955) and after (1956) stronger enforcement of speed limits. It appears to show a strong and favorable event—a dramatic decline in traffic deaths once enforcement became stronger. The message of graph (a) is strong and clear: Deaths dropped from 325 in one year to somewhere around 280 the next year.

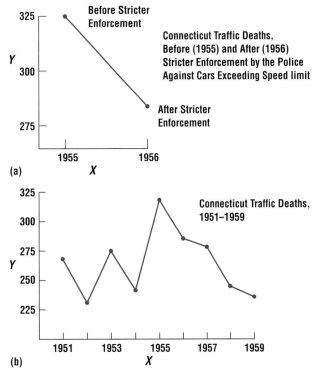

Figure 3.9 Connecticut Traffic Deaths Before and After Speed Limit Enforcement

Note: Graphs (a) and (b) were taken from Tufte (1983), page 74

But wait a moment. Take a look at graph (b) in Figure 3.9. The addition of more contextual information—the number of deaths a few years *before* and *after* the stricter speed limit enforcement tell us more. Yes, there were fewer deaths in 1956, but there were actually *many fewer deaths still* in the years 1951 through 1954 *before* enforcement began in earnest. In fact, the decline continues beyond 1954 to levels approximating the earlier mortality rates. Thus, *context matters: As critical students of behavioral science, we must always ask, "Compared to what?"*

Our search for useful contextual information is not over yet, however. The researchers who actually worked with these data wondered if the decline in traffic fatalities was unique to Connecticut or if adjacent states were in any way affected (Campbell, 1969; Campbell & Ross, 1970). Figure 3.10 provides even more contextual information because it shows the fatalities for three states plus Connecticut pre and post speed limit changes in the latter. What can we learn from the data? Figure 3.10 clearly shows that Connecticut was *not* the only state to experience declines in traffic deaths between 1955 and 1956. We would not have known that by examining graph (a) or (b) in Figure 3.9. A change may *appear* to be a dramatic one, but a good graph must provide adequate information for readers to concur with—and critically accept—such a judgment.

Care must be taken whether you are a producer or consumer of graphs, and developing a constructive but appropriately skeptical regard for graphs can be healthy. Some guidelines for developing accurate graphs are provided in Table 3.7. I recommend that you consult these guidelines whenever you are creating or evaluating a graph.

New Alternatives for Graphing Data: Exploratory Data Analysis

John W. Tukey (1977) coined the term **exploratory data analysis (EDA)** to refer to various straightforward approaches to working with data and to make initial work with a data set effective. Little math is involved in EDA; instead, it is a precursor to the typical,

> Cultivate the habit of asking "Compared to what?" whenever you examine any data presentation—including your own.

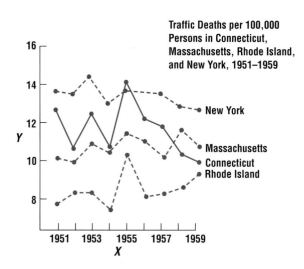

Figure 3.10 Traffic Deaths in Connecticut, Massachusetts, Rhode Island, and New York (1951–1959)

Note: This graph was taken from Tufte (1983), page 75, which in turn was drawn from Campbell (1969).

Table 3.7   Some Guidelines for Graphs

1. Tradition holds that in the behavioral sciences, the independent variable is plotted on the *x* axis and the dependent measure is plotted on the *y* axis.
2. Both the *x* and the *y* axis must be clearly labeled. Quantity marks, too, should be labeled with numbers.
3. The *y* axis is always a continuous scale, and it usually begins at zero. The scale can be "broken," that is, values are skipped, only when absolutely necessary.
4. A graph must have a clear and concise label describing the variables and/or relationship it illustrates.
5. A graph must have a clearly written caption or note underneath it. Readers should be guided to and through the graph by accompanying text.
6. Graphs should never have extraneous information or excess detail. As in prose, when in doubt cut it out.
7. Graphs are only used to convey important information, and they should be used sparingly.

traditional, and advanced statistical procedures (what Tukey calls confirmatory data analyses) that are later applied to the data. In other words, EDA is used before a researcher even determines whether a study's results confirm his or her hypotheses. You will learn many confirmatory analyses later in this book.

What is involved in EDA? Taking a fresh look at one's data by getting a preliminary feel for it. EDA is comprised of guidelines for quickly organizing, summarizing, and interpreting data from a piece of research. We will not—indeed, we cannot—review all of the procedures entailed in EDA, but we can learn to use two of them. These procedures are a novel way to present numbers in a frequency distribution and a quick way to tally numbers. Both procedures will help you think about the rest of the material in this book, and no doubt they will prove to be useful for any research you do in the future. If you become interested in EDA, I heartily recommend that you consult Tukey's (1977) now classic work.

Stem and Leaf Diagrams

Previously, we tried to make sense out of the LOT scores shown in Table 3.1, and we concluded that if such data were not organized, it would be difficult to quickly and efficiently point to the high and low, most frequent scores, and so on. We organized the LOT scores into a frequency distribution, which enabled us to answer these (and other) questions with greater ease. There is yet another way to organize the same sorts of data for quick perusal, a technique that Tukey (1977) calls a *stem and leaf diagram*.

KEY TERM   **Stem and leaf diagrams** are numerical graphs that promote exploration of a data set while retaining the values of the original observations.

Imagine that you are working with the test scores shown in Table 3.8. These are scores on a 100-point Introductory Psychology test given to 50 students. These scores have been converted into the stem and leaf diagram shown in Figure 3.11. The vertical line between the two sets of numbers divides the "stems" from their "leaves." The numbers to the left of the line are the stems, which represent the first or base digit of a two-digit number (e.g., the stem of 5 accounts for all of the numbers between 50 and 59). The numbers to the right of the vertical line, the leaves, are the second digits in these two-digit numbers.

DATA BOX 3.B

Biased Graphical Display—Appearances Can Be Deceiving

Why would anyone want to "lie" with a biased graph? The creators of a deceiving graph may not be out to lie to people but, rather, to persuade them to adopt some point of view. Deceptive data displays are often used to convince an audience—a jury, a school board, some trustee group—to commit to one choice and not another. A good way to persuade people is by presenting them with graphic evidence that appears simple, logical, and incontrovertible. Not only should you avoid persuading people with untruthful data, you should also avoid being persuaded by others.

Let's consider a hypothetical example. Imagine you are reading the newspaper and you see an advertisement for a new medically supervised "wonder" diet guaranteed to help people lose unwanted pounds. Placed squarely in the center of the page is a graph purporting to show dramatic weight loss [see graph (a)]. The x axis shows three nominally scaled diet groups and the y axis plots the average number of pounds lost after 1 month. As you can see, clients on the "wonder" diet appear to have lost much more weight than those on a competitor's diet program or a control group.

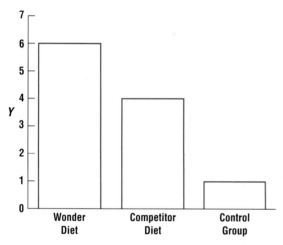

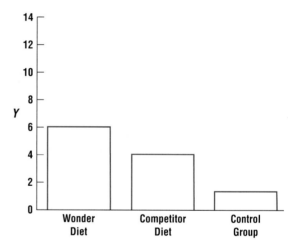

But was the weight loss actually dramatic? To answer that question, take a look at graph (b), which presents the *same* information but the height of the bars is not as great so that the weight loss does *not* appear as great. In fact, graph (b) indicates that weight loss on the "wonder" diet was not miraculous; indeed, it was only a couple pounds higher than the competing diet.

Is one graph better than another is? No, not really. Graph (a) exaggerates the relationship between diet and weight loss, while graph (b) indicates that the between-group differences are slight and not at all interesting. If truth rather than deception were the goal, a better route for the researcher would be to place numerical information in a table rather than a bar graph.

The string of numbers 334455 represents the 6 scores that fell in the 50 to 59 range (i.e., 53, 53, 54, 54, 55, and 55).

The stem and leaf diagram's virtue is that all the original scores are still visible in the distribution. Readers still receive the desired information about the relative frequency of scores in several ways. One can see the actual data, as well as the range of scores where the most frequent (i.e., scores in the 80 range) or least frequent (i.e., scores in the 30 range) observations fell (see Figure 3.11). With one glance, too, the high and the low scores can be readily discerned (here, 99 and 34, respectively). The shape of the distribution is also apparent, and a reader can get a sense of whether the

Table 3.8   Fifty Test Scores on an Introductory Psychology Examination

55	34	66	87	85	88	54	44	39	84
74	88	92	55	70	63	41	90	88	72
66	65	91	53	40	99	81	73	65	87
92	88	70	86	74	90	88	54	87	73
88	45	92	84	76	53	76	74	80	85

3	49
4	0145
5	334455
6	35566
7	002334466
8	014455677788888
9	0012229

Figure 3.11 Stem and Leaf Diagram of Introductory Psychology Test Scores

Note: These data are from Table 3.8.

data are uniformly distributed or grouped in one or more areas. As shown by Figure 3.11, the scores appear to be weighted toward the high end, as most scores are above 60 (as they should be!).

Can we do more with these data using the stem and leaf diagram approach? Absolutely. For instance, we need not look at ranges of scores in a stem and leaf diagram by units of 10 (i.e., 0 to 9 values). Following Tukey's (1977) encouragement to get a feel for the data, we can divide the leaves, if you will, in half: that is, we look at score values from 0 to 4 in one stem and those ranging from 5 to 9 in another stem. This "breakpoint" effectively divides each potential range of scores in half, and enables us to examine a distribution of scores with a still finer eye. These new breakpoints are shown in Figure 3.12. The asterisk (*) next to the first stem for 4 indicates that the leaf values can range from 40 to 44. The dot (•) next to the second stem for 4, then, covers values from 45 to 49.

What do we know now? As shown by Figure 3.12, we can now see that most scores fell into the low 70 range and the high 80 range. Looking closer, it is apparent that there is a concentrated clustering of scores from the high 60s to the low 70s, and then again from the high 80s to the low 90s (notice the two "peaks" represented by the leaf spreads in these ranges). As shown by the shape of the distribution, the majority of the test scores are still shown to fall in the 60 and above range (cf., Figure 3.11), while fewer scores are found in the lower or "tail" of the distribution. Note, too, that with the use of breakpoints in Figure 3.12, the high and low scores in the distribution are now even more apparent. There is a certain advantage, then, to looking at a data distribution from a variety of perspectives before the actual analyses get underway, and EDA is particularly helpful in this regard.

3 *	**4**
3 •	**9**
4 *	**014**
4 •	**5**
5 *	**3344**
5 •	**55**
6 *	**3**
6 •	**5566**
7 *	**0023344**
7 •	**66**
8 *	**0144**
8 •	**55677788888**
9 *	**001222**
9 •	**9**

Figure 3.12 Stem and Leaf Diagram of Introductory Psychology Test Scores

Note: These data are from Table 3.8.

As you might guess, it is possible to make even smaller breakpoints than are shown if Figure 3.12. The stems in a stem and leaf diagram can be made into interval classes like those we reviewed earlier in the chapter, causing their leaves to reflect the greater or lesser width of the classes. Further, the digits in a stem and leaf diagram are not restricted to two—they can be expanded to account for observations in the hundreds or even thousands. It all depends on what the data are like and if they lend themselves to an EDA display—remember to let simplicity be your guide.

Tukey's Tallies

What happens if the observations within a stem and leaf diagram become too numerous? Tukey (1977) suggests that once 20 or more leaves appear on a stem, the data analyst is apt to feel cramped. Stem and leaf diagrams, then, are very useful for examining smaller sets of data, but what about larger distributions? Can we retain their information but render them easy to handle visually? Tukey recommends relying on a tallying system that used dots first, then lines that form boxes, and then crossed lines that represent a final symbol for 10. **Tukey's line box tally system** is shown in Figure 3.13. It is much easier to use than the old fashioned method of counting by lines of five:

Why is the line box system better? Because even the most careful data analyst can make a mistake as he or she adds yet another line to make a bundle of five lines to count. I used the older tallying system more times than I care to remember—invariably I would miscount, make an error, and have to start all over again. I became frustrated by my error and annoyed when I noticed the time I wasted trying to correct it. The Tukey (1977) tallying system prevents such mistakes, is pleasing to the eye, and reveals accurate counts of observations quickly.

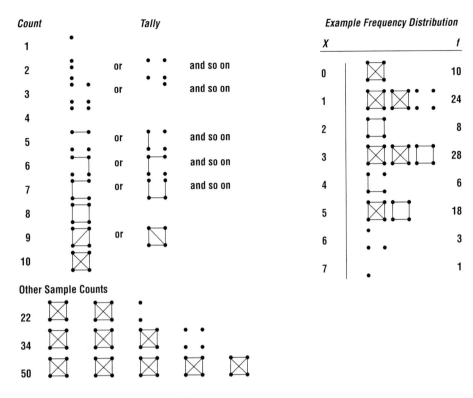

Figure 3.13 Tukey's (1977) Tallying System

Tukey's tallying system prevents counting errors, a bane of good data analysis.

Consider the simple frequency distribution shown in the upper right section of Figure 3.13. The X observation values are noted to the left of the vertical line and the symbols for the tally counts of the observations are shown to its right. For your convenience, the actual frequency (f) of the tallies is shown to the far right. Notice how quickly you can pick up the tallying symbols and know what the count is with a glance. As with the stem and leaf diagram, the graphic quality of the tallies enables viewers to get a sense of what the distribution of scores is like and where the heaviest concentration of scores falls. Other larger sample counts are shown in the bottom left of Figure 3.13.

By the way, it makes no difference where you start a box with four dots, nor which line you draw first when you want to connect two points (see the column labeled *Tally* in Figure 3.13). An added virtue of this system for tallying is that there is no correct order—like most EDA procedures, this one is very flexible for both researcher and data.

Knowledge Base

1. Traditionally, which axis is used to plot the dependent measure? Which one plots the independent variable?
2. True or False: A histogram and a frequency polygon based on the same data set convey the same information.
3. Using the data from the frequency distribution that follows, plot a histogram and a frequency polygon.

x	f
7	0
6	8
5	4
4	5
3	5
2	2
1	2

4. True or False: In a bar graph, both the x and the y axes are based on quantitative scales.
5. Why is contextual information important in graphs?
6. How do stem and leaf diagrams differ from other types of graphs?
7. Place the following data in a stem and leaf diagram:
    33 22 24 35 47 50 53 33 30 29 22 41 40 33 21 42 59 20 43 27
8. How many observations are represented by the following tally:

Answers

1. The y axis; the x axis
2. True
3.

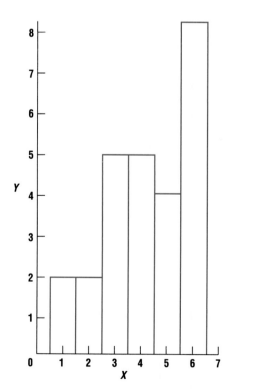

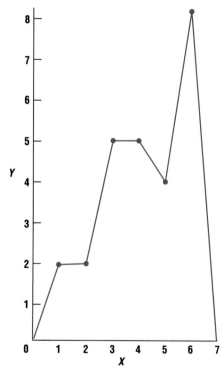

4. False: In a bar graph, only the y axis is quantitative; the x axis is qualitative.

5. Critical reviewers should be able to ask, "compared to what?" about any particular result shown in a graph. To do so, context is important—one result cannot be properly understood in isolation from other relevant information.

6. Stem and leaf diagrams retain and display the actual raw scores in a set of data.

7.

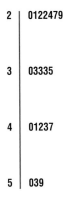

2	0122479
3	03335
4	01237
5	039

8. 26

Envisioning the Shape of Distributions

What do distributions look like? Smaller distributions can be understood in any one of several ways that we have explored in this chapter. You can think of a grouped frequency distribution in terms of numbers, for instance, as a histogram, or even as a frequency polygon. In the case of smaller data sets, which, granted, are both easy to work with and envision, these characterizations of the distributions tend to be linear, angular, and, at times, even "spikey."

What if the data set we were working with—more likely *from*—were very large and theoretical, so that we would need to speculate about its size and characteristics. What would the shape be like then? To begin with, if the data set were large, say, infinitely large, then observations would be so plentiful and close together that the shape of any given distribution would be actually be relatively smooth, not angular. Yet, depending on the relationships in the data, these smoother curves would still suggest the (angular) hills and valleys shown in any graph—they would just be more fluid-like in appearance.

Frequency distributions can come in any number of varieties and shapes. As you will learn later in this book; however, one form of distribution is ideal for performing statistical analyses. This distribution is called the *normal distribution*.

KEY TERM A **normal distribution** is a hypothetical, bell-shaped curve wherein the majority of observations appear at or near the midpoint of the distribution.

A typical normal distribution is shown in (a) of Figure 3.14. As you can readily see, the distribution is symmetric around its midpoint; that is, if you split the bell curve in half, each side is the mirror image of the other. Most of the observations or scores fall at or around the midpoint of the distribution, and fewer and fewer fall away from this center—the observations occur less frequently—as you move into what are usually referred to as the "tails" of the distribution. We will review the statistical properties of the normal distribution that make it so helpful to psychologists and other behavioral scientists later in the book.

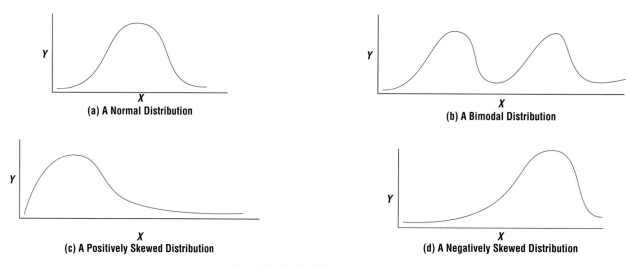

Figure 3.14 Four Distribution Shapes

The classic example of the normal distribution is apt to induce fear and trembling in most students, and memories of things long past in the minds of many former students. I refer, or course, to the distribution of grades within the typical college class of yore: The majority of students earned grades in the C (i.e., average) range, which is represented by the bulk of observations underneath the "bell" in the normal curve. Moving outward to the left and right of the bell, a smaller number of students received grades of D and B, respectively. Finally, in the tails of the distribution fall the fewest students—those receiving the highest (i.e., As) and lowest (i.e., Fs) grades. Some readers will be surprised to learn that it used to be assumed that a portion of students enrolled in any given class would be anticipated to fail it, just as the vast majority were expected to pass it with only average grades. Fortunately, student goals and desires, as well as faculty teaching philosophies, have moved away somewhat from the tenets of the normal curve where grading is concerned.

It is also possible to have a distribution that looks like two normal distributions put together. This two "humped" distribution is still deemed symmetrical, and it is called a **bimodal** distribution. "Bi" means two and "modal" refers to the frequency of scores, an issue we will take up again in the next chapter. For the present, think of a bimodal distribution as one that has two more or less symmetrical curves in it (if the distribution has more than two score clusters or curves, it is sometimes described as being **multimodal**). Chances are that you have been part of a bimodal distribution at one time or another. Have you ever taken a test where half of the students score either very highly (A or B range) or very poorly (D or F range)? Few or no students receive an average grade of C on this all or nothing test. In this case, the range of test scores is said to be bimodal, as one of the humps corresponds to very high grades and the other to very low grades. A bimodal distribution is shown by (b) in Figure 3.14.

Do the distributions of data that behavioral scientists work with tend to be normal ones? Not necessarily. In fact, statisticians have developed various descriptions for the different forms distributions can take. One of the chief features of a distribution is a property called *skew*, which refers to the lack of symmetry within a distribution.

▽

Anything that can be measured—from behaviors to beliefs—will have a distribution of scores comprising some shape.

KEY TERM   **Skew** refers to a nonsymmetrical distribution whose observations cluster at one end.

When a distribution has a **positive skew,** its observations tend to be clustered at the lower end of the distribution—very few observations fall into the upper region of the scale, which has a long but low tail. An example of positive skew is shown in (c) of Figure 3.14. Positive skew can occur, for example, when a test is so difficult that the distribution of scores reveals that the majority of people who took it performed poorly—only a relative handful scores highly [see (c) in Figure 3.14]. **Negative skew,** then, occurs when many observations fall at the upper end of the scale, which can be seen in (d) in Figure 3.14. As shown in (d), the tail in a negatively skewed distribution is long and low to the left of the scale. A test that is too easy will show negative skew in its distribution of scores—most everyone scores relatively highly on it, and only a few test-takers receive poor or failing scores [see (d) in Figure 3.14]. The distribution shown in the stem and leaf diagrams in Figures 3.11 and 3.12 also has a negative skew. Normal distributions do not have skew, of course, because the observations are symmetric about the midpoints of these distributions [see (a) in Figure 3.14]. Another prominent feature of some distributions is discussed in Data Box 3.C.

DATA BOX 3.C

Kurtosis, or What's the Point Spread?

Distributions of observations can be normal or they can be skewed. In either case statisticians sometimes like to further characterize what sort of clustering of scores takes place within a given distribution. Is a distribution "skinny" or "fat"? This relative peakedness or the flatness of a curve is called **kurtosis.** There are three categories of kurtosis.

a. A normal distribution is called **mesokurtic** because most scores appear in its middle (*"meso"* refers to middle). The normal curve shown in curve (a) is mesokurtic.
b. When a curve is very tall and skinny with only a quasi-normal shape, it is referred to as **leptokurtic.** Curve (b) is leptokurtic ("lepto" refers to thin).
c. Fatter curves that still possess a somewhat normal shape [see curve (c)] are said to be **platykurtic.** As you can see, the spread of scores is broad or flat, the definition of "platy."

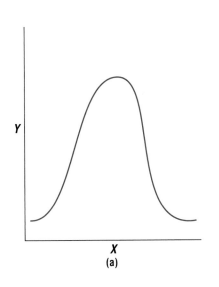

(a)

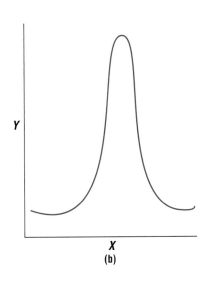

(b)

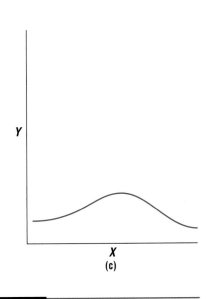

(c)

DATA BOX 3.D

Elegant Information—Napoleon's Ill-fated March to Moscow

Information can be presented in elegant and informative ways. An example of such graphical elegance is shown below. The image represents Napoleon Bonaparte's ill-fated march to Moscow in the war of 1812. It was created by a French engineer, Charles Joseph Minard (1781–1870). Minard deftly shows what happened to Napoleon's army as it marched from the Polish-Russian border near the Niemen river toward Moscow and then back again. The thick band at the top of the graphic represents the army (which began with 422,000 men) as it invaded Russia during June of 1812. As the band moves to the right, notice that it reduces in width, Minard's way of illustrating Napoleon's losses—indeed, by the time the army reaches Moscow in September, there are only 100,000 soldiers remaining (see the far right of the graphic). By then, Moscow was sacked and deserted.

The black band in the lower portion of the graphic is Napoleon's army in retreat—black is appropriate, of course, because as your eye follows the band back toward the Niemen River, it grows ever smaller in width. Why? The winter was bitterly cold, as noted by the temperatures and months Minard provided at the bottom of the graphic. Soldiers died or were lost by the thousands. The numbers running along the bottom of the black band represent the number of soldiers left as the army returns to its point of origin—only 10,000 men remained alive at the campaign's end.

Minard's presentation of the data is simple but staggering. This tragic tale is conveyed graphically through five variables—the army's size, it's location, the direction of travel, and the temperatures and dates during the retreat from Moscow. Tufte (1983, p. 40) remarked about this graphic that, "It may well be the best statistical graphic ever drawn." I want to draw your attention to this and similar data displays (cf., Dr. Snow's map of cholera in central London; see p. 86) to remind you relationships between variables can be powerful. Such presentations can—and should—be portrayed in ways that capture a viewer's attention, even imagination, but that the integrity and factual basis of the data must not be sacrificed. Although you will probably not create images like Snow's or Minard's, allow their careful work to inspire you to develop meaningful graphs and tables for your own data.

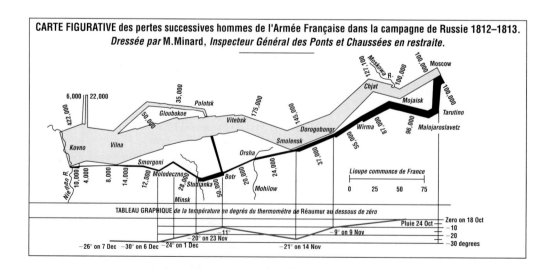

Percentiles and Percentile Ranks

When we examined the distribution of optimistic versus pessimistic transfer students earlier in this chapter, we considered their scores on the Life Orientation Test (LOT) within the framework of a frequency distribution. Our concern was to develop a sense of what the data were like—how many individuals received the same score, for example—and to identify the most and least frequent scores on the personality measure. Whether they appear in the form of a table, a histogram, a frequency polygon, or a stem and leaf diagram, frequency distributions provide "the big picture," if you will, about a data set.

What frequency distributions do not usually provide, however, is precise information about the relative position of a given score on a dependent measure; that is, how does one observation compare to all others? Is a given LOT score high (i.e., optimistic) or low (i.e., pessimistic)? In the absence of information indicating the average LOT score or how many respondents had higher or lower scores on this personality measure, readers really do not know much about what a given score means. Indeed, it is the equivalent of getting back an exam with a numerical score on it, but your instructor neglects to share the grading distribution with the class. Did you do well, merely pass, or fail miserably? One of my college roommates, an electrical engineering major, routinely had exams and homework assignments with scores less than 30 out of a possible 100 points—I remember once he had an 11. I was shocked, as I assumed he was failing the class, indeed, perhaps the entire semester. I offered support and sympathy. He laughed: Compared to the class average, his grades were *actually quite high—he was doing well on the assignments!* Thus, some indication of a score's relative position within a distribution is desirable. As I was unaware of the grading distribution, I could not make such relative—and in this case, accurate— judgments about my friend's performance.

The statistic used to disclose relative position within a data distribution is called *percentile rank.*

KEY TERM   A **percentile rank** is a number indicating what percentage of scores fall at or below a given score on a measure.

If you know an individual's score on a measure such as the LOT, it is relatively easy to determine where that score stands in relation to the rest of the sample's scores. For example, a score of 30 might be equal to or higher than 75% of the LOT scores in the sample. Percentile ranks are informative. In this case, you know that a score of 30 is relatively high, higher, say, than 3/4 of the other scores in the sample. Take note that percentile rank is another technique that enables researchers to ask, "compared to what?"

When a score's percentile rank is known, the score itself is called a *percentile.*

KEY TERM   When a score is defined by its percentile rank, it is called a **percentile.**

If a LOT score is 30 and it has a percentile rank of 75, then the score of 30 would be at the 75th percentile.

▽

The virtue of percentile information is that it provides the relative placement of one score to all others above and below it.

You may not realize it, but chances are you have encountered percentile rank information and not even been aware of it. If you took any standardized test for admission to your undergraduate institution, your score (or *scores* if the test had subscales) was probably accompanied by its percentile rank (i.e., how did your score on the test fare when compared to scores of others who took the test simultaneously). At the time, you probably either ignored this percentile rank information or you did not really understand what it meant. I hope to rectify that situation shortly; indeed, such knowledge will probably prove to be helpful if applying to graduate or professional school is in your future —standardized tests are still required for entry into most postbaccalaureate programs. Moreover, many standardized psychological inventories—the kind you might read about or use in a research project—usually have copious amounts of documentation, much of which refers to percentiles.

Cumulative Frequency

Before any percentile rank or percentile can be calculated, however, we first need to determine the *cumulative frequency* for the data we are analyzing.

Cumulative frequency refers to the number of values within a given interval added to the total number of values that fall below that interval.

Cumulative frequencies are organized into what are called **cumulative frequency distributions.**

Table 3.9 shows a cumulative frequency distribution for the LOT data we examined earlier in the chapter. As you can see, we created the intervals previously and their original frequencies were retained. The third column of Table 3.9 is labeled "*cf*" for "cumulative frequency." The convention associated with creating cumulative frequencies is to begin with the frequency of the lowest class interval (see 1 in interval 4.5–8.5)—this is the base value of the *cf.* This base value of 1 is then added to the value in the class interval immediately above it (here, 6 in 8.5–12.5) to create the *cf* for this next-to-the-lowest class interval, which is 7. The same procedure is used to determine the *cf* for the next highest (the third one from the bottom) interval (i.e., 7 + 1 = 8), and so on, until all of the frequencies are accounted for in the top most class interval. Note that the total *cf* = 30, which is equal to the $\sum f$ and, in turn, *N.* Please make sure you understand why this is—and must be—so.

What can we learn from the *cf* of the LOT scores? Take another look at Table 3.9. For example, consider the 6 respondents who had LOT scores falling in the interval 20.5–24.5. We know that 17 (i.e., the *cf* for that class interval) respondents in the sample received LOT scores that were less than or equal to 24.5, the upper true limit of the interval. We also know, then, that 13 people in the sample had LOT scores that were greater than 24.5, the lower true limit of the above interval. How so? If we know that the $\sum f$ is 30, then all we need to do is subtract 17 from that sum (i.e., 30 − 17 = 13). Thus, our reliance on

Table 3.9 Cumulative Frequency Distribution of LOT Scores with True Limits and Class Intervals

Class Intervals of X	f	cf
36.5–40.5	1	30
32.5–36.5	5	29
28.5–32.5	5	24
24.5–28.5	2	19
20.5–24.5	6	17
16.5–20.5	3	11
12.5–16.5	1	8
8.5–12.5	6	7
4.5–8.5	1	1
	$\sum f = 30$	

Note: The intervals in this table are based on the frequency distribution shown in Table 3.2, which in turn is based on the raw scores from Table 3.1.

cumulative frequencies provides a bit more information about the relative positions of scores than was available through a grouped frequency distribution.

Please note that cumulative frequencies need *not* be calculated using data that are already organized into class intervals. One could determine cumulative frequencies for frequencies of individual scores. Thus, for example, a column of cumulative frequencies could be added to the frequency distribution of LOT scores shown back in Table 3.2. Because larger samples of data are usually presented in class intervals (with or without true limits), however, it is likely that any cumulative frequencies you work with will already be in some sort of grouped frequency distribution. As a result, I feel it is more beneficial for you to see and work with examples that present cumulative frequencies for data that are already organized into class intervals.

Cumulative Percentage

Once they are available, cumulative frequencies, in turn, can be converted into *cumulative percentages.*

KEY TERM   A **cumulative percentage** is the percentage of values within a given interval added to the total number of percentage values that fall below that interval.

Cumulative percentages enable you to consider a distribution of data as having 100 equal parts, and can be determined from cumulative frequencies with ease. A cumulative frequency can be changed into a cumulative percentage simply by dividing the *cf* value by *N* and multiplying the resulting product by 100, or:

[3.10.1]   *cumulative percentage* = cumulative frequency/total number of scores (i.e., *N*) × 100.

Thus, if we want to know the cumulative percentage corresponding to the *cf* of 17 in the class interval 20.5–24.5 in Table 3.9, the calculation would be:

[3.10.2]   *cumulative percentage* = 17/30 × 100,

[3.10.3]   *cumulative percentage* = 0.5667 × 100 = 56.67%.

In other words, 56.67% of the LOT scores in the sample fall below the upper true limit of 24.5. Naturally, it is possible to also determine what percentage of the scores appear *above* the upper true limit of 24.5. This percentage—which can be determined by subtracting 56.67% from 100%—is 43.33%.

Table 3.10 repeats the information from Table 3.9 but a fifth column is added to reflect the cumulative percentages of the distribution of data (for convenience, the fourth column displays the percentage of LOT scores within each class interval). As was true for the cumulative frequencies, the cumulative percentages accumulate as you move from the bottommost interval to the top most class interval. In the case of percentages, of course, the total cumulative percentage must equal 100%, not *cf* or the Σf or *N*. Once again, please be sure you understand why this must be true. Be sure to keep in mind, as well, that the cumulative percentages are simply another way of considering the data—in terms of their meaning, the relationships shown by cumulative frequencies and cumulative percentages are identical.

Finally, as was the case for cumulative frequencies, the data need not appear in a grouped frequency distribution in order to be converted into cumulative percentages. A fifth column labeled "*c*%" could be added with little difficulty to the relative frequency distribution shown back in Table 3.3. Indeed, the percentage values for each score are already present (see the column labeled % in Table 3.3); starting at the bottom of that column, the percentage values would just need to accumulate interval by interval in a new (fifth) column.

Table 3.10

Cumulative Frequency and Cumulative Percentage Distribution of LOT Scores with True Limits and Class Intervals

Class Intervals of X	f	cf	%	c%
36.5–40.5	1	30	3.33%	100%
32.5–36.5	5	29	16.67%	96.67%
28.5–32.5	5	24	16.67%	80.00%
24.5–28.5	2	19	6.67%	63.33%
20.5–24.5	6	17	20.00%	56.67%
16.5–20.5	3	11	10.00%	36.67%
12.5–16.5	1	8	3.33%	26.67%
8.5–12.5	6	7	20.00%	23.33%
4.5–8.5	1	1	3.33%	3.33%
	$\sum f = 30$			

Note: The intervals in this table are based on the frequency distribution shown in Table 3.2, which in turn is based on the raw scores from Table 3.1.

Cumulative percentage information provides a good approximation of the relative position of a known or given score as compared to the remaining scores within a distribution. The shortfall of cumulative percentage information, however, is its relative lack of precision. By examining the class interval for LOT scores between 28.5 and 32.5 in Table 3.10, for example, we know that 16.67% of the distribution's scores were in that interval (see the *f* for the interval), and that 80% of the scores were equal to or less than the upper true limit of the score 32.5 (see the *cf* for the interval). We also know that 5 LOT scores fall inside this interval—but we only know information about the class interval *as a whole,* not any individual score's relative position with respect to the rest of the scores in the distribution. To address more precise questions, we must calculate a given score's percentile rank.

Calculating Percentile Rank

The calculation of a percentile rank is not difficult if you keep in mind what you are trying to accomplish—a necessary act anytime you are performing any statistical calculation—and you rely on a straightforward formula. To calculate percentile rank, I will use a formula suggested by Runyon, Haber, Pittenger, and Coleman (1996, p. 83). There are two reasons to use this and not alternative means to calculate percentile ranks. First, the formula results in a precise answer. Second, the formula is detailed, requiring you really think about and get a feel for the distribution of data with which you are working. Here is the formula:

[3.11.1]
$$PR = \frac{cf_{11} + \left[\frac{(X_i - X_{11})}{w}\right]f_i}{N} \times 100,$$

where

cf_{11} = cumulative frequency of the class interval below X,

X_i = the score to be converted to a percentile rank,

X_{11} = score at the lower true limit of the class containing X,

w = width of the class interval,

f_i = number of scores within the class interval containing X,

N = the number of scores within the distribution.

To determine the actual percentile rank for one of the LOT scores, say, a score of 35, we will need to replace the variables in formula [3.11.1] with numbers from or based on the data in Table 3.10. To simplify the process, we will follow Runyon et al.'s (1996) lead and perform the calculation in two steps (be certain to check the math as we proceed and that you are absolutely sure you know where all the numbers came from!).

1. What is the percentile rank for a LOT score of 35? We need to begin by entering all the values into the formula. To begin, we know that X_i is 35 (we selected it above) and the width (w) of the class intervals in Table 3.10 is 4. Where is X? Take a look at Table 3.10 and locate it in the class interval for scores between 32.5 and 36.5. We now know that the lower true limit of the class interval containing $X = 35$ (i.e., X_{11}) is 32.5. How many scores are in this interval? There are 5, so $f_i = 5$. The cumulative frequency of the class below that containing X, the score of 35, is 24 (i.e., $cf_{11} = 24$). Our N is 30 because the sample contains 30 LOT scores.

   These numbers are substituted for the variables in the formula that appears below—it is essential that you make certain that you know where they came from. Be sure to not only review the formula above in [3.11.1], but also to locate these numbers in Table 3.10.

   [3.11.2]
   $$PR = \frac{24 + \left[\frac{(35 - 32.5)}{4}\right]5}{30} \times 100.$$

2. Recalling the order of operations from chapter 1, we then continue to solve the formula. Please make certain that you understand the information at each consecutive step.

   [3.11.3]
   $$PR = \frac{[24 + (0.625)5]}{30} \times 100,$$

   [3.11.4]
   $$PR = \frac{27.125}{30} \times 100,$$

   [3.11.5]
   $$PR = 0.9042 \times 100,$$

   [3.11.6]
   $$PR = 90.42 \cong 90.$$

What do we know about a LOT score of 35? The score is quite high, indeed, it reflects a high degree of optimism (see Data Box 3.A). Further, of course, we can say that 90% of the people in the sample received a score of 35 or below on the LOT.

Reversing the Process: Finding Scores from Percentile Ranks

On occasion, you may know the percentile rank of a score on some inventory or standardized test, but you have no idea what score corresponds to it. Fortunately, the percentile rank formula shown in [3.11.1] can be reversed. That is, as long as you possess percentile rank information and the distribution of data it was drawn from, the score can be determined. For consistency, we will again work with the distribution of LOT scores shown in Table 3.10, and we will convert the percentile rank we found in the last section back into its original score. Once again, we will rely on a useful formula and series of steps provided by Runyon and colleagues:

[3.12.1]
$$X_{PR} = X_{11} + \frac{w(cf_{PR} - cf_{11})}{f_i},$$

where

cf_{PR} = the cumulative frequency found by multiplying the known percentile rank (*PR*) by the sample *N* and then dividing by 100,

cf_{11} = the cumulative frequency of the class below the one containing the known *PR*,

X_{11} = the score at the lower true limit of the class containing the known *PR*,

w = the width of the class intervals,

f_i = number of scores within the class interval containing the *PR*.

1. The first step involves converting the known percentile rank (here, 90.42) into a cumulative frequency. The percentile rank is multiplied by the *N*, and the resulting number is divided by 100, or

[3.13.1]
$$cf_{PR} = PR(N)/100,$$

[3.13.2]
$$cf_{PR} = (90.42)(30)/100 = 2712.60/100,$$

[3.13.3]
$$cf_{PR} = 27.126.$$

2. Using information provided in Table 3.10, we then substitute numbers for the variables shown in formula [3.12.1]. First, we now know that the cf_{PR} falls within the class interval of 32.5–36.5. Thus, we know that the value of X_{11} is 32.5. The *cf* below this class interval is 24, so that $cf_{11} = 24$. Finally, the f_i of the class containing the *PR* is 5, and the width (*w*) of the class intervals remains 4.

3. Once the numbers are entered into formula [3.12.1], it can be solved:

[3.12.2]
$$X_{PR} = 32.5 + \frac{4(27.126 - 24)}{5},$$

[3.12.3]
$$X_{PR} = 32.5 + \frac{4(3.126)}{5},$$

[3.12.4]
$$X_{PR} = 32.5 + 2.5008,$$

[3.12.5]
$$X_{PR} = 35.008 \cong 35.$$

We have come, as it were, full circle where percentile ranks are concerned. The LOT score of 35 was previously found to fall around the 90th percentile, and now we have reversed the process—the 90th percentile was shown to correspond to a score of 35 on the LOT. There are two lessons to be learned here. First, once you know a score or its percentile rank, you can determine the other. Second, knowing both of these formulas gives you flexibility and enables you to *verify* any answer. Thus, when you calculate the percentile rank of a known score, you can "check your math" by reversing the process to prove the answer is correct (and vice versa). Never underestimate the importance of checking your work, and do not miss any opportunity to do so!

Exploring Data: Calculating the Middle Percentiles and Quartiles

This chapter includes a variety of ways a researcher can examine a set of data—from graphing to EDA. The consideration of percentiles and percentile ranks adds yet another dimension. There is one final set of approaches that should not be overlooked, and it is good preparation for issues we will discuss in chapter 4. These approaches entail exploring percentiles as indicators of a distribution's dispersion—how the scores are scattered through the distribution or about some midpoint. In the next chapter, we will delve into great detail about what are called measures of central tendency, or statistical indicators that identify the most common or average scores in a data set. For the present, however, we can obtain a sense of dispersion and central tendency in a distribution by examining *quartiles*.

KEY TERM When a data distribution is divided into four equal parts, each part is labeled a **quartile.** By convention, these quartiles are sometimes referred to as Q_1, Q_2, and Q_3.

The 25th and 75th percentiles are called quartiles, and would be called Q_1 and Q_3, respectively. Scores that fall between these two demarcations in the data can be used as a general measure of dispersion (Runyon et al., 1996). In fact, the scores between the quartiles from a distribution representing one sample can be used for comparison with the similar scores from another sample. As we progress through the book, such comparisons between or among distributions will become more frequent and necessary for the data analysis we will be learning.

Table 3.11 shows Q_1 and Q_3 for the LOT data. These quartiles were calculated as percentiles (i.e., 25 and 75) using formula [3.13.1]. I have provided the specific numbers that were entered in this formula so that you can check my work and your understanding of where the numbers came from. Note, too, that the actual answers (i.e., X_{PR}) were rounded, as scores on the LOT must be whole numbers (see the review of this personality measure presented at the start of the chapter). How do we use the scores that fall at Q_1 and Q_3—that is, 13 and 36 (see Table 3.11)? To point out that *approximately* or *around* 50% of the distributions score's fall between LOT scores of 13 and 36. Why do hedge the description by using the word "approximately" or "around"? Simply because we rounded the X_{PR} values for both scores.

But there is more to it than rounding. If you were to calculate the actual percentage of scores that fall between these two scores, you would find it is equal to 73%. That's correct, our estimate was off by 13%, but remember that we are exploring the distribution and, in the spirit of John Tukey, trying to get a sense of it—accuracy is not (yet) the point. Such minor "errors" happen—the point is that we have nonetheless gotten a rough and ready sense of what the distance between the two quartiles is like. If you are at all troubled by the magnitude of this error, then you are well on the way to becoming a good data analyst. As a mental exercise, let me suggest that you consider a compelling reason for it that was introduced in chapter 2—the relatively small sample of LOT

Table 3.11   The Median and Quartiles of the LOT Scores

	Percentiles		
	25th (Q_1)	**50th (Q_2)**	**75th (Q_3)**
LOT score (X)	$\cong 13$	$\cong 26$	$\cong 36$
X_{PR}	12.83	25.83	35.5
c_{PR}	7.5	15	22.5
cf_{11}	7	11	19
f_i	6	3	2
X_{11}	12.5	20.5	28.5
w	4	4	4

Source: Adapted from Table 3.7 on p. 82 of Runyon, Haber, Pittenger, and Coleman (1996).

scores; that is, smaller samples are apt to be more affected by changes in frequency than are larger samples. Why? Because in a larger sample, any given score creates very little percentage change, whereas in a small sample like this one, any given score contributes 3.33% (i.e., 1/30). If the sample size were 100, then a given score would represent only 1% change (i.e., 1/100), and so on for even larger samples.

What about the 50th percentile, also known as Q_2? Well, the 50th percentile has a special name—the **median.** We will spend considerable time discussing the median in the next chapter but for now, know that the median divides a distribution of data exactly in half—that is, half of the scores fall above a median point and half below it. The median LOT score was determined to be 26 (see Table 3.11). Thus, we can say that half of the LOT scores were higher than 26 and half were lower.

Writing About Percentiles

When do behavioral scientists write about percentiles and percentile ranks? How do they write about these concepts? As noted earlier, percentile information is very often reported in connection with psychological tests and measures. Percentile information is usually presented in technical reports or summaries about new or existing tests. For many of these tests, the respondent samples are very large—there may be hundreds, possibly even several thousand respondents whose scores form the distributions from which percentile information is drawn. Psychologists often consult these published reports in order to learn how a given score (or even set of scores) they collected compares to one of these normative or "standard" samples.

What should be written about percentile information? Typically, written comments about percentiles and percentile ranks are quite brief. Basically, a researcher will want to note that a given score corresponded to a particular percentile rank, and that the score was equal to or higher than some percentage of other scores on the measure. If you review the previous sections dealing with the LOT scores, you can see how one score can be written about—that is, described and compared to other scores in a distribution. *The main point here is that a percentile or percentile rank must be written about in relation to some group.* If no comparisons are made in the narrative, then readers will not understand the points the researcher is trying to convey.

In general, the best way to write about percentile information is by referring to the appropriate entries within a data table—text and table must be linked (see the related discussion in a later section on *Constructing Tables and Graphs*). Specifically, you must refer the reader to the percentile rank of interest within a table, identify the score corresponding to it, and then discuss the import of these two pieces of information. Here is a brief excerpt about the School Form (i.e., children's version) of the Self-Esteem Inventory (SEI; Coopersmith, 1987). As a measure of general self-approval or disapproval, the SEI was designed to identify individuals' beliefs relating to social, academic, family, and personal life experiences. When discussing a study of public school children (Kimball, 1972), the SEI manual (Coopermith, 1987, p. 17) notes that

> The SEI was administered to 7593 public school children in grades 4 through 8. The sample included all socioeconomic ranges and Black and Spanish surnamed students. Derived percentiles (see Table 5) showed a consistency of score values at a given percentile regardless of the population considered.

The written text refers to a table (I have not provided the table of data here because I want to emphasize the writing side of the link between data and explanation). What do we know from this brief passage? We know that across grades 4 through 8, the SEI scores in every percentile (1 to 99 for the SEI) were consistent with one another so that the

Percentiles and percentile rank information directly answer the question, "Compared to what?"

reader knows what to expect when she reviews the percentile data in the table. The author presents this information clearly and succinctly. If any score or scores stood out—were aberrant, for instance—they would be discussed in greater detail. Let me close this section by encouraging you to treat describing percentile results as a guide for writing about data—create links between what you know and what you must tell readers, and do so in a judicious manner.

Knowledge Base

1. A group of clinically depressed individuals completes a self-esteem inventory, and most of the scores cluster at the low end of the scale (i.e., most members of the sample have low self-esteem). The distribution of scores is best described as
   a. positively skewed   b. negatively skewed   c. bimodal
   d. normal
2. A score on a psychological inventory is observed to be at the 85th percentile. Explain what this fact means.
3. Calculate the percentile rank for a score of 8 using the following data:

X	f	cf
25.5–30.5	8	36
15.5–20.5	7	28
10.5–15.5	5	21
5.5–10.5	10	16
0.5–5.5	6	6

4. Using the data set in 3, find the score corresponding to a percentile rank of 70.

Answers

1. a. Positively skewed
2. Eighty-five percent of the inventory scores fall at or below the observed score.
3. Percentile rank of a score of $8 = 30.5556 \cong 31$.
4. Score corresponding to a percentile rank of $70 = 15.02 \cong 15$.

Constructing Tables and Graphs

Quite a bit of the material in this chapter focuses on how to present and interpret information in graphs. As you know by now, the presentation of data within a clear graph is an important way to convey results to an audience of readers or listeners. We have not, however, spent much time reviewing tables or how to present information in tabular form. I have not neglected this topic—on the contrary, most chapters in this book contain numerical information presented within tables. Due to the frequency with which tables appear throughout the book, however—and compared to the relative paucity of graphs—I felt that emphasis in this chapter should be placed on the latter.

   I do want to close this chapter with some suggestions that can improve the construction and the presentation of data in tables as well as graphs. Some information will be a continuation of themes raised by our earlier review of Tufte's (1983) comments on graphic images, while the remainder deals with guidelines for data display advocated by the American Psychological Association (APA), notably its rules of style. For continuity, we close the chapter with a project exercise dealing with a historical use of data reminiscent of Dr. Snow's cholera map of central London; old information can be presented in relatively new and powerful ways.

Less is More: Avoiding Chartjunk and Tableclutter, and Other Suggestions

Whether data appear in a table or a graph, they should be readily interpretable. A good graph should have the qualities of accuracy, brevity, and clarity (e.g., Tufte, 1983). Where data displays are concerned, less *really is* more. In my view, a good table should aspire to these same qualities except that it can have a tad more information than a graph. Why? Viewers should ponder tables. In their ideal form, tables highlight numerical relationships that invite viewers to proceed at a slower pace than do graphs. In general, then, tables are assumed to possess a higher degree of complexity than most graphs.

No table or graph should slow readers too much, however. One particular form of graphic complexity slows readers down considerably—the presence of what Tufte (1983) calls **chartjunk.** Chartjunk refers to those parts of a graphic image that are not useful or even necessary for representing data. In fact, Tufte calls chartjunk the "interior decoration of graphics" that "generates a lot of ink that does not tell the viewer anything new" (Tufte, 1983, p. 107). A classic example of chartjunk is shown in Figure 3.15. What is the problem with this image? The eye is drawn all over the place by too many colors (here, too many shades of pink), overlapping textures, and what we might call "printed noise"—this graph is just *too busy*. For example, should the different "layers" in Figure 3.15 be understood as appearing on *top* of one another or *in front* of each other? Can you interpret this graph? Possibly, but not until you have studied it for a while, a situation that is antithetical to the intent and purpose of a good graph.

Relevant perception research demonstrates that extraneous details, such as three-dimensional effects and other "gewgaw" embellishments, actually make graphs more difficult to interpret (Barfield & Robless, 1989; Carswell, Frankenberger, & Bernhard, 1991; see also Pittenger, 1995). In fact, simple but good two-dimensional graphs are much easier to interpret than are most three-dimensional displays, despite their "professional" appearance and frequent use in popular magazines and daily newspapers of dubious quality. Two-dimensional images tend to be interpreted more quickly and with less error. Moreover, viewers are more confident in the conclusions they draw from two- rather than three-dimensions (for a list of references on graphs and graphing; see Pittenger, 1995).

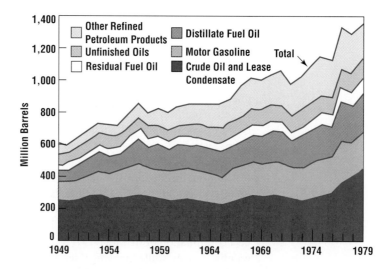

Figure 3.15 A Classic Example of Chartjunk

Source: Reprinted from Tufte (1983). Original Source : Energy Information Administration, U.S. Department of Energy, *Annual Report to Congress,* 1979 (Washington, DC, 1979), vol. 2, p. 64.

What about tables? Can they also have chartjunk or, to coin a term, **tableclutter?** Of course. Any table that contains too many unnecessary numbers, labels, categories, and footnotes is probably suffering from tableclutter. If a reader must spend more than a minute or two reviewing the contents of a table in order to understand it or to gain his or her bearings, as it were, something is wrong with both its conception and construction. Many complex and detailed relationships are appropriately displayed through numerical entries and headings in a table, but when too much numerical information appears within a table, its message will be lost on readers. To be useful, data tables must be informative but not encyclopedic. The best guide when creating a table is to determine the minimal information needed for readers to understand the main point(s) the table is presenting. In this sense, a good table is like a good paragraph—it says what it is supposed to say and no more.

A second consideration in a good graph or table is the *link* between it and the accompanying written text. A graph or a table can be wonderfully clear and meaningful, but it will go unheeded if the author does not make direct, guiding reference to it in the text. In most cases, it is not sufficient to tell a reader to "See Table 2" if you do not bother to explain either before or after this directive what the fuss is all about. If you plan to take the time to create informative tables and graphs, then you must also explain what relationships—numerical or otherwise—you want viewers to notice. Keep in mind that graphs and tables are supplements supporting a researcher's ideas and insights, and that they stand alone only in the sense that their contents should be interesting to look at or consider. Researchers must still write clear and cogent prose that leads readers through this distilled information, pointing to interesting or suggestive trends along the way. Readers' imaginations are best left to fiction, not to scientific writing in the behavioral sciences—some link between text and table or graph must be established.

A third and final consideration is *redundancy.* A moment ago I advocated having written text complement tables and graphs—this still holds true—but the issue here is the amount of detail involved. A table or a graph should provide some new information, not repeat the same information presented in the text. Of course, there will be some small degree of overlap. A researcher will want to specifically point to numbers that stand out or a line that portrays a crucial pattern, but this should be done carefully and sparingly. Experience is the best teacher here. As you gain experience presenting and discussing data in graphs and tables, you will acquire a sense that what to leave out of the written text is as important as what you put into it.

American Psychological Association (APA) Style Guidelines for Data Display

The APA has very decided views on what should and should not appear in a graph or a table. Indeed, the APA specifically dictates what constitutes a graph or a table. For the record, the *Publication Manual* (APA, 1994) stipulates that a *table* contains numbers *only,* and no graphics of any kind. (By the way, if you do not yet own a copy of the *Publication Manual,* you should obtain one at your earliest opportunity.) You will probably be surprised to learn that APA style does not use the term *graph* or *graphic* in any official sense. Graphs, histograms, stem and leaf diagrams, bar graphs, pie charts, maps, pictures—indeed, almost anything else you can name—are technically referred to as *figures.* (Perhaps you have noticed that all the graphs in this book are labeled figures and that most tables are comprised of numbers exclusively—I have been more liberal with the term "table," as I think some textual information is best described as tabular in nature).

When you plan to organize some data into a table or figure, it is a very good idea to review pertinent sections of the *Publication Manual* before you begin (APA, 1994; for

Table 3.12   Some Considerations for Creating High-Quality Tables and Figures

1. Be certain that a table or figure absolutely necessary. Does it add—not detract from—the point you want to make?

2. A table or figure must be double-spaced.

3. Tables and figures must be consistent with other tables and figures in a text or presentation.

4. Titles, notes, and footnotes accompanying tables and figures must be brief but explanatory.

5. Entries in columns or rows must have headings.

6. Any abbreviations or acronyms appearing in a table or figure must be defined or explained in a note or a footnote.

7. Tables and figures must be connected to material in the text.

8. Spelling in any table or figure must always be checked.

9. A table or figure must appear on a separate page in a manuscript or a report.

Source: Some entries were adapted from the *Publication Manual of the American Psychological Association,* 4th ed. (1994).

tables, see sections 3.62 to 3.74; for figures, see 3.75 to 3.86; see also section 4.21). For your convenience, I have distilled several of the *Publication Manual*'s key points, as well as some intuitive observations, about table and graph construction into Table 3.12. Study this table before you create or evaluate any tables or figures. Finally, you should also consult Appendix C in this book, which is focused on presenting results (including tables and figures) in APA style.

Project Exercise   DISCUSSING THE BENEFITS OF ACCURATE BUT PERSUASIVE DATA DISPLAY

In our day and age, we take many things for granted, including the high quality of health care. Prenatal care and childbirth are a good case in point. In the middle of the last century, for example, maternal mortality following a birth was often quite high and physicians had only vague speculations as to its causes (Wertz & Wertz, 1977). The work of Dr. Ignaz P. Semmelweis, a Hungarian doctor, stands out as a clear example where casual observation led to the systematic collection of convincing data. Semmelweis noted a link between a contagious fever—then called puerperal fever—and an antiseptic environment as a means to prevent it. Working in Vienna's largest maternity hospital, Semmelweis discerned an interesting pattern of maternal mortality. In a ward where medical students delivered infants, the maternal mortality rate was 437% higher than in a ward where midwives did the deliveries (in the year 1846, the former ward had 459 deaths versus 105 losses in the latter). He knew that training and experience were not the key, as women who delivered babies on the hospitals' steps or in the corridors before reaching the wards never contracted the fever.

Semmelweis developed a hypothesis when a colleague died from puerperal fever after completing an autopsy. He believed—correctly—that women who survived childbirth had not been touched by student doctors whose hands had been contaminated from the handling of decomposed matter (i.e., the student doctors worked with and learned from cadavers in the hospital's autopsy ward). Those mothers who died, however, had been infected by disease lingering on the hands or person of the physicians who delivered their children.

Medicinal hygiene, a given in our century, was the key. Following his deduction, Semmelweis required anyone helping with births to wash their hands in a chloride of lime solution before ever touching the mothers. Two years later, only 45 women out of 3,556 died in the medical students' ward (43 died the same year in the midwives care). The drop in maternal mortality was dramatic, though you may be surprised to learn that the medical community still did not universally accept that cleanliness was necessary for health after childbirth (or many other medical procedures; see Wertz & Wertz, 1977).

Can some of the remaining deaths in the medical students' and midwives' wards be accounted for? Indeed, they can. Wertz and Wertz (1977) note that even the insightful Dr. Semmelweis did not understand the full importance of hygienic hospital conditions. He did not know, for instance, that it was necessary for each mother-to-be to have clean sheets on her bed! Other opportunistic infections beyond puerperal fever were still present when hospital beds were vacated by one patient in order to make room for the next one.

Think about Semmelweis' data: He had no tabular or graphic knowledge to call on when he set out to convince his medical colleagues that they were infecting their patients and indirectly causing their deaths. For your *project exercise,* think about and then answer the following questions by calling on the skills you have developed in the course of reading this chapter:

1. What makes the link between hygiene and maternal mortality a problem for behavioral science? How was Semmelweis acting like a behavioral scientist?
2. Knowing what you now know about graphs, for example, how could you reasonably use the mortality data cited above to make Semmelweis' case a convincing one?
3. If you were to construct a table linking mortality to the medical student ward but not the midwives' ward, how would you do it?
4. Are there other ways to break the mortality totals for 1846 down into other meaningful units? What units would you use? How would you use them to make your case regarding the link between disease and hygiene?
5. How would you link your data display to your arguments for creating and maintaining hygienic conditions?
6. Do you think your ideas for displaying data would be as convincing as (a) Semmelweis' numerical observations or (b) Snow's cholera map? Why or why not?

LOOKING FORWARD THEN BACK

he decision trees gracing the opening page of this chapter are very practical in scope. The first three trees are designed to help you determine, respectively, whether a data display is properly called a figure or a table, choosing to make a graph of some data, or deciding between creating a table or a graph. The fourth decision tree will help you to characterize the shape of a distribution of data (i.e., normal or skewed), a matter of grater or lesser importance depending on the nature of the data and the statistical tests used for analysis. In each case, these decision trees promote clarity when organizing research results into written form—a report, say, or a paper—or readying them for formal presentation in a classroom or conference setting. After you use these guidelines a few times, selecting and then creating an appropriate mode for presenting or describing information will become second nature to you.

Summary

1. There are two reasons for examining frequencies and graphing display data: To get a feel for the data and to present it to others.

2. The best way to organize and summarize data is a frequency distribution. A frequency distribution is a table of scores organized into numerical categories. Frequency distributions indicate how many times some particular type of response was made. Scores in a frequency distribution are ranked from the highest to the lowest observation.

3. Proportions and percentages, indices of relative position, are often included in frequency distributions. Percentages are readily calculated from proportions (and vice versa). Because both illustrate the relationship of frequency to the total number of available observations, they are often called relative frequencies, and thus, they appear in relative frequency distributions.

$$proportion = p = f/N,$$

$$percent = p(100).$$

4. Grouped frequency distributions collapse the data into class intervals of a set size. Each interval contains a group of scores, the origin of the name "grouped frequency distribution." Depending on the range of values in a data set, most grouped frequency distributions will have around 10 class intervals—larger data sets will require more intervals, smaller ones fewer. The width of the class intervals will be a fixed whole number (e.g., 6, 8), and no gaps must exist between the intervals, nor should they overlap one another.

5. The class intervals in most grouped frequency distributions will have upper and lower true limits. In general, the true limits will be determined by adding or subtracting one half of the unit of measure, respectively, from upper and lower class interval values.

6. The x axis in a graph of a frequency distribution has scores running horizontally, where the y axis has scores running vertically. In most graphs, the two axes meet in the bottom-left corner at the value of 0. By convention, the dependent measure is graphed along the y axis and the independent variable is graphed on the x axis.

7. Bar graphs are used to show data from ordinal or nominal scales. Bar graphs illustrate simple group differences in terms of frequency. Nonoverlapping bars are drawn above labeled or "named" groups on the x axis, and the height of a group's bar corresponds to its frequency on the y axis.

8. Histograms and frequency polygons plot data from interval or ratio scales. A histogram is similar to a bar graph except that a given bar is attached to a score on a measure. Bars are drawn above their corresponding scores on the x axis until they reach the heights of their frequencies on the y axis. When the bars are drawn extending up from the x axis, they should touch one another because each bar has upper and lower true limits. Frequency polygons are graphs of connected lines. The lines meet at points placed above a score or the midpoint of a class interval along the x axis. The height of any point is determined by its frequency on the y axis.

9. Graphs can be misleading if their data are not accurately presented or represented. Good behavioral scientists always examine relationships portrayed in graphs by asking, "Compared to what?" That is, what other pertinent information does a viewer need to know in order to be sure the graph is both accurate and honest?

10. Exploratory data analysis refers to initial, nonmathematical work with data that gives the researcher a sense of the data before any testing for hypothesized relationships begins. Stem and leaf diagrams allow the researcher to quickly graph a data set while retaining the original scores for examination. A "stem" is the first digit or digits in some array of scores, and a leaf is the last digit or digits of a score within the array. Stems appear in a column (usually ranked from lowest to highest) and the leaf or leaves appear to the right of each stem. Stem and leaf diagrams present a quick "picture" of the data, but become less useful if too many scores are present. In that case, a "tally" of scores using Tukey's line box tally system is useful because it allows for accurate counts of observations quickly.

11. The shape of a distribution tells a story about a sample's data. A symmetrical or bell-shaped curve is called a normal distribution. When distributions are symmetrical but they have two "bells" or "lumps," they are described as "bimodal." If there are more than two clusters of scores, then the distribution may be "multimodal." When a distribution is not symmetrical, it is skewed; that is, its scores are clumped either at the high end or the low end. When scores appear predominantly at the left or low end of the distribution, positive skew is present. When the scores clump at the high end, negative skew is said to have occurred.

12. A percentile is a statistic disclosing the relative position of a score within a distribution. Percentile rank is a number indicating the percentage of scores that fall at or below a given score (e.g., a score at the 80th percentile means that it is higher than or equal to 80% of the remaining scores on the test). Percentile information is useful because it places the score in context—only 20% of test scores were higher than one at the 80th percentile.

13. Cumulative frequency refers to the total number of frequencies falling at or below a given point in a distribution. Cumulative percentage, the percent of responses or respondents at or below a given point in a distribution, can be determined from cumulative frequency. Both can be used to determine percentiles and percentile ranks.

14. Data distributions can be divided into four equal parts called quartiles. By convention, the 25th and 75th percentiles in a

distribution are called Q_1 and Q_3. The 50th percentile (Q_2) is called the median.

15. Quality graphs and tables should strive for accuracy, brevity, and clarity. Graphs that are too complex and weighted down with extra (largely useless) information have an abundance of chartjunk. Tables with too many numbers and categories that making discerning meaning and patterns difficult suffer from tableclutter. Any graph or table should be clearly linked to accompanying text, but that text should complement—not be redundant with—the data display.

Key Terms

Bar graph *(p. 98)*
Bimodal *(p. 112)*
Chartjunk *(p. 124)*
Cumulative frequency *(p. 116)*
Cumulative frequency distribution *(p. 116)*
Cumulative percentage *(p. 117)*
Exploratory data analysis (EDA) *(p. 104)*
Frequency *(p. 87)*
Frequency distribution *(p. 87)*
Frequency polygon *(p. 100)*
Graph *(p. 97)*
Grouped frequency distribution *(p. 92)*

Histogram *(p. 99)*
Kurtosis *(p. 113)*
Leptokurtic *(p. 113)*
Median *(p. 122)*
Mesokurtic *(p. 113)*
Multimodal *(p. 112)*
Negative skew *(p. 113)*
Normal distribution *(p. 111)*
Percent *(p. 91)*
Percentage *(p. 91)*
Percentile *(p. 115)*
Percentile rank *(p. 115)*

Platykurtic *(p. 113)*
Positive skew *(p. 113)*
Proportion *(p. 90)*
Quartile *(p. 121)*
Relative frequency *(p. 92)*
Relative frequency distribution *(p. 92)*
Skew *(p. 112)*
Stem and leaf diagram *(p. 105)*
Tableclutter *(p. 125)*
Tukey's line box tally *(p. 108)*
x axis *(p. 97)*
y axis *(p. 97)*

Chapter Problems

1. Place the following data into a relative frequency distribution. Be sure to add columns for proportion and percent.

   3, 1, 4, 2, 1, 3, 1, 5, 6, 3, 2, 3, 4, 1, 2, 2, 3, 5, 3, 2

2. What is a proportion? What is its relationship to percent? How can percent be calculated from proportion?

3. Place the following data into a relative frequency distribution.

   10, 11, 13, 13, 15, 13, 10, 11, 11, 12, 14, 13, 15, 16, 13, 12, 12, 11, 10, 10, 11, 12, 12, 13, 15

4. Using the data shown in problem 1, draw a histogram and a frequency polygon.

5. Using the data shown in problem 3, draw a histogram and a frequency polygon.

6. What is the difference between a bar graph and a histogram? When should you use a bar graph instead of a histogram?

7. The following are quiz scores from a high school physics class. The maximum score possible is a 10:

   8, 8, 9, 7, 5, 3, 3, 5, 7, 8, 9, 10, 3, 2, 3, 8, 9, 6

   a. Put the scores into a frequency distribution.

   b. Graph the scores using a histogram.

   c. If the usual score on this quiz is a 6, how would you describe the performance of the students on this quiz?

8. An anthropology professor assigns numerical grades to the term papers she receives. Here are the scores:

   79, 85, 88, 72, 65, 89, 94, 75, 72, 82, 80, 89, 92, 96, 75, 70, 81, 69

   a. Place these scores into a frequency distribution.

   b. Graph the scores using a histogram.

   c. The anthropologist usually gives an average grade of 77 on term papers. Compared to that standard level of performance, how well did this class do on the term paper?

9. Examine the following frequency distribution:

X	f
5	10
4	7
3	3
2	5
1	6

a. What is the N of this distribution?
b. What is the $\sum f$?
c. What is the $\sum X$ for the distribution?

10. Examine the following frequency distribution:

X	f
5	12
4	0
3	5
2	7
1	2

a. What is the N of this distribution?
b. What is the $\sum f$?
c. What is the $\sum X$ for the distribution?

11. Using the data provided in problem 9, draw a frequency polygon.

12. Using the data provided in problem 10, draw a frequency polygon.

13. Review the following data:

30	28	20	25	18	15
12	20	10	28	17	8
22	16	12	13	27	25
6	10	18	17	18	27
29	30	22	16	11	9

Place the data into a grouped frequency distribution using
a. An interval width of 2
b. An interval width of 5

14. Using the data from problem 13, determine the true limits of each class interval when
a. The interval width is 2
b. The interval width is 5

15. Using the data from problem 13, draw a histogram (using true limits) when
a. The interval width is 2.
b. The interval width is 5.

16. Using the data from problem 13, draw a frequency polygon (using true limits) when
a. The interval width is 2.
b. The interval width is 5.

17. Describe some of the ways that a graph can misrepresent data. What should a critical researcher or viewer do to verify that a graph's data are presented accurately?

18. You are planning to graph some data—what are some of the steps you should take to ensure you present them accurately?

19. What is exploratory data analysis (EDA)? Why do researchers find it useful?

20. Using a unit of 10, construct a stem and leaf diagram of these data:

20	32	43	52	67	77	81
83	65	23	33	72	80	79
45	31	27	35	48	71	76
89	72	65	63	42	41	30
44	31	22	29	56	70	79

21. Using the data from problem 20, construct a stem and leaf diagram using units of 5.

22. Examine the following frequency distribution and then recreate it using Tukey's tally system of dots, lines, and boxes:

X	f
6	15
5	11
4	20
3	3
2	8
1	5

23. Using the following table of data, add a column for cumulative frequency (cf) and one for cumulative percentage ($c\%$):

X	f
10	8
9	5
8	0
7	4
6	9
5	6
4	8
3	5
2	3
1	6

24. Using the data shown in problem 22, add a column for cumulative frequency (cf) and one for cumulative percentage ($c\%$).

25. Examine this data table and then answer the questions that follow.

X	f
18–20	3
15–17	7
12–14	8
9–11	6
6–8	2

a. What is the percentile rank for a score of 13 (i.e., $X = 13$)?
b. What score (X) corresponds to the 65th percentile?
c. What is the median score (i.e., 50th percentile)?

26. Complete the following table and then answer the questions that follow:

X	f
26–30	12
21–25	15
16–20	10
11–15	5
6–10	11
1–5	2

a. What is the percentile rank for $X = 27$?

b. What is the percentile rank for $X = 9$?

c. What score (X) falls at the 35th percentile?

d. What scores (X) fall at Q_1, Q_2, and Q_3?

27. Assume that the data presented in problem 25 represent achievement tests scores for fifth-graders (higher scores indicate better mastery of grade-level materials). Put the per-

centile results into words; that is, write about the answers you gave to parts a, b, and c in the problem.

28. Assume that the data presented in problem 26 are scores on measure of introversion–extraversion (higher scores correspond to more extroverted behavior). Put the percentile results into words by writing about the answers you gave to parts a through d in the problem.

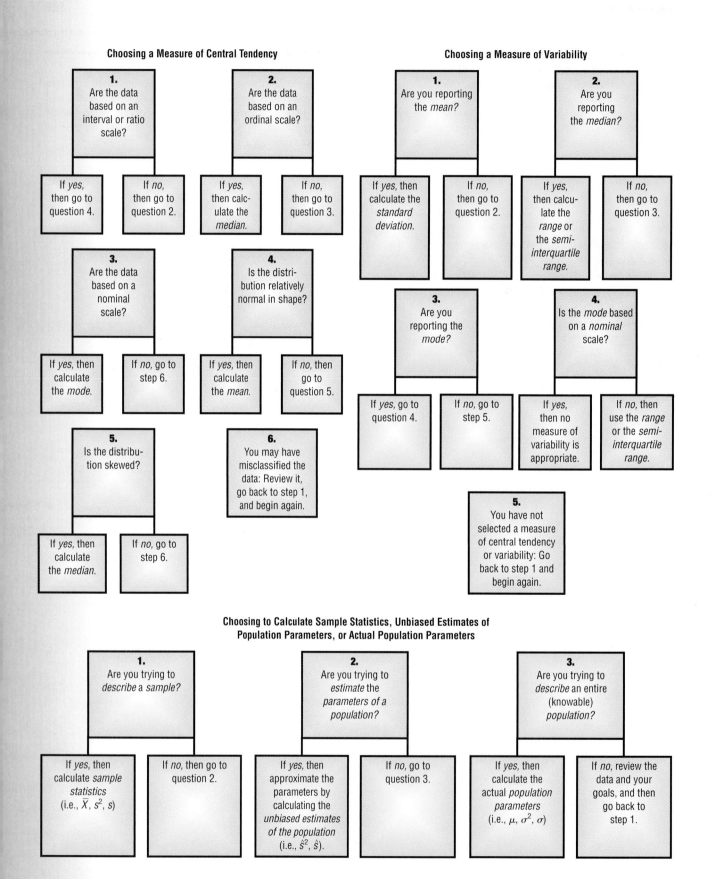

DESCRIPTIVE STATISTICS: CENTRAL TENDENCY AND VARIABILITY

Do you do especially well at playing cards, chess, fly-fishing, or basketball—or whatever activity you wish to name? That is, when doing the activity, would you describe your performance as adept (above average), typical (average), or novice (below average)? When making such judgments, how do you decide whether you are similar to or different from others? Where do you fall on a hypothetical skill continuum, and how does your performance compare with that of others on the same dimension? Indeed, how can the differing skills—the behavior—of many different people be taken into account?

This chapter is devoted to the exploration of two classes of basic descriptive statistics—what are called measures of central tendency and measures of variability. In concrete terms, of course, we refer to the average score in a distribution and how the scores are spread throughout that distribution. These two classes of measures are often introduced in separate chapters in statistics books, but conceptually, they are bound together, each related to the other. Why present central tendency and variability together? When behavioral scientists ask about one, they necessarily ask about the other. You will shortly learn that there are no more important statistical indices in the behavioral scientist's arsenal than measures of central tendency and variability.

Before we begin to explore these measures in great detail, though, I want you to answer the following questions. Your answers will have some bearing on the material we cover in this chapter, so please answer them before proceeding to the next section. We will review your answers later in the chapter.

Compared to other students the same age and sex as you, what are the chances that the following events will happen to you? (Circle the number that best corresponds to your view of each event.)

Central tendency and *variability* are inextricably linked—in order to make sense of one you must know the other.

A. Like your postgraduate job:
   1—Much less likely for me
   2—Somewhat less likely for me
   3—Slightly less likely for me
   4—Neither more nor less likely for me
   5—Slightly more likely for me
   6—Somewhat more likely for me
   7—Much more likely for me
B. Divorce a few years after marriage:
   1—Much less likely for me
   2—Somewhat less likely for me
   3—Slightly less likely for me
   4—Neither more nor less likely for me
   5—Slightly more likely for me
   6—Somewhat more likely for me
   7—Much more likely for me
C. Live past age 80 years:
   1—Much less likely for me
   2—Somewhat less likely for me
   3—Slightly less likely for me
   4—Neither more nor less likely for me
   5—Slightly more likely for me
   6—Somewhat more likely for me
   7—Much more likely for me
D. Have a heart attack:
   1—Much less likely for me
   2—Somewhat less likely for me
   3—Slightly less likely for me
   4—Neither more nor less likely for me
   5—Slightly more likely for me
   6—Somewhat more likely for me
   7—Much more likely for me

Why Represent Data by Central Tendency

In chapter 3, we began to discuss how a given score or observation is not really very telling or meaningful unless it can be examined within some larger context. The contexts we considered were frequency distribution tables and graphs, as well as a relative statistical index, percentile rank. In each case, our discussion revealed the necessity and desirability of seeing how some score compared to other scores—whether it was higher than some but lower than others, for instance. We also considered the shape of distributions, particularly where scores cluster or group together at certain points in a distribution.

We are now going to expand this discussion by considering ways to describe—really, summarize—the behavior expressed in a distribution of scores with a single statistic. Specifically, we are going to look for a numerical value that indicates how the average or typical individual in a given sample felt, responded, or behaved. Why focus on the typical or the average? The goal of using a measure of *central tendency* is to identify a numerical value that is the *most representative one* within a distribution or set of data.

KEY TERM   Measures of **central tendency** are descriptive statistics that identify the central location of a sample of data. The *central tendency* of a data set is the best single indicator describing the representative value(s) of any sample.

The most representative value in a given distribution is its *central tendency.*

The search for an indicator of central tendency, then, is an exercise in data reduction. We are not altering the data; rather, we are beginning to explore one of its most basic characteristics by working with—really, manipulating—its raw values. Instead of discussing the various qualities of a distribution, we want to first hone in on one characteristic—usually that area of the distribution where the majority of scores appear to "clump" or cluster together. In a perfectly normal distribution (which was introduced in chapter 3), the observations cluster in its center, where they form a bell. The most representative numerical value in a normal distribution is apt to be at the center of this bell shape, where the curve can be split into two symmetric halves. In distributions of other shapes, particularly those lacking symmetry, the index of central tendency may move around a bit, but we should still be drawn by the clustering of observations as an initial guide to its location.

But we are getting ahead of ourselves. Before we review some specific measures of central tendency, it is important to discuss the meaning of the word **average.** This word has a clear meaning to statisticians and behavioral scientists; namely, it refers to "a mathematical quantity indicating the most typical or representative number in a set of observations." True enough. No doubt this definition (or words to that effect) come to mind when we hear televised reports or read news stories about the "average rainfall in the Mississippi basin," "the average compensation package of CEOs of major corporations," "the grade point average," "the average number of emergency calls the local 911 number receives each week," and so on.

The meaning of the word average in everyday language, however, has a somewhat different connotation, one that is sometimes deemed pejorative. In my experience, few professionals want to be evaluated as average by their employers, just as few students—most readers of this book included—want to earn C or "average" grades in college. The term average has, as it were, fallen in with bad company. Indeed, many people equate the term average with mediocrity or being "second rate." In some quarters, notably athletics, average performance is erroneously seen as evidence of poor or even failing efforts. American culture and our educational systems (largely unknowingly, perhaps) encourage this view, so that people bristle if they are deemed average. Many aspire to be citizens of humorist Garrison Keillor's community, Lake Wobegone, where "all the women are strong, all the men are good-looking, and all the children are above average."

Statistically and mathematically, of course, we cannot *all* be above average on any given dimension—if we were, there would be no average per se. Think back to the normal distribution for a moment. The bell-shaped curve illustrates the problem precisely: Although some observations will fall below the bell (i.e., below the average) and others above it (i.e., above average), the preponderance of the data will be found at a central, thereby representative, point. The idea of being average should not have any stigma attached to it—as we will see, the concept has a great deal of utility. In practical terms, being average should not be seen as an odd or troublesome circumstance either, as one is in good company (i.e., with most other people). To be sure, people should excel on some dimensions (for instance, I hope you are excelling in your study of statistics and data analysis), but assuming that one is above average on a host of skills is misguided, if not foolhardy. Keep this in mind the next time you witness the idea of average performance being derided or criticized. (While you are at it, you might begin to think about your answers to the four questions that opened the chapter, as well; see also, Data Box 4.B.)

The term *average* has a statistical as well as a colloquial meaning. Be aware of which one is being used in a given situation.

Our job, then, is not to change people's understanding of the word "average"—that is too tall an order—but to acknowledge that perception of what the word means has changed. Be advised, though, that the term average means different things to different people, and it has finer shades of meaning in various contexts. Let's turn back to central tendency. There are three common measures of central tendency—the mean, the median, and the mode—and we will review each in turn. We will use the term average with the first statistical measure of central tendency we learn—the mean. Keep in mind that the term average should be used appropriately, accurately, and judiciously when discussing statistical relationships—to do otherwise is to forget the linguistic baggage it carries.

The Mean: The Behavioral Scientist's Statistic of Choice

With few exceptions, whatever literature in the behavioral sciences you read, you will encounter the *mean,* the statistical or arithmetic average. The mean is by far the single most useful measure of central tendency available, and it can be used to analyze data from interval or ratio scales of measurement. It is not too far from the truth to note that the extensive literature in psychology, for example, is largely based on the study of means. That is, how does the average behavior in one group of participants differ from the average behavior found in other groups? The classic example here is the model of the standard experiment we reviewed in chapter 2: Did the manipulation of an independent variable lead to a different average level of behavior in the dependent measure for the experimental group than the control group? The mean, then, is critical to the experimental tradition in psychology and related fields.

KEY TERM   The **mean** is the arithmetic average of a set of scores. The *mean* is calculated by summing the set of scores and dividing by the *N* of scores.

▽

In statistical terms, the *mean* is an *average* (and vice versa).

If the data were drawn from a sample, the mean is denoted statistically as $\overline{X}$ ("ex-bar"). When it appears in APA style reports, however, it is written as M (for "mean"). Here is the formula for calculating the mean for a sample of data:

[4.1.1]
$$\overline{X} = \frac{\sum X}{N}.$$

In words, "X-bar is equal to the sum of the values of X divided by the number of values in the sample," or

[4.1.2]
$$\overline{X} = \frac{X_1 + X_2 + X_3 + \cdots + X_N}{N}.$$

If we have an array of scores from a sample that were randomly drawn, say, 12, 15, 10, 14, and 8, their mean would be:

[4.1.3]
$$\overline{X} = \frac{12 + 15 + 10 + 14 + 8}{5},$$

[4.1.4]
$$\overline{X} = \frac{59}{5},$$

[4.1.5]
$$\overline{X} = 11.8.$$

When we are working with sample statistics, the symbols are based on the Roman alphabet (i.e., X leads to $\overline{X}$), but when we are considering population parameters, we switch to Greek letters. (If you need to review the distinctions between samples and populations, please turn back to chapter 1 before proceeding.) Thus, the population mean is symbolized as μ (pronounced "mew" or "mu").

The formula for calculating the mean of a population would be:

[4.2.1]
$$\mu = \frac{\sum X}{N}.$$

Some of the populations that behavioral scientists and students work with are said to be finite; that is, the number of observations (N) is known and it is small enough that the observations can be counted. Other populations are infinitely large and their Ns are unknowable. These populations contain so many observations—real or potential—that counting or keeping track of them all is not possible. In the case of infinite populations, we rely on $\overline{X}$ to *estimate* the value of μ. We will learn a bit more about estimation later in this chapter and in greater detail in chapter 9. For the present, we will focus on finite populations.

If we have a population of six observations, for example,

> 34   22   12   20   24   26

the mean is calculated as

[4.2.2]
$$\mu = \frac{X_1 + X_2 + X_3 + X_4 + X_5 + X_6}{N},$$

[4.2.3]
$$\mu = \frac{34 + 22 + 12 + 20 + 24 + 26}{6},$$

[4.2.4]
$$\mu = \frac{138}{6},$$

[4.2.5]
$$\mu = 23.$$

As you can see, the formulas are virtually identical—only the symbol at the start of the equation changes. This change is by no means a minor one, as the data analyst and readers of the research must know whether the data are based on a sample or represent an entire population. *You* must know whether your statistics are based on sample data, which is drawn from a presumably larger, possibly theoretical population, or the actual population itself. This distinction will become increasingly important in subsequent chapters of this book. To recap briefly: When we work with sample data, we use sample statistics—for populations we use population parameters.

Table 4.1 contains symbols representing other sample statistics and their corresponding population parameters—to this point you have only been exposed to $\overline{X}$ and μ. This table also contains what are referred to as "unbiased estimates of population parameters," statistics we will learn about later in this chapter. Table 4.1 is presented here so that you can anticipate subsequent material—it will also serve as a good reference point for you later on when you actually perform calculations.

▽

$\overline{X}$ denotes a sample's average and μ identifies a population's mean.

Some Symbols for Sample Statistics, Population Parameters, and
Table 4.1   **Unbiased Estimates of Population Parameters**

	Sample Statistic	Population Parameter	Unbiased Estimate of Population Parameters
Mean	$\overline{X}$	μ	—
Variance	s^2	σ^2	$\hat{s}^2$
Standard deviation	s	σ	$\hat{s}$
Pearson correlation *coefficient*	r	ρ	—

DATA BOX 4.A

How Many Are There? And Where Did They Come From? Proper Use of *N* and *n*

Consistency is said to be the hobgoblin of little minds, but any adequate data analyst wants to know when to use *N* or *n* to refer to the number of observations available for a calculation. Though it is not the stuff of high drama, there are minor inconsistencies in the way statistics books present how and when to use *N* and *n*. In chapter 1, *N* was introduced as a way to designate the number of observations in a population. What about *n*? Different texts introduce *n* differently. Some books indicate that *n* refers to the number of known observations in a sample of data (e.g., $n = 6$ means there 6 raw scores in the sample). The use of *n*, then, is reserved for sample data. Other books, including this one, often refer to sample data using *N* in lieu of *n*. Instead, the latter books often reserve *n* for those occasions where there is more than one sample of data; that is, an experimental group might have 10 observations ($n_1 = 10$) and the control group might have 12 ($n_2 = 12$). Still other books use N_1 and N_2 to denote the same circumstance—it all depends on the analytic temperament of the author.

Chances are that you will be able to figure out *N* or *n*'s meaning in a particular context by determining whether you are working with a sample or a population. To make that determination is usually quite straightforward—just answer this question: Is the symbol for the test statistic you are considering written using a Roman (sample data) or Greek (population) letter? Because we will spend relatively little time dealing with population parameters in this book, I elected to use *N* wherever possible, as its meaning is by now both familiar and intuitive. In those few situations where *n* is employed, I will draw your attention to its presence and identify the appropriate interpretation.

Calculating Means from Ungrouped and Grouped Data

The psychoanalytic worldview has lost much of its luster for academic psychologists, but many of its ideas still spawn research. Suppose you were interested in exploring the link between hostility and humor that Sigmund Freud posited over 90 years ago (Freud, 1905/1960). Freud was interested in what he called "tendentious" jokes, or jokes that reveal something about the joke teller as well as the people who laugh at the jokes. Freud believed that some jokes were told to release pent-up impulses normally trapped in the unconscious. To Freud, our unconscious might desire, even enjoy, expressing violent actions; jokes enable us to be aggressive in socially sanctioned, if not necessarily constructive, ways. Some jokes deal more or less directly with aggression—they contain obvious insults or, by their nature, are satirical—they poke fun at human foibles. Other jokes disguise their hostility, frequently involving subtle commentary about ethnic groups and social conflict, or marriage and marital fidelity (or the lack thereof).

You decide to hit the matter head on, as it were, by exploring whether people do indeed find hostile humor to be funnier than other types of humor. A prior study, for example, found that participants rated cartoons from the "Far Side" and "Herman" strips to be funnier when the characters were in some way injured than when no violent themes were evident (Deckers & Carr, 1986). Other research reached similar conclusions about the comic portrayal of pain and violence (e.g., Kuhlman, 1985; McCauley, Woods, Coolidge, & Kulick, 1983).

Following the lead of earlier researchers, you scour magazines and newspapers for cartoons that contain situations where the characters experience pain or violence in

Table 4.2   Hypothetical Humor Ratings of Hostile and Non-Hostile Cartoons

Experimental Group (Rated Hostile Cartoons) X_e	Control Group (Rated Nonhostile Cartoons) X_c
7	5
6	4
7	4
5	3
6	5
7	4
6	3
4	4
$\sum X_e = 48$	$\sum X_c = 32$
$N_e = 8$	$N_c = 8$
$\overline{X}_e = 6.0$	$\overline{X}_c = 4.0$

Note: Hypothetical ratings are based on a 1 ("not at all funny") to 7 ("very funny") scale. Higher scores indicated greater perceived funniness.

what are supposed to be humorous circumstances. You conceptually replicate these prior research efforts by randomly assigning participants to two groups, an experimental group and a control group. The experimental group rates a cartoonist's work containing characters experiencing painful pratfalls. Cartoons lacking violent themes but drawn by the same artist were evaluated by the control group. Exposure or nonexposure to hostile cartoons was the independent variable, and the participants' ratings of how funny the cartoons actually were constituted the dependent measure. Table 4.2 contains the ratings for both groups, and these data are not grouped in any particular way—the raw humor ratings are simply listed within the respective group.

As you can see, there were eight participants in each group. Please note that for convenience, the subscripts "e" for "experimental" and "c" for "control" are attached to the symbols shown in Table 4.2 (use of subscripts as labels for keeping track of information will become more frequent and necessary as illustrative examples become more complex; see Data Box 4.B). By eyeballing the raw scores in the groups, you can see that the ratings are slightly higher in the experimental group. The means shown at the bottom of the two columns confirm this expectation: The experimental group rated the cartoons with hostile content as funnier on average ($\overline{X}_e = 6.0$) than did the control group, which rated cartoons lacking the theme ($\overline{X}_c = 4.0$). The means were calculated using the formula for sample means presented back in [4.1.1]. As descriptive statistics, the two means are suggestive—they appear to support Freud's theory of hostile humor because we know the typical reactions of the members of both groups. We need to confirm this prediction, though, by determining if the difference between the two means is a reliable one (i.e., the mean humor rating of the hostile cartoons is actually higher than the mean associated with the nonhostile cartoons), a topic we explore in later chapters.

What happens if the data you are working with are arranged in a frequency distribution? Is it possible to determine the mean with relative ease and accuracy? Fortunately, yes. We can capitalize on the working knowledge of frequency distributions we developed in chapter 3.

Table 4.3   Frequency of Spatial Errors Made by Rats in a Radial Arm Maze

X	f	fX
8	3	24
7	5	35
6	6	36
5	8	40
4	10	40
3	4	12
2	2	4
1	5	5
0	1	0
	$N = 44$	$\sum fX = 196$

Note: *X* refers to the number of possible errors rats could make while navigating the radial arm maze.

Table 4.3 shows a frequency distribution of errors from a radial arm maze used in an animal learning experiment. Experimental psychologists often measure spatial ability in rats by using a maze that has eight "corridors," or arms, extending outward from a central chamber (e.g., Suzuki, Augerinos, & Black, 1980). A rat must navigate its way through space to find a food reward in each arm. If a rat navigates all eight arms successfully, it makes no errors and can eat all the food rewards. If the animal goes down a given arm twice (i.e., once after the first trial when it ate the food available in the arm), the behavior counts as an error. If it backtracks through the same arm three or four times, it counts as two and three errors, respectively. The rats in this study were allowed a maximum of eight errors before they were removed from the maze. As you can see in Table 4.3, only one of the 44 rats in the study made no errors in the maze, just as only three animals managed to make eight errors. The remaining 40 animals had errors ranging between these two extremes—but what was the mean error rate for the sample of rats?

How can we calculate the mean number of errors from the data shown in Table 4.3? Recall that in chapter 3, we learned how to find the $\sum X$ by multiplying each value of X by its frequency (f) and then summing the products (i.e., $\sum fX = \sum X$; see [3.2.1]). Once we know $\sum fX$, we can determine the $\overline{X}$ of this frequency distribution by dividing the $\sum fX$ by N, or

[4.3.1]
$$\overline{X} = \frac{\sum fX}{N}.$$

We need to enter only the numbers from Table 4.3 to find the mean:

[4.3.2]
$$\overline{X} = \frac{196}{44},$$

[4.3.3]
$$\overline{X} = 4.4545 \cong 4.46.$$

Rats running the radial arm maze made an average of 4.46 errors.

Caveat Emptor: Sensitivity to Extreme Scores

The Latin phrase "caveat emptor" translates as "let the buyer beware," and as we have said on prior occasions, consumers of statistical data must always evaluate it carefully and critically. We noted earlier that the mean is the most useful measure of central tendency, yet one of its characteristics should encourage a bit of interpretive caution—the mean is *sensitive to extreme scores*. By extreme scores, I refer to any observations in a data set that

The mean of a frequency distribution is usually relatively easy to calculate.

are very far away—either high or low in value—from the central tendency of the distribution. Such scores are often called **outliers** because they lie very far outside the central part of a distribution. Outliers that are high in value can inflate the mean; the opposite effect—deflating the average—occurs when an outlying score (or scores) is very low in value. We will consider the effect of outlying scores conceptually as well as through a practical example.

Let's do the conceptual work first. Think about a balance beam or a playground seesaw. It is possible to put several smaller weights on one side of a balance beam and a larger, heavier one on the opposite side—despite the presence of several smaller weights, the bigger weight can still tilt the beam to one side. In the same way, two or three smaller toddlers on one side of a seesaw cannot balance the weight of a full-grown adult. Can balance ever be achieved when weight magnitudes vary? Yes. Lighter weights can balance a heavier weight when the latter is moved closer to the fulcrum, the support that balances the beam or seesaw. If our hypothetical adult moved closer to the fulcrum (and the toddlers), the children can balance his or her weight.

In virtually the same way, the presence and magnitude of any outliers can influence the mean of a distribution of numbers. Now we can turn to a practical illustration near and dear to the hearts of any people who have ever been employed—average salaries. Imagine that you worked in a small business, one that had seven employees and one owner. Hypothetical salaries for this business are shown in Table 4.4. As you can see, the owner makes a very high salary compared to the modest but generally similar salaries of the employees. When the mean of these salaries—a figure of $57,000—is calculated, the problem is apparent: No one in the business actually *earns* a salary near the mean; indeed, the figure closest to it is $42,000.00, a difference of $15,000.00. The owner's salary exceeds this average by $143,000.00! Why is the average inflated? Like the heavy weight on a balance beam, the owner's salary drags value of the mean away from where the preponderance of salaries lay. If one read about the average salary of employees working in this small business in a trade report or a newspaper article, the impression received would be quite different than the financial reality. Caveat emptor!

We may not be able to examine the salary data for privately held companies, but we can assuredly examine our own data or those published in behavioral science books and journals. The utility of the mean as an index of central tendency is not offset by its sensitivity to extreme scores—on balance, as it were, it is still the best indicator. We must be vigilant, however, and always carefully review any distribution of data in search of outliers that could substantially influence the magnitude of a mean. In general, extreme scores pose greater problems when they appear in data sets with fewer observations (see Table 4.4) than in larger ones—once again, larger samples are apt to be more representative of

▽

The mean of a distribution can be inflated or deflated when an extreme or outlying score is present.

Table 4.4 Hypothetical Annual Salaries for a Small Business

Owner's salary	$200,000.00
Employees' salaries	$38,000.00
	$42,000.00
	$36,000.00
	$41,000.00
	$32,000.00
	$31,000.00
	$36,000.00
	$\overline{X} = \$57,000.00$

population than smaller ones. It is also true that more representative scores will appear in larger samples, a property we will revisit in later chapters.

Weighted Means: An Approach for Determining Averages of Different-Sized Groups

What happens if a researcher wants to know the average of more than one distinct but related group? Can the averages of such separate groups be combined together? When a researcher has more than one group that shares the same dependent measure, it is possible to calculate an average using what is called the weighted means approach.

KEY TERM   A **weighted mean** is based on different-sized groups of data using the same dependent measure. The calculation of the *weighted mean* takes into account the respective contributions—weights— of each group.

Here is a relatively common situation where calculating a weighted mean would be both appropriate and, where accuracy is concerned, advantageous. Imagine you were an instructor teaching two sections of the same course, a rather common occurrence at many colleges and universities. One class has an enrollment of 60 students, the other 45. If both classes had the same N, you would simply add all the observations together and divide the sum by the total N of observations (i.e., $N_1 + N_2 = N$) to know the mean test score. When samples have different Ns, however, you must rely on the weighted means approach precisely because it takes into account that the average must acknowledge the influence of samples of different sizes. Here is the formula for determining the weighted mean:

[4.4.1]
$$\overline{X}_w = \frac{\sum (N\overline{X})}{\sum N},$$

where $\overline{X}_w$ is the symbol for the weighted mean. This formula indicates that the user must multiply the mean of each sample by the its respective N, sum the products, and then divide the resulting total by the number of observations available.

Here are the hypothetical data for the two statistics classes:

$$N_A = 60 \qquad N_B = 45$$
$$\overline{X}_A = 82.0 \qquad \overline{X}_B = 87.0$$

Class A had an average of 82.0 on the test and class B had an average of 87. What was the test average across both classes? We simply enter the numerical information into [4.4.1] for:

[4.4.2]
$$\overline{X}_w = \frac{(60)(82.0) + (45)(87.0)}{60 + 45},$$

[4.4.3]
$$\overline{X}_w = \frac{4,920 + 3,915}{105},$$

[4.4.4]
$$\overline{X}_w = \frac{8,835}{105},$$

[4.4.5]
$$\overline{X}_w = 84.14 \cong 84.0.$$

Thus, the mean score on the test across both classes was 84.0. Note that if we did *not* use the weighted mean approach—that is, if we simply calculated the average of 82.0 and 87.0 (i.e., $82 + 87/2 = 169/2 = 84.5$), we would have overestimated the true mean by a slight amount. Imagine how the overestimation could increase, however, if the sample sizes were more disparate from one another. Avoiding the bias inherent in such overestimation is the primary reason for relying on the weighted means approach.

DATA BOX 4.B

Self-Judgment Under Uncertainty—Being Average is Sometimes OK

Take a few moments and look back at the answers you gave to the questions on page 134. Now that you have read a great deal about central tendency, would you change any of your answers?

If you answered these questions like most students do, then you probably indicated that:

- You are *more* likely to like your postgraduate job.
- You are *less* likely to divorce a few years after marriage.
- You are *more* likely to live past age 80 years.
- You are *less* likely to have a heart attack.

Note that I have not indicated whether your estimate was slightly, somewhat, or much more (or less) likely than your peers, rather, I am interested to see if you rated yourself above or below the average response (i.e., "Neither more nor less likely for me"). Weinstein (1980; see also, Weinstein, 1989) finds that most people—even students like yourself—demonstrate this sort of *unrealistic optimism* regarding their future life events. Specifically, most individuals rate their chances of experiencing positive outcomes as above average, while the likelihood of encountering negative outcomes is portrayed as below average. Unrealistic optimism is a belief in one's own efficacy and relative invulnerability—in short, good things happen to us, bad things happen to other people. This sort of optimism is erroneous precisely because it is implausible intellectually and statistically: All people cannot claim that good things are more likely and bad things are less likely to happen to them. We do not live in Lake Wobegone!

Weinstein (1980) asked college students to rate how their chances of experiencing 42 life events—18 positive and 24 negative—differed from those of their classmates. Results indicated that the students rated themselves about 15% more likely to experience positive events and over 20% less likely to encounter negative events than their peers. These percentages represent the averages of the two event categories. Here are a few extreme observations: students assumed they were 44% more likely to own their own home and 35% more likely to travel to Europe than peers. They also believed they were 58% less likely to have a drinking problem and almost 32% less likely to be fired from a job (see Weinstein, 1980, for estimates of good and bad outcomes).

What about you? Are you really so different from the students who participated in this study? Do you want to readjust your future prospects, or at least your answers to the questions that opened this chapter? More to the point, what should *you* say in answer to such questions? When in doubt, the best answer to such questions is the average or mid-point—in other words "Neither more nor less likely for me." Unless you have striking and definitive evidence that you will be an outlier on some dimension or dimensions (and despite their richness and familiarity, family lore and anecdotes are usually not convincing in this regard), stick with the average and chances are that you won't go wrong. Sometimes being average is OK, then, and in the present circumstance it is the best estimate you can make about the future. (Note that we are *not* considering the potential benefits of unrealistic optimism, such as heightened perceptions of control; see Dunn & Wilson, 1990; Langer, 1983; Taylor & Brown, 1988).

How did the study's participants respond to the questions you answered? They believed that they were 50% *more* likely to like a postgraduate job and over 12% *more* likely to live past age 80. They also believed that they were almost 49% *less* likely to divorce a few years after marriage and 23% *less* likely to have a heart attack than their peers. As an exercise, why not summarize and calculate your statistics class's percentage responses to these questions and then compare them to the published data? Did the members of your class—including you—respond the same way that the participants in Weinstein's (1980) research did? Why or why not?

Don't be disappointed if you fell for the siren's song of unrealistic optimism, but do try to consider the virtues of assuming you are apt to be average in some of life's dimensions in the future.

We will leave our review of the mean, its applications and properties, for the time being so that the remaining measures of central tendency can be introduced. We will return, however, to consider two mathematical properties of the mean later in the chapter. Chapter 4's *Project Exercise* entails having you prove that these properties make the mean the most useful gauge of central tendency.

The Median

You may remember being introduced to the *median* in chapter 3 when the calculation of quartiles was introduced. At that time, I promised to discuss the median in some detail at the proper place, which is here by virtue of its utility as a measure of central tendency. The median can be used for calculations involving ordinal, interval, or ratio scale data.

The **median** is a number or score that precisely divides a distribution of data in half. Fifty percent of a distribution's observations will fall above the *median* and fifty percent will fall below it.

One way to think about the median is that it represents a particular case of percentile rank—a median score that falls at the 50th percentile of a given distribution. Thus, you could determine the median for a grouped frequency distribution of data by calculating Q_2, the 50th percentile (see formula [3.13.1] and the related distribution in chapter 3).

Many times, of course, the distribution of data is relatively small and not grouped into a frequency distribution. The formula for determining the median score in this case is surprisingly easy.

For an Odd Number of Scores.   Here is a data set of 15 scores to consider:

26   32   21   12   15   11   27   16   18   21   19   28   10   13   31

To calculate the median, arrange the scores from the lowest to the highest:

10   11   12   13   15   16   18   19   21   21   26   27   28   31   32

When you have an odd number of scores, find the score that splits the distribution into two halves. The location of the median score can be found by using this simple formula:

[4.5.1]
$$median\ score = \frac{N + 1}{2},$$

[4.5.2]
$$median\ score = \frac{15 + 1}{2},$$

[4.5.3]
$$median\ score = \frac{16}{2} = 8.$$

Locate the 8th score in the original array, which is 19 (see below):

10   11   12   13   15   16   18   19   21   21   26   27   28   31   32

As you can see, 7 scores appear on either side of this median score.

For an Even Number of Scores.   What happens if we are confronted with an even number of scores? Consider a new array of 8 scores:

55   67   78   83   88   92   98   99

We need to calculate the median, which will fall half way between the two middle scores in the previous array. We can again employ formula [4.5.1] to find the median score:

$$median\ score = \frac{8+1}{2} = \frac{9}{2} = 4.5.$$

The median score can be found 4.5 scores into the array, which places it between the scores of 83 and 88:

55   67   78   *83   88*   92   98   99

The average of these two middle scores is the median score: $(83 + 88)/2 = 171/2 = 85.5$.

The median has one important characteristic that sometimes makes it a better indicator of central tendency than the mean. Unlike the mean, the median is *not* particularly sensitive to extreme scores. Recall the data we examined back in Table 4.4. The mean we calculated from those data was inflated by the relatively large, outlying salary of the owner—what if we instead determined the median annual salary of that small business? If you follow the above instructions for calculating a mean when there is an even number of scores present, you will discover that the median salary based on the data in Table 4.4 is $37,000.00. Here are the salaries (ranked low to high) from Table 4.4:

$31,000.00 $32,000.00 $36,000.00 $36,000.00 $38,000.00 $41,000.00
$42,000.00 $200,000.00

To locate the median score, we use formula [4.5.1] and calculate a value of 4.5, which means that the median salary falls half way between score 4 ($36,000.00) and score 5 ($38,000.00)—hence, we know that the median is $37,000.00. Clearly, the median provides a much more realistic figure of central tendency for this relatively small distribution than the biased mean of $57,000.00 we calculated previously.

Further, we can extrapolate from this small business example to the work done by demographers when they report "average" income in the United States. Demographers study what are called vital and social statistics, such as the number of births, deaths, marriages, and so forth, within a given population. They are also concerned with employment and salary data. Demographers routinely eschew reporting *mean* income because—similar to the small business example—the distribution of data is unduly influenced by the relatively small number of citizens who make salaries of incredible size. That is, most households in our nation probably earn somewhere around $40,000.00 per year or less, but this majority of offset by other members of the population who make salaries in the hundreds of thousands, even multimillions, of dollars. If we determined mean household income in the United States, we would no doubt see the same problem we witnessed with the data from Table 4.4—the mean would be so inflated that it would not numerically represent the compensation experience of most Americans. As we discussed, the median is not as sensitive to extreme scores, so demographers usually report *median* household income when they portray the average economic experience of the population.

A final note: There is no Roman letter designating the median. In APA style, however, the word "median" is abbreviated and then written as *mdn*. This abbreviation can appear in written text or within a table.

The Mode

The third and final measure of central tendency is the *mode*. The mode is not calculated, rather, it is simply reported once the various frequencies within a distribution of data are known. The mode is the most frequently occurring observation within a distribution.

Although it can be used to describe the most frequent observation based on any one of the four scales of measurement, it is usually associated with nominal scales.

The **mode** of a distribution is the score or category that has the highest frequency.

Take a second look at the definition of the mode and be sure you understand a subtle but defining point: the mode is the *most frequent score or category*—it is *not* the frequency associated with the score or category. Thus, if we reexamine a sample of scores from our previous review of the median:

10 11 12 13 15 16 18 *19* 21 21 26 27 28 31 32

Which score (or scores) occurs with the most frequency? As you can see, the score 21 appears twice, as all the other scores appear only once. The mode of this simple distribution, then, is 21.

The mode is usually quickly and easily discerned from any frequency distribution. Imagine you wanted to know the modal or most frequently declared major among a group of prospective first-year college students. You could form a frequency distribution like the one shown in Table 4.5, subsequently locating the mode with alacrity. As you can see, psychology is the modal prospective major in this hypothetical distribution—97 prospective first-year students indicated they were interested in majoring in that field. Its next closest rival in terms of student interest is economics. For the sake of argument, what if both psychology and economics had the same frequency of expressed interest—let's say that each had 110 students say they were interested in both fields—can there be more than one mode? Absolutely. Psychology and economics could both be the mode; that is, the simple distribution in Table 4.5 could be bimodal. Indeed, if three or four or

Table 4.5 Frequency Distribution of Prospective First-Year Students' Choice of Majors (*N* = 858)

College Major	*f*
Art	20
Art history	8
Biology	65
Chemistry	28
Classics	15
Computer science	40
Economics	75
English	96
Foreign language	58
History	74
Mathematics	45
Music	35
Philosophy	36
Physics	15
Political science	52
Psychology	97
Religion	37
Sociology	62

even five majors had the same frequency, they would all constitute the mode, which would mean that the distribution is multimodal. It really does not matter as long as the most frequent score (or scores) is identified as the mode. The chief advantage of using this measure of central tendency is that no calculations need to be performed. The data just need to be organized and "eyeballing" by the data analyst can take over from there.

Because the mode only relies on one aspect of central tendency—frequency—its use is rather limited. It is the least flexible and applicable of the three measures we reviewed here. Finally, the mode does not have any special statistical abbreviation or symbol to identify it, and APA style has no separate designation for it. When writing about the mode of some distribution, just write "mode," along with the score or category name.

In contrast to its definition, the *mode* is the least frequently used measure of central tendency.

The Utility of Central Tendency

Shapes of Distributions and Central Tendency

Here are a few things to think about regarding central tendency and the shape of distributions. As you read this section, try to visualize the relations among the three measures of central tendency and be sure to carefully review the accompanying figures. First, know that if a given distribution is normal and symmetric, the mean, the median, and the mode will all have the same value. This possibility is shown in panel (a) in Figure 4.1. Think about it—doesn't it make sense that the average of a normal distribution—that is, the mean appearing in the center of the distribution is equal to the distribution's 50th percentile, which splits it into two symmetric halves? If you look at panel (a) in Figure 4.1, it also follows that the mode—the most frequently occurring score in the distribution—would also fall at exactly the same point as the mean and the median (i.e., the most frequent score would appear at the peak, here, the central point, of the distribution).

What happens when a distribution is unimodal but skewed? Kirk (1999) notes that the three measures of central tendency usually fall into a predictable order in nonsymmetric distributions. The mean will almost always fall onto the side of the distribution

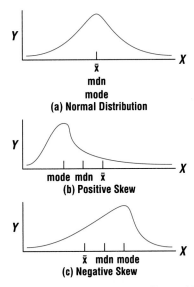

Figure 4.1 Relation of Measures of Central Tendency to the Shape of Distributions

that has the longest tail, and the median will appear approximately one-third of the distance between the mean and the mode (Kirk, 1999). Why this and not other orderings? Extreme scores, which fall into the longer tail of a given distribution, will pull the mean toward their positions. The median, in turn, is affected by the relative position of these outliers but not their magnitudes. The mode remains unaffected by the presence of extreme scores unless one or more of them happen to have the greatest frequency of occurrence. Kirk notes that the ordering can be remembered as an alphabetical mnemonic—*mea*n, *medi*an, and *mo*de—as long as the user begins the ordering in the longer of a distribution's two tails.

A distribution's departure from symmetry can be tracked by the magnitude of the discrepancy existing between the mean and the median. A smaller discrepancy implies greater symmetry; less symmetry occurs when there is a greater discrepancy. In most cases, the actual ordering of the mean and median can indicate whether a distribution is positively or negatively skewed (Kirk, 1999). As introduced in chapter 3, positively skewed distributions show a clustering of scores toward the low end of the scale of measurement—the opposite pattern occurs in negatively skewed distributions. Where central tendency is concerned, a positively skewed distribution will have a mean with a higher value than its median. As shown in panel (b) in Figure 4.1, $\overline{X} > mdn$, and the mode falls below the latter measure. In negatively skewed distributions, however, medians tend to be of greater value than means. Panel (c) in Figure 4.1 illustrates that the $mdn > \overline{X}$, and that the mode lies above the median.

The fact that the values of the three measures of central tendency can vary widely depending on the shape of a distribution should serve as ample warning to any data analyst or reader of the behavioral science literature. Relatively few distributions are completely normal—indeed, depending on the research topic, nonsymmetric distributions may be, if you will, the relative "norm." Let me encourage you to carefully examine your own data as well as what you read in the published literature, and to know the value and location of *each* measure of central tendency before drawing any psychological or behavioral conclusions dependent on them.

In the wrong hands, an asymmetric distribution of data can be used to distort factual information (e.g., Campbell, 1974). If you were trying to negotiate a higher salary for yourself or your coworkers, for instance, you would want to know whether the mean, median, or modal salary in your company was the highest one. If the distribution of salaries were positively skewed, you would want to argue for the mean, but a disingenuous but savvy management would probably suggest the median or even the mode. If the data were negatively skewed, however, you would be undercutting yourself if you took the mean salary, as the median and modal salaries, respectively, would be relatively higher (see also, Kirk, 1999, p. 87). Caveat emptor with a vengeance!

When to Use Which Measure of Central Tendency

When a behavioral scientist—a psychologist, sociologist, or political scientist—begins to plan a piece of research, which measure of central tendency should she plan to use, and why? Despite its sensitivity to extreme scores, the arithmetic mean is still the measure of choice—the mean is the one you will read about the most in the literature and it makes the most intuitive sense (i.e., what was the average response?). Still, the measure one chooses to use or report can depend on other issues, some of which are noted in Table 4.6. I recommend that you refer back to Table 4.6 when you are planning a piece of research or when you want to decide if the measure of central tendency you are using— or reading about—is the appropriate one.

A given piece of behavioral science research is apt to use the *mean* before either the *median* or the *mode*.

Table 4.6   Issues to Consider When Selecting a Measure of Central Tendency

The mean $(\overline{X})$	The arithmetic average
	For quantitative, not qualitative, data
	The most commonly reported and calculated statistic
	Used extensively in advanced statistical procedures
	Very sensitive to the values of extreme scores, unlike the median or mode
	Dependent on the value of every observation in a distribution should be examined carefully if the distribution is skewed
The median (mdn)	The 50% marker for any distribution
	For quantitative, not qualitative, data
	Relatively insensitive to the values of extreme scores, though the number of scores can affect it
	Used infrequently in advanced statistical procedures
The mode	The most frequently occurring score or observation in a distribution
	Quantitative in nature, but can be used with qualitative data
	Rarely used
	Not used in advanced statistical procedures

Source: Adapted from Kirk (1999), page 85.

Writing About Central Tendency

Writing about the three measures of central tendency is not difficult, but there is a cardinal rule to remember: Describe the behavior represented by the mean, the median, or the mode as clearly and vividly as possible (cf., Bem, 1987). Keep in mind that measures of central tendency are descriptive statistics—*they describe things.* As a researcher who is writing up the results of a study you conducted or summarizing the results of studies previously reported in the literature, your job is to tell the reader *what happened,* and to do so in concrete terms. Readers will want to know about supporting inferential statistics later (i.e., did the hypothesis pan out?), but your first goal or line of defense is to describe behavior using the measures of central tendency.

Use descriptive statistics, especially the measures of central tendency, to describe behavior in the most concrete terms possible.

If you were writing about participants' responses to some rating scale, for example, it is not sufficient to merely note that, "After viewing the stimulus photograph once, the participants' mean rating was 5.4 on the 7-point scale of attractiveness." What does that mean? Provide a bit of context for the mean and describe the scale. "After viewing the stimulus photograph, the participants' mean rating of the image was 5.4, which fell between 'slightly attractive' and 'very attractive' in appearance. Their ratings were based on a 7-point scale (1 = 'extremely unattractive' to 7 = 'extremely attractive')." If the behavior was physical instead of self-report, you can be still more concrete: "When the confederate made a great deal of noise in the adjacent room, participants looked toward the door an average of 6 times. The mean amount of time that passed before the participants began to investigate the odd noises—trying to open the locked door, looking around for a key—was 2.5 minutes."

Means can be reported within the narrative of the results of a piece of research. In the following example, the means delineate the effects of different levels of an independent variable (type of tutor) on a dependent measure (frequency with which help is offered):

> Each peer tutor offered academic assistance to his or her learning group more times ($M = 7.2$) during the work session than did the traditional tutors ($M = 4.3$) or the teacher, who worked with students in the control group ($M = 4.0$).

If there is a relatively large number of means to report, you will probably want to place them into a table (see chapter 3). If you do so, just be sure to explain the table to readers and to lead them carefully through it. Describing the mean relationships in the text is important, of course, and you will presumably need to repeat a mean or two from the table. Avoid repeating all the numbers shown in the text, however; such redundancy defeats the legitimate purpose of using a data table.

Data concerning the median and the mode are similarly descriptive in nature. In an animal learning experiment, an author might note that, "The median pecking rate of the pigeons placed in the operant chamber was 127." The mode might best be linked to the median or the mean within a research summary. Consider a hypothetical sociological investigation of the smoking habits of middle school students:

> Sixth-, seventh-, and eighth-graders were asked to indicate whether they ever smoked cigarettes and, if so, how many per day. Forty percent of the students said they had smoked at least one cigarette, and 26% of these indicated they smoked daily. The mean number of cigarettes smoked per day was 8.0. For comparison purposes, the mode was 4.0 cigarettes per day.

In this study, the presence of the mode told readers a bit more about the students' smoking habits than the solo mean level would have accomplished. A statistically sophisticated reader like you would posit that the distribution of cigarettes consumed in the middle school sample was probably positively skewed. If you are not certain why this should be so, review the earlier discussion concerning the shape of distributions and likely positions of the central tendency measures.

Because they are somewhat less flexible than the mean, the median and the mode appear less often in the Results section of an APA style article. The two measures are much more likely to appear in the Method section of the article, where they often accompany pretest information (e.g., "The *mdn* of practice trials was 5."), brief descriptions of standardized psychological measures (e.g., "High and low agoraphobia groups were created by using the median score on the Public Space Scale as a guide."), and participant sample descriptions (e.g., "The most frequent participant category was divorced mother with two children. This modal group had 12 members."). Of course, the mean can also be a useful statistic for a Method section (e.g., "Mean age of respondents was 27.5 years"). It all depends on what information appropriately but concisely helps to clarify the scopes and goals of the research in question.

Please understand, then, that there is no pressing need to report more than one or even all three measures of central tendency unless you have a good reason for doing so. The descriptive quality of these measures is important, but only when they support a conclusion or fact the researcher wishes to highlight—otherwise they serve as excess writerly baggage that detracts from the main points of the research.

Knowledge Base

1. Calculate the mean of the following scores:

    19   22   8   14   25   17   6   16   9   2

2. Calculate the mean of this frequency distribution:

X	f
5	12
4	8
3	11
2	5
1	3

3. What is the median of the following array of scores?

    11   3   17   12   6   3   10   20   16   8

4. What is the mode of the frequency distribution shown above in item 2? What is the mode of the array of scores shown in question 3?
5. Why calculate any measure of central tendency?
6. If you knew that the mean of a distribution was *greater* than the median, is it likely that the distribution is positively or negatively skewed?

Answers

1. The mean is 13.8.
2. The mean is 3.54.
3. The median is 10.5.
4. The modes are 5 and 3, respectively.
5. Measures of central tendency enable us to characterize data with one representative or typical number.
6. The distribution is apt to be positively skewed.

Understanding Variability

Measures of central tendency, particularly the mean, characterize a sample or population of observations with one number. To be sure, this indexing of central tendency—where does the general behavior tend to fall and what is it like?—is useful, but researchers need contextual information in order to properly evaluate it. Context is provided by the manner in which the observations within a distribution disperse themselves. Are the scores clustered close together, right on top of one another, or spread very far apart? Clustering, spread, dispersion—each word is a synonym for the concept of *variability.*

KEY TERM   **Variability** refers to the degree to which sample or population observations differ or deviate from the distribution's measures of central tendency.

When the values in a distribution are very similar to the distribution's average value—that is, the spread of the observations around the mean is small—then variability is said to be low. When a distribution's values are dissimilar from its mean—that is, the spread of observations around the mean is large—variability is high.

For the moment, using numerical values to illustrate variability may seem a bit abstract. In more concrete terms, how can we construe variability in a sample or population? Imagine that you wanted to compare recall rates for two participant groups, an experimental group that relied on a particular memory strategy and a control group that did not. Cognitive psychologists have studied what is called the method of loci (Hayes, 1981), a strategy for remembering a list of unrelated items sequentially.

The clustering, spread, or dispersion of data emphasize the relative amount of *variability* present in a distribution.

Participants are coached to mentally "walk through" a familiar place (e.g., home, campus) and to associate each item (e.g., "umbrella") with an object ("I will visualize the 'umbrella' on the chair in my living room") found along the "path." To recall the items, you simply "retrace" your steps. The loci method is very effective and easy to use, so much so that a list of 20 items can be recalled with ease (Hayes, 1981). The participants in the experimental group could learn the loci strategy in a few minutes, whereas the control group would receive no special instruction before hearing and then recalling the item list.

Behaviorally, low variability in the experimental group's recall scores could mean that most participants recalled all the items—that is, they more or less acted or responded in the same way (i.e., on average, individual recall rates were close to the group's mean). Perhaps members of the experimental group were found to recall an average of 18 out of 20 words. Higher variability in the control group's behavior could indicate that recall rates were relatively freewheeling, that without a common memory strategy, some people tended to remember fewer words—make more errors than others (i.e., generally, recall scores were far away from the group's mean). The hypothetical study might find that the mean recall rate for the control group was 12 words.

Thus, the loci method appears to be superior—the mean number of items recalled in the experimental group ($M = 18.0$) was higher than the control group ($M = 12.0$). Please note, however, the importance of knowing about the variability within the distribution of each group. A mean tells you only part of the behavioral story. You need to know how close or far away from one another—*how variable*—the scores were in the respective groups in the experiment.

You may not realize it, but in a statistical sense, you already have some working knowledge of variability. In chapter 3, the concepts of skewness and kurtois were introduced (skewness was also reviewed here in chapter 4). Both concepts deal with the shape of distributions, or how the observations in a set of data are spread along a continuum. When a distribution is positively or negatively skewed, the scores cluster, respectively, on the lower and higher ends of the measurement scale. Skewed distributions, too, have a longish "tail" that increases their variability. In contrast, a normal distribution will have two much shorter tails and observations falling in its center, two factors that contribute to its relatively lower variability.

What about kurtosis? If you look back to Data Box 3.C, you will recall that kurtosis refers to the peakedness or flatness of a curve. Three types of kurtosis—meso-, lepto-, and platykurtic—were introduced to characterize whether the spread of scores in a given distribution was relatively normal, tall and skinny, or broad and flat (see Data Box 3.C). That is, a mesokurtic distribution is apt to have relatively low variability, a leptokurtic one will have almost no variability, and a platykurtic curve will have a great deal. Again, it is important for you to envision the degree to which values in a set of data deviate from the mean, as the amount of deviation indicates the relative amount of variability present. Keep the shapes of distributions in mind as you learn the quantitative indices used to indicate variability.

Generally speaking, what do researchers in the behavioral sciences desire where variability in their research is concerned? As we will see in later chapters where inferential statistics are reviewed, researchers usually want a low degree of variability within a given condition in an experiment. In other words, an investigator hopes that the level of an independent variable presented to the experimental condition will cause most people in it to behave similarly to one another (i.e., close to some mean level). Accordingly, the members of a control group, too, should act like one another (i.e., close to another mean level, one differing in value from the experimental group). Further, researchers hope that the variability between the two groups is relatively high; that is, the independent variable

The shape of a distribution, its *skewness* or *kurtosis,* often characterizes its variability.

truly had an effect because the behavioral differences between the two groups are pronounced. We will review this research desideratum many times. Here is a simple mnemonic, a memory aid, you can learn to describe the desired pattern of variability in experimental groups: Low within, high without.

The Range

The most basic index of variability is called the *range* or, on occasion, the crude range or even the simple range. When it is used to describe the variability of a distribution, the range is reported with the mean, the median, or the mode.

KEY TERM   The **range** is the difference between the highest and the lowest score in a distribution.

The range entails subtracting a smaller number from a larger one, and it identifies the distance between the two extreme points in a distribution. The formula for the range is:

[4.6.1]
$$range = X_{\text{high}} - X_{\text{low}}.$$

If the lowest observation is a sample of data were 20 and the highest was 75, then the range would be 55, or:

[4.6.2]
$$range = 75 - 20 = 55.$$

Please note that we are calculating the range—represented by only one number—and not the *range of scores* (i.e., 20 to 75), which entails two values.

The *range* is the most basic index of variability.

The range is readily capable of accommodating a distribution's true limits. In the prior example, the true limits of the scores 20 and 75 might be 19.5 and 75.5, respectively (i.e., 1/2 the unit of measure added to the highest and subtracted from the lowest scores in a distribution). In this case, the range would be 56 (i.e., 75.5 − 19.5 = 56) instead of 55, which was found for the raw scores.

The range is a rough-and-ready way to get the sense of a distribution, but it has a decided limitation: Like the mean, extreme scores easily affect it. Similar to the mean, the range is subject to instability when extreme scores are present. Outlying scores, particularly one aberrant score that is very far away from any other, can artificially inflate the range, giving a false sense of what the data are really like. The majority of the scores, for example, might fall into a somewhat normal distribution, but the presence of even one outlying score will obscure the distribution's balance.

Checking the *ranges* of variables is a good way to catch errors in a data set.

As a practical matter, however, calculating or checking the range of a measure with a limited number of possible values is an excellent way to catch mistakes. If a given measure, say, a 7-point rating scale, is used and the range is found to be 10 (e.g., a high score of 11 minus a low score of 1), some error occurred; logically, this range cannot exceed 6 (i.e., 7 − 1). The error in this case is apt to be a data entry error or "typo"—perhaps the number 7 was being entered and 11 was substituted by mistake. Thus, checking ranges to make certain that the values make sense is a straightforward way to catch errors in a data set.

The Interquartile Range and the Semi-Interquartile Range

The instability of the range led statisticians to develop related but better indicators of dispersion for situations when distributions are not normal. The **interquartile range** indicates the range of scores that fall between the 75th and 25th percentiles—the middle 50%—of a distribution. You will remember that these two percentiles are often referred to as quartiles, or Q_1 and Q_3. The formula for the interquartile range is easy to calculate:

[4.7.1]
$$interquartile\ range = Q_3 - Q_1.$$

In practice, the interquartile range is less likely to be used than the *semi-interquartile range,* which characterizes the distance between 75th and the 25th percentiles, and then divides the distance in half.

KEY TERM   The **semi-interquartile range** overcomes the instability of the range by providing a numerical index of half the distance between the first (Q_1) and third (Q_3) quartiles in a distribution.

Larger values representing the semi-interquartile range indicate a greater distance between Q_1 and Q_3; that is, a greater spread of scores. Smaller values, then, would point to less spread. Here is the formula used to calculate the semi-interquartile range, which can be abbreviated as SIQR:

[4.8.1]
$$\mathrm{SIQR} = \frac{Q_3 - Q_1}{2}.$$

In symmetric distributions, when the semi-interquartile range is added to and subtracted from the median, the location of 50% of the observations in the distribution can be identified. If the median score in a distribution was 55 and the value of the semi-interquartile range was 15, then 50% of the scores in the distribution would fall between the scores of 40 and 70 (i.e., 55 ± 15; see panel (a) in Figure 4.2). Interestingly, even when a distribution is skewed, use of the semi-interquartile range can still capture the middle 50% of the observations available. This possibility is shown by panel (b) in Figure 4.2. If the median score was 27 and the semi-interquartile range was 8.5, then fully half of the distribution's observations would fall between the scores of 18.5 and 35.5 (see panel (b) in Figure 4.2). The semi-interquartile range is the ideal index of dispersion when the median is used, which often happens when distributions are skewed, precluding the use of the mean.

The interquartile range and the semi-interquartile range are of limited use beyond situations where a distribution is skewed and its median is known, however. If necessary, for example, the semi-interquartile range can indicate the variability when a distribution's mode is the focus of inquiry. Neither the interquartile range nor the semi-interquartile range is employed in any advanced statistical tests, however. We turn next to dispersion indices that have greater applicability to behavioral science data, variance and standard deviation.

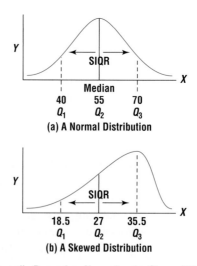

Figure 4.2   The Semi-Interquartile Range in a Normal and a Skewed Distribution

Variance and Standard Deviation

If the mean is the chief measure of central tendency, then the standard deviation is the choice measure of dispersion. Before we learn about the standard deviation, however, we need to examine its parent statistic, *variance*.

KEY TERM   **Variance** is equal to the average of the squared deviations from the mean of a distribution. Symbolically, sample *variance* is s^2 and population *variance* is σ^2.

This definition for variance seems all too technical, but bear with me for a few minutes. You already have a conceptual knowledge regarding variability, but it does need to be bolstered with a bit of technical knowledge. As you will see, working through this technical knowledge will help you appreciate the utility of statistics generally and, more specifically, the virtues of the standard deviation—but now back to explaining variance.

Variance is the numerical index of variability, being based on the average of the *squared deviations* from the mean of a data set.

What is meant by a *deviation from the mean?* One way to explain the fundamental role the mean plays in statistics is to acknowledge that its value is completely dependent on every single score in a distribution—adding or subtracting an observation will change the value of the mean. There is more to the mean than such numerical sensitivity, however. Let's examine the role of deviation from the mean in a simple data set. Below is a frequency distribution that notes the values of X in column 1, the $\overline{X}$ [mean] of the distribution in column 2, and deviation scores—each value of X minus the $\overline{X}$ in column 3.

X	$\overline{X}$	$X - \overline{X}$
6	4	2
5	4	1
3	4	-1
2	4	-2
		$\sum (X - \overline{X}) = 0$

What stands out here? When calculating the sum of the deviation scores, or $\sum (X - \overline{X})$, you will discover that it is always equal to 0. What does this mean? Two things, really. First, the mean is the balance point between the high and the low scores in this (or any) distribution. Second, statistically speaking, we cannot work with the deviation scores in their present form precisely because they are positive and negative numbers that always sum to 0. The deviation scores must be transformed in some way so they can be entered into formulas and used in calculations.

When squared and summed, *mean deviation* scores yield positive numbers that are useful in a variety of statistical analyses.

Our statistical recourse is to square the deviation scores so that we will always be working with relatively large and positive numbers. Unless you are working with 0, 1, or with decimals between 0 and 1, squaring a number will always increase its value. By squaring the deviation scores, we create a fundamental and helpful number—the sum of the squared deviations from the mean, otherwise know as the *sum of squares*, which is always abbreviated in statistical works as *SS*.

KEY TERM   The **sum of squares (SS)** is the sum of the squared deviations from the mean of a distribution. The *SS* is fundamental to descriptive and inferential statistics.

Symbolically, the *SS* looks like this:

[4.9.1]
$$SS = \sum (X - \overline{X})^2.$$

The *SS* will be used extensively in the calculation of inferential statistics that appear later in this book, so I advise you to become familiar with it now. This frequency distribution is modified somewhat by $(X - \overline{X})^2$. As you can see immediately below, summing the squared deviations results in a positive number (i.e., $SS = 10$). Please make certain that you understand where the SS came from before you proceed:

X	$\overline{X}$	$(X - \overline{X})^2$
6	4	4
5	4	1
3	4	1
2	4	4
		$\sum (X - \overline{X})^2 = SS = 10$

There is a second formula that is used to calculate the SS, and it, too, is useful for working with a table of data. It is often referred to as the "computational formula" for the SS. Here it is:

[4.10.1]
$$SS = \sum X^2 - \frac{(\sum X)^2}{N}.$$

There are no unfamiliar calculations here. We can use the data table from above and recalculate the SS using the computational formula. All we need to do is calculate the $\sum X^2$ and $(\sum X)^2$. As we noted back in chapter 1, remember that $\sum X^2 \neq (\sum X)^2$. Here is the revised data table:

X	X^2
6	36
5	25
3	9
2	4
$\sum X = 16$	$\sum X^2 = 74$

The values of $\sum X$ and $\sum X^2$, as well as N, are then entered into [4.10.1]:

[4.10.2]
$$SS = 74 - \frac{(16)^2}{4},$$

[4.10.3]
$$SS = 74 - \frac{256}{4},$$

[4.10.4]
$$SS = 74 - 64,$$

[4.10.5]
$$SS = 10.$$

As must be the case, the same answer for the calculation of the SS is found using [4.9.1] and [4.10.1].

Now, consider what happens when we have a larger number of observations than what is shown in the frequency distribution, and these observations have values great and small. If we use them all to calculate the SS of squares of their distribution, we will discover something interesting. If the scores are spread out and relatively far from the mean—that is, they have a relatively high degree of variability—then the total SS for the distribution will be a relatively large number. On the other hand, if the scores are close to the mean, even clustered, then there will be less variability and a smaller total for the SS. Intuitively, then, we know that scores that are more deviant from the mean will result in higher SS and be indicative of greater variability (people behaved somewhat differently than each other). The reverse will hold true for scores

There will generally be more than one procedural formula available for calculating statistics like the *sum of the squares* (SS).

that fall closely around the mean of a distribution (people behaved similarly to one another).

The size of the *SS*, then, is influenced by the magnitude of the deviation scores around the mean. A second factor, the number of observations available, also plays a role in the *SS*'s size. Generally speaking, the more scores available in a distribution, the larger the *SS* will be, especially if some of the scores diverge greatly from the mean. As we acknowledged on earlier occasions, the more observations we have in a data set the better, but in that case, we need a way to make *SS* a good indicator of dispersion. We need—so to speak—to get the *SS* under our control. The most direct way to do so is by dividing the *SS* by the number observations (i.e., *N*) available. By doing so, we are calculating a number that represents the average of the squared deviations from the mean, that is, the variance. (At this point, you might want to review the definition of variance presented at the start of this section of the chapter.) We now turn to the measurement of variance in samples, then populations, and finally, where and how sample statistics are used to estimate population parameters.

Sample Variance and Standard Deviation

Most students and many researchers are apt to calculate variance for sample data. The results of an experiment need to be analyzed, and the investigator is interested in the variance of the dependent measure in the sample data. Please note that in this case, the investigator is not necessarily interested in whether the variance of the sample reflects that of its parent population, nor is any attempt made (yet) to estimate the population variance from this sample data.

The symbol for sample variance is s^2 and here is the formula that statistically defines it:

[4.11.1]
$$s^2 = \frac{\sum (X - \overline{X})^2}{N}.$$

Due to its derivation from the *SS*, the s^2 can also be represented by:

[4.12.1]
$$s^2 = \frac{SS}{N}.$$

Because we already calculated the *SS* above, we need only enter the relevant numbers into [4.12.1] to determined the variance:

[4.12.2]
$$s^2 = \frac{10}{4},$$

[4.12.3]
$$s^2 = 2.5.$$

It follows that the variance can also be calculated by incorporating the *SS* information from [4.10.1], except that now the formula, which already includes division by *N*, must itself be divided by *N*:

[4.13.1]
$$s^2 = \frac{\sum X^2 - (\sum X)^2/N}{N}.$$

Let's enter the numbers we know into [4.13.1] to illustrate that we can obtain the same variance shown previously in [4.12.3]. We can simply repeat the information found in [4.10.2] and then divide by $N = 4$ again.

[4.13.2]
$$s^2 = \frac{74 - (16)^2/4}{4},$$

Greater variability means less consistency (larger deviations between X and $\overline{X}$) in behavior, whereas less variability leads to greater consistency (smaller deviations between X and $\overline{X}$).

[4.13.3]
$$s^2 = \frac{74 - 256/4}{4},$$

[4.13.4]
$$s^2 = \frac{74 - 64}{4},$$

[4.13.5]
$$s^2 = \frac{10}{4},$$

[4.13.6]
$$s^2 = 2.5.$$

The variance, then, can be calculated directly if the *SS* is known (i.e., using [4.12.1]) or with a few more steps if the *SS* must be determined from scratch (i.e., using [4.13.1]).

As a measure of dispersion, the variance is useful for averaging the effects of greater and lesser deviations from the mean. However, the variance represents the average of the sum of the *squared deviations* between each observation *X* and the mean of a distribution. It does *not* represent the *average deviation between an observation and the mean using the original scale of measurement.* In other words, we need to transform the squared deviations to average deviations—and the way to achieve this goal is by taking the square root of the variance, which converts the variance to what is called the *standard deviation.*

KEY TERM   The **standard deviation** is the average deviation between an observed score and the mean of a distribution. *Standard deviation,* symbolized *s,* is determined by taking the square root of the variance, or $\sqrt{s^2} = s$.

The formula for the standard deviation of a sample is:

[4.14.1]
$$s = \sqrt{s^2}.$$

We can easily determine the standard deviation for the variance shown in [4.13.6]:

[4.14.2]
$$s = \sqrt{2.5},$$

[4.14.3]
$$s = 1.5811.$$

As can be seen from [4.14.1], once you know the value of the variance, the standard deviation is also known once the square root of the variance is taken—an easy feat with a calculator. It follows, of course, that if you know the standard deviation, you can determine the variance by squaring *s,* or:

[4.15.1]
$$s^2 = (s)^2,$$

[4.15.2]
$$s^2 = (1.5811)^2,$$

[4.15.3]
$$s^2 = 2.5.$$

As we will see, the idea of standard deviation and the descriptive statistic, *s,* are essential to many of the inferential statistics that researchers use. The basic idea behind the concept and the numerical value is actually rather straightforward: Standard deviation describes the typical distance—the average deviation—between a given score in a distribution and the mean. It is a very useful index of variability, and as you gain experience calculating and thinking about it, you will develop an intuitive sense of what it means in terms of any given data set. For now, conceptualize it the same way we conceptualize other indicators of variability—smaller standard deviations indicate that observations fall closer to the mean and larger standard deviations suggest that, on average, observations fall farther away from the mean.

Homogeneity and Heterogeneity: Understanding the Standard Deviations of Different Distributions

The standard deviation is the most common and, arguably, the best single index of a distribution's variability.

Low dispersion = homogeneous observations; high dispersion = heterogeneous observations.

Smaller standard deviations indicate that observations fall close to a distribution's mean. These low average deviations from the mean also indicate that the observations in the distribution tend to be similar to one another. Statisticians refer to high degrees of similarity—that is, low dispersion—as **homogeneity,** and the observations in such a distribution are said to be **homogeneous.** When data are spread farther apart in a distribution, when observations tend to be dissimilar in value, a distribution is classified as **heterogeneous. Heterogeneity** occurs when a distribution's values show a relatively high degree of dispersion around a mean.

These twin concepts are very useful when it comes to characterizing and comparing distinct distributions. Figure 4.3 shows two distributions, each with a different mean. Their standard deviations, too, vary: panel (a) has a relatively low degree of spread around the mean (i.e., the standard deviation is 2.0) and panel (b) shows greater dispersion around the mean (i.e., the standard deviation is 5.0). As you can see, panel (a) in Figure 4.3 would best be described as homogeneous—the observations are closely clustered around the mean. Notice that the numbers around the mean in panel (a) represent the standard deviation, which is small—this fact is also shown by the rather tight curve surrounding the mean. The spread in panel (b) in Figure 4.3 is much wider, just as this distribution's standard deviation is much larger. As you can see, the standard deviation intervals around the mean of panel (b) cause the curve to be much shorter and more spread out than panel (a). Thus, especially when it is compared to panel (a), the panel (b) distribution is clearly heterogeneous.

Besides serving as a good index of dispersion and providing a base for comparison among different distributions, the standard deviation serves one other function: It locates the bulk of the scores in any distribution. As can be seen in Figure 4.3, both distributions contain shaded areas around the mean and, as you know, these areas were created by taking each mean and then adding and subtracting their respective standard deviations. More to the point, though, by "bulk" of the scores in each distribution, I mean that about 68% of the available observations fall within the first standard deviation intervals around each mean, leaving about 32% of the remaining observations in the distributions' tails (i.e., in the second and third standard deviation intervals

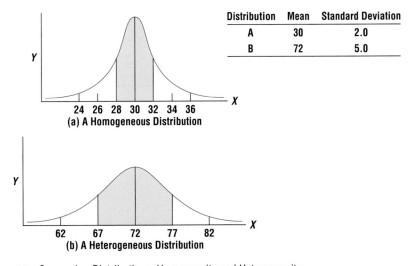

Distribution	Mean	Standard Deviation
A	30	2.0
B	72	5.0

24 26 28 30 32 34 36
(a) A Homogeneous Distribution

62   67   72   77   82
(b) A Heterogeneous Distribution

Figure 4.3 Comparing Distributions: Homogeneity and Heterogeneity

extending outward to the left and right of the mean). Why do distributions possess this sort of standardization? We will explore this matter in chapter 5, when we learn about the consistency of standard deviation intervals and their utility for locating observations in a distribution.

Calculating Variance and Standard Deviation from a Data Array

We have seen that the variance and standard deviation are not difficult to calculate from a small sample of data, but what if the data we are analyzing appear in a larger array of observations with different frequencies? We simply build on the knowledge of frequency distributions we gained earlier. Table 4.7 shows scores on a 10-point social anxiety scale, where higher scores indicate greater levels of discomfort associated with public speaking and other extraverted activities. The first step is to take note of X and to then calculate X^2, which is placed in the second column of the table. Column 3 represents the frequencies (f) of the different values of X and because some values occur more than once, we multiply both X and X^2 by f. As you can see in Table 4.7, the $\sum fX$ is the same as $\sum X$ (this fact was noted back in chapter 3), just as $\sum f(X^2)$ is the same value as $\sum X^2$. Once these relationships are noted, it is simply a matter of entering the appropriate

Table 4.7   Hypothetical Scores on a Social Anxiety Scale

X	X^2	f	$f(X)$	$f(X^2)$
10	100	6	60	600
9	81	8	72	648
8	64	7	56	448
7	49	6	42	294
6	36	6	36	216
5	25	5	25	125
4	16	9	36	144
3	9	2	6	18
2	4	8	16	32
1	1	2	2	2
		$N = \sum f = 59$	$\sum fX = 351$	$\sum f(X^2) = 2{,}527$
			$\sum X = 351$	$\sum X^2 = 2{,}527$
			$(\sum X)^2 = 123{,}201$	

$$s^2 = \frac{\sum X^2 - (\sum X)^2/N}{N}$$

$$s^2 = \frac{2527 - (123{,}201)/59}{59}$$

$$s^2 = \frac{2527 - 2088.1525}{59}$$

$$s^2 = \frac{438.8475}{59}$$

$$s^2 = 7.4381 \cong 7.44$$

$$s = \sqrt{s^2}$$

$$s = \sqrt{7.4381}$$

$$s = 2.7272 \cong 2.73$$

numbers into the respective equations for variance and standard deviation shown at the bottom of Table 4.7.

Population Variance and Standard Deviation

On occasion, a researcher will be working with a complete and intact population, making it entirely possible to describe its characteristics with accuracy and precision. An educator, for example, might be exclusively interested in how the students enrolled in a nontraditional college class perform on written assignments. The educator is genuinely interested in one and only one group of students—no attempt is made to generalize their experience to that of other students. Similarly, a rural sociologist might study the health of residents of a very small town (population around 500 persons) in the American midwest to learn how repeated, familiar contact among the same people promotes their well-being (cf., Egolf, Lasker, Wolf, & Potvin, 1992). The sociologist, too, is only interested in this one population of people.

In such circumstances, the true values—the population's parameters—could be measured and known. Instead of relying on the sample statistics we reviewed in the previous section, an investigator would calculate population parameters (see Table 4.1). When actual values are known and not estimated, the formulas for the variance and standard deviation are mathematically identical with those used to calculate sample statistics. In fact, the sample data examples reviewed in the previous section could be recast here in population terms and their answers would not change. Why? As was the case with the population mean (see formula [4.2.1]), only the symbols involved change. Thus, I want you to get a conceptual understanding of population parameters here—we will do calculations concerning populations later when we discuss how sample statistics are used to estimate population parameters.

The symbol for the population variance is σ^2, or "lowercase sigma squared." The formula for determining the variance of a population is:

[4.16.1]
$$\sigma^2 = \frac{\Sigma(X - \mu)^2}{N}.$$

That is, the population variance is the sum of the squared deviations between all observations (X) in the population and the mean of the population (μ), which is then divided by the total number of available observations. If we want to "unpack" this formula a bit, we remember that the population SS would be based on:

[4.17.1]
$$SS = \Sigma(X - \mu)^2.$$

Because this relationship holds true here as well as for sample data, it follows that the population variance can also be calculated by:

[4.18.1]
$$\sigma^2 = \frac{SS}{N},$$

or by

[4.19.1]
$$\sigma^2 = \frac{\Sigma X^2 - (\Sigma X)^2/N}{N}.$$

As you can see, these three formulas (ie., [4.17.1], [4.18.1], [4.19.1]) are mathematically similar to [4.9.1], [4.12.1], and [4.13.1], respectively, because the relationships being examined among the variables are the same. The only difference is that we are now considering describing the variance of a "knowable" population.

What about calculating the standard deviation of a knowable population? The symbol for a population's standard deviation is σ, or "lowercase sigma." As you no doubt discerned already, it is simply a matter of taking the square root of the population variance, or:

[4.20.1]
$$\sigma = \sqrt{\sigma^2}.$$

We showed above that when the standard deviation of a sample is known, by squaring it the variance also can be known. This relationship holds true for population data as well, therefore:

[4.20.2]
$$\sigma^2 = (\sigma)^2.$$

Finally, the population standard deviation can also be determined by taking the square root of the *SS* divided by *N:*

[4.21.1]
$$\sigma = \sqrt{\frac{SS}{N}}.$$

Practically speaking, then, accessible, intact populations are treated no differently than sample data—only the symbolic relations within the appropriate formulas change. What happens when we try to use sample statistics to infer the characteristics of larger, potentially unknowable populations? We must estimate population characteristics by using slightly adjusted formulas for working with sample data, the topic of the next section.

Looking Ahead: Biased and Unbiased Estimators of Variance and Standard Deviation

We need to look ahead. By looking ahead, I mean introducing and reviewing some concepts and practical calculations that will be of great use when we read later chapters and learn inferential statistics. My intention is to continue to build on your conceptual understanding of the relations between samples and populations so that when complex inferential tests are eventually introduced, these relations will be second nature to you. I will only need to remind you of the conceptual partnership existing between samples and populations—you will, as it were, fill in the blanks. By learning this background material now, I guarantee that your introduction to inferential tests will be a smooth one.

When working with sample data—when we specifically want merely to *describe* a sample—the basic formulas for calculating the sample variance and the standard deviation we introduced earlier in this chapter are both appropriate and useful. I repeat them here to refresh your memory—we will also compare them with alternative formulas in a moment. Sample variance (based on formula [4.11.1]) is:

$$s^2 = \frac{\sum (X - \overline{X})^2}{N}.$$

If we place a radical or square root sign over the equation from [4.11.1], we have the formula for the sample standard deviation. Written more simply, of course, we can rely on [4.14.1]:

$$s = \sqrt{s^2}.$$

What if we are not describing a sample but, rather, trying to *estimate* the population variance and standard deviation? We must use modified formulas to do so because [4.11.1] and [4.14.1] provide what is called a *biased estimate* of these population parameters.

KEY TERM　A **biased estimate** (sometimes called a "biased estimator") is any descriptive statistic that will reliably overestimate or underestimate a corresponding population parameter.

The term "reliable" in statistical or methodological contexts is usually a synonym for "consistent." In other words, the formulas for variance and standard deviation shown above will consistently and incorrectly portray the characteristics of their parent population. In fact, statisticians have found that these particular formulas error on the side of *underestimating* the actual parameters.

What is the origin of this bias toward underestimation? Can it be corrected? When calculating the population variance (and, therefore, the population standard deviation), the bias occurs when N divides the sum of the squares (SS). The use of N as the denominator for the sum of the squares formula results in a number that is, on average, *smaller* than the population's actual variance. To circumvent this underestimation problem, statisticians use $N - 1$ as the denominator instead of N. On average, this minor correction results in a *larger* but more accurate estimate of the population variance and population standard deviation.

Use of the $N - 1$ correction in a formula results in what statisticians refer to as an *unbiased estimate* of the population variance and standard deviation.

KEY TERM　An **unbiased estimate** (sometimes referred to as an "unbiased estimator") is any descriptive statistic that reliably approximates the value of a population parameter.

"Unbiased" means that any calculated sample statistics are closer to actual population parameter values than would be the case if a biased estimate formula were used.

This is another occasion when the size of a sample affects the accuracy of a statistic; where sampling is concerned, bigger is better. When the N of a sample is relatively small (e.g., < 20 observations) estimates based on the unbiased population variance and standard deviation will still differ somewhat from the actual parameters. For a larger N (e.g., 100 or 200 observations), however, unbiased estimates will approach the actual values of the population parameters. Errors in estimation, then, will be greater when samples are small, gradually decreasing as sample sizes grow.

New symbols will indicate when unbiased estimates are being used (recall Table 4.1). The unbiased estimate of the variance is $\hat{s}^2$ and the unbiased estimate of the standard deviation is $\hat{s}$. The "caret" or $\wedge$ means that the correction factor of $N - 1$ was used as the denominator in the respective formulas. The formulas for the unbiased estimate of the population variance and population standard deviation, respectively, are:

Biased estimators consistently *overestimate* or *underestimate* parameters, whereas *unbiased estimators* tend to *approximate* parameters.

$$[4.22.1] \qquad \hat{s}^2 = \frac{\sum (X - \overline{X})^2}{N - 1} = \frac{SS}{N - 1},$$

$$[4.23.1] \qquad \hat{s} = \sqrt{\hat{s}^2}.$$

It is important to remind yourself what the unbiased estimates mean symbolically. If a population is virtually infinite in size or so large that an investigator will never be able to adequately sample it, using unbiased estimates can approximate the population parameters. In general, then, it should be true that unbiased estimates of the population variance should be approximately equal to the true population variance:

$$\hat{s}^2 \cong \sigma^2, \text{ or:}$$

$$\hat{s}^2 = \frac{\sum (X - \overline{X})^2}{N - 1} \cong \sigma^2 = \frac{\sum (X - \mu)^2}{N}.$$

It follows that the unbiased estimate of the population standard deviation should approximate the population's true standard deviation:

$$\hat{s} \cong \sigma, \text{ and thus:}$$

$$\hat{s} = \sqrt{\frac{\sum (X - \overline{X})^2}{N - 1}} \cong \sigma = \sqrt{\frac{\sum (X - \mu)^2}{N}}.$$

The presence of a caret (^) indicates that an estimate is *unbiased*, one usually involving a correction factor of $N-1$ in a formula's denominator.

We can work through one example to illustrate how the unbiased estimates for the population parameters differ from the (biased) estimates provided by sample statistics. Imagine that we draw a sample of $N = 6$ observations. These X observations, ranked from high to low scores, are shown below. A second column provides the X^2. The calculation of SS is shown underneath the data table. Please beware of a potential error when calculating the SS using the computational formula: N, *not* $N - 1$, is first used to determine the SS; $N - 1$ (or, in the case of sample variance, N) is subsequently used as a denominator after the SS is known.

X	X²
9	81
7	49
5	25
4	16
3	9
1	1
$\sum X = 29$	$\sum X^2 = 181$

$$SS = \sum X^2 - \frac{(\sum X)^2}{N},$$

$$SS = 181 - \frac{(29)^2}{6},$$

$$SS = 181 - \frac{841}{6},$$

$$SS = 181 - 140.1667,$$

$$SS = 40.833.$$

Once we know that the SS is 40.833, we are free to calculate the variance and the standard deviation for the data. If we want to estimate the parameters of the population where these data were drawn from, then formula [4.22.1] should be used to calculate the variance:

$$\hat{s}^2 = \frac{SS}{N - 1} = \frac{40.833}{5} = 8.167.$$

The unbiased estimate of the population standard deviation would be based on formula [4.23.1]:

$$\hat{s} = \sqrt{\hat{s}^2} = \sqrt{8.167} = 2.8578.$$

On the other hand, if we only wish to describe the variance and standard deviation of the sample, we could rely on the biased estimate formula. For the variance, we use [4.12.1]:

$$s^2 = \frac{SS}{N} = \frac{40.833}{6} = 6.0855.$$

Using formula [4.14.1], the sample standard deviation is:

$$s = \sqrt{s^2} = \sqrt{6.8055} = 2.6087.$$

As you can see, the unbiased estimates of the population variance and standard deviation are indeed larger than the corresponding sample statistics.

Skeptical readers and researchers—you should be the former working toward becoming the latter—will wonder whether the $N - 1$ correction for unbiased estimates is truly necessary. As behavioral scientists are wont to say, "it's an empirical question," meaning that we need to see some actual data demonstrating the presumed effect to reduce or eliminate any skepticism. As modern statistics developed, statisticians found that over many, many trials employing observations from real as well as theoretical populations, the $N - 1$ correction lessened the distance between estimated and actual parameters. Is the correction perfect? No, but it reaches a level that statisticians find to be descriptively acceptable and satisfactory for subsequent applications or analyses.

Keep in mind that statistics and data analysis are tools that provide guidance to behavioral scientists, not definitive answers—an estimate is always just an estimate, and a researcher or student must decide if it seems to be a reasonable one. What matters here is how close these approximations are to parameters that are sometimes knowable, other times not. When analyzing data using formulas for unbiased estimates, we assume that our results are close, if not entirely accurate, the majority of the time. In other words, statistical estimates enable us to approximate reality, to close in on the relative location of a parameter, not to define it with absolute certainty. Later, we will learn how this assumption is very important for the testing of research hypotheses within experiments.

DATA BOX 4.C

Avoid Computation Frustration: Get to Know Your Calculator

In chapter 1, we acknowledged that some calculators are more complicated to use than others. This observation is especially true for calculators that have statistical functions already programmed into them. There is a good chance you have one—and I am guessing that there is an equally good chance that you never bothered to read the instruction manual that accompanied it. You should remedy this oversight quickly, right now.

Why? Do you know whether your calculator uses the biased estimate formula or the unbiased estimate formula when it calculates the variance and the standard deviation? I have taught more than my fair share of students who become understandably frustrated when the variance they calculated by hand does not match the answer on their calculator's screen. Why the error or apparent confusion? The students might be trying simply to *describe* a sample's variance (denominator of N) while the calculator is seeking to *estimate* the variance of the population the sample hailed from (denominator of $N - 1$).

To add to the confusion, some calculators have a variance key (labeled s^2, S^2, or σ^2) or a standard deviation key (labeled s, S, or σ), and still others use a key symbol like "$s - 1$" or even "$\sigma - 1$". What do these various keys mean? Presumably, the presence of a "-1" indicates the calculator's standard routine is to provide unbiased estimates of parameters. Yet some calculators will give unbiased estimates but their keypad lacks the telltale "-1," and some machines provide both sample statistics as well as population estimates (users just need to know which keys to push in what sequence!). Avoid being plagued by wrong answers and frustration—before you check your homework or analyze any data, be sure that you know which formulas for variance and standard deviation your calculator relies on.

Knowledge Base

1. Determine the range for the following data:

   10 12 16 19 22 23 28 32 34

2. Turn to Table 3.11 on page 121. Using the quartile information from this distribution of scores on the Life Orientation Test (LOT):
   a. Calculate the semi-interquartile range.
   b. If the mean LOT score is 22.83, between what two scores do half of the distribution's observations fall?

3. Consider the following table of sample data:

   X

   8
   5
   4
   2
   1

   a. What is the SS for this distribution?
   b. What is the s^2?
   c. What is the s?

4. Assume the data in item 3 represent a population. What are the values for μ, σ^2, and σ?

5. Using the data from item 3, calculate the unbiased estimates for the population variance and standard deviation.

Answers

1. *range* $= 34 - 10 = 24$
2. a. SIQR $= 36 - 13/2 = 11.5$ b. $22.83 \pm 11.5 = 11.33$ and 34.33
3. a $SS = 30$ b $s^2 = 6$ c $s = 2.5$
4. $\mu = 4.0$; $\sigma^2 = 6.0$; $\sigma = 2.5$
5. $\hat{s}^2 = 7.5$; $\hat{s} = 2.74$

Factors Affecting Variability

You now have a good understanding of what variability means conceptually, as well as ways in which measures of dispersion—range, variance, and standard deviation—can be used to quantify it. Variability's role in the research process remains to be discussed, however. Specifically, what factors in a piece of research, such as an experiment or a field study, can affect whether the variability of a measure is small or large? As noted previously, researchers usually want a relatively small amount of variability within the conditions of a research project, though larger amounts of variability between the conditions are desirable. There are six factors that can influence variability in research projects: sample size, participant selection, sample characteristics, independent variables, dependent measures, and time.

Sample Size.   Generally speaking, greater variability is apt to be found in studies employing smaller sample sizes than research based on larger numbers of observations (see also, Data Box 4.D). Although the utility of larger samples will be discussed in detail in chapter 9, a short preview can be made here. Unlike smaller samples, larger samples of data are more likely to reflect the characteristics of their parent populations. In this chapter, for example, larger samples were shown to result in closer matches between unbiased parameter estimates and actual population parameters. Larger samples, too, are likely to actually take on the shape of the parent distribution; indeed, as we will see later,

Bigger samples are generally better samples where the reliability of inferential statistics is concerned.

large enough samples can even approximate normal distributions, making them ideal for inferential statistics.

Selection Process.   All else being equal, random sampling and random selection are more likely to result in distributions containing relatively low amounts of variability. If every member of a given population has the same chance of being selected as all the others, there is no bias in the formation of the sample. That is, the randomization process will probably yield a distribution of observations that adequately portray the parent population's characteristics. In the absence of any randomization, researchers can unknowingly draw on biased subsamples of a population or include nonrepresentative members, resulting in higher than desired levels of variability in their responses. Randomization is the raison d'être—the reason or justification—for a quality selection process in any research effort.

Sample Characteristics.   Behavioral scientists hope research participants' behavior is influenced by the experiment or study—did the independent variable affect participants' responses to the dependent measure? There is always a danger, though, that participant characteristics are unknowingly leading to the observed results. How so? First, if randomization is absent, a researcher cannot be sure that a study's participants do not share some common but unidentified feature (e.g., a personality trait, shared experiences) that is causing the low variability in the study, as well as its outcome. Conversely, a heterogeneous sample used with no randomization can lead to aberrantly large, conceptually unmanageable amounts of variability within and between measures.

Second, what if all the participants in a study are highly similar to one another? Many psychologists worry that the bulk of the field's published research is based on the behavior of men and women between the ages of 18 and 22 years of age, for example (e.g., Dawes, 1991; Sears, 1986). This relatively privileged "sample" of people is hardly representative of the general population; indeed, it is largely homogeneous, so much so that one could question whether random assignment is adversely affected by the participants' "sameness." Where variability is concerned, then, it may be artificially low due to sample characteristics, not the experimental variables per se.

Independent Variables.   In an experiment, the different levels of the independent variable should lead to different sources of variability in behavior. In other words, the variability of behavior in the experimental group(s) should be different than that found in the control group, though both should reflect the hypothesis. Even if the research question is a good one, the hypothesized pattern of variability within the respective research groups will occur only if the independent variable is a strong one. By "strong," we refer to whether its manipulation—the clarity of its presence or absence—had a discernable effect on participants' behavior. If the manipulation was "weak," that is, neither participant group, on average, noticed it, then the variability within and between conditions will probably be the same. In other words, both groups will behave similarly. The quality and magnitude of the independent variable, then, is linked in a pronounced way to the variability in an experiment.

Dependent Measures.   Where independent variables should be strong, dependent measures should be sensitive. Contextually, sensitivity means that the measures should clearly differentiate between fine shades of meaning (self-report measures) or subtle behavioral distinctions and actions (behavioral measures). Insensitive measures are likely to show low levels of variability for the wrong reasons—participants give the same response, say, because alternative responses are unavailable. The opposite problem, too much variability, could occur if dependent measures are *too* sensitive, leading to many outliers, as well as inconsistent responses to even related ideas. Ideal dependent measures cut a middle course between these extremes by allowing participants, as well as investigators, a moderate degree of response flexibility—change, reaction, response, action— all must be measured appropriately.

Passage of Time Between the Presentation of the Independent Variable and Dependent Measure.   The passage of time is a practical matter than can influence judgment and behavior in the lab or in everyday life: How long does the effect of a given independent variable last? In most experiments, only a few minutes pass between the manipulation of the independent variable and the measurement of the dependent variable. Although the latter may have greater or lesser amounts of variability, it is not likely to be due to time passage or related problems (e.g., fatigue, memory loss; see also, Cook & Campbell, 1979). If the time between the presentation of one and then the other is longer—days or weeks pass, even months, before a dependent measure is administered—then variability in response is less likely to be attributed to the independent variable. As demonstrated by Elizabeth Loftus' (Loftus & Palmer, 1974; see also, Loftus, 1979) research on constructive memory processes for events occurring during an accident, for example, people fill any vacuums in recall with stereotypic expectations (see also, Nisbett & Wilson, 1977). As an extraneous variable, then, time can affect variability in ways that are not necessarily desirable where predicted results are concerned.

Writing About Range, Variance, and Standard Deviation

Within APA style, there are no statistical abbreviations for range or variance. If either term is used within text or a table, it must be written out. In practice, reporting ranges or the variance of a measure does not occur very often. When these descriptive statistics are specifically noted, they tend to appear in the Method or Results section of an APA style paper. In the former case, the range and variance usually provide readers with contextual information about self-report measures (e.g., "The range of participant aggression scores was 50"). When these statistics are reported in a Results section, they are often used to draw attention to unusual aspects of the data (e.g., "The variances observed within in the experiment's three groups were too similar to allow for an adequate test of the hypothesis").

In contrast, the standard deviation is really the empirical coin of the realm; that is, it is the measure of dispersion most frequently reported in APA style reports. No doubt it acquired this status by serving as the best indicator of average deviation from a mean, and because, as will be shown later, it features prominently within the calculation of inferential statistics. Within tables and parenthetical comments included in text, the standard deviation is abbreviated as *SD* in APA style. Similar to the range and variance, the standard deviation, too, is apt to appear primarily in Method and Results sections.

One pronounced difference, though, is that the standard deviation is most likely to appear in consort with the mean. As noted at the outset of this chapter, this combination of descriptive statistics makes a great deal of sense—you cannot really make sense of an average without knowing the dispersion of the observations around it. When reporting a mean, it is almost obligatory to also report its standard deviation. There are really two ways to report this information. If a researcher is interested in discussing one or two observations in relative isolation from others, then these descriptive statistics are placed (usually parenthetically) into sentences appearing in the text:

Standard deviation rather than *variance* is usually reported in research summaries.

DATA BOX 4.D

Sample Size and Variability—The Hospital Problem

Here is a challenging problem to read and then think about, one calling on your new found knowledge of variability (from Tversky & Kahneman, 1974):

> A certain town is served by two hospitals. In the larger hospital about 45 babies are born each day, and in the smaller hospital about 15 babies are born each day. As you know, about 50% of all babies are boys. However, the exact percentage varies from day to day. Sometimes it may be higher than 50 percent, sometimes lower.
>
> For a period of 1 year, each hospital recorded the days on which more than 60% of the babies born were boys. Which hospital do you think recorded more such days? Check one:
>
> The larger hospital? _____
>
> The smaller hospital? _____
>
> About the same (that is, within 5% of each other) _____

What is the correct answer? Across a year, the smaller hospital is apt to have more days that diverge from the 50% male and 50% female birth norm. Why? Think about the relationship between variability and sample size: Larger samples are likely to be more representative of any given population (here, 50:50) than are smaller samples. In statistical contexts, this fact is called the **law of large numbers.** Tversky and Kahneman (1971) note that people appear to fall prey to what they dubbed (tongue in cheek) the *law of small numbers,* which renders even skeptical researchers insensitive to the statistical problems present in small samples. Indeed, smaller samples are usually *not* representative of their parent populations—they often contain extreme or outlying scores. Thus, we should expect that because fewer births occur at the small hospital, anyway, it should be the one to show the greatest divergence from the expectation of equal male and female births. Put another way, smaller samples usually show higher variability or heterogeneity than large samples.

If you missed the problem, please go back and read it again—do you see why the smaller hospital is the correct choice? Congratulations to readers who selected the right answer, but don't worry if you missed it, as psychologists, mathematicians, and even statisticians have been known to get such problems wrong. Tversky and Kahneman (1974; see also, Tversky & Kahneman, 1971) report that most people who encounter this problem are *insensitive* to the effects sample size has on outcomes; that is, they assume that each hospital should show about the same number of days diverging from the 50:50 split.

Problems like this one, as well as real-life situations where some form of sampling occurs, should demonstrate to you the powerful way that the size of a sample can sway its variability. The lesson is clear: It is always a good idea to consider the size of a sample before drawing any conclusions from it or answering any questions about it.

> On the 7-point rating scale ("extremely uninteresting" to "extremely interesting"), most members of the experimental group rated the task as being very interesting ($M = 6.25$, $SD = 1.1$). In contrast, participants in the control condition gave a mixed account of their task; some liked it, others did not, leading to a neutral evaluation ($M = 4.1$, $SD = 4.5$).

Please take note that when reporting such relationships, APA style dictates that values inside the parentheses be separated by a comma.

The second way to report means and accompanying standard deviations is, of course, as entries displayed in a table of data. Instead of reporting the central tendency and variability information in sentence form, it can be summarized in a table.

Table 4.8 Ratings of Two Task Types within an Experiment as a Function of Participant Gender

| | Task Type | |
	Experimental	Control
Males		
M	6.50	4.05
SD	1.10	3.30
Females		
M	6.00	4.15
SD	3.60	1.60

Note: Higher numbers indicate the task was rated as more interesting on a 7-point rating scale (extremely uninteresting to extremely interesting).

Table 4.8 contains the male and female participants' mean ratings of two different tasks, as well as the standard deviation within each participant group (for related suggestions about presenting information in tabular form, see chapter 3). As shown by the relatively small size of the respective standard deviations, males tended to rate the experimental task the same, while females rated the control task similarly to one another. In contrast, greater variability was found for the males' ratings of the control condition and the females' evaluation of the experimental task (see Table 4.8)

Specific mention should be made somewhere regarding the number of participants in each condition in the experiment, as well as the total participating in the research. Some writers prefer to make note such numerical information in the method section (e.g., "There were 40 participants in the study; 20 were placed in the experimental condition and 20 in the control condition") or in a *Note* appearing under a figure or table. Other writers prefer to insert specific numerical information into a table. Under each of the 4 *SD*s in Table 4.8, for example, one could add an "$n = 10$." Note that the use of n in this circumstance refers to the number of participants appearing in subgroups comprising the larger N (recall Data Box 4.A).

Remember, N = the total number of observations comprising a sample; n = the number of observations within a given subsample of N.

Project Exercise PROVING THE LEAST SQUARES PRINCIPLE FOR THE MEAN

Early on in this chapter, the mean—the arithmetic average—was identified as the single best measure of central tendency for research in the behavioral sciences. Various explanations for the ubiquity and utility of the mean were offered, but the supporting arguments were more rhetorical than quantitative. I want to change that perspective somewhat now that you have a relatively solid understanding of the relation between central tendency and variability. Several properties of the mean were discussed, but one was postponed until now: the *least squares principle* for the mean. In fact, once I introduce and define the least squares principle, I will leave it to you to prove its importance using a distribution of data.

KEY TERM The **least squares principle** refers to the fact that within a distribution, the sum of the squared deviations between the mean and individual scores will be smaller than the sum of squared deviations between a given score and any other individual scores from that distribution.

Table 4.9 | Demonstration of the Least Squares Principle

X	$(X - 1)^2$	$(X - 2)^2$	$(X - \bar{X})^2$	$(X - 6)^2$	$(X - 7)^2$
1	0				
2	1				
4	9				
6					
7					
$\Sigma X = 20$ SS =		SS =	SS =	SS =	SS =

$$\bar{X} = \frac{\Sigma X}{N} = \frac{20}{5} = 4.0$$

$\Sigma (X - 1)^2 = 71; \Sigma (X - 2)^2 = 26; \Sigma (X - \bar{X})^2 = 46; \Sigma (X - 6)^2 = 46; \Sigma (X - 7)^2 = 71$

Another way to define the mean is that it represents the *smallest average squared difference between itself and the individual observations in a distribution*—hence, the term "least squares." As we will see later, this minimal amount of squared deviation is one of the primary reasons that the mean features so large in the family of inferential statistics.

What must be shown for the present, though, is that the sum of the squares (*SS*) around the mean of a distribution must be smaller than the *SS* for all other observations (or possible observations) in a distribution. Table 4.9 presents a small distribution of scores (*X*). There is space provided for you to calculate the squares and the sum of the squared deviations from the distribution's mean as well as the other scores in the distribution. Your object here is to demonstrate the least squares principle, that $\Sigma (X - X)^2$ is less than the difference between *X* and any of the other scores in the distribution. To help you get started, a few entries already appear in the column under $(X - 1)^2$. Be sure to record the *SS* under each of the columns so that you show the one corresponding to the mean is indeed less than the others.

This *project exercise* is by no means difficult or time consuming, but it will give you first hand experience with one of the main reasons that the mean is the statistic of choice for the majority of analyses performed in inferential statistics. The calculated answers appear upside down under Table 4.9, but please do not look at them until you have tried to prove the least squares principle on your own.

LOOKING FORWARD ⟳ THEN BACK

entral tendency and variability are two powerful, as well as intertwined, statistical concepts. An average is not meaningful unless you know how the data disperse themselves around it, just as the spread of a distribution is not very useful unless its point of central tendency is identified. When the scale (i.e., interval, ratio, ordinal, nominal) used and the shape of a distribution are known, the decision tree opening this chapter will help you to select an appropriate measure of central tendency. Once a measure of central tendency is known, the second decision tree will guide your choice of an index of variability (an important choice, especially when it and the central tendency are presented in the context of a research summary).

The third and final decision tree serves as a reminder regarding the difference between—and appropriate use of—the sample statistics $(\overline{X}, s^2, s)$ and population parameters (μ, σ^2, σ). Whether to report sample statistics or to estimate population parameters (biased or unbiased) depends on the source of the data (sample, population) and whether the research goal is description or statistical inference. In later chapters, too, the role and use of unbiased estimators will become more important. At present, however, consider how this decision tree, as well as the two noted immediately above, can be used to characterize typical responses and the relative level agreement with them, as well as to accurately portray such information to interested others.

Summary

1. Measures of central tendency and variability comprise two classes of basic, descriptive statistics. The two topics are bound together because when behavioral scientists ask about one, they necessarily need to know about the other.

2. A measure of central tendency is used in order to identify one numerical value that is the most representative one within a distribution. A given measure of central tendency is the best single indicator of what a sample or population is like.

3. The word "average" originally was reserved for describing some numerical value that was the most typical or representative one in a data set. Unfortunately, the word average has developed other connotations, some pejorative. As a result, it is often a good idea for researchers and students to make clear whether they are interpreting the word in a statistical or a cultural sense.

4. The mean, the arithmetic average, is the most useful measure of central tendency. Much of the literature in the behavioral sciences, especially psychology, is based on the relationship among mean observations in experiments. The mean is symbolized $\overline{X}$ in statistical formulas and M in text written in APA style.

5. The formula for calculating the sample mean is similar to that used to determine the population mean—one relies on symbols denoting sample statistics (i.e., $\overline{X}$), the other population parameters (i.e., μ).

6. Although the mean is very useful, extreme or outlying scores in a distribution can unduly influence its value. To combat this sensitivity, the median, another index of central tendency is sometimes reported in place of the mean.

7. The median (abbreviated in APA style as *mdn*) is the number or score in a distribution that precisely divides into two equal halves. Fifty percent of the scores fall above the median in a distribution, and 50% fall below it. It is not sensitive to extreme scores, so its value tends not to shift dramatically when scores (including outliers) are added to or subtracted from the distribution.

8. The mode is the most frequently occurring value in a distribution and, as such, is not calculated. Typically, the mode is based on a nominal scale. As it highlights frequency exclusively, use of the mode is rather limited.

9. In normal, that is, symmetric distributions, the mean, median, and mode will share the same value. In positively skewed distributions, the mean will be higher than the median and mode, respectively. The median and mode—in that order—will fall higher than the mean in negatively skewed distributions.

10. Measures of central tendency should be written about in clear, descriptive terms. Readers should get a real sense of what the mean, median, or modal behavior was like.

11. Measures of dispersion or variability account for the ways data in samples or populations deviate from the relevant measure(s) of central tendency. When the spread of scores around a mean is small, for example, variability is low. Variability is high when scores around the mean are far apart from one another.

12. The range is the simplest index of variability, and it is based on the difference between the highest and lowest scores in a distribution. Similar to the mean, however, the range's value can be inflated by extreme scores.

13. When a distribution is not normal, the interquartile range or the semi-interquartile range (SIQR) can be employed as measures of dispersion. The latter measure overcomes the instability of the range by numerically indexing half of the distance between a distribution's first and third quartiles. A larger SIQR value implies a greater spread of scores, just as a smaller value indicates lower variability.

14. The most flexible measures of variability are the variance and the standard deviation. The variance is the average of the squared deviations from a distribution's mean. Taking the square root of the variance yields the standard deviation, or the average deviation between an observed score and the mean of a distribution.

15. Although they contain different symbols, the formulas used to describe the variance and standard deviation of a sample or population are mathematically equivalent. When sample data is used to infer the characteristics of a population, however, formulas for making unbiased estimates of the population parameters are used. $N - 1$ serves as the denominator in the variance and standard deviation formulas for unbiased estimates, as N routinely underestimates population values.

16. Homogeneous distributions contain a preponderance of similar values, generally pointing to response unanimity and low dispersion. When values are spread far apart and tend to be dissimilar in value, such high variability distributions are labeled heterogeneous.

17. Within behavioral science research, variability can be influenced by sample size, how participants were selected, participant characteristics, the clarity of the independent variable(s), the sensitivity of dependent measure(s), and the passage of time between the manipulation and measurement of variables.

18. Measures of variability tend to be reported in the Method and Results sections of APA style articles and, inevitably, they accompany measures of central tendency. If a study's variability is not summarized in the text, then it is noted within a table.

19. The fact that the sum of the squared deviations between a distribution's mean and its individual scores is smaller than the sum of squared deviations between the individual scores themselves is called the least squares principle for the mean.

Key Terms

Average *(p.135)*
Biased estimate *(p.163)*
Central tendency *(p.134)*
Heterogeneous *(p.159)*
Heterogeneity *(p.159)*
Homogeneous *(p.159)*
Homogeneity *(p.159)*
Interquartile range *(p.153)*

Law of large numbers *(p.169)*
Least squares principle *(p.170)*
Mean *(p.136)*
Median *(p.144)*
Mode *(p.146)*
Outlier *(p.141)*
Range *(p.153)*
Semi-interquartile range *(p.154)*

Standard deviation *(p.158)*
Sum of squares (*SS*) *(p.155)*
Unbiased estimate *(p.163)*
Variability *(p.151)*
Variance *(p.155)*
Weighted mean *(p.142)*

Chapter Problems

1. Define the term "central tendency." Explain the concept's utility for statistics and data analysis, as well as research in the behavioral sciences.

2. Calculate the mean, the median, and the mode of each group of scores:
   a. 10, 16, 8, 9, 20, 15, 21, 6, 13, 18, 12, 10
   b. 3, 1, 3, 4, 7, 2, 1, 7, 8, 2, 3, 1, 5, 7, 3, 7, 6, 2, 3
   c. 20, 34, 21, 45, 32, 33, 16, 84
   d. 13, 13, 13, 11, 10, 9, 14, 16, 15, 15, 12, 11

3. Review your answers to problem 2. Would reporting the mean for any of the four distributions pose a problem for an investigator? Why?

4. Select one of the distributions from problem 2 and use it to demonstrate the least squares principle. (*Hint:* Repeat the procedure used for the *Project Exercise* presented at the end of the chapter.)

5. You have a distribution of scores and most of them are relatively close in value to one another. There is, however, an outlying score that is very far from main cluster of scores. What measure of central tendency should you report? Why?

6. Why is the mean sensitive to extreme scores? How can researchers reduce the interpretive problem posed by outlying scores? In such situations, is one of the other measures of central tendency a better choice than the mean? Why?

7. An investigator wants to report the average score on a standardized personality measure that was administered to three

different groups of participants. Calculate the mean based on these data: The 32 members of group A had a mean of 27.5; the 48 members of group B had a mean of 23.0; and the 12 members of group C had a mean of 25 on the personality measure.

8. When should a researcher use the weighted means approach to analyze data? Why was the weighted means approach the appropriate one for analyzing the data presented in problem 7? Would it make any difference if an investigator simply calculated the mean of the three means in problem 7—in other words, what makes the weighted average a better statistics for this example?

9. Most people who need welfare tend to receive this form of public assistance for a very short time (6 months or less), and the number of people who review welfare for the long term is relatively small. If you were a government demographer who was researching welfare, which measure(s) of central tendency—the mean, the median, or the mode— would probably be the best one to use for your analyses. Why?

10. Examine the following information and then indicate whether these hypothetical distributions are apt to be normal, or positively or negatively skewed:
    a. $\overline{X} = 34$, *mdn* = 36, mode = 39
    b. $\overline{X} = 12$, *mdn* = 12, mode = 12
    c. $\overline{X} = 5$, *mdn* = 3, mode = 2

11. Create examples of data where the appropriate measure of central tendency is:
    a. The mean
    b. The median
    c. The mode
12. How would you characterize the following hypothetical distribution? $\overline{X} = 53$, median $= 57$, mode $= 63$
13. Which measure of central tendency is most affected by skew in a distribution? Which one is least affected? Why?
14. Compute the mean of the following table of data:

X	f
7	10
5	8
3	11
2	9
1	7

15. Calculate the range for distributions a to d in problem 2.
16. Calculate the semi-interquartile range for distributions a to d in problem 2.
17. Calculate the sum of the squares (SS) for the following distribution:

X
11
8
7
6
5
4
2

18. Assume the distribution shown in problem 17 is sample data and you want to describe it. Calculate the mean, range, sample variance, and standard deviation.
19. Assume the distribution shown in problem 17 represents a population. Calculate μ, σ^2, and σ.
20. Imagine that you want to use the sample data shown in problem 17 to estimate the parameters of the population from which it was drawn. Calculate the unbiased estimates of the population's variance and standard deviation.
21. Explain the difference between so-called "biased" and "unbiased" estimates of population parameters. Which type of estimate is used in what sort of situation?
22. Review the SS and N information provided below, then calculate the biased and unbiased estimates of the variance and standard deviation for each one.
    a. $SS = 127, N = 30$
    b. $SS = 78, N = 40$
    c. $SS = 100, N = 15$
    d. $SS = 45, N = 10$

23. Calculate the biased and unbiased estimates of the variance and standard deviation for distributions a to d in problem 2.
24. Although the two measures of dispersion are intimately related, why is the standard deviation preferred over the variance? Explain the concept underlying the standard deviation as a measure of variability.
25. Explain the role variability plays in both homogeneous and heterogeneous distributions.
26. What measure of dispersion is usually reported with the median? Why?
27. Review the four distributions presented in problem 2 and then answer this question for each one: Between what two scores do half of a distribution's observations fall? (*Hint:* Use the semi-interquartile ranges calculated in problem 16.)
28. You are a psychologist who is about to conduct a social psychology experiment on interpersonal attraction. Name three factors that can affect variability in a research project.
29. What is the relationship between sample size and variability? Is it better to have data from a larger or a smaller sample? Why?
30. Consider these two samples:
    Sample X: 3, 4, 6, 8, 9, 12, 14, 18
    Sample Y: 2, 8, 17, 25, 26, 27, 35, 36
    a. Intuitively, which sample do you think has greater variability? Why?
    b. Calculate the mean and standard deviation for each sample.
    c. Does either mean convey a better sense of the data it is based on? What does each standard deviation convey about the data?
31. Assume that you want to use samples X and Y in problem 30 to infer the characteristics of their respective populations of origin. Calculate the unbiased estimates of the variance and standard deviation for each one.
32. Examine the following data:
    11, 14, 15, 15, 12, 10, 8, 11, 12, 14, 47, 18, 20, 25, 27, 20, 42,
    a. Calculate the mean, variance, and standard deviation.
    b. Calculate the median and semi-interquartile range.
    c. Does either combination of central tendency and variability provide a better sense of the data? Explain your answer.
33. Use the decision tree(s) at the start of this chapter to answer the following:
    a. The data are based on an interval scale, and the distribution is skewed. Which measure of central tendency should be used?
    b. The data are based on an ordinal scale. Which measure of central tendency should be used?
    c. The data are based on a nominal scale. Which measure of central tendency should be used?
    d. The data are based on a ratio scale, and the distribution is normal. Which measure of central tendency should be used?
34. Use the decision tree(s) at the start of this chapter to answer the following:

a. A median is being reported. Which measure of variability should be used?

b. A mode is being reported, but it is *not* based on a nominal scale. Which measure of variability should be used?

c. A mean is being reported. Which measure of variability should be used?

35. Use the decision tree(s) at the start of this chapter to answer the following:

a. A researcher plans to estimate the characteristics of a population. Should statistics or parameters be calculated? Why?

b. A researcher plans to describe the characteristics of a sample. Should statistics or parameters be calculated? Why?

c. A researcher plans to describe the characteristics of an entire population. Should statistics or parameters be calculated? Why?

Describing the Placement of Observations

1.
Do you want to know an observation's location relative to the *mean*?

If *yes*, then convert the raw score to a *z* score.

If *no*, then go to step 2.

2.
Do you want to know the score's standing relative to other *scores*?

If *yes*, then convert the raw score to *z* score and determine its *percentile rank*.

If *no*, then go to step 3.

3.
Do you want to summarize the entire *distribution of scores*?

If *yes*, then select measures of *central tendency* and *variability* (see chapter 4)

If *no*, then review your goals and go back to step 1.

Converting a Raw Score to a *z* Score

1.
Is the raw score from a *population*?

If *yes*, then go to step 3.

If *no*, then go to step 2.

2.
Is the raw score from a *sample*?

If *yes*, then go to step 4.

If *no*, then go to step 7.

3.
Do you know the μ and the σ of the *population*?

If *yes*, then go to step 5.

If *no*, determine these population parameters and then to go to step 5.

4.
Do you know the $\bar{X}$ and the *s* of the *sample*?

If *yes*, then go to step 6.

If *no*, then determine these *sample statistics* and then go to step 6.

5.
Enter the appropriate numbers into the following formula and then report the *z* score's location relative to the population μ: $z = (X - \mu)/\sigma$

6.
Enter the appropriate numbers into the following formula and then report the *z* score's location relative to the sample $\bar{X}$: $z = (X - \bar{X})/s$

7.
A *z* score cannot be calculated unless information about the raw score's parent distribution is available.

Determining the Percentile Rank of a *z* Score

1.
Is the *z* score *above* the mean of 0.0?

If *yes*, then go to step 3.

If *no*, then go to step 2.

2.
Is the *z* score *below* the mean of 0.0?

If *yes*, then go to step 4.

If *no*, then go to step 5.

3.
Locate the *z* score in column 4 of Table B.2 in Appendix B, then:

a. Find the area between the mean and *z* by reading across to column B;

b. Convert the column B proportion to a percentage by multiplying it by 100;

c. Add the percentage to 50%— the resulting (total) percentage is the *percentile rank* of the *z* score.

4.
Locate the *z* score in column A of Table B.2 in Appendix B, then:

a. Find the area below the *z* by reading across to column C.

b. Convert the column C proportion to a percentage by multiplying it by 100.

c. The resulting percentage is the *percentile rank* of the *z* score.

5.
Is the *z* score equal to 0.0?

a. If *yes*, then the *percentile rank* of the mean is 50%.

b. If *no*, you have made an error; go back to step 1.

STANDARD SCORES
AND THE NORMAL
DISTRIBUTION

ne of the great lessons taught by research methods, statistics, and life is the importance of asking a particular question: Compared to what? The methodology used by behavioral scientists reminds them to constantly compare the behavior of one group with that of another, usually a control group. Comparing what research participants do within the various conditions of an experiment is reinforced when the data are analyzed. As we learned in chapter 4, most statistics are meaningless unless they compare the measures of central tendency and dispersion observed in one group with those drawn from others. We will broaden our conceptual understanding of the process of drawing meaning from descriptive statistics by starting to compare them in this chapter. Actual, inferential statistics will be presented later in the book, but their underlying foundations begin in earnest here.

But wait a moment, what about life—how does life teach us to ask about or to make various comparisons? The act of comparing ourselves to others is ubiquitous and ongoing in the social world. In the language of social psychology, for example, the act of evaluating our own opinions and abilities against those of other people is called social comparison (Festinger, 1954). We do it all the time, no doubt because other people—their acts, abilities, feelings—are such a good source of information for us. In fact, we cannot seem to help ourselves, as we almost effortlessly, seemingly automatically, look to others for information about what we should do or how we should feel in a particular situation.

There is no more obvious realm for comparing ourselves to others than the classroom. Take a moment and think about how often you spend time comparing your academic performance to that of others, whether real (e.g., roommate, friends, family, classmates) or imagined (e.g., the "perfect" student, the "struggling" peer). There is a good chance that your social comparing in the educational realm has been a minor preoccupation since middle or high school, if not earlier (in my experience, even the most laid back college student has a competitive streak, one prompted by comparing the self to others).

Here is a past example of your drive to compare, one that may still be a source of mild pride or subtle discomfort for your conscious self: What were your scores on the Scholastic Aptitude Test (SAT)? Way back when you received two main scores, one for verbal ability and one for math. Despite the fact that the College Board and the Educational Testing Service cautioned against adding these subtest scores together, your primary concern was presumably whether their combination put you in the "admit range" of the college or university of your choice. After that, you probably shared (and compared!) your scores—and the hopes and dreams you had for those scores—with friends and peers who had similar plans for their futures.

Back in chapter 3, we established that you were probably unaware that the percentile rank information accompanying your SAT scores provided a relative sense of how your scores compared to those of other people who took the test at the same time you did. If your verbal score was at the 70th percentile, for instance, then you performed better than or equal to 70% of predominantly high-school-aged peers who took the test. But there was also some other information that you probably did not know or really attend to—that the test was standardized so that individuals evaluating performance on the SAT would have a sense of where a given verbal or math score fell along the distribution of possible scores. In other words, people evaluating your scores were able to ask—and to answer—compared to what?

The SAT is a single but important component of student applications to college, one that has been used for admissions purposes for over 70 years, and not without its share of controversy (Schwartz, 1999; for a related discussion, see Bowen & Bok, 1998). The verbal and mathematical subtests each can have scores ranging between 200 and 800 or, if you prefer, combined scores ranging from 400 to 1,600 (but see Data Box 5.B and the end-of-chapter *Project Exercise*). The mean of each subtest was set at 500: scores falling above this point were deemed above average and scores falling below were said to be below average. Different educational institutions determine different admissions standards for acceptable test scores (i.e., how many students within a given range of scores would be considered for admission at the college or university).

Your understanding of central tendency (mean scores on the SAT), dispersion (range of possible values on the two subtests or the combined score), and percentile rank (relative standing of a given score within the distribution of SAT scores) should—albeit with some hindsight—render your own SAT scores a bit more meaningful. What remains to be explained, however, is how scores on the SAT or any other standardized test, psychological inventory, or personality measure can be compared to past, present, and yes, even *future* test takers. How are such comparisons, really extrapolations, possible? We will touch on these and related issues throughout the chapter.

To do so, we will apply knowledge acquired in the first four chapters of the book to examine what are called standard or *z* scores and their relation to the normal distribution. Both *z* scores and the normal distribution will provide us with a meaningful context for understanding how a given score or statistic can be interpreted in light of the distribution it was drawn from, an excellent preparation for the inferential statistics to come. To begin, however, we must discuss the matter of standardizing measures.

▽

When examining actual behavior or descriptive statistics referring to it, be a critical observer by asking, "Compared to what?"

DATA BOX 5.A

Social Comparison Among Behavioral and Natural Scientists: How Many Peers Review Research Before Publication?

A hallmark of the scholarship and publication in the behavioral and natural sciences is peer review. Manuscripts—primarily journal articles but some books, as well—are anonymously reviewed by peers before they are deemed worthy of publication. Many authors routinely ask peers who work in the subfield of their discipline to read and comment on their work before it is submitted to a journal editor or a publisher. Suls and Fletcher (1983) wondered to what extent researchers from physics, chemistry, psychology, and sociology were apt to consult with colleagues in advance of submitting work for publication.

Following the work of philosopher of science Thoman Kuhn (1970), Suls and Fletcher (1983) argued that behavioral scientists would be more likely to seek colleagues' counsel about the contents of their research than would natural scientists. Kuhn persuasively suggested that the natural sciences are "mature" disciplines—they have agreed on theories, research methodologies and codified knowledge—relative to the behavioral sciences, which still seek intellectual unity. As a result, behavioral scientists deal with a higher degree of uncertainty in their work than do natural scientists and such uncertainty promotes a need to communicate and validate one's views with those of others. Suls and Fletcher posited that this difference would manifest itself rather obviously in publications—behavioral scientists would exhibit greater social comparison by acknowledging or thanking a higher average number of peers in published articles than would natural scientists.

Using an archival procedure—that is, examining, coding, and analyzing preexisting records—Suls and Fletcher (1983) counted the number of colleagues cited in footnotes, author notes, or other acknowledgment sections of published physics ($n = 220$), chemistry ($n = 209$), psychology ($n = 115$), and sociology ($n = 89$) articles (more studies from the former two disciplines were included because many more articles are published in the natural than behavioral sciences). The results indicated that natural scientists tended to cite the same number of peers, which, as predicted, fell below the number cited by either the psychologists or the sociologists. In turn, sociologists tended to thank more peers than the psychologists (see the table shown below). Further, natural science articles tended to have more authors relative to those published in the behavioral sciences, a fact that emphasizes both the collaborative nature and shared perspective of physics and chemistry (see the table shown below).

What can we conclude from these data? Behavioral scientists are more motivated to compare their scholarship with their colleagues prior to the usual round of peer review, and the certainty of knowledge in one's discipline plays a part in the process. Natural scientists appear to be more certain of the knowledge promulgated by their fields, and psychologists seem somewhat more certain of disciplinary conclusions than their colleagues in sociology. Following Suls and Fletcher (1983), a good question to ask is whether this higher level of consultation among behavioral scientists will lead to less uncertainty and, in the long run, disciplinary maturity?

Mean Number of Acknowledgements and Authors by Scientific Discipline

Variable	Physics	Chemistry	Psychology	Sociology
N acknowledged[a]	0.55	.52	1.24	2.07
N of authors[b]	3.16	2.79	1.98	1.62

Note: [a]Higher numbers reflect more peers acknowledged per article; [b]higher numbers indicate more authors per article.

Source: Adapted from Suls & Fletcher (1983).

DATA BOX 5.B

Explaining the Decline in SAT Scores: Lay Versus Statistical Accounts

Pundits have noticed a steady but modest decline in the SAT verbal and math scores for years, puzzling over the meaning and significance of the changes in these averages. Are students becoming dumb or dumber? Or, has the SAT been "dumbed down"? If these two possibilities are both false, how else can the noted decline in SAT scores be explained? To answer this question, we need to examine the lay or nonstatistical explanation for the decline, as well as a more data-driven, statistical account for the change in scores.

Lay explanations for the decline in SAT scores focus on social themes that can quickly become politicized. One popular explanation is that today's students are less intellectual or motivated than the students of past generations, having been raised on television and rock videos rather than books and newspapers. A companion theme of this "anti-intellectual" youth argument is that our public schools, teachers as well as administrators, are doing a worse job at educating students than they did 20 or 30 years ago (i.e., "in the good old days"). This latter argument tends to appear in the context of test scores or whenever school taxes are levied or increases are contemplated. You have probably seen national and local politicians of various stripes make political hay with these sorts of arguments.

Stop and think for a moment: Given the educational and technological booms the United States has enjoyed for the past few decades, is it really possible that students are becoming, as it were, "dumber"? What else might be going on to make a decline in SAT scores be more apparent than real? Well, consider the fact that in 1941, 10,000 predominantly white males from the Northeastern United States took the test—recently, more than 1 million— indeed, closer to 2 million—men and women take the SAT in a given year. These men and women hail from diverse ethic, racial, and social backgrounds as well as educational experiences (College Board, 1995).

Can you guess what a statistician might say about the SAT data and the purported decline in scores? Consider what you know about sample size and populations. First, the relative size and composition of the yearly population of college bound students has grown dramatically in size. This fact might bring to mind the law of large numbers introduced in chapter 4—the apparent decline in scores may be a false one because the performance of (recent) larger samples of students taking the SAT may be more representative of the population's parameters. In other words, the "decline" in average scores is really a better reflection of the μ of the distribution of possible SAT scores.

Second, and in a related way, the population of students now taking the test is diverse—more heterogeneous—than the homogeneous student samples from decades past. More students, different subpopulations of students, taking the test should result in some shift in the test scores—the one that has occurred just happens to be in a downward direction, which may more appropriately capture or represent the population parameters of the test. The College Board and the Educational Testing Service have actually addressed this artificial decline by performing what is called a "recentering" of the scores, a simple transformation that returns the verbal and math subscale means back to 500 each. We will examine this transformation procedure in more detail in the *Project Exercise* at the end of this chapter.

Score realignments aside, I hope that the lesson here is clear. You should always be suspicious of claims that skills are changing—for better or worse—when at the same time the population based on which those skills are assessed is also changing. Remember the lessons taught by larger samples, as well as the theme of this chapter—compared to what?

Why Standardize Measures?

The logic behind standardizing measures is really quite simple. By the term "standardize," we refer to a process whereby a given object or measure can be interpreted or used in a consistent way across time, setting, and circumstance. Standardization enables us to understand and compare similar objects or measures on the same continuum, rendering them familiar and easy to understand. When heating the oven to 350 degrees in preparation for baking a cake, for example, you do not have to worry that the oven's heat settings somehow differ from the recipe's author (that is, unless your oven is on the fritz or you live at a high altitude). Similarly, if your shoe size is 8 and your shirt size is medium, you can walk into virtually any clothing store and find shoes and shirts that fit. Our monetary system, too, is a form of standardization—a dollar in rural Nebraska is equivalent in value to one in midtown Manhattan, despite the fact it might stretch a bit farther in the former than the latter setting. More to the point, perhaps, two disparate items can be equivalent in value—say, a book and a hair dryer—because they have been standardized on the dimension of price. Oven temperature, shoe and clothing sizes, and money, then, are all standardized.

In the same way, behavioral scientists often create standardized measures that produce scores that mimic the universality of heat settings or shoe sizes. Beyond the now familiar SAT example, the other common instrument to cite in this vein is the intelligence or IQ (for "intelligence quotient") test. Like the SAT, most IQ tests are composed of more than one subtest, the contents of which sometimes vary. Some entail mathematical or verbal components, but others tap into memory, the ability to assemble or to deconstruct objects, general comprehension, and gross and fine motor skills among numerous other possibilities.

Most IQ tests yield a single score—a standard score—said to reflect the performance of an individual. In fact, the standard IQ scores form a distribution possessing a population mean (μ) of 100 and a population standard deviation (σ) of 15. Thus, an individual with a measured IQ of 110 is said to score in the above average range or in the first standard deviation around the mean (i.e., $100 + 15 = 115$, the boundary of the first standard deviation above the mean; see Figure 5.1). Someone scoring an 84 would be below average, falling just inside the second standard deviation below the mean. The first standard deviation below the mean falls at a score of 85 (i.e., $100 - 15$), while the second falls between scores of 85 and 70 (i.e., $85 - 15 = 70$). As scores fall away from the mean in either

▽

Standardization involves consistent forms of measurement and interpretation, an attempt to consider the relative position of objects on a single dimension.

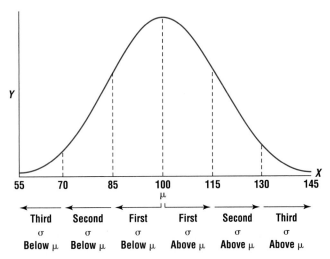

Figure 5.1 Hypothetical Distribution of Scores on an IQ Test

direction—that is, in the so-called "tails" of the distribution—they occur less frequently as compared to those scores that cluster close to the mean (note that in Figure 5.1, the median and the mode would share the population mean's value; see chapter 4). Thus, for example, a person who scores a 142 on an IQ test is certainly not unheard of, but by falling way in the distribution's upper tail, neither is she commonplace.

Various and sundry IQ tests and the SAT are by no means the only standardized tests you may know of or encounter. Other common standardized tests include the Law School Admissions Test (LSAT), the Graduate Record Exam (GRE), the Graduate Management Admissions Test (GMAT), and the Medical College Admissions Test (MCAT). There are also a host of psychological tests and inventories with unfamiliar names or acronyms that also yield standard scores.

Standardization of IQ scores or, for that matter, any measure, enables researchers to precisely locate where a particular score falls in a distribution and to describe how it compares to other scores in the distribution. This achievement involves converting a raw *score* into a *standard score.*

KEY TERM   A **raw score** is any score or datum that has *not* been analyzed or otherwise transformed by a statistical procedure.

A raw score, then, is any basic score, rating, or measurement in its pure form.

KEY TERM   A **standard score** is derived from a raw score. *Standard scores* report the relative placement of individual scores in a distribution and are useful for various inferential statistical procedures.

Raw scores are turned into standard scores so that they can be used for comparison purposes (e.g., Is one score closer to the mean than another?) or to make inferences (e.g., How likely is it that a given score is from one rather than another population?). When raw scores are converted into standard scores, their apparent value will change but *no* information is lost; rather, the conversion renders the score easier to work with and to compare with other scores along a distribution.

In order for standard scores to be truly useful, however, the mean of the relevant distribution must also be taken into account. Does a given score fall above, at, or below the mean of its distribution? The mean continues to serve as the main reference point, the anchor, if you will, of any distribution. Any mean, of course, provides limited information unless it is accompanied by its standard deviation. We rely on the standard deviation to inform us whether a given score is similar to or divergent from the mean, as well as other scores in the distribution. For example, does a particular score fall into the first or the second standard deviation above or below a mean? To begin to answer these questions more concretely, we turn to the *z* score.

Converting raw scores to standard scores promotes comparison and inference.

The *z* Score: A Conceptual Introduction

When percentile rank was presented in chapter 3, we discussed the utility of knowing what percentage of scores fell at or below a given point, a score, within a distribution. The *z* score, too, provides placement information about the location of a score within a distribution but, unlike percentile rank, it relies on the mean and the standard deviation. Specifically, the *z* score provides information about the relative position between some observed score and the mean, and it is reported in terms of relative deviation (i.e., the mean deviation is reported in standard deviation units, a topic that was introduced in chapter 4).

Let's begin with a straightforward example. Imagine that you have a score of 55 drawn from a distribution with a mean of 50. We know that the absolute difference between these numbers is 5 (i.e., $55 - 50 = 5$), that the observed score is greater than the known mean—but how much greater? In other words, we want to know the *relative*

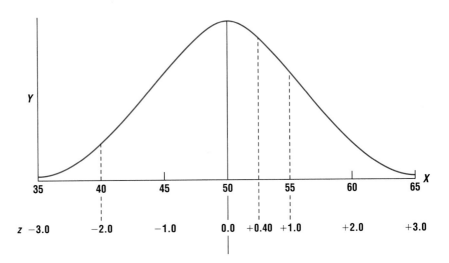

Figure 5.2 Distribution of Raw Scores and Corresponding z Scores Where $\mu = 50$ and $\sigma = 5$

difference between the mean and the observed score. Imagine, then, that we also know the standard deviation, which is equal to 5. If we divide the absolute difference between the mean and the observed score (i.e., 5) by the standard deviation of 5, we will know the relative deviation of the observed score from the mean. That is, $5/5 = +1.0$, indicating that a score of 55 lies 1.0 standard deviation above the mean of 50 (see Figure 5.2). In fact, anytime a relative deviation is positive in value, we know that the score falls above the mean—and we know where it falls in terms of standard deviation units.

What if the observed score were equal to 40? This time, although we know the absolute difference between the mean and the observed score is 10, we will have a negative number (i.e., $40 - 50 = -10.0$). If we divide -10.0 by the standard deviation of 5, we find that a score of 40 lies 2.0 standard deviations below the mean (i.e., $-10.0/5 = -2.0$; see Figure 5.2). Anytime a relative deviation is negative, then, we know how many standard deviation units below the mean it is located.

What have we accomplished? We have just calculated two *z scores,* common types of standard scores derived from raw scores.

KEY TERM   A descriptive statistic, the **z score** indicates the distance between some observed score (X) and the mean of a distribution in standard deviation units.

The z score tells us one very important thing: *How many standard deviations away from the mean is a given score?* As we just learned in the above examples, a score of 55 was 1.0 standard deviation above the mean, while a score of 40 happened to be 2.0 standard deviations below the mean. Put another way, we know that the first score was relatively closer to the mean than the second score (see Figure 5.2). In fact, a defining characteristic of any z distribution is that the width of the standard deviation around the mean will *always* be equal to 1.0.

▽

The standard deviation of a z

distribution is *always* 1.0.

Please note that a z score need not fall precisely on a standard deviation as the two scores in this example did. I used numbers that fell precisely on the standard deviations for convenience. If we have an observed score of 52, for example, then the corresponding z score would be equal to $+0.40$ (i.e., $52 - 50/5 = 2/5 = +0.40$), which falls less than halfway across the first standard deviation above the mean (see Figure 5.2). That is, $+0.40$ is less than $+1.0$, which tells us that a score of 52 is very close to the mean of 50, just as $+0.40$ is very close to the z distribution's mean of 0.

The mean of the *z* distribution is always equal to 0.0.

That's right—the mean of any distribution of *z* scores is always equal to 0. Students can initially be put off by the mean of the *z* distribution always being equal to 0 because they assume that means it is equal to "nothing." Don't be put off in this way: Think of a *z* score, any *z* score, as a guidepost that tells you an observed (raw) score's relative location within a distribution of scores. When you calculate a *z* of 0, it simply means that an observed score is equal to the mean, just as negative *z*s fall below the mean and positive *z*s place themselves above it.

Key Points Regarding *z* Scores.   Let's review these three important characteristics of *z* scores:

1. The mean of any *z* distribution is always 0.
2. The standard deviation of the any *z* distribution is always 1.0.
3. When the value of a *z* score is positive (+), then the score falls above the mean of 0; when it is negative (−), it falls below it. The only time a *z* score lacks a sign is when it is equal to 0 (i.e., the raw score is equivalent to the original mean of the distribution).

The third point merits more emphasis and explanation. When we use the + and − signs, we again use them as guideposts for the relative placement of a score above or below the mean. We do not treat these signs as being indicative of value per se. Although it is true that a *z* of +1.50 is greater than a *z* of −1.2, it is appropriate to think of the former as being higher in value or magnitude than the latter by virtue of its location relative to the mean.

But wait, there is one more point to add to this list:

4. The distribution of *z* scores will always retain the shape of the distribution of the original raw scores.

Standardization ≠ normalization; conversion to *z* scores does not alter the shape of a distribution in any way.

Students—and many faculty members, actually—often forget this last one because they misunderstand the definition of standard scores. Specifically, they may erroneously believe that the conversion to *z* scores somehow "sanitizes" or "normalizes" the data, taking an any-old-shaped distribution of raw scores and turning it into that paragon of statistical virtue, a normal distribution (see below). Not so. The conversion to relative deviation provides a much better indication of where scores lie relative to one another, but it does *not* change the shape of the distribution in any way—any skew or kurtosis present, as well as any outlying scores, remains intact.

A Brief Digression on Drawing *z* Distributions for Plotting Scores.   Despite the likelihood of an irregular shaped distribution, I have always found it useful to draw a normal shaped distribution when I work with *z* scores. Figure 5.2 is a formal example of what I have in mind, as it enables you to visualize the placement of one score relative to another, and to identify their relation to the mean of 0 and the 1-unit standard deviations surrounding it. Again, few distributions of scores you encounter will actually be normal, but jotting down a bell-shaped curve is a heuristic convenience, a short cut or rule of thumb, that makes interpreting the converted raw scores easier to conceptualize.

Your bell-shaped curve need not be elegantly drawn, perfectly symmetric, or even particularly neat to look at—but it should enable you to "see" how scores in the data relate to one another. A simple way to proceed is to sketch what I call a "volcano" shape first (see panel (a) in Figure 5.3), and then to draw a semicircle over its top (see panel (b) in Figure 5.3). Once you add this lid, you can erase the lines underneath it (see panel (c) in Figure 5.3) and draw in lines representing the mean and standard deviations (see panel (d) in Figure 5.3). It then becomes a snap to mark in the *z* score or

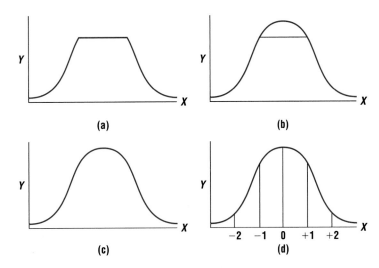

Figure 5.3 Sketching a Simple Bell-Curve to Represent a Distribution of *z* Scores

scores on the distribution for ready reference. I promise you that these quick curve drawings will come in handy in later sections of this chapter and for solving the problems at its end.

Comparing Different Measures and Distributions.   There is a conceptual as well as practical advantage associated with the conversion of raw scores to *z* scores that must be mentioned here. The use of *z* scores enables researchers to compare measures from different distributions with one another, despite the fact they have different means and standard deviations. Because any different measures—besides SAT or IQ scores, self-esteem, depression, grade point average (GPA) are obvious candidates—can be converted to *z* scores, an individual's relative placement on one measure can be compared with any other (see the *Application* discussion later in this chapter). Conceptually, then, these various measures represent variables available for comparison, and instead of only comparing one person's relative level of self-esteem with his GPA, we can perform the same comparison for many people. This advantage will become increasingly important, and we will revisit it directly in the next chapter when we discuss correlational relationships among variables in detail.

Formulas for Calculating *z* Scores

In general, we talk about *z* scores in terms of populations, but they are also frequently calculated from sample data. Here is the formula used to calculate a *z* score from sample data:

z Scores can be calculated from sample or population data.

[5.1.1]
$$z = \frac{X - \overline{X}}{s}.$$

As you can see, *X* represents the known raw score, $\overline{X}$ is the sample mean, and *s* is the sample's standard deviation. The formula for calculating a *z* score from population data is conceptually identical—only the symbols change:

[5.2.1]
$$z = \frac{X - \mu}{\sigma}.$$

Once again, *X* is the known raw score, but now μ represents the mean of the population and σ is its standard deviation.

What if you know a z score and you want to transform it back to its original raw score form? This reverse conversion is really quite simple. Besides the z score itself, you must know the value of the mean and the standard deviation of the distribution of raw scores, and then it becomes a simple matter of multiplication and addition. Here is the transformation formula back to a sample's raw score:

[5.3.1] $$X = \overline{X} + z(s).$$

As shown in [5.3.1], the original raw score can be determined by multiplying the z score times the sample standard deviation, which is then added to the sample mean. Let's use sample data from earlier in the chapter to demonstrate this reconversion. Recall that we earlier calculated that a score of 55 from a distribution with a mean of 50 and a standard deviation of 5 corresponded to a z score of 1.0. If we enter the z, the mean ($\overline{X}$), and the standard deviation (s) into [5.3.1] we can show that the raw score of X is indeed 55:

[5.3.2] $$X = 50 + 1.0(5),$$
[5.3.3] $$X = 50 + 5,$$
[5.3.4] $$X = 55.$$

The transformation formula for converting a population-based z score back to its raw form is conceptually identical but symbolically different:

[5.4.1] $$X = \mu + z(\sigma).$$

In this version of the transformation formula, the population standard deviation (σ) is multiplied by the z score, the product of which is then added to the population mean (μ).

Conceptually, of course, both the sample and population formulas achieve the same end. The distance between an observed score and the mean of its distribution is divided by the standard deviation of that mean. Before we learn more about the statistical utility of z scores, we need to review the standard normal distribution, which will help us to work with the information the scores provide.

The Standard Normal Distribution

In chapter 4, the basic shape of distributions, notably the normal distribution, was introduced. You will recall that the normal distribution is bell-shaped, featuring a preponderance of observations about its middle (the center of the bell) and gradually fewer as you move in either direction away from the center area into the tails surrounding it. One half of the normal distribution is the mirror image of the other half; that is, 50% of the available observations can be found on either side. In its idealized form, the mean, median, and mode of the normal distribution will share the same values.

Most people tend to think of the normal distribution as a two-dimensional image, as a line that is drawn left to right, but one that rises up halfway into a bell shape before it begins a symmetric decline. In fact, the normal curve can be thought of in three-dimensional terms, like a symmetric half-bubble or gradual hump rising from an otherwise flat surface. Due to convenient displays, such as blackboards and texts like this one, however, we are used to thinking of the normal curve in flat terms—when, in fact, only if we were to split a three-dimensional curve in half would it appear this way. My point is that although we cannot presently look at a three-dimensional normal distribution together, we can try to think three-dimensionally about it while learning its properties.

The normal distribution was created as an abstract ideal useful to mathematicians and statisticians. These two groups used the normal curve as a way to account for numerical relationships, notably the relative likelihood of some numerical events occurring instead of others, or probability (see chapter 8). In reality, there is not one normal distribution but rather a "family" of curves that can be defined as normal (Elifson, Runyon, & Haber, 1990). The reason so many exist is the endless potential for different combinations of population means (μ) and population standard deviations (σ). As we will see, all normal curves share some basic characteristics, but they are not "cookie-cutter" constructs; some are larger than others, flatter in shape, or have a steeper peak (recall the discussion of distribution shapes in chapter 3).

Across time, researchers realized that the normal distribution had a wide variety of applications and that it was a very effective way to describe the behavior of various naturally occurring events. Natural and behavioral scientists were quick to realize that the normal curve was useful for studying phenomena germane to their respective areas of inquiry. A wide variety of sociological, psychological, and biological variables distribute themselves normally or in an approximately normal fashion, or they lend themselves to transformation to a normal curve (e.g., Rosenthal & Rosnow, 1991). The discipline of psychology, for example, would be at a loss if the properties of the normal distribution—notably its usefulness for hypothesis testing (see chapter 9)—were not available. Of course, some everyday variables are also normally distributed. Height and weight represent everyday examples of variables that qualify in this regard.

Although we will not be using it directly, there is a formula that specifies the shape of the normal distribution. Here it is:

[5.5.1]
$$f(X) = \frac{1}{\sqrt{2\pi\sigma^2}} \, e^{-(x-\mu)^2/2\sigma^2}.$$

Take a good look at it—it won't bite you. Forgive me, but I merely want you to think about the following information pertaining to this formula and not be intimidated by it. The conceptual information the formula provides will be useful background material for the rest of this section of the chapter. For statisticians, the main advantage of having this formula is that although available data can change or vary, this formula can always be used to determine what a normal distribution looks like, no matter what the value of its mean and standard deviation. What we see in [5.5.1] is that the relative frequency or function of any score (X) is dependent upon the population mean (μ) and variance (σ^2), the constant π (which is $\cong 3.146$), and the constant e (the base of the natural logarithm, which is $\cong 2.7183$). In other words, if the relative frequencies of X were entered into the equation, we would be able to see how they must form the now familiar normal curve.

Of course, such plotting of scores is not our purpose here, because we already know—or at least assume—that the normal distribution provides us with certain statistical advantages. Chief among these advantages is the ability to partition the area under the normal curve to identify what proportion or percentage of observations must fall within given ranges.

Standard Deviation Revisited: The Area Under the Normal Curve

In some sense, normal distributions are "standardized" because particular percentages of observations occur in a predictable pattern. (For ease of comparison, we will rely on percentages, but discussing proportions under the curve is equally appropriate; recall the relation between percentages and proportions introduced in chapter 3.) When the area under the curve was described as being predictable in chapter 4, you did not know anything about z scores or greater detail about the utility of the normal distribution. We noted then that approximately 68% of the available observations fall within the first standard deviation interval above and below the mean, or 34.13% in each one. Formula [5.5.1] actually enables us to specify what percentage of observations fall within each of these standard deviation intervals occurring to the left and the right of the mean.

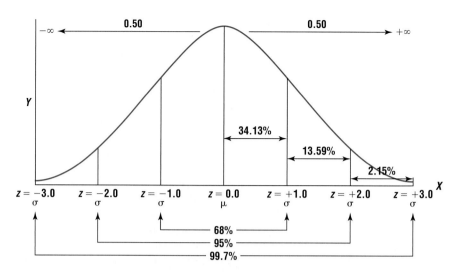

Figure 5.4 Area Between Standard Deviation Intervals Along a *z* Distribution

Our understanding of *z* scores and their fixed standard deviation interval widths of 1.0 will now pay off. Theoretically, the total area under the normal curve is equal to 100%. Figure 5.4 illustrates a standard normal distribution with *z* scores running along the *x* axis. As you can see in Figure 5.4, on either side of the mean of 0 is one standard deviation interval equal to 34.13% of the area under the normal curve (i.e., 2 × 34.14% = 68.26%, the available area under the curve). The area between the first and second standard deviation on either side of the mean is equal to 13.59% (i.e., 2 × 13.58% = 27.18% of the available area; see Figure 5.4). In the third standard deviation from the mean resides 2.15% of observations (i.e., 2 × 2.15% = 4.30% of the available area; see Figure 5.4). If you add the total area accounted for under the curve in Figure 5.4—you have accounted for 99.74% of the available observations or *z* scores.

What about this less than 1% of other (potential) observations? They appear to remain but are not accounted for under the curve—why? In practical terms, these observations fall relatively far in either tail, the resting place of true outliers. But there is a theoretical consideration regarding the normal curve that must be noted as well. The normal curve never "closes" because its two tails do not end (asymptotic to the x-axis)— that is, it is comprised of a potentially infinite number of cases (Elifson et al., 1990). As a result, notice that the sign for infinity—both positive ($+\infty$) and negative ($-\infty$)—is included in Figure 5.4. These signs serve as theoretical reminders about the nonclosing nature of the normal distribution, but they also have some practical significance. These signs reinforce the idea that researchers are actually trying to generalize findings to populations that are large and subject to change, but still measurable.

Contrary to expectation, a normal distribution never ends (theoretically) because its tails remain open.

Beyond the uniformity of observations falling in standard deviations, what else do we know about normal distributions? For most practical and theoretical purposes, the standard normal distribution is treated as having outer boundaries that end at ±3.0 standard deviations (see Figure 5.4). Normal distributions are symmetric (lack any skew) and are described as generally mesokurtic (see chapter 4). Finally, using a normal distribution, the percentile ranking of any given *z* score is easily determined.

Application: Comparing Performance on More than One Measure

It may have dawned on you that because *z* scores are standard scores, they can allow researchers to compare empirical "apples," as it were, with "oranges." That is, different measures can be compared with one another even if they have different numbers of

Table 5.1   Scores on Three Hypothetical Measures of Psychological Well-Being

Measure	Raw Score	Population Parameters	z Score
Depression	80	$\mu = 110, \sigma = 15$	−2.00
Self-esteem	90	$\mu = 75, \sigma = 8$	+1.88
Life-satisfaction	25	$\mu = 40, \sigma = 5$	−3.00

items, as well as different means and standard deviations. The ability to covert disparate measures to comparable scores is invaluable for researchers, as it frees them to consider how all kinds of variables can affect one another.

We can consider a simple example in this vein. A clinical psychologist might be interested in examining a client's scores on a few standardized measures, say, a depression inventory, a self-esteem scale, and a life satisfaction scale. Perhaps the clinician wants to confirm her assessment that the client is not depressed, but merely dissatisfied with some life circumstances involving both home and work. The client's raw scores on the standardized measures, the population mean and sample deviation for each measure, and the z scores are shown in Table 5.1.

As shown in Table 5.1, the z score for the client's depression level ($z = -2.00$) is relatively far below the mean, which indicates a low likelihood of depression (i.e., higher scores reflect a greater incidence of depression). The z score corresponding to self-esteem ($z = +1.88$), however, falls fairly high above the mean (i.e., the client has a relatively high level of self-esteem). In contrast, the z score representing life satisfaction ($z = -3.00$) is not in the desired direction—the client is clearly dissatisfied with salient aspects of his life—as it is three standard deviations below the mean. As shown by this simple example, then, scores from different scales can be compared relative to one another once they are converted to standard scores. The psychologist can now focus on helping the client to recognize which aspects of his life need to be addressed, and the comparison of some empirical "apples" and "oranges" allowed that to happen.

When converted to z scores, different, even disparate, variables can be compared to one another.

Knowledge Base

1. What are the characteristics of any distribution of z scores?
2. You have a sample with a mean of 25 and a standard deviation of 3. What are the z scores corresponding to the following raw scores?
   a. 18   b. 26   c. 25   d. 32   e. 15
3. You have a population with a μ of 65 and a σ of 6. Convert the following z scores back to their raw score equivalents.
   a. +1.2   b. −2.5   c. −1.0   d. 0   e. +2.9
4. In percentage terms, what is the total area under the normal curve? What percentage of the observations fall in the first standard deviation below the mean?

Answers

1. Any z distribution has a mean of 0 and a standard deviation of 1.0. Positive z scores are always greater than the mean, whereas negative z scores are less than the mean in value. A distribution of z scores will retain the shape of the original raw score distribution.

2. a. -2.33 b. $+0.33$ c. 0 d. $+2.33$ e. -3.33
3. a. 72.2 b. 50 c. 59 d. 65 e. 82.4
4. 100%; 34.13%

Working with *z* Scores and the Normal Distribution

In general, working with statistics entails not only performing some calculations but also learning to work with—that is, to read—statistical tables. Earlier in the book, for example, you learned to understand how to use a table of random numbers (see the *Project Exercise* in chapter 2 and Table B.1 in Appendix B). In this section of the text, you will learn to use Table B.2 from Appendix B, which contains the approximate proportions of the area under the normal curve (for convenience, proportions will be converted to percentages). Table B.2 can be used to address questions regarding the relative placement of a given *z* score in relation to the mean (i.e., the percentage of cases existing between the mean and the *z*), to specify the percent of cases falling above the *z* score, and finally, to identify the percentage of cases occurring between two *z* scores.

Learning to use Table B.2 really serves two purposes. It will address the obvious need posed by this section of the chapter—how to locate *z* scores and identify the area they delineate under the normal curve. Working with this table will also prepare you for what is to come later, a variety of other statistical tables that can be read and understood with the same ease. Remember, statistical tables exist to make data analysis easier, not to hinder you or to create undue anxiety. Whenever I begin to use any statistical table, I always remind myself what its purpose is, while at the same time I ask myself, "What am I doing now?" That is, I make sure that I know what I am reading in the table—and why—and that I am not simply going through the motions of flipping pages and locating numbers without really understanding the rationale for doing so.

To begin, please turn to Table B.2 in Appendix B. As you can see, Table B.2 has three columns—one for *z* scores (A), one indicating the area between the mean and *z* (B), and one denoting the area beyond *z* (C). The *z* scores in column A all appear to be positive—what happened to the negative scores in the distribution? Recall that the *z* distribution is symmetric; in other words, except for the plus ($+$) or minus ($-$) signs, each side of the distribution is equal to the other. In practical terms, then, when working with a negative *z* score, we need only to attach a negative sign ($-$) to an entry in column A.

The entries in columns B and C are proportions. To convert them to percentages, we simply multiply them by 100 (i.e., the decimal point is moved two places to the right). A proportion of .3389, for example, would be equal to 33.89%. When rounded, this number could be reported as 34%.

Before we review several examples incorporating *z* scores and our knowledge of the normal curve, we need to be sure of our interpretive bearings regarding Table B.2. Locate the entry for a *z* of 0.0 in column A (see the top left corner of the table's first page). As we know, a *z* of 0.0 corresponds to the mean of the distribution. What percentage of the cases should fall between the mean and itself? None, of course. This intuitive fact can be confirmed by examining the proportion shown in column B, which is .0000. By looking at column C, the cases occurring in the area *beyond* the *z* of 0.0—that is, above or below the mean—is shown to be .5000, or 50%. This percentage should make sense to you, as 50% of the cases *must* fall to the right and to the left of the mean in this symmetric distribution. If the logic of these facts does not make sense to you, please stop and reread the previous chapter sections explaining *z* scores and their relation to the normal curve.

Finding Percentile Ranks with *z* Scores

Imagine that a student earns a score of 35 on a test that is normally distributed. The μ of the test is 28 and the σ is 4. Using formula [5.2.1], the *z* score for a raw score of 35 would be:

$$[5.6.1] \qquad z = \frac{35.0 - 28.0}{4.0} = \frac{7.0}{4.0} = +1.75.$$

By locating $z = +1.75$ in column A of Table B.2 and then reading across to column B, we find that the area between the mean and *z* is .4599. Thus, 45.99%, really 46%, of the available scores lie between the students score and the mean (see Figure 5.5). Because we also know that 50% of the scores fall below the mean, we can say that 95.99% (i.e., 50% + 46.99%) of the area under the curve falls at or below the student's score of 35. In other words, by using the *z* distribution, we know the percentile rank of a score of 35 on this particular test.

If you examine the entry in column C corresponding to the *z* score of $+1.75$, you can see that 4.01% of the cases fall above it (see Figure 5.5). In other words, about 4% of the people who took the test could have scores greater than a score of 35.

What if a second student received a score of 23 on the test? Where does this score fall? Calculate a *z* score using the now familiar formula:

$$[5.7.1] \qquad z = \frac{23.0 - 28.0}{4.0} = -\frac{5.0}{4.0} = -1.25.$$

As noted earlier, negative *z* scores share the exact same proportion (and percentage) information as positive *z* scores. Turn to Table B.2 in Appendix B and locate the $z = -1.25$ entry in column A. This time, we know that our work will take place *below* the mean of 0.0 because the *z* is negative. Column B in Table B.2 indicates that the area between the mean and $z = -1.25$ is .3944 or 39.44%. This area between the mean and *z* is also highlighted in Figure 5.6. The numerical entry in column C now gives us the percentile rank of a score of 23 on the test. How so? Column C's entry—.1056 or 10.56%—represents

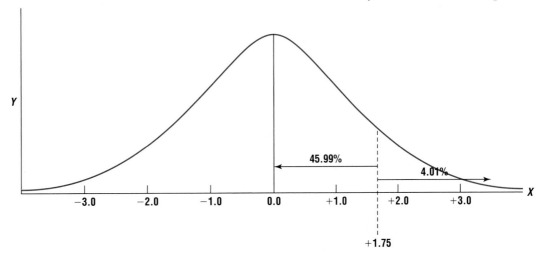

Figure 5.5 Location of $z = +1.75$ in a *z* Distribution with $\mu = 28.0$ and $\sigma = 4.0$

Note: In percentage terms, the area between the mean and the *z* score of $+1.75$ is 45.99%. The area in the curve beyond the *z* score of $+1.75$ is 4.01%.

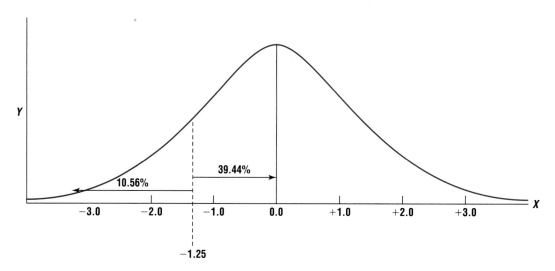

Figure 5.6   Location of $z = -1.25$ in z Distribution with $\mu = 28.0$ and $\sigma = 4.0$

Note: In percentage terms, the area between the mean and a z score of -1.25 is 39.44%. The area in the curve beyond the z score of -1.25 is 10.56%.

the available area of the curve that falls below $z = -1.25$ (see Figure 5.6). Thus, a score of 23 on the test fell at approximately the 11th percentile—11% of the scores fell at or below the score of 23.

Further Examples of Using z Scores to Identify Areas Under the Normal Curve

Besides using z scores to determine the percentile rank of raw scores, z scores can also be used to delineate the area between two raw scores. We will consider two illustrative examples, one using z scores falling on either side of the mean and one involving standard scores appearing on the same side of the mean.

Area Between z Scores on Either Side of the Mean.   An investigator wants to know what percentage of the cases on a standardized instrument fall between scores of 85 and 111. The standardized test, which measures people's knowledge of geography, has a μ of 96 and a σ of 7. The first step is to convert both test scores to zs using formula [5.2.1]. The test score of 85 is equal to:

$$[5.8.1] \qquad z = \frac{85 - 96}{7} = -\frac{11}{7} = -1.57,$$

and the score of 111 is equal to:

$$[5.9.1] \qquad z = \frac{111 - 96}{7} = \frac{15}{7} = +2.14.$$

To begin, of course, we draw a diagram of a z distribution similar to the one shown in Figure 5.7. As you well know, the z of -1.57 is just over one and one half standard deviations below the mean and the z of $+2.14$ is slightly over the boundary of the second standard deviation to the right of the mean (see Figure 5.7). How do we proceed?

Well, because we want to know the area—the percentage of the cases—falling between scores falling on either side of the mean of 0.0, intuitively, we can (1) first determine the percentage distance between each score and the mean, and then (2) add these percentages together. Using column B in Table B.2, we learn that 44.18% of the cases fall between a z of -1.57 and the mean, and that 48.38% of the cases fall between a z of

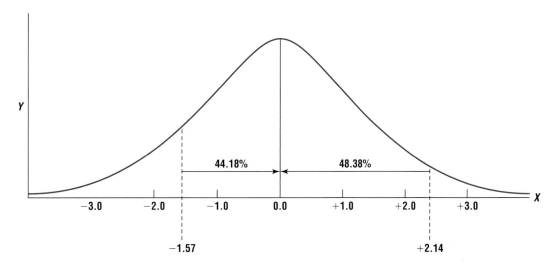

Figure 5.7 *z* Distribution Representing Geographic Knowledge Test with $\mu = 96$ and $\sigma = 7$

Note: The raw scores of 85.0 and 111.0 are shown as *z* scores of −1.57 and +2.14, respectively. The area between $z = -1.57$ and the mean is 44.18%, and between +2.14 and the mean is 48.38%. The total area between these scores is 95.52% (i.e., 44.14% + 48.38% = 95.52%). Thus, 95.52% of the area under the normal curve falls between scores of 85.0 and 111.0.

+2.14 and the mean (see Figure 5.7). To describe the total area between these two scores, then, we add 44.14% to 48.38% and learn that 92.52% of the area under curve falls between the raw scores of 85 and 111. As long as you understand the logic behind working with *z* scores and the *z* distribution, and you bother to draw a diagram similar to Figure 5.7 (for guidance, see Figure 5.3), answering the question is not at all difficult.

Area Between Two *z* Scores on the Same Side of the Distribution. Let's do a second example. This time, however, we will delineate the area between two scores that happen to fall on the same side of the mean. A teacher of gifted middle school students wants to know what percentage of IQ scores in the population fall between 132 and 138. As you may recall, standardized IQ tests usually have a μ of 100.0 and a σ of 15.0.

Right at the start, we know that these two scores are well into the right (upper) tail of the distribution. Before we begin to perform any calculations, a pressing issue of planning must be addressed: How can we determine the percentage distance between two scores that fall on the *same side of the distribution* (here, the positive side)? Previously, we have added relative distances together. Now, however, we must identify the area between the mean and where the two scores overlap one another—the remaining area under that section of the curve will represent the percentage of cases existing between the two IQ scores.

As always, begin by drawing a *z* distribution like the one shown in Figure 5.8 and then calculate the *z* scores corresponding to the two IQ scores. An IQ score of 132 is equal to a *z* of +2.13, or:

[5.10.1] $$z = \frac{132.0 - 100.0}{15} = \frac{32}{15} = +2.13.$$

The *z* score corresponding to an IQ score of 138 is:

[5.11.1] $$z = \frac{138.0 - 100.0}{15} = \frac{38}{15} = +2.53.$$

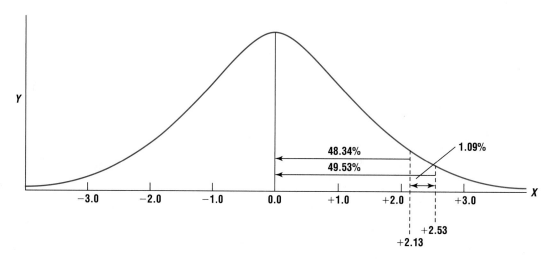

Figure 5.8   *z* Distribution Representing IQ Test with with $\mu = 100$ and $\sigma = 15$

Note: The raw scores of 132 and 138 are shown as *z* scores of +2.13 and +2.53, respectively. The area between +2.13 and the mean is 48.34%, and that between +2.53 and the mean is 49.43%. The total area between these scores is defined by subtracting the smaller area from the larger area (i.e., 49.43% − 48.34% = 1.09%). Thus, approximately 1% of the area under the curve—the possible cases—falls between scores of 132.0 and 138.0.

DATA BOX 5.C

Intelligence, Standardized IQ Scores, and the Normal Distribution

What is intelligence? How can it be measured and reduced to one score? What does the distribution of IQ scores look like?

Defining the term "intelligence" is an old problem for educators and researchers, especially psychologists. Robert J. Sternberg, a prominent researcher who studies intelligence, defines it as the ability to learn from past experiences, to understand and control one's own thinking to promote learning, and to adapt to environments containing varied cultural and social elements (Sternberg, 1999; Sternberg & Detterman, 1986). To some extent, intelligence means different things to different people who find themselves (or the people they notice or, for psychologists, formally study) in varied contexts. A doctor diagnosing a medical problem can display a different type of diagnostic intelligence than a plumber repairing a drain or a mechanic fixing a plane engine, but each one demonstrates what can be called a contextual "intelligence."

Historically, psychology has been interested in assessing human intelligence via various intelligence tests, subsequently ranking people based on their scores. Although this practice has been subject to stark and accurate criticism (e.g., Gould, 1996), the use of intelligence testing and scores—notably the IQ score—continues. The original IQ score was devised by Stern (1912, cited in Sternberg, 1999), who argued that intelligence should be based on the ratio of an individual's mental age (MA) divided by chronological age (CA), multiplied by 100, or:

$$IQ = \frac{MA}{CA} \times 100.$$

If a teenager's mental age was the same as his chronological age (e.g., 13 years) then his IQ score would be 100—the exact average on the scale (i.e., IQ = [13/13] × 100 = 1.0 × 100 = 100). When mental age is greater than chronological age, the IQ score exceeds the average; when the reverse is true, the IQ score will fall below the mean of 100. This type of IQ score is called a *ratio IQ* (Sternberg, 1999).

Table 5.1 Normal Distribution of Deviation IQs

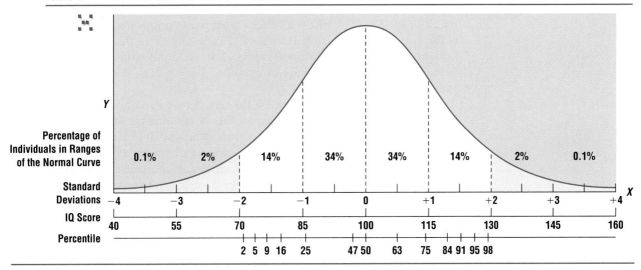

This figure shows a normal distribution as it applies to IQ, including identifying labels that are sometimes used to characterize different levels of IQ. It is important not to take these labels too seriously, as they are only loose characterizations, not scientific descriptions of performance.

Ratio IQs turned out to pose practical and conceptual measurement problems, so in recent decades they were replaced by *deviation IQ* scores. As you might guess, deviation IQ scores are based on the normal distribution and its assumptions for large populations. "Deviation" in this context means scores that deviate from the mean score within a normal distribution of IQ scores. The normal distribution of deviation IQs is shown in Table 5.1.

With any luck, you remain blissfully unaware of your measured IQ score and the above distribution is a mere curiosity for you. If you know your IQ score, however, then you are probably locating it on this curve to see how your performance compares to the population at large. In either case, you would do well to heed the sage wisdom of many research psychologists as well as intelligence test critics: The IQ score is but *one* measure of intelligence and an imperfect, incomplete one at that—no skill or behavior can be adequately reduced to one numerical index. As the definition provided earlier suggests, intelligence is comprised of various abilities. In other words, you are more than one score.

For further discussion of intelligence, its definition, and measurement, as well as accompanying controversies, see Ceci (1996), Gardner (1983), Gould (1996), and Sternberg (1985).

Locate and then plot where the two *z*s fall on your sketch of the *z* distribution (see Figure 5.8). Before proceeding any further, think about what relationship the plotted scores should disclose. First, both IQ scores are at least two standard deviation units away from the mean, placing both almost into the tail of the distribution. As a result, we should anticipate that the area between the two scores is probably quite small because few cases exist at the extreme of any distribution.

Turn to Table B.2 in Appendix B and locate the area between the mean and each of the two *z* scores. The percentages for +2.13 and +2.53, respectively, are 48.34% and 49.43%. As shown in Figure 5.8, then, a considerable amount of area is shared by the two scores (see the arrows pointing left from the *z* scores back to the mean)—only a small area exists between the scores (see the double-headed arrow pointing to both the scores). This small area represents the answer to the original question: What percentage of IQ scores on the test fall between 132 and 138?. To determine its numerical value, we sub-tract the smaller area associated with the z of $+2.13$ from the larger area for the z of $+2.53$, or $49.43\% - 48.34\% = 1.09\%$. In other words, only about 1% of the IQ scores in the distribution fall between scores of 132 and 138. Given that we know that rela-tively few people score in the upper ranges of the scale, this result makes sense. (As an aside, try to develop the practice of questioning any result—does it make statistical sense? Is it too large or too small?)

What if you needed to determine the area between two z scores that fell *below* the mean? The logic is the same as that used in the last example—you would simply be using negative z scores. To begin, of course, you would plot the standard scores, determine the area of overlap between each z and the mean, and then subtract the smaller area under the curve from the larger area. As an exercise, take a moment and make the sign on the z scores from the above example negative, sketch a z distribution, and then enter the scores on to it. Redo the above example using scores that now fall below the mean to verify that you understand the process and obtain the same answers.

A Further Transformed Score: The T Score

A variety of psychological and educational tests were created to adhere to the normal dis-tribution and to yield z scores. Researchers, practitioners, and educators use such tests for academic as well as research purposes. Many times, use of actual z scores from these dis-tributions is a problematic enterprise. Despite their benign qualities, some users can become confused by the presence of negative signs with some z scores. Moreover, these users will have forgotten—or perhaps never learned—the properties of z scores and the z distribution. Users can also be put off by the presence of numbers beyond the decimal point found even in many positive z scores, preferring to deal with whole numbers instead.

To deal with these and related concerns, tests originally based on transformations to z scores can be easily changed yet again to what are commonly called "transformed" or *T scores* (*not* to be confused with the t test, an inferential test reviewed extensively later in the book).

KEY TERM   A **T score** is a standard score which usually has a set μ and σ. Unlike z scores, *T scores* are re-ported as positive, whole numbers.

▽

Transformed (T) scores are reported as positive, whole numbers.

A T score deals with the aforementioned decimal point problem by multiplying the z score by 10.0 or 100.0. The negative number problem, in turn, is eliminated by taking the resulting product and then adding it to or subtracting it from a positive whole number.

An example will demonstrate the efficacy of the T score concept. If we wished to work with a scale that had a set mean of 100.0, we could use the following T score for-mula from Runyon et al. (1996):

[5.12.1] $$T = \overline{T} + 10(z),$$

[5.12.2] $$T = 100 + 10(z).$$

where T is the transformed score, $\overline{T}$ is the mean of some scale determined by its creator or an investigator and $10(z)$ is a given z score multiplied by 10.

The formula shown above in [5.12.1] and [5.12.2] transforms any entered z scores into a new distribution with a mean of 100.0. Negative signs from negative zs are changed to positive values. Please note that this transformation simply presents the information in a different, easier to comprehend, way—the shape of the distribution and the relationships among the relative placement of scores on the test remain intact.

We can demonstrate the T score transformation by imagining an individual with a z score of -1.28 on some educational test. What is the corresponding T score? We sim-ply enter the known z score into the T score formula, or:

[5.12.3] $T = 100 + 10(-1.28),$

[5.12.4] $T = 100 - 12.8,$

[5.12.5] $T = 87.2.$

Procedurally, the resulting *T* score is rounded to the nearest value of the whole number. Thus, a score of 87.2 would be reported as 87.0. Again, please note that the value of $\overline{T}$ will vary depending on the characteristics of the measure being used.

Can *T* scores be converted back to their *z* score equivalents? Yes, with little difficulty. The formula for this transformation back is:

[5.13.1] $z = \dfrac{T - \overline{T}}{10.0}.$

If we enter the original (nonrounded) *T* score, as well as $\overline{T}$, we find:

[5.13.2] $z = \dfrac{87.2 - 100.0}{10.0}$

[5.13.3] $z = -\dfrac{12.8}{10.0}$

[5.13.4] $z = -1.28$

Thus, we are back to the original *z* score.

Naturally, *z* scores derived from *T* scores are no different than any other *z* score. They, too, can be plotted on a *z* distribution or used to determine the percentile rank of a corresponding *T* score.

As noted by Runyon et al. (1996), the main contribution of *T* scores is that they permit researchers to compare the performance of test-takers from different subpopulations, such as disparate age groups. On a given test of motor skills, for instance, the test parameters of a college-aged population may differ from those associated with a much older group (age range 50 to 60 years). Once the *z*s for both groups are known, a *T* score transformation can convert them to the same distribution, allowing researchers to compare relative performance at one age with that found at another (e.g., Did younger individuals score higher on selected motor tasks relative to older persons?).

Writing About Standard Scores and the Normal Distribution

In a way, standard scores—whether *z* scores or *T* scores—are really the work horses, if you will, of descriptive statistics. Researchers and students are actually apt to *use* these standard scores in calculations more often than they are to *write* about them. When standardized measures are written up in a report or article, however, it is important to include either accompanying sample statistics ($\overline{X}$, *s*) or population parameters (μ, σ). Further, *z* and *T* scores must be appropriately used to answer, "compared to what?"

In a rare instance where you might be called on to write about *z* scores, for example, you would indicate the raw score and describe the test it was based on (i.e., statistics or parameters), and then indicate the score's use (e.g., to determine the area under the curve between the score and its mean, between two scores). If you were to describe a single score from a measure it might be structured as follows:

> The client received a raw score of 180 on the Youth Stress Index (YSI), a personality measure with a mean of 150 and a standard deviation of 15. Once converted to a standard score ($z = +2.00$), the client's YSI score was found to be two standard deviations above the mean, indicating a high level of adolescent stress. A score of 180 is at the 98th percentile of the YSI; only 2% of the adolescent population have been documented to have higher levels of reported stress at any point in time.

When writing about a z or T score, the goal is *not* to draw attention to the statistics per se, but to focus on the properties of the measure in question and the observations drawn from it.

Knowledge Base

1. You have a raw score of 220 drawn from a sample with a $\overline{X}$ of 215 and an s of 11.
   a. What is the z score corresponding to the raw score of 220?
   b. What proportion and percentage of cases occur between the mean and z?
   c. What proportion and percentage of cases exist beyond z?
2. What is the percentile rank of the raw score from question 1?
3. Using the sample statistics from question 1, determine the percentage of the area under the curve falling between scores of 210 and 218.
4. Using the sample statistics from question 1, determine the percentage of the area under the curve falling between scores of 200 and 213.
5. Using the z score transformation to a T score shown in formula [5.12.1] and [5.12.2], determine the T score for a z score of -2.20.

Answers

1. a. $+0.46$ b. .1772, 17.72%   c. .3228, 32.28%
2. 67.72% of the cases fell at or below a score of 220.
3. 28.0%
4. 34.17%
5. T score $= 78.0$

Looking Ahead: Probability, z Scores, and the Normal Distribution

Probability is an attempt to predict the likelihood of particular events, usually those in the future. The study of probability is the formal examination of what event X is likely to happen given particular condition Y or Z. We will learn about probability in some detail in chapter 8. For the present, however, it is useful to know that z scores and the z distribution can be used to identify probabilities. We will introduce this topic in brief, conceptual terms here, supplying the numerical elements later.

Think about how the position of a given z score—its proximity to the mean, how many standard deviation units above or below the mean it falls—can define its typicality. In general, scores closer to the mean—the average—are more common, occur with greater frequency, than those further out in the tails (exceptions to this rule include bimodal distributions, among others). In a real sense, scores that lie closer to the mean are more likely to occur than any observations that fall in either tail. As we saw in an example from the previous section of the text, IQ scores falling between 132 and 138 are few and far between, comprising less than 2% of the scores in the entire population. Finding someone with an IQ of, say, 136 is a relative rarity; you are simply more likely to run into someone with an IQ of 102 because there are more people with IQs close to the distribution's average.

As standard scores that disclose relative placement within distributions, z scores are also used to discuss the typicality of observations. Think about it: If I randomly select a score from the z distribution, is it likely to be one that is within one, two, or three standard deviations of the mean in either direction? Given the bell shape of the normal distribution, I am relatively likely to draw an observation from the first standard deviation rather than the other two, just as I am more likely to select a score from the second rather than the third standard deviation from the mean (see Figure 5.4 to recall the percentages associated with each standard deviation under the normal curve).

Note the presence of the qualifying phrases "relatively likely" and "more likely" that get to the heart of the matter of probability. Probability is not certainty, so despite the fact that more scores cluster close to the mean, I might still randomly select one that lies two standard deviations or more away. In terms of chance, though, I am less likely to pick an extreme score. The relative likelihood underlying the selection of particular observations is the basis of probability theory. We will discuss how *z* scores can be used to determined specific numerical probabilities associated with the normal distribution in detail in chapter 8.

Project Exercise   UNDERSTANDING THE RECENTERING OF SCHOLASTIC APTITUDE TEST SCORES

There is a good chance that some readers of this textbook took the SAT I reasoning test prior to April 1995, when scores on the test were recentered. What does the term "recentering" mean? Essentially, recentering the SAT scores placed the average score on both the verbal and math subtests back to 500, the midpoint of the 200 to 800 scale. Why was this necessary? As noted in Data Box 5.B, the population of students taking the test has expanded greatly since 1941, the year that the scores of 10,000 college-bound students were used to establish norms—performance expectations and comparison scores—for the test.

Prior to this 1995 recentering of scores, the average SAT verbal had "fallen" from 500 to 424 and the math score changed from an average of 500 to 478. In other words, the distribution of test scores changed from 1941 to the 1990s. As shown graphically in Figure 5.9, the average score shifted from the 1941 midpoint to a point well below it. The distribution for the current (pre-1995) scale shown in Figure 5.9 appears to be showing some

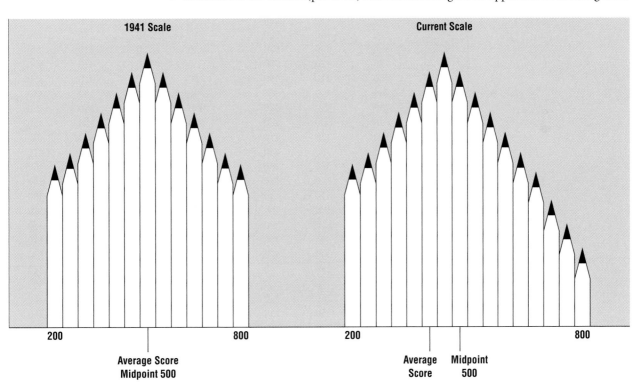

Figure 5.9 Shape of Distributions of Test Scores for 1941 and 1990s Student Samples

Note: The average score on the 1941 version of the verbal and math subscales of the SAT was 500. The average scores on these subscales in the early 1990s were 424 (verbal) and 478 (math), indicating that the population of test takers changed in the intervening years.

positive skew; that is, test scores appear to be clustering toward the lower end of the distribution. Recentering of the SAT made the distribution of scores once again appear like the normal (original) distribution shown in the left side of Figure 5.9.

By balancing scores on the SAT, the College Board returned the scores to a standard normal distribution. Following the logic of transforming scores presented in this chapter, "old" SAT scores were transformed into "new" ones. The difference here, of course, is that the shape of the distribution was changed somewhat—it was "normalized" once again, presumably by a transformation formula similar to one used for calculating T scores. Although the exact formula is not public information, I do have two equivalence tables that quickly illustrate how pre-April 1995 SAT scores on the verbal and math subtests can be changed to the "new" SAT scores (see Table 5.2).

Table 5.2 | Conversion Tables From "Old" to "New" SAT I Scores

SAT verbal: original scale to recentered scale				SAT mathematical: original scale to recentered scale			
Equivalence Table				Equivalence Table			
Original Scale	Recentered Scale	Original Scale	Recentered Scale	Original Scale	Recentered Scale	Original Scale	Recentered Scale
800	800	500	580	800	800	500	520
790	800	490	570	790	800	490	520
780	800	480	560	780	800	480	510
770	800	470	550	770	790	470	500
760	800	460	540	760	770	460	490
750	800	450	530	750	760	450	480
740	800	440	520	740	740	440	480
730	800	430	510	730	730	430	470
720	790	420	500	720	720	420	460
710	780	410	490	710	700	410	450
700	760	400	480	700	690	400	440
690	750	390	470	690	680	390	430
680	740	380	460	680	670	380	430
670	730	370	450	670	660	370	420
660	720	360	440	660	650	360	410
650	710	350	430	650	650	350	400
640	700	340	420	640	640	340	390
630	690	330	410	630	630	330	380
620	680	320	400	620	620	320	370
610	670	310	390	610	610	310	350
600	670	300	380	600	600	300	340
590	660	290	370	590	600	290	330
580	650	280	360	580	590	280	310
570	640	270	350	570	580	270	300
560	630	260	340	560	570	260	280
550	620	250	330	550	560	250	260
540	610	240	310	540	560	240	240
530	600	230	300	530	550	230	220
520	600	220	290	520	540	220	200
510	590	210	270	510	530	210	200
		200	230			200	200

Source: The College Board, 45 Columbus Avenue, New York, NY 10023.

What happened to student scores? Generally, the conversion appeared to increase the scores of most students. Thus, someone who took the test in 1993 and scored a 510 verbal and a 560 math would now have scores of 590 and 570, respectively. On average, the College Board reports that most student scores increased as a result of the transformation. The rank and percentile rank of the scores remained virtually unchanged, however. Why? Recall what you know about relative placement in a distribution and conversion to standard scores—a given scores changes but the relative percent of test takes who score higher or lower remains the same.

Many admissions officers and educators feared that the recentering of scores meant that the SAT was suddenly an easier test to score well on. This fear was unfounded, of course, because the recentering merely placed the subtest means back to 500. Neither the inherent difficulty of the questions on the test nor the rank order of student scores on the test changed. Because everyone's score was readjusted, the relative placement of a given score compared to all other scores remained the same.

Here are some questions to think about and discuss regarding the transformation of scores and the normal distribution.

1. An admission's officer at a small university is worried that the recentering of the SAT will hurt student recruitment. Specifically, this professional is worried that potential applicants will be scared to apply because his institution's averages have increased—the scores printed in the university's admission's material seem to be much higher on the "new" SAT. As a student of statistics, what would you say to reduce his fears?
2. A college graduate happens to see the SAT conversion table, Table 5.2, converts her "old" verbal and math scores from 1992 to their "new" score equivalents. She then remarks to you that, "I always knew that they messed up my score on that test. I knew that I scored higher on that verbal test, especially—and look, I was right!" What do you tell this former student about the SAT transformation, as well as standard scores and the normal distribution more generally?
3. A peer examines the two distributions shown in Figure 5.9. Your peer comments that the two curves only confirm what he has always known—American students are getting dumber. "Just look at the clump of low scores in the curve on the right—and there are so few people who are at the upper end of the scale!," he says. What do you say in response? How can you cogently and concisely explain the statistical shift in scores from 1941 to the 1990s?

LOOKING FORWARD   THEN BACK

C onceptually, standard or *z* scores are an integral part of statistical inference, helping to represent distinct variables with different qualities in a common frame of reference. The decision trees that open this chapter will help you to recall the role of *z* scores when working with distributions of data (decision tree one), converting raw scores into their *z* score equivalents (decision tree two), or using a *z* score to determine a percentile rank (decision tree three). Keep in mind that one of the *z* distribution's capabilities is the way it allows the data analyst to generalize. Knowing a score's placement enables analysts to make an inference about its relative relationship with other scores in a distribution. The decision trees will prove to be helpful whether you are in need of a quick refresher to recall the characteristics of *z* scores or to use them for descriptive purposes.

Summary

1. When evaluating any score or measure, it must always be compared to other observations—including the mean and standard deviation—within the distribution.
2. Standardizing scores or measures enables researchers to understand and compare them to other objects or observations along a single continuum.
3. Raw scores can be transformed into standard scores, which are an important part of various inferential statistical procedures. The apparent value of standard scores can change but no information, including their relation to other scores, is lost.
4. The z score is a descriptive statistic that identifies the distance between a raw score (X) and a distribution's mean, and it is reported in standard deviation units. A z score can be calculated as long as sample statistics $(\overline{X}, s)$ or population parameters (μ, σ) are known. A given z score indicates how many standard deviations away from the mean the score is placed.
5. The z distribution has a mean of 0.0 and a standard deviation of 1.0, and it is symmetric; negative values fall below the mean and positive values lie above it. Conversion to z scores changes the value of scores but not their placement on or the shape of their parent distribution.
6. The standard normal distribution, a bell-shaped curve, contains observations laid out in a predictable pattern. The area under the curve (which can be known in proportion or percentage terms) is delineated in standard deviation units, such that the bulk of available observations are found—in descending order of magnitude—in the first, second, and third standard deviations to the right and left of the mean.
7. When allied with the standard normal distribution, z scores enable investigators to compare different types of measures, variables, or scores with one another on the same distribution. Such comparison is possible even when the means and standard deviations of the raw scores differ substantially from one another.
8. Due to their respective properties, z scores and the normal curve can be used to determine the percentile rank of a given raw score.
9. T scores are another form of standard score that usually converts z scores into positive, whole numbers.
10. Probability—predicting the likelihood of particular outcomes—is conceptually and numerically linked to z scores and the normal distribution.

Key Terms

Raw score *(p.182)*   Standard score *(p.182)* T score *(p.196)*
                                                                             z score *(p.183)*

Chapter Problems

1. What are the properties of the z distribution? Why are z scores useful?
2. Explain why comparison between one observation and another is so important for statistics and data analysis, as well as the behavioral sciences.
3. What are the properties of the standard normal distribution? Why is the normal curve useful for statisticians and behavioral scientists?
4. Explain what role the statistical concept of standard deviation plays in understanding z scores and the area under the normal curve.
5. Why do researchers standardize data? What is a standard score? Why are z scores and T scores standard scores?
6. If z scores appear to have such a wide range of applicability to statistical analysis, why did behavioral scientists find it necessary to develop T scores? What is the relationship between z and T scores?
7. What is probability? How does probability conceptually relate to z scores and the normal distribution?
8. A researcher examines her data and notices that its distribution is negatively skewed, and that its $\mu = 342.0$ and its $\sigma = 21.0$. If she converts all the data to z scores, what will be the numerical value of the mean and the standard deviation? What will the shape of the distribution of scores look like now?
9. Imagine you have a distribution with a $\mu = 78.0$ and its $\sigma = 12.5$. Find the z score equivalents of the following raw scores: 54.0, 63.5, 66.0, 77.0, 78.5, 81.0.
10. Imagine you have a distribution with a $\mu = 78.0$ and its $\sigma = 12.5$. Convert the following z scores back to their raw score equivalents: $-3.10, -1.55, -1.0, +0.55, +1.76, +2.33, +3.9$.
11. Sketch a z distribution and plot the z scores from problem 9. Determine the area under curve (in percent) between each z and the mean of the distribution.
12. Imagine you have a sample with a $\overline{X} = 35$ and an $s = 3.5$. Find the z score equivalents for the following raw scores: 27, 29.5, 34.3, 35, 45, 47.5.

13. Imagine you have a sample with a $\overline{X} = 35$ and an $s = 3.5$. Convert the following z scores back to their raw score equivalents: $-3.01, -2.56, -1.21, +1.40, +2.77, 3.00$.

14. Sketch a z distribution and plot the z scores from problem 12. Determine the area under curve (in percent) between each z and the mean of the distribution.

15. You have a very large distribution of IQ scores. As you know, the IQ test has a $\mu = 100.0$ and its $\sigma = 15.0$. Find the percentage of the curve falling between each of the following scores and the mean: 85, 88, 98.0, 112, 120, 133.

16. You have a very large distribution of IQ scores. As you know, the IQ test has a $\mu = 100.0$ and its $\sigma = 15.0$. Find the percentage of the curve falling between each of the following pairs of scores: 85 and 88; 92 and 96; 98 and 108; 115 and 128; 130 and 140; 141 and 143.

17. You have a data set with a $\overline{X} = 50.0$ and an $s = 7.0$. Find the percentage of the curve falling between each of the following scores and the mean: 38.0, 39.5, 45.0, 52.0, 57.0, 66.6.

18. You have a data set with a $\overline{X} = 50.0$ and an $s = 7.0$. Find the percentage of the curve falling between each of the following pairs of scores: 39.0 and 43.0; 44.5 and 56.5; 51.0 and 61.0; 62.0 and 63.0; 65.0 and 75.0; 76.0 and 80.0.

19. Determine what percentage of the cases under the normal curve are beyond each of the z scores calculated in problem 9.

20. Determine what percentage of the cases under the normal curve are beyond each of the z scores calculated in problem 12.

21. Determine what percentage of the cases under the normal curve are beyond each of the z scores calculated in problem 15.

22. Calculate the percentile rank of each of the z scores found in problem 9.

23. Calculate the percentile rank of each of the z scores found in problem 12.

24. Calculate the percentile rank of each of the z scores found in problem 15.

25. Are z scores normally distributed? Why or why not?

26. Is there one normal curve or many normal curves? Can there be more than one? How? Explain.

27. A student has taken four area tests designed to measure particular intellectual abilities. The following table identifies each test, summarizes its characteristics, and provides the student's score on it. Assume that the possible scores on each test are normally distributed.

Area Test	μ	σ	Student's Score
Verbal ability	58.5	6.50	63.0
Visualization	110.0	15.0	102.5
Memory	85.0	11.5	98.0
Spatial relations	320.0	33.5	343.0

a. Change each of the student's score to its z score equivalent.

b. On which test did the student receive a high score? A low score?

c. What is the percentile rank of the student's verbal ability score? What percentage of the students who took the spatial relations test scored higher than the student?

28. Envision a normal distribution with $\mu = 88$ and $\sigma = 14$.
a. Identify the scores at the 25th, 75th, and 95th percentiles.
b. What percentage of cases fall below a score of 74.0?
c. What percentage of scores are higher than a 93.0?
d. What percentage of cases lie between the mean and a score of 99.0?
e. What percentage of cases fall between scores of 86.5 and 92.5?

29. Using the T score formula of $T = 75 + 10(z)$, transform the following z scores into T scores. Round your answers to the nearest whole number: $-1.12, -2.30, +1.18, +2.67, +3.58$.

30. A transformation to T scores resulted in the following values when the formula $T = 400 + 100(z)$ was used. Convert these T scores back to their original z scores: 420, 373, 510, 485, 624.

31. Use the decision trees opening this chapter to answer the following questions:
a. An investigator wants to know a data point's location relative to the mean of its (large) distribution. What should the investigator do?
b. A researcher draws an observation from an intact population whose parameters are known. How can this observation be converted to a z score?
c. What is the percentile rank of a z score equal to 1.76?

Choosing a Measure of Association

1.
Are the data organized into *pairs of scores* (i.e., *X, Y*)?

If *yes*, then go to step 2.

If *no*, then go to step 5.

2.
Are both variables *X* and *Y* measured on *interval* or *ratio* scales?

If *yes*, then calculate a Pearson *r*.

If *no*, then go to step 3.

3.
Are both variables *X* and *Y* measured on *ordinal scales*?

If *yes*, then calculate a Spearman r_s (see chapter 14).

If *no*, then go to step 4.

4.
Are both variables *X* and *Y* measured on *nominal scales*?

If *yes*, then select a measure of association from Table 6.6.

If *no*, then go to step 5.

5.
You *cannot* perform correlational analyses on these data. Consider an alternative method of analysis or presentation of results.

Factors to Review in Order to Prevent Spurious Correlations

1.
Is the range of values for variable *X* or *Y* "truncated" or restricted?

If *yes*, then the correlation may be *spurious*.

If *no*, then go to step 2.

2.
When graphed in a scatter plot, does the relationship between variables *X* and *Y* appear to be *nonlinear*?

If *yes*, then the correlation may be *spurious*.

If *no*, then go to step 3.

3.
Are there any *extreme* or *outlying* scores in the data set?

If *yes*, then the correlation may be *spurious*.

If *no*, then go to step 4.

4.
Is the size of the sample small (i.e., <20 pairs of observations)?

If *yes*, then the correlation may be *spurious*.

If *no*, then go to step 5.

5.
Has the examination of scatter plots involving all the main measures and subject variables ruled out the presence of any *preexisting subpopulations* in the data?

If *yes*, then the correlation may be spurious.

If *no*, then a correlation based on the data may be trustworthy.

CORRELATION

ll of us search for predictable, stable patterns in our experience. By seeing or recognizing connections between events, we can make sense of the world around us. Generally, we are drawn to make connections between two events or variables, and we probably make conjoint judgments in this vein with great regularity. If you have ever lived with another person for any length of time, you probably began to recognize associations between certain events and your roommate's behavior. A phone call from an old flame, for example, might elicit happy reminiscences for an hour or two, or a sullen demeanor for the rest of the day. A mountain of homework, in turn, could elicit considerable grumbling and procrastination or extraordinary feats of efficient study.

When these same events happen more than once, we begin to detect a pattern between one event (an old flame's call) and another (a bad mood), or what statisticians call a *correlation* between the two variables. Literally, we create our own hypotheses about how and why one variable "co-relates" with another variable. An ironic aspect of our desire to seek and identify predictable, consistent correlations in everyday experience is that we are actually not very proficient at picking them out (e.g., Nisbett & Ross, 1980). That is, sometimes we *believe* that we see a pattern when, in fact, the association between variables is illusory and nonexistent (e.g., Chapman & Chapman, 1982). Other times we sense that a pattern is present but, as intuitive rather than formal scientists, we are not by nature well-calibrated enough to recognize its strength or magnitude (e.g., Dawes, 1988; Plous, 1988).

A classic series of studies by Jennings, Amabile, and Ross (1982) illustrate the real obstacles people run into when they try to detect correlations. Research participants encountered paired stimuli from three data sets—10 pairs of numbers, sketches of 10 male figures of different heights with canes of varied lengths, and a tape recording of 10 people reciting a letter from the alphabet and singing a musical note. Participants tried to determine if any association existed between the variables in each data set. In other words, for example, did tall figures tend to have long walking sticks and short figures have short sticks (a positive relationship)? Or did figures with greater heights seem to have shorter sticks, and vice versa (a negative relationship)? Alternatively, there might be no discernable pattern between height and stick length (a zero relationship). As we will see later in this chapter, correlations can take on a value ranging between −1.00 and +1.00 and, as values move toward either extreme, they become stronger (i.e., more predictive). Jennings et al. (1982) purposefully created patterns within each data set so that the objective correlations ranged between 0 (no relationship) and 1.00 (a perfect, predictable relationship).

Correlation refers to whether the nature of association between two (or more) variables is positive, negative, or zero.

Did the participants do a good job at identifying the presence and strength of the correlations for each data set? Not really. Jennings and colleagues (1982) found that the participants did not really begin to notice any positive relationships in any of the three data sets until they were "strong," that is, with objective numerical values ranging between +.60 and +.70. In fact, participants generally viewed objectively "strong" relationships as "moderate," while objectively "moderate" relationships in the data were missed altogether.

Sometimes, of course, we are capable of recognizing that two variables share a relationship, one that we can readily seek (e.g., Hard work usually leads to rewards) or avoid (e.g., If you touch a hot stove, you will burn yourself). Under relatively controlled conditions, there is also some evidence indicating that people can recognize everyday life correlations with some accuracy, such as the degree to which social behavior is consistent across occasions (e.g., If Jill is more honest than Jane once, how will she behave in the future?; see Kunda & Nisbett, 1986). The world is a complex place much of the time, however, and it can be difficult for the person on the street to isolate which variable is linked with which variable, and in what way. To circumvent this complexity, statisticians and behavioral scientists rely on a straightforward procedure enabling them to convert variables to numbers, which are then entered into a formula that provides an objective index of correlation. Correlational research, which was introduced in chapter 2, can be a powerful tool for identifying heretofore unnoticed relationships in the behavioral sciences, engaging in exploratory research, or examining associations between variables when experimental research is not a possibility. This chapter reviews the conceptual material underlying one of the more common correlation statistics, as well as practical advice about its calculation and application.

▽

Calculating correlations is necessary, if only because humans are not "calibrated" to recognize objective empirical relationships unless they are obvious ones.

◖ Association, Causation, and Measurement

The 18th century philosopher David Hume can be credited with setting the stage for the behavioral sciences' interest in the association between or among variables (e.g., Hume, 1974). Following a grand tradition in Western philosophy, Hume argued that ideas become associated with one another, but unlike earlier thinkers, he emphasized association as a tool for addressing fundamental questions of psychology and philosophy (Leahey, 1997). To Hume, the link between cause and effect was the most important principle governing the association of ideas. He was quick to point out, however, that we never perceive causes directly, rather, we infer cause based on observing the conjoining of two events. I press a button, for example, and then hear a bell ring, but I do *not* "see" the electrical current that causes the clapper to strike the bell and create the sound. Our belief in causes, then, is based on our experiences or, more to the point, the association of one event (pressing a button) with another (hearing a bell's ring). Hume called this form of association a habit, whereby we come to believe that a first event caused a second one. Subsequent efforts by Galton and Pearson moved from philosophical speculation to attempts at objective measures of association occurring out in the world.

Galton, Pearson, and the Index of Correlation

Sir Francis Galton was one of the widest ranging intellects of the 19th century. A relative of Charles Darwin, Galton is hailed as the first individual to systematically rely on statistics to examine psychological data (Leahey, 1997), and he is distinguished as being the creator of the first correlation coefficient. Galton was curious about heredity and later, regrettably, eugenics, the pseudoscience of regulating reproduction among persons possessing supposedly "desirable" genetic endowments (e.g., intelligence). Whether breeding peas or speculating about biological inheritance in human families, he needed a straightforward means to describe the similarity of parents and their offspring on various traits. Still later, when planning to critique a novel system of criminal identification, the concept of correlation came to him in a flash (Vadum & Rankin, 1998).

Galton chose the letter *r* to represent his "index of co-relation," which later became the now familiar spelling "correlation." Here are Galton's own words on the matter (Galton, cited in Vadum & Rankin, 1998, p. 117):

> Two variable organs are said to be co-related when the variation of the one is accompanied on the average by more or less variation of the other, and in the same direction. Thus the length of the arm is said to be co-related with that of the leg, because a person with a long arm has usually a long leg, and conversely. If the co-relation be close then a person with a very long arm would usually have a very long leg; if it be moderately close then the length of his leg would only be long, not very long; and if there were no co-relation at all then the length of his leg would on the average be mediocre. . . . Between these two extremes are an endless number of intermediate cases, and it will be shown how the closeness of co-relation in any particular case admits of being expressed by a simple number.

The simple number, of course, is the correlation coefficient. An ardent admirer and junior colleague of Galton, the statistician Karl O. Pearson, enlarged the mathematical background and precision of the index of correlation. The official name of this, the most frequently used index of correlation, is the **Pearson product-moment correlation coefficient,** or *Pearson r* (the Greek letter *rho*) for short. The word "moment" is a synonym for the mean and, as you well know, the multiplication of two numbers results in a product. "Coefficient" is a mathematical term specifying an operation on some data. "Product-moment," then, refers to the average of the multiplied numbers in the coefficient's calculation (Runyon et al., 1996). Before we examine the conceptual underpinnings of the Pearson *r*, we must review a general but powerful aspect of all correlational relationships—that they are not causal.

A Brief But Essential Aside: Correlation Does Not Imply Causation

Correlation does not imply causation. First mentioned in chapter 2, this statement is one of the fundamental dictums shared by the behavioral and natural sciences, and it is also one of the most important ideas any educated person can ever learn. It serves to remind us that relationships in the world are not always what they seem to be. Unless we actively intervene into a situation by manipulating variables and measuring their affect on one another, we cannot assume that we know the causal order involved.

To illustrate this interpretive problem, we can consider an intriguing, if offbeat, anthropological example. Li (1975, cited in Stanovich, 1998) reports that a research team composed of behavioral scientists and physicians conducted a correlational study examining contraceptive use on the island of Taiwan. The team collected extensive data pertaining to the inhabitants' public and private lives, and the environments in which they

Note well: correlational relationships are not causal relationships.

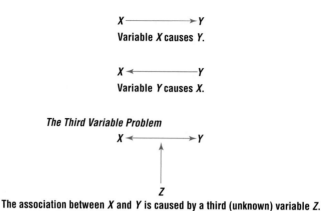

Figure 6.1 Graphic Representation of Possible Causal Links Between Variables *X* and *Y*, and the Third Variable Problem

lived. What was the single best predictor of whether birth control methods were adopted and used? The number of electrical appliances (e.g., toasters, fans, blenders) found in the home: more appliances, more birth control—fewer or no labor-saving devices, less or no contraceptive practice.

Despite the correlation's implication, as Stanovich (1998, p. 73) wryly observes, we are not apt to conclude that teenage pregnancy can be discouraged by passing out free toasters in Taiwan's schools. Intuitively, this conclusion cannot be correct, that is, there is a noncausal relationship lurking hereabouts. Can you think of an explanation that can parsimoniously explain this quirky anthropological observation? While you do that, let's focus on thinking about the relations between variables identified by any correlation.

First, variable *X* (presence or absence of appliances) can lead to a change in variable *Y* (use or nonuse of birth control). The problem, however, is that correlational relationships are bidirectional—that is, *Y* might also be creating the change in *X*. Both of these possibilities are illustrated graphically in Figure 6.1. This lack of certainty in directional relationships—the origins of cause and effect—is the reason that correlations are not causal.

Understanding the relation between variables is more complicated still due to what is sometimes referred to as the **third variable problem** in correlational analysis. A third variable (or fourth or fifth, for that matter) is a variable that exercises an unrealized effect in a correlational result. Why is this third variable a problem? Perhaps *X* does not lead to *Y* nor *Y* to *X*. Instead, it may be that the apparent relationship between *X* and *Y* is actually the result of some third, unknown variable *Z* (see Figure 6.1). The problem, of course, is there can be an infinite number of candidates for variable *Z*. And so we return to the question of how birth control and electric appliances are linked—have you developed any hypotheses about the probable causal agent here?

The mediating variable—the one that ties the relationship between the two represented by the correlation—is probably education or socioeconomic status (SES to behavioral scientists), two variables that, in turn, are highly correlated. In other words, individuals with more education are also apt to earn more money, which in turn is spent on electric appliances. Persons with more education, then, are more likely to know about and exercise birth control; they also happened to have a higher disposable income to spend on food processors and related items. This account is plausible, but consider how long it took us to get here. More to the point, we still lack definitive (i.e., causal) proof. Only when some controlled intervention is created—a manipulation in an experiment

Correct causal ordering is difficult to recognize, let alone prove—be on the lookout for mediating variables driving the association between two seemingly related variables.

(see chapter 2), perhaps—can we actually determine what factors increased or inhibited the use of birth control on the island of Taiwan. Other examples of correlations exhibiting the third variable problem can be found in Stanovich (1998) and Abelson (1995).

If correlation does not imply causation, then should such analyses be avoided? Not at all. Correlational research, the examination of associations among variables, is extremely valuable and very often revealing, even enlightening. After all, few people would posit a link between toasters and birth control out of the blue! More seriously, however, correlations are a start. They can be highly suggestive, pointing researchers in the right direction so that experiments identifying the actual causal ordering among known and unknown variables can be designed and subsequently executed. As a critical consumer of behavioral science research, one who is becoming well versed in data analysis, however, you must always avoid confusing *correlated variables* with *causal variables*.

The Pearson Correlation Coefficient

Conceptual Definition of the Pearson *r*

The Pearson *r* is used to advance research beyond the arena of descriptive statistics we covered in the first five chapters of the book. Specifically, the Pearson *r* enables investigators to assess the nature of the association between two variables, *X* and *Y*. Correlations, then, are based on *pairs of variables*, and each pair is based on the responses of one person. In fact, a correlation cannot be calculated if each participant in a sample does not have a pair of *X* and *Y* scores (or the *N* used in the calculation can only include those participants with intact pairs).

A convention is to treat the *X* variable as the independent or predictor variable, so that changes in *X* lead to changes in *Y*. The *Y* variable, then, is sometimes described as the dependent or criterion variable—the variable that is influenced by *X*. In many correlational research designs, the *X* variable is presumed to cause the observed change in *Y* (i.e., the change in one precedes the corresponding change in the other). This reasoning is certainly useful for hypothesizing about the character of relationships existing between variables, but it must be tempered by the aforementioned dictum: correlation does not imply causation. In practice, of course, many researchers do not bother specifying that *X* is the independent variable or that *Y* is the dependent variable. As we will see, the formula used to calculate the correlation does not split such empirical hairs and, in any case, the correlational relationships can be described in any number of ways.

When calculating a correlation, the *X* and *Y* variables can represent any number of psychological tests and measures, behaviors, or rating scales—the only requirement for the scaling of a given variable is that it be based on an interval or a ratio scale (see chapter 1 for a review of the characteristics of scales of measurement). Indeed, as an index of association, the Pearson *r* is facile enough to help researchers speculate about the relationship between empirical "apples" and "oranges" (recall the advantages of *z* scores in this regard; see chapter 5). Why? Simply because the statistic's formula standardizes the *X* and *Y* variables so that their degree of association—their relative positions on a continuum—can be determined (see the discussion of *r*'s relation to *z* scores below).

▽

A correlation is calculated on paired observations (*X, Y*), and only intact pairs can be used.

▽

In a conventional correlational relationship, *X* is the independent variable (predictor) and *Y* is the dependent (criterion) measure.

KEY TERM The **Pearson *r***, a correlation coefficient, is a statistic that quantifies the extent to which two variables *X* and *Y* are associated, and whether the direction of their association is positive, negative, or zero.

We will review this conceptual definition for the Pearson r in the context of an example here and then learn how to calculate it in the subsequent section. Conceptually, the Pearson r assesses the degree to which X and Y *vary together*—this shared information is then divided by the degree to which X and Y *vary separately* from one another.

Imagine that a personality psychologist is interested in developing a new inventory to measure extraversion (e.g., Jung, 1931/1971; Myers, 1962). As you know, extraverts are individuals who display highly sociable characteristics—they are drawn to form connections with others, to seek new experiences, and are generally "outgoing" in their demeanor. In contrast, persons with introverted personalities appear to be shy, less outgoing, and are much less sociable, particularly in novel or public settings. Introverts are usually hesitant to form new social connections, holding back until they become comfortable in a situation. The new inventory contains 20 questions, each of which requires respondents to rate whether their reaction to a hypothetical situation would be introverted or extraverted. Thus, scores on the inventory can range between 1 and 20, and higher scores indicate a greater degree of extraversion.

Column 2 in Table 6.1 shows the extraversion score for the 10 participants who took part in a small scale validation study (for convenience, column 1 assigns a number to each participant). The third column in Table 6.1 is a behavioral measure employed to test whether the inventory is adequately measuring the personality construct of introversion-extraversion. One week after the 10 participants completed the inventory, they returned to the laboratory to take part in a staged social interaction. Specifically, the 10 participants met 12 confederates in a cocktail party setting, and their instructions were simply to greet and meet new people for 30 minutes. Unbeknownst to the participants, their sociability was carefully monitored by the investigator—the whole numbers in column 3 of Table 6.1 represent the number of "new" people they interacted with during the party (the numerical value of these interactions could range between 0 ["met no one"] to 12 ["met everyone"]). The personality psychologist predicts that higher levels of extraversion will be linked with higher levels of sociability; that is, extraverts will tend to meet more new people relative to introverts. If the inventory is valid, then the direction of the correlational relationship between the personality scores (X) and the observed social behavior (Y) should be a positive one.

Table 6.1 Extraversion Scores and Interaction Behavior in a Hypothetical Validation Study

Participants	Extraversion Score[a] (X)	Interaction Behavior[b] (Y)
1	20	8
2	5	2
3	18	10
4	6	3
5	19	8
6	3	4
7	4	3
8	3	2
9	17	7
10	18	9

Note: [a]Higher scores indicate higher level of extraversion (range: 1 to 20); [b]higher number indicates more social contacts made in the 30-minute get-acquainted session (range 0 to 12).

Direction of Relationship. What is a *positive correlation?* For that matter, what is a *negative* or a *zero correlation?* Before we proceed further with the extraverted behavior example, let's define these terms.

KEY TERM
A **positive correlation** is one where as the value of X increases, the corresponding value of Y also increases. Similarly, a *positive correlation* exists when the value of X decreases, the value of Y also decreases.

In short, a positive correlational relationship exists when higher values of one variable tend to be associated with higher values of the other, or lower values on one correspond to lower values on the other. When does this occur? Consider an example that may be familiar to you: How is study time associated with grades? Casual observation suggests that people who study more hours per week tend to have higher grades in college. Conversely, individuals who study less usually have lower grade point averages. This positive relationship is correlational, not causal; however, think of those individuals who never study and still earn remarkably high grades, or those who study consistently but nonetheless have a mediocre academic record.

Positive correlation: As X increases in value, so does Y; alternatively, as X decreases, so does Y.

What will a positive relationship between the extraversion inventory and displayed social behavior be like? The investigator would anticipate that extraverts (those with higher scores) would interact with more people during the "get acquainted" session. The personality psychologist would necessarily also be predicting that individuals with lower inventory scores (i.e., introverts) would mingle with relatively fewer of the study's confederates. A positive correlation implicates both relationship patterns between X and Y.

Negative correlations entail what are often called inverse relationships between two variables.

KEY TERM
A **negative correlation** identifies an inverse relationship between variables X and Y—as the value of one increases, the other necessarily decreases.

In the academic realm, a negative correlation can occur between the number of hours spent watching television and the grades one earns. Logically, an inverse relationship would exist between these variables—more hours spent watching TV potentially leads to lower grades, while fewer hours propped in front of the tube would be associated with higher grades. Bear in mind that although these examples seem to be intuitive, even plausible, they cannot be treated as identifying causal relationships. Many students who do well scholastically spend untold hours watching television, while others avoid any such leisure activity and still receive lower grades. Correlation does not imply causation!

Negative correlation: As X increases, Y decreases (and vice versa).

A negative correlational relationship between extraversion and the number of people engaged during the 30-minute study would be counterintuitive to the goals of the study, not to mention what is known about the personality constructs involved. Nonetheless, of course, a researcher must anticipate what pattern of results an (unexpected and unwanted) negative correlation would reveal, as planful investigators always envision alternative results and consider their impact on theory (Dunn, 1999). A negative correlation would occur if extraverted participants introduced themselves to relatively few confederates, while the introverts in the study ended up meeting many more people by comparison.

Finally, a *zero correlation* occurs when there is no discernable pattern of covariation—how things vary together—between two variables.

KEY TERM
A **zero correlation** indicates that there is no pattern or predictive relationship between the behavior of variables X and Y.

Quite simply, a zero correlation—occasionally called a "zero relationship"—means that there is no association between the variables. Thus, time spent watching television or hours studying is not linked in any way with academic performance. As for the extraversion inventory's relationship to the participants' sociability in the lab, scores on the personality measure would not correspond in any interpretable fashion with the number of persons one did (or did not) meet.

Signs and Strength of Correlational Relationships.

Aside from describing examples between variables to illustrate a positive, negative, or zero correlation, how else can these relationships be recognized? As a statistic, the correlation coefficient provides guidance because whatever number results from a given calculation has either a positive (+) or a negative (−) sign accompanying it. Just as the sign accompanying a z score informs the user which side of the mean it falls on, the sign for the r indicates the nature of the relationship between variables X and Y.

The range of values for the Pearson r also indicates the relative strength of the correlational relationship between the variables. Values for the statistic are $-1.00 \leq r \leq +1.00$. As a calculated value for r approaches either extreme (± 1.00), the strength of the positive or negative relationship between the variables becomes more predictive. As an r moves closer to 0 in value, there will be little or no apparent relationship between variables X and Y. Indeed, as noted earlier, a zero relationship means that any change in variable X is not accompanied by any predictable change in Y.

Is it possible to calculate a Pearson r-value of -1.00 or $+1.00$? Yes, but such a "perfect" correlational relationship is understandably rare, if not suspect. Such relationships are earmarked by the fact that every change in variable X is accompanied by a corresponding change in Y. A positive correlation of $+1.00$, then, would indicate every value of X had a Y value of the same magnitude matching it (e.g., a person scoring 20 on the extravert inventory would meet all 12 people, a person scoring 1 would meet no one). Similarly, a negative correlation of -1.00 would indicate that every value of X was matched by an opposing value of Y (i.e., a person scoring 20 on extraversion would meet no one, a person scoring a 1 would meet everyone). Perfect correlations do happen, but savvy data analysts are suspicious of them and quick to confirm that the data were coded and analyzed properly.

Linear Relationships and Scatterplots of Variables *X* and *Y*.

When variables X and Y result in an r of $+1.00$ or -1.00, they are said to exhibit a perfect linear relationship. By "linear," we mean that the relationship between the two variables is best represented by a straight line on a diagram. The diagram of choice for plotting variables is called a *scatter plot* or scatter diagram.

KEY TERM   A **scatter plot** is a particular graph used to present correlational data. Each point in a *scatter plot* represents the intersection of an X value with its corresponding Y value.

Panels (a) and (b) of Figure 6.2 illustrate near perfect linear relationships denoting a positive and a negative correlation, respectively. As you can see in panel (a), as the value of X increases, the corresponding value of Y increases. Conversely, a decrease in value by one variable is marked by a similar decrease in another. As positive correlations become stronger, their values become higher and, when plotted, their data become more linear. Positive linear relationships are easily identified by the fact that the plotted points in space move to the right of a graph in a northeasterly direction—the drawn slope of the line moves increasingly to the right and up (see panel (a) in Figure 6.2).

The value of r falls between -1.00 and $+1.00$ (inclusive).

Mood as Misbegotten: Correlating Predictors with Mood States

Do you know what factors put you into a good mood? Pleasant conversation? A sunny day? Is happiness *really* a warm puppy, or is it more likely to come to you in the form of a rich cup of real (caffeinated) coffee?

Wilson, Laser, and Stone (1982) had 50 students complete daily questionnaires regarding their moods and various predictor variables (e.g., how much they slept, the quality of the food they ate, the weather) for 5 weeks. Correlations between the predictors and mood ratings were determined for each participant, and these were subsequently compared with the participants' estimates of what the relationships were like (i.e., positive, negative, or zero). A second group of observer participants (who did not know the first group) estimated how much each of the aforementioned variables predicted mood.

Were the actual participants more accurate than the observers were when it came to knowing what affected their moods? Wilson et al. (1982) found that although the participants achieved a moderate level of accuracy at judging how their moods covaried with the predictors (the average *r* between estimated and actual mood predictors was +.42), the peer observers who had no direct experience were *equally accurate*. How so? Wilson et al. correlated the observers' estimates of how predictors were linked to mood with the participants' actual estimates, yielding an *r* of +.45! In other words, the observers who had *no* experience with judging what does or does not affect mood were as accurate as individuals who carefully monitored predictor variables and their own moods for over a month!

How can this intriguing event be explained? Wilson and colleagues (1982) suggest that instead of basing mood judgments on the actual data they collected, the 5-week participants relied on cultural beliefs and theories about what causes moods (e.g., "Rainy days and Mondays always get me down."). These same shared beliefs and theories were used by the observers when they were asked to predict to what extent each factor was linked to people's moods. Both groups, then, relied on what some researchers have called a priori causal theories (e.g., Nisbett & Wilson, 1977) and not the data found in their actual experiences (for further reading, see Wilson, 1985; Wilson & Stone, 1985).

Now, do you think you really know what factors predict whether you will be in a good mood or a bad one? Would you be any more (or less) accurate than the students who tracked their moods for 5 weeks? To test your accuracy, try your hand at the *Project Exercise* presented at the end of the chapter.

▽

Plotting the X and Y pairs on a scatterplot is a good way to visualize a correlational relationship.

Negative correlations routinely show a downward sloping plot of points moving from the top left of the graph to its bottom right side (see panel (b) in Figure 6.2). When a negative relationship is apparent, then, its points appear to move in a southeasterly direction as you look from the left to the right of a graph. When a given value *X* is low, for example, the accompanying *Y* value is high due to the inverse nature of negative relationships. It follows, then, that higher values of *X* are found with lower values of *Y*.

If a liner relationship were *truly perfect*, one where every value of *X* and *Y* either shared identical values (i.e., a positive correlation) or met its opposite (i.e., a negative correlation), the points in the space of the graph would form a perfectly straight line. These largely theoretical possibilities—behavioral data almost never achieve such clean

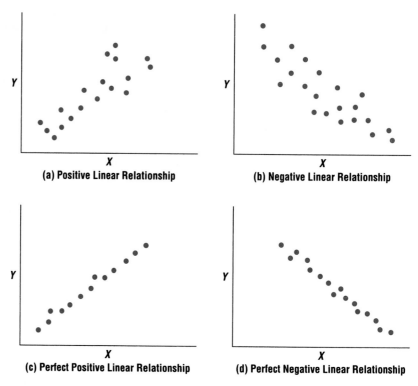

Figure 6.2   Linear Scatter Plots Illustrating Positive and Negative Correlations

linearity—are shown in panels (c) and (d), respectively, in Figure 6.2. In other words, the known value of each variable would predict its complement; if you knew one value, you would necessarily know the other. In practice, such perfect prediction rarely occurs, though the ideal prediction of points will be the goal of a technique called linear regression, which is based on correlation. We will learn about this technique—one that gives life, as it were, to correlations—in chapter 7.

☑

Greater linearity in a scatter plot's points indicates a stronger correlation.

Of course, scatter plots are not used only to plot perfect linear relationships. They are at home, as it were, plotting any correlational data. Figure 6.3 is a scatter plot representing the relationship between the scores on the personality inventory and the participants' social interaction with the study's confederates (the data were taken from Table 6.1). As shown in Figure 6.3, each of the plotted points represents the intersection of pairs of *X* and *Y* values from our hypothetical study. Thus, for example, participant 6 had an inventory score of 19 and he or she met 8 confederates during the 30-minute session (see Figure 6.3). What sort of relationship does the scatter plot in Figure 6.3 suggest? It looks to be quite a strong positive relationship—extraverts tended to meet many of the confederates, while introverts sought out relatively few. We will see if our supposition of a strong, positive relationship is borne out by the correlation between these variables below.

What about correlational relationships between *X* and *Y* that hover near 0? What do these patterns look like when they are graphed? As shown by the data presented in Figure 6.4, there is not much to see by way of any discernable pattern. This lack of consistency between values *X* and *Y* is, of course, the point of a zero correlation. No meaningful, interpretable pattern should appear (see Figure 6.4). In general, weaker correlations between variables can be known by a broader scattering of points in space.

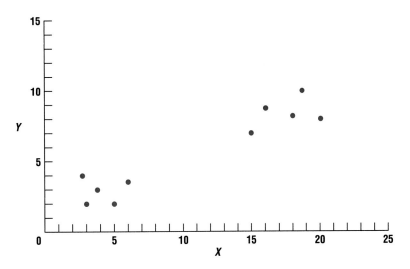

Figure 6.3 Scatter Plot of Personality Inventory Scores and Interaction Behavior

Note: These data were taken from Table 6.1.

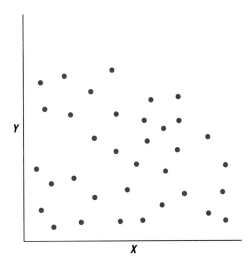

Figure 6.4 Scatter Plot of a Zero Correlational Relationship

Scatter plots can appear in an endless variety falling between the strict linearity of perfect correlations and the spatial disarray of zero correlations. Figure 6.5 illustrates a few other (hypothetical) possibilities. In each case, the value of X is matched with another value Y. Some scatter plots can illustrate a curvilinear relationship, as shown by panel (a) in Figure 6.5. Such a pattern of points will yield a correlation close to 0 because the Pearson r does not detect covariation that does not conform to a linear relationship. Panel (b) in Figure 6.5 illustrates how scores on a dichotomous variable—one with only two levels or values, such as gender where M stands for male and F stands for female (X)—can be plotted with a variable, say test scores (Y) that can take on many values. Finally, panel (c) presents a scatter plot representing the effects of practice. As time (X) passes, for instance, the memorization of novel information (Y) gradually

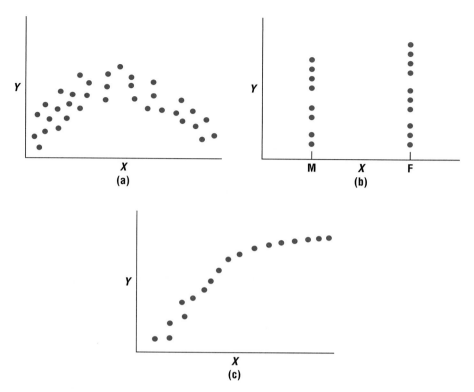

Figure 6.5   Other Possible Scatter Plots Showing Relationships Between Some Variables *X* and *Y*

improves until it eventually levels off (note that the curve in panel (c) eventually becomes "flat").

The scatter plot of a data set allows a researcher to think about what the relationship between two variables is apt to be like. By examining the pattern of points, one can get a feel for whether the relationship between the variables is positive, negative, or zero, as well as the probable strength of the actual correlation statistic (i.e., are the points relatively close together or far apart). Of course, the only way to truly understand the nature of the relationship is by actually calculating the *r* statistic, the matter we turn to next.

Calculating the Pearson *r*

Calculating the Pearson *r* involves briefly reviewing *z* scores and the sum of the squares, two familiar statistical concepts. A new concept, "covariance," will also be introduced, as it is integral to determining *r*. Two ways to calculate *r* will be presented, the raw score method and the mean deviation method.

The Pearson *r*'s relation to *z* scores.
In chapter 5, we learned that the distinct advantage posed by *z* scores is their ability to standardize variables. Once a score is converted to a *z*, we can see how close it lies to the *z* distribution's mean of 0, as it is now represented in standard deviation units (if these facts seem unfamiliar to you, please turn back to chapter 5 before proceeding with your reading here). By using a *z* score, we can precisely locate the placement of an individual score in a distribution.

The Pearson *r* capitalizes on this standardization by assessing and reconciling, as it were, the relative locations of *X* and *Y* simultaneously. In other words, the Pearson *r* actually employs z scores to specify the locations of X and Y, and then it measures the relationship between them. This relationship—positive, negative, or zero—is based on the location of each score X in what relative proximity to its Y partner. Not surprisingly, the r statistic can be expressed in a formula that uses only z scores:

$$[6.1.1] \qquad r = \frac{\sum z_X z_Y}{N},$$

where each of the z scores from X is multiplied by each z score for Y, and their products are summed and then divided by the number of XY pairs. These calculations are somewhat involved, though not at all difficult (Gravetter & Wallnau, 1996), and we will rely on alternative conceptual and computational formulas for r later in the chapter. What you should retain from the present discussion is that the Pearson r incorporates the logic and statistical advantages of z scores, though we will learn to calculate it using the sum of the squares.

Sum of the Squares Revisited.   Back in chapter 4, you will recall learning that the sum of the squared deviations from the mean—the "sum of the squares" for short—played an essential role when it came to the calculation of the variance and the standard deviation. As we noted then, the sum of the squares is integral to many, if not most, inferential statistical tests. You will see in a moment that the formula for the Pearson r is no exception, that the sum of the squares is prominent within it.

Here is a second conceptual formula for the Pearson r:

$$[6.2.1] \qquad r = \frac{\sum (X - \bar{X})(Y - \bar{Y})}{\sqrt{\sum (X - \bar{X})^2 \sum (Y - \bar{Y})^2}}.$$

The numerator of the formula is based on the sum of the mean deviations from X and Y multiplied by one another. With the possible exception of the square root radical, however, the denominator should look somewhat more familiar. The $\sum (X - \bar{X})^2$ and $\sum (Y - \bar{Y})^2$ are the sums of squares for variables X and Y, respectively. The formula we use to compute the sum of the squares is [4.10.1], or:

$$SS = \sum X^2 - \frac{(\sum X)^2}{N}.$$

This formula can certainly be used to determine the sum of squares for X, but we also need to remind ourselves that we must calculate the same information for Y. To simplify matters, we can revise [4. 10.1] by making two versions of it, one for X and one for Y, or:

$$[6.3.1] \qquad SS_X = \sum X^2 - \frac{(\sum X)^2}{N}.$$

and

$$[6.4.1] \qquad SS_Y = \sum Y^2 - \frac{(\sum Y)^2}{N}.$$

Once we think of the denominator of [6.2.1] in terms of SS_X and SS_Y it no longer seems so forbidding. Now, take another look at the numerator of [6.2.1]—it, too, is another form of the sum of squares, one that assesses what is called the *covariance* of X and Y. Statistically, the covariance is defined as the average of the sum of products of deviations from the mean, or $(X - \bar{X})(Y - \bar{Y})$. The calculation formula for the covariance of X and Y is:

$$[6.5.1] \qquad \text{cov}_{XY} = \sum XY - \frac{(\sum X)(\sum Y)}{N}.$$

If we place [6.5.1] in the position of the numerator and then put [6.3.1] and [6.4.1] under the radical, the original Pearson r formula shown in [6.2.1] can be rewritten as the common computational formula:

[6.6.1]
$$r = \frac{\sum XY - \dfrac{(\sum X)(\sum Y)}{N}}{\sqrt{\left[\sum X^2 - \dfrac{(\sum X)^2}{N}\right]\left[\sum Y^2 - \dfrac{(\sum Y)^2}{N}\right]}} \;.$$

As noted above in the conceptual introduction, the correlation coefficient r is based on taking the numerical index of how variables X and Y *vary together* (i.e., covariance) and then dividing it by numerical information representing how X and Y *vary separately.*

We can now return to the example that opened this section of the chapter—whether a personality inventory that measures extraversion is linked with sociable behavior—and actually calculate the r between the two variables. To calculate r, we will use what is commonly referred to as the "raw score" method to determine the values to be entered into formula [6.6.1]. Table 6.2 extends the information originally provided in Table 6.1 by adding columns of numbers that enable us to determine the sums of squares for X and Y, as well as the covariance between X and Y. Each of the X and Y observations has been squared and placed in the second and fourth columns, respectively, of Table 6.2. The fifth column of Table 6.2 contains the products resulting from multiplying each observation X by its paired Y observation.

The bottom of Table 6.2 summarizes information about the paired variables X and Y. Under column 2 are shown the summary statistics for X, the psychological inventory, including $\sum X$, $\sum X^2$, $\overline{X}_X$, and s_X. The corresponding information for the Y variable, which represents social interaction, is shown beneath column 4. Finally, the $\sum XY$ is

Table 6.2 **Data Prepared for Calculation of the Pearson r (Raw Score Method)**

Participants	X	X^2	Y	Y^2	XY
1	20	400	8	64	160
2	5	25	2	4	10
3	18	324	10	100	180
4	6	36	3	9	18
5	19	361	8	64	152
6	3	9	4	16	12
7	4	16	3	9	12
8	3	9	2	4	6
9	17	289	7	49	119
10	18	324	9	81	162
	$\sum X = 113$		$\sum Y = 56$		$\sum XY = 831$
	$\sum X^2 = 1{,}793$		$\sum Y^2 = 400$		
	$\overline{X}_X = 11.3$		$\overline{X}_Y = 5.6$		
	$s_X = 7.57$		$s_Y = 3.10$		
	$N = 10$				

Note: Hypothetical data were drawn from Table 6.1; $\overline{X}_Y = \overline{Y}$.

Table 6.3	Step-by-Step Calculations for the Pearson r (Raw Score Method) Using Data from Table 6.2

$$r = \frac{\sum XY - \frac{(\sum X)(\sum Y)}{N}}{\sqrt{\left[\sum X^2 - \frac{(\sum X)^2}{N}\right]\left[\sum Y^2 - \frac{(\sum Y)^2}{N}\right]}}$$

$$r = \frac{831 - \frac{(113)(56)}{10}}{\sqrt{\left[1793 - \frac{(113)^2}{10}\right]\left[400 - \frac{(56)^2}{10}\right]}}$$

$$r = \frac{831 - \frac{6,328}{10}}{\sqrt{\left[1793 - \frac{12,769}{10}\right]\left[400 - \frac{3,136}{10}\right]}}$$

$$r = \frac{831 - 632.8}{\sqrt{[1,793 - 1,276.9][400 - 313.6]}}$$

$$r = \frac{198.20}{\sqrt{[516.10][86.4]}}$$

$$r = \frac{198.20}{\sqrt{44,591.04}}$$

$$r = \frac{198.20}{211.1659}$$

$$r = +.9386 \cong +.94$$

shown under the last column of Table 6.2. If you have any questions regarding how any of these sums or statistics were determined, please review the appropriate sections of chapter 1 or 4.

We now calculate the Pearson r between scores on the psychological inventory and the number of social interactions during the 30-minute get-acquainted session. This calculation is shown in Table 6.3. For convenience, formula [6.6.1] is repeated there. The sums entered into the second step of the calculation here were taken from Table 6.2. Be sure that you can follow each of the steps shown in Table 6.3. The computed $r = +.9386$. The convention is to round the correlation coefficient to two places behind the decimal, thus $r = +.94$.

What about the second method for calculating the Pearson r? The second method—the mean deviation approach—is no more difficult than the raw score method. Here is the computational formula for the mean deviation method:

[6.7.1]
$$r = \frac{\sum (X - \bar{X})(Y - \bar{Y})}{\sqrt{SS_X \cdot SS_Y}}.$$

As you can see in formula [6.7.1], this approach also relies on the sum of squares and the covariance of X and Y.

Table 6.4   Data Prepared for Calculation of the Pearson r (Mean Deviation Method)

Participants	X	$X - \bar{X}$	$(X - \bar{X})^2$	Y	$Y - \bar{Y}$	$(Y - \bar{Y})^2$	$(X - \bar{X})(Y - \bar{Y})$
1	20	8.7	75.69	8	2.4	5.76	20.88
2	5	−6.3	39.69	2	−3.6	12.96	22.68
3	18	6.7	44.89	10	4.4	19.36	29.48
4	6	−5.3	28.09	3	−2.6	6.76	13.78
5	19	7.7	52.29	8	2.4	5.76	18.48
6	3	−8.3	68.89	4	−1.6	2.56	13.28
7	4	−7.3	53.29	3	−2.6	6.76	18.98
8	3	−8.3	68.89	2	−3.6	12.96	29.88
9	17	5.7	32.49	7	1.4	1.96	7.98
10	18	6.7	44.89	9	3.4	11.56	22.78

$$SS_X = 516.10 \qquad\qquad SS_Y = 86.4$$

$$\sum (X - \bar{X})(Y - \bar{Y}) = 198.20$$

$$\bar{X}_X = 11.3 \qquad\qquad \bar{X}_Y = 5.6$$

$$s_X = 7.57 \qquad\qquad s_Y = 3.10$$

$$N = 10$$

Note: Hypothetical data were drawn from Table 6.1. $\bar{X}_Y = \bar{Y}$.

Calculating r using the mean deviation method is really no more difficult than the raw score method. The data for X and Y from Table 6.1 are shown in Table 6.4 (see the second and fifth columns, respectively). Column 3 contains the deviation scores based on subtracting the mean of X (i.e., $\bar{X}_X = 11.3$) from each of the values of X. Column 4, in turn, shows the square of the mean deviation scores for X, the sum of which, of course, is the sum of squares ($SS_X = 516.10$; see the bottom of column 4). Columns 6 and 7 repeat these respective procedures for variable Y ($\bar{X}_Y = 5.60$). The sum of squares for Y, which is equal to 86.4, can be found at the bottom of column 7. The sum of the last column in the far right of Table 6.4 shows the covariance of X and Y, or 198.20. This number is based on the deviation scores for both variables. Multiplying the values in column 3 by those in column 6, and then summing the resulting products calculates the covariance of X and Y.

Once the covariance of X and Y and their respective sums of squares are known, they can be entered into formula [6.7.1]. For your convenience, each of the steps used to calculate r using this formula is summarized in Table 6.5. Naturally, the same result—$r = +.94$—is found using the mean deviation method (see Table 6.5). To verify that you understand how all the numbers were determined, please compare the contents of Tables 6.3 and 6.5 with one another.

Which of the two calculation methods should you use? The choice is your own; some individuals prefer the raw score method, others the mean deviation method. Both approaches will provide the same answer and probably take approximately the same amount of time to perform.

Regardless of which formula you select, there are couple pitfalls to be wary of when calculating r. An easy to forget feature of the Pearson r is that N refers to the number of

☑

In correlational analyses, N refers to the number of X, Y pairs, *not* the total number of observations present.

Table 6.5 Step-by-Step Calculations for the Pearson r (Mean Deviation Method) Using Data From Table 6.2

$$r = \frac{\sum (X - \bar{X})(Y - \bar{Y})}{\sqrt{SS_X \cdot SS_Y}}$$

$$r = \frac{198.20}{\sqrt{(516.10)(86.4)}}$$

$$r = \frac{198.20}{\sqrt{44,591.04}}$$

$$r = \frac{198.20}{211.1659}$$

$$r = .9386 \cong .94$$

pairs of variables X and Y (here, $N = 10$), *not* the total number of observations available (i.e., 20—10 for X and 10 for Y). It is easy to make this mistake because you are not (yet) used to working with pairs of observations. Further, it is important to keep the *mise en place* philosophy from chapter 1 in mind when calculating a correlation. As you can see by the amount of information that must be kept track of (see Tables 6.2 and 6.4) and then entered into an r formula (see Tables 6.3 and 6.5), it pays to be organized. None of the calculations are particularly difficult or even time consuming, but with so many numbers, it is easy to write down the right number in the wrong place. To avoid computational errors, then, it is essential for you to keep track of which number goes where by carefully writing them down on a separate sheet with column headings like those shown in Tables 6.2 and 6.4.

We now turn to the important matter of interpreting a correlational result.

Interpreting Correlation

Based on our analysis of the scatter plot (see Figure 6.3) and the correlation calculated in Tables 6.3 and 6.5, what do we know? The scatter plot provided us with graphic evidence that the correlation was positive in nature and the r-statistic of $+.94$ confirmed it. We know that extraverts—those individuals who had higher scores on the personality inventory—were apt to meet many more confederates during the staged "get acquainted" session than their introverted counterparts. The latter, as predicted, tended to meet fewer confederates, that is, to engage in less social contact. In short, particular personalities were correlated with particular social behaviors.

Correlation and Causation—A Reprise. It is tempting to say that personality "caused" behavior in this instance, but we cannot rule out that (past) social behavior—meeting or not meeting others—did not "cause" extraverted or introverted personalities. The fact that the inventory was completed *prior* to social interaction is not sufficient justification for making a causal claim. Nor have we ruled out the possibility that some third variable is not responsible for mediating the relationship between personality and social interaction in this instance. Perhaps good or bad social experiences rooted in childhood led to both the scores on the inventory and the social behavior (or lack thereof) with the confederates. Remember, correlation does not entail causation.

Beyond discounting causal accounts, however, there are other considerations that must be examined before any correlational result is to be relied on. These considerations include examining the magnitude of the correlation, its predictive accuracy, and ruling out factors that can preclude an accurate interpretation of the statistic.

Magnitude of *r*

Beyond indicating the sign and strength of a correlational relationship, researchers typically also describe the magnitude of the association between the two variables. Different researchers use different descriptors, but what follows is a helpful guide of arbitrary labels for ranges of *r* values (based on Evans, 1996, p. 146):

Range of r	Descriptive label for r
±.80 to 1.00	Very strong
±.60 to .79	Strong
±.40 to .59	Moderate
±.20 to .39	Weak
±.00 to .19	Very weak

These ranges and descriptions are not writ in stone. One investigator might describe an *r* of +.75 as very strong, while another might say that one equal to −.35 is moderate. The choice of label depends on the data, the context of the scientific argument, and the investigator's temperament.

How can our hypothetical study's Pearson *r* of +.94 be classified? It is clearly a very strong correlation, indeed, falling in the +.80 to +1.00 range. An investigator could legitimately describe this correlation as "very strong" in a written summary of the project (see below). In most cases, however, it is not sufficient to just note the value of the correlation and to describe its magnitude—readers will also want to know how accurately it portrayed the data. The issue of accuracy is wrapped up with how knowing the variability of one variable can allow you to predict the change in another.

☑

Though conventions exist, adjectives describing the magnitude of correlational relationships are somewhat arbitrary.

Coefficients of Determination and Nondetermination

More can be learned from a correlational result by determining its predictive accuracy, which is contextually defined as the percentage of variance in one variable within a correlation that can be described by the second member of the pair. This type of variability can be known by squaring the *r* value, resulting in r^2, a statistic known as the *coefficient of determination*.

KEY TERM   The **coefficient of determination** (r^2) indicates the proportion of variance or change in one variable that can be accounted for by another variable.

In our personality-social behavior example, squaring the *r* value of +.94 gives us an r^2 value of +.88, or:

$$[6.8.1] \qquad r^2 = (r)^2 = (.94)^2 = +.88.$$

Thus, the coefficient of determination for $r = +.94$ is +.88. (Note that r^2 will *always* be a positive number—any number that is squared is positive—and that an r^2 value *must* be smaller than *r*, as any decimal value that is squared becomes smaller.) How is r^2 interpreted? We can say that 88% of the variance or the change in social behavior (Y) can be predicted by the participants' introverted or extraverted personalities (i.e., the relationship shared with X).

A second, complementary statistic, the *coefficient of nondetermination*, symbolized as *k*, can also be calculated when *r* is known. The coefficient of nondetermination provides the proportion of the variance in one variable that is not attributable to any change within the other variable in a correlational relationship. It is easily calculated simply by subtracting r^2 from 1.

KEY TERM The **coefficient of nondetermination** (k, or $1 - r^2$) indicates the proportion of variance or change in one variable that *cannot* be accounted for by another variable.

In the present example, $1 - r^2$ would be equal to:

[6.9.1] $$k = 1 - r^2 = 1 - .88 = +.12.$$

Thus, 12% of the social interaction that took place in the lab can be explained by factors *other than* the extraverted or introverted personalities of the study's participants. (Note that if you add the values of r^2 and k together—here $(+.88) + (+.12)$—they must sum to $+1.00$.)

Another way to think about the statistical relationships portrayed by the coefficient of determination and the coefficient of nondetermination is to represent them graphically. Figure 6.6 employs circles to represent variables X and Y, and the circles' relative degree of overlap to illustrate correlation. As the overlap between the two circles increases, so does the magnitude of their correlation with one another. The actual shaded area—the overlap—graphically portrays r^2. Greater correlation leads to greater overlap, which in turn yields a relative high value for the coefficient of determination (and a correspondingly low value for the coefficient of nondetermination, which is

When r^2 is known, so is k (i.e., $1 - r^2$), and vice versa.

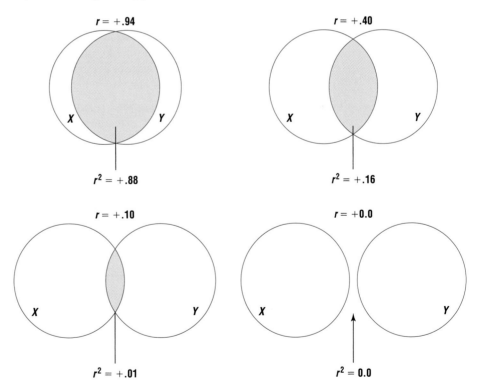

Figure 6.6 Graphic Illustration of Correlation and the Coefficients of Determination and Nondetermination

Note: Overlapping circles indicate the extent of the correlation between variable X and Y. The shaded area shared between circles can be quantified as the coefficient of determination (r^2). Nonoverlapping areas of circles can be quantified as the coefficient of nondetermination ($1 - r^2$).

graphically represented by the nonoverlapping sections of the circles). As shown in Figure 6.6, when two circles (variables) do not share space with one another, their correlation is equal to 0.0.

The coefficients of determination and nondetermination are the first indices designed to support statistics that we have encountered so far. These "supporting" statistics tell us more about a correlational result than the result does all by itself (for limitations associated with r^2, see Rosnow & Rosenthal, 1996; Rosenthal & Rubin, 1982). Increasingly, statisticians and researchers are relying on such supporting statistics to broaden the interpretation and quantify the strength of a given result. As we learn additional inferential tests, we will learn to use supporting statistics that will help us gauge the size of their effects.

Factors Influencing *r*

Before one can conclude definitively that a correlation is trustworthy, several factors should be examined. These factors are the range of values used to compute a result, the extent of a linear relationship between variables, the presence of any outlying scores, the size of a sample, and the potential for preexisting subpopulations within a data set. Each of these factors can lead to abnormally high or low correlations masking any real effects within a set of data.

Restricted Range and Its Effects on Correlation.   A restricted—sometimes called a "truncated"—range occurs when the range of the values for one or both of the variables in a correlation is limited. Allowing for considerable variability, variable X might have a possible range of values from 0 to 20; variable Y, however, might be limited to values ranging from 1 to 3. The presence of a restricted range for a variable like Y often leads to what is called a *spurious,* low correlation between X and Y.

KEY TERM   A **spurious correlation** is one that is either artificially high (inflated) or low (deflated) due to the particular characteristics of some data or the methodology used to collect it.

When do behavioral scientists encounter restricted ranges? More often than you might expect, especially if they work with particular subgroups of people with traits possessing restricted ranges. A developmental psychologist, for example, might work exclusively with infants and toddlers, thereby risking problems with truncated ranges if the age (in months) of research participants was too close together (e.g., 6 to 8 months, 20 to 24 months). The same sort of range problem might occur if another researcher studied a particular age range in adolescence (e.g., 13 to 14 years) or old age (e.g., 80 to 90 years).

Despite the fact that other variables one might measure—say, scores on a personality inventory or performance on a cognitive task—have reasonable amounts of variability or change across a sample of scores, limited age ranges often preclude using or trusting the results of a correlational analysis. The moral here is an obvious one: Always make certain that both the X and Y variables have a fairly wide range of responses by scanning their respective distributions prior to performing any correlational analyses.

Limited Linear Relationship Between *X* and *Y*.   As noted earlier, the Pearson *r* is designed to detect the linear relationship between two variables. If the data of interest depart too much from a straight-line orientation in space (see the earlier discussion of scatter plots of data), then the size and the magnitude of the correlation will be adversely affected. Curvilinear relationships between X and Y—when plotted they form a U shape or an inverted U—will result in very low

Pearson *r* values, for example, *despite* the fact that a scatter plot makes the data appear to be predictable (see panel (a) in Figure 6.5). The reason for low predictability is that the positive and negative values on either side of the curve tend to cancel one another out, resulting in a low, often spurious, correlation. A savvy researcher always examines the scatter plot of any data before beginning an analysis or drawing conclusions from one that has already been completed.

Outlying Scores and Correlation.   Extreme scores—those with aberrantly high or low values—have a similar deleterious effect on correlations as they do on descriptive statistics like the mean. Outlying scores can artificially increase (or decrease) the apparent size of a correlation; just one or two "deviant" scores in a small or medium-sized sample can wield a great influence.

Researchers really have two choices to make to reduce the deleterious effects of extreme scores. First, increasing the size of the sample can usually diminish the effects of any given outlier (i.e., recall the law of large numbers introduced in chapter 4). Second, an investigator can examine the scatter plot of scores for variables *X* and *Y* to determine if any outliers are present and, therefore, if they should be removed from subsequent analyses. Given a choice, increasing a sample's size seems to be a more ethically compelling maneuver than dropping problematic observations on a whim. On the other hand, removing outliers is often easier to carry out than widening the size of a sample. Whichever alternative is chosen, researchers must be honest with themselves and to their readers by providing a full account of how they dealt with the problem of outlying scores.

Sample Size and Correlation.   On occasion, sample size can influence whether a correlation reveals a spurious relationship between two variables. Whenever possible, investigators should recruit sufficiently sized samples of participants for research purposes. The goal, of course, is to obtain enough participants so that their responses, and correlations between pairs of particular responses, will adequately represent their population of origin. Do not fall prey to a common myth, however, that larger samples yield larger correlations and that smaller samples necessarily result in smaller correlations. Sample size and the strength of a given correlation are actually independent of one another; that is, one does not predict the other (e.g., Runyon et al., 1996). This qualification is not an invitation to run correlational analyses on small samples, though, rather it is encouragement to seek adequately sized samples in order to reduce the risk of uncovering spurious correlations in your data.

What is a reasonably sized sample? How many participants will you need for your research? Answers to these questions involve exploring (a) *available resources* and (b) the *effect* you hope to demonstrate (Dunn, 1999). Resources can be divided into two components, the time available to you to collect data and the number of participants available to you. If you have a large amount of time and a corresponding number of research participants, then you are probably in good shape. If you have a shortage of either resource, beware of the heightened potential for spurious correlations. Indeed, where correlational analyses are concerned, you should endeavor to have around 30 or so participants before running any Pearson *r*s.

What about the particular effect, some positive or negative relationship between two variables, you hope to demonstrate? There are several techniques available to researchers that can help them to determine how many participants they need in order to demonstrate a statistical effect that reaches a particular magnitude. Collectively, these techniques are called **power analysis** (e.g., Cohen, 1988, 1992; Rosenthal & Rosnow, 1991), a topic we will return to later in the book. Until that time, follow the general rule that larger samples are apt to be helpful toward testing for the presence of desired effects in data.

Preexisting Subpopulations and Correlation.   The final factor that can preclude a clear and accurate interpretation of a correlation between variables *X* and *Y* is the presence of preexisting subpopulations within a sample of data. By preexisting subpopulations, I refer to any groups of participants who share some common feature or trait that escapes being noticed by a researcher. Subject variables such as age, gender, marital status, ethnic or religious background, as well as any number of personality traits (e.g., self-esteem), can reduce the overall correlation between two variables. How so? Imagine that a researcher was interested in women's self-esteem and how well it correlated with life satisfaction, among other indices of psychological well-being. Other investigators routinely document strong relationships between these variables, yet the researcher finds a relatively low correlation (i.e., *r* = .15).

Why did the researcher fail to replicate the usual correlational results? When examining a scatter plot of data, the researcher notices two distinct clusters of scores, either of which might be predictive on its own but, in combination, cancel out each other's effects. She quickly realizes that the upper cluster contains mostly scores of married professional women, while the lower cluster is composed primarily of divorced women heading single-parent households. In other words, the investigator neglected to consider the effects of marital status, its potential link to economic well-being and, in turn, how it affects self-esteem. Had she examined scatter plots displaying self-esteem and its relation to various other variables (including marital status) before running any analyses, she would have anticipated the distinct and problematic subgroups. Thus, it is always beneficial to search for patterns in your data *before* actually sitting down to analyze them in earnest (recall the spirit of exploratory data analysis introduced in chapter 3; see, for example, Tukey, 1977).

Writing About Correlational Relationships

Writing about correlational results is not at all difficult as long as a few basic principles are followed. First, always describe the relationship a correlation posits in clear prose and interpret the correlation for your readers. Do not assume they will discern its importance or readily recognizing the positive or negative relationship existing between the variables it identifies. If you were noting that "higher levels of aggression were linked with more impatient or awkward behaviors exhibited by the participants," be sure to remind readers that the reverse—"lower levels of aggression corresponded to fewer impatient or awkward behaviors"—was also (necessarily) found. These opposite results need not be reported in a "sing-song" or mirror image fashion as long as you convey that both possibilities occur within the context of a positive correlation.

When reporting the actual value of a correlation in APA style, you should note the statistic used (the Pearson *r* is denoted simply as *r*, or an underlined "r"; symbols for other types of correlations can be found in section 3.58 of the *APA Publication Manual* [APA, 1994]); its value to two places (occasionally three) behind the decimal point (e.g., +.45, −.32, +.021, −.654); and usually the number of pairs of scores (e.g., *N* = 20) used in the calculation.[1] Regarding the latter, be certain to alert the reader if there were any incomplete pairs of scores in the data, as this fact will change the *N* from analysis to analysis.

---

[1] A correlation is also usually accompanied by a probability or *p* value, which indicates whether the *r* is statistically significant. Significance testing and *p* values are introduced in chapters 8 and 9, and I will postpone discussing their relation to *r* until then.

Correlational results can be presented in several ways. First, a correlation can be reported in the heart of a sentence:

> The Pearson correlation between number of children and marital satisfaction was −.35, suggesting that couples with more children tend to experience lower levels of contentment. Those with fewer or no children report greater marital compatibility with their spouses.

Alternatively, a correlational relationship between two variables can be described by a sentence, and the actual statistical results can be noted either parenthetically or at the end of the sentence:

> **Parenthetically.** Number of children and marital satisfaction were inversely related to one another at a moderate level ($r = −.35$, $N = 60$), indicating that contentment in marriage declines as couples elect to have more children.

> **End of a Sentence.** Number of children and marital satisfaction were inversely related to one another at a moderate level, indicating that contentment in marriage declines as couples elect to have more children, $r = −.35$, $N = 60$.

Finally, correlational results can be described in the body of the text, but the actual numerical information is placed in a table, often in the form of a correlation matrix (see Data Box 6.C for suggestions about reading and interpreting a correlation matrix). Such matrices are very useful, especially when several correlations are reported. In practice, a matrix will show the correlation values computed between all of the possible variable pairings. Although only some of the correlations represented by these pairings will be of primary interest to researchers and readers alike, the scientific convention is to disclose them all for public scrutiny. Indeed, astute readers sometimes identify relationships neglected by the researcher or pose alternative hypotheses for the data when viewing a given pattern of correlations.

If you do place correlational data into a table, be sure to follow the guidelines for describing tabular information within the body of a paper (see chapter 3; see also, Dunn, 1999). You must guide readers to correlational relationships that are of particular interest to you or that support your arguments rather than assuming they will find them on their own.

Knowledge Base

1. What are the three types of directional relationships that can be found in a correlational analysis?
2. A middle-aged man begins to exercise regularly because he read a newspaper study identifying an inverse correlation between heart disease and physical activity. He proudly announces to his spouse, "Well, I'll *never* have a heart attack." What is wrong with his reasoning?
3. True or False: An $r = +.47$ is stronger than an $r = −.47$.
4. What is the coefficient of determination for $r = −.40$? What is the coefficient of nondetermination for $r = −.40$?
5. A scatter plot reveals scores falling close together into a well-defined U-shaped curve, but the researcher is surprised to learn that the Pearson r is only equal to $+.12$. Why is the correlation so low?

Answers

1. A correlation can reveal a positive, a negative, or a zero relationship.
2. Although exercise is certainly beneficial, correlation does not imply causation—there is no guarantee that he will or will not have a heart attack at some point.

3. False: The $+$ or $-$ sign denotes directionality in the relationship. The shared numerical value of these correlations makes them equally strong.
4. The $r^2 = +.16; 1 - r^2 = +.84$.
5. The Pearson r is designed to detect linear, not curvilinear, relationships within a set of data.

Correlation as Consistency and Reliability

Reliability is a methodological concept that has an important statistical component. As defined in chapter 2, reliability is a clear methodological strength, referring to the extent to which a given measure provides a stable or consistent reading each time it is used. The expectation is that a satisfactory measure will *consistently measure* the construct it was designed to measure. As a desirable quality of measures employed by behavioral scientists, then, reliability ensures that a personality inventory given to a group of participants at one point in time should yield similar results if it is readministered to them later. We would never anticipate that every person in the sample would obtain the exact same score on the inventory during both administrations, of course, but we would ex-

DATA BOX 6.B

Personality, Cross-Situational Consistency, and Correlation

Are warm and friendly people warm and friendly regardless of the circumstance? Think about the one or two personality traits that best describe you. Are they stable; that is, do these traits manifest themselves across situations?

What could be more obvious than the fact that people (including ourselves) behave in consistent, seemingly predictable ways. Our personalities and the individual traits that comprise them seem to be pronounced, recognizable, and consistent or, as personality psychologists are wont to say, "stable," from setting to setting. Such everyday beliefs jibe well with some formal psychological theories of personality, but both perspectives encounter difficulties under the careful scrutiny of controlled research.

The Pearson r plays a very prominent role in what turns out to be one of the great debates in American psychology—the cross-situational consistency (or lack thereof) of personality traits and behavior. Surprisingly, considerable research demonstrates that correlations between measured personality traits at one point in time (e.g., honesty) and behaviors (e.g., stealing, cheating) measured at other points usually range between $r = +.20$ to $+.30$, almost never exceeding what appears to be the ceiling of $+.30$ (Mischel, 1968; Peterson, 1968). In other words, the strength of association between many traits and related behaviors can be described as weak; indeed, an r^2 of $+.09$ is what one finds at the *high end* of the correlation range (i.e., when r reaches $+.30$; but see Rosenthal & Rubin, 1982, for another view).

Mischel (1968) provocatively suggested that such low correlations did not indicate that the study of trait-behavior linkages be abandoned, rather that researchers should consider the possibility that people are apparently motivated to perceive higher degrees of consistent behavior across situations than is generally warranted. This perceptual bias, then, opens an interesting avenue of exploration for social-personality psychologists, one that has been pursued in various ways for the last 30 years. If nothing else, the consistency controversy generated new life in the field of personality and some lessons were learned (Kenrick & Funder, 1988). Many researchers generally supported Mischel's position (e.g., Ross & Nisbett, 1991), others critiqued it (e.g., Funder, 1983; Funder & Ozer, 1983), and some staked out a middle ground (e.g., Bem & Allen, 1974). In each case, however, the correlation and its interpretive power were put to good use in the development and subsequent peer review of personality theories.

pect that, on the average, each member of each pair of scores would not differ substantially from one another (recall the discussion of observed versus true scores presented in chapter 2).

What is the statistical component of reliability? The reliability of any given measure can be quantified or assessed using the Pearson correlation coefficient. All a researcher has to do, for example, is to correlate one set of scores on a measure with another set from the same measure as long as they were collected at a different point in time. This simplest form of reliability, referred to as **test-retest reliability,** involves giving the same test or measure twice to the same group of respondents. If the measure in question were truly reliable, then the Pearson r between the scores on the first and second administration should be relatively high, say, between +.80 and +.90. When a Pearson r is used to demonstrate reliability, it is often called a **reliability coefficient.**

In order to be deemed reliable, a measure must display a positive correlation (reliability coefficient) that reaches or exceeds an r of +.70. A correlation lower than this minimal value suggests that the responses across the two administrations vary considerably from one another (i.e., consistency from time 1 to time 2 is low). By definition, measures that show low levels of consistency cannot be considered reliable for research purposes.

A reliable measure provides consistent or similar measurements each time it is used.

Other Types of Reliability Defined

Although it is popular, test-retest reliability is not the only statistical way to determine if a measure is reliable by using the Pearson r. In fact, giving the same test to participants twice can be problematic, as many respondents may recall the answers they gave on the first administration. Parroting an earlier response on a later administration of a measure only serves to inflate the test-retest reliability coefficient. To combat this problem, some researchers rely on **alternate form reliability** where participants complete different measures containing the same sort of items on two separate occasions. Their two scores are then correlated and a higher r value indicates whether the alternate form reliability is successful.

Reliability need not necessarily be assessed using the same measure given at two points in time—under certain conditions a single administration can actually be sufficient. To do so, behavioral scientists occasionally rely on what are collectively called **internal consistency measures of reliability.** The main condition for this form of reliability is that the measure in question must be comprised of a reasonably large number of items. The rationale for this condition will be articulated shortly.

The first form of internal consistency reliability is called **split-half reliability** because it entails literally "splitting" a test in half so that respondents' total scores on the first half of the test can be correlated with their total scores on the second half. A second, related form is called **odd-even reliability.** As you might guess, responses to the odd numbered items on a test are totaled and then correlated to the total scores of the even numbered items. A third method of internal consistency reliability is labeled **item-total reliability,** and it requires a bit more effort for researchers than the previous two approaches. Scores on each item of a test are correlated with the total score on the test. A test with 100 items, for instance, would require that 100 correlation coefficients be computed, the mean of which would serve as the reliability coefficient.

A Brief Word About Validity

Correlational analysis can also be used to establish the validity of a measure or construct. In chapter 3, validity was defined as the degree to which some observation or measure corresponds to the construct it was designed to gauge. Many times a researcher will want to verify that some novel test or measure for a psychological construct (e.g., chronic

DATA BOX 6.C

Examining a Correlation Matrix: A Start for Research

A correlation matrix provides investigators with a precise indication of how each variable is associated with every other variable in a given data set. When beginning to analyze data, many researchers routinely create a correlation matrix so that they can see how each variable relates to all the others. This "eyeballing" of relationships among variables can be an invaluable starting point for data analysis. Researchers have the opportunity, for example, to learn if their predictions were borne out: Were certain variables positively or negatively associated with certain other variables?

Researchers can also see unexpected patterns or relationships within their data. In other words, studying a correlation matrix sometimes entails a bit of serendipity—some novel findings may be worthy of further study. Unexpected, interesting relationships are not taken immediately to the "empirical bank," of course; correlations are not causal, and a good researcher indicates that even when a serendipitous result merits further study, it cannot be trusted outside the confines of a theoretically driven, controlled experiment. Still, correlation matrices can provide food for thought.

The table of descriptive statistics and the accompanying correlation matrix shown below is from a pilot study on social inhibition among people with HIV/AIDS (Dunn, Stoudt, & Vicchiullo, 1999). Research in health psychology demonstrates that the failure to disclose negative events undermines health and well-being through active inhibition—the conscious restraint or suppression of emotion—which increases bodily stress (e.g., Traue & Pennebaker, 1993). Due to stigma, people with HIV/AIDS may constitute a group that is particularly susceptible to social inhibition. The data shown here are based on responses to a questionnaire completed by 33 clients at a hospital's AIDS clinic. Some of the correlational results suggest that higher levels of inhibition (self-concealment) are related to greater risk of depression ($r = +.31$). The tendency to conceal uncomfortable information is also associated with lower levels of disclosure to men ($r = -.50$) and women ($r = -.35$), less self-esteem ($r = -.60$), a more pessimistic outlook ($r = +.40$), and more AIDS-related symptoms ($r = +.26$). Take a look at the matrix to see how these preliminary conclusions were determined. What other correlational relationships can you see in these data? Consider generating a similar matrix when you have a reasonably large set of data available to analyze.

Means, Standard Deviations, and Ranges for the Correlated Variables

	M	*SD*	**Range (Low to High)**	*N*
CES-D[1]	19.46	12.67	1.0–48.0	33
Self-esteem[2]	30.55	5.89	14.0–37.0	33
Self-concealment[3]	22.53	10.77	10.0–49.0	32
Self-disclosure (male)[4]	22.13	12.38	1.0–40.0	32
Self-disclosure (female)[5]	24.03	12.67	0.0–40.0	31
Symptom checklist[6]	53.06	16.97	30.0–106.0	33
LOT-R[7]	9.72	4.35	1.0–19.0	33

Note: CES-D is a depression scale (Radloff, 1977); LOT-R is the revised Life Orientation Test, a measure of dispositional optimism (Scheier, Carver, & Bridges, 1994).

[1]Higher scores indicate greater risk for depression (a score above 16 is considered "at risk").

[2]Higher scores indicate greater levels of self-esteem (Rosenberg, 1965).

[3]Higher scores reflect a tendency to conceal uncomfortable thoughts, feelings, and information about the self from others (Larson & Chastain, 1990).

Correlation Matrix

	1	2	3	4	5	6	7
1. CES-D	1.00	−.55	.31	−.26	.02	.61	.41
2. Self-esteem		1.00	−.60	.64	.26	−.35	−.55
3. Self-concealment			1.00	−.50	−.35	.26	.40
4. Self-disclosure (male)				1.00	.43	.05	−.39
5. Self-disclosure (female)					1.00	.41	−.24
6. Symptom checklist						1.00	.15
7. LOT-R							1.00

Note: Only negative entries have a sign (−); positive entries do not. Please note that the entries of 1.00 in the matrix indicate the correlation between a given variable and itself (i.e., a correlation matrix shows every variable correlated with every other variable).

shyness) is related to existing measures of the construct (e.g., social reticence). A straightforward way to verify the relation between new and existing measures of any construct is to correlate each measure's total score with the scores on every other measure and to then examine the strength of the relationships (see Data Box 6.C on interpreting a correlation matrix). In most cases, a researcher would prefer to find a moderate correlation between a new and an existing measure or measures (i.e., convergent validity; see chapter 2). Why? If the correlation were too high ($r > .70$), then it would effectively mean that the new measure was no different than the old one, as it measured the same construct in (apparently) the same way. Conversely, if the correlation were too low ($r < .40$), one would conclude that the new measure was not tapping into the intended construct. For validity purposes, then, most investigators would desire a correlation in the .40 to .70 range (see also, Campbell & Fiske, 1959).

Beyond correlating a new measure with existing similar measures of the same construct, an investigator would also want to see how it correlated with *unrelated* measures or constructs (i.e., discriminant validity; see chapter 2). Ideally, the new measure of shyness would be predicted to have a negative relationship with some measures (e.g., sensation seeking) and a near zero relationship with others (e.g., work involvement). This predictive pattern of noncorrelations or inverse correlations helps to bolster a researcher's claims about the contents—the validity—of any new measure.

What to Do When: A Brief, Conceptual Guide to Other Measures of Association

As an undergraduate student, you are most likely to work with interval-scale data in any research you read about, conduct, or analyze, hence it is logical for you to learn about the Pearson r in some detail. Despite its ubiquity in behavioral science research, however, the Pearson r is not the only available index of association between two variables. Later, in chapter 14, we will learn about Spearman's rho (denoted r_S), a correlation coefficient specifically designed to assess association between paired measures of ordinal (ranked)

[4]Higher scores indicate greater willingness to disclose to a male friend (Miller, Berg, & Archer, 1983).

[5]Higher scores indicate greater willingness to disclose to a female friend (Miller, et al., 1983).

[6]Higher scores indicate greater incidence of health symptoms associated with HIV/AIDS within the past week (Reed, Taylor, & Kemeny, 1993).

[7]Higher scores indicate higher levels of optimism, a belief that future outcomes will be positive (Scheier & Carver, 1985).

DATA BOX 6.D

Perceived Importance of Scientific Topics and Evaluation Bias

According to Wilson, DePaulo, Mook, and Klaaren (1993), scientists are just as susceptible to making biased judgments as everyone else, particularly when it comes to recognizing methodological flaws in research on topics perceived to be important. Wilson and colleagues identified two related biases that can impact on scientists' judgments. The *leniency bias* entails the fact that a flawed study is more likely to appear in the published literature if it presents data on an important than an unimportant topic. Editors and peer reviewers can be more lenient in assessing a piece of research if it deals with pressing matters such as AIDS or cancer than, say, procrastination or nail biting. When a research question is seen as addressing a critical problem, evaluators may be so impressed by its relative importance that they overlook a study's methodological weaknesses. In short, they fall prey to the *oversight bias*.

Two groups of participants, research psychologists and medical school faculty members, read identical vignettes describing flawed studies. There were two versions of six vignettes, and one version in each pair examined an important (e.g., cardiovascular disease) or unimportant (e.g., heartburn) topic. Participants randomly received three important and three unimportant vignettes to read. They then rated each study's perceived importance, its publishability, rigor, and the soundness of the researchers' conclusions.

As predicted, Wilson and colleagues found that participants rated the important vignettes as being *more* important than the unimportant vignettes (i.e., heart disease was seen as a more significant concern than heartburn). Scientists were also lenient when it came to recommending publication—important projects were rated as more worthy of publication than unimportant projects. Finally, the oversight bias was present in full force: Both the psychologists and the medical school faculty perceived the (flawed) vignettes dealing with important topics to be methodologically superior to identical vignettes covering unimportant topics. The authors suggest these results are cause for pause, as perception and expectation guided judgment instead of the critical powers of appraisal usually attributed to scientists.

Why are biased judgments of research relevant to a chapter on correlation? Simply due to the fact that one of the most common errors people—including students, professors, and scientists—make is to assume that *correlational relationships are causal relationships*. They are not, but our best critical intentions can be disrupted by the perceived importance of a topic.

Keep the warning issued by Wilson and colleagues (1993) in mind: Topic importance can have a decidedly biasing influence on scientific judgments. In much the same way, correlational research can sway opinions and impressions by promoting reliance on inappropriate inferences. Correlations can suggest how research might proceed, but no definitive conclusions can be drawn from them.

---

data. The Spearman r_S is probably the second most common measure of association to which students are exposed.

What about other measures of association? Is it possible to "correlate" nominally scaled data? Are there other statistics for analyzing ordinal data besides the Spearman correlation? There are a variety of other measures of association available, many of which are amenable to nominal as well as ordinal data. It is beyond the scope of the present book to provide you with detailed instructions regarding how to calculate all of the alternative approaches to measuring association. Later in the book, we will review two of these indices in some detail because they support other statistics (recall the role of r^2 in explaining the strength of association between correlated variables). I do, however, want

Beyond the Pearson and Spearman Correlation Coefficients:
Table 6.6 Alternative Measures of Association

Scale Type	Name and Symbol	Applicable to What Kind of Data?
Nominal	Contingency coefficient (C)	Two nominal variables with equal rows and columns
	Lambda (λ)	Two nominal variables
	Phi coefficient (ϕ)	Two dichotomous variables[*]
	Cramer's V (V)	Two nominal variables[*]
Ordinal	Somer's d (d)	Two ordinal variables
	Goodman and Kruskal's gamma (G)	Two ordinal variables
	Kendall's tau-b (tau-b)	Two ordinal variables
Interval/Ratio	Multiple correlation coefficient (R)	Three or more interval and/or ratio variables

Note: Adapted from Table 9.1 in Elifson, et al. (1990).

[*]This statistic serves as a supporting measure (strength of association) to another statistic presented later in chapter 14.

to provide you with a resource where some of the other measure of association are concerned, a summary guide to rely on in the future when confronted with data that cannot be analyzed by the Pearson or Spearman statistics.

Table 6.6 lists the four scales of measurement and then some recommended, alternative measures of association under each one. The specific formulas for these statistics can be found in any number of advanced statistics texts (e.g., Agresti & Finlay, 1997; Elifson, Runyon, & Haber, 1990; Rosenthal & Rosnow, 1991). I hope that Table 6.6 will be a useful for resource for you in the future, especially if you develop a strong interest in statistics and data analysis.

Project Exercise IDENTIFYING PREDICTORS OF YOUR MOOD

Did you read Data Box 6.A? If not, then please go read it now before proceeding. If you read Data Box 6.A, then you no doubt found yourself wondering whether you could identify what aspects of your daily experience affect how you feel. Such questions are always interesting, if not provocative, because they motivate us to wonder how well we know ourselves. Is it possible that you don't know what affects your mood each day, or to what degree given factors like the weather or physical exercise actually influence how you feel?

The following *Project Exercise,* designed by Timothy D. Wilson of the University of Virginia, enables you to effectively replicate the Wilson et al. (1982) study by keeping track of your daily moods for a few weeks. You can perform this project by yourself and then share and compare your results with your classmates. While tracking your moods, you can also record how you believe that each of several factors influenced your mood each day.

When this data collection period is over, you will have the opportunity to judge the degree to which each of the tracked factors covaried with your mood. You will also learn how well each of the factors is actually correlated with your mood. Finally, you will compute a correlation that will indicate your relative judgment accuracy—in other words, how well did you identify what factors influence why you feel the way you do.

Answer the following set of questions at the same time each day. Complete one questionnaire daily. You should complete at least 7 (i.e., one week s worth) of these questionnaires; the results will be more stable if you record data for 3 or more weeks, however. If you miss a day, do *not* try to recall how you felt just skip it until the next week.

Today s date _____

1. How would you describe your *overall mood* today?
   Very Bad   Very Good
      1   2   3   4   5   6   7

2. What is the day of the week (e.g., Tuesday?)_____

3. How would you rate the *weather* today?
   Pleasant   Unpleasant
      1   2   3   4   5   6   7

4. How would you rate your *physical health* today?
   Very Bad   Very Good
      1   2   3   4   5   6   7

5. How were your relations with your *romantic partner/spouse/friends* today?
   Very Bad   Very Good
      1   2   3   4   5   6   7

6. How was the *food* you ate today?
   Very Bad   Very Good
      1   2   3   4   5   6   7

7. How much *work* did you have today?
   Very Little   Very Much
      1   2   3   4   5   6   7

8. How much *physical exercise* did you get today?
   Very Little   Very Much
      1   2   3   4   5   6   7

9. How many *hours of sleep* did you get last night?_____

10. *Other* (your question and rating): _____
      1   2   3   4   5   6   7

11. *Other* (your question and rating): _____
      1   2   3   4   5   6   7

Figure 6.7   Daily Mood Rating Sheet

Step 1.   Figure 6.7 contains a short questionnaire that you should fill out each day for a week or two. You can either write down your responses or ratings to answer the questions in Figure 6.7 on a separate sheet of paper each day or use a copy machine to make the number of copies you think will be necessary (7 for a week, 14 for 2 weeks, and so on). Be advised that the correlational results will be more stable if you collect data for a longer period of time, say, 3 weeks or more (the original study was 5 weeks long; see Data Box 6.A). Be sure to follow the instructions shown in Figure 6.7. Please note that questions 10 and 11 in Figure 6.7 encourage you to keep track of two factors of your own choosing—just be consistent in your record keeping! When your week or two is up and you are finished collecting data, go on to step 2.

Step 2.   Complete the questionnaire shown in Figure 6.8 and then go on to step 3.

Step 3.   Compute the correlation coefficient between your daily mood ratings (the first question in Figure 6.7) and each of the factors that might predict your mood (see

Read the following questions and then rate the relationship you believe exists between the cited factors and your mood *during the time you completed the Daily Questionaire* shown in Figure 6.7. Each question asks you to determine whether there was a positive relationship between each factor (e.g., amount of exercise, the weather) and your mood, a negative relationship, or no relationship. A positive relationship occurred when a factor was given a high rating (e.g., amount of exercise) and your mood was relatively high (i.e., positive), or when the factor was rated as being low and so was your mood. A negative relationship would indicate that as a factor tended to be rated as high, mood was rated as low (or vice versa). No relationship exists when you believe that a given factor and your mood were unrelated to one another.

Use the following scale to rate each of the factors cited below:

−3 = **Strong negative relationship**
−2 = **Moderate negative relationship**
−1 = **Slight negative relationship**
 0 = **No relationship**
+1 = **Slight positive relationship**
+2 = **Moderate positive relationship**
+3 = **Strong positive relationship**

1. **How was your daily mood related to whether it was *Monday*?** _____
   (negative relationship = mood tends to be lower on Mondays than on other days; positive relationship = mood tends to be higher on Mondays than on other days)
2. **How was your daily mood related to whether it was *Tuesday*?** _____
3. **How was your daily mood related to whether it was *Wednesday*?** _____
4. **How was your daily mood related to whether it was *Thursday*?** _____
5. **How was your daily mood related to whether it was *Friday*?** _____
6. **How was your daily mood related to whether it was *Saturday*?** _____
7. **How was your daily mood related to whether it was *Sunday*?** _____
8. **How was your daily mood related to the *weather*?** _____
9. **How was your daily mood related to your *physical health*?** _____
10. **How was your daily mood related to your *relations with your romantic partner/spouse/friends*?** _____
11. **How was your daily mood related to the *food* you ate?** _____
12. **How was your daily mood related to your *workload*?** _____
13. **How was your daily mood related to your amount of *physical exercise*?** _____
14. **How was your daily mood related to the *amount of sleep you had the night before*?** _____
15. **Your Question 1:** _____
16. **Your Question 2:** _____

questions 2 to 11 in Figure 6.7). Here are brief instructions illustrating how to correlate your recorded mood with the amount of sleep you got each night. The same procedure, then, can be used to correlate your rated mood with the remaining ten predictors. As you finish calculating each correlation coefficient, enter it into the appropriate place in column 2 of Figure 6.9.

To determine the Pearson r between mood and number of hours of sleep per night, use formula [6.6.1], where:

X = your daily mood ratings,

Y = number of hours of sleep the previous night,

N = the number of days you filled out the *Daily Mood Rating Sheet* (i.e., Figure 6.7).

Please note that for the days of the week, such as Monday, enter $Y = 1$ only when it is Monday; enter $Y = 0$ when it is *not* Monday, and do the same for the remaining 6 days (i.e., for Tuesday, $Y = 1$ and for *not* Tuesday, $Y = 0$).

Step 4.   You should end up with a correlation between your daily mood ratings and each of the 16 predictor variables shown in column 1 of Figure 6.9. Be certain that the correlations are properly entered into the second column of Figure 6.9.

Step 5.   Take the estimates of how much you believe each factor predicts mood from Figure 6.8 (*Reviewing the Daily Mood Questionnaires*) and write them into column 3 of Figure 6.9.

Step 6.   Compute the correlation between columns 2 and 3 of Figure 6.9 (*Mood Rating Worksheets*) and record it in the space provided at the bottom of the figure. This correlation represents your accuracy score. If it falls between $+.50$ and $+1.00$, then you are fairly accurate when it comes to judging how each variable affects your mood state. If the correlation is less than $+.50$, then you are either fairly inaccurate or there are

(1) Predictor Variable	(2) Correlation Between Mood Ratings and Variable (values from -1.0 to $+1.0$)	(3) Subjective Weights of this Variable (values from -3 to $+3$)
Monday	_____	_____
Tuesday	_____	_____
Wednesday	_____	_____
Thursday	_____	_____
Friday	_____	_____
Saturday	_____	_____
Sunday	_____	_____
Weather	_____	_____
Physical Health	_____	_____
Relationships	_____	_____
Food	_____	_____
Workload	_____	_____
Amount of Exercise	_____	_____
Amount of Sleep	_____	_____
Other 1	_____	_____
Other 2	_____	_____

Correlation between columns 2 and 3 _____

Number of days you filled out daily questionnaires _____

Figure 6.9   Mood Rating Worksheet

problems with the data (e.g., there was not enough variance in your mood—perhaps due to truncated ranges—during the time you completed the daily questionnaires).

Step 7.   Using the correlational results now written into Figure 6.9, as well as the Wilson et al.'s (1982) research (see Data Box 6.A), write a brief explanation wherein you discuss how the correlational results relate to your self-beliefs (e.g., how well do you seem to know what predictor variables influence your moods). Discuss the role the correlation coefficient plays in this type of research: What are the advantages and disadvantages of correlation as a technique for behavioral scientists?

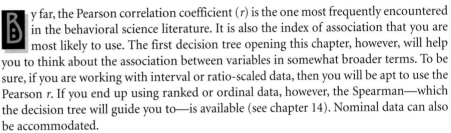

LOOKING FORWARD   THEN BACK

By far, the Pearson correlation coefficient (*r*) is the one most frequently encountered in the behavioral science literature. It is also the index of association that you are most likely to use. The first decision tree opening this chapter, however, will help you to think about the association between variables in somewhat broader terms. To be sure, if you are working with interval or ratio-scaled data, then you will be apt to use the Pearson *r*. If you end up using ranked or ordinal data, however, the Spearman—which the decision tree will guide you to—is available (see chapter 14). Nominal data can also be accommodated.

The second decision tree is designed to help you get your hands a bit dirty with your data. In other words, it is often important to verify that a correlation's numerical value is informative. The second decision tree invites you to check the range of values used to calculate the Pearson—is there some degree of difference or are the observations too close together? Plotting the observations can also reveal the absence of a linear relationship—the only relationship the Pearson *r* is designed to detect—but the presence of some other (e.g., curvilinear) pattern that could give you empirical pause. Finally, any outlying scores or preexisting subpopulations lurking in the data must be reckoned with, which serves as a reminder that statistical analysis is all about data analysis.

Summary

1. The term "correlation" refers to the association between two variables, that is, how they vary or relate to one another.

2. Because the variables are measured and not manipulated in any experiment, a correlational result is not a causal result. In a correlational relationship, variable *X* can lead to *Y*, *Y* can lead to *X*, or an unknown third variable *Z* can mediate the relationship between the two. Correlations can be suggestive, pointing to relationships between variables that are worthy of experimental investigation.

3. The Pearson product moment correlation coefficient, or Pearson *r*, is the most commonly used index of correlation. Conceptually, this statistic assesses the degree to which variables *X* and *Y* vary together, as well as the degree to which they vary separately from one another.

4. The direction of a correlational relationship is described as being positive, negative, or zero. In a positive relationship, as the value of one variables increases (or decreases), the value of the second variables behaves in a similar fashion. In a neg-

ative relationship, the variables' values are inverted: As the value of one increases, the other necessarily decreases. In a zero relationship, no pattern or predictable relationship exists between the variables.

5. Correlational values range from −1.00 to +1.00. The positive and negative signs indicate the direction of the relationship, where the strength of association between the variables is known by the correlation's numerical value. Values close to 0.0 indicate that the variables are not related to one another, but as values move away from 0.0, their strength, as well as the predictability and association increase.

6. A scatter plot is a graph used to represent correlational data. The points in a scatter plot indicate the intersection of each *X* value with its corresponding *Y* value. As points become more linear within the graph, the strength of the correlation will increase.

7. When an *r* value is squared (i.e., r^2), it can be used to learn what proportion of the variance in one variable within a

correlation is accounted for by the other variable. This statistic is known as the coefficient of determination. The correlation of nondetermination, which is equal to $1 - r^2$, reveals the proportion of changes in one variable that cannot be accounted for by the other variable.

8. Spurious correlations can possess unusually high or low values that disguise any real (or nonreal) effects within a data set. Such correlations occur due to several factors: a truncated range of values in one or both variables, nonlinear relationships in the data, the presence of extreme scores, problems with sample size, and preexisting subgroups within the data.

9. The Pearson r can be used to determine the consistency of a measure (i.e., its reliability), as well as its relationship with other similar and dissimilar instruments (i.e., its validity).

10. The Pearson r is the most popular index for measuring the strength of association between two interval or ratio-scaled variables. There are, however, a variety of other types of correlations that can be used for ordinally or nominally scaled variables.

Key Terms

Alternate form reliability *(p. 229)*
Coefficient of determination *(p. 222)*
Coefficient of nondetermination *(p. 223)*
Correlation *(p. 206)*
Internal consistency measure of reliability *(p. 229)*
Item-total reliability *(p. 229)*

Negative correlation *(p. 211)*
Odd-even reliability *(p. 229)*
Pearson product-moment correlation coefficient *(p. 207)*
Pearson r *(p. 209)*
Positive correlation *(p. 211)*
Power analysis *(p. 225)*

Reliability coefficient *(p. 229)*
Scatter plot *(p. 212)*
Split-half reliability *(p. 229)*
Spurious correlation *(p. 224)*
Test-retest reliability *(p. 229)*
Third variable problem *(p. 208)*
Zero correlation *(p. 211)*

Chapter Problems

1. Conceptually, correlation assesses the association between two variables. Why isn't the association causal in nature?
2. What is the third variable problem in correlational analyses? Provide a concrete example.
3. Describe the possible directions of relationships between two variables in correlational analyses. What role do positive (+) and negative (−) signs play?
4. What is the possible range of values for the Pearson r? Is an $r = +.35$ stronger than an r of $-.35$?
5. Describe a scatter plot showing a positive correlation, a negative correlation, and a zero correlation.
6. Describe a scatter plot of a perfectly linear positive correlation and a perfectly linear negative correlation.
7. In what way is the Pearson r related to z scores? What advantage does the z score provide to the Pearson r?
8. Provide descriptive labels for the magnitudes of the following r-values: $-.67, +.98, -.03, +.25, -.81, +.79, -.55, +.37$.
9. Conceptually define the coefficients of determination and nondetermination. How do these coefficients aid researchers?
10. Provide the coefficient of determination corresponding to each of the r values shown above in problem 8.
11. Provide the coefficient of nondetermination corresponding to each of the r values shown above in problem 8.
12. Some factors lead to abnormally high or low correlational values. Briefly describe three of the factors that can have deleterious effects on correlations.

13. Examine the following set of data:

X	Y
4	7
3	2
8	5
7	6
8	7
2	5

a. Draw a scatter plot for the X and Y variables and then describe the relationship, if any, between them.
b. Calculate a Pearson r between X and Y. Does the r fit the relationship you described in part a?
c. What are the coefficients of determination and nondetermination for these data?

14. Examine the following set of data:

X	Y
1	3
5	5
3	2
4	5
5	4
2	3

d. Draw a scatter plot for the X and Y variables and then describe the relationship, if any, between them.

e. Calculate a Pearson r between X and Y. Does the r fit the relationship you described in part a?

f. What are the coefficients of determination and nondetermination for these data?

15. A health psychologist is interested in the relationship between self-reported stress (X) and objective health ratings (Y). Higher scores on each measure indicate more stress and better health, respectively. Using the following data, determine the nature of this relationship by calculating a Pearson r and then interpreting the result in words.

X	Y
2	10
9	3
10	4
11	5
4	13
5	11
1	10
3	4

16. Read each of the following descriptions of correlations. Evaluate whether each description is a reasonable account of what the correlation means. If the description is not accurate, then suggest how it should be corrected.

a. An educator correlates the number of course books students purchase in a semester with their grade point averages (GPA). This r is +.56, and the educator concludes that using more books in a given semester leads to higher grades (and vice versa).

b. A negative correlation exists between number of visits to the student health center per year and GPA. Healthier students appear to have better grades than those who are frequently ill.

c. GPA in college and scores on the Scholastic Aptitude Test (SAT) are moderately correlated. We cannot conclude, however, that higher scores on the SAT cause better grades later on.

17. How is the Pearson r used to determine the reliability of a measure? What range of r values is appropriate for demonstrating reliability?

18. How is the Pearson r used to determine the validity of a measure? What range of r values is appropriate for demonstrating validity?

19. You are an industrial/organizational psychologist who wants to develop a new measure of job stress for use in corporate settings. How would you go about assessing the reliability of your new measure?

20. You are an educational psychologist who has developed a new intelligence test for use in elementary school grades 1–3. How would you go about assessing the validity of this new intelligence test?

21. The following scores represent a personality test that was given to the same group of participants on two separate occasions. Calculate an r to represent the test's reliability. Does the test appear to be reliable? Why or why not?

X	Y
9	9
8	6
6	7
9	8
7	10
8	5
9	9
3	8

22. Draw a scatter plot of the X and Y data provided in problem 21. Does plotting the data provide any further evidence for the reliability of the measure? Why or why not?

23. Use the decision trees opening this chapter to answer the following questions:

a. A researcher wants to assess the correlation between temperature and rainfall. Which measure of association is appropriate?

b. A student wants to determine the correlation between his rankings of national league baseball teams and those of a friend. Which measure of association is appropriate?

c. An investigator discovers a correlation of +.75 between five pairs of test scores. Is this correlation apt to be reliable? Why?

d. Before calculating a correlation between two variables, a student notices that one of them is dichotomous—the score for X is either "1" or "2," but Y has a relatively wide range of values. Should the student be concerned? Why?

Deciding to Perform a Linear Regression Analysis

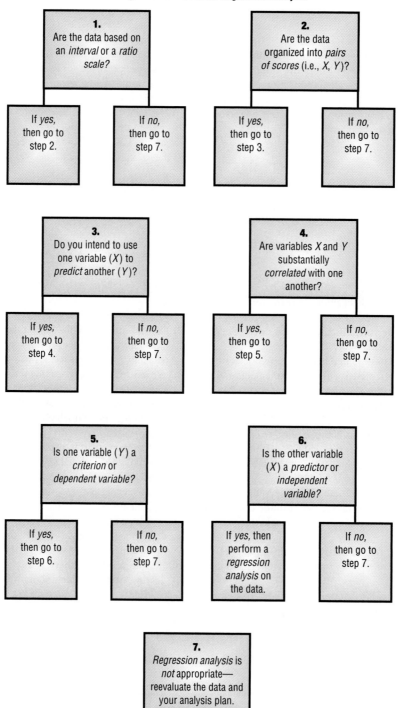

LINEAR REGRESSION

W hen do you make predictions? What are they like? Are your predictions better described as educated guesses or "off-the-cuff" hunches?

As a semester's final examinations draw near, for example, do you take stock of your performance in each class and estimate your final course grades? When two tall friends have a baby, do you assume their child will be quite tall, as well? Why are we so quick to link the amount a new activity is practiced with better future performance? Sports like tennis or golf, as well as professional skills such as writing or public speaking, come to mind. While watching two professional sports teams compete on the field, why do most of us routinely act like sportscasters trying to predict a game's winner?

In each of these cases, we often use one variable (e.g., grade at midterm) to predict the value of another variable (e.g., final course grade). On occasion, we may rely on more than one variable—say, class participation and attendance in addition to midterm grade—to predict an outcome. We have an intuitive understanding, then, that certain variables are quite useful when it comes to predicting outcomes. Our intuitive predictions are sometimes in error (e.g., Kahneman & Tversky, 1973), however, just as in chapter 6 we learned that contrary to perception and wishful thinking, correlation does not imply causation. Despite my belief that I can earn an A in a class if I do well on the final, for example, I may still receive a B; sometimes, too, tall parents have short offspring (and we will learn why such apparently reasonable predictions sometimes go awry). Sometimes, too, a game's outcome changes dramatically in the last few seconds of play. Fortunately, we can rely on a statistical technique called linear regression to improve or counter the shortcomings of many personal predictions, as well as to help us predict behavior in research contexts.

Linear regression is intimately related to correlation. In fact, regression gives a bit of life to the concept of correlation by using it for predictive purposes. Regression is a technique for predicting a score on variable *Y* based on what we already know to be true about the value of some variable *X*. Indeed, unless one variable is substantially correlated with the other, there is no reason to use regression to predict a score on *Y* from a score on *X*. For example, it makes sense that a positive correlation exists between the amount of study time and subsequent performance on an examination. If I know that you studied 10 hours (*X*) for the exam, then, can I predict your actual score on the exam (*Y*)? Regression analysis helps in this regard by essentially searching for a pattern in the data, usually a scatter plot of points representing hours studied (X) by exam scores (Y). In effect, this statistical technique seeks to find the best fit for a straight line projected among the points on the scatter plot, one that "captures" as many of them as possible (if necessary, you may wish to review the discussion of scatter plots introduced in chapter 6 before proceeding). In the process of doing so, linear regression can provide a viable estimate for the each individual's exam score, given the number of hours he or she studied for the test.

Of course, regression analysis does *not* guarantee that a given prediction will match the reality imposed by the available data, but it can help us to approximate actual observations, as well as to identify reasons for the error between our estimates and reality. Remember that regression is only *one* tool that guides us through the process of drawing inferences. It cannot provide absolute or definitive answers. As you will see, regression is a powerful technique that enables us to apply skills and concepts learned from earlier chapters—especially knowledge about correlation and the standardization of z scores—toward developing more precise accounts of human reasoning and behavior.

Simple Linear Regression

The most basic form of *regression analysis* is called simple linear or bivariate ("two variable") regression.

KEY TERM   **Regression analysis** is based on correlational analysis, and it involves examining changes in the level of Y relative to changes in the level of X.

Variable Y is the dependent measure, which in regression analysis is termed the **criterion variable.** The independent or **predictor variable** is represented by variable X. Thus, if we were trying to predict people's income levels based on the number of years they spent receiving an education (i.e., in kindergarten to 12th grade, college, and graduate or professional school), income is the criterion variable and education is the predictor variable. Presumably, higher income is predicted by more years of education (and vice versa).

The z Score Approach to Regression

By now, you have had some experience thinking about the mathematical relations underlying several statistical concepts. Recall from chapter 5 that standard or z scores are integral to inferential statistics. Although this section may seem a bit mathematically complex, take a few minutes to carefully read it and think about the z score equation for regression. The computational formulas in the subsequent section will be much easier for you to use following a careful review of the z score concept applied to regression.

As was the case for correlation, regression can also be understood using z scores. A variable Y can be predicted from X using the z score regression equation, which is:

[7.1.1]
$$z_{\hat{Y}} = r_{XY} z_X$$

where $z_{\hat{Y}}$ is a predicted score for variable Y. Hereafter, $\hat{Y}$ ("Y caret" or "Y hat") will be used to indicate a predicted or estimated value for Y. The correlation between variables X and Y is denoted by r_{XY}, and z_X is an actual z score based on variable X.

The z score equation for regression is noteworthy for two reasons. First, when r_{XY} is positive in value, z_X will be multiplied by a positive number—thus, $z_{\hat{Y}}$ will be positive when z_X is positive and it will be negative when z_X is negative. Why is this characteristic important? When r_{XY} is positive, then $z_{\hat{Y}}$ will have the same sign as z_X, so that a high score will covary with high scores and low scores will do so with low scores (see [7.1.1]).

Correlation = association; regression = prediction.

Y is the criterion or dependent variable; X is the predictor or independent variable.

A note on notation: Besides $\hat{Y}$, the other common way to designate a predicted value is by use of the prime (') symbol. Thus, $\hat{Y} = Y'$.

When r_{XY} is negative, however, the sign of $z_{\hat{Y}}$ will be opposite of z_X; low scores will be associated with high scores and high scores with low scores (see [7.1.1]).

The second point regarding the z score equation for regression is that when $r_{XY} = \pm 1.00$, $z_{\hat{Y}}$ will have the same score as z_X. As we know, of course, such perfect correlation is rare in behavioral data. Thus, when $r_{XY} < \pm 1.00$, $z_{\hat{Y}}$ will be closer to 0.0 than z_X. Any z score that approaches 0.0 is based on a raw score that is close to a distribution's mean, implying that a predicted score will always be closer to a mean than the raw score on which the prediction was based. The most extreme example in this vein occurs when $r_{XY} = 0.0$. When this happens, z_X is multiplied by 0.0 and $z_{\hat{Y}}$ becomes equal to 0.0, the mean of the z distribution (see [7.1.1]).

Computational Approaches to Regression

Linear relationships between variables X and Y can also be represented by this well-known computational equation:

[7.2.1] $$Y = a + b(X),$$

where Y is the criterion variable—what we are trying to predict—and a and b are constants with fixed values. Variable X, of course, is the predictor variable that can take on different values. As in correlational analyses, variables X and Y are pairs of scores that will vary or change from individual to individual within a given data set, whereas the values of a and b will not change.

Some of you may remember having seen this formula (or a variation) earlier in your educational career, where it was probably used as an equation for plotting points into a straight line. If so, then you will remember that b is also called the **slope** of the line, the purpose of which is to link Y values to X values. The slope of any straight line defines its angle in space. Conceptually, the slope of a line represents changes occurring in Y that take place when X is changed 1 unit, or

[7.3.1] $$b = \frac{\text{change in } Y}{\text{change in } X}.$$

If you recall our discussion of the direction of correlational relationships from chapter 6, whether a slope is deemed *positive* or *negative* will make sense to you. Similar to a positive correlation, a positive slope indicates that changes in X are directly related to changes in Y. As X increases (or decreases) in value, Y behaves the same way. It follows that a negative slope will act like a negative correlation because it points to an inverse relationship between X and Y—as the value of one variable increases the other decreases (and vice versa). When plotted, lines with positive slopes move from the bottom left of a graph in a northeasterly direction to its top right. In contrast, negatively sloping lines move from the top left of a graph to the bottom right, proceeding to that point in a southeasterly direction.

What about a? In a regression equation, a is called the intercept of the line or the y-intercept. The **intercept** is the point in a regression of Y on X where the line crosses the Y axis.

Let's look at a straightforward example showing how X can predict Y, and see how numbers can be entered into the regression formula in the process. Imagine that we create a measure of procrastination, the tendency to postpone or defer completion of some activity (e.g., Boice, 1996). As you know, procrastination is a real problem for many students, typically manifesting itself as the inability to complete academic work (e.g., homework, term papers, projects) or other achievement-oriented activities (e.g., job or graduate school applications).

▽

When two variables are uncorrelated with one another, the best predictor of any individual score on one of the variables is the mean. The mean is the predicted value of X or Y when the correlation between these variables is 0.

▽

$Y = a + b(X)$ is the formula for a straight line.

Assume that the measure is behavioral—it is a problem-solving task requiring the manipulation of several objects—but test takers receive a numerical score indicating their inclination to procrastinate (i.e., higher scores indicate a relatively high level of the trait's presence). The minimum score on the measure is 20 points, and test takers receive 5 additional points for each minute it takes them to complete the task. In this example, the 20-point minimum would represent a and the 5 additional points would be b. Variable Y is the score being predicted by changes in X, the number of minutes used to complete the procrastination measure. The formula describing the relationship among these variables looks like this:

[7.4.1] $$Y = 20 + 5(X).$$

We can compute Y values using [7.4.1] and then plot them to confirm that they fall into a straight line. Let's assume that one research participant spends 3.0 minutes (i.e., $X = 3.0$) on the procrastination task. Her score would be,

[7.4.2] $$Y = 20 + 5(3.0),$$

[7.4.3] $$Y = 20 + 15,$$

[7.4.4] $$Y = 35.$$

A second participant spends 5.5 minutes on the task. His procrastination score is:

[7.4.5] $$Y = 20 + 5(5.5),$$

[7.4.6] $$Y = 20 + 27.5,$$

[7.4.7] $$Y = 47.5.$$

What if a third participant took 2 minutes to complete the task? What is the value of this individual's Y? Use the formula shown in [7.4.1] and calculate the Y value now.

Because the slope of the equation (b) is positive, we expect a graph of the computed criterion scores (Y) plotted with the predictor scores (X) to indicate a direct relationship. Figure 7.1 illustrates the relationship between scores on the procrastination task and number of minutes spent performing its behavioral component. As you can see, the plotted data reveal a straight line, which begins at the Y intercept of $a = 20$. Did you calculate the value for Y when X is equal to 2? Note that when $X = 2.0$ minutes, $Y = 30$ (see Figure 7.1).

As seen here—and as we learned in chapter 6—a straight line is often an excellent way to portray the relationship between two variables. Regression analysis effectively tries to determine the best fitting straight line that can be projected among a set of points for any set of data. This line is referred to as the *regression line*.

KEY TERM   A **regression line** is a straight line projecting through a given set of data, one designed to represent the best fitting linear relationship between variables X and Y.

What is meant by a "best fitting" line? We must first recognize that scatter plots of data points rarely look as organized and linear as those plotted in Figure 7.1. In fact, behavioral data are typically not very neat and tidy, let alone linearly predictable. Indeed, if we actually had a scatter plot of points that fell into perfect alignment with one another, we would know that the correlation between X and Y was either $+1.00$, -1.00, or 0!

Generally, scatter plots of data look like those shown back in chapter 6 (e.g., see Figure 6.2 on page 214)—there are many points in a graph's space that can suggest a positive or a negative pattern, but they rarely fall into an orderly, let alone straight, shape or pattern. Of course, a straight line can be drawn among plotted points that

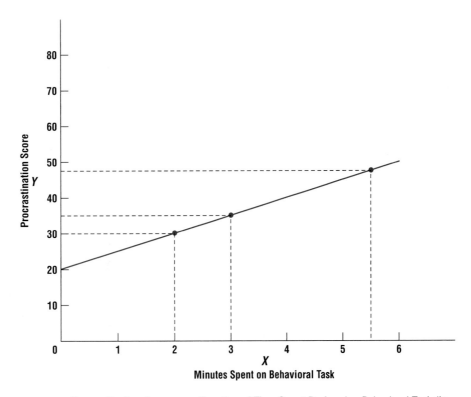

Figure 7.1 Procrastination Scores as a Function of Time Spent Performing Behavioral Task (in Minutes)

Note: Higher scores indicate a greater predisposition for procrastination. The plotted points were determined using the formula $Y = 20 + 5(X)$, where Y is the score on a behavioral procrastination measure and X is the minutes spent performing the procrastination task. As shown above, the formula reveals a linear relationship between X and Y.

are either close together or very far apart from one another, and such a line can be drawn by using our own best guess or (now) by haphazardly using the formula $Y = a + b(X)$. Still, both of these methods lack precision—one is too intuitive, the other somewhat unwieldy. A preferable alternative, of course, is finding a way to *consistently* determine a best fitting straight line tailored to a given set of data.

The Method of Least Squares for Regression

In order to determine the best fit among a set of data points, statisticians rely on what is called the method of least squares. You will recall the "least squares" concept from chapter 4's *Project Exercise*, where you proved that the mean was the specific point in a distribution of scores where the sum of the squared deviations reached a minimum level (i.e., calculating $\sum (X - \overline{X})^2$ results in a smaller number compared to any other value of X that is substituted for $\overline{X}$).

When the least squares method is used in the context of regression, the best fitting line is the one drawn (out of an infinite number of possible lines) so that the sum of the squared distances between the *actual Y values* and the *predicted Y values* is minimized. Symbolically, Y continues to denote the actual or observed value of Y and, as noted earlier, $\hat{Y}$ is used to indicate the predicted or estimated value for Y. Ideally, then, a regression line will minimize the distance between Y and $\hat{Y}$, which in sum of squares terms can be represented as:

[7.5.1] $$\sum (Y - \hat{Y})^2.$$

Any best fitting regression line minimizes the distance between actual and predicted values of *Y*.

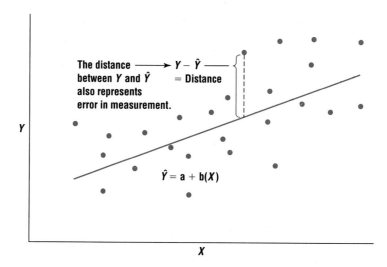

Figure 7.2   Hypothetical Scatter Plot of Scores with Accompanying Regression Line

This formula calculates the total squared difference between the actual values for Y and the predicted values for Y, and a better fitting straight line will result when $Y \cong \hat{Y}$. In the meantime, we must recast the formula for a straight line as:

[7.6.1] $$\hat{Y} = a + b(X).$$

When we say the "distance" between Y and $\hat{Y}$, what do we mean exactly? Figure 7.2 shows a hypothetical scatter plot of points with a regression line drawn among them. As you can see, one X,Y data point falling above the line has been highlighted. The broken line drawn between this point and the regression line represents the distance between an actual Y value and the value predicted by the regression line (i.e., $\hat{Y}$). The distance or difference between these two values represents *error*, or the how measured reality differs from a prediction, a topic we will explore in the next section of the chapter. Obviously, a desirable state of affairs entails minimizing error or, put another way, having predicted $\hat{Y}$ values that closely match actual Y values. Some of the distances between Y and $\hat{Y}$ will be positive, others negative—by squaring these distance values we ensure that we have a positive measure of error, one that can be used for subsequent analytic purposes. (Recall that in chapter 4, we learned that such deviation values *must* be squared, otherwise the positive and negative values will sum to 0.)

Now that we will rely on revised regression formula [7.6.1] for a best fitting line, we need to learn how to determine specific numerical values for a and b within the formula. The mathematics involved is actually rather complicated, providing much more detail than we need for present purposes. Fortunately, however, the results of the mathematics can be presented in familiar terms we can both understand and use. Let's begin with b, which is equal to:

[7.7.1] $$b = r \frac{s_Y}{s_X}$$

That is, the slope of the regression line can be determined by multiplying the correlation between X and Y by the product of the standard deviation of Y divided by the standard deviation of X.

The value of the intercept, a, in turn, can be determined by:

[7.8.1] $$a = \overline{Y} - b\overline{X}.$$

Table 7.1 Practice and Actual Aptitude Test Scores

Participant	Practice Scores (X)	Actual Scores (Y)
1	75	82
2	83	86
3	92	88
4	95	98
5	74	75
6	80	86
	$\overline{X} = 83.17$	$\overline{Y} = 85.83$
	$s_X = 8.70$	$s_Y = 7.55$
	$r_{XY} = .8925 \cong .89$	
	$N = 6$	

In other words, intercept a can be determined by subtracting the product of b multiplied by the mean of X from the mean of Y.

The math involved in formulas [7.7.1] and [7.8.1] is not difficult, though it can be somewhat time consuming to solve. By combining these formulas with revised regression formula [7.6.1], a more straightforward formula for calculating $\hat{Y}$ is available. This formula is sometimes referred to as the raw score method for regression:

[7.9.1]
$$\hat{Y} = \overline{Y} + r\left(\frac{s_Y}{s_X}\right)(X - \overline{X}).$$

Indeed, this formula produces the same result as formula [7.6.1], but it does so in a way that will probably make more sense to you as we work through an example.

Table 7.1 presents X and Y scores for six people. The X scores represent performance on a practice aptitude test and the Y values are scores on the actual aptitude test given a week later. Can we use X to predict Y? Take a few moments and look over the data in the table. The respective means and standard deviations for X and Y are provided here for you, and you will recall how these values were calculated from chapter 4.

As shown in Table 7.1, participant 2 scored an 83 on the practice aptitude test. Using the information available in Table 7.1, we can see what score he is predicted to receive ($\hat{Y}$) and then compare it with the score that we know he did receive ($Y = 86$). We simply enter the relevant information from Table 7.1 into formula [7.9.1], or:

A rule of thumb for selecting $r(s_X/s_Y)$ or $r(s_Y/s_X)$ for the raw score regression formula: The standard deviation for the variable you wish to predict is the numerator and the standard deviation for the predictor variable is in the denominator.

[7.9.2]
$$\hat{Y} = 85.83 + .89\left(\frac{7.55}{8.70}\right)(83 - 83.17),$$

[7.9.3]
$$\hat{Y} = 85.83 + .89(.8678)(-.17),$$

[7.9.4]
$$\hat{Y} = 85.83 + .89(-.1475),$$

[7.9.5]
$$\hat{Y} = 85.83 - .1313,$$

[7.9.6]
$$\hat{Y} = 85.698 \cong 85.70.$$

As you can see, the second participant is predicted to earn an 85.7 on the actual test, which is approximately equal to the actual score of 86.

Do not assume that a regression prediction will always be so close, however. Let's repeat the same estimation procedure for the first participant. She received a 75 on the practice test—what is her predicted score on the actual test? We once again use formula [7.9.1], entering the necessary values from Table 7.1 into:

[7.9.7]
$$\hat{Y} = 85.83 + .89\left(\frac{7.55}{8.70}\right)(75 - 83.17),$$

[7.9.8]
$$\hat{Y} = 85.83 + .89(.8678)(-8.17),$$

[7.9.9]
$$\hat{Y} = 85.83 + .89(-7.0899),$$

[7.9.10]
$$\hat{Y} = 85.83 - 6.31,$$

[7.9.11]
$$\hat{Y} = 79.52.$$

Although the estimate of 79.5 is close to the actual score of 82 (see Table 7.1), it is not as close as the score we predicted for the second participant. Still, the regression equation's predicted scores for both participants 1 and 2 were quite close to their actual scores. Can you think of any reasons why this might be the case?

Take a look at the correlation between the X and Y variables. This correlation, $r = +.89$, is very high, indicating that a change in one variable had an almost synonymous change in the other. If the correlation between these two sets of aptitude test scores were much lower (i.e., their reliability was lower), then we could anticipate that our predicted Y values ($\hat{Y}$) would match the actual Y scores much less frequently. This conclusion is a general rule to keep in mind about regression: Errors in prediction, or $\sum(\hat{Y}-Y)^2$, the sum of the squared differences between the predicted and actual scores of Y, will be *less frequent* as r approaches ± 1.00 and *more frequent* as r gets closer to 0.0.

Can we determine the regression equation for the data shown in Table 7.1? In actuality, we already have determined these values above when we calculated $\hat{Y}$ using formula [7.9.1]. We can now isolate the values for the intercept (a) and the slope of the regression line (b) by solving formulas [7.7.1] and [7.8.1]. The slope of the regression line for these data is:

[7.10.1]
$$b = r\frac{s_Y}{s_X},$$

[7.10.2]
$$b = +.89\frac{7.55}{8.70},$$

[7.10.3]
$$b = +.89(.8678),$$

[7.10.4]
$$b = +.7723 \cong +.77.$$

In turn, the intercept for Y is:

[7.11.1]
$$a = \bar{Y} - b\bar{X},$$

[7.11.2]
$$a = 85.83 - (.77)(83.17),$$

[7.11.3]
$$a = 21.789 \cong 21.8.$$

By entering these values for a and b into equation [7.6.1], the regression formula for the data in Table 7.1 is:

[7.12.1]
$$\hat{Y} = 21.8 + .77(X).$$

This formula and the plotted data it is based on are shown in Figure 7.3.

Y Can Also Predict X.   As you no doubt recall from our discussion of correlation in chapter 6, the relationship between variables X and Y is a reciprocal one. Thus, in

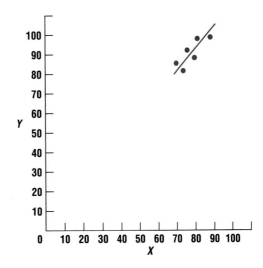

Figure 7.3   Scatter Plot with Regression Line for Practice and Actual Aptitude Test Scores

Note: The line projected through the above points is the best fitting straight (regression) line. Predicted values for $\hat{Y}$ fall onto the line. The points shown around the line are the actual values for Y. As long as the correlation between X and Y is less than ± 1.00, there will be some degree of error between the predicted and actual values of Y.

regression analysis, X can be used to predict Y—but X can also be predicted *from Y* (i.e., X becomes $\hat{X}$). The formula for predicting X is:

[7.13.1]
$$\hat{X} = \overline{X} + r\left(\frac{s_X}{s_Y}\right)(Y - \overline{Y}).$$

Beside the fact that X is now being predicted instead of Y, the main differences between this formula and [7.9.1] are that the standard deviation of X is being divided by the standard deviation of Y, and that Y and $\overline{Y}$ have been substituted for the respective complements of X. Like correlation, regression is flexible, so that researchers need not necessarily always denote the independent variable as X and dependent variables as Y.

X can predict Y or Y can predict X.

One final point about regression lines and the calculation of $\hat{Y}$ or $\hat{X}$ values. You should avoid calculating any predicted values for Y or X that do not fall within the range of the original data. Why not? Simply because we do not know the quality of the relationship between pairs of X and Y values beyond their known boundaries. The X values in Table 7.1 range between 75 and 95, but it would not be appropriate to calculate $\hat{Y}$ values for X = 62 or X = 121, for example, as both fall outside the data set's boundaries.

Knowledge Base

1. Within this equation, $\hat{Y} = 10 - 4.5(X)$, what are the respective values of the intercept and the slope of the line?
2. Using the equation $\hat{Y} = 20 - 2.8(X)$, calculate $\hat{Y}$ when X = 3, 5, 6, 8.
3. What does $\sum (\hat{Y} - Y)^2$ represent?
4. True or False: As r approaches -1.00, the amount of error in a regression analysis will increase.

Answers

1. Intercept = 10; slope = -4.5.
2. The values of $\hat{Y}$ are 11.6, 6.0, 3.2, and -2.4.

3. Error in the prediction of Y, or the sum of the squared differences between the predicted and actual values of Y.

4. False: As r approaches -1.00 or $+1.00$, the amount of error decreases (i.e., $\hat{Y}$ will increasingly approximate Y). Error increases as r gets closer to 0.0.

DATA BOX 7.A

Predicting Academic Success

Can a linear regression model be used to predict academic success? Dawes (1979) describes how variables such as grade point average (GPA), scores on the Graduate Record Exam (GRE), and ratings of undergraduate institutions' selectivity can be used to develop formulas for graduate admissions committees. Such formulas determine which applicants are apt to succeed in a given graduate program. As Dawes and Corrigan (1974, p. 105) put it, "the whole trick is to know what variables to look at and then to know how to add." Developing useful regression equation involves a bit more work than this wry observation suggests, but the point is well taken.

Humor aside, however, many people become upset at the thought that a mere formula rather than a flesh-and-blood judge or committee decides who is (or is not) granted admission to a graduate program. Are such reactions justified, especially if the method proves to be successful, that is, accurate in its predictions? Knowing what you now know about linear regression, for example, how would you feel about your future being decided by the outcome of an equation? Is it more or less fair than the decision reached by a committee evaluating the same information, which the latter would do in a much less formal and systematic manner?

Dawes (1979) persuasively argues that linear models are better at making important judgments in a fair and decisive manner because they are more objective and technically superior to human judges. Many people—including some behavioral scientists—are loath to abdicate their right to admit students on subjective grounds, however. There are also a variety of psychological arguments against linear models, notably the persistent, if erroneous, belief that clinical intuition regarding admission decisions will be correct with greater regularity (see Data Box 7.B). Finally, Dawes addresses the ethical implications of relying on linear models. Is making an important choice about graduate admissions—or any other decision forum—"dehumanizing" if no interview occurs? Dawes (1979, pp. 580–581) addresses this matter cogently.

> I think that the question of whether people are treated in a fair manner has more to do with the question of whether or not they have been dehumanized than does the question of whether the treatment is face to face. (Some of the worst doctors spend a great deal of time conversing with their patients, read no medical journals, order few or no tests, and grieve at funerals.) A GPA represents 3½ years of behavior on the part of the applicant. (Surely, not all the professors are biased against his or her particular form of creativity.) The GRE is a more carefully devised test. Do we really believe that we can do a better or a fairer job by a 10-minute folder evaluation or a half-hour interview than is done by these two numbers? Such cognitive conceit (Dawes, 1976, p. 7) is unethical, especially given the fact of no evidence whatsoever indicating we can do a better job than does the linear equation. (And even making exceptions must be done with extreme care if it is to be ethical, for if we admit someone with a low linear score on the basis that he or she has some special talent, we are automatically rejecting someone with a higher score, who might well have had an equally impressive talent had we taken the trouble to evaluate it.)

Before you decide that admitting people based on "mere numbers" is too extreme, take a few minutes and think about Dawes's comments and their implications for the use of regression in decision making (see also, Dawes, 1971, 1975).

Residual Variation and the Standard Error of Estimate

The formulas for the regression line and the calculation of the predicted values of Y in the previous section enable us to find a best fitting line for virtually any set of data. Our best fit, or course, is dependent on how well predicted values match up to actual values, or the relative amount of error in our regression analysis. In other words, we know how to make predictions, but how do we characterize their relative accuracy?

We can characterize the accuracy of prediction by considering error in regression akin to the way scores deviate from some average. Think about how the observations fall on or near the regression line in the same way that observations cluster closer or farther away from the mean of a distribution—minor deviation entails low error and a better fit of the line to the data, greater deviation indicates more error and a poorer fit. The information leftover from any such deviation—the distance between a predicted and actual Y value—is called a **residual,** literally the remainder between two points. This residual information around a regression line can be understood in terms conceptually akin to the variance and standard deviation of the mean of some sample of data.

The variance around the regression line is termed *residual variance.*

KEY TERM **Residual variance** refers to the variance of the observations around a regression line.

The residual variance can be determined from the sum of squares of the distance between actual Y values and predicted Y values (i.e., $\hat{Y}$), which we introduced previously in [7.5.1] as $\sum (Y - \hat{Y})^2$. The symbol for the residual variance is $s^2_{\text{est } Y}$ and, in formula terms, it looks like this:

[7.14.1]
$$s^2_{\text{est } Y} = \frac{\sum (Y - \hat{Y})^2}{N - 2}.$$

Conceptually, then, residual variance—also known as **error variance**—is based on the sum of the squared deviations between the actual Y scores and the predicted or $\hat{Y}$ scores divided by the *number* of pairs of X and Y scores minus two (i.e., $N - 2$). As you can imagine, this calculation is a bit cumbersome to determine. Fortunately, we are much more interested in identifying a standardized measure of the error variability around a regression line. The amount of error in a given regression analysis can be presented in a standardized way by calculating what is called the *standard error of estimate.*

KEY TERM The **standard error of estimate** is a numerical index describing the standard distance between actual data points and the predicted points on a regression line. The *standard error of estimate* characterizes the standard deviation around a regression line.

The standard error of the estimate is similar to the standard deviation, as both measures provide a standardized indication of how close or far away observations lie from a certain point—the regression line in the case of the standard error of the estimate and a mean in the case of the standard deviation. The standard error of the estimate—symbolized $s_{\text{est } Y}$—can be conceptually presented as the square root of the residual variance:

[7.15.1]
$$s_{\text{est } Y} = \sqrt{s^2_{\text{est } Y}} = \sqrt{\frac{\sum (Y - \hat{Y})^2}{N - 2}}.$$

For ease of calculation, however, we rely on this simpler computational formula:

[7.16.1]
$$s_{\text{est } Y} = s_Y \sqrt{\frac{N(1 - r^2)}{N - 2}}.$$

Take a good look at [7.16.1] and then think about these properties. First, when r is equal to -1.00 or $+1.00$ (or very close to either value), then $s_{est\ Y}$ will be equal to 0.0. In other words, there are no predictive errors because the regression line perfectly matches up to the actual values of Y. As the value of r draws closer to 0.0, however, then the corresponding value of $s_{est\ Y}$ will increase (i.e., error will increase as variables X and Y are shown to be less associated with one another). In fact, when $r = 0.0$, errors in prediction will be at their maximum for a given distribution of scores, drawing close to the value of the standard deviation for Y, or s_Y. In symbolic terms,

[7.17.1] $$s_{est\ Y} \cong s_Y \sqrt{\frac{N}{N-2}}.$$

As the sample size becomes increasingly large, $s_{est\ Y} \cong s_Y$ because $\sqrt{N/(N-2)}$ will be approximately equal to 1.0.

What is the standard error of the estimate for the aptitude test data presented earlier in the chapter? We need only to turn back to Table 7.1 to collect the information we need to enter into [7.16.1] for:

[7.18.1] $$s_{est\ Y} = s_Y \sqrt{\frac{N(1-r^2)}{N-2}},$$

[7.18.2] $$s_{est\ Y} = (7.55)\sqrt{\frac{6(1-.89^2)}{6-2}},$$

[7.18.3] $$s_{est\ Y} = (7.55)\sqrt{\frac{6(1-.7921)}{4}},$$

[7.18.4] $$s_{est\ Y} = (7.55)\sqrt{\frac{6(.2079)}{4}},$$

[7.18.5] $$s_{est\ Y} = (7.55)\sqrt{\frac{1.2474}{4}},$$

[7.18.6] $$s_{est\ Y} = (7.55)\sqrt{.3119},$$

[7.18.7] $$s_{est\ Y} = (7.55)(.5584),$$

[7.18.8] $$s_{est\ Y} = 4.2162 \cong 4.22.$$

Thus, the standard error of estimate for Y, the actual aptitude test scores, is equal to 4.22. Similar to the standard deviation, the standard error of estimate indicates that there is some dispersion of Y scores around the regression line shown in Figure 7.3. As the standard error of estimate increases in magnitude, this statistic indicates a relatively greater amount of dispersion around the regression line. Further, we now know more about a prediction than simply where a regression line is plotted—we also have a sense of how well it captures the observations in a set of data.

DATA BOX 7.B

The Clinical and the Statistical: Intuition Versus Prediction

A long-running debate in the discipline of psychology concerns the proper role, if any, of statistical formulas for use in diagnosing and predicting psychological disorders or making other clinically related decisions (e.g., Meehl, 1977). These statistical—sometimes called "actuarial"—methods do not involve human judges, rather such judges identify diagnostic criteria for inclusion in the formulas. The term actuarial means computed statistics, which are usually based on large samples of people. Clinical conclusions based on such formulas, then, focus entirely on empirically valid relations between predictor variables and outcomes. In contrast, clinical judgments rely entirely on human judges (e.g., psychiatrists) and their intuitions. Such human judges must carefully observe, collect, and codify clinically related information in their heads to diagnose clients.

Close to 100 behavioral science studies on various topics indicate that where accuracy is concerned, statistical predictions are equal to or better than clinical judgments made by humans (see Dawes, Faust, & Meehl, 1989). The fact is that statistical predictions remain superior *even when* human judges have access to all the available actuarial information (e.g., diagnostic test scores, personality inventory results) that is entered into the formula. Such data indicate rather conclusively that our intuitions are not nearly as good as formal statistical models, which raises an important question: Why don't we rely on these models consistently?

Presumably, people do not like the idea of allowing a nonhuman entity to make decisions about the fate or treatment of people. More than this understandable concern, of course, may be another human concern—taking the role of decision-maker away from human experts (psychiatrists, psychologists, and social workers, among others)—who have years of training and vested interests in making clinical decisions. A way out, of course, is *not* to assume that the data indicate human judges do a mediocre job compared to actuarial formulae, rather we should focus on what a difficult job it is to assess a variety of variables in order to reach a decision (Nisbett & Ross, 1980). Human experts should be lauded for developing accurate formulas and for subsequently treating people based on a formula's diagnosis. After all, what shame can there be in using a tool that is consistently shown to actually help people?

Research continues to demonstrate the actuarial method's superiority to clinical method (for a review, see Dawes, Faust, & Meehl, 1989; see also, Chapman & Chapman, 1971; Dawes, 1979), yet many people cannot abide allowing a decision to be made by formulas, not people—even when the former consistently matches or outperforms the latter (see also, Goldberg, 1970). What do you think about the trade-off between accuracy and who (or in this case, *what*) is making a decision? If a formula consistently and correctly diagnoses clinical conditions or points to appropriate decisions in other realms, should it be favored over the (sometimes flawed) opinions of human judges? Or, are such formulae admittedly useful tools that must still be necessarily displaced by the final judgment of human experts?

Assumptions Underlying the Standard Error of Estimate

There are a few important assumptions underlying the use of the standard error of estimate and, more generally, reliance on regression analysis. First, although any standard error of estimate you calculate will be based on sample data, it is meant to represent the larger population from which the sample data were drawn. In other words, we assume that the best fitting regression line created for one set of data, as well as its standard error of estimate, is theoretically applicable to other, similar sets of data

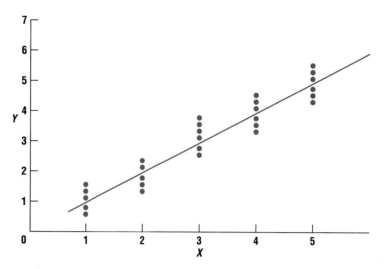

Figure 7.4   Scatter Plot of Hypothetical Data Illustrating the Assumption of Homoscedasticity

collected at other times and based on the responses of other participants. Indeed, one motivation for researchers is to develop regression equations that become increasingly predictive as they are applied to various data sets (and such equations are frequently revised based on new data). A college or university might create a regression model—a term often used to describe an equation that is repeatedly tested and revised—for predicting the qualifications students need to academically succeed at the institution.

Second, as was the case for correlational analysis, variables X and Y presumably share a linear or straight-line relationship with one another.

Third, we assume that in theory, every X value has a possible distribution of Y values associated with it; $\hat{Y}$ is equal to the mean of each distribution of Y values, which vary around it. The standard deviation of each of these distributions is said to be equal to $s_{est\,Y}$. The spread of Y values around $\hat{Y}$ values should be the same up and down a regression line, then, meaning that $s_{est\,Y}$ will have the same value for each and every predicted ($\hat{Y}$) value. Put another way, the distribution of Y scores for each X value will have the same variance. This particular condition is called **homoscedasticity,** which basically means that the variability associated with one variable (Y) remains constant at all of the levels of the other variable (X).

Essentially, it is as if small but relatively normal distributions of scores occur at regular intervals all along the regression line. Figure 7.4 portrays some hypothetical data that adhere to the assumption of homoscedasticity of variance. As you can see, various small distributions of Y values appear to "line up" in a regular fashion above each value of X. A scatter plot of data violating the homoscedasticity assumption would show irregular spreadings of Y values for each value of X along a regression line—some of these Y distributions would contain closely aligned Y scores whereas others would illustrate scores widely apart from one another. This condition, which is the opposite of homoscedasticity, is referred to as **heteroscedasticity.** When heteroscedasticity occurs, the homoscedasticity assumption is violated precisely because the value of $s_{est\,Y}$ varies from distribution to distribution along the regression line.

When homoscedasticity is present and each of the distributions of Y corresponding to some value of X is normal (i.e., Y is normally distributed at every level of X), the standard error of estimate is known to share some characteristics with the standard normal

Heteroscedasticity is the opposite of homoscedasticity. It refers to the condition where Y observations vary in differing amounts at different levels of X.

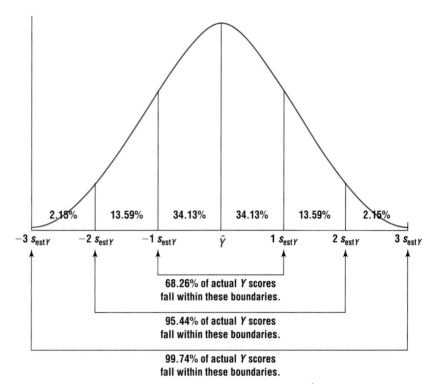

Figure 7.5 Normal Distribution of Y Values Spread Around a Given $\hat{Y}$ Value on a Regression Line

Note: A distribution of actual Y values is assumed to exist for each predicted value of $\hat{Y}$.

curve. In particular, once we predict a value of Y from a value of X, we can identify an interval or range of values where the true value of $\hat{Y}$ is apt to be. Using the logic of the standard normal distribution we learned in chapter 5, we can create a normal distribution that represents any given $\hat{Y}$ value along a regression line.

Imagine that we arbitrarily choose one hypothetical $\hat{Y}$ value on the regression line. Figure 7.5 illustrates a normal distribution of Y scores around this given value of $\hat{Y}$. Instead of standard deviation units around a mean, Figure 7.5 displays standard error of estimate units around $\hat{Y}$—yet the logic underlying both is analogous. As you can see, 68.26% of the values for Y lie between -1 standard error of estimate unit ($s_{est\ Y}$) below $\hat{Y}$ and $+1$ standard error of estimate unit ($s_{est\ Y}$) above it. When we go to $\pm 2\ s_{est\ Y}$ out, 95.44% of the values for Y are assumed to fall therein (see Figure 7.5). Relatively few (extreme) Y values would fall $\pm 3\ s_{est\ Y}$ units without from $\hat{Y}$; that is, less than 5% of the observations would be anticipated to vary that much from $\hat{Y}$.

Due to these properties of the standard error of estimate, what do we assume is true whenever a regression analysis is performed? First, we can assume that approximately 95% of the participants whose data are used in any linear regression obtain Y scores that do not differ from their $\hat{Y}$ by more that $2\ s_{est\ Y}$ (i.e., approximately 95% of measured Y scores will fall within two standard error units of $\hat{Y}$).

Second, the standard error of estimate can constructively be used for assessing the relative margin of error in the predictions made by any regression analysis. Within reasonable limits, then, we can point to how much actual Y values could deviate from predicted (i.e., $\hat{Y}$) values. *We are only justified in drawing such conclusions, however, if the homoscedasticity assumption and the assumption that Y is normally distributed at every level of X are true.*

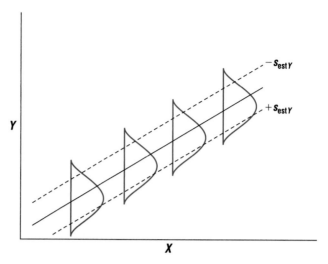

Figure 7.6   Standard Error of Estimate with Assumptions of Homoscedasticity and Normal Distributions of Y at Every Level of X Being Met

Note: Approximately 68.3% of the Y scores fall within $\pm 1\ s_{est\ Y}$ of $\hat{Y}$. This condition will hold true as long as the distribution of Y scores at every score of X is approximately normally distributed and all the distributions have the same pattern of dispersion (i.e., homoscedasticity).

Figure 7.6 nicely illustrates these two assumptions and their theoretical effects on the standard error of estimate. The mean of each of the theoretical distributions along the regression line (i.e., the middle line in Figure 7.6) is equal to $\hat{Y}$, and the boundaries for $\pm 1\ s_{est\ Y}$ are shown to the left and right of this point (see Figure 7.6).

Partitioning Variance: Explained and Unexplained Variation

Any data set used in a regression analysis provides two basic sources of variation—explained and unexplained variation. Explained variation is the proportion of variance in variable Y that is said to be "explained" or accounted for by changes in variable X. To return to the earlier aptitude test example, how much of the variation in the actual aptitude test scores is predictable from the information provided by the practice test? Unexplained variance (i.e., error), in turn, is the proportion of variance in Y that is *not* accounted for by any change in X. What proportion of the variation in the aptitude test scores is not explained by earlier performance on the practice test? Dividing the available variance into these two components is usually called *partitioning*, that is, allocating, variance.

To begin to partition variance, we need to think about any regression analysis as being comprised of three separate sums of squares calculations: One for explained, one for unexplained, and the third for the total sum of squares.

1. *Sum of squares for the explained variance in variable Y.* The variance of the predicted scores around the mean of a distribution can be known by determining the differences between $\hat{Y}$ and $\bar{Y}$, or symbolically as: $\sum (\hat{Y} - \bar{Y})^2$. This sum of squares is often called the **regression sum of squares.**
2. *Sum of squares for the unexplained variance in Y.* The variance of the scores around the regression line, otherwise known as the variance between actual and predicted scores for Y. This form of sum of squares is also called the **error sum of squares,** and

it is symbolically shown as: $\sum (Y - \hat{Y})^2$. We reviewed this formula earlier in the chapter when it was used to calculate error variance (see [7.14.1]).

3. *Total sum of squares for Y.* The total available sum of squares can be determined by subtracting $\overline{Y}$ from every actual value of Y, or symbolically: $\sum (Y - \overline{Y})^2$. When all of these deviation scores are squared and summed to form the total sum of squares (SS_{tot}), the variance and standard deviation for Y are easily known (i.e., SS_{tot}/N and $\sqrt{SS_{tot}/N}$, respectively; see chapter 4).

In mathematical terms, we can show that Total sum of squares = Unexplained variation in Y (i.e., error sum of squares) + Explained variation in Y (i.e., regression sum of squares), or:

[7.19.1] $$\sum (Y - \overline{Y})^2 = \sum (\hat{Y} - \overline{Y})^2 + \sum (Y - \hat{Y})^2.$$

$SS_{tot} = SS_{unexplained} + SS_{explained}.$

Though it is time consuming, it is entirely possible to take a data set and calculate each of these different variances in order to demonstrate that the above relations are true. Table 7.2 displays the partitioned variance for the practice and aptitude test data from Table 7.1. As shown in Table 7.2, the explained and unexplained variation do sum to the total sum of squares (SS_{tot}). Please note that the SS_{tot} and the sum of the explained variation and the unexplained variation are *approximately* equal to one another due to rounding (see Table 7.2). Such minor rounding error illustrates the real nature of data analysis, that calculations do not always add up perfectly. As long as the values involved are relatively close to one another, such approximations are fine.

Is there an easier way to conceptualize the explained variation versus the unexplained variation in a regression analysis? Yes, indeed, and instead of actually performing calculations like the ones shown in Table 7.2, we can rely on the coefficients of determination and nondetermination to help us achieve the same end.

A Reprise for the Coefficients of Determination and Nondetermination

Back in chapter 6, we learned that the coefficient of determination, r^2, was used to identify the proportion of variance shared between two variables, In contrast, the coefficient of nondetermination, k, denoted the proportion of variance not shared between two variables because it is calculated by the formula $1 - r^2$. In regression terms, r^2 can be described as:

Table 7.2 Partitioned Variance for Actual Aptitude Test Scores

X	Y	$\hat{Y}$	Explained Variation $(\hat{Y} - \overline{Y})^2$	Unexplained Variation $(Y - \hat{Y})^2$	Total Variation $(Y - \overline{Y})^2$
75	82	79.52	39.82	6.15	14.67
83	86	85.7	0.017	0.09	0.029
92	88	92.65	46.51	21.62	4.71
95	98	94.97	83.54	9.18	148.11
74	75	78.75	50.13	14.06	117.29
80	86	83.38	6.00	6.86	0.029
Sum of Squares			226.02	57.96	284.84

$\overline{X} = 83.17$ $\overline{Y} = 85.83$ Mean of $\hat{Y} = 85.83$

Explained variation (226.02) + Unexplained variation (57.96) = 283.98 $\cong SS_{tot}$ (i.e., 284.84)

Note: Based on data shown in Table 7.1.

$$[7.20.1] \qquad r^2 = \frac{\text{Regression sum of squares}}{\text{Total sum of squares}} = \frac{\sum (\hat{Y} - \overline{Y})^2}{\sum (Y - \overline{Y})^2}.$$

We need not do all these calculations if we already know the correlation between variables X and Y. Thus, if we know that the correlation between the practice aptitude test scores and the actual aptitude test scores in the earlier example was $+.89$, then $r^2 = (r)^2 = (+.89)^2 = .7921$. In other words, about 79% of the variance in the actual aptitude test can be predicted from the practice exam. We know this to be true because r^2 is the proportion of variance in Y accounted for by X.

Naturally, we can just as easily and quickly determine the variation in Y *not* accounted for by X by calculating k, the coefficient of nondetermination. In regression terms, then:

$$[7.21.1] \qquad k = 1 - r^2 = \frac{\text{Error sum of squares}}{\text{Total sum of squares}} = \frac{\sum (Y - \hat{Y})^2}{\sum (Y - \overline{Y})^2}.$$

As was true for the coefficient of determination, we do not need to perform laborious calculations to determine k if we know the correlation between X and Y or the value of r^2. Because we already know the value of r^2, we need only to subtract it from 1, or $k = 1 - r^2 = 1 - (.7921) = .2079 \cong .21$. Thus, about 21% of the variation in the actual aptitude test scores cannot be predicted from the practice exam scores (i.e., other unmeasured factors, systematic as well as random, are responsible).

Proper Use of Regression: A Brief Recap

Any linear regression equation will plot the best fitting straight line through some data, as well as make some predictions about the relationship between variables X and Y. To truly understand the accuracy of these predictions, however, a researcher must be sure to examine the magnitude of r^2 and the relative size of the standard error of estimate (i.e., $s_{\text{est } Y}$). Failure to consider the latter indices will result in lower accuracy and limit the applicability of research results obtained through regression analysis.

Knowledge Base

1. True or False: When performing a regression analysis, investigators generally want a larger standard error of estimate ($s_{\text{est } Y}$).
2. Define *homoscedasticity*.
3. The total sum of squares (SS_{tot}) can be partitioned into two sources of variation. What are these sources called?
4. The correlation between the X and Y variables in a regression analysis is $+.55$. What percentage of the variability in Y is explained by changes in X? What percentage of variability in Y is not accounted for by changes in X?

Answers

1. False: Investigators generally want a smaller standard error of estimate, as it involves less dispersion of Y sores around the regression line.
2. Homoscedasticity indicates that the variability associated with one variable (Y) remains the same or constant at all levels of another variable (X) all along the regression line.
3. Sum of squares for explained variance in Y and the sum of squares for unexplained variance in Y.
4. $r^2 = (+.55)^2 = .3025 \cong .30$ or 30% of the variability in Y is explained by X; $k = 1 - r^2 = 1 - .3025 = .6975 \cong .70$ or 70% of the variability in Y is not explained by X.

Regression to the Mean

Have you ever had the odd experience of receiving an unusually high or low score on a quiz or a test? What happened? Why did you perform unexpectedly well or so poorly? Like most people, your unexpectedly high or low score probably surprised you. You probably also wondered how you would perform on the next quiz or test; that is, would you do equally well or poorly? Statisticians would theorize that your next score would probably fall closer to your typical (i.e., mean) level of academic performance. If you normally score in the B rather than the A range, your future quiz performance should be less extreme (i.e., closer to your average level of performance). Conversely, if you normally score in the B rather than the D or lower range, you should expect to see a rebound from the low quiz score to your usual level of performance.

Sir Francis Galton dubbed this tendency for new scores following relatively extreme scores to move to an average level *regression toward the mean.*

KEY TERM   Regression toward the mean refers to situations where initially high or low observations are found to move closer to or "regress toward" their mean after subsequent measurement.

Do you recall the tall parent and child example presented at the opening of the chapter? One reason we might anticipate two tall parents to have somewhat shorter children is regression to the mean. Why? As you know, regression analysis is based on the examination of relative deviation scores from a mean, the point in any distribution that is closest to the largest number of scores. This is not to say that our hypothetical parents will absolutely *have* a shorter child, rather, any offspring are simply more likely to be shorter (i.e., closer to a mean height) than their parents. Note that this regressive prediction is an educated guess—sometimes taller parents *do* have an equally tall (or even taller) child, but the best prediction is to assume that the child will be somewhat shorter (i.e., closer to the mean) in height.

Why does regression to the mean occur? To begin, we know observations in any distribution tend to cluster around a mean. If variables X and Y are more or less independent of one another (i.e., $r_{XY} \cong 0.0$), then some outlying score on one variable is likely to be associated with either a high or a low score on the other variable (recall the earlier review of the z score formula for regression). More to the point, though, if we obtain an extreme score on X, the corresponding Y score is likely to regress toward the mean of Y. If, however, X and Y are highly correlated with one another (i.e., $r_{XY} \cong \pm 1.00$), then an extreme score on X is likely to be associated with an extreme score on Y, and regression to the mean will probably not occur. Regression to the mean, then, can explain why an unexpected or aberrant performance on one exam does mean subsequent performance will be equally outstanding or disastrous.

Regression toward the mean can be a particular problem for research, especially when participants are recruited precisely because they appear to possess relatively high or low degrees of some trait. For this reason, Cook and Campbell (1979) list regression toward the mean as a potential threat to the internal validity of experiments or quasi-experiments. That is, an unknown regression effect can mask the effect (or noneffect) of an independent variable on some dependent measure.

Regression effects are especially apt to occur in studies that recruit participants exhibiting extreme qualities—very high or very low—on dimensions critical to the research hypothesis. Studies concerned with the effects of intensive remedial education, for example, involve students whose academic performance is particularly low on standard grading scales (e.g., below a GPA of 2.00). Regression to the mean becomes a problem if these low performing students are recruited based on poor performance on

DATA BOX 7.C

Reinforcement, Punishment, or Regression Toward the Mean?

Regression to the mean is often an elusive phenomenon, one that can lead to errors in judgment. Can it also hamper insight into the human condition? Kahneman and Tversky (1973) offered the following problem, which was based on an actual experience. Read the following problem and formulate your answer before consulting the explanation that follows:

A Problem of Training

The instructors in a flight school adopted a policy of consistent positive reinforcement recommended by psychologists. They verbally reinforced each successful execution of a flight maneuver. After some experience with this training approach, the instructors claimed that contrary to psychological doctrine, high praise for good execution of complex maneuvers typically results in a decrement of performance on the next try. What should the psychologist say in response?

A group of graduate students was asked to explain the performance of the pilots. Although they suggested a number of possible explanations (e.g., verbal reinforcement is ineffective for some pilots, the instructors' observations were biased), not one nominated regression to the mean. Kahneman and Tversky (1973, p. 251) remarked that, "Regression is inevitable in flight maneuvers because performance is not perfectly reliable and progress between successive maneuvers is slow. Hence, pilots who did exceptionally well on one trial are likely to deteriorate on the next, regardless of the flight instructors' reaction to the initial success." They also waggishly note that even well-trained students can be thrown by regression examples that do not involve descriptions of tall parents and their children, a comment that should motivate all of us to be on the look out for regression to the mean effects with greater vigilance!

Oddly, perhaps, this real-life example of regression to the mean actually illustrates how teachers can be led to see punishment as being a more efficacious course for learning novel skills than reinforcement; effects of the former are overestimated while the latter's impact is underestimated. The danger, of course, is that we can generalize from experiences where rewards and punishments appear to switch places (Tversky & Kahneman, 1973). Due to regression to the mean, we may see evidence that behavior is most likely to get better after punishment and to decline after praise or reward (perhaps this is one reason that people who work hard and well are so often rewarded with still more work). Like Tversky and Kahneman (1973), do you ever wonder if the chance elements in human experience often lead to rewards for those who punish others and to punishment for those who reward them?

---

initial (screening) measures, then subjected to remediation, and then tested again. Many of the recruits might demonstrate a rebound in performance on subsequent testing. Such improvement might *not* be due to remediation but, instead, to statistical regression—the students are simply returning to their own average level of performance. Any cited improvement, then, might be artificial, but unless regression is controlled for in the research design (e.g., adequate control groups are used), the investigators might conclude that intensive remediation *caused* the scores on the subsequent test to rise.

Cook and Campbell (1979) suggest that extreme performance in any domain is anomalous because it is influenced by chance factors. As time passes and new but similar events occur, people will return to their more typical or mean levels of performance. And you should not assume that regression toward the mean only occurs in testing-related environments. A variety of everyday events can probably accurately be described as regression phenomena, though we are more likely to seek special explanations for them. Plous (1993) cites some superstitious behavior in the context of sport as reactions to regression phenomena, as when a baseball team is having a winning streak and a player elects to wear the same clothing for weeks running so as not to "disrupt" it. In fact, almost any extreme run of events—sudden changes in crime rates, heavy weather for weeks straight, a dramatic rise in demand for a good or service—is quite likely to be an instance of regression to the mean. Nisbett and Ross (1980) note that one discomfiting aspect of implementing actions to address these problems is the intervention's illusory impact—the return to "normal" or average events is regression to the mean, not entirely the results of one's good work or intentions.

Under what circumstances does regression to the mean dissipate? Regression effects are less likely to pose any problems for research based on a true experiment, one where participants are randomly assigned to two or more levels of an independent variable. Within a true experiment, regression to the mean is assumed to affect all participant groups equally—that is, relatively—so that the effect is spread across conditions and with no adverse effects.

Regression as a Research Tool

The utility of regression analysis as a research tool can be most easily understood by comparing it to correlational analysis. Correlational analysis is often used to develop behavioral science theories. Researchers often look for patterns of association between variables in exploratory research. In contrast, regression analysis is often used in research applications. We already know, for example, that regression is frequently used for admissions purposes in higher education. An admissions officer might want to learn whether and to what degree variables such as IQ, aptitude test scores, socioeconomic status (SES), hobbies, and athletic participation are helpful in predicting future academic achievement (Pedhazur, 1982).

Harris (1998) points out that with effort and planning, regression is a research tool that could advise people to select appropriate careers or create programs designed to help individuals with special needs excel in some domain. In theory, one could use empirically derived scores pertaining to success or failure in any number of professions to develop predictive models. Models for competitive sports (e.g., football, golf), musical performance (e.g., pianist, violist), service industry (e.g., cook, waiter), or medicine (e.g., doctor, nurse, surgeon), among many others, could be developed. Imagine how helpful linear regression could be in directing people toward situations where their skills and abilities could be channeled in constructive, beneficial ways.

Some investigators already use linear regression to predict an individual's future performance based on his or her responses to some test. Corporations routinely employ industrial-organizational psychologists to help select new employees from large applicant pools. Some of these psychologists simplify the hiring process by using regression analysis to make decisions about which applicants should receive job offers. Job candidates, for example, are sometimes asked to complete aptitude tests related to work and job performance as part of the interview process in a company. Candidates' scores on such measures can then be entered into a regression equation in order to determine if their future performance is projected to be sufficient for the needs of the corporation.

Researchers usually rely on regression only when relatively large samples—often numbering in the hundreds—of respondents are available. In fact, regression equations based on small samples are rarely useful (i.e., predictive), as they cannot be applied from sample to sample with reasonable rates of success. Reliance on large samples makes a

▽

In practice, we forget that there is really little to be gained from thinking about regression as a way to predict Y from X when we have all the actual values of Y. *Regression is really for predicting the behavior of individuals in samples beyond the original sample.*

great deal of sense when we remember that such samples tend to be more representative of populations than small samples. In regression terms, then, larger samples ensure a greater degree of predictive accuracy than small samples. By comparison, correlational analyses tend to be performed on relatively small data sets (we noted in chapter 5 that values of N greater than 30 are desirable).

In sum, then, linear regression is used when one variable is being used to predict the value of another variable. Prediction, then, is the watchword. Both of the variables entered into any regression analysis must be based on either interval or ratio scales. The working assumption of investigators using regression is that an equation derived from a sufficiently large sample can be applied in the future to other similar samples. This assumption is valid only when the samples are representative of a larger population of origin.

Other Applications of Regression in the Behavioral Sciences

There are a wide variety of applications for linear regression in the behavioral sciences. Here are some other examples to think about:

- Economists use linear regression to demonstrate the relation between income as a predictor variable and criterion variables like consumption and savings. In economic terms, consumption refers to the things that people spend money on—everything from the bills they pay to the consumer goods (e.g., toys, cars, books, vacations) they buy. Larger incomes predict greater levels of consumption. Similarly, higher income also predicts greater levels of savings, the amount of income that consumers reserve for future uses or expenses.

- Management professionals rely on regression to link skill, effort, responsibility, and job conditions to wages (e.g., Cascio, 1991). Each of these factors contains several categories that can be awarded points. People's skill level can be awarded more or less points based on their education, ingenuity, and work experience, for example, just as fewer points would be assigned for safe rather than hazardous job conditions. The more total points accrued by an individual based on these employment factors would predict higher wages, whereas fewer earned points would be linked to relatively lower wages. Regression, then, can be one tool used to create and administer a wage structure for hourly employees (see also, Milkovich & Newman, 1987).

- Regression is often used by employment professionals to verify that a personnel decision—who is hired from a group of applicants—is fair. Fairness is especially important when minority applicants are present in an applicant pool, as the person doing the hiring must demonstrate that discrimination due to gender or race, for example, did not occur. Thus, regression is often used to establish that the subgroups present in an applicant pool performed similarly to one another on a given screening test—bias is present when a given subgroups' performance is either *over-* or *under*predicted because of their group membership (Cleary, Humphreys, Kendrick, & Wesman, 1975). Using regression, the performance of minority students in academic settings can be studied in much the same way (e.g., Cleary, 1968).

- Finally, a computer science instructor I know likes to show students how doing homework actually predicts their exam performance. After an exam, he often uses students' total scores on their homework to predict their exam scores. There is an obvious motivational component here, of course, that working hard on homework can improve test scores. Let me gently suggest that the same relationship no doubt holds true for statistics homework and exams, as well.

Writing About Regression Results

When writing about regression results, it is important to specify the criterion (i.e., dependent) variable (Y) and the predictor (i.e., independent) variable (X). The convention in journal articles is to sometimes describe the variables in a regression analysis as follows, "A regression of academic achievement on grade point average (GPA) was performed." Note that the word *on* in this sentence implies that academic achievement is the criterion variable (Y) and GPA is the predictor (X).

Most authors include the actual regression formula, placing it within the written text or possibly in a table of data. You do not need to explain which values in the equation are the y intercept and the slope, as most readers should understand such information. It is certainly appropriate to remind readers what variable X represents (i.e., what values were entered into the equation in order to obtain values for $\hat{Y}$). You will want to be sure to provide the means and standard deviations for X and Y, as well as the correlation (r) between X and Y. Finally, it is a good idea to note the range of values for the two variables.

Once a regression equation is presented, it is a good idea to indicate how well it fits the data. Demonstrating the best fit of a line can be done in at least two ways. First, you might create a scatter plot showing the relationship between variables X and Y. Remember to be judicious in your use of graphics, however; avoid having more than one or two in any research report you write (see chapter 3 for guidelines on data display). Second, of course, you should report the standard error of estimate so that readers will have a sense of how close the Y scores fall near the regression line. Beyond providing the numerical value for $s_{\text{est } Y}$, be certain to explain what it means—does the $s_{\text{est } Y}$ suggest that the observations are dispersed widely around the regression line or rather close in to it? If you do decided to show a scatter plot of the data along with the $s_{\text{est } Y}$, then you can use one to support the other.

The remaining pertinent piece of information that should be shared with readers is the coefficient of determination. As a practical matter, I would not note its value until the end of your review of regression results, the point where you reflect on how well the equation predicted $\hat{Y}$. Despite the fact one could report r^2 at the same time r is presented, conceptually, it belongs toward the end of the review of results. What about k, the coefficient of nondetermination? Because its presence is implied and can be readily known once r^2 is identified (i.e., $k = 1 - r^2$), it is not necessary to report k. I think that reporting both r^2 and k involves a bit of overkill unless you have an important reason for doing so.

Multivariate Regression: A Conceptual Overview

This chapter focuses exclusively on linear regression, how one independent variable can be used to predict one dependent variable. In practice, most students in a first statistics course or those conducting a research project will need little more than linear regression. Many of the journal articles and book chapters you will read for your disciplinary studies, however, will sometimes present research based on more advanced regression procedures. You should know that researchers use advanced regression techniques, notably what is usually called *multiple regression,* to examine complex, predictive relationships.

KEY TERM   **Multiple regression** is a statistical technique for exploring the relationship between *one* dependent variable (Y) and *more than one* independent variable ($X_1, X_2, \ldots, X_N$).

Multiple regression is widely used in the behavioral and natural sciences, where relationships are complex and a more detailed sense of how variables work together is necessary. Thus, for example, a multiple regression equation with two independent variables would look like this:

[7.22.1] $$Y = a + b_1(X_1) + b_2(X_2).$$

As you can see, this equation contains an intercept (a), but there are two slopes (b_1 and b_2), each of which is aligned with two independent or predictor variables, X_1 and X_2. This particular equation could be the basis for predicting respondents' stress scores on some standardized measure (Y), so that variable X_1 could be a self-reported rating of job pressure and X_2 might be a score on a measure of physiological arousal. Please understand that formula [7.22.1] is still a formula for a straight line, but the line is somewhat harder to conceptualize than those presented earlier in the chapter. Indeed, a line based on [7.22.1] would be three-dimensional and best represented by a plane (Allison, 1999) or perhaps a vector passing through a plane.

Within the behavioral and natural sciences, multiple regression is used in two general ways: prediction and causal analysis (Allison, 1999). You are already familiar with the idea of prediction, as we have discussed it extensively in linear regression terms. Where multiple regression is concerned, prediction is based on the combination of many variables, which often results in the optimal forecasting of a dependent measure. Causal analysis refers to the use of multiple regression to identify the underlying causes of some observed dependent measure. Researchers are drawn to the causal analysis side of regression because it allows them to separate and explore the unique contributions of each independent variable to the prediction of some dependent measure (Allison, 1999).

Similar to linear regression, multiple regression also develops an equation for predicting respondents' scores ($\hat{Y}$). More than this, however, multiple regression is also used to learn how well some predictor variables (X) actually do predict the criterion variable (Y). Any multiple regression analysis yields what is called a *multiple correlation coefficient,* which is symbolized by the letter R and can range in value from .00 to +1.00. The multiple R, or simply R, indicates the degree of relationship between a given criterion variable (Y) and a set of predictor variables (X). As R increases in magnitude, the multiple regression equation is said to perform a better job of predicting the dependent measure from the independent variables.

Similar to the relationship between r and r^2, a multiple R value can also be squared to illustrate the percentage of variance in Y that is accounted for by the set of predictors, that is, X variables. The job of the researcher is to empirically determine which combination of predictor variables yields the best fitting regression equation. Those predictor variables that add little to the value of R are usually dropped from the analysis.

There is a great deal to learn about multiple regression, much more than can be described here, as it is beyond the scope of this text. Interested readers are encouraged to consult the variety of advanced texts available on the topic (e.g., Allison, 1999; Cohen & Cohen, 1983; Newton & Rudestam, 1999; Pedhazur, 1982).

Project Exercise | PERCEIVING RISK AND JUDGING THE FREQUENCY OF DEATHS

As noted earlier, regression analysis is an appropriate analytic technique when relatively large data sets are available. In the absence of many observations, correlational analysis is an appropriate substitute for gaining a sense of the level to which one variable predicts another (i.e., the degree of association between X and Y). Still, the concepts underlying regression—how well one variable predicts the value of another and with what

Table 7.3 | Estimating Causes of Death

Which of the following are the most frequent causes of death in the United States? Circle one answer in each pair and then rate your level of certainty (50% to 100%).

1. Homicide or diabetes?   I feel _____ percent certain of my answer.*

2. Floods or infectious hepatitis?   I feel _____ percent certain of my answer.

3. All accidents or strokes?   I feel _____ percent certain of my answer.

4. All cancers or heart disease?   I feel _____ percent certain of my answer.

5. Tornadoes or asthma?   I feel _____ percent certain of my answer.

6. Drowning or leukemia?   I feel _____ percent certain of my answer.

7. Lightning or appendicitis?   I feel _____ percent certain of my answer.

8. Motor vehicle accidents or cancer of
    the digestive system?   I feel _____ percent certain of my answer.

Note: This table is based on an exercise from Bolt (1993), which in turn is based on Fischhoff, Slovic, and Lichtenstein (1977).

*Certainty judgments can range from 50% ("I'm guessing—it's a 50-50 chance that I'm correct") to 100% ("I am absolutely certain that I am correct in my choice").

accuracy—can be applied toward our understanding (if not always our actual analysis) of a variety of real life domains.

The perception of risk is one real life domain that has wide ranging social implications, as it involves psychological as well as behavioral dimensions—what hazards we think exist and what we do (or fail to do) to avoid them. Our perception of hazards, too, is easily compared to the actual incidence of risk, and regression analysis can help in this regard. Chapter 7's *Project Exercise* entails risk perception and its conceptual link to linear regression. Before reading any further in this section of the chapter, however, please answer the questions concerning risk listed in Table 7.3. This short exercise requires you to circle which of two causes of death you believe is the most frequent in the United States, and to then indicate how certain you are about your choice. Certainty judgments can range from 50% ("I'm guessing—it's a 50-50 chance that I'm correct") to 100% ("I am absolutely certain that I am correct in my choice").

Did you complete the questions in Table 7.3? No doubt these questions seemed a bit odd to you. Chances are (I hope) that you have not spent much time thinking about causes of death, let alone relative mortality rates in the United States. Yet questions like those listed in Table 7.3 are not entirely unreasonable because we are all exposed to television, radio, newspaper, and magazine reports describing any number of natural or man-made disasters. Most of us buy auto, home, and life insurance, an act that is linked at least in some way to our thinking about risks. We also have health insurance to cover or defray the high costs associated with the diagnosis and treatment of numerous health problems, and the cost of such coverage, too, is predicated on risk.

When most people answer questions like those in Table 7.3, they are usually misled by what is called an availability bias, the tendency to recall information that is more readily available in memory (e.g., Tversky & Kahneman, 1973). In this case, an availability bias usually leads people to select the more vivid cause of death in each pair and to be (over) confident in their choice (Fischhoff, Slovic, & Lichtenstein, 1977). Most of us can recall news coverage of tornadoes wreaking havoc, killing

Table 7.4 | Causes of Death and Their Actual Relative Frequencies

Cause of Death	Number of Deaths per 100 Million People
Smallpox	0
Poisoning by vitamins	0.5
Botulism	1
Measles	2.4
Fireworks	3
Smallpox vaccination	4
Whooping cough	7.2
Polio	8.3
Venomous bite or sting	23.5
Tornado	**44**
Lightning	**52**
Nonvenomous animal	63
Flood	**100**
Excess cold	163
Syphilis	200
Pregnancy, childbirth, and abortion	220
Infectious hepatitis	**330**
Appendicitis	**440**
Electrocution	500
Motor vehicle and train collision	740
Asthma	**920**
Firearm accident	1,110
Poisoning by solid or liquid	1,250
Tuberculosis	1,800
Fire and flames	3,600
Drowning	**3,600**
Leukemia	**7,100**
Accidental falls	8,500
Homicide	**9,200**
Emphysema	10,600
Suicide	12,000
Breast cancer	15,200
Diabetes	**19,000**
Motor vehicle (car, truck, or bus) accident	**27,000**
Lung cancer	37,000
Cancer of the digestive system	**46,400**
All accidents	**55,000**
Stroke	**102,000**
All cancers	**160,000**
Heart disease	**360,000**
All diseases	849,000

Note: These data were taken from Fischhoff et al. (1977). The entries appearing in **bold** are those also shown in Table 7.3.

people, and damaging property, say, in the Midwest with little or no difficulty. Instances of people succumbing to asthma do not leap to mind, however, despite the fact that more people die (on average) each year from asthma (920 deaths per 100 million U.S. residents per year) than tornadoes (44 deaths per 100 million people). As you may have guessed by now, the second cause of death in each pair in Table 7.3 is far more prevalent than the first cause—and not coincidentally, these second causes

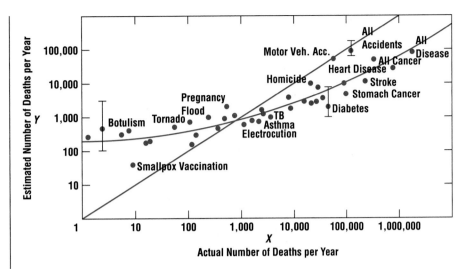

Figure 7.7   Estimates of Lethal Deaths by Actual Incidence Rates

Note: This figure was taken from Slovic, Fischhoff, and Lichtenstein (1982). To index variability across respondents, the vertical bars were drawn to depict the 25th and 75th percentiles of judgments for botulism, diabetes, and all accidents. The range of responses was similar for the other 37 fatalities shown above.

are also usually much more subtle, even quiet killers, compared to the first member of a pair. For comparison purposes, Table 7.4 lists all of the causes of death (and their relative rates) from Table 7.3, plus several other lethal events (these data were taken from Fischhoff et al., 1977). Please note that the causes of death (and their incidence) from Table 7.3 appear in boldface in Table 7.4.

How accurate were the predictions you made in Table 7.4? Did you behave like most respondents—that is, did the availability bias guide your selections and boost your confidence in them? If you made some accurate choices in Table 7.4, what guided your selection? Were your confidence ratings appropriately gauged to any correct choices?

What if we considered the estimated frequency of deaths per year to be Y and the actual frequency of deaths attributable to lethal events to be X? In other words, can we treat the estimates people make as a regression problem? Figure 7.7 illustrates the relationship between the judged frequency and actual frequency of death due to lethal events. If people's estimates and the actual death rates matched, then the data points would fall on the straight line shown in Figure 7.7. The points plotted in Figure 7.7, as well as the curved line that is more or less fitted to them, represent the average responses of laypeople who took part in research conducted by Lichtenstein, Slovic, Fischhoff, Layman, and Combs (1978). As shown in Figure 7.7, hazards that occur with greater regularity were generally estimated to occur more often, yet the data points are sometimes above, other times below, the line of accurate judgment.

How can the data shown in Figure 7.7 be characterized? Generally speaking, participants appeared to inflate the frequency of rare causes of death and to minimize the incidence of common fatalities. Table 7.5 summarizes the participants' judgmental biases regarding the relative frequencies of death. As an exercise, compare the answers you recorded in Table 7.4 to the respondents' data shown in Table 7.5. Do you see why peoples' predictions often over- or underestimate the actual incidence of some events? It should be clear that regression analysis is very useful when it comes to linking predicted scores with actual observations.

Table 7.5	Bias in Judged Frequencies of Death	
	Most Overestimated Fatalities	**Most Underestimated Fatalities**
	All accidents	Smallpox vaccination
	Motor vehicle accidents	Diabetes
	Pregnancy, childbirth, and abortion	Stomach cancer
	Tornadoes	Lightning
	Flood	Stroke
	Botulism	Tuberculosis
	All cancers	Asthma
	Fire and flames	Emphysema
	Venomous bite or sting	
	Homicide	

Source: Adapted from Slovic, Fischhoff, & Lichtenstein (1979).

LOOKING FORWARD   THEN BACK

L inear regression is used to predict changes in a dependent (criterion) variable based on changes in an independent (predictor) variable. Regression is a powerful technique, one that researchers can use in traditional experimental situations (where change in two or more groups can be compared) as well as in less controlled field settings (where change in only one group is studied). The chapter opened with a decision tree that will enable you to maximize the predictive power of regression analyses (e.g., if the two variables involved are not substantially correlated with one another, there is little reason to do this analysis). Indeed, you might be drawn to regression techniques if any research you read or conduct involves estimating the incidence of some behavior in the future given prior knowledge (e.g., depression at one point is often linked with health problems later; a team's performance early in a season is often linked to whether it makes it to the playoffs). This decision tree will also serve as quick review of regression, as the necessity for paired scores, as well as a predictor and a criterion variable, are also noted.

Summary

1. Linear regression involves predicting the value of one variable (Y) from another variable (X). Regression is related to correlation: Unless one variable is correlated with the other, a reasonable degree of prediction is not possible.

2. Regression attempts to locate patterns within data, which are usually shown in a scatter plot. Specifically, linear regression projects a "best fitting" straight line through the plotted points representing X and Y. Ideally, this line is placed so as to minimize the distance between the predicted and actual values of Y.

3. Regression analysis examines changes in the level of variable Y to corresponding changes in the levels of X. By convention, variable Y is designated the criterion or dependent variable,

whereas variable X is the predictor or independent variable in most regression analyses.

4. Although regression can be both understood and performed using z scores, it is usually more practical to rely on one of the computational formulas. The most common computational formula is $\hat{Y} = a + bX$, the formula for a straight line, where $\hat{Y}$ is a predicted score, a is equal to the y intercept, b is the slope of the line, and X is a predictor variable whose value varies.

5. Any variance found around a regression line is termed residual or error variance, and it is symbolized $s_{est\ Y}^2$. The index most frequently used to describe the distance between actual data points and those points predicted from a regression line

is called the standard error of estimate, or $s_{est\ Y}$. In essence, the standard error of estimate is a standard deviation found around any regression line.

6. As the correlation between variables X and Y draws closer to ± 1.00, the $s_{est\ Y}$ will move closer to 0.0 (i.e., no error exists between actual and predicted scores). As the correlation becomes closer to 0.0, however, errors in prediction will increase, closing in on the value of the standard deviation of Y (i.e., s_Y).

7. Homoscedasticity refers to the fact that variability associated with one variable (Y) remains constant at all of the levels of another variable (X). In theory, homoscedasticity involves small distributions of Y scores lining up in a regular fashion above each value of X along the regression line. This condition must be met before a regression analysis can properly be performed (in practice, heteroscedasticity—irregular Y distributions—will result in poor or no prediction of $\hat{Y}$).

8. In sum of squares terms, the variation in a regression analysis can be partitioned into two components: explained variation and unexplained variation. When summed, these components equal the total sum of the squares (SS_{tot}).

9. The coefficient of determination (r^2) is used to identify the percentage of variance in Y explained by changes in X, whereas the coefficient of nondetermination (k) indicates the percentage of variance in Y *not* explained by changes in X.

10. Regression toward the mean occurs when extreme observations are later found to regress or move toward a distribution's mean after subsequent measurement. In research, regression toward the mean can be a particular problem when participants who score very high or very low on measures of interest are recruited. Subsequent increases or decreases in some behavior can be erroneously attributed to an intervention when regression to the mean is actually the source of the perceived change. For this reason, regression to the mean is considered to be a serious threat to the internal validity of research projects lacking adequate control groups.

11. Linear regression is best used in research that involves very large data sets, where observations can number in the hundreds or even thousands. Although it is often associated with data analysis in achievement settings (e.g., college admissions, hiring decisions), regression can be used in any forum where predicting future behavior from past behavior is desired.

12. Multiple regression predicts one dependent variable (Y) from more than one independent variable (X). As an analytic technique, multiple regression is used for prediction when a combination of variables is available. This technique can also be used for causal analysis, that is, to separate and identify the unique contributions of each independent variable in the prediction of a dependent variable.

Key Terms

Criterion variable *(p. 242)*
Error sum of squares *(p. 256)*
Error variance *(p. 251)*
Heteroscedasticity *(p. 254)*
Homoscedasticity *(p. 254)*
Intercept *(p. 243)*

Multiple regression *(p. 263)*
Predictor variable *(p. 242)*
Regression analysis *(p. 242)*
Regression line *(p. 244)*
Regression sum of squares *(p. 256)*
Regression toward the mean *(p. 259)*

Residual *(p. 251)*
Residual variance *(p. 251)*
Slope *(p. 243)*
Standard error of the estimate *(p. 251)*

Chapter Problems

1. What is the nature of the relationship between correlation and regression?

2. Define each of the variables and constants in the formula $Y = a + bX$.

3. Explain the relationship between a "best fitting" regression line and the "the method of least squares."

4. Explain the relationship between r, residual variance, and errors in prediction. That is, describe the relative incidence of error when $r \cong \pm 1.00$ and when $r \cong 0.0$.

5. What is residual variance and how is it related to the standard error of estimate? Why are lower values for the standard error of estimate more desirable than larger values?

6. Define homoscedasticity and heteroscedasticity. Why is homoscedasticity an important assumption for regression analysis?

7. What does it mean when statisticians "partition" variation? How and why is the variation around a regression line partitioned?

8. What roles do the coefficients of determination and nondetermination play in regression analysis?

9. A college athlete plays very well in a series of games, but his performance drops off late in the season. The team's coach explains the change in performance by noting that his star player is under a lot of pressure, as he must choose between

professional sports or graduate school. Can you offer the coach a statistical explanation for the player's slump in performance?

10. Regression to the mean is said to be a common threat to the internal validity of experiments and quasi-experiments. How and why is it a threat? Can anything be done to reduce or eliminate the deleterious effects of regression to the mean?

11. Conceptually, how does multiple regression differ from linear regression? In what ways is multiple regression used?

12. Suggest two real world applications for regression analysis.

13. Sketch a graph showing the linear equation $Y = 5 + 4X$.

14. Using the equation $Y = -5 + 6.3X$, calculate $\hat{Y}$ when $X = 7$, 12, 14, 20, and 21.

15. Using the equation $\hat{X} = 15 + .87Y$, calculate $\hat{X}$ when $Y = 2.8$, 3.7, 4.5, 5, and 6.

16. Determine the regression equation for these data:

X	Y
1	2
3	4
6	4
3	2
2	6
1	3

Compute each of the $\hat{Y}$ values based on each of the X values. What is the standard error of estimate for $\hat{Y}$?

17. What percentage of the Y scores lie between ± 1 $s_{est\ Y}$ around any given $\hat{Y}$ value? What percentage of the Y scores lies between ± 3 $s_{est\ Y}$ around any given $\hat{Y}$ value?

18. A sociologist believes that there is a relationship between hours spent exploring the Internet and grade point average (GPA). Specifically, the sociologist believes that lower grades can be predicted from increasing amounts of time spent "surfing" the Internet. She surveyed 80 college students, asking them to indicate their GPAs (Y) and the number of hours per week spent on the Internet (X). Here are the data:

Hours on Internet	GPA
$\overline{X} = 20$	$\overline{Y} = 2.75$
$s_X = 5.0$	$s_Y = .45$

$$r = -.70$$
$$N = 80$$

a. Determine the regression equation of Y on X for these data.

b. Biff uses the Internet for 30 hours a week—estimate his GPA.

c. Susan has a GPA of 3.25. Estimate the number of hours she spends on the Internet.

d. What is the standard error of estimate of Y?

19. Researchers believe that positive mood is related to work productivity. The following data were collected in an office:

Positive Mood	Productivity
$\overline{X} = 15.5$	$\overline{Y} = 25$
$s_X = 3.0$	$s_Y = 6.0$

$$r = .66$$
$$N = 50$$

a. Determine the regression equation of Y on X for these data.

b. Sam's recorded mood is a 12. What is his projected productivity level?

c. Andrea's productivity level is 33. What level of mood led to such a high level of productivity?

d. Calculate the standard error of estimate for both X and Y.

e. What percentage of total variation in productivity is accounted for by positive mood?

20. For each of the following data sets, what is the value of the slope of a regression line?

a. $r = +.43$, $s_X = 2.5$, $s_Y = 4.0$.

b. $r = -.72$, $s_X = 4.0$, $s_Y = 5.4$.

c. $r = +.83$, $s_X = 1.0$, $s_Y = 1.8$.

d. $r = -.53$, $s_X = 2.8$, $s_Y = 2.1$.

21. Assume that each of the data sets in problem 20 is based on an N of 90. What is the value of $s_{est\ Y}$ for each one? Which data set has the largest $s_{est\ Y}$? The smallest $s_{est\ Y}$?

22. Report the coefficients of determination and nondetermination for each of the data sets shown above in problem 20.

23. A psychologist examines the link between a measure of depression (Y) and one for stress (X). Based on a random sample of students from a very large state university, the psychologist obtains the following data:

Stress Test	Depression Measure
$\overline{X} = 22.5$	$\overline{Y} = 45.0$
$s_X = 2.0$	$s_Y = 4.5$

$$r = +.73$$
$$N = 400$$

a. If a student's stress score is 32, what is his or her depression score apt to be?

b. A new student receives a 20 on the depression measure. What is her estimated score on the stress test?

c. What percentage of the variation in the depression measure is not explained by scores on the stress test?

24. The psychologist introduced in problem 23 creates an intervention program designed to reduce stress and alleviate depression. He recruits 20 highly stressed freshmen and meets in private and group sessions with them for 1 month. At the end of that time, their depression scores drop by an average of 8.5 points. The psychologist presents his results to the university's administration in order to ask for funding to undertake a larger intervention project. Are the psychologist's conclusions about the intervention program justified? Why or why not? How could he improve his intervention project?

25. A gerontologist wants to see if age predicts declines in scores on a particular intelligence test. Despite having a large number of research participants who range in age from 25 to 85, age is not highly correlated with performance on the intelligence test. Is a regression analysis appropriate? (*Hint:* Use the decision tree at the start of this chapter to answer this question.)

26. A student wonders if birth order (firstborn, secondborn, and so on) predicts shyness, such that first or only children tend to be shyer than later born children are. The student gives a standardized measure of shyness to 60 participants (30 males, 30 females), asking each one to indicate their number of siblings and their birth orders. Is a regression analysis appropriate? (*Hint:* Use the decision tree at the start of this chapter to answer this question.)

27. A researcher conducts a field study under trying conditions, so that she has some data from each participant. It is the case, however, that some participant records lack a criterion variable, others a predictor—few have both pieces of data. Is a regression analysis appropriate? (*Hint:* Use the decision tree at the start of this chapter to answer this question.)

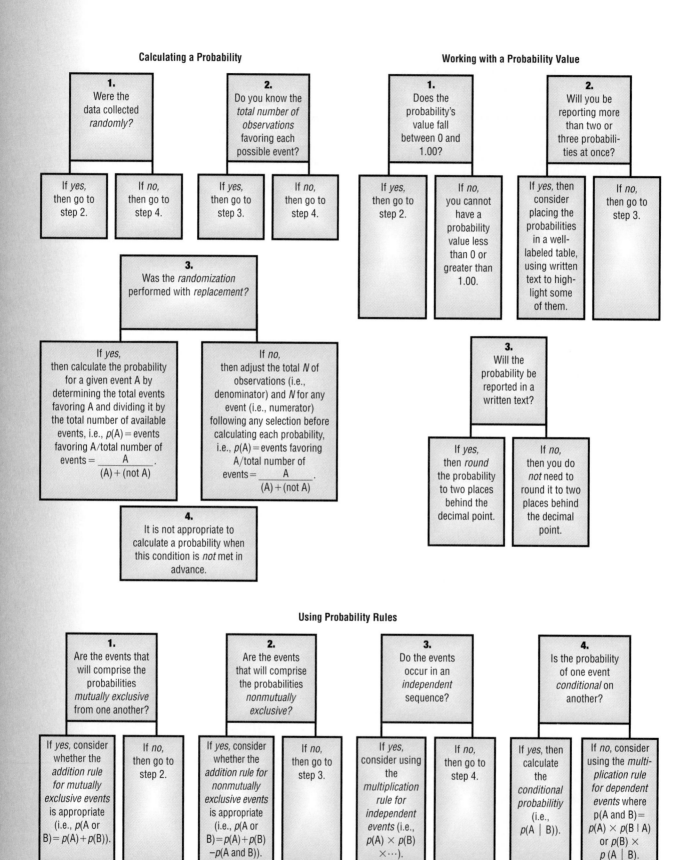

Calculating a Probability

1. Were the data collected *randomly?*

If *yes,* then go to step 2.

If *no,* then go to step 4.

2. Do you know the *total number of observations* favoring each possible event?

If *yes,* then go to step 3.

If *no,* then go to step 4.

3. Was the *randomization* performed with *replacement?*

If *yes,* then calculate the probability for a given event A by determining the total events favoring A and dividing it by the total number of available events, i.e., $p(A)$ = events favoring A/total number of events = $\dfrac{A}{(A) + (\text{not } A)}$.

If *no,* then adjust the total N of observations (i.e., denominator) and N for any event (i.e., numerator) following any selection before calculating each probability, i.e., $p(A)$ = events favoring A/total number of events = $\dfrac{A}{(A) + (\text{not } A)}$.

4. It is not appropriate to calculate a probability when this condition is *not* met in advance.

Working with a Probability Value

1. Does the probability's value fall between 0 and 1.00?

If *yes,* then go to step 2.

If *no,* you cannot have a probability value less than 0 or greater than 1.00.

2. Will you be reporting more than two or three probabilities at once?

If *yes,* then consider placing the probabilities in a well-labeled table, using written text to highlight some of them.

If *no,* then go to step 3.

3. Will the probability be reported in a written text?

If *yes,* then *round* the probability to two places behind the decimal point.

If *no,* then you do *not* need to round it to two places behind the decimal point.

Using Probability Rules

1. Are the events that will comprise the probabilities *mutually exclusive* from one another?

If *yes,* consider whether the *addition rule for mutually exclusive events* is appropriate (i.e., $p(A$ or $B) = p(A) + p(B)$).

If *no,* then go to step 2.

2. Are the events that will comprise the probabilities *nonmutually exclusive?*

If *yes,* consider whether the *addition rule for nonmutually exclusive events* is appropriate (i.e., $p(A$ or $B) = p(A) + p(B) - p(A$ and $B)$).

If *no,* then go to step 3.

3. Do the events occur in an *independent* sequence?

If *yes,* consider using the *multiplication rule for independent events* (i.e., $p(A) \times p(B) \times \cdots$).

If *no,* then go to step 4.

4. Is the probability of one event *conditional* on another?

If *yes,* then calculate the *conditional probability* (i.e., $p(A \mid B)$).

If *no,* consider using the *multiplication rule for dependent events* where $p(A$ and $B) = p(A) \times p(B \mid A)$ or $p(B) \times p(A \mid B)$.

PROBABILITY

ames of chance are very popular. Some people like to gamble, placing bets or wagers on the outcomes of particular events, including team sports, horse races, and boxing matches. Other people prefer to be more actively involved in the gambling process, frequenting casinos in places such as Las Vegas or Atlantic City. Still others choose games of chance where participation is sure but short—they buy tickets or various game cards from state-sponsored lotteries, hoping to win a great deal of money for the relatively modest investment of a dollar or two spent while buying bread and milk at the convenience store.

In each of these situations, playing a game of chance involves being aware of probability, or the relative frequency with which some event actually occurs or is likely to occur again in the future. The general concept of probability is not foreign to most of us. We buy car insurance to guard against the probability of having an accident and paying for repairs. We exercise, eat a reasonably healthy diet, and get proper amounts of sleep to reduce the likelihood (probability) of becoming ill. And we are at least peripherally aware that roughly one out of every two marriages ends in divorce, leading to a divorce rate hovering around 50% (i.e., the odds of staying married are about 50:50). In everyday life, too, we make what are effectively small-scale probability judgments involving our best guess about future events (e.g., "If I accept the job, will I be satisfied with the salary?" "If I order seafood for dinner while visiting Ohio, what are the chances that it will be fresh?" "If I ask her, will Sheila go out with me on a date?").

Despite our general awareness of its applicability, most of us are not armed with any formal understanding of probability and its properties. Statisticians who study probability theory and behavioral scientists who rely on probabilistic concepts share an interest in making quantitative statements about the likelihood or occurrence of uncertain events. We already quantified aspects of uncertainty in different ways earlier in this book. In the last chapter, for example, we discussed how linear regression is used to make particular predictions that are often uncertain (e.g., Will information collected at one time estimate future performance?). Similarly, a correlation indicates whether the relationship between two variables is positive, negative, or zero, but it does not specify the causes of the relationship (see chapter 6)—such factors remain unknown unless an experimental investigation is undertaken. Even the results of such experiments remain uncertain until independent variables are manipulated, dependent measures are measured, and data are collected and appropriately analyzed.

Probability involves the degree to which some event is likely to happen in the future.

In the course of this chapter, we will explore some basic aspects of probability theory, and our goals in doing so will be two fold. First, familiarity with some formal properties of probability theory will help us to understand the statistics derived from them. Generally, we will learn that probability entails examining the ratio of the number of *actual occurrences* of some event to the total number of *possible occurrences* for the event.

Second, we will use probability in connection with a main theme of statistics, inferring the characteristics of a population based on a sample drawn from it. The link shared between samples and populations is often described in probabilistic terms—how likely is that sample A was drawn from population B rather than population C? When a sample is established as originating from a given population, empirical research and statistical analysis can be used to make inferences about the characteristics of the population. These inferences are based on inferential statistics, which enable investigators to use the limited information from a sample to draw broad conclusions about a population.

Let's consider an example that will illustrate these two goals in microcosm:

> Consider the letter V and its placement in words in the English language. Is V more likely to appear as
>
> ___the first letter in words?
> ___the third letter in words?

How can we explore this problem in the context of the chapter's first goal, the examination of the ratio of actual to possible occurrences of some event? When people answer this problem by treating it as a **subjective probability** judgment—a reliance on belief, opinion, or intuition—most select the first option. My guess is that most readers solved this problem by making a subjective probability judgment—V was perceived to occur more frequently as the first rather than the third letter of words. A more empirical approach, of course, would be to randomly select words from a book or newspaper, comparing how often V appeared in the first or third position of the sampled words. Using this method, one would not know the actual number of possible occurrences, but the relative frequency of first letter V words to third letter V words could be assessed (i.e., counted) through this sort of sampling.

Such sampling and subsequent examination of words from some text would, of course, involve the second of the stated chapter goals. You would be using the sample of words containing V in the first or third position to try to characterize the quality of the larger population of words—does it contain more words with V in the first or third position? No inferential statistics would be involved in this case, but inference assuredly would, as a limited sample of information would be used to estimate the characteristics of the larger (and largely unknown) population.

As you almost certainly guessed by now, actual word counts reveal that the letter V is more frequently the third rather than the first letter of English words. Tversky and Kahneman (1973) explain the pronounced tendency for placing V in the first position as another case of availability bias, the ease with which examples can be brought to mind. This heuristic or inferential shortcut was introduced in chapter 7's *Project Exercise*. Thus, it is by far easier to mentally retrieve words starting with V (e.g., verb, vendetta, victory, viper, vim) than it is to think of words having V in third place (e.g., live, love, dive). Availability biases aside, we are clearly familiar with probability judgments—but we must learn ways to make them properly and, therefore, more accurately.

The Gambler's Fallacy or Randomness Revisited

At some point in your experience, you have probably had the opportunity to flip a coin and then to call out either "heads" or "tails." Any fair coin is assumed to provide players with a "50-50" chance of "winning" a given toss. The team who wins the toss of a coin at the start of a football game, for example, chooses how the game begins (e.g., who receives or kicks off first). A coin is tossed, too, before the start of a soccer match. The team winning the toss can select which of two goals they want to defend. I would guess that most of us have flipped a coin to determine the outcome of some mundane but necessary task (e.g., who will take out the trash, go grocery shopping, pay for the next round of drinks).

Imagine that you were flipping a coin several times and you received the following sequence of tosses (H = "heads" and T = "tails"):

H–T–H–H–H–T–T–H–H–H–H

What face of the coin should occur next in the sequence, an H or a T?

If you responded *either* an H or a T—*neither* is more or less likely—you are quite right. In the case of a fair coin, there is always an equal chance that either an H or a T will occur on any given toss. If you said a T because there are too many Hs—that is, a T is somehow "due" next—you were incorrect. Despite its lower comparative frequency in the above distribution, there is no unseen force setting out to maintain the relative ratio of Hs to Ts. You would be equally wrong, of course, if you said an H would come up next because there were more Hs than Ts in this sequence—both are equally probable.

Why do some people misconstrue the role of chance when predicting the outcome of the next flip of a coin? As discussed back in chapter 2, humans often misperceive the role of randomness and its effects on a variety of outcomes (see Data Box 2.A; see also Data Box 8.D). We may recognize that randomness is present, but we frequently impose order where it does not belong. Kahneman and Tversky (1972) argue that people anticipate that a sequence of events that is generated by some random process (e.g., coin flips) will exemplify the characteristics of that process even when a sequence is short (i.e., few rather than many observations on which to base inferences). Randomness or, rather, people's idealized but erroneous version of it is the characteristic of interest in this example. Consider the following two sequences of coin flips—is one more likely than the other?

H–H–H–T–T–T

H–T–H–T–T–H

We commit the gambler's fallacy when we assume that one chance event will cause another chance event.

Neither one is more likely than the other, but many people will nonetheless select the second array because it appears to be relatively more "random" than the first one. In fact, the first one appears to many people to be *too ordered* or *sequenced*—nature, after all, should be choppy or somewhat haphazard, shouldn't it? Not in this case, nor in many similar cases.

When we fall prey to seeing order amidst randomness, order where it does not apply, we are being influenced by what is traditionally called the *gambler's fallacy*.

KEY TERM The **gambler's fallacy** entails the erroneous belief that one randomly determined event will affect the outcome of another randomly determined event.

A fallacy is a delusion, an untruth, one that is disruptive to the extent that people follow or believe it. Misconstruing chance is called the gambler's fallacy for very good reason—individuals actively involved in risking their money while gambling "see" unrealized patterns in outcomes where none exist or impute cause, effect, and order where it is absent. Thus, people who lose several hands of black jack believe that a win is now due, just as individuals playing roulette see a run of red as ripe for a change to black. We want chance—that is, nature and its random parts—to be a self-correcting process, and it is not. "[D]eviations are not 'corrected' as a chance process unfolds, they are merely diluted" (Tversky & Kahneman, 1974, p. 1125).

▽

Chance is *not* a self-correcting process.

Yet even as you read and understand the explanation of the gambler's fallacy, I am guessing that some readers are saying to themselves something like the following: "Well, OK, but at some point when you toss a coin and you get a run of heads, a tail *should* appear." That's right. A tail should appear—it just so happens that it has the same odds of appearing as a head, which should also appear. Coins obey the **law of averages,** meaning that if a coin is fair, there is an equal chance that the next flip will result in a head or a tail (Runyon, Haber, Pittenger, & Coleman, 1996). Statisticians note that in the case of coin tosses or other random events, each event is *independent* of every other event.

KEY TERM   **Independence** exists when the probability of one event is not affected by the probability of any previous events.

In other words, one coin flip has nothing whatsoever to do with the next or previous coin flip—each one is independent of every other one. Put more simply still, coins have no memory—only coin flippers do.

As we discuss probability theory in its myriad forms, you would do well to remember that people routinely misperceive the role chance plays in variety of events. To some degree, this misperception is understandable. First, we are not intellectually "hardwired," as it were, to always detect the subtle nuances of probability in daily life. As we established at the chapter's outset, we have an intuitive sense of probability and an abundance of relevant experience, but little formal understanding. Even when we possess a formal understanding of probability, there is no guarantee we will use it appropriately when confronting real-world situations where it applies (e.g., Gilovich, 1991; Kahneman, Slovic, & Tversky, 1982; Nisbett & Ross, 1980).

Second, many of the settings where chance operates probably affect our moods or outlooks in positive ways. When I buy a lottery ticket or play a slot machine, I may know in a general sense that the odds of winning are against me, but I enjoy the moment. There is a positive feeling associated with the possibility of winning, and I can deny the objective probabilities of winning or losing as long as I do not lose much in the process (Dunn & Wilson, 1990). No doubt this process is extended to less objective settings, as well.

Third, whether probabilities are known or not, we have a real need to explain events, and otherwise random events are not exempt. It will help, I think, to keep one last very interesting example in mind as we begin to review the quantitative side of probability. During the Nazi bombing blitz on London during World War II, city residents developed rather elaborate theories to explain the pattern of destruction caused by the V-1 rockets (Feller, 1968, cited in Fischhoff, 1982). Such theories were used to guess what the Germans were aiming at as well as to decide when it was time to take cover. A later analysis of the frequency of hits revealed that they were random (see Figure 8.1)—they had no pattern per se—but understandably, perhaps, humans are prone to see order in disasters just as we hope to see it at the craps table, the slot machine, or any other event (see Clarke, 1946). Keep this desire in mind—and in check—as we study probability.

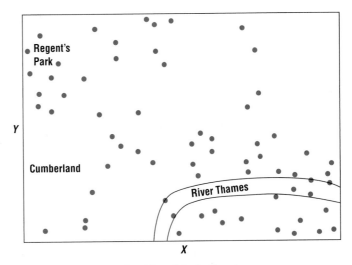

Figure 8.1   Random Pattern of V-1 Bombing of Central London

Source: Johnson (1981).

Probability: A Theory of Outcomes

> Probability is like the cane that the blind man uses to feel his way. If he could see, he would not need the cane, and if I knew which horse was the fastest, I would not need probability theory.
>
> ——Stanislaw Lem

The quotation from Lem illustrates that the study of probability is used to predict what is likely to happen in the future given that some information is already known. Such information usually concerns the characteristics of a sample, which are used to infer the actual nature of the larger population from which they were drawn (for a review of samples and populations, see chapter 1). Probability, then, serves as a guide to understanding what could happen in the future, and it is based on assessing the nature of the relationships among the variables found within a sample.

A person could spend a lifetime learning all there is to know about probability theory, as it is a special area of study within the discipline of statistics. Thus, our review of probability theory and probabilistic concepts will necessarily be a selective one. We will begin with the so-called "classical approach" to probability, which will be linked with our working knowledge of proportions and frequency distributions.

Classical Probability Theory

When we speak of the classical approach to probability, we refer to a mathematical account of the likelihood that one event will occur in the context of all other, possible events. In this case, probability is usually determined by the frequency with which the event of interest and the other events can occur within a *sample space.*

KEY TERM   A **sample space** is the frame of reference for any probability, as it is defined as all the potential outcomes that can be observed or measured.

The students in my statistics class comprise not only a sample but also a sample space. When I call on any one of them, I am sampling their opinion—one student is an observation from the larger sample space of students.

DATA BOX 8.A

"I Once Knew A Man-Who . . .": Beware Man-Who Statistics

As you begin your study of probability, you would do well to keep in mind that people often debate the accuracy of probabilities (or any statistical information) by calling on anecdotal evidence. All of us, for example, have been bombarded for years with news and advertising demonstrating the link between smoking and cancer, as well as numerous other health problems. Recent successful litigation against the tobacco industry underscores the health risks associated with smoking and the tremendous cost in health care and loss of life than can be laid at its doorstep. Yet, I will hazard a guess that most readers have encountered a smoker (or a defender of smoking) who will attest to a version of the following: "They say that smoking causes cancer, but I know a man who has smoked 2 packs of cigarettes every day since he was 15 years old. Now, he's in his eighties and he still *doesn't* have cancer!"

Discussing welfare and welfare recipients is another arena where anecdotes are employed to fend off disquieting truths (Dunn, 1999). A common myth is that most welfare recipients are members of urban minority groups who want to be paid for *not* working for years at a time. In actuality, most welfare recipients in the late 1990s are white residents of rural and suburban areas—and about one third of these people leave the welfare rolls within 12 months (Keil, 1996). Yet, we hear about the "guy on welfare who picked up his check driving a Cadillac sedan," as well as other stock characters who abuse the system (see also, Hamill, Wilson, & Nisbett, 1980).

Such defending (and defensive) comments about welfare or smoking are often called **"man-who" statistics** because an anecdote, usually one or two salient cases, is held up as evidence that some otherwise compelling scientific explanation is potentially fraught with error. Nisbett and Ross (1980) suggest that many people seem driven to offer up these counterexamples as a way to contradict the meaning and message found in statistical results. Any reasonable person knows that a "man-who" statistic cannot outweigh empirical evidence (i.e., not all smokers get cancer—but a high percentage do; some welfare recipients are African-American or Hispanic—but most are white). To be sure, "man-who" statistics are intriguing—just as any unexpected tales are intriguing—but they are not substitutes for facts. One fact is that smoking increases the probability of health problems for smokers, and one smoker, a "man who . . . ," does not change an abstract statistical relationship borne out by the data. Nor does one welfare recipient driving an expensive car change the facts about typical welfare recipients and their respective characteristics.

Remember that our goal is to use statistics and the careful analysis of data to generalize from samples back to a population. Any conclusion we draw from the relationships among variables in a sample is not a definitive statement, rather it is a probabilistic statement—a best estimate of what is likely to be true or to occur given other conditions. The Latin phrase *ceteris paribus*—which means "all else being equal" or "other things remaining the same"—applies well here. When we encounter probability information relating to the incidence of some disease or event, we should keep in mind that, *all else being equal,* the highlighted relationship is likely to occur to the degree specified by the probability—but it is only a certainty if that probability is 1.00. For further discussion of "man-who" statistics and general biases in human perception and judgment, see Nisbett and Ross (1980), Gilovich (1991), and Plous (1993).

Statisticians conventionally refer to the probability of interest in any sample space as "A." Traditionally, we examine the frequency of outcomes favoring the event of interest (A) and the frequency of outcomes *not* favoring this event (not A) within a sample space. Thus, the probability of event A, or symbolically $p(A)$ (for "the probability of event A," or "p of A" for short), is:

$$[8.1.1] \qquad p(A) = \frac{\text{number of outcomes favoring event A}}{\text{total number of possible outcomes}}$$

which is conceptually equivalent to:

$$[8.2.1] \qquad p(A) = \frac{\text{number of outcomes favoring event A}}{\text{total number of outcomes favoring A} + \text{those not favoring A}}$$

because the "total number of possible outcomes" can be broken down into those events "favoring A" and those events "not favoring A."

Please note that the "number of outcomes" in each case refers to the *known* frequencies of the events, which can be defined as $f(A)$ for "the frequency of A" and $f(\text{not A})$ for "the frequency of not A" (i.e., the frequencies of those events that are not related to event A; for a review, see chapter 3). Or, symbolically:

$$[8.3.1] \qquad p(A) = \frac{f(A)}{f(A) + f(\text{not A})}.$$

Let's look at a straightforward example. Imagine that you have a small bag and inside of it you place 6 red marbles and 10 black marbles. You then shake the bag up so that the marbles become mixed together. This "mixing" is an important and not at all trivial act. Randomization is a critical assumption associated with the calculation of any probability—it must be present in some form or the resulting probability is meaningless (for a review of different methods of randomization, see Table 2.1). In the present situation, we assume that a simple random sampling procedure for choosing a marble ensures that every member of the population—here, the 16 marbles—has the same chance of being selected as all the other members.

▽

A probability has no meaning unless it is based on a sample that was drawn using some random process.

Sampling with Replacement. What is the probability that you will draw a red marble? We know there are 6 red marbles and 10 black ones. If we designate the red marbles "A" and the black marbles "not A," then based on [8.3.1], the probability of A can be determined by:

$$[8.3.2] \qquad p(A) = \frac{6}{6 + 10},$$

$$[8.3.3] \qquad p(A) = \frac{6}{16},$$

$$[8.3.4] \qquad p(A) = .375.$$

Thus, the probability of event A, the selection of one red marble from the population of 16 marbles, is .375. We will explain how to interpret this numerical probability below—let's continue to focus on calculation for a bit longer.

Whether it is red or black, if we return a marble drawn from the sack, the probability associated with selecting a red marble remains constant. Why? Note that 6 out of the 16 marbles are red—if we return whatever marble we select back into the sack, the denominator in the probability calculation, 16, stays the same. This procedure—selecting an observation from some sample, determining its probability, returning the observation to the sample, and then randomizing the sample before drawing again—is called **sampling with replacement.** When you replace an observation before proceeding to the next draw, all of the probabilities remain constant, that is, unchanged.

What is the probability of selecting a black marble? Remember that in this example, we have designated the event of selecting a black marble as "not A." If we follow the same formula (i.e., [8.3.1]) and logic, the $p(\text{not A})$ is:

$$[8.4.1] \qquad p(\text{not A}) = \frac{f(\text{not A})}{[f(\text{not A}) + f(A)]}.$$

Please note that we are still using the conceptual information from formulas [8.1.1] and [8.2.1]. We are simply treating "not A" or the choice of black marbles as the probability of interest. (If so desired, we could redefine the black marbles as "A" or even call them "B" or whatever—it is the numerical relationships between the probabilities that matters, not the nomenclature. Just be sure to keep the chosen variable designations in mind as you proceed with any probability calculations.) To continue:

[8.4.2] $$p(\text{not A}) = \frac{10}{10 + 6},$$

[8.4.3] $$p(\text{not A}) = \frac{10}{16},$$

[8.4.4] $$p(\text{not A}) = .625.$$

Thus, the probability of selecting one of the 10 black marbles (.625) is greater than selecting one of the 6 red marbles (.375). If we continue to sample in this manner—with replacement—the probability associated with selecting a red or a black marble will not change.

Here is an important lesson we can point to now and come back to later:

[8.5.1] $$p(A) + p(\text{not A}) = 1.00.$$

This mathematical relationship must be true and we can certainly demonstrate it with the probabilities we have already determined. The probability of selecting a red marble plus the probability of selecting a black marble is equal to 1.00, or:

[8.5.2] $$.375 + .625 = 1.00.$$

Sampling Without Replacement.   Imagine that we repeated this example but used **sampling without replacement,** that is, once a marble was drawn from our hypothetical sack, it is not replaced therein. Let's say that we chose a red marble on the first draw—we know that our probability of doing so was .375. What is the probability of selecting a red marble on the next draw? When sampling without replacement, we need to take into account that there is one less red marble (i.e., now 5, *not* 6) and one less marble overall (now 15, *not* 16); thus, the $f(A)$ changes, as does the denominator (i.e., $f(A) + f(\text{not A})$) used to determine the $p(A)$, or

[8.6.1] $$p(A) = \frac{5}{5 + 10},$$

[8.6.2] $$p(A) = \frac{5}{15},$$

[8.6.3] $$p(A) = .333.$$

As you can see, the likelihood of selecting a red marble decreases somewhat—from .375 to .333—but we have taken into account the fact that we removed the original red marble. The probability of selecting a black marble, too, is affected due to sampling one red marble without replacement.

[8.7.1] $$p(\text{not A}) = \frac{10}{10 + 5},$$

[8.7.2] $$p(\text{not A}) = \frac{10}{15},$$

[8.7.3] $$p(\text{not A}) = .667.$$

The likelihood of selecting a black marble increases once a red marble is removed from the sample. Naturally, the two probabilities—$p(A) + p(\text{not } A)$—still sum to 1.00 (i.e., .333 + .667).

Anytime you sample without replacement, you must be sure to account for the removal of an observation from the denominator of a probability formula, and possibly its numerator, as well (see [8.6.1]). Whether you are examining marbles, people, or personality test scores, just be sure to keep track of what observations are drawn from a sample each time and to account for them after every round.

At this point, you have a very basic working knowledge of classical probability. There are a few key points we need to highlight here before proceeding to the next topic. These points are:

Probability refers to an event that is likely to happen, not than event *must* happen. Higher probabilities indicate what events are apt to take place in the long run.

1. *Any probability discloses a pattern of behavior that is expected to occur in the long run.* A probability value does *not* mean that a behavior is actually going to happen at any given point in time, just that it is more (or less) likely to happen depending upon its strength. In fact, it is a good idea to think about probability as if you were repeatedly sampling for a given behavior *across some period of time* in order to understand how it is truly likely to occur.

2. *A given probability can take on a value ranging from 0 to 1.00.* An event that is never expected to occur has a probability of 0 and one that is absolutely certain to occur has a probability equal to 1.00. In the previous example, the probability of selecting a blue marble is 0 because there are no blue marbles in the sample. The probability of selecting a red *or* a black marble is 1.00 because all 16 of the marbles are either black or red. The individual probabilities of selecting red or black, of course, were around .300 and .600, respectively, varying somewhat due to whether sampling occurred with or without replacement.

Probability values can range from 0 to 1.00.

3. *Probabilities can but need not be rounded.* If a probability is determined to be, say, $p(A) = .267$, it can be reported as .267 or rounded to .27. For pedagogical purposes and issues of calculation accuracy, the convention in this book is to report a probability to three places behind the decimal point. Be advised that the convention of the *American Psychological Association* (1994) is to report such information to only two places behind a decimal point. Both approaches are correct, and here is a compromise to help you accommodate to their difference: When doing a calculation, go out to three places—when reporting a result based on a calculation, round to two places. Please also note that APA style eschews placing a 0 in front of the decimal point of probabilities and any numbers that will never have a value greater than 1.00.

We can now turn to interpreting numerical probabilities, which is linked to proportions and percentages, two familiar topics.

Probability's Relationship to Proportion and Percentage

As you were reading the previous material, you probably realized that the probabilities we calculated were done the same way that we learned to determine proportions and percentages back in chapter 3. In fact, a probability can be expressed as a proportion— the comparative relation or magnitude between parts of a whole—precisely because it *is* a proportion. Recall that a probability is defined as the relative likelihood that one event will occur in the context of all other possible events. Identifying and explicating these events involves determining their proportion within some range of possibilities. Thus, the proportion of red marbles (with replacement) in the example described in the last section was .375, the same value as the probability of selecting a red marble at random from the sack. It follows, then, that the proportion of black marbles from this same example is equivalent to its probability (i.e., .625).

DATA BOX 8.B

Classical Probability and Classic Probability Examples

We have already examined one of the classic tools used to teach probability, coin flips, but it is worth revisiting it for a moment in the context of classical probability theory. What is the probability of flipping a coin and having it come up "heads"?

If $p(A)$ = heads, then $p(\text{not } A)$ = tails, so:

$$p(A) = \frac{p(A)}{p(A) + p(\text{not } A)} = \frac{1}{1 + 1} = \frac{1}{2} = .50.$$

What is the probability of tossing a coin and having "tails," or $p(\text{not } A)$, come up?

$$p(\text{not } A) = \frac{p(\text{not } A)}{p(\text{not } A) + p(A)} = \frac{1}{1 + 1} = \frac{1}{2} = .50.$$

It follows, then, that $p(A) + p(\text{not } A) = .50 + .50 = 1.00$

Another common domain for demonstrating examples of probability is the standard deck of 52 cards. Once the deck has been thoroughly shuffled (i.e., the cards are randomized), what is the probability of drawing the ace of spades? As there is only 1 ace of spades in a deck,

$$p(A) = \frac{p(A)}{p(A) + p(\text{not } A)} = \frac{1}{1 + 51} = \frac{1}{52} = .0192.$$

What is the probability of selecting a queen from the same deck after the ace of spades is returned and the cards are reshuffled? There are four queens in any deck, so

$$p(A) = \frac{p(A)}{p(A) + p(\text{not } A)} = \frac{4}{4 + 48} = \frac{4}{52} = .0769.$$

Thus, the odds of picking the ace of spades or a queen on any given draw are few and far between. After shuffling and drawing from a deck of cards 100 times, you can expect to select the ace of spades once or twice, and to pick a queen approximately seven or eight times.

▽

Probabilities in any data table must always sum to 1.00.

In practice, it is easy to convert a probability or proportion into a percentage, especially when such information is being discussed in a report or a presentation. One way to accomplish this conversion is to recall that on any given draw (with replacement) from the sack of 16 marbles, the probability of selecting a red one is .375. If we replace the drawn marble, shake the bag up, and then repeat the same process 100 times, we can expect to draw a red marble 37.5% of the time. Naturally, we never actually perform this feat 100 times—we do not need to because we can use the probability as an estimate of what should happen over a long run of observations. As was true for proportions and percentages, then, one need only to multiply an obtained probability by 100 (i.e., move the decimal point two places to the right) to know its percentage equivalent. Similarly, we can expect to select a black marble about 62.5% of the time across 100 random draws from the sack.

Now that we have discussed the relationship among proportion, percentage, and probability, we can turn to how probabilities can be known from any simple frequency distribution. Developing a working knowledge of how to use probability within such distributions will prepare us to understand the more complex probabilistic relationships presented later in the chapter.

Probabilities Can Be Obtained from Frequency Distributions

Consider this simple frequency distribution of scores, which can be treated as a population:

X	f
10	2
8	4
6	3
5	7
3	4
2	5
	$\sum f = 25$

We can determine the simple probability of any event X within a frequency distribution by using this formula:

[8.8.1]
$$p(X) = \frac{f}{N},$$

where f is the frequency of any given value for X and N is equal to the $\sum f$ (here, 25), the total number of observations available. Let's do an example. What is the probability of randomly selecting a 10 from this population?

[8.8.2]
$$p(X = 10) = \frac{2}{25} = .080.$$

Note once again that this probability value is also a proportion.

Besides determining the probability of any single event X, we can also explore the probability associated with sampling a range of possible values within a population. In other words, if we randomly select an observation X from the above frequency distribution, what is the probability it will be less than ($<$) 6? If you look at the above frequency table, you can see that X is less than 6 when X is equal to 5, 3, or 2. We need only sum the frequencies (fs) associated with these three observations (X) to determine the probability of selecting an observation less than 6, or:

[8.9.1]
$$p(X < 6) = \frac{16}{25} = .640.$$

This probability was determined by summing the fs of 7, 4, and 5, which correspond to $X = 5, 3,$ and 2, respectively.

What is the probability of drawing an observation that is less than or equal to ($\leq$) 6? This time, of course, we need to account for the frequency associated with $X = 6$, which, as shown above, is $f = 3$. This additional frequency would be added to the 16 observations already accounted for in [8.9.1], or

[8.10.1]
$$p(X \leq 6) = \frac{19}{25} = .760.$$

What is the probability of randomly selecting an observation greater than 8? Only one observation is greater than ($>$) 8 (i.e., $X = 10$), and the frequency associated with it is $f = 2$, so

[8.11.1]
$$p(X > 8) = \frac{2}{25} = .080.$$

Knowledge Base

1. A bag contains 10 marbles—4 red, 2 green, and 4 blue. When sampling with replacement, what is the probability of selecting a blue marble? A green marble?

DATA BOX 8.C

A Short History of Probability

How old is the study of probability? When did humans begin to recognize—and to exploit—probability, as well as to develop theories to account for the occurrence of events?

In a fascinating book called *The Emergence of Probability*, Hacking (1975) discusses the relative absence of any theories of probability until the middle of the seventeenth century, when it suddenly emerged. He writes that, "Probability has two aspects. It is connected with the degree of belief warranted by evidence, and it is connected with the tendency, displayed by some chance devices, to produce stable relative frequencies. Neither of these aspects was self-consciously and deliberately apprehended by any substantial body of thinkers before the time of Pascal [the philosopher-mathematician (1623—1662)]"(p.1).

To be sure, various randomizing devices, such as dice, and randomizing activities, such as the drawing of lots, have been around since antiquity, and presumably earlier still. Humans have always engaged in some form of gambling—throwing the knuckle or heel bones of a horse or deer was the precursor to the die, for instance, though it could only land in one of four, not six, ways. Interestingly, however, there were no clear theories of betting, randomness, or our concern, probability. Indeed, Hacking (1975, p. 3) only half-jokingly suggests that, "Someone with only the most modest knowledge of probability mathematics could have won himself the whole of Gaul [what we think of as Western Europe] in a week."

Why did an interest in probability emerge during the Renaissance? Hacking (1975) suggests the time was ripe because of two intellectual themes that effectively joined forces. First, philosophers settled on an epistemology, a theory of knowledge, entailing varying degrees of belief in ideas that had no statistical background. Second, an understanding of statistics developed that focused on "stochastic"—subject to unexplained variability—laws of chance determined processes. A representative problem for this time involving both of the aforementioned themes is Pascal's famous justification for the belief in God despite the absence of evidence that the belief is a true one.

In a historical sense, probability is a modern concept, modernity being defined as the period of time from 1600 or so forward. Probability is an essential part of inferential statistics, of course, which did not become commonplace until well into the 20th century. Without probability, there would be no conceptual and practical "bridge" between sample data and estimating how well it describes the population from which it was drawn. For other historical perspectives on statistics and measurement, see Stigler (1986) and Crosby (1997).

2. A bag contains 12 marbles—4 red, 3 green, 3 blue, 2 yellow. You draw a green marble. Using sampling without replacement, what is the probability of drawing a green marble again? What is the probability of subsequently drawing a yellow marble, and then another green marble on a third round?

3. Examine the following frequency distribution:

X	f
9	4
8	1
5	1
3	3
2	6
1	5

Determine the following probabilities: $p(X = 3)$; $p(X > 5)$; $p(X \leq 3)$.

Answers

1. p(blue) $= 4/10 = .400$; p(green) $= 2/10 = .200$
2. p(green) $= 2/11 = .182$; p(yellow) $= 2/11 = .182$; p(green) $= 2/10 = .20$
3. $p(X = 3) = 3/20 = .150$; $p(X > 5) = 5/20 = .250$; $p(X \leq 3) = 14/20 = .70$.

Calculating Probabilities Using the Rules for Probability

Besides the classical approach to probability, there are two basic rules of probability that will provide us with more flexibility as we examine real and potential relationships among randomly determined variables or observations. These rules are the addition rule and the multiplication rule, and each can be applied with ease in appropriate circumstances. As you read this section of the text, I am more interested in having you understand why the probabilities we determined behave the way they do—I am less interested in having you memorize the basic rules and their accompanying variations, as you can always refer back to this section of the book. Remember that our interest here is in the logic behind and utility of probability theory for examining inferential relationships between samples and populations.

The Addition Rule for Mutually Exclusive and Nonmutually Exclusive Events

The *addition rule* for probability is used when considering the "union" or intersection of two events. We will introduce the formal definition for the addition rule and then demonstrate its use in an example.

KEY TERM   The **addition rule** for probability indicates that the probability of the union of two events, A and B, that is, p(A or B), is equal to: p(A or B) $= p$(A) $+ p$(B) $- p$(A and B).

Imagine, for example, that we have a small class of 20 elementary school students. Eight of the children have blond hair, 6 have blue eyes, and 4 have both blonde hair and blue eyes. What is the probability of selecting a child who has blond hair or blue eyes? (*Not* both.)

In evaluating this sample, we notice a few things. First, we are considering a subset of the children, not all 20, though we will use 20 as the denominator for our probability calculations. Second, we know the probability of having blond hair is equal to 8/20 (i.e., p(A) $= .400$) and that associated with blue eyes is equal to 6/20 (i.e., (B) $= .300$). Third, we know that a *joint probability*—having both blond hair and blue eyes—is also present.

KEY TERM   A **joint probability** is the mathematical likelihood of selecting an observation wherein two conditions—p(A) and p(B)—are present. In formula terms, a *joint probability* is equal to p(A and B).

In the present example, the joint probability of hair and eye color can be known by determining p(A and B). If the question were "What is the probability of selecting a child from the sample who has blond hair and blue eyes?" we could readily answer it using the information presented: p(A and B) $= 4/20 = .20$.

Because we were asked to provide the probability of having blond hair *or* blue eyes, however, we need to take into account that some of the children in the sample have both conditions—there are four of them—and then, in effect, we do not want to count them twice. Figure 8.2 shows an example of what is called a Venn diagram to illustrate the relationship between hair color and eye color (there is a good chance you encountered Venn diagrams at some earlier point in your education). As you can see, the circle on the left represents blond haired children and the one on the right those with blue eyes. The shaded intersection of the two circles indicates the overlap—the joint

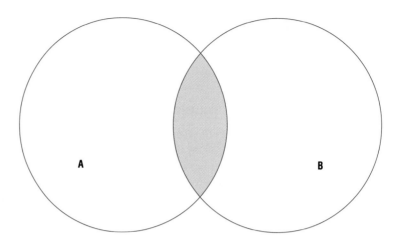

Figure 8.2　Venn Diagram of Sample of Elementary School Children

Note: The shaded area indicates the joint probability (i.e., p(A and B)), the overlap between p(A) and p(B) representing the four children in the sample who have both blond hair and blue eyes.

probability—between the two groups (i.e., the four blond-haired, blue-eyed children). By using the addition rule we can develop a probability estimate that partials out this joint probability.

The probability of selecting a blond-haired or a blue-eyed child from the sample (and *not* a blond haired, blue eyed child), then, would be:

[8.12.1]　　　　$p(\text{A or B}) = p(\text{A}) + p(\text{B}) - p(\text{A and B})$,

[8.12.2]　　　　$p(\text{A or B}) = (.400 + .300) - .200$,

[8.12.3]　　　　$p(\text{A or B}) = .700 - .200$,

[8.12.4]　　　　$p(\text{A or B}) = .500$.

As you can see, the probabilities of A and B are added together, and then the joint probability of A and B is subtracted from the resulting sum. Thus, when randomly selecting a child from the sample, we know that the probability is .50 that the child will have either blond hair or blue eyes.

The addition rule is also applicable to probabilistic events that are said to be *mutually exclusive*.

KEY TERM　　Two events are **mutually exclusive** when they have no observations within a sample in common. *Mutually exclusive* events cannot occur simultaneously.

In contrast to a joint probability and its points of overlap or intersection, when two events are described as being mutually exclusive, they are disjoint from one another. A person is either male or female; one cannot be both because gender is a mutually exclusive construct. Similarly, the U.S. government does not permit its citizens to hold dual citizenship in another nation. If you are a U.S. citizen, for example, you cannot also be a citizen of Canada.

When the addition rule is used to identify probabilities for mutually exclusive events, it is simplified somewhat. Specifically, the joint probability of A and B, that is, p(A and B), is equal to 0. Imagine that we revisited the same elementary school introduced above and went to a different room of children. In this room there are 18 children, 7 with blond hair and 5 with blue eyes—none of the children have both blond hair and blue eyes. What is the probability of having blond hair or blue eyes? We follow the same

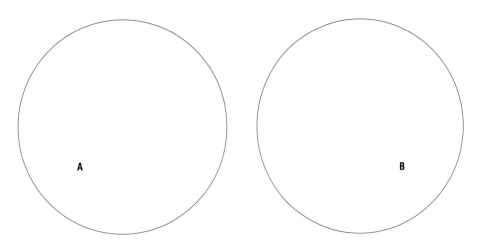

Figure 8.3   Venn Diagram of Second Sample of Elementary School Children

Note: The probabilities of A and B are said to be mutually exclusive; that is, they share not overlapping space with one another. No children in the sample have both blond hair and blue eyes (i.e., p(A and B) = 0).

procedure for calculating simple probabilities—f/N—so that the likelihood of having blond hair in this group is 7/18 (i.e., p(A) = .389) and that of having blue eyes is 5/18 (i.e., p(B) = .278). In the face of such mutually exclusive events, then, our addition rule becomes

[8.13.1] p(A or B) = p(A) + p(B),

[8.13.2] p(A or B) = .389 + .278,

[8.13.3] p(A or B) = .667.

Please note that [8.13.1] is the same as [8.12.1] except that the p(A and B) is obviously absent. The p(A and B) is *implied,* however, but because it is equal to 0, there is no need to represent it in the formula. If we randomly select a child from the second classroom, then, we know that the probability he or she will be blond haired or blue eyed is .667. Figure 8.3 shows a Venn diagram for the mutually exclusive events of having blond hair or blue eyes (note that the two circles never intersect, as their probabilities are disjoint from one another).

The Multiplication Rule for Independent and Conditional Probabilities

The second basic rule of probability is called the *multiplication rule,* which is used for estimating the probability of a particular sequence of events. In this case, a sequence of events refers to joint or cooccurrence of two or even more events, such as a particular pattern of coin tosses (e.g., what is the probability of flipping H–T–H–H–T?).

Determining the probability of a precise sequence of coin flips involves recognizing the independence of each flip from every other flip. To determine this probability, we rely on the multiplication rule for independent events.

KEY TERM   When a sequence of events is independent, the **multiplication rule** entails multiplying the probability of one event by the probability of the next event in the sequence, or p(A then B then $\cdots$) = p(A) x p(B) x p($\cdots$).

If we want to know the probability of a sequence of coin flips, such as the aforementioned pattern H–T–H–H–T, we need only remember that the probability of an H or a T on any toss is .500. Thus,

DATA BOX 8.D

Conjunction Fallacies: Is Linda a Bank Teller or a Feminist Bank Teller?

Read the following description and then select your answer:

> Linda is 31 years old, single, outspoken, and very bright. She majored in philosophy. As a student, she was deeply concerned with issues of discrimination and social justice, and also participated in anti-nuclear demonstrations. Which of the following statements is apt to be true about Linda? Check one.
>
> Linda is a bank teller. _____
>
> Linda is a bank teller and is active in the feminist movement. _____

At first blush, many people immediately decide that Linda must be a bank teller who is also a feminist—after all, she appears to be something of an activist, doesn't she? The descriptive information about Linda is socially interesting but it has no bearing (that is, it *should* have no bearing) on the decision at hand. Yet after reading the above (brief) description, the majority of respondents in a study by Tversky and Kahneman (1983) were quite willing to predict that she was more likely to exhibit both characteristics than just one. These researchers labeled this judgment bias the *conjunction fallacy* (for related efforts, see Abelson, Leddo, & Gross, 1987; Leddo, Abelson, & Gross, 1984; Morier & Borgida, 1984).

What do they mean by conjunction fallacy? The conjunction of events is a key concept in elementary probability. The conjunction or joint occurrence of two events (e.g., "bank teller" *and* "active in the feminist movement") *cannot* be more likely than the probability of either event on its own (e.g., "bank teller" *or* "active in the feminist movement"). The veracity of the conjunction rule is easily demonstrated by the probabilistic relationships portrayed in the Venn diagram shown below. As you can readily see, the shaded area shared by the two circles represents the joint probability of being a "bank teller and active in the feminist movement." The probability of the two events cooccurring *must* be lower than either event—being a "bank teller" (see the left circle) or being "active in the feminist movement" (see the circle on the right)—separately. Why? Well, not all bank tellers are feminists nor do all feminists have careers as bank tellers.

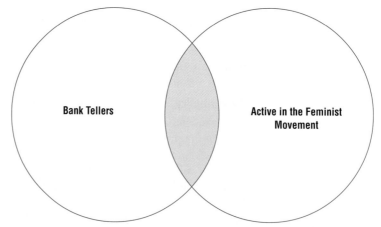

According to Tversky and Kahneman (1983), then, we frequently violate the conjunction rule when making everyday judgments. Ironically, we see specific, detailed scenarios as being more likely to occur than general events, despite the fact that the latter are by definition much more likely to happen. Indeed, as the detail associated with a projected event or a person's behavior increases, the objective probability linked to the event or act actually decreases. In our minds, however, detailed, even wild, scenarios take on a life of their own, and our belief in the likelihood that they will occur actually increases.

Plous (1993, p. 112) provides another compelling example that reinforces Tversky and Kahneman's conclusion that we see specific scenarios as more likely than general events because they are representative of the ways we imagine particular events occurring. Which of the following is more likely to occur:

Scenario 1:   An all-out nuclear war between Russia and the United States
Scenario 2:   A situation in which neither country intends to attack the other side with nuclear weapons, but an all-out nuclear war between the United States and Russia is triggered by the actions of a third country such as Iraq, Libya, Israel, or Pakistan

Similar to the Linda problem, most respondents believe that a specific crisis (a third country triggers a war between the United States and Russia) is more likely than a general one (an all-out war between the United States and Russia). Plous (1993) notes that Pentagon planners behaved like most respondents for decades—they committed the conjunction fallacy by developing incredibly detailed war plans to deal with any number of improbable chains of events in spite of the fact that the two nation conflict is more likely.

[8.14.1] $p(\text{H then T then H then H then T}) = p(\text{H}) \times p(\text{T}) \times p(\text{H}) \times p(\text{H}) \times p(\text{T}),$

[8.14.2] $p(\text{H then T then H then H then T}) = (.500) \times (.500) \times (.500) \times (.500) \times (.500),$

[8.14.3] $p(\text{H then T then H then H then T}) = .031.$

What is the probability of obtaining a pattern like T–T–T–T–T? As long as we are concerned with five coin tosses, the probability should be the same as that found for H –T–H–H–T, shouldn't it? Certainly.

[8.15.1] $p(\text{T then T then T then T then T}) = p(\text{T}) \times p(\text{T}) \times p(\text{T}) \times p(\text{T}) \times p(\text{T}),$

[8.15.2] $p(\text{T then T then T then T then T}) = (.500) \times (.500) \times (.500) \times (.500) \times (.500),$

[8.15.3] $p(\text{T then T then T then T then T}) = .031.$

In the case of coin tosses, then, any combination of heads and tails across five tosses will have the same likelihood of occurrence, that is, $p = .031$.

We need not restrict the application of the multiplication rule for independent events to coin flips. It can also be applied to situations where the independent probabilities vary in magnitude from one another at the outset and when more than two events exist. Perhaps we have a collection of 20 marbles. Ten are red, 6 are blue, and the remaining 4 are green. Using random sampling with replacement, what is the probability of selecting a red marble, then a green marble, and then a blue marble? We treat the selection of marbles in the same manner the independent coin flips were examined. By using the same logic and formula, we find that

[8.16.1] $p(\text{red then green then blue}) = p(\text{red}) \times p(\text{green}) \times p(\text{blue}),$

[8.16.2] $p(\text{red then green then blue}) = p\dfrac{10}{20} \times p\dfrac{4}{20} \times p\dfrac{6}{20},$

[8.16.3] $p(\text{red then green then blue}) = .50 \times .20 \times .30,$

[8.16.4] $p(\text{red then green then blue}) = .030.$

In spite of the fact that each draw of a marble is independent of the others, the likelihood of first selecting a red marble, then a green one, and finally a blue one is really quite low.

What happens if we sample without using replacement? The events are still independent of one another but it is necessary to take into account that the number of marbles in the population is reduced *after* each draw. Using random sampling without replacement, what is the probability of selecting a blue marble, then a red marble, and then a blue marble once again? Following the same procedure as before, we set the probability up as

[8.17.1] $p(\text{blue then red then blue}) = p(\text{blue}) \times p(\text{red}) \times p(\text{blue}),$

[8.17.2] $p(\text{blue then red then blue}) = p\dfrac{6}{20} \times p\dfrac{10}{19} \times p\dfrac{5}{18}$

[8.17.3] $p(\text{blue then red then blue}) = .300 \times .526 \times .278,$

[8.17.4] $p(\text{blue then red then blue}) = .044.$

The probability, then, of drawing one blue, one red, and a second blue marble—in that order—is rather low (i.e., $p = .044$). Please take another look at [8.17.2] in order to be sure you understand that sampling without replacement means that one observation is subtracted from the value of the denominator after each draw. Please also note that because we assumed that we would select a blue marble on the first draw, the numerator for selecting a blue marble again on the third round is also reduced by 1 (i.e., there are now five blue marbles to choose from as the sixth was drawn on the first round).

Probabilistic relationships can be more complex than the ones we have reviewed so far. In fact, behavioral scientists often examine what are called *conditional probabilities* precisely because the probability of one event can be better understood by taking into account the likelihood of another.

KEY TERM   A **conditional probability** exists when the probability of one event is conditional—that is, it depends on—the role of another event.

Can you recall the last time you visited your family doctor because you were ill? Chances are that your doctor asked you to describe your particular symptoms before treatment was recommended or any prescription was written. As you described your ailments, your doctor was listening intently so as to rule out various diagnoses in favor of the one that seemed to be the most plausible "fit," that is, the most probable account. Making one diagnosis might have been dependent on the presence of a fever, but perhaps it was ruled out in favor of another when you mentioned that you also had a sore throat. The final diagnosis depended on the pattern of symptoms present.

In the same way, conditional probabilities involve portraying more complex relationships among two variables of interest when you know something about one of them. Before we learn to work with conditional probabilities, however, we need to work through an example in order to build up to the examination of these complex relationships. Imagine that the director of a university's admissions office is interested in how the presence of a personality construct influences upper-class students' ability to serve as tour guides for prospective freshmen on campus visits. The personality construct of interest is called self-monitoring, which refers to the degree one expends effort toward creating and maintaining a social impression in the minds of others (e.g., Snyder, 1987). High self-monitors are "social chameleons," that is, they are very attuned to social situations and the people in them. In contrast, low self-monitors are less inclined to worry or even think about the reactions of other people. Presumably, high self-monitors would show off the qualities of the campus better, as well as be more persuasive about why applicants should attend the institution, compared to low self-monitors.

Table 8.1   Observed Frequencies of Students by Self-Monitoring Type and Gender

Gender	High Self-Monitors	Low Self-Monitors	Row Total
Male	55	23	78
Female	25	47	72
Column Total	80	70	150

Students were invited to apply for tour guide positions and part of the application process entailed completing a self-monitoring questionnaire. Table 8.1 shows the observed frequencies of male and female students subsequently classified as either high or low self-monitors. In this sample, relatively more men than women were classified as high self-monitors, whereas the reverse pattern was true in the case of low self-monitors (see Table 8.1).

By relying on the inherent relationship between proportion and probability, the frequencies shown in Table 8.1 can be readily converted into probabilities. Each entry of the four cell entries in the center of the table, as well as the two column totals and the two row totals, were divided by the overall N of the sample (which is 150; see the bottom right corner of the table). The resulting probabilities are presented in Table 8.2.

Please note that I use subscripts to denote the two levels of variables A and B in Table 8.2. Where self-monitoring is concerned, for example, I could just as easily have used "A" and "not A" instead of "A_1" and "A_2" to denote "high" and "low" self-monitors, respectively, which would mean that the former personality type would be "A." In this and similar contexts, however, I find such designations to be arbitrary, if not confusing—after all, low self-monitoring personalities are on the *same* continuum with high self-monitors, so designating one group as "not A" seems to me to be odd, even inaccurate.

Table 8.2 contains two important types of probability information. First, the four entries in the center of the table are joint probabilities shared between the two levels of A (self-monitoring type) and B (gender). The probability of being a high self-monitor and a male ($p(A_1$ and $B_1)$), for example, is .367, just as the relative likelihood of being a low self-monitor and a female ($p(A_2$ and $B_2)$) is .313 (see Table 8.2). Please note that the sum of the four joint probability cells must sum to 1.00 (i.e., .367 + .153 + .167 + .313 = 1.00). It is always a good idea to perform this quick check for calculation errors before using or reporting the probabilities.

Table 8.2 also includes what are called *marginal probabilities,* probabilities based on collapsing across one of the two variables shown in the table. For example, by glancing *down* columns A_1 and A_2, the probability of being a high or a low self-monitor, respectively, can be known. In the same way, reading *across* the two rows representing gender will reveal the probability of being a male or a female in the sample.

▽

A proportion is also a probability; a probability is also a proportion.

Table 8.2   Joint and Marginal Probabilities of Students by Self-Monitoring Type and Gender

Gender	High Self-Monitors A_1	Low Self-Monitors A_2	Marginal Probability A
Male, B_1	.367	.153	.520
Female, B_2	.167	.313	.480
Marginal Probability, B	.533	.467	1.00

A **marginal probability,** sometimes known as an "unconditional probability," indicates the likelihood of an independent event's occurrence.

As shown in the far right of Table 8.2, the marginal probability of being a male in the sample ($p(B_1)$) is .520. Similarly, the marginal probability of being a high self-monitor ($p(A_1) = .533$) is slightly higher than the probability of being a low self-monitor ($p(A_2) = .467$; see Table 8.2). The sum of the marginal probabilities for either personality type ($A_1 + A_2$) or gender ($B_1 + B_2$) must also sum to 1.00 (see Table 8.2). As noted above, it is always appropriate to determine that each respective set of marginal probabilities do sum to 1.00 to eliminate any errors that could plague later calculations.

What about conditional probabilities? Can we go beyond the joint and marginal probabilities provided here and create more specific—that is, conditional—probability estimates? Keep in mind that the conditional probability of a given event is one that depends upon the presence of some other event. Our hypothetical admissions director might ask a question like the following: Given that we know a student in the sample is a male, what is the probability he is also a high self-monitor? In other words, the student's gender—here, male—is a "given" piece of information, one that makes any subsequent probability information conditional (i.e., we can only determine probabilities involving men). This conditional probability estimate is written in the following symbolic terms: The probability of being a high self-monitor ($p(A_1)$) given he is a male ($p(B_1)$), or

[8.18.1]
$$p(A_1 \mid B_1) = \frac{p(A_1 \text{ and } B_1)}{p(B_1)}.$$

When you see (or use) a line like this one (|), you know you are working with a conditional probability. The line means "given," so that the probability is read as "the probability of A_1 given B_1." Notice that the probability of being male ($p(B_1)$)—the given information—is the denominator. The numerator is conditional on this information: If we want to know the probability that the person is a high self-monitor, we can assume that this high self-monitor must be male because it is given information. Thus, we will use the joint probability of being a high self-monitor and male ($p(A_1 \text{ and } B_1)$). If we take these probabilities from Table 8.2 and enter them into [8.16.1], we get

[8.18.2] $$p(A_1 \mid B_1) = \frac{.367}{.520},$$

[8.18.3] $$p(A_1 \mid B_1) = .706.$$

Thus, if we already know that a person drawn from the sample is a male, there is a relatively high likelihood that the person is also a high self-monitor. Note that this particular conditional probability is also much higher than either the individual probability of being male or that of being male *and* a high self-monitor. Because in a sense we know more (i.e., the conditional information), we can make a more confident probability judgement.

Let's look at another example of conditional probability based on the data shown in Table 8.2. Please try to do the calculation on your own first before you read ahead to see my solution. Here is the conditional probability: Given that you select a student who is a high self-monitor, what is the probability that the student is female?

This time, the given information pertains to being a high self-monitor, so the denominator in the probability calculation will be A_1. The likelihood that this high self-monitor is also female moves us to look at the joint probability for being female and a high self-monitor (i.e., $p(A_1 \text{ and } B_2)$). We need only set the probability up symbolically and then enter the relevant probabilities from Table 8.2 for

[8.19.1]
$$p(B_2 \mid A_1) = \frac{p(A_1 \text{ and } B_2)}{p(A_1)}.$$

That is, given that we know the selected student is a high self-monitor, what is the probability the student is also female? Or

[8.19.2]
$$p(B_2 \mid A_1) = \frac{.167}{.533},$$

[8.19.3]
$$p(B_2 \mid A_1) = .313?$$

Thus, if we select a person at random and know that the person is a high self-monitor, the chance that the person is also female is not terribly high. Please note that this conclusion makes sense because we established earlier that males in the sample were apt to be high self-monitors, whereas females were more likely to be low self-monitors.

Conditional probabilities are not interchangeable: $p(A \mid B) \neq p(B \mid A)$.

There is one final important thing you should know about conditional probabilities—they are not interchangeable with one another. As a general rule, then, $p(A \mid B) \neq p(B \mid A)$. We can demonstrate this fact by determining specific conditional probabilities from Table 8.2. Thus, for example, the $p(B_2 \mid A_2) \neq p(A_2 \mid B_2)$ because the former conditional probability (.670) is not equal to the latter (.652). As an exercise, go back and perform the calculations to prove this fact and to verify that you understand how to determine conditional probabilities.

Multiplication Rule for Dependent Events

At the opening of this section of the chapter, you were introduced to the multiplication rule for independent events, one we examined against the background of coin tossing and the random selection of various combinations of colored marbles. There is also a variant of the *multiplication rule for dependent events*, one that enables us to determine joint probabilities by using marginal and conditional probabilities.

KEY TERM   The probability of a specific combination of dependent events can be known by using the **multiplication rule for dependent events**. A specific combination is determined by multiplying the probability of a given event by the event's conditional probability, or $p(A \text{ and } B) = p(A) \times p(B \mid A)$.

We can easily demonstrate the effectiveness of this rule using the data in Table 8.2. What, for example, is the probability of selecting a low self monitor who is also female? We know that we are looking to calculate the $p(A_2 \text{ and } B_2)$. There are two ways to determine this joint probability. We can use $p(A_2) \times p(B_2 \mid A_2)$ or, alternatively, $p(B_2) \times p(A_2 \mid B_2)$. The answer will be the same in both instances. We previously noted that the $p(B_2 \mid A_2)$ was equal to .670, just as we know from Table 8.2 that the $p(A_2)$ is .467, thus, we can determine the probability using $p(A_2) \times p(B_2 \mid A_2)$.

[8.20.1]
$$p(A_2 \text{ and } B_2) = p(A_2) \times p(B_2 \mid A_2),$$

[8.20.2]
$$p(A_2 \text{ and } B_2) = .467 \times .670,$$

[8.20.3]
$$p(A_2 \text{ and } B_2) = .313.$$

The accuracy of this probability can be verified by looking at the joint probability of A_2 and B_2 given in Table 8.2—as you can see, it is indeed equal to .313.

Knowledge Base

1. A jar contains 30 marbles. Nine of the marbles are green, 8 are pink, 8 are brown and white, and 5 are pink and green. What is the probability of selecting a marble that is pink or green?

2. A jar contains 20 marbles. Ten are yellow, 6 are blue, 2 are pink, and 2 are brown. What is the probability of selecting a yellow or a pink marble? Using sampling with

replacement, what is the probability of selecting a blue and then a brown marble? Using sampling without replacement, what is the probability of selecting a blue, a pink, and then a yellow marble?

3. You are flipping a coin. What is the probability of obtaining the following sequence of heads (H) and tails (T): H–H–T–T–T–H–T?

4. You are a developmental psychologist who is interested in humor. Two age groups of children hear a joke, and you classify whether they found it to be funny. Examine the following table of data and answer the questions that follow it

Age	Funny	Not Funny
Five year olds	20	8
Ten year olds	4	23

   a. What is the probability of selecting a 5-year-old from the sample?
   b. What is the probability a 10-year-old thought the joke was funny?
   c. Given you select a child who is age 10, what is the chance the child did not think the joke was funny?

5. Using the multiplication rule for dependent events, demonstrate how to determine the joint probability of being a 5-year-old and finding the joke unfunny.

Answers

1. p(pink or green) $= 8/30 + 9/30 - 5/30 = .267 + .300 - .167 = .400$
2. p(yellow or pink) $= 10/20 + 2/20 = .500 + .100 = .600$; ; p(blue then brown) $= 6/20 \times 2/20 = .300 \times .100 = .030$; p(blue then pink then yellow) $= 6/20 \times 2/19 \times 10/18 = .300 \times .105 \times .556 = .018$.
3. p(H–H–T–T–T–H–T) $= (.500) \times (.500) \times (.500) \times (.500) \times (.500) \times (.500) \times (.500) = .0078$.
4. a p(5-year-old) $= 28/55 = .509$
   b p(10-year-old and funny) $= 4/55 = .073$
   c p(not funny and 10 $|$ 10) $= .418/.490 = .853$
5. p(5 and not funny) $= p(5) \times p$(not funny $|$ 5) $= (.51) \times (.286) = .146$ or p(not funny) $\times p$(5 $|$ not funny) $= (.564) \times (.259) = .146$.

Using Probabilities with the Standard Normal Distribution: z-Scores Revisited

Back in chapter 5, we noted that z scores could be used to determine the probabilities associated with areas under the standard normal ("bell-shaped") curve. In other words, investigators can ask focused questions concerning the probability of randomly selecting an observation or individual possessing some quality or characteristic that is less than, greater than, or equal to a particular range of values. As we learned in chapter 5, any measure can be converted to a z score as long as the mean and standard deviation of its distribution are known. Once a score on a measure is transformed into a z score, its relative position is understood in terms of the z distribution's mean of 0 and standard deviation of 1.0. If these ideas seem unfamiliar to you or your recollection of the z distribution's properties is a bit hazy, then you should review chapter 5 before proceeding with the remainder of this section.

One other matter must be discussed before we firmly establish the link between probability and the area under the normal distribution. Most of the probabilities we have calculated so far in this chapter have involved discrete rather than continuous variables. With the exception of calculating the probability that a score within a grouped frequency distribution was above or below a certain point or range of scores (see page 283), our work in this chapter has focused largely on counting the number of observations favoring one outcome and dividing that number by the total number of available observations. To be sure, discrete probabilities are quite useful, but our interest in behavioral science research and its need to generalize results from one sample to other samples and populations will be hampered unless we are concerned with a continuum of probabilities, with ranges of probabilities therein.

Our interest, then, turns toward learning to determine the probability that an observation or score can be shown to fall within a certain area under the normal curve. The probability for a continuous variable—one that has no gaps between values—can be expressed as the proportion of the area under the normal curve. Thus, we can ask the probability that some score, X, falls within a range of values represented by A and B. In conceptual terms, we mean that

$$[8.21.1] \quad p(A \le X \le B) = \frac{\text{the area under a section of the curve between A and B}}{\text{total area under the curve}}.$$

In this case, A and B represent the lower and upper true limits of some class containing X (for a review of true limits, please see chapter 1).

Let's use a familiar example—scores on an intelligence test—to illustrate how we can delineate probabilities under the normal curve using a continuous variable. An educational psychologist wants to know the probability of randomly selecting a person from the population with an IQ score of 125 or higher. You may recall than most IQ tests have a fixed μ of 100 and a σ of 15. Using this information, we can convert the IQ score to a z score using formula [5.2.1] from chapter 5:

$$[5.2.1] \qquad\qquad z = \frac{X - \mu}{\sigma}.$$

That is, the population mean is subtracted from some known score X, and the resulting difference is divided by the population standard deviation. Using the information for the present example, we find that

$$[8.22.1] \qquad z = \frac{125 - 100}{15},$$

$$[8.22.2] \qquad z = \frac{25}{15},$$

$$[8.22.3] \qquad z = +1.67.$$

We know, then, that an IQ score of 125 lies 1.67 standard deviation units above the mean. The top curve in Figure 8.4 illustrates a normal distribution of IQ scores with a μ of 100 and σ of 15. A score of 125 is highlighted in Figure 8.4, and the area under the curve at or beyond 125 is shaded. The curve representing the z distribution in the bottom half of Figure 8.4 portrays the same relationships as those in the upper curve—this time, however, the observed z score of +1.67 is highlighted; the area at or beyond this z, too, is shaded.

Turning to Table B.2 in Appendix B, we want to determine the probability of selecting a score equal to or greater than 125. As you can see, the z score of +1.67 is located in the upper left corner of the second page of Table B.2. Because we are interested in the probability of selecting a score that is *greater than or equal* to 125, we look to column C, which is labeled "area beyond z." The entries in Table B.2 are proportions under the curve, but we already know that proportions are interchangeable with probabilities. Thus, the probability (proportion) of randomly selecting an IQ score of 125 or higher is equal to .0475, or $p(X \ge 125) = .0475$ (which is equal to the shaded area under the z

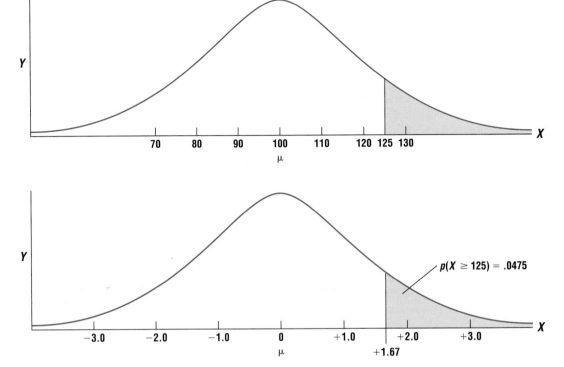

Figure 8.4 Normal Distribution of IQ scores ($\mu = 100$, $\sigma = 15$) and Corresponding z Distribution

Note: The shaded area under each of the curves represents the proportion (probability) of scores equal to or greater than an IQ score of 125.

distribution shown in the lower half of Figure 8.4). In other words, there is a less than 5% chance of randomly selecting a person whose IQ score is 125 or higher.

In our second example, we can rely on the addition rule for mutually exclusive events that was presented earlier in this chapter. What is the probability of randomly selecting someone from the population whose IQ falls below 75 or above 130? The upper curve in Figure 8.5 illustrates the two areas of the curve—the lower and upper tails of the distribution—that are relevant to answering this question. All that we need to do is to identify the two proportions (probabilities) under the curve corresponding to the shaded areas shown in the upper curve in Figure 8.5, and then sum these values.

We first convert each of the IQ scores to their z score equivalents. Using formula [5.2.1], the z score corresponding to an IQ score of 75 is

[8.23.1] $$z = \frac{75 - 100}{15},$$

[8.23.2] $$z = -\frac{25}{15},$$

[8.23.4] $$z = -1.67.$$

The z for an IQ of 130 is

[8.24.1] $$z = \frac{130 - 100}{15},$$

[8.24.2] $$z = \frac{30}{15},$$

[8.24.3] $$z = +2.00.$$

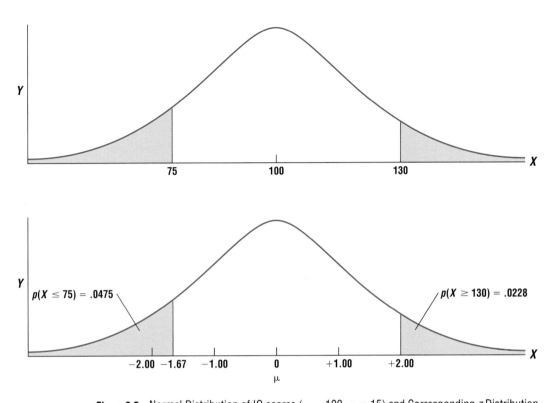

Figure 8.5 Normal Distribution of IQ scores ($\mu = 100$, $\sigma = 15$) and Corresponding z Distribution

Note: The shaded area to the left under each of the curves represents the proportion (probability) of scores less than or equal to an IQ score of 75. The shaded area to the right under each of the curves represents the proportion (probability) of scores greater than or equal to 130.

As shown by the shaded areas in the z distribution presented in the lower half of Figure 8.5, we need to determine the proportion of the curve that is *equal to or below* $z = -1.67$ and the area *equal to or greater than* $+2.00$. Recall that when we turn to Table B.2 in Appendix B, no negative signs accompany the z scores in the table because the z distribution is symmetric. Turning to Table B.2, then, we conceptually want to know the proportion (probability) of the area beyond (that is, below) $z = -1.67$. We look, then, to column C for $z = +1.67$ and learn that $p(X \leq 75) = .0475$. When then look to see the area beyond $z = +2.00$ (again, column C) and find that $p(X \geq 130) = .0228$. The respective probabilities are noted in the z distribution presented in the bottom of Figure 8.5. If we add these two probabilities together, we will know the likelihood of selecting an individual whose IQ is less than or equal to 75 or greater than or equal to 130, or

[8.25.1] $p(X \leq 75 \text{ or } X \geq 130) = p(X \leq 75) + p(X \geq 130),$

[8.25.2] $p(X \leq 75 \text{ or } X \geq 130) = (.0475) + (.0228),$

[8.25.3] $p(X \leq 75 \text{ or } X \geq 130) = .0703.$

In other words, there is about a 7% chance of randomly selecting a person whose IQ falls at or below 75 or at or beyond 130.

Our third example concerns an IQ score that falls below the mean of 100. What is the probability of randomly selecting an individual with an IQ score of 89 or higher? First, we sketch a normal curve for the IQ scores and identify where 89 falls in relation to the mean of the distribution (see the upper curve in Figure 8.6). Note that the probability we are looking for is associated with a "score of 89 or higher," thus besides the area under curve

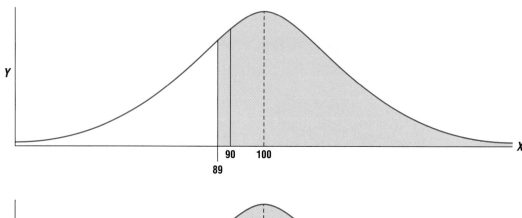

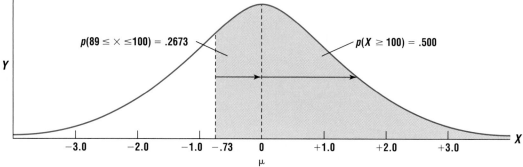

Figure 8.6   Normal Distribution of IQ scores ($\mu = 100$, $\sigma = 15$) and Corresponding z Distribution

Note: The shaded area under each of the curves represents the proportion (probability) of scores equal to or greater than an IQ score of 89.

falling between 89 and 100, we must also take into account the entire area from the mean and beyond (see the shaded areas in the upper curve shown in Figure 8.6).

For our next step, we calculate the z score corresponding to an IQ score of 89, or

[8.26.1] $z = \dfrac{X - \mu}{\sigma}$,

[8.26.2] $z = \dfrac{89 - 100}{15}$,

[8.26.3] $z = -\dfrac{11}{15}$,

[8.26.4] $z = -.73.$

The bottom curve in Figure 8.6 highlights the location of $z = -.73$. The shaded area in this curve indicates the proportion (probability) under the curve associated with randomly selecting a person who has an IQ score of 89 or higher. Before we proceed to Table B.2 to determine the area between the mean and the observed z score, by looking at the bottom curve in Figure 8.5, we know that we will be adding .50 to this area precisely because the original probability question asked for the probability of selecting a score of 89 or higher. In this case, "higher" entails the whole upper half of the z distribution, which you will remember is equal to .50 (if you do not recall why this must be so, please stop now and review chapter 5, especially Figure 5.4).

We locate the entry for $z = +.73$, keeping in mind that we are working with $z = -.73$. Following the logic developed in the bottom curve shown in Figure 8.5, we need to know the proportion of the area (probability) under the curve falling between $z = +.73$ and the mean. Looking in the center section of the first page of Table B.2, we learn that the area between the mean and $z = +.73$ is equal to .2673 (see the bottom curve in Figure 8.6). In symbolic terms, of course, we are describing the probability that an IQ score is greater than or equal to 89 but less than or equal to the mean IQ of 100, or $p(89 \leq X \leq 100) = .2673$. Symbolically, in turn, the probability of having an IQ score equal to or greater than 100 is $p(X \geq 100) = .50$. (Please note that this fact can be verified by looking up the mean of 0.00—the first entry—in the top left section of the second page of Table B.2, where the area beyond the mean, that is, $z = 0.00$, is .500.)

The probability of randomly selecting an individual who has an IQ score of 89 or greater can be known by adding the $p(89 \leq X \leq 100)$ to $p(X \geq 100)$. Symbolically, this probability is

[8.27.1] $p(X \geq 89) = p(89 \leq X \leq 100) + p(X \geq 100)$,

[8.27.2] $p(X \geq 89) = (.2673) + (.500)$,

[8.27.3] $p(X \geq 89) = .767$.

Thus, the probability of sampling a person who has an IQ equal to 89 or greater is actually quite high. If you sampled 100 people, you would expect to find that about 77% of them would have IQ scores at or above 89.

We will close this section of the chapter with a final example, one that relies on the multiplication rule for independent events. Imagine that we are sampling with replacement. What is the probability of selecting a person with an IQ less than or equal to 75, followed by one with an IQ equal to or greater than 130? To simplify matters, we can use the information we collected when working with the second example. Through random sampling, we learned that the probability of selecting someone with a score at or below 75 is .0475, or $p(X \leq 75) = .0475$. We know, too, that the likelihood of drawing an individual with an IQ of 130 or greater is .0228, or $p(X \geq 130) = .0228$.

Using the multiplication rule for independent events, the probability of randomly selecting two people—one with an IQ less than or equal to 75 and one with an IQ equal to or above 130 is,

[8.28.1] $p(X \leq 75)$ then $p(X \geq 130) = (.0475) \times (.0228)$,

[8.28.2] $p(X \leq 75)$ then $p(X \geq 130) = .0011$.

There is little likelihood that we would randomly sample two people in a row who fell in the lower and upper tail, respectively, of the distribution of IQ scores. Indeed, there is about a 1 in a thousand chance that we would do so!

Determining Probabilities with the Binomial Distribution: An Overview

As a counterweight to the emphasis placed on determining discrete probabilities, the last section of the chapter demonstrated how z scores are used to examine probabilities based on a continuum. In the present section, we will return to using discrete probabilities but in concert with the normal distribution and the advantages it offers to answering focused questions about data. To do so, we will work with the *binomial distribution*, where data are divided into two categories.

KEY TERM   A **binomial distribution** is one where events can have only two possible outcomes. The probabilities associated with each event need not be equal, though when added together, they must sum to 1.00, the area under the *binomial distribution*.

We already worked with binomial data when we discussed tossing a coin to predict a particular pattern of heads (H) and tails (T). Coin tossing is a binomial process because there are two possible outcomes involved. Answers to Yes or No questions (e.g.,

"Do you speak a foreign language fluently?" "Are you married?"), too, are binomial, as are any variables that can be categorized into two groups. One's gender—male or female—is obviously binomial because it naturally falls into one of two possible classes.

Other variables can become binomial through reclassification. Earlier in the chapter we mentioned the personality construct called self-monitoring (Snyder, 1987), noting that based on their scores on a self-monitoring scale, people can be classified as either high or low self-monitors (e.g., Snyder, 1974). That is, a score below a designated cutoff point (e.g., the median score) indicates one is best described as a low self-monitor—a score above a cutoff would be placed in the high self-monitoring group. As you can imagine, any personality or other measure with a continuum of possible scores (e.g., high versus low, present versus absent) can probably be divided into two discrete groupings (e.g., self-esteem, intelligence, reading ability, anxiety).

When behavioral scientists work with binomial data, they typically know or can determine the probabilities associated with the two categories of the variable in question. To simplify matters and to demonstrate the basic idea, let's return to a coin tossing example. When tossing a fair coin, the probability of heads is the same as the probability of tails: $p(\text{heads}) = p(\text{tails}) = .500$. When working with such binomial data, we usually want to know how often each category is anticipated to occur across time—that is, across a number of trials (here, coin tosses). What is the probability of getting 20 tails out of 30 flips of a fair coin?

Now, if we leave coin tosses for a moment, we can ask a similar binomial question regarding data based on some personality construct. What, for example, is the probability of finding 25 high self-monitors in a sample of 40 research participants? Alternatively, if I have a colony of lab rats, what is the probability that 35 out of 100 research animals will be abnormally aggressive? To answer a questions like these, we can rely on the normal distribution but we will do so in a way that enables us to determine probabilities with binomial data.

Working with the Binomial Distribution

Any binomial distribution has two categories, A and B. To work with A and B, their probabilities (proportions) are designated by p and q, respectively. Specifically,

[8.29.1] $p = p(A) =$ the probability of event A occurring,

[8.30.1] $q = p(B) =$ the probability of event B occurring.

As you would expect when there are only two possible outcomes, the $p(A)$ added to the $p(B)$ must sum to 1.00, or $p(A) + p(B) = 1.00$. When working with binomial probabilities, it is always necessary to identify the number of observations or individuals within a sample, and to do so n (the convention is to use lower case n, *not N*) is used. Finally, variable X denotes the frequency with which variable A occurs within a sample. In practical terms, then, X can range from no occurrence (i.e., 0) to n, the total number of observations available.

Returning to coin tosses, let's consider the binomial distribution for the potential number of tails observed in two tosses of a fair coin. Think about it: If you flip a coin twice, you could get T–T, H–H, T–H, or H–T. In binomial terms, you could get as few as no tails or as many as two tails across two tosses.

Let's move the discussion to the consideration of specific probabilities and rely on the binomial terms we introduced above. Using [8.29.1], the probability of tossing a tail on any given coin flip is

[8.29.2] $p = p(T) = .500.$

Using [8.30.1], it follows that the probability of obtaining a head on any given flip is

[8.30.2] $q = p(H) = .500.$

Table 8.3   Binomial Probabilities for $n = 2$ Coin Tosses

Toss 1	Toss 2	Pattern	Probability
Tail (.500)	Tail (.500)	T–T ("2 tails")	$(.500) \times (.500) = .250$
Head (.500)	Head (.500)	H–H ("0 tails")	$(.500) \times (.500) = .250$
Tail (.500)	Head (.500)	T–H ("1 tail")	$(.500) \times (.500) = .250$
Head (.500)	Tail (.500)	H–T ("1 tail")	$(.500) \times (.500) = .250$

Probability of 1 tail on 2 tosses $= (.25) + (.25) = .500$

If the sample size is $n = 2$ and X is the number of tails, we can create a table of the possible outcomes and their accompanying probabilities. Table 8.3 illustrates the precise probabilities for the four possible combinations of outcomes. These probabilities were determined by using the multiplication rule for independent events, as well as the addition rule for mutually exclusive events. Using the multiplication rule, we know that the probability of tossing two tails in a row (i.e., T–T) is .250, as is the probability of tossing no tails twice (i.e., H–H) (see the upper portion of Table 8.3). We again use the multiplication rule to determine the likelihood of tossing one tail and one head in either order (see the lower portion of Table 8.3). In both cases, the probability is again .250, but this time we must use the addition rule for mutually exclusive events—*two of the four* possible outcomes have one tail, so these probabilities must be added together (i.e., $p(T–H) + p(H–T) = (.250) + (.250) = .500$). In short, the likelihood of obtaining one tail out of two tosses is .500. (Please note that the probabilities for the four possible binomial outcomes shown in Table 8.3 sum to 1.00.)

The binomial probabilities shown in Table 8.3 can be used to answer other questions, as well. What, for example, is the probability of tossing *at least one* tail in two tosses? To answer this question, we must take note of the three possible sequences in Table 8.3 that include at least one tail, and then sum the probabilities together. That is, $p(T–T) + p(T–H) + p(H–T) = (.250) + (.250) + (.250) = .750$. Do you see why the probability of tossing at least one tail on two coin flips is equal to .750? A tail occurs in three of the four possible binomial sequences—adding the probability of each independent sequence together gives .750 (see Table 8.3).

Relying on the same logic presented here, you could develop binomial distributions that would allow you to determine probabilities associated with 3, 5, 6, or even 10 tosses of a fair coin. If you did so, you would witness an important aspect of the binomial distribution, one that should not surprise you: As the size of the sample (n) increases, the binomial distribution becomes more normal in shape. Across 10 coin tosses, for example, the most likely outcome is 5 tails and 5 heads. In contrast, if the coin were fair, the probabilities associated with tossing 10 tails (or 10 heads) across 10 tosses would be very low indeed. Ten tails or 10 heads occurs in the tail of either side of the probability distribution, areas that represent the least likelihood of occurrence.

Think about it: A binomial distribution approximates a normal distribution because the highest probabilities occur in the center of the distribution (i.e., 5 tails *and* 5 heads); other binomial patterns become less frequent as you move toward either tail (i.e., 10 tails *or* 10 heads).

Approximating the Standard Normal Distribution with the Binomial Distribution

Before we can proceed with using the binomial distribution to approximate the normal distribution, we need to introduce a few more facts about the links between these distributions. We already know that as n increases in size, the binomial distribution will approximate the normal distribution very well. It turns out that the binomial distribution will fit the normal distribution best when pn and qn are both *greater than or equal to* a value of 10. When this requirement is met, the μ and the σ of the binomial distribution, respectively, can be known by using the following formulas. The mean or

[8.31.1] μ of a binomial distribution $= pn$.

The standard deviation is determined by

[8.32.1] σ of a binomial distribution $= \sqrt{npq}$.

Because the binomial distribution is approximately normal under these circumstances, we are free to use Table B.2 in Appendix B to answer questions about the probability of occurrence of particular binomial events. We will again rely on z scores to use Table B.2, thus we need a formula to convert a given binomial observation into a z score. Here is a formula that enables us to perform such conversions (for comparison purposes, the familiar z score conversion—formula [5.2.1]—appears first):

[8.33.1] $$z = \frac{X - \mu}{\sigma} = \frac{X - pn}{\sqrt{npq}}.$$

True limits are necessary when the normal distribution is used to approximate probabilities for the binomial distribution.

There is one important difference between the normal distribution and its binomial counterpart—the latter has gaps between observations. The normal distribution is continuous, so we need not worry than any gaps appear between observations along the continuum. Although the binomial distribution is generally a good fit to the normal distribution, its observations are discrete, not continuous—gaps exist. We deal with this minor discrepancy here in the same way we learned to do so when working with discrete data in any grouped frequency distribution—we rely on true limits (for a review, see page 95 in chapter 3). Thus, if we want to know the probability of getting a score of $X = 18$ on some measure, we set its boundaries as 17.5 and 18.5. We then find the proportion of the area under the curve (probability) falling between these two true limits. (As an aside, I hope you realize the cumulative nature of the material you have learned in the first eight chapters of this book. The material really builds on itself, and earlier ideas are central to understanding and working with later ones. Please do not hesitate to review any concepts that you cannot remember—what you read will mean more to you and, more importantly, you will retain it better if you take a few minutes to reread earlier sections of the book.)

By taking all the properties of the binomial distribution into account, we can now work through a complete example. Imagine that you are an industrial organizational psychologist who is interested in developing a screening measure for potential employees. This screening measure is designed to identify those persons who have a predilection for telling lies or being otherwise deceptive in their responses. The instrument contains 60 multiple choice questions, and each question has 3 possible answers. One of each of three answers to a question is deemed to be a deceptive (i.e., lie prone) response. You constructed the instrument so that a respondent is considered to be potentially untruthful if 25 deceptive responses out of 60 questions are endorsed.

If a respondent were just answering randomly, the chance of selecting a deceptive answer would be 1 out of 3 (i.e., $p = 1/3 = .333$) and the probability of selecting a nondeceptive response would be 2 out of 3 (i.e., $q = 2/3 = .667$). If we have 60 questions, then we can calculate both pn and qn to ascertain whether they are greater than or equal to 10, the aforementioned requirement that must be met before we can use the normal distribution.

[8.34.1] $pn = (.333)(60) = 19.98,$
[8.35.1] $qn = (.667)(60) = 40.02.$

Both pn and qn clearly exceed the criterion of 10, so we can proceed to the calculation of the population mean and standard deviation for this binomial distribution. We will use formulas [8.31.1] and [8.32.1], respectively, for determining μ and σ.

[8.31.2] μ of a binomial distribution $= pn = (.333)(60) = 19.98.$

(Please note that we already calculated this number earlier using [8.34.1], however, we did so for a different reason.)

[8.32.2] σ of the binomial distribution $= \sqrt{npq} = \sqrt{(60)(.333)(.667)}$,

[8.32.3] σ of the binomial distribution $= \sqrt{13.33}$,

[8.32.4] σ of the binomial distribution $= 3.65$.

Thus, the distribution of 60 questions is normal, and it has a μ of 19.98 and a σ of 3.65. Our interest is to determine the area of the distribution where $X = 25$. As shown in the upper curve in Figure 8.7, $X = 25$ falls into the region bounded by the lower true limit of 24.5 and the upper true limit of 25.5. How do we determine the probability associated with the highlighted area in upper curve shown in Figure 8.7? We simply calculate the z scores corresponding to 24.5 and 25.5 using [8.33.1], or

[8.36.1] $z = \dfrac{X - pn}{\sqrt{npq}}$,

[8.36.2] $z = \dfrac{24.5 - 19.98}{3.65}$,

[8.36.3] $z = \dfrac{4.52}{3.65}$,

[8.36.4] $z = 1.24$.

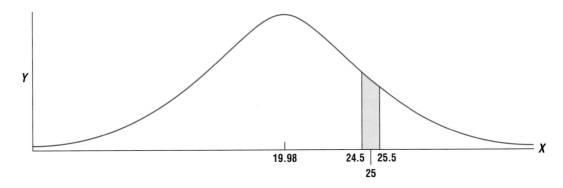

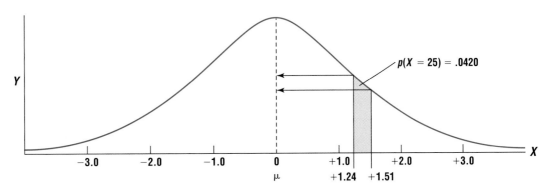

Figure 8.7   Binomial (Normal) Distribution Representing the Number of Deceptive Answers (X) on a 60-item Employment Instrument

Note: The shaded portion in the upper and lower curves represents the probability of giving 25 (X) out of 60 deceptive answers. The score of 25 is bounded by the true limits 24.5 and 25.5.

DATA BOX 8.E

Control, Probability, and When the Stakes are High

Back in chapter 2, the illusion of control—the tendency to believe that one can exercise control over otherwise random events—was introduced (see Data Box 2.A). People frequently try to exert illusory control in those situations where skill-related behaviors (e.g., choosing a lottery ticket from a stack of tickets) become confused with the random nature of the situation (e.g., the winning lottery ticket number is chosen at random). Clearly, probability plays a prominent role in situations where illusory control is apt to be exercised, though individuals who believe they can control outcomes may ignore or overlook the relative likelihood involved in winning.

Timothy Wilson and I wondered whether we could reduce people's tendency to fall prey to illusions of control by making them aware that their probability of winning was actually quite low (Dunn & Wilson, 1990). Our participants wagered poker chips on the roll of a die, the object of which was to either win money or to reduce the amount of time they would have to spend performing an unpleasant task (e.g., alphabetizing lists of words). Each poker chip represented either a small (low cost) or large (high cost) amount of money or task time. We induced illusory control in half the participants by allowing them to choose the face of a fair die they would bet on, and they were also told they would get to roll the die. The remaining participants were assigned a face of the die and told an experimenter would roll for them.

What did we find? When the potential costs associated with gambling were low, participants who perceived illusory control wagered more and were more confident of winning than were those without illusory control. When the costs were high, however, illusory control dissipated, such that it had no effect on wagers or confidence. Increasing the stakes involved, then, may have dampened the desire to take risks by exerting illusory control because there was more to lose—higher costs—in doing so.

What is the moral of the research? We may ignore the probabilities involved in decisions whose outcomes have little consequence for us. We know that the chances of actually winning a multi-million dollar lottery are infinitesimally small, but we buy a ticket anyway—a dollar or two for a few minutes of fantasy costs little. As one lottery ad is wont to say, "Hey, you never know . . .," while another promotes, "Practice saying, 'I'm a winner.'" On the other hand, we can become appropriately aware that the odds of winning are against us when the potential costs involved in losing are great. The illusion of control's hold on probabilistic reasoning, then, can be diminished when the stakes are high (for a recent review of the illusion of control literature, see Thompson, Armstrong, & Thomas, 1998).

The z score equal to 25.5 would be,

[8.37.1] $$z = \frac{X - pn}{\sqrt{npq}},$$

[8.37.2] $$z = \frac{25.5 - 19.98}{3.65},$$

[8.37.3] $$z = \frac{5.52}{3.65},$$

[8.37.4] $$z = 1.51.$$

Please note that these two z scores have been plotted in the z distribution shown in the lower half of Figure 8.7. As you can see, we need to determine the proportion (probability) of the curve falling between these two boundaries. To do so, we need to (a) determine the area between the mean and *z* for each *z* score and then (b) calculate the amount of overlapping area between the two. That overlapping area can be calculated by subtracting the smaller proportion (probability) of $z = 1.24$ from the larger proportion (probability) of $z = 1.51$. Turning to Table B.2 in Appendix B, we find that the area between the mean and *z* for 1.24 is .3925 and the area between the mean and *z* for 1.51 is .4345. The difference between these two probabilities represents the likelihood of getting a deception score of 25 on the instrument, or $.4345 - .3925 = .042$. Thus, the probability of getting a lie score of 25 is very low—less than 5%—and if a respondent did obtain such a score, the industrial organizational psychologist would be appropriately concerned about extending that person a job in the corporation.

What is the probability of obtaining a lie score of less than 25 on the same deception scale used for applicant screening? The industrial organizational psychologist also needs to be aware of the relative likelihood of not being considered a deceptive applicant. If you look back at Figure 8.7, we are interested in the area under the curve that falls at or below $z = 1.24$. Why $z = 1.24$? Precisely because it is the lower true limit associated with a score of 25 on the lie scale, and the question cited above specifies a score *less than 25.*

Notice that we need to use the proportion of the curve falling between the mean and *z*, which we already determined was equal to .3925. To this, of course, we must add .50, the proportion (probability) of the curve falling at or below the mean of the *z* distribution (see the lower curve shown in Figure 8.7). Why? Because the question asked the probability of obtaining a score less than 25 on the deception scale. Thus, $.3925 + .500 = .893$. In other words, the majority of people who take the deception scale are not likely to be identified as potential liar—indeed, over 89% will "pass" the test without ever raising concern about the nature of the answers they provided on it.

Knowledge Base

1. A personality test has a μ of 50 and a σ of 10. What is the probability of obtaining a score of 62 or higher on the test?
2. Using the parameters presented in question 1, what is the probability of obtaining a score less than or equal to 40 and greater than or equal to 55?
3. When can the normal distribution be used to approximate the binomial distribution?
4. There are 50 multiple choice questions on a quiz, and each question has four possible responses. What is the probability that a person would get 20 questions right just by guessing?

Answers

1. $p(X \geq 62) = .1151$
2. $p(X \leq 40) + p(X \geq 55) = (.1587) + (.3085) = .467$
3. When both *pn* and *qn* are greater than or equal to 10.
4. $p = .25$, $q = .75$; *pn* and $qn \geq 10$; $\mu = 12.5$, $\sigma = 3.06$; $p(X = 20) = .0065$

p Values: A Brief Introduction

In the next chapter, we will explore hypothesis testing, the necessary preparation for using the inferential statistical tests that are the focus of subsequent chapters. A working understanding of probability is necessary to frame a hypothesis adequately, as well as to determine if a hypothesized relationship is observed to occur within some data set.

Every hypothesis and each statistic used to evaluate or test its efficacy is accompanied by what is called a **probability value** or ***p* value.** The role *p* values play in hypothesis testing will be conceptually introduced here—their actual use will be taken up in the next several chapters.

Any *p* value helps a researcher determine whether the likelihood of the results obtained in an experiment or other research investigation deviate from a conservative expectation of no difference. Thus, the baseline expectation in any research venture is that the independent variable will create no observed difference between an experimental and a control group. We use probability in the guise of a *p* value to gauge the likelihood that a favored research hypothesis defies this conservative expectation, that a difference between groups is detected. What is the likelihood that a difference between groups is actually found? How do we know that the observed difference is actually due to an independent variable (i.e., a systematic factor) rather than chance (i.e., random, uncontrollable factors)?

When a *p* value is linked to a test statistic, the *p* value indicates the observed relationship between some independent variable and its influence on a dependent measure. Specifically, the *p* value reveals the degree of the likelihood that the test statistic detected any difference between the two (or more) groups represented by different levels of the independent variable (e.g., the mean level of behavior in one differed from the mean behavior observed in a second group). In the behavioral sciences, the convention is to rely on a *p* value equal to or lower than .05. A *p* value of .05 (read as "point oh-five") tells an investigator that there is a 95% chance that an observed difference is real—that is, the independent variable presumably caused the observed difference between group performances on the dependent measure. At the same time, the *p* value reminds us that there is a probability of 5% (or less) that the observed difference is due to chance factors—random variation in the sample—and not the effect of the independent variable on the dependent measure.

To be more conservative in the sense of making it more difficult to detect a difference between two groups, one can use a *p* value of .01 (read as "point-oh-one"). A *p* value equal to .01 means that there is a 99% chance that a test statistic is identifying a reliable effect and only a 1% chance that the difference is due to influences beyond an experimenter's control. Reducing the level of a *p* value makes it harder to detect a difference between groups, so that when a difference is detected under these strenuous conditions, we are reassured that it is apt to be a reliable one. One can even rely on still lower *p* values, a matter we will discuss later in this book.

For the time being, however, I want you to think about how probability can help investigators to determine the likelihood of obtaining particular research results. Probability helps researchers decide whether a particular event is likely to occur due to some intervention or the degree to which a treatment can be seen as actually creating verifiable change in behavior.

Writing About Probability

When writing about probabilities, you must be certain to let readers know about the sampling process used to generate them. Was it a random process? Was the sampling done with or without replacement? Beyond reporting the actual numerical probability value associated with an event (e.g., selecting a person with some characteristic, observing a test score with a particular value), it is also important to explain what the probability value means using words. Your readers should always have some context or background for the points you are trying to make. Thus, you might write, "The probability of selecting an individual with a score on the instrument exceeding the mean value was .345. Given that 34.5% of a sample of 100 respondents could be expected to perform above average, the criterion for inclusion was deemed to be too low. . . ."

Naturally, readers should be informed if a particular type of probabilistic relationship is reported. One might write that, "The marginal probability of being male in the sample was .54" or that the "joint probability of being both male and a fraternity member was equal to .26." When writing about a conditional probability, I would err on the side of caution. In addition to reporting the actual probability value, I would also be sure to describe the conditional quality of the relationship among the variables: "Given that we knew that a respondent was male, the probability that he was also an active member of a fraternity chapter was .64."

When reporting several probabilities at once, it is a very good idea to place them into a well-labeled table. By using a table, you can describe the main points or gist of the probability results in the text and then direct readers to consider examining specific probabilities in the table. If you try to report more than a handful of probabilities in the text, readers will become bored or distracted—they will skip the presumably important probability information and go on to other material. In fact, reading about more than a few probabilities at one point in time *is* boring, as the tendency to present them is unavoidably done in a "sing song"sort of fashion (e.g., "The probability of being a female was .46, while the probability of being female and on the Dean's list was .24. On the other hand, the probability of . . ."). Like more than one or two correlational relationships, multiple probabilities should be placed in a table so they can be examined or referred to when a reader's pace or level of interest allows. Only the most important or otherwise salient probabilistic relationships need to be described in the actual text.

A final suggestion: When you have occasion to write about probability several times in the same paper, try to break up the descriptive monotony for the reader (and yourself as writer) by using probabilistic synonyms such as "likelihood," "expectation," or even "chance." It may seem to be a minor point but repeated use of the word "probability" can grow tiresome—judicious use of synonyms will spice up the prose and maintain reader interest.

Project Exercise

FLIPPING COINS AND THE BINOMIAL DISTRIBUTION

The purpose of this *Project Exercise* is to give you practical rather than exclusively theoretical experience with a binomial distribution and probability's link to it. The exercise is based on one developed by Tanner (1990) and it involves the binomial process of flipping and spinning a coin.

Flipping. In order to *flip* a coin, place your thumb in between your middle and index fingers. Place the coin on the top of your thumbnail and then "flick" your thumb in an upward motion so that the coin flips upward into the air.

Spinning. In order to *spin* a coin, place the edge of the coin on a flat surface—a table top, for example—and balance it there with the tip of one of your index fingers. Using the other index finger, tap the coin off center so as to create a spinning motion and then remove your finger from the upper edge of the coin (relatively strong force is often necessary to get the coin to really spin). If the coin does not spin for at least 4 seconds, repeat the spin.

Whether you are flipping or spinning, a trial does not count if the coin rolls away or falls off a table where you are working—repeat the flip or spin when this happens. Here are the initial directions:

1. *Flip* the coin 30 times and record the results of each trial (using H for "heads" and T for "tails") in the space provided in Table 8.4. *Spin* the coin 30 times and record the

| Table 8.4 | Data Record for Coin Flips and Spins |

	Flips	Spins
1.	———	———
2.	———	———
3.	———	———
4.	———	———
5.	———	———
6.	———	———
7.	———	———
8.	———	———
9.	———	———
10.	———	———
11.	———	———
12.	———	———
13.	———	———
14.	———	———
15.	———	———
16.	———	———
17.	———	———
18.	———	———
19.	———	———
20.	———	———
21.	———	———
22.	———	———
23.	———	———
24.	———	———
25.	———	———
26.	———	———
27.	———	———
28.	———	———
29.	———	———
30.	———	———
Total number of heads by flipping ————		Total number of heads by spinning ————

results (again, H or T) in the space provided in Table 8.4. Be sure to total the number of "heads" for the respective categories at the bottom of Table 8.4.

2. Be prepared to hand in the results shown in Table 8.4, as you will need to combine your results with those found by your classmates. For convenience, your instructor may want to pool the class results and distribute a master data set to everyone in your class (see Figure 8.8).

3. Create a simple matrix with four columns (see Figure 8.8). The number of rows should correspond to the number of students (i.e., 1 to N) who share the results of their 30 flips and 30 spins from Table 8.4. The information in the columns of Figure 8.8 should contain the following information in this order: number of "heads" obtained by flipping; total number of flips; number of "heads" obtained by spinning; and the total number of spins (see Figure 8.8). Create a master record like the one shown in Figure 8.8 and then make the appropriate number of copies for all students who collected data.

Students' Names	*N* of "Heads" Flipped	*N* of Flips	*N* of "Heads" Spun	*N* of Spins
1. Jane Doe	10	30	14	30
2. _____	_____	_____	_____	_____
3. _____	_____	_____	_____	_____
.				
.				
.				
N. _____	_____	_____	_____	_____

Figure 8.8   Master Data Record for Project Exercise

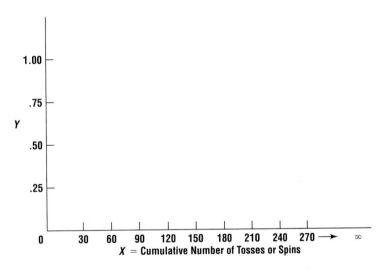

Figure 8.9   Proportion (Probability) of Heads Across *N* Flips/Spins of a Coin

4. Every student should have flipped a coin 30 times, as well as indicated the number of heads that appeared in 30 flips. Using the results from the *N* students, compute the cumulative proportion of "heads" (*Y*) and plot this value versus the total number of flips (*X*) (see Figure 8.9). Imagine that your class had three students, for example, and if the first student obtained 10 heads in 30 flips, the second had 16 heads in 30 flips, and the third had 14 heads across 30 flips, then the cumulative proportions would be 10/30, 26/60, and 40/90, respectively. These proportions (probabilities) would then be plotted on the *Y* axis versus the number of flips (e.g., 30, 60, and 90) shown in Figure 8.9. *What does your plot of these data reveal about the probability of observing heads as you flip a coin across an increasing number of trials?*

5. Using the spin data from Table 8.4, repeat the steps presented in question 4. Compare the plot of the spin data to the plot of the flip data. Are these plots similar? How so? *How would you characterize the proportion (probability) of "heads" as the N of tosses or spins increases?*

6. In your class, everyone flipped a coin 30 times and then spun a coin 30 times. Explain the advantages and disadvantages of this research design as compared to a study where (a) each student is randomly assigned to either flip a coin 30 times or spin a coin 30 times and (b) everyone is randomly assigned to *either* flip a coin 30 times and then spin a coin 30 times *or* to spin a coin 30 times and then to flip a coin 30 times.

LOOKING FORWARD THEN BACK

A lthough it stands as a statistical topic in its own right, the concept of probability is an essential part of inferential statistics. Indeed, it is impossible to interpret the results of an experiment—and the statistical analyses supporting it—without making a nod to probability theory, the likelihood that events will occur given particular conditions. The three decision trees opening this chapter will remind you how to calculate and interpret a probability, as well as to select from among the available probability rules. In the future, for example, you may need to determine the probability of some event occurring during an experiment (e.g., the likelihood that a participant will favor one alternative over another) so that a comparison between an actual and a probable outcome can be examined. If so, then the first decision tree will be helpful to you. The second decision tree is apt to be useful when preparing probabilistic information for presentation—some probabilities are better reported in a table rather than in written text. Finally, the third decision tree will prove to be useful when you require a quick review of the probability rules and when they are applicable. Though useful, such abstract information is quickly forgotten unless it is used with some regularity—a quick glance at the third decision tree can trigger your memory for the rules guiding this essential statistical concept.

Summary

1. A probability is a quantitative statement about the likelihood that some event will occur in the future. Probabilities range between 0 and 1.00, and higher probabilities indicate a relatively greater likelihood that some event will take place in the long run.

2. Probabilities usually entail examining the ratio of the number of actual occurrences of some event to the total number of possible occurrences. Probability is also used to determine the likelihood that a sample is drawn from one population rather than another. To make such judgments, probability is linked with inferential statistics.

3. The gambler's fallacy refers to the erroneous belief that one randomly determined event will influence the outcome of another randomly determined event. Examples of the gam-

bler's fallacy include any game of chance where players assume that a run of one event must necessarily change to another event (e.g., a string of tossing "heads" means that "tails" must occur next).

4. Independence refers to situations where the probability of one event remains unaffected by the probability of some other event. When flipping a coin, for example, a "head" is just as likely to be followed by another "head" as it is a "tail."

5. Classical probability theory calculates the probability of some event A to be $p(A)$ = the number of outcomes favoring event A/the total number of available outcomes (i.e., A + not A).

6. Sampling with replacement entails selecting an observation

from a sample, determining the probability, and then returning the observation before drawing the next observation. When sampling with replacement, the probabilities associated with a given sample remain constant. Sampling *without* replacement follows the same process except that the observation is never returned to the sample—thus, the numerator(s) and denominator(s) in subsequent probability calculations must be adjusted to reflect the removal of observations from the sample.

7. Proportion and probability are related concepts; indeed, both are calculated the same way. Thus, the area under the normal curve can be discussed interchangeably as proportion or probability information. Standard or *z* scores can be used to determine various proportions (probabilities) associated with various areas under the normal curve.

8. Two events are mutually exclusive from one another when they share no observations in common (e.g., a person is either male or female). An event is said to be nonmutually exclusive then two events occur simultaneously (e.g., a person can be male and a Yankees fan). Two rules for probability—the addition rule and the multiplication rule—were introduced, and variations of each rule were applied to mutually exclusive and not mutually exclusive events.

9. A joint probability is the numerical likelihood of selecting some observation that shares two characteristics or events (i.e., *p*(A and B)). A conditional probability occurs when the probability of one event is dependent upon the role of another event (e.g., given that a student is a freshmen, what is the probability he will be placed on academic probation, or *p*(A|B)). Finally, a marginal or "unconditional" probability provides the likelihood of some independent event's occurrence.

10. Binomial data occur when information can be divided into or changed into two discrete groupings. A binomial distribution is one wherein events can have one of two possible outcomes. When particular conditions are met, the binomial distribution can approximate the standard normal distribution.

11. Probability or *p* values were briefly introduced. These *p* values will become increasingly important as we review inferential statistical tests in subsequent chapters. For present purposes, *p* values were described as guides to determining whether some inferential statistical test actually found that the independent variable created some observed change in the dependent measure.

12. When reporting probabilistic information, the numerical value should be explained in concrete terms—it is not sufficient to rely exclusively on numbers, as readers require a context for understanding results. When several probabilities are presented, they should appear in a table, whereas three or fewer probabilities can probably be discussed within the text. Judicious use of synonyms for the word "probability" will retain readers' attention, while overuse of the latter term can quickly become monotonous.

Key Terms

Addition rule *(p. 285)*
Binomial distribution *(p. 299)*
Conditional probability *(p. 290)*
Gambler's fallacy *(p. 275)*
Independence *(p. 276)*
Law of averages *(p. 276)*
Joint probability *(p. 285)*

"Man-who" statistics *(p. 278)*
Marginal probability *(p. 292)*
Multiplication rule *(p. 287)*
Multiplication rule for dependent events *(p. 293)*
Mutually exclusive *(p. 286)*
p value *(p. 306)*

Probability value *(p. 306)*
Sample space *(p. 277)*
Sampling with replacement *(p. 279)*
Sampling without replacement *(p. 280)*
Subjective probability *(p. 274)*

Chapter Problems

1. What are some examples of the sort of probability judgments you make in daily life? Even if they are difficult to quantify, can they still be probability judgments? Why or why not?

2. You are standing outside on a dark and cloudy day. You remark to a friend, "I am fairly certain that it is going to rain." Why is your remark best described as a subjective probability?

3. Steve is playing a slot machine in one of the major hotels in Las Vegas. His friend, Paul, tries to convince him to leave it and join other friends in the main casino. Steve refuses, noting that "I've spent 20 bucks on this thing so far—I've primed it. I

know that I'm due to win soon!" Characterize the inherent flaws in Steve's reasoning. What do statistician's call this sort of thinking and behavior?

4. A sociologist presents data on the average life span of male and female adults in the United States, noting than the average age of death for men is about 72 years and that for women is about 74. A student raises her hand and says she cannot believe those statistics because "my grandmother is 92 and my next door neighbor, Mr. Smith, is 97!" What sort of statistic is the student citing? Why is it problematic? What should the sociologist say in response?

5. When flipping a coin and obtaining a string of either "heads"

or "tails," why do some people assume that they can accurately predict what the next flip will be?

6. Why isn't one flip of a coin, say a "head," affected by the flip that occurred just before it? Does chance "correct" itself? Why or why not?

7. In your opinion, what does the quote from Stanislaw Lem on page 277 mean about the role probability plays where human judgments and decisions are concerned?

8. A sack contains 30 blue marbles, 10 green ones, and 20 red ones. Using sampling with replacement, what is the probability of selecting a green marble? A red marble? Two blue marbles in a row? A green, then a red, and then a blue marble?

9. Using sampling without replacement, provide the probabilities listed in question 8.

10. An upper-level seminar class offered by the Psychology Department enrolls 15 students, 8 of whom are juniors and the rest are seniors. Six of the juniors are female and 3 of the seniors are female. The remaining students are males. What is the probability of being a male in this class? A female? What is the probability of being a junior and female? A senior and male?

11. Examine the following frequency distribution:

X	f
12	8
11	10
8	11
6	10
5	6
4	3
3	5

Determine the following probabilities: $p(X = 4)$; $p(X = 11)$; $p(X > 5)$; $p(X < 3)$; $p(X \geq 8)$; $p(X \leq 8)$.

12. Examine the following frequency distribution:

X	f
15	7
12	13
7	10
3	8
2	6

Determine the following probabilities : $p(X = 3)$; $p(X = 15)$; $p(X > 7)$; $p(X < 15)$; $p(X \geq 5)$; $p(X \leq 3)$.

13. A sack contains 13 black marbles, 16 white marbles, 4 pink marbles, and 8 pink and white marbles. What is the probability of selecting a marble that is black? What is the probability of selecting a marble that is pink? What is the probability of selecting a pink or a white marble? What is the probability of selecting a marble that is pink and white?

14. You are flipping a coin. What is the probability of obtaining each of the following sequences: H–H–H–T–H–H–T; H–H–H; T–T–T–T–T–T–T–T; H–H–T–T–H.

15. Which of the following distributions of coin tosses is more likely to occur than any of the others: H–H–H–T–T–T or H–H–H–H–H–H or T–H–T–T–H–H?

16. A social psychologist studies helping behavior when a person is either alone or when others are present. She performs a study in the field—an older woman appears to fall and hurt her leg. Sometimes only one participant witnesses the event, other people besides the participant are present the remainder of the time. Examine the following data table and then answer the questions that follow it.

Participant	Help Given to Confederate	No Help Help Given to Confederate
Alone	30	8
With others	6	42

What is the probability a person waiting alone offered to help the confederate? What is the probability that a someone waiting with others did not offer to help the confederate? Given that a person was with others, what is the probability that the person offered to help the confederate?

17. Using the data provided in question 16, show how the multiplication rule for dependent events can be used to calculate the joint probability of being alone and not offering to help the confederate.

18. An intelligence test has a μ of 100 and a σ of 15. What is the probability of obtaining a score of 103 or higher? What is the probability of obtaining a score of 85 or lower? What is the probability of obtaining a score less than or equal to 95 and greater than or equal to 115?

19. A measure of romantic attraction has a μ of 75 and a σ of 8. What is the probability of obtaining a score between 76 and 82? What is the probability of obtaining a score greater than or equal to 90? What is the probability of obtaining a score of less than 50?

20. In what ways is the binomial distribution similar to the standard normal distribution? How is the former different than the latter? Under what specific conditions can the binomial distribution be used to approximate the standard normal distribution?

21. A multiple-choice test has 100 questions, and four possible responses to each question. Only one out of each of the four responses is correct. If a respondent is just guessing, what is the probability of getting 48 questions correct by chance?

22. A true–false quiz has 50 questions, and a student needs to get 30 of them correct to pass. What is the probability of earning a passing grade by guessing?

23. A statistician calculates the probability that an event will occur to be $-.35$. How likely is it that this event will occur? (*Hint*: Use the decision tree(s) at the start of the chapter to answer this question properly.)

24. A researcher calculates 20 separate probabilities to include in a research report. How should these probabilities be presented to readers? (*Hint*: Use the decision tree(s) at the start of the chapter to answer this question properly.)

25. A students wants to calculate the likelihood that several events will occur but she does not know the number of possible observations favoring each event. Can she still calculate the

probabilities? (*Hint:* Use the decision tree(s) at the start of the chapter to answer this question properly.)

26. A statistics instructor wants to demonstrate probability theory to his class. He dumps 10 red marbles, then 5 green marbles, and then 40 yellow marbles into a can. He wants to explain to his class the likelihood that if he reaches into the can he will select a yellow marble. Is he ready to demonstrate the probability of selecting a yellow marble? Why or why not? Properly speaking, does he need to do anything else in order to prepare this

demonstration? (*Hint:* Use the decision tree(s) at the start of the chapter to answer this question properly.)

27. Which probability rule is appropriate for each of the following situations (*Hint:* Use the decision tree(s) at the start of the chapter to answer this question properly):
    a. Events are conditional on one another.
    b. Events occur in an independent sequence.
    c. Events are mutually exclusive.
    d. Events are not mutually exclusive.

Performing a One-Sample Hypothesis Test

1.
Is there more than one separate *sample* available?

If *yes*, then a *one-sample hypothesis test* is not appropriate; consult a later chapter (e.g., chapters 10, 11, 12, or 13) for guidance.

If *no*, then go to step 2.

2.
Is there information regarding *population parameters* (especially σ, but perhaps μ or ρ, as well)?

If *yes*, then go to step 3.

If *no*, then you cannot perform a *one-sample hypothesis test*.

3.
Will a *two-tailed significance test* be used to test the null hypothesis?

If *yes*, then go to step 4.

If *no*, then provide a clear rationale for using a *one-tailed test* before proceeding to step 4.

4.
Is the *significance level* for the statistical test appropriately conservative (i.e. $p = .05$ or less)?

If *yes*, then consider whether the *significance level* is sufficient to guard against *Type I errors*; go to step 5.

If *no*, then consider lowering the *significance level* for the test while reviewing its potential impact on the test's *power*; go to step 5.

5.
Is the value of the test (z or r) greater than or equal to an obtained *critical value*?

If *yes*, then *reject the null hypothesis of no difference* and interpret the result.

If *no*, then *accept the null hypothesis of no difference* and interpret the result.

Selecting a Significance Level for a Test Statistic

1.
Is the research topic a novel one (i.e., little related research is available)?

If *yes*, then rely on the conventional *significance level* of .05.

If *no*, then go to step 2.

2.
Does the available research indicate that the same or similar *independent variables* routinely find significant differences between experimental and control groups?

If *yes*, then use a more stringent *significance level* (.01, .001) for the test statistic.

If *no*, retain the conventional .05 *significance level* and take steps to enhance the *power* available for the test statistic.

Avoiding Making a Type I Error

1.
Is the study's *sample size* reasonably large (i.e., ≥ 30)?

If *yes*, then go to step 2.

If *no*, then consider collecting more data before beginning analyses.

2.
Will a *two-tailed significance test* be used?

If *yes*, then go to step 3.

If *no*, provide a clear rationale for using a *one-tailed test before* going to step 3.

3.
Does the research cover an established topical area?

If *yes*, then to avoid making a *Type I error*, consider using a *p* value lower than .05.

If *no*, then use the conventional *p* value of .05 but consider replicating any significant effect(s) before any publication or presentation.

Enhancing a Study's Power

1.
Will the *sample size* be reasonably large (i.e., ≥ 30)?

If *yes*, then go to step 2.

If *no*, then recruit more participants before beginning data collection.

2.
Is the *dependent measure* sensitive enough to reveal differences between groups?

If *yes*, then go to step 3.

If *no*, then consider using a more established *dependent measure*; go to step 3.

3.
Is there evidence to indicate that the *independent variable* will be salient to research participants?

If *yes*, then go to step 4.

If *no*, then consider verifying the *independent variable's* effectiveness in a pilot study before actual data collection begins; go to step 4.

4.
Can a *one-tailed significance test* be used?

If *yes*, then be sure to balance its use against the threat posed by *Type I errors*; go to step 5.

If *no*, then go to step 5.

5.
Will a conventional *significance level* (.05) be appropriate for the statistical test used to analyze the data?

If *yes*, then be sure to balance its use against the threat posed by *Type I errors*.

If *no*, then be advised that more conservative *significance levels* (e.g., .01, .001) restrict *power*.

INFERENTIAL STATISTICS:
SAMPLING DISTRIBUTIONS AND
HYPOTHESIS TESTING

The first eight chapters in this book were a necessary preamble to prepare readers for this chapter. These earlier chapters introduced and explained a variety of statistical theories and concepts, which will render this chapter's material—the logic underlying the testing of hypotheses—comprehensible and doable. Your understanding of sampling, populations, and probability will all be brought to bear in the exploration of hypotheses, which were previously defined as testable questions or focused predictions. Once a hypothesis is identified, the research is executed, and the data are collected, inferential statistics are used to test the viability of the hypothesis; that is, was an anticipated relationship found within the data?

Here are a few examples of the sorts of hypotheses behavioral scientists investigate:

- A clinical psychologist who treats obsessive-compulsive (OC) disorder—recurrent, persistent thoughts concerning cleanliness and rule governed behavior—believes that the link between obsessive thoughts (e.g., "My hands are still dirty") and behavior (e.g., repeated hand washing) can be disrupted with a combination of behavioral and cognitive therapies. A control group of OC patients receives standard behavior therapy while at the same time a comparable patient group is exposed to the same therapy coupled with work on reducing obsessive thoughts. The clinical psychologist wants to learn if the two-prong treatment is more beneficial than behavior therapy alone.
- A political psychologist studies how higher education affects college students' voting behavior in national elections. The researcher hypothesizes that students generally become more liberal and politically aware across their four college years. She sets out to compare the voting behavior of first-year students with that of fourth-year students in a mock national election. Students from both classes read a series of mock candidate profiles and then answer questions about their beliefs concerning

a variety of public and social policy issues. The political psychologist wants to determine if fourth-years students are more likely to vote for liberal candidates, while first-year students will tend to endorse conservative candidates.

■ A health psychologist believes that middle-aged individuals who care for elderly parents are at greater risk for illness than similarly aged persons with no caregiver responsibilities. The investigator interviews the two sets of adults and then gains permission to examine their medical records at the end of a 1-year period, hypothesizing that the caregiver group will show more frequent illnesses, visits to the doctor, hospitalizations, and medicine prescriptions than the noncaregiver group.

■ An experimental psychologist is interested in the role that zinc, a nutrient in a normal daily diet, plays in learning and memory processes. The psychologist exposes two groups of laboratory rats—a control group of "normal" animals and an experimental group of nutritionally zinc-deprived animals—to a novel maze. After a few baseline trials, the animals are individually returned to the maze and the number of errors made prior to the discovery of a food reward is recorded. The psychologist wants to demonstrate that the zinc-deprived group will show a higher average number of search errors relative to the control group.

In each of these four scenarios, the procedures involved in testing the respective hypotheses are similar. None of these researchers can ever hope to measure the responses of every possible respondent in their population of interest, so such data are usually collected in the form of some random sample, one that is presumed to be representative of a larger population. This random sample is then generally randomly divided into two (or, on occasion, more) distinct groups—a control group and an experimental group. Each group is then exposed to one level of the independent variable—the variable manipulated by or under the control of the investigator. As suggested above, not every variable of interest can be manipulated (e.g., time to acquire sociopolitical sophistication, the stress of caregiving)—some are naturally occurring, but their effect on the members of a distinct subgroup can still be examined. But in every case, the collected data are the participants' responses to a dependent variable, usually some verbal or behavioral measure, an identical version of which is presented to each group in each of the respective studies.

Hypothesis testing entails comparing the groups' reactions to the dependent measure following the introduction of the independent variable. The practical matter is this: Did the independent variable create an observed and systematic change in the dependent measure? Specifically, did the experimental group behave or respond differently than the control group after both were exposed to the independent variable? The theoretical matter is this: Following exposure to the independent variable, is the μ of the experimental group verifiably different from the μ of the control group? In other words, can we attribute the differential and measured between group differences to the fact that the control and experimental groups now effectively represent *different* populations with *different* parameters? We turn now to the importance of establishing a link among the questions researchers pose, the samples they draw, and issues of estimation and experimentation.

Samples, Population, and Hypotheses: Links to Estimation and Experimentation

Before asking any question, a researcher must identify a population of interest. As you know from previous chapters, especially chapter 1, it is rare to know much about the characteristics of any population. A sample—preferably a random sample—is then drawn from this population. The investigator hopes that the sample is representative of the population from which it was drawn, that the typical or average behavior witnessed in the sample reflects what is usually true of the population. In chapter 1, we learned that the first question to ask of any sample is whether its sample statistics (i.e., the sample mean and standard deviation) are similar to those of the population's parameters (i.e., the population mean and standard deviation). Thus, our first matter of concern is the role of inferential statistics in the *estimation of population parameters*.

Point Estimation

Can we characterize the parameters of a population based on a single sample? Yes, we can—or we can at least try—and when we do so, we are engaging in what statisticians refer to as *point estimation*.

KEY TERM   **Point estimation** is the process of using a sample statistic (e.g., $\overline{X}$, s) to estimate the value of some population parameter (e.g., μ, σ).

Anytime we calculate the mean of some sample of data in preparation for use in some statistical test, we are also, in effect, asking whether that mean ($\overline{X}$) is close to or equal in value to the μ of the population from which it came (to refresh your memory on the link between sample statistics and population parameters, see Table 4.1). Indeed, we truly hope that $\overline{X} \cong \mu$.

The obvious drawback to point estimation is that only *one* sample is used to estimate the characteristics of a population that could very well be infinite in size and scope. To phrase the problem in the language you acquired in the last chapter, what is the probability that one sample statistic is going to provide an adequate estimate of a given population parameter? The chances that a sample statistic will closely match a population parameter are few and far between—one sample is simply not sufficient, though it is often all that a behavioral scientist has to go on. We assume, then, that any given sample statistic is apt to contain some degree of error (i.e., the difference between estimated and actual reality) and there is little we can do to improve the situation besides using random sampling and ensuring that the size of the sample is reasonably large. This form of error—called **sampling error**—was introduced in chapter 2, where we acknowledged that there will always be *some* degree of sampling error. The question is, how much sampling error is reasonable or acceptable?

Overcoming point estimation's limitations can be achieved through a somewhat more laborious process known as *interval estimation*. Where point estimation focuses on comparing *one* statistic and *one* parameter, as it were, interval estimation relies on repeated sampling and repeated generation of statistics in order to characterize a population of interest, as well as some parameter (usually μ). The repeated sampling, though, is for the express purpose of examining the amount of variability observed to occur among the sample statistics.

KEY TERM   **Interval estimation** involves careful examination and estimation of the variability noted among sample statistics based on the repeated sampling of the same population.

Interval estimation provides a range within which sample statistics can fall by allowing behavioral scientists to project by how much these statistics would be expected to vary through repeated sampling of the population. If repeated sampling reveals sample $\overline{X}$s of similar value, then a researcher can be reasonably confident that any given sample is representative of the population. If the sampling process reveals sample $\overline{X}$s that vary somewhat from one another in value—in other words, there is some degree of variability among the observed means—then the researcher will want to report the sampling error around the mean of the sample means.

You probably do not realize it, but you frequently hear or read about interval estimates when public opinion surveys are reported. When a scientific study reports that "62% of Americans favor shoring up the Social Security program," the written text or televised voice-over will also typically note that the study is "accurate to within 3 percentage points." This accuracy reading refers to the fact that not *every* American was actually polled, so that "majority" opinion actually falls within ±3 percentage points, or between 59% and 65%. This interval estimate, then, provides an adequate cushion or set of boundaries, really, for any sampling error in measurement. We will discuss how to calculate a similar sort of interval later in the chapter.

Statistical Inference and Hypothesis Testing

Once a sample is assumed to be representative of the desired parent population, the second step is to randomly assign half of the sample's members to a control group and the other half to an experimental group. The research project then presents each group with a distinct level of some independent variable and measures subsequent reactions based on changes to the dependent variable. The second, key question here is whether the sample data—now divided into two groups—show detectable differences due to the influence of some independent variable. This process of detection centers on the role inferential statistics plays in *hypothesis testing*, which is generally to demonstrate mean differences.

KEY TERM   **Hypothesis testing** compares sample data and statistics to known or estimated population parameters.

Statistical inference is an essential part of hypothesis testing, as it enables a researcher to determine the probability that a sample is from one population and not another. Similarly, a sample statistic can appear to be so different in value from some population parameter that it is highly likely that the statistic is representative of some other population. This process of determining whether a sample or sample statistic fits one or another population better or worse is, of course, the heart of the hypothesis testing enterprise. If a behavioral scientist can show that a sample statistic from an experimental group is no longer similar to its counterpart in a control group (see Figure 9.1), then there is some evidence that the observed change could be due to experimental intervention (i.e., the independent variable caused a difference in the dependent measure). On the other hand, the researcher must also be wary—there remains the possibility (and probability) that the observed change is due to chance, not experimental intent.

Statistical inference enables researchers to do more than infer the presence or absence of change regarding an independent variable's impact on a dependent measure. It also enables researchers to make educated guesses when limited information is available to guide judgment. Hypotheses are generated in order to account for the behavior of relatively larger groups—in the behavioral sciences, the responses of humans or animals—yet no experiment, quasi-experiment, or other form of investigation will involve but a few participants representing humanity or the animal kingdom (for a review of research approaches, see chapter 2 and Appendix F). Generalization from a sample to the larger population is necessary, and this goal cannot be achieved without estimating the potentially wider effects of what results are observed in a sample. Involving every person or animal is impossible, impractical, and nonsensical. Yet if we could do so, we would be *directly* evaluating the reasonableness or the explanatory power of the hypothesis—in the same way that we directly evaluate a single person's behavior or that of a solitary animal.

Statistical inference enables researchers to evaluate the veracity of a hypothesis *as if* a whole population of participants were available instead of merely a small (but hopefully)

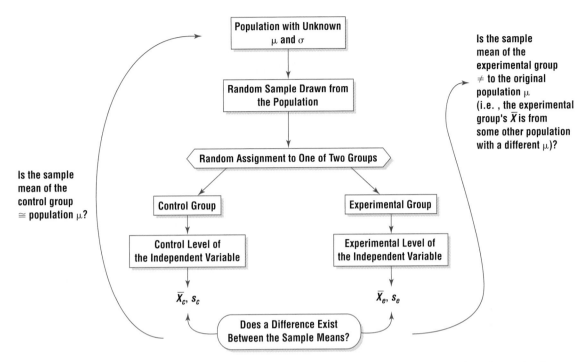

Figure 9.1 The Process of Sampling and Inferring Whether a Statistic is from One or Another Population

representative sampling. This "as if" hypothesizing enables behavioral scientists to evaluate the strength of hypotheses in an *indirect* manner; that is, given what the sample data show, how likely is it that the same effects hold true in the population at large?

This review of hypothesis testing and point estimation is a conceptual introduction. We will learn their practical side—how to calculate and apply them—later in the chapter. No doubt some of the material reviewed so far can sometimes seem redundant, as we discussed much of it earlier in the book. Some ideas merit repetition, however, and I think that later you will agree that it is better to err on the side of repetition to ensure understanding than to assume that understanding already exists or that your memory of the eight previous chapters is flawless. We turn now to some critical theoretical topics concerning sampling, probability, and estimating the characteristics of unknown populations.

The Distribution of Sample Means

Data analysis and reliance on samples is akin to looking through a glass darkly, as the samples rarely match the characteristics of the population from which they were drawn. More troubling still, of course, is the fact that the samples themselves tend to be variable in the qualities they display (hence, for example, the reliance on interval estimation noted above). How, then, can we know or even trust that a given sample is actually from a given population? We need to establish a few basic rules about sampling, rules that will bring order and reason to the way we think about sampling's relationship to hypothesis testing and statistical inference.

Imagine a very large population of observations. If we drew a couple of random samples with fixed sample sizes of N (say, $N = 40$), we might notice that each of the two samples displayed somewhat different characteristics (i.e., not only are the samples composed of different respondents, they also possess a different $\overline{X}$ and s). What if we continued to draw samples of the same fixed sample size N—could we begin to discern any pattern or shared characteristics among the samples? Yes, and in fact, we could even make some predictions based on all of these sample means. If we did so, we would be using what is known as the *distribution of sample means*.

KEY TERM   A **distribution of sample means** is a group or collection of sample means based on random samples of a fixed size N from some population.

Theoretically, the distribution of sample means can be exhaustive—that is, all possible sample means based on an infinite number of samples—but in a conceptually more manageable way, it is possible to think of this distribution as being based on a very large number of samples.

Please take careful notice of one important aspect of the distribution of sample means: It is a distribution comprised of sample statistics (here, $\overline{X}$s) rather than individual scores or observations, a clear departure from the familiar sorts of frequency distributions we have encountered previously. This distinction is an important one to keep in mind as you continue reading.

Any time a researcher works with a distribution that is based on some sample statistic like the mean or the standard deviation, such a distribution is labeled a *sampling distribution*.

▽

Sampling distributions are different than frequency distributions, as they are comprised of an array of a single sample statistic (e.g., $\overline{X}$), not raw scores.

KEY TERM   A **sampling distribution** is a distribution comprised of statistics (e.g., $\overline{X}$, s) based on samples of some fixed size N drawn from a larger population.

The distribution of sample means, then, is a sampling distribution, and there is a theoretical sampling distribution for every statistic that exists. Besides one for means, then, there is one for variances, standard deviations, correlations, proportions or probabilities, and so on. Any statistic that can be calculated from some sample of data has its own sampling distribution.

What would the sampling distribution of means look like if we plotted it? That is, what shape would its distribution adopt or take on? Given its ubiquity in our discussions in this book, it will come as no shock that a sampling distribution of means of some fixed size N will take on the shape of the standard normal distribution (see Figure 9.2). As shown in Figure 9.2, most of the sample means will be similar in value to one another—they will cluster under the bell in the normal curve (for a review of the normal distribution and its properties, see chapter 5). A few stray or aberrant sample means will fill out the tails of the normally shaped sampling distribution (see Figure 9.2). What *will* probably surprise you is the enormous importance the bell-shaped assumption for any sampling distribution takes on in inferential statistics, leading us to carefully consider what is called the central limit theorem in the next section of the chapter. Before we proceed to review this critical theorem, however, let's pause for a moment to consider two important concepts that are part of any sampling distribution, expected value and standard error.

Expected Value and Standard Error

If you treat the sample means (or whatever statistic) comprising a sampling distribution as an array of scores, it is not at all difficult to calculate their mean. Note that we can talk about such a calculation in theoretical terms—the mean of the distribution of sampling means shown in Figure 9.2—or we could actually determine the mean of the means of some random samples from a larger population. The mean of the sample statistics of any sampling distribution is called its *expected value*.

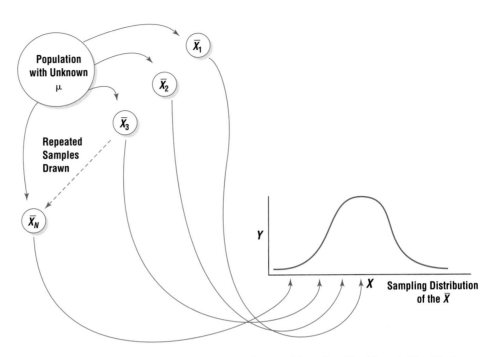

Figure 9.2 A Sampling Distribution Created by Repeated Sampling (Fixed Sample Size *N*) of a Population

The mean of any sampling distribution of a sample statistic is referred to as the sampling distribution's **expected value**.

Thus, the mean of a sampling distribution of means is called the *expected value of the sampling distribution of the mean,* which is symbolically known as $\mu_{\bar{X}}$. The formula for calculating $\mu_{\bar{X}}$ is:

[9.1.1]
$$\mu_{\bar{X}} = \frac{\sum \bar{X}}{N_k},$$

where the expected value of the sample mean can be known by summing all the sample means and then dividing them by the *number of samples* (N_k), not the *size of the samples.* Please be aware that formula [9.1.1] is meant to conceptually present how $\mu_{\bar{X}}$ *could* be known. Given that most sampling distributions of means are presumably composed of an infinite number of samples, we will not actually be using [9.1.1] to perform any calculations.

The standard deviation of any sampling distribution of sample statistics is also known by a particular name, the *standard error.*

The standard deviation of any sampling distribution of a sample statistic is referred to as the sampling distribution's **standard error**.

When working with a sampling distribution of means, then, the standard deviation of that distribution would be known as the **standard error of the mean.** The symbol for the standard error of the mean is $\sigma_{\bar{X}}$. Please note that $\sigma_{\bar{X}}$ does not mean the same thing as σ, the symbol for the standard deviation of a population. The standard error of the mean can be calculated using:

[9.2.1]
$$\sigma_{\bar{X}} = \frac{\sqrt{\sigma^2}}{N} = \frac{\sigma}{\sqrt{N}}.$$

Besides the sample size (N), this formula assumes that the population variance (σ^2) or the population standard deviation (σ) is known.

We will learn more about the expected value of the mean and its standard error shortly. We now turn to a review of the central limit theorem and its implications for sampling, hypothesis testing, and inferential statistics.

The Central Limit Theorem

I am going to postpone providing you with a formal definition for the *central limit theorem* for a moment and simply describe its importance to the discipline of statistics and, more broadly, any empirically driven research discipline. The central limit theorem is part of the statistical catechism of statisticians or really any researcher who uses data analysis in his or her work. By catechism, I mean that one must take it on faith (or, if you prefer, theory) that sampling distributions behave in consistent, predictable ways that allow investigators to ask focused questions of them.

▽

The central limit theorem applies to continuous variables, whose values have no gaps between them.

The central limit theorem is a theorem—a principle or theoretical proposition—enabling statisticians to work with continuous variables on a relatively large scale. The central limit theorem can readily describe the qualities of a sampling distribution of means based on a fairly large but fixed sample size. For our purposes, the central limit theorem is the rationale behind point estimation, interval estimation, and hypothesis testing.

KEY TERM   The **central limit theorem** proposes that as the size of any sample, N, becomes infinitely large in size, the shape of the sampling distribution of the mean approaches normality—that is, it takes on the appearance of the familiar bell-shaped curve—with a mean equal to μ, the population's mean, and a standard deviation equal to $\sigma/\sqrt{N}$, which is known as the standard error of the mean. As N increases in size, the standard error of the mean or $\sigma_{\bar{X}}$ will decrease in magnitude, indicating that the sample will be close in value to the actual population μ. Thus, it will also be true that $\mu_{\bar{X}} \cong \mu$ and that $\sigma_{\bar{X}} \cong \sigma/\sqrt{N}$.

Two main points stand out in the definition of the central limit theorem:

■ Despite a parent population's shape, mean, or standard deviation, the central limit theorem can be used to describe *any* distribution of sample means. Thus, a population does *not* have to be normally distributed in order for the central limit theorem to be true. The central limit theorem, then, can be applied to any population as long as samples can be randomly drawn and be of a reasonable, fixed size.

■ As N increases in size, the shape of the distribution of sample means quickly approaches normality. When an $N = 30$ observations or greater, a sampling distribution will take on the familiar, symmetric bell-shaped curve. Interestingly, if a population is normally distributed to begin with, then even small fixed size N samples (i.e., < 30) will create a normally shaped sampling distribution of means.

Law of Large Numbers Redux

The law of large numbers was introduced in Data Box 4.D in the context provided by variability and sample size. At that time, we simply noted that larger samples are apt to be more representative of their parent populations than are smaller samples. No doubt you now recognize the link between the central limit theorem and the law of large numbers, which can now be formally defined.

DATA BOX 9.A

The Law of Small Numbers Revisited

The law of large numbers and the central limit theorem are essential to hypothesis testing, but do not assume that their influence is assured in every circumstance. Keep an open mind as you read and then answer the following problem from Tversky and Kahneman (1971):

> The mean IQ of the population of eighth graders in a city is *known* to be 100. You have se-lected a random sample of 50 children for a study of educational achievements. The first child tested has an IQ of 150. What do you expect the mean IQ to be for the whole sample?

Given our previous experience with IQ and sampling issues, my guess is that most readers guessed that the mean IQ should still be 100. Although that guess is a good one, the actual average should be 101. Why? Well, despite the fact that the first child selected has an IQ of 150, the 49 remaining children are still anticipated to have an IQ of 100 each. To calculate the expected mean IQ score, we would have to determine the average of the total number of IQ points available. To do so, mul-tiply the 49 children $\times$ 100 points = 4,900 points, which is added to the 150 points we know about from the first child (i.e., 150 + 4,900 = 5,050). The mean of the available IQ scores would be based on dividing the 5,050 points by the 50 children, which is equal to 101. The expected IQ average of the class, then, is 101.

Why, then, do people say the average IQ for the above problem should be 100? Think about what you know about the normal distribution—it is symmetric on both sides of the mean of the distribution. Many readers who answer the IQ problem assume that the aberrantly high IQ score of 150 will necessarily be *balanced out* by a very low score (or group of scores) on the other side of the distribution so that the mean will remain 100. In other words, people erroneously assume that chance is self-correcting, but as you know from chapter 8, it is not! To paraphrase Tversky and Kahneman (1971), chance is not self-correcting but rather it is self-diluting; the effects of extreme or high scores are diluted by other scores that are closer to the mean (here, the IQ average of 100).

Samples, then, are not always representative. Remember that the law of large numbers simply states that the larger samples drawn from their parent populations will generally—*not absolutely*—be close to the true population average. Beware, then, the *law of small numbers* whereby people assume that that any random sample (a) *must* resemble all other random samples and that (b) any random sample *will* necessarily approximate the true population average. On av-erage, any random sample of sufficient size is expected to be representative of the parent popula-tion, but this expectation is easily violated by chance—a given sample may not be representative.

KEY TERM

The **law of large numbers** proposes that the larger the size of a sample (N), the greater the proba-bility that the sample mean ($\overline{X}$) will be close to the value of the population mean (μ).

▽

The $\overline{X}$ of a larger sample is more likely to approximate μ that the $\overline{X}$ of a smaller sample.

Why is the law of large numbers important? Precisely because it reminds us of the virtues behind and importance of obtaining an adequately sized sample. Anytime you conduct a piece of research or read a published summary, one of the first questions you should ask yourself is whether the sample size is adequate for the inferential task in-volved. In a more concrete way, think back to the David L. problem that was introduced in chapter 1. If you were looking at a college again or searching for an appropriate grad-uate or professional school, would you want to know the opinions of 2 students or 20 students? Without going to Herculean efforts or bothering too many passersbys on your campus visits, I think that you will agree that bigger samples are better samples when an inference is being made, especially because such samples are apt to more accurately re-flect the true values inherent in a population—or the opinions of the indigenous mem-bers of college and university communities!

Standard Error and Sampling Error in Depth

The standard error of the mean is the standard deviation of the distribution of sample means. In more practical terms, the standard error represents the typical or average distance between a sample mean ($\overline{X}$) and the mean of a population. The standard error is linked to sampling error—in fact, standard error can be used to both define and accurately measure sampling error.

In concrete terms, sampling error is the difference between a given sample mean and a population mean ($\overline{X} - \mu$), and this difference can be great or small. What causes the sampling error to be great or small? Really, any number of possible influences can lead a sample mean to deviate from the population mean. Unless proven to be otherwise, the events that affect sampling error are presumed to be random and unsystematic. Due to its random nature, then, sampling error can artificially increase or decrease the size of a particular sample mean when it is used to estimate μ. Similar to the distribution of sample means, the distribution of sample errors is also assumed to be normally distributed; theoretically, then, if we have a distribution of sufficient size, we could readily show that the $\sum (\overline{X} - \mu) = 0$. That is, the sum of the sampling errors—the positive as well as negative differences between sample means and a population mean—would be equal to 0. In theory, these random deviations would cancel one another out.

When sampling error is not random but, instead, systematic, then a real problem exists in the form of some intervening variable (or variables), one that is beyond the experimenter's control. Such uncontrolled factors disrupt the goal of identifying causality within a research context by undermining an adequate test of a hypothesis. Although these non-random factors exert a systematic influence, their origins, effects, and potential impact are often unknown—what *is* known is that they are antithetical to the process of making clean and clear inferences about which independent variable causes anticipated change in a dependent measure. For these reasons, then, researchers work to ensure that any research effort is free from sampling error that is caused by unknown, systematic factors.

Estimating the Standard Error of the Mean

Knowing the standard error of the mean provides a researcher with a very important advantage: the standard error indicates the how well a sample mean estimates the value of a population mean. A smaller standard error specifies a close match between a sample mean and a population mean, a larger error points to considerable disparity between the two indices. To determine standard error, we need to review what we previously learned about estimating population variance and standard deviation from known values of sample variance and standard deviation.

In chapter 4, we discussed the difference between biased and unbiased estimators of variance and standard deviation (see pages 162 to 165). In the course of our detailed review of variability, we learned that the standard formula for calculating sample variance, formula [4.11.1], routinely underestimates the population variance. Here it is, renumbered to reflect its placement in this chapter:

[9.3.1]
$$s^2 = \frac{\sum (X - \overline{X})^2}{N}.$$

We noted that this version of the sample variance formula is known as a biased estimator when used for any purpose besides describing sample data; when used as an estimate of the actual population variance, it falls short of the mark. It follows, then, that a standard deviation (formula [4.14.1]) based on taking the square root of s^2, too, would underestimate the standard deviation of the population, or:

[9.4.1] $$s = \sqrt{s^2} = \sqrt{\frac{\sum (X - \overline{X})^2}{N}}.$$

The solution to the problems posed by biased estimators was a simple one. Statisticians learned that a biased estimate can be corrected, that is, converted into an unbiased estimate by reducing the value of the denominator by one observation—in formula terms, N becomes $N-1$. The formulas for sample variance and standard deviation are easily recast into unbiased estimates that more closely approximate population values. The unbiased estimate of population variance (σ^2) can be determined by using formula [4.22.1], recast as:

[9.5.1] $$\sigma^2 = \hat{s}^2 = \frac{\sum (X - \overline{X})^2}{N - 1}.$$

As you will recall, the caret ($\wedge$) over s^2 indicates that the statistic is an unbiased estimate. The population's standard deviation (σ) can then be determined by formula [4.23.1], or:

[9.6.1] $$\sigma = \hat{s} = \sqrt{\hat{s}^2} = \sqrt{\frac{\sum (X - \overline{X})^2}{N - 1}}.$$

By relying on the formulas and logic behind these unbiased estimators, we can now approximate the variance of the population ($\sigma_{\overline{X}}^2$) as well as the standard error of the mean ($\sigma_{\overline{X}}$). To do so, of course, we need to rely on the estimated variance of the population ($s_{\overline{X}}^2$) and the estimated standard error of the mean ($s_{\overline{X}}$). Please note that although these symbols appear to be "new," you can readily interpret them by their content—the s^2 and the s indicate the use of sample data, and the subscript $\overline{X}$ refers to the sampling distribution of the mean. Given that we do not know the true values of σ^2 and σ, we must use estimates provided by $\hat{s}^2$ and $\hat{s}$, respectively.

The formula for estimating the variance of the sampling distribution of the mean from a set of sample data is:

[9.7.1] $$\text{Estimated } \sigma_{\overline{X}}^2 = s_{\overline{X}}^2 = \frac{\hat{s}^2}{N}.$$

It follows, then, that the standard error of the mean can be estimated by using:

[9.8.1] $$\text{Estimated } \sigma_{\overline{X}} = s_{\overline{X}} = \sqrt{\frac{\hat{s}^2}{N}} = \frac{\hat{s}}{\sqrt{N}}.$$

On occasion, of course, unbiased estimates of $\hat{s}^2$ and $\hat{s}$ may be unavailable. If so, the standard error of the mean can be estimated using the following formula, which corrects for the use of biased estimates:

[9.9.1] $$\text{Estimate } \sigma_{\overline{X}} = s_{\overline{X}} = \frac{s}{\sqrt{N - 1}} = \sqrt{\frac{\sum (X - \overline{X})^2}{N(N - 1)}} = \sqrt{\frac{SS}{N(N - 1)}}.$$

Given your prior experiences with their component parts, I very much hope that you feel that the preceding set of formulas is not difficult to follow. I also hope that you appreciate how interrelated each of the formula variations is with the others—by now, you should be able to see how one formula can be derived from (is related to) another. If you are feeling a bit overwhelmed at this moment, please take a break for a few minutes and then reread this section of the chapter. You must have a solid grasp of the theoretical nature and computational derivation of the standard error of the mean before proceeding to the next section.

Standard Error of the Mean: A Concrete Example Using Population Parameters

The utility of the standard error of the mean is the way it concretely demonstrates how much variability is apt to occur in a distribution of sample means. Keep in mind that the standard error of the mean is simply the standard deviation of the sample distribution of means that happens to be estimated by use of sample statistics. In practice, we will rely on $s_{\overline{X}}$ to estimate $\sigma_{\overline{X}}$.

Imagine for the present, however, that we know the parameters of some normally distributed population, say, one where $\mu = 50$ and $\sigma = 15$. Using these parameters, we can readily demonstrate why a smaller standard error is theoretically desirable and to a researcher's advantage. How so? We can show that sample size directly affects the sampling accuracy of the standard error of the mean. We learned earlier, for example, that the central limit theorem predicts that as sample sizes increase, the standard error of the mean should decrease.

The standard error of the mean can be determined from population information using this formula:

$$[9.10.1] \qquad \sigma_{\overline{X}} = \sqrt{\frac{\sigma^2}{N}} = \frac{\sigma}{\sqrt{N}}.$$

Because we know $\sigma = 15$ already, we can simply divide this value by the square root of N.

Let's begin with a sample size of one ($N = 1$) observation. Obviously, when we draw only one observation, the mean of this distribution of 1 will be that observation (i.e., $X = \overline{X}$). Put another way, when $N = 1$, the standard error for the distribution of sample means will be equal to the population's standard deviation. We can show this using the latter half of formula [9.10.1], or

$$[9.11.1] \qquad \sigma_{\overline{X}} = \frac{\sigma}{\sqrt{N}},$$

$$[9.11.2] \qquad \sigma_{\overline{X}} = \frac{15}{\sqrt{1}},$$

$$[9.11.3] \qquad \sigma_{\overline{X}} = 15.$$

As you can see, when $N = 1$, the standard error of the mean is identical to the population standard deviation.

As the sample size increases, however, we should see a smaller standard error. If we make $N = 20$, what happens to the value of $\sigma_{\overline{X}}$?

$$[9.12.1] \qquad \sigma_{\overline{X}} = \frac{15}{\sqrt{20}},$$

$$[9.12.2] \qquad \sigma_{\overline{X}} = \frac{15}{4.47},$$

$$[9.12.3] \qquad \sigma_{\overline{X}} = 3.36.$$

Clearly, the expected standard error of the mean for a sample size of 20 is much smaller than that for $N = 1$. What if we make $N = 100$?

$$[9.13.1] \qquad \sigma_{\overline{X}} = \frac{15}{\sqrt{100}},$$

$$[9.13.2] \qquad \sigma_{\overline{X}} = \frac{15}{10},$$

$$[9.13.3] \qquad \sigma_{\overline{X}} = 1.5.$$

Thus, when a sample size increases to 100 observations, the standard error of the mean can be expected to drop substantially to only 1.5 standard error units. In other words, the width of the bell-shaped curve narrows when sample size rises, thereby confirming the central limit theorem and the law of large numbers, as well as demonstrating the usefulness of the standard error concept. As N increases, then, the error between a given $\overline{X}$ and μ readily decreases, so that the standard error of the mean serves as an index of how well a sample mean represents or stands in for a μ.

▽

As N increases, the measurement error between the $\overline{X}$ and μ decreases.

Defining Confidence Intervals Using the Standard Error of the Mean

We can now return to a practical application of the standard error of the mean, one dependent on the estimated standard error of the mean, or $s_{\overline{X}}$. Once we know one sample mean, can we predict how similar the *next* sample mean will be to it? Many times, researchers want to establish a range of values where they can be relatively certain that sample means will fall. Statisticians call this range of values a *confidence interval*.

A **confidence interval** contains a range of values wherein subsequent samples drawn from a population are likely to fall.

For example, the likelihood that a subsequent sample mean will fall within a particular range can be estimated in terms of some specific probability.

A researcher draws a sample of 75 participants from a population. The sample's mean is 65 and the unbiased estimate of its standard deviation is 4.5. The first thing we do is calculate the standard error of the mean, which is:

[9.14.1]
$$s_{\overline{X}} = \frac{\hat{s}}{\sqrt{N}}.$$

We then enter the standard deviation and the N of 75 for:

[9.14.2]
$$s_{\overline{X}} = \frac{4.5}{\sqrt{75}},$$

[9.14.3]
$$s_{\overline{X}} = \frac{4.5}{8.66},$$

[9.14.4]
$$s_{\overline{X}} = .52.$$

Using this value for the standard error of the mean, a confidence interval for the mean can be created. To begin the next step, we remember that the sampling distribution for the mean is normally distributed. As a result, we can use standard or z scores to create a confidence interval. Do you remember that back in chapter 5 we examined the percentage of the area under the normal curve that fell within standard deviation units around the mean of 0 of the z distribution? Figure 5.4 on page 188 illustrates the areas between the standard deviation intervals along the z distribution. You will remember, for example, that approximately 68% of the area under the curve falls between ± 1.0 standard deviation units around the mean.

The formula for calculating the confidence around the mean is:

[9.15.1]
$$\text{confidence interval}_{\overline{X}} = \overline{X} \pm z_{\text{CI}}\left(\frac{\hat{s}}{\sqrt{N}}\right) = \overline{X} \pm z_{\text{CI}}(s_{\overline{X}}).$$

A z score representing some area (in percent) under the normal curve is multiplied by the value of the standard error of the mean, the product of which is then added to and subtracted from the mean of the sample. This process of adding and subtracting the same product from the known sample mean outlines the confidence interval.

DATA BOX 9.B

Standard Error as an Index of Stability and Reliability of Means

Gravetter and Wallnau (1996) highlight standard error as a measure of stability and reliability, two important ways this statistic can be used in research in the behavioral sciences.

Standard error as stability. Back in chapter 4, we learned that one of the properties of the mean as a measure of central tendency is its sensitivity, especially when a distribution of scores is small and an extreme score is introduced. In general, when a new score is added to an existing array, the mean of the array will change somewhat unless the array is quite large. It turns out that the standard error behaves in a synonymous manner. When a standard error is small, the introduction of any new observation into the population—say, you add another respondent to the group being surveyed—then the value of the $\overline{X}$ on the measure of interest is not apt to change much. That is, a small standard error indicates that the sample mean is a stable one. A larger standard error score, however, suggests that the introduction of any new observation can have a decided effect on the sample mean precisely because it is not stable. In short, then, the standard error can also serve as a very useful guide to judging the degree to which a sample mean is apt to change in value if new data are introduced or existing data are removed.

How would the law of large numbers factor into the stability question? As you might guess, larger samples are more likely to display smaller and more stable standard errors. Thus, adding a data point or two to sample with 600 observations is not going to make much difference, whereas the addition or subtraction of some observations from a sample comprised of 20 data points could matter a great deal

Standard error as reliability. Reliability refers to the consistency of measure across some period of time. Thus, does an individual's score on a personality measure at time 1 predict or correspond to his or her score at time 2? A high, positive correlation between two sets of scores on the same measure is usually taken to be a sufficient indicator of a measure's reliability (see chapter 6). In a similar way, the standard error can be treated as a measure of a sample mean's reliability. Think about it: If the means repeatedly drawn from some population are very close to one another in value, then they appear to provide a reliable measure of the population and its μ. More to the point, of course, is the fact that the standard error corresponding to all of these similar means would of necessity be very small. Thus, a small standard error would indicate a high degree of reliability where the similarity of means is concerned. By the same token, a larger standard error would suggest a lower degree of reliability (i.e., the sample means are relatively dissimilar from one another in value).

How do we determine the appropriate z score to use? Turn to Table B.2 in Appendix B and locate $z = 1.00$. As you can see, the entry in column B corresponding to this z score is .3413, indicating that approximately 34% of the area under the curve falls between the mean of 0 and the first standard deviation. If we take into account the same percentage area falling below the mean (i.e., $z = -1.0$), then we have accounted for the aforementioned 68% of the area under the curve. To define the confidence interval for the mean, all that remains is to enter the z score of ± 1.0, the $s_{\overline{X}}$, and the sample's mean into [9.15.1], or:

[9.15.2]   confidence interval$_{\overline{X}}$ = 65 $\pm$ 1.00 (.52).

Thus, the lower boundary of the confidence interval is:

[9.15.3]   confidence interval$_{\overline{X}}$ = 65 $-$ .52 = 64.48,

and the upper boundary is:

[9.15.4]   confidence interval$_{\overline{X}}$ = 65 $+$ .52 = 65.52.

The 68% confidence interval for the mean is between 64.48 and 65.52. The width of this confidence interval should make intuitive sense to you, as it represents where the bulk of the sample means should fall—within 1 standard deviation on either side of the mean.

In general, researchers tend to rely on confidence intervals that capture a greater amount of area under the curve than just 1 standard deviation unit on either side of the mean. It is common, for example, to see 95% and 99% confidence intervals cited in the research literature. Using the hypothetical sample data here, we can determine the confidence intervals for these more frequently used ranges for the mean. The z scores corresponding to 95% and 99% of the area under the curve can be found in Table B.2, and they are 1.96 and 2.58, respectively. I encourage you to examine the area between the mean and z for each of these z scores (see their column B entries in Table B.2), remembering to double the value to take into account the symmetric nature of the normal distribution.

Using [9.15.1], the 95% confidence interval for a mean of 65 and an $s_{\bar{X}}$ of .52 is:

[9.16.1] $$\text{confidence interval}_{\bar{X}} = 65 \pm 1.96\,(.52),$$

which yields a confidence interval ranging between 63.98 and 66.02. The 99% confidence interval, then, is based on:

[9.17.1] $$\text{confidence interval}_{\bar{X}} = 65 \pm 2.58\,(.52),$$

resulting in confidence interval boundaries of 63.66 and 66.34.

We must keep in mind what information a confidence interval does and does not supply. A confidence interval defines only an interval where the population mean is believed to fall, but it does not specify the likelihood that the mean we have is the correct one. Confidence intervals like the ones we have just identified are often misinterpreted—and misrepresented—to mean that an investigator can be, say, 95% confident that the population mean is 65. This is an incorrect statement—please read it one more time so that you will remember that confidence intervals do *not* specify the accuracy of observed means.

Neither do confidence intervals suggest that the likelihood a population mean falls within a specified interval is .68, .95, .99, or whatever probability you choose. Why not? Keep in mind that population parameters are unknown constants; sample data we use to create confidence intervals for them will vary from sample to sample, and from sample size to sample size. We should anticipate that the accompanying sample statistics, too, will vary substantially, implying that our confidence interval estimates will vary, as well. What, then, does a confidence interval establish? A confidence interval means that if repeated samples of a given size are drawn from a population, then 95% or 99% of the confidence interval estimates will include the population mean. In a sense, we know where the population mean is apt to be much of the time, but we still do not know its true value.

Knowledge Base

1. Assuming that a fixed sample size is sufficiently large, what will the shape of a sampling distribution of means be like?
2. How do sampling distributions differ from the distributions we have previously studied in this book?
3. What is the law of large numbers? How does it relate to the central limit theorem?
4. What are the mean and the standard deviation of a sampling distribution called?
5. You have a population with $\mu = 82$ and $\hat{s} = 5.0$, and you have 100 observations. What is the $s_{\bar{X}}$? What is the 95% confidence interval for the mean?

Answers

1. Normal; it will appear to be a bell-shaped curve.
2. Sampling distributions are made up of statistics (e.g., means), whereas the other distributions we have reviewed contain raw scores or observations.

DATA BOX 9.C

Representing Standard Error Graphically

The reporting of standard errors of the mean is by no means standardized in the behavioral sciences. Some disciplines report standard errors with greater regularity than others do. Within the discipline of psychology, for example, the subfield often referred to as psychobiology—the direct or indirect examination of physiological systems underlying human and animal behavior—relies on standard error a great deal. Besides simply reporting standard error values, however, psychobiologists often represent them graphically through what are commonly referred to as "error bars." You should learn to recognize these error bars so that when you read within various behavioral science literatures, you will be able to recognize when the standard error of the mean is being highlighted in a data display. We will consider illustrative two figures from a piece of research in psychobiology.

Stewart and Brunjes (1990) examined growth-related changes in the olfactory (i.e., sense of smell) system of the goldfish. Different areas of the brain are composed of different types of neurons. Some neurons process information locally whereas others send information to other distant brain regions. Stewart and Brunjes were interested in how developmental timing affects olfactory structures (i.e., the fish's olfactory bulb, the part of the fish brain that receives and interprets odor information). Figures A and B contain different representations of error bars showing the standard error of the mean for data gleaned from the olfactory bulbs of goldfish at various developmental stages.

The goldfish olfactory bulb is a three-layered (or "laminated") structure, divided into an olfactory nerve layer (ONL), a cell-sparse glomerular layer (GL), and an inner granule cell region (GR). The layering inherent in this brain region makes it possible for psychobiologists to see where different types of neural processing occur. Figure A (see immediately below), a histogram, shows the mean laminar volumes—layers of cells—in the olfactory bulb of small, medium, and large goldfish. In this example, the standard error bars are incorporated right into the figure's bars (S.E.M. is "standard error of the mean"). Note that the top of each bar represents a mean level of cell volume, so that the standard error extending above each one appears to be a "T." The inverted "T" inside and below the mean level of each bar indicates the standard error below the mean.

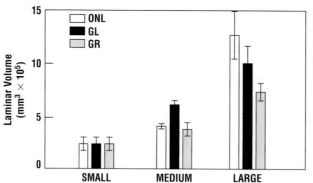

Figure A   Mean laminar volumes of the 3 individual layers of the olfactory bulb for small, medium, and large fish (bars represent ± 1 S.E.M.).

A second style of standard error representation is shown in Figure B. Each dot represents a fish's average granule cell density, and the "Ts" rising above and below the dot are the standard error around the mean. Granule cells—so-called due to their granular appearance—process local information in the brain. Stewart and Brunjes (1990) were interested in seeing how the size and stage of development of the goldfish would influence the development of the olfactory bulb's granule cell population.

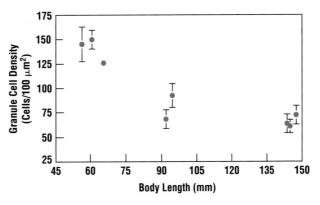

Figure B Changes in olfactory bulb granule cell density with increasing fish size. Plot of granule cell density (each point represents one animal's average score) vs fish body length (bars represent ±1 S.E.M.).

3. The law of large numbers posits that larger sample sizes increase the chance that a sample mean ($\overline{X}$) will approximate μ. In part, the central limit theorem proposes that the mean of a sampling distribution based on a large, fixed size N will be equal to μ.

4. The expected value and the standard error.

5. $s_{\overline{X}} = .50$; confidence interval ranges between 81.02 and 82.98.

Asking and Testing Focused Questions: Conceptual Rationale for Hypotheses

It is the first duty of a hypothesis to be intelligible.

——Thomas Henry Huxley (1825–1895)

When behavioral scientists conduct research, they formulate hypotheses or testable questions. Hypotheses can be divided into two types, one focusing on conceptual or theoretical matters, the other emphasizing statistical matters. You are already familiar with conceptual hypotheses, especially if you are a veteran of a course in research methodology. A conceptual hypothesis outlines the predicted relationship between the independent variable and dependent measure of interest. To be sure, it represents the scientific statement of some problem or question, and it can contain abstract or operational elements (for a review, see chapter 2).

We might be interested in a hypothetical construct called environmental sensitivity, the extent to which people notice aspects of their immediate surroundings. In particular, we embark on research concerning what search strategies people use to navigate their environments. As a starting point, we develop an abstract statement regarding the adaptive nature of environmental sensitivity, defining it as the tendency to readily recognize change in the immediate environment. In operational terms, we define environmental sensitivity as recognizing particular changes in the placement of objects in a cluttered room. Operationally defining the dependent measure could entail the number of correctly identified changes from time 1 (seeing a display of objects during a learning phase) to time 2 (recognizing changes made to the original display). As for an independent variable, we could manipulate the amount of clutter (number of distinct objects) present in the room, so that participants encounter either a relatively large or small display of objects. The number of absolute changes in object placement made after initial exposure would be the same for both participant groups. Participants exposed to the small objects display could be designated the control group, while those encountering the larger display would constitute the experimental condition.

DATA BOX 9.D

What Constitutes a Good Hypothesis?

Whether you are developing a hypothesis for your own research or evaluating one that already appears in the behavioral science literature, it should satisfy the following list of criteria (adapted from Dunn, 1999). A good hypothesis:

1. *Is a clear statement, not a question.* Despite the fact that a hypothesis is a testable question, it should appear as a declarative statement (e.g., crowded environments promote aggressive behavior).

2. *Identifies specific relationships between or among variables.* In general, some independent variable (e.g., the presence or absence of crowded conditions) should be expected to create an observable change in some dependent measure (e.g., physically or verbally aggressive behavior directed from one person to another).

3. *Is theory-based or somehow linked to existing knowledge.* There are few new psychological ideas under the sun. Chances are that some literature exists pertaining to a hypothesis or at least the general area it touches on (e.g., there are extensive literatures on human as well as animal aggression).

4. *Is concise and to the point.* Less is more (or at least less is better). Most hypotheses should be no more than one or perhaps two clear sentences in length. Supporting details should be saved for the theory underlying a hypothesis (see points 1 and 3 above).

5. *Can be tested.* The variables within a hypothesis should be operationalized with relative ease and, as a declarative statement, the hypothesis should lend itself to empirical examination in an experiment, quasi-experiment, observational study, or other form of investigation (see point 2).

6. *Is readily understood by others.* People interested in the behavioral sciences—researchers, scholars, teachers, students, and outside observers—should be able to interpret a hypothesis with little difficulty. Some hypotheses will be more technical than others will, but an ideal hypothesis expresses an empirical relationship that can be understood by educated persons.

We now turn to the *statistical hypothesis*, which concerns quantifying the relationship between the variables involved in the conceptual and operational hypotheses.

KEY TERM   A **statistical hypothesis** represents the mathematical relationship presumed to exist between two or more population parameters.

We might specify, for example, that the group of participants exposed to the small display of objects would notice more changes (i.e., make fewer recall errors) than those presented with the larger object display. Thus, the statistical hypothesis highlights the mathematical relationship presumed to exist between the two groups—exposure to a small array of objects leads to a higher number of correctly recognized changes than exposure to a larger array of objects.

Statistical hypotheses are usually represented in symbolic as well as written form. Thus, the average number of correctly recognized changes for the control group (μ_c) is anticipated to be higher than the changes noted by the experimental group (μ_e), or $\mu_c > \mu_e$. Why are we using μ to designate population means? Precisely because we anticipate that changes observed in the respective groups of research participants (who were randomly assigned to one or the other condition) are representative of changes in population parameters. Indeed, the symbolic use of population means reminds us that the results of one experiment are meant to generalize beyond the original participant sample to the larger population of participants, extant as well as potential.

Directional and Nondirectional Hypotheses

The hypothesized mathematical relations existing between the population parameters identified in any statistical hypothesis can be one of two types, *directional* or *nondirectional*. The prediction from our hypothetical study on environmental sensitivity is directional because the control group is anticipated to identify a higher number of perceived changes than the experimental group.

KEY TERM   A **directional hypothesis** specifies the exact nature or direction of the relationship between population parameters.

When using a control group and an experimental group, a directional hypothesis will be either $\mu_c > \mu_e$ or $\mu_c < \mu_e$. Most of the hypotheses that behavioral scientists entertain and investigate are directional. Before conducting any actual research, most investigators have a strong sense of what relationship between the manipulated and measured variables is specified by a theory. Note that the explicit use of the "greater than" ($>$) or "less than" ($<$) sign provides the directionality in any hypothesis. Naturally, the mathematical signs representing "less than or equal to" ($\leq$) and "greater than or equal to" ($\geq$) can also be used to represent relationships in, as well as to test, directional hypotheses.

In contrast, a nondirectional hypothesis does not specify the direction of a difference, merely that *some* difference will exist between two population parameters. If we employed a nondirectional hypothesis in the environmental sensitivity study, we would simply note that there would be a difference in the number of changes noted by the control group versus the experimental group. We would not, however, speculate about which group would have a higher recall rate.

KEY TERM   A **nondirectional hypothesis** anticipates a difference will exist between population parameters but does not specify the nature, or direction, of that difference.

Researchers elect to use nondirectional hypotheses when they are uncertain or unwilling to characterize the difference between the population means, often when the relevant research is novel or the investigator is new to the area of inquiry. Symbolically, a nondirectional hypothesis can be represented as $\mu_c \neq \mu_e$, but the representative magnitudes of the population means are not specified by this relationship—all we know is that a difference should exist between them. The "not equal to" ($\neq$) sign reminds us that either population could be larger than the other one.

The Null and the Experimental Hypothesis

Philosophers, logicians, scientists, and statisticians generally agree that empirical statements can never be proved to be true, but they can be demonstrated to be false. A simple example will suffice to illustrate this important touchstone of hypothesis testing. Consider this declarative statement: All dogs bark. Do all dogs—that is, does *every* dog—bark? Well, in *your* experience perhaps all dogs bark, but you have not met every dog, nor is it possible for you to do so. Think beyond the present time, too, because the supposition that "all dogs bark" necessarily implicates all dead as well as living dogs, as well as those yet to be.

Is it possible, then, to prove the statement "all dogs bark" to be true in a literal sense? Not at all. And you need only encounter one counterexample—a nonbarking dog—to render it a false statement. Therein lies the empirical rub, as it were. It is clearly much easier to prove a statement to be false than to ever determine it to be true. This realization guides virtually all the empirical research in the behavioral sciences, as well as that performed in the natural sciences.

The process of formulating and testing hypotheses, then, becomes one of systematically disproving or falsifying hypotheses. Under these conditions, a theory about behavior is never regarded as ultimately true but merely a useful, even reliable guide until it is proven to be false, at which time another, better account replaces it. This process then repeats itself virtually endlessly (a variation of this theme was introduced as the research loop of experimentation in chapter 2). How, then, do we go about the business of creating, testing, and falsifying hypotheses?

When testing any hypothesis, researchers actually develop two competing hypotheses and effectively pit one against the other. These hypotheses are typically labeled the *null hypothesis* (H_0) and the *alternative hypothesis* (H_1). In experimental terms, the null hypothesis specifies that an independent variable does not have any effect on a dependent measure. In the parlance of statistics, the population mean of one group (e.g., the control group) is the same as the population mean of the other group (e.g., the experimental or "research" group)—indeed, these groups are said to behave the same or in very similar ways. In other words, the groups share the same population mean because they are from—and remain a part of—the same population because the treatment or intervention represented by the different levels of the independent variable had no effect.

KEY TERM The **null hypothesis** traditionally indicates all the population parameters in an experiment, which are represented by sample statistics, are equal. The *null hypothesis* predicts that a given independent variable or other intervention will *not* cause a change in some dependent measure. The *null hypothesis* is symbolically presented as H_0.

The null hypothesis (H_0 is pronounced "H-oh" or sometimes "H-naught") of the environmental sensitivity study would be that there would be no difference between the average number of changes recalled by the control group and the experimental group, or:

$$H_0: \text{as } \mu_c = \mu_e.$$

For heuristic reasons, the null hypothesis is sometime referred to as "the hypothesis of no difference," highlighting the fact that it usually posits than no discernable differences exist between means at the level of the samples tested or from which population(s) they hail.

The alternative hypothesis (H_1 is pronounced "H-one"), sometimes called the experimental hypothesis, is the idea actually being examined or tested by a piece of research. The alternative hypothesis embodies the researcher's expectation of what will happen when an independent variable is manipulated and a dependent measure is measured.

KEY TERM The **alternative** or **experimental hypothesis** specifies that a difference exists between the population parameters identified by the null hypothesis. The *alternative hypothesis* predicts that a given independent variable or other intervention will cause a change in some dependent measure. The *alternative hypothesis* is symbolically presented as H_1.

We already specified the alternative hypothesis of the environmental sensitivity study earlier, but it merits mention once more. The control group—those exposed to the small array of objects—should identify a higher number of perceived changes than the experimental group, which was confronted with a relatively larger number of objects, or:

$$H_1: \mu_c > \mu_e.$$

The projected results of any experiment are compared to the results anticipated by its null hypothesis. In other words, the experimental results (e.g., a verified difference between sample means) are used to demonstrate that the null hypothesis is false—the groups specified by the null hypothesis are in fact *not* equal to one another. When the hypothesized relationship is found in the analysis of an experiment's data, statisticians say that we can *reject the null hypothesis as false and accept the alternative hypothesis as an adequate explanation for the time being*. Please note that we specifically did not say that the alternative hypothesis was *true*—remember we can disprove a statement (i.e., render it false) but we cannot prove a statement (i.e., declare it to necessarily be true and accurate). When the hypothesized relationship (H_1) is *not* found in the course of the data analysis, statisticians say that we can *accept or retain the null hypothesis*. Here again, we do not say that we are rejecting the alternative hypothesis (though, in effect, we are) because the null hypothesis represents the touchstone for hypothesis testing—every statistical conclusion is understood in terms of the null hypothesis.

⊽

Any statistical conclusion is based exclusively on the null hypothesis, which is either accepted or rejected.

When we accept the null hypothesis, however, please do not assume that the sample means representing the control and the experimental groups are *literally* equal in value to one another (see Table 9.1). There will always be some degree of observable sampling error, and such superficial differences between these means are readily attributable to random influences. At the level of the population parameters, of course, the population means represented by the samples means are equal to one another because we are concluding that the two groups come from the same population. We retain or accept the null hypothesis to show that the independent variable did not achieve its intended or desired effect on the dependent measure. Moreover, our statistical analysis does not literally demonstrate that $\mu_c = \mu_e$ is absolutely true, rather the research is unable to show that it is *not* true in the present situation (see Table 9.1).

What about the statistical import of the alternative hypothesis? We know that by showing the null hypothesis to be an incorrect account in this instance, the observed sample means are different from one another due to the affect of the independent variable. More to the point, by rejecting the null hypothesis we are claiming that the population mean of the control group (μ_c) is not equivalent to that of the experimental group (μ_e)—the behavior observed in one sample is from a different population than the behavior exhibited by the other sample. The statistical difference portrayed by the rejection of the null hypothesis is one where the observed difference between two sample means

Table 9.1   What Are We Doing When We *Accept* the Null Hypothesis?

Accepting the null hypothesis (H_0)—the hypothesis of no difference—is *not necessarily* and *not always* the same thing as declaring it to be *true*. Here are some reasons that the null hypothesis is not rejected:

1. The null hypothesis is actually true (i.e., no mean difference exists) and therefore it should *not* be rejected.

   But it is also possible that:

2. The null hypothesis is actually false (i.e., a mean difference actually exists) and therefore it should be rejected, however, the obtained sample of participants is not representative of the true population. A biased sample, then, leads to the acceptance of the null hypothesis.

   Or:

3. The null hypothesis is actually false (i.e., a mean difference actually exists) and therefore it should be rejected, however, the experimental methodology is insufficient to detect the true situation (i.e., the mean difference). Experimental methodology can fail to detect differences because the manipulation of the independent variable is weak, the dependent measure is insensitive, randomization is flawed or absent, the sample size is too small, an unknown but influential "third variable" is present, and so on.

Thus, the null hypothesis is *accepted as an appropriate conclusion* until more data are collected, a new experiment(s) is performed, experimental methodology is improved—whatever additional information can be gathered to execute another test of the alternative hypothesis (H_1) or some other alternative hypothesis.

Source: Adapted from Kirk (1999, pp. 303–304).

is too great to be due to chance alone, an issue we will discuss in detail shortly. Some systematic influence—presumably the hypothesized effect represented by the independent variable—is the cause and the sample means are described in statistical terms as being *significantly different* from one another.

Statistical Significance: A Concrete Account

How can two means be "significantly different" from one another? What is statistical significance? A difference between means is described as being statistically significant—one mean is larger in value than another—when only a very low probability exists that the results are due to random error rather than the systematic influence of an independent variable. Although significance is examined locally, at the level of sample means, the inferential process involves making judgments about population parameters. A **significant difference** between group averages, for example, is unlikely to occur when population means are actually equal to one another. Any significant difference, then, suggests that each sample mean represents a distinct and different population. Inferential statistics rely heavily on this form of *significance testing*.

KEY TERM   **Significance testing** entails using statistical tests and probabilities to determine whether sample data can be used to accept or reject a null hypothesis involving population parameters.

In practical terms, when a test statistic is said to be significant, a mathematical difference—say, one mean is larger in magnitude than another—is observed to occur between the two (or more) groups within an experiment (i.e., the sample means represent different populations with different parameters). If a difference is in the predicted direction, then it is attributed to the independent variable and the null hypothesis of no difference is rejected. When a test statistic is not significant, then no mathematical difference exists between the means of the two groups—both are similar in magnitude (i.e., they presumably represent the same population and its parameters). Lack of a significant difference promotes retention of the null hypothesis. We will learn how to assess significance using particular test statistics later in this chapter as well as in four subsequent chapters in this book.

Regrettably, the word significance has a great deal of conceptually confusing baggage attached to it. In everyday language, the word "significant" is used as a synonym for "important," "meaningful," "notable," or even "consequential." In the context provided by statistics and data analysis, however, the word means something quite different, and it possesses much narrower, even modest, applications. It refers to whether a result is *statistically reliable*, one that is sufficiently trustworthy so that an investigator can *reasonably reject the null hypothesis*. Wright (1997) sagely observes that researchers would be better served if the word *detected* were used in place of the word significant. For example, did some inferential statistical test detect a difference between groups? The word "detect" is certainly a less confusing choice, and it does not imply whether a difference is great or small—merely that the difference exists. In contrast, the word significant raises expectations in the minds of naïve readers and novice data analysts—they erroneously assume that a difference is big, powerful, and sometimes even dramatic.

Significance is directly related to probability or *p* values, which were briefly introduced at the end of chapter 8. In statistical jargon, probability values are often referred to as **significance levels** or *levels of significance* because they indicate the degree to which an observed difference between sample means is a reliable one. An alternative term that is frequently used to denote a *p* value or a significance level is **alpha level,** which is symbolized by the Greek letter α. (Although these three terms are largely interchangeable,

▽

Statistical significance is *not* synonymous with scientific importance or the strength or size of a result. A significant result is one that is reliable and detectable through statistical means.

DATA BOX 9.E

Distinguishing Between Statistical and Practical Significance

"Significant" results are reported in journals as though they are important, although to whom and why are left to the reader's imagination. Let us replace the term *significance* with the more accurate term *reliability* immediately!

—— SCARR (1997, p. 17; EMPHASIS ADDED)

Scarr's point is well taken. Whenever you evaluate the results of a statistical test, one you perform or one you read, ask yourself whether any obtained differences should be considered to be reliable differences. In a related way, you should also remind yourself about the valuable distinction between statistical significance and practical significance, a distinction that many users of statistics all too easily forget.

Statistical significance refers to whether a test detected a reliable difference between two (or more) groups, one caused by the effect of an independent variable on a dependent measure. Keep in mind that significance testing deals only with the analysis of measures according to the groupings dictated by the hypothesis—it has absolutely nothing to do with whether the theory underlying the hypothesis is reasonable, tenable, absurd, or clever. Indeed, significance tests are mute where theory is concerned—they only deal with the numbers based on samples, which in turn reflect the relationships that are present or absent in their populations of origin.

In contrast, the *practical significance* of results refer to what they mean in the context of theory. Practical significance also addresses the implication of results for the understanding of behavior. Does a result disclose something new and dramatic about why people or animals behave the way they do? Does it tell us what we already knew to be true? Or, in the worst of cases, does it reveal something that is in the "big picture" of behavior, rather trivial? Sad but true—one can observe a significant statistical result that is ultimately not terribly meaningful, a point that should reinforce for you the distinction between statistical and practical significance (e.g., Abelson, 1995).

α-levels are often discussed in connection with inferential errors, a matter we will take up at the end of this chapter.)

At the conclusion of chapter 8, two of the more conventional p values or levels of significance were introduced—.05 and .01. When a test statistic is said to be significant at the .05 level, for example, the likelihood that the difference it detected is due to chance (i.e., random error) is less than 1 in 20. In other words, if the experiment were repeated 100 times, we would expect to observe the same results *by chance*—not due to the effect an independent variable exerts on a dependent measure—5 time or less. Indeed, when reporting the differences detected by test statistics, no difference is deemed to be a reliable one unless it reaches (or is still lower than) this conventional 5 percent mark or, in statistical terms, the .05 ("point oh-five") level of significance.

If a researcher or data analyst chooses to use a more stringent requirement for detecting a statistically significant difference, then a result could be deemed acceptable or reliable ("significant") only when it was apt to be due to chance once in 100 trials, the 1 percent or .01 level of significance. Some investigators rely on the even more demanding p value of .001, which indicates that there over 1,000 trials, there is only 1 chance of obtaining a predicted difference when the null hypothesis is actually true.

Most behavioral scientists choose to use the .05 level of significance as the minimum acceptable level of significance and, in fact, a p value is invariably reported with any test statistic. These p values are commonly reported as $p < .05$ ("pee less than point oh-five"), $p < .01$ ("pee less than point oh-one"), and $p < .001$ ("pee less than point oh-oh-one"). In truth, of course, it is actually possible to determine a precise p value

▽

The terms p value, significance level, level of significance, and alpha (α) level are generally interchangeable. They all refer to some predetermined probability level (e.g., .05, .01, .001) used to assess the null hypothesis.

corresponding to any test statistic (e.g., $p = .026$)—many statistical software packages provide such information routinely—but the convention is to report the p value to the nearest conventional level (i.e., .026 is less than .05, yet still greater than .01—the observed relationship is reliably less than the required cutoff for significance—but .05 is reported).

Please understand, however, that the .05 level is an arbitrary cutoff point. What happens if a result is determined to be significant at the .06 level? Well, practically speaking we know that the probability of obtaining the same result due to chance will occur 6 or fewer times across 100 trials. Is the .06 level of significance really *so* different than .05? No, of course not, but 6 times is one more time than 5, which is—among statisticians, and behavioral as well as natural scientists—the generally agreed upon cutoff point. In fact, any result where $p > .05$ (watch that "greater than" sign) is technically described as *not* statistically significant. A related convention, though, is to describe any results falling between the .06 and .10 levels of significance as "marginal," meaning that though they are suggestive (i.e., interesting but potentially unreliable because the .05 boundary is exceeded), they should be interpreted and used with caution in written results or further theorizing and research.

Any result where is $p > .10$ is said to be "nonsignificant"—.10 is beyond the statistical pale—because an investigator cannot be sure that the independent variable had any effect at all on the dependent measure employed in the research. Harris (1998) constructively notes that any researcher could choose another minimum significance level besides $p < .05$, such as $p < .14$, for example. Deviations from this conventional cutoff rarely occur, however, presumably because researchers would not want to appear capricious rather than careful; they fear conveying the impression that their statistical decisions and inferences were in any way subjective. One argument for using a more liberal p value like .14 is that when few facts are known about a research area, investigators could hedge their empirical bets, as it were, by not overlooking any potential relations in a data set (Harris, 1998). More traditional (i.e., conventional) p values could be used in future studies as the observed effects were understood better and made more predictable as a research program grows and develops.

Let's conclude this section by highlighting an important characteristic of any inferential statistical result and its link to significance testing: Either it *is* significant in the statistical sense or it is *not* significant. In other words, investigators detect a difference (between two or more means) and reject the null hypothesis, or no difference is detected and the null hypothesis is retained. When performing significance testing, researchers are limited to these two choices and only these two choices. Please note that a statistical test is never "insignificant" (a word meaning petty, trifling, or minor), "almost significant" (close to but not quite at the magical level of .05—try "marginal" instead), or "highly significant" (the result exceeds expectations, and even the extreme .001 significance level)—it is merely significant or not significant. Nor should we characterize our results as "wildly significant," "unbelievably significant" or, at the other end of the spectrum, "depressingly insignificant" (Dunn, 1999). Why? Because our goal as data analysts and researchers is to focus on whether a reliable relationship was (or was not) detected between samples representing one or possibly more populations.

A result *is* or *is not* significant; that is, a reliable difference exists or it does not exist.

Critical Values: Establishing Criteria for Rejecting the Null Hypothesis

The process of determining whether the result of a statistical test is significant involves comparing its calculated value to the value of a pre-established cutoff. These cutoff values are called *critical values*. When compared with a critical value, the magnitude of a test statistic determines the presence or absence of a significant difference.

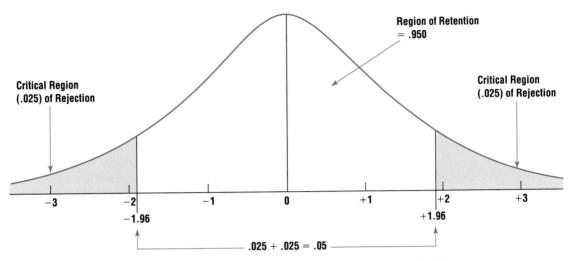

Figure 9.3   Two-Tailed Critical Values and Critical Regions of a *z* Distribution

KEY TERM   A **critical value** is a numerical value that is compared to the value of a calculated test statistic. When a test statistic is less than a *critical value,* the null hypothesis is accepted or retained. When a test statistic is equal to or higher than a *critical value,* then the null hypothesis is rejected.

A critical value is the minimum value that a calculated test statistic must match or exceed in order for a statistically significant difference to be realized. Critical values are usually organized into a table of values wherein statistical significance is indicated for any given sample size (Appendix B contains several examples we will use shortly and in later chapters). Naturally, these critical values correspond to one of the conventional significance levels, such as .05, .01, or .001, used to test hypotheses.

Figure 9.3 portrays the graph of a sampling distribution similar to those discussed previously. This version of the standard or *z* distribution highlights two critical values that serve as cutoff points for regions of the distribution where statistically significant and statistically nonsignificant results are found. The *z* values of -1.96 and $+1.96$ correspond to the .05 significance level because each one "cuts off" .025 of the scores at either end of the distribution (i.e., .025 + .025 = .05). Why is this so? Turn to Table B.2 in Appendix B and locate the entry for a *z* score of 1.96. Now check the value found in column C, to the right of where $z = 1.96$ is located. As you will remember, column C represents the area under the curve that is beyond *z,* and here it turns out to be equal to .0250. Because the *z* distribution is symmetric, we can account for both -1.96 and $+1.96$—hence, we add the probabilities associated with the areas beyond each *z* and achieve .05 (see Figure 9.3).

The region of the sampling distribution lying at and beyond these two *z* scores is referred to as the **critical region** or sometimes the **region of rejection.** This region or, if you prefer, either region, is one leading to the rejection of the null hypothesis. When the value of a test statistic is equal to or greater than $+1.96$ (or less than or equal to -1.96 in the case of a test statistic with a negative value), the null hypothesis of difference is rejected. Thus, for example, if an observed statistic were $z = +2.21$ (or -2.21), then the null hypothesis could be rejected because these values fall into the rejection regions (see Figure 9.3). Any critical region contains relatively rare or extreme values that are not likely to be found when a null hypothesis is true, thus, any test statistic falling inside a critical region is sufficient grounds to reject a null hypothesis.

A critical value is a cutoff, a guide to whether a test statistic is or is not significant.

When a test statistic is found to have a value less than $+1.96$ (or greater than -1.96), then the null hypothesis is accepted. Retention of the null hypothesis occurs because the test statistic falls into the **region of retention** (see Figure 9.3) or, in other words, it neither reaches nor exceeds the required critical value. A z score of $+1.34$ (or -1.34) would fall into the region of retention, so that the alternative hypothesis it represented would be found wanting (i.e., the null hypothesis of no difference would be accepted, instead; see Figure 9.3).

One- and Two-Tailed Tests

☑

Similar to choosing an appropriate test statistic, *p* values (.05, .01, .001) must be determined in advance, usually before any data are collected.

The example using Figure 9.3 concerns what is called a **two-tailed significance test** (also known as a two-tailed probability test) because *two* critical regions appear under the curve. As noted previously, each of these critical regions is determined by dividing the *p* or alpha level in half (i.e., $.05 \div 2 = .025$). When a two-tailed significance test is employed, there are three possible outcomes that can occur in terms of a hypothesis:

- The control group mean exceeds the experimental group mean: $\mu_c > \mu_e$.
- The control group mean is lower than the experimental group mean: $\mu_c < \mu_e$.
- The null hypothesis of no difference is accepted: $\mu_c = \mu_e$.

The first two outcomes represent the critical regions of rejection located in the two tails of the distribution (see Figure 9.3), and the third outcome, of course, deals with the retention region in the center of the distribution (see Figure 9.3).

One-tailed significance tests, or one-tailed probability tests, rely on a single critical value and region of rejection. The placement of this value and its rejection region are dependent upon the direction of the relationship between groups specified by the hypothesis. Two normal curves with one-tailed significance tests representing the .05 level of significance are shown in Figure 9.4. Note that the same critical value of z (here, -1.65 in the upper curve and $+1.65$ in the lower one) is identified in both, and that the shaded areas representing the critical regions of rejection in each curve represent 5% of the scores in the representative distribution (i.e., those score lying above $+1.65$ or below -1.65). Notice that the remaining region above or below these cutoffs represents the region of retention, which is equal to .95. (To verify this fact, turn to Table B.2 in Appendix B and locate the entry for $z = 1.65$. Note that the area between the mean and z is equal to .4500 (column B) and the area beyond z (column C) is equal to .0500. Where does the .950 retention region come from? Recall that the distribution is symmetric, so that an entire half of it is equal to .5000. In the case of $z = +1.65$, the lower half of the curve (.5000) is added to the upper half (.4500) to obtain .950; see Figure 9.4.)

Take a moment and compare these z scores with those used for the two-tailed test (i.e., $+1.96$ and -1.96) shown above. The one-tailed test scores are necessarily *lower* in value because they represent only *one* critical region of rejection (each) under a curve, and each distinct area corresponds to .05 of the scores under a curve (see Figure 9.4). The two-tailed scores are higher in value—that is, they are further "out" in either tail—because they represent still smaller areas under the curve (i.e., .025) that, when combined, sum to .05.

Given the choice, should you use a one-tailed or a two-tailed significance test? Different researchers offer various rationales for making such a choice, but the scientific perspective on the matter really involves two main issues: an appropriate level of rigor and a healthy dose of curiosity. By rigor, I mean that you do not want to make things too easy on yourself. In many cases, a two-tailed test is seen as more exacting than a one-tailed test precisely because its region of rejection is narrower (i.e., the *p* value is split in two), making it more difficult to reject H_0. Regarding curiosity, I mean that the two-

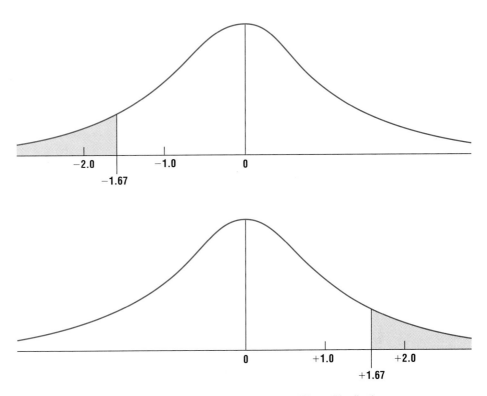

Figure 9.4   One-Tailed Critical Values and Critical Regions of Two *z* Distributions

tailed test can detect differences on both sides of a distribution, so that an observed difference between sample means can be found in the predicted direction or its exact opposite—but it would always be found. In contrast, one-tailed tests emphasize a single direction, so that if an observed difference does not conform to that direction, it is not found. Many researchers, for example, want to know why a significant difference was observed on one rather than the other side of a distribution, speculating about a result's cause in the process. In other words, two-tailed significance tests allow researchers to be a bit more exploratory about their results. When a result is opposite from a prediction, then a researcher can consider whether some revision to the existing theory is warranted, if a methodological innovation is the culprit, and so on—interesting, plausible possibilities abound.

What about using a one-tailed test? One-tailed tests appear to be more rigorous because they are restricted to one side of a test statistic's distribution, but remember that their region of rejection is larger because it covers one tail, not two. Some researchers (e.g., Harris, 1998) suggest that a one-tailed test should only be undertaken when the investigator is *willing to retain* the null hypothesis if the obtained results fall very far in the opposite direction from an alternative hypothesis's prediction. According to a one-tailed test, such an odd result would be completely unexpected and therefore could not be accommodated by the hypothesis test. An investigator would be placed in the bizarre position of assuming a certain result would be found, and in its absence, being unable to explore the obtained results. In general, then, two-tailed significance tests are favored over one-tailed tests.

Degrees of Freedom

One final component of most inferential hypothesis tests remains to be presented, a statistical concept called *degrees of freedom*. The conceptual details involved are actually

Two-tailed significance tests promote rigor, as well as satisfy curiosity when predictions go awry.

One-tailed tests should be used with care. Unlike two-tailed tests, one-tailed tests cannot accommodate unexpected results.

DATA BOX 9.F

When the Null Hypothesis is Rejected—Evaluating Results with the MAGIC Criteria

When you evaluate the meaning of the statistical results of any piece of research, you should consider them in light of Abelson's (1995) **MAGIC criteria.** The five criteria are presented in the form of questions and definitions below:

Magnitude. In statistical terms, are the results reliable? How strong are they in terms of supporting the alternative hypothesis? Magnitude also addresses issues of effect size and what is known as statistical power, topics considered later in this chapter.

Articulation. Are the results presented in clear, concise, and cogent terms? In general, shorter explanations are better than longer explanations as long as crucial details are not lost or overlooked. Qualifications—too many *ifs, buts,* and *but alsos*—undermine readers' interest and confidence in research conclusions.

Generality. Are the results externally valid, that is, can they be applied toward understanding behavior in other settings (see chapter 2 for more detail on validity issues)? Are the results broad or narrow in scope?

Interestingness. Will behavioral scientists care or be interested in the results? Is anything about the results surprising or counterintuitive? Will existing theories need to be reevaluated in light of the findings? Abelson suggests that results satisfy this criterion to the extend that they alter what people currently believe to be true about important research issues (see also Data Box 9.E).

Credibility. In the end, are the results believable? Was the research methodology—everything from sampling to the last statistical test—appropriate? Do the results "hang together" in support of or to advance a theory?

Source: Adapted from Abelson (1995).

rather complex, but here is a relatively straightforward account. The degrees of freedom in any set of data are the number of scores that are free to take on any value once some statistical test is performed. Generally, the degrees of freedom for a test can be known by taking the total number of available values—the sample size—and then subtracting the number of population parameters that will be estimated from the sample. Statisticians described this as N minus the number of restrictions researchers place on any data by asking focused questions in the form of hypotheses.

Here is a simple example illustrating the concept behind degrees of freedom. Perhaps you know that a sample's mean is 25, and you have six observations—five of them can take on any value whatsoever. Once the values of those five observations are known, however, the sixth observation can have *one* and *only one* possible value in order for the distribution's mean to be equal to 25. Thus, the degrees of freedom would be 5—based on $N - 1$—because the value of the sixth observation is no longer free to vary.

KEY TERM   **Degrees of freedom** are based on the number of available observations or scores minus the number of parameters that are being estimated from the data. Virtually all inferential statistical tests have accompanying calculations for their *degrees of freedom*.

▽

A good rule of thumb for thinking about degrees of freedom is this: You lose one degree of freedom for every mean that you calculate.

In more practical terms, degrees of freedom are numerical guides that enable the data analyst to select the appropriate critical value from a statistical table. Indeed, most statistical tables have a column labeled "degrees of freedom," enabling users to quickly and efficiently select a proper critical value once the corresponding degrees of freedom are calculated or identified. (We will calculate the degrees of freedom for the Pearson correlation coefficient [r; see chapter 6] and use an appropriate table of critical values in the next section of this chapter.)

As we conclude our discussion of statistical significance, let me remind you how important it is to link statistical results with their meaning. Too many first-time data analysts become overly focused on the finer details of testing hypotheses and, in the process, they lose sight of what their results are telling them about behavior. To combat this analytical myopia, I urge you to develop the habit of thinking about results in terms of Abelson's (1995) MAGIC criteria. MAGIC is an acronym standing for *m*agnitude, *a*rticulation, *g*enerality, *i*nterestingness, and *c*redibility, five evaluative criteria that are defined in Data Box 9.F. Abelson suggests that these criteria should be kept in mind when deciding whether a set of results adequately supports a research hypothesis. When analyzing a study's data, develop the practice of asking the questions associated with each criterion (see Data Box 9.F). This simple practice will remind you to always link calculations with their meaning and, in turn, to think about whether this linkage is strong enough to convincingly persuade others that the results merit their attention (see also the later section of this chapter on *Writing* about hypotheses and results).

Knowledge Base

1. Which of the following hypotheses is a directional hypothesis? A nondirectional hypothesis?
    a. $\mu_c \neq \mu_e$
    b. $\mu_c < \mu_e$
    c. $\mu_c \geq \mu_e$
2. When a null hypothesis is accepted, what does a researcher conclude about a population?
3. Why is the null hypothesis either accepted or rejected? Why isn't the alternative or research hypothesis accepted or rejected?
4. True or false: A statistically significant difference is a meaningful difference.
5. What is a critical region?

Answers

1. a. Nondirectional
    b. Directional
    c. Directional
2. When H_0 is accepted, the researcher concludes that the independent variable did not create any observable change in the dependent variable meant to represent the population.
3. Although empirical statements can be falsified, they can never be deemed true. Thus, the null hypothesis of no difference serves as a researcher's comparison point—it is rejected when differences are found and retained when no differences are found. An alternative hypothesis is assumed to provide an adequate description of events only until another, more complete explanation is identified.
4. False: Statistical significance refers to the detection of some difference—a reliable one—between groups, not whether a finding is meaningful or noteworthy.
5. A critical region or region of rejection is the area of a sampling distribution that contains "cutoff" values that are unlikely to be obtained unless a difference between groups exists (i.e., H_0 can be rejected). When a test statistic based on sample data falls at or inside a critical region, the null hypothesis of no difference is rejected.

Single Sample Hypothesis Testing: The *z* Test and the Significance of *r*

Using the knowledge and skills acquired earlier in this chapter, we can test actual hypotheses involving sample means and population parameters, as well as decide whether a correlation demonstrates a reliable relationship between two variables. In each case,

Table 9.2   Steps for Testing a Hypothesis

1. State the null (H_0) and the alternative hypotheses (H_1), and select a significance level (p value or α level) for the statistical test.

2. Calculate the standard error of the mean (if any) and decide whether to use a one-tailed or a two-tailed significance test, which will determine the critical region(s) and critical value(s) for rejecting or accepting H_0.

3. Calculate the test-statistic and degrees of freedom (if any), and then determine whether to accept or reject H_0.

4. Interpret and evaluate the results in light of the null and the alternative hypotheses.

Note: The steps outlined in this table are meant to be flexible and adaptive. Some statistical tests will use all the steps, others only one or two.

the hypothesis tested will involve making inferences about a population from a single sample of data (e.g., is a mean representative of one population or another?). In keeping with the *mise en place* philosophy of analysis espoused in chapter 1, we follow a series of flexible steps that will make hypothesis testing a straightforward, orderly procedure. These steps are summarized in Table 9.2, and they will be loosely—*not* absolutely— followed in the examples of hypothesis testing presented below, as well as in those appearing in later chapters. Take a moment and review Table 9.2 before going on to the examples, and remember that these are flexible, not lockstep, guidelines. Once all the necessary numerical information is available and organized, the required calculations are actually rather simple. I think you will be surprised to see how material you previously learned comes together in the process.

What Is the Probability a Sample Is from One Population or Another?

The z test, which is derived from the z or standard distribution (see chapter 5), tests hypotheses about parameters based on sample data drawn from populations whose standard deviations are known. The z test is used in these circumstances to test a hypothesis involving one sample mean. Calculating a z test statistic is not terribly different than calculating a z score. Where a z score is determined by subtracting a population mean from some observation, and then dividing the difference between these scores by the population standard deviation, or $(X - \mu)/\sigma$, the z test examines the difference between a sample mean ($\overline{X}$) and μ, divided by the standard error of the mean, $\sigma_{\overline{X}}$, or:

[9.18.1]
$$z = \frac{\overline{X} - \mu}{\sigma_{\overline{X}}}.$$

Once a z score is calculated, its value can be looked up in Table B.2 in Appendix B in order to see the probability of observing a score that extreme (cf., chapter 8). The probability of the observed z helps a researcher decide the likelihood that some sample mean really came from a distribution of scores where the hypothesized value of μ is the same as the population mean. If the observed z score is not found to originate from a population with the hypothesized value of μ, then the researcher assumes that the sample mean is from some other population with a different μ. In other words, there is a statistically significant difference between the sample mean and the hypothesized value of μ.

Let's look at a concrete example so that you can see that there is little difference here compared to your prior work with the z distribution. Imagine that an instructor of 75 gifted students knows that the mean IQ of the group is 132. She also knows that the IQ distribution of all school children has a μ of 100 and a σ of 15. How likely is it that the sample mean of 132 is reflective of a random sample from the population of school children?

Step 1.   Following Table 9.2, the first step involves identifying the null and alternative hypotheses, and then deciding upon a significance level. We are essentially asking if the μ of the gifted students μ is greater than or equal to the general population μ (or, if you prefer, that the general population μ is less than μ_g). Thus, the null and alternative hypotheses, respectively, are:

$$H_0: \mu = \mu_g,$$
$$H_1: \mu < \mu_g.$$

Relying on conventional wisdom, the gifted student instructor decides to set the significance level at .05.

Step 2.   This step involves calculating the standard error of the mean, which is easily determined by using formula [9.2.1]. Entering the known population standard deviation of 15 and the gifted sample's size of 75 into it, we find that:

[9.19.1] $$\sigma_{\overline{X}} = \frac{\sigma}{\sqrt{N}},$$

[9.19.2] $$\sigma_{\overline{X}} = \frac{15}{\sqrt{75}},$$

[9.19.3] $$\sigma_{\overline{X}} = \frac{15}{8.66},$$

[9.19.4] $$\sigma_{\overline{X}} = 1.73.$$

The instructor then decides to use a two-tailed significance test (each tail of the distribution covers a critical region equal to .025). Because we are determining a probability based on the *z* distribution, no critical values or regions of rejection are necessary.

Step 3.   We can now calculate the *z* test statistic using formula [9.18.1]. We simply need to enter the sample mean (132), the known μ (100), and the standard error of the mean (1.73):

[9.20.1] $$z = \frac{132 - 100}{1.73},$$

[9.20.2] $$z = \frac{32}{1.73},$$

[9.20.3] $$z = 18.50.$$

This *z* is very, very large and, in fact, it does not even appear in Table B.2 (please turn there now), which indicates that the likelihood of obtaining a *z* of this size by chance is far less than .05 (i.e., .025 in the upper tail because we used a two-tailed test); indeed, it is much less than .001! Therefore, we conclude that the sample of gifted students do not constitute a random sample from the population that has a mean IQ of 100. The gifted students have an IQ that is far above the average, so they are not representative of the general population of school children. The null hypothesis is rejected.

Step 4.   There is not much more to conclude here beyond the fact that the group of 75 gifted students cannot be considered a random sample within the larger population of school children. This conclusion should come as no surprise, yet it nicely illustrates the basic procedures and underlying logic of testing the likelihood a sample is from some given population.

Is One Sample Different from a Known Population?

A developmental psychologist believes that the transition from elementary school to middle school is a definitive one. The researcher argues that students in their first year of middle school (sixth graders) show rapid growth in social and emotional development as compared to peers who are only one grade below them in elementary school. An established measure of socioemotional development, one tested on generations of elementary school students, has a μ of 45 and a σ of 6. The researcher decides to give the same measure to a sample of 60 sixth-graders. He assumes that their scores on the developmental measure will be abnormally high, suggesting a level of maturity beyond that typically found in the elementary school population. The mean score of the sixth grade sample turns out to be 48.

Step 1.   We again follow the steps laid out in Table 9.2, so that formulating the statistical hypotheses is a rather straightforward exercise. The researcher wants to determine if the μ of known population of elementary school students is lower than the μ of the middle school group (μ_m). The null and alternative hypotheses can be readily expressed as:

$$H_0: \mu = \mu_m,$$
$$H_1: \mu < \mu_m.$$

Given that the developmental measure is an established instrument, the investigator elects to use a conservative significance level of .01 instead of the usual .05.

Step 2.   Using a two-tailed significance test, each of the tails will be equal to .005 (i.e., $.01/2 = .005$). The researcher then determines the standard error of the mean using formula [9.2.1]. The population standard deviation of 6 and the N of 60 are entered into this formula:

[9.21.1] $$\sigma_{\overline{X}} = \frac{\sigma}{\sqrt{N}},$$

[9.21.2] $$\sigma_{\overline{X}} = \frac{6}{\sqrt{60}},$$

[9.21.3] $$\sigma_{\overline{X}} = \frac{6}{7.75},$$

[9.21.4] $$\sigma_{\overline{X}} = .775.$$

The critical z value for a two-tailed significance test can be obtained by finding the z score corresponding to .005 percent of the area under the z curve. A close examination of Table B.2 in Appendix B reveals that $z = 2.58$ is the critical value for .0049, which, when rounded up, is equal to .005. Figure 9.5 illustrates the (shaded) critical regions of rejection for a two-tailed significance test with a critical value of ± 2.58.

Step 3.   The z test is then used to determine if the sixth-graders' mean score on the developmental measure is higher than the established mean of the elementary school-aged population. Following formula [9.18.1], the population mean (45) is subtracted from the sample mean (48), and the difference is then divided by the value of the standard error of the mean (.775), or:

[9.22.1] $$z = \frac{\overline{X} - \mu}{\sigma_{\overline{X}}},$$

[9.22.2] $$z = \frac{48 - 45}{.775},$$

[9.20.3] $$z = \frac{3}{.775},$$

[9.20.4] $$z = 3.87.$$

Is the observed z of 3.87 greater than or equal to the previously established critical value of ± 2.58? Yes, indeed it is, so the researcher rejects the null hypothesis of no difference.

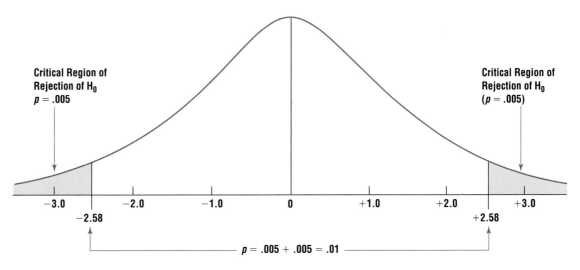

Figure 9.5 Two-Tailed Significance Test of *z* where *p* = .01

The observed *z* of 3.87 falls well into the upper critical region of rejection for H_0 (see Figure 9.5).

Step 4. Based on their average scores on the maturity measure, the developmental psychologist is justified in arguing that the socioemotional development of the middle school children is significantly higher than the population of elementary school children—the sixth-graders represent a different population because they responded at a higher level of development. How would the researcher succinctly report this result? He might write something like this: "After completing a standardized instrument, middle school students displayed higher levels of socioemotional development than their elementary school peers, *z* = 3.87, *p* < .01." Make careful note of the statistical nomenclature appearing at the end of the sentence—the researcher provides information about (a) the test statistic (*z*) and its obtained value (3.87) as well as (b) specific indication of the significance level (the *p* value or *α* level of .01) used to successfully reject the null hypothesis. Throughout the remainder of the text, we will learn to present statistical results in this common reporting style (see also, Appendix C).

When is a Correlation Significant?

Why consider correlational relationships again? Because we postponed discussing their utility in testing hypotheses about single samples until now. Before proceeding to hypothesis testing, however, a brief review of the qualities ascribed to the correlation coefficient may jog your memory. The Pearson *r*, a measure of the strength of association between two variables, was introduced in chapter 6. A correlation coefficient can range in value from −1.00 to +1.00. As *r* approaches +1.00, the values of variables *X* and *Y* share a direct relationship—as one variable increases or decreases in value, the other behaves similarly. A negative correlation—one where *r* moves toward −1.00—is indicative of an inverse relationship: As the value of one variable increases, the other variable necessarily decreases. When *r* hovers around 0, there is no predictable relationship between *X* and *Y*. If these facts seem unfamiliar or "fuzzy" to you, please take a few minutes and review chapter 6 before proceeding with the rest of the material.

One issue that we did not discuss in chapter 6 is how to determine when a positive or negative correlational relationship is significant, that is, one where *r* is reliably different from 0 (i.e., the absence of any measurable association between X and Y). In fact, the null hypothesis for testing whether a correlation is significant assumes that its value is equal to 0, while the alternative hypothesis posits that the association is detected as different from 0. A statistically significant correlation, then, is one that is large enough in value that a researcher anticipates obtaining the same result in other, similar samples. A significant correlation (r) is assumed to reflect a true positive or negative correlation existing in a population (ρ; see Table 4.1), one greater than 0, so that the researcher must be interested in generalizing the relationship portrayed by the correlation beyond the current sample. Sociologists and demographers, for example, routinely find a positive correlation between years of education and income in any reasonably large sample of adults—more education tends to result in higher earned income, just as abbreviated schooling is linked to generally lower earnings.

Once a correlation is calculated (see chapter 6), determining whether it is significant is relatively easy. Generally, two criteria must be met: the value of r must be relatively far from 0 and the statistic should be based on a reasonably large sample. Some balancing can be achieved using these two criteria: smaller correlations can still be declared significant if they are based on very large samples and, in turn, very large correlations—those close to ± 1.00—can compensate for smaller samples. It is rare, however, to observe a significant correlation that is based on fewer than 10 pairs of observations.

To demonstrate how to determine a correlation's significance, we can return to an example from chapter 6 and consider it in light of the steps for hypothesis testing outlined in Table 9.2. A personality psychologist was interested in validating a new inventory designed to measure extraversion. Ten participants completed the inventory and then, a week later, they took part in a staged social interaction—a cocktail party—where they were instructed to meet and greet 12 new people (confederates of the investigator) for 30 minutes. The correlation between their scores on the extraversion measure and the number of confederates they met was $+.94$ (to review the data and the calculation of r, please see tables 6.1–6.3). Is this correlation significantly different from 0?

Step 1. The personality researcher decides to use the .05 level of significance for testing whether the observed correlation is different from 0. The null hypothesis is that the population correlation coefficient (ρ) is equal to 0, while the alternative hypothesis is that the population the sample was drawn from is greater than 0, or:

$$H_0: \rho = 0,$$
$$H_1: \rho > 0.$$

Step 2. The value of the correlation coefficient was calculated previously, so there is no need to calculate any other statistics, including standard error. The personality researcher elects, however, to rely on a two-tailed significance test.

Step 3. The formula for determining the degrees of freedom for r is $N - 2$. There were 10 participants in the study, so the degrees of freedom are equal to 8 (i.e., $10 - 2 = 8$). To determine whether $r = +.94$ is statistically significant, we turn to Table B.3 in Appendix B — please turn there now—which contains critical values for the Pearson r. We look for the critical value that represents the intersection between the row containing 8 degrees of freedom (located in the far left column) and the column labeled .05 under the heading "Level of Significance for Two-Tailed Test." As you can see, the critical value of r—usually called r_{crit}—is equal to .632. Is the calculated r of $+.94$ greater than or equal to the r_{crit} of .632? Yes, it is, so we can reject the null hypothesis. The observed correlation coefficient of $+.94$ is from a population whose ρ is greater than 0.

Step 4. The personality researcher successfully demonstrated a significant, positive correlation between the trait of extraversion and the number of people participants met socially. The correlation could be reported as: "A significant correlation between extra-

A correlation representing sample data is symbolized r; one representing a population is symbolized ρ.

version and sociability was found, $r(8) = +.94$, $p < .05$. Extraverts tended to meet more confederates during the staged social interactions, while introverts met relatively fewer persons." Please note that the degrees of freedom are noted parenthetically (8) after the r and before the actual value of the test statistic ($+.94$), and that the significance level used (.05) to reject the null hypothesis is also provided for readers. One other important note: Despite the fact that this correlation is significantly different from 0, we still do not know if the relationship it identifies is a causal one. Even a significant correlation does not imply causation.

Learning to test hypotheses is not difficult, but it is detailed. These are but three different hypothesis tests illustrating whether a sample is from one sample or another. There is clearly quite a bit of detail associated with hypothesis testing and, even with the guidelines presented in Table 9.2, you still may have felt a bit at sea. Learning to test hypotheses takes a bit of practice and, with more experience and review of the relevant concepts, it will gradually become familiar and less threatening. Identify any concept you are still not sure about and resolve to reread that section of this chapter again soon, if not right at this moment. We will pick up with hypothesis testing immediately in the next chapter—before that, however, a few collateral issues remain to be considered in this chapter, notably identifying and avoiding inferential errors.

> ☑
>
> The formula for calculating the
>
> degrees of freedom of the Pearson r
>
> is $N - 2$.

Inferential Errors Types I and II

Every researcher who uses statistics and data analysis is well aware of one important fact—whether you decide to accept or to reject H_0, there is always the chance that you are making an inferential error. By inferential error, I mean a situation where you accept H_0 as true when you should reject it (i.e., a true difference is missed), or one where you reject H_0 as false when the appropriate decision is to accept it (i.e., a false difference is located). In fact, anytime a significance test is performed, there are four possible outcomes with which a researcher must knowingly contend. These outcomes are:

- The H_0 is *not* rejected because H_0 is *true:* This is a correct decision.
- The H_0 is rejected because H_0 is *false:* This is a correct decision.
- The H_0 is rejected *but H_0 is true:* This is an incorrect decision known as a *Type I error.*

KEY TERM A **Type I error** involves rejecting the null hypothesis—a researcher believes that a significant difference is found—when, in fact, there is actually no difference, so that the null hypothesis is true. A *Type I error* occurs when a researcher finds a difference where one does not exist.

- The H_0 is *not* rejected *but H_0 is false:* This is an incorrect decision known as a *Type II error.*

KEY TERM A **Type II error** involves accepting the null hypothesis—a researcher believes that no significance difference is present—when, in fact, there actually is a difference, so that the null hypothesis is false. A *Type II error* occurs when a researcher fails to "find" a difference where one exists.

A data analyst has two chances to make correct decisions and two opportunities to draw faulty inferences. These four decision possibilities are summarized in Table 9.3. Please take a few minutes to review each cell carefully.

Type I Error. Sometimes a researcher incorrectly rejects the null hypothesis, thereby believing in results that only appear to contain statistically reliable differences. How can such an error occur? Unknowingly, for instance, a researcher can draw an unrepresentative sample that shows a difference or effect that does not occur at the level of the

Table 9.3   Statistical Decisions and Reality: Making Correct Decisions or Inferential Errors

		Statistical Decision	
		Accept H_0	Reject H_0
Reality	H_0 is True	*Correct* decision probability $= 1 - \alpha$	*Incorrect* decision Type I error probability $= \alpha$
	H_0 is False	*Incorrect* decision Type II error probability $= \beta$	*Correct* decision probability $= 1 - \beta$ (power $= 1 - \beta$)

population. The Type I error, then, can be due to unlikely but extant random variation. When a null hypothesis is actually true, the probability of making a Type I error is equal to α, that is, the significance level used for rejection. Thus, if a researcher is using a .05 significance level, then there is a 5% chance of rejecting a true null hypothesis (see the upper right cell in Table 9.3). A researcher would be making a Type I error by concluding that an herbal dietary supplement helped people feel more alert when, in actuality, it had no effect on mental acuity whatsoever. As shown in Table 9.3, the probability of making a correct decision—accepting the null hypothesis when it is true—is equal to $1 - \alpha$ or, here, .95 (see the upper left cell in Table 9.3).

What can be done to avoid a Type I error? Researchers can hedge their empirical bets by using a more stringent level of significance to reject the null hypothesis. In other words, the probability of making a Type I error can be reduced by lowering α. Thus, for example, a researcher reduces the risk of making this inferential error by changing α from .05 to .01—to be sure, this change decreases the likelihood of incorrectly rejecting the null hypothesis, just as it increases the probability of correctly accepting the null hypothesis when it is actually true (i.e., $1 - \alpha = .99$). There is an empirical price to be paid for this careful logic, however: By reducing the risk of making a Type I error, the chance of making a Type II error increases.

Type II Error.   Type II errors happen when researchers accept the null hypothesis when it is actually false, that is, they fail to reject it and miss identifying an actual statistical effect in the data. What causes this error? Lowering the level of α to protect against making a Type I error decreases the area available in a sampling distribution used for detecting significant differences—if the critical region is smaller, the likelihood of obtaining a test statistic of sufficient magnitude to fall within its confines becomes more difficult. In fact, by decreasing α you necessarily decrease the chance of rejecting the null hypothesis whether it is actually true *or* false. Thus, an investigator out to rigorously test for the mood enhancing effects of an herbal dietary supplement might miss documenting the effects entirely by decreasing α to .01 or .001—reliable differences become harder to detect while accepting the null hypothesis becomes a stronger possibility.

Can we determine the probability of making a Type II error? Although it is called a β (the Greek letter "beta") error (see the lower left cell in Table 9.3), the actual likelihood of making a Type II error is theoretical and, therefore, very hard to determine (and if we knew β, we could also know the probability of correctly rejecting the null hypothesis, or $1 - \beta$; see the bottom right cell in Table 9.3). Indeed, a Type II error is influenced by several factors besides the level of α, including sample size, random variation present in the data set, and the size of the effect the study's independent variable has on the

The probability of making a Type I error is equal to a test's predetermined significance (α) level.

Protecting against Type I errors (reducing α) increases the likelihood of making a Type II error.

dependent measure. Although we cannot readily pinpoint a probability value for β, it is certainly the case that making a Type II error becomes *less likely* when a larger sample size is available, α is increased (i.e., .01 is moved "up" to .05), and the independent variable's effect size—a matter we take up in the next section—is pronounced. When there is a great deal of error variance present, however, the probability of making a Type II error remains high.

Which error—Type I or Type II—is worse? A cursory analysis of the question leads many people to reply that a Type II error is the worse of the two because a researcher's effort is not rewarded. A good idea is operationalized and tested in an experiment, but the hypothesized effect never pans out empirically—the researcher moves on to other projects, unaware that his or her research expectation is actually true.

Although this scenario is no doubt frustrating, Type I errors are actually assumed to be much worse than Type II errors (e.g., Bakan, 1966). Think about it for a moment—what could be worse than having faith in a research result that is not actually true? Once a Type I error finds itself into a scholar's program of research, his or her subsequent publications and presentations will spread the contaminated result to other investigators who, in turn, will use it in their theorizing, writings, and teaching. The false result quickly becomes established wisdom within the research literature (Dunn, 1999) and, across time, false theories and dubious findings mislead future generations of students and researchers. When a result appears in the published literature, most researchers assume it is valid, if not the gospel truth. When they cannot replicate it in their own studies, researchers are apt to blame themselves because the false effect is already known to be "true"—after all it appeared in the literature, didn't it?

Unless they are caught early in the research process, then, Type I errors can haunt a research literature for quite some time. Type II errors are frustrating and the damage caused by *not* knowing about whether a result could benefit a topical area is hard to assess. Still, most behavioral scientists agree that it is better to forgo a good idea (Type II error) than to perpetuate a potentially destructive falsehood (Type I error). One thing all researchers can do to combat both types of errors is perform more than one experiment to examine a hypothesized relationship between an independent variable and a dependent measure. Replicating an effect is certainly more work, but it is one of the best ways to avoid making inferential errors that can be damaging and costly in the long run. We now turn to a related issue, ensuring that we do what we can statistically to identify real differences and to avoid locating spurious ones.

▽

Type I errors are considered to be more harmful to the research enterprise than Type II errors.

Statistical Power and Effect Size

Similar to the word significant, *power* is another word that has a special meaning in statistical contexts. Where data are concerned, power is not strength or authority, nor is it the persuasiveness of a result or set of findings. Instead, power refers to the ability to achieve research goals, in particular, the likelihood that one can successfully reject the null hypothesis when it is truly false (Aron & Aron, 1997).

KEY TERM **Power** is defined as the probability that a statistical test correctly rejects a null hypothesis.

Earlier we noted that the probability of making a Type II error is equal to β (see the lower left cell in Table 9.3). It follows, then, that the probability of correctly rejecting a true null hypothesis is defined by $1 - \beta$ (see the lower right cell in Table 9.3, especially the parenthetical comment beneath it defining power as $1 - \beta$). If a researcher knew, for example, that the probability of committing a Type II error was .30 (i.e., β), the likelihood of correctly rejecting the null hypothesis—the power of the test being used—would be equal to .70 (i.e., $1 - \beta$).

Power is the ability to accomplish research goals, to correctly reject the null hypothesis.

Determining probabilities like these is actually a very complex process, one that is beyond the scope of our present discussion and the level of this book. We will, however, consider practical steps that you, as a researcher and data analyst, can take to enhance the level of power in experiments and in the analyses used to interpret experimental results. You should be aware, too, that there are power tables containing values associated with various statistical procedures based on different sized samples. Such tables are very useful when it comes to estimating the power necessary for a particular research design, and they can be found in various advanced statistics texts (e.g., Cohen & Cohen, 1983; Cohen, 1988; see also, Aron & Aron, 1997).

There is one simple but important lesson to be learned about the concept of power and whether to accept or reject a null hypothesis. Many budding researchers assume that if an alternate or research hypothesis is true, then a significant result—one based on the rejection of a null hypothesis—will be found. Although this scenario is very desirable, the data and the results based upon it will not always cooperate. Why not? Well, the sample data drawn from a population of interest may not contain values extreme enough to reject the null hypothesis—that is, the statistical power associated with the analysis of a particular sample may not be sufficient. Thus, just because a research hypothesis is tenable—it is routinely replicated—do not assume that a significant difference will actually be found; indeed, steps should always be taken to enhance the likelihood that predicted, significant differences will be observed.

Experienced researchers and savvy data analysts are well aware of the important role that power plays in research efforts. As a result, they try to maximize the power available within any study—great or small—by taking concrete action before any data are collected. Power, then, is not something to worry about when analysis begins (i.e., when it is too late), rather it is a concern when the research begins, when it is in its planning stages. Despite the fact that researchers are usually unable to measure power precisely, there are several ways to increase power. Some of these actions were mentioned earlier as factors influencing Type II errors, but they merit broader discussion here:

Increase a Study's Sample Size.   As you know by now, larger samples are apt to be representative of their parent populations to a much higher degree than smaller samples. If a result actually exists at the level of a population, then a hypothesized effect is likely to be found if the sample size is sufficiently large. More to the point, increasing a sample's size is often the most straightforward, easy method to augment a study's power. How large a sample is "big enough?" As unsatisfying as it may sound, "it depends" on the circumstance. As noted earlier in the book, always strive to obtain as many participants as possible. As a general rule of thumb, it is difficult to detect trustworthy significant differences with fewer than 30 participants and, as a study's N moves toward 100, the probability of rejecting a null hypothesis is enhanced dramatically.

Figure 9.6 illustrates how a larger N can increase the probability (i.e., $1 - \beta$) of rejecting the null hypothesis. Drawing (a) in Figure 9.6 represent two hypothetical, somewhat overlapping distributions when $N = 20$. Note the two-tailed critical regions shaded in the null distribution, especially that the lower tail shares some overlap with the experimental distribution. The shaded portion of the experimental distribution in drawing (a) corresponds to power of the test being used to detect a difference between the control and experimental groups. Now look at drawing (b) in Figure 9.6, which illustrates two narrower, less overlapping distributions based on $N = 100$. Two-tailed critical regions are again noted for the null (control) distribution, but notice that the relative overlap of the two distributions in drawing (b) is much less—a larger sample size leads to less variability in a sampling distribution. More important for present purposes, of course, is the fact that the shaded area under the experimental curve—the area indi-

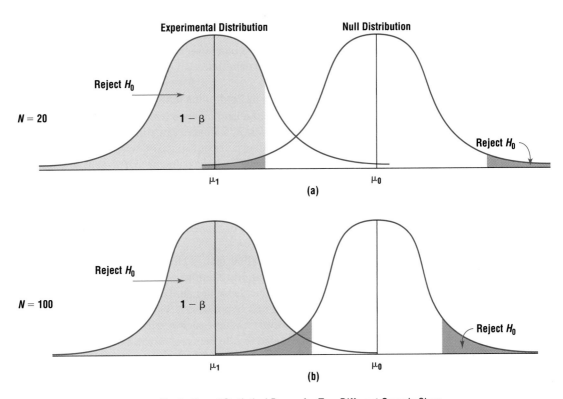

Figure 9.6 Illustration of Statistical Power for Two Different Sample Sizes

Note: Based on Figure 8.11, page 255, in Gravetter & Wallnau (1996).

cating the power available to reject the null hypothesis—is greater than that found in drawing (a). In general, then, a larger sample size increases the amount of power available to reject the null hypothesis.

Use Precise Dependent Measures.   Harris (1998) advocates using sensitive or precise dependent measures. These terms usually implicate relying on established or well-tested instruments, such as published questionnaires or valid inventories, as well as concrete behavioral indices, found to reliably demonstrate differences among groups in prior research. I am not trying to stifle your creativity where developing novel measures is concerned, but tried and true dependent variables are likely to show lower levels of error variance than instruments being given a trial run. The goal is to avoid increasing measurement error, which unduly inflates standard deviations within groups, making it more difficult to locate any significant differences between them. In contrast, sensitive measures possess lower levels of error, thereby increasing the chance of identifying even small—but reliable—differences between groups.

Make Independent Variables Salient to Research Participants.   Just as a dependent measure should be sensitive to change, any variable you manipulate must create change in the attitudes or behavior of research participants exposed to it. By salient, of course, I mean that the level of the independent variable presented to each group (e.g., control versus experimental) within a research design must be distinct—literally standing out as the only factor responsible for eliciting group-based differences in participant responses. Research methods books are better suited to this sort of troubleshooting, and several offer sage guidance about how to enhance the impact of independent variables (e.g., Cozby, 1997; Dunn, 1999; Martin, 1996; Rosenthal & Rosnow, 1991). One good way to determine the effectiveness of a novel independent variable is to pilot test it *prior* to the start of a project's actual data collection (Dunn, 1999).

Reduce Error Variation by Controlling for Random Factors.   Obviously, using sensitive dependent measures and salient independent variables will go far toward reducing error variance, but only so far. Researchers can still take other steps to enhance power by keeping all aspects of an experiment constant except exposure to a level of an independent variable. These steps include reducing participant attrition or determining its cause, using trained experimenters who memorize a research script (i.e., the "lines" and "blocking" in an experimental production), balancing gender across conditions in the experiment, and tracking—measuring—any potentially influential variables for inclusion in subsequent analyses or discussion (Dunn, 1999).

Consider Using a One-Tailed Test.   This piece of advice will seem contradictory given the earlier recommendation to employ exclusively two-tailed significance tests. To be sure, such rigor will reduce, even negate, Type I errors, but the power of the statistical test used to examine the null hypothesis is also reduced in the process. The truth of the matter is clear, however; it is far easier to reject a null hypothesis by using a one-tailed rather than a two-tailed test. In concrete terms, a one-tailed z test at the .05 level relies on a critical value of ± 1.65, while its two-tailed counterpart requires a z equal to ± 1.96. Assuming the one-tailed test's hypothesized direction pans out, it is much simpler to reject the lower (one-tailed) than the higher (two-tailed) z in an analysis.

Avoid Reducing Significance Levels.   Similar to considering a one-tailed test as an option, maintaining a relatively liberal significance level (e.g., .05) in the face of Type I errors will appear to be odd advice. Indeed, the researcher's best defense against making a Type I error is *reducing* a significance level to make it more conservative (e.g., .05 to .01)—why fight success, as it were? In the same way a one-tailed test is easier to reject than a two-tailed test, a .05 critical value is easier to reject than a .01 or a .001 critical value. Why? Reducing the significance level of a statistical test reduces that test's power. Just as you are less likely to reject a true null hypothesis (i.e., commit a Type I error) with a lower α level, you are also less likely to reject a false null hypothesis—which is what you really want to do (see the upper left and lower right cells, respectively, in Table 9.3). Informed researchers and data analysts know they must wrestle with the virtues of trying to avoid making a Type I error at the same time they are vigorously seeking to reject a false null hypothesis.

Attention to any one or several of these steps can enhance the power of almost any statistical test. Yet there is another, key factor that can affect power—the magnitude of the actual effect created by an independent variable.

Effect Size

The power of a statistical test is not dependent exclusively on sample size, the clarity or sensitivity of variables, level of significance tests, controlling error variance, or any of the other influences noted above. Power is also affected by what statisticians call *effect size*. Conceptually, the degree to which two populations—one for the control group, the other for the experimental group—do *not* overlap with one another is indicative of effect size, as the measurable disparity reveals whether the manipulation of an independent variable truly separated the values of the populations from one another.

KEY TERM   **Effect size** is the measured strength of association among variables within a study or the magnitude of an experimental effect. *Effect size* influences power, such that the greater the *effect size,* the greater the power within a study.

In practical terms, effect size refers to how far apart group means are from one another, and how much variance occurs within each group (e.g., Aron & Aron, 1997). Effect size is usually reported in standardized units—the mean difference between the groups is divided by the standard deviation of the control group.

Effect size is not difficult to calculate and there are a variety of different indices available to researchers. We will learn to calculate several effect size indices in subsequent chapters in this book. Many investigators now routinely report effect sizes in their presentations and publications, allowing interested observers to learn the magnitude of an independent variable's effect and how difficult it was to obtain. In fact, some journal editors now require that authors include effect size statistics in articles they submit for peer review and publication. Presumably, larger effect sizes point to larger effects, which are more detectable than smaller effects (but see the *Project Exercise* concluding this chapter). Reporting effect size in this manner is very helpful to the scientific community because other researchers can plan related studies knowing the level of difficulty entailed in finding a particular result (e.g., during a study's planning stage, effect sizes can be used in consort with the aforementioned power tables; see Cohen, 1988; see also Rosenthal & Rosnow, 1991). Such studies are more likely to succeed—legitimately reject a null hypothesis—when researchers can determine how difficult it is to find significant differences between the groups in an experiment.

Although it is usually determined afterward, Cohen (1988) persuasively argues that researchers should consider the effect size they plan (or hope) to obtain before they perform the research. Cohen's extensive research concerning the analysis of power in numerous studies led to the identification of conventional values for effect size. Effect size is usually reported as a coefficient ranging between 0 and 1.00, and higher values indicate that an independent variable had greater influence on a dependent measure. Cohen suggests that an effect size value is labeled small (.20), medium (.50), or large (80), a matter we will explore in detailed examples beginning in the next chapter.

Writing About Hypotheses and the Results of Statistical Tests

Inferential statistics are used to make general statements about a population through reliance on sample data. When a hypothesis is tested, the statistical predictions concern the population parameters, which sample statistics estimate. When researchers write about hypotheses and results, however, they usually focus on what happened between the conditions in the sample—how did the participants in each of the groups behave or respond? Were their actions consistent with the alternative hypothesis? Were the means in each of the experiment's groups consistent with the hypothesis?

Sometimes it is difficult to keep the technical aspects of the data analysis in mind at the same time you are trying to write a convincing, interesting story about what happened in a piece of research. Indeed, many students and faculty see statistical analysis and the reporting of results as separate rather than complementary activities. As Abelson (1995, p. xiii) put it:

> [S]tatistical analysis also has a narrative role. Meaningful research tells a story with some point to it, and statistics can sharpen the story. Students are often not mindful of this. Ask a student the question, "If your study were reported in the newspaper, what would the headline be?" and you are likely to receive in response a rare exhibition of incoherent mumblings, as though such a question had never been even remotely contemplated.

Let me add that the word "student" should be read as "student of statistics," and this includes instructors, statisticians, and the author whose words you are now reading. Everyone can easily miss the "forest"—a clean and clear summary of a hypothesis and its link to a study's results—for the "trees," all the small details and asides that can be spun off from a hypothesis and supporting results.

As you analyze the homework problems presented in the remaining chapters in this book, do calculations for your next statistics exam, or when the opportunity arises, conduct your own research project from start to finish, keep Abelson's (1995) admonition in mind. It is essential that you learn to quickly and efficiently link up the results of a given statistical analysis with a clear, relatively concise interpretation of what those results *actually* mean. Making this link is no small feat because we often become bogged down in the technical details or minutiae of "doing the math" required for a statistical test, or we neglect to think about what a test's results tell us about behavior. Please keep in mind that statistics and data analysis are tools designed to help investigators to draw more clear conclusions about events that take place in the world, but the interpretation and articulation of the events is still much more important than the number crunching involved (see chapter 1).

From this point forward, then, cultivate the habit of expressing each result you calculate in terms of Abelson's (1995) "headline" approach. Alternatively, adopt a "bumper sticker" point of view by effectively but efficiently getting across the essence of some research results succinctly. That is, put the result into simple terms that someone who is *not* the veteran of a statistics class—a close friend, your grandmother—can understand. Your explanation should be no more than a sentence or two in length. Why such a short summary? After more than 12 years of classroom teaching, I've observed that if students cannot define a concept briefly or summarize it concisely, they rarely understand the concept very well. Regrettably, our culture fosters the impression that lengthy (and too often windy) explanations, "big" multisyllabic words, and overly technical jargon correspond to expert understanding of some phenomenon. Don't you believe it! The best explanation is still the simplest explanation. Strive to explain complex concepts in straightforward prose as long as you do not lose any important meaning in the process. If some technical information is needed, then by all means use it, jargon and all—just be sure to properly explain what any complex relationship or unusual terms mean for readers. One good way to make technical information less dry is to explain it in the context provided by an example, so that you will give the reader something to latch onto in the midst of a detailed account.

Concern about making the technical more comprehensible nicely leads to the concluding point I want to make in this section. When reading behavioral science journal articles that employ statistical analysis, you will notice a curious thing—generally, authors do not discuss predictions, analyses, or results in terms of either the null or the alternative hypothesis. Inferential statistical tests are certainly performed and significant differences are noted, even discussed at length, but the technical terms we learned in this chapter—whether to "accept" or "reject," for example—rarely appear. Many students find the absence of this (now) familiar material a bit disconcerting (though others rejoice!)—what is going on?

Behavioral scientist authors and journal editors assume that general readers of the literature are already initiated into the mysteries of statistics and data analysis, that educated consumers of research "know" the null or alternative hypothesis is implied in any published piece of research. Readers who are unfamiliar with the symbolic and mathematical language of statistics, too, can skip over any sections of a research report containing overly technical material in favor of details provided in more accessible sections. Journal articles written in APA style, for example, are crafted in such a way that readers can get the "gist" of what a researcher did and found by reading any single section of a text, from the Abstract to the Discussion section (see Appendix C). Why? Because each section of an APA style paper is meant to "stand alone," that is, it should be readily interpretable to almost any level of reader with little effort (Bem, 1987; Dunn, 1999).

Statistically sophisticated readers know whether a null hypothesis is accepted or rejected based on the statistical information provided by an analysis and any accompanying prose explanations. Thus, an author might report that,

> The intensive treatment group reported lower anxiety scores than are generally observed in clinical populations, $z = 3.75$, $p < .05$.

In this case, the "$p < .05$" indicates a significant difference was obtained—here, the intensive treatment group appears to represent the characteristics of another population—so that the null hypothesis of no difference was rejected. If the intensive treatment proved to be ineffective, then you might read a summary like this one:

> The intensive treatment group reported mean anxiety scores that were similar to those observed in clinical populations, $z = 1.20$, $p > .05$.

Here, the "greater than" sign ($>$) linked with the p value informs the reader that the result did *not* reach the conventional level of significance. Some authors choose to report the same result by using "$p = $ ns" instead, where "ns" translates as "not significant." In both cases, of course, the message to readers is that the null hypothesis was accepted, that no reliable difference from the known population was discerned. By literally learning to read the signs and their link to descriptive accounts of what took place in a study, you can determine whether a null hypothesis was accepted or rejected with relative ease.

Knowledge Base

1. What is a Type I error? A Type II error?
2. What is the probability of correctly rejecting a true null hypothesis?
3. True or False: Lowering a significance level from .05 to .01 increases the chance of rejecting a null hypothesis.
4. True or False: Increasing power reduces the chance of making a Type II error.
5. Name any three steps a researcher can perform to increase the power of a statistical test.

Answers

1. A Type I error occurs when a researcher finds a significant effect that does not really exist. A Type II error occurs when a researcher does not find a significant effect that does exist.
2. $1 - \beta$, which is also known as power
3. False. Lowering a significance level reduces the power of a test.
4. True. Increasing power reduces the incidence of "missed" effects.
5. Increase sample size; use sensitive dependent measures or salient independent variables; reduce error variance by controlling for random factors; use a one-tailed significance test; avoid reducing significance levels.

Project Exercise | THINKING ABOUT STATISTICAL SIGNIFICANCE IN THE BEHAVIORAL SCIENCE LITERATURE

This chapter is devoted to reviewing the key components that enable researchers to formulate and subsequently test hypotheses using statistics and data analysis. A great deal of material was covered in the course of this chapter, everything from sampling distributions to standard error, from the null hypothesis to power and effect size. When used

Table 9.4 | Some Guidelines for Reading for Meaning in Journal Articles

1. *Read actively, not passively.* Identify the main message behind the author's research and summarize it in a sentence or two. What does the article's title reveal about the research and its results? What are the main points highlighted in the study's Abstract?

2. *What do you know about the author?* Is the author a noted expert on the topic or in the field? Has the author written similar publications? Do the current findings complement or oppose earlier findings? Is the author affiliated with a college or university, a research institution, or an organization that might espouse a particular political philosophy or point of view that might color any conclusions drawn from the results?

3. *What do you know about the article and the journal where it appears?* Is the article recent or several years old? Are the data new (sometimes called "cutting edge") or somewhat dated? Is the journal reputable, that is, is it cited regularly by scholars in the field? Is the journal subject to peer review via an editorial board? Is the journal known to be rigorous (e.g., it has a high rejection rate for submissions, only high quality articles appear in it) or is it relatively easy to publish there (e.g., acceptance rate is high, submissions vary in quality)?

4. *How is the article organized?* After a quick perusal of the article, is the author's organizational plan—the paper's outline—apparent? Do the article's main points seem to be represented by the headings and subheadings in the text?

5. *Read for knowledge, read for notes.* Read the article at least twice, once to get a sense of the article's main points and a second time for careful notetaking. The first reading can be quick—you can skim the article in order to get a sense of the whole. The second reading, however, needs to be relatively slow and deliberate so that you can really highlight the main points being made by the research, especially how the results fit into what is already known about the topic.

Source: Adapted from Hult (1996, pp. 41–42).

in consort with one another, these components enable researchers to ask focused questions of their data, and to use the resulting answers to build or revise theories in the behavioral sciences. Teaching you to use and understand these components and how they work together will enable you to perform analyses for assignments in your statistics class and for any independent piece of research you choose to conduct. The knowledge you are acquiring, too, can be used to think about research that has already been published.

When reading and evaluating a published piece of research, you should begin by thinking about whether the study's results are meaningful—important or consequential for research and theory—as well as whether significant or nonsignificant relationships exist among the study's independent and dependent variables. Table 9.4 offers some suggestions about how to read for meaning when you review an empirical article. The suggestions in Table 9.4 are meant to remind you that an article is more than just its statistical results, that you must get a sense of the whole text—from the topic of the study to the author's intentions in conducting the work and writing it up.

Once an article is read for meaning, the statistical results can be considered. By reviewing the four possible outcomes of any statistical analysis, Table 9.5 is meant to provide you with some perspective when you evaluate data published within an article. As shown by the entries in Table 9.5, the fact that a study obtains a significant result is not necessarily grounds for assuming the result is particularly noteworthy. If the sample size is small and the result is significant, then that result could be an important one (see possibility 1 in Table 9.5). On the other hand, a significant result that is based on a large sample size might or might not be interesting or prove to be useful for advancing knowledge about a topic. Possibility 2 is likely to motivate researchers to collect (or want) more data, while it can remind readers to be appropriately critical, even skeptical consumers.

Table 9.5

Relationships Between Significance and Sample Size for
Interpreting Research Results

	Is Result Significant?	Sample Size	Conclusion
Possibility 1	Yes	Small	Potentially important result
Possibility 2	Yes	Large	Could be important; collect more data
Possibility 3	No	Small	Inconclusive result; collect more data
Possibility 4	No	Large	Research (alternative) hypothesis is probably false

Source: Based on Aron and Aron (1997), Table 7–5, p. 148.

What happens when a predicted result is not found? The absence of a result can be tricky to interpret when a sample size is small—you cannot be sure if the null hypothesis is actually true or really false at the level of the population (see possibility 3 in Table 9.5). Nonresults and large samples do conspire together, as it were, highlighting the fact that even a favored research hypothesis is likely to be false (see possibility 4 in Table 9.5).

This chapter's *Exercise* involves having you search for empirical articles on a topic that interests you. You will then judge each article's hypothesis, read the article for meaning, and then evaluate the reported data—the results and the statistical analyses that led to them. A series of suggested steps follow:

1. Select a well-defined *area of research* within the behavioral science literature (e.g., social psychology, experimental psychology, sociology of the family).
2. Select a well-defined *topic* within the area of research (e.g., deceiving and detecting deceit in social psychology; divided attention research in experimental psychology; divorce and remarriage in the sociology of the family).
3. Search the topic's *literature* for recent, representative experimental or quasi-experimental investigations. To do so, visit your institution's reference library and use one of the online databases for your search (e.g., PsycLIT, Sociological Abstracts, ERIC; for search tips, see Hult, 1996; Dunn, 1999).
4. Obtain copies of two or three articles, read each one for meaning (follow the suggested guidelines in Table 9.4), determine whether the hypotheses are appropriate (rely on the criteria listed in Data Box 9.D), and then evaluate any statistical results based on the possibilities listed in Table 9.5. As you perform these activities, answer the questions listed below to the best of your ability. At this point in time, you probably feel uncertain about your knowledge of hypothesis testing; indeed, you may be hesitant to use what you know to critique a published article. Your reservations are understandable, but there is no better way to learn the utility and limits of hypothesis testing than to "leap in" and apply what you know. I promise you that this exercise will help you to learn the material that is presented in the next few chapters. Base the answers to the following questions on your reactions to the articles you collected:

■ Are the published results important? What makes the results important—the research topic(s), the question(s) asked, the statistical conclusions about the results, and/or the author's opinion? What is *your* opinion about the meaning and statistical reliability of the results?

■ What makes each study's hypothesis a good one? Do the hypotheses have any shortcomings? If so, what are they?

- What makes the study's hypothesis, methodology, and results meaningful? Do the results have practical as well as statistical significance?
- Is the sample size of the study large or small? Is your judgment a relative one (i.e., is a study based on 25 participants really very different than another with 30 people), or is the sample truly substantial (i.e., close to or over 100 participants)?
- Did you find a study that lacked significant results? If so, how did the author(s) explain the absence of results? Do you agree with the explanation? If not, how do you think that the absence of results can or should be explained?
- Chances are that you had difficulty locating studies lacking significant results, presumably due to the publication bias inherent in the behavioral sciences—usually only those studies with significant differences between groups ever get published. The search for significance is important, but do you think it is sometimes short-sighted where theory development and hypothesis testing are concerned?
- What else would you like to know about the significance testing used by the authors of the studies you collected? Can you think of any competing or complementary hypotheses the researchers might have tested using their data? If such hypotheses were tested, what statistical results would you anticipate? Try answering this question using the four possibilities outlined in Table 9.5.

LOOKING FORWARD THEN BACK

This chapter represents the first major step into hypothesis testing using inferential statistics, and the decision trees appearing at the start of the chapter emphasize this point. The first decision tree provides a concise overview of the steps needed to adequately—and accurately—perform a one-sample hypothesis test, which involves determining whether observed sample data hail from a known population.

Practical as well as conceptual issues presented in this first tree resonate with the three others; indeed, if you forget some important detail, you need only look to one of these subsequent trees for guidance. The second decision tree is a quick guide to selecting an appropriate significance level for a test statistic. The decision is one of the most important ones a data analyst makes, as it entails choosing convention (i.e., $p < .05$) or being more conservative (i.e., $p < .01$ or $.001$); only on a rare occasion would one be more liberal than the tree's guidelines suggest (i.e., $p > .05$). The third decision tree cautions the data analyst from being too quick to perform a hypothesis test and risk drawing an error in inference. Please note that the tree is flexible in that it can be used to evaluate analyses you perform or those available in the published literature. Finally, the fourth decision tree summarizes important considerations in thinking about statistical power, whether a given test on some data will allow you to demonstrate a desired result. Power concerns are important for effective hypothesis testing, and so we are brought back full circle to the main point of this chapter, as well as most research conducted in the behavioral sciences.

Summary

1. Hypothesis testing compares the reactions of distinct groups to a dependent measure following exposure to a level of an independent variable. Any resulting systematic change in a group's reaction to a dependent measure is attributed to the independent variable.

2. Statistical differences are examined at the level of sample data, but any observed differences between groups are assumed to originate at the population level. Such differences indicate that one population (represented by a control group) is different from another (represented by the experimental group).

3. The use of a sample statistic (e.g., $\overline{X}$, s) to estimate a population parameter (e.g., μ, σ) is called point estimation. In contrast, interval estimation provides a range of values for sample statistics based on repeated sampling of a population of interest.

4. Sampling error refers to a distribution of sample means that vary somewhat from one another in value.

5. Inferential statistics are used in hypothesis testing, generally to demonstrate mean differences. Hypothesis testing compares sample data and statistics to either known or estimated population parameters.

6. A distribution of sample means is a gathering of sample means that are all based on some random sample of a fixed size N of some population. A sampling distribution contains statistics based on samples of some fixed size N that were drawn from a larger population.

7. The mean of a sampling distribution of any sample statistic is called its expected value. The mean of a sampling distribution of means ($\mu_{\overline{X}}$) is called the expected value of the sampling distribution of means.

8. The standard deviation of a sampling distribution of sample statistics is called its standard error. The standard deviation of a sampling distribution of means is known as the standard error of the mean.

9. The central limit theorem states that as the size (N) of a sample becomes increasingly large, the shape of the sampling distribution of the mean becomes normal or bell-shaped. The mean of this distribution is equal to μ, and its standard deviation—the standard error of the mean—is equal to $\sigma/\sqrt{N}$.

10. The so-called law of large numbers states that as a sample increases in size, the value of a sample mean ($\overline{X}$) will close in on the value of the population mean (μ).

11. Although it is based on a population, the standard error of the mean can be estimated using sample data and accompanying statistics. As the N of a sample increases in size, the error between the observed $\overline{X}$ and a known μ substantially decreases. The standard error of the mean, then, reveals how closely a sample mean approximates μ.

12. The range of values where a sample mean is expected to fall is called a confidence interval.

13. There are two types of hypotheses, conceptual/theoretical and statistical. Conceptual hypotheses identify predicted relationships among independent variables and dependent measures. Statistical hypotheses test whether the predicted relationships are mathematically supported by the existing data, that is, do differences based on sample statistics reflect differences among population parameters.

14. Statistical hypotheses can be directional or nondirectional. A directional hypothesis identifies the precise nature, the ordered difference, between population parameters. No precise or ordered difference is specified by a non-directional hypothesis, simply that some difference between parameters will occur.

15. Any experiment pits a null hypothesis (H_0) against the researcher's prediction, which is embodied in the alternative or research hypothesis (H_1). The null hypothesis posits that no discernable differences exist among population parameters, while the alternative hypothesis specifies that some difference exists between population parameters.

16. The null hypothesis is the touchstone or guide for any statistical test. When no predicted difference is found by a test statistic, the researcher retains or accepts the null hypothesis of no difference. When a predicted difference is found by a test statistic, the researcher rejects the null hypothesis of no difference. Note that the alternative hypothesis is neither accepted nor rejected.

17. Significance testing relies on statistical tests and probabilities to decide whether to accept or reject a null hypothesis. A significant difference is one where a mathematically reliable, detected difference exists between two (or more) sample means that reflect distinctions between two (or more) population means. The word "significant" does *not* refer to "meaningful" or "important," rather it simply indicates that some difference was "detected."

18. Statistical significance is guided by probability or p values, which are also called significance levels or α levels. The most common p values employed in statistical tests are .05, .01, and .001; indeed, the p value of .05 is taken to be the conventional cutoff distinguishing between significant (i.e., $p < .05$) and non-significant (i.e., $p > .05$) differences between means and the populations they approximate.

19. Critical values are numerical values that a calculated test statistic must match or exceed in value in order for statistical significance to be realized. Critical values are usually presented in tabular form, and such tables of values exist for virtually all inferential statistics. When the value of a test statistic falls at or above a designated critical value and into a critical region, the null hypothesis is usually rejected. When a test statistic falls below a critical value, inside what is called the region of retention, then the null hypothesis is accepted.

20. Significance tests can be either one- or two-tailed. A one-tailed significance test relies on a single critical value and region of rejection. Two critical values and regions of rejection, however, are used for a two-tailed significance test.

21. Degrees of freedom are numerical guides that help researchers to select critical values for comparison with calculated test statistics. Technically, degrees of freedom are the number of scores that are free to vary or take on different values once a statistical test is performed on a data set.

22. Single sample hypothesis testing is usually used to determine whether a sample of data is consistent in value with a known population or another different population. The z test is frequently used in single sample hypothesis tests where population values are known. Testing whether a correlation coefficient (r) is significantly different than 0, too, is a single sample hypothesis test.

23. There are two types of inferential errors, Type I and Type II. A Type I error takes place when a null hypothesis is rejected but it is actually true—in other words, an effect is found but it is not really a true result. A Type II error happens when a

null hypothesis is accepted but it is actually false—an effect is missed when it actually exists. Type I errors are considered worse because false, misleading results affect future theorizing, research, and education concerning a topic.

24. Statistical power is the probability that a statistical test will correctly reject a null hypothesis. Power is defined as $1 - \beta$. Concrete steps, such as increasing sample size, will enhance a test's power to reject a null hypothesis.

25. Effect size is the degree to which two populations (represented by control and experimental groups) do not share overlapping distributions. Greater effect size is linked to higher levels of statistical power, leading to an increased likelihood of rejecting a null hypothesis. Practically speaking, effect size involves how far apart two sample means are from one another, as well as how much variance occurs within these respective groups.

Key Terms

Alpha (α) level *(p. 336)*
Alternative hypothesis *(p. 334)*
Central limit theorem *(p. 322)*
Confidence interval *(p. 327)*
Critical region *(p. 339)*
Critical value *(p. 339)*
Degrees of freedom *(p. 342)*
Directional hypothesis *(p. 333)*
Distribution of sample means *(p. 320)*
Effect size *(p. 355)*
Expected value *(p. 321)*
Experimental hypothesis *(p. 334)*

Hypothesis testing *(p. 318)*
Interval estimation *(p. 317)*
Law of large numbers *(p. 323)*
MAGIC criteria *(p. 342)*
Nondirectional hypothesis *(p. 333)*
Null hypothesis *(p. 334)*
One-tailed significance test *(p. 340)*
Point estimation *(p. 317)*
Power *(p. 351)*
Region of rejection *(p. 339)*
Region of retention *(p. 340)*
Sampling distribution *(p. 320)*

Sampling error *(p. 317)*
Significance level *(p. 336)*
Significance testing *(p. 336)*
Significant difference *(p. 336)*
Standard error *(p. 321)*
Standard error of the mean *(p. 321)*
Statistical hypothesis *(p. 332)*
Two-tailed significance test *(p. 340)*
Type I error *(p. 349)*
Type II error *(p. 349)*

Chapter Problems

1. What is point estimation? Is point estimation different than interval estimation? How so? What role do these two forms of estimation play in hypothesis testing?

2. Explain the difference between a distribution of sample means drawn from a population and a sampling distribution.

3. How do frequency distributions differ from sampling distributions?

4. What are the specific labels used to denote the mean and standard deviation of a sampling distribution? What is the name used for the standard deviation of a sampling distribution of means?

5. If fixed, reasonably large sample sizes are repeatedly and randomly drawn from a population, what will the shape of the sampling distributions of means be like? Why?

6. What is the central limit theorem? Why is this theorem so important to inferential statistics? What is the central limit theorem's particular relationship with the standard error of the mean?

7. Why is the law of large numbers relevant to the central limit theorem?

8. A normally distributed population has a μ of 43 and a σ of 16. Determine the standard error of the mean ($\sigma_{\bar{X}}$) for each of the following sample sizes: $N = 10, 30, 55, 70, 100$.

9. A normally distributed population has a μ of 80 and a σ of 20. Determine the standard error of the mean ($\sigma_{\bar{X}}$) for each of the following sample sizes: $N = 15, 40, 65, 80, 110$.

10. A sample of 85 participants is drawn from a population. The mean of the sample is 30 and the unbiased estimate of its standard deviation is 6. Calculate 75%, 95%, and 99% confidence intervals for the mean.

11. A sample of 100 participants is drawn from a population. The mean of the sample is 56 and the unbiased estimate of its standard deviation is 12.5. Calculate 80%, 95%, and 99% confidence intervals for the mean.

12. What is a statistical hypothesis? How does it differ from a conceptual or theoretical hypothesis?

13. Name several of the components comprising a good hypothesis.

14. Define directional and nondirectional hypotheses. Is there any advantage to favoring one type over the other? Why?

15. An educational psychologist develops a new reading program she believes will accelerate reading skills and comprehension of the population of at risk readers in grades 1 and 2. A sample of at risk readers takes part in the reading program for 4 months. The researcher decides to determine if the sample's scores on a reading and comprehension test exceed the population average for at risk readers. Formulate H_0 and H_1 using a directional test and then a nondirectional test.

16. Explain the status of the null hypothesis within statistical analysis and science more broadly.

17. Statistical analysis is guided by the null hypothesis and not the alternative hypothesis—why is this so? Why is it difficult to prove an alternative or research hypothesis? How does this difficulty enhance the utility of the null hypothesis?

18. An investigator can accept (retain) the null hypothesis or she can reject it—why can't a researcher accept the alternative hypothesis?

19. Define the word significant, as well as its use, in statistical contexts.

20. Explain the difference between statistically significant research results and those possessing practical significance. Are these research terms opposites or complements of one another?

21. Review the following p values and indicate which, in conventional statistical terms, are significant, marginal, or non-significant: .031, .040, .003, .076, .051, .120, .250, .098, .0001, and .046.

22. What is a critical value? What role do critical values play in hypothesis testing? In general, is it easier to reject a null hypothesis using one-tailed or two-tailed critical values? Explain your answer.

23. Explain the difference between one-tailed and two-tailed significance tests. Is one test considered to be more statistically rigorous than the other? Why? Which test enables researchers to satisfy their curiosity regarding relationships among variables in a statistical analysis?

24. Assume that the educational psychologist cited above in problem 15 analyzed her data using a z test. What critical value(s) for z would be used for a one-tailed significance test at the .05 and .01 levels? For a two-tailed test at the .05 and .01 levels?

25. In conceptual terms, what are degrees of freedom? More practically, how are degrees of freedom used by data analysts?

26. Using the study described in problem 14 for context, review and summarize the four steps for testing a hypothesis.

27. What does the acronym MAGIC mean? Why should researchers adhere to its criteria when conducting research?

28. An herbal dietary supplement is believed to enhance the short-term memory capacity of individuals who are age 85 and over. A gerontologist dispenses the supplement to a group of 65 elderly persons living in a nursing care facility. Four months later the gerontologist tests their short-term memory, observing that the group's mean performance on a standardized measure is 35. The researcher knows that the performance distribution for individuals 85 years and older has a μ of 30 and a σ of 10. What is the probability that the group's sample mean of 35 is different from the general performance distribution? Use a two-tailed significance test where $\alpha = .05$.

29. A developmental psychologist studies moral awareness in male and female adolescents. Casual observation suggests that girls develop moral awareness earlier than boys, though most published research contains male participants. A standard measure of moral awareness, one validated using only male samples, has a μ of 72 and a σ of 18. The psychologist administers the measure to 58 13-year-old girls, whose mean score is 76. Test the hypothesis that the known μ representing males is different from the sample mean for females. Use a two-tailed test where $\alpha = .01$.

30. In statistical terms, what does a significant correlation (r)

between two variables reflect? What criteria promote the likelihood of observing a significant correlation?

31. The correlation between self-esteem and weight in a sample of 50 people is equal to $-.37$. Using a two-tailed test, determine if this correlation is significant. What are the degrees of freedom and the value of r_{crit}? Report what this result means in words and using statistical nomenclature.

32. What is a Type I error? Why do Type I errors occur? Provide an example.

33. What is a Type II error? Why do Type II errors occur? Provide an example.

34. As inferential errors, both Type I and Type II errors are disruptive to the research process. Is one worse than the other? Why? Provide an example to support your answer.

35. What can be done to reduce the incidence of making a Type I error? What can be done to reduce the incidence of making a Type II error? How can a researcher balance the demands of these competing concerns in a research project?

36. An experimental psychologist finds a significant difference at the .05 level between an experimental and a control condition in a highly technical study. What is the probability the investigator is committing a Type I error? What can the researcher do to reduce the chances a Type I error is being committed?

37. Define the word power, as well as its use, in statistical contexts.

38. A clinical psychologist is planning a yearlong intervention study on alleviating depression among elderly women whose spouses died of medical complications following surgery. What are some concrete steps the researcher can take to enhance the power of her statistical analyses at the study's conclusion? (Hint: Consider using the decision trees that open the chapter to answer this question.)

39. Define the word effect size, as well as its use, in statistical contexts.

40. How does sample size affect power, critical regions for rejection and retention, and a researcher's ability to reject the null hypothesis?

41. A researcher acquires some sample data and wants to determine whether it comes from a larger population of interest. Unfortunately, there is no information available regarding the population's parameters—can the researcher still perform the appropriate hypothesis test? Why or why not? (Hint: Consider using the decision trees that open the chapter to answer this question.)

42. An investigator wants to select a significance level for a topic where little information is available. What significance level should she choose? (Hint: Consider using the decision trees that open the chapter to answer this question.)

43. A researcher wants to avoiding making a Type I error when analyzing the data from a recent project where the $N = 24$. She intends to use a one-tailed test. Can you give her any specific analytic guidance before the analyses begin? (Hint: Consider using the decision trees that open the chapter to answer this question.)

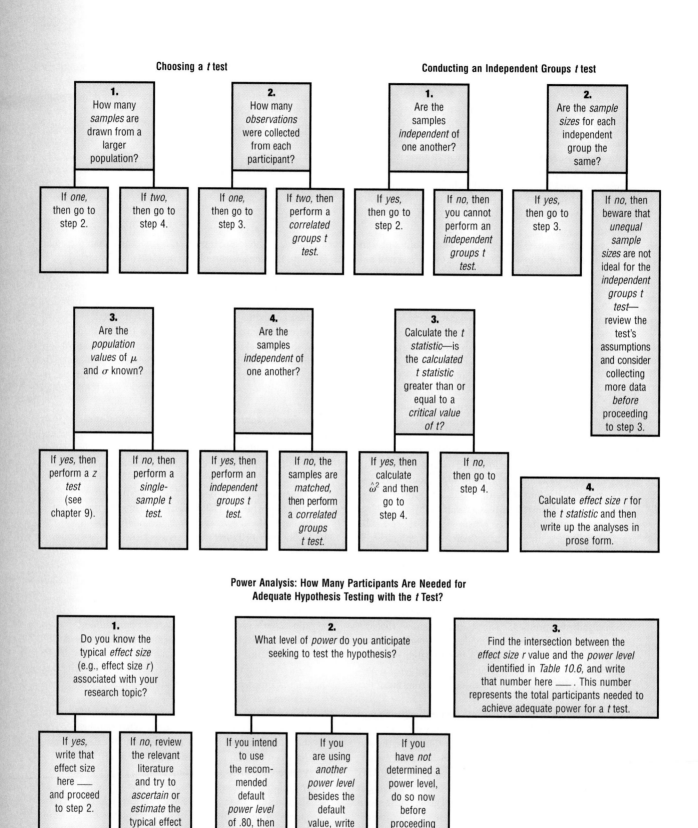

Choosing a *t* test

1. How many *samples* are drawn from a larger population?

If *one*, then go to step 2.

If *two*, then go to step 4.

2. How many *observations* were collected from each participant?

If *one*, then go to step 3.

If *two*, then perform a *correlated groups t test*.

3. Are the *population values* of μ and σ known?

If *yes*, then perform a *z* test (see chapter 9).

If *no*, then perform a *single-sample t test*.

4. Are the samples *independent* of one another?

If *yes*, then perform an *independent groups t test*.

If *no*, the samples are *matched*, then perform a *correlated groups t test*.

Conducting an Independent Groups *t* test

1. Are the samples *independent* of one another?

If *yes*, then go to step 2.

If *no*, then you cannot perform an *independent groups t test*.

2. Are the *sample sizes* for each independent group the same?

If *yes*, then go to step 3.

If *no*, then beware that *unequal sample sizes* are not ideal for the *independent groups t test*—review the test's assumptions and consider collecting more data *before* proceeding to step 3.

3. Calculate the *t statistic*—is the *calculated t statistic* greater than or equal to a *critical value of t?*

If *yes*, then calculate $\hat{\omega}^2$ and then go to step 4.

If *no*, then go to step 4.

4. Calculate *effect size r* for the *t statistic* and then write up the analyses in prose form.

Power Analysis: How Many Participants Are Needed for Adequate Hypothesis Testing with the *t* Test?

1. Do you know the typical *effect size* (e.g., effect size *r*) associated with your research topic?

If *yes*, write that effect size here ___ and proceed to step 2.

If *no*, review the relevant literature and try to *ascertain* or *estimate* the typical effect size and then go to step 2.

2. What level of *power* do you anticipate seeking to test the hypothesis?

If you intend to use the recommended default *power level* of .80, then proceed to step 3.

If you are using *another power level* besides the default value, write it here ___ and then go to step 3.

If you have *not* determined a power level, do so now before proceeding to step 3.

3. Find the intersection between the *effect size r* value and the *power level* identified in *Table 10.6*, and write that number here ___ . This number represents the total participants needed to achieve adequate power for a *t* test.

MEAN COMPARISON I: THE t TEST

tatistical tests are rarely born out of high drama, but they often originate because of human interest, ingenuity, and simple necessity. The chances are very good that you are already familiar with the inferential test reviewed in this chapter, one created by a young scientist working in an Irish brewery. Neither a pure mathematician nor a brewer, this scientist grappled with the same problem all behavioral scientists (and statistics students!) struggle with—how to make inferences from sample data when the samples are small and the variability of the larger population is unknown. The scientist devised a statistical test enabling the brewery to detect differences between different grains and hops, as well as kegs of beer. Prior to this innovation, objective analysis of reasonable production questions was difficult (e.g., Is one strain of barley superior to another? Is one batch of beer darker in color or richer in flavor than a separate batch?). Have I piqued your interest in the *t* test, or merely made you thirsty? More details on the birth of the test and its creator appear later, in Data Box 10.A.

Historical fact and humor aside, the *t* test (or "Student's *t*") was created to deal with small samples when the parameters and variability of larger, parent populations remain unknown. Where hypothesis testing is concerned, the material presented here represents a minor departure from the previous chapter. From this point forward, our reliance on explicit information about parameters is over, as the inferential tests we use will presume little or nothing is known about population characteristics. To be sure, we will use sample statistics ($\overline{X}$, *s*) to make inferences about populations, but the fact is that analytical efforts are more properly directed toward perfecting experimental design and correctly applying statistics and data analysis within it. We are still asking focused questions of our data, but we must take care to be sure that the questions are asked in experimentally appropriate and rigorous ways.

This is the first of four chapters introducing inferential statistical tests designed to identify significant differences among group means or average levels of behavior. The focus of this chapter, the *t* test, examines differences existing between two—and *only* two—means. Three variations of the *t* test, each with a slightly different use, are presented in this chapter:

- One variation of the *t* test is used for hypothesis testing about a sample mean when the relevant population mean (μ) and standard deviation (σ) are unknown. **Application:** A developmental psychologist wants to test the prediction that highly reactive ("choleric") infants show more stranger anxiety than the general population of children. This form of the *t* test is similar to the one-sample *z* test introduced in chapter 9.
- A second variation of the *t* test is probably the most common inferential test taught to and used by undergraduate behavioral science students. Often referred to as the *t* test for independent groups, it is specifically designed to detect significant differences between a control group and an experimental group in any classic two-group randomized experiment. **Application:** A marital therapist speculates that, following divorce, women maintain larger social networks (i.e., family and friend connections) than do men. In order to collect data for the analysis, the therapist interviews male and female clients about the relative number and frequency of former contacts as well as newly initiated social relationships.
- The third variation appears less frequently in the behavioral science literature, but it is a powerful addition to any data analyst's repertoire. The *t* test for dependent groups enables an investigator to demonstrate the presence of measurable change in the average attitudes or behavior of a group from one point in time (time$_1$) to another (time$_2$). **Application:** Following an intensive intervention, the average amount of social anxiety reported by a group of chronically shy people is found to decrease across a two-month period, suggesting that the treatment was successful.

These three variations of the *t* test are presented graphically in Figure 10.1.

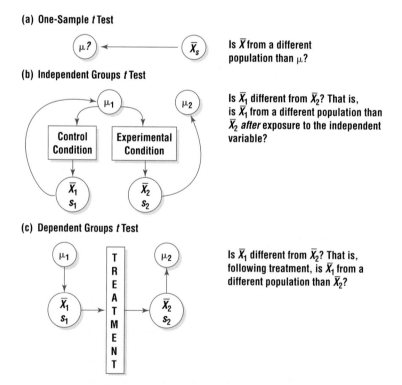

Figure 10.1   Experimental Logic Underlying the Three Variations of the *t* Test

Before we learn how to appropriately calculate and apply each of these two group inferential tests in experimental and quasi-experimental settings, a brief review of the important role of mean comparison in the behavioral sciences is needed.

Recapitulation: Why Compare Means?

> Observations are different copies of one original; statistics are different originals affording one "generic portrait."
>
> ——Edgeworth (1887, p. 139)

As this quote from Edgeworth suggests, statistics are used to represent possibilities—what might be true given the conditions found within some situation or, in behavioral science terms, a controlled research setting. The statistic most often used to represent the behavior of many observations is, of course, the mean. In chapter 4, we learned that the mean is the best single indicator for describing an array or sample of observations. This singular status is awarded because the mean identifies the typical or average response in a group—how Edgeworth's "generic portrait" of the average individual responds to some particular circumstance or influential stimulus.

Researchers cannot study every person's singular reactions to an event, so people's collective response is examined in the form of a mean, just as samples are meant to stand in for larger populations. The mean possesses a canonical—that is, a sanctioned or authoritative—place in the behavioral sciences, so much so that discipline-based books and journal articles rarely bother to explain *why* it is used with such regularity or that such faith is attached to any results based upon it. Beyond its mathematical properties (e.g., the least squares principle; see chapter 4) and ubiquity, most statistics texts never mention other beneficial aspects of the mean. Indeed, on occasion, just the opposite occurs—the "tyranny" of the mean within the behavioral sciences is decried (Aron & Aron, 1997) and the dearth of alternative approaches in general is mentioned, instead, implying everyone implicitly understands the unique status of the mean (some alternative, more qualitative, approaches are introduced in Appendix F).

Think about it: what does the mean actually *mean*, as it were? You don't often "see" people's average behavior or learn their average opinions in some topical domain (e.g., politics, religion, women's issues), rather, you *infer* a group's typical response by sifting through and thinking about what several people did or said. On rare occasions, of course, responses unite or are highly similar to one another, and this low variability clues us into actually recognizing a mean or average reaction. More often than not, however, we are left to our own judgment devices where mean reactions are concerned—in a real sense, we make inferences about averages in much the same way inferential statistical tests do. We judge whether one sample of an act or opinion is similar to or distinguishable from another. Our judgments of significance where mean performance is concerned, too, are simply less formalized and somewhat subjective when compared against the objective methods of statistics (e.g., Kahneman, Slovic, & Tversky, 1982; Nisbett & Ross, 1980).

As you acquire the skills for comparing means statistically, try to keep in mind the hypothetical but general behaviors they are meant to represent. Do not simply focus on the means as numbers; focus on what they refer to, what story they tell within a research context. When you compare one mean with another to learn if some reliable, detectable difference exists between them, you are really speculating about whether what was said or done in one group is substantially different from the acts performed in another group. Following the outline of the standard experiment summarized in chapter 2 and noted selectively thereafter, then, did the manipulation of some independent variable create a different average level of behavior in the dependent measure for an experimental and control group, respectively?

The Relationship Between the *t* and the *z* Distributions

At this point, I can imagine many student readers asking themselves, "Oh no—why do we need to learn about *another* distribution? Can't we just use the *z* distribution—I already know it!" Although it is often desirable to stick with what you already know well, continuing to rely on the standard normal distribution would not be beneficial educationally or, where research is concerned, empirically. To begin with, the *z* distribution is limited—it cannot be used when population parameters remain unknown, for example. Using sample statistics to estimate population parameters is fine to a degree, but when we run into smaller samples—a reality for most behavioral scientists and student researchers—we run into some inferential difficulties.

Use a *z* test to detect mean differences when σ is known; otherwise, use one of the three *t* test variations.

Samples with 30 or fewer observations rarely provide accurate estimates. Based on such smaller samples, even an unbiased standard deviation ($\hat{s}$) will *underestimate* σ much of the time, usually in 50% of the cases where it is applied (Runyon, Haber, Pittenger, & Coleman, 1996). This fact leads to a broad but important conclusion for researchers: The standard normal distribution will not adequately reflect a sampling distribution of means when the sample size is a fixed value lower than 30. When you have the opportunity to take a research methods course, conduct an experiment on your own, or work on a faculty member's project, you will learn firsthand the real but challenging truth that the typical research enterprise in the behavioral sciences runs on less than 30 participants.

The *z* distribution provides unreliable estimates of differences between samples when the number of available observations is less than 30.

The *t* Distribution

Enter the *t* distribution—or, actually, *t distributions*—which were derived to specifically deal with the inherent shortcomings posed by small samples and the statistics based upon them.

KEY TERM   The *t* **distributions** are sampling distributions of means designed for use with small samples. Any *t distribution* has a mean of 0 and a standard deviation that decreases as the available degrees of freedom or number of observations increase.

To begin with, then, no *t* distribution is a standard normal distribution, though it possesses a characteristic "bell-shape" and, thus, is symmetric on both sides of its mean. As shown by the overlaying curves in Figure 10.2, the *t* distribution looks somewhat squat compared to the *z* distribution—it is shorter, flatter, and broader. In fact, *t* distributions tend to have a greater spread than the standard normal distribution, especially when sample sizes are relatively small.

Why is this so? Despite the fact that both *t* and *z* distributions have a mean of 0, they have different standard deviations. Where the standard normal distribution has fixed standard deviations equal to 1.0 (for a review, see chapter 5), the standard deviations of any *t* distribution vary in size; indeed, there is a distinct distribution for all possible degrees of freedom. The spread of the *t* distributions and their standard deviations do *decrease* in size as the available degrees of freedom *increase* in value (remember that *z* tests do not have or need degrees of freedom; see chapters 5 and 9).

t tests are used to compare one or two sample means—but *not* more than two.

The distributions are similar where probabilities are concerned, however; similar to the *z* distribution, a *t* distribution can be used to determine the relative likelihood a sample mean differs from a population mean. Later, we will see that directional and nondirectional hypotheses can be posed and tested in a similar fashion using either distribution. Both the *t* and *z* distributions test hypotheses involving either one or two sample means, but no more than two (other, more advanced tests are used to compare more than

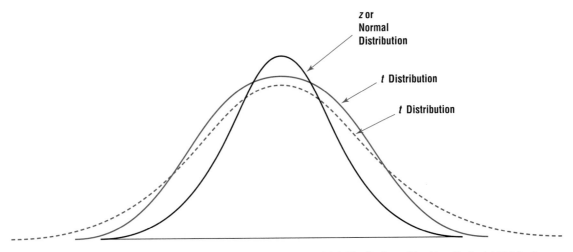

Figure 10.2 Comparing the Standard Normal (*z*) Distribution with a Hypothetical *t* Distribution

Note: The *z* distribution is more compact than the *t* distribution, which tends to display greater variability under its curve.

two means simultaneously; see chapters 11, 12, and 13). Finally, when a sample size is quite large, the statistical procedures and conclusions drawn from them are identical (and some researchers routinely rely on *t* tests when a *z* test would suffice; Harris, 1998).

Assumptions Underlying the *t* Test

Because it is a parametric test, the *t* test was designed for data analysis only when certain conditions are met. These conditions are:

- The population (or populations) the sample data are drawn from is normally distributed.
- The data are either (a) randomly sampled from a larger population or (b) individually sampled from a larger population. In both cases, the sample data are used to generalize back to a population of origin.
- Means can be calculated from the data, so that the dependent measures involved must be based on either interval or ratio scales (for a review of scales of measurement and their properties, see chapter 1).
- When two independent samples are used to test a hypothesis, the samples are presumed to come from populations that have equal variances.

Please do not read this list of assumptions as a checklist of requirements. Why? Because we already acknowledged that the *t* test is for use in those situations where information about population parameters is scarce (e.g., how can a researcher know if two populations have equal variances when little is know about either one?). Similarly, an investigator will not necessarily be able to verify—only hope or assume—that a population he or she is sampling from is actually normally distributed. As in most analytical situations, performing analyses with the *t* test requires a bit of faith, if not a leap of faith.

Violating the *t* Test's Assumptions. Seasoned researchers and well-intentioned novices frequently violate the assumptions underlying the *t* test. Why do such violations occur? Are some violations more typical than others are? In many cases, there is no practical way to acquire the necessary information to avoid violating one or another assumption. We acknowledged earlier in the book that true random sampling is rarely used, and that random selection is treated as an adequate, though less-than-perfect, substitute for it. If one knew a great deal about a population—that it was normal, for instance—the need to conduct experimental research relying on the *t* test would be much less pressing. Violation of the *t* test's assumptions is acceptable in most situations (though trying to perform an analysis without calculating a sample mean(s) would surely be problematic) because the test is said to be *robust*.

KEY TERM   A statistical test is described as **robust** when it provides reasonably valid portrayals of data (and relationships therein) when some of the test's assumptions are not met during its application.

▽

The robust nature of the *t* test ensures that results remain reliable even when one of the test's assumptions is violated.

In particular, the robustness of a test lies in its ability to hold the probability of making a Type I error relatively constant. When some of the test's assumptions are violated (e.g. no random sampling, nonnormal parent populations), the *t* test holds the likelihood of incorrectly rejecting the null hypothesis to the predetermined *p* value (e.g., .05, .01). A robust test, then, provides researchers with a decided advantage—they are no more likely to detect a false effect when conditions for the statistical test are fair than when conditions are ideal.

Across time and frequent application, the *t* test has proven itself to be relatively immune to the general violations of some of its assumptions. As a statistical procedure, then, it still indicates reliable, valid differences between a sample mean and a population parameter or two-sample means from potentially different populations when conditions are less than ideal. Naturally, no researcher should actively seek to violate any of the test's assumptions, nor should an investigator assume that every detected difference is real—it pays to be cautious and conservative when reporting any observed difference, even when no assumption was violated. (By now, I hope your reflex is to think about why replicating results from any experiment or other piece of research is so important.)

Is there a situation where a researcher should not calculate a *t* test? Yes, there is one clear case for worry. Harris (1998) suggests that the *t* test will provide less than trustworthy results when two samples are being compared and (a) they have an unequal number of observations in each, (b) the respective distributions are not all normal in shape, and (c) the sample variances differ from one another by a factor of 10 or more (e.g., $s_1^2 = 15.5$ and $s_2^2 = 27.0$). When these three problems coincide, then, the *t* test will not be robust—some other statistical test or an alteration in the data will be required (see also, Coombs, Algina, & Oltman, 1996).

What Does the *t* Test Actually Do?   The practical, mathematical mechanics of the *t* test are introduced shortly, but I want you to have a conceptual foundation for the statistic before you do any calculations. The *t* test assesses whether any measurable difference exists between means—any difference found with sample data reflects a difference at the population level. When no difference occurs, the value of the *t* statistic will be equal to 0, suggesting that the distributions being examined are identical. As the distributions are measured as being different from one another, the value of the *t* statistic deviates from 0 in either a positive or a negative direction.

Because *t* distributions are symmetric (recall Figure 10.2), the positive or negative sign accompanying the test statistic lets the user know which mean was larger than the other (i.e., a negative *t* value indicates that the second mean was greater—subtracting a larger number from a smaller one provides a negative number; the first mean, then, is identified as the larger one when the *t* value is positive). Similar to the *z* distribution, the negative sign is a guidepost for locating and working with the regions of rejection and retention under the *t* distribution (but see Data Box 10.B for a discussion of what to do when a negative *t* value is obtained).

The number representing the measurable difference between means is then divided by the standard error of the difference between the means. Because the value of the population standard deviation(s) (σ) is unknown, we rely on a sample standard deviation (*s*) to calculate the value of the standard error (recall that standard error is reviewed extensively in chapter 9). Larger values of *t*, which point to significant mean differences, occur when:

- The difference between means is relatively large, and this difference serves as the numerator for calculating any *t* statistic.
- The standard deviation, which is used to estimate the standard error of the difference between the means, is relatively small. As the denominator for the *t* statistic, a smaller standard error will result in a larger value of *t*.
- As always, larger sample sizes are desirable because they lead to smaller standard deviations, which in turn leads to a smaller standard error for the difference between the means.

When any one or a combination of these circumstances occur within sample data based on an experiment or other investigation, a researcher's chance of successfully and legitimately rejecting the null hypothesis of no difference is quite good.

> A *t* test detects a significant difference between means when the difference is large, the sample standard deviation is small, and/or the sample size is large.

DATA BOX 10.A

Some Statistical History: Who was "A Student"?

William S. Gosset (1876–1937), who published his work under the pseudonym "A Student," studied chemistry and math at New College, Oxford. After leaving Oxford, Gosset was one of several scientists hired by the Guinness Brewing Company, where he examined how brewing outcomes (e.g., beer quality) were influenced by variability in the quality and type of ingredients, as well as temperature fluctuations (Peters, 1987; Tankard, 1984).

Prior to Gosset's innovations, most such quality control analyses relied on the standard normal distribution, which, as you know, has wide and correct applications when samples are large. Because he necessarily contended with small samples, however, Gosset set out to devise ways to make adequate inferences when the standard normal distribution could not be used. Gosset developed a new distribution by combining mathematics with what is now referred to as simulation, systematically creating a sampling distribution of means and then examining the ratios of the differences between sample means and the (known) mean of the population they were drawn from (Peters, 1987). The resulting ratios fit the new distribution but not the normal distribution. Gosset's work drew the attention of the great statistician Ronald A. Fisher, who offered mathematical proofs for the new distribution, later deriving the formula most often recognized as the *t* test from it. (Fisher, one of the 20th century's foremost experimentalists, is profiled in the next chapter.)

Student's *t* is ubiquitous in the behavioral sciences and elsewhere—today, it is even a common fixture on the keypad of many pocket calculators, a fact that would no doubt surprise the modest Gosset (Vadum & Rankin, 1998). But why did Gosset publish under "Student" and not his own name? Gosset wanted to save the Guinness Brewery from the embarrassment of admitting that it sometimes produced a less than potable batch or two of ale (Aron & Aron, 1997). Generations of statisticians, researchers, and students—not to mention distillers and consumers—are forever in his debt.

Hypothesis Testing with *t*: One-Sample Case

The *t* test and the *z* test are based on similar formulas. The only difference is that the denominator in the *t* test is the estimated standard error of the mean ($s_{\overline{X}}$), whereas the denominator in the *z* test is the standard error of the population ($\sigma_{\overline{X}}$). Both statistics are based on this formula:

$$t \text{ or } z = \frac{\text{observed sample mean} - \text{population mean}}{\textit{estimated} \text{ or } \textit{known} \text{ standard error}}.$$

Symbolically, then, a *t* statistic is determined using:

[10.1.1]

$$t = \frac{\overline{X} - \mu}{s_{\overline{X}}}.$$

The *single- or one-sample t test* links populations and samples together by way of mean comparison.

KEY TERM   The **single- or one-sample *t* test** is used to compare the observed mean of one sample with a hypothesized value assumed to represent a population. One-sample *t* tests are usually employed by researchers who want to determine if some set of scores or observations deviate from some established pattern or standard.

Imagine that a memory researcher is interested in determining whether careful and consistent training can extend the normal limitations of working (occasionally called short-term) memory. An undergraduate participant in a prior extended memory experiment increased his ability to recall strings of digits from the typical average of 7 to an unbelievable 79 (Ericsson, Chase, & Faloon, 1980). This rare and unusual mnemonic feat was performed by one person, who spent about 5 hours a week for over 1 1/2 years learning random sequences of digits (e.g., 5–4–8–2–1).

In contrast to this intriguing case study demonstration, our cognitivist chooses a more modest classroom demonstration. He trains a group of 20 students (10 males, 10 females), randomly selected from his class list, to increase their memory for digits across three sessions in a one-week period. The final session occurs during class, enabling the researcher to collect data from the trainees, perform an analysis, and immediately present results to the class. The students' recall accuracy for digits ranged from 8 to 13 digits, with a mean of 10 digits and an unbiased standard deviation of 2.5. The cognitive researcher wants to show that their mean recall is significantly higher than the presumed population average of 7 digits.

We begin to analyze these data by following the four steps for testing a hypothesis outlined in the last chapter (for a step-by-step guide, see Table 9.2). *Step 1* entails identifying the null and alternative hypotheses and then selecting a significance level for the test statistic. If the null hypothesis is true, then the training does not enhance the students' memory spans for digits—in other words, their average recall for digits should fall with the range of the population, or

$$H_0: \mu_{\text{recall}} \leq 7.0.$$

Please notice two things about the null hypothesis shown here. First, I added the word "recall" as a subscript to the population mean. Hypotheses should always be presented in terms of the parameter μ, but adding a label to it is very useful because it will always remind you about the dependent measure (i.e., mean recall for digits) you are actually testing. Second, the "less than or equal to sign" ($\leq$) is used here to indicate that although the normal outer limit for memory span is 7 digits—some people remember fewer, hence it is reasonable to indicate that recall of "7 or fewer" digits reflects the population average.

A directional hypothesis is used, of course, because the researcher specifically predicted that the three training sessions would *increase* recall accuracy for digits. Thus, the alternative or research hypothesis could be:

$$H_1: \mu_{recall} > 7.0.$$

Following usual practice, the significance level for the test will be held at .05.

Step 2. As always, the second step involves calculating the standard error of the mean and choosing whether to use a one- or a two-tailed test (see Table 9.2). Because we do not know the values of any population parameters, we must calculate the estimated standard error of the mean using the sample standard deviation, the sample *N*, and formula [9.8.1], which is renumbered here for consistency:

[10.2.1] $$s_{\overline{X}} = \frac{\hat{s}}{\sqrt{N}},$$

[10.2.2] $$s_{\overline{X}} = \frac{2.5}{\sqrt{20}},$$

[10.2.3] $$s_{\overline{X}} = \frac{2.5}{4.47},$$

[10.2.4] $$s_{\overline{X}} = .559.$$

Should we use a one- or a two-tailed significance test? In chapter 9, I encouraged you to rely on two-tailed tests due to their rigor, counseling that one-tailed tests be used only when the direction of a relationship is unquestionably certain or to increase available power. Let's assume the memory researcher never conducted a memory training program before, thus he decides to follow a more conservative approach and employ a two-tailed significance test here.

Step 3. We can now calculate the actual value of the one-sample *t*, as well as the test's degrees of freedom, and then determine whether to accept or to reject the null hypothesis. The formula for *t* is:

[10.3.1] $$t = \frac{\overline{X} - \mu}{s_{\overline{X}}}.$$

Calculating the *t* test is straightforward—we need only to enter the sample mean of 10 ($\overline{X}$), the population mean of 7 (μ), and, from step 2, the estimated standard error of .559:

[10.3.2] $$t = \frac{10 - 7}{.559},$$

[10.3.3] $$t = \frac{3}{.559},$$

[10.3.4] $$t = 5.37.$$

The formula for degrees of freedom for the one-sample *t* test is:

[10.4.1] $$\text{degrees of freedom} = N - 1.$$

Because there were 20 participants in the sample, the degrees of freedom for this test are:

[10.4.2] $$\text{degrees of freedom} = 20 - 1 = 19.$$

In order to decide whether to accept or reject H_0, we must learn to read and use a new statistical table, one containing critical values of *t*. Table B.4 in Appendix B

Table 10.1   Excerpt of Table B.4 (Selected One- and Two-Tailed Critical Values of *t*)

df	Level of Significance for One-Tailed Test					
	.10	.05	.025	.01	.005	.0005
	Level of Significance for Two-Tailed Test					
	.20	.10	.05	.02	.01	.001
16	1.337	1.746	2.120	2.583	2.921	4.015
17	1.333	1.740	2.110	2.567	2.898	3.965
18	1.330	1.734	2.101	2.552	2.878	3.922
19	1.328	1.729	2.093	2.539	2.861	3.883
20	1.325	1.725	2.086	2.528	2.845	3.850

Critical Values of *t*

For any given df, the table shows the values of *t* corresponding to various levels of probability. The obtained *t* is significant at a given level if it is equal to or *greater than* the value shown in the table.

contains various critical values of *t* for samples with various degrees of freedom. A portion of Table B.4 is reproduced in Table 10.1. To read Table 10.1, locate the .05 column shown under the heading "Level of Significance for Two-Tailed Test" toward the top of the table. Now, look over to the left most column, which is labeled *df* ("degrees of freedom"), and locate 19, the number of degrees of freedom available for this test. Read across in the table from the number 19 until you locate a number under the .05 column for two-tailed tests—what is the critical value? If you selected 2.093, you are correct (see Table 10.1; to verify that you have your bearings, as it were, please find this same critical value in Table B.4 in Appendix B now).

Is the calculated *t* value greater than or equal to the critical value of *t*? The observed *t* value of 5.37 is clearly greater than the critical value of 2.093, so we can reject the null hypothesis. What can we conclude about the training, which was the whole point of this statistical exercise anyway? We can conclude that the training group displayed a significantly higher average recall score for digits than is found in the general population (we will return to the proper way to report this below in step 4).

Symbolically, the decision to reject H_0 is shown as:

$$t_{calculated}(19) = 5.37 > t_{crit}(19) = 2.093: \textit{Reject } H_0.$$

Both *t* values have 19 degrees of freedom available, and these are shown in parentheses immediately following the statistic's symbol. Please note that I added the abbreviation "crit" as a superscript to the second or critical *t* value. I prefer to add such superscripts to avoid forgetting which value was calculated and which came from a table of critical values (another reminder of the *mise en place* philosophy).

Step 4.   The memory researcher effectively demonstrated to his class that three training sessions across a one-week period were sufficient to increase the participants' memory for digits. The mean recall of the sample ($\overline{X} = 10.0$) was significantly higher than the population average of 7 digits. Put another way, the training was effective where memory for digits is concerned.

Writing Up the Result of a One-Sample *t* Test.   How can this result be presented in accordance with APA style? The memory researcher could write that, "A one-sample *t* test found that the training group of 20 students displayed a significantly

▽

Superscripts on calculated test statistics and critical values reduce confusion by organizing results.

higher recall for digits ($M = 10.0$, $SD = 2.5$) compared to the average recall, said to be around 7 digits, $t(19) = 5.37$, $p < .05$." The format for reporting the results of a *t* test, then, is:

$$t(\mathrm{df}) = t_{\text{calculated}}, p < \alpha.$$

If you calculated the *t* statistic using a software program or a calculator rather than by hand and with the use of a table, you could report the actual significance value associated with it. The format is:

$$t(\mathrm{df}) = t_{\text{calculated}}, p = p,$$

where the value of *p* is provided by the printout on a screen or paper. In practice, most researchers report the standard range significance levels along with a result (i.e., .05, .01) rather than the actual probability value (e.g., $p = .022$). You should know, however, that you do have different reporting options available to you.

Note that it is not necessary to indicate that the test is two-tailed because this choice is the default option—educated readers and researchers expect that this more rigorous test will be used. In contrast, the choice of a one-tailed test would need to be explained in some detail, and an explicit statement that the test was one-tailed would be included along with the above explanation.

Please also note that both the observed sample mean and the usual population mean of recall memory for digits were reported. There is no use in reporting any statistical result unless readers are able to *ask* and *answer* the ever-important question, "Compared to what?" As a parametric test, the *t* test searched for—and found—a probable difference between the sample mean of 10 and the population mean of 7. Readers need to know what the respective mean recall levels for digits are so that they can intuitively understand what difference the test is identifying. Indeed, critical readers (and you are becoming one) also want to verify for *themselves* the directional relationship portrayed by the means. One of the worst sins of data analysis is the failure to report the means (and their accompanying standard deviations) along with a significance test. Such omission leads more critical readers to assume that the researcher either is sloppy or is hiding something, both of which are unfavorable impressions to create in the minds of others.

When evaluating means or mean differences using inferential statistics, cultivate the important habit of asking,"Compared to what?"

Confidence Intervals for the One-Sample *t* Test

As presented in chapter 5, confidence intervals identify sets of limits where population parameters are estimated to be located in probability terms. A 95% confidence interval, for example, indicates that 95% of all 95% confidence intervals will contain a parameter they are being used to estimate.

A confidence interval is easily constructed for the one-sample *t* test. The computational formula is:

[10.5.1] $$\overline{X} \pm t_{\text{crit}} (s_{\overline{X}}),$$

where the critical value of *t* under the null hypothesis is multiplied by the standard error of the mean. The resulting product is then added to and subtracted from the known sample mean to form the confidence interval for the one-sample *t* test. We will use the information from the memory for digits example here, but you could determine the confidence interval for a sample mean without previously conducting a one-sample *t* test (i.e., determine the degrees of freedom based on sample size and then look up the corresponding critical *t* value in Table B.4).

Because we used a critical value of *t* at the .05 level for the previous problem, we will be calculating a 95% confidence interval for the sample mean from the training

DATA BOX 1⁰.B

The Absolute Value of *t*

Yet another connection exists between *t* and *z*—neither of the tables for these respective distributions (see Tables B.4 and B.2) contain any negative values. Earlier, we noted that positive and negative values serve as guideposts for determining the direction of relationships within statistical hypotheses (i.e., will the hypothesis be tested in the upper or lower tail of the distribution)—but that's all.

Where hypothesis testing is concerned, what happens when a negative *t* statistic is calculated? To begin with, anytime you calculate a *t* statistic, you should always take its absolute value. Why? Because the decision rule for rejecting or accepting the null hypothesis is whether the magnitude of the calculated *t* is *greater than or equal to* the critical value of *t* (from Table B.4) or, Is $|t_{calculated}| \geq |t_{crit}|$? Develop the habit of thinking of any *t* statistic as $|t|$—the vertical or absolute value lines mean that any number lying therein is treated as positive. This straightforward procedure is conceptually easier, I think, than the other (still appropriate) alternative, which is to add a negative sign to a critical value from Table B.4.

One practical issue remains: Should a researcher report the (original) negative value of a *t* statistic *or* the statistic's absolute value, which was used to accept or reject H_0? Many researchers routinely report the absolute values of all *t* statistics, a choice that is entirely correct. Whether a *t* statistic is positive or negative, however, my own preference is to report the original value of the statistic so that the analysis is kept "intact" for readers. Which reporting style to follow is up to you—just be consistent in your reporting style and rely on the absolute value of *t* for the hypothesis-testing portion of your work.

---

project (i.e., $1 - \alpha = 1 - .05 = 95\%$). The known sample mean (10), the two-tailed critical value of *t* at the .05 level (2.093), and the standard error of the mean (.559) are all entered into formula [10.5.1], or:

[10.5.2] $$10 \pm 2.093(.559).$$

The first step is to calculate the lower limit of the confidence interval:

[10.5.3] $$10 - 2.093(.559),$$
[10.5.4] $$10 - 1.17 = 8.83.$$

The upper limit of the confidence interval, then, is:

[10.5.5] $$10 + 1.17 = 11.17.$$

What can we conclude? Remember, we *cannot* conclude that there is a 95% chance that the population mean is 10. Rather, the confidence interval establishes boundaries for the range of possible means that might be observed if repeated samples of the same size were drawn from the population. By relying on the observed sample mean and standard deviation, which are based on a population whose parameters are unknown, an interval is identified where other means selected from this population are likely to fall. Means representing mean digit recall should appear in the interval ranging between 8.83 and 11.17. We cannot be more precise here because we do not know much about the parent population. We are also limited by the reality of working with relatively small samples of observations, which increase the chance of sampling error. If we continued to sample in this fashion, we would no doubt learn that subsequent sample statistics—means and standard deviations—would all vary somewhat in value from one another.

Table 10.2   Criteria Affecting the Power of the *t* Test

Significance (α *or* p) *level*—less conservative p values (e.g., .05 instead of .01) increase the likelihood of rejecting H_0. Bear in mind that concerns about power must be balanced against concerns regarding Type I errors (i.e., less conservative p values increase the probability of making a Type I error; see chapter 9).

Variability within the sample data—all else being equal, less variability in the form of a lower standard deviation(s) will lead to a lower standard error of the mean (or the standard error of the difference between means).

Sample size—bigger samples are better samples. The more observations available, the greater the chances of rejecting H_0. Larger samples, too, mean that more degrees of freedom are available for a *t* test.

Mean differences—The larger the difference between a sample mean and a population mean (or two independent or dependent sample means), the larger the resulting *t* statistic, thereby increasing the chance of rejecting H_0. When there is little difference between means, a calculated *t* statistic will be close to 0, indicating the absence of any significant difference.

Note: These criteria are meant to apply to the one-sample, as well as the independent and dependent group *t* tests.

Remember: Power helps to achieve research and data analytic goals by enabling investigators to reject H_0 when H_0 is true.

Power Issues and the One-Sample *t* Test

Do you remember some of the criteria that enhance the power of a statistical test? Several criteria affecting the degree of power available to reject a null hypothesis were introduced in chapter 9. Naturally, these criteria are relevant to the *t* test, including the one-sample variety. Table 10.2 lists four key criteria that influence the viability of the one-sample *t* test's power. Please take a moment to examine the criteria listed in Table 10.2 and refresh your memory about power issues. You can refer back to this table as necessary when planning a study and its analyses or reviewing statistical results.

Knowledge Base

1. When is it appropriate to use the *t* test and the *z* test, respectively?
2. How does sample size affect the standard deviations and degrees of freedom associated with *t* distributions?
3. True or False: One of the assumptions of the *t* test is that means are based on interval or ratio scales of measurement.
4. True or False: A robust test is one that applies to many different types of data.
5. When is it appropriate to use a one-sample *t* test?
6. A sample comprised of 30 participants has a mean of 27 and a standard error of 1.2. Calculate a 99% confidence interval for the mean.

Answers

1. The *t* test is used when population parameters remain unknown and the *z* test is used when parameters are known.
2. As sample sizes increase, the standard deviation decreases and the available degrees of freedom increase. Smaller sample sizes are associated with larger standard deviations and fewer degrees of freedom.
3. True.
4. False. Robust tests can be used when a test's assumptions are violated. Under these circumstances, too, the likelihood of making a Type I error remains constant.

5. One-sample *t* tests are used for hypothesis tests comparing a sample mean to a related population where the population mean and standard deviation are unknown.

6. $27 \pm 2.756(1.2) =$ interval between 23.69 and 30.31.

Hypothesis Testing with Two Independent Samples

The independent groups *t* test is ideal for hypothesis testing within experiments, as an experimental group can be compared to a control group.

The *t* test for independent samples is the ideal test for experimental research—it verifies whether a difference exists between the mean of a control group and the mean of an experimental group. This variation of the *t* test is useful because behavioral scientists rarely know much about the two populations that the respective groups originate from, as their parameters are unknown. To proceed, a researcher randomly assigns participants to one of the two groups, presents one level of the independent variable to each one, and then measures the groups' reactions to a dependent measure (see part [b] of Figure 10.1). An independent groups *t* test is then used to compare the mean reaction of one group to the other, thereby assessing whether the independent variable elicited an anticipated behavioral change in one group but not the other. By checking to see if a mean difference occurs between the two samples, the researcher is trying to determine whether a corresponding difference exists between the populations.

The particular research design that relies on the comparison of two independent groups of participants is often referred to as a *between-subjects* or *between-groups design*.

KEY TERM   A **between-subjects (between-groups) design** is one where the data are obtained from independent participant samples, each of which is exposed to one—and only one—level of an independent variable.

Each participant in a between-subjects design is exposed to one—and *only* one—level of an independent variable or other experimental treatment. In terms of the standard experiment, a participant encounters *either* the control or the experimental level of the independent variable (in chapter 11, we will see that between-subjects designs sometimes have more than two groups). Any observed difference between the levels of the independent variable on the dependent measure necessarily reflects behavioral or attitudinal differences between the control and experimental groups of participants. Please note that some authors refer to between-subjects designs as "independent-measures" designs (e.g., Gravetter & Wallnau, 1996).

What about the nature of the independent variables used in between-subjects designs? As noted in chapter 2, when we traditionally think of an independent variable, we think of the variable that is *manipulated* by an experimenter. The experimenter has control over what stimulus or other piece of information a group of participants (or a single participant) is exposed to. By comparing the average behavioral response of one group to that of another to the independent variable, the experimenter tries to assess causality—did the independent variable create the differential group change associated with the dependent measure (see chapter 2 for a more thorough review of these issues)?

A second category of independent variable—one not discussed until now—is called a *subject variable*.

KEY TERM   **Subject variables** (also known as organismic variables) are individual characteristics that research participants bring to an experiment that cannot be influenced—changed or manipulated—by an experimenter.

Gender, age, any number of personality traits, intelligence, race, and religion are all examples of subject variables (for a more detailed discussion, see Dunn, 1999). Experimenters cannot control subject variables—a participant cannot be randomly assigned to one or the other gender, for example; the participant is *already* a male or a female. The experimenter, however, can compare the presence or absence of a subject variable's influence on participant reactions to something (e.g., male reactions to a given stimulus—say, a film of violent behavior—are compared to the reactions of women). Subject variables provide a "lens" through which other behaviors can be evaluated or compared, though causal conclusions cannot be drawn.

As you may recall from chapter 2, though, a researcher cannot determine the causal ordering of events *unless* a variable is manipulated, thus, identifying causality is always indirect—and potentially problematic—when subject variables are present. Instead, the investigator must be content with making an inference about the affect the presence of a subject variable *may* have on some behavioral outcome. Perhaps males are generally attracted to violent images due to socialization processes. These same social influences, in turn, lead most females to be repelled by violent images, a proposition that is worth considering but one that can never be fully tested because of the limitations posed by subject variables.

An experimenter manipulates independent variables, but subject variables can only be measured for making between-groups comparisons.

Standard Error Revised: Estimating the Standard Error of the Difference Between Means

You are already familiar with the role the standard error of the mean plays in hypothesis testing involving one sample. We assume that a sampling distribution of means will show some variability where individual means and standard deviations are concerned. Theoretically, for example, we can create a sampling distribution of means by drawing a number of samples with a fixed size N and then plotting the mean of each one. The standard error is the standard deviation of the resulting sampling distribution.

What happens when two groups are involved? How can we conceptualize a sampling distribution based on two independent groups? These are important questions and the material used to answer them is conceptually challenging but understandable if you take your time to read through it and to think about it carefully. The attention and energy you commit to reading and, more importantly, learning the logic laid out in this section of the chapter will pay off in the future. If you find yourself losing the thread of the argument, take a break for a few minutes before proceeding with the rest of the section leading up to the actual calculation of the t test for independent groups.

Here we go: Figure 10.3 illustrates the theoretical perspective underlying sampling distributions for two independent groups. Two population distributions with unknown parameters are shown at the top of Figure 10.3, and the hypothesis test we perform will determine whether their means are equal to (H_0 is accepted) or different from (H_0 is rejected) one another. Immediately beneath the population distributions are two sampling distributions of means (see Figure 10.3). We could determine the respective standard errors for each of the sampling distributions following procedures we learned in chapter 9.

Instead, however, we extend the original idea behind sample means in the following way: Imagine that we randomly draw pairs of samples from the two populations shown in Figure 10.3, calculate the mean of each one, and then determine the *difference* between the means associated with each pair *(i.e., $\overline{X}_1 - \overline{X}_2$)*. We then create a distribution by plotting these *differences between the means*. This theoretical sampling distribution is called the **sampling distribution of the difference between means,** and it is shown beneath the two sampling distributions of means in Figure 10.3. Please note that it is a sampling distribution like any other—it just so happens that it is made up of the differences between means rather than, say, the means themselves. As shown in

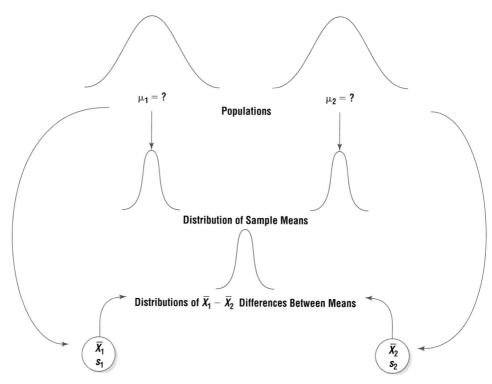

Figure 10.3   Understanding the Origins of the Sampling Distribution of the Difference Between Means

Source: Adapted from Figure 9-1 in Aron and Aron (1997, p. 180).

the bottom of Figure 10.3, the sampling distribution of the difference between means is theoretically derived from the respective samples and their statistics (i.e., sample means and sample standard deviations) which, in turn, were drawn from the populations with the unknown parameters.

Adopting an apt metaphor from Henry David Thoreau, Aron and Aron (1997, p. 180–181) note that the theory behind this sampling procedure is "really a kind of complicated castle in the air." We never actually create the sampling distribution of the difference between means, but we behave *as if* we did by following the logical implications derived from sampling theory. The only mortar of our castle, as it were, the only concrete realities involved here, are the data we collect after two samples are randomly created and exposed to one or another level of some independent variable. The data comprising each sample are then used to estimate the variances of the respective populations, which in turn are used to estimate the variances of the two distributions of sample means that lead to the sampling distribution of the difference between means.

You are probably anticipating what this sampling distribution's characteristics are like and no doubt guessed correctly that it will be normal (congratulate yourself now if this thought occurred to you when you began reading this section). Because it is a normal distribution composed of difference scores, the sampling distribution of the difference between means will have a mean of 0. Here is an important aspect of this normally shaped sampling distribution—we can describe it even when the pairs of samples we use to create it are *not* from the same population. Symbolically, the mean of this sampling distribution is shown as $(\mu_{\bar{X}_1} - \mu_{\bar{X}_2})$ and it is used to approximate the actual population mean of $(\mu_1 - \mu_2)$.

The standard deviation of this sampling distribution, symbolically represented as $\sigma_{\overline{X}_1 - \overline{X}_2}$, is known as the *standard error of the difference between means.*

KEY TERM The **standard error of the difference between means** is the standard deviation of the sampling distribution of mean differences derived from two independent samples presumed to represent two separate populations.

Similar to any index of standard error, standard error of the difference between means enables us to determine how well a sample statistic approximates a population parameter. In this case, of course, we are trying to determine how well the difference between two means $(\overline{X}_1 - \overline{X}_2)$ approximates the difference between two parameters $(\mu_1 - \mu_2)$. In fact, when we know the population parameters involved, the sampling distribution can be described using z, or

[10.6.1] $$z = \frac{(\overline{X}_1 - \overline{X}_2) - (\mu_1 - \mu_2)}{\sigma_{\overline{X}_1 - \overline{X}_2}}.$$

The resulting distribution will be normal and because the population parameters are known, hypotheses can be tested using the standard normal distribution.

Given that we will probably not know the value of any population parameters, we will need to estimate the standard error of the difference between means and substitute its value for the denominator shown in [10.6.1]. As you will see, doing so converts this z test into the t test for independent groups. Before we get to that point, however, we first need to estimate $\sigma_{\overline{X}_1 - \overline{X}_2}$ from sample data.

Using $s_{\overline{X}_1 - \overline{X}_2}$ to estimate $\sigma_{\overline{X}_1 - \overline{X}_2}$. The *estimated* standard error of the difference between means is known as $s_{\overline{X}_1 - \overline{X}_2}$ and we will review its utility in conceptual and then computational terms. To begin, the estimated standard error of the difference between means can be determined by taking the square root of the combined variances for each of the two samples, or

[10.7.1] $$s_{\overline{X}_1 - \overline{X}_2} = \sqrt{s_1^2 + s_2^2}.$$

There is a shortcoming to this formula, however, in that it provides a biased estimate of $\sigma_{\overline{X}_1 - \overline{X}_2}$ whenever the respective sample sizes (i.e., N_1 and N_2) are not equal to one another. As an aside, maintaining equal sample sizes between conditions in any experiment is no small feat, and it must always be a concern for data analysts. Ideally, the conditions or groups in any experiment will have the same number of participants randomly assigned to them (another desirable factor is to have the same number of males and females in each condition), but the reality of experimentation often disrupts this goal—participants drop out, neglect to attend research sessions, equipment fails—any number of tragedies great and small can prevent a researcher from achieving equal Ns across conditions. As a result of this real concern, a variation of formula [10.7.1] provides an unbiased estimate of the standard error of the difference between means:

[10.8.1] $$s_{\overline{X}_1 - \overline{X}_2} = \sqrt{\frac{(SS_1 + SS_2)}{(N_1 + N_2 - 2)} \cdot \left(\frac{1}{N_1} + \frac{1}{N_2}\right)}$$

The advantage of formula [10.8.1] is that it takes into account the biasing influence of unequal groups by providing a more balanced—and unbiased—estimate. Take a moment to examine formula [10.8.1] and to refresh your memory about the source of the numbers shown within it. The sums of the squares (i.e., SS_1 and SS_2) are calculated separately by using formula [4.10.1], which was introduced back in chapter 4. This formula is renumbered here for each of the two groups (note that the calculations are precisely the same, *except* that the data entered into each is from one sample or the other):

[10.9.1]
$$SS_1 = \sum X_1^2 - \frac{(\sum X_1)^2}{N_1},$$

and

[10.10.1]
$$SS_2 = \sum X_2^2 - \frac{(\sum X_2)^2}{N_2}.$$

If you feel a bit rusty where calculating the sum of the squares is concerned, take a minute and examine the relevant portion of chapter 4.

Besides being an unbiased estimate, what statistical information is formula [10.8.1] actually providing? Formula [10.8.1] estimates $\sigma_{\overline{X}_1 - \overline{X}_2}$ by "pooling"— or combining— the separate sums of squares and degrees of freedom representing the two samples that, when their square root is taken, yield a pooled estimate of the standard error of the difference between means (i.e., $s_{\overline{X}_1 - \overline{X}_2}$).

Why does this pooling procedure to estimate the standard error of the difference between means make sense? Think about it for a moment. If you were working with one sample drawn from a larger population, you could calculate sample statistics from it. By dividing the unbiased estimate of the variance (i.e., $\hat{s}^2$) by the available N and then taking the square root of the resulting product, you could determine the standard error of the mean for that sample. In effect, formula [10.8.1] is doing the *same thing* except that it combines the separate standard errors for *two samples into one* useful numerical index—the standard error of the difference between means.

Formula [10.8.1] is readily reduced to a simpler version when the available Ns for the two samples are equal to one another. When N_1 and N_2 are equal to one another, use the following formula to estimate $s_{\overline{X}_1 - \overline{X}_2}$:

[10.11.1]
$$s_{\overline{X}_1 - \overline{X}_2} = \sqrt{\frac{(SS_1 + SS_2)}{N(N - 1)}},$$

where N is equal to the *equivalent* number of observations in each group, *not* the total number of observations available (i.e., $N_1 + N_2$). When unbiased estimates of the sample variances are available, an alternative formula can be used:

[10.12.1]
$$s_{\overline{X}_1 - \overline{X}_2} = \sqrt{\frac{\hat{s}_1^2}{N_1} + \frac{\hat{s}_2^2}{N_2}}.$$

Please remember that the caret ($\wedge$) not only indicates that a statistic is unbiased, its presence specifically means that $N - 1$ rather than N was the denominator in the formula used to calculate the respective sample variance estimates (i.e., $\sum(X - \overline{X})^2/N - 1$). The variance estimates are then divided by the respective sample sizes, the resulting products are summed, and the square root of the sum is taken.

When sample sizes and their population variances are approximately equal to one another (i.e., $\sigma_1^2 \cong \sigma_2^2$), the standard error of the difference between means ($s_{\overline{X}_1 - \overline{X}_2}$) is ideally suited for use in the t test for independent groups. Many statistics books and some research methods texts refer to this form of standard error as an *error term*. In other words, the standard error of the difference between means serves as a numerical gauge of how much random error—the degree to which observations deviate from a population's true characteristics—is present when samples are drawn from a population.

▼

The standard error of the difference between means ($s_{\overline{X}_1 - \overline{X}_2}$) is often referred to as the error term, the denominator in statistical calculations.

KEY TERM

The **error term** is a synonym for the standard error of the difference between means, one used to estimate the random error that is found anytime samples are drawn from a population.

The error term is always used as a denominator in statistical calculations. Keep in mind, too, that the standard error of the difference between means is just a different incarnation of the standard deviation—it just so happens that this standard deviation lets data analysts estimate how much random samples differ from population values. Armed with this statistic, we are almost ready to test a hypothesis involving two independent groups. Before we do so, however, a short overview of the relationship between error terms and mean differences is in order.

Comparing Means: A Conceptual Model and an Aside for Future Statistical Tests

This section is a very important one, so much so that if you read it carefully and think about it critically, I assure you that the statistical tests that follow in this and even the next chapter will make a great deal of sense. Take your time reading and refer back to previous sections as needed, but remember that by comparing means we are trying to assign a numerical value to how people behave under various conditions. The disparity or similarity of behavior within and between groups of people allows us to determine whether and where any statistically significant differences lie.

Various statistical tests used to compare means—especially those relying on two samples—are based on the following conceptual model:

$$Statistical\ test = \frac{Difference\ between\ sample\ means}{Standard\ error}.$$

Given that we just learned that error term is a substitute phrase for standard error, this formula is easily recast as:

$$Statistical\ test = \frac{Difference\ between\ sample\ means}{Error\ term}.$$

This model indicates that the measured difference between sample means (numerator) is divided by estimated random error of the difference between means (denominator). When the observed difference between the means is great—so great that it exceeds the estimated random error—then the difference between these sample means is presumably due to some influence *beyond* random variation in the samples. A researcher, of course, hopes that the influence is the independent variable, one that created a measurable difference in behavior between the samples. When an observed difference between means is sufficiently large, that is, greater than would be anticipated by chance, the sample means—and the result they represent—are said to be significantly different from one another.

Earlier, we discussed what is meant by a between-subjects design, a designation we can return to here to describe what occurs between samples. The mean of each sample represents an average level of behavior within that group, so that if we examine the *difference* between the averages of the two groups, we identify what statisticians call **between-groups** or **between-samples variation.** The difference in variability between the groups—literally, a difference in average behavior—is attributed to the independent variable.

Let's turn back to the error term for a moment. It represents a combined index of average deviation from the mean behavior within each sample. When the error term is relatively small, it means that behavior within each sample was similar to the mean of the sample (i.e., low variability within each respective group). On the other hand, when the error term is larger, behavior within either group deviated from what was typical for the group. Where mean comparisons are concerned, statisticians refer to the standard error or error term in a test statistic as **within-group** or **within-sample variation.**

Within-group variation—deviation from a group's average—is explained by examining two sources: random error and experimental error. Random error is ascribed to a host of minor influences, chief of which is that people are simply different from one another (many investigators refer to this as **individual differences** within a sample). Random error is expected and there is little or nothing to be done about it. Experimental error is more problematic—indeed, it is often systematic, originating from equipment failure, environmental conditions, poorly presented instructions, or any other disruption in what should ideally be a smoothly running study (for more detailed discussion of such biases, see Dunn, 1999; Rosenthal & Rosnow, 1991).

Within-group variation—the error term—is comprised of random error and experimental error.

As you might imagine, a researcher's goal is to control experimental error and to reduce random error as much as possible. The practical reason for doing so is statistical. By doing so, the error term is kept small so that when it is divided into the observed mean difference, the resulting test statistic should be numerically large enough to exceed some critical value so that the null hypothesis of no difference between the means is thereby rejected. When the error term is large, its utility as a denominator suffers; any resulting test statistic is unlikely to even reach a critical value and the null hypothesis of no difference must be retained.

What, then, is the conceptual "take home" message from this section? In order to find a statistically significant difference between two means, a researcher desires a relatively large amount of between-groups variation and a relatively small amount of within-groups variation. Put another way, due to the affect of the independent variable, each sample should behave somewhat differently from the other, whereas the behavior displayed within each sample should be similar. We can now recast the relationship between error terms and mean differences as:

$$Test\ statistic = \frac{Between\text{-}groups\ variation}{Within\text{-}groups\ variation}.$$

In yet more practical terms, the numerator in this conceptual formula should be large and the denominator should be small so that the resulting ratio is large—sufficiently large so that H_0 can be rejected. We can now use this conceptual material to guide an actual hypothesis test between two independent groups.

The *t* Test for Independent Groups

The ***t* test for independent groups** is used for hypothesis testing when a researcher does not know the parameters of the populations of interest, as well as when the size of the samples used to estimate the populations is relatively small. The *t* test is applied to null hypotheses in which $\mu_1 = \mu_2$; that is, the difference between the respective means of two populations is equal to 0, which effectively indicates that the two samples are not independent of one another—they are presumed to come from the same population.

The complete formula for the *t* test for independent groups looks like this:

[10.13.1]
$$t = \frac{(\overline{X}_1 - \overline{X}_2) - (\mu_1 - \mu_2)}{s_{\overline{X}_1 - \overline{X}_2}}.$$

You may remember this version of the *t* formula, as you encountered it back in chapter 1's project exercise. Let's review each part of formula [10.13.1] before using it to actually test a hypothesis. As you can see, the denominator is the standard error of the difference between means or error term that we just reviewed in detail. The magnitude of the error term will depend on the size of the two samples and the variability within each one, though two general rules of data analysis apply: Larger sample sizes will usually result in a smaller error term, as will lower variance within each sample.

The numerator presented in [10.13.1] is unusual because it has two components, one representing sample means and one representing population means. Actually, the second component is literally symbolic—$(\mu_1 - \mu_2)$ points to the null hypothesis, which will equal 0 if no difference between the population means exists. When H_0 is true, any minor difference between the observed means is attributed to sampling error, not the intervention of any independent variable. The first component in formula [10.13.1], then, is the actual numerator, so that the numerical difference between $\overline{X}_1$ and $\overline{X}_2$ is assessed and then divided by the error term. A simplified way to present the t test for independent groups is:

[10.14.1]
$$t = \frac{\overline{X}_1 - \overline{X}_2}{s_{\overline{X}_1 - \overline{X}_2}}.$$

Statistically, what are we doing when H_0 is rejected? The observed t statistic is deemed to be too great (i.e., exceeding some critical value) to be due to chance alone. In other words, the distance between the two means is too improbable—too disparate—to be a random event. Instead, as researchers, we assume that mean difference is being driven by some other factor—an independent variable, for example—*besides* the anticipated amount of sampling error (as noted earlier in this book, there is *always* some degree of sampling error).

Perhaps an educational researcher wants to determine whether cooperative learning—two or more students working together to achieve some educational goal—is beneficial. Sixteen middle school students are randomly assigned to a control or a cooperative learning group (8 students—half males and half females—are placed in each). Students in the control group work alone to study a novel academic topic (e.g., reducing industrial pollution), while those in the cooperative learning group are placed in mixed-sex pairs to learn the same information. The learning phase continues for one week, at the end of which a test is given to all 16 students. The students' scores (broken down by group) are shown in Table 10.3.

Using these data, we can determine whether the control group's mean test score was lower than the cooperative learning group's mean test score (i.e., working with others enhances learning relative to studying alone). To do so, we will again follow the steps for testing a hypothesis outlined in Table 9.2.

Table 10.3 Test Scores from Control and Cooperative Learning Groups

	Control Group	Cooperative Learning Group
	3	6
	5	7
	3	7
	5	8
	4	6
	3	8
	3	8
	3	7
N	8	8
$\sum X$	29	57
$\sum X^2$	111	411
$\overline{X}$	3.63	7.13
SS	5.88	4.88
s	.916	.835

Step 1. The null hypothesis for the present study is that neither group has a higher test score, or:

$$H_0: \mu_1 = \mu_2.$$

The alternative or research hypothesis would be that the control group would exhibit a lower test score than the cooperative learning group, or:

$$H_1: \mu_1 < \mu_2.$$

As always, the significance level for rejecting H_0 will be .05.

Step 2. We need to calculate the standard error of the difference between means (error term), but we will do that in the course of calculating the t statistic in step 3. What we can do now is to decide to use a one- or a two-tailed significance test. To be appropriately conservative, a two-tailed test will be performed.

Step 3. We can now perform the t test for independent groups using formula [10.14.1]. Because the sample sizes are equal, we can use formula [10.11.1] to determine the error term (denominator).

[10.14.2]
$$t = \frac{(\overline{X}_1 - \overline{X}_2)}{\sqrt{\frac{(SS_1 + SS_2)}{N(N - 1)}}}.$$

Information drawn from the bottom of Table 10.3 can now be entered into this formula for:

[10.14.3]
$$t = \frac{(3.63 - 7.13)}{\sqrt{\frac{(5.88 + 4.88)}{8(8 - 1)}}},$$

[10.14.4]
$$t = \frac{-3.5}{\sqrt{\frac{10.76}{8(7)}}},$$

[10.14.5]
$$t = \frac{-3.5}{\sqrt{\frac{10.76}{56}}},$$

[10.14.6]
$$t = \frac{-3.5}{\sqrt{.1921}},$$

[10.14.7]
$$t = \frac{-3.5}{.4383},$$

[10.14.8]
$$t = -7.99.$$

Because this is the first statistical test used to compare independent samples, I provided more detailed steps for performing the calculation than usual. Please note that I did not demonstrate how to calculate the sum of the squares here, as we have reviewed it numerous times before (see formulas [10.9.1] and [10.10.1]).

Before we can identify a critical t value, enabling us to accept or reject the null hypothesis, we need to calculate the degrees of freedom for this t test. Degrees of freedom for an independent group t test are calculated using:

[10.15.1]
$$degrees\ of\ freedom\ (df) = (N_1 + N_2) - 2.$$

There were 8 students in each group, so:

[10.15.2] $df = (8 + 8) - 2,$

[10.15.3] $df = 16 - 2,$

[10.15.4] $df = 14.$

We then turn to Table B.4 in Appendix B (please turn there now, as you need to develop the habit of using this table). Locate the number 14 in the left most row under the column (labeled "df"), as well as the .05 column under the heading "level of significance for two-tailed test." What critical value for t meets your gaze as you read across the row for 14 degrees of freedom and down the .05 column? You should locate 2.145. Did you?

We now compare the calculated t against this critical t value—but wait, the calculated t is negative? Recall the guidance provided in Data Box 10.B and "drop" the negative sign (for now) and compare the absolute value of the calculated statistic with the critical value from Table B.4. Is the absolute value of the calculated t greater than the critical t? Yes, indeed:

$$t_{calculated}\ (14) = 7.99 > t_{crit}\ (14) = 2.145: \textit{Reject } H_0.$$

Thus, we can reject the null hypothesis of no difference—there is a significant difference between the means representing the test scores of the two student groups.

Step 4. What is the nature of this difference? Take one more look at the group means shown in Table 10.3. The control group had a lower mean score ($\overline{X} = 3.63$) on the pollution knowledge test than the cooperative learning group ($\overline{X} = 7.13$). An important quality of the independent groups t test is that when a significant difference is established statistically, its nature is obvious. How so? Keep in mind that the t test—any t test—compares two and only two means. When a significant difference is found, a researcher knows that one mean is greater than the other (i.e., $\overline{X}_1 > \overline{X}_2$ or, if you prefer, one mean is less than the other: $\overline{X}_1 < \overline{X}_2$). The only remaining matter is to verify that the relationship revealed by the analysis is consistent with the hypothesis. Clearly, when more than two means are present, identifying where the significant difference or *differences* lie is a bit more complex (we will learn to pinpoint more than one difference in chapter 11).

Writing up the Result of an Independent Groups *t* Test. What can the educational researcher conclude? Reporting the results in APA style, the researcher would briefly remind the reader about the hypothesis and then highlight the obtained results. Here is one way to achieve these ends:

> Did those students who learned about industrial pollution while working together learn more than those who studied the material alone? At the end of the week, a 10-point knowledge test concerning pollution reduction was given to all 16 students. As expected, students in the control group received lower scores ($M = 3.63$, $SD = .916$) than did those in the cooperative learning group ($M = 7.13$, $SD = .835$), $t(14) = -7.99$, $p < .05$, two-tailed.

Please note a few things about how the result is reported. First, I elected to report the means and respective standard deviations within a single sentence. As noted earlier in this book, this style is preferable when there are few means to review—if several means were being tested, a tabular format would be appropriate. Second, the parenthetical means use "M" for mean rather than "$\overline{X}$" and "SD" for standard deviation in lieu of "s" —APA style abbreviation conventions that subtly emphasize average behavior, not statistical analysis, as the key point when results are presented. Third, the actual result of the test statistic is presented at the end of the sentence *describing what happened.* By placing the statistical information here, it can easily be examined by interested researchers or safely ignored by lay readers. Finally, note that in the interest of reporting accurate analyses, I retained the negative sign on the calculated t value.

When comparing calculated t values with critical values of t, always drop any negative signs.

DATA BOX 10.C

Language and Reporting Results, or (Too) Great Expectations

On occasion, using a thesaurus—a dictionary of synonyms and antonyms—is fine, just as long as the user does not become dependent on it (Dunn, 1999). Where data analysis is concerned, any collection of available word equivalents can get even the most careful writers, researchers, and students into trouble. How so? The temptation to "jazz up" one's prose, especially the often dry reporting of statistical relationships, is a strong one (recall the perils associated with use of euphemisms for the phrase "statistically significant"; see chapter 9). This warning works two ways: beware of writing dramatic statistical prose, but also when you read it—many writers who are unfamiliar with statistics and data analysis publish attention-getting but fundamentally inaccurate material.

Mauro (1992) particularly warns against words that are misused in order to make numerical relationships "appear to be what they are not" (p. 21). His warning is helpful, motivating us to be on the lookout for unreliable news stories and advertisements that misrepresent data by strategic use of modifiers—words used to inflate or deflate the meaning attached to numerical relationships and often our expectations about them. Here are some words and phrases Mauro identifies as both representative and problematic (note that there is space to write in examples you come across in the future):

Inflaters (words used to describe "dramatic" positive change or strong improvement): *astonishing growth, zoomed, skyrocketed, spiraled, shot up, lunged, as much as, as many as, bounced,* _____

_____

Deflaters (words used to describe "dramatic" negative change or poor performance): *only, meager growth, poor performance, mere, nose dived, tumbled, deteriorated, slipped, collapsed, disintegrated, toppled, shrank, as little as,* _____

_____

On first blush, these words and phrases appear to be associated with the mass media, but some of them find their way into the behavioral science literature, as well. As you read articles, books, and book chapters containing statistical analysis and interpretation, watch for strategic use of inflaters and deflaters to emphasize the magnitude of mean differences or other results. Remember that the relationships observed within a set of data may not be as strong or as weak as they are said to be!

Are we finished with the analysis? We are actually not finished yet, as the opportunity to examine the obtained effect remains. What information are we missing? We need to have an index for the cooperative learning effect, one that denotes its relative strength.

Effect Size and the *t* Test

The first of Abelson's (1995) MAGIC criteria is *magnitude*, which can refer to the effect size associated with an independent variable (recall Data Box 9.F). Effect size addresses whether an observed effect is relatively strong, moderate, or weak (see chapter 9). In other words, what is the magnitude of the relationship in a population? Or, how great is the observed departure from the null hypothesis of no difference between the groups? Knowing the size of an effect in one study is a valuable piece of information for planning the next piece of research in a program.

In the present example, what was the magnitude of the effect of the experimental-level of the independent variable (i.e., cooperative learning) on the dependent measure (i.e., test scores)? Statistical effect size is readily calculable—different indices for various test statistics are available—and higher values generally indicate that the independent variable had a stronger influence on the dependent measure. One effect size formula for the independent groups t test is *effect size r*, which is derived from the Pearson correlation coefficient introduced in chapter 6 (e.g., Rosenthal, 1991; Rosenthal & Rosnow, 1991; see also, Cohen, 1988):

[10.16.1] $$\text{effect size } r = \sqrt{\frac{t^2}{t^2 + df}}.$$

We need only enter the calculated t statistic, which is then squared, and its accompanying degrees of freedom, or:

[10.16.2] $$\text{effect size } r = \sqrt{\frac{(-7.99)^2}{(7.99)^2 + 14}},$$

[10.16.3] $$\text{effect size } r = \sqrt{\frac{63.84}{63.84 + 14}},$$

[10.16.4] $$\text{effect size } r = \sqrt{\frac{63.84}{77.84}},$$

[10.16.5] $$\text{effect size } r = \sqrt{.8201},$$

[10.16.6] $$\text{effect size } r = .9056 \cong .91.$$

Clearly, the effect size of .91 in this hypothetical example is very strong (in the neighborhood of what Rosnow and Rosenthal [1996] refer to as "jumbo-sized"), indicating that the cooperative learning of material between pairs of students enhanced their later test performance.

How is effect size r reported along with the main test statistic? Rather easily, actually. As a data analyst, you can assume that some of your readers will be familiar with—even knowledgeable about—effect size, and so you do not need to go to great pains to explain it within the Results section of an APA style paper. Readers who are unfamiliar with statistical analysis will be looking for the "gist" or take-home message of your results, which will appear in clear prose, anyway. To indicate that the effect size of the t statistic in the cooperative learning study was strong, we need only add an additional sentence to the results paragraph (excerpted from above):

> . . . students in the control group received lower scores ($M = 3.63$, $SD = .916$) than did those in the cooperative learning group ($M = 7.13$, $SD = .835$), $t(14) = -7.99$, $p < .05$, two-tailed. The size of this effect was large (effect size $r = .91$).

Note that by presenting the result in this manner, the context provided by the descriptive portion of the results will help people who know little about statistics understand the result's importance.

Characterizing the Degree of Association Between the Independent Variable and the Dependent Measure

By quantifying and reporting effect size, a researcher informs interested readers about whether an obtained result is relatively large (as in our example) or small (remember that a statistically significant difference does *not* say anything about the magnitude of an effect; but see Data Box 10.D). Neither the t test nor effect size r tells us anything

Small Effects Can Be Impressive Too

The concept of effect size, or the magnitude of some statistically significant result, was conceptually introduced in the last chapter, and a particular formula for its calculation (effect size *r* derived from *t*) was presented here. Behavioral scientists now routinely note that effect size is as important and informative as the statistical significance denoted by a *p* value. Data analysts are now encouraged to report effect size along with standard inferential tests as a matter of course (e.g., Rosenthal & Rosnow, 1991). Still, it is reasonable to ask whether there are other ways to think about effect size besides statistical indices.

Prentice and Miller (1992) persuasively argue for the long tradition of examining effects from a methodological rather than a merely statistical perspective. Indeed, generations of researchers in psychology approached issues of effect size by way of research design strategies, not data analysis. An intriguing quality inherent in these strategies is their emphasis on statistically small effects that are nonetheless "impressive demonstrations" (Prentice & Miller, p. 161) Two strategies are prominent: minimally manipulating an independent variable and choosing difficult-to-influence dependent measures.

Minimal manipulations.   The minimalist approach is impressive because even the relatively minor manipulation of an independent variable can account for change in the variability of a corresponding dependent measure. An obvious, classic example in this vein is Tajfel's minimal group experiments (e.g., Billig & Tajfel, 1973; Tajfel & Billig, 1974), where arbitrary assignment to a group leads to displays of ethnocentrism, a pronounced preference for one's own group and a decided distrust of outsiders. Even when group assignment is done *explicitly* by some randomizing procedure, individuals still demonstrate a clear preference for the members of their own group (Locksley, Ortiz, & Hepburn, 1980).

This undue preference is all the more sobering when observers consider the complete arbitrariness of the exercise—a group member may literally have nothing whatever in common with group peers *except* the accident of assignment to one rather than another collection of individuals. Yet that group assignment is sufficient to engender loyalty and commitment to one's compatriots in the arbitrary group, as well as a strong tendency to favor this ingroup at the expense of individuals randomly assigned to the (other) outgroup (see also, Tajfel, 1981). Beyond these group assignment effects, of course, other independent variables adhering to the minimalist approach can be found in Prentice and Miller (1992).

Difficult dependent measures.   On the surface, some dependent measures appear less open to influence by particular independent variables than others. What independent variable, for example, could be expected to show clear and consistent effects where people's subjective ratings of intelligence, success, sociability, kindness, and sensitivity are concerned? Prentice and Miller (1992) point to the pronounced effect that physical attractiveness has on social perceivers—more attractive people are readily perceived to be more intelligent, successful, sociable, kind, and sensitive, among other positive qualities, than are less attractive people (see Berscheid & Walster, 1974, for a review).

More to the point, physical attractiveness is repeatedly demonstrated to influence human judgment in socially important domains, such as mock jury trials. Attractive defendants, for example, are given lighter sentences and judged guilty less often than their less physically appealing counterparts (e.g., Efran, 1974; Sigall & Ostrove, 1975). As Prentice and Miller wryly observe, if personal attractiveness has such subtle but powerful effects in what should be the paradigm example of objectivity, the courtroom, then there may be no social setting that is immune to its influence.

The moral to the effect size story? Prentice and Miller (1992) remind us that our statistical zeal for searching out strong effect sizes is all to the good, but that we should not neglect alternative research strategies in the process. Minimal manipulations and difficult-to-influence dependent measures highlight roles for independent variables and psychological processes, respectively, even when neither source provides particularly impressive results in statistical terms. As behavioral science researchers and data analysts, we can learn a valuable lesson from these observations and supporting studies—even small effects can be impressive where understanding human behavior is concerned.

---

about the effect of the independent variable (e.g., the presence or absence of cooperative learning) on the dependent measure (e.g., follow-up knowledge test score). To be sure, the significant difference identified by the independent groups t test indicates that there is *some* degree of association between these two variables, but it does not quantify it.

Presumably, the educational researcher would like to characterize the relationship between cooperative learning and subsequent test performance as an important one. Generally speaking, the greater the degree of association between an independent variable and a dependent measure, the more the finding can be designated an important one. A straightforward index of the association between an independent variable and a dependent measure is $\hat{\omega}^2$ (estimated omega-squared).

KEY TERM   As a statistical index, **estimated *omega-squared*** ($\hat{\omega}^2$) indicates the degree to which an independent variable accounts for variation or change in a dependent variable.

Calculating $\hat{\omega}^2$ for an independent groups t test is done using:

[10.17.1]
$$\hat{\omega}^2 = \frac{t^2 - 1}{t^2 + N_1 + N_2 - 1}.$$

Once again, we need only insert the value of the calculated t statistic (it will be squared) and, in addition, the number of participants appearing in both groups. Thus,

[10.17.2]
$$\hat{\omega}^2 = \frac{(-7.99)^2 - 1}{(-7.99)^2 + 8 + 8 - 1},$$

[10.17.3]
$$\hat{\omega}^2 = \frac{63.84 - 1}{63.84 + 15},$$

[10.17.4]
$$\hat{\omega}^2 = \frac{62.84}{78.84},$$

[10.17.5]
$$\hat{\omega}^2 = .7971 \cong .80.$$

How do we interpret an $\hat{\omega}^2$ of .80? This statistic is interpreted in the same way we learned to interpret r^2 (see chapter 7), that is, the degree to which the independent variable accounts for the dependent variable. In concrete terms, we can say that approximately 80% of the variance in the test scores (dependent measure) is accounted for by the learning method (independent variable). This amount of variation is considerable, suggesting that the degree of association between the variables is very high.

Unlike r^2, however, $\hat{\omega}^2$ can have a positive *or* a negative value (r^2 values only range between 0 and 1.0; see chapter 7). Very small t statistics—those falling below 1.00 in magnitude—can lead to a negative $\hat{\omega}^2$. Negative values for $\hat{\omega}^2$ are not at all meaningful; indeed, there is no reason to calculate this statistic if the t test does not reveal a significant between-group difference, anyway (Runyon, Haber, Pittenger, & Coleman, 1996).

Thus, we use $\hat{\omega}^2$ for the same reason that we rely on effect size r: Despite their utility for research, inferential statistics like the t test only identify the presence or absence of a difference between means. To more fully understand the empirical quality of the relationship between variables, these additional indices are used. But wait, how do we report $\hat{\omega}^2$ in the results of the t test for independent groups? We need only add another clause to our growing account:

> Students in the control group received lower scores ($M = 3.63$, $SD = .916$) than did those in the cooperative learning group ($M = 7.13$, $SD = .835$), $t(14) = -7.99$, $p < .05$, two-tailed. The size of this effect was large (effect size $r = .91$), as was the degree of association between the independent variable and the dependent measure ($\hat{\omega}^2 = .80$).

An index like $\hat{\omega}^2$ is an important supplement to inferential statistical tests. In a way, these additional statistics keep researchers honest. Runyon and colleagues (1996), for example, point out that it is possible to observe a significant difference between means while discovering that the $\hat{\omega}^2$ is quite small (e.g., less than .10). This relative lack of association between the independent and dependent variable suggests any differences between the participant groups are probably due to random error, not the desired systematic variation created by experimental intervention. Rejecting H_0 is important, but it is by no means the entire enterprise of data analysis. An understanding of $\hat{\omega}^2$ and related statistics enables you—a developing critical reader and data analyst—to challenge inflated claims of significance.

Knowledge Base

1. True or False: Similar to traditional independent variables, subject variables are also manipulated by researchers.
2. In contrast to the one-sample t test, when is the t test for independent groups used?
3. Where the sources of variation are concerned, most inferential test statistics are based on _____ groups variation divided by _____ groups variation.
4. A health psychologist exposes two groups of randomly selected student volunteers to a common flu virus. One group is comprised of 10 athletes who get regular exercise and the other is made up of 10 students who do not exercise regularly. The researcher measures the average number of days each group stays ill with a cold. Here are the data:

Athletes	Nonathletes
$\overline{X} = 6.0$	$\overline{X} = 8.0$
$SS = 10$	$SS = 18$

Can the researcher argue that regular exercise decreases the amount of time one is ill?
5. What is the effect size and the value of $\hat{\omega}^2$ for the study described in question 4?

Answers

1. False: Subject variables (also known as organismic variables) are individual differences that cannot be changed or otherwise manipulated.
2. An independent groups t test is used in traditional or standard experiments where two randomly assigned groups are exposed to one of the two levels of an independent variable. Any between-group difference in the sample data is assumed to reflect a real difference between respective populations and their parameters.
3. *Test statistic = between-groups variation/within-groups variation.*

4. Reject H_0: $t(18) = -3.76$, $p < .05$ (two-tailed). The athletes were sick for fewer days on average ($M = 6.0$) than the nonathletes ($M = 8.0$).

5. Effect size $r = .66$; $\hat{\omega}^2 = .40$.

Hypothesis Testing with Correlated Research Designs

Not all questions a researcher wants to address lend themselves to examination through the traditional comparison of two group means after exposure to an independent variable. An alternative approach relies on the third and final t test, one used to test hypotheses where some change is anticipated to occur in the *same* group of participants or between two *related groups* of participants following exposure to an independent variable. This two-group inferential test is known as the *t test for correlated groups* or, occasionally, the *t test for dependent groups* or the *"paired" t test.*

KEY TERM

The *t* **test for correlated groups** (also known as the *t* **test for dependent groups** or **paired *t* test**) assesses whether an observed difference between two conditions for the same (or a matched) group of participants is significant.

As was true for the two previous variations of the t test, the assumptions underlying use of the t test for correlated groups include random selection of research participants and that their data are normally distributed. When these assumptions are violated, there is an increased chance of making a Type I error (the assumptions behind the t test are reviewed in detail earlier in this chapter).

Note that the t test for correlated groups is used to analyze data collected in one of two types of research design, a **correlated groups design** or a **matched groups design.** A correlated groups design is referred to as "correlated" precisely because there is an established association between the two groups involved—the same people appear in both groups (i.e., their responses to a dependent variable are measured at least twice). In contrast, the groups used in an independent design are presumed to be uncorrelated with one another (i.e., there are two distinct groups of participants). Correlated designs usually measure a group's response to some dependent measure at time_1, subsequently exposing the group to some independent variable or other treatment, and then measuring their responses to the original (or a highly similar) dependent measure again at time_2. It is sometimes referred to as a *before-after design* because participant reactions are measured before and after the introduction of an independent variable or some equivalent treatment.

When the reactions of the same group of participants are measured twice, any observed change in the dependent measure is attributed to the influence of the experimental treatment. This research design is ideal for examining how some treatment or intervention—perhaps a new exercise regimen coupled with a diet—alters some measurable variable (e.g., weight, caloric intake) across time. Some authors refer to a correlated groups design as a **repeated measures design** or a **within-subjects design,** appropriate labels I prefer to reserve for projects where the same group of participants responds to a dependent measure more than twice (see chapter 12).

Use of a correlated research design can create conditions of special concern for researchers and data analysts. Any research design assessing the same group of participants more than once can introduce what is known as a **carryover effect.** Carryover effects occur when a previous treatment (time_1) condition alters the observed behaviors or verbal responses in a subsequent treatment condition (time_2). Thus, some observed change from time_1 to time_2 might not be due to any independent variable; rather, it may be due to the simple experience of being in the study—aspects of the first testing encounter "carryover" and affect responses given during the second testing. These carry-

Carryover effects are potential threats to internal validity.

Table 10.4   Carryover Effects Categorized

Learning—When participants learn to perform a task (e.g., learning to solve a puzzle) during the first treatment of an experiment, their subsequent performance on the same (or similar) tasks is likely to artificially improve in a subsequent treatment(s).

Habituation—Repeated exposure to the same stimulus leads to reduced responsiveness to that stimulus (e.g., people are often startled by an unexpected noise but after they hear it a few times, they no longer react to it). If participants encounter the same stimuli throughout a study, their attention—including what could be directed at an independent variable—may wane.

Sensitization—On occasion, being exposed to one stimulus can lead participants to respond more strongly to a subsequent stimulus (this carryover effect is the functional opposite of habituation). An unsettling aspect of an experimental procedure (e.g., noxious stimuli, unpleasant physical environment, difficult instructions, unfriendly experimenter) met earlier can influence responses that come later.

Fatigue—When a participant's performance in the first part of a study induces fatigue—the participant becomes tired, easily distracted, or even bored—performance in a later treatment(s) is apt to deteriorate despite the clear presence of an independent variable. Difficult experimental tasks (e.g., solving puzzles, word or math problems) can reduce or even hinder concentration across time.

Adaptation—When participants go through a period of adaptation—adjusting to some situational factor (e.g., novel stimuli are presented on a small computer screen), then earlier measures can differ from later measures due to adaptive changes (e.g., participants' eyes eventually adjust), *not* the influence of any independent variable.

Contrast—When one condition in an experiment contrasts with a later condition(s), responses provided later can vary from earlier ones because the research conditions are perceived differently. Note that such response variation is due to the contrast effect and not necessarily any independent variable. A contrast effect can occur when participants are given a break or some refreshments relatively early in a study—they may work less hard or approach the task less seriously when no additional rewards are forthcoming.

Note: Carryover effects can plague any correlated or repeated measures design where two or more measures are administered to the same group of research participants.

over effects are threats to the internal validity of the research because the investigator is not always sure that the observed change is exclusively due to the effect of the independent variable on the dependent measure (for a review of internal validity, see chapter 2).

Table 10.4 lists six of the most common types of carryover effects observed in correlated research designs. Depending on the nature of the research, one or more of the sources listed in Table 10.4 can plague a correlated design. Plan to consult this list of common carryover effects anytime you are reading about, planning, or analyzing data from a correlated groups design. When presenting or writing about such results, you should always acknowledge the potential presence of carryover effects by discussing them in detail. Beyond such acknowledgement—and depending on the data's source or use—you may want to assure yourself, as well as those learning about your research, that carryover effects were either controlled for or ruled out in your work insofar as it was possible to do so.

Counterbalancing is one methodological maneuver experimenters can use to prevent carryover effects. Counterbalancing is a form of experimental control where each participant encounters all stimulus materials but in a *different* order than any of the other participants (e.g., Campbell & Stanley, 1963). Imagine that before a pretest is administered, three stimuli—call them A, B, and C—are presented to a given participant. At the same time, a second and a third participant view the same stimuli, but in still *different orders* than the first (e.g., B, C, A; C, A, B). Why is this counterbalancing beneficial? Alternating stimulus presentation evenly spreads the effect of any *particular* order across all the participants in a study, so that no experimental confound favoring one ordering over another occurs.

In contrast to the standard correlated groups design, a matched groups design entails recruiting participants who are paired together on some matching variable, one a researcher believes is highly related to the study's dependent measure. Participants who have approximately the same scores on the matching variables are paired together at the project's outset. One participant in each pair is then randomly assigned to either an experimental *or* a control condition, and the remaining participant is placed in the other condition. The chief advantage of a matched groups design is that it enables an investigator to assume that the two participant groups were *more or less* identical at the study's outset.

Perhaps a psycholinguist is interested in how age and intelligence are linked to language learning under intensive and normal educational conditions. A general observation is that learning a foreign language becomes more difficult as people age, but heretofore no one controlled for the role of intelligence in the presumed relationship. The researcher recruits participants who are matched by chronological age (in years) and intelligence (measured IQ). One member of each resulting pair (e.g., two 15-year-olds with IQs of 110, two 40-year-olds with IQs of 105, etc.) is randomly assigned to an intensive language learning program and the other is placed in a traditional language class.

At the end of a semester, the psycholinguist gives both groups a language test to assess whether the intensive learning treatment was more effective than the traditional mode, while controlling for the effects of age and intelligence. By matching participants on two variables that are clearly linked (i.e., correlated) with language learning, the investigator can offer a strong and clear test of whether the intensive language learning is superior to the standard approach. One final methodological note: Matched groups designs are especially ideal when only a relatively small number of research participants are available, as careful matching actually reduces the need for a large sample (for more detail on matched groups designs, see Martin, 1996; Shaughnessy & Zechmeister, 1997).

The Statistical Advantage of Correlated Groups Designs: Reducing Error Variance

The relatively low error variance associated with correlated groups designs increases the chance of finding a significant research result.

The correlated group design enables us to build on the knowledge we gained earlier in this chapter when we reviewed the conceptual model for comparing means. Statistically, the great advantage of the correlated group design is that the same participants experience any and all treatments. Thus, assessing participants' states before and after the presentation of the independent variable establishes a firm basis for comparison. In a very real sense, each participant serves as his or her own control group. How so? Because participant experiences both levels of the independent variable; that is, each person encounters the study's control level (pretest measure) as well as experimental level (posttest measure). Think about it: Assuming that carryover effects pose no interpretive threat (see Table 10.4), the correlated research design is ideal because *any* measurable change from one measure to the next is attributed to the influence of the independent variable.

Correlated group designs effectively keep error variation—the error term in the denominator of the correlated groups *t* test—*relatively* low by using the same (or carefully matched) participants before and after the treatment is introduced. What keeps the magnitude of the error term small? Because the same participants are measured twice, any subject-related factors (e.g., age, IQ, personality, gender, religion) are identical (or nearly so in the case of matched groups) at time$_1$ *and* time$_2$. All else being equal, then, the within-group variation for the correlated groups *t* test should be relatively low because there is only one source of error—the one group of participants or carefully matched subject pairs—rather then the two sets of (different) participants associated with the independent groups *t* test.

If the independent variable is at all effective in eliciting behavioral change, then there will be an observed difference between the obtained means at time$_1$ and the time$_2$ (i.e., between-groups variation represented by the numerator in the *t* test). With a smaller error term in the denominator, a larger calculated *t* value is likely to be found when it is divided into the numerator. Simply put, a smaller denominator generally leads to a larger *t* value, thereby increasing the likelihood of rejecting H_0 and identifying a significant positive or negative change in the means from time$_1$ to time$_2$. In the next section we turn to calculation procedures for the correlated groups *t* test, where we will see how a reduced error term pays off empirically. (We will revisit this statistical advantage in another guise later in chapter 13, when a dependent measure is administered on more than two occasions.)

The *t* Test for Correlated Groups

The actual formula for the correlated groups *t* test looks like this:

$$[10.18.1] \qquad t = \frac{(\overline{X}_1 - \overline{X}_2) - (\mu_1 - \mu_2)}{\sqrt{s_{\overline{X}_1}^2 + s_{\overline{X}_2}^2 - 2rs_{\overline{X}_1}s_{\overline{X}_2}}}.$$

To be sure, this formula looks a bit forbidding, though parts of it should certainly be recognizable. Similar to the two prior *t* test variations, the numerator in formula [10.18.1] denotes the comparison between means—here they happen to be from the same or similar group of people, of course—and, as in the *t* test for independent groups, the parameter notation involving μ is strictly symbolic. The denominator, the error term, is not very different from what you already know, except that a correlation between the standard errors of the two dependent measures is indicated.

Fortunately, another, much less laborious formula (with accompanying calculation procedures) is available, one based on raw scores resulting from the mean differences between time$_1$ and time$_2$:

$$[10.19.1] \qquad t_D = \frac{\overline{X}_D}{\dfrac{s_{\overline{D}}}{\sqrt{N - 1}}},$$

▽

The t test for correlated groups assesses the average change between a measure taken at time$_1$ and another taken at time$_2$.

where $\overline{X}_D$ is the mean of the difference scores—the average change—between the before and after measures, and $s_{\overline{D}}/\sqrt{N - 1}$ is the standard error of these difference scores. As was the case for the Pearson *r*, please note that N refers to the number of pairs of difference scores and *not* the total number of observations available. One other note before we work through a sample problem: To avoid confusing this variation of the *t* test with the other two we know, I prefer to identify it as t_D when performing a calculation (the subscript D refers to "difference scores" or, if you prefer, "dependent" groups). When reporting a result in written form, just be certain to let the reader know that a *t* test for correlated group designs was used to analyze the data.

Let's consider a straightforward example involving attitude change, one adapted from Dunn (1999). An applied social psychologist wants to determine if an antismoking campaign aimed at high school students is effective when it comes to making existing attitudes toward cigarettes less positive. *Following* some intervention (e.g., a month-long series of speakers, class discussions on the perils of smoking, a poster campaign in school hallways), a group of high school students is anticipated to perceive smoking more negatively than *before* the intervention was initiated. Imagine that participants are eight randomly-selected high school students (four males, four females) who rate their attitudes toward cigarette smoking at time$_1$ (preintervention) and then one month later at time$_2$ (postintervention). Naturally, we will follow the four steps for testing a hypothesis outlined in Table 9.2.

Step 1. What is the null hypothesis we are testing? By using formula [10.19.1], we are assessing a mean difference in an unusual way. How so? We treat two samples—pre- and posttest attitudes—as one sample (i.e., the calculated difference score based on a raw score at time$_1$ minus a raw score at time$_2$). In effect, the population we are sampling from is comprised of difference scores, and we are trying to determine whether an observed mean difference ($\overline{X}_D$) is greater than 0. A larger average difference indicates the presence of attitude change, while a smaller average change implies relative constancy of belief. This logic is somewhat similar to that used to test hypotheses involving the Pearson r in chapter 9 (i.e., is an observed value for r different from 0?). The hope, of course, is that the obtained difference is in a direction consistent with the study's hypothesis.

Thus, the null hypothesis regarding attitude change toward the cigarette smoking is:

$$H_0: \mu_{\overline{D}} = 0.$$

In other words, no change in attitude is expected to occur under H_0; the responses collected before and after the antismoking campaign would essentially be from the same population of attitudes. The alternative or research hypothesis is that some attitude change occurred so that the difference between the observed means is greater than 0. In particular, the social psychologist expects that the mean attitude will decrease (become less positive) from time$_1$ to time$_2$. Symbolically, however, the alternative hypothesis is:

$$H_1: \mu_{\overline{D}} > 0.$$

Following standard convention, our significance level for the correlated groups t test will be .05.

Step 2. This second step usually entails calculating the standard error of the mean or, in this case, the standard error of the difference between means. We must postpone this calculation until step 3, when the standard error is determined after the standard deviation of the difference scores becomes known. At this point, however, we can decide to use a two-tailed significance test.

Step 3. Now we can get down to the actual hypothesis testing. The upper portion of Table 10.5 illustrates how to set up the t test for correlated groups. As you can see, there are eight participants (see the column labeled "participants" on the far-left side of Table 10.5). Raw scores representing the pre- and the posttest attitude measures are displayed in the second and third columns of Table 10.5. As shown by the means beneath the respective columns, the average attitude before the antismoking campaign ($\overline{X}_1 = 5.58$) was more favorable than the average attitude ($\overline{X}_2 = 3.75$) after it. How do we know this is so? The participants completed the same seven-point rating scale twice, where higher scores indicate greater tolerance for smoking. Our interest, though, is not in these two means per se but in the average difference between them. By performing the correlated groups t test, we can determine if the average difference between these means is significant (i.e., attitudes toward smoking became more negative—the mean dropped—from time$_1$ to time$_2$).

Table 10.5 Tabular Presentation of Smoking Attitudes for Correlated Measures Design and *t* Test

Participant	Pretest[a]	Posttest[a]	Difference (D)	$\overline{X}_D$	$X_D - \overline{X}_D$	$(X_D - \overline{X}_D)^2$
1	6	4	2	2.13	−.13	.017
2	5	2	3	2.13	.87	.757
3	7	4	3	2.13	.87	.757
4	6	3	3	2.13	.87	.757
5	5	5	0	2.13	−2.14	4.54
6	6	4	2	2.13	−.13	.017
7	5	2	3	2.13	.87	.757
8	7	6	1	2.13	−1.13	1.28

$$\overline{X}_1 = 5.88 \qquad \overline{X}_2 = 3.75 \qquad \sum D = 17 \qquad \sum (X_D - \overline{X}_D)^2 = 8.88$$
$$\overline{X}_{\overline{D}} = 2.13$$

$$\overline{X}_D = \frac{\sum D}{N} = \frac{17}{8} = 2.13$$

Note: Data are hypothetical attitudes concerning smoking collected before (pretest) and after (posttest) an antismoking campaign.

[a]Ratings are based on a seven-point scale where higher numbers indicate more favorable attitudes toward cigarette smoking.

How do we begin the calculations? The first step is to calculate the difference (*D*) between the pretest and posttest scores. These difference scores are shown in column 4 of Table 10.5 (please note that the $\sum D$ and the mean of *D* (i.e., $\overline{X}_{\overline{D}}$) are shown at the bottom of this fourth column). The formula for calculating the mean of *D* is shown in the lower portion of Table 10.5. The $\overline{X}_D$, equal to 2.13, is then entered into column 5, and the difference between each entry in columns 4 and 5 is subsequently entered into column 6 (i.e., $X_D - \overline{X}_D$; see Table 10.5). These difference scores are then squared (see the entries in column 7) and the sum of the squared differences scores (i.e., $\sum (X_D - \overline{X}_D)^2 = 8.88$) is shown below column 7 (see Table 10.5).

The next step is to determine the standard deviation of the difference scores by using:

$$[10.20.1] \qquad s_{\overline{D}} = \sqrt{\frac{\sum (X_D - \overline{X}_D)^2}{N}}.$$

We need only enter the number noted at the bottom of column 7, which is 8.88, as well as the *N*. Again, please note that *N* refers to the number of participants or, if you prefer, paired measures—but *not* the total number of observations available.

$$[10.20.2] \qquad s_{\overline{D}} = \sqrt{\frac{8.88}{8}},$$

$$[10.20.3] \qquad s_{\overline{D}} = \sqrt{1.11},$$

$$[10.20.4] \qquad s_{\overline{D}} = 1.0536 \cong 1.05.$$

In order to calculate the actual *t* statistic, this standard deviation is then entered into formula [10.19.1] (it will become the standard error of the difference scores), along with the $\overline{X}_D$ and $N - 1$, for:

$$[10.19.2] \qquad t_D = \frac{2.13}{\frac{1.05}{\sqrt{8-1}}},$$

$$[10.19.3] \qquad t_D = \frac{2.13}{\frac{1.05}{\sqrt{7}}},$$

$$[10.19.3] \qquad t_D = \frac{2.13}{\frac{1.05}{2.646}},$$

$$[10.19.4] \qquad t_D = \frac{2.13}{.3969},$$

$$[10.19.5] \qquad t_D = 5.367 \cong 5.37.$$

Do you see how small the error term—the denominator—is in the calculation of t_D? Despite the fact that the value of $\overline{X}_D$ is relatively small, when it is divided by the still smaller error term, a quite large t ratio is the result. Remember: A small error term generally leads to a large t ratio. I hope that this concrete example is sufficient to convince you that the correlated groups t test really capitalizes on the low amount of within-group error available, thereby increasing the chance of obtaining a significant difference between the two means.

We now need to verify whether the observed t ratio is, indeed, statistically significant. In order to identify a critical value for the t test for correlated measures, we need to calculate the degrees of freedom for this statistic. The formula for degrees of freedom for this test is:

$$[10.21.1] \qquad degrees\ of\ freedom\ (df) = N - 1,$$

$$[10.21.2] \qquad df = 8 - 1,$$

$$[10.21.3] \qquad df = 7.$$

Please turn to Table B.4 in Appendix B and look for a two-tailed critical t value at the .05 level with 7 degrees of freedom. What value did you find? You should identify this value as $t_{crit}\ (7) = 2.365$. Armed with this critical value, what statistical decision should you make? Can you accept or reject the null hypothesis of no difference? We reject H_0 because:

$$t_{calculated}\ (7) = 5.37 > t_{crit}\ (7) = 2.365:\ Reject\ H_0.$$

Writing Up the Result of a Correlated Groups *t* Test.

What, then, do we know? We know that the attitudes of the eight high school students became more negative across 1 month—the mean attitude toward smoking became less positive from time$_1$ ($\overline{X}_1 = 5.88$) to time$_2$ ($\overline{X}_2 = 3.75$). The applied social psychologist could report this result as follows:

> As anticipated, student attitudes toward cigarette smoking did become less favorable following the month long antismoking campaign. A correlated groups t test revealed that the difference between attitudes measured before and after the intervention was significant ($M = 2.13$, $SD = 1.05$), $t(7) = 5.37$, $p < .05$), two-tailed.

Following the precedent started with the independent groups t test, we need to expand our understanding of this result by calculating its effect size and determining the degree of association between the independent variable and the dependent measure.

Calculating Effect Size for Correlated Research Designs

Effect size for the correlated groups t test is calculated the same way it is for an independent groups t test. Using formula [10.16.1] (renumbered here), we find the study's effect size by entering the correlated groups t ratio we calculated (this value will be squared), as well as its degrees of freedom:

[10.22.1] $$effect\ size\ r = \sqrt{\frac{t^2}{t^2 + df}},$$

[10.22.2] $$effect\ size\ r = \sqrt{\frac{(5.37)^2}{(5.37)^2 + 7}},$$

[10.22.3] $$effect\ size\ r = \sqrt{\frac{28.84}{28.84 + 7}},$$

[10.22.4] $$effect\ size\ r = \sqrt{\frac{28.84}{35.84}},$$

[10.22.5] $$effect\ size\ r = \sqrt{.8047},$$

[10.22.6] $$effect\ size\ r = .8970 \cong .90.$$

As shown by the value of effect size *r*, the difference between the two means is quite pronounced. Put another way, the change in attitude from before and after the intervention is quite pronounced, even meaningful.

We can now add an account of effect size to the correlated groups *t* test results presented above:

> As anticipated, student attitudes toward cigarette smoking did become less favorable following the month long antismoking campaign. A correlated groups *t* test revealed that the difference between attitudes measured before and after the intervention was significant ($M = 2.13$, $SD = 1.05$), $t(7) = 5.37$, $p < .05$, two-tailed. The size of the intervention's effect was large (effect size $r = .90$).

Use of this supplemental statistical information provides readers with a clearer sense of what happened in the research project, one that extends beyond the province of the mean difference. We turn now to the final topic in this chapter, one that will help us to think about predicting differences when a research topic is still on the drawingboard or merely the seed of an interesting idea.

A Brief Overview of Power Analysis: Thinking More Critically About Research and Data Analysis

For many years, two psychologists—Robert Rosenthal and Ralph L. Rosnow—have gone to great lengths to encourage researchers and students to pay close attention to the power of statistical tests (e.g., Rosenthal & Rosnow, 1991). Power—the probability of rejecting the null hypothesis when it is truly false and should be rejected—was introduced and defined in chapter 9. In quantitative terms, power is defined as $1 - \beta$, the likelihood of not making a Type II error (i.e., missing a result that actually exists; see chapter 9 for a review).

By drawing our attention to issues of statistical power, Rosnow and Rosenthal (1996) want us to always think about whether a given significance test is sensitive enough to provide the opportunity to reject a null hypothesis that should be rejected. The term **power analysis** was coined to motivate researchers to think beyond the presence or absence of significant differences in their results. For instance, power analysis sometimes involves analyzing null results with an eye to learning whether it was *ever* reasonable to anticipate finding any significant differences between conditions in an experiment. Power analysis also entails planning for how many research participants are needed in order to detect a given effect at a predetermined level of significance (e.g., .05, .01).

When an inferential statistic such as the *t* test is used to accept or reject the null hypothesis, three factors affect the test's power:

- The probability of making a Type I error (i.e., the *p* value or significance level of the test)
- The sample size used in the piece of research
- The effect size of the inferential test.

Rosnow and Rosenthal (1996) remind us that these three factors are so interconnected that when two are known, the third is more or less established. Why is this fact important? Because we usually know the first factor and can estimate or guess the third from prior research efforts, our own or those performed (and published) by others. When these two factors are known, we can *approximate* the sample size we need in order to increase the chance of obtaining a significant result in a project we are planning (or hoping to conceptually replicate in the case of a "failed" study).

Power analysis can entail examining the existing relations among significance levels, sample sizes, and effect sizes.

It turns out that given a particular effect size *r*, we can identify how large a sample we will need to approach a desired level of significance—and we can do so with some level of probable success (i.e., power) in mind. Table 10.6 provides an easy way to estimate the total number of participants necessary to detect various effects at the .05 (two-tailed) level of significance. As you can see, the column headings in Table 10.6 are various effect sizes ranging from .10 to .70 (no doubt you notice that the effect sizes reported in our hypothetical examples are usually larger than .70, a fact attributable to the contrived nature of the numbers—real data are rarely so cooperative). Various power levels are provided at the start of the rows in the leftmost column of Table 10.6.

A power level of .80 is both reasonable and recommended for behavioral science research efforts.

How do we begin? Imagine that you choose to work with a power level of .80, a desirable, recommended level for behavioral research (see Cohen, 1965) and that published research in your topical area of interest typically finds medium-sized effects (e.g., effect size *r* = .40). If you find the table entry representing the intersection between power = .80 and effect size *r* = .40, you will find that 45 participants are needed in order to reject the null hypothesis at the .05 (two-tailed) level of significance. What if you stayed with the same power level but were anticipating a much smaller effect size, say, *r* = .20? You would need a total of 195 participants in order

Table 10.6 Rounded Sample Sizes (Overall *N*) Required to Detect Various Effects (*r*) at the .05 (Two-Tailed) Significance Level

Power	Effect Sizes (*r*)						
	.10	.20	.30	.40	.50	.60	.70
.15	85	25	10	10	10	10	10
.20	125	35	15	10	10	10	10
.30	200	55	25	15	10	10	10
.40	300	75	35	20	15	10	10
.50	400	100	40	25	15	10	10
.60	500	125	55	30	20	15	10
.70	600	155	65	40	25	15	10
.80	800	195	85	45	30	20	15
.90	1000	260	115	60	40	25	15

Source: Rosnow and Rosenthal (1996, p. 263), which was adapted from Cohen (1998, pp. 92–93).

to have a reasonable shot at rejecting H_0—that is quite a few participants, coupled with a great deal of hope!

This table and others like it (see Cohen, 1988) are excellent resources that can help you to plan a project or to try to discern why one went awry. I encourage you to consult such resources as you design studies, evaluate them, or analyze their data. Like many of the data analytic tools we have learned so far, power analysis is meant to take some of the mystery out of statistics, and to make your thinking about data and results more precise.

Knowledge Base

1. What does the word "correlated" refer to in correlated group designs?
2. True or False: Carryover effects are threats to the internal validity of correlated group designs.
3. True or False: In a matched groups design, the same group of participants appears in both the control and experimental condition.
4. Why is the error term in the correlated groups *t* test usually relatively low?
5. What is the nature of the mean difference assessed by the *t* test for correlated groups?
6. An investigator is planning an experiment on a topic that usually finds effect sizes around $r = .30$, and she assumes a power level of .70. How large should her participant sample be in order to have a reasonable chance of rejecting the null hypothesis?

Answers

1. The dependent measures are said to be correlated because the same participants respond to them at least twice (e.g., before and after exposure to an independent variable).
2. True.
3. False: Similar participants are paired together on some matching variable, one highly correlated with the dependent measure. One member of each matched pair is then randomly assigned to a control or an experimental condition; the other member is then placed in the remaining condition.
4. The error term remains low because the research participants are measured more than once or matched so that any subject-related factors (i.e., individual differences that are sources of error) are more or less identical.
5. The *t* test for correlated groups assesses whether the mean of the difference scores $(\overline{X}_D)$—the average change between a before and after measure—is greater than 0.
6. Using Table 10.6, a total of 65 participants would be needed.

Project Exercise

PLANNING FOR DATA ANALYSIS: DEVELOPING A BEFORE AND AFTER DATA COLLECTION ANALYSIS PLAN

We began this chapter by discussing the statistical exploits of William Gosset, a creative researcher who developed an effective statistical alternative—the *t* test—enabling him to cope with the research vagaries endemic to the brewing industry (e.g., small samples). Fortunately, similar problems were noticed in the behavioral sciences, and an alliance between the *t* test and experimental research was forged. We closed the chapter by touting the use of power analysis tables as effective tools for increasing the chance of obtaining significant results by creating relatively ideal research conditions (e.g., ample sample size of participants). Such tools decrease a researcher's risk and render expenditures of time, effort, and energy worthwhile.

Besides the ubiquitous statistical theme, what else do these topics have in common? Both illustrate the need for careful and thoughtful planning where statistical analyses are concerned. An unsung but important part of becoming a skilled researcher and savvy data analyst is planning the statistical analysis you will use at the same time you are planning the experiment that will use it. By "planning the analysis," I mean thinking about all the necessary parts of a research project from start to finish, from idea conception to the sharing of results, with an eye on how the collected data will be analyzed.

You would be surprised (if not shocked) by the number of researchers—students and faculty alike—who do not bother to think about what statistical test will be used to analyze what data until after the study is over, when it is usually always too late to do anything about the empirical sins committed along the way (e.g., Dunn, 1999; Martin, 1996; McKenna, 1995). Despite entreaties and earnest warnings, I still encounter students who design and execute a semester's research project without ever thinking about how to analyze their data. To our mutual regret, many times the student and I discover that the data are not analyzable by conventional tests—indeed, the data often cannot be understood by *any* statistical test! Once data are collected, salvage missions are hard to launch and, in any case, they rarely lead to behavioral insight or salvation for researchers (or in the case of students, their grades).

Why don't people plan their analyses more carefully? Fear and loathing of statistics, time constraints, disorganization, and general sloth all conspire to keep students and researchers from planning what they will do with the information they gather at a project's outset. To combat this problem, I encourage—sometimes exhort—my students to develop what I refer to as a *Before and After Data Collection Analysis Plan before* they begin a project in earnest.

An analysis plan identifies and defines independent and dependent variables, as well as the statistical test(s) used to analyze the relationship(s) between them. Chapter 10's *Project Exercise* is designed to help you to plan your analyses—literally or hypothetically—while avoiding the research fate of less organized peers. This *Project Exercise* can be performed for (a) an experiment you *are* actually conducting or (b) a hypothetical experiment you *could* conduct. In either case, I encourage you to follow the steps outlined in Table 10.7 and to think about the issues highlighted therein. The questions provided will help you to think more critically about the links among the available literature on a topic, research methodology, and data analysis. Table 10.7 makes these links more apparent by outlining four steps that should be followed *before* any data are collected and four steps guiding research activities once the data are in hand. Please note that only step 5 in Table 10.7 refers to conducting the actual project; there is more to research planning than just data collection.

If you are creating an analysis plan for a project you intend to conduct (option a above), then obviously you can use the steps in Table 10.7 with any number of different statistical tests in mind. If you develop an analysis plan for a hypothetical study (option b above), however, I encourage you to create a study where one of the three variations of the *t* test presented in this chapter would be appropriate. By using your knowledge of mean comparison and the *t* test in this way, you are increasing the chance that you will remember information about this test and its applications for the future.

Your instructor may ask you to share your research topic and analysis plan with the class. Before you do so, be sure to think about how your choice of statistical analyses can be used to support the ideas underlying your research.

Table 10.7	A Before and After Data Collection Analysis Plan

Before

Step 1. Select a topic and search the relevant literature.
  a. Identify the average effect sizes (e.g., *r*) for research on the topic.
  b. Develop a hypothesis.

Step 2. Determine the quality of the dependent measure(s) and research design.
  a. Continuous or discontinuous data?
  b. Independent (administered once) or correlated (administered more than once) design?

Step 3. Using effect size identified in step 1 and a reasonable power level (e.g., .80), determine the total number of participants necessary for the project (see Table 10.6).

Step 4. Select the appropriate statistical test to analyze the data (e.g., *t* test for independent groups, *t* test for correlated measures).[*]

Step 5. Begin the project and collect the data.

After

Step 6. Summarize the data and perform descriptive statistics.
  a. Copy data onto record sheets or enter into a computer file.
  b. For continuous data, calculate means and standard deviations.
  c. For discontinuous data, calculate frequencies or percentages.

Step 7. Perform statistical analysis based on the test selected back in step 4.
  a. Follow Table 9.2's four steps for hypothesis testing in order to accept or reject H_0.
  b. Determine the effect size of the result. (e.g., effect size *r*).
  c. If H_0 is rejected, then calculate $\hat{\omega}^2$, if appropriate.

Step 8. Interpret result(s).
  a. Write results in prose form but include descriptive and inferential statistics when appropriate.
  b. Create a data display (e. g., table, figure, graph), if necessary (see chapter 3 for guidance).

Step 9. Integrate the results into a paper or a presentation.
  a. See Appendix C for guidelines.

---

[*]The decision tree that opens chapter 15, as well as that chapter's *Project Exercise*, provide guidance for choosing an appropriate statistical test.

Source: Adapted from Dunn (1999) and McKenna (1995).

Here are the *Project Exercise* questions you should answer as you link options (a) or (b) to the guidelines shown in Table 10.7:

1. What is your research topic? What behavioral science discipline (e.g., psychology, sociology, education) does the topic fall under?

2. What types of studies—experiments, quasi-experiments, observational research—are published on your topic? Characterize the usual research design(s), independent and dependent variable(s), and statistical analyses employed. What differences were found? How strong were they?

3. What will your study be like? What question will you address empirically? Operationally define your variables, characterize the research design, and explain who will take part in the study. How many participants will be necessary for your research? Who will they be?

4. What statistical hypothesis will you test? What statistical analysis will you use to test it? Describe the results in behavioral and statistical terms you anticipate observing.

5. Are there any special issues for your research that do not appear in Table 10.7? If so, what are they? Why do they matter?

LOOKING FORWARD   THEN BACK

his chapter represents the first group of inferential statistical tests designed for use with sample data drawn from one or two populations. The *t* test is probably the most common statistical test used in the behavioral sciences, and it is one with more applicability than many students and researchers realize. The three decision trees at the beginning of this chapter attest to this fact. The first decision tree is useful because it will help you to decide which of the three possible *t* tests (i.e., single-sample, independent groups, or correlated groups) is best suited to your data. The second decision tree reinforces the fact that the independent groups *t* test is by far the most familiar one, and its test statistic is the one students are apt to encounter in their reading or analyses for a research project they undertake. More to the point, perhaps, this second tree can guide you from start to finish through any analysis requiring the independent groups *t* test.

The third and final decision tree is designed to encourage you to think about key data analytic issues *before* you start an experiment to test some hypothesis. Effect size and power are two essential considerations that can "make or break" the results from a piece of research. As noted on previous occasions in this book, planning and forethought where statistical analyses are concerned enhances the chance of success—here, correctly rejecting the null hypothesis of no difference.

Summary

1. The *t* test—Student's *t*—was born out of necessity to deal with small samples when the parameters and variability of larger populations remain unknown. The *t* test is used to detect significant differences between two sample means, which are either independent or dependent, or between a sample mean and an estimated population mean.

2. The *t* distribution substitutes for the *z* distribution because the latter is of limited use when small samples (<30 participants) are examined. The *t* distributions are a family of bell-shaped sampling distributions with a mean of 0 and standard deviations that reduce in magnitude as sample sizes increase.

3. Several assumptions underlie the *t* test: (a) the data are drawn from a normally distributed population(s); (b) the data are either randomly sampled from a larger population or individually selected from a larger population; (c) dependent measures must be based on an interval or a ratio scale; and (d) when independent samples are used, they are presumed to originate in populations with equal variances.

4. The *t* test is said to be statistically robust; that is, it can still provide reliable answers when some of its assumptions are violated. Robust tests generally guard against Type I errors.

5. The *t* test assesses whether a difference exists between two means, and this difference serves as the numerator in a calculation. The standard deviation(s) of a sample(s) is used to estimate the standard error of the mean or the difference between means, which acts as the denominator. Smaller standard error values tend to occur when sample sizes are large, two conditions that lead to larger *t* statistics.

6. The single- or one-sample *t* test is used to compare an observed sample mean with a hypothesized value thought to be representative of a population. This variation of the *t* test is often used to measure deviation from some known behavioral pattern or standard.

7. The power of a *t* test is influenced by the selected significance level, variability within the sample data, the size of a sample(s), and the magnitude of the difference between means.

8. Hypothesis testing aimed at assessing whether a significant difference exists between two independent samples is the most common—and familiar—application of the *t* test. The independent groups *t* test compares the mean reaction of one group (e.g., experimental condition) to another (e.g., control condition). This inferential statistic is commonly used to analyze data from two-group between-subjects designs.

9. Independent variables are either manipulated, as in traditional or standard experiments, or measured as a subject variable. A subject variable is an individual characteristic a participant possesses, a trait or characteristic (e.g., age,

gender, height, IQ) that is beyond the control of the experimenter. For example, subject variables can be used for comparing one group showing the trait to another group where the trait is absent.

10. Various inferential statistical tests, including the *t* test, are based on a conceptual model where between-groups variation (attributable to an independent variable) is divided by within-groups variation (the error term or the degree of behavioral similarity observed in each group). Generally, researchers want to obtain a large amount of between-groups variation relative to a small amount of within-groups variation.

11. Beyond reporting a mean difference revealed by an independent groups *t* test, it is also important to index any significant effect size (e.g., effect size *r*) and to indicate the degree of association existing between the relevant independent variable and dependent measure (e.g., $\hat{\omega}^2$).

12. The *t* test for correlated groups is used to assess an observed difference between two conditions for the same or a matched group of participants. This test is used to analyze correlated group designs, where participant responses are assessed before and after exposure to an independent variable. The test can also analyze data from matched group designs, where pairs of participants are equated on some dimension that is highly related to the dependent measure.

13. Carryover effects involve response bias, where prior responses to a dependent measure influence reactions to the same measure on a subsequent occasion(s). These carryover effects are common in correlated group designs and can mislead investigators by mimicking, masking, or eliminating the effects of an independent variable. As a result, carryover effects serve as a threat to internal validity.

14. Correlated group and matched group designs pose a distinct statistical advantage, the reduction of error variance. In contrast to between-groups research designs, these correlated designs draw error variance from one source (e.g., one group of participants) rather than two (e.g., two independent samples of participants). When a smaller error term is present in the denominator of the *t* test, there is a greater likelihood of rejecting the null hypothesis even when the difference between means is modest.

15. Power analysis is a tool to enhance a researcher's probability of correctly rejecting a null hypothesis. By planning an experiment in advance (i.e., identifying effect sizes in the relevant research literature and selecting a power level), a researcher can identify the total number of participants needed to have a reasonable chance of detecting a statistically significant result.

16. Before collecting one datum, every student and researcher should complete an analysis plan, a guiding "game plan" that promotes identifying necessary statistical tests in advance.

Key Terms

Between-groups design (*p. 378*)
Between-groups variation (*p. 383*)
Between-samples variation (*p. 383*)
Between-subjects design (*p. 378*)
Carryover effects (*p. 393*)
Correlated groups design (*p. 393*)
Error term (*p. 382*)
Estimated $\hat{\omega}^2$ (*p. 391*)
Individual differences (*p. 384*)

Matched groups design (*p. 393*)
Paired *t* test (*p. 393*)
Power analysis (*p. 400*)
Repeated measures design (*p. 393*)
Robust (*p. 370*)
Sampling distribution of the difference
   between means (*p. 379*)
Single- or one-sample *t* test (*p. 372*)
Standard error of the difference between
   means (*p. 381*)

Subject variables (*p. 378*)
t distributions (*p. 368*)
t test for correlated groups (*p. 393*)
t test for dependent groups (*p. 393*)
t test for independent groups (*p. 384*)
Within-group variation (*p. 383*)
Within-sample variation (*p. 383*)
Within-subjects design (*p. 393*)

Chapter Problems

1. Why is the *t* test used in place of the *z* test?
2. How do *t* distributions differ from the *z* distribution?
3. List the assumptions underlying use of a *t* test. What happens when one of these assumptions is violated? Can the *t* test still be used—why or why not?
4. What does it mean when a statistical test is described as "robust"? Is the *t* test robust? Under what particular condi-

tions does use of the *t* test become problematic, that is, a result based on it becomes less robust?
5. Why are larger samples desirable? How do larger samples influence the size of a sample's standard deviation and standard error?
6. When should a researcher use the single sample *t* test? Describe a hypothetical but concrete example.

7. A personality researcher wants to know if students attending smaller colleges are more introverted that those going to larger universities. The researcher selects a sample of $N = 32$ 19-year-old students from a small liberal arts college. These students complete a standardized introversion-extroversion scale, one whose scale characteristics were developed using university populations (lower scores indicate higher levels of introversion). The scale's $\mu = 65$. The mean of the sample $\overline{X} = 62$ and the standard deviation is 7. Using a significance level of .05, can the personality researcher assume that the college students are more introverted than the general population?

8. What is 95% confidence interval for the mean reported in problem 7.

9. An organization of middle school educators believes that students' geographical knowledge has improved over the past five years. To verify this belief, a sample of 26 middle school students completes a world geography test ($\overline{X} = 53$, $s = 8.5$). The middle school average on this measure is 50. Using a significance level of .01, have the educators demonstrated that geographical knowledge is actually improving? Why or why not?

10. What is the 99% confidence interval for the mean reported in problem 9.

11. A random sample is drawn and observed to have a $\overline{X} = 45$ and an $s = 11$. Use this sample data to test the null hypothesis that $\mu = 42$ when:
   a. The sample size is 40 and the significance level for the test is .05.
   b. The sample size is 25 and the significance level for the test is .01.
   c. The sample size is 62 and the significance level is .05.

12. A random sample is drawn and observed to have an $\overline{X} = 77$ and an $s = 7.5$. Use this sample data to test the null hypothesis that $\mu = 80$ when:
   a. The sample size is 30 and the significance level for the test is .01.
   b. The sample size is 43 and the significance level for the test is .05.
   c. The sample size is 20 and the significance level is .05.

13. A campus psychologist is starting a weekly group to discuss low level depression, the type often triggered by stressful, academic events. The psychologist knows that the population mean of the screening test is 35, and that scores at or above this level indicated the probable presence of low level depression. His sample of students obtained screening test scores of 30, 36, 34, 34, 38, 40, 32, 30, 28, 37, 36, and 37. Can the psychologist label this group of students as having low level depression so that he can begin the therapy group? Use a .05 level of significance and perform a one-tailed test.

14. A teacher of gifted students believes that her sample of students have IQs still higher than the superior gifted cutoff of 134. Her students' scores on the IQ test were 132, 130, 136, 137, 135, 136, 133, 135, and 137. Is the teacher correct?

Can she claim that as a group, her students exceed the superior level? Use a significance level of .01 and perform a one-tailed test.

15. What are the confidence intervals for the sample means based on the data reported in problems 13 and 14. Base the confidence interval on the appropriate significance level provided in each problem.

16. Discuss the factors affecting the statistical power of a t test.

17. Why is the t test for independent groups ideal for hypothesis testing in experimental research?

18. How do traditional independent variables differ from subject variables?

19. What is a subject variable? How are subject variables used in concert with between-groups designs and the independent groups t test?

20. How does the standard error of the difference between means differ from the usual measures of standard error?

21. Explain the nature of the conceptual model for comparing means presented in this chapter. Why is this model an appropriate prelude for most inferential statistical tests?

22. Unbeknownst to his class, an instructor decides to replicate a classic study on experimenter expectancy effects (Rosenthal & Fode, 1963). In an experimental psychology lab, each student was given a rat to teach to run a standard maze. However, half of the students were told their rats were specially bred to be "maze bright" while the remaining students were told their rats were "maze dull." In actuality, of course, all the rats were of the same breed and possessed no special talents. The following data represent the rats' skill-level at running the mazes, where lower numbers represent fewer errors (i.e., higher skill). Did the students with the maze bright rats transmit that expectancy to the animals, so that they outperformed the "maze dull" animals? Use a one-tailed test with a significance level of .05.
   Maze bright scores: 15, 10, 11, 10, 12, 13, 10, 13, 12, 11
   Maze dull scores: 17, 18, 17, 16.5, 17, 19, 13, 12, 18, 17

23. What is the effect size for the result obtained in problem 22? If the t statistic calculated in problem 22 reached significance, then determine the value of $\hat{\omega}^2$.

24. Using the examples presented earlier in the chapter, write a paragraph or two summarizing the results obtained in problems 22 and 23.

25. Participants took part in a study on aversive noise and its affect on performing skilled tasks. An experimental psychologist believes that the predictability of the aversive noise is key to understanding its influence on performance. Specifically, predictable noise—noise occurring at fixed intervals of time—is less disruptive than random noise, which reminds participants that they lack control in the situation. Two groups of participants solved moderately difficult math problems while listening to a loud noise. One group heard the loud noise at fixed intervals, the other heard it at random intervals. The following data are the total number of math problems that participants in each group got correct. Determine

whether the experimenter was right, that random noise is more disruptive to skilled performance than fixed noise (use a .05 significance level for a one-tailed test).

Random noise: 10, 9, 8, 8, 9, 10, 9, 8, 7, 8.

Fixed noise: 6, 7, 8, 8, 7, 7, 6, 5, 8, 6.

26. What is the effect size for the result obtained in problem 25? If the *t* statistic calculated in problem 25 reached significance, then determine the value of $\hat{\omega}^2$.

27. Using the examples presented earlier in the chapter, write a paragraph or two summarizing the results obtained in problems 25 and 26.

28. When teaching about science, instructors are assumed to rely on less descriptive or flowery language because the natural sciences contain topical information that is relatively fixed in content. Classroom instructors in the humanities, however, rely on much more descriptive language because the topics are open to debate and multiple interpretations. An educational researcher sits in several natural science and humanities classes at several high schools and monitors the teaching styles of instructors. What follows are the number of different words and phrases used by the respective sets of instructors to convey course material: Did the humanities teachers use more descriptive language than the natural science instructors? Use a .01 significance level and perform the appropriate one-tailed test, and take note that the groups are not of equal size.

Humanities instructors' speech: 34, 28, 27, 32, 33, 30, 38, 32, 30, 28, 34, 32

Natural science teachers' speech: 27, 26, 23, 30, 25, 26, 27, 26, 27

29. What is the effect size for the result obtained in problem 28? If the *t* statistic calculated in problem 28 reached significance, then determine the value of $\hat{\omega}^2$.

30. Using the examples presented earlier in the chapter, write a paragraph or two summarizing the results obtained in problems 28 and 29.

31. Are there any advantages to conducting a correlated groups design rather than an independent groups design? If so, what are they?

32. How does a correlated groups design differ from a matched groups design? When is it appropriate to use one design rather than the other?

33. What is a carryover effect? Why do such effects pose concerns for correlated groups designs?

34. An educational psychologist believes that relaxation training can help students to improve their performance on standardized tests. A group of high school students completes two grade-appropriate reading comprehension tests, one before the relaxation training and the other a week later, after the training is complete. Using the following data, demonstrate whether reading comprehension scores increased following the training. Use a significance level of .05 as well as a one-tailed test.

Participant	Test Score$_1$	Test Score$_2$
A	8	10
B	6	7
C	6	8
D	5	6
E	9	10
F	8	9

35. Review the research project described above in problem 34. Do you think this project could be susceptible to any carryover effects? If so, which one(s) and why?

36. An industrial psychologist is concerned that a recent round of layoffs at a plant may have increased the stress felt by employees who retained their positions. To measure whether this survivor stress actually exists, the psychologist administered a stress measure to a sample of employees before and after the layoffs occurred. Evaluate whether self-reported stress increased from time$_1$ to time$_2$ by using a .01 significance level and a one-tailed test.

Employee	Stress Score$_1$	Stress Score$_2$
A	21	23
B	24	26
C	15	15
D	18	22
E	19	20
F	20	19
G	18	21

37. Review the research project described above in problem 36. Do you think this project could be susceptible to any carryover effects? If so, which one(s) and why?

38. A social psychologist is interested in how emotional contagion—adopting the affective state of people after hearing them describe positive or negative experience—affects people who have an optimistic disposition. The psychologist is particularly interested in whether the number of people sharing their emotional experiences makes any difference in the affective transfer (e.g., perhaps two people sharing a happy event with a third enhance her mood to a greater degree than one person talking about the same experience). The social psychologist recruits a group of people who are matched on their measured level of optimism, age, and gender. One member of each pair is then exposed to three people who discuss the same emotion eliciting experience, while the other matched participant meets with one person for emotion sharing. The following data are emotion ratings on a 1 to 7 scale, where higher numbers indicate greater emotion transfer. Evaluate whether the participants who met with a group rather than a single person showed a greater degree of emotional contagion. Use a .05 significance level for a one-tailed hypothesis test.

Matched Pair	Solo-Emotion Encounter	Group Emotional Encounter
A	4	6
B	3	5
C	7	6
D	5	7
E	2	4
F	6	6
G	5	7
H	5	6

39. Why should investigators learn to perform a power analysis? Should a power analysis be performed before or after a study? Why?

40. Examine the following effect sizes and power levels, and then determine how many total participants are needed for each of the studies represented. (Hint: Consider using the decision trees that open the chapter to answer this question.)

a. effect $r = .30$, power $= .40$; b. effect size $r = .20$, power $= .60$; c. effect size $r = .70$, power $= .15$; d. effect size $r = .30$, power $= .50$.

41. Which t test is most appropriate for each of the following situations? (Hint: Consider using the decision trees that open the chapter to answer this question.)
   a. Samples are not independent of one another.
   b. Population parameters are known.
   c. Two observations at different points in time were gathered for each participant.
   d. Two independent samples were drawn.
   e. One observation was drawn for each participant, and population parameters were not known.

42. Two independent samples of data are available, but their sample sizes are unequal. What should the data analyst do? (Hint: Consider using the decision trees that open the chapter to answer this question.)

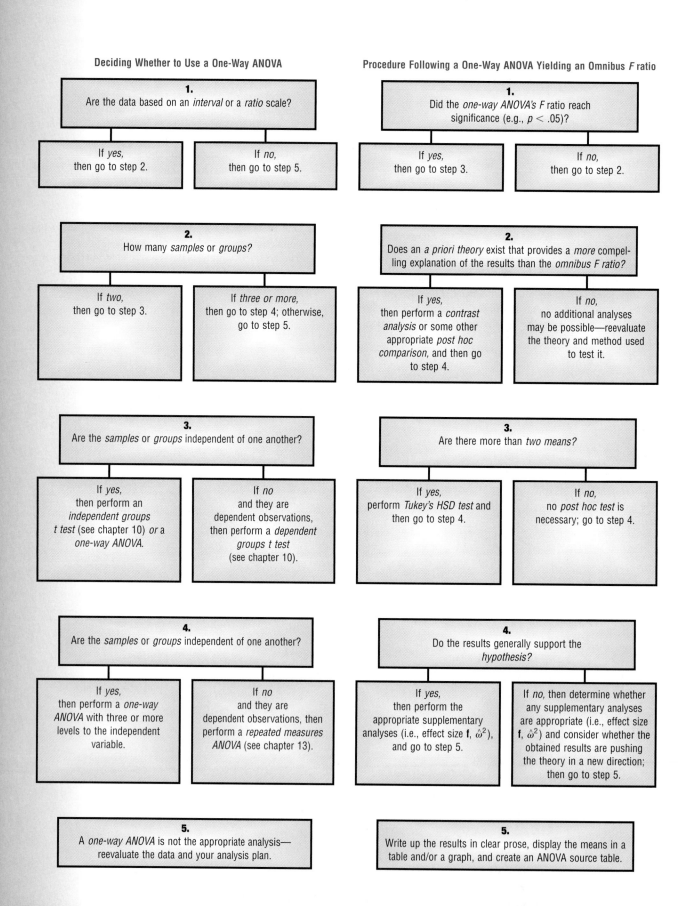

Deciding Whether to Use a One-Way ANOVA

1.
Are the data based on an *interval* or a *ratio* scale?

If *yes,*
then go to step 2.

If *no,*
then go to step 5.

2.
How many *samples* or *groups?*

If *two,*
then go to step 3.

If *three or more,*
then go to step 4; otherwise,
go to step 5.

3.
Are the *samples* or *groups* independent of one another?

If *yes,*
then perform an
*independent groups
t test* (see chapter 10) *or a
one-way ANOVA.*

If *no*
and they are
dependent observations,
then perform a *dependent
groups t test*
(see chapter 10).

4.
Are the *samples* or *groups* independent of one another?

If *yes,*
then perform a *one-way
ANOVA* with three or more
levels to the independent
variable.

If *no*
and they are
dependent observations, then
perform a *repeated measures
ANOVA* (see chapter 13).

5.
A *one-way ANOVA* is not the appropriate analysis—
reevaluate the data and your analysis plan.

Procedure Following a One-Way ANOVA Yielding an Omnibus *F* ratio

1.
Did the *one-way ANOVA's F* ratio reach
significance (e.g., $p < .05$)?

If *yes,*
then go to step 3.

If *no,*
then go to step 2.

2.
Does an *a priori theory* exist that provides a *more* compelling explanation of the results than the *omnibus F ratio?*

If *yes,*
then perform a *contrast
analysis* or some other
appropriate *post hoc
comparison,* and then go
to step 4.

If *no,*
no additional analyses
may be possible—reevaluate
the theory and method used
to test it.

3.
Are there more than *two means?*

If *yes,*
perform *Tukey's HSD test* and
then go to step 4.

If *no,*
no *post hoc test* is
necessary; go to step 4.

4.
Do the results generally support the
hypothesis?

If *yes,*
then perform the
appropriate supplementary
analyses (i.e., effect size **f**, $\hat{\omega}^2$),
and go to step 5.

If *no,* then determine whether
any supplementary analyses
are appropriate (i.e., effect size
f, $\hat{\omega}^2$) and consider whether the
obtained results are pushing
the theory in a new direction;
then go to step 5.

5.
Write up the results in clear prose, display the means in a
table and/or a graph, and create an ANOVA source table.

MEAN COMPARISON II: ONE-VARIABLE ANALYSIS OF VARIANCE

I want to open this chapter by issuing a small challenge, one designed to help you to think about situations where the data cooperate (i.e., an experiment succeeds and significant differences are found) and where they do not (i.e., no predicted differences are found). I want you to focus more on the importance of performing an appropriate statistical analysis, however, than worrying about whether a hypothesis is confirmed. These words may seem anathema to many readers (e.g., what *could* be more important than finding a significant result?), but my point is a simple one: We have low tolerance for null results. By virtue of the courses students take in the behavioral sciences, they are used to reading about the results of experiments that uniformly *succeeded* (achieved statistical significance) in some way. One rarely reads about research that *failed* to achieve statistical significance; indeed, given the quantitative orientation of empirical journals in the behavioral sciences, it is very difficult—if not impossible—to publish work that lacks reliable, verifiable differences in line with carefully articulated hypotheses.

This artifact of the publication process sets many students up, so to speak, to be distressed when a research effort and its accompanying statistical analysis do not confirm a cherished hypothesis. As seasoned researchers are well aware from personal experience, projects and their analyses rarely adhere to every predicted detail—serendipity and random error, after all, have an effect, as well. (More candid investigators will admit that most research ideas do not pan out on the first trial, anyway.) In fact, I would like you to think for a moment about all the everyday situations where serendipity and random error do affect us—or at least the perceptions we draw. As you read the following scenario, think about the power of expectations and how they make us feel when things do not work out as planned (from Kahneman & Tversky, 1982, p. 203):

> Mr. Crane and Mr. Tees were scheduled to leave the airport on different flights, at the same time. They traveled from town in the same limousine, were caught in a traffic jam, and arrived at the airport 30 minutes after the scheduled departure time of their flights.

Mr. Crane is told that his flight left on time.

Mr. Tees is told that his flight was delayed, and just left 5 minutes ago. Who is more upset? Mr. Crane *or* Mr. Tees?

Ninety-six percent of a group of students reported that Mr. Tees would be more upset—after all, he *just* missed the plane by a scant 5 minutes, whereas Mr. Crane missed his by a full 30 minutes. In the minds of perceivers, that 25-minute difference looms large—but should it? Is the travel plight of the two men so different?

Consider the fact that the situation of these two hypothetical figures is identical—both missed their planes and no doubt fully expected to do so when they were stuck in traffic (i.e., the departure time came and went). As Kahneman and Tversky (1982, p. 203) point out, the "only reason for Mr. Tees to be more upset is that it was 'more' possible for him to reach his flight." These investigators point out that this scenario invites us to run a mental simulation, a "what-if" exercise where reality and fantasy, hope and desire, meet—we (and Mr. Tees) feel "upset" because we can imagine arriving 5 minutes sooner; it is much harder to imagine being there 30 minutes earlier, the less reasonably imaginable event that would help Mr. Crane.

My point here is that doing more complex data analyses like those presented in this chapter—especially with our own data—can sometimes put us in a mental place analogous to Mr. Tees. Our study "almost" reached significance, for example, or our results were close to the pattern predicted by the hypothesis and so on. It can be difficult to fight the tendency to be disappointed when fate—and *our* hard-won data—is less than cooperative, but it can and *will* happen to most of us. As you read this chapter and learn a new set of statistical procedures, bear in mind that you may be faced with a situation like the hypothetical Mr. Tees, one where you are faced with, say, a significance level of .06 rather than the "magical" (predetermined) significance level of .05. When a situation like this comes to pass, try to imagine a researcher whose *p* value was .07 or even .09—are you in such a different place with .06, or even the magical .05? No, not really, and in any case, you can still focus on a practical matter: discerning why the experiment and the analyses did not work out, then focusing on how to rectify the problem(s) in a future study. Armed with this philosophy and, I hope, the ability to run mental simulations about data in their proper perspective, we can move on to the main topic of this chapter.

As you know by now, the statistical analysis of data is an eminently practical enterprise. The *t* test, the focus of the last chapter, was originally developed to ensure consistency and maintain quality in the brewing of beer and ale. That statistical procedure is now an ubiquitous tool in the natural and behavioral sciences, one at home in the laboratory as well as the classroom. This chapter's topic, the *F* test, had an equally propitious start in the analysis of agricultural data—crop yields, in particular—in England and later the United States. By studying the growth of wheat and other crops in carefully planted fields, the statistician Sir Ronald A. Fisher (see Data Box 11.A) examined how varied soil quality, as well as the presence or absence of fertilizer, had an effect on the amount and quality of a harvest. Given the agricultural origins of Fisher's work on the *F* test, you should never take the term "field experiment" for granted again!

By linking statistical reasoning with modern farming techniques, Fisher almost single-handedly created a detailed theory of experimentation, a variety of experimental designs, and most important for our purposes, a method of data analysis capable of working with *more* than two means at once. The *F* test is at the heart of this method, which is formally known as the *analysis of variance* but commonly recognized by the acronym "ANOVA." If the *t* test is indeed the inferential statistic most often recognized by students, then the ANOVA is arguably the most familiar procedure for behavioral scientists, and you will learn why as you read this chapter. For the last half-century, the

ANOVA, as well as many of Fisher's other contributions, has exerted widespread influence over the basic and applied research conducted in many disciplines. Without these statistical and experimental innovations, disciplines in and outside of the behavioral sciences would literally be at a loss—the very existence of some would probably be threatened—and most fields would certainly lack the intellectual maturity and analytic sophistication they currently enjoy.

The ANOVA is based on another statistical distribution, the *F* distribution (named, as you might guess, for Fisher), which is used to test hypotheses regarding significant differences among two or more means. Where the *t* test was limited to identifying whether the average of one group of scores was larger or smaller than the average of a second group of scores, the ANOVA and its *F* test can search for reliable differences among the magnitudes of two, three, four, or even more means simultaneously. As we will see, the ability to examine more than two means at once is a boon for experimentation in the behavioral sciences, as more complex questions about behavior and its underlying causes can be asked. Indeed, this is the second chapter in this book explicitly dealing with issues involving comparing means from different groups or experimental conditions. Because more than two means can be examined at one time, the scope and the complexity of the hypotheses being tested by the ANOVA, too, are on the rise.

Why do we need to move beyond the *t* test and its two-group comparisons? Despite the fact that the two group standard experiment is the *raison d'être*—the reason for being—for experimental research, its impact is necessarily limited. How many interesting questions consistently lend themselves to this form of dichotomous examination? Life, as well as the human behavior represented by it, is not exclusively an either/or process or one governed by the precise, if limited, comparison afforded by control and experimental groups. Many important topics require an investigator to consider how *more than* two levels of an independent variable affect a dependent measure. For example, which of four seating patterns maximizes group discussion and decision making in an organizational setting? What is the optimal number of students for an undergraduate research team—2, 4, or 6? Can short-term depression observed in newly retired males be most effectively reduced by psychotherapy, group counseling, a combination of the two therapies, or no intervention at all? As you can see, moving beyond simple two group comparisons opens up many other research possibilities.

What will you learn in this chapter? Beyond acquiring the ability to compare more than two groups at one time, I think you will learn—and be surprised by—how much knowledge about statistics and data analysis you are now carrying around in your head. In other words, the bulk of what you will learn in this chapter is about thinking more broadly about the relationships portrayed in data—you already have a firm grasp on variance (as in the analysis of variance), the sum of squares we use to calculate variation, and the logic underlying hypothesis testing and comparing means. We are simply fleshing out the important skills you currently possess. Let's get down to it, shall we?

In contrast to the independent groups *t* test, for example, the ANOVA can compare more than two means at the same time.

The ANOVA enables investigators to analyze data addressing complex questions (i.e., beyond those posed by standard two-group experiments).

Overview of the Analysis of Variance

The ANOVA is an inferential statistical procedure for analyzing the results of experimental or nonexperimental data (e.g., quasi-experiments; see chapter 2).

KEY TERM   The **analysis of variance (ANOVA)** is a statistical test used to identify differences between or among distinct sample means. As a statistical technique, the *ANOVA* partitions or divides variability, attributing portions of it to the effect of an independent variable on a dependent measure.

Imagine that we decide to conduct a simple experiment with one independent variable and one dependent measure. Twenty-four research participants are recruited and

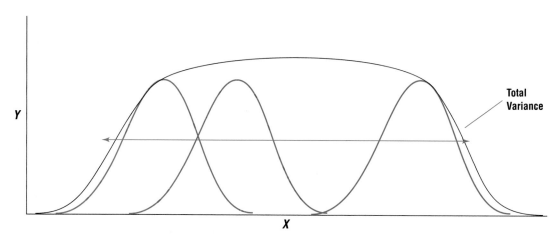

Figure 11.1   Total Variance of Three Independent Samples in an Experiment

Note: Each of these samples was exposed to a different level of an independent variable. The large bell-shape encompassing the other three distributions covers their total variance.

randomly assigned to three groups or samples, eight in each one. Each sample is then exposed to one—and only one—level of the independent variable. To begin with, we can think of the three samples of research participants as a collective source of variation. In fact, the variance of *all* the participants' scores from the three samples combined would be labeled the *total variance* or total variation.

KEY TERM   Total variance entails the combined variance of all the scores or observations within an experiment.

Figure 11.1 shows three distinct distributions corresponding to the three levels of the independent variable in our hypothetical study. Two of these distributions are relatively close together and the third is located farther away from them (see Figure 11.1). Do you see the larger bell-shape surrounding the three smaller distributions? That larger bell is covering the total variance present in the experiment. We could determine the total variance by summing the squared deviations from the mean of the entire sample of 24 participants (the mean of a larger sample that is comprised of smaller samples is sometimes called the **grand mean**). Please note that the total variation indicated in Figure 11.1 is greater than the variance in any one of the three samples.

     Our next consideration is to partition or divide the total variation into smaller amounts of variability that are due to (a) the effect of an independent variable creating change in a dependent measure and (b) error due to random or chance influences. How does the ANOVA partition variance when some hypothesis is being tested? Conceptually, the ANOVA pits some alternative hypothesis against a null hypothesis that two or more samples of randomly assigned participants hail from populations sharing the same means. The ANOVA provides a statistic, the F ratio, comprised of two elements:

▽

The ANOVA yields an F ratio, a test statistic that is determined by dividing between-groups variance (largely based on an independent variable) by within-groups variance (random error).

- The numerator of the F ratio indicates the variability between or among the means of two or more samples (i.e., between-group variance).
- The denominator of the F ratio identifies the variability among the observations within each sample (i.e., within-group variance).

Thus, we can construe the relationship between these two elements as:

[11.1.1]
$$F = \frac{between\text{-}group\ variance}{within\text{-}group\ variance}.$$

These elements should be familiar to you, as they are virtually identical with those we encountered in the conceptual and procedural reviews of the *t* test (see chapter 10). Similar to the *t* test, the within-group variance can also be referred to as the error term or, more precisely in this case, the *error variance.*

KEY TERM **Error variance,** which is estimated by within-group variance, refers to the idiosyncratic, uncontrollable, unknown factors or events that create differences among the observations within a group.

The error variance represents the differential behavior of participants (i.e., individual differences) within the samples as well as experimental error (e.g., misunderstood directions, equipment problems). If all the participants in a given sample behaved exactly alike, then there would be *no* error variance in that sample. In fact, we would be apt to attribute their common reactions exclusively to the influence of the independent variable. As people act more differently from one another, however, the error variance increases, so we know that individual differences and possibly experimental error are present.

Figure 11.2 shows the familiar three distributions from Figure 11.1, each of which represents a different independent group of randomly assigned participants who were exposed to a single level of an independent variable. As you can see, the within-group or error variance is identified within each distribution. Keep in mind that the observed differences within a sample are not—*should not be*—systematic, but instead are due to chance. When calculating an *F* ratio, the estimate of within-group variance or error variance is based on the *average variance of the observations within each sample.*

The between-group variance also adopts a particular name in the context of the ANOVA—it is frequently referred to as *treatment variance.* Each level of an independent variable can be construed as a "treatment," literally a manipulation designed to elicit some reaction or response from research participants. A paradigmatic example of

▽

Treatment is another name for an independent variable.

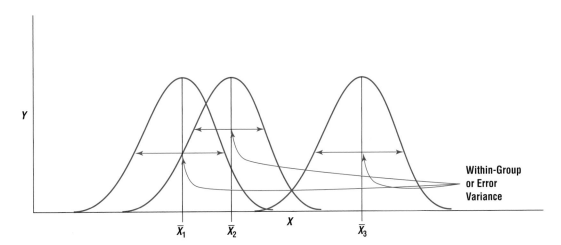

Figure 11.2 Within-Group or Error Variance Within Three Independent Samples in an Experiment

Note: Each of the three samples contains scores or observations that vary from their sample mean. Each sample was exposed to a different level of an independent variable.

a treatment, of course, is when one group is given an experimental drug, another takes a current prescription used for the ailment, and a third group is administered a placebo. Naturally, a treatment does not need to be a drug—it can just as easily be more conceptual, as when some stimulus (e.g., an unexpected gift) elicits some psychological state (e.g., positive mood; Isen, 1987)—some *X* causes a change in some *Y*.

Besides the variability attributable to some independent variable, treatment variance is also comprised of error variance, that is, individual differences and experimental error. Why? Simply because not all of the behavioral change within a sample can be attributed to the influence of an independent variable—some change is neither predictable nor controllable. Ideally, most of the between-groups or treatment variance will be due to the impact of an independent variable and only a small portion will be error variance.

KEY TERM   **Treatment variance** is based on the systematic influence of different levels of an independent variable on a dependent measure, combined with error variance.

Figure 11.3 shows the same three independent samples from Figure 11.2. This time, however, we are interested in the variance existing *between the three group means,* which makes each of the groups distinct from the others. As the treatment variance increases, the three samples appear to stand out from one another—in other words, the respective levels of the independent variable lead to distinct behaviors and accompanying treatment variance. The lines drawn from each mean to the other two means in Figure 11.3 represent this type of variance. We can now recast the *F* ratio shown in formula [11.1.1] slightly differently:

[11.1.2]
$$F = \frac{\text{treatment variance} + \text{error variance}}{\text{error variance}}.$$

Naturally, the two formulations are identical, but it will help you to think about what the ANOVA actually does with data by being exposed to them both.

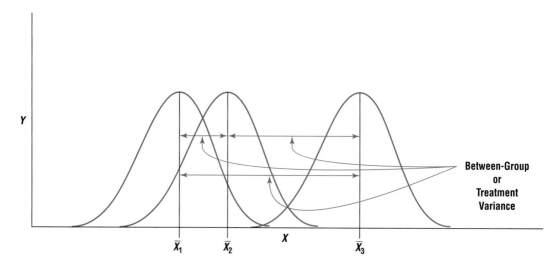

Figure 11.3   Between-Group or Treatment Variance Shared Among Three Independent Samples in an Experiment

Note: Each of the three samples can be described by its respective mean. Each sample was exposed to a different level of an independent variable. The between-group or treatment variance is based on variation among the three sample means.

When the numerator of the F ratio is larger (i.e., manipulating an independent variable led to behaviorally distinct groups with different means; see Figure 11.2) than the denominator (i.e., the behavior of participants within a given group is relatively consistent; see Figure 11.1), then the null hypothesis of no difference is rejected. Any significant difference between or among particular means is then explored and interpreted in the framework provided by an appropriate scientific theory. Practically speaking, a calculated F ratio must be somewhat greater than 1.00 in order to be declared "significant."

Describing the *F* Distribution

In the past, we learned about the shape and characteristics of the t and the z distributions. What is the F distribution like? How does it compare to these other distributions? The F distribution is different from these other distributions by virtue of the fact it is based on the ratio of two independent estimates of variance. As noted above, one variance represents an F statistic's numerator and the other its denominator. At the population level, the F ratio is readily described as:

[11.2.1]
$$F = \frac{\sigma^2_{\text{between}}}{\sigma^2_{\text{within}}}.$$

Of course, we will always be working with sample data so it is probably better to think of the F ratio in terms of sample variance:

[11.3.1]
$$F = \frac{s^2_{\text{between}}}{s^2_{\text{within}}}.$$

Because any F ratio is based on separate variance estimates—one divided by another—you know that calculations involving sums of squares will be involved. Why is this issue worth mentioning? When we began to calculate variance in chapter 4, we learned that the sum of squares is an integral part of the calculation process—without squaring any numbers, the mean deviations called for in the variance formula sum to 0. Because the square of any number is positive, the value of any F ratio, too, will always be positive. Whatever its magnitude or significance, an F ratio must be positive, a fact that will serve you well when checking your statistical calculations for errors. You know that you cannot have any negative numbers entering into the calculation of an F ratio (unlike the t and the z distributions, then, the F distribution lacks negative values).

A second characteristic of the F distribution concerns the logic underlying the actual ratio calculation. In theory, when the null hypothesis is true, the two variance estimates representing the numerator and the denominator, respectively, should be *equal* in value to one another. Under such conditions, the resulting F ratio is equal to 1.00. In practice, of course, obtaining a perfect 1.00 ratio does not occur very often because of sampling error—even if the two variance estimates are equal at the population level, they are unlikely to match one another precisely when they are based on sample data.

What happens when an F ratio *exceeds* 1.00? When an F statistic is greater than 1.00, it is a clear indication that the null hypothesis of no difference between or among a set of means may be false. In other words, two or more means might actually be reliably different from one another, and the pattern of the difference(s) will ideally reflect the theory linking the levels of a treatment variable to changes in a dependent measure. Again, obtaining a value greater than 1.00 indicates that there is more between-groups

▽

Because they are based on variance estimates, which in turn are determined by sum of squares, *F* ratios are always positive numbers.

variability (presumably due to the effect of an independent variable) and less within-groups variability (participants within a given condition in the experiment behaved more or less alike). As F ratios increase in value (i.e., > 2.00 or 3.00), the probability of rejecting H_0 increases accordingly.

Comparing the ANOVA to the *t* Test: Shared Characteristics and Assumptions

Besides the fact that the ANOVA can detect significant differences between two means, there is another similarity between it and the *t* test. Neither the *t* nor the F statistic is based on *one* distribution, rather, each one is comprised of a *series* of distinct distributions, one for every possible number—or combination of numbers—of degrees of freedom. Any given F distribution differs from a *t* distribution in that it has *two* different degrees of freedom rather than just one. One of these degrees of freedom represents the variance estimate for the numerator and the other corresponds to the denominator.

Why mention this fact now, before we learn to calculate either the statistic or its accompanying degrees of freedom? Precisely because the degrees of freedom influence the shape of the F distribution. The family of F distributions tends to be positively skewed (for a review of skew, see chapter 3); however, when both the degrees of freedom for a given F ratio are relatively large, the distribution will be approximately normal in shape.

A typically shaped F distribution is shown in Figure 11.4. This distribution is based on 3 (numerator) and 14 (denominator) degrees of freedom. The critical values of F at the .05 level ($F = 3.34$) and the .01 level ($F = 5.56$) are also shown in Figure 11.4. These respective critical values demonstrate that of all the values in the distribution, only 5% exceed $F = 3.34$ and only 1% are greater than $F = 5.56$. Following our usual practice with critical values, the null hypothesis of no difference is rejected when a calculated F ratio is equal to or greater than 3.34 at the .05 level or 5.56 at the .01 level. Critical values like these can be obtained from Table B.5 in Appendix B, a table of guiding F ratios that we will use in earnest later in the chapter.

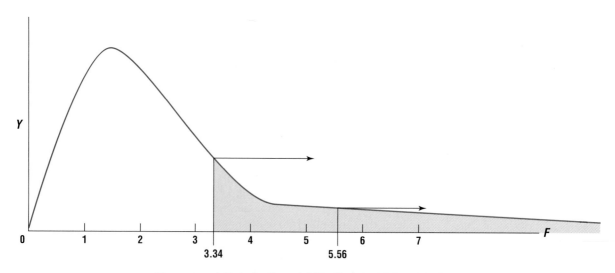

Figure 11.4 A Typically Shaped F Distribution with 3 and 14 Degrees of Freedom

Note: This distribution represents F ratios with 3 (numerator) and 14 (denominator) degrees of freedom. Only 5% of the distribution's values exceed 3.34 and only 1% are greater than 5.56.

When only two sample means are involved, an independent groups t test and a one-way—one independent variable—ANOVA (to be reviewed in detail shortly) will reach the same empirical conclusion: either there *is* or *is not* a reliable difference between two averages. Naturally, the actual values for a t statistic and an F ratio will differ, but in the two-sample (two-means) case, both are related to the normal distribution, a relationship providing statistical as well as conceptual links. When an independent groups t test yields a statistic (which, as you will recall from chapter 10, has $N - 2$ degrees of freedom), the corresponding F ratio has 1 and $N - 2$ degrees of freedom (remember, the F distribution, which the ANOVA is based on, supplies two numbers for degrees of freedom—one corresponding to a numerator, the other a denominator). The relationship between a t value and a two-group F ratio is verifiable by squaring the obtained t statistic:

[11.4.1] $$t^2 = F.$$

Thus, if we knew that $t = 2.0$, then F would be equal to 4.0 because:

[11.4.2] $$(2.0)^2 = 4.00.$$

It follows, of course, that if we take the square root of a known F ratio based on two groups (i.e., 1 and $N - 2$ degrees of freedom), then the corresponding t value (with $N - 2$ degrees of freedom) is equal to:

[11.5.1] $$\sqrt{F} = t.$$

Our simple example will again suffice here. If we knew that an F ratio was equal to 4.0, then the corresponding t would be equal to 2.0, or:

[11.5.2] $$\sqrt{4.0} = 2.0.$$

An advantage to knowing the link between t and F is recognizing that the factors that influence the size of a t statistic (i.e., generally, larger t values enable an investigator to reject a null hypothesis) will also have an impact on the size and significance of an F ratio. When an ANOVA is calculated, then, an F ratio is likely to achieve significance when:

■ The sample size of each condition or group in the experiment is relatively large.
■ The variability (sample variance or standard deviation) within each condition or group in the experiment is relatively small.
■ The observed difference between the means for each condition or group in the experiment is relatively large (remember that the ANOVA can be used to identify differences existing among more than two means).

Establishing these similarities—and reminding yourself of what you already know about the t test—will help you to retain information about the ANOVA, as well.

The statistical assumptions underlying the ANOVA are identical to those pertaining to the t test. These assumptions include:

■ The populations the samples were drawn from have equal variances.
■ The dependent measure's data are normally distributed in their populations of origin.
■ The data were either (a) randomly sampled or (b) individually sampled.
■ Means can be calculated from the data, so the dependent measure is based on either an interval or a ratio scale (for a review of scales of measurement and their characteristics, see chapter 1).

▽

When two samples are analyzed by an independent groups t test or an ANOVA, the results will be the same because the respective test statistics are related to one another in the two group case.

Unless there is a considerable amount of research available on a topic of interest, an investigator is unlikely to know whether the first two assumptions are ever met. Fortunately, the ANOVA is similar to the *t* test in that one or more assumptions can be violated without a great deal of worry. Like its cousin the *t* test, the ANOVA is a relatively robust test. The one case where a researcher needs to worry about relying on the ANOVA occurs when the population variances are *not* equal, the dependent measure is *not* normal, and the sample sizes are small and unequal across the different levels of the independent variable (for more detail, see Coombs, Algina, & Oltman, 1996). When these four problems crop up at the same time, then a researcher should consult a statistician for guidance or rethink whether the project can be completed.

Where sample size is concerned, I'd like to add a fifth point to this list of assumptions, one that is more of a guideline than purely a statistical matter. Whenever possible, a researcher should strive to obtain an equal number of participants for each condition or group in an experiment.

- Each sample or group should contain an equal number of participants or observations.

As an addendum to this guideline, it is also wise to balance the gender composition of each sample or group. Unless there is a compelling theoretical reason to use exclusively male or female participants in a research design, then, 50% of each gender per condition is a desirable goal. Given that some disciplines in the behavioral sciences, notably psychology, currently enroll fewer male than female undergraduate students, researchers must occasionally revise this goal. (The field of psychology relies heavily on college students to serve as research participants—some critics believe the field is overly reliant on this subject source; see Dawes, 1991; Sears, 1986.) A researcher might reasonably expect to populate 30% of each group in an experiment with males, for example, filling the remaining slots with female participants. In terms of analytic considerations, I urge you to keep the size and composition of samples or groups as similar to one another as possible.

▽

Similar to its relation to the *t* test, the ANOVA is a robust test—it tolerates having one or more of its assumptions violated.

Problematic Probabilities: Multiple *t* Tests and the Risk of Type I Error

At this point in the review of the ANOVA, many students are often moved to ask whether it is entirely necessary to bother learning the steps for calculating an *F* ratio. "After all," they usually say, "if the *t* test and the *F* test are so similar, why not just perform several *t* tests and have done with it?" There are two problems with this seemingly innocent but fundamentally misguided strategy. First, depending on how many sample means are available, calculations for quite a few *t* tests would need to be performed. In fact, the following formula can identify just how many *t* tests would be necessary for a given number of samples means:

[11.6.1]
$$C = \frac{k(k-1)}{2},$$

where *C* is the number of possible comparisons between 2 means given *k*, the number of treatments or samples in an experiment.

Thus, if there were four conditions (levels of an independent variable) in an experiment, then a data analyst would have to perform six separate *t* tests, or:

[11.6.2]
$$C = \frac{4(4-1)}{2},$$

[11.6.3]
$$C = \frac{4(3)}{2},$$

$$[11.6.4] \qquad C = \frac{12}{2},$$

$$[11.6.5] \qquad C = 6.$$

Six separate t tests! That is quite a bit of calculation. Imagine how easily one could make a calculation error given the repetitive nature of the exercise. The possibility of making a simple but inferentially disruptive error should give any researcher or data analyst pause (of course, relying on a statistical software package eliminates this fear).

The second problem with performing multiple t tests is much more insidious than mere math errors, however. In normal circumstances, when only one comparison between two independent means is being performed, the risk of making a Type I error is equal to the level of α, the significance level of the statistical test (e.g., .05). This form of comparison between two means using the t test is called a *pairwise comparison α*.

KEY TERM   **Pairwise comparison α** is the probability of making a Type I error (e.g., $\alpha = .05$) when two sample means are assessed using the t test.

⬇

Performing multiple independent t tests on the same data set increases the probability of committing a Type I error—reliance on the ANOVA reduces this problem to an acceptable level of risk.

By performing numerous, even repeated, analyses of the same data set, a researcher substantially increases the risk of committing a Type I error. In other words, the more similar tests you perform—each based on the same significance level, say, $\alpha = .05$—the greater the chance of making a Type I error when the null hypothesis is actually true. Table 11.1 shows the probability of making *at least one* Type I error when all pairs of means are examined using separate, independent t tests. Notice that when the difference between two means is examined, the probability of making a Type I error is equal to α (i.e., $p = .05$). So far, so good. But notice what happens when three means are examined—performing the necessary three independent t tests increases the probability of making one Type I error (there may be more!) to .14. As shown in Table 11.1, once you go beyond three means, the likelihood increases still more dramatically. In short, performing more than one legitimate pairwise comparison α inflates the probability of identifying a false difference between means.

The probability of committing one or more Type I errors under these conditions has a special name—statisticians refer to it as *experimentwise error*.

KEY TERM   **Experimentwise error** refers to the likelihood of making one or more Type I errors in the course of performing multiple pairwise comparisons with independent t tests in the same data set.

The probability of committing experimentwise error under particular conditions—known significance level of a statistical test and the number of two mean comparisons being contemplated—is easily calculated. The following formula was used to estimate the probabilities of making a Type I error shown in Table 11.1:

$$[11.7.1] \qquad p(experimentwise\ error) = 1 - (1 - \alpha)^C,$$

Table 11.1   Probability of Making at Least One Type I Error When All Pairs of Means Are Examined by Independent t Tests

Number of Means (k)	Number of Two Mean Comparisons (C)	Probability[1] of Making At Least *One* Type I Error
2	1	.05
3	3	.14
5	10	.40
10	45	.90

[1]Note that $p(experimentwise\ error) = 1 - (1 - \alpha)^C$ if the C comparisons are independent of one another.

DATA BOX 11.A

R. A. Fischer: Statistical Genius and Vituperative Visionary

Ronald A. Fischer (1890–1960) was a gifted student of mathematics who revolutionized the discipline of statistics. His contributions were largely developed in the years he spent at England's Rothamstead Agricultural Experimental Station. Expecting to stay for only a short time—his original position at the Station was a temporary one—Fisher arrived in 1919 and stayed 14 years (his sponsor realized Fisher's genius and worked to keep him there). During his tenure there, Fisher developed fundamental ideas about the appropriate design of experiments (with particular emphasis on randomization) and the analysis of their data.

Fisher was always busy and productive. He presented the analysis of variance in 1924, publishing his instant classic text *Statistical Methods for Research Workers* the next year. This difficult book—Fisher was not a very good or interesting writer—altered the teaching and conduct of statistical analysis for the next quarter century (Peters, 1987). Indeed, William Gosset, the *t* test's creator, once remarked about the complexity of Fisher's thinking that "when I come to 'Evidently' [in one of Fisher's papers] I know that means two hours hard work at least before I can see why" (Gosset, 1970, cited in Tankard, 1984). It took George Snedecor, a statistician at Iowa State University, to popularize Fisherian concepts for agricultural researchers and academics in his own more accessible text *Statistical Methods* (the second edition of which sold over 100,000 copies—yes, that's right, a statistical bestseller!).

According to the statistician Harold Hotelling, Fisher made three major contributions to the discipline: improving the theory underlying the estimation of parameters via statistics, symbolically and conceptually clarifying the difference between sample statistics and population parameters, and the derivation of particular distributions (e.g., the *F* distribution) for hypothesis testing (Peters, 1987). Beyond these statistical innovations, Fisher made highly successful intellectual contributions to the field of genetics, so much so that in 1943 he was appointed professor of genetics at Cambridge University.

By all accounts, Fisher was interpersonally unpleasant—he was all too aware of his great intellect—and demanding on those around him. Although he worked closely with many of the giants in the field of statistics at one time or another, it was rare for a relationship with him to remain a placid one. Several intellectual feuds with his peers went on for years, though to be fair, the battles were largely intellectual, not personal. Recurring feuds took place with Karl Pearson, the creator of the correlation coefficient, who described them as "titanic arguments" and "titanic battles" (E. Pearson, 1968, p. 416).

Fisher's temperamental nature came through in the most everyday of situations, as when the statistician William G. Cochran was trying to cross a busy street with him. The traffic was heavy and Fisher's eyesight was quite poor. Cochran (1967, p. 1462) writes that:

> Finally there was a gap, but clearly not large enough to get us across. Before I could stop him he stepped into the stream, crying over his left shoulder "Oh, come on, Cochran. A spot of natural selection won't hurt us."

Fortunately for statisticians and experimentalists of all stripes, Fischer led a long and productive life that changed the way the business of research is conducted and scientific inferences are drawn from data.

---

where α is the significance level employed in a given pairwise comparison and C is the number of two mean comparisons being made (recall that we learned to calculate C using formula [11.6.1]). Suffice it to say that as the number of comparisons increases, the probability of making at least one Type I error accelerates rather dramatically.

Can anything be done to alleviate this problem? The usual practice of lowering the significance level of the test (e.g., changing .05 to a more rigorous .01) makes some sense, but is ultimately counterproductive. You no doubt remember that reducing the significance level for a test statistic necessarily leads to a reduction in the power available to reject the null hypothesis of no difference (see chapters 9 and 10).

What is the moral of the story? A researcher is unwise, even foolhardy, to perform multiple *t* tests on the same data set. This foolhardiness is not limited to the possibility of inferring the existence of a relationship in the data that is not, in fact, real or true (i.e., committing a Type I error). More damaging still is the ethical implication of performing multiple *t* tests—any researcher should know better than to risk drawing false conclusions that could potentially harm the welfare of others if the results were unknowingly used as if they were accurate. The mind reels when considering the great damage the publication of faulty research results can incur. In fact, I encourage you to be highly skeptical of any published piece of research you encounter that relies on multiple *t* tests in the analysis of results. Please keep in mind that any test statistic—not just the *t* test—needs to be used carefully, appropriately, and judiciously in the analysis of data.

How is the ANOVA Distinct from Prior Statistical Tests? Some Advantages

In spite of its frequent appearance in everyday language, the word "unique" is a tough one to use correctly. It literally means solo, solitary, or without peers—in other words, when something is unique, it is one of a kind; there really is nothing else like it. In some ways, the ANOVA is unique from the tests we studied before, but there is more than one type of ANOVA—we will learn the most basic version in this chapter and then some variations on it in the next one. Thus, we cannot properly describe the ANOVA as unique, but we can say that it is distinct from the other tests we have examined.

How does the ANOVA differ from prior statistical tests we have studied? In three ways, really—by virtue of the way it compares means, protects against Type I errors, and enables us to think about complex causal relationships among variables.

Omnibus Test: Comparing More than Two Means Simultaneously

The ANOVA is classified as an **omnibus statistical test,** a term used to characterize any test that deals with multiple variables or several levels of the same variable at the same time. A wonderful but rarely used word, "omnibus" is an adjective that means "pertaining to or dealing with numerous objects or items at the same time." But what does this unusual word mean in a statistical context?

As you are already aware, the ANOVA enables an investigator to detect significant differences between two means or among more than two means. There is an important aspect to this search for significant differences among a collection of means, however. Unless there are two means—and only two means—being compared, the omnibus ANOVA is an unfocused test. That is, the resulting *F* ratio from an ANOVA will inform the researcher as to whether *any* difference is present in a collection of means representing different levels of one or more independent variables, but it will *not* specify the exact nature of the difference(s) except when there are only two means (i.e., when the *F* ratio is akin to the independent groups *t* test; see above). Any careful and critical researcher (yourself included) will "eyeball" or examine the pattern of means in order to locate any possible or apparent between-group differences—but such visual examination is not reliable, of course, and must be verified statistically. Still, it is an excellent idea to see if the pattern of means adheres to the experimental hypothesis before any supplementary analyses are undertaken.

DATA BOX 11.B

Linguistically *Between* a Rock and *Among* Hard Places

When is it correct to substitute the preposition *among* for *between*? Grammarians recommend that *between* be used for comparing or contrasting two things, and that *among* be reserved for those times when more than two things are at issue. Correct usage turns out to be a bit more complicated than this simple rule suggests, however. The language maven William Safire recently wrote about the use of *between* and *among* in his weekly *On Language* column in *The New York Times* (Safire, 1999, p. 24).

> Although I fuzzily warned about the trickiness of the relationship of several items considered a pair at a time, [the late linguist James] McCawley came thundering back with the vivid examples that bring his theories to life: "Only *between* is appropriate when you say, 'He held four golf balls *between* his fingers' or 'He has a fungus *between* his toes.'"
>
> No arguing with that, even as I try the four-golf-ball stretch; it is not in the grammar that is hard-wired in our heads to say, "The golf balls are *among* my fingers." Jim then zinged home the lesson: "What determines the choice of the preposition isn't whether its object denotes two entities or more than two, but whether the entities are being referred to in twos or in combinations of more than two." Therefore, I will follow the simple rule of style (*between* two, *among* several), remembering the exception's complexity every time I feel an itch in my shoes. (Italics in original.)

In much the same way, statisticians stretch the use of *between,* referring to relationships between means rather than *among* them. Statisticians prefer to always use *between,* but I think that it is possible to rely on *among,* as well, and I have tried to do so at various points throughout this chapter and book. When writing about the process of comparing means, I encourage you to try your hand at using both of these prepositions, learning by doing to see which one is better suited to what sort of descriptive situation or set of results. The main point, of course, is to be consistent in your usage and to recognize that many authors will stick to *between* when *among* might well suffice.

We will learn a statistical procedure used to identify the precise differences between or among means later in this chapter. Such procedures are referred to as **post hoc** ("post hoke") or "after the fact" **tests** because the data are already collected and analyzed in a preliminary fashion by the ANOVA or some other test. For the present time, think about the advantages posed by omnibus statistical tests, especially the way they enable investigators to entertain and explore complex questions that are prevented by most two-group experiments.

Experimentwise Error: Protecting Against Type I Error

We already established that conducting a series of *t* tests on the same data set is a bad idea, and that the ANOVA affords us the opportunity to check for the presence of means differences all at once. Table 11.1, for example, clearly demonstrated the problems inherent in conducting more than one comparison using a *t* test for independent groups, which we defined earlier as experimentwise error. The ANOVA is an ideal antidote to the experimentwise error problem because it simultaneously compares the means of all the available independent samples or groups in a single statistical test. Thus, the ANOVA is a revelation for experimenters—they can ask more complex questions—and for data analysts—they are protected from making

Type I errors beyond the usual level of risk (i.e., the α level or significance level chosen *before* the analysis is undertaken).

Causality and Complexity

The third way that the ANOVA differs from previous statistical tests we have encountered is its utility for examining causal relationships. Research methods used in the behavioral sciences teach us that the systematic manipulation of causal factors, chiefly independent variables, allows us to develop increasingly complex descriptions of events. With time and thought, these descriptions evolve into detailed theories about the causal relationships among variables that affect behavior.

The ANOVA can help us to develop more detailed, even intricate, theories because it enables us to examine the empirical relationship existing among several means, not just two. One could build a complex theory by repeatedly experimenting with two group studies and analyzing their data with the *t* test, but it would be time consuming and quite difficult, not to mention tedious. More to the point, complex questions examining the relations among, say, five means could not be entertained simultaneously. Research on human experience must be more than merely comparing the reactions of control and experimental groups with respect to some dependent measure.

The availability of the ANOVA as an analytic tool invites researchers to theorize more broadly, to tackle more complex questions empirically.

Particular variations of the ANOVA can be used to plan and analyze these more complex accounts of behavior. To be sure, learning all of the detailed analytic procedures is beyond the scope of this book, as well as the purview of most introductory statistics courses. Still, it is important to be aware of the various complex causal relations that potentially exist between or among variables. To that end, I have included Table 11.2 here, which catalogs various causal processes and their descriptions. The causal processes in

Table 11.2 Food for Analytical Thought: Causal Processes Categorized

Causal Process	Process Description
Necessary *and* sufficient	Variable Y will change if X changes and will never change if X does not.
Necessary *but not* sufficient	Variable Y will not change unless X does, but changing X only works under the right conditions.
Sufficient *but not* necessary	Changing X will change Y, but there are factors other than X that can also change Y.
Neither necessary *nor* sufficient	Changing X under the right conditions can change Y, but other factors can also change Y.
Threshold effects	(a) Changing X will affect Y only if the initial value of X is large enough. (b) Changing X will affect Y only if the initial value of Y is large enough.
Ceiling effects	(a) Changing X will affect Y only if the initial value of X is not too large. (b) Changing X will affect Y only if the initial value of Y is not too large.
Interactive effects	A change in X has differential effects on Y *depending* on the conditions of other variables.
Developmental effects	A change in X has differential effects on Y *depending* on when the change occurs, in terms of age, growth rate, etc.

Source: Adapted from Exhibit 1.6 in Leik (1997), p. 14.

Table 11.2 generally move from relatively simple relationships to more complex ones. I want you to view this table as a resource for your thinking about and planning of research efforts, as well as their analyses. You may never actually conduct a study that hypothesizes the presence of ceiling effects, say, or developmental effects, but being aware of the behavioral patterns they reflect can help you to think more critically about the work you do conduct and the data you analyze. The ANOVA, then, will help you to see causal relations in somewhat broader strokes than prior opportunities allowed.

One last point: The ANOVA is still only one tool for pinpointing cause and effect between independent variables and dependent measures, just as no one experiment—no matter how complex its design—can answer every question. The ANOVA is very useful, though, for analyzing studies that empirically bring together points of view based on prior research (i.e., using an old operationalization of an independent variable) and novel approaches (i.e., use of a new operationalization)—and the ability to compare more than two participants groups means that an adequate control group need not be sacrificed in the process.

Knowledge Base

1.   What is the source of the variability in the F ratio's numerator? The denominator?
2.   What makes the F distribution different than the t or the z distributions?
3.   When does the t statistic bear a special relationship to the F ratio? What is the nature of the relationship?
4.   Why is it a bad idea to use multiple t tests to assess whether significant differences exist among more than two means?
5.   What makes the ANOVA distinct from previous statistical tests reviewed in this book?

Answers

1.   The numerator of the F ratio is comprised of between-groups or treatment variance (i.e., variance attributable to an independent variable and error variance). The denominator is based on within-group or error variance, which is made up of variance from individual differences and experimental error.
2.   The F distribution has two degrees of freedom (one for the numerator, the other for the denominator in the F ratio) based on two independent sources of variance; it is nonnormal in shape except when these two degrees of freedom are large; the F ratios comprising the distributions are always positive in value.
3.   The value of a t statistic can be determined from an F ratio (and vice versa) only when both statistical tests are used to analyze data from two independent samples, in which case $t^2 = F$ and $\sqrt{F} = t$.
4.   Multiple pairwise comparison α tests inflate the probability of making at least one Type I error, known as experimentwise error. Use of the ANOVA is prescribed instead because it simultaneously evaluates whether any differences exist among a collection of means while holding the risk of Type I error constant.
5.   The ANOVA (a) is an omnibus statistical test, (b) protects against experimentwise error, and (c) assesses more complex causal relationships than prior statistical tests we have learned.

One-Factor Analysis of Variance

We are now ready to learn to perform an ANOVA on some actual data. Following the usual custom laid out in this book, we will explore the statistical test through a detailed example from start to finish. Before we begin by learning about formulating the null hypothesis and learning the notation associated with the ANOVA, I must issue a practical warning. The ANOVA involves more steps and a bit more calculation than you are used to—*yet*. As you read through the next several pages, this statistical technique may even look a bit daunting—but it only looks that way; in statistics, appearances really are deceiving.

As you work through the example in a step-by-step manner, you will discover that the ANOVA is no more difficult a technique than any of the others we have already learned. As always, keep focused on what you are doing so that if you stop at any point, you will know how and why you got to that point. Keep the *mise en place* philosophy in mind here, as it will serve you well—there is quite a bit of quantitative information to organize and interpret, but you will have little difficulty if you take your time with this section of the chapter and think about what you are doing every step of the way.

We can begin defining the statistical test that is the focus of the remainder of this chapter, the so-called *one-way analysis of variance* or one-way ANOVA, for short. It is called a one-way ANOVA because it involves the use of one—and only one—independent variable (treatment), which must have two or more levels to it.

KEY TERM   A **one-way analysis of variance (one-way ANOVA)** is a statistical technique for analyzing the variation found within the various levels of a single independent or treatment variable. A *one-way ANOVA* will compare the means of two or more levels with one another in order to determine if any significant difference(s) exist(s) between or among them.

An environmental psychologist, for example, might be concerned with identifying the proper amount of ambient light that should be prevalent in public structures—an office building or a public library—where work or study take place. Ambient light would be the treatment or independent variable, and the psychologist would simply manipulate the amount of light (measured in lumens) different samples of participants are exposed to in the setting. The psychologist might use four different levels of illumination—these correspond to the levels of treatment or of the independent variable—so that some aspect of people's behavior (e.g., work productivity, books read or checked out) could serve as a dependent measure.

Within any ANOVA, the independent variable is assigned a different name than is commonly used anywhere else. Independent variables are referred to as *factors,* which contain different levels, the components or values that serve to differentiate what one sample of participants experiences and another—or others—do not.

KEY TERM   A **factor** is a synonym for a treatment or independent variable within an ANOVA. To be analytically viable, a *factor* must have two or more levels within in it.

In the previous example, ambient light was a factor, and the four distinct amounts of illumination were its levels.

Identifying Statistical Hypotheses for the ANOVA

There is relatively little novelty in the formulation of the null and alternative hypotheses for an ANOVA. In fact, their formulation and supporting logic is virtually identical with the information provided for the *t* test in chapter 10. The one difference, of course, is that a null and an alternative hypothesis for an ANOVA usually make provision for more than two means (as discussed earlier, one could examine two means with an ANOVA but, all else being equal, an independent groups *t* test is much easier and quicker to calculate).

When writing the null hypothesis for an ANOVA, an investigator is assuming that a treatment variable (and its distinct levels) has no effect on a dependent measure. In other words, the null hypothesis of no difference specifies that the means of each of the

Factor is a term used to denote an independent variable or treatment used almost exclusively when calculating an ANOVA.

samples are functionally equivalent to one another (i.e., conceptually, they hail from the same population, therefore, each μ is equal to all the others), or:

$$H_0: \mu_1 = \mu_2 = \cdots = \mu_j,$$

where j is the individual number of the k means (or samples) present. If there were three sample means (i.e., $k = 3$) representing three levels of a treatment variable (i.e., $j = 1, 2,$ and 3) then the null hypothesis would specify their presumed equivalence as:

$$H_0: \mu_1 = \mu_2 = \mu_3.$$

Naturally, there is no reason to anticipate that the three means (or however many are present) actually share precisely similar magnitudes—we are dealing with sample data and so we assume that any observed differences among the means are superficial, created by chance or sampling error.

Runyon, Haber, Pittenger, and Coleman (1996) offer a compelling substitute for this traditional formulation of the null hypothesis. These authors suggest emphasizing the fact that through the F ratio, the ANOVA literally looks at the ratio of between-groups variance to within-groups variance. As we noted earlier, when an independent variable fails to create marked differences between samples or groups, then the variance estimate for the numerator is treated as being equivalent to the denominator—the F ratio is equal to 1.00 (or thereabouts due to measurement or sampling error). Thus, the null hypothesis could be convincingly recast as:

$$H_0: \sigma^2_{\text{between}} = \sigma^2_{\text{within}}.$$

What about the alternative hypothesis? How do we present it using these two schemes? To begin with, we acknowledge—and remind ourselves—that the ANOVA is an omnibus statistical test, one that indicates whether at least one mean is significantly different from another mean; this test does *not* (except in the case of two means) identify where or how many differences exist. We will learn a technique to tease this important matter out of the data later. For now, we simply want to note that the alternative hypothesis implies that at least one difference exists (keeping in mind, though, that an investigator will have a desired, theory-based pattern of results in mind).

We can achieve this end in a few ways. First, we can broadly state that the alternative hypothesis does *not* conform to H_0, suggesting some lack of equivalence among the means stipulated by the null hypothesis, or:

$$H_1: \text{not } H_0.$$

A second possibility is to indicate that some difference will exist, as in:

$$H_1: \text{One treatment mean, at least, will be different than another treatment mean.}$$

Note that both alternative hypotheses are identical in their meaning.

The third possibility, one advanced by Runyon et al. (1996), compliments the variance comparison made for H_0 above:

$$H_1: \sigma^2_{\text{between}} \neq \sigma^2_{\text{within}}.$$

Note that this alternative hypothesis is nondirectional, though we hope that a relatively large amount of estimated variance exists in the numerator and a smaller amount of variance is found in the denominator. If the empirical tables turn—there is more variance in the denominator than the numerator—then the F ratio will not detect any significant difference between any means. We will come back to hypothesis formulation again when we work thorough an ANOVA example in detail.

Some Notes on Notation and the ANOVA's Steps

Because the ANOVA has more steps than many statistical procedures, a notation—a set of guiding symbols—is frequently used to help the data analyst (and any interested observers) perform (or follow) the required calculations. You may not realize it, but you picked up quite a bit of notation already in the course of this book—thus, the notation for the ANOVA should pose little difficulty for you. To make you a bit more comfortable with the process, however, I am going to introduce the notation here, before we actually rely on it in the next section of the chapter.

First of all, there is no one universally agreed upon notation. Different statisticians, as well as different statistics texts, rely on different styles of notation—and the mathematical procedures they represent—to perform an ANOVA. There is no "right," "perfect," or "correct" way to proceed. In a sense, all roads lead to Rome, or at least to an F ratio. Remember that we are out to find two variance estimates corresponding to the numerator and the denominator of an F ratio. Whether this F ratio is greater than or equal to a critical value, in turn, determines the acceptance or rejection of H_0. All calculations, including those for the degrees of freedom, are oriented toward this goal.

Here is a conceptual overview of the steps necessary to perform an ANOVA, including the formulas and their specific notation. We will review these steps now and then put them together with actual data in the next section of the chapter:

1. **Calculate the total sum of squares.** Before we begin the process of partitioning the total variance into its between- and within-group components, we need to know the total sum of the squares. The computational formula for the total sum of squares (SS_{total}), which involves all the observations without regard to treatment level, is:

   [11.8.1]
   $$SS_{total} = \sum X_{ij}^2 - \frac{(\sum X_{ij})^2}{N},$$

   where i refers to the number of a given participant (e.g., participant 6) and j identifies the level of the factor (e.g., level 1 of the independent variable might correspond to the control group). Please note that formula [11.8.1] is no different from the formula for the sum of squares we learned back in chapter 4 (see formula [4.10.1]) *except* that subscripts are used to denote each participant and the factor level the participant encountered. This formula directs (a) that each of the raw scores in the data is squared and *then* summed ($\sum X_{ij}^2$) and (b) that all the raw scores are summed and *then* squared (($\sum X_{ij})^2$), and divided by the total number of available observations or participants (N). The number resulting from this second calculation (i.e., $(\sum X_{ij})^2/N$) is usually referred to as the *correction term* (e.g., Harris, 1998); then the product of (b), the correction term, is subtracted from the product of (a) (see [11.8.1]). The degrees of freedom associated with the total variance (df_{total}) is known by:

   [11.9.1]
   $$df_{total} = N - 1.$$

2. **Calculate the between-groups variance estimate.** The between-group variance is the basis for the numerator of the F ratio, and to begin to estimate it we calculate the between-group sum of squares ($SS_{between}$) using this formula:

   [11.10.1]
   $$SS_{between} = \sum \left[\frac{(\sum X_j)^2}{n_j} \right] - \frac{(\sum X_{ij})^2}{N}.$$

This formula prescribes that (a) the observations within a factor level (j) are summed and then squared ($(\sum X_j)^2$), and this result is then divided by the number of observations or participants with that level (n_j). In turn, each of the products is then summed—if there are three levels in a factor, for example, then three products are summed ($\sum [(\sum X_j)^2/n_j]$). Finally, (b) the correction term (i.e., the same number from the previous step) is subtracted from the sum of the products from (a) (see formula [11.10.1]).

The degrees of freedom for the between groups variance estimate ($df_{between}$) is:

[11.11.1] $$df_{between} = k - 1,$$

where k is the total number of levels in the study's factor (and the total number of j levels should equal k, of course).

The between-groups variance estimate, $\sigma^2_{between}$, is also called the mean squares between-groups or $MS_{between}$. "Mean squares" refers to the fact that it is based on the mean or the average of the sum of the squared deviations between the groups. Thus, the estimated variance between groups is based on:

[11.12.1] $$MS_{between} = \frac{SS_{between}}{df_{between}}.$$

3. **Calculate the within-groups variance estimate.** The third and last calculation for the one-way ANOVA is the within-groups variance estimate (σ^2_{within}). As always, we begin by calculating the within-groups sum of squares (SS_{within}) using this formula:

[11.13.1] $$SS_{within} = \sum X_{ij}^2 - \sum \left[\frac{(\sum X_j)^2}{n_j} \right].$$

If you look closely at both parts of this formula, you will recognize the fact that we already did the requisite calculations in the course of the previous two steps. Thus, all of the raw scores were squared and summed back in (a) in step 1 (i.e., $\sum X_{ij}^2$), just as $\sum [(\sum X_j)^2/n_j]$ was determined in (a) in step 2. We need only calculate the difference between the numbers corresponding to each to know SS_{within}—I hope you appreciate the virtue provided by the quick substitutions of prior calculations (you will shortly).

The formula for the degrees of freedom for the within-group variance estimate is:

[11.14.1] $$df_{within} = N - k.$$

That is, the number of groups or samples is subtracted from the total number of participants available. We can then determine the within-group variance estimate—known as the mean squares within-groups—using:

[11.15.1] $$MS_{within} = \frac{SS_{within}}{df_{within}}.$$

4. The final step, of course, is the calculation of the F ratio, which is based on the between-groups variances estimate ($\sigma^2_{between}$) divided by the within-groups variance estimate (σ^2_{within}), or:

[11.16.1] $$F = \frac{MS_{between}}{MS_{within}}.$$

DATA BOX 11.C

Yet Another Point of View on Variance: The General Linear Model

Earlier in this chapter, we discussed how to partition the total variance into two components: between-groups and within-groups variance. Schematically, the division of total variance looks like this:

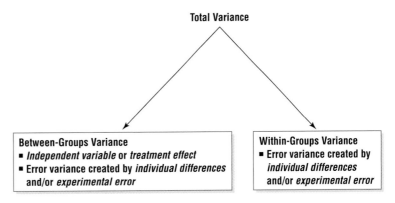

Total Variance

Between-Groups Variance
- *Independent variable* or *treatment effect*
- Error variance created by *individual differences* and/or *experimental error*

Within-Groups Variance
- Error variance created by *individual differences* and/or *experimental error*

There is yet another way to construe variability. We are so accustomed to thinking about variability in group terms (i.e., behavioral differences between groups and behavioral similarity within groups) that we lose sight of the fact that any behavioral change begins in each individual in a given experiment. In theory, a score corresponding to each individual in a data set can be described by a single equation. This equation is known as the *general linear model* (GLM).

The GLM posits that any observed score is based on the sum of the population mean, the specific level of some independent variable and random or chance influences. Symbolically, the GLM for a one-way ANOVA looks like this:

$$X_{ij} = \mu + \alpha_j + \varepsilon_{ij},$$

where

X_{ij} = is the score of one person (i) in a given group (j)

μ = the population mean of the domain of interest

α = the positive or negative effects of a specific treatment condition (note that this α is not the one we associate with significance testing)

ε_{ij} = the Greek letter ε (epsilon) denotes random error (e.g., individual differences and experimental error).

This alternative approach to variability and the ways it is partitioned should help you to construe behavioral change in individual rather than exclusively group terms. To be sure, the ANOVA model encourages us to think of behavioral change occurring as a group phenomenon, but the GLM nicely illustrates how change actually occurs one person at a time. This individualized approach should remind you of one important truth—an independent variable affects each person slightly differently, just as random vagaries of personal experience will have different effects, as well.

▽

Think about it: As an error check, the $SS_{between}$ added to the SS_{within} must sum to the SS_{total}. If not, then you have made a calculation error.

One-Way ANOVA from Start to Finish: An Example with Data

Eyewitness testimony and the role that memory plays within it continues to generate interest. In a simple but clever experiment, Loftus and Palmer (1974) demonstrated how the phrasing of questions regarding a perceived event could readily influence witnesses' memories of the event. In other words, memory is malleable depending on what and how we are asked to recall or describe a past event. The implications are obvious—people who witness a crime, an auto accident, or some other emotionally charged event can be led to draw certain conclusions about what they recall, even to make memory errors (i.e., false recall), due to the specific content of questions posed by police or lawyers.

To demonstrate this sort of memory error, Loftus and Palmer (1974) showed a film of two cars crashing into each other to a group of participants. Later, some participants were asked to estimate, "About how fast were the cars going when they *smashed* into each other?" Others were invited to make an estimate in response to similar questions containing different action verbs, such as, "About how fast were the cars going when they *bumped* into each other?" By manipulating the action verb (the level of the independent variable) in an otherwise innocent question, the researchers found that people's speed estimates (in miles per hour) varied widely, with more dramatic verbs (i.e., *smashed*) eliciting greater speed estimates than less dramatic ones (i.e., *contacted*)—but everyone initially saw the *same* collision on film!

Suppose that a student investigator decides to replicate this classic result in a simpler design, one using only three levels of the independent variable (i.e., action verb choice). A group of 12 participants views the film of the crash, and they are then randomly assigned to one of three verb groups (4 participants in each) before responding to the dependent measure. The three verbs (levels of the independent variable) are *smashed*, *bumped*, and *contacted*. The student researcher predicts a decline in estimated speeds (miles per hour) as a function of the action verb presented; participants who encounter *smashed* will estimate a greater speed than those reading *bumped*. Both groups' speed estimates, in turn, will be higher than that reported by the third group, whose verb was *contacted*.

The raw data from the experiment, as well as basic descriptive statistics (i.e., sample means and standard deviations) and preliminary calculations, are shown in Table 11.3. By eyeballing the means for the three different verbs, you can see that the data appear to replicate prior results, thereby conforming to the hypothesis. Participants who were asked about speed when the cars *smashed* into one another ($\overline{X}_1 = 26.0$) provided a higher estimate than the *bumped* group ($\overline{X}_2 = 18.0$), and in turn, both of these estimates appear

Table 11.3   Hypothetical Speed Estimates (in Miles per Hour) from a Replication of Loftus and Palmer's (1974) Language and Memory for Auto Accidents Study

Verb	Group 1 "Smashed"	Group 2 "Bumped"	Group 3 "Contacted"
	$X_{1,1} = 30$	$X_{1,2} = 20$	$X_{1,3} = 10$
	$X_{2,1} = 25$	$X_{2,2} = 16$	$X_{2,3} = 14$
	$X_{3,1} = 22$	$X_{3,2} = 18$	$X_{3,3} = 12$
	$X_{4,1} = 27$	$X_{4,2} = 18$	$X_{4,3} = 10$
	$\sum X_1 = 104$	$\sum X_2 = 72$	$\sum X_3 = 46$
	$\sum X_{i1}^2 = 2{,}738$	$\sum X_{i2}^2 = 1{,}304$	$\sum X_{i3}^2 = 540$
M	26.0	18.0	11.5
SD	3.37	1.63	1.92

$N = 12$
$\sum X_{ij} = 222$
$\sum X_{ij}^2 = 4{,}582$

Table 11.4 Steps for Testing a Hypothesis Using an ANOVA

1. State the null (H_0) and the alternative (H_1) hypotheses.

2. Select a significance level (p value or α level) for the statistical test.

3. Perform the analyses for the ANOVA, complete an ANOVA source table, and then determine whether to accept or reject H_0 for each F ratio. Interpret and evaluate the results in light of the hypothesis or go to step 4.

4. Perform any necessary post hoc test(s), and then interpret and evaluate the results in light of the hypothesis.

to be greater than the one reported by the *contacted* group ($\overline{X}_3 = 11.5$). By analyzing these data with an ANOVA, the student researcher will determine (a) whether any differences exist between (or among) the means representing the three levels of the independent variable and (b) verify if the replication of Loftus and Palmer's (1974) work was successful.

Similar to the previous detailed examples we conducted from start to finish, we are going to rely on guidance from Table 9.2's list of steps for testing a hypothesis—however, that list of steps needs to be revised a bit to conform to the constraints of the ANOVA. A suitable revision is shown in Table 11.4, which contains four steps for testing a hypothesis with an ANOVA. The first step and part of the second step in Table 11.4 are identical with their counterparts in Table 9.2—the differences occur in steps 3 and 4, primarily because the ANOVA involves more detailed steps than the t or the z tests. In addition, Table 11.4 is meant to accommodate other forms of ANOVA beyond the one-variable case we are introducing in this chapter (other ANOVA designs are introduced in chapters 12 and 13).

We will now begin the actual ANOVA analyses of the data in Table 11.3. Following step 1 of Table 11.4, we state the null and alternative hypotheses for the replication experiment. Naturally, the student researcher assumes that H_0 entails no difference among the sample means and the populations they hail from (i.e., use of a different action verb in each group will have no effect on the participants' estimates of how fast the filmed cars were traveling when they crashed), or:

$$H_0: \mu_1 = \mu_2 = \mu_3.$$

On the other hand, the alternative hypothesis will stipulate that the use of three different action verbs will lead to at least one difference between means, or:

$$H_1: \text{not } H_0.$$

Step 2 in Table 11.4 invites us to choose a significance level for the ANOVA. Following the tenets of rigor as well as convention, we will rely on a p value of .05.

As we begin to perform step 3 in Table 11.4, we know that it will take us some time—and quite a few calculations—to finish. There is a statistical aid in this process, however, one designed to make the work easier and to organize results as we proceed. This aid is mentioned in Table 11.4—its unfamiliar presence may have confused you—and it is called an ANOVA **source table** or, occasionally, an ANOVA summary table. The results of any ANOVA are conventionally reported within a source table, enabling interested readers and data analysts to follow along and even check their work. For the data analyst, the ANOVA source table is a boost toward organization and, as we will see, it can also be a great help in catching the minor errors than can disrupt any analysis. Whenever you perform an ANOVA hereafter, you will want to create a source table to record and order the results of the calculations done along the way.

Conducting an ANOVA requires some different steps than are used to calculate the t or the z test.

Table 11.5   A One-Way ANOVA Source Table with Symbolic Entries

Source of Variation	Sum of Squares	df	Mean Square	F	p
Between groups	$SS_{between}$	$df_{between}$	$MS_{between}$ $= \dfrac{SS_{between}}{df_{between}}$	$\dfrac{MS_{between}}{MS_{within}}$	.05
Within groups	SS_{within}	df_{within}	MS_{within} $= \dfrac{SS_{within}}{df_{within}}$		
Total	SS_{total}	df_{total}			

☑

The ANOVA source or summary table organizes various statistics in preparation for calculating an *F* ratio.

Table 11.5 illustrates the basic source table used for any one-way ANOVA, though it only contains the statistical symbols we reviewed previously—the actual statistics (numbers) will be entered into a copy of this summary table that comes later, after the calculations. Take a moment to look over this table so that you are familiar with the logic involved in its construction. In terms of making entries, we move from the left (*source* of the variation) to the right (the actual *F* ratio and its accompanying *p* value). We will refer back to Table 11.5 as we proceed with the analyses here in step 3. Each of the calculations we perform will be entered in the appropriate place in completed source Table 11.6.

We begin by calculating the *sum of squares of the total variance* and then the *degrees of freedom* associated with it. (Please note that for the most part, we are using the formulas and repeating the formula numbers presented earlier in the chapter.) To calculate the total sum of squares, we use:

[11.8.1]
$$SS_{total} = \sum X_{ij}^2 - \frac{(\sum X_{ij})^2}{N}.$$

The numbers corresponding to formula [11.8.1]'s entries are readily found in Table 11.3, so that:

[11.8.2] $SS_{total} = 4{,}582 - \dfrac{(222)^2}{12}$,

[11.8.3] $SS_{total} = 4{,}582 - \dfrac{49{,}284}{12}$,

[11.8.4] $SS_{total} = 4{,}582 - 4{,}107$,

[11.8.5] $SS_{total} = 475$.

The SS_{total} of 475 is then entered at the bottom of the second column in Table 11.6.

Calculating the degrees of freedom for the SS_{total} is readily accomplished using formula [11.9.1]:

[11.9.1] $df_{total} = N - 1$.

Because there are a total of 12 participants,

[11.9.2] $df_{total} = 12 - 1$,

[11.9.3] $df_{total} = 11$.

These 11 degrees of freedom are then entered at the bottom of the third column in Table 11.6.

We now perform the three calculations for the *between-groups variance estimate*. The first step is identifying the *sum of squares between groups*, or $SS_{between}$:

[11.10.1] $$SS_{between} = \Sigma \left[\frac{(\Sigma X_j)^2}{n_j} \right] - \frac{(\Sigma X_{ij})^2}{N}.$$

Once again, the requisite information is easily obtained from the prior work done in Table 11.3:

[11.10.2] $$SS_{between} = \Sigma \left[\frac{(104)^2}{4} + \frac{(72)^2}{4} + \frac{(46)^2}{4} \right] - 4,107.$$

Please stop for a moment here and verify that you recognize where each of the numbers shown in [11.10.2] came from in Table 11.3, and that you know how they were calculated. (Remember, too, that we simply tacked 4,107—the correction term, or $(\Sigma X_{ij})^2/N$—on to the end of [11.10.2] *without* recalculating it; we determined its value earlier when we calculated the SS_{total}.) By proceeding with the calculation for the $SS_{between}$, we see that:

[11.10.3] $$SS_{between} = \Sigma \left[\frac{10,816}{4} + \frac{5,184}{4} + \frac{2,116}{4} \right] - 4,107,$$

[11.10.4] $$SS_{between} = \Sigma \left[2,704 + 1,296 + 529 \right] - 4,107,$$

[11.10.5] $$SS_{between} = 4,529 - 4,107,$$

[11.10.6] $$SS_{between} = 422.$$

The $SS_{between}$ of 422 is then entered into the upper slot of column 2 in Table 11.6.

The *degrees of freedom* for the between-groups sum of squares is known by:

[11.11.1] $$df_{between} = k - 1,$$

where k is the total number of levels of the independent variable (factor) or:

[11.11.2] $$df_{between} = 3 - 1,$$

[11.11.3] $$df_{between} = 2.$$

These 2 degrees of freedom are entered into the top place in column 3 in Table 11.6.

By dividing the $SS_{between}$ by the $df_{between}$ we can determine the *mean square between-groups*, that is, the between-groups variance estimate:

[11.12.1] $$MS_{between} = \frac{SS_{between}}{df_{between}}.$$

We need only enter the two numbers we just calculated for:

[11.12.2] $$MS_{between} = \frac{422}{2},$$

[11.12.3] $$MS_{between} = 211.$$

The $MS_{between}$ of 211 is then entered into the top entry place in column 4 of Table 11.6.

The final variance estimate, the *within-groups variance estimate*, is based on a process similar to the one used to obtain the between-groups variance estimate. We first determine the *sum of squares within-groups*, then the *within-group degrees of freedom*, followed by the *within-groups variance estimate* (MS_{within}). The SS_{within} is based on:

[11.13.1]
$$SS_{within} = \sum X_{ij}^2 - \sum \left[\frac{(\sum X_j)^2}{n_j} \right].$$

Again, the necessary numerical information for the first half of the formula is drawn from Table 11.3 (verify you know how and where it came from, please), whereas the second part —$\sum [(\sum X_j)^2/n_j]$— is taken from the previous calculation of $SS_{between}$, for:

[11.13.2] $SS_{within} = 4{,}582 - 4{,}529,$

[11.13.3] $SS_{within} = 53.$

The SS_{within} is then entered into the middle of column 2 in Table 11.6. Before we proceed to the calculation of the degrees of freedom for the within-groups variance estimate, however, we can perform a quick *error check* involving the sources of the three sums of squares. Specifically, using the three entries in column 2 of Table 11.6, we can verify that the $SS_{between}$ and SS_{within} sum to the SS_{total}, or:

[11.17.1] $(SS_{between} + SS_{within}) = SS_{total},$

[11.17.2] $(422 + 53) = 475,$

[11.17.3] $475 = 475.$

Be sure to perform any and all error checks—they will save time and increase accuracy in the long run.

As you can see, the sum of squares corresponding to the two variances estimates does add up to the total sum of squares—thus, we can be confident that no math error was made.

The degrees of freedom within-groups is known by:

[11.14.1] $df_{within} = N - k,$

[11.14.2] $df_{within} = 12 - 3,$

[11.14.3] $df_{within} = 9.$

The degrees of freedom within groups can be entered into the middle of column 3 in Table 11.6, enabling us to perform a second *error check*. We must verify that the degrees of freedom for the between- and within-groups variances estimates add up to the total degrees of freedom shown at the bottom of column 3 in Table 11.6. Do they?

[11.18.1] $(df_{between} + df_{within}) = df_{total},$

[11.18.2] $(2 + 9) = 11,$

[11.18.3] $11 = 11.$

They do, so that once again, we can assume that no errors have been made.

The within-groups variance estimate or mean square within groups is based on:

[11.15.1]
$$MS_{within} = \frac{SS_{within}}{df_{within}}.$$

If we enter the numbers we just calculated we find that:

[11.15.2] $MS_{within} = \dfrac{53}{9},$

[11.15.3] $MS_{within} = 5.89.$

The MS_{within} can be now placed into the second entry place in column 4 in Table 11.6. As a third *error check*, it is helpful to verify that the $MS_{between}$ and MS_{within} were calculated correctly the first time. To do so, simply check the numbers shown in the first two

Table 11.6   Completed (Hypothetical) One-Way ANOVA Source Table with Entries

Source of Variation	Sum of Squares	df	Mean Square	F	p
Between groups	422	2	211		
				35.82	.05
Within groups	53	9	5.89		
Total	475	11			

columns of rows 1 and 2 in Table 11.6 (i.e., When $SS_{between}$ is divided by $df_{between}$, does the resulting number equal $MS_{between}$? When SS_{within} is divided by df_{within}, does the resulting number equal MS_{within}?). If the numbers check out—as they should—then the final calculation in the source table, the F ratio, is a snap.

We now calculate the F ratio for this one-way ANOVA, the test statistic that will indicate whether any reliable difference exists between (among) any of the speed estimates corresponding to the three action verbs (represented by the three means shown in Table 11.3). Be sure to remember that an F ratio for a one-way ANOVA is based on the ratio of between-group variation to within-group variation—and that more of the former is preferred relative to a small amount of the latter. Using formula [11.16.1] and the two variance estimates from column 5 in Table 11.6, we find this to be the case:

[11.16.1] $$F = \frac{MS_{between}}{MS_{within}},$$

[11.16.2] $$F = \frac{211}{5.89},$$

[11.16.3] $F = 35.82.$

How do we report this F ratio and determine whether it is significant? The F ratio is correctly reported with the degrees of freedom taken from both its numerator and denominator (remember that any F distribution is based on both these number sources), as well as the statistic itself:

$$F(2, 9) = 35.82.$$

Make careful note that these two numbers for the degrees of freedom were taken from column 3 in Table 11.6, as they represent—in order—the between-group variance estimate (i.e., 2) and the within-group variance estimate (i.e., 9).

We now need to locate a critical value for F, a number whose magnitude indicates whether we can accept or reject the null hypothesis of no difference. To achieve this end, we must learn to use a new table of critical values—you guessed it, a table of F values. A section of Table B.5 is reprinted in Figure 11.5 (the complete table may be found in Appendix B). The F table is not at all difficult to use: All we need to do is find the intersection between the column corresponding to the numerator (here, 2) and the row for the denominator (here, 9; see where the arrows are drawn and meet in Figure 11.5). The *lighter entries* in Figure 11.5 (and Table B.5 in Appendix B) are critical values at the .05 level, while the *darker ones* represent the .01 level. Back in step 2 (following the guidelines shown in Table 11.4), we chose .05 as the significance level, so the critical value of F for this experiment is 4.26, written as:

$$F_{crit}(2, 9) = 4.26.$$

Following the usual statistical convention, we determine that if the calculated statistic is *greater than or equal to* the critical value, then H_0 is rejected—otherwise, it is

Degrees of freedom for denominator	Degrees of freedom for numerator																
	1	②	3	4	5	6	7	8	9	10	11	12	14	16	20	24
1	161	200	216	225	230	234	237	239	241	242	243	244	245	246	248	249
	4052	4999	5403	5625	5764	5859	5928	5981	6022	6056	6082	6106	6142	6169	6208	6234
2	18.51	19.00	19.16	19.25	19.30	19.33	19.36	19.37	19.38	19.39	19.40	19.41	19.42	19.43	19.44	19.45
	98.49	99.01	99.17	99.25	99.30	99.33	99.34	99.36	99.38	99.40	99.41	99.42	99.43	99.44	99.45	99.46
3	10.13	9.55	9.28	9.12	9.01	8.94	8.88	8.84	8.81	8.78	8.76	8.74	8.71	8.69	8.66	8.64
	34.12	30.81	29.46	28.71	28.24	27.91	27.67	27.49	27.34	27.23	27.13	27.05	26.92	26.83	26.69	26.60
4	7.71	6.94	6.59	6.39	6.26	6.16	6.09	6.04	6.00	5.96	5.93	5.91	5.87	5.84	5.80	5.77
	21.20	18.00	16.69	15.98	15.52	15.21	14.98	14.80	14.66	14.54	14.45	14.37	14.24	14.15	14.02	13.93
5	6.61	5.79	5.41	5.19	5.05	4.95	4.88	4.82	4.78	4.74	4.70	4.68	4.64	4.60	4.56	4.53
	16.26	13.27	12.06	11.39	10.97	10.67	10.45	10.27	10.15	10.05	9.96	9.89	9.77	9.68	9.55	9.47
6	5.99	5.14	4.76	4.53	4.39	4.28	4.21	4.15	4.10	4.06	4.03	4.00	3.96	3.92	3.87	3.84
	13.74	10.92	9.78	9.15	8.75	8.47	8.26	8.10	7.98	7.87	7.79	7.72	7.60	7.52	7.39	7.31
7	5.59	4.74	4.35	4.12	3.97	3.87	3.79	3.73	3.68	3.63	3.60	3.57	3.52	3.49	3.44	3.41
	12.25	9.55	8.45	7.85	7.46	7.19	7.00	6.84	6.71	6.62	6.54	6.47	6.35	6.27	6.15	6.07
8	5.32	4.46	4.07	3.84	3.69	3.58	3.50	3.44	3.39	3.34	3.31	3.28	3.23	3.20	3.15	3.12
	11.26	8.65	7.59	7.01	6.63	6.37	6.19	6.03	5.91	5.82	5.74	5.67	5.56	5.48	5.36	5.28
⑨	5.12	4.26	3.86	3.63	3.48	3.37	3.29	3.23	3.18	3.13	3.10	3.07	3.02	2.98	2.93	2.90
	10.56	8.02	6.99	6.42	6.06	5.80	5.62	5.47	5.35	5.26	5.18	5.11	5.00	4.92	4.80	4.73

Figure 11.5 Excerpt from Table B.5—Critical Values of F

Source: Reprinted from Snedecor & Cochran (1980).

accepted (i.e., retained). Because the obtained value is greater than critical value, the null hypothesis of no difference is rejected, or:

$$F_{\text{calculated}}(2, 9) = 35.82 \geq F_{\text{crit}}(2, 9) = 4.26: \textit{Reject } H_0.$$

> ▽
>
> A significant omnibus ("big, dumb") F encourages the data analyst to undertake the (post hoc) search for where precise differences between or among means are found.

What does this significant F ratio tell the student researcher who set out to conceptually replicate Loftus and Palmer (1974)? More specifically, where exactly *is* (or *are*) the difference(s) between (among) the three means shown in the middle of Table 11.3? In actuality, we cannot say—*yet*—where any given difference lies. Why not? Remember that earlier in the chapter we learned that except in the two-sample case, the F test yields an omnibus statistic; that is, it partitions the variance and detects the presence or absence of a reliable difference(s) but it does *not* pinpoint where it is (except in the two sample—two mean—case when the difference is *obvious;* recall the independent groups t test). In a real sense, then, the omnibus F statistic is effectively a "hunting license," one that, when significant—as it is here—entitles the data analyst to use supplemental statistics to determine the precise nature and location of the significant difference(s). This possibility was mentioned before when the idea of post hoc tests was introduced, as well as being noted in step 4 of the guidelines in Table 11.4.

In other words, we are not yet finished with the one-way ANOVA. We know that some difference exists between or among the three speed estimates, but we cannot be certain where it lies until we perform the requisite post hoc analysis. We cannot begin to write up the results in detailed prose yet either—we need more information before any concrete behavioral conclusions can be drawn. At this point in time, the F ratio is mute about the true nature of the results. In fact, some researchers only half-jokingly refer to a significant *F* ratio for more than two sample means as a "big, dumb *F*," a surprisingly odd but apt and even memorable name for it. I assign the *F* this *nom de guerre*—an assumed name—because it helps me (as it will help you) to remember the nature of significant differences in the ANOVA and the necessity of post hoc tests, matters we take up in earnest in the next section.

Post Hoc Comparisons of Means: Exploring Relations in the "Big, Dumb *F*"

An omnibus or "big, dumb *F*" lets an investigator know that some difference between the means in a study exists, one where the variability attributed to the influence of the treatment variable exceeds that associated with sampling error or chance variation. To locate where the difference or differences exist, a data analyst will rely on what is called a *comparison*, one usually but not necessarily performed between pairs of means.

KEY TERM   A **comparison** is a statistical procedure wherein a researcher tests a particular hypothesis regarding how various means compare to one another.

The logic of the comparison process is similar to that used by the independent groups *t* test, except that most comparison procedures are designed to protect the researcher from making a Type I error.

Statistical comparisons can be further subdivided into two approaches: *a priori* and *post hoc comparisons*. We already mentioned the latter in passing, so we will define the approach advocated by *a priori* (pronounced "aye pry-or-ee") comparisons first. An a priori comparison is created prior to the collection of any data, one that is usually an integral part of the study's hypothesis. These types of comparisons are often called "planned comparisons" or even "planned contrasts" (see Rosenthal & Rosnow, 1985). A priori comparisons are often based on existing theories and the weight of data from the published literature, or at least the certainty assured from an ongoing program of research.

To be sure, almost any piece of research conducted involves some degree of hypothesizing about the relationships between or among levels of a treatment variable before the data are collected. The key issues are the relative amount of certainty a researcher has in those relationships and the degree of statistical rigor desired in a given set of analyses. In many situations, unexpected, even serendipitous patterns between means do show up, rendering an *a priori* comparison untenable as well as inappropriate. When this sort of event occurs—and it does fairly often, as data rarely meet a hypothesis in a perfect one-to-one match—the researcher must rely on the aforementioned *post hoc comparison*.

Post hoc comparisons are identical to planned comparisons in computational terms. Where they differ from planned comparisons is in the ease with which a critical value delineating a significant difference from a nonsignificant one can be reached or exceeded. In other words, post hoc tests make it tougher on the data analyst to find a reliable difference, thereby increasing the level of confidence or faith one can have in a result. To be sure, a priori comparisons are statistically more powerful than post hoc comparisons, but the latter have the advantage of being useful when (a) no firm hypotheses are established (a proverbial "fishing expedition" where one is fishing around in the data in order to "catch" some result—other authors [e.g., Kirk, 1999] refer to this process as "data snooping") or (b) unanticipated relationships are uncovered in the data.

Other points of comparison, as it were, between these two approaches include:

- A researcher undertakes post hoc tests only when the initial pass of the ANOVA indicates a null hypothesis is rejected. In contrast, an a priori comparison can

Comparisons can be planned (a priori) or developed after the fact (post hoc), and either type is appropriate, depending on the particular circumstance.

actually be done without doing an ANOVA (see the later section introducing contrast analysis).

■ Post hoc tests control the experimentwise error rate via the possible number of comparisons one could perform rather than the number actually performed. A priori tests control experimentwise error in terms of the specific number of comparisons being conducted.

■ Each of these types of statistical procedures protects data analysts from inflated alpha or Type I errors, and can compare pairs of means or groups of means.

We focus on post hoc comparisons in this section of the chapter for two reasons. First, as a student of ANOVA, you should learn the logical progression of steps a researcher follows when a significant *F* ratio is found—and the next step is usually a post hoc comparison. Second, most researchers rely on the ANOVA in a more or less exploratory fashion, anyway, so it will be important for you as a producer and consumer of behavioral science data to comprehend the whys and wherefores of post hoc tests. I will, however, close this chapter with an example of how one sort of planned comparison can be liberating and enlightening for researchers, but I offer it there as food for thought and future statistics courses, as it covers advanced terrain. Here, in a basic introductory course, it is more important for you to acquire the necessary background for understanding what is typically done with statistics and data analysis in mainstream behavioral science research (but see the controversies regarding mainstream approaches in chapter 15). If you are interested in exploring *a priori* comparisons further than the descriptive overview provided here or at the end of the chapter, there are very good references available to do so (Harris, 1998; Kirk, 1994; Rosenthal & Rosnow, 1985).

Tukey's Honestly Significant Difference Test

Different authors select or promote different post hoc tests. In truth, some post hoc tests are better suited to certain kinds of data than others, but Tukey's honestly significant difference (*HSD*; some texts refer to the test as *Q*) test is ideal because of its wide range of applicability. This test is most appropriately used when the results of an ANOVA like the one conducted in the previous section leads to the rejection of an overall null hypothesis (and as a reminder, no post hoc test is properly used unless a significant *F* ratio is found). In the search for differences between means, the HSD test enables a researcher to conduct any and all pairwise comparisons between means in a data set (see Hancock & Klockars, 1996). By "pairwise," I refer to comparisons made between two means at a time. Some post hoc tests (e.g., the Scheffé test; see Kirk, 1999) permit an investigator to compare combinations of means with one another, or combinations of means with one mean.

The *HSD* is also a good candidate for beginning data analysts to learn because the computations are straightforward and the use of the test is quite intuitive once an example is demonstrated. There are different ways to perform the *HSD* test and the one I will present is adapted from Runyon and colleagues (1996; see also, Harris, 1998; Kirk, 1999; Kramer, 1956). Using the Tukey's *HSD* test, the absolute difference between two means (e.g., $|\overline{X}_1 - \overline{X}_2|$) is determined to be statistically significant at a selected level of α if the absolute difference is greater than or equal to an *HSD* value derived from the information in the ANOVA's source table. The version of the Tukey *HSD* formula we will use is:

[11.19.1]
$$HSD = q_\alpha \sqrt{\frac{MS_{\text{within}}}{n}},$$

where *HSD* is a critical difference between means that must be reached or exceeded in order to identify a reliable difference between pairs of means. The value of q_α, which is based on *k* (the number of means or groups in a study) and the df_{within} drawn from the ANOVA, is taken from Table B.6 in Appendix B. The within-groups variance estimate, or MS_{within}, is taken directly from the ANOVA source table. Finally, *n* refers to the number of participants within each sample or group—a data analyst need only be concerned about whether the *n* is equivalent across groups. If not, then *n'* ("n-prime"), the mean of various different values of n_j, is substituted in the *HSD* formula, where

$$[11.20.1] \qquad n' = \frac{number\ of\ means}{\sum (1/n_j)}.$$

If there were three means with respective sample sizes of 6, 5, and 8, then *n'* would be

$$[11.20.2] \qquad n' = \frac{3}{1/6 + 1/5 + 1/8},$$

$$[11.20.3] \qquad n' = \frac{3}{.167 + .20 + .125},$$

$$[11.20.4] \qquad n' = \frac{3}{.492},$$

$$[11.20.5] \qquad n' = 6.10.$$

This value of *n'* would be entered into the *HSD* formula (i.e., [11.19.1]) in place of an equal *n*.

The three groups in the replication of Loftus and Palmer (1974) study, however, had an equal number of participants—four—per group. We can now finish that ANOVA analysis by calculating an *HSD* value and determining where, precisely, differences between pairs of means lie. As a first step, we need to identify q_α using Table B.6 in Appendix B (please turn there now—the table is on page 605). Table B.6 is titled "Percentage Points of the Studentized Range," and it has three main column headings—one labeled "error *df*" (for the within-groups degrees of freedom), one for α (the desired significance level; here, .05 or .01), and *k* (for the number of means being considered). Based on the results of the ANOVA shown in Table 11.6, we know to locate the row for 9 degrees of freedom under the "error *df*" column. We then read down the *k* column corresponding to 3 (for the three sample means in the study). Please locate the intersection point for row 9 and column 3—you should see 2 values, 3.95 and 5.43. We select 3.95 as the q_α value because it corresponds to the .05 significance level (i.e., the significance level chosen using step 2 in Table 11.4).

Now that q_α is known, we can calculate the *HSD* value using formula [11.19.1]. Besides substituting 3.95 for q_α, all we need to do is enter MS_{within} from Table 11.6, as well as the *n* of 4, for:

$$[11.19.2] \qquad HSD = (3.95)\sqrt{\frac{5.89}{4}},$$

$$[11.19.3] \qquad HSD = (3.95)\sqrt{1.4724},$$

$$[11.19.4] \qquad HSD = (3.95)(1.21),$$

$$[11.19.5] \qquad HSD = 4.78.$$

What do we do with this *HSD* value? The first thing to do is recall what the value means—any absolute difference between a pair of means that is 4.78 or greater

Table 11.7   Pairwise Comparisons Between All Means Using the Tukey *HSD* Test

Action Verb Mean Estimates		Action Verb Mean Estimates (in Miles per Hour)		
		Smashed	Bumped	Contacted
		26.0	18.0	11.5
Smashed	26.0	—	8*	14.5*
Bumped	18.0	—	—	6.5*
Contacted	11.5	—	—	—

Note: The table contains absolute differences between all possible pairs of means in the replication of Loftus and Palmer (1974). An asterisk (*) indicates that the absolute difference between the means (pairwise comparison) is significant at the .05 level using the Tukey *HSD* test.

is statistically significant at the .05 level. The second thing to do is to create a simple matrix of the three means so that we can identify the absolute differences between every possible pair. The matrix shown in Table 11.7 fits the bill—note that the three means are presented in both the columns and the rows of this table. (The upper-right and lower-left portions of a matrix like this one are always symmetric. To avoid confusion, the absolute differences are shown only in the upper right of Table 11.7.) Inside the table, you can see that the absolute differences between each possible pair of means are indicated (remember, when you take the absolute value of any number, the negative sign is dropped). How many of the absolute differences presented in Table 11.7 reach or exceed the *HSD* of 4.78? In this particular case, they all do—thus, we know that each of the sample means was significantly different than each of the others at the .05 level (the asterisk [*] shown by each entry in Table 11.7 indicates that the pairwise comparison is statistically reliable according to the *HSD* test).

In practical terms—how use of a particular action verb influenced speed estimates—what do we now know based on the results of the Tukey *HSD* test? As hypothesized, speed estimates tended to increased as a function of the action verb used in the question, "About how fast were the cars going when they_____-ed into each other?" Participants who encountered the most dramatic verb, "smashed" ($\overline{X} = 26.0$), offered significantly greater speed estimates than those who read the verbs "bumped" ($\overline{X} = 18.0$) or "contacted" ($\overline{X} = 11.5$). In turn, the speed estimates for the "bumped" sample were significantly higher than those made by participants in the "contacted" group. In short, the student researcher successfully replicated the Loftus and Palmer (1974) study.

How are these statistical results reported into an APA-style narrative? We will postpone this important matter until after we perform two supplementary analyses that support the results of the one-way ANOVA—effect size, and the degree of association existing between the treatment variable and the dependent measure.

Remember to compare the *HSD* value with the absolute value of any difference (drop all negative signs!) between a pair of means.

Effect Size for the *F* Ratio

Cohen (1988) developed a straightforward index of effect size for the *F* ratio, and it is referred to as **f**. Cohen provided ranges for **f** to indicate when an effect size is small (**f** = .10), medium (**f** = .25), and large (**f** = .40 and beyond). Of course, these ranges are only guidelines—as noted before, some statistically small effects can have great import for describing complex behavior in the behavioral sciences (but recall

Data Box 10.D). The formula for **f** is:

[11.21.1]
$$\mathbf{f} = \sqrt{\frac{\eta^2}{1 - \eta^2}},$$

where

[11.22.1]
$$\eta^2 = \frac{SS_{between}}{SS_{total}}.$$

We can readily determine the value of η^2 ("eta-squared") by taking the respective sums of squares from the ANOVA source table (see Table 11.6):

[11.22.2]
$$\eta^2 = \frac{422}{475},$$

[11.22.3]
$$\eta^2 = .8884.$$

This value for η^2 can then be entered into formula [11.21.1] so that **f**, too, can be known:

[11.21.2]
$$\mathbf{f} = \sqrt{\frac{.8884}{1 - .8884}},$$

[11.21.3]
$$\mathbf{f} = \sqrt{\frac{.8884}{.1116}},$$

[11.21.4]
$$\mathbf{f} = \sqrt{7.96},$$

[11.21.5]
$$\mathbf{f} = 2.82.$$

Data analysts speak of effect sizes for ANOVA results as being small, medium, or large, though **f**s above .50 are rare in behavioral science data.

This effect size statistic is clearly quite large—in fact, it is off Cohen's (1988) scale—though you must keep in mind that these data are hypothetical. I do, however, want you to get a feel for the magnitude of the differences that can exist between means. The effect size in this hypothetical replication study is quite large, alerting us to the fact that where verbs are concerned, how a question is phrased has a powerful effect on resulting judgments—at least where speed estimates are concerned. I must point out, though, that Cohen argued that effect sizes above .50 are rarely observed in real behavioral science data. I mention this fact so that you can make a realistic appraisal when you collect and analyze your own data or evaluate the research of others.

Estimating the Degree of Association Between the Independent Variable and the Dependent Measure

When an *F* ratio is declared statistically significant and we know that the null hypothesis is rejected, we know there is at least one difference between some set of means. A post hoc test, such as the Tukey *HSD* test, then identifies the nature of the mean difference(s). We still do not know, however, anything about the relationship between the independent variable and the dependent measure.

We can determine the degree to which the three levels of the treatment variable (the action verbs "smashed," "bumped," and "contacted") affected changes in participants' speed estimates (the dependent measure) by relying on information from the ANOVA source table. We first learned about $\hat{\omega}^2$ in chapter 10, where it was used to indicate the degree of association between the independent and dependent variable in a *t* test. There is also a version of $\hat{\omega}^2$ for use when an *F* ratio is significant.

DATA BOX 11.D

A Variance Paradox—Explaining Variance due to Skill or Baseball is Life

Robert Abelson (1985), a statistically savvy social psychologist and baseball fan, drew attention to an intriguing paradox involving $\hat{\omega}^2$ and America's favorite pastime. In your opinion, how much does a player's skill affect his batting record? Now, answer this same question in variance terms—how much variability in performance at any given time at bat is due to skill, how much is due to chance and other factors?

Using baseball "stats" as they are called, Abelson examined the percentage of variance in batting performance attributable to skill differences among major league baseball players. In a typical year, the batting averages of major league baseball players range between the low .200s and the low .300s. A batting average is determined by dividing a player's number of hits by the number of times he has batted; a team average can be calculated using the same logic. Abelson estimated an $\hat{\omega}^2$ of .00317 for the average major league baseball player, a minuscule figure suggesting that the variability in any single batting performance accounted for by skill is equal to *one third of 1%* (or, if you prefer, over 99% of the available variation is *not* explained by a player's abilities)!

This result should give you pause, just as it did Abelson and his interested colleagues who found it surprising, even unbelievable. The casual observation of countless fans, as well as coaches, teams, and team owners—not to mention sportswriters—is at odds with this sort of conclusion, or is it? Abelson explains the baseball skill versus variance paradox this way: A given player's batting prowess is measured across a long season, not on a particular trial at bat. As Abelson (1985) put it, "a way to understand the paradox is to realize that in the major leagues, skills are much greater than in the general population. However, even the best batters make outs most of the time" (p. 131).

Furthermore, Abelson's (1985) calculation of $\hat{\omega}^2$ takes into account players of all skill levels, and most of them, of course, are average (see chapter 4). When people think of a player's skill at batting, they are usually reflecting on his entire career, not the single time at bat entailed in this statistic. As observers, we frame perceived athletic performance in different terms than those measured by a statistic like $\hat{\omega}^2$. Should we belittle this statistic, then? Not according to Abelson (p. 132):

> The single at bat is a perfectly meaningful context. I might have put the question this way: As the team's manager, needing a hit in a crucial situation, scans his bench for a pinch hitter, how much of the outcome is under his control? Answer: one third of 1%. Qualification: This assumes that the standard deviation of the batting averages against a given pitcher is the same as the standard deviation of batting averages in general.

Are there any statistical implications of this sort of variance analysis? Yes, indeed there are some implications. Teams score runs as a result of a conjunction of events (e.g., a prior hit by player A is linked to a current hit by player B), and teams with better-than-average batters should perform better across time than those with lower than average players. A team's athletic success is affected more by the *average batting skill* of its players than any individual's successful performance on a given try at bat. Skill, then, is cumulative, and this is true for any given player and for an entire team. What matters is the *process* whereby variables like these operate in real world settings—they may have an additive quality so that their effects are not salient or influential in any given circumstance. Belief that the variance in batting averages is related to skill is intuitively correct but only in the long run—skill is not very powerful or even consequential in a single situation.

Abelson's (1985) point is a powerful one—relying on $\hat{\omega}^2$ or a similar index that accounts for variability can be inappropriate in situations where small changes become cumulative across time. Despite appearances and belief to the contrary, some meaningful outcomes (e.g., a player's batting prowess, a winning team), then, develop or unfold gradually, and though skill is clearly a part of the process—it is more apparent than real at any point time. Explaining variance via $\hat{\omega}^2$ is not always the best indicator on systematic influence. Like so many things in life, skill is in the eye of the beholder. Some social processes, such as educational interventions or the effects of persuasive communication on consumer behavior, as well as baseball, take some time—and a longer perspective—to arrive at an adequate understanding of their operations (Abelson, 1985).

Here it is:

[11.23.1]
$$\hat{\omega}^2 = \frac{df_{between}\,(F - 1)}{df_{between}\,(F - 1) + N}.$$

Once again, all the information we need to perform the necessary calculations can be drawn from the ANOVA source table we created (see Table 11.6) and knowledge about the study (i.e., we know that 12 participants took part in the replication, so $N = 12$). Entering the appropriate statistical information we find that:

[11.23.2]
$$\hat{\omega}^2 = \frac{2(35.82 - 1)}{2(35.82 - 1) + 12},$$

[11.23.3]
$$\hat{\omega}^2 = \frac{2(34.82)}{2(34.82) + 12},$$

[11.23.4]
$$\hat{\omega}^2 = \frac{69.64}{69.64 + 12},$$

[11.23.5]
$$\hat{\omega}^2 = \frac{69.64}{81.64},$$

[11.23.6]
$$\hat{\omega}^2 = .8530 \cong .85.$$

▽

An $\hat{\omega}^2$ based on ANOVA results is interpreted in the same manner as a $\hat{\omega}^2$ for a *t* test, though the calculations differ.

The student researcher can conclude that the independent variable (action verb choice) accounted for approximately 85% of the variance in the dependent measure (speed estimates). In short, there was a very high degree of association between the independent variable and the dependent measure.

Writing About the Results of a One-Way ANOVA

As always, a researcher's goal is to convey the statistical results and their behavioral implications in clear language. Similar to the *t* test, the one-way ANOVA is used to identify any mean differences existing between or among the levels of an independent variable. When writing up the results from a one-way ANOVA, a researcher can capitalize on this important feature of the analysis—literally, one can point to the concrete behavioral differences existing between the groups. In behavioral terms, what did the participants actually *do?* Where did any *specific* differences occur between independent groups? Remember, too, the importance of reminding the reader about the hypothesis—a brief recapitulation is always helpful.

Results from an ANOVA—a one-way design or the more complex designs we will explore in chapters 12 and 13—differ from those of the *t* test in that there are usually several (i.e., more than 2) means and, therefore, multiple mean relationships to examine. Depending on the complexity of the research design and the number of levels in an independent variable, you might want to show the means in tabular form in lieu of presenting them in the text. It is often easier for readers to follow a general descriptive summary of what happened behaviorally in the text before being referred to a table, where the precise mean differences can be shared. This is by no means a hard and fast rule. With practice as a researcher and data analyst, you will develop an intuitive sense of how to best present some data, whether it makes more sense to see it in numerical form in a text or table, or in a more graphic presentation—a figure of some sort (see chapter 3 for relevant guidelines). Just remember to provide thorough statistical information for critical readers to follow and, if they so desire, to verify the logic of your arguments.

Here is one way that the student researcher could summarize the replication of Loftus and Palmer (1974). Please note that any supporting statistics (e.g., effect size) are reported following the main results:

> Previous research indicated that the language used in a question can be as important as the question itself. Participants in the present study all saw the same car crash and were later asked to estimate how fast the cars were traveling when they hit one another—however, the three groups of participants encountered three different action verbs embedded in the speed question. Were these eyewitnesses as prone to memory-related errors due to language as Loftus and Palmer (1974) suggest? Preliminary analyses indicated that participants' speed estimates varied according to how dramatic the action verb embedded in the dependent measure happened to be. The means and standard deviations for the three action verb groups are shown in Table 1. A one-way analysis of variance revealed a significant difference among the three groups, $F(2, 9) = 35.82$, $p < 0.5$. Tukey's *HSD* test indicated that the average speed estimate for the "smashed" group was significantly higher than the other two groups; in turn, the mean of the "bumped" group was statistically greater than that observed in the "contacted" group (see Table 1). The effect size of this result was quite large ($\mathbf{f} = 2.82$), and there was a high degree of association between the changes in the action verbs and participants' speed estimates ($\hat{\omega}^2 = .85$).

Table 1   Speed Estimates (in Miles Per Hour) as a Function of Action Verbs Used in the Dependent Measure

	Action Verb		
	Smashed	**Bumped**	**Contacted**
M	26.0	18.0	11.5
SD	3.37	1.63	1.92

Note: All of the mean entries are significantly different from one another at the .05 level.

Knowledge Base

1. True or False: *Factor* is another term for independent or treatment variable.
2. You conduct an experiment where the independent variable has five levels. The data are analyzed with a one-way ANOVA and a significant *F* ratio is found. Does the *F* ratio indicate where the difference(s) between means are? Why or why not?
3. What is meant by the term "big, dumb *F*"?
4. True or False: A post hoc test can be undertaken when an ANOVA's *F* ratio is not significant.

Answers

1. True
2. For more than two independent groups, the one-way ANOVA yields an omnibus *F* ratio, one that indicates the presence of a difference but not its precise location. A follow-up comparison, for example, one relying on a post hoc test (e.g., Tukey *HSD* test) must be conducted to specify the nature of any difference(s) between means.

When writing about the results of any analysis–ANOVA or otherwise–be sure to describe what happened in behavioral terms.

3. This nontechnical but apt term refers to the omnibus nature of the F ratio when more than two groups are being analyzed by an ANOVA—the statistic cannot identify where any precise difference occurs so that additional analysis is necessary.

4. False. Some a priori comparisons can be performed under these circumstances, but a post hoc test is only proper when the F ratio reaches significance.

An Alternative Strategy for Comparing Means: A Brief Introduction to Contrast Analysis

I do not want to conclude your first exposure to the ANOVA by directly leading into more complex research designs, the topics of chapters 12 and 13. Rather, I want you to think about a one-variable research design beyond the confines of the typical one-way ANOVA and the necessary reliance on its omnibus F test and subsequent post hoc analyses. I would be greatly surprised if some readers did not wonder what happens when a specific pattern of means is anticipated, but the one-way ANOVA is either not the appropriate analytic tool or the F ratio turns out to be less in value than its appropriate critical value. What is a conscientious researcher to do? Give up, go back to the drawing board (or lab), and collect more data?

An alternative strategy relies on a priori hypothesis testing using what is called **contrast analysis** (Rosenthal & Rosnow, 1985, 1991). A contrast is another name for the statistical comparison of means, albeit in a planned manner as opposed to a post hoc approach. Rosnow and Rosenthal (1989) go so far as to argue that contrast analysis should almost always be used in favor of the omnibus F tests usually associated with the various approaches to ANOVA. The exploratory nature of so much research (especially student research)—that is, one specific pattern of means is not necessarily anticipated over another—keeps me from wholeheartedly endorsing this position, though I am sympathetic to it, having used it myself (Dunn & Wilson, 1990).

In my opinion, Rosenthal and Rosnow (1985, 1991) do offer convincing evidence that contrast analysis is a strong antidote to overreliance on the results of standard ANOVA analyses. We will review a hypothetical example used by these authors to demonstrate how a thoughtful investigator can overcome the constraints of a typical one-way ANOVA design. My interest here is to briefly introduce this alternative approach to you, not to review it in an exhaustive and detailed manner. Even if you never have occasion to use contrast analysis, you are likely to appreciate being aware that its power and logic are available to you.

Here is the example adapted from Rosenthal and Rosnow (1991). Imagine that an educational researcher administers a measure of cognitive activity to 50 children in a cross-sectional research design (i.e., all participants are measured at one point in time rather than repeatedly). There are five age levels (8, 9, 10, 11, and 12), and 10 children in each age group. The upper portion of Table 11.8 shows the average performance score for the five age groups. Below the data is an ANOVA source table for the one-way analysis, wherein you will notice that there is *no* significant difference between any two (or more) of the five group measures (i.e., $F[4, 45] = 1.03$, $p = .40$; see the source table in Table 11.8). This lack of result is somewhat puzzling given that the means shown in the top of Table 11.8 appear to increase in a somewhat progressive, linear fashion (i.e., as the children age, their performance on the cognitive activity improves accordingly; see the means in Table 11.8, as well as a graph of these means in Figure 11.6).

What ever is wrong with these data? The means shown in Table 11.8 appear to increase with age and Figure 11.6 graphically confirms this speculation—why are the

▽

A contrast is another name for a planned comparison that is theory-based.

Table 11.8   Hypothetical Data and ANOVA Source Table from Children's Age and Cognitive Ability Study

Mean Performance Scores at Five Age Levels

	Age Levels				
	8	**9**	**10**	**11**	**12**
	2.0	3.0	5.0	7.0	8.0

ANOVA Source Table for Performance Scores by Age

Source	*SS*	*df*	*MS*	*F*	*p*
Age levels	260	4	65		
				1.03	.40
Within-groups	2,835	45	63		

Source: Adapted from Rosenthal and Rosnow (1991, pp. 467–468).

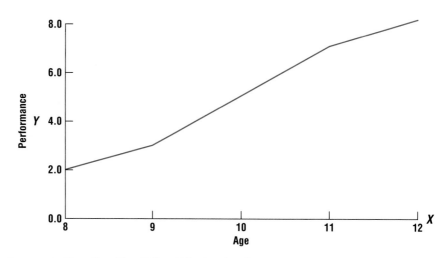

Figure 11.6   Mean Cognitive Ability at Five Age Levels

Source: Adapted from Rosenthal and Rosnow (1991, p. 468).

visually apparent differences not significant? The omnibus *F* based on the one-way ANOVA looks for *any* mean differences, and it does so in an unfocused, diluted manner—the arrangement of means by increasing age, for example, is not considered by this omnibus test. Rosenthal and Rosnow (1991) advocate that a better test of the hypothesis that task performance is enhanced by age can be tested by a **contrast,** a focused comparison where weights for each mean are used to compare obtained results against some predetermined pattern (i.e., one based on theory, a hypothesis, or even an educated guess). These weights are called λ ("lambda") weights and they adopt numerical values such that the sum of λ ($\sum \lambda$) is equal to 0 for any given contrast (the rationale for this procedure will become clear shortly).

Any contrast has one (1) degree of freedom corresponding to the numerator.

Any contrast has one (1) degree of freedom for the numerator, while the denominator is linked to the error degrees of freedom found in the ANOVA source table. An F ratio based on a contrast can be determined using this formula:

[11.24.1]
$$MS_{\text{contrast}} = SS_{\text{contrast}} = \frac{L^2}{n \sum \lambda^2},$$

where L is the sum of all the condition totals (T), each one of which is multiplied by a λ-weight based on some hypothesis, or:

[11.25.1]
$$L = \sum (T\lambda) = T_1\lambda_1 + T_2\lambda_2 + \cdots + T_k\lambda_k,$$

where

> k = the number of conditions (i.e., means),
>
> n = the number of observations within each level of the independent variable

(here, we assume an equal number of 10 per group; if the group sizes were unequal, we would substitute n' using formula [11.20.1]),

> $T = n\overline{X}$, which is called the condition total,
>
> λ = the contrast weights linked to a particular hypothesis, weights that necessarily sum to 0.

Rosenthal and Rosnow (1991) note that the necessary contrast is actually already hardwired into the example. The means shown at the top of Table 11.8 can each be multiplied by 10 (i.e., the n in each condition) in order to determine the T for each condition[1] (see Table 11.9). The T value of 20 for the 8-year-old group was determined by multiplying the group mean (2.0) by n (10; see Table 11.9). In turn, each T must be multiplied by a λ-weight based on the educational researcher's theory (i.e., cognitive skill increases with age). The weights corresponding to this linear trend can be determined by subtracting the mean age of the five groups (i.e., $\overline{X}_{\text{age}} = 8 + 9 + 10 + 11 + 12/5 = 50/5 = 10$) from each age group (i.e., $8 - 10 = -2$; $9 - 10 = -1$; $10 - 10 = 0$; $11 - 10 = +1$; $12 - 10 = +2$). (Tables of different contrast weights can be found in Rosenthal & Rosnow, 1985; Snedecor & Cochran, 1967.) These weights are shown in the second row of Table 11.9; as required, the weights sum to 0 (see the 0 entry at the

Table 11.9   Table of Calculations for Age Level and Performance Contrast

| | Age Level | | | | | |
	8	9	10	11	12	$\sum$
$T(n\overline{X})$	20	30	50	70	80	250
λ	-2	-1	0	$+1$	$+2$	0
$T\lambda$	-40	-30	0	70	160	160

Source: Adapted from Rosenthal and Rosnow (1991, p. 470).

[1]If the number of observations per group were unequal, then T would be calculated using n'.

end of the row). Each T is then multiplied by its appropriate λ-weight (see row three in Table 11.9), and the resulting products are summed:

[11.25.2] $L = \sum T\lambda = 20(-2) + 30(-1) + 50(0) + 70(+1) + 80(+2),$

[11.25.3] $L = \sum T\lambda = (-40) + (-30) + (0) + (70) + (160),$

[11.25.4] $L = \sum T\lambda = 160.$

For convenience, the $\sum T\lambda$, that is, L, is also shown in the lower right corner of Table 11.9.

By entering L into formula [11.24.1], we can calculate the sum of squares and then the variance estimate for the contrast and, in turn, an F ratio that will reveal whether the means are significantly different from one another in a linear fashion. The only other entry into [11.24.1] that we need to calculate is $\sum \lambda^2$, which is:

[11.26.1] $\sum \lambda^2 = \lambda_1^2 + \lambda_2^2 + \lambda_3^2 + \lambda_4^2 + \lambda_5^2,$

[11.26.2] $\sum \lambda^2 = (-2)^2 + (-1)^2 + (0)^2 + (+1)^2 + (+2)^2,$

[11.26.3] $\sum \lambda^2 = 4 + 1 + 0 + 1 + 4,$

[11.26.4] $\sum \lambda^2 = 10.$

Thus, we can finish formula [11.24.1]:

[11.24.2] $MS_{\text{contrast}} = SS_{\text{contrast}} = \dfrac{(160)^2}{(10)(10)},$

[11.24.3] $MS_{\text{contrast}} = SS_{\text{contrast}} = \dfrac{25{,}600}{100},$

[11.24.4] $MS_{\text{contrast}} = SS_{\text{contrast}} = 256.$

As always, the F ratio is determined by dividing the variance estimate for the numerator (MS_{contrast}) by that for the denominator (MS_{within}; see Table 11.8) for:

[11.27.1] $F_{\text{contrast}} = \dfrac{MS_{\text{contrast}}}{MS_{\text{within}}},$

[11.27.2] $F_{\text{contrast}} = \dfrac{256}{63},$

[11.27.3] $F_{\text{contrast}} = 4.06.$

Turning to Table B.5, we find a critical value corresponding to 1 and 45 degrees of freedom (remember that any contrast has 1 df in the numerator—the denominator df is from the source table in Table 11.8). When you turn to Table B.5, however, you will find that there are error degrees of freedom entries for 44 and 46, but not 45 degrees of freedom. Using what is called *interpolation*, literally estimating or finding a value between two others (here, Fs of 4.06 and 4.05), we identify the critical F as being equal to 4.055. We find, then, that:

$$F_{\text{calculated}} (1, 45) = 4.06 > F_{\text{critical}} (1, 45) = 4.055$$

What does this significant F tell us? It indicates that the linear trend of means shown in Table 11.8 is significant, such that children's performances on a cognitive activity increased in a steady manner as they aged. Literally, the contrast shows us that the 8-year-olds scored lower than the 9-year-olds, who in turn did less well than the 10-year-olds, and so on up to the 12-year-old group, which had the highest average score of all (see the display of means in Table 11.8).

How would the educational researcher report these results? There are two options. The more conservative approach would be to first report the (nonsignificant) findings from the traditional one-way ANOVA before presenting the (significant) contrast results. The newer approach, that advocated by Rosnow and Rosenthal (1989), would be to focus exclusively on the results of the contrast and to not even bother reporting the one-way ANOVA findings as, strictly speaking, germane. The choice is ultimately your own, though you may be asked by an instructor or editor to follow the more conservative approach in the interest of thoroughness. Here is one way to present the data in that more inclusive spirit:

> Did the older children perform better than the younger ones? The mean performance scores appeared to adhere to a linear trend, where ability increased systematically with age (see Table 1). This developmental question was addressed by analyzing the performance scores with a one-way analysis of variance (ANOVA), with age level serving as the independent variable. The ANOVA did not reach significance, $F(4, 45) = 1.03$, $p = ns$.[2] The more appropriate analysis, however, entails a planned contrast where performance was predicted to increase with age. As hypothesized, this contrast was significant, indicating that cognitive ability improved with age, $F(1, 45) = 4.06$, $p < .05$ . . . .

Table 1   Mean Cognitive Ability Scores by Age Group

Age	8	9	10	11	12
M	2.0	3.0	5.0	7.0	8.0

Note: All of the mean entries are significantly different from one another at the .05 level, and the n for each age group is 10. These data were adapted from Rosenthal and Rosnow (1991, p. 467).

Project Exercise

WRITING AND EXCHANGING LETTERS
ABOUT THE ANOVA

Throughout this book, I try to create strong connections between writing and statistics, as well as data analysis. This *Project Exercise* continues forging these connections but in a slightly different way, one that involves communicating about the complexity and utility of the one-way ANOVA in the form of a personal letter. It is based on an exercise I've used successfully in my classes and reported elsewhere (Dunn, 2000). I believe that letter writing is one way to make concepts from statistics and data analysis more meaningful (Dunn, 2000; see also Konzem & Baker, 1996). How so? By enabling you, the letter writer, to put conceptually challenging ideas into your own words and then sharing them in the form of a letter to another person.

Why is it necessary to write about statistics and data analysis in the form of a letter? In my experience, students sometimes learn statistical procedures by rote, drawing little real meaning from them. By writing a letter, you have the opportunity to explain abstract concepts to others using terms that make sense to you (ideally, of course, by highlighting examples to support your ideas). Johnson (1989), too, observes that many students understand statistical topics at a concrete level of interpretation rather than one where abstract thought and reasoning can really bring the topic to life—and make its techniques seem to be clear and applicable to real questions found within a set of

---

[2]Some writers use "*ns*" for "not significant," whereas others either report the actual p value (here, .40) or indicate $p > .05$ (note the direction of the sign). I happen to prefer "*ns*."

data. Writing about a complex topic requires you to really think about how to "marry" abstract and concrete elements to one another in a coherent way where others can understand your point of view.

Here are step-by-step instructions for writing a letter on what you know about the one-way ANOVA. Chances are that as you write your letter, some aspects of the ANOVA will become clearer to you, others less so. I want you to know that this sort of mixed reaction is perfectly normal, as it will motivate you to ask particularly focused questions and to reread portions of this chapter so that your understanding of one-way ANOVA is relatively complete.

1. **Identify your intended audience.** You can write a letter describing what you know about the ANOVA to your statistics instructor, a peer in your class, or a peer in some other class (Dunn, 2000; Konzem & Baker, 1996). Often times, it can be constructive to write to someone who knows little about the subject, as you will need to explain any technical issues carefully and thoroughly.

2. **Choosing the content and focus of the letter.** Your goal is to write a letter wherein you explain one or two things you have learned about the one-way ANOVA that are interesting, compelling, confusing, or otherwise noteworthy (Dunn, 2000). Describe why it was important to learn the ANOVA, for example, particularly where it can aid students in the behavioral sciences. You could also describe some hypothetical experiment whose results illustrate either *very little* or *considerable* between-groups variability, and how this variability impacts on the presence or absence of statistical significance via the F ratio (Johnson, 1989). Alternatively, you could write about the nature of the F ratio and what it means to obtain an F ratio close to 1.00. The choice of what to write about is entirely up to you—just be somewhat creative and detailed.

3. **Sharing letters: Writing, reading, and responding.** A variation of this exercise entails exchanging letters with a peer in or outside of the class. That is, you not only write about the ANOVA, you also read what another student thought about this analytical tool and, in addition, have the opportunity to write back to him or her in the form of a second letter. Exchanging letters can be a helpful exercise because it allows you to see—and sometimes critique—the ideas of others while they comment on the point of view espoused in your letter. (Your instructor may want copies of any letters you share with or receive from a peer.)

4. **Other suggestions.** Your letter can be printed out and mailed to your instructor or a peer, or sent directly via e-mail. If your instructor is interested or you are particularly motivated, a chat room could be created for the members of your statistics class on your campus network. How long should your letter be? I would strive for two or so typed, double-spaced pages. Remember, the best way to really learn something is to write about it!

LOOKING FORWARD THEN BACK

The one variable or "one-way" analysis of variance (ANOVA) builds on the logic of hypothesis testing that began with the z test and the t test, respectively. The one-way ANOVA enables the data analyst to simultaneously compare two or more means, where these previous tests restricted such comparisons to two sample means (see chapter 10) or a sample mean and a known population average (see chapter 9). The two decision trees at the start of this chapter promote the idea of moving beyond simple two-group comparisons. In fact, there are many steps involved in the calculation of a one-way ANOVA, and these trees provide an excellent review of procedures, thereby ensuring that no important issues are neglected. In this spirit, the first decision tree is designed to help you, the investigator or data analyst, decide whether a one-way ANOVA is the appropriate tool for the available data and research design. By answering a few questions concerning how the data are scaled and whether the samples or groups are independent, one can quickly determine the best way to proceed with an analysis.

What happens after the one-way ANOVA is performed? The second decision tree opening the chapter is a guide to the procedures that follow the calculation of an F ratio. Beyond determining whether the test statistic is significant, the data analyst must also decide to proceed with any necessary post hoc test or the calculation of supplementary analyses (i.e., effect size, degree of association between independent and dependent variables). When correctly performed, the one-way ANOVA and these supplementary procedures can provide a detailed portrayal of behavior, which can help you to build more specific theories of why people act the way they do.

Summary

1. The F ratio, the test statistic based on the analysis of variance (ANOVA), was originally used to analyze agricultural data.
2. The ANOVA is probably the most commonly recognized statistic used by behavioral scientists. It is used to test hypotheses involving two or more means.
3. Statistically, the ANOVA "partitions" or divides variance into portions that can be attributed to the effect of an independent variable on a dependent measure. Total variance refers to the combined variance of all available data in an experiment, which can be broken down into between-groups variance (usually caused by the manipulation of an independent variable) and within-groups variance (caused by random error or chance events).
4. Between-group variance is often called treatment variance, and it involves examining how some treatment (e.g., drug, novel stimulus) affects some outcome (e.g., elimination of disease, learning). Within-group variance is referred to as error variance, as its source is largely uncontrollable as unknown elements affect people. Error variance, then, creates the usually minor behavioral differences that occur within a group of people.
5. Conceptually, the F ratio is based on between-groups variance/within-groups variance, or treatment variance + error variance/error variance.
6. The F distribution is generally skewed in a positive direction, though it approaches normality when both the sample sizes for the numerator and the denominator are large. Unlike the t and z distributions, then, the F distribution lacks negative values.
7. When an F ratio equals 1.00, then the between-groups and the within-groups variances are equal—in other words, the

null hypothesis of no difference is appropriately accepted. As the F ratio becomes greater than 1.00 in value, the probability of rejecting H_0 increases substantially.
8. The t statistic and the F ratio share a specific relationship when two—and only two—means are present. Specifically, the square root of an F ratio yields a t statistic for a two-group comparison, while squaring a t value from an independent groups t test results in a comparable F ratio.
9. The statistical assumptions underlying the ANOVA match those related to the t test. Similar to the t test, the ANOVA provides quite a robust statistic. The t test is limited, however, when it comes to comparing multiple means. Practically speaking, only two means can be compared at one time and, as the number of t tests is increased due to interest or need, the probability of making a Type I error increases dramatically. Where multiple means are concerned, the ANOVA is a more appropriate analytical tool in that it provides adequate protection against Type I errors.
10. Pairwise comparison α, the probability of making a Type I error when two samples are compared, increases as the number of t tests increases. Experimentwise error is the likelihood of making one or more Type I errors when performing multiple t tests in the same data set.
11. The F test is an appropriate antidote to the problem posed by using multiple t tests, especially since the ANOVA is designed to hold Type I error rates constant. The F test is called an omnibus test precisely because it can assess the presence of any statistically significant differences among more than two means, but it cannot pinpoint these differences (or difference) until some post hoc test is performed.

12. A one-way analysis of variance searches for behavioral differences among more than two sample means. The term "one-way" refers to the fact that the analysis can only handle one independent variable with two or more levels.

13. The term "factor" is a synonym for a treatment or independent variable in any type of ANOVA.

14. The one-way ANOVA compares the null hypothesis of no difference, which stipulates that all samples or groups come from the same population, against a flexible alternative hypothesis. The alternative hypothesis can be precisely stated in terms of predicted relations among means or, as is more typical, simply noted as "not H_0" or that at least one treatment mean will differ from the others.

15. The one-way ANOVA can be calculated in a variety of different ways, and different texts promote different formulas. In most cases, however, some notation or symbol system is introduced to make the data analysts' work easier. The notation is used to keep track of observations for between- and within-group (sample) analyses necessary to determine the variance estimates that eventually yield an F ratio.

16. The conceptual steps that make up the ANOVA analysis reflect the partitioning of variation noted previously. The between-groups sum of squares ($SS_{between}$), degrees of freedom ($df_{between}$), and mean square or between-groups variance estimate ($MS_{between}$) are calculated initially, followed by the same statistics corresponding to the within-groups or error perspective (i.e., SS_{within}, df_{within}, MS_{within}). The F statistic is then calculated by dividing the $MS_{between}$ by the MS_{within} estimates. The resulting F ratio is significant—some mean difference or differences exists—when it equals or exceeds a critical value of F (drawn from Table B.5 in Appendix B) determined by the respective degrees of freedom for the numerator (between-groups variance estimate) and the denominator (within-groups variance estimate).

17. When an F ratio is determined to be significant with more than two means present, the location of the difference(s) must wait until some a priori (i.e., planned) or post hoc (after the fact) comparisons are performed. In other words, the omnibus or "big, dumb F" indicates the presence of difference but does not specify the location between or among the means. In general, most students and many researchers rely on post hoc tests rather than planned comparisons.

18. Tukey's honestly significant difference (*HSD*) test is frequently used by investigators because its calculations are straightforward and it can be applied to most data sets. Essentially, the researcher calculates an *HSD* statistic, a numerical value, based on statistical information drawn from the ANOVA source table. The *HSD* statistic is then compared to all possible absolute differences between pairs of means. When the difference between any pair of means is equal to or greater than the *HSD*, the two means are significantly different from one another.

19. Supplementary analyses that support the interpretation of ANOVA results include effect size **f** and a variation of $\hat{\omega}^2$ based on the F ratio and related ANOVA information. These supplementary measures allow a researcher to flesh out what is known about the effect of an independent variable on a dependent measure when an obtained difference(s) is significant.

20. When writing about the results of an ANOVA, one should be sure to connect the numerical information (i.e., means and mean differences) with actual behavior—in other words, what participants actually *did* is as important the statistical interpretation being proffered.

21. Contrast analysis—an a priori, theory-based comparison of means—is an alternative strategy one can use in lieu of post hoc analyses. An advantage of contrast analysis is that obtaining a significant omnibus F ratio in an ANOVA design is not necessary. A researcher can pose a 1 degree of freedom contrast using weights to compare the magnitude of the obtained means against a hypothesis. If the resulting F ratio is found to be significant, then the investigator knows that the pattern of the means conforms to the hypothesis.

Key Terms

Analysis of variance (ANOVA) (*p. 413*)
Contrast (*p. 448*)
Contrast analysis (*p. 447*)
Comparison (*p. 439*)
Error variance (*p. 415*)
Experimentwise error (*p. 421*)

Factor (*p. 427*)
Grand mean (*p. 414*)
Omnibus statistical test (*p. 423*)
One-way analysis of variance (One-way ANOVA) (*p. 427*)
Pairwise comparison α (*p. 421*)

Post hoc test (*p. 424*)
Source table (*p. 433*)
Total variance (*p. 414*)
Treatment variance (*p. 416*)

Chapter Problems

1. Why should any researcher—student or professional—avoid becoming overly focused on finding statistical significance when conducting behavioral science research?

2. How is the ANOVA similar to other statistical tests used to establish mean differences? How is the ANOVA distinct or different from these tests?

3. What are some advantages of the ANOVA that make it a versatile and useful statistical test? Is it more versatile or useful

than the other statistical tests used for mean comparison? Why or why not?

4. In what ways are the ANOVA and the independent groups t test related to one another? Can they be used interchangeably? Why or why not?

5. Explain the source of the variation used to calculate the F ratio in a one-way ANOVA. Is the partitioning of variance for the ANOVA similar to the way it is divided by the analysis performed by the t test?

6. What is treatment variance? What is error variance? How do these terms relate to between-group and within-group variance?

7. Briefly describe the F distribution—how is it similar to or different from the t and z distributions?

8. In terms of variance and the behavior of participants, explain what it means when a data analyst obtains an F ratio equal to 1.00.

9. Is it possible to calculate an F ratio with a negative value? Why or why not?

10. Explain the statistical assumptions underlying the ANOVA. How are these assumptions similar to or different from those associated with the t test?

11. Under what particular circumstances do the independent groups t test and the F ratio share a special relationship with one another? Explain the nature of this relationship.

12. Is it advisable to conduct numerous t tests when, say, six means are involved? Why or why not? What analysis should be performed with this many means, that is, levels of an independent variable?

13. Given the number of means cited in question 12, what is the risk of committing at least one Type I error using multiple t tests? What would the probable risk be if there were 8 means?

14. How is the ANOVA distinct from prior statistical tests?

15. A student uses an independent groups t test to compare the number of hours per week men versus women spend studying in the library. She finds a t statistic of -3.22. Another student analyzes the same data using an ANOVA. What does he find?
    a. $F = 10.37$ b. $F = 9.2$ c. $F = -9.2$ d. $F = 3.22$
    e. $F = 5.23$

16. Under what circumstances is it appropriate to conduct a post hoc test following an ANOVA? How do post hoc tests differ from a priori comparisons?

17. Examine the following ANOVA summary table and complete the missing information. (Hint: use the numbers shown and the formula provided in the chapter.)

Source	Sum of Squares	df	MS	F
Between-groups	15	___	7.5	$F =$ ___
Within-groups	___	27	___	
Total	72.5	29		

18. Calculate the effect size f and the $\hat{\omega}^2$ using the information provided in question 17.

19. Examine the following ANOVA summary table and complete the missing information. Hint: use the numbers shown and the formula provided in the chapter. The independent variable is comprised of three groups, and each group has 15 participants.

Source	Sum of Squares	df	MS	F
Between-groups	___	___	20	$F =$ ___
Within-groups	90	___	___	
Total				

20. Calculate the effect size f and the $\hat{\omega}^2$ using the information provided in question 19.

21. Examine the following ANOVA summary table and complete the missing information. (Hint: use the numbers shown and the formula provided in the chapter.) The independent variable is comprised of four groups, and each group has 10 participants.

Source	Sum of Squares	df	MS	F
Between-groups	100	___	___	$F =$ ___
Within-groups	___	___	5.00	
Total				

22. Calculate the effect size f and the $\hat{\omega}^2$ using the information provided in question 21.

23. These data are based on an experiment comprised of three independent groups. Perform a one-way ANOVA using $\alpha = .05$. Can you accept or reject H_0? If you reject H_0, perform the appropriate post hoc test in order to identify where the differences lie.

Treatment A	Treatment B	Treatment C
10 8 10 9	6 6 7 6	5 4 5 6
11 9 10 8	7 7 6 5	4 5 7 6

24. These data are based on an experiment comprised of two independent groups. Perform a one-way ANOVA using $\alpha = .01$. Can you accept or reject H_0? Once you complete the ANOVA, use an independent groups t statistic to verify a significant difference (if one is found).

Treatment A	Treatment B
12 10 10 8	8 9 8 7
11 11.6 10 7	7 9 8 7
12 11 10 11	8 7 6 6.6

25. Calculate the effect size and degree of association between the independent variable and dependent measure for the data presented in question 23.

26. Calculate the effect size and degree of association between the independent variable and dependent measure for the data presented in question 24.

27. Nursing students are taught clinical skills in various ways—some learn from nursing texts, others rely on computer simulations of patient condition profiles, still others learn by observing staff, and some learn by lecture. Imagine that you are the member of a nursing school and are interested in learning which method of acquiring clinical skills is the best. Here are clinical quiz scores for each of the four methods (NOTE: lower scores mean poorer performance):

Texts	Simulations	Observation	Lecture
3	5	6	2
4	6	4	1
3	7	5	1
5	6	4	3
2	6	5	4
3	5	4	1

   a. Perform a one-way ANOVA using $\alpha = .05$. Be sure to prepare an ANOVA source table.
   b. If the F ratio is significant, conduct the Tukey HSD test to determine the character of any differences.
   c. If appropriate, calculate the effect size and $\hat{\omega}^2$.
   d. Write up all the results in prose form, supplying any tables or graphs as needed to support the text.

28. A student believes that undergraduates become more sociable across their 4 years of college. To test this hypothesis, the student recruits a random sample of students from each of the four classes at his college, asking them to complete a measure of sociability. The scores from this measure (by class membership) are shown below (Note: higher scores reflect greater levels of sociability):

Freshmen	Sophomores	Juniors	Seniors
2	4	6	10
4	5	7	9
2	4	5	8
5	5	6	9
1	4	6	8
1	3	7	7

   a. Do students become more sociable across 4 years? Perform a one-way ANOVA using $\alpha = .05$. Be sure to prepare an ANOVA source table.
   b. If the F ratio is significant, conduct the Tukey HSD test to determine the character of any differences.
   c. If appropriate, calculate the effect size and $\hat{\omega}^2$.
   d. Write up all the results in prose form, supplying any tables or graphs as needed to support the text.

29. A researcher is interested in people's reactions to having their personal space violated by strangers. In our culture, the norm is to maintain a distance of approximately 2 feet between others and ourselves in public settings. Only those with important social connections—spouses, family members, and friends, are permitted to be any closer physically. Below are the self-reported comfort levels (where 1 = very uncomfortable to 7 = very comfortable) of 25 people based on measured distances between themselves and a stranger. Is it true that personal space violations by strangers leads to higher levels of discomfort?

Distance:	3 inches	1 foot	1.5 feet	2 feet	3 feet
	1	2	4	5	7
	1	3	3	4	7
	1	3	4	5	7
	1	2	4	5	6
	1	3	1	6	7

   a. Perform a one-way ANOVA using $\alpha = .01$. Be sure to prepare an ANOVA source table.
   b. If the F ratio is significant, conduct the Tukey HSD test to determine the character of any differences.
   c. If appropriate, calculate the effect size and $\hat{\omega}^2$.
   d. Write all the results in prose form, supplying any tables or graphs as needed to support the text.

30. A student is reading an empirical journal article. In the results section, she encounters the following sentence: "Once the data were coded, they were subjected to a one-way analysis of variance (ANOVA), which was found to be significant, $F(3, 27) = 3.86, p < .05$." Using this summary statistic, answer the following questions:
   a. How many levels did the treatment or independent variable possess?
   b. What is the total number of participants who took part in the testing?
   c. What is the value of $\hat{\omega}^2$ for this experiment?

31. A student is reading an empirical journal article. In the results section, he encounters the following sentence: "Once the data were coded, they were subjected to a one-way analysis of variance (ANOVA), which was found to be significant, $F(2, 45) = 5.63, p < .01$." Using this summary statistic, answer the following questions:
   a. How many levels did the treatment or independent variable possess?
   b. What is the total number of participants who took part in the testing?
   c. What is the value of $\hat{\omega}^2$ for this experiment?

32. A researcher conducts an experiment wherein two independent samples must be compared. Participant responses are based on a ratio scale. Is a one-way ANOVA the appropriate statistical test to analyze these data? Why or why not? (Hint: Use the decision tree(s) at the start of this chapter to answer these questions.)

33. Four independent groups with ordinal responses must be compared. Is a one-way ANOVA the appropriate statistical test to analyze these data? Why or why not? (Hint: Use the decision tree(s) at the start of this chapter to answer these questions.)

34. An F ratio based on an analysis of three independent groups reaches statistical significance ($p < .05$). What is the next step the data analyst must undertake? Is a one-way ANOVA the appropriate statistical test to analyze these data? Why? (Hint: Use the decision tree(s) at the start of this chapter to answer these questions.)

35. Once the results of a one-way ANOVA are found to support a hypothesis, what should a researcher do next? Why? (Hint: Use the decision tree(s) at the start of this chapter to answer these questions.)

Deciding Which ANOVA to Use

1.
Are the data based on an *interval* or a *ratio* scale?

If *yes*, then go to step 2.

If *no*, then go to step 9.

2.
How many independent variables are there?

If there is *one* independent variable, then go to step 5.

If there are *two* independent variables, then go to step 3.

3.
Are *both* variables between-groups factors?

If *yes*, then perform a *two-way ANOVA*.

If *no*, then go to step 4.

4.
Is one of the variables a *repeated-measures factor* while the other is a *between-groups factor*?

If *yes*, then perform a *mixed-design ANOVA*—consult an appropriate source for guidelines (see also chapter 13).

If *no*, then the answer to the previous question may be incorrect—go back to step 1 and begin anew.

5.
Are there *three* or more levels in the *independent variable*?

If *yes*, then go to step 6.

If *no*, then go to step 7.

6.
Are the samples or groups represented by a *single independent variable* so that they are *independent* of one another?

If *yes*, then perform a *one-way ANOVA* (see chapter 11).

If *no*, they are *dependent observations*, then perform a *repeated-measures ANOVA* (see chapter 13).

7.
Are there at least *two* levels in the *independent variable*?

If *yes*, then go to step 8.

If *no*, then go to step 9.

8.
Are the *two* levels *independent of one another*?

If *yes*, then perform an *independent groups t test* (see chapter 10).

If *no*, then perform a *dependent groups t test* (see chapter 10).

9.
No *ANOVA* is appropriate for the analysis—please *reevaluate* the data and your *analysis plan*.

Procedure Following a Two-Way ANOVA

1.
Did any of the *three F* ratios reach significance (e.g., $p < .05$)?

If *yes*, then go to step 2.

If *no*, then go to step 5.

2.
Answer the following questions and perform the accompanying steps for *each significant F ratio* (examine the interaction first, then the main effects): Did the *F* ratio support the hypothesis?

If *yes*, then go to step 3.

If *no*, then go back to step 2 and consider the next *F* ratio; if no significant *F* ratio remains, then go to step 5.

3.
Perform the appropriate supplementary analyses (i.e., effect size **f** and $\hat{\omega}^2$) and then go back to step 2 if *any* other significant effect remains; otherwise, go to step 4.

4.
Did the *interaction* reach significance?

If *yes*, perform a *mean polish* and display the characteristic X-plot; go to step 5.

If *no*, then go to step 5.

5.
Write up the results in *clear prose*, report any *supplementary analyses* (as appropriate), display *means in a table*, create an *ANOVA source table*, and *revise theory* as necessary.

CHAPTER 12

MEAN COMPARISON III:
TWO-VARIABLE ANALYSIS
OF VARIANCE

 n odd bit of statistical history: Ronald A. Fisher (Cowles, 1989; see Data Box 11.A) once illustrated his principles of research design by entertaining the following "experiment":

> A lady declares that by tasting a cup of tea made with milk she can discriminate whether the milk or the tea infusion was first added to the cup. We will consider the problem of designing an experiment by means of which this assertion can be tested (Fisher, 1966, p. 11).

Fisher went on to describe how to test this assertion, which was prompted by a Dr. B. Muriel Bristol's refusal of a cup of tea because the tea was added *before* the milk (Fisher Box, 1978). Fischer's colleague at the Rothamsted Agricultural Research Station insisted that the order by which milk or tea is added to a cup affects the taste of the beverage favored by the British. There will always be an England!

In terms of topics presented in the last chapter, "tea first" or "milk first" into the cup, represents the two levels of an independent variable, perhaps for a one-way analysis of variance (ANOVA). Where the topic of this chapter is concerned—complex ANOVA designs—we might complicate matters by adding a second independent variable, whether a cube of sugar is added to the cup *before* or *after* the tea or milk is poured. In other words, we are interested in whether the effects of these two independent variables (tea then milk versus milk then tea, and sugar before versus sugar after the second liquid is introduced) on some dependent measure—mean ratings of the taste of tea—can be observed simultaneously. Preferences about the preparation of hot drinks may seem trivial, but Fisher's real interest was not this experimental domain per se, but rather that inferences from multivariable questions could be drawn in the first place.

This is the third chapter devoted exclusively to comparing means in this book. We began with simple two group comparisons using the *t* test in chapter 10 and moved onto the simultaneous comparison of more than two independent samples in chapter 11. This chapter builds on the logic and empirical framework found in the previous two, but its goal is to demonstrate how introducing a relatively minor degree of change in a standard experiment enables researchers to ask questions containing higher levels of complexity. The change I refer to here involves introducing a second independent variable into a research design and its accompanying analysis. In the language of statistics and experimentation, we will learn to think about and analyze data using the two-way ANOVA.

The two-way ANOVA is used to analyze data from experiments wherein each participant is exposed to one level from each of *two* treatment variables instead of just *one*. An investigator might be curious about the effects of room temperature (e.g., ambient versus hot) and time pressure (e.g., pressure versus no pressure) on people's problem-solving abilities. Instead of running two different experiments—one examining how temperature affects the number of problems correctly solved, the other how time pressure influences the same outcome—and then conducting two separate one-way ANOVAs on the resulting data, both variables can be investigated and analyzed in one study. As we will see, research time and effort are not the only advantages—conclusions about the nature of relationships between variables are positively enhanced, as well.

◖ Overview of Complex Research Designs: Life Beyond Manipulating One Variable

It is a cliché, but still true, that modern life is complex. Each and every day, most of us encounter a host of different people across a variety of different settings, just as we are barraged with media influences from the time our clock-radios go off or, later on, as we listen to the news on our commute to and from daily destinations. Quite a lot happens to the average person on a daily basis; some of it is extraordinary and much of it, no doubt, is rather mundane. Yet our consideration of how to go about studying life through the methods and techniques of behavioral science has been rather unidimensional. In other words, we spent almost two thirds of this book acquiring the knowledge necessary for comparing multiple means representing different levels of the same independent variable (see chapter 11). At that time, we noted that life was more than a two group research design, and now we are saying, in turn, that there is more than comparing means representing several levels of the same independent variable with one another. What more can we learn about analyzing complex situations? Why should we bother learning it?

Human behavior is complex and varied, and it cannot be completely understood—only approximated—by isolating the influences of one or two independent variables and some dependent measure.

As we just acknowledged, life is more complex than the one-way ANOVA; indeed, it is more varied, even infinite, than can be properly grasped, measured, or analyzed in the most complex experiment imaginable. Poets and philosophers are more comfortable addressing such questions from the heart, and they have long-standing traditions the typical sociologist or political scientist cannot follow. Still, however, the behavioral scientist must enter the breach by relying on the tools he or she has available. In the present situation, we can try to capture a slice of life, as it were, through undertaking more complex research designs and analyses. By examining how two (or even more) independent variables affect a single dependent measure, we develop a broader sense of how human behavior is influenced by people, situations, or thoughts. Such complex experiments can tell us whether a given variable has a pronounced effect, no effect, or an effect that becomes apparent only in combination with another variable. Studying one variable in isolation, then, tells us something about its characteristics, but its role in concert with others or how it changes across time tells us still more.

Here are some reasons to manipulate more than one variable in a factorial experiment. This list of reasons is by no means an exhaustive one, but it should help you to see beyond the mere mechanics of the analyses we will undertake shortly, to remember that there is actually a larger purpose to these statistical exercises:

- **Economy.** Manipulating more than one factor introduces a tremendous savings in terms of time, energy, and resources. By performing only one rather than several studies addressing a series of questions, a researcher can gain knowledge more quickly, is apt to maintain interest in and enthusiasm for the topic, and will not overtax available materials (e.g., space where the research will occur, creation and production of any questionnaires, funding for experimenter[s] to aid with the project, modest payment [if any] to participants).
- **Efficiency.** Economic considerations aside, it is simply easier to run one—not several—empirical investigations. When designed correctly, a complex investigation will answer more than one pertinent question.
- **Elegance.** Two-factor designs are more elegant—gracefully concise, admirably succinct—than the basic two-group, one independent-variable design because they cover a bit more empirical terrain without a great deal of additional effort or expense. These complex designs are often ideal candidates for developing the broader theories of behavior so prized by behavioral scientists.
- **Generality of effects.** Two-factor designs not only tell us more without making additional taxing investments of time, effort, or expense, they also enable investigators to offer a more comprehensive account of behavior, one that aspires to portray life's intricacies. We are back to accurately characterizing the aforementioned slice of life while emphasizing that the presence of multiple independent variables or repetitions of a dependent measure enhances external validity. Regardless of its complexity, no laboratory experiment can ever be said to approach the complexity of real life, but the juxtaposition of more than one variable or measure clearly approximates real life in spirit more than a single independent variable.
- **Interaction of variables.** Finally, where experiments with two or more independent variables are concerned, there is a statistical concept called interaction, which will be discussed in detail shortly. An interaction occurs when the effect of one independent variable changes at different levels of another independent variable. Why is this a matter of design complexity? As we will see, an *interaction* can occur only in the presence of two (or more) independent variables, one hallmark of more complex designs.

Please keep these characteristics in mind as we review the two-way ANOVA.

Two-Factor Analysis of Variance

Similar to its one-variable counterpart, the *two-factor* or *two-way ANOVA* is an inferential statistical procedure that can analyze data from experimental or quasi-experimental research projects. The two-factor ANOVA, however, examines the between-group differences resulting from two independent variables, not one.

KEY TERM — A **two-factor** or **two-way ANOVA** is a statistical test used to identify differences between sample means representing the independent effects of variables A and B, as well as the interaction between the two variables. As a statistical technique, the *two-factor ANOVA* partitions variability, attributing portions of it to the respective independent variables and the interaction between them.

In order to get an accurate sense of the scope and utility of the two-factor ANOVA, we will review a classic two-factor study conduced by Glass, Singer, and Friedman (1969). In study 1, Glass and his colleagues were interested in the aftermath of being exposed to an uncontrollable, distracting—even irritating—noise. These researchers were interested in a psychological construct generally labeled "tolerance for frustration," which is generally operationalized as how long a participant will continue working on a more or less impossible task before giving up. While being exposed to loud (110 decibels) or soft (56 decibels) noise that was either predictable (i.e., appeared at fixed intervals) or random (i.e., appeared at random intervals for varied amounts of time), college women worked on a collection of puzzles, two of which (unbeknownst to them) were insoluble. The dependent measure was tolerance for frustration as measured by the number of attempts participants made to solve the insoluble puzzles before they displayed frustration and quit their efforts.

The design of the Glass et al. (1969) experiment is shown in Figure 12.1. As you can see, factor A (noise predictability) is shown on the left side of the matrix in Figure 12.1 and factor B (noise level) is shown across the top of the matrix. The experience of the women in the four groups is noted within the cells shown in the matrix. Thus, for example, participants in cell A_1B_2 heard soft noise at random intervals across the course of the experiment.

This particular research design is probably the most common one for two-factor experiments. It is called a 2×2 ("two by two") design because there are two independent variables, each of which has two levels. Research designs that involve more than one independent variable are called *factorial designs*.

KEY TERM

KEY TERM   A **factorial design** is an experimental design where each level of one factor is administered in combination with each level of another (or every other) factor.

Within a research design, multiplying the number of levels found in one independent variable by those found in another indicates the number of unique experimental conditions (e.g., $2 \times 3 = 6$ separate conditions).

A characteristic of any factorial design is that the number of levels for one independent variable multiplied by the number available for each of the other variables yields the total number of treatment combinations. Thus, a 2×2 factorial design has four treatment conditions (i.e., $2 \times 2 = 4$; see Figure 12.1 and Data Box 12.A).

Notice that the advantage of this particular factorial research design is that we do *not* need to conduct two separate experiments—one on the effects of predictable noise on tolerance for frustration and the other on the effects of noise level on tolerance for frus-

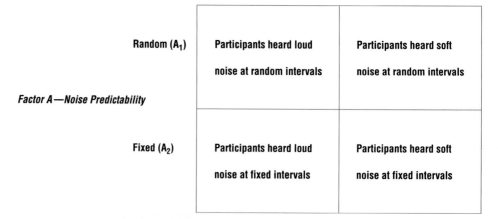

Figure 12.1   Design of Two-Factor Study of Noise Predictability and Noise Level on Tolerance for Frustration (after Glass, Singer, & Friedman, 1969)

DATA BOX 12.A

Thinking Factorially

Factorial designs assess the effects of more than one independent variable on the same dependent measure. The most basic factorial design is the so-called 2 × 2 design, one that replicates the format of the simplest possible one-factor study twice. A researcher can examine how variables A and B affect a dependent measure separately (main effects) and together (the A × B interaction). A key idea behind factorial design—the presence of more than one independent variable in an experiment or study—is the creation of different combinations of variable packages. We know that a 2 × 2 design has four possible combinations of variables a participant could experience (i.e., A_1B_1, A_1B_2, A_2B_1, and A_2B_2).

The combinations here are easy to envision, but what about more complex combinations? Here is a simple problem to think about in this vein:

> Any student buying lunch can have one and only one item from the main course, drink, and dessert categories. How many possible combinations of items from these three categories are there?

Main Course	Drink	Dessert
Hamburger	Milk	Chocolate cake
Hot dog	Juice	Vanilla ice cream
Salad		

Number of combinations of three items _____

If you think about the three categories as independent variables with two or three levels each, the combination question becomes much easier to answer. Some readers will be tempted to write out the combinations in a systematic manner (e.g., hamburger, milk, cake; hamburger, milk, ice cream; and so on), but there is an easier way, one used by researchers all the time. When planning or conducting a factorial design, you simply multiply the number of levels of each independent variable times the number of levels in the other independent variable(s). Thus, there are 12 possible meal combinations because 3 × 2 × 2 is equal to 12 (just as the ubiquitous 2 × 2 design has four groups). That is all there is to it!

Despite the fact that we are not going to analyze complex research designs with more than two variables in this book, you can now readily identify the number of distinct groups such designs possess. Use the factorial multiplication rule to determine the number of groups for the following designs:

2 × 3

2 × 4 × 2

3 × 3 × 2

2 × 2 × 2 × 2

5 × 2

[*Answers:* 6, 16, 18, 16, 10]

tration—just one where both variables are represented. (For convenience, assume that each of the four cells has an equal number of female participants—here,10—within it.)

We will consider some actual data resulting from this design in a moment. In the meantime, let's review the two-factor ANOVA's link to the F distribution and the ratios derived from it. Like the one-way ANOVA, the two-factor ANOVA relies on the F

distribution for hypothesis testing (for a review of the F distribution's qualities, see chapter 11). Instead of testing for the significance of a single F ratio, however, the two-factor ANOVA actually provides three F ratios, each of which must be compared against some critical value (or, depending on the degrees of freedom calculations required, two or three critical values). Using the experiment performed by Glass et al. (1969) to provide context, the respective F ratios test for:

1. A mean difference due to variable A (noise predictability): Does predictable noise lead to greater tolerance for frustration (more attempts to solve puzzles) than unpredictable noise?

2. A mean difference due to variable B (noise level): Does soft noise lead to greater tolerance for frustration (more attempts to solve puzzles) than loud noise?

3. An interaction between variables A and B, or differences among group means that are not a result of the main effects or random variability. An interaction occurs when the influence of one variable on a dependent measure is affected by the presence of a second variable (e.g., perhaps soft noise is linked with greater tolerance for frustration [more attempts to solve puzzles] when the noise is predictable rather than unpredictable). Please note that there are always several possible interaction patterns for a given research design—the actual one found by Glass et al. (1969) will be presented later.

A two-way ANOVA provides three F ratios, two corresponding to variables A and B, and one for the interaction between the variables.

Statistically, the F ratios for the two independent variables are calculated essentially the same way an F ratio based on a one-way analysis is determined. The difference, of course, is that two variables yield three Fs, not just one. Conceptually, the F ratio for the noise predictability or A factor is:

$$F_A = \frac{\textit{variance differences between the sample means}}{\textit{error variance for variable A}}.$$
(due to variable A + error variance for variable A)

Similarly, the F ratio for the noise level, or factor B, is:

$$F_B = \frac{\textit{variance differences between the sample means}}{\textit{error variance for variable B}}.$$
(due to variable B + error variance for variable B)

As always, the error variance is comprised of variability presumably due to individual differences possessed by the participants and experimental error.

What about the interaction between the two variables? In what way does noise predictability interact with noise level, if at all? How should we construe the variability partitioned within it? We can think of the variance attributable to an interaction in a couple of ways. First, we can think of it as the interaction between noise predictability and noise level (symbolized A $\times$ B for "A by B," *not* "A times B"):

$$F_{A \times B} = \frac{\textit{variance differences between the sample means due to A} \times \textit{B}}{\textit{error variance for A} \times \textit{B interaction}}.$$
(interaction + error variance for variable for A × B interaction)

This formation is another way of identifying the residual or leftover variance that is *not* explained by either noise predictability or noise level alone, or:

$$F_{A \times B} = \frac{\textit{variance differences between the sample means not due to}}{\textit{error variance not due to variable A or B}}.$$
(variable A or B + error variance not due to variable A or B)

At base, of course, each of the three F ratios that are derived from any two-factor ANOVA is based on the conceptual formulation we rely on for exploring mean differences:

$$F = \frac{between\text{-}groups\ variation}{within\text{-}groups\ variation},$$

where the bulk of the between-groups variation is presumed to be systematic, caused by factor A (noise predictability), factor B (noise level), or the A × B (noise predictability × noise level) interaction, as well as individual differences (each participant displays some idiosyncratic behavior), and experimental error (e.g., less-precise measurement, deviation from experimental script, equipment problems). The within-groups variation, in contrast, should be random, not systematic, being caused by the aforementioned combination of individual differences and experimental error.

As was true for the one-way ANOVA, as the value of any of the three F ratios exceeds 1.00, there exists the possibility that an observed difference between sample means is not due to chance but, rather, either variable or the interaction between the two variables. In order to determine if one or more of the F ratios is significant, each calculated value must be compared to a critical value of F drawn from Table B.5 in Appendix B.

Reading Main Effects and the Concept of Interaction

Let's turn to considering data from the Glass et al. (1969) experiment so that we can learn to understand what the three F ratios resulting from a two-way ANOVA identify statistically. Data representing the participants' average number of trials attempted on the first insoluble puzzle are shown in Table 12.1. Take a moment and look over these data carefully, both the entries inside the matrix as well as those in the margins. Remember that it is always helpful to get a "feel" for your data before proceeding to draw any strong conclusions or even beginning the main analyses. What can we learn by this brief examination? First, notice that the women who were exposed to the loud or random noise gave up the earliest ($\overline{X}_{A_1B_1} = 3.67$), while those who encountered the soft or fixed-interval noise made the most attempts ($\overline{X}_{A_2B_2} = 19.90$). The average number of attempts of *every person* who took part in the study—$\overline{X} = 12.93$—is shown by the grand mean in the lower right corner of the table.

We can now begin to examine the means that correspond to each of the F ratios that would result from a two-way ANOVA. Because our current purpose is to help you to read the data table and to understand how a given F links up to the means displayed within it, we are not going to focus on any conceptual or actual statistical calculations. We will get to these respective concerns in a later section on notation and formulas, as well as a sample problem that is analyzed from start to finish. Data analytic strategy, then, is the important issue here—we will get to the statistical matters a little later.

Table 12.1 Average Number of Attempts to Solve First Insoluble Puzzle as a Function of Noise Predictability and Noise Level

Factor A—Noise Predictability		Factor B—Noise Level		
		Loud (B₁)	**Soft (B₂)**	*Predictability Average*
	Random (A₁)	3.67	9.60	6.64
	Fixed (A₂)	18.55	19.90	19.23
	Noise Average	11.11	14.75	12.93

Note: Data are drawn from Table 3 in Glass et al. (1969, p. 204).

To begin, an advantage of the two-way ANOVA is its ability to isolate the effects of one independent variable from the other, a process that identifies what is called a *main effect* for each independent variable.

KEY TERM   A **main effect** occurs when an independent variable has an overall and significant effect on a dependent measure. A *main effect* is likely to exist when there are mean differences between or among the levels of a factor.

Take a look at the far right column of two means in Table 12.1. These means represent the effect of factor A (noise predictability) on the number of tries participants made to solve the puzzle. What do we know? Participants exposed to the random noise ($\overline{X}_{A_1}$ = 6.64) made fewer attempts than those who heard the noise in the fixed pattern ($\overline{X}_{A_2}$ = 19.23). The difference between these means indicates that there was *a main effect for noise predictability*—unpredictable noise was more frustrating for the women than predictable noise. Of course, this main effect would only be considered a reliable one if the aforementioned F ratio for factor A (i.e., F_A) reached statistical significance. If the means were the same or similar—and the resulting F ratio was close to 1.00—then no main effect for noise predictability would be present, and any superficial mean differences would be attributed to sampling error or other random variation.

Please take note of one other important fact: In examining the main effect for noise predictability, we have collapsed across the noise level factor B (see Table 12.1). In other words, in order to determine the marginal means for noise predictability, we had to take the average of cells A_1B_1 and A_1B_2 (i.e., $\overline{X}_{A_1}$) as well as the average of cells A_2B_1 and A_2B_2 (i.e., $\overline{X}_{A_2}$). No information regarding factor B (noise level) is lost in the process of examining the main effect for factor A (noise predictability)—we are merely interested in isolating the effects of factor A before examining factor B.

Now, what about factor B? This time, we will be collapsing *downward* across factor A—noise predictability—in order to examine whether noise level has any influence on tolerance for frustration. Look at the bottom row of marginal means in Table 12.1. As you can see, there also appears to be a main effect for factor B (noise level), though the magnitude of the mean difference is more modest than that for factor A. Women who heard the loud noise ($\overline{X}_{B_1}$ = 11.11) were frustrated more easily than those who heard the soft noise ($\overline{X}_{B_2}$ = 14.75). Once again, we say there appears to be a main effect because of the mean difference—note the importance of linking the means in question to participants' behavior—but we cannot be sure unless we determined that the F ratio for factor B (F_B) was statistically significant.

Because each main effect represents the independent effect of one independent variable—here noise predictability and level—it is as if you conducted two separate experiments. In fact, this is precisely one of the advantages I raised earlier: one experiment reveals that predictability matters where tolerance is concerned (i.e., the main effect for factor A) and another suggests that noise level, too, affects performance (i.e., the main effect for factor B). Fortuitously, however, we discover these two effects by performing only one experiment!

Although these two main effects are informative, they can be *qualified* by the presence of an interaction between the two variables in the experiment. As we will see, an interactive effect between two variables—here, noise predictability and noise level—actually supersedes the simpler information disclosed by the ANOVA's two main effects. There are several issues to consider when looking for an *interaction*. Let's get a precise definition out of the way first, and then consider whether one exists in the data from the experiment performed by Glass and colleagues (1969). Recall that an interaction results from some unique combination of the independent variables and their effects on a dependent measure.

KEY TERM   A statistical **interaction** involves the combined effect of two or more factors on a dependent variable, one that is independent of the separate effects of the two or more factors. In a two-way ANOVA, an A $\times$ B *interaction* exists when the effect of one factor depends on the level of the second factor. A statistically significant interaction between two or more variables qualifies the results identified by one or more main effects.

Take another look at Table 12.1. This time, we are interested in the four cell means shown *inside* the table because the focus is on whether the two variables affect one another in some unique fashion. The easiest way to begin to determine if an interaction exists is to plot the data. A simple plot of the four cell means is shown in Figure 12.2. The mean number of puzzle solving attempts, a quantitative scale, is noted on the Y axis, while the second index—loud noise versus soft noise (i.e., factor B)—appears on the X axis (the choice of placing factor A or B on this axis is an arbitrary one). The upper line graph in Figure 12.2 links the two-cell means (loud and soft) reflecting predictable noise. This line reveals something interesting about the predictable means—the cell means are very similar (i.e., 18.55 and 19.90), so the line connecting the means is almost level. In the presence of the fixed noise, then, level of the noise did not seem to affect the number of attempts to solve the puzzles. The cell means for unpredictable noise (loud and soft) are shown in the lower line graph. This line has a relatively steep slope, one indicating that fewer attempts occurred when the unpredictable noise was loud than when it was soft.

Is there an interaction between factors A and B? The accurate way to determine whether the F ratio for the A $\times$ B interaction is statistically significant, of course, involves comparing its value to an established critical value. There is a quicker way to estimate the likelihood that an interaction is present, however—simply examine the two lines shown in Figure 12.2 and then answer one simple question: *Are the lines parallel?* If the answer is "yes, the lines *are* parallel," then there is not likely to be an interaction between the two variables. If the lines are *not* parallel, however—they either intersect with one another at some point or they could intersect with one another if their respective lengths were extended— then an interaction is probably present. The parallel test is a quick guide for examining obtained data and then making an educated guess as to whether an interactive relationship exists between the variables.

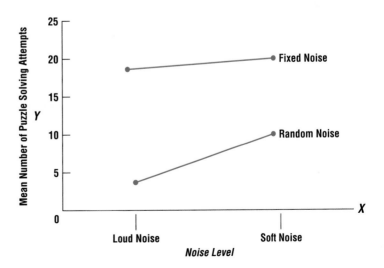

Figure 12.2   Graph of Cell Means from Table 12.1

Note: Graph of tolerance for frustration means from Table 12.1. Higher means indicate more tolerance for frustration (i.e., participant attempts to solve first insoluble puzzle).

▽

Plotting cell means in a line graph can suggest whether an interaction is present: parallel lines = no interaction, whereas nonparallel lines = potential interaction.

Based on this quick guide to reading the nonparallel line graph shown in Figure 12.2, we can say that there appears to be an interaction between noise level and noise predictability. Specifically, Glass and colleagues (1969) found that the number of attempts to solve the insoluble puzzle was greater than when the noise was soft than when it was loud—but this relationship held only when the noise was unpredictable. When the noise was predictable, the number of attempts was relatively high, between an average of 18 and 20 tries, regardless of the noise intensity (see the cell means in Table 12.1 and the graph in Figure 12.2). Changing the noise predictability altered the relationship between noise intensity and the attempts to solve the puzzle—thus, noise intensity and noise predictability interacted with one another. As noted earlier, then, the presence of this interaction qualifies—limits the interpretive power—of the two main effects. We know more about people's tolerance for frustration reactions based on the interaction between noise predictability and noise level than considering the effects of either variable in isolation.

If no interaction were present, the simple plot of the means might have looked like any one of the line graphs shown in the top row of Figure 12.3. Each line in a given pair is parallel to the other, thereby indicating the absence of any interaction (see the top row of Figure 12.3). The bottom row of Figure 12.3, however, illustrates some other possible interaction patterns. Each of these line graphs suggests the presence of an interaction (note that some of the lines actually cross over or connect with one another—others do not cross but would eventually if the lines were extended). Naturally, many other graphic patterns illustrating the presence or absence of interactions are also possible. The examples presented in Figure 12.3 are suggestive, not exhaustive.

Any two-way ANOVA will test three separate hypotheses—one for factor A, another for B, as well as one for the A × B interaction. Each of these hypothesis tests is independent of the others, which means that the result of any one of the tests is not related to the outcome of the other two. In other words, the results of any two-way ANOVA

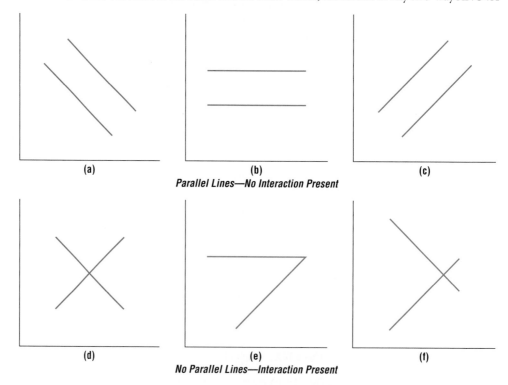

Figure 12.3   Some Line Graphs Illustrating the Presence or Absence of Interaction Between Hypothetical Variables A and B

can display several combinations of significant or nonsignificant main effects and interactions. In the present example, we found a main effect for factors A and B, and an A $\times$ B interaction. We could just as easily have found a main effect for A, none for B, and no interaction. How many possible combinations of present or absent main effects and interactions exist? Think about it: If we have three effects with two levels (i.e., effect present or effect absent) each, how many possible combinations are there? That's right—there are eight (i.e., 2 $\times$ 2 $\times$ 2; see also Data Box 12.A).

Figure 12.4 presents four data tables illustrating means that do or do not yield main effects and interactions. Please take a few minutes and examine these data tables to make certain that you know how to spot main effects, and to plot and identify interactions. We will learn to read and take apart data tables like these using a more advanced technique later in this chapter's *Project Exercise*. In the meantime, remember that a thorough data analyst will always examine each and every effect in a two-way ANOVA. Any significant main effect must yield, however, to the more detailed interpretation offered by a significant interaction (see Data Box 12.B).

Statistical Assumptions of the Two-Factor ANOVA

The statistical assumptions underlying any two-way ANOVA are the same as those associated with the one-way ANOVA (see chapter 11) and the *t* test (see chapter 10). The assumptions are that:

- Data analyzed by a two-way ANOVA are based on either an interval or a ratio scale (i.e., means can be computed from the data).
- The data within each sample are either (a) randomly or (b) independently sampled.
- The parent populations from which data samples—responses to a dependent measure—are drawn are assumed to be normal.
- The parent populations from which samples are drawn have equal variances (homogeneity of variance criterion).

Similar to the one-way ANOVA, the two-way ANOVA is a robust statistical test. Even when the normality assumptions or need for equal variance is violated, the two-way ANOVA can still provide relatively reliable results. Whenever possible, of course, acquiring larger sample sizes helps to support these assumptions.

Although it is not technically an assumption—more of a goal, really—we can add:

- The ANOVA design should be fully factorial (i.e., all possible combinations between the two independent variables are represented by distinct experimental conditions), and each cell in the design should have the same number of participants represented within it. If possible, desirable, or necessary, the membership in any given cell should have equal representation by male and female participants.

Hypotheses, Notation, and Steps for Performing for the Two-Way ANOVA

How do we present the null and alternative hypotheses for the two main effects and the interaction found in any two-way ANOVA? We proceed really no differently than we have done for any other inferential statistical test, notably the one-way ANOVA, of course. We will briefly present the null and alternative hypotheses for each of the three effects provided by any two-way ANOVA. For continuity and ease of understanding, the Glass et al. (1969) study's design will provide some context for our hypotheses; indeed, you may want to turn back to examine the data in Table 12.1 as you review each one.

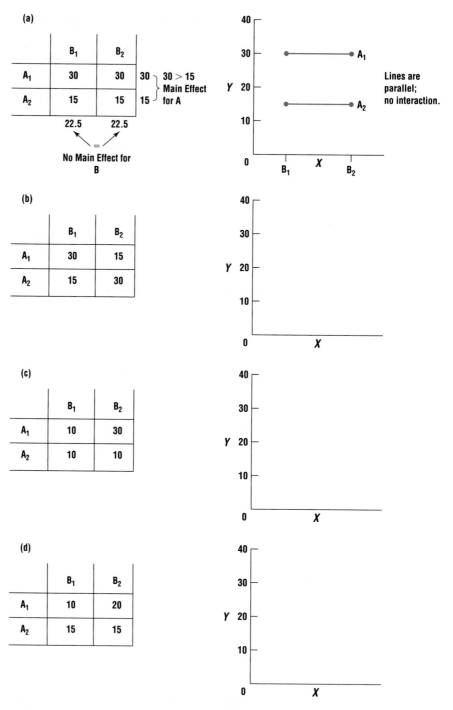

Figure 12.4 Reading Data Tables for Main Effects and Interactions

Four data sets illustrating the presence or absence of main effects and interactions for studies involving two independent variables are shown above. The numbers in each cell of a table represent the mean values found within a condition. To illustrate the task involved, the first data table (a) is done for you. Determine whether each of the remaining three tables have a main effect for A, one for B, and an interaction.

DATA BOX 12.B

Interpretation Qualification: Interactions Supersede Main Effects

What happens when both main effects and the interaction in a two-way ANOVA are significant? How do we go about reporting the results? Are the main effects as important as the interaction?

Statistically speaking, a significant interaction *qualifies*—that is, modifies or limits—any conclusions drawn from either of the separate main effects in a two-way ANOVA. How so? Consider the Glass et al. (1969) tolerance for frustration results for a moment. We know that relatively fewer attempts were made when the noise was loud than when it was soft (main effect for factor B), just as we know that fewer tries took place when the noise was random than when it was fixed (main effect for factor A) (see Table 12.1). Despite the fact that these two main effects provide a clear and relatively concise portrayal of the participants' behavior, we know still more when we examine the interaction between them. The interaction revealed that noise level only mattered when it was unpredictable—tolerance for frustration was lowest in the presence of loud noise—but not when it was predictable (i.e., the number of attempts for the loud and soft noise conditions were approximately equal) (see Figure 12.2). Thus, we know more about both variables when they interact together, much more than is apparent in the information provided by either main effect.

As Harris (1998) put it, a significant interaction invites us to interpret results by reporting that "it all depends" (p. 419). Any effect of factor A must be understood in terms of the level of factor B, and any effect of factor B is dependent on the level of factor A. Here, then, are some rules to follow when reviewing the results of a two-way ANOVA: *Report any and all significant main effects and any interactions, but remember that a significant interaction captures more of the available information than either or both of the main effects.* Thus, the more complex relationship revealed by a significant interaction should be the focus of any discussion—consideration of either or both main effects must be subordinate to that given to the interaction. When an interaction is not significant, emphasize the results provided by the significant main effect(s) and then speculate about why an interaction was not found. Keep in mind, too, that researchers do not necessarily always want to find an interaction—it all depends on the theory or hypothesis they are testing.

The null hypothesis for factor A (noise predictability) is that there is no difference between the effects of random or fixed noise on tolerance for frustration, or:

$$H_0: \mu_{A_1} = \mu_{A_2}.$$

The alternative hypothesis, then, is that predictability *would* matter, a between-group relationship that can be portrayed as nondirectional,

$$H_1: \mu_{A_1} \neq \mu_{A_2},$$

or directional—where, for example, random noise might be predicted to lead to fewer tries than noise presented at a fixed interval:

$$H_1: \mu_{A_1} < \mu_{A_2}.$$

In turn, the null hypothesis for factor B (noise level) is that noise level has no effect on people's tolerance for frustration:

$$H_0: \mu_{B_1} = \mu_{B_2}.$$

As was true for factor A, the alternative hypothesis for the effect of loud versus soft noise on the number of attempts to solve the puzzle can be presented as nondirectional or directional (i.e., loud noise leads to fewer tries than soft noise):

$$H_1: \mu_{B_1} \neq \mu_{B_2},$$
$$H_1: \mu_{B_1} < \mu_{B_2}.$$

Where the hypothesis for the A $\times$ B interaction is concerned, we could specify some particular pattern of results involving the two variables. It usually makes more sense, though, to be general where both the null and the alternative hypothesis is concerned, as in:

H_0: The effect of one factor is not dependent on the levels of the other factor.

H_1: The effect of one factor depends on the levels of the other factor.

The notation and formulas used to perform a two-way ANOVA are virtually identical to those used for the one-way ANOVA calculations in chapter 11. The goal is to identify and partition the variance attributable to each of the two main effects (A and B), the interaction (A $\times$ B), and the within-group or error variance. Each of these variance estimates is found by carving up the total sums of squares based on the two-way ANOVA (see Data Box 12.C):

$$SS_{\text{total}} = SS_A + SS_B + SS_{A \times B} + SS_{\text{within}}.$$

In addition, the degrees of freedom for each of the variance estimates must also be determined. All of this information will be placed into a two-way ANOVA source table, a convenient method for organizing and interpreting the obtained F ratios from any investigation. Keep in mind that the notation and formulas presented here are but one of several methods available to perform a two-way ANOVA; other writers and texts present alternative approaches that will yield the same answers.

1. **Calculate the total sum of squares.** Prior to assigning variation to main effects, an interaction, or an error term, we need to determine the total sum of squares. Here is the computation formula for SS_{total}:

   [12.1.1]
   $$SS_{\text{total}} = \sum X_{ijk}^2 - \frac{(\sum X_{ijk})^2}{N},$$

   where i refers to the number of a given participant (e.g., participant 2), j identifies the level of factor A (i.e., 1 = random noise and 2 = fixed noise), and k identifies the level of factor B (i.e., 1 = loud noise and 2 = soft noise). The content and mechanics of formula [12.1.1] are no different than any other formula we have previously used to find the total sum of squares—we are just highlighting two independent variables as well as the number of a participant. The formula directs us to (a) square and then sum all of the raw scores in the data ($\sum X_{ijk}^2$); (b) and to then sum all of the raw scores, square them (($\sum X_{ijk})^2$), and then divide the product by the total number of available observations or participants (N). As was true for the one-way ANOVA, the second half of the equation for the total sum of squares— (b)—(i.e., $(\sum X_{ijk})^2 / N$) is referred to as the *correction term* (Harris, 1998), and it is subtracted from the product found in (a) (see [12.1.1]).

   The degrees of freedom associated with the total variance is found by

   [12.2.1]
   $$df_{\text{total}} = N - 1.$$

2. **Calculate the between-group variance estimate for factor A.** In order to calculate the variance estimate for factor A, we first need to determine the sum of squares for A using:

$$[12.3.1] \qquad SS_A = \sum \left[\frac{(\sum X_j)^2}{n_j} \right] - \frac{(\sum X_{ijk})^2}{N}.$$

This formula prescribes that (a) the observations within each level j of factor A are summed and then squared $((\sum X_j)^2)$, and that this result is then divided by the number of observations or participants within that level of factor A (n_j). Please note that the n of each level j of factor A might differ. In turn, each of the resulting products is summed—if factor A had three levels, for example, then all three products would be summed $(\sum [(\sum X_j)^2/n_j])$. Once we know the product of (a), then we can subtract (b) the correction term (i.e., the same numerical value from step 1) from it (see formula [12.3.1]).

The degrees of freedom for factor A are determined by:

$$[12.4.1] \qquad df_A = j - 1,$$

where j is the total number of levels found in factor A.

The mean square or variance estimate for factor A is then based on:

$$[12.5.1] \qquad MS_A = \frac{SS_A}{df_A}.$$

3. **Calculate the between-group variance estimate for factor B.** The between-group variance for factor B is calculated by the same logic used to find the sum of squares, degrees of freedom, and mean square for factor A. Only the notation for the sum of squares for B differs slightly, as k denotes the levels of factor B:

$$[12.6.1] \qquad SS_B = \sum \left[\frac{(\sum X_k)^2}{n_k} \right] - \frac{(\sum X_{ijk})^2}{N}.$$

This time, of course, we are collapsing downwards across factor A in order to calculate the necessary components for B.

The degrees of freedom for factor B are equal to:

$$[12.7.1] \qquad df_B = k - 1,$$

where k refers to the total number of levels in factor B.

The mean square or variance estimate for factor B, then, is known by:

$$[12.8.1] \qquad MS_B = \frac{SS_B}{df_B}.$$

4. **Calculate the variance estimate for the interaction.** Calculating the interaction sum of squares is only slightly more complicated than either of the main effect estimates. Here is the formula:

$$[12.9.1] \qquad SS_{A \times B} = \sum \left[\frac{(\sum X_{jk})^2}{n_{jk}} \right] - \frac{(\sum X_{ijk})^2}{N} - (SS_A + SS_B).$$

This looks like quite a bit of work, but there is actually not much calculation here because the values for two thirds of the formula were determined earlier. Notice, for example, that we already know the (b) correction term—the middle of formula [12.9.1]—and the (c) respective sum of squares for factors A and B from the two previous calculations. All that we really need to calculate is the first third of the equation. Notice that the first part of formula [12.9.1] indicates that we should (a) take the sum of the observations for each cell in the design $(\sum X_{jk})$, square each sum (i.e., $(\sum X_{jk})^2$), and then divide each squared sum by the number of observations found in the appropriate cell (n_{jk}). The resulting products representing each cell of the design are then summed ($\sum [(\sum X_{jk})^2 / n_{jk})]$) together, and the rest of the equation can be solved (i.e., the [b] correction term and the [c] sum of squares for the two main effects are subtracted from the product of [a]).

The degrees of freedom for the interaction are based on:

[12.10.1]
$$df_{A \times B} = (j - 1)(k - 1),$$

where j and k refer to the total number of levels of factors A and B, respectively.

The mean square or variance estimate for the interaction is calculated using:

[12.11.1]
$$MS_{A \times B} = \frac{SS_{A \times B}}{df_{A \times B}}.$$

5. **Calculate the within-group or error variance estimate.** The within-group or error variance estimate is not difficult to determine, especially because we already know the values of both its components:

[12.12.1]
$$SS_{within} = \sum X_{ijk}^2 - \sum \left[\frac{(\sum X_{jk})^2}{n_{jk}} \right].$$

We can complete the first half of formula (a) by inserting the value for $\sum X_{ijk}^2$, which was calculated back in step 1. Similarly, the second half of the formula (b), $\sum [(\sum X_{jk})^2 / n_{jk})]$, can be found in step 4. We need only subtract (b) from (a) (see [12.12.1].

The degrees of freedom for the within-group variance estimate are equal to:

[12.13.1]
$$df_{within} = N - c,$$

where c refers to the total number of cells in the research design. In a 2 × 2 design, for example, c is equal to 4 (recall Data Box 12.A).

The mean square for within-groups or error term is based on:

[12.14.1]
$$MS_{within} = \frac{SS_{within}}{df_{within}}.$$

6. **Calculating the F ratios for the main effects and the interaction.** The final calculations for the two-way ANOVA involve the F ratios for the two main effects (factors A and B), and the A × B interaction. These calculations entail dividing the appropriate mean square for each of the three separate effects by the mean square representing the within-groups variance estimate. Thus, the F ratio for factor A is equal to:

[12.15.1]
$$F_A = \frac{MS_A}{MS_{within}}.$$

The F ratio for factor B, then, is known by:

[12.16.1]
$$F_B = \frac{MS_B}{MS_{within}}.$$

Finally, the F ratio for the interaction between factors A and B is determined by:

[12.17.1]
$$F_{A \times B} = \frac{MS_{A \times B}}{MS_{within}}.$$

Naturally, all of these calculations are systematically entered into a source table designed for the two-way ANOVA. We will complete one from start to finish in the next

Table 12.2   A Two-Way ANOVA Source Table with Symbolic Entries

Source	Sum of Squares	df	Mean Square	F	p
Between groups					
Factor A	SS_A	df_A	MS_A	$\dfrac{MS_A}{MS_{within}}$	.05
Factor B	SS_B	df_B	MS_B	$\dfrac{MS_B}{MS_{within}}$	.05
A × B	$SS_{A \times B}$	$df_{A \times B}$	$MS_{A \times B}$	$\dfrac{MS_{A \times B}}{MS_{within}}$	.05
Within groups	SS_{within}	df_{within}	MS_{within}		
Total	SS_{total}	df_{total}			

section of the chapter. In the meantime, however, it will be good preparation for you to examine one that includes all of the symbolic entries we just reviewed. Table 12.2 contains these symbolic entries and, as was true for the one-way ANOVA source table, the calculations build from the left to the right, from the sum of squares for each effect to the three resulting F ratios. This table can serve as a resource to remind you where a particular calculation is placed. We will review the simple error checks you can perform as you proceed through a two-way source table in the next section, as we perform a two-way ANOVA from start to finish.

Knowledge Base

1. List the reasons it is sometimes desirable to manipulate more than one independent variable.
2. How many conditions would a 3 × 4 design have? A 2 × 2 design?
3. How many main effects and interactions does a two-way ANOVA provide?
4. What is a quick method to determine if two variables interact with one another?

Answers

1. *Economy* of time, energy, resources; *efficiency,* as more than one question can be addressed; *elegance* of design; *generality of effects,* which leads to more comprehensive portrayals of behavior; *interaction of variables,* such that one independent variable changes at different levels of another independent variable.
2. A 3 × 4 design would have 12 separate conditions. A 2 × 2 design has 4 separate conditions.
3. A two-way ANOVA provides two main effects—one for factor A, the other for factor B—as well as one interaction between factor A and B.
4. Plot the cell means in a line graph. If the two lines are parallel, there is no interaction. If the lines are not parallel (i.e., they intersect or could intersect), then an interaction may be present.

The Effects of Anxiety and Ordinal Position on Affiliation: A Detailed Example of a Two-Way ANOVA

The late social psychologist, Stanley Schachter, conducted a detailed series of studies examining the psychology of affiliation, people's desire to be in close proximity to or

DATA BOX 12.C

The General Linear Model for the Two-Way ANOVA

When it was first introduced in chapter 11, the general linear model (GLM) was described as another way to think about partitioning the variance in the one-way ANOVA (see Data Box 11.C). As you will recall, the novelty of the GLM is that it enables us to think about the component parts of a single observation within some research design. The GLM's logic can also be extended to the two-way ANOVA. Thus far in this chapter, we have grown accustomed to partitioning the variation in a two-way ANOVA into the following components:

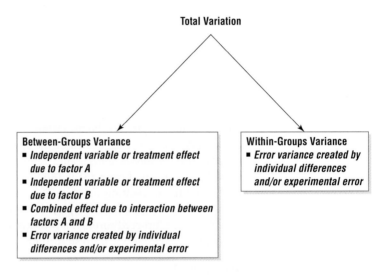

Using the GLM, we can think of any participant's score obtained in a research project as being based upon this formulation:

$$X_{ijk} = \mu + \alpha_j + \beta_k + \alpha\beta_{jk} + \varepsilon_{ijk},$$

where

X_{ijk} = the score of one person within one cell (combined treatment condition).

The i refers to an individual observation, the j is the particular level of factor A, and the k is the level of factor B.

μ = the mean of the population mean of the domain of interest.
α_j = effects due to a specific level of factor A.
β_k = effects due to a specific level of factor B.
$\alpha\beta_{jk}$ = effects due to the interaction between factors A and B.
ε_{ijk} = random error caused by individual differences and experimental error.

contact with others (Schachter, 1959). His research examined a variety of situational and personal variables influencing the degree to which people prefer the company of others, particularly when they feel under duress. Using a variation of one Schachter's studies and some hypothetical data, we will illustrate the utility of the two-way ANOVA for data analysis.

Schachter's basic paradigm entailed presenting research participants with an anxiety-producing communication regarding an experiment they were to take part in, and then observing whether they preferred to wait alone or with others (i.e., engage in affiliation) who would be undergoing the same experience. In general, Schachter found that the desire to affiliate was stronger when participants felt a high rather than a low degree of anxiety about the upcoming experiment. To examine individual differences in affiliation, Schachter then considered a second variable—birth order—positing that firstborn children would show a stronger desire to affiliate relative to later-born children. Why? Casual observation as well as empirical research suggests that parents dote on firstborn children (a group that includes "only" children, as well) more than later-born children, possibly creating a pronounced degree of dependence in the process (e.g., Schachter, 1959).

Imagine that a group of 24 college-aged men (run in groups of 6) sign up to take part in an experiment. Half of the participants are firstborn children, the other half are the second- or later-born children within their families. Once a participant arrives at the psychology laboratory, he and the other members of his group are told they will be taking part in an experiment on the effects of electric shock. When the preliminary instructions are over, participants in the high-anxiety condition are informed by a somewhat authoritarian experimenter that, "I do want to be honest with you and tell you that these shocks will be quite painful but, of course, they will do no permanent damage" (Schachter, 1959, p. 13). From a somewhat friendlier researcher, the low-anxiety participants learn that, "what you feel will not in any way be painful. It will resemble more a tickle or a tingle than anything unpleasant" (pp. 13–14).

Participants were then told that they would wait 10 minutes before the actual experiment would begin, and that they were welcome to wait alone or with others. The prediction, of course, is that participants in the high anxiety condition would want to wait with others rather than be alone (i.e., "misery loves company"), and that firstborns would have a generally higher affiliative desire than later-borns. To see if these predictions were borne out, the participants then completed the main dependent measure, a simple rating scale that looked like this:

1	*2*	*3*	*4*	*5*
I very much prefer being alone.	I prefer being alone.	I don't care very much.	I prefer being together with others.	I very much prefer being together with others.

Participants circled the number corresponding to how they felt about being alone or with others. The data resulting from the four experimental conditions are shown in Table 12.3. Please take a moment and familiarize yourself with these data, as we will be using them to complete the subsequent calculations for the two-way ANOVA.

What does a preliminary review of the data in Table 12.3 reveal? By eyeballing the main effect for birth order, participant reactions appear to be consistent with the hypothesis: firstborns ($\overline{X}_{A_1} = 3.67$) wanted to wait with others more than later-borns ($\overline{X}_{A_2} = 2.25$)(see Table 12.3). Similarly, participants exposed to the high anxiety communication ($\overline{X}_{B_1} = 3.58$) rated their desire to wait with others as higher than the low anxiety group ($\overline{X}_{B_2} = 2.33$) (see Table 12.3). The means corresponding to the interaction are in the four cells inside Table 12.3. Figure 12.5 shows a simple plot of these cell means. Because the lines are more or less parallel, we anticipate that no interaction is present as we begin the calculations for the two-way ANOVA. We will see if this speculation is borne out by the data analysis.

As usual, we will follow the four steps for testing hypotheses using the ANOVA outlined in Table 11.4 (which is a revised version of Table 9.2). Step 1 involves identifying the null and alternative hypotheses for the two main effects and the interaction. As you review these three sets of hypotheses, please make certain you understand how and

Table 12.3   Hypothetical Data for Birth Order, Anxiety, and Affiliation Study

Factor A (Birth Order)	Factor B (Anxiety) High (B_1)	Factor B (Anxiety) Low (B_2)	Marginal Means
Firstborn (A_1)	$X_{111} = 5, X_{111}^2 = 25$ $X_{211} = 4, X_{211}^2 = 16$ $X_{311} = 5, X_{311}^2 = 25$ $X_{411} = 3, X_{411}^2 = 9$ $X_{511} = 5, X_{511}^2 = 25$ $X_{611} = 4, X_{611}^2 = 16$	$X_{112} = 3, X_{112}^2 = 9$ $X_{212} = 2, X_{212}^2 = 4$ $X_{312} = 4, X_{312}^2 = 16$ $X_{412} = 4, X_{412}^2 = 16$ $X_{512} = 3, X_{512}^2 = 9$ $X_{612} = 2, X_{612}^2 = 4$	
	$\sum X_{11} = 26, \sum X_{11}^2 = 116$ $n_{11} = 6$ $\overline{X}_{11} = 4.33$	$\sum X_{12} = 18, \sum X_{12}^2 = 58$ $n_{12} = 6$ $\overline{X}_{12} = 3.00$	$\sum X_{A_1} = 44$ $n_{A_1} = 12$ $\overline{X}_{A_1} = 3.67$
Later-born (A_2)	$X_{121} = 3, X_{121}^2 = 9$ $X_{221} = 2, X_{221}^2 = 4$ $X_{321} = 4, X_{231}^2 = 16$ $X_{421} = 3, X_{241}^2 = 9$ $X_{521} = 3, X_{251}^2 = 9$ $X_{621} = 2, X_{261}^2 = 4$	$X_{122} = 1, X_{122}^2 = 1$ $X_{222} = 2, X_{222}^2 = 4$ $X_{322} = 2, X_{322}^2 = 4$ $X_{422} = 3, X_{422}^2 = 9$ $X_{522} = 1, X_{522}^2 = 1$ $X_{622} = 1, X_{622}^2 = 1$	
	$\sum X_{21} = 17, \sum X_{21}^2 = 51$ $n_{21} = 6$ $\overline{X}_{21} = 2.83$	$\sum X_{22} = 10, \sum X_{22}^2 = 20$ $n_{22} = 6$ $\overline{X}_{22} = 1.67$	$\sum X_{A_2} = 27$ $n_{A_2} = 12$ $\overline{X}_{A_2} = 2.25$
Marginal means	$\sum X_{B_1} = 43$ $n_{B_1} = 12$ $\overline{X}_{B_1} = 3.58$	$\sum X_{B_2} = 28$ $n_{B_2} = 12$ $\overline{X}_{B_2} = 2.33$	$\sum X_{ijk} = 71$ $N = 24$ $\overline{X}_{jk} = 2.96$

Additional Preliminary Calculations for the Two-Way ANOVA
$\sum X_{ijk} = X_{11} + X_{12} + X_{21} + X_{22} = (26 + 18 + 17 + 10) = 71$
$\sum X_{ijk}^2 = X_{11}^2 + X_{12}^2 + X_{21}^2 + X_{22}^2 = (166 + 58 + 51 + 20) = 245$

why they match up with the conceptual discussion of the means we just had. The null and alternative hypotheses for birth order (factor A) are:

$$H_0: \mu_{A_1} = \mu_{A_2},$$
$$H_1: \mu_{A_1} > \mu_{A_2}.$$

In turn, the null and alternative hypotheses for the anxiety communication (factor B) are:

$$H_0: \mu_{B_1} = \mu_{B_2},$$
$$H_1: \mu_{B_1} > \mu_{B_2}.$$

Finally, the null and alternative hypotheses for the A $\times$ B interaction entail:

H_0: The effect of one factor is not dependent on the levels of the other factor.

H_1: The effect of one factor depends on the levels of the other factor.

Step 2 from Table 11.4 requires us to select a significance level for rejecting the null hypotheses for the two-way ANOVA. Following convention, we rely on a p value of .05.

As we begin step 3—the actual calculation of the sums of squares, degrees of freedom, variance estimates (mean squares), and the three F ratios—we acknowledge that there is quite a bit of procedure to be followed and information to be organized. The *mise en place* philosophy must be followed to the letter—any and all calculations we

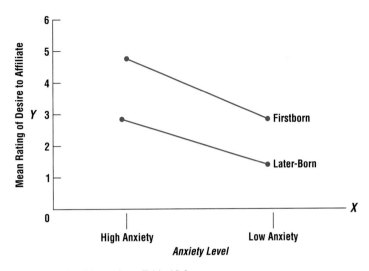

Figure 12.5   Graph of Cell Means from Table 12.3

Note: Graph of mean rating of desire to affiliate on 1 to 5 rating scale, where higher numbers reflect a greater desire to be with others.

perform and information we track must be neatly arranged. To that end, Table 12.4 represents the completed two-way ANOVA source table for the birth order and anxiety data. Please refer back to it as we proceed with each step in each calculation—that way, you will see where each entry is placed and how it fits into the calculations of the three F ratios. I will draw your attention to a few error checks that will help us avoid common mistakes along the way.

One last reminder: Please read the following pages carefully and critically so that you know where each and every number came from and why—the moment you feel uncertain or confused, stop where you are and backtrack immediately until you identify where and why you got lost. I realize that you will be tempted to speed read the next few pages, maybe even skip them, with an eye to reading them "later" when you have to do so in order to complete homework problems. Fight this temptation—the time and effort you expend now will save you time in the long run—and you will also have the satisfaction of knowing what you are doing now rather than having some doubts later.

As always, we begin by calculating the *sum of squares of the total variation* and then the accompanying *degrees of freedom.* I will be using the formulas introduced earlier in the chapter, hence I will be repeating formula numbers you encountered earlier. The total sum of squares (SS_{total}) is equal to:

[12.1.1] $$SS_{\text{total}} = \sum X_{ijk}^2 - \frac{(\sum X_{ijk})^2}{N}.$$

Remember that the value of $\sum X_{ijk}^2$ is found by squaring the individual observations in each of the four cells in the design (see the squared values of X and the resulting $\sum X^2$ values representing each of the cells in Table 12.3). The four $\sum X^2$ values are then summed to form $\sum X_{ijk}^2$, which is equal to 245 (this calculation is shown in the preliminary calculations section at the bottom of Table 12.3). The value of $\sum X_{ijk}$ is also obtained from Table 12.3, as the four $\sum X$ values are summed and found to be equal to 71 (the calculation for this sum appears at the bottom of Table 12.3—be sure you see where the values came from in the upper portion of this table). Finally, N is equal to the total number of participants, which we already know is equal to 24 (i.e., 6 participants per cell, and there are 4 cells; see Table 12.3). All of these numbers are then entered into [12.1.1] for:

[12.1.2] $SS_{total} = 245 - \dfrac{(71)^2}{24}$,

[12.1.3] $SS_{total} = 245 - \dfrac{5{,}041}{24}$,

[12.1.4] $SS_{total} = 245 - 210.04$,

[12.1.5] $SS_{total} = 34.96$.

The SS_{total} is entered into the bottom of the second column of Table 12.4, and we proceed to calculate the accompanying degrees of freedom based on the 24 participants in the study:

[12.2.1] $df_{total} = N - 1$,

[12.2.2] $df_{total} = 24 - 1$,

[12.2.3] $df_{total} = 23$.

We then enter the 23 degrees of freedom at the bottom of the third column in Table 12.4.

We now begin to partition the *between-groups variation* by calculating the *sum of squares* for each of the two main effects and the interaction, their respective *degrees of freedom,* and the three separate *variance estimates*. Let's start with the *sum of squares for factor A*, the main effect for birth order, using:

[12.3.1] $SS_A = \sum \left[\dfrac{(\sum X_j)^2}{n_j} \right] - \dfrac{(\sum X_{ijk})^2}{N}$.

Note that the correction term—the second half of the formula (i.e., $(\sum X_{ijk})^2/N$)—was already determined when SS_{total} was calculated previously (see the second half of [12.1.1]); we need not do this math a second time, rather, we can simply insert its known value, 210.04 (this value was found in [12.1.4]). The information for the first half of the formula—the $\sum X$ for each of the two levels of factor A (i.e., $\sum X_{A_1}$ and $\sum X_{A_2}$)— can be drawn from the leftmost column in Table 12.3. Please take careful note of the fact, too, that each level of A is based on 12 observations (n_j), *not* 6 observations, because we are collapsing across the B factor (see Table 12.3):

[12.3.2] $SS_A = \sum \left[\dfrac{(44)^2}{12} \right] + \left[\dfrac{(27)^2}{12} \right] - 210.04$,

[12.3.3] $SS_A = \sum \left(\dfrac{1{,}936}{12} \right) + \left(\dfrac{729}{12} \right) - 210.04$,

[12.3.4] $SS_A = \sum (161.33) + (60.75) - 210.04$,

[12.3.5] $SS_A = 222.08 - 210.04$,

[12.3.6] $SS_A = 12.04$.

The SS_A can now be entered into the upper slot in column 2 of Table 12.4.

The *degrees of freedom* for the sum of squares for factor A are known by:

[12.4.1] $df_A = j - 1$.

Remember, there are two levels (j) to the birth order factor, so:

[12.4.2] $df_A = 2 - 1$,

[12.4.3] $df_A = 1$.

This 1 degree of freedom is entered in the first slot in column 3 of Table 12.4.

Because we know SS_A and df_A, we can also calculate the mean square or variance estimate for birth order (factor A) using:

$$[12.5.1] \qquad MS_A = \frac{SS_A}{df_A}.$$

Please note that in this case the MS_A will be equal to SS_A because df_A is equal to 1 (i.e., a number divided by 1 is equal to that number). By entering the two values we just calculated we find:

$$[12.5.2] \qquad MS_A = \frac{12.04}{1},$$

$$[12.5.3] \qquad MS_A = 12.04.$$

The MS_A is then entered in the first slot of column 4 of Table 12.4. Please do not assume that the degrees of freedom for any factor A will always be equal to 1, as there can be more than two levels to factor A (i.e., $j > 2$).

The calculations for the *sum of squares for factor B*, the main effect for anxiety level, is analogous to those performed for factor A—except that we are collapsing downward across factor A—using:

$$[12.6.1] \qquad SS_B = \sum \left[\frac{(\sum X_k)^2}{n_k} \right] - \frac{(\sum X_{ijk})^2}{N}.$$

Once again, the correction term—the end of the formula—is based on a previous calculation, and each level of factor B will is based on 12—not just 6—observations. The first portion of formula [12.6.1] is based on information provided in the lower margin of Table 12.3, for:

$$[12.6.2] \qquad SS_B = \sum \left[\frac{(43)^2}{12} \right] + \left[\frac{(28)^2}{12} \right] - 210.04,$$

$$[12.6.3] \qquad SS_B = \sum \left(\frac{1,849}{12} \right) + \left(\frac{784}{12} \right) - 210.04,$$

$$[12.6.4] \qquad SS_B = \sum (154.08) + (65.33) - 210.04,$$

$$[12.6.5] \qquad SS_B = 219.41 - 210.04,$$

$$[12.6.6] \qquad SS_B = 9.37.$$

The value of SS_B can now be entered into the second row of column 2 in Table 12.4.

The degrees of freedom for SS_B are calculated using:

$$[12.7.1] \qquad df_B = k - 1,$$

where k is equal to the two levels of factor B:

$$[12.7.2] \qquad df_B = 2 - 1,$$

$$[12.7.3] \qquad df_B = 1.$$

This degree of freedom can be placed in the second row of column 3 in Table 12.4. While we are here, we can quickly calculate the variance estimate (MS_B) for factor B, which will be equal to SS_B because of this 1 degree of freedom:

$$[12.8.1] \qquad MS_B = \frac{SS_B}{df_B},$$

[12.8.2] $MS_B = \dfrac{9.37}{1},$

[12.8.3] $MS_B = 9.37.$

This number for the MS_B is then entered in the second row of column 4 of Table 12.4.

Our next calculation concerns the variance estimate for the A × B interaction. As noted previously, the actual calculation is rather straightforward—we already know two of the terms in the formula—but, as I will show you, there is at least one part of the formula requiring vigilance to prevent a math error. Here is the formula for $SS_{A \times B}$:

[12.9.1] $SS_{A \times B} = \sum \left[\dfrac{(\sum X_{jk})^2}{n_{jk}} \right] - \dfrac{(\sum X_{ijk})^2}{N} - (SS_A + SS_B)$

We can readily enter the known correction term as (b) the second part of the formula, and we can insert the recently calculated sums of squares for the respective main effects (c) at the end of the formula. In order to complete the first part of the formula (a), all that we need to do is to take the sum of each of the four cells in the design, square it, divide the squared value by the number of observations in the cell, and then add the resulting products together. Parts (b) and (c) are then subtracted from (a). As you will see when you check the numerical entries, all of them can be found in Table 12.3:

[12.9.2] $SS_{A \times B} = \sum \left[\dfrac{(26)^2}{6} \right] + \left[\dfrac{(18)^2}{6} \right] + \left[\dfrac{(17)^2}{6} \right]$

$+ \left[\dfrac{(10)^2}{6} \right] - 210.04 - (12.04 + 9.37),$

[12.9.3] $SS_{A \times B} = \sum \left(\dfrac{676}{6} \right) + \left(\dfrac{324}{6} \right) + \left(\dfrac{289}{6} \right) + \left(\dfrac{100}{6} \right) - 210.04 - 21.41.$

Here is the tricky part of the calculation: Treat the last two numbers in the equation (210.04 and 21.41) as negative, so that you *add* the numbers together to form a larger negative number, as in:

[12.9.4] $SS_{A \times B} = \sum \left(\dfrac{676}{6} \right) + \left(\dfrac{324}{6} \right) + \left(\dfrac{289}{6} \right) + \left(\dfrac{100}{6} \right) - 231.45,$

[12.9.5] $SS_{A \times B} = \sum (112.67 + 54 + 48.17 + 16.67) - 231.45,$

[12.9.6] $SS_{A \times B} = 231.51 - 231.45,$

[12.9.7] $SS_{A \times B} = .060.$

The $SS_{A \times B}$ is rather small, confirming our suspicion that little variability is available for a statistical interaction. Before the $SS_{A \times B}$ is entered into Table 12.4, we can also determine the degrees of freedom and the variance estimate for the A × B interaction.

The degrees of freedom are based on:

[12.10.1] $df_{A \times B} = (j - 1)(k - 1),$

where j and k, respectively, refer to the number of levels in factors A and B—each is equal to 2:

[12.10.2] $df_{A \times B} = (2 - 1)(2 - 1),$

[12.10.3] $df_{A \times B} = (1)(1),$

[12.10.4] $df_{A \times B} = 1.$

Due to this single degree of freedom, the $MS_{A \times B}$ will be equal to the $SS_{A \times B}$ following this formula:

[12.11.1] $MS_{A \times B} = \dfrac{SS_{A \times B}}{df_{A \times B}}$,

[12.11.2] $MS_{A \times B} = \dfrac{.060}{1}$,

[12.11.3] $MS_{A \times B} = .060$.

The $MS_{A \times B}$, as well as the 1 degree of freedom, and the $SS_{A \times B}$ are now entered into their proper columns in row 3 of Table 12.4. Please look at row 3 in Table 12.4 now to verify that you understand the rationale behind their placement.

The final set of variance estimate calculations concerns the within-group or error sum of squares. The formula for SS_{within} is:

[12.12.1] $$SS_{within} = \sum X_{ijk}^2 - \sum \left[\dfrac{(\sum X_{jk})^2}{(n_{jk})} \right].$$

Numerical values for both portions of the formula are already known. The first of the formula (a)—the sum of all the squared values of X in the sample ($\sum X_{ijk}^2$)—was calculated when the SS_{total} was determined (see [12.1.1], as well as the additional preliminary calculations at the bottom of Table 12.3). The $\sum X_{ijk}^2$, which is equal to 245, was found by adding the individual $\sum X^2$ from each of the four cells (see Table 12.3). We just calculated the second part of the formula (b)—$\sum [(\sum X_{jk})^2 / n_{jk}]$—when the $SS_{A \times B}$ was identified (see [12.9.1]). The value of $\sum [(\sum X_{jk})^2 / n_{jk}]$, which is equal to 231.51, was found by squaring each of the four $\sum X$ values from Table 12.3, dividing each by the number of observations per cell (i.e., 6), and then summing the resulting products together (see [12.9.2] to [12.9.6]). Taking the values from these prior procedures, we find that:

[12.12.2] $SS_{within} = 245 - 231.51$,

[12.12.3] $SS_{within} = 13.49$.

The accompanying degrees of freedom are:

[12.13.1] $df_{within} = N - c$,

where c is the number of cells or conditions in the research design. Here, there are four (see Table 12.3):

[12.13.2] $df_{within} = 24 - 4$,

[12.13.3] $df_{within} = 20$.

Table 12.4   Two-Way ANOVA Source Table for Birth Order, Anxiety, and Affiliation Data

Source	Sum of Squares	df	Mean Square	F	p
Between groups					
Factor A (birth order)	12.04	1	12.04	17.84	$p < .05^*$
Factor B (anxiety)	9.37	1	9.37	13.88	$p < .05^*$
A × B (birth order × anxiety)	.06	1	.06	.089	$p > .05$
Within groups	13.49	20	.675		
Total	34.96	23			

*Statistically significant effect

The value of MS_{within} is known by dividing the SS_{within} by df_{within}, or:

[12.14.1] $$MS_{within} = \frac{SS_{within}}{df_{within}},$$

[12.14.2] $$MS_{within} = \frac{13.49}{20},$$

[12.14.3] $MS_{within} = .675.$

These three values—SS_{within}, df_{within}, and MS_{within}—are then entered into the respective places in Table 12.4 (see the three entries in row 4).

All that remains is to calculate the three F ratios corresponding to the two main effects and the interaction. Before we perform these calculations, however, we should first verify that we have not made any calculation errors when determining the various sum of squares values or the variances estimates. Here are three quick error checks using the completed two-way ANOVA source table shown in Table 12.4:

By employing any and all error checks, data analysts increase the chance that the observed results are actually correct.

- First, using the entries from Table 12.4, make certain that partitioned sum of squares for the main effects, the interaction, and the error term actually add up to the total sum of squares, or:

$$SS_{total} = SS_A + SS_B + SS_{A \times B} + SS_{within},$$
$$34.96 = (12.04 + 9.37 + .06 + 13.49),$$
$$34.96 = 34.96.$$

In this case, the SS_{total} precisely matched the sum of the partitioned sum of squares values. Keep in mind, however, that some rounding error often occurs—the point is that the SS_{total} and the sum of the remaining sums of squares should be approximately equal to one another.

- Second, be sure that the individual degrees of freedom for the respective variance estimates actually add up to the df_{total} using:

$$df_{total} = df_A + df_B + df_{A \times B} + df_{within},$$
$$23 = (1 + 1 + 1 + 20),$$
$$23 = 23.$$

Once again, our calculations prove to be accurate—the error check is successful.

- A third possible error check involves checking the accuracy of the four variance estimates based on the division of each sum of squares value by its accompanying degrees of freedom. When a 2×2 design is used, each of the degrees of freedom for the main effects and the interaction will be equal to 1 (as noted previously, each SS value will necessarily be the same as its MS value). It is a good idea, however, to verify that the MS_{within} is actually equal to SS_{within}/df_{within}, or:

$$MS_{within} = \frac{SS_{within}}{df_{within}},$$

$$.675 = \frac{13.49}{20},$$

$$.675 = .675.$$

We can now calculate the three F ratios and determine which one, if any, is statistically significant. All the information we need is easily gleaned from the right side of Table 12.4, the far end of which contains space where the F ratios are entered (with the accompanying significance levels, if any).

The F ratio for the main effect of factor A (birth order) is known by:

[12.15.1] $$F_A = \frac{MS_A}{MS_{within}},$$

[12.15.2] $$F_A = \frac{12.04}{.675},$$

[12.15.3] $$F_A = 17.84.$$

The F ratio for the main effect of factor B (anxiety level) is calculated using:

[12.16.1] $$F_B = \frac{MS_B}{MS_{within}},$$

[12.16.2] $$F_B = \frac{9.37}{.675},$$

[12.16.3] $$F_B = 13.88.$$

Finally, the F ratio for the A $\times$ B interaction is calculated, despite the fact that the extremely small magnitude of $SS_{A \times B}$ assures us that the effect will not be a significant one:

[12.17.1] $$F_{A \times B} = \frac{MS_{A \times B}}{MS_{within}},$$

[12.17.2] $$F_{A \times B} = \frac{.060}{.675},$$

[12.17.3] $$F_{A \times B} = .089.$$

To determine whether any of the F ratios reach significance, we first report each one by recording its numerical value and accompanying degrees of freedom—the numerator df corresponds to the effect's variance estimate df (see the first three rows in column 3 in Table 12.4) and the denominator degrees of freedom is the df_{within} (see row 4 in column 3 in Table 12.4), for:

$$F_A(1, 20) = 17.84,$$
$$F_B(1, 20) = 13.88,$$
$$F_{A \times B}(1, 20) = .089.$$

We now turn to Table B.5 (critical values of F) in Appendix B in order to determine the critical value at the .05 level for an F ratio with 1 and 20 degrees of freedom. We locate the column for numerator 1 across the top of Table B.5 and then read down the table's left-most rows until we find the denominator value of 20. When we find the intersection between row and column, we choose the lighter type-faced value of 4.35, which is the .05 critical value (recall step 2). We now compare this number with each of the obtained Fs in order to determine if they equal or exceed it in value, in which case they can be declared significant:

Is $F_A(1, 20) = 17.84 \geq F_{crit}(1, 20) = 4.35$? Yes, *reject* H_0.
Is $F_B(1, 20) = 13.88 \geq F_{crit}(1, 20) = 4.35$? Yes, *reject* H_0.
Is $F_{A \times B}(1, 20) = .089 \geq F_{crit}(1, 20) = 4.35$? No, *accept or retain* H_0.

Thus, the two main effects in the affiliation study reached significance but the interaction between the two variables did not. What do we know? Look back at Table 12.4. We know that there was a main effect for birth order (factor A), such that firstborn participants rated the desire to wait with others ($\overline{X}_{A_1} = 3.67$) as significantly greater than later-born participants ($\overline{X}_{A_2} = 2.25$) (see the marginal means in the far-right side of Table 12.4). There was also a main effect for anxiety level, so that participants in the high anxiety group rated the desire to wait with others ($\overline{X}_{B_1} = 3.58$) as significantly greater than those who heard a less anxiety provoking communication from the experimenter ($\overline{X}_{B_2} = 2.33$) (see the marginal means in the bottom row of Table 12.4). There was no interaction between these two variables, however, as was originally shown by the parallel plots of cell means in Figure 12.5.

Please notice that no post hoc tests are necessary with two-way ANOVA when it is used to analyze a 2×2 research design. All the mean comparisons for the main effect and the interaction are, as it were, "hardwired." We need only to examine the marginal means or the cell means in a table similar to Table 12.4 in order to determine the direction of any effect and whether it is consistent with or in opposition to a relevant hypothesis. We will postpone further interpretation of these data, as well as advice on how to write up the results, until after we consider issues of effect size and the degree of association between the independent variables and the dependent variable in this study.

Effect Size

How can we characterize the effect sizes of the significant results, the main effects, we found? We can use Cohen's (1988) **f**, which was first introduced in chapter 11. Recall that we use **f** to label a significant effect as small (**f** = .10), medium (**f** = .25), or large (**f** = .40). To calculate **f**, we use formulas [11.21.1] and [11.22.1], respectively:

$$\mathbf{f} = \sqrt{\frac{\backslash\eta^2}{1 - \eta^2}},$$

where

$$\eta^2 = \frac{SS_{\text{effect}}}{SS_{\text{total}}}.$$

We are only interested in the effect sizes of the main effect for birth order (factor A) and anxiety level (factor B), as they were both statistically significant. All of the information we need can be drawn from the ANOVA source table in Table 12.4. The effect size for birth order is:

[12.18.1] $$\eta_A^2 = \frac{SS_A}{SS_{\text{total}}},$$

[12.18.2] $$\eta_A^2 = \frac{12.04}{34.96},$$

[12.18.3] $$\eta_A^2 = .34.$$

This value of η_A^2 is then entered into the formula for **f**:

[12.19.1] $$\mathbf{f}_A = \sqrt{\frac{\eta_A^2}{1 - \eta_A^2}},$$

[12.19.2] $$\mathbf{f}_A = \sqrt{\frac{.34}{1 - .34}},$$

[12.19.3] $$\mathbf{f}_A = \sqrt{\frac{.34}{.66}},$$

[12.19.4] $$\mathbf{f}_A = \sqrt{.5152},$$

[12.19.5] $\mathbf{f}_A = .71.$

Thus, the main effect for birth order is quite large.

What about the effect size of anxiety level? We repeat the same analyses, now substituting the symbols for factor B as well as SS_B:

[12.20.1] $\eta_B^2 = \dfrac{SS_B}{SS_{total}},$

[12.20.2] $\eta_B^2 = \dfrac{9.37}{34.96},$

[12.20.3] $\eta_B^2 = .268.$

This value of η_B^2 is then entered into the formula for $\mathbf{f}$:

[12.21.1] $\mathbf{f}_B = \sqrt{\dfrac{\eta_B^2}{1 - \eta_B^2}},$

[12.21.2] $\mathbf{f}_B = \sqrt{\dfrac{.268}{1 - .268}},$

[12.21.3] $\mathbf{f}_B = \sqrt{\dfrac{.268}{.732}},$

[12.21.4] $\mathbf{f}_B = \sqrt{.3661},$

[12.21.5] $\mathbf{f}_B = .61.$

The main effect for anxiety level, too, is quite large.

Estimated Omega-Squared ($\hat{\omega}^2$) for the Two-Way ANOVA

By calculating $\hat{\omega}^2$, we can determine how much variability in the desire to affiliate with others is due to experimental factors like birth order and induced anxiety level. As was true for effect size $\mathbf{f}$, we calculate an $\hat{\omega}^2$ for significant effects only. We can use formula [11.23.1] to do so, which is modified here to reflect that we are not yet specifying which result is being analyzed:

[12.22.1] $\hat{\omega}^2_{result} = \dfrac{df_{result}\,(F_{result} - 1)}{df_{result}\,(F_{result} - 1) + N}.$

The degree of association between birth order (factor A) and affiliative desire, then, would be:

[12.23.1] $\hat{\omega}^2_A = \dfrac{df_A(F_A - 1)}{df_A(F_A - 1) + N}.$

Using information drawn from Table 12.4 we find that:

[12.23.2] $\hat{\omega}^2_A = \dfrac{(1)(17.84 - 1)}{(1)(17.84 - 1) + 24},$

[12.23.3] $\hat{\omega}^2_A = \dfrac{(1)(16.84)}{(1)(16.84) + 24},$

[12.23.4] $\hat{\omega}_A^2 = \dfrac{16.84}{16.84 + 24},$

[12.23.5] $\hat{\omega}_A^2 = \dfrac{16.84}{40.84},$

[12.23.6] $\hat{\omega}_A^2 = .41.$

This statistic suggests that approximately 41% of the variance in the participants' affiliative tendencies are attributable to their birth order.

Where anxiety level (factor B) is concerned, the value of $\hat{\omega}_B^2$ is:

[12.24.1] $\hat{\omega}_B^2 = \dfrac{df_B \, (F_B - 1)}{df_B(F_B - 1) + N}.$

Once again, we draw on numerical information provided in Table 12.4 and complete the formula:

[12.24.2] $\hat{\omega}_B^2 = \dfrac{(1)(13.88 - 1)}{(1)(13.88 - 1) + 24},$

[12.24.3] $\hat{\omega}_B^2 = \dfrac{(1)(12.88)}{(1)(12.88) + 24},$

[12.24.4] $\hat{\omega}_B^2 = \dfrac{12.88}{12.88 + 24},$

[12.24.5] $\hat{\omega}_B^2 = \dfrac{12.88}{36.88},$

[12.24.6] $\hat{\omega}_B^2 = .35.$

About 35% of the variance pertaining to participants' affiliative tendencies, then, can be ascribed to their anxiety level. This variation is not explained by birth order or the interactive effects (which are virtually absent) between birth order and anxiety. We can now take this information, along with the effect size and the main two-way ANOVA results, and report the results in written form.

Writing About the Results of a Two-Way ANOVA

As always, our goal is to follow APA style guidelines and to report the results in a clear, coherent, and consistent manner. Reporting results from a two-way ANOVA is really not much more complicated than reviewing findings from a one-way ANOVA—there are three F ratios to report rather than just one, however. Emphasizing the meaning of the results, recapitulating the hypothesis and, where appropriate, highlighting data in tabular or graphic form, remain important. Tables are especially appropriate when there is a relatively large number of means to contend with, and a simple line graph—especially when an interaction is present—is a good idea, as well. Here is one way to summarize the results of the birth order, anxiety, and affiliation study:

> Schachter (1959) demonstrated that birth order and anxiety both affect the degree to which people seek out the company of others. The present piece of research generally replicated these prior observations with one difference: the participants in the original study were all women, while the present effort involved males exclusively. Using the same research paradigm, first- or later-born men were exposed to a high or low anxiety-provoking communication and then asked to rate the degree to which they preferred to wait alone or to be with others.

Their ratings, which were based on a 1 to 5 rating scale (higher numbers reflect a greater desire to affiliate with others) were analyzed by a 2 (first- vs. later-born) $\times$ 2 (high vs. low anxiety) analysis of variance (ANOVA). Table 1 presents the means separated by birth order and anxiety level. A significant main effect for birth order was found, indicating that as expected, first born men ($M = 3.67$) rated their desire to affiliate as greater than later born men ($M = 2.25$), $F(1, 20) = 17.84$, $p < .01$. The main effect for anxiety level was also significant. Participants who heard the high anxiety communication ($M = 3.58$) wanted to wait with others more than those in the low anxiety condition ($M = 2.33$), $F(1, 20) = 13.99$, $p < .01$. There was no interaction between these two factors, however, $F(1, 20) = .089$, $p = ns$. The effect sizes for birth order ($\mathbf{f} = .71$) and anxiety level ($\mathbf{f} = .61$) were both quite large. The degree of association between the desire to affiliate and birth order ($\hat{\omega}^2 = .41$) and anxiety level ($\hat{\omega}^2 = .35$), were quite strong, as well.

Table 1 Desire to Affiliate as a Function of Birth Order and Anxiety Level

	Anxiety Level		
Birth Order	High	Low	*M*
Firstborn M	4.33	3.00	3.67
SD	(.817)	(.894)	
Later-born M	2.83	1.67	2.25
SD	(.753)	(.817)	
M	3.58	2.33	

Note: Means are based on a 5-point scale. Higher values reflect a greater desire to affiliate with others.

Please notice that I elected *not* to include a line graph of the cell means (but see Figure 12.5) because the interaction did not reach significance. Had an interaction been found, then I would want to draw the reader's attention to it. Instead, I chose to highlight the marginal means when the main effects were reported in the text (see above). There is no one right way to report these or any set of data. As the data analyst, the choice is your own. As you gain experience writing and presenting results, you will acquire intuition about which results to highlight and which ones to downplay a bit—just be sure to be honest and report all of the main results from any multi-factor ANOVA design.

Coda: Beyond 2 × 2 Designs

The lion's share of our discussion of the two-way ANOVA focused on two factors with two levels each. If you will forgive me a small joke, this choice was a calculated one. The 2 $\times$ 2 design is not only ubiquitous in the behavioral science literature, I believe that it is still the best introduction to how to think about and interpret factorial data tables when learning ANOVA. I could have described the analysis of a 2 $\times$ 3 or even a 3 $\times$ 3 design instead, but the clarity and precision associated with the 2 $\times$ 2 design—and your first exposure to factorial analysis—would have been sacrificed in the process. You now have the knowledge and tools available to perform any two-factor ANOVA—all that you need to do is to extend the logic of the 2 $\times$ 2 ANOVA by adding the necessary number of cells means, adjusting the sum of squares, degrees of freedom, and variance estimate calculations in the process.

Although we will not examine them in this book, you should be aware that there are still more advanced multifactorial ANOVA designs. On occasion, a researcher can elect to manipulate three or even four independent variables in the same experiment. We could have extended the affiliation study, for example, by adding a third factor. In addition to looking at birth order (firstborn vs. later-born) and anxiety level (high vs.

Higher order ANOVA designs—those beyond the typical 2 × 2 design—can contain three or even four independent variables. Such complexity can sacrifice interpretability, however.

low), we might have added gender (male vs. female). Recall that Schachter's (1959) original work used women and our replication study employed men. If we included both men and women in the study, then our research design would be a 2 × 2 × 2 design. Not only would we have three main effects—one each for birth order (A), anxiety level (B), and participant gender (C)—we would also have three interactions (i.e., A × B, B × C, and A × C) and what is known as a triple interaction (i.e., A × B × C) to analyze.

As more variables are added, the designs become more complex to carry out and to interpret, and their practical value is sometimes questionable (Gravetter & Wallnau, 1996; but see Rosenthal & Rosnow, 1991). Indeed, one must be quite practiced at evaluating more basic two-variable designs before tackling anything on a grander scale. Higher order factorial designs are best saved for advanced statistics classes, though I will encourage you to look for comprehensible examples as you read in the behavioral science literature (for some cases, see Rosenthal & Rosnow, 1991). In the next chapter, we will examine another advanced ANOVA technique—the repeated measures ANOVA—that is neither difficult to perform or understand.

Knowledge Base

Examine the following table of means and then answer the questions that follow.

| Variable B | Variable A | | Marginal Means |
	A_1	A_2	
B_1	10	20	15
B_2	20	10	15
Marginal means	15	15	

1. Is there a main effect for factor A? Why?
2. Is there a main effect for factor B? Why?
3. Is there an interaction between factors A and B? Why?

Answers

1. No. The means for A_1 and A_2 are both 15.
2. No. The means for B_1 and B_2 are both 15.
3. Yes. A plot of the cell mean indicates that there is a classic crossover interaction.

Project Exercise

MORE ON INTERPRETING INTERACTION—
MEAN POLISH AND DISPLAYING RESIDUALS

Psychologists Ralph Rosnow and Robert Rosenthal (1989; Rosenthal & Rosnow, 1991) launched something of minor crusade to decrease the widespread misunderstanding surrounding the concept of statistical interaction within the ANOVA. Interactions are the bread-and-butter results of many areas of the behavioral sciences, and yet many researchers, data analysts, and readers remain unaware of a major problem in how such effects are presented—interaction effects are rarely separated from the main effects (Rosenthal & Rosnow, 1991). We already noted that a significant interaction qualifies any accompanying main effect (see Data Box 12.B), but what do these researchers mean by "separating" the two effects from one another? How will such separation help you to interpret interactions in the future?

Rosenthal and Rosnow (1991) point out that when an interaction from a 2 × 2 ANOVA is significant, the pattern of results will *always* be the classically "X"-shaped

Table 12.5   Test Scores as a Function of Subject Matter and Classroom

	Subject Matter		
Environment	English	Math	*Mean*
Computer-enhanced classroom	7	13	10
Traditional classroom	7	5	6
Mean	7	9	8

pattern. At this point, you should be wondering how this observation could be true when we learned earlier that an interaction can take on any number of forms. Both points are true—Rosenthal and Rosnow are simply drawing attention to the fact that most researchers never actually display the "true" interaction effect (i.e., those we examined earlier still had the main effects embedded within them). Let's quote the authors on this matter before we move onto an illustrative example: "The diagram of the interaction is X-shaped; indeed, it is true *in general* that in any 2 × 2 analysis of variance the display of any nonzero (i.e., significant) interaction will be X-shaped" (Rosenthal & Rosnow, 1991, p. 366).

In other words, before an accurate interpretation of an interaction can be offered, the interaction itself must be identified and then displayed. To do so, Rosenthal and Rosnow (1991) advocate that researchers calculate the **residual values** within a research design that point to the interaction. The term "residual" usually refers to something that is left over when something else has been removed. In the context of interactions, the residuals are guiding numbers that remain once the main effects have been removed. Perhaps we have some data from an education project on the use of computer-enhanced classrooms and learning in traditional high school subjects. In other words, do computer classrooms generally enhance learning or does the subject matter make a difference (e.g., English, mathematics)?

Take a look at the hypothetical test scores shown in of Table 12.5. As you can see, there appears to be a main effect for environment (i.e., students score higher when learning occurred in the computer-based rather than traditional class setting) and one for subject matter (i.e., math scores were slightly higher than English scores). (If you feel a bit rusty about reading this data table, turn back to the relevant section on reading tables presented earlier in this chapter before proceeding with the rest of the discussion.) There also appears to be an interaction, which is plotted in Figure 12.6. Imagine that the interaction is statistically significant—how do we interpret it following Rosenthal and Rosnow (1991)?

To uncover the interaction, we must first subtract the row and the column effects (i.e., the means) from each of the cells in the experiment using a technique that Rosenthal and Rosnow (1991) refer to as the mean polish.

KEY TERM   The *mean polish* is a technique whereby row, column, and grand mean effects are removed from a table of means in order to illustrate residuals that define an interaction.

A *row effect* is based on subtracting the grand mean, the average of all the observations, (here, the number 8 shown in the lower right portion of Table 12.5) from each of the row means for the computer-enhanced and traditional environment, respectively, or: $10 - 8 = 2$ and $6 - 8 = -2$ (see the far right column in Table 12.6). We then subtract the respective row effects from each of the conditions found within its row. For the computer-enhanced row, the cell value of 7 becomes 5 (i.e., $7 - 2$) and the cell value of 13 becomes 11 ($13 - 2$; see the upper row in Table 12.7). We then subtract the row

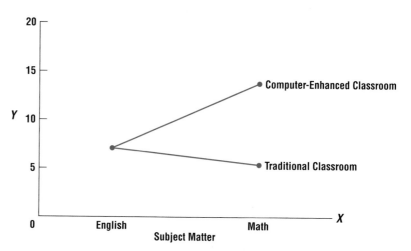

Figure 12.6   Figure Illustrating Two Main Effects and Interaction Involving Learning Environment and Subject Matter

effect from the cells representing the traditional environment and find the new cell values of 9[7 − (−2) = 9] and 7[5 − (−2) = 7] (see the lower row in Table 12.7). Finally, each of the row means is also corrected by subtracting its respective row effects (see the new means of 8 and 8, respectively, in Table 12.7).

The next step involves removing the column effects from the data table of means. We use the same procedure that was used to remove the row effects. To begin, we identify the column effects, which are based on subtracting the grand mean of 8 from each of the two column means. The column effects are 7 − 8 = −1 for the English course and 9 − 8 = 1 for math (these values are identified in the bottom row of Tables 12.6 and 12.7). Removal of a given column effect means that the effect's value must be subtracted from each of the cells within its own column (remember that the cell values being used have had the row effects already removed; see Table 12.7). Thus, the two values in the first column in Table 12.7 now become 6[5 − (−1) = 6] and 10[9 − (−1) = 10)]. The two values in the second column of Table 12.7, in turn, now are 10(11 − 1 = 10) and 6(7 − 1 = 6). We must also subtract the respective column effects from the column means, yielding values of 8[7 − (−1) = 8] and 8(9 − 1 = 8), respectively. Test scores corrected for both row and column effects are shown in Table 12.8.

What are we left with in Table 12.8? Once the row and column effects are removed, we are left with a set of residuals that define an interaction effect, yet one last calculation remains. We must remove the effect of the grand mean from the residuals because

Table 12.6   Test Scores as a Function of Subject Matter and Classroom with Row and Column Effects Identified

Environment	Subject Matter		*Mean*	**Row Effect**
	English	Math		
Computer-enhanced classroom	7	13	10	2
Traditional classroom	7	5	6	−2
Mean	7	9	8	
Column effect	−1	1		

Table 12.7 Test Scores as a Function of Subject Matter and Classroom Corrected for Row Effects

| Environment | Subject Matter | | *Mean* | Row Effect |
	English	Math		
Computer-enhanced classroom	5	11	8	0
Traditional classroom	9	7	8	0
Mean	7	9	8	
Column effect	−1	1		

this number inflates their values. To remove the grand mean—we already know that its value is 8 (see Table 12.5)—we subtract its value from each of the cells, as well as each of the row and column means. If you subtract the grand mean of 8 from all of the numbers shown in Table 12.8, then you end up with the numbers presented in Table 12.9. The positive and negative *pattern* shown by the numbers in the cells in Table 12.9, not the numbers per se, reveal the descriptive nature of the interaction. That is, positive and negative signs indicate the relative magnitude of the relationships between the cell means.

What do these numbers suggest about the relationship between learning environment and subject matter? Take a closer look at Table 12.9: Math test scores were higher than English test scores when learning took place in the computer-based classroom; however, English scores were higher than math scores when the traditional classroom settings were utilized. Put in still simpler terms: Math scores are higher when learning is computer-enhanced, whereas English scores are higher when learning occurs in the traditional classroom. Compare these statements with the residuals shown in Table 12.9. This interpretation of the interaction is not only simple, it is also completely accurate. To plot the means disclosing this relationship, we need only go back to the corrected means provided in Table 12.8 (remember that these means are all positive because the grand mean was not yet removed from them). As you can see in Figure 12.7, the plot of the mean is X-shaped, just as Rosenthal and Rosnow (1991) promised, and it does illustrate the interaction once the main effects due to learning environment and subject matter are removed from the data.

That is all there is to it! The calculations involved are not at all difficult and once you have the concepts down, you can polish the means of any 2 × 2 study quickly and efficiently in order to make certain that you are reporting the accurate interaction, one based on the actual pattern of the residuals.

Here is the *Project Exercise*, one designed to give you some practice with using the mean polish procedure and displaying residuals.

Table 12.8 Test Scores as a Function of Subject Matter and Classroom Corrected for Row and Column Effects

| Environment | Subject Matter | | *Mean* | Row Effect |
	English	Math		
Computer-enhanced classroom	6	10	8	0
Traditional classroom	10	6	8	0
Mean	8	8	8	
Column effect	0	0		

Table 12.9   Test Scores as a Function of Subject Matter and Classroom Corrected for Row and Column Effects and for the Grand Mean

Environment	English	Math	Mean	Row Effect
	Subject Matter			
Computer-enhanced classroom	−2	2	0	0
Traditional classroom	2	−2	0	0
Mean	0	0	0	
Column effect	0	0		

1. Locate some data based on a 2 × 2 between-groups research design. You can locate studies published in the behavioral science literature, reanalyze data from tables presented earlier in this chapter (see Table 12.1 or Figure 12.4, for instance), or ask your instructor for some data. Alternatively, create a data table demonstrating an interaction—make up some data similar to what we just reviewed.

2. Perform the mean polish from start to finish. Be sure to create progressive data tables like those we reviewed above in order to carefully track your calculations (i.e., remove the row effects first, then the column effects, then the grand mean, etc.). Keep the *mise en place* philosophy in mind here, as it is relatively easy to make a simple math error, one that will disrupt the inherent symmetry of the residual patterns.

3. Once you have the residuals from the mean polish, describe what they mean in the simplest terms possible—be sure to write out your interpretation and then practice simplifying it still more, if necessary. Finally, plot the mean residuals *before* the grand mean is removed so that you can get a real sense of the X-shape of the interaction, as well as to verify that your calculations were correct. (Keep in mind that you cannot perform the mean polish and expect to get tidy residuals, as well as a neat X-plot, if there is no interaction present in the data.)

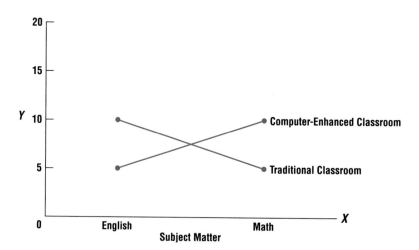

Figure 12.7   Figure Illustrating Interaction Between Learning Environment and Subject Matter Once the Two Main Effects Are Removed

Note: The data here are taken from Table 12.8.

LOOKING FORWARD THEN BACK

The decision tree that opens this chapter is designed to help you differentiate among the various ANOVAs and to choose the one that best fits a research design and its data. (For continuity, this same tree is reprinted at the opening of chapter 13, the last chapter devoted to mean comparisons). When, for example, is it appropriate to use a one-way (chapter 11) or a two-way ANOVA (this chapter's topic) rather than a one-way repeated-measures ANOVA or a mixed-design ANOVA (topics covered in the next chapter)? Such decisions should not—indeed, cannot—be taken lightly by researchers; there is little worse than choosing an incorrect statistic or collecting data that cannot be analyzed.

Assuming that a two-way ANOVA is identified as appropriate, the second decision tree will help you to decide which supplementary analyses (if any) should accompany the main results of an analysis, as well as to pinpoint what additional information (e.g., tables, graphs, source tables) should also be included in any writeup of research data. Remember, a good data analyst tries to portray a complete picture of the results—*how* results are presented matter as much as *what* they mean in the context of a theory or an application. Thus, tables and graphs must accompany the main analyses which, in turn, are supported by supplementary statistics. The whole "package" of results should provide readers with a coherent framework within which to think about the implications of and future directions for the findings.

Summary

1. Two-variable ("two-way") analysis of variance (ANOVA) designs involve two independent variables.

2. Human behavior is complex, and no single research design with an accompanying method of analysis can hope to capture it entirely. Complex ANOVA designs enable investigators to explore multivariable relationships, thereby extending knowledge beyond conventional one-variable studies.

3. Multivariable—factorial—designs present advantages where economy, efficiency, elegance, generality of effects, and interaction between variables are concerned.

4. A two-way ANOVA provides three effects: a main effect (mean difference) due to variable A, a second main effect (mean difference) caused by variable B, and an A × B interaction. An interaction between two variables reveals how a change in one variable influences changes in the other variable.

5. The most common factorial design is the 2 × 2 ("two by two") design, which involves two independent variables with two levels in each one. By multiplying the number of levels in one variable by those in another, a researcher can identify the number of unique experimental conditions. Thus, a 2 × 2 has four conditions (i.e., 2 × 2 = 4) and a 2 × 3 design has six (i.e., 2 × 3 = 6), and so on.

6. The statistical assumptions of the two-way ANOVA are identical with those associated with the traditional one-way ANOVA or the independent groups *t* test. An additional assumption is that any two-way ANOVA should be fully factorial (all combinations existing between the two independent variables are displayed).

7. Partitioning variability in the two-way ANOVA is analogous to the procedure used for the one-way ANOVA—the chief difference, of course, is that variability for two independent variables and their interaction are explained. Though they include a few more steps, the calculations for the two-factor ANOVA are no more difficult than those associated with the one-factor ANOVA.

8. Once the significant *F* ratios are identified in a two-way ANOVA, it is advisable to calculate their respective effect sizes (f) as well as the association between the significant independent variables and dependent measure ($\hat{\omega}^2$). Such supplementary information is routinely included in the writeup of the results, along with a table or graph of a study's means.

9. Multifactorial designs—studies where 3 or more independent variables are manipulated—are possible to conduct, but interpreting their results becomes increasingly difficult as their complexity increases.

Key Terms

Factorial design (*p. 462*)

Interaction (*p. 467*)

Main effect (*p. 466*)

Mean polish (*p. 491*)

Residual values (*p. 491*)

Two-way or two-factor ANOVA (*p. 461*)

Chapter Problems

1. Conceptually, how does a two-way ANOVA differ from a one-way ANOVA? (Hint: Use examples to illustrate your points.)
2. Why manipulate more than one independent variable? What are the advantages of using a two-way ANOVA design?
3. What is a *factorial* design? How can you tell how many different levels are present in a given factorial design?
4. How many separate conditions exist in the following designs: 3×2; 3×4; $2 \times 2 \times 2$; 2×4; $2 \times 2 \times 2 \times 2$.
5. What is a *main effect?* Define this term and provide an example.
6. What is an *interaction?* Define this term and provide an example. Why are interactions often graphed?
7. Why are interactions only associated with factorial designs?
8. What is the quickest, simplest method to determine if an interaction is present in a set of data?
9. How many *F* ratios result from a two-way ANOVA? What is the purpose of each of the *F*s?
10. In the context of the two-way ANOVA, what is a *residual?* How are residuals used for interpreting results from an ANOVA?
11. A developmental psychologist believes that language learning in preschool girls differs from boys, such that the former use more complex sentence constructions earlier than the latter. The researcher believes that a second factor affecting language skills is the presence of older siblings; that is, preschool children with older siblings will generate more complex speech than only children. The researcher carefully records the speech of a classroom of 40 preschool children (20 males, 20 females), half of whom have older siblings. The speech of each child is then given a complexity score in preparation for analysis—what method of analysis should the researcher use? Why? Use the decision trees that open this chapter to answer and to guide your thinking about these questions.
12. Assume that the sentence complexity result(s) from the analysis of identified in question 11 were statistically significant. Using prose, describe what the main effects for gender and the presence of older siblings, respectively, might be like. Speculate about the nature of the interaction between gender and the presence of older siblings on children's sentence complexity—what might it reveal? What next step(s) should the investigator take? Use the appropriate decision tree provided at the opening of this chapter to answer these questions.
13. Examine the following data table and indicate the presence of any main effect(s) or interaction:

	Factor B	
	B₁	**B₂**
A₁	5	10
A₂	10	5

14. Examine the following data table and indicate the presence of any main effect(s) or interaction:

	Factor B	
	B₁	**B₂**
A₁	10	10
A₂	10	5

15. Examine the following data table and indicate the presence of any main effect(s) or interaction:

	Factor B	
	B₁	**B₂**
A₁	20	10
A₂	5	20

16. Create your own data table wherein:
    a. There is a main effect for variable A and B, but no interaction.
    b. There is a main effect for variable A but not B, and an interaction.
    c. There is no main effect for A or B, but there is an interaction.
17. The following data were collected in a 2×2 between-groups research design. Perform the appropriate analyses and be sure to include a data table, a source table, and, if necessary, a graphical display of the relationship between the variables.

	Factor B	
	B₁	**B₂**
A₁	5, 6, 7, 5, 7, 6	3, 3, 2, 4, 5, 5
A₂	10, 11, 10, 7, 8, 8	5, 6, 7, 7, 7, 8

18. The following data were collected in a 2×2 between-groups research design. Perform the appropriate analyses and be sure to include a data table, a source table, and, if necessary, a graphical display of the relationship between the variables.

	Factor B	
	B₁	**B₂**
A₁	7, 7, 8, 7, 7	5, 6, 3, 4, 3
A₂	6, 5, 6, 6, 6	7, 6, 7, 7, 6

19. Calculate the effect size and association between the independent variable and dependent measure (if appropriate) for the results presented in question 17.
20. Calculate the effect size and association between the independent variable and dependent measure (if appropriate) for the results presented in question 18.
21. A student taking a cognitive psychology class decides to conduct a memory experiment examining recall for nonsense (e.g., sleemta) versus real (e.g., sleeve) words. Half of the participants in his study learn nonsense words while the other half study real ones. The students decide to also see how the environment where the learning occurs affects recall, so that half the students learn their words in a very warm room (i.e., 82 de-

grees F) while the remaining students are placed in an ambient room (70 degrees F) during the study. The data (number of correctly recalled words) are shown below. Using the appropriate ANOVA, determine whether word type or learning environment had any discernable effect on recall. Be sure to create any appropriate tables or graphs, calculate supplementary statistics as appropriate, and to write up the results of the analysis in APA style. (Hint: you may find the decision trees appearing at the opening of the chapter to be helpful.)

Learning Environment	Word Type	
	Nonsense	**Real**
Warm room	2, 3, 4, 3, 4, 2	3, 4, 2, 4, 4, 3
Ambient room	5, 5, 4, 5, 6, 4	7, 8, 4, 7, 6, 8

Note: There are six participants per condition.

22. Complete the following ANOVA source table and answer the accompanying questions:

Source	Sum of Squares	*df*	*MS*	*F*
Between groups				
Factor A	125	—	125	—
Factor B	225	—	225	—
A × B	65	—	65	—
Within groups	1,100	—	—	
Total		51		

a. How many levels are there in factor A? Factor B?
b. If the cells sizes are equal, how many participants are in each cell?
c. Did any of the *F* ratios reach significance?
d. What are the critical values associated with each of the *Fs*?

23. Complete the following ANOVA source table and answer the accompanying questions:

Source	Sum of Squares	*df*	*MS*	*F*
Between groups				
Factor A	85	1	—	—
Factor B	93	1	—	—
A × B	52	1	—	—
Within groups	—	36	—	
Total	570			

a. How many levels are there in factor A? Factor B?
b. If the cells sizes are equal, how many participants are in each cell?
c. Did any of the *F* ratios reach significance?
d. What are the critical values associated with each of the *Fs*?

24. Calculate the effect size and association between the independent variable and dependent measure (if appropriate) for the results presented in question 22.

25. Calculate the effect size and association between the independent variable and dependent measure (if appropriate) for the results presented in question 23.

26. What is the procedure known as a "mean polish"? Why is it a more useful procedure than simply looking at a data table and guessing the nature of an interaction?

27. Create a 2 × 2 data table that you believe illustrates an interaction between some variables A and B, and perform a mean polish on the table of means using the procedure outlined in the *Project Exercise*.

28. An experiment has two between-groups factors with two levels in each one, and the data are based on an interval scale. Which type of ANOVA should be used for the analysis? Why? (Hint: Use the decision tree(s) at the start of this chapter to answer these questions.)

29. The following data were collected in a 2 × 3 between-groups research design. Perform the appropriate analyses and be sure to include a data table, a source table, and, if necessary, a graphical display of the relationship between the variables.

	Factor B		
	B₁	**B₂**	**B₃**
A₁	10, 11, 10, 12, 11, 10	8, 8, 7, 9, 8, 7	5, 4, 5, 4, 5, 4
A₂	5, 5, 5, 6, 4, 4	7, 8, 8, 9, 8, 7	11, 10, 9, 12, 11, 10

30. Calculate the effect size(s) and association between the independent variable and dependent measure (if appropriate) for the results from question 29.

Deciding Which ANOVA to Use

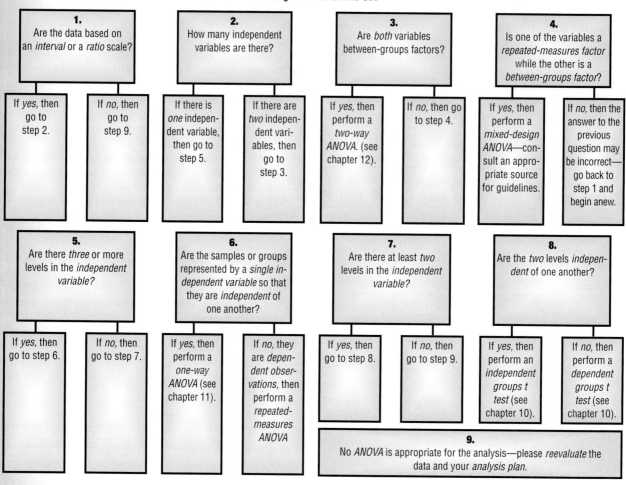

1. Are the data based on an *interval* or a *ratio* scale?

If *yes*, then go to step 2.

If *no*, then go to step 9.

2. How many independent variables are there?

If there is *one* independent variable, then go to step 5.

If there are *two* independent variables, then go to step 3.

3. Are *both* variables between-groups factors?

If *yes*, then perform a *two-way* ANOVA. (see chapter 12).

If *no*, then go to step 4.

4. Is one of the variables a *repeated-measures factor* while the other is a *between-groups factor*?

If *yes*, then perform a *mixed-design* ANOVA—consult an appropriate source for guidelines.

If *no*, then the answer to the previous question may be incorrect—go back to step 1 and begin anew.

5. Are there *three* or more levels in the *independent variable*?

If *yes*, then go to step 6.

If *no*, then go to step 7.

6. Are the samples or groups represented by a *single independent variable* so that they are *independent* of one another?

If *yes*, then perform a *one-way* ANOVA (see chapter 11).

If *no*, they are *dependent observations*, then perform a *repeated-measures ANOVA*

7. Are there at least *two* levels in the *independent variable*?

If *yes*, then go to step 8.

If *no*, then go to step 9.

8. Are the *two* levels *independent* of one another?

If *yes*, then perform an *independent groups t test* (see chapter 10).

If *no*, then perform a *dependent groups t test* (see chapter 10).

9. No *ANOVA* is appropriate for the analysis—please *reevaluate* the data and your *analysis plan*.

Procedure Following a One-Way Repeated-Measures ANOVA

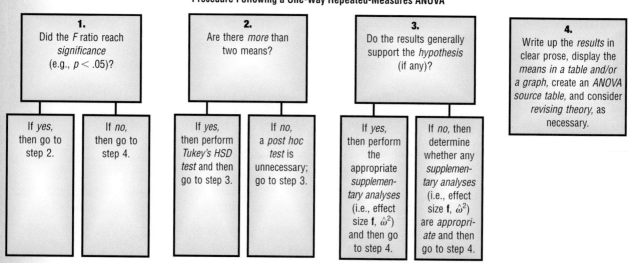

1. Did the *F* ratio reach *significance* (e.g., $p < .05$)?

If *yes*, then go to step 2.

If *no*, then go to step 4.

2. Are there *more* than two means?

If *yes*, then perform *Tukey's HSD test* and then go to step 3.

If *no*, a *post hoc test* is unnecessary; go to step 3.

3. Do the results generally support the *hypothesis* (if any)?

If *yes*, then perform the appropriate *supplementary analyses* (i.e., effect size **f**, $\hat{\omega}^2$) and then go to step 4.

If *no*, then determine whether any *supplementary analyses* (i.e., effect size **f**, $\hat{\omega}^2$) are *appropriate* and then go to step 4.

4. Write up the *results* in clear prose, display the *means in a table and/or a graph*, create an *ANOVA source table*, and consider *revising theory*, as necessary.

MEAN COMPARISON IV: ONE-VARIABLE REPEATED-MEASURES ANALYSIS OF VARIANCE

Any honest researcher or statistician will admit that it is virtually impossible to control for or rule out every conceivable variable that could influence the results of a study. Still, researchers and data analysts alike exert reasonable efforts to identify, reduce, and, ideally, eliminate any obvious influences that could jeopardize a study's outcome—or at least render its interpretive character murky rather than clear. The patron saint of this effort to control the research situation turns out to be none other than Ivan Pavlov, the Nobel prize winning physiologist who performed the original, classic research on the conditioned reflex (Pavlov, 1927/1960; see also, Pavlov, 1928). As the father of classical conditioning, Pavlov holds a revered place in the discipline of psychology but, ironically, he held the field (and presumably the other behavioral sciences, as well) in such low esteem that his assistants were fined or fired for using mentalistic terms (e.g., mind, thought) while carrying out his research program!

Pavlov examined the salivary reflex of dogs, noting that saliva production initially associated with the presentation of food (meat powder, actually) could be *conditioned* to occur when a bell rang. The food served as the unconditioned stimulus for salivation, the unconditioned response; later, the ringing sound became the conditioned stimulus for salivation, a (now) conditioned response. Pavlov compared the rate of salivation to the bell before conditioning (i.e., the control condition) with the rate of salivation to the bell after the conditioning sessions (i.e., the experimental condition) within a single subject.

Vadum and Rankin (1998) report that Pavlov tackled the problem of uncontrolled variables by attempting to literally control all aspects of the experimental situation his participants, the dogs, encountered. Pavlov expended great effort to ensure that the dogs' experiences were completely under his control, thereby demonstrating the hypothesized relations between experimental variables and behavioral responses. The laboratory building housing the dogs was known as the "tower of silence" because it was sound-proof, a feature designed to eliminate any potential effects from outside (i.e., uncontrolled) noise. Aside from those times when an experimental procedure was running, it was rare for anyone to directly interact with the animals. Instead, the dogs' behavior was often observed via periscope to prevent any unplanned contacts with their human caretakers or experimenters. As you can see, Pavlov was somewhat obsessed with the idea of total control and its possible link to accurate inference about the causes of behavior. Vadum and Rankin (1998) note that his obsession for control led to the development of the so-called "$n = 1$" or single-subject designs (for discussion of these research designs, see Dunn, 1999; Shaughnessy & Zechmeister, 1994).

It is much easier to impose absolute control in animal studies than the sort typically involving people, as practical, methodological, and ethical issues abound in human research. Substitute methods reinforcing the Pavlovian desire for control have developed, however, not the least of which is the one-variable repeated-measures or within-subjects research design, the topic of this chapter. This statistical technique tests for mean differences in participants' responses to the same measure, one that is assessed multiple times—usually following the presentation of some level of an independent variable—in the course of a study. The repeated measures ANOVA, then, serves the same purpose as the dependent groups *t* test (see chapter 10)—it assesses change in people's reactions to the same dependent measure across some period of time. Where the dependent variant of the *t* test could only explore change between two means measured at two distinct points in time, however, the repeated-measures ANOVA examines change in the same measure at *more* than two points in time.

A researcher might study how and why people's emotional reactions shift depending on the nature of what they encounter. Thus, how the same group of people react, feel, or act toward some stimulus—say, an exciting or distressing film—can be tracked so that distinct changes (if any) can be noted. Such repeated measures enable the researcher to estimate when and if a change occurred, as well as its direction (i.e., positive, negative, or zero). Repeatedly assessing participants' reactions to varied stimuli provides us with a more coherent picture of how changes in thought and behavior occur.

As we will see, a researcher can introduce participants to all levels of an independent variable using a repeated-measures design, a huge savings in time and materials. Instead of running, say, *four* independent groups and exposing each to one level of an independent variable, *one* group is presented with all four levels of treatment. Not surprisingly, repeated-measures designs capitalize on several of the advantages associated with factorial experiments cited in chapter 12. That is, repeated-measures designs are generally:

■ **Economical.** Measuring a dependent variable more than once in a piece of research saves time, energy, and resources, especially because fewer participants are usually required.
■ **Efficient.** Where participants' responses are concerned, change can be studied as an ongoing rather than a discrete process. This quality, too, often heightens the external validity of a research effort—life is perhaps more similar to a within-than a between-subjects design.
■ **Elegant.** The ability to explain how a response changes across some period of time leads to more detailed theorizing about the processes underlying behavior.
■ **Generalizable.** As acknowledged previously, life is complex and, sometimes, repeated-measures (within-subjects) approaches do a better job at capturing or

characterizing complexity than do between-subjects designs. Occasionally, then, examining how behavior unfolds across time can be more informative than simply reviewing responses to a once-and-done dependent measure.

We conclude the chapter with a short discussion of the mixed design ANOVA, an advanced analysis used for experiments where different levels of one factor (i.e., some between-subjects variable) are presented to independent groups of participants, all of whom are exposed to every level of some other variable (i.e., a repeated-measures or within-subjects variable). Naturally, this design requires that a dependent measure is repeatedly presented to assess any change(s) in participants' verbal or behavioral reactions to stimuli. A cognitive psychologist, for example, could examine whether gender (between-subjects factor) is related to the recall of different types of verbal stimuli (within-subject or repeated-measures factor). Although we will not present the actual formulas and calculations for the mixed design ANOVA in this book, this brief overview of yet another analytic alternative will encourage you to think about the advantages of manipulating and measuring more than one variable in a research design. We begin by considering how to analyze data from a dependent measure that is administered more than twice in the course of an experiment.

One-Factor Repeated-Measures ANOVA

In some cases, an investigator is not interested in conducting an experiment or other piece of research where there are several discrete groups of participants, each one receiving a different combination of levels of independent variables. That is, there are some questions that do not require between-group comparisons—instead, they require within-group comparisons, where the same group of participants encounters all the different levels of the available independent variables. These research designs are commonly called *repeated-measures designs* or *within-subjects designs* because the same type of dependent measure is administered to the same group of participants at several different points during the experiment. These sort of designs—their logic and methodology—were introduced in chapter 10 in the context provided by the dependent groups *t* test (please turn there now if you find you do not remember the major issues involved in the repeated-measures approach).

☑

"Within-subjects" design is another name for a repeated-measures design.

Just as the correlated groups *t* test was appropriate for assessing change in one group of participants at two distinct points in time (see chapter 10), the *one-variable repeated-measures analysis of variance (ANOVA)* considers the reactions of a group of participants at *three or more* points in time. Each reaction—the administration of the same dependent measure—is assessed after a given level of an independent variable is presented to the participants. The assessed reactions, of course, are not independent of one another so a distinct statistical test must be used, one that compares observed mean differences against differences anticipated by chance.

KEY TERM   A **one-variable or one-way repeated-measures ANOVA** is a statistical test used to identify differences between or among three or more sample means representing the corresponding (different) levels of a single independent variable.

The statistical advantage of the one-variable repeated-measures ANOVA is that the random error resulting from individual differences is all but eliminated because only one group of participants takes part in the research design. That is, each participant appears in each and every experimental condition, so that the variability attributable to a given person—his or her unique variability—can be statistically removed from the study's random error. For this reason, each participant in a repeated-measures design is sometimes said to serve as his or her own "control group." The only available source of error, then, should be that due to unsystematic but uncontrolled experimental error (e.g., environmental variables such as heat, lighting, or room temperature; inconsistent instructions).

As a result, the F ratio of interest in a one-variable repeated-measures design is based on the effect of the independent variable in question and experimental error *only*, or:

$$F_{\text{between}} = \frac{\begin{array}{c}\textit{variance differences between sample means due to the}\\ \textit{independent variable} + \textit{variance differences due to experimental error}\end{array}}{\textit{variance differences due to experimental error}}.$$

This F ratio represents a between-groups or treatment factor in that each of its levels is systematically presented to the same group of participants, and a different sample mean results from each exposure to a given level. For this reason, we continue to refer to the statistic as a "between-groups" F ratio but it is a "within-subjects" or repeated-measures statistic because it determines the presence or absence of mean differences based on the responses of the *same* participants across some period of time.

Do make careful note that a repeated-measures design only has experimental error in the denominator—there is no error attributable to individual differences, unlike the between-subjects designs reviewed previously. What happens to the error due to individual differences? This error—which is typically quite low in a repeated-measures design—is removed separately from the analysis. Typically, the lower error variance in the denominator of the F ratio will yield a larger statistic (i.e., even modest between-groups differences based on an independent variable are often significant when a denominator is small).

How does the one-variable repeated-measures ANOVA separate or partition variability? With one exception—the inclusion of a new sum of squares term—the variability components will be familiar to you. The total sum of squares (SS_{total}) is comprised of:

$$SS_{\text{total}} = SS_{\text{between}} + SS_{\text{subjects}} + SS_{\text{within}}.$$

The only new component of variability here is SS_{subjects}, which statistically represents the change within the group of participants *across* the given number of measures. When a considerable aspect of a study or experiment of interest is devoted to individual difference issues, then the SS_{subjects} will be relatively large (Runyon, Haber, Pittenger, & Coleman, 1996). Research that is not focused on individual differences per se, however, will generally yield values for SS_{subjects} that are low in value.

When researchers employ a repeated-measures design, they must necessarily be concerned about the sequencing used to present any stimuli (i.e., levels of the independent variable) to research participants. If all the participants experienced the same material in the same order of presentation, an inherent bias or confound might develop (e.g., participants might attend more readily to the early items and pay less or no attention to information coming later in the study). This particular problem and its antidote, counterbalancing, were discussed in the context provided by the dependent groups t test (please see chapter 10 for a review; but see the *Project Exercise* at the end of this chapter).

> ▽
>
> Error variance in a repeated-measures ANOVA is based on experimental error exclusively, as individual difference variation is partialed out of the analysis.

Statistical Assumptions of the One-Way Repeated-Measures ANOVA

The statistical assumptions behind the one-way repeated-measures ANOVA are almost identical to those underlying the one-way ANOVA used to assess between-group differences (see chapter 11). Specifically, when using a one-way repeated-measures ANOVA, data analysts assume:

■ The dependent measures are based on either a ratio or an interval scale of measurement (i.e., means can be calculated from the data).

- The data collected *within* each level of the independent variable are independent of one another (although the dependent [repeated] measures are *not* independent of one another—a participant's response to measure$_1$ is necessarily related to her response to measure$_2$, and so on).
- The distribution of the population from which the measures in each level of the independent variable are drawn is assumed to be normal. Concern over the normality assumption is only appropriate, however, when the sample of participants and the number of observations drawn from them are both very small.
- The distribution of the populations within each level of the independent variable are homogeneous (i.e., homogeneity of variances requirement).

A fifth and somewhat novel assumption exists for the repeated-measures ANOVA:

- The effects of each level of the independent variable on behavior should be consistent across a study's participants and, as noted previously, no carryover or other order-related effects should be present in the data (Gravetter & Wallnau, 1996).

Hypothesis, Notation, and Steps for Performing the One-Variable Repeated-Measures ANOVA

Given that the procedure for performing a one-variable repeated-measures ANOVA is highly similar to the procedures used for one- and two-way ANOVAs, we will truncate our presentation of hypotheses, notation, and steps for performing this statistical test. In contrast to past chapters, we will review the data from a hypothetical study at the *same* time we state a null and alternative hypothesis, learn proper notation, and actually perform the analysis (including completing and interpreting its ANOVA source table).

Imagine that a clinical researcher is interested in reducing the amount of time a group of six clients spends ruminating about uncontrollable life events (e.g., imagined future health problems, death of a loved one). Active rumination is linked to a variety of anxiety symptoms, including depression and sleep disorders (e.g., Nolen-Hoeksema, 1990, 1993). The clinician asks the participants to record how often they ruminate—that is, anxiously think about something over and over—during a typical week. The daily average for a week per participant from this record-keeping exercise serves as a baseline measure (see Table 13.1). Following this baseline week, the participants were taught to use meditation in order to relax, hopefully reducing their relative amount of daily rumination. The participants then recorded how often they ruminated daily about uncontrollable events for the subsequent two weeks, and the daily average for each of those weeks served as a postmeasure of success for the relaxation therapy (see Table 13.1).

The clinical researcher decided to perform a one-way repeated-measures ANOVA on the average rumination scores. The analysis compared the baseline week's daily rumination average (per day premeditation) with the daily averages from the following two weeks (meditation phase) in order to determine whether the meditation actually reduced the incidence of anxiety-driven thinking. As shown in Table 13.1, participants ruminated much more frequently during the baseline week ($\overline{X}_1 = 9.25$ ruminative thoughts per day) than either the first ($\overline{X}_2 = 5.75$ ruminative thoughts per day) or second ($\overline{X}_3 = 5.08$ ruminative thoughts per day) week following the meditation therapy. A one-way repeated-measures ANOVA will help the clinical researcher determine whether any differences between these weekly averages exist, as well as where they occur.

Table 13.1   Hypothetical Data from a Study on Rumination and Therapeutic Meditation

Subject	Baseline Week	Meditation Week$_1$	Meditation Week$_2$	Subject Totals
1	$X_{11} = 10$ $X_{11}^2 = 100$	$X_{12} = 5$ $X_{12}^2 = 25$	$X_{13} = 4$ $X_{13}^2 = 16$	19
2	$X_{21} = 8$ $X_{21}^2 = 64$	$X_{22} = 5.5$ $X_{22}^2 = 30.25$	$X_{23} = 6$ $X_{23}^2 = 36$	19.5
3	$X_{31} = 10$ $X_{31}^2 = 100$	$X_{32} = 6$ $X_{32}^2 = 36$	$X_{33} = 5$ $X_{33}^2 = 25$	21
4	$X_{41} = 9.5$ $X_{41}^2 = 90.25$	$X_{42} = 7$ $X_{42}^2 = 49$	$X_{43} = 6$ $X_{43}^2 = 36$	22.5
5	$X_{51} = 7$ $X_{51}^2 = 49$	$X_{52} = 5$ $X_{52}^2 = 25$	$X_{53} = 5.5$ $X_{53}^2 = 30.25$	17.5
6	$X_{61} = 11$ $X_{61}^2 = 121$	$X_{62} = 6$ $X_{62}^2 = 36$	$X_{63} = 4$ $X_{63}^2 = 16$	21

Measure totals	$\sum X_1 = 55.5$ $\sum X_1^2 = 524.25$	$\sum X_2 = 34.5$ $\sum X_2^2 = 201.25$	$\sum X_3 = 30.5$ $\sum X_3^2 = 159.25$	
Means	$\overline{X}_1 = 9.25$	$\overline{X}_2 = 5.75$	$\overline{X}_3 = 5.08$	

Additional Calculations for the One-Way Repeated-Measures ANOVA:

$\sum X_{ij} = 55.5 + 34.5 + 30.5 = 120.5$

$\sum X_{ij}^2 = 524.25 + 201.25 + 159.25 = 884.75$

Note: Each table entry (X) represents the average (mean) number of ruminative thoughts across a 7-day period.

We will again follow the basic steps for testing a hypothesis laid out in Table 11.4. Step 1 entails the identification of the null and the alternative hypotheses. The null hypothesis posits that no differences exist among the means representing participant responses to the different levels of an independent variable. In the context of our example, the null hypothesis would be:

$$H_0: \mu_{\text{baseline week}} = \mu_{\text{meditation week 1}} = \mu_{\text{meditation week 2}}.$$

The most straightforward alternative hypothesis involves assuming that some mean difference between the repeated measures will be found, or:

$$H_1: \text{There will be at least one mean different from another mean.}$$

The second step in the process of testing a hypothesis involves choosing a significance level for rejecting the null hypothesis. Following precedent, we will rely on a p value of .05.

We begin the actual analyses of the data here in step 3. As we proceed with the analyses, we will complete a source table for the one-way repeated-measures ANOVA (see Table 13.2 later in this section). The number of calculations involved in this statistical test is far fewer than the two-way ANOVA you learned in chapter 12, but still more than is found with the one-way ANOVA introduced in chapter 11. Please be certain that you always know the origin of any entries within a given formula (*hint:* following along by comparing the numbers and answers shown in the formula with the numbers in Tables 13.1 and 13.2, respectively, will help in this regard). If you ever become confused or uncertain, please stop and review the appropriate portions of the text *before* proceeding—a moment's delay is a small price to pay where accurate understanding is concerned! Moreover, your careful review now will pay dividends in the future, when homework or review for an exam is necessary.

As always, we begin by calculating the total sum of squares (SS_{total}):

[13.1.1]
$$SS_{\text{total}} = \sum X_{ij}^2 - \frac{(\sum X_{ij})^2}{N},$$

where $\sum X_{ij}^2$ is based on squaring and then summing all of the individual observations shown in Table 13.1 (please notice that this particular calculation is shown there under the heading "Additional Calculations for the One-Way Repeated-Measures ANOVA" at the bottom of the table). The error or correction term—$(\sum X_{ij})^2/N$—is based on summing all of the observations, squaring the sum (this calculation is also shown at the bottom of Table 13.1), and then dividing the resulting product by N. *Here is an important note:* In any repeated measures ANOVA, N refers to the total number of observations available, rather than the number of participants (see the 18 entries in the middle of Table 13.1); n is used to denote the number of participants in this kind of research design (there are six here—see the leftmost column in Table 13.1).

We can now enter the numbers from Table 13.1 and calculate SS_{total}:

[13.1.2] $$SS_{total} = 884.75 - \frac{(120.5)^2}{18},$$

[13.1.3] $$SS_{total} = 884.75 - \frac{14,520.25}{18},$$

[13.1.4] $$SS_{total} = 884.75 - 806.68,$$

[13.1.5] $$SS_{total} = 78.07.$$

Once the value of the SS_{total} is entered at the bottom of column 2 in Table 13.2, its accompanying degrees of freedom are calculated:

[13.2.1] $$df_{total} = N - 1.$$

Again, do not forget that N refers to the number of available observations and not the number of participants in the study:

[13.2.2] $df_{total} = 18 - 1,$

[13.2.3] $df_{total} = 17.$

The df_{total} is then entered at the bottom of column 3 in Table 13.2.

Our next goal is to calculate the between-groups variance estimate. To obtain this value, we first need to calculate the between-groups sum of squares and its degrees of freedom. The $SS_{between}$ is known by:

[13.3.1] $$SS_{between} = \frac{(\sum X_j)^2}{n} - \frac{(\sum X_{ij})^2}{N}.$$

The first half of the formula (a) involves summing the observations within each of the treatment periods (i.e., the 3 weeks; $\sum X_j$), squaring the 3 sums separately $((\sum X_j)^2)$, and then dividing each product by the number of observations within its treatment (here, $n = 6$)—the resulting 3 values are then added together. The second half of the formula (b) is the correction term, whose value was determined when we calculated the SS_{total} (the value—806.68—is first shown above in [13.1.4]). All of the numerical information we need for this calculation can be obtained from the preliminary work done in Table 13.1. Thus,

[13.3.2] $$SS_{between} = \left[\frac{(55.5)^2}{6} + \frac{(34.5)^2}{6} + \frac{(30.5)^2}{6} \right] - 806.68,$$

[13.3.3] $$SS_{between} = \left(\frac{3,080.25}{6} + \frac{1,190.25}{6} + \frac{930.25}{6} \right) - 806.68,$$

[13.3.4] $$SS_{between} = (513.38 + 198.38 + 155.04) - 806.68,$$

[13.3.5] $SS_{between} = 866.80 - 806.68$,

[13.3.6] $SS_{between} = 60.12$.

The $SS_{between}$ can then be entered into the first row under column 2 in Table 13.2. The degrees of freedom corresponding to the $SS_{between}$ are equal to:

[13.4.1] $df_{between} = k - 1$,

where k is the number of levels of the independent variable (here, the 3 weeks).

[13.4.2] $df_{between} = 3 - 1$,

[13.4.3] $df_{between} = 2$.

The value of the $df_{between}$ can be recorded under column 3 in the first row of Table 13.2.

Given that we now know the $SS_{between}$ and the $df_{between}$, we can determine the $MS_{between}$ using:

[13.5.1] $MS_{between} = \dfrac{SS_{between}}{df_{between}}$,

[13.5.2] $MS_{between} = \dfrac{60.12}{2}$,

[13.5.3] $MS_{between} = 30.06$.

The $MS_{between}$ can then be written into row 1 under column 4 of Table 13.2.

The next set of calculations concerns the portion of the analysis that is unique to the one-way repeated measures ANOVA—the variability associated exclusively with the subjects themselves; that is, the $SS_{subjects}$, $df_{subjects}$, and $MS_{subjects}$.

[13.6.1] $SS_{subjects} = \dfrac{(\sum X_i)^2}{k} - \dfrac{(\sum X_{ij})^2}{N}$.

The second part of the formula (b) is simply the correction factor used in the previous calculations. In contrast, the first portion of this formula can seem to be unfamiliar until you realize that it merely entails squaring and then summing each of the "subject totals" (i.e., $(\sum X_i)^2$) shown in the far right side of Table 13.1. Once these values are squared and summed, the resulting product is divided by the number of levels in the independent variable (k), which is equal to 3 in the present analysis, or:

[13.6.2]

$$SS_{subjects} = \left[\dfrac{(19)^2 + (19.5)^2 + (21)^2 + (22.5)^2 + (17.5)^2 + (21.5)^2}{3} \right] - 806.68,$$

[13.6.3]

$$SS_{subjects} = \left[\dfrac{361 + 380.25 + 441 + 506.25 + 306.25 + 441}{3} \right] - 806.68,$$

[13.6.4] $SS_{subjects} = \left(\dfrac{2{,}435.75}{3} \right) - 806.68$,

[13.6.5] $SS_{subjects} = 811.92 - 806.68$,

[13.6.6] $SS_{subjects} = 5.24$.

As you can see, there is very little variation in this study that is linked with individual differences. The value of $SS_{subjects}$ is entered into row 2 under column 2 of Table 13.2.

The df_{subjects} is calculated by the following formula before its value is placed in row 2 under column 3 of Table 13.2:

[13.7.1] $df_{\text{subjects}} = n - 1$.

There are six participants, so:

[13.7.2] $df_{\text{subjects}} = 6 - 1$,

[13.7.3] $df_{\text{subjects}} = 5$.

The value of MS_{subjects} can then be readily determined using:

[13.8.1] $MS_{\text{subjects}} = \dfrac{SS_{\text{subjects}}}{df_{\text{subjects}}}$,

[13.8.2] $MS_{\text{subjects}} = \dfrac{5.24}{5}$,

[13.8.3] $MS_{\text{subjects}} = 1.05$.

The MS_{subjects} is then recorded in row 3 under column 4 in Table 13.2.

The final set of calculations for the ANOVA source table deal with within-groups variability. We begin by calculating the SS_{within} using:

[13.9.1] $SS_{\text{within}} = \sum X_{ij}^2 - \dfrac{(\sum X_i)^2}{k} - \dfrac{(\sum X_j)^2}{n} + \dfrac{(\sum X_{ij})^2}{N}$.

There are a few more numbers in this formula than the others, but all of the values are already available, either from prior calculations or Table 13.1. The first part of the formula (a) is readily found in Table 13.1 (i.e., $\sum X_{ij}^2 = 884.75$), for example, and the second part (b) was just determined in the previous set of calculations ($(\sum X_i)^2/k = 811.92$; see [13.6.5]). The third entry (c) can be taken from the between-groups sum of squares calculation ($(\sum X_j)^2/n = 866.80$; see [13.3.5]) and the last entry (d), of course, is the correction term, which was originally determined in [13.1.4]. Entering the appropriate values we find:

[13.9.2] $SS_{\text{within}} = 884.75 - 811.92 - 866.80 + 806.68$.

Do not be put off by all these numbers—just perform the addition or subtraction as appropriate to find SS_{within}:

[13.9.3] $SS_{\text{within}} = 12.71$.

This value is then placed into the third row of column 2 in Table 13.2.

We then calculate the degrees of freedom for the within-groups variance estimate:

[13.10.1] $df_{\text{within}} = (n - 1)(k - 1)$,

[13.10.2] $df_{\text{within}} = (6 - 1)(3 - 1)$,

[13.10.3] $df_{\text{within}} = (5)(2)$,

[13.10.4] $df_{\text{within}} = 10$.

The df_{within} is then recorded in the third row of column 3 in Table 13.4.

The variance estimate within-groups is determined by:

[13.11.1] $MS_{\text{within}} = \dfrac{SS_{\text{within}}}{df_{\text{within}}}$,

[13.11.2] $MS_{\text{within}} = \dfrac{12.71}{10}$,

[13.11.3] $MS_{\text{within}} = 1.27$.

DATA BOX 13.A

Cell Size Matters, But Keep the Cell Sizes Equal, Too

Throughout this book, the importance of obtaining an adequately sized sample is stressed again and again. Larger samples are much more likely to approximate or even closely characterize populations than smaller ones. This truth is evident whether one is performing a t test or one of the various types of ANOVAs we have learned about in this and the previous two chapters.

So, size matters, but should we also worry about whether each cell in a simple or complex research design has an equivalent number of observations in it? In a word, yes. A one-way ANOVA can have differing numbers of participants in each level of the independent variable with no ill effects where the results are concerned, but a two-way ANOVA is another story. Performing a factorial ANOVA with unequal numbers of observations in each cell is a problematic but, unfortunately, rather common practice; conducting an actual research project from start to finish is not always a tidy enterprise (Dunn, 1999). Thus, obtaining all the participants you need is a desirable goal, but often a difficult one to realize.

You will notice that most of this book's hypothetical examples are based on equal sample sizes within cells. As a writer and data analyst, this choice was not simply made for convenience or to create order in data—I also wanted to illustrate the methodological importance of what otherwise might be seen as a small detail. Why does equivalent cell size matter? The explanation is rather technical but the simple fact of the matter is that the results one obtains are generally somewhat distorted (e.g., Aron & Aron, 1999).

What is a conscientious researcher to do where unequal cell sizes are concerned? Here are a few possibilities.

1. **Never work with unequal cell sizes!** Do your best to balance the number of participants in each cell in a factorial design. Make certain that all of the cells in your 2×2 design, for example, have equal membership and representation.
2. **Drop extra data or collect some more.** Some researchers use a random selection procedure to remove the "extra" data from a cell in order to keep its size equivalent to the others in the research design. This procedure seems to be a bit drastic and even wasteful—why would one want to literally throw data away (and statistical power in the process)? A better idea might be to recruit a few more participants in order to "fill up" those cells that have lower membership than the others.
3. **Learn a new ANOVA technique.** Finally, there is a regression-based statistical procedure called least squares analysis of variance. This computer-based data analysis procedure effectively equalizes each cell's respective influence on any main effects and interactions (Aron & Aron, 1999). Many software packages rely on this procedure—indeed, Aron and Aron note that when cell sizes are unequal, it may automatically be used in lieu of the more conventional ANOVA procedures. If you use statistical software, be sure to consult a manual to learn how unequal cell sizes are handled.

This value, too, is entered into Table 13.2 (see row 3, column 4).

Before we calculate the F ratio indicating whether any difference(s) existed between the average number of ruminative thoughts across the 3 weeks, we must be certain that no errors exist in the calculations we just performed. Here are two quick error checks to verify what you have already done:

■ Using information from Table 13.2, check whether the individual sum of squares estimates add up to the SS_{total}:

Table 13.2   ANOVA Source Table for Rumination and Therapeutic Meditation Study

Source	Sum of Squares	df	Mean Square	F	p
Between-groups	60.12	2	30.06	23.67	.05
Subjects	5.24	5	1.05	.827	
Within-groups	12.71	10	1.27		
Total	78.07	17			

$$SS_{total} = SS_{between} + SS_{subjects} + SS_{within},$$

$$78.07 = 60.12 + 5.24 + 12.71,$$

$$78.07 = 78.07.$$

■   Using information from Table 13.2, check whether the individual entries for degrees of freedom are equal to df_{total}:

$$df_{total} = df_{between} + df_{subjects} + df_{within},$$

$$17 = 2 + 5 + 10,$$

$$17 = 17.$$

Always perform any requisite error checks before calculating the F ratios—otherwise, computational errors can affect the results.

We can now calculate the F ratio for the one-way repeated measures ANOVA. To calculate the appropriate F ratio, we divide $MS_{between}$ by MS_{within}:

[13.12.1] $F_{between} = \dfrac{MS_{between}}{MS_{within}},$

[13.12.2] $F_{between} = \dfrac{30.06}{1.27},$

[13.12.3] $F_{between} = 23.67.$

We report this F ratio in the usual way, being careful to select the appropriate degrees of freedom representing the between-groups variance estimate (numerator df) and within-groups variance estimate (denominator df):

$$F(2, 10) = 23.67.$$

To locate a critical value for this F statistic, we turn to Table B.5 in Appendix B and search for the value lying at the intersection of the column labeled 2 (for the numerator df) and the row labeled 10 (for the denominator df). Two critical values are available and we select the one shown in the lighter typeface—4.10—as it corresponds to $\alpha = .05$. Invoking the statistical convention, we ask ourselves whether the observed F ratio is greater than or equal to this critical value—if so, then H_0 can be rejected:

Is $F_{calculated}$ (2, 10) = 23.67 ≥ $F_{critical}$ (2, 10) = 4.10? *Yes: Reject H_0.*

Thus, we can reject the null hypothesis of no difference, indicating that at least one mean difference exists among the means representing daily ruminative thoughts across the 3-week period. Please note that the F ratio for this one-way repeated-measures ANOVA is an omnibus F because there are more than two groups (means) present. If there were only two means present, the nature of the difference would be apparent (though it is likely that we would have used a dependent groups t test in lieu of the repeated-measures ANOVA; see chapter 10). Given that we have a "big, dumb F," our only recourse is to conduct a post hoc comparison before we can properly complete step 4 of the analysis, the interpretation of the results.

Before we perform this post hoc comparison, however, one other calculation remains involving Table 13.2. Despite the fact that we are only interested in the presence of differences between the means representing the 3 weekly averages—the between-groups factor—we should also calculate the F ratio linked to the subjects factor. As I will show you later on, this other F ratio plays a particular role in a supplementary measure. Calculating the F for the subjects is done the same way as any other F ratio:

[13.13.1] $$F_{\text{subjects}} = \frac{MS_{\text{subjects}}}{MS_{\text{within}}}.$$

The necessary information is drawn from Table 13.2 for:

[13.13.2] $$F_{\text{subjects}} = \frac{1.05}{1.27},$$

[13.13.3] $$F_{\text{subjects}} = 0.827.$$

No post hoc comparison or other procedure will be carried out on this statistic—for the time being, we just note that its location is in the second row of the fifth column of Table 13.2. We can now get back to the business of identifying the location of the mean difference(s) for the between-groups factor using Tukey's HSD test.

Remember, the F_{between} statistic indicates if there are mean differences involving the repeated measures factor. The F_{subjects} statistic must also be calculated, but it is reserved for another purpose.

Tukey's *HSD* Test Revisited

The virtue of Tukey's HSD test is that it specifies the location of each and every mean difference within a given data set (for a review, see chapter 11). The HSD test performs pairwise comparisons involving the absolute value of the differences between all the means in a given data set. A mean difference is said to be significant if its value is greater than or equal to an HSD value, which is derived from information from an ANOVA source table and formula [11.19.1] (renumbered here for convenience and continuity):

[13.14.1] $$HSD = q\alpha \sqrt{\frac{MS_{\text{within}}}{n}},$$

where $q\alpha$ is a value drawn from Table B.6 in Appendix B. The value of $q\alpha$ is determined by locating a number at the intersection of a column representing k (i.e., the number of means or groups being compared) and a row value corresponding to df_{within} drawn from an ANOVA source table. Based on the means for the 3 weeks ($k = 3$) and 10 degrees of freedom ($df_{\text{within}} = 10$), the value of $q\alpha$ from Table B.6 is 3.88 (please turn there now to verify that you know how to find this value in the table). The value of MS_{within}, of course, is readily found in Table 13.2, just as n refers to the number of participants who took part in the relevant study. Entering the requisite numbers into the HSD formula we find:

[13.14.2] $$HSD = (3.88)\sqrt{\frac{1.27}{6}},$$

[13.14.3] $$HSD = (3.88)\sqrt{0.212},$$

[13.14.4] $$HSD = (3.88)(0.460),$$

[13.14.5] $$HSD = 1.79.$$

The next step involves creating a simple 3×3 matrix of the mean ruminative thoughts from Table 13.1, calculating the absolute values of the differences between the possible pairings of the 3 means, and then indicating which difference(s) is greater than or equal to the HSD value of 1.79. Such a matrix is shown in Table 13.3.

Table 13.3   Pairwise Comparisons Between All Means Using the Tukey *HSD* Test

Average Daily Ruminations		Average Daily Ruminations		
		Baseline Week	Week$_1$	Week$_2$
		9.75	5.75	5.05
Baseline week	9.75	—	4.00*	4.70*
Week$_1$	5.75	—	—	0.700
Week$_2$	5.05	—	—	—

Note: This table contains absolute differences between the three possible pairs of means. An asterisk (*) indicates that the absolute difference between the means (pairwise comparison) is significant at the .05 level using Tukey's *HSD* test.

By interpreting the results shown in Table 13.3, we can complete the interpretation and evaluation portions of step 4 of Table 11.4's hypothesis testing process. As you can see by the values shown inside the matrix in Table 13.3, only two of the three absolute differences between the means are significant: More ruminations occurred daily during the baseline week ($\overline{X}_1 = 9.75$)—before the meditation therapy—than in either the first ($\overline{X}_2 = 5.75$) or the second week ($\overline{X}_3 = 5.05$) *after* its introduction (see Table 13.3). There was no difference, however, between the number of daily ruminative thoughts during the two weeks after the therapy was taught to the six research participants (see Table 13.3).

As was true for the other variations of the ANOVA, we can compute the usual supplementary indices—effect size **f** and $\hat{\omega}^2$—to provide more meaningful context for the results. Once these two indices are known, we can tie everything together into a written summary for this one-way repeated-measures ANOVA.

▽

Remember that an absolute difference between two means must be greater than or equal to the *HSD* value in order for a difference to be significant.

Effect Size and the Degree of Association Between the Independent Variable and Dependent Measure

The effect size for the introduction of meditation therapy to combat ruminative thoughts can be known by using formulas [11.21.1] and [11.22.1], which are renumbered here for our present purposes:

[13.15.1]
$$\mathbf{f} = \sqrt{\frac{\eta^2}{1 - \eta^2}},$$

where

[13.16.1]
$$\eta^2 = \frac{SS_{\text{between}}}{SS_{\text{total}}}.$$

We begin by calculating η^2 by drawing the values of SS_{between} and SS_{total} from Table 13.2 (remember, we are only interested in the between-groups effect, which corresponds to how the number of daily ruminative thoughts varied across the 3 averages):

[13.16.2] $\eta^2 = \dfrac{60.12}{78.07},$

[13.16.3] $\eta^2 = 0.77.$

The value of η^2 can then be entered into [13.15.1] to complete the effect size calculation:

[13.15.2] $\mathbf{f}_{\text{between}} = \sqrt{\dfrac{0.77}{1 - 0.77}},$

[13.15.3] $\mathbf{f}_{\text{between}510} = \sqrt{\dfrac{0.77}{0.23}},$

[13.15.4] $\mathbf{f}_{\text{between}} = \sqrt{3.35},$

[13.15.5] $\mathbf{f}_{\text{between}} = 1.83.$

According to Cohen (1988), this effect size is very large—real data rarely exhibit such a strong effect size, though keep in mind that the nature of the repeated measures analysis (i.e., individual difference variance is not used to calculate the F statistic) enhances whatever statistical differences are present.

How do we calculate the degree of association between the independent variable and the dependent measure? First of all, we must rely on a particular variation of $\hat{\omega}^2$, one designed for results based on a one-way repeated measures ANOVA. The following formula demonstrates the extent to which an independent variable affects a dependent measure, but the effects of individual differences created by participants are appropriately removed in the process (from Runyon et al., 1996):

[13.17.1]

$$\hat{\omega}^2 = \frac{df_{\text{between}}\,(F_{\text{between}} - 1)}{df_{\text{between}}\,(F_{\text{between}} - 1) + F_{\text{subjects}}\,(df_{\text{subjects}}) + df_{\text{between}}\,(df_{\text{subjects}}) + 1},$$

Now you know why we bothered to calculate the F ratio representing the subjects effect—we need it to calculate $\hat{\omega}^2$. In any case, all of the information we need to complete the formula is easily obtained from our prior work shown in the ANOVA source table. Here is the completed formula:

[13.17.2] $\hat{\omega}^2 = \dfrac{2(23.67 - 1)}{2(23.67 - 1) + 0.827(5) + 2(5) + 1},$

[13.17.3] $\hat{\omega}^2 = \dfrac{2(22.67)}{2(22.67) + 4.135 + 10 + 1},$

[13.17.4] $\hat{\omega}^2 = \dfrac{45.34}{45.34 + 15.14},$

[13.17.5] $\hat{\omega}^2 = \dfrac{45.34}{60.475},$

[13.17.6] $\hat{\omega}^2 = 0.7497 \cong 0.75.$

Thus, approximately 75% of the difference between the 3 ruminative means can be attributed to the effects of the meditation therapy.

Writing About the Results of a One-Way Repeated-Measures Design

Writing up the results of a repeated-measures analysis is not very different than summarizing the findings associated with a one-way ANOVA. It is incumbent on the writer, however, to make it clear that only one group of participants took part in all phases (levels of the independent variable) of the study. As always, a brief review of the study's hypothesis or underlying theory is necessary to prime the reader's memory about the material previously read in an APA-style introduction and Method section. Draw the reader's attention to the nature of the design, highlight any mean differences, and then make note of the supplementary statistics (if any) used. Here is one way the hypothetical meditation therapy study could be reported:

Table 1 shows the average number of daily ruminative thoughts for the six clients across a 3-week period. As hypothesized, these data suggest that more ruminative thoughts occurred during the baseline period, prior to the introduction of the meditation therapy for the second and third weeks of the study. Indeed, participants reported experiencing far less anxiety-based cognition on a daily basis during weeks 2 and 3 (see Table 1).

A one-way repeated measures analysis of variance (ANOVA) revealed a significant decreases in the number of ruminative thoughts following the introduction of meditative therapy, $F(2, 10) = 23.67$, $p < .01$. Post hoc comparisons of means based on Tukey's *HSD* test indicated that participants reported a higher number of daily ruminative thoughts in the baseline period than in either of the subsequent weeks, where lower but equivalent numbers of ruminations were reported (see Table 1).

Based on this clinical sample, the effects of meditation therapy show great promise. The effect size for the therapeutic intervention is extremely large ($\mathbf{f} = 1.83$), and there was a high degree of association between the independent variable the dependent (repeated) measures of rumination ($\hat{\omega}^2 = 0.75$).

Table 1 Mean Number of Daily Ruminative Thoughts Across Three Weeks

| | Baseline Week | Post-Therapy | |
		Week 1	Week 2
M	$9.75_{1,2}$	5.75_1	5.05_2
SD	(1.48)	(0.758)	(0.917)

Note: Means sharing the same subscripts are significantly different from each other at the .05 level.

Knowledge Base

1. Why is it sometimes said that a participant in a repeated-measures design serves as his or her own control group?
2. Complete the following ANOVA source table for a one-way repeated-measures design:

Source	Sum of Squares	*df*	Mean Square	*F*
Between-groups	60	—	20	—
Subjects	—	9	—	—
Within-groups	30	—	—	
Total	130	39		

Answers

1. Because each participant appears in every level (k) of an independent variable, the variability attributable to that person is apt to be low, and it can be statistically removed from the study's random error. The remaining error will generally be small because it is due exclusively to experimental error, not individual differences *and* experimental error. As a denominator, the experimental error will be small, leading—through division into the numerator of the between-groups variability—to a relatively large F ratio.

2.

Source	Sum of Squares	*df*	Mean Square	*F*
Between-groups	60	3	20	18.02
Subjects	40	9	4.44	3.996
Within-groups	30	27	1.11	
Total	130	39		

DATA BOX 13.B

Improved Methodology Leads to Improved Analysis—Latin Square Designs

Although Sir Ronald A. Fisher (see Data Box 11.A and chapter 12's opening section) is usually associated with statistical innovations, his intellectual stature is also assured by his methodological contributions. Fisher can be credited with developing the "Latin square," a research design wherein restricted randomization is used to prevent bias in the assignment of participants to experimental treatments. (Originally, however, Latin squares were used in agriculture, where predetermined treatments were applied to plots of soil.) By "restricted randomization," we mean that the design is an alternative to a full-blown, repeated measures design where all possible (i.e., counterbalanced) orders of treatment combinations are run (Dunn, 1999). Why use a Latin square? Too few research participants may be available, for example, or there may be some compelling reason to avoid representing all possible treatment combinations in a given study.

In a Latin square design, the number of rows and columns correspond to the number of treatments being compared. A research design with two treatments, then, would have two rows and two columns; one with six treatments would have six rows and six columns, and so on. A Latin square's treatments are so arranged that one—and only one—treatment falls into a given row or column. Here is an example of a three-treatment Latin square:

	Order of Treatment		
Group 1	A	C	B
Group 2	B	A	C
Group 3	C	B	A

As you can see, each of the three treatments—A, B, and C—appear once in each of the three order positions, yielding three distinct treatment orders. By the way, the term "group" can refer to an actual group comprised of several people *or* it can denote only one person who receives a particular treatment combination. Although this form of randomization eliminates systematic bias, the measurement of error and the calculation of statistical tests for within- and between-groups differences are more advanced than those presented in this book. Guidance on creating or selecting particular Latin square designs, as well as advice on analyzing their data, can be found in Kirk (1982) and Winer, Brown, and Michels (1991).

Wolraich and colleagues (1994) used a three-treatment Latin square like the one shown above to examine the effect of sugar intake on children's hyperactivity. Many parents and educators believe that some children are highly reactive to sugar, so that aggressive behavior, attentional problems, and poor academic performance can be attributed to a sugar-laden diet. To verify the accuracy of this perception, 48 children and their families were assigned to one of three groups. The groups followed three different diets (A, B, & C; see above Latin square design), each for a period of three weeks. Here is a description of the diets:

Diet A—high in sugar but no artificial sweeteners (e.g., aspartame, saccharin)
Diet B—low in sugar; aspartame used as a sweetener
Diet C—low in sugar; saccharin used as a sweetener

Across the 9 weeks of the study, the children completed various tests and measures weekly, and their parents, teachers, and the researchers rated their behavior for evidence of hyperactivity and aggression. What did the investigators find by using this Latin square design? The children's behavior was *not* linked to diet or sugar intake—observers (parents, teachers) believe in a link between sugar and hyperactivity that is more apparent than real. The origin of this widespread fallacy is the intriguing question for future research efforts.

Mixed Design ANOVA: A Brief Conceptual Overview of Between-Within Research Designs

Just as between-groups designs can take on greater degrees of complexity beyond the classic 2×2 approach, within-subjects or repeated-measures designs come in more complicated varieties, as well. One of these designs combines the elegance of the repeated-measures approach with the pragmatism of the between-groups approach—the best of these two statistical worlds, as it were, in one data analytic tool. It is commonly called a *mixed design*—between- and within-groups designs are "mixed" together—though some authors refer to it as a "between-within" design or an IV $\times$ SV ("independent variable by subject variable") design (e.g., Cozby, 1997).

KEY TERM   A **mixed design** contains both a between-groups variable and a repeated measures factor, such that a given participant experiences one level of a first (between) independent variable and each level of a second (within) independent variable.

A *mixed design ANOVA* is used to analyze data from mixed designs.

KEY TERM   A **mixed design ANOVA** statistically examines mean differences caused by the between- and within-groups factors (i.e., main effects), as well as interactions between these two types of variables.

The computations for the mixed design are beyond the scope of this book (but see Runyon, Coleman, & Pittenger, 1999, for guidelines). A brief overview of the logic underlying the mixed design ANOVA, however, will illustrate how this type of advanced research design can aid investigators. Such aid encompasses the ability to ask complex—and often subtle—questions involving mean differences, questions that expand knowledge in the behavioral sciences.

We start by considering the repeated measures design that was introduced in the last section of the chapter. Was it an ideal research design? That is, can we be sure that the decrease in ruminative thoughts is attributable to the therapeutic intervention? Not necessarily. Why? That particular research example actually had a flaw built into it—there was no control group of clients who ruminated but did *not* receive the meditative therapy. In the absence of such a control group, for example, we cannot be sure that the frequency of rumination did not taper off in spite of the therapy. By including a control group in the study, we would be creating a mixed design—the between-groups factor would be the client groups (therapy vs. control) and the within-groups factor would be the measured incidence of ruminative thoughts across the three weeks. As I am sure you will agree, a mixed design would make the interpretive power of the research design—and the trustworthiness of its results—much more compelling.

Let's consider another example to illustrate a mixed design. Imagine, for example, that a researcher is interested in whether caffeine enhances memory. To test the hypothesis that this common ingredient in coffee, tea, and many soft drinks promotes learning and retention of information, an investigator recruits 32 college students (16 males, 16 females) for a project. The first between-groups factor is whether a student is or is not a coffee drinker—let's assume that half of the participants drink coffee regularly, while the others never do (for convenience, assume that this preference is evenly divided along gender lines). The participants are then assigned to one level of the second between-groups factor, caffeine administration (i.e., 8 participants, balanced by gender and coffee vs. noncoffee drinkers):

- Coffee group (participants drink a cup of caffeinated coffee before the memory trials)

■ No drink group (participants are not given anything to drink before the memory trials)

■ Placebo group (participants are given decaffeinated coffee and told that it is caffeinated).

■ Alternate beverage group (participants are given water to drink)

What about the repeated-measures factor? The repeated-measures factor in a mixed design is usually, but not always, temporal (e.g., measurement across hours, days, weeks, months, number of trials). The investigator has all of the participants complete four separate memory tasks designed to examine their ability to retain stimulus items in short- and long-term memory. Participants might learn a word list, for example, and after a fixed time interval, be tested to see how many items they recalled. To control for any order effects, the order of the 4 memory tasks is counterbalanced across the 32 participants (see Dunn, 1999; Shaughnessy & Zechmeister, 1994; for counterbalancing recommendations).

The advantage of a mixed design ANOVA is that it can compare mean recall for items on each of the four memory tasks between coffee drinkers and noncoffee drinkers (factor A), between the four types of caffeine administration (factor B), and across the four different memory tasks (factor C). This is a 2 × 4 (between-groups factors) × 4 (repeated measures factor) design, and you are no doubt already probably using knowledge gained in this and the last chapter to identify what particular effects emerge from the analysis. In terms of specific results, this mixed design ANOVA would reveal three main effects—one each for coffee drinking status, caffeine administration, and recall, as well as the following interactions: A × B, B × C, A × C, and a triple interaction—A × B × C. Explaining the interpretation of these main effects and interactions—even in the context of a hypothetical example—is a somewhat complex exercise. I offer this closing example to chapter 13 as a teaser, an invitation, really, for you to pursue learning advanced statistical techniques like the mixed design ANOVA in future classes.

Project Exercise

REPEATED-MEASURES DESIGNS: AWARENESS OF THREATS TO VALIDITY AND INFERENCE

In a now classic work on experimental design, Campbell and Stanley (1963) identified several major threats to the internal validity—the unambiguous influence of an independent variable on a dependent measure (see chapter 2)—of repeated-measures research designs. By use of the term "threats," the authors were referring to possible rival explanations for the observed outcomes of experiments. In other words, a researcher might assume that some obtained mean difference based on a repeated measures ANOVA was reliable when, in fact, it might have resulted from some unknown—and uncontrolled—factor *other than* the intended independent variable.

This *Project Exercise* involves examining repeated-measures research designs that employ (or could do so) a one-variable repeated-measures ANOVA, and then identifying any potential threats to accurate inference where internal and external validity are concerned (see chapter 2 for a review of validity issues). According to Campbell and Stanley (1963), the four threats that are apt to occur when a repeated-measures design is employed include:

Testing. After completing any sort of test, the original testing affects the scores an individual obtains at any subsequent testing (e.g., standardized test scores often improve across time as respondents become familiar with the question format, time demands, and the like).

Instrumentation. Any changes—planned or otherwise—in the way measures, equipment, or even observers are used in a study can lead to changes in subsequent measurements. A scale for measuring weight or a computer program for storing data must be reliable, otherwise the information both provide is corrupted. In the same way, experimenters must scrupulously maintain the same procedure throughout the life of a study, even when the routine is tiresome or boring—even minor changes to a script can alter later research results.

History. What happens across an experiment's "life"? Aside from an independent variable, things happening in the environment in which a study is performed can be threats of history. Consider a longitudinal study that is 3 months in length rather than a traditional experiment that is 30 minutes long—many uncontrolled or unknown environmental factors are a greater threat to causal inference in the former relative to the latter.

Maturation. Maturation involves individual, time-related processes occurring within research participants. These processes include growing more tired or bored, becoming hungrier, and even growing older; indeed, any such process that could impinge on the accurate interpretation of research results is said to be due to maturation.

A fifth threat (or collection of possible threats), one we have learned about before, can affect the external validity—the generalizability—of research results. The threat of carryover effects was previously introduced in the context of the dependent groups *t* test in chapter 10:

Carryover effects. Carryover effects refer to the interference that sometimes occurs when research participants encounter multiple treatments and/or dependent measures in the course of a study. In simpler terms, the effects of being measured early on in a study can unduly influence responses to later measures, independent of any experimental intervention. Some particular carryover effects—learning, habituation, sensitization, fatigue, adaptation, and contrast—were defined and reviewed in Table 10.4. For a broader discussion of threats to internal validity, including those that can affect between-subjects designs, please consult Campbell and Stanley (1963), Cook and Campbell (1979), or Judd and Kenny (1981).

Here are some options for the *Project Exercise,* which can be presented in written form or discussed during class:

1. Review the hypothetical repeated-measures design presented earlier in this chapter. Evaluate the design based on the threats to internal validity highlighted above, as well as the carryover effects found in Table 10.4. What specific threats, if any, might affect this design? Why? Could any methodological, interpretive, or even statistical action be taken to reduce or eliminate any threat?

2. Go to the Reference Department of your institution's library and search the behavioral science literature for studies employing repeated measures designs and analyses. Obtain copies of the journal articles, books, or book chapters wherein the research is presented, and then evaluate the designs based on the threats to internal validity noted above, as well as the carryover effects found in Table 10.4. What specific threats, if any, might affect these designs? Why? Did the author(s) make note of these threats or take any action to reduce, prevent, or eliminate them? Could any methodological, interpretive, or even statistical action been taken to reduce or eliminate these threats?

3. Create a hypothetical experiment using a repeated measures design, one based on some underlying theory (i.e., your own or one found in the behavioral science literature). Evaluate the design based on the threats to internal validity presented, as

well as the carryover effects found in Table 10.4. What specific threats, if any, might affect this design? Why? Could any methodological, interpretive, or even statistical action be taken to reduce or eliminate any threat?

LOOKING FORWARD THEN BACK

nce again, the first decision tree opening this chapter enables you to identify differences among the four types of research designs amenable to analysis by the ANOVA (note that the independent and dependent groups *t* tests are highlighted there, as well). As a statistical test for locating mean differences, the ANOVA is a routine analytic procedure within the behavioral sciences. Unless such analyses are performed with some regularity, however, it is always helpful to have a guide like the first decision tree available when questions arise. If you decide to conduct experimental research involving more than a basic two group comparison, my guess is that you will probably rely on one of these ANOVAs to analyze your data.

The second decision tree will prove to be helpful after you perform a one variable repeated measures ANOVA. As always, it is important to perform post hoc comparisons of means when more than two are present, just as supplementary analyses—effect size and degree of association between independent and dependent variables—add to our understanding of any obtained results. Keep in mind that it is not merely results per se that are of interest to readers—as a data analyst, you must endeavor to provide a theoretical context for any findings. Thus, be certain to present your results in a clear, concise written summary, and to support such explanation with any necessary tables, graphs, or other aids. Such attention to detail will make you a better researcher and data analyst, as well as an informed consumer of the behavioral science literature.

Summary

1. A one-way repeated-measures ANOVA is often referred to as a within-subjects ANOVA, as the same group of participants is exposed to all the levels of a single independent variable. This statistical test is a close relative of the dependent groups *t* test—the difference between the two tests is that the latter can only examine the difference between two means.

2. There is a distinct statistical advantage to a repeated-measures ANOVA: Because each participant serves as his or her own control group, the variability in the denominator of the *F* ratio is exclusively due to experimental error—variability due to individual differences is partialed out separately in the analysis.

3. The statistical assumptions of the one-way repeated-measures ANOVA differ from those associated with other ANOVA techniques in one respect only—it is assumed that the effects of each independent variable are consistent across the study's

participants and that no carryover or other order-related effects are present.

4. Partitioning variability in the one-way repeated-measures ANOVA is analogous to the procedure associated with the other ANOVA techniques, however, the variability due to the subjects ($MS_{subjects}$) is kept separate and distinct from that associated with the independent variable ($MS_{between}$). This separation leads to a smaller denominator, which frequently enhances the likelihood of finding a significant *F* ratio associated with the repeated-measures factor.

5. When the *F* ratio for a repeated-measures factor is found to be significant, some post hoc test—such as Tukey's *HSD* test—must be employed to locate differences between means when more than two are present. Although the *F* ratio for the "subjects" factor is calculated, it is used to determine the value of a supplementary measure and not as a result per se.

6. Supplementary measures (e.g., effects size f and $\hat{\omega}^2$) should be included in any write up of one-way repeated-measures results, along with a table illustrating how the means representing the different levels of the independent variable changed (if at all) across time.

7. A mixed design is one comprised of at least one between-groups factor and one repeated-measures factor, and data from it are analyzed by the mixed design ANOVA. Calculation of this test is beyond the scope of this chapter, though it is important to be aware that a main effect for each variable, as well as an interaction between all variable pairs, results.

Key Terms

Mixed design (*p.* 515)

Mixed design ANOVA (*p.* 515)

One-variable or one-way repeated-measures ANOVA (*p.* 501)

Chapter Problems

1. How does a one-way repeated-measures ANOVA differ from a one-way ANOVA? (*Hint:* Use examples to illustrate your points.)

2. Why measure a dependent variable more than once? What are the advantages of using a repeated-measures ANOVA design?

3. Why would a data analyst elect to use the dependent groups *t* test instead of a one-variable repeated-measures ANOVA? Illustrate your points through an example(s).

4. A one-variable repeated-measures ANOVA is conducted on data collected from eight participants whose responses were measured at four different points in time. What is the value of the degrees of freedom for the *F* ratio?

5. A one-variable repeated-measures ANOVA is conducted on data collected from 10 participants whose responses were measured at three different points in time. What is the value of the degrees of freedom for the *F* ratio?

6. An educational psychologist is interested in how students' moods vary across a given school day. The researcher is interested in identifying stable mood patterns among middle school students, as such patterns may reveal the "best" or "worst" time for teaching and learning particular academic topics. Twenty students complete a mood scale at six intervals during a typical day (i.e., about every 2 hours). The measures are administered at home (when they wake up and just before bed), as well as in school. What type of analysis should the educational psychologist use to analyze the data from the mood scales? Why? Use the decision trees that open this chapter to answer and to guide your thinking about these questions.

7. Assume that the result(s) of the analysis proposed in question 6 reached significance. What is the next step(s) the investigator should take? Use the appropriate decision tree provided at the opening of this chapter to answer this question.

8. An investigator performs a one variable repeated measures ANOVA and finds an *F* ratio with 4 and 36 degrees of freedom. How many participants took part in the study? How many times was the dependent measure administered?

9. An investigator conducts a study where 4 dependent measures are administered to 10 participants. The investigator analyzes the data using a one variable repeated measures ANOVA. What are the degrees of freedom associated with the resulting *F* ratio for the repeated measures variable?

10. A guidance counselor is interested in how student motivation changes across time. She tracks six students from 10th through 12th grade in order to document any change in their academic motivation. To do so, the students complete the Student Academic Motivation (SAM) scale during the second week of school in each of the three grades (higher scores indicate greater scholastic motivation; the data are provided below). Calculate the average SAM scores for the three years and then use the appropriate ANOVA to determine whether (and how) the scores changed across the 3-year period (use a significance level of .05). If any significant differences are observed, perform the required post hoc tests and supplementary statistics. (*Hint:* You may find the decision trees appearing at the opening of the chapter to be helpful.) Be sure to write up the results of your analysis in APA style.

SAM Scores

Students	10th grade	11th grade	12th grade
1	10	6	11
2	9	8	12
3	8	6	10
4	10	5	9
5	9	6	10
6	8	8	9

11. Are there any advantages that repeated-measures designs have over between-groups designs?

12. How does the calculation of a repeated-measures ANOVA's error term (i.e., the denominator in the F ratio) differ from the one associated with a between-groups ANOVA?

13. The following data were collected in a repeated-measures design. Analyze these data using the appropriate test and explain whether (and where) any significant differences lie (use a significance level of .05):

Treatments

Participants	1	2	3	4
A	2	4	5	7
B	1	2	4	5
C	2	5	3	6
D	1	4	3	6

14. The following data were collected in a repeated-measures design. Analyze these data using the appropriate test and explain whether (and where) any significant differences lie (use a significance level of .05):

Sessions

Participants	1	2	3	4
A	8	7	5	2
B	9	8	4	2
C	8	7	4	1
D	8	6	5	3
E	7	4	4	2

15. Calculate the effect size and association between the independent variable and dependent measure (if appropriate) for the results presented in question 13.

16. Calculate the effect size and association between the independent variable and dependent measure (if appropriate) for the results presented in question 14.

17. The following source table represents the results of an experiment, the data from which were analyzed by a one-way repeated-measures ANOVA. Assume that there were 10 participants in the study and then complete the source table's entries.

Source	Sum of Squares	df	MS	F
Between-groups		2	15	—
Subjects	8.00	—	—	
Within-groups		—		
Total	88.00	—		

18. The following source table represents the results of an experiment, the data from which were analyzed by a one-way repeated-measures ANOVA. Assume that there were six participants in the study and then complete the source table's entries.

Source	Sum of Squares	df	MS	F
Between-groups	48	3	—	—
Subjects	—	—		—
Within-groups	35	—		
Total	90	—		

19. Calculate the effect size and association between the independent variable and dependent measure (if appropriate) for the results presented in question 17.

20. Calculate the effect size and association between the independent variable and dependent measure (if appropriate) for the results presented in question 18.

21. An industrial organizational psychologist examines the productivity scores of a trainee group at a manufacturing plant. The trainees' performance is assessed weekly for the first three weeks of their employment. The psychologist wants to learn whether there are any significant changes in performance across the training period. Here are the data:

Trainee	Week 1	Week 2	Week 3
A	5	8	9
B	4	7	10
C	2	4	8
D	6	9	10

Calculate an ANOVA to determine whether any differences in productivity occur across the training period (use a significance level of .05 in your analysis). If appropriate, determine effect size as well as the degree of association between the independent variable and the dependent measures.

22. A coach examines the hours per week her players devote to weight training. She wants to see whether the time devoted to weight training increases steadily over a period of one month. Here are the data:

Player	Week 1	Week 2	Week 3	Week 4
A	1	2	2.5	4
B	2	3	4	6
C	3	3	4	7
D	1	1.5	3	5
E	2	3	3	5
F	0.5	2	4	5.5

Calculate an ANOVA to determine whether any differences in training time occur across the month (use a significance level of .05 in your analysis). If appropriate, determine effect size as well as the degree of association between the independent variable and the dependent measures.

23. Under what sort of circumstances would an investigator elect to use a mixed design ANOVA? How does a mixed design ANOVA differ from the other forms of ANOVA reviewed in this and the previous chapter?

24. A research project on weight loss and health follows a group of dieters for one year. During the year, their weight is measured monthly, so each participant has 12 recorded weights. What sort of analysis should be performed on these weight scores in order to determine whether dieting led to weight loss across the year? Why? (*Hint:* Use the decision tree(s) at the start of this chapter to answer these questions.)

Choosing Which Nonparametric to Use for Data Analysis

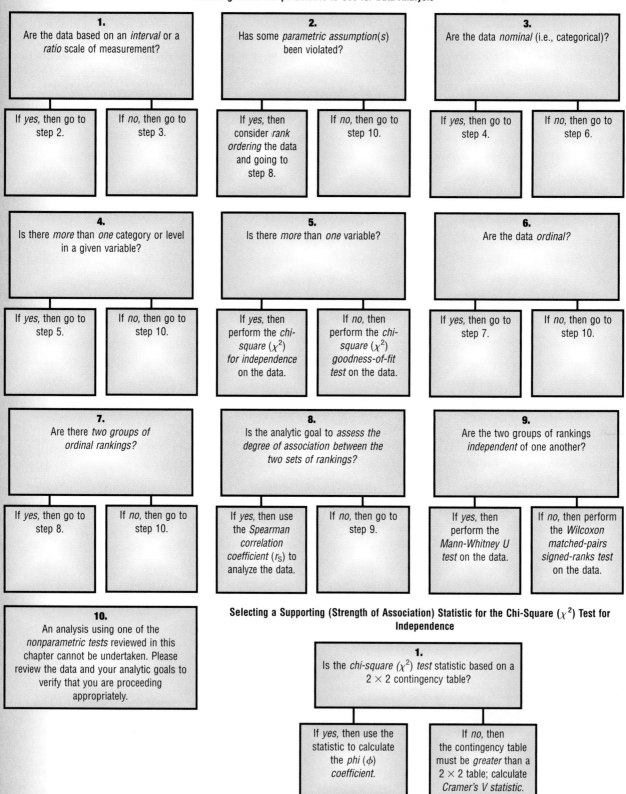

1.
Are the data based on an *interval* or a *ratio* scale of measurement?

If *yes*, then go to step 2.

If *no*, then go to step 3.

2.
Has some *parametric assumption(s)* been violated?

If *yes*, then consider *rank ordering* the data and going to step 8.

If *no*, then go to step 10.

3.
Are the data *nominal* (i.e., categorical)?

If *yes*, then go to step 4.

If *no*, then go to step 6.

4.
Is there *more* than *one* category or level in a given variable?

If *yes*, then go to step 5.

If *no*, then go to step 10.

5.
Is there *more* than *one* variable?

If *yes*, then perform the *chi-square* (χ^2) *for independence* on the data.

If *no*, then perform the *chi-square* (χ^2) *goodness-of-fit test* on the data.

6.
Are the data *ordinal*?

If *yes*, then go to step 7.

If *no*, then go to step 10.

7.
Are there *two groups of ordinal rankings*?

If *yes*, then go to step 8.

If *no*, then go to step 10.

8.
Is the analytic goal to *assess the degree of association between the two sets of rankings*?

If *yes*, then use the *Spearman correlation coefficient* (r_S) to analyze the data.

If *no*, then go to step 9.

9.
Are the two groups of rankings *independent* of one another?

If *yes*, then perform the *Mann-Whitney U test* on the data.

If *no*, then perform the *Wilcoxon matched-pairs signed-ranks test* on the data.

10.
An analysis using one of the *nonparametric tests* reviewed in this chapter cannot be undertaken. Please review the data and your analytic goals to verify that you are proceeding appropriately.

Selecting a Supporting (Strength of Association) Statistic for the Chi-Square (χ^2) Test for Independence

1.
Is the *chi-square* (χ^2) *test* statistic based on a 2×2 contingency table?

If *yes*, then use the statistic to calculate the *phi* (ϕ) *coefficient*.

If *no*, then the contingency table must be *greater* than a 2×2 table; calculate *Cramer's V statistic*.

SOME NONPARAMETRIC STATISTICS FOR CATEGORICAL AND ORDINAL DATA

ome years ago, I had an officemate who worked in a developmental research laboratory where children's social behavior was observed and coded. The codings were often used to create frequency tables wherein the behavioral styles of families (e.g., nurturing, distracted, abusive) and their impact on the children's social and emotional development could be studied. The leader of this laboratory was a dedicated researcher who kept a close watch on incoming data as they were coded for later analysis. She was known to closely eyeball a table of frequencies, sometimes remarking that, "a visual chi-square [an inferential statistical test] tells me this pattern is significant."

Of course, this researcher did not seriously trust her intuition in place of actual statistical analyses, nor was she actually performing an analysis with just a glance (but note that I always implore you to eyeball your data before beginning any analyses). The spirit of the researcher's remark, however, is important for our present purposes. She identified an appropriate statistical test for the data that is not very complicated to calculate; indeed, the chi-square test—and others like it—are much less complex than the inferential tests presented earlier in this book. These tests, some of which will be discussed in this chapter, represent a collection of alternative approaches to hypothesis testing.

This chapter represents a departure from our careful and thorough examination of how to statistically test for mean differences, the focus of the previous four chapters. We are still very much interested in asking focused questions of data through hypothesis testing, but now we will use different sorts of data. Previously, our emphasis was on measuring things—observations, participants' reactions to some stimulus—using either an interval or ratio scale, and then determining whether any significant between- or within-groups differences involving the measurements existed. To be sure, the behavioral sciences have something of a mania for measurement, invoking a philosophy only half-jokingly referred to as the "if-it-moves, then-measure-it" approach. It is also true, however, that there are many other interesting questions that are not at all dependent on measurement per se—and these questions, too, are well within the purview of the behavioral sciences.

Questions that do not lend themselves to analysis by the usual inferential statistical tests require an altogether different set of statistical techniques, which are collectively referred to as nonparametric statistics. Here are some nonmeasurement questions that are amenable to analysis by the nonparametric approach:

■ A campus physician is interested in determining whether male and female students are equally aware that regular workshops on wellness, fitness, and diet are offered by the health center. She randomly samples 200 students (half male, half female) and asks whether they are aware of these programs, subsequently comparing the frequencies of their responses. Here are the data:

	Aware Workshops are Offered?	
Gender of Student	**Yes**	**No**
Male	30	70
Female	80	20

As you can see, their responses are readily categorized as raw frequencies—"Yes, I know about the workshops" or "No, I didn't know about the workshops"—so that no rating scales or other types of measurement are needed. As you look over the table, the obvious question to ponder is whether the university's women are more aware of the health initiatives than men—the pattern of their "yes" and "no" answers certainly points to this conclusion. A nonparametric test performed on such data enables us to take any speculation a step further, to consider whether the observed pattern of responses is statistically valid (i.e., women *are* more aware of available campus health initiatives than men). Such a significant finding serves as an invitation for the physician to embark on research designed to reveal the possible reasons for and implications of the disparity in knowledge between the two groups.

■ A professor of decision sciences wants to demonstrate that the problem-solving efforts of groups generate better, more creative solutions than individuals working alone. To test this idea empirically, the researcher gives groups of five people or solo individuals a complex task involving describing a government for a hypothetical society. All participants are given 1 hour to develop mock bureaucratic systems on paper, each of which is then rated (in rank order) by a political scientist who is unaware of the study's intent. The decision researcher wants to show that more complex but possible structures are likely to originate in groups rather than being thought up by persons working alone. The decision sciences professor will need to employ a method of data analysis enabling him to determine whether group solutions will be ranked more highly than the plans of individual thinkers.

■ A perception researcher is interested in people's similarity judgments where texture gradients are concerned. She provides two participants with a collection of 10 different grades of sandpaper, asking each to rank order the sandpaper samples from the most fine-grained to the coarsest texture. The researcher wants to determine the degree of overlap between the rankings made by each of the participants: Were their rankings of texture unanimous, somewhat similar, or rather diverse? To adequately address this question, the researcher must assess the degree of association (correlation) between the respective sets of rankings (note again that the data are *rankings* rather than *ratings*).

In the course of this chapter, then, we will examine a variety of statistical tests that stretch our general conception of hypothesis testing, enabling us to think about data in new ways. These new ways chiefly entail working with ordered rankings of observations or critically examining frequency information to determine if either reveals any clear conclusions about behavior. Before we learn the actual statistical tests, however, we must be certain we understand the underlying difference between the inferential tests we learned in earlier chapters and those we are studying now.

How Do Nonparametric Tests Differ from Parametric Tests?

At this point, you are thoroughly immersed in the "whys" and "wherefores" of *parametric statistics*, as most of the previous chapters in this book focus on them.

KEY TERM   A **parametric statistic** is an inferential test that, prior to its use, assumes that certain specific characteristics are true of a population—particularly the shape of its distribution—from which data are drawn for analysis.

Parametric tests concern population parameters (e.g., μ, σ) and making inferences about those parameters, requiring that certain assumptions be met before they can properly be used for data analysis. One of the most common parametric assumptions we visited over and over in recent chapters is normality. The majority of inferential statistics used to test for mean differences, for example, presume that observations are drawn from bell-shaped or normal distributions. (In spite of the fact that some of these tests are "robust" enough to provide trustworthy results when their distributions are not normal, the normality assumption is a basic principle of parametric statistics and theory.)

Another characteristic of parametric tests, one so obvious that it is routinely overlooked, is that a single number must be associated with each observation or participant in a data set. These numbers are then mathematically manipulated—squared, summed, divided, multiplied, averaged, and so on—in the course of calculating a parametric statistic. Thus, parametric tests generally require that *something* be done to the data, and often many steps are involved in calculating or otherwise transforming the available numbers.

When a set of data are not normal in shape (i.e., a distribution is skewed; see chapter 3) and they violate various other parametric assumptions, a different group of statistics must be employed when inferential analyses are required. These tests are usually referred to as *nonparametric statistics* because they lack the relatively rigid assumptions of their parametric cousins.

KEY TERM   A **nonparametric statistic** is an inferential test, one that makes few or sometimes no assumptions regarding any numerical data or the shape of the population from which the observations were drawn.

Nonparametric statistics are often labeled "distribution-free tests of significance" precisely because a constraint like normality need not be met before the tests are applied to some data. Indeed, researchers can use these tests to search for or to verify statistically significant differences between groups, but they can often do so without having to satisfy a set of strictures before analyzing the data. More to the point, nonparametric tests often serve a worthy function for researchers—they are often the only statistical recourse when a traditional parametric test cannot be used (e.g., too few observations exist, a distribution is skewed). Generally, then, parametric tests are powerful when their assumptions are met, but nonparametric tests are excellent choices when such assumptions are violated.

Advantages of Using Nonparametric Statistical Tests Over Parametric Tests

Why use nonparametric tests when there are so many parametric tests to choose from? Despite their ubiquity and flexibility, parametric tests cannot do everything a researcher needs—their applicability is widespread in carefully controlled experiments but notably less so out in the field, quasi-experimental investigations, or naturally occurring behavioral events composed of few observations. Siegel (Siegel & Castellan, 1988) lists four clear advantages of nonparametric tests for behavioral scientists to carefully consider:

- **Nonparametric statistical tests are usually "distribution free."** As already noted, the tests do not possess any underlying assumptions that must be met before they can be applied to data. Unlike the bulk of the parametric tests we studied, nonparametric tests do not adhere to the normal distribution nor do they necessarily require that the data be collected in any particular manner.
- **Nonparametric tests can be used to analyze data that are not precisely numerical.** Parametric tests generally analyze only interval or ratio data, where values have a relatively precise meaning along some given dimension. In contrast, many nonparametric tests are less focused on numerical values per se than they are on how the values can be categorized (i.e., nominally scaled) or ranked (i.e., ordinally scaled) for comparison with one another.
- **Nonparametric tests are ideal for analyzing data from small samples.** Most—perhaps all—of the parametric tests we reviewed really require that a relatively large number of observations comprise a data set. Nonparametric tests are not so hindered by sample size—indeed, they are arguably most useful in those situations that are rare and by their nature contain few observations. Nonparametric tests, then, can play a large role in happenstance situations that present themselves to researchers (e.g., unusual behavioral or attitudinal samples from a singular cultural group, or some rare event, mental illness, or disease).
- **Nonparametric tests are generally easy to calculate.** As we have seen throughout most of this book, parametric tests usually require a variety of relatively detailed steps be performed before a statistic's value is known. To use Siegel's (1988, p. xv) phrasing, nonparametric tests possess a "computational simplicity." Because nonparametric tests can be calculated with relative ease, researchers can fruitfully spend their timesavings on the careful formulation of solid, testable questions and the collection of appropriate data (cf. Evans, 1996).

Despite these advantages, however, keep in mind that it is also true that:

- Nonparametric tests are less statistically powerful than parametric tests.
- The scales of measurement analyzed by nonparametric tests (i.e., chiefly nominal or ordinal data) are less sensitive than those analyzed by parametric tests (i.e., chiefly interval and ratio data).

Still, Siegel's (1988) advantages are worth keeping in mind, though we need to step back a moment and ask a pressing question: "How do I know when to use one nonparametric test rather than another?" I will provide a few guidelines in the next section, as well as in the presentation of each nonparametric test introduced in this chapter. Please be aware that my presentation of the nonparametric tests is selective rather than exhaustive—there are many nonparametric tests one could learn. Chances are good, however, that you will use only one or two of them for analyzing data unless some unusual research design or collection of observations materialize. Indeed, given the way behavioral science research is taught and generated, an individual is more likely to need to know all (or most, anyway) of the basic parametric tests but only a handful of the nonparametric offerings. Fortunately, there are excellent references where one can search out appropriate nonparametric tests when unusual research needs crop up(see Gibbons, 1971; Hollander & Wolfe, 1973; Kirk, 1990; Moses, 1952; Siegel & Castellan, 1988; Sprent, 1989).

Choosing to Use a Nonparametric Test: A Guide for the Perplexed

We have repeatedly seen that data analyzed by parametric statistics must be based on either an interval or a ratio scale (for a review, see chapter 1). Except when parametric assumptions are violated, nonparametric statistics are rarely used to analyze data from interval or ratio scales. Instead, nonparametric tests are frequently employed when making inferences from nominally or ordinally scaled data. As noted in chapter 1, nominal data are usually based on observations that are placed into one (and only one) category. Nonparametric tests used to analyze nominal data basically infer whether the pattern discerned across some number of categories is anticipated by chance (the available categories have approximately the same number of observations in each one) or not (one or more of the categories contains significantly more observations than the others).

What about ordinal data? Ordinal data have some implicit order or ranking built within them. When nonparametric tests are applied to ordinal data, they are often used to discern whether one sample of observations has higher rankings than another sample—perhaps one group was exposed to some experimental treatment but the other was not. The fact that one sample had a consistently higher set of rank orderings than another could indicate an obvious and significant difference between the two samples.

Table 14.1 illustrates several types of research designs, and the nonparametric (for nominal and ordinal data, respectively) and parametric statistical tests used to analyze data collected within them. Please notice that this table includes *only* those statistical tests reviewed in this text—there are many other appropriate tests that could analyze the same designs and accompanying data. (Naturally, the decision trees presented at the opening of this chapter should also be used to decide which nonparametric test, if any, is appropriate for a given situation.)

Consider the second row of Table 14.1. The research design involves comparing two independent samples to determine whether a difference exists between them. By

Table 14.1 Research Designs and the Nonparametric and Parametric Tests Available to Analyze Their Data

| Research Design | Nonparametric Tests for | | Parametric Tests |
	Nominal Data	Ordinal Data	
One sample	χ^2 goodness-of-fit	—	One-sample t or z test
Two independent samples	χ^2 test of independence	Mann-Whitney U test	Independent groups t test
Two dependent samples	—	Wilcoxon matched-pairs signed-rank test	Dependent groups t test
More than three independent samples	χ^2 test of independence	—	One-way ANOVA
Correlation	—	Spearman r_s	Pearson r

Note: The entries in this table are selective. Various other nonparametric and parametric tests are not included in this table. The blank entries indicate that an appropriate test(s) is not reviewed in this book.

DATA BOX 14.A

The Nonparametric Bible for the Behavioral Sciences: Siegel and Castellan (1988)

Every student of the behavioral sciences should be aware of a classic reference work, *Nonparametric Statistics for the Behavioral Sciences*. I use the word "aware" because you are not likely to use this book unless a particular need arises, but when one does, you need to know where to go for guidance.

Written by Sidney Siegel, the first edition of this guide to nonparametric statistics appeared in 1956 (Siegel, 1956). The decided strengths of the book include its focus on presenting nonparametric techniques in concert with the research designs they were developed to analyze. To his great credit, Siegel employed a step-by-step calculation method throughout the book. A revised version of the book—Siegel died in 1961—appeared in 1988 (Siegel & Castellan, 1988). This revision, undertaken by John Castellan, preserves the best aspects of the original text while incorporating newer techniques from the ever-expanding repertoire of nonparametric tests (contrary to popular opinion, the discipline of statistics is not static, but changing, growing, and developing like any other academic field).

The Siegel and Castellan (1988) text is best described as the bible for nonparametric statistics. Why? Simply because the authors put together a clearly written reference tool that aids researchers who must decide which statistic is most appropriate for their particular circumstances—and data. The chapters in the Siegel and Castellan text guide readers through tests for single samples, one sample with two measures, two independent samples, two or more dependent samples, two or more independent samples, and measures of association. I urge you to keep this key reference work in mind should you find yourself with data that do not conform to the expectations of parametric tests.

now, you should reflexively think of employing the independent groups *t* test (for a review, see chapter 10) to analyze interval or ratio scaled data from such a design. As you can see, the independent groups *t* test is identified as the parametric test of choice. When the available data are nominal, however, the χ^2 (chi-square, which is pronounced "kie-square") test of independence is the correct analytic tool (we will learn to calculate this statistic in the next section). On the other hand, ordinal data placed into two independent groups would be examined using what is called the Mann-Whitney *U* test, a statistic that will be introduced later in the chapter. Table 14.1 will serve as a valuable reference for you when you must decide which nonparametric test is appropriate for a given research design.

The Chi-Square (χ^2) Test for Categorical Data

Categorical or nominal data involve calculating or keeping track of frequencies. As you learned back in chapter 3, a frequency refers to the number of observations or items that can be meaningfully grouped under some heading or label. If we had a group of 20 people, for example, we could describe them—and group them—based on arbitrary frequency information (e.g., How many had blue eyes? Green eyes? How many of the women are over 6 feet tall? How many group members have advanced degrees?). Such information is usually easy to follow and interpret, but when we want to make inferences about the presence or absence of some pattern (e.g., Are there more women over 6 feet than under that height in the sample?) within the frequencies, then we need to rely on a statistical tool for analyzing frequencies. The chi-square, which compares *observed* frequencies against *expected* frequencies, is such a tool.

Statistical Assumptions of the Chi-Square

The chi-square distribution is not a single distribution but rather a collection of similar curves, each of which is based on some number of degrees of freedom. The chi-square distribution is similar to the t distribution in that it is based on one degree of freedom value; in contrast, for example, recall that an F statistic is always based on two separate degrees of freedom values.

Given its nonparametric nature, the chi-square test need not be applied to data that conform to any particular shape (i.e., normal distribution), though the observations must be nominal. The data are usually organized as frequencies placed within a relatively small range of categories. As a result, the shape of the data's distribution is unlikely to resemble the familiar bell-shaped curve.

One underlying assumption the chi-square does have is that observations are randomly selected from some larger population. If the observations are not randomly selected—and many times they will not be—then a researcher must be very cautious about generalizing from the data set's results back to the larger population. After all, you cannot learn the social climate of a college campus by speaking to fraternity and sorority members exclusively—so-called "independent" students must be polled, as well. Naturally, this random sampling assumption is not novel—it is shared by virtually every inferential test we have reviewed.

A second assumption is that the number of expected observations within a given category should be reasonably large. A good rule of thumb is to have few (preferably no) categories with less than an expected frequency of 5 observations in any given analysis. In general, however, the link between statistical power and sample size is much less obvious in chi-square calculations than is true for parametric tests.

The Chi-Square Test for One-Variable: Goodness-of-Fit

With most parametric tests, we were concerned with examining how the mean value of a dependent measure varied as a function of the levels of some independent variable. The means, of course, were "stand-ins," proxy values representing parameters from some theoretical population that we wanted to describe or make inferences about. When working with nominal, also known as categorical, data, however, we are interested in exploring the relative frequencies or proportions present in some distribution (e.g., How many experimental psychologists are males rather than females? Of the four most popular majors at the college, which one do sophomores choose most often?).

Questions like these involve collecting frequency data and then making comparisons based on how the observations are categorized. The statistical test designed to make such comparisons is commonly referred to as the *chi-square test for goodness-of-fit*.

KEY TERM   Using sample data, the **chi-square test for goodness-of-fit** tests whether obtained observations conform to (i.e., "fit") or diverge from the population proportions specified by a null hypothesis.

The phrase "goodness-of-fit" literally points to the comparison of what pattern or distribution of frequencies would be anticipated due to chance versus the one that is actually obtained. When the fit between "observed" and "expected" observations is good, then we know that the distribution of observations across the available categories is more or less equal. When the discrepancy between observed and expected observations is sufficiently large, however, then a significant difference is likely to be found between (or among) the categories. The departure of observed from expected results means that the fit is not "good," that some influential factor or factors is presumably causing it.

Let's consider a specific example to illustrate the chi-square test for goodness-of-fit. A statistics instructor asks the 35 students in her class to complete a standard course evaluation. One of the key questions of interest to this instructor was: "Statistics was my favorite class this semester." To respond to the statement, a student simply circled one (and only one) of the rating options (i.e., strongly agree, agree, undecided, disagree, strongly disagree). Here is a breakdown of the students' responses ($N = 35$):

Observed Data

Strongly Agree	Agree	Undecided	Disagree	Strongly Disagree
17	8	3	2	5

Please note that the instructor elected to treat the responses as categorical data—she might just have easily calculated a mean rating based on the 35 responses.

What can we conclude from these categorical data? By casually "eyeballing" the data, it appears that the majority of the students in the sample (those comprising the "strongly agree" and "agree" categories) affirmed the sentiment that this was their favorite course that particular semester. (As an aside, I wonder how you would answer this question, and whether you and your classmates agree with the positive sentiment!) The statistical issue, of course, involves demonstrating that this positive pattern of agreement deviates from what would be expected by chance (i.e., if the students were responding more or less randomly to the question).

Thus, the chi-square test statistic (χ^2) indicates whether there is a difference between some observed set of frequencies—the data drawn from a piece of research—and a set of expected frequencies. These expected frequencies constitute the prediction made under the null hypothesis. We will review the null hypothesis for the chi-square test in some detail momentarily.

Before we do so, however, we should review the necessary steps for testing a hypothesis using a nonparametric statistic. I say "review" because the steps involved do not diverge much from those we followed for previous inferential tests (recall Tables 9.2 and 11.4). The five basic steps for performing a nonparametric test are shown in Table 14.2. The main difference here is that it is advisable for you to first verify that the data are either nominal or ordinal, as well as to select a test statistic (see step 1 in Table 14.2). (We already completed this step when we began to talk about the data presented earlier in this section. When you perform this step "solo," you can rely on Table 14.1 as well as the decision trees that open the chapter.) Once this step is completed, the next few steps—stating a null and alternative hypothesis (step 2), choosing a significance level (step 3), performing requisite calculations in order to accept or reject H_0, as well as interpreting and evaluating the results (step 4), follow the standard pattern. Nonparametric tests do

Table 14.2   Steps for Testing a Hypothesis Using a Nonparametric Test

1. Verify that the available data are based on a *nominal* or an *ordinal* scale, not on an *interval* or a *ratio* scale. (Note, however, that the latter two types of data can be analyzed by a nonparametric test when a parametric assumption(s) is violated.) Select an appropriate test using chapter 14's first decision tree, Table 14.1, or a reference work (e.g., Siegel & Castellan, 1988; see Data Box 14.A).

2. State the null (H_0) and the alternative (H_1) hypotheses.

3. Select a significance level (p value or α level) for the nonparametric test.

4. Perform the analyses using the statistic, determining whether to accept or reject H_0. Interpret and evaluate the results in light of the hypothesis, and if necessary, go to step 5.

5. Compute any supporting statistics.

not require any post hoc tests, though some supporting statistics are sometimes calculated (this flexibility is provided by step 5 in Table 14.2). We will refer back to this table through the remainder of this chapter.

We can now return to the null hypothesis for the chi-square test for goodness-of-fit. This null hypothesis can take one of two forms: *no frequency difference* among a set of different categories or *no frequency difference from a comparison population*.

To return to our example, the H_0 for no frequency difference among a set of different categories would be:

> H_0: No difference in course ratings across the five rating categories
> (i.e., strongly agree to strongly disagree).

Because there are 35 students, the expected frequency for each category when no difference exists would be 7 (i.e., 35 students divided by the five possible categories equals 7 students in each one), or:

Expected Data Under H_0

Strongly Agree	Agree	Undecided	Disagree	Strongly Disagree
7	7	7	7	7

Thus, the general rule of thumb for determining the expected frequencies for the chi-square test for goodness-of-fit test is simply *dividing N by the number of available categories*. The alternative hypothesis, then, is:

> H_1: There is a statistically reliable difference between the
> observed and the expected frequencies.

What if a comparison population existed? In that case, you would simply compare the observed data with some existing comparison data. To continue our example, it is possible that a faculty member wanted to compare student ratings from a prior semester (say, one where a different textbook was used) with the current semester. The comparison data might look like this:

Comparison Data Under H_0

Strongly Agree	Agree	Undecided	Disagree	Strongly Disagree
4	10	11	5	5

The null hypothesis for the no frequency difference from a comparison population, then, could look like this:

> H_0: No difference in course ratings from prior semester across the
> five rating categories (i.e., strongly agree to strongly disagree).

The expectation of this null hypothesis is that the observed data would not depart significantly from the ratings gathered in the previous semester. If a difference were found to exist between the observed data and the comparison data, then perhaps—depending on the pattern of the frequencies—the instructor could conclude that the new book led to more favorable ratings. More simply, however, the alternative hypothesis could be:

> H_1: There is a statistically reliable difference between the
> observed and the comparison frequencies.

In general, most chi-squares tests focus on testing the first null hypothesis, where some set of observed data is compared to a pattern expected by chance. Thus, we will finish this example by testing just this hypothesis and so complete step 2 in Table 14.2. Before we proceed, however, what other information do we need? Beyond identifying the hypotheses, we must choose a significance level for the test statistic (step 3 in Table 14.2; as usual, the alpha-level of .05—two-tailed—is fine), which will later help us to pinpoint the critical value for accepting or rejecting H_0.

We can now move on to step 4 in Table 14.2, the actual calculations for the test statistic. Here is the formula for calculating the chi-square test:

[14.1.1]
$$\chi^2 = \frac{\sum (f_O - f_E)^2}{f_E},$$

where f_O refers to the observed frequency in a given category and f_E is the expected frequency under H_0 for that category. The numerical difference between these two frequencies is calculated, its value is squared, and then divided by the f_E. The process is repeated for each of the remaining cells, and then all of the products are summed to create the chi-square test statistic.

Before we proceed with the actual calculations, pause for a moment and think about what intuitively must be true about the process of assessing differences between observed and expected frequencies: When the respective frequencies are similar to one another, the value of the χ^2 test statistics will be relatively small (i.e., the null hypothesis is apt to be accepted). As the differences between the observed and expected values increase, there is an increased likelihood that the null hypothesis can be rejected (i.e., a statistically reliable difference is identified).

An easy way to organize the calculation of the χ^2 test statistic is by using a tabular format. Table 14.3 illustrates each of the observed (f_O; see column 2) and expected (f_E; see column 3) frequencies, the difference between them ($f_O - f_E$; see column 4), the squared value of the difference (($f_O - f_E)^2$; see column 5) and the final product resulting once each squared-difference score is divided by f_E(($f_O - f_E)^2/f_E$; see column 6). The value of the χ^2 test statistic is determined by summing each of these final products together. Once summed (see the bottom of column 6 in Table 14.3), the value of the χ^2 test statistic is known. (Please take a moment and review the calculations presented in Table 14.3 and assure yourself that you know where all the numbers came from and why. Take special note of the fact that both $\sum f_O$ and $\sum f_E$ must be equal to N—here, 35.)

Table 14.3   Calculating a χ^2 Test Statistic Using a Tabular Format

	f_O	f_E	$(f_O - f_E)$	$(f_O - f_E)^2$	$(f_O - f_E)^2/f_E$
Strongly agree	17	7	10	100	14.29
Agree	8	7	1	1	0.143
Uncertain	3	7	−4	16	2.29
Disagree	2	7	−5	25	3.57
Strongly disagree	5	7	−2	4	0.571
	$\sum f_O = 35$	$\sum f_E = 35$	$\sum (f_O - f_E) = 0$		$\sum (f_O - f_E)^2/f_E = 20.86$

$\chi^2 = \sum (f_O - f_E)^2/f_E = 14.29 + 0.143 + 2.29 + 3.57 + 0.571 = 20.86$

Note: $N = 35$ (i.e., $\sum f_O$) respondents. These data are based on hypothetical responses to the statement "Statistics was my favorite class this semester."

In any χ^2 analysis, the Σf_O and the Σf_E must both be equal to N.

Using [14.1.1] (repeated here for consistency) and entering the values from Table 14.3, we can calculate the χ^2:

[14.1.1]
$$\chi^2 = \frac{\Sigma (f_O - f_E)^2}{f_E},$$

[14.1.2]
$$\chi^2 = \frac{(17 - 7)^2}{7} + \frac{(8 - 7)^2}{7} + \frac{(3 - 7)^2}{7} + \frac{(2 - 7)^2}{7} + \frac{(5 - 7)^2}{7},$$

[14.1.3]
$$\chi^2 = \frac{(10)^2}{7} + \frac{(1)^2}{7} + \frac{(-4)^2}{7} + \frac{(-5)^2}{7} + \frac{(-2)^2}{7},$$

[14.1.4]
$$\chi^2 = \frac{100}{7} + \frac{1}{7} + \frac{16}{7} + \frac{25}{7} + \frac{4}{7},$$

[14.1.5]
$$\chi^2 = 14.29 + 0.143 + 2.29 + 3.57 + 0.571,$$

[14.1.6]
$$\chi^2 = 20.86.$$

In this example, the value of the χ^2 test statistic—20.86—is quite large.

Once the value of the test statistic is known, you can calculate the degrees of freedom for the χ^2, which are based on:

[14.2.1]
$$df_\chi = k - 1,$$

where k is equal to the number of available categories. The original rating scale is based on five categories, so the degrees of freedom for this χ^2 test statistic are:

[14.2.2] $df_\chi = 5 - 1,$

[14.2.3] $df_\chi = 4.$

Once the degrees of freedom are identified, we can turn to Table B.7 in Appendix B, a table of critical values of χ^2. Please turn to Table B.7 now and locate the row corresponding to 4 degrees of freedom in the table's leftmost column. Read across that row until you find the value under the column labeled ".05." What value did you find? If you located the χ^2 critical value of 9.488, then you are correct. As we have done with all other hypothesis testing ventures, we ask a straightforward question: Did the observed test statistic exceed or equal the value found in the table? Or,

Is $\chi^2 (4) = 20.86 \geq \chi^2_{\text{critical}} (4) = 9.488$? *Yes, so Reject H_0.*

As shown here, the degrees of freedom are included (parenthetically) along with the reported test statistic and critical value. To report this significant χ^2 in APA style, you would write:

$$\chi^2 (4, N = 35) = 20.86, \quad p < .05.$$

The statistic is reported in the standard APA manner but with one important exception: Because the degrees of freedom bear little resemblance to a study's sample size, N is always included for clarification. Please note that there is no supporting statistic (i.e., step 5 in Table 14.2) for the chi-square test for goodness-of-fit.

Interpreting and Writing About the χ^2 Goodness-of-Fit Result. What does this significant test statistic mean? As shown by the original data, students enrolled in statistics that semester generally (and strongly) agreed with the sentiment that it was their favorite course. When a χ^2 test statistic is significant, "what you see is what you get" where interpretation is concerned. Can we conclude that all students share this belief? Certainly not. Aside from required courses—and statistics may be one—anytime students take a class they generally elect to be there, so they were not randomly selected from the larger population. We can be reasonably confident that students in this sample defied expectations—they did indeed like the course—but we cannot generalize beyond this sample.

Just as there is relatively little to say where the interpretation of the χ^2 is concerned, there is not that much to write about, either. This virtue enables the researcher/data analyst to get right to the point. Here is one way this example could be shared with others:

> Students enrolled in the statistics class were asked to indicate their level of agreement with the statement that "Statistics was my favorite course this semester." Five rating categories were available for participant responses, which were in general agreement with the statement (see Table 1). A chi-square test for goodness-of-fit revealed that the observed data departed from the expectation of no difference across the categories, χ^2 (4, $N = 35$) = 20.86, $p < .05$ (two-tailed). Thus, the students generally felt that statistics was their favorite course that semester.

Table 1

Strongly Agree	Agree	Undecided	Disagree	Strongly Disagree
17	8	3	2	2

The Chi-Square Test of Independence of Categorical Variables

There are many instances where a behavioral scientist is interested in more than one variable (recall the discussion of two-way and mixed design ANOVAs in chapters 12 and 13, respectively). When there are two categorical variables, researchers are often interested in knowing whether these variables are *independent* of one another or *dependent* on each other. By independent, each of the variables—and its influence—can be understood in isolation from the other. Is more of a story revealed, however, when the association between the two variables is examined? In other words, perhaps, understanding one of the variables really depends on being aware of its relationship to the other. Thus, is the size of first-graders' vocabularies at all related to whether their parents read to them daily? Put another way, is the size of a child's vocabulary *independent* of being read to, or does verbal fluency *depend* on this regular activity?

The chi-square test for the independence of categorical variables examines two variables with two or more categories in each one.

KEY TERM   The **chi-square test for independence** indicates whether the frequencies associated with two variables (with two or more categories each) are statistically independent of or dependent upon one another.

Each observation is placed in one—and only one—cell representing a joint relationship between one category from each variable. Let's consider an example in some detail. Imagine that a media specialist wants to find out how people learn about major news events—generally, do they read the newspaper or watch television? In turn, does their level of education influence which source they rely upon for the news? The specialist randomly samples 206 adult residents from a community, asking them to indicate their educational status (i.e., high school diploma or college diploma) and their primary source of news (i.e., television or the newspaper). Their responses are tallied in the following contingency table:

News Source

Educational Status	Television	Newspaper	Row Totals
College	47	62	109
High School	58	39	97
Column Totals	105	101	206

A glance at the cell entries *inside* the table suggests that college graduates are more likely to rely on the newspaper as their source for news, where high school graduates tend to use the television predominantly for gathering information. Note that the row totals and the column totals representing the respective variables are very similar in magnitude. The chi-square test for independence will reveal whether this apparent relationship between the two categorical variables is a dependent one—that is, both variables need to be considered simultaneously—or whether they are actually independent of one another.

Given that we are dealing with two categorical variables, we know to apply the chi-square test for independence, thereby satisfying step 1 of Table 14.2. Step 2 entails identifying the null and the alternative hypotheses. In this case, the null hypothesis is that the participants' level of education is independent of their mode of news acquisition. The varying pattern of frequencies shown above in the contingency table, then, is due to chance rather than any dependent relationship. In contrast, the alternative hypothesis tests whether a dependent relationship exists between education and mode of news gathering. In other words, more education is associated with whether people select a more active mode of news acquisition (i.e., *reading* the paper versus *watching* the television). Before we test the veracity of this alternative hypothesis, we can complete step 3 by selecting .05 as the significance level for rejecting H_0.

Step 4 entails the actual calculation of the nonparametric statistic, and here is the formula for doing so:

[14.3.1]
$$\chi^2 = \sum_{r=1} \sum_{c=1} \frac{(f_O - f_E)^2}{f_E},$$

where r is the number of rows and c is the number of columns, and f_O *and* f_E refer to the observed and expected frequencies, respectively. This formula directs the data analyst to determine the difference between the observed (f_O) and expected (f_E) frequencies in a given cell (i.e., $f_O - f_E$), square that difference ($(f_O - f_E)^2$), and then divide it by the expected frequency ($(f_O - f_E)^2/f_E$)—each of the product's corresponding four cells are then summed to create the chi-square statistic for independent events. If the χ^2 value equals or exceeds a critical value, then the null hypothesis of independence is rejected and the two variables are said to be in a dependent relationship with one another.

So far, the steps involved in calculating this form of the chi-square are identical to those used for the goodness-of-fit variation (recall [14.1.1]). We now introduce a pronounced difference from the latter statistic, however, by illustrating the procedure for determining the cell values expected under the null hypothesis of no difference. Please recognize that because there are two variables, the expected cell frequencies cannot be identified by simply dividing the number of participants by the number of cells available. Instead, we use a simple procedure called the "cell A" strategy to calculate the expected frequencies for the four cells. By cell A, we refer to the somewhat arbitrary identification of the upper left cell in any 2 × 2 table (see below):

	Television	*Newspaper*
College	A	B
High school	C	D

The remaining three cells are labeled B, C, and D, accordingly. Our goal is to calculate the expected frequency corresponding to each of these four cells.

Here is the formula for the cell A strategy:

[14.4.1] $$Cell\ A = \frac{column\ total}{N} \times row\ total.$$

Going back to the original contingency table presented above, we simply need to enter the column total found under cell A, divide that number by N, and multiply the result by row total found to the far right of cell A. Entering the appropriate numbers from the contingency table, we find:

[14.4.2] $$Cell\ A = \frac{105}{206} \times 109,$$

[14.4.3] $$Cell\ A = 0.5097 \times 109,$$

[14.4.4] $$Cell\ A = 55.56.$$

Thus, the expected frequency for cell A (i.e., college grads who watch the television for news) is 55.56. Please note that we would get the same result if we switched the placement of the row and column totals, or:

[14.5.1] $$Cell\ A = \frac{row\ total}{N} \times column\ total,$$

[14.5.2] $$Cell\ A = \frac{109}{206} \times 105,$$

[14.5.3] $$Cell\ A = 55.56.$$

How do we calculate the expected frequencies for the remaining three cells? There are really two ways. First, we could simply use the cell A strategy for each of the remaining cells; that is, dividing a given row (column) total by N and then multiplying the product by the column (row) total. Based on the relevant entries from the contingency table, the expected frequency for cell B, then, would be:

[14.6.1] $$Cell\ B = \frac{column\ total}{N} \times row\ total,$$

[14.6.2] $$Cell\ B = \frac{101}{206} \times 109,$$

[14.6.3] $$Cell\ B = 0.4903 \times 109,$$

[14.6.4] $$Cell\ B = 53.44.$$

This procedure is then repeated the same way for cells C and D, a relatively easy feat requiring the data analyst to select only the appropriate row and column totals.

Alternatively, the original expected value for cell A (i.e., 55.56) and some relatively easy subtraction can be used to determine the expected values for cells B, C, and D. Here's how. Once the value of cell A is fixed at 55.56, we need only subtract this value from the row total of 109 (see the original contingency table) to determine cell B (i.e., $109 - 55.56 = 53.44$). Note that this is the same value we just calculated with formula [14.6.1]. Using the same logic, cell C's value can be known by subtracting the value of cell A from the column total of 105 (see the contingency table). Thus, cell C's value is 49.44 (i.e., $105 - 55.56 = 49.44$). To calculate the expected frequency of cell D, we have a choice. We can subtract the value of cell C from the row total of 97 or cell B's value can be subtracted from the column total under it, which is 101. Either calculation will yield the same result of 47.56 (as an exercise, show that this claim is true). Here, then, are all the expected frequencies alongside the four lettered cells:

	Television	*Newspaper*		*Television*	*Newspaper*
College	A	B	College	55.56	53.44
High school	C	D	High school	49.44	47.56

Once again, please note that the sum of all the expected frequencies for the 4 cells must be equal to N (here, 206—remember that in any chi-square test, the sum of the observed data must always equal the sum of the expected frequencies). Another error check, of course, is to verify that when both row totals or both column totals are summed together, their values should both be equal to N, as well (check this assertion by going back to the original contingency table).

Using these expected frequencies, we can now continue with the chi-square analysis using formula [14.3.1], repeated here for convenience:

When computing a χ^2 test for independence, be certain that the row totals and the column totals each sum to N—any discrepancy from N indicates that a math error is present.

[14.3.1] $$\chi^2 = \frac{\sum\limits_{r=1}^{}\sum\limits_{c=1}^{}(f_O - f_E)^2}{f_E},$$

[14.3.2] $$\chi^2 = \frac{(47 - 55.56)^2}{55.56} + \frac{(62 - 53.44)^2}{53.44}$$
$$+ \frac{(58 - 49.44)^2}{49.44} + \frac{(39 - 47.56)^2}{47.56},$$

[14.3.3] $$\chi^2 = \frac{(-8.56)^2}{55.56} + \frac{(8.56)^2}{53.44} + \frac{(8.56)^2}{49.44} + \frac{(-8.56)^2}{47.56},$$

[14.3.4] $$\chi^2 = \frac{73.27}{55.56} + \frac{73.27}{53.44} + \frac{73.27}{49.44} + \frac{73.27}{47.56},$$

[14.3.5] $$\chi^2 = 1.3188 + 1.3711 + 1.4821 + 1.5407,$$

[14.3.6] $$\chi^2 = 5.71.$$

Once we have the χ^2 statistic, we need to determine its degrees of freedom before we can declare whether it is statistically significant. The formula for degrees of freedom for the chi-square test for independence is:

[14.7.1] $$df_\chi = (r - 1)(c - 1),$$

where r is the number of rows (i.e., categories) and c is the number of columns (i.e., categories) representing the respective variables shown in the original contingency table. In our example, there are two of each, so:

[14.7.2] $df_\chi = (2 - 1)(2 - 1),$
[14.7.3] $df_\chi = (1)(1),$
[14.7.4] $df_\chi = 1.$

This chi-square statistic, degrees of freedom, and—remembering APA style—the study's sample size, are reported as:

$$\chi^2 (1, N = 206) = 5.71.$$

To determine if the value reaches significance, we turn to Table B.7 in Appendix B, locating the row on the left side of the table corresponding to 1 degree of freedom. We then

DATA BOX 14.B

A Chi-Square Test for Independence Shortcut for 2 × 2 Tables

Instead of computing expected frequencies using either of the two procedures presented in the text, the following simple procedure can be used. The other two procedures can be expanded for contingency tables that are larger than 2 × 2 (e.g., 2 × 3, 3 × 3)—however, the following method can *only* be used for 2 × 2 tables. We will review the necessary steps using the data from the example problem presented in the text:

1. Organize the data as follows:

A	B	A + B	47	62	109
C	D	C + D	58	39	97
A + C	B + D	N	105	101	206

2. Enter the organized numbers into this formula (and do not be put off by unusually large numbers!):

$$\chi^2 = \frac{N(AD - BC)^2}{(A + B)(C + D)(A + C)(B + D)},$$

$$\chi^2 = \frac{206[(47)(39) - (62)(58)]^2}{(109)(97)(105)(101)},$$

$$\chi^2 = \frac{206(1{,}833 - 3{,}596)^2}{112{,}126{,}665},$$

$$\chi^2 = \frac{206(3{,}108{,}169)}{112{,}126{,}665},$$

$$\chi^2 = \frac{640{,}282{,}814}{112{,}126{,}665},$$

$$\chi^2 = 5.71.$$

3. The observed χ^2 has the same value as that found using formula [14.3.1].

---

read down the column of .05 values, thereby finding the critical value of 3.84 (please turn to Table B.7 and verify that you would select the same critical value). Is the observed chi-square statistic greater than or equal to the critical value? Yes, in symbolic terms:

$$\chi^2(1) = 5.71 \geq \chi^2_{\text{critical}}(1) = 3.84 - \textit{Reject } H_0.$$

The significant χ^2 statistic is then reported as:

$$\chi^2(1, N = 206) = 5.71, p < .05.$$

How do we interpret this result? Clearly, the two variables are *not* independent of one another—source of news acquisition *depends* on level of education. College graduates tend to read the newspaper for news, where high school graduates are more likely to watch a news program on television.

When reporting the result of any chi-square test, be sure to indicate which type of test (i.e., goodness of fit or independence) was performed.

Supporting Statistics for the Chi-Square Test of Independence: Phi (ϕ) and Cramer's *V*

The chi-square test for independence reveals whether two variables have a statistically significant relationship with one another, but not the strength of their mutual relationship.

The strength of the relationship between two variables can be assessed using one of two supporting statistics, the *phi* (ϕ) or *Cramer's V statistic*.

Phi (ϕ) coefficient.   The phi coefficient can be calculated when an investigator is performing a chi-square analysis on a 2 × 2 contingency table. In a manner similar to the Pearson *r*, the phi coefficient provides a measure of association between two dichotomous variables. The formula for this supporting statistic is:

[14.8.1]
$$\phi = \sqrt{\frac{\chi^2}{N}}.$$

Using the data from the education and news acquisition, we find that:

[14.8.2] $$\phi = \sqrt{\frac{5.71}{206}},$$

[14.8.3] $$\phi = \sqrt{.0277},$$

[14.8.4] $$\phi = .17.$$

The value of the phi coefficient can range between 0 and 1, where higher values indicate a greater degree of association between the variables. Values closer to 0 suggest that there is little or no relationship between the variables. In the present case, we see that the strength of association between education and news acquisition is not very pronounced, despite the fact that the chi-square value is significant. Once again, we must remind ourselves that significance per se is not the issue—just because a result reaches conventional statistical significance does not give us license to claim its effect is strong. In the present example, the two variables share only a minor relationship with one another.

Cramer's *V* statistic.   When is Cramer's *V* preferred over the phi coefficient? Cramer's *V* statistic is used only when a contingency table is larger than the standard 2 × 2 size. The formula for Cramer's *V* is:

[14.9.1]
$$V = \sqrt{\frac{\chi^2}{N(n-1)}},$$

where *n* refers to the *smallest* number of rows *or* columns present in a contingency table. If the table were a 3 × 4 design, then *n* would be equal to 3. One last suggestion: Neither the phi coefficient nor Cramer's *V* should be calculated unless the χ^2 is statistically significant.

Writing About the Results of a Chi-Square Test for Independence

The results of a chi-square test for independence are written up in essentially the same manner as the goodness-of-fit test. You need not report the actual raw frequencies, however; instead, many authors will convert the frequency data into percentages for inclusion in a simple table. Thus, a researcher might report that:

> A chi-square test for independence was performed to determine whether participants' level of education was at all related to the manner in which they acquired news. Table 1 presents the percentage of respondents broken down by educational background and news source (i.e., television or newspaper). As anticipated, the test revealed that college graduates were more likely to learn about current events from the newspaper, where high school graduates identified the television as their preferred media source, χ^2 (1, $N = 206$) = 5.71, $p < .05$ (see Table 1). Although the two variables are not independent of one another, the strength of association between them is relatively modest ($\phi = 17$). Reasons for this inconsistency in the results are presented later in the Discussion.

Table 1 News Acquisition as a Function of Educational Level (in Percentages).

| | News Source | | |
Educational Status	Television	Newspaper	Row Totals
College	22.82	30.1	52.91
High school	28.16	18.93	47.09
Column Totals	50.97	49.03	100

DATA BOX 14.C

Research Using the Chi-Square Test to Analyze Data

Does nonhuman companionship—caring for a dog or a cat, for instance—promote health and well-being? Can the presence of animal companions positively enhance the 1-year survival rate for people who have had a heart attack? Friedman, Katcher, Lynch, and Thomas (1980) argued that similar to human beings—a spouse, a close friend or other family member—pets provide an important source of companionship that may mitigate subsequent health problems associated with heart disease. Pets must serve some important function in the lives of many people, as almost half of the homes in the United States report having some kind of pet (Friedman et al., 1980).

The researchers interviewed 67 male and 29 female patients diagnosed with heart attack (myocardial infarction or angina pectoris) and then admitted to a hospital, contacting them again a year later. The survival rate of the patient group after one year was 84%. Of the original sample, 58% claimed they had one or more pets at the time of their heart attack. The relationship between owning a pet and the survival rate following a year after hospital admission was examined in the following contingency table (from Friedman et al., 1980, p. 308):

| | Number of Patients with | |
Patient Status	No Pets	Pets
Alive	28	50
Dead	11	3

A chi-square test for independence performed on these data proved to be significant, $\chi^2 (1, N = 92) = 8.90$, $p < .002$. Of the 39 patients who did not own pets, 11 of them (28%) died within that first year following their heart attacks, compared to only 3 (6%) of the 53 pet-owning patients. Thus, pet ownership was linked with an increased survival rate 1 year after heart attack. The authors are quick to note that the increased survival rate is presumably not due to the beneficial effects of physical activity associated with pet care (i.e., walking a dog regularly), as a subsequent analysis showed that owners of pets other than dogs also had a higher survival rate than individuals who had no pets.

Did Friedman et al. (1980) conclude that the presence of pets definitively reduces mortality following heart disease? Certainly not, but these authors did use the chi-square test (as well as other, related statistical analyses) to make a case to researchers and health care professionals that pets, like other social factors, can have a potentially important effect on people's health following debilitating illness. Questions concerning the presence of pets, too, can be easily added to standard patient questionnaires, yielding a ready source of potentially insightful data.

Knowledge Base

1. Name a few ways in which nonparametric statistics differ from parametric tests.
2. What does Σf_O always equal? What does Σf_E always equal?
3. Examine the following contingency table and determine the expected frequencies for cells A and D.

	A_1	A_2
B_1	10	25
B_2	15	10

4. A chi-square test for independence is performed on a 3×4 contingency table. Assuming the test finds a significant result, which supporting statistic should be calculated?

Answers

1. Nonparametric tests are distribution free, generally require nominal or ordinal data, and tend to require less complex calculations. When parametric assumptions are violated, interval or ratio scale data can sometimes be analyzed by nonparametric statistics.
2. Both sums must be equal to the N of the observations available.
3. Cell A $= 14.58$; cell D $= 14.58$
4. Cramer's V is the appropriate supporting statistic for any contingency table larger than a 2×2 table.

Ordinal Data: A Brief Overview

In every day life, we are used to rank ordering our preferences ("Peach ice cream is tastier than chocolate, which I prefer in any case to vanilla" or "I didn't like that movie as much as the one I saw last Wednesday") and sharing them with others. In fact, relative rankings exist for any number of objects, particularly in the consumer realm (e.g., any given bestseller list for books, movies, or music; the infamous but popular published rankings lists of "top 100" or "best buys" colleges and universities). On occasion, too, a researcher may be interested in how participants rank order some set of stimuli within the context of an experiment.

How can ordinal or "ranked" data be analyzed? Ordinal data cannot be analyzed by the chi-square or by any of the other inferential (parametric) tests we examined previously in this book. Instead, we will learn to use three tests that allow us to test hypotheses with ordinal data (the Mann-Whitney *U* test, the Wilcoxon signed-ranks test) or to examine the degree of association between ordered rankings (the Spearman correlation coefficient, or Spearman *r*).

The Mann-Whitney *U* Test

As shown in Table 14.1, the Mann-Whitney *U* test is the statistic of choice for ordinal data that conceptually mirror the independent groups *t* test.

KEY TERM The **Mann-Whitney *U* test** is a nonparametric statistic used to identify a difference between two independent samples of rank-ordered (ordinal) data.

Here are the statistical assumptions underlying this test:

- The data are based on an ordinal scale of measurement.
- The observations were drawn or selected independently of one another.
- There are no "ties" (i.e., same values with different ranks) between rankings (ties *do* occur, however, and a quick procedure for dealing with them is presented in

Data Box 14.D). When the majority of ranks in a data set are tied, however, consult statistical works like Hays (1988) or Kirk (1990) for guidance.

The Mann-Whitney U test is employed when two independent samples exist—the presence of noninterval scale data precludes using the independent groups t test—and different participants appear in each of the two samples. Let's review an example in some detail. Perhaps a linguist is interested in comparing the effectiveness of traditional, classroom-based language learning versus total immersion learning where elementary students are concerned. The linguist randomly assigns a group of 18 fourth-graders to either a traditional Spanish language class (i.e., the teacher gives directions in English, though the emphasis is on learning to speak Spanish) or a total immersion class (i.e., the teacher speaks exclusively in Spanish). At the end of the school year, a panel of judges gives an age-appropriate Spanish-language test to the students, subsequently using the scores to rank the children's linguistic skills from 0 to 100 (the judges remain unaware of which learning technique each child was exposed to). The rankings were then categorized by the respective teaching techniques the students were exposed to (see Table 14.4).

The goal of any nonparametric test is to establish overall differences between two (or possibly more) distributions, *not* to identify the differences between any particular parameters (e.g., Evans, 1996). The Mann-Whitney U test assumes that if two collections of rankings originate from the same parent population, then the rankings from each group will be unsystematically "mixed" with one another. If, however, one group's rankings (say, group A) are found to be localized in *upper* or *lower* positions relative to the other group's ranks (group B), then we can reasonably assume that the ranks of one group come from a different population than the other. Let's follow the usual steps for testing a hypothesis using this nonparametric test.

Following Table 14.2, we have already completed step 1 by recognizing that the data are ordinal, rather than nominal, interval, or ratio-scaled. Stating the null and alternative hypothesis for the Mann-Whitney U test is not at all difficult (step 2); indeed, it only entails noting whether a systematic difference exists between the language skills of the two groups (based, of course, on their respective rankings), or:

H_0: There will be no systematic difference between the Spanish-speaking skills of the traditional-learning group and the total immersion group.

The Mann-Whitney U test is the nonparametric analog of the t test for independent groups.

Table 14.4   Spanish-Speaking Skills Resulting from Linguistic Pedagogy

Traditional Classroom (English and Spanish spoken)	Total Immersion (Spanish only spoken)
35	75
56	83
42	77
78	92
82	85
72	95
62	73
42	88
51	
38	

Note: Each number represents the relative ranking of a student's ability to speak Spanish after 1 year of receiving one mode of instruction.

The alternative hypothesis will suggest that such a difference exists, as in:

H_1: There will be a systematic difference between the Spanish-speaking skills of the traditional-learning group and the total immersion group.

Following the convention associated with step 3, we will rely on a significance level of .05 for the Mann-Whitney *U* test. Naturally, step 4 requires the lion's share of our efforts, as we must learn the calculation procedures for a new statistical test. We begin by noting that N_A, the number of students in the traditional learning group, is equal to 10; N_B is equal to 8 (i.e., the overall *N* for the study is 18, or $N_A + N_B$; see Table 14.4). We then sort the raw ordinal rankings into a new table, one where they are listed in *ascending* order, and next to these raw data are rankings from 1 (lowest score) to *N* (i.e., $N_A + N_B$, the highest score; see Table 14.5). Any tied ranks—a situation where two or more observations receive the same ranking—must be resolved using the straightforward procedure outlined in Data Box 14.D.

The third column in Table 14.5 identifies whether a given score is from group A (traditional learning) or B (total immersion). This labeling is accomplished in order to separate the rankings in the subsequent steps in the calculation of the Mann-Whitney *U* statistic. Columns 4 and 5 in Table 14.5 identify the respective rankings for groups A and B. As you can see, the former's ranks tend to be lower relative the latter's ranks, suggesting that a between-group difference is present (see columns 4 and 5 in Table 14.5).

We now select what is called the $U_{critical}$ value for the Mann-Whitney *U* test. To do so, we need to know the sample sizes of groups A ($N_A = 10$) and B ($N_B = 8$), as well as the predetermined significance level from step 2 (i.e., .05). Armed with this information, we turn to Table B.8 in Appendix B, which is the table of critical values for the

Table 14.5 Combined Ranks for Spanish-Speaking Skills Resulting from Linguistic Pedagogy

1 Ordered Raw Scores of Two Groups	2 Ranks of Scores of Two Groups	3 Group Identification	4 Ranks for Group A	5 Ranks for Group B
35	1	A	1	
38	2	A	2	
42	3.5	A	3.5	
42	3.5	A	3.5	
51	5	A	5	
56	6	A	6	
62	7	A	7	
72	8	A	8	
73	9	B		9
75	10	B		10
77	11	B		11
78	12	A	12	
82	13	A	13	
83	14	B		14
85	15	B		15
88	16	B		16
92	17	B		17
95	18	B		18
			$\sum R_A = 61$	$\sum R_B = 110$

DATA BOX 14.D

Handling Tied Ranks in Ordinal Data

When analyzing ordinal data, it is common to come across two or more ranks that are tied with one another. The following straightforward procedure can be readily used to "break the ties" and determine appropriate ranking values for substitution in whatever ordinal procedure you are conducting.

In the case of the Mann-Whitney U test performed in the text, for example, two scores of 42 represented tied ranks (see column 1 in Table 14.5). These two identical ranks held places 3 and 4 in the rankings of scores shown in column 2 of Table 14.5, but because the scores are indeed the same, we cannot call them 3 and 4! Instead, we rely on this simple formula to rectify the problem:

$$Rank\ of\ tied\ scores = \frac{sum\ of\ rank\ positions\ possessed\ by\ tied\ scores}{number\ of\ tied\ scores\ present}.$$

Because the two 42s held positions 3 and 4, their shared ranking becomes:

$$Rank\ of\ tied\ scores = \frac{3 + 4}{2},$$

$$Rank\ of\ tied\ scores = \frac{7}{2},$$

$$Rank\ of\ tied\ scores = 3.5.$$

As shown in column 2 of Table 14.5, both scores of 42 are assigned the shared rank of 3.5, thereby "breaking the tie," as it were.

What if we had three tied scores, say, in the fifth, sixth, and seventh places in a data set? We would simply add these places and divide by 3, or:

$$Rank\ of\ tied\ scores = \frac{5 + 6 + 7}{3},$$

$$Rank\ of\ tied\ scores = \frac{18}{3},$$

$$Rank\ of\ tied\ scores = 6.$$

The number of rankings needed to break any tie(s) can be expanded or contracted for the analysis of ordinally scaled data.

Mann-Whitney U test (the **boldface** entries in this table indicate two-tailed critical values at the .05 level and then the .01 level—we are interested in the .05 critical values, which comprise the first half of Table B.8). Table B.8 permits one-tailed (directional) hypothesis tests, too, but most research questions will be presented in a two-tailed (nondirectional) manner. Table B.8 requires a user to locate the intersection between a column heading corresponding to the value of N_A (10) and a row heading corresponding to the value of N_B (8)—when reading down and across, the **boldface** $U_{critical}$ value is 17. If the subsequent analysis, the actual U test, produces a statistic *that is less than or equal to this $U_{critical}$ value, then we can reject H_0.* Please note that this procedure is different—indeed, opposite of—the usual hypothesis testing logic, as an observed value should be lower than or equal to a critical value in order to reject the null hypothesis of no difference.

To compute the value of U, we must first determine the sum of the ranks of the two groups shown in Table 14.5. For convenience, the respective sums are shown at the bottom of columns 4 and 5 in Table 14.5 (i.e., 61 and 110, respectively). We now compute a U statistic for groups A and B. The formula for U_A is:

[14.10.1] $$U_A = N_A N_B + \frac{N_A(N_A + 1)}{2} - \sum R_A.$$

This formula requires us to enter the number of rankings for group A ($N_A = 10$) and group B ($N_B = 8$), as well as the sum of the ranks for group A (i.e., $\sum R_A = 61$; see Table 14.5). Entering the values for these sample sizes and the sum of the ranks for A, we find:

[14.10.2] $$U_A = (10)(8) + \frac{10(10 + 1)}{2} - 61,$$

[14.10.3] $$U_A = 80 + \frac{10(11)}{2} - 61,$$

[14.10.4] $$U_A = 80 + \frac{110}{2} - 61,$$

[14.10.5] $$U_A = 80 + 55 - 61,$$

[14.10.6] $$U_A = 135 - 61,$$

[14.10.7] $$U_A = 74.$$

The value of U_B is determined by:

[14.11.1] $$U_B = N_A N_B + \frac{N_B (N_B + 1)}{2} - \sum R_B.$$

We again enter the number of ranks for groups A ($N_A = 10$) and B ($N_B = 8$); instead of the sum of the ranks for group A, however, we substitute the sum of the ranks for group B (i.e., $\sum R_B = 110$). Entering these values we find:

[14.11.2] $$U_B = (10)(8) + \frac{8(8 + 1)}{2} - 110,$$

[14.11.3] $$U_B = 80 + \frac{8(9)}{2} - 110,$$

[14.11.4] $$U_B = 80 + \frac{72}{2} - 110,$$

[14.11.5] $$U_B = 80 + 36 - 110,$$

[14.11.6] $$U_B = 116 - 110,$$

[14.11.7] $$U_B = 6.$$

To determine whether we can reject H_0, we compare the *smaller* of the two values of U_A and U_B against the $U_{critical}$ value of 17. The value of U_B, 6, is smaller than U_A, which is equal to 74. Because the U_B of 6 is *less than* the $U_{critical}$ value of 17, we reject H_0. The two groups of ranks represent different populations, such that students in the language immersion group had higher language proficiency rankings than those students who learned in the traditional manner (see the relative rankings of groups

A and B in columns 4 and 5, respectively, of Table 14.5). Apparently, then, the language immersion group demonstrated relatively greater proficiency speaking Spanish than did the traditional learning group.

Mann-Whitney *U* Test for Larger (*Ns* > 20) Samples: A Normal Approximation of the *U* Distribution

Table B.8 in Appendix B only includes N values up to 20. When larger sample sizes (i.e., both N_A and N_B are 20 or higher) are available, the Mann-Whitney U test can be performed using a formula that transforms U to a z score within the standard normal distribution. There are three basic steps for performing this transformation and it is possible to use smaller samples, as well, though the results can sometimes be less reliable (Evans, 1996). We will perform these steps using the data from the U test we just completed. As you follow the steps, keep the hypothesis testing routine used with the z test in mind (for a review, see chapter 9).

To begin, we first calculate the population mean (μ_U) and then the population standard deviation (σ_U) for U. To determine the population mean, multiply the number of ranks available for group A by the number available for group B, and then divide the resulting product by 2 (see step 1 below).

Step 1. Calculate the population mean:

$$[14.12.1] \qquad \mu_U = \frac{N_A N_B}{2},$$

$$[14.12.2] \qquad \mu_U = \frac{(10)(8)}{2},$$

$$[14.12.3] \qquad \mu_U = \frac{80}{2},$$

$$[14.12.4] \qquad \mu_U = 40.$$

To calculate the population standard deviation, we multiply the number of rankings for group A by those in group B (i.e., $N_A N_B$), and then multiply the resulting product by the sum of the ranks for A and B, plus 1 (i.e., $N_A + N_B + 1$). The resulting product is then divided by 12 (i.e., $[N_A N_B(N_A + N_B + 1)]/12$)—a constant in this formula—and the square root of this final product is then found. These steps are summarized in step 2.

Step 2. Calculate the population standard deviation:

$$[14.13.1] \qquad \sigma_U = \sqrt{\frac{N_A N_B(N_A + N_B + 1)}{12}},$$

$$[14.13.2] \qquad \sigma_U = \sqrt{\frac{(10)(8)(10 + 8 + 1)}{12}},$$

$$[14.13.3] \qquad \sigma_U = \sqrt{\frac{(80)(19)}{12}},$$

$$[14.13.4] \qquad \sigma_U = \sqrt{\frac{1,520}{12}},$$

$$[14.13.5] \qquad \sigma_U = \sqrt{126.67},$$

$$[14.13.6] \qquad \sigma_U = 11.26.$$

The third step involves computing a z ratio by entering the (now) known values of the population mean and the population standard deviation into [14.14.1]. Please note that either U_A or U_B can be used as U in this formula.

Step 3. If we use $U_B = 6$, then:

$$[14.14.1] \qquad z_U = \frac{U - \mu_U}{\sigma_U},$$

$$[14.14.2] \qquad z_U = \frac{6 - 40}{11.26},$$

$$[14.14.3] \qquad z_U = \frac{-34}{11.26},$$

$$[14.14.4] \qquad z_U = -3.02.$$

We then proceed as if a standard z test were being conducted (see chapters 5 and 9). As you will recall, when $\alpha = .05$, z_{critical} is equal to ± 1.96. The value of z_U exceeds -1.96 —it is more extreme, falling within the region of rejection. Thus, we can reject H_0 and draw the same conclusion that we did when relying on the standard Mann-Whitney U test (bearing in mind, of course, that we again follow standard hypothesis testing rules with z_U, as we are interested in whether the computed U is equal to or *exceeds* z_U in value). As an exercise to check your understanding of the three steps used to transform a U value to a z score, redo the steps using the value of U_A instead of U_B. Using a two-tailed test, do you obtain the same result? Why or why not?

Writing About the Results of the Mann-Whitney U Test

A singular virtue of most parametric tests is the ease with which their results can be reported. There are no hard-and-fast rules for reporting results from a Mann-Whitney U test in APA style, however, reasonable advice is to keep the explanation simple but thorough. Here is one way to report the results of the comparison of the Spanish-teaching techniques:

> The students' performance on the age-appropriate Spanish language proficiency test were rank ordered by Spanish-speaking judges, and then a Mann-Whitney U test compared the ranks for the traditional teaching approach ($n = 10$) and total immersion ($n = 8$) approach. The test revealed a significant difference between the groups, where students in the total immersion group tended to rank higher in language proficiency than those who were taught traditionally, $U = 6$, $p < .05$, where the sum of ranks was equal to 110 for the former group and 61 for the latter group.

The Wilcoxon Matched-Pairs Signed-Ranks Test

The Wilcoxon matched-pairs signed-ranks test—the Wilcoxon test for short—analyzes ordinal data from a basic one-group, repeated measures experiment.

KEY TERM The **Wilcoxon matched-pairs signed-ranks test** is a nonparametric statistic used to identify a difference between two dependent samples of rank-ordered (ordinal) data.

As noted in Table 14.1, the parametric analog of the Wilcoxon test is the dependent groups t test. Like the dependent groups t test, the data used to perform the Wilcoxon test are comprised of differences scores (i.e., the difference between how each participant reacted during a first treatment and then again in a second treatment) or observations collected in a matched-pairs research design (i.e., two separate participant groups are matched on some variable or variables). This nonparametric test involves ranking these difference scores from the smallest to the largest one in *absolute value terms* (i.e., without attending to the presence of a positive or negative sign), and it follows the same statistical assumptions associated with the Mann-Whitney U test (see previous page). The Wilcoxon test produces a test statistic referred to as T (please note that the letter is *always* capitalized so that it is not confused with the t reserved for its parametric cousin—please also note that the Wilcoxon T is not a T [transformed] score; see chapter 5).

A clinical researcher interested in decreasing social phobias might rely on the Wilcoxon test to analyze data resulting from an intervention involving a therapy group. The clinician is running a weekly group comprised of seven people who fear meeting new people, public places, and having to engage in conversations with strangers for protracted periods of time. The clinician has a colleague who is a social worker rate the social acumen and competence of these group members before the first group meeting occurs (this rater is only asked to perform the rating—the true purpose of the study is not revealed to her). This pretest rating was based on a 20-point social competence scale, where a higher score indicates greater competence. The rater was explicitly asked to compare the social competence of each participant with that displayed by all the other participants.

After the group therapy took place for 2 months, the clinician asked the social worker to again rate the social competence displayed by the participants. Thus, the rater used the same scale to assess the perceived social competence of the therapy group members after 8 sessions (i.e., posttest rating). The pretest and posttest ratings are shown below in Table 14.6.

Why is the Wilcoxon test a more appropriate analytic choice than the dependent groups t test? For a couple of reasons, actually. First, the participants and their behavior do not constitute a normal population where social competence is concerned; if anything, their social reticence would best be described as extreme (i.e., far away from average). Second, the rater was asked to make a comparison of each person to all the others while executing the ratings, a request that built a ranking component directly into the exercise. Thus, the only way to adequately assess the difference between pretest and posttest behavior is through using the Wilcoxon T test.

Following Table 14.2, this line of reasoning leads us to complete step 1, the identification of an appropriate test statistic. Although the content of their research designs vary from one another, the style or format of the null and alternative hypotheses of the

▽

The Wilcoxon test is symbolized T, not t—be certain not to confuse the two statistics (here is a mnemonic: "Capital T is used when lowercase t cannot be").

Table 14.6 Rated Social Competence of Eight Socially Phobic Therapy Group Members

(1) Participant	(2) Pretest	(3) Posttest	(4) Difference[*]
1	8	11	3
2	14	15	1
3	7	12	5
4	8	6	−2
5	2	8	6
6	13	11	−2
7	10	14	4
8	9	9	0

[*]Each difference score is based on a posttest score minus a pretest score.

Wilcoxon test is almost identical to the Mann-Whitney U test. Thus, the null hypothesis for this group therapy study might be:

H_0: There will be no systematic difference between the pretest
and posttest social competency skills.

It follows that the alternative hypothesis would be:

H_1: There will be a systematic difference between the pretest
and posttest social competency skills.

Once step 2 is completed and we then decide on a significance level of .05 for the test (i.e., step 3), we can perform the actual analysis for step 4.

To begin the analysis, each pretest rating is subtracted from its posttest rating, and this difference score is placed in column 4 of Table 14.6. Because these difference scores are the basic observations in this correlated or dependent-groups research design, only this single set of difference scores will be ranked in lieu of ranking the two original sets of scores (see columns 2 and 3 in Table 14.6). We now prepare the rankings for the analysis by:

- Changing all the difference scores to absolute values (i.e., ignore the sign of the difference score; see column 3 in Table 14.7).
- The difference scores are then reordered from the *lowest* to the *highest* in value (see column 3 in Table 14.7).
- Beginning with "1," a ranking is then assigned to each difference score until N is reached.
- Difference scores with a value of 0 are not, however, included further in the analysis (see the data for participant 8 in the top row of Table 14.7), and any ties are broken using the procedure presented in Data Box 14.D (see the two differences scores with values of -2 in Table 14.7).
- The ranks showing positive differences are then placed into one column and those illustrating negative differences are placed into another column (see columns 5 and 6, respectively, in Table 14.7).
- Once the positive and negative ranks are separated in two columns, the sum of each column should be noted beneath it (see the $\sum R_+$ and the $\sum R_-$ under columns 5 and 6).

Table 14.7 Calculating the Wilcoxon T Statistic from Difference Scores

(1) Participant	(2) Difference Score	(3) Absolute Difference	(4) Ranks Without 0	(5) Ranks of $+$ Differences	(6) Ranks of $-$ Differences
8	0	0	—		
2	1	1	1	1	
4	-2	2	2.5		2.5
6	-2	2	2.5		2.5
1	3	3	4	4	
7	4	4	5	5	
3	5	5	6	6	
5	6	6	7	7	
				$\sum R_+ = 23$	$\sum R_- = 5$

DATA BOX 14.E

Even Null Results Must Be Written Up and Reported

We have not had occasion to discuss an important but often overlooked aspect of writing-up statistical results—what happens when we accept the null hypothesis, when we find that no statistically reliable results were obtained in our analyses? Many novice data analysts become frustrated when expected results are not found (e.g., means are in the wrong directions, frequencies spread across categories are almost identical to one another), so much so that they may be moved to "shelve" the data and the analyses. In truth, there are many prominent behavioral scientists who effectively do the same thing—they box up and file away (mentally as well as physically) the null findings and move on to the next project.

There is nothing wrong with this understandably human reaction, but I advocate that you should still try to learn from analyses yielding nonsignificant results, anyway. Here are some reasons—guidelines, really—as to why you should write up results *before* putting them away:

■ Null results are *still* results, and they can sometimes tell you something true or useful about behavior that you heretofore overlooked. Writing up null results can help you to identify or consider possibilities that you missed when you designed the project and executed the analyses.

■ It is incumbent on any researcher or data analyst to tell the true story about his or her research, warts and all. You should not write endlessly about "what might have been" or speculate in too great a detail in an article or paper about why some statistically reliable difference was not found. You should, however, report null results as a matter of course alongside those findings that do match up to their hypotheses.

■ A careful reading of the behavioral science literature will reveal that many, if not most, publications contain at least some null findings. Such empirical honesty is worthy of your congratulation and emulation.

■ An honestly written research summary can shed light on why a desired result was not found (e.g., low power, small sample size, an odd sampling procedure).

■ A research summary can point investigators and readers to consider new directions for the research. Theory revision, then, becomes a possibility.

■ By the same token, a written summary can help a researcher to see how subsequent studies on the same or similar topics can be improved.

■ Although it is difficult, if not impossible, to publish research results that are entirely null (see chapter 15), researchers and data analysts will want to maintain a record of "failed" studies for future reference. Such studies can often be "imported" into other work (e.g., a multi-study publication, grant writing, conference presentations).

■ Finally, sometimes the null hypothesis is actually false.

Suggested Guidelines for Reporting Null Results

1. Report all test statistics (e.g., t, F, χ^2, U, T, r_S) and include their actual p values (if known), as in $p = .26$ *or* report $p = ns$ ("not significant").
2. Describe the original hypothesis and clearly acknowledge that the current results were not consistent with it. Briefly speculate as to why this might be the case (remaining cognizant that you cannot prove whether any explanation for a null result is compelling outside an experiment designed to test its tenability).
3. Provide a table of means or in the case of categorical data, frequencies or percentages. Link the table to the statistical results (see point 1 above).

Remember that you are in good company. Getting a study to "work" takes practice, patience, experience, and time (see Dunn, 1999, for further discussion of this issue). Congratulate yourself for having collected the data and/or performed the statistical analyses.

Unlike the Mann-Whitney U test, no further computations are necessary. The value of Wilcoxon's T is equal to the *smaller* of the two sums of the ranks. In this case, $T = \sum R_- = 5$ (see Table 14.7). To determine the critical value of T (i.e., $T_{critical}$), turn to Table B.9 in Appendix B. This table of critical values simply requires the user to identify the value at the intersection of α (recall our previously determined significance level of .05) and N—but N in the context of the Wilcoxon T statistic means the *number of nonzero differences found within the data*. Thus, although we began with eight participants, one of them did not show any change from the pretest to the posttest (a zero difference), so that our N becomes 7 (cf. Gravetter & Wallnau, 1996). Following Table B.9, then, the $T_{critical}$ value (two-tailed) is equal to 2.

Can we accept or reject the null hypothesis? Similar to the Mann-Whitney U test, the observed T statistic must be *equal to or less than the $T_{critical}$* value. Because 5 is *not* less than 2, we cannot reject H_0, or:

$$T = 5 \geq T_{critical} = 2; \; Accept \; H_0.$$

The observed T is greater than the critical value for T, suggesting that the two months of group therapy were not successful in reducing social phobia or enhancing social competence.

Writing About the Results of the Wilcoxon (*T*) Test

Like the Mann-Whitney U test, there is no prescribed format for presenting the results of a Wilcoxon (T) test in APA style. Once again, though, a good rule of thumb is to present the results in simple terms and to provide as much statistical information as necessary. I hasten to add one more point: even the null results of the test we just reviewed should be written up for later use in a written report or oral presentation (see also Data Box 14.E):

> The eight members of a social phobia therapy group had their social competence rated by an independent, expert judge prior to the start of the therapy (pretest) and then again after two months (posttest). The magnitude of change in social competence from $time_1$ to $time_2$ was examined by a Wilcoxon T test. Despite the group therapy, the results revealed no significant change in social competence rankings, $T = 5$, $p = ns$, where positive change in ranks totaled 23 and negative change totaled 5.

The Spearman Rank Order Correlation Coefficient

Back in chapter 6 we learned to calculate and to interpret the degree of association existing between two interval or ratio-scaled measures. The Pearson correlation coefficient, or Pearson r, was introduced as the statistic appropriate to that task. Later, in chapter 9, the method for determining whether a Pearson r was significantly different from 0 was presented. Is it possible to assess the correlation between two ordinally scaled variables? Yes, indeed. Another type of correlation coefficient, which is called the *Spearman rank order correlation coefficient,* is used to examine the nature of association found between two ordinally scaled variables. The Spearman correlation is actually an application of the Pearson r formula to rank-ordered data.

KEY TERM   The **Spearman rank order correlation coefficient** assesses the strength of association between ordinal data. It is symbolized r_S (occasionally ρ, or "rho").

The Pearson r is ideal for measuring associations that are linear (e.g., as X increases in value, a corresponding increase in Y occurs). When relationships are not particularly linear, however, the Spearman r_S is a much better choice for analyzing the data than the

---

Why sum ranks for both positive and negative difference scores? The Wilcoxon test assumes that an effective treatment will show consistent effects (mostly + or −) on difference scores, but that chance—no effect—will be apparent when inconsistent difference scores appear (about equal numbers of + and −).

Pearson. Indeed, it is usually the case that interval or ratio-scaled data can be converted into ordinal rankings with relative ease, making the Spearman r_S a viable alternative in many nonlinear situations.

When two variables are related to one another in a uniform manner, a rank ordering of their values will be linearly related (Gravetter & Wallnau, 1996). How so? Consider the data for 5 individuals (denoted as A through E) shown below:

Individuals	Variable X	Variable Y
A	27	17
B	6	9
C	43	20
D	32	19
E	12	15

As you can see, the third person (C) has the highest scores on both variable X (i.e., 43) and variable Y (i.e., 20), while the second person (B) has the lowest scores corresponding to these two variables (i.e., 6 and 9, respectively). Actually, these data portray a consistent relationship between the two variables, but if we plotted the X and Y scores shown above, they would not appear to be linear because of the different scales involved.

What if we convert the raw scores for X and Y into rankings (i.e., 1, 2, 3, and so on)? The lower ranks for both the X and Y values can be assigned a "1", the next lowest a "2", and so on up through the rank of 5 for each variable. Once these data are converted to ranks (see table below), a different picture—a linear relationship between the two variables—emerges.

Individuals	Variable X	Variable Y
A	3	3
B	1	1
C	5	5
D	4	4
E	2	2

Thus, the second person (C) is ranked first on both variables, the fifth person (E) is ranked second, the first (A) is ranked third, and so on. When these ranks are plotted and labeled, the linear relationship inherent in the data becomes clear:

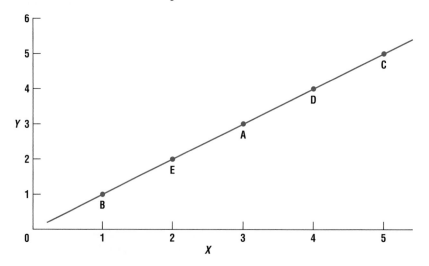

Table 14.8 Calculating a Spearman r_S Using Ordinal Data

Actor	Judge 1's Rankings	Judge 2's Rankings	D	D^2
Adam	1	3	-2	4
Bill	2	1	1	1
Cara	3	2	1	1
Deena	4	5	-1	1
Ernesto	5	4	1	1
Fran	6	7	-1	1
Gerald	7	8	-1	1
Helen	8	6	2	4
$\sum$	36	36	$\sum D = 0$	$\sum D^2 = 14$

We can now apply the logic of the Spearman correlation and the linearity of rankings in an example. In preparation for conducting an experiment on detecting deception, a social psychologist recruited a group of eight actors and asked them to tell a collection of truths and lies while being filmed by a camera. The film was then shown to two judges who were asked to rank order the actors from "best" to "worst" liar. The judges' rankings are shown in Table 14.8, accompanied by the differences between the each of the two rankings (i.e., D = Judge 1's rank $-$ Judge 2's rank). When any tied ranks appear, follow the guidelines outlined in Data Box 14.D.

In order to assess the level of agreement expressed by these two judges, the social psychologist performed a Spearman r_S on their rankings. You will no doubt be pleased to learn that calculating the Spearman r_S is quicker and easier than the Pearson r. Here is the formula for the Spearman r_S:

[14.15.1] $$r_S = 1 - \frac{6 \sum D^2}{N(N^2 - 1)},$$

where D^2 is equal to the difference between ranks, squared (see the last column in Table 14.8), and N refers to the number of *pairs* of data (here, 8; *not* the total number of observations).

Notice that the sum of each of the judges' rankings must be equal, while the sum of the difference scores must equal 0 (see these respective sums shown under columns 2, 3, and 4 in Table 14.8). The sum of the squared differences, which will be included in the Spearman r_S formula, is shown at the bottom of the last column in Table 14.8 (i.e., $\sum D^2 = 14$). We can now complete the calculations for the Spearman r_S:

[14.15.2] $$r_S = 1 - \frac{6(14)}{8[(8)^2 - 1]},$$

[14.15.3] $$r_S = 1 - \frac{84}{8(64 - 1)},$$

[14.15.4] $$r_S = 1 - \frac{84}{8(63)},$$

[14.15.5] $$r_S = 1 - \frac{84}{504},$$

▽

Be careful: The value determined on the right side of the Spearman formula is *subtracted* from 1, which appears on the left side of the formula. The number 1 should *not* appear in the formula's numerator!

[14.15.6] $r_S = 1 - .1667,$

[14.15.7] $r_S = .83.$

Thus, there appears to be a very high degree of association between the judges' rankings of the actors' skills at lying. Put another way, there is a relatively high degree of consistency between the judges' rankings of the actors' lying skills.

Before we report this statistic in APA style, however, we need to determine whether it is statistically significant. To do so, we turn to Table B.10 in Appendix B (please do so now). Table B.10 contains both one-tailed and two-tailed critical values for r_S. To determine a critical value for comparison, we need to locate the N associated with the calculation in the leftmost column of Table B.10 (once again, please remember that N refers to the number of pairs of ranks included in the analysis). As usual, we will perform a two-tailed test at the .05 level, so we read across the row for $N = 8$ and locate the critical value of .738 (please verify that you can locate this critical value in Table B.10 before proceeding).

When the Pearson r does not reach statistical significance, it is unlikely that the Spearman r_S will either (and vice versa).

Is the observed r_S of .83 greater than or equal to the $r_{S\ critical}$ value of .738? Yes, so we can reject the null hypothesis of no difference, or:

$$r_S(8) = .83 \geq r_{S\ critical}(8) = .738;\ Reject\ H_0.$$

The judges' ranks reached a level of agreement that was greater than chance (i.e., significantly different from 0). In the interests of thoroughness, the number of pairs of rankings is included in parentheses following the r_S in both the test statistic and the critical value.

Writing About the Results of a Spearman r_S Test

The Spearman r_S is reported in the same manner as the Pearson correlation. In spite of the fact that the Spearman r_S is used exclusively to analyze rank-ordered data, it is always a good idea to subtly remind readers of this fact. Similar to other nonparametric tests, the Spearman r_S is neither used nor seen as frequently as the Pearson r, thus some contextual reminders are helpful. The results of the prestudy on rating "liars" could be reported this way:

> After viewing the filmed actors lie on camera, two expert judges rank ordered the perceived skill of these "liars" (two random orders of the actors' taped performances were prepared). There was a high level of agreement between the two judges regarding the rankings of lying skills of the actors, $r_S(8) = .83, p < .05$.

Congratulate yourself—you made it! The Spearman r_S is the last statistic and set of calculations presented in this text.

Knowledge Base

1. Rank these scores and be sure to take any tied ranks into account: 2, 5, 8, 3, 1, 6, 8, 4, 12.
2. When performing a Mann-Whitney U test, should U_A or U_B be used to test a hypothesis?
3. Under what conditions is it proper to use the z transformation for the Mann-Whitney U test?
4. What hypothesis testing procedure associated with the Mann-Whitney U test and the Wilcoxon test renders them different from all other testing procedures introduced in this book?
5. How does the Spearman correlation coefficient differ from the Pearson correlation coefficient?

DATA BOX 14.F

Research Using an Ordinal Test to Analyze Data

Since early in this century, social psychologists have argued that people's attitudes should predict their subsequent actions, though demonstrating this empirical link has been a challenge (Eagly & Chaiken, 1993; Wicker, 1969). Within this well-established research tradition, Wilson, Dunn, Bybee, Hyman, and Rotondo (1984) used the Spearman correlation coefficient (r_S) to demonstrate the disruptive effects of analyzing reasons on attitude-behavior consistency.

Wilson and colleagues (1984) had research participants become familiar with a variety of paper-and-pencil puzzles (e.g., letter series completion task) for 5 minutes (see Fazio & Zanna, 1981, for a review of research on direct experience with such attitude objects). During this "get acquainted" session, half of the participants were instructed to analyze *why* they felt the way they did about the puzzles ("I liked the maze because it was challenging"), while those comprising the control group were given no additional directions. When the time was up, participants in the reasons analysis condition wrote down the reasons they found each of the puzzles to be interesting or boring. The control participants, on the other hand, were given a filler questionnaire to complete. Later, all participants rated how interesting they found each of the puzzles to be on a (1) extremely boring to (7) extremely interesting rating scale. They were then left alone for 15 minutes with several packets containing the five puzzle types, which the experimenter told them they could play with while waiting for the next part of the study. Unbeknownst to the participants, trained coders behind a one-way mirror recorded the amount of time they played with each of the types of puzzles.

Of chief interest to Wilson and colleagues (1984) was the within-subject Spearman rank order correlation computed between participants' interest ratings of the five puzzles and the amount of time they spent playing with each one during the 15-minute free play period. In the control group, the average attitude-behavior correlation (i.e., rated level of interest in a puzzle with amount of actual time spent playing with that puzzle) was $r_S = .54$, $p < .001$. The average correlation in the reasons analysis conditions, however, was not significantly different from 0 ($r_S = .17$, $p = $ ns), but it was significantly lower than the mean correlation found in the control group, $t(24) = 2.23$, $p < .05$.

Wilson and colleagues concluded that analyzing the reasons for one's feelings toward an attitude object can change attitudes in a less accurate direction and that, as a result, the expressed attitude does not correspond very well with their subsequent actions (i.e., the observed discrepancy found in attitude-behavior consistency). These investigators confirmed and elaborated on these basic findings in a series of subsequent studies (see Wilson, Dunn, Kraft, & Lisle, 1989, for a review).

Answers

1. Ranks: 1 2 3 4 5 6 7.5 7.5 9
2. Whichever value of U is smaller is used to test whether to accept or reject H_0.
3. When both groups of ordinal data have ns that are greater than or equal to 20.
4. Both the Mann-Whitney U test and the Wilcoxon test must show statistics (i.e., U or T) that are *less than or equal to* some critical value—all other statistical tests in this book require that the observed statistic equal or exceed some critical value.
5. The Spearman correlation coefficient assesses the degree of association between ordinally ranked data, whereas the Pearson is used with interval or ratio-scaled data.

Project Exercise

SURVEY SAYS–USING NONPARAMETRIC
TESTS ON DATA

There are two straightforward *project exercises* for this chapter, one dealing with the χ^2 and the other involving the Spearman correlation coefficient. Both exercises are designed to give you a bit of experience collecting and analyzing some simple data using these nonparametric tests. The first exercise, adapted from Tanner (1990), requires that you collect data from your entire class (your instructor may assign this one) or some other group of people, whereas the second entails performing a straightforward survey with one of your peers.

Using the χ^2 to Check for a Number Generation Bias

The goal of this simple *Project Exercise* is to illustrate how the chi-square goodness-of-fit test and the chi-square test for independence can be used to identify a bias in people's ability to generate numbers. You and a group of students should complete the questions shown in Table 14.9. The answers to these questions should then be organized into the data sheet shown in Table 14.10, a copy of which should be given to each of the students in your class (again, your instructor may have you do this *Project Exercise* in class). Once you have a data sheet, follow the steps outlined below, perform the appropriate analyses, and then compare your answers with those found by your peers. Where and when did any bias(es) appear in the process of generating numbers? Does gender have a role? How so? Be sure to consult the guidelines for calculating the two types of χ^2 tests presented earlier in the chapter.

The following instructions are based on Tanner (1990, p. 187).

1. Take a look at the first round of number generation (see column 1 in Table 14.10) and then assess whether the digits 1, 2, and 3 were generated in an *equally likely* manner. Is there any evidence that the digits were *not* generated in an *equally likely* manner? How so?
2. Repeat the analysis performed for question 1 using data from the second round of number generation (see column 2 in Table 14.10).
3. Repeat the analysis performed for question 1 using data from the third round of number generation (see column 3 in Table 14.10).
4. Combine the three rounds of data in Table 14.10 and then test whether the digits 1, 2, and 3 were generated in an *equally likely* manner. Based on your answers to

Table 14.9 | Data Sheet for *Project Exercise* on Number Generation

1. Close your eyes and think of an integer between 1 and 3, inclusive. Check that value below: 1 _____ 2 _____ 3 _____

2. Close your eyes and think of an integer between 1 and 3, inclusive. Check that value below: 1 _____ 2 _____ 3 _____

3. Close your eyes and think of an integer between 1 and 3, inclusive. Check that value below: 1 _____ 2 _____ 3 _____

4. Check your gender (1 = male, 2 = female): 1 _____ 2 _____

Note: Your instructor may collect your responses to these questions so they can be pooled with those given by the other members of your class.

Adapted from Tanner (1990, p. 185).

Table 14.10 | Number Generation Survey Results Sheet*

Summarize and organize the data from the Data Sheets (i.e., Table 14.9) below before beginning the analyses:

Student Number	Round 1	Round 2	Round 3	Student Gender
1				
2				
3				
4				
5				
6				
7				
8				
.				
.				
.				
N				

*Entries in columns 2 through 4 should be 1, 2, or 3; entries in column 5 can be 1 for male respondents or 2 for female respondents.

questions 1 through 4, did you and your peers have trouble generating numbers in an equally likely manner?

5. Now compare the responses of the men ("1" = male) and the women ("2" = female) (see column 5 in Table 14.10) based on the data collected in the first round of number generation. To do so, you will need to construct a 2 × 3 contingency table. Is there any reason to believe that men and women differ with regard to number generation? If so, explain how they differ—does one group show a preference for a given digit, for example?

6. Compare the responses of the men and the women when the three rounds of data from Table 14.10 are combined (see question 4). Construct a 2 × 3 contingency table to answer this question. Is there any reason to believe that men and women differ with regard to number generation? If so, explain how they differ—does one group show a preference for a given digit, for example?

Ranking Favorite Films and Assessing Agreement with the Spearman r_S

How well does your assessment of the top 10 films of all time correlate with the list identified by the American Film Institute (AFI)? Turn to Table 1.3, where you will see the AFI's rankings (from "Citizen Kane," the number 1 film of all time to number 10, "Singin' in the Rain"). Develop your own rankings from 1 to 10 for these classic films, and then use the Spearman r_S to assess the degree of association between the two sets of ratings. Does the correlation between these two sets of rankings achieve statistical significance? Have a peer rank the same films and then correlate these new data with your rankings. Does the correlation between these two sets of rankings achieve statistical significance?

Alternatively, create a list of 10 or so films you have seen in the last few years and then rank them. (If you would prefer another domain of interest, rank popular songs, rock groups, actors and actresses, music videos, books, etc., instead.) Have a peer review your list, asking him or her to rank order the same stimuli. Perform the Spearman correlational analysis and evaluate the result.

LOOKING FORWARD THEN BACK

Not all of the data a researcher will encounter or collect can be analyzed using parametric tests. Fortunately, a class of inferential tests, collectively referred to as nonparametric tests, is available for the analysis of nominal (categorical) and ordinal (ranked) data. The first decision tree appearing at the opening of this chapter will help you to correctly select the nonparametric test that best fits the research design you are working with or the data you are gathering. The second decision tree will prove to be useful when you want a supporting measure of strength of association for the chi-square test of independence.

Do keep in mind that nonparametric tests tend to be used when researchers and data analysts discover that their data do not adhere to the traditional assumptions of parametric tests. Thus, there is sometimes a post hoc ("after the fact") flavor to these tests, as if they are being consulted as a last resort. Try to avoid creating or reinforcing this unfortunate impression. Nonparametric statistics are powerful tests in their own right, and the fact that they are less well known or applied relatively infrequently speaks more to available statistical training than the inherent qualities of the tests themselves. Should any of the nonparametric tests reviewed in this chapter seem inappropriate for your research needs, consult one of the references cited in this chapter (e.g., Siegel & Castellan, 1988) to track down a test statistic best suited to your situation.

Summary

1. Research questions that cannot be analyzed by conventional inferential statistics can often be examined by nonparametric statistics.
2. Nonparametric statistics generally test hypotheses involving ordinal rankings of data or frequencies.
3. Where parametric tests require that certain assumptions be met, especially the shape of a population's distribution, nonparametric tests are said to be "distribution free." That is, nonparametric tests make no assumptions regarding parent populations or the shape of their distributions.
4. Parametric tests are very powerful when their assumptions are met, but nonparametric tests make worthy substitutes.
5. The advantages of nonparametric tests include that they are distribution free; can analyze data that are not precisely numerical; are applicable when sample sizes are small; and tend to be relatively easy to calculate.
6. Categorical or nominal data are analyzed by the chi-square (χ^2) test, which compares observed frequencies against expected frequencies. The one variable chi-square test, known as the chi-square test for goodness-of-fit, determines whether the obtained observations in each level of a variable are approximately equal (i.e., chance determined) or if they adhere to a pattern (i.e., a significant difference exists between the observed and expected observations).
7. The degrees of freedom for the chi-square goodness-of-fit test are based on the number of available categories rather than the total number of observations available.
8. The chi-square test for the independence of categorical variables indicates whether two variables are independent of one another (i.e., can be understood separately) or dependent (i.e., the effect of one variable cannot be properly understood without taking the other variable into account).
9. The degrees of freedom for the chi-square test for independence are based on both the number of rows (levels) representing one variable and the number of columns (levels) representing the other.
10. The chi-square test for independence reveals whether two variables have a statistically significant relationship with one another but *not* the strength of that relationship. The phi (ϕ) coefficient is used to measure the strength of association between variables from a 2 × 2 contingency table, whereas Cramer's V statistic is used when a contingency table exceeds this standard size.
11. The Mann-Whitney U test is a nonparametric test used to assess whether a statistically significant difference exists between two independent samples of rank ordered data. It is the nonparametric equivalent of the independent groups t test.
12. The Mann-Whitney U test can be applied when the data are ordinal; were randomly selected; and no ties are present within the rankings (or those ties have been dealt with using a standard procedure presented in the chapter; see Data Box 14.D).
13. Unlike previous inferential statistics, the Mann-Whitney U test only identifies a significant difference when the lower of

its two U values is still less than or equal to some critical value of U.

14. When large sample sizes are available (i.e., both of the groups contain 20 or more rankings), then the normal approximation of the Mann-Whitney U test, one based on a z transformation, can be used for hypothesis testing.

15. The Wilcoxon matched-pairs signed-ranks test examines whether a difference between two dependent samples of ordinal rankings is significant. This test is based on the same statistical assumptions as its cousin, the Mann-Whitney

U test; indeed, it also shares the same hypothesis testing procedure (i.e., the observed statistic—Wilcoxon's T—must be less than or equal to a critical T-value in order to reject a null hypothesis).

16. Wilcoxon's T statistic is different from the t test (see chapter 10) or a transformed score, or T-score (see chapter 5).

17. The Spearman rank order correlation coefficient (r_S) assesses the degree of association between two sets of ordinally ranked data. The Spearman r_S is ideally used when the available rankings are not linear.

Key Terms

Chi-square (χ^2) test for goodness-of-fit (*p. 529*)
Chi-square (χ^2) test for independence (*p. 534*)
Cramer's V statistic (*p. 539*)

Mann-Whitney U test (*p. 541*)
Nonparametric statistic (*p. 525*)
Parametric statistic (*p. 525*)
Phi (ϕ) coefficient (*p. 539*)

Spearman rank order correlation coefficient (r_S) (*p. 551*)
Wilcoxon matched-pairs signed-ranks test (*p. 547*)

Chapter Problems

1. What is a nonparametric statistical test? How do nonparametric tests differ from parametric tests?

2. What is a parametric test? Do parametric tests share the same statistical assumptions with nonparametric tests? Why or why not?

3. How do interval and ratio scales differ from nominal and ordinal scales? Provide an example of each scale type.

4. What are some advantages associated with using nonparametric tests?

5. Why should researchers in the behavioral sciences be open to learning to use nonparametric statistical tests?

6. A researcher performs a study that yields no statistically reliable differences. What should the researcher do with these null results? Why?

7. Which nonparametric tests are most similar to the t test for independent groups?

8. What is the nonparametric test that is most similar to the t test for dependent groups?

9. Which nonparametric test can be used to analyze data from one sample only?

10. Which nonparametric test can analyze data based on two variables?

11. What is the nonparametric counterpart of the Pearson r?

12. A chi-square test performed on a 2×2 contingency table reaches statistical significance. Which supporting statistic can be used to describe the strength of association between the two variables? Why? (*Hint:* Use one of the decision trees presented at the opening of this chapter.)

13. Under what conditions is it preferable to use Cramer's V statistic instead of the phi (ϕ) coefficient?

14. A researcher creates a contingency table of frequencies based

on the intersection of two variables, each of which has three levels. What nonparametric statistic should the researcher use to analyze the data? Why? (*Hint:* Use one of the decision trees presented at the opening of this chapter.)

15. Two restaurant critics for the same newspaper rank order the top 30 places to dine in the city. What nonparametric test will allow them to quickly determine their level of agreement? Why? (*Hint:* Use one of the decision trees presented at the opening of this chapter.)

16. The office of the dean of students wants to examine whether the priorities of freshmen change across their first year in college. The first year students ranked their priorities (e.g., grades, dating) during the first week of school and then again during the last week of the academic year. What test should be used to demonstrate that the students' rankings changed across time? Why? (*Hint:* Use one of the decision trees presented at the opening of this chapter.)

17. A pizza parlor wants to determine whether one of its "special" pizzas is ordered more frequently than two other special pies. The owner of the shop examines the phone orders for the three types of pizza for a week. What test should be used to demonstrate that requests for the three special pizzas varied? (*Hint:* Use one of the decision trees presented at the opening of this chapter.)

18. Rank order the following data and be certain to "break" any ties in the process: 12, 4, 3, 6, 8, 3, 4, 5, 9, 11, 3, 6, 7, 0, 1, 21, 45.

19. Rank order the following data and be certain to "break" any ties in the process: 99, 67, 32, 12, 100, 23, 33, 11, 6, 78, 34, 56, 22, 32, 70, 89, 99.

20. What are the expected frequencies for this contingency table?

	A_1	A_2
B_1	10	23
B_2	30	8

21. What are the expected frequencies for this contingency table?

	A_1	A_2
B_1	9	10
B_2	10	9

22. What are the expected frequencies for this contingency table?

	A_1	A_2	A_3
B_1	5	10	3
B_2	8	4	10

23. What are the expected frequencies for this contingency table?

	A_1	A_2	A_3
B_1	5	10	20
B_2	20	5	10

24. Use the chi-square test for independence shortcut presented in Data Box 14.B on the contingency table presented in problem 20. What is the value of the χ^2 statistic? Is it significant?

25. Use the chi-square test for independence shortcut presented in Data Box 14.B on the contingency table presented in problem 21. What is the value of the χ^2 statistic? Is it significant?

26. A professor wonders whether an unusual number of upper-class students are enrolled in his introductory psychology class, which is usually populated primarily by first, second, and third-year students. Here are the enrollment data:

Freshmen	Sophomores	Juniors	Seniors
15	12	14	27

Is there any significant preference by senior class standing? Use an α level of .05 to test the appropriate hypothesis.

27. A university health center tracks the number of flu-related visits during each month of the fall semester. The center director wonders whether students come down with the flu more often around midterm (mid-October) and final (mid-December) exams. Can these data shed any light on this issue?

Flu-Related Visits to the University Health Center
(by months)

September	October	November	December
20	48	27	56

Is there any significant difference among the flu-related visits during the fall semester? Use an α level of .05 to test the appropriate hypothesis.

28. The chair of a psychology department wants to determine if student gender is linked with area of interest in the field of psychology. She distributes a survey to a random sample of

majors within the department, noting that each person can endorse one—and only one—interest area. Evaluate the data using an α level of .05 to determine if gender is linked with preference for an area of study:

	Clinical	Social	Biopsychology
Male	15	23	10
Female	8	25	40

29. A researcher wonders whether self-esteem is linked with willingness to persist at a difficult task. Evaluate the data using an α level of .05 to determine if self-esteem is linked with persistence:

	Continue Working on Task	Quit
High self-esteem	30	10
Low self-esteem	14	25

30. What is the strength of association between the two variables in problem 28?

31. What is the strength of association between the two variables in problem 29?

32. A clinical psychologist wonders whether individuals with Type A personality answer the telephone faster (fewer rings) than those with the Type B personality. Use a Mann-Whitney U test with $\alpha = .05$.
Type A: 2, 5, 4, 3, 2, 3, 6, 3, 2, 4
Type B: 5, 6, 3, 6, 7, 6, 5, 3, 5, 6, 4, 6, 8, 4

33. An animal behaviorist wonders whether one strain of rats runs in a play-wheel more often than another species. The researcher observes the number of times 8 rats from each species run in a wheel for a 5-day period. Do the following data suggest that one species runs more often than the other? Use the Mann-Whitney U-test at the .05 level of significance to examine these data.
Species 1: 12, 32, 10, 20, 22, 19, 8, 8
Species 2: 3, 4, 2, 1, 1, 3, 4, 7

34. Use the normal approximation of the U distribution to test the significance of the following research results. Use an α level of .05: $N_A = 46$, $N_B = 34$, $U_A = 312$, $U_B = 332$.

35. Use the normal approximation of the U distribution to test the significance of the following research results. Use an α level of .01: $N_A = 38$, $N_B = 42$, $U_A = 252$, $U_B = 236$.

36. A study on prejudice reduction assessed perceived changes in students' attitudes toward members of minority groups. A clinical psychologist rated the students' prejudicial attitudes before and after they participated in a weeklong encounter group with members of various minority groups. Examine the following data—pre- and posttest prejudice ratings for each of the students—and then use the Wilcoxon matched-pairs signed-ranks test ($\alpha = .05$) to determine if there was a significant change from pre- to posttest attitudes.

Student	Pretest	Posttest
A	21	17
B	17	13
C	20	18
D	23	16
E	17	18
F	25	19
G	18	15
H	19	13

37. Student teachers were rated on their classroom presence before and after being filmed teaching an elementary school class. All of the students watched themselves on film before teaching—and being rated again—in a subsequent class. Did the film appear to improve the new teachers' classroom presence? Use an α level of .05.

Student Teacher	Before Seeing Film	After Seeing Film
A	3	2
B	5	3
C	4	3
D	7	5
E	2	2
F	6	4
G	8	5

38. Two instructors are team-teaching a high school science class. In order to make certain that they are grading the students consistently, the instructors each rank the students in terms of their perceived ability from 1 to 10. Using an α level of .05, determine their level of agreement.

Teacher A's ranking	Teacher B's ranking
1	3
2	2
3	1
4	6
5	7
6	5
7	4
8	8
9	10
10	9

39. Rank the following scores and then compute the Spearman rank-ordered correlation between X and Y (use $\alpha = .05$ to test the hypothesis that r_s is significantly different from 0):

X	Y
6	12
7	10
9	14
1	4
5	7
7	10

40. Two variables are arranged into a 3×4 table, one where the entries—nominal data—appear in each of the 12 cells. Which nonparametric test should be used to analyze the data? Why? (*Hint:* Use the decision tree(s) at the start of this chapter to answer these questions).

41. Imagine that the analysis described in question 40 reaches statistical significance. What is the next step the researcher should take? Why? (*Hint:* Use the decision tree(s) at the start of this chapter to answer these questions).

42. A researcher wants to assess the degree of association between two sets of ordinal rankings. Which nonparametric test should be used to analyze the data? Why? (*Hint:* Use the decision tree(s) at the start of this chapter to answer these questions).

43. A researcher wants to determine whether a difference exists between two sets of ordinal rankings that are not independent of one another. Which nonparametric test should be used to analyze the data? Why? (*Hint:* Use the decision tree(s) at the start of this chapter to answer these questions).

44. After calculating a significant χ^2 test statistic based on a 2×2 contingency table, what should the data analyst do next? Why? (*Hint:* Use the decision tree(s) at the start of this chapter to answer these questions).

Matching a Statistical Test to a Research Design

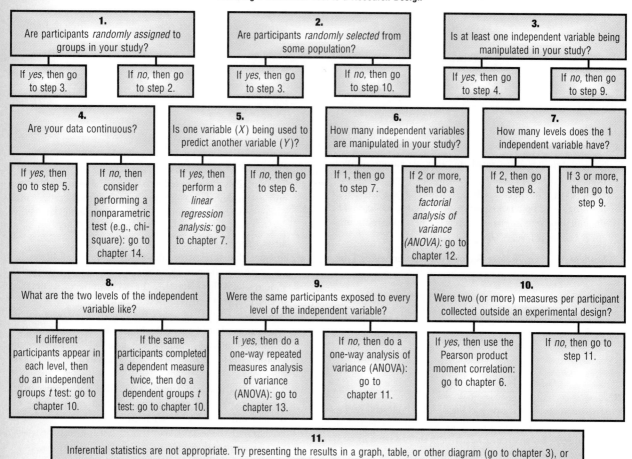

1.
Are participants *randomly assigned* to groups in your study?

If *yes*, then go to step 3.　　　If *no*, then go to step 2.

2.
Are participants *randomly selected* from some population?

If *yes*, then go to step 3.　　　If *no*, then go to step 10.

3.
Is at least one independent variable being manipulated in your study?

If *yes*, then go to step 4.　　　If *no*, then go to step 9.

4.
Are your data continuous?

If *yes*, then go to step 5.　　　If *no*, then consider performing a nonparametric test (e.g., chi-square): go to chapter 14.

5.
Is one variable (X) being used to predict another variable (Y)?

If *yes*, then perform a *linear regression analysis:* go to chapter 7.　　　If *no*, then go to step 6.

6.
How many independent variables are manipulated in your study?

If 1, then go to step 7.　　　If 2 or more, then do a *factorial analysis of variance (ANOVA):* go to chapter 12.

7.
How many levels does the 1 independent variable have?

If 2, then go to step 8.　　　If 3 or more, then go to step 9.

8.
What are the two levels of the independent variable like?

If different participants appear in each level, then do an independent groups *t* test: go to chapter 10.　　　If the same participants completed a dependent measure twice, then do a dependent groups *t* test: go to chapter 10.

9.
Were the same participants exposed to every level of the independent variable?

If *yes*, then do a one-way repeated measures analysis of variance (ANOVA): go to chapter 13.　　　If *no*, then do a one-way analysis of variance (ANOVA): go to chapter 11.

10.
Were two (or more) measures per participant collected outside an experimental design?

If *yes*, then use the Pearson product moment correlation: go to chapter 6.　　　If *no*, then go to step 11.

11.
Inferential statistics are not appropriate. Try presenting the results in a graph, table, or other diagram (go to chapter 3), or consider adopting a qualitative approach (go to Appendix F).

Implementing Some Recommendations from APA's Task Force on Statistical Inference

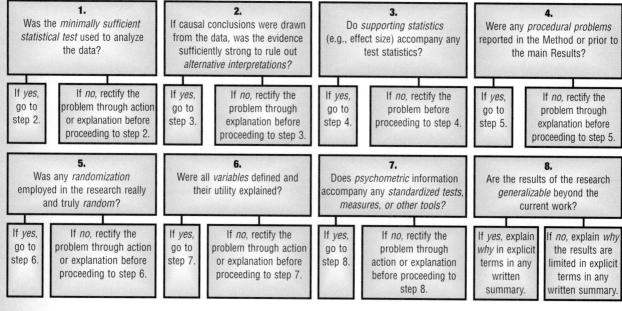

1.
Was the *minimally sufficient statistical test* used to analyze the data?

If *yes*, go to step 2.　　　If *no*, rectify the problem through action or explanation before proceeding to step 2.

2.
If causal conclusions were drawn from the data, was the evidence sufficiently strong to rule out *alternative interpretations?*

If *yes*, go to step 3.　　　If *no*, rectify the problem through explanation before proceeding to step 3.

3.
Do *supporting statistics* (e.g., effect size) accompany any test statistics?

If *yes*, go to step 4.　　　If *no*, rectify the problem before proceeding to step 4.

4.
Were any *procedural problems* reported in the Method or prior to the main Results?

If *yes*, go to step 5.　　　If *no*, rectify the problem through explanation before proceeding to step 5.

5.
Was any *randomization* employed in the research really and truly *random?*

If *yes*, go to step 6.　　　If *no*, rectify the problem through action or explanation before proceeding to step 6.

6.
Were all *variables* defined and their utility explained?

If *yes*, go to step 7.　　　If *no*, rectify the problem through action or explanation before proceeding to step 7.

7.
Does *psychometric* information accompany any *standardized tests, measures, or other tools?*

If *yes*, go to step 8.　　　If *no*, rectify the problem through action or explanation before proceeding to step 8.

8.
Are the results of the research *generalizable* beyond the current work?

If *yes*, explain *why* in explicit terms in any written summary.　　　If *no*, explain *why* the results are limited in explicit terms in any written summary.

CONCLUSION: STATISTICS AND DATA ANALYSIS IN CONTEXT

W hen planning to write this book, I had occasion to examine many existing statistics books in and outside of the behavioral sciences. Admittedly, I did not read every book I came in contact with from cover to cover, but I did form some lasting impressions of many works, taking notice of some of their more salient characteristics. One aspect of practically all the books I looked at stood out more than any other—rarely did a book have any sort of concluding chapter. Indeed, within my haphazard collection of 20 or so statistics books (I admit the possibility of selection bias in this nonrandom sample) only two texts bothered to include a conceptual parting shot—only two! The majority of the texts actually ended rather abruptly, most final chapters being devoted to reviewing some nonparametric statistics.

Why the paucity of concluding chapters? Why no final words of wisdom or direction, or at least an appeal to properly use, not abuse, statistics in the course of conducting behavioral science research? I cannot speak for my fellow authors, but in my opinion some closing comments designed to put what you have learned into perspective are truly required. I want you to leave your course and this book with an awareness that statistics and data analysis are for something, not just means to inferential ends. Thus, we will conclude what is probably your first exposure to statistics and data analysis by discussing the recent fuss over null hypothesis testing, a public discussion that is likely to influence how statistics and data analysis are used in the future. We will then consider how to avoid allowing statistical analysis to determine rather than merely steer your thinking, emphasizing once more that good interpretation always supersedes a right answer. I will suggest some ways to forge links between analysis and behavioral science research. We will also consider computers as research tools, as well as some educational, social, and ethical implications of statistics and data analysis. The book's final *Project Exercise* provides a checklist of statistical issues to consider when evaluating or planning a piece of research.

The Fuss Over Null Hypothesis Significance Tests

After reading an entire book on the statistical analysis of data, it may surprise you to learn of a growing controversy surrounding the proper use of null hypothesis significance testing. Many professional researchers claim that the statistical techniques we reviewed throughout this book are often misunderstood and, worse still, misused in the classroom, the lab, and out in the field. Concerns about the appropriate use of statistical methods are leading to new guidelines for students, teachers, and researchers in psychology and the other behavioral sciences. We will review the fruits of this controversy as a reminder that statistics are helpful tools for behavioral science research but that they must not be used dogmatically.

Various researchers have questioned the wisdom of the prevailing reliance on null hypothesis significance tests (e.g., Cohen, 1994; Loftus, 1993, 1996; Shrout, 1997). These researchers highlight concerns including the inappropriate, even "slavish," reliance on significance tests when other—often simpler—ways of discerning differences among research groups are available; failing to consider issues of power and effect size before planning and executing a study; and neglecting to view the presence or absence of an observed difference as somewhat arbitrary. In addition, there is the simple failure to educate a lay public that still erroneously equates phrases like "statistical significance" with "truthful," "powerful," and "meaningful" (e.g., Scarr, 1997; recall Data Boxes 9.E and 10.C). These various and sundry problems suggest that researchers become "distant" from their data when they rely too heavily on statistics for statistics' sake. To borrow an observation from John W. Tukey (1969, p. 83), a staunch advocate for analytic clarity, "There really seems to be no substitute for 'looking at the data.'"

▽

Though critics decry their overuse or misuse, null hypothesis significance tests are the analytic method of choice for most behavioral scientists.

Fortunately, Tukey's is not a lone voice. Geoffrey Loftus (1991, 1993, 1996), a cognitive psychologist and journal editor, jumped into the statistical fray by suggesting several alternatives to the usual null hypothesis-testing program found in the average journal article. His modest proposals for improving the way data are analyzed and presented include (adapted from Loftus, 1996):

■ Plotting data for visual examination in lieu of presenting table after table of test statistics (e.g., F, t) with their accompanying p values. The heuristic value of this suggestion is obvious—it is easy to see the meaning (e.g., presence or absence of a predicted difference) in a graph of data (recall chapter 3; see also Tukey, 1977).

■ Performing planned comparisons or contrasts, which can lead to more focused research questions and, eventually, agendas (see the discussion of contrast analysis in chapter 11).

■ Reporting confidence intervals for any sample statistics. Smaller confidence intervals around a sample mean, for example, indicate greater statistical power; wider intervals point to less power (Loftus, 1996).

■ Combining the effects of independent research efforts in order to isolate and identify consistent, predictable patterns of behavior. The advanced statistical technique used to achieve this synthesis is called **meta-analysis,** and it is beyond the scope of this book (but see, for example, Rosenthal, 1991). In a related vein, it is also important to assess the effect sizes (e.g., strength of association between independent and dependent variables) found within these efforts, as well.

These recommendations are by no means that dramatic or surprising—we have embraced most of them or their spirit in previous chapters in this book. They are by no means universally accepted or even known in many quarters, however. A convergence of forces and concerns like those raised by Loftus led the American Psychological Association (APA) to recently revisit the role of significance testing in psychology journals (Wilkinson & The Task Force on Statistical Inference, 1999).

Panel Recommendations: Wisdom from the APA Task Force on Statistical Inference

A task force of statistical and methodological experts was recently convened by the APA to develop a list of recommendations for the use and reporting of statistical techniques (Azar, 1999). The APA Task Force on Statistical Inference originally convened to address the concern that too many investigators were relying exclusively on null hypothesis significance tests in their research, that other useful statistical or data analytic techniques were being overlooked (other analytic matters were subsequently examined as well). One of the most historically contentious issues has been the faulty perception that a study failing to reject a null hypothesis at the .05 (or less) level is "not significant" so it is not worth publishing (e.g., Locascio, 1999). The presence or absence of significance, of course, is not the point—any inferential light a statistic sheds on the *meaning* of a result is the point.

Remember, statistics are only tools—their interpretive meanings rather than their numerical values are what matter.

Although the recommendations were developed for the psychological community, their importance is both valid and useful for other behavioral science disciplines. In general, the points raised by the task force will come as no surprise to researchers, educators, and students who are conscientious about conducting and reporting about research. One of the main points raised in the report is the importance of carefully and clearly describing a study's methodology, acknowledging any related limitations in its design or execution, and providing a sufficient amount of data for readers to critically evaluate the effort (Azar, 1999). In addition, researchers should describe the characteristics of any research populations as well as the membership in any control or comparison groups. Following the lead of Loftus (1996), researchers are also encouraged to carefully examine their data, plotting or graphing it whenever possible, so as to identify consistency as well as any aberrations within the observations. As one of the coleaders of the task force, Robert Rosenthal, stated the matter, researchers should "make friends with their data" (quoted in Azar, 1999).

A particularly important message of the report is one that I have tried to emphasize throughout this book: Select the simplest or most straightforward statistical test or approach to answer a question. It is never a good idea to become enslaved to powerful but complicated computer packages or statistical software that removes the user from his or her data. Any result should be cross-checked by hand calculation or another program, and then conveyed in the most clear prose possible. The goal, as always, is to focus on describing and interpreting behavior by using statistics as a tool (recall chapter 1); data, *not* data analytic techniques, must be the focus of the work.

The APA Task Force on Statistical Inference (Azar, 1999; Wilkinson & the Task Force on Statistical Inference, 1999) also recommends that researchers and students alike:

Select a Minimally Sufficient Analytic Technique.   Complexity is not impressive. Simpler statistical tests are generally better tests for almost any set of data. When a more advanced technique is appropriate, it is the data analyst's responsibility to explain its use, function, and meaning to readers in the most straightforward language possible.

Be Wary When Making Conclusions About Causality.   It is often difficult to determine when one variable truly causes change in another variable. In any case, it is also important to identify and discuss any possible alternative explanations or rival hypotheses that could account for results.

Provide Supporting Statistics Along with Any Main Statistics.   As we learned in previous chapters, any main statistical result should be bolstered by appropriate supporting statistics. When a mean difference is found, for example, be sure to include an accompanying effects size statistic and/or a statistic demonstrating the amount of variance accounted for by the observed difference.

Account for Problems in Research Procedure Before Presenting Any Results.   Any number of problems can occur in the course of conducting a piece of research; some are merely annoying while others are potentially hazardous to the drawing of meaningful conclusions from the work. Be sure to report any problems (e.g., research protocol violations, missing data, participant attrition) *before* presenting the results so that readers can consider the magnitude of the complication's effects on the data.

Document That Randomizing Procedures Are Truly Random.   When participants are described as being "randomly assigned" or "randomly selected," and so on, verify for yourself and any readers that these terms are being used truthfully and accurately. If not, then discuss what statistical or methodological controls were used to reduce potential bias in the actual research and any conclusions drawn from it.

Define Any Variables in Detail and Explain Their Relevance.   Independent and dependent variables must be explicitly defined and presented contextually. Why was one variable rather than another chosen for inclusion in a given project? The use of any and all variables in any study must be justified, and their presence must support the goals of the research effort.

Provide Psychometric Information About Any Measures, Tests, or Other Research Tools.   Whether a published test or measure is used or you develop your own, it is essential to provide basic psychometric evidence about it (e.g., test-retest reliability). Beyond reporting statistics drawn from reports about standardized measures, of course, appropriate psychometric statistics should also be run on standardized measures when they are used with current research populations. It is not sufficient to rely only on published (i.e., past) evidence—verification must also be established with newer participant groups.

Consider the Generalizability, Applicability, and Robust Nature of Results.   Instead of rushing to report or publish one's findings, step back and carefully evaluate whether they replicate or extend what is already known about some behavior. Do the results apply to existing findings or related research from other areas? Can the obtained results be described as "robust" or are they marginal at best? Honesty with oneself as a researcher is as important as that demonstrated in the process of presenting or publishing the work for wider audiences in the behavioral science community.

Other, more technical issues are presented in the task force's recommendations (Wilkinson & the Task Force on Statistical Inference, 1999; for related views, Bailar & Mosteller, 1988), but what really matters is the place of statistics and data analysis in behavioral science research. Despite their utility and importance, statistics and data analysis are guiding tools, not sacred objects. Interest in and excitement about the thoughtful study of human behavior must be the emphasis of researchers—becoming sidetracked by excessive focus on statistical methods is counterproductive to that end.

Knowledge Base

1. True or False: Complex statistical analyses are better than simple ones because they can address difficult research questions.
2. True or False: There is a growing consensus that there are viable alternatives to null hypothesis significance tests.

Answers

1. False: Simpler statistical tests are easier to use, more familiar to users and readers, and more readily interpretable.
2. True.

Statistics as Avoidable Ideology

For the past several years, I have been an instructor in a team-taught course on Western culture. During the class, we spend considerable effort getting students to identify some of the larger socioeconomic, historical, and political forces influencing people's collective behavior over the last 500 years. When considering the 19th and 20th centuries, we discuss the perspective of the philosopher-economist, Karl Marx (1818–1883), who wrote about the power of what he termed an *ideology*.

KEY TERM   An **ideology** is any system of symbols, images, or ideas that serve to be legitimate and preserve the status quo—an existing state or condition—of power.

By power, of course, we are referring to a nation, monarchy, group of elites, or bureaucracy desirous of maintaining control over some large number of people.

Generally, an ideology benefits a small controlling group while it is internalized by a (usually) larger, powerless one. As an ideology pervades a culture, it becomes the consciousness of the people. Prior to the Civil Rights Movement, for example, an ideology separated the experiences, roles, and advantages of white from black Americans. More recently, the Feminist movement's critical reaction to traditional gender identity reduced people's reliance on a masculine ideology. To Marx, ideologies like these pose a problem because they represent a "false" consciousness or set of beliefs, one leading to a condition of *alienation*. By alienation, Marx meant that people become estranged from or indifferent to their true natures because they adopt the ideology being promulgated by the small but powerful minority controlling their fate. Thus, for instance, African-Americans and women rightly rebelled against social, political, and economic constraints that curtailed their rights and welfare.

What, you ask, does political philosophy have to do with statistics and data analysis? Quite a bit, actually. Whenever we discuss Marx, I invariably feel that his ideas are as appropriate to the process of conducting research and performing statistical analyses as they are to the understanding of some sociopolitical systems. Ideologies provide ways of looking at or construing reality, just like research, statistics, and data analysis. Unwavering belief in and overreliance on statistical analysis is clearly a type of ideology, one that has advanced the interests of science and technology, but not without some costs (e.g., see the discussion of "status wars" of the behavioral sciences presented in Appendix F).

Automatic or even mindless use of statistical methods and data analytic techniques does not advance real science, nor does it shed light on the causes of behavior. Scientific minds are flexible, watchful minds. Good researchers remind themselves about why one statistical test is preferable to another in a particular circumstance, avoiding intellectual stagnation in the process. With apologies to Marx, unless you work to remain an open-minded, interested researcher, there is always the danger that you will become

Statistics and data analysis—and quantification more generally—are influential ways of construing and interpreting reality.

alienated from your data, merely going through the motions of an analysis. The survey researcher who continually collects data in the same way study after study, for example, is no different than the psychologist who uses the same paradigm in every experiment—not only is innovation lacking, but it is likely than novelties (real or potential) in the data are being missed.

Alienation is also inevitable when statistics and data analysis are placed on a high intellectual pedestal, one where quantification is portrayed as an unassailable authority ("If it's a number, it must be true"). Regrettably, such quantitative worship occurs when students—and all too many teachers and researchers—become empirical zealots who see rigorous statistical analysis as the sole way to discern cause and effect relationships in the world. Anything that does not conform to the dominant rules of evidence—formulas, Greek letters, p values, or any form of quantification—is deemed less worthy or, worse, less "correct" than observations made using some other technique (see the discussion of qualitative methods in Appendix F). Once again, I am not trying to debunk the arguments I made throughout this book—yes, statistical analysis is an important part of the research process, but it is only one part of the process. To unduly inflate the importance of statistics at the cost of other aspects of the research process is not only misguided, it reduces a researcher's flexibility and creativity.

Finally, alienation from data and even the research process occurs when statistics and data analysis are viewed from a "been there, done that" frame of reference. Some students feel that a statistics class is something to be suffered through once and that no return engagement is necessary—statistics was a requirement for a major or for graduation, one that merely needed to be checked off the list with all those other distribution requirements. Others see statistical analysis as a ritual to be performed in a set way forever, one where no deviation from the script (or the old class notes or user-friendly statistical software) is permitted. Believe it or not, some spontaneity in the planning and execution of research is to be welcomed—and the field of statistics is one that actually continues to advance and grow. In any case, I hope that what you learned about statistics and data analysis in this book is more than some rite of passage for you, that exposure to quantitative methods will help you to be an active thinker, producer, and consumer of research.

Reprise: Right Answers Are Fine, but Interpretation Matters More

Every picture tells a story, and so does every statistical result. In the same way that I hope you avoid becoming alienated from your data, I hope that you will see beyond a result. In other words, learn to focus on what the result of an analysis reveals about behavior rather than the numbers present in the analysis. Similar to selecting the appropriate test, getting the right or correct answer to a statistics question is a desirable goal. Remember, though, not to become too fixated on the value of a test statistic or whether its level of significance is .03 or .003. Your concern is better directed at discerning what a significant or nonsignificant test statistic tells you about people's behavior. How does a given statistical analysis inform or change your thinking about some behavior? The statistic itself is mute on this matter—you must use a combination of theory and inference in order to develop a coherent explanation for what people do under particular conditions, and why.

As noted above, statistics provide credibility in the form of technical support, but such support is incidental to the goal of describing *what happened* behaviorally. The meaning underlying a statistical result matters much more than the result itself. I encourage you to keep Abelson's (1995) MAGIC criteria in mind whenever you are considering the meaning and importance of a statistical result based on your own work or

Remain open to (and open-minded about) new analytic techniques and research methods.

Numerical results are secondary to behavioral results.

one you come across in the published literature (see Data Box 9.F; see also Dunn, 1999). You may recall that MAGIC stands for a result's *magnitude, articulation, generality, interestingness,* and *credibility.* How strongly does a result support a hypothesis? Can a finding be explained clearly and succinctly? Does a result apply to other contexts? Who will care about a finding? Is there sufficient evidence to believe what a result reveals? Abelson exhorts researchers to examine results through the critical lens of these five criteria, which also serve as reminders that numerical results represent only a superficial part of the story. It is the relationships among variables in a set of data—the stories the numbers tell about the interplay between or among the variables—which matter more than any clean, correct statistical result.

Linking Analysis to Research

Knowledge transfer from one domain to another, from recognition of a concept to its successful application, is the mark of understanding. Now that you have basic statistics and data analysis under your intellectual belt, do you know how to apply what you know? Students often learn about statistics and data analysis separate from research methods and design and, as a result, they are uncertain about how to match one with the other. I have tried to establish guidelines within each of the chapters in this book (i.e., decision trees) that will enable you to correctly apply the "right" test to the "right" data. Those guidelines tend to focus on a particular test's characteristics, however, rather than an overview of many tests available.

The first decision tree opening this chapter is designed to help you narrow your search and to give you a bird's-eye view of the process of matching statistical tests to research design. Once you identify the appropriate statistical test from this tree, you can turn to the appropriate chapter for more specialized information including, of course, more specialized decision trees and step-by-step directions for calculating the chosen statistic. For your convenience, the relevant chapter is noted along with each of the statistics. In the future, I hope that you will consult the final decision tree when conducting or evaluating a piece of research.

Do Something: Collect Some Data, Run a Study, Get Involved

Being able to link a statistical test to a research design is important but not, perhaps, as important as having the occasion to actually make a link happen. Will you have chances to forge this sort of link—and what happens, for example, if you do not have such opportunities? How much information about statistics and data analysis will you retain in the weeks, months, and years to come? My fervent hope is that you will remember many of the practical and conceptual tools presented in this book. Quite honestly, particular statistical tests and their precise meanings are apt to fade from your memory unless you have occasion to use them with some regularity (the "use it or lose it" syndrome). Such knowledge loss is common to any subject matter but more apparent, perhaps, to first-time students of statistics, who typically lack opportunities to regularly apply what they learned.

Is there anything you can do to reduce this knowledge loss and keep your skills sharp? Certainly. First, you can consult this book when the need arises. Rely on the decision trees presented at the opening of each of the chapters, as well as relevant tables and figures in the chapters, to jog your memory as to what test is employed under what conditions, how to locate information you need, and so on.

Second, take heart in some research on transfer of statistical knowledge from one setting to others. One study, for example, demonstrated that students majoring in the

Statistical and data analytic skills are best maintained through use and application, especially in the context of actual research.

behavioral sciences improved their statistical and methodological reasoning across their four undergraduate years (Lehman & Nisbett, 1990). Foundation courses in statistics and research methods favorably affected students' inferential reasoning across time, so much so that they outperformed peers in the humanities and the natural sciences (Lehman & Nisbett, 1990; see also Data Box 15.B; Lehman, Lempert, & Nisbett, 1988; Nisbett, Fong, Lehman, & Cheng, 1987). Another study, one emphasizing methodological issues (dependent in part on statistical knowledge), corroborates these results. VanderStoep and Shaughnessy (1997) found that students enrolled in a one-semester research methods course improved their inferential reasoning (e.g., generalizing from samples to populations, recognizing regression to the mean) regarding real-life events compared to a control group enrolled in a different behavioral science course.

Third—and arguably most important—you can pledge to conduct some independent piece of research that relies on statistics and data analysis at your earliest opportunity. There is really no better way to reinforce what you learned than by applying these skills in a project run from start to finish. Research projects run by individuals or groups of students can be conducted in the context of almost any content course (e.g., social psychology, cognitive psychology), as an independent study guided by a faculty member, or a senior or honors project. There are a variety of books available that can help you to develop ideas for a project, prepare the necessary groundwork, and then actually run the study (e.g., Cozby, 1997; Dunn, 1999; Martin, 1996; Pelham, 1999).

Alternatively, you could hone your research skills by volunteering to work in a faculty member's lab on his or her program of research. Many faculty members are delighted to have help with their work, and they truly enjoy teaching students about their research passions outside the classroom. It is not uncommon for such volunteer efforts to blossom into collaborative ones where students serve as coinvestigators—indeed, many prominent behavioral scientists began their careers in this fashion. This sort of "behind the scenes" experience is excellent preparation for graduate study, as well as a meaningful way to make an informed choice about your future.

Knowing When to Say When: Seeking Statistical Help in the Future

Experience is a great teacher in the lives of most people, but sometimes they need a nudge in the right direction. Despite the fact that you now have a good, solid background in basic statistics and data analysis, there is still much to learn—much more, in fact, than you will have access to unless you take other statistics courses at the undergraduate or graduate level. As you might expect, I have high hopes that you will pursue an interest in statistics and data analysis, availing yourself of other courses in order to build on the foundation you now have. Before registering for next semester's classes, for example, be sure to peruse the available research design courses and any statistically related offerings in the behavioral sciences (e.g., survey research, multiple regression, advanced ANOVA). You should also see if your institution's mathematics or statistics departments offer any accessible courses that pique your interest.

If you pursue any independent research now or in the future, there is a good chance that you will design a project or encounter a situation where the proper statistical analysis does not immediately present itself. When you are uncertain about how to proceed, should you wait for fate, inspiration, or insight to strike? Should you plod along alone by applying some familiar test to data that are only remotely applicable? Absolutely not. Suffering in silence is not noble; it's foolish. Avoid taking this path of least resistance—the same one leading to a potentially failed project—by seeking professional counsel about your work. Many statistics instructors are more than happy to troubleshoot questions regarding the marriage of design with analysis. Others will point you to an

DATA BOX 15.A

Statistical Heuristics and Improving Inductive Reasoning

Back in chapter 1, you read about the plight of David L., a hypothetical high school student who had to choose between attending an Ivy League university and a small liberal arts college. The scenario was used to illustrate how a statistical framework could be used to think about the matter of college choice. Issues such as sample size (e.g., how much could David learn about each school after only one visit?) and sample bias (e.g., were his conclusions after one day less diagnostic than the opinions of his friends who lived there 9 months each year?) were touted not only as statistically relevant but also as relevant for improving inductive inference.

The David L. problem was developed by social psychologist Richard Nisbett and his colleagues (see Nisbett, Krants, Jepson, & Kunda, 1983) as part of a program to examine what they dubbed *statistical heuristics*. A statistical heuristic is any rough and ready judgmental tool or guide that approximates some statistical principle. Nisbett and colleagues suggest that some statistical principles are intuitive—really hardwired—into human thinking, and that they can be applied when certain conditions are present. These conditions include (a) recognizing defined sample spaces and sampling procedures, (b) being aware of chance's influence on events, and (c) seeing statistical reasoning as culturally appropriate to a decision or task.

What is the importance of this work? Nisbett and his colleagues concluded that because statistical heuristics are apparently preexisting ideas in humanity's intellectual repertoire, any formal training in statistics increases the likelihood that people will use them (and do so properly much of the time). In other words, your experience reading this book and taking a class in statistics and data analysis has—to a degree—forever changed the quality of the inferences you are apt to make where data are concerned. There is a reasonably good chance that when the three conditions noted previously are met and an inferential situation is reasonably well defined, you will give a statistically sound answer. By "well defined," we mean that some cue is present to trigger your memory about issues of sampling, for example. Some statistical ideas may be too abstract to be reliably depended on in everyday situations (e.g., statistical regression). If nothing else, these findings should bolster your confidence that learning about statistics was a worthwhile activity—it will have some staying power for you.

With these results in mind, let's consider one more inferential problem and see how you do with it (from Nisbett et al., 1983, p. 356):

Championship Selection Problem

Two sports fans are arguing over which sport—baseball or football—has the best (most accurate) playoff system. Charlie says that the Super Bowl is the best way of determining the world championship because, according to him, "the seven games of the World Series are all played in the home cities of the two teams, whereas the Super Bowl is played in a neutral city. Since you want all factors not related to the game to be equal for a championship, then the Super Bowl is the better way to determine the world championship." Which procedure do you think is a better way to determine the world champion—World Series or Super Bowl? Why?

Statistical answers to this question suggested that the World Series was the better test of athletic acumen: "Anyone can get lucky for one game [the Super Bowl], but it is harder to be lucky for four. Besides, being home or away is a part of the game, you don't play on neutral ground during the season" (Nisbett et al., 1983, p. 356). A nonstatistical answer would highlight the Super Bowl as a "one-shot" opportunity to demonstrate a team's prowess under pressure.

How did you do? Did your training help you consider the sampling issues involved in this problem? Do you believe Nisbett and colleagues' argument that aspects of your training in statistics (and no doubt data analysis, as well) will stay with you, affecting future inferences?

appropriate reference book, a seminal article on design issues, or know of an investigator who dealt with a question or problem similar to your own.

Many colleges and universities also employ statistical consultants, usually researchers or graduate students, who have training in advanced statistics and data analysis. These professionals are paid to help students and faculty iron out the wrinkles in research designs and analyses. The only inviolate rule is this one: Request statistical consultation as soon as possible, preferably before, *not* after, data collection. Even the most gifted statistician cannot turn empirical dross into gold if the data are flawed (Dunn, 1999). So, do not be shy or prideful about seeking help. The mark of a mature intellect is the willingness to learn from others, especially experts, when opportunities present themselves.

Data Analysis with Computers: The Tools Perspective Revisited

Computers armed with statistical software are desirable helpmates when performing many statistical analyses, and they are virtually essential for studies with hundreds or even thousands of cases. Imagine doing a census by hand, for example, or conducting a phone poll without a computer to store respondent responses. The ideological concern expressed earlier is germane to reliance on computers, however, as well as the statistical and data analytic strategies stored within them. It is very easy to become overly dependent on sophisticated software that "does everything" for you. Indeed, the problem with some software is that it does entirely too much, really more than you will need. Earnest but novice users often assume that "more" is a good thing, so they run every possible analysis with every possible option the software package makes available. And why not? After all, even most of the outmoded desktop computers can usually perform even the most esoteric or complicated analyses in a few seconds. Remember, though, that less is generally more where analyses are concerned. Consider this appropriate analogy: Why use a between-groups analysis of variance (ANOVA) to analyze the data from a two-group experiment when the independent groups *t* test will suffice quite nicely? (If your memory is vague regarding these two tests, consult chapters 10 and 11 to recall why the latter test is more appropriate for two-group studies.)

Wading through an ocean of detailed statistical printouts, too, can be confusing to the data analyst, but worse for his or her readers who are bogged down by Results sections with too many superfluous details serving as distractions. Indeed, it is probably intellectually unsound and ethically compromising for students or professionals to report analyses and results they do not fully understand (sadly, though, it happens all too frequently). All the bells and whistles in sophisticated software can seem impressive but, in the end, the data analyst's goal is simplicity and clarity where results are concerned (Wilkinson & the Task Force on Statistical Inference, 1999). Even the best software in the world does you no good if you cannot interpret its output or use its information in clear, meaningful ways.

One must always know where the numbers entered into or emerging from any calculation came from, for example; statistical analysis should not be a "mystery hour" where information disappears, reappears in a new form, and is accepted without verification. You will recall that the original motivation for teaching you to perform statistical calculations by hand was so that you had a real sense of what happened to the data in the course of analysis (see chapter 1). To paraphrase an important message from the Task Force on Statistical Inference, computers afford researchers the opportunity to control their thinking about analyses—the computer is not a substitute for that thinking, however (Wilkinson & the Task Force on Statistical Inferences, 1999). When it is used wisely and well, then, the computer is a valuable ally, but in the end it is still a tool designed to support, not replace, the data analyst's efforts.

Wise researchers capitalize on the statistical skills and data analytic knowledge of others.

Computers and statistical software should help, not hinder, data analysis; however, they should not become crutches or substitutes for thinking and creativity.

Knowledge Base

1. True or False: Statistical analysis remains the best method available for drawing conclusions about behavior.
2. Why is the interpretation of a result more important than the statistics used to find it?
3. How can students maintain their statistical knowledge base?
4. True or False: Less is generally more where reliance on computer software is concerned.

Answers

1. False: Statistical analysis is but one perspective on behavior. Although it is certainly a dominant mode of inquiry, others (e.g., qualitative approaches) serve as compelling alternatives.
2. Statistical analysis is an important tool used to *discern* or *support* the interpretation of a research result. Such statistics are not as important as the result, however.
3. Students can keep their knowledge of statistics fresh by relying on chapter decision trees, by remembering that transfer of learned material does occur, or by conducting an independent project or volunteering to work on scholarly projects with active researchers. Learning to ask for help, too, can enhance recall of course material.
4. True. Computers are extremely useful tools, but data analysts should avoid becoming dependent on them.

(Thinking Like a Behavioral Scientist: Educational, Social, and Ethical Implications of Statistics and Data Analysis

Learning to perform statistics and data analysis is certainly learning to do something with numbers. The measurement, manipulation, and transformation of data enable researchers to see patterns, even occasional surprises, while working in the behavioral sciences. Uncovering and then interpreting results is part of the analytic process—as we have said all along, it is really the important end result of that process. Is the process over, the researcher's job complete, when the calculations end and the interpretations are offered in the form of a presentation or publication?

No, not just yet—what remains is the critical matter of thinking about the implications of any statistical analysis a behavioral scientist performs, what it means, and to whom it will be relevant. As data analysts, behavioral scientists (and students like yourself) have a responsibility to use statistics wisely and well in three distinct but related ways: to educate, to improve the social welfare, and to uphold ethical standards where scientific conduct is concerned. We will consider each one in turn.

Education is perhaps the most straightforward of the three areas, particularly because it is related to matters we have touched on repeatedly in this book. In the first place, behavioral scientists have a responsibility to use statistics and data analysis to inform people—students, fellow researchers, as well as the person on the street—about what a statistical result means, why it means one thing and not another, and what remains to be learned. Interpretation of a result—assuming it was based on the appropriate statistical analysis—matters most, of course, but a researcher must make the effort to explain to an audience what a given test statistic reveals in light of the properties of the data and, where appropriate, the context provided by a theory.

Let me explain what I mean by pointing to an example from a recent newspaper article. Some researchers at the University of Michigan examined the emotional effects of having an unwanted birth on the relationship between the mother and the child (Barber, Axinn, & Thornton, 1999). The statistical analysis of two sets of survey data revealed that mothers who had intended births were less likely to slap or spank their children than were other mothers. Moreover, these mothers were also likely to participate in various activities with their intended children, including taking them places outside the home. The lead researcher, Dr. Jennifer Barber, told an interviewer that "mothers with intended births engaged in fun stuff like going to the movies or the zoo with their children 3.7 times a week" (Berger, 1999). Mothers with unintended births, however, reported doing such pleasurable activities only an average of 3.5 times per week. Dr. Barber commented that, "Over the lifetime of a child, that's a huge difference" (Berger, 1999, p. F8).

Many readers, even the most sophisticated ones, might have stopped short of saying that the difference between a mean of 3.7 and 3.5 was a particularly "huge" one because the article was short—only a handful of paragraphs—and written for the lay public (the data were originally published in an issue of the *Journal of Health and Social Behavior;* see Barber et al., 1999). As a statistically knowledgeable individual, however, you understand the meaning the researchers were trying to convey, that it is not the means per se that matter, but their direction and magnitude. The difference begins to be more powerful, if not sobering, when we learn that the survey data contained 13,000 respondents who were interviewed between 1987 and 1988.

Remember: data are meaningless without context.

Furthermore, we need to move beyond the numbers, as it were, to think about what the occurrence (or relative absence) of pleasurable outings represents in the context of familial relationships. Emphasizing context enables us to examine the effects of relationship quality in childhood and its impact on later socioemotional development, a feat that cannot be achieved when results are not "unpacked" for readers. Unless attention is given to the educative nature of statistics and data analysis in situations like this one, there is the unfortunate possibility that the implications of results can be missed—or at least misconstrued.

The possibility of misconstruing statistical results, especially controversial ones, is related to the second area, social welfare. Some readers might wonder what statistics could possibly have to do with the welfare of society but, again, behavioral scientists have a responsibility to present their work in constructive ways—even when the fruits of their labors are not greeted warmly. At the same time I read the article on unintended births, I read a second, longer one discussing some data that have not yet been published. Because the data are so controversial, however, they began to attract attention before appearing in any peer-reviewed publication.

The investigators, two economists, suggest that a portion of the large drop in the national crime rate in the 1990s—maybe as much as 50%—is attributable to the distinct rise in the number of abortions since the *Roe v. Wade* ruling made by the Supreme Court in 1973 (Goode, 1999; see also Perman, 1999). In other words, at least some of the reduced level of crime is due to the fact that children who might have grown up to perpetrate the crime were never born. The constitutionally guaranteed right to abortion led to approximately ¼ of all pregnancies being aborted within a few years of the *Roe v. Wade* ruling.

The conceptual details and technical aspects of the economists' argument is beyond the scope of our present discussion, but the factual side of their work—and its controversial if unintended effects—is not. The two researchers conducted their research in the spirit of interested economic inquiry, as many writers, scholars, politicians, and pundits have tried to account for the drop in crime rates over the last decade. The economists simply wanted to demonstrate that a given social factor (i.e., legal right to abortion) could be legitimately linked with a second social factor (i.e., reduced crime rates). They never intended to make any controversial splash with their work, nor did they think anyone would react to it as a public policy piece, something it was never intended to be (the authors were never out to advocate abortion). According to Goode (1999), however, both liberal and conservative observers were outraged by the "implications" of the work, implications like using abortion to curtail crime or the promotion of eugenics! These ideas have nothing whatever to do with the research or the data analysis involved in it, but they readily illustrate how even dispassionate behavioral scientists can become embroiled in larger debates (e.g., the politics of abortion, the Pro-Choice movement vs. Right to Life) beyond their control but related to their work.

The moral where social welfare and statistics are concerned is this one: Be prepared to explain and sometimes defend your choice of and the meaning underlying your analyses. Just as behavioral scientists go before a jury of their peers when they seek to publish their research in reviewed journals, they must effectively be "tried" when they go before the public in interviews, on televised talk shows, or through some other medium. In both instances, they are accountable and they must, indeed, explain themselves to everyone's satisfaction. To do otherwise is to be disingenuous—why analyze data in the first place unless you are prepared to explain your conclusions—if not unethical. The public is free to criticize behavioral science research, a right and privilege in a democracy, but it remains the behavioral scientist's sacred duty to make that research accessible and interpretable, even when its message is not terribly palatable.

Finally, we turn to the necessity of upholding ethical standards, the third issue confronting behavioral scientists who rely on statistics and data analysis. We have already highlighted the main ethical standard that comes to mind—telling the truth with data—but we have not yet touched on scientific fraud. Fraud in the scientific community tends to involve deceit and trickery where presenting accurate results are concerned. Back in 1830, Charles Babbage, Lucasian Professor of Mathematics at the University of Cambridge, England, identified four classes of scientific fraud (Babbage, 1989). Although Babbage was specifically interested in criticizing problems with science (broadly defined) in England during his lifetime, his points are easily translated into ethical quandaries relevant to statistics and data analysis. We will mention each one in turn.

1. **Hoaxing** involves claiming that some novel result has been found when there is no concrete evidence for it. A researcher perpetrates a statistical hoax by claiming to have measured some behavior or detected some significant difference when nothing of the kind actually occurred. Hoaxing is, of course, pure fabrication and, therefore, a form of intentional fraud.

2. **Forging** is a close cousin of hoaxing, but it is worse because the false claim—the hoax—is supported by fabricated ("forged") data. A behavioral scientist practicing forging would make up some data and then perform statistical analyses on it so as to show results confirming some favored hypothesis. Sadly, this type of forging occurs, even among eminent scientists (see the case of Cyril Burt and arguments for the heritability of intelligence; Gould, 1981).

3. **Cooking** data entails selecting (and perhaps selectively presenting or publishing) only those observations that confirm a cherished hypothesis or theory. A behavioral scientist guilty of cooking his or her data would simply drop, overlook, or otherwise remove any offending (usually extreme) observations from the analysis, perhaps pushing the (recalculated) difference between or among a group of means toward significance. To be sure, removing problematic observations from a data set is acceptable, but only under stringent, clear, and proscribed conditions— conditions normally determined *prior* to the start of data collection and *absolutely* before any analysis was undertaken (for further discussion, see Dunn, 1999). Cooking is perhaps less dramatic than hoaxing or forging, but it is just as insidious and, in any case, careful readers are always suspicious of data that look *too* perfect.

Researchers and data analysts are responsible for correctly interpreting the meaning and (where possible) implications of results for the public, but not necessarily how the public chooses to construe findings.

DATA BOX 15.B

Recurring Problems with Fraudulent, False, or Mistaken Data Analysis: The Dracula Effect

I often think of fraudulent or false data that manage to get published as being like a lot like Dracula. Think of all those vampire movies you have ever seen—generally, even after Dracula has a stake driven through his heart, he comes back, maybe not in that movie, but certainly in a host of sequels. In much the same way, false results—whether erroneous due to chance or through calculated fakery—do not "go away," either. It is very hard to "kill" a false result once it is published in the scientific literature. Here's why:

- It might never be caught or recognized as false; for example, as when other researchers try to publish results conflicting with the accepted (but false) ones. Peers may reject these competing works as "wrong," or challenging data may simply be deemed inconsistent with the existing (unknowingly false) data.
- Alternatively, a false result might be acknowledged as such, as when the original author publishes a retraction and apology. There is still a problem, however, because not everyone who is aware of the original "result" will ever learn of the retraction!
- A false result can spur an ongoing series of research exchanges designed to prove or disprove the veracity of the result. On the one hand, such intellectual police actions are probably a good idea to the extent they alert readers to the questionable findings of some study. On the other hand, however, the authors of such follow-up investigations lose valuable time and energy in this diversion—their efforts are thus drawn away from their own research agendas.
- Finally, false findings affect the research programs of committed investigators, leading them down blind empirical alleys, and wasting their efforts and funding in the process. This resource drain probably sets researchers and sciences back for quite some time, as everyone involved—researchers, teachers, students, and members of the general public—lose out when false results are perpetrated or perpetuated.

4. **Trimming,** the fourth of Babbage's instances of scientific fraud, is directly relevant to statistics and data analysis. By trimming, the mathematician meant removing any extreme observations—high or low in value—that would unduly increase the variability of some variable (e.g., group mean) or reduce the level of error in some measurement. Trimming, then, is a subtle form of sanitizing or "prettying up" the data to make it look better. Too much trimming leads right to cooking, of course, but you can understand why many "innocent" researchers would claim that there is nothing wrong with cleaning up some data, especially if the obtained result becomes that much more convincing.

The road to hell, as they say, is paved with good intentions, and so is unethical behavior where statistics and data analysis are concerned. Many otherwise conscientious students and researchers can be seduced by the opportunity to make an empirical splash by cleaning up their data or altering it for a better result. Of course, such actions are not only unethical on a personal level—they lack principle or moral justification because they are selfish—they undermine the very goals of proper statistics and data analysis, the identification and explication of verifiable relationships among variables. If the relationships among variables are tainted, then imagine the damage that is created when the same variables are used to develop, build, or extend theorizing in the behavioral sciences. Science and the search for truth and understanding are truly at risk (for extended discussion of scientific misconduct, see Grinnell, 1992).

"That's the gist of what I want to say. Now get me some statistics to base it on."

Figure 15.1 According to Professor Babbage: The Danger Posed by Hoaxing, Forging, Cooking, and Trimming

In the end, you must make a concerted effort to be an honest researcher whose integrity and work ethic precludes committing the sort of transgression shown by Figure 15.1. The humorous intent of Figure 15.1 belies a larger problem, however: As Babbage knew, some people misuse statistics and data analysis for inappropriate ends. Avoid being one of them, and do your best to combat erroneous statistics and data analysis whenever you encounter them. It is your responsibility as an educated person, data analyst, and producer and consumer of statistics.

One final ethical concern for the data analyst is worth mentioning: Should one report all the statistics that were computed or only those that reached statistical significance? If I did my job well earlier in the book, then your automatic response to this question should be something like, "well, it all depends." Why? Just because a statistic is significant does not mean it is worth reporting; by the same token, some nonsignificant statistics can be informative. What to report or leave out all depends. The point, then, is to be honest with readers by specifying what statistical tests were conducted (and why). You may not need or want to report all the results from the data that were analyzed, but you are honor bound to disclose what sort of analyses were actually conducted even when the specific findings are not provided. Following the advice of

Kromrey (1993) and other researchers, you do not want to give the misleading impression that the reported (mostly significant) tests were the only ones actually performed (but recall Data Box 14.E).

Conclusion

I closed the first chapter of this book by reciting a fortune appropriate to an individual's first exposure to statistics and data analysis, so it is only fitting to do the same here and now, at the journey's end. Whatever your goals are now or in the future, I know that the quantitative knowledge presented in this book will serve you well, teaching you to look at the world around you from a different perspective. Maintaining this different point of view will refine the judgments you make because, in the spirit of the slip of paper found in a recent fortune cookie, "You should be able to undertake and complete anything."

Project Exercise

A CHECKLIST FOR REVIEWING PUBLISHED RESEARCH OR PLANNING A STUDY

This final *Project Exercise* is designed to supplement the decision tree that opened the chapter, as well as to build on the aforementioned goal of applying the statistical knowledge you acquired in the course of reading this book. You can review three aspects of your knowledge by performing this *Project Exercise:* characterizing what existing or potential data are like, identifying the purpose of a piece of research, and reviewing or reporting statistical information. The *Project Exercise* consists of a series of simple questions (and accompanying checklists) designed to help you evaluate published data and analyses appearing in a journal article, chapter, or book. The questions are designed to refresh your memory about a test, as well as to verify the proper use of an analysis and the presence (if any) of supporting statistics.

As you review some published data, for example, you can compare the authors' analyses and results with those proscribed by the checklist shown below. Alternatively, the following questions can also be used as a checklist during the analysis planning stages of a research project you are conducting (e.g., to keep track of completed analyses, to plan any remaining ones). When you set out to plan analyses—preferably in advance of any actual data collection—the questions and checklist provided below will help you to frame your thinking appropriately. You can also rely on the three sets of questions to organize your presentation of data and any analyses you have already completed.

1. **Characterizing the data**
   a. What scale of measurement is being used?
      ـــــ nominal
      ـــــ ordinal
      ـــــ interval
      ـــــ ratio
   b. What is the shape of the distribution of data?
      ـــــ normal
      ـــــ positively skewed
      ـــــ negatively skewed
      ـــــ bi- or multimodal
   c. Is the sample size reasonable?
      ـــــ very small—potential for bias
      ـــــ small

_____ adequate

_____ large

2. **Purpose of the research**

    a. Is the research descriptive?

        _____ summary or descriptive statistics (i.e., mean, variance, standard deviation, range)

        _____ tables (e.g., frequencies)

        _____ graphs (e.g., bar graphs, Tukey's tallies)

    b. Is the research focused on associations between variables?

        _____ continuous data are analyzed by the Pearson correlation coefficient (r)

        _____ discontinuous data (discrete) data are analyzed by the Spearman rank-order correlation coefficient (r_S)

    c. Is the research predictive?

        _____ continuous data are analyzed by linear regression

    d. Is the research inferential, generally focused on mean comparison?

        _____ one independent variable

            _____ one mean—single-sample t test or z test

            _____ two means

                _____ independent groups t test

                    _____ estimated $\hat{\omega}^2$

                _____ one-way ANOVA (F test) for two means

                    _____ estimated $\hat{\omega}^2$

                    _____ **f** (effect size)

                _____ dependent groups t test

            _____ three or more means

                _____ one-way ANOVA (F test)

                    _____ Tukey's _HSD_ for post hoc comparison of means

                    _____ estimated $\hat{\omega}^2$

                    _____ **f** (effect size)

                _____ one-way repeated measures ANOVA (F test)

                    _____ Tukey's _HSD_ for post hoc comparison of means

                    _____ estimated $\hat{\omega}^2$

                    _____ **f** (effect size)

         _____ two independent variables

            _____ two-way ANOVA (F test)

                _____ estimated $\hat{\omega}^2$

                _____ **f** (effect size)

    e. Is the research focused on nonparametric differences?

        _____ discontinuous (discrete) data are:

            _____ ordinal

                _____ association between ranks—Spearman rank-order correlation coefficient (r_S)

                _____ independent rankings—Mann-Whitney U test

                _____ dependent rankings—Wilcoxon matched-pairs signed-ranks test

            _____ categorical

                _____ one variable—chi-square (χ^2) goodness-of-fit test

                _____ two variables—chi-square (χ^2) test for independence

                    _____ phi coefficient (ϕ)

                    _____ Cramer's V

    f. Other _____

3. **Reviewing or reporting statistical information**
   a. What information is reported along with a test statistic?
      ____ symbol for test statistic (i.e., t, F, χ)
      ____ degrees of freedom for the statistic
      ____ numerical value of a test statistic
      ____ accompanying significance level (e.g., .05, .01) or indication of nonsignificant result
      ____ data (i.e., means, categorical or ordinal information) or data display to demonstrate relationship examined by test statistic
   b. Is there any interpretation?
      ____ concise verbal interpretation of what test statistic reveals
      ____ verbal explanation is accompanied (where necessary) by descriptive statistics (e.g., means)

LOOKING FORWARD THEN BACK

I encourage you to make use of both the decision trees opening this chapter and the most recent *Project Exercise* when reading about, evaluating, planning, or conducting any statistical analysis. Coupled with the decision trees provided in earlier chapters, you will be well prepared to tackle statistical matters in the future. To close the book, my parting wisdom is simple: Whether you conduct behavioral science research or think about everyday events from a more critical vantage point, your statistical and data analytic skills will serve you well.

Summary

1. Traditional null hypothesis significance tests have been repeatedly criticized as being too confining, limited in scope, or flagrantly misapplied by many researchers. The APA's Task Force in Statistical Inference recommends that researchers be more flexible and less dogmatic where statistics and data analysis are concerned.

2. Meaning is more important than method, and researchers are encouraged to examine their data more closely and with more of an eye to replication than has heretofore been the case. Generalizing results from one setting to another is as dependent on the practical matter of replication as it is on the statistical significance of results.

3. Readers were warned to not treat statistics as an ideology or too stringent a set of beliefs or procedures for working with data. A statistical ideology can lead to alienation by reducing a researcher's analytic flexibility, promoting mere analysis over the importance of interpretation, or curtailing openness to new analytic techniques.

4. The results of any statistical analysis should be viewed from their interpretive utility first and foremost—does a finding increase understanding of behavior? Whether a calculation leads to a right or correct answer is less important than what the answer reveals about behavior. Data analysts should always keep Abelson's (1995) MAGIC (magnitude, articulation, generality, interestingness, and credibility) in mind.

5. Learning about statistics and data analysis is more than plugging numbers into formulas. A prepared, thoughtful data analyst knows which statistical test to use under what condition, tries to retain statistical knowledge by being involved in research, and knows when to seek advice or assistance.

6. Computers are valuable aids, but like statistical analysis itself, they ideally serve as tools to help the research process run smoothly. Budding statisticians should avoid becoming overly dependent on computers and their statistical software—it is too easy (and problematic) to let a program do your thinking for you.

7. In order to truly think like a behavioral scientist, one must consider the educational, social, and ethical implications of statistics and data analysis. A researcher must educate audiences about the interpretation, meaning, and application of any result by placing it in context. When a result has social implications—even controversial ones—a researcher must

defend the choice of an analysis and its meaning, and be accountable for both.

8. Ethical standards in statistics and data analysis require researchers to acknowledge and avoid four forms of scientific fraud identified by Babbage (1989). These include pointing to findings that do not exist (hoaxing), fabricating data and analyses (forging), selectively presenting information (cooking), and removing extreme scores from samples (trimming).

9. The chapter and book concludes by encouraging readers to undertake behavioral science research and the statistical analysis of data with confidence.

Key Terms

Ideology (*p.* 567)   Meta-analysis (*p.* 564)

Chapter Problems

1. Identify some of the problems or concerns linked to the use of null hypothesis significance testing in the behavioral sciences, especially psychology.

2. What are some of the remedies proposed to improve the use of significance testing and the reporting of results in the behavioral sciences?

3. Discuss six of the specific recommendations made by the American Psychological Association's (APA) Task Force on Statistical Inference (TFSI). How can these recommendations improve the use of statistics and data analysis, as well as the reporting of written results?

4. In lieu of exclusive reliance on statistical results, what alternative do Loftus and others recommend? In your opinion, why have researchers been relatively slow to embrace this alternative?

5. How can replication be used to demonstrate generalizability?

6. Why should researchers avoid treating statistics as an ideology? How can investigators become alienated from their data?

7. In your opinion, is it possible for a researcher to become overly dependent on statistics? How?

8. Are right answers to statistical calculations more or less important than their interpretation?

9. How do Abelson's (1995) MAGIC criteria impact on the tension between obtaining right answers and offering accurate interpretation?

10. Why is it important to transfer statistical knowledge from one setting to another?

11. What evidence supports the contention that statistical or data analytic skills acquired in one domain can be transferred to others? Explain.

12. How can first-time data analysts retain the statistical knowledge and skills they have acquired after reading a book like this one or taking a statistics course?

13. As a novice data analyst, how will you keep your statistical skills sharp?

14. Characterize the proper role of computers and statistical software in data analysis.

15. When planning to analyze some data using statistical software, what are some of the *dos* and *don't*s a data analyst should follow?

16. Why is the computer a "tool"? Explain.

17. Why should behavioral scientists be concerned about the educational implications of the analyses used to support their research?

18. Why should behavioral scientists be concerned about the social implications of the results and analyses based on their research?

19. You are a behavioral scientist whose research and analyses have led to some controversial finding that is upsetting to the general public. How should you react? What are your responsibilities to the public and to your research, including the statistical analyses?

20. Identify, define, and explain the four classes of scientific fraud identified by Babbage (1989).

21. Why do you suppose some investigators might see "trimming" as more acceptable than the other three classes of fraud? Is it more acceptable—why or why not?

22. Why is scientific fraud so dangerous to the scientific enterprise, including statistics and data analysis?

23. Why are fraudulent, false, or otherwise misleading data so problematic where the scientific literature is concerned?

24. What is the "Dracula effect"? What problem does it present to behavioral science?

25. Is a researcher ethically bound to report the results of all statistical analyses performed on a data set? Why or why not?

26. In your opinion, what is the proper role of statistics and data analysis in the behavioral sciences?

27. In your opinion, what contributions do statistics and data analysis make to the behavioral sciences?

28. A criminologist studies the decrease in juvenile delinquency and petty crime in a group of middle school students following an intensive educational intervention. Delinquent behavior was measured before and then 6 months after the intervention. The criminologist wants to demonstrate a decrease in mean crimes committed by the children across the 6-month period. Which statistical test is best suited to test the researcher's hypothesis? Why? (*Hint:* Use the decision tree at the opening of the chapter to answer this question.)

29. An animal breeder compares the rated temperaments of four different breeds of dogs (Labrador retriever, rottweiler, fox

terrier, Jack Russell terrier). How can the breeder determine which breed has the least reactive (i.e., emotional) temperament, which one has the most, and so on? Which statistical test is best suited to test the breeder's hypothesis? Why? (*Hint:* Use the decision tree at the opening of the chapter to answer this question.)

30. A college admissions director wants to compare the mean achievement test scores of this year's entering class with the average of the previous year. The director believes that the entering class has a higher mean score than last year's average. Which statistical test is best suited to test the director's hypothesis? Why? (*Hint:* Use the decision tree at the opening of the chapter to answer this question.)

31. Imagine that the admissions director described in question 30 was interested in comparing the class rank of the entering class against that of the rank found in the previous year's class. The director believes that last year's class has a lower rank than this year's class. Which statistical test is best suited to test the director's hypothesis? Why? (*Hint:* Use the decision tree at the opening of the chapter to answer this question.)

32. A family practice physician examines the link between age, gender, and the incidence of motion sickness in children. She recruits three groups of children (ages 4, 10, and 14). Each group has an equal number of males and females in it. The doctor believes that motion sickness decreases with age, but that the decrease is especially pronounced in female children. Which statistical test is best suited to test the doctor's hypothesis? Why? (*Hint:* Use the decision tree at the opening of the chapter to answer this question.)

33. A developmental psychologist studies whether the details young children leave out of stories are linked to the well-known serial position effect associated with memory research (i.e., items appearing at the start or finish of a list are recalled better relative to those appearing in the middle). The re-searcher has a group of children listen to a story and then each child (separately from the others) is asked to repeat the story from start to finish. The children's recall is then checked for accuracy (i.e., how many errors occur at the beginning, middle, or end of the story). The psychologist assumes that most errors will occur in the middle of the children's stories. Which statistical test is best suited to test the researcher's hypothesis? Why? (*Hint:* Use the decision tree at the opening of the chapter to answer this question.)

34. A medical researcher looks at the incidence (number of cases) of meningitis in a large city, categorizing the occurrence of the disease by age (i.e., 25 and under, 26 to 50, and 51 and above). The researcher wants to determine whether meningitis risk is linked to any particular age group. Which statistical test is best suited to test for this link? Why? (*Hint:* Use the decision tree at the opening of the chapter to answer this question.)

35. A demographer believes that the number of siblings (X) people have is inversely related to intellectual outlook of the family environment (Y). The researcher rates the intellectual atmosphere of a large number of families and then tries to see if fewer siblings predict a more favorable intellectual family environment. Which statistical test is best suited to test the researcher's hypothesis? Why? (*Hint:* Use the decision tree at the opening of the chapter to answer this question.)

36. A professor of nursing has male and female college students categorize themselves as light, medium, or heavy (binge) drinkers of alcoholic beverages. This nursing researcher wants to see whether gender is linked to how students categorize themselves as drinkers. Which statistical test is best suited to test the researcher's question? Why? (*Hint:* Use the decision tree at the opening of the chapter to answer this question.)

BASIC MATHEMATICS REVIEW AND DISCUSSION OF MATH ANXIETY

 ## Overview

This appendix presents the basic mathematical operations that are used throughout the calculations presented in this book (i.e., addition, subtraction, multiplication, division, exponentiation and square roots, absolute values, and elementary algebra). Many readers will be very familiar with the operations presented here, needing only to skim the following material. Other students might feel a bit rusty, however, so this review should be useful in jump-starting their memories of basic math and algebra. To help spur recall, I include a *Knowledge Base* at the end of each section, which can serve as a short quiz of material that was just presented. If you find yourself having difficulty with particular but consistent sorts of problems within a given review section and/or *Knowledge Base,* you should seek help from your instructor, a teaching assistant, or a tutor. Alternatively, consider looking up the relevant topics in one or more of the references in basic mathematics provided at the end of the first half of this appendix.

The second half of Appendix A briefly discusses math anxiety—the fear of doing poorly in math or activities requiring mathematics (including, naturally, statistics)—and what can be done about it. I sincerely regret that I cannot dedicate a large amount of space to addressing ways to combat math anxiety in this book. What I can do, however, is to identify the symptoms and consequences of math anxiety and then encourage you to seek appropriate assistance if you believe you are experiencing it. To that end, some references on the topic are provided at the end of this appendix.

Where possible, I consciously try to avoid repeating information that I presented elsewhere in the book. Thus, you will need to turn to chapter 1 for a review of the order of mathematical operations and see Table 1.1 for a comprehensive list of mathematical symbols, their meaning, and an example illustrating each one.

Addition and Subtraction

In the course of adding numbers together, the order of addition makes no difference to determining the value of a sum. Thus, the equation

[A.1.1] $$2 + 7 + 3 = 12$$

yields the same sum as this equation:

[A.2.1] $7 + 3 + 2 = 12.$

Note, too, that although the presence of parentheses indicates which numbers should be summed first, this imposition of order has no effect on the final sum, as in:

[A.3.1] $(2 + 7) + 3 = 12,$
[A.3.2] $9 + 3 = 12,$
[A.3.3] $12 = 12.$

Adding positive and negative numbers together has no effect on a sum, either. Consider this equation, where the negative sign is treated as a subtraction sign:

[A.4.1] $4 + (-2) + 3 = 5,$
[A.4.2] $4 - 2 + 3 = 5,$
[A.4.3] $2 + 3 = 5,$
[A.4.4] $5 = 5.$

What happens when a long string of positive and negative numbers is present? An easy way to proceed is to (a) add all the positive numbers together, (b) add all the negative numbers together, and then (c) subtract the negative sum from the positive sum. Thus, for instance, we might have:

[A.5.1] $4 + (-1) + 6 + 2 + (-5) + 1 + (-4).$

The positive sum is determined first:

[A.5.2] $4 + 6 + 2 + 1 = 13,$

followed by the negative sum:

[A.5.3] $-1 - 5 - 4 = -10.$

Subtracting the negative sum from the positive sum, we find:

[A.5.4] $13 - 10 = 3.$

Naturally, if the negative sum were -13 and the positive sum were 10, you would subtract 13 from 10, which is equal to -3.

When subtracting negative numbers, however, keep in mind that two adjacent negative signs convert to a positive sign, meaning that addition is taking place. Thus,

[A.6.1] $10 - (-6) = 16,$
[A.6.2] $10 + 6 = 16,$
[A.6.3] $16 = 16.$

Knowledge Base

Perform the following calculations to check your understanding of addition and subtraction.

1. $10 - (-4) + 3 + (-6) =$
2. $3 + 5 + 6 + 1 + 9 =$
3. $(3 + 5) + 2 =$
4. $(10 - 5) + (-5) + 2 =$
5. $7 - 5 + 9 - (-3) + 1 + 3 + 5 + (-5) =$
6. $-5 + 3 - 5 - (-2) + 4 - 3 =$

Answers

1. 11
2. 24
3. 10
4. 2
5. 18
6. -4

Multiplication

The order or placement of numbers in multiplication has no influence on a product's value. Thus,

[A.7.1] $$4 \times 5 \times 2 = 40$$

is equivalent to

[A.8.1] $$2 \times 4 \times 5 = 40.$$

The presence of parentheses, too, has no effect on a resulting sum:

[A.9.1] $(2 \times 5) \times 4 = 40,$

[A.9.2] $10 \times 4 = 40,$

[A.9.3] $40 = 40.$

It is the case, however, that the placement of a decimal point matters a great deal where correct answers are concerned. Thus,

[A.10.1] $$5.0 \times 3.0 = 15$$

is *not* the same as

[A.11.1] $$5.0 \times 0.3 = 1.5.$$

One of the most common errors occurring in the calculation of statistics is the dropping or misplacing of a decimal point. As shown by [A.10.1] and [A.11.1], placement of a decimal point (i.e., 3.0 vs. 0.3) has a dramatic effect on the magnitude of an answer (i.e., 15 vs. 1.5).

Knowledge Base

1. $3 \times 5 \times 7 \times 5 =$
2. $(7 \times 4) \times 3 \times 2 =$
3. $5 \times 1 \times (2 \times 9) =$
4. $2.5 \times 25 =$
5. $10.0 \times 1.0 =$
6. $5.0 \times 4.0 =$

Answers

1. 525
2. 168
3. 90
4. 62.5
5. 10.0
6. 20.0

Division

Division involves two numbers—one is divided by the value of the other—and the *order of these numbers in an equation makes a difference.* Thus, for example,

[A.12.1] $6 \div 2 \neq 2 \div 6,$

[A.12.2] $3 \neq 0.33.$

Although division is usually designated by the symbol $\div$, most division in this book is denoted by one number appearing on top of another, with a straight line separating the two, or:

[A.13.1] $\dfrac{6}{2} = 3,$

[A.13.2] $3 = 3.$

Similarly, it must be true that:

[A.14.1] $\dfrac{2}{6} = 0.33,$

[A.14.2] $0.33 = 0.33.$

The number appearing on top of the line is called the *numerator,* whereas the one under the line—the number that does the actual dividing—is called the *denominator.* As acknowledged previously in the discussion of multiplication, the presence of a decimal point has an effect on an answer, and you must be vigilant about where it is placed. If you are not careful, you can easily make a miscalculation. Consider, for instance,

[A.15.1] $$\frac{18}{15} = 1.2$$

versus

[A.16.1] $$\frac{18}{1.5} = 12.$$

Knowledge Base

1. $\dfrac{100}{25}$

2. $\dfrac{100}{2.5}$

3. $\dfrac{10}{25}$

4. $\dfrac{10}{2.5}$

5. $\dfrac{8}{8}$

6. $\dfrac{8.0}{0.8}$

Answers

1. 4
2. 40
3. 0.40
4. 4
5. 1.0
6. 10

Exponents and Square Roots

An exponent involves a number or symbol being placed above and after another number or symbol, denoting the power to which the latter is to be raised. Exponentiation is often used to "square" a number, which is a shorthand way of indicating that the number is multiplied by itself. Thus,

[A.17.1] $$9^2 = 9 \times 9 = 81.$$

The number presented as a superscript indicates the number of times the larger number is to be multiplied by itself. To continue with the number 9, we can take 9 to the third power, or:

[A.18.1] $$9^3 = 9 \times 9 \times 9 = 729.$$

Taking 9 to the fourth power results in:

[A.19.1] $$9^4 = 9 \times 9 \times 9 \times 9 = 6,561.$$

And so on, depending on the exponent being used.

Most calculators have a "square" function key (e.g., x^2) or a more generic exponent key (i.e., x^y). Calculators vary as to how they present the exponent function, so you should check the one you intend to use before working with exponents.

Square root is the reverse of the squaring function, and it is symbolized by a radical sign, or $\sqrt{}$. Thus,

[A.20.1] $$\sqrt{81} = 9,$$

or

[A.21.1] $\sqrt{9} = 3$

or

[A.22.1] $\sqrt{227} = 15.07.$

Calculating all but the simplest (i.e., usually memorized) square roots by hand is tedious. Fortunately, most calculators have a square root key (i.e., $\sqrt{x}$), and you should make certain that your calculator is equipped with one.

Knowledge Base

1. $5^2 =$
2. $10^2 =$
3. $6^3 =$
4. $\sqrt{28} =$
5. $\sqrt{0.10} =$
6. $\sqrt{100} =$

Answers

1. 25
2. 100
3. 216
4. 5.29
5. 0.3162
6. 10

Absolute Values

Taking the absolute value of a positive or a negative number means that you are converting the number—regardless of its value—to a positive number. Symbolically, the number is placed between two horizontal lines (i.e., $|x|$). Here are a few examples:

[A.23.1] $|-224| = 224,$

[A.24.1] $|12| = 12,$

[A.25.1] $|-76.55| = 76.55.$

Knowledge Base

Find the absolute value of each of the following numbers:

1. -45
2. $-2,765$
3. 67
4. 2
5. -70
6. 0

Answers

1. $|-45| = 45$
2. $|-2,765| = 2,765$
3. $|67| = 67$
4. $|2| = 2$
5. $|-70| = 70$
6. $|0| = 0$

Algebra: Solving Equations

When calculating statistics or performing a statistical test, knowing basic algebra—how to solve an equation in order to determine the value of an unknown variable—can be very helpful.

Transposition.   Transposition is the mathematical operation where a number or other mathematical term is moved from one side of an equation to the other. You may remember the common refrain that generations of teachers have passed on to their students: "What you do to one side must also be done on the other side." Words to live by when doing algebra. With this dictum in mind, recognize that each of the following mathematical statements are actually equal to one another:

$$x + y = z,$$
$$y = z - x,$$
$$x = z - y,$$
$$0 = z - x - y,$$
$$0 = z - (x + y).$$

Transposition enables us to fill in the blanks, the unknown values, of any equation. Consider the following:

[A.26.1] $30 + x = 8.$

If we subtract 30 from both sides of the equation, we get:

[A.26.2] $x = 8 - 30,$

which, in turn, is equal to:

[A.26.3] $x = -22.$

As an error check, plug the obtained answer into the original formula shown above in [A.26.1] (but renumbered here for consistency). Replacing x with -22, we find:

[A.27.1] $30 + (-22) = 8,$
[A.27.2] $30 - 22 = 8,$
[A.27.3] $8 = 8.$

Some equations involve subtracting a value from x. Here is an example:

[A.28.1] $x - 6 = 14.$

In this case, 6 must be added to both sides of the equation in order to isolate the value of x, as in:

[A.28.2] $x = 14 + 6,$
[A.28.3] $x = 20.$

Once again, we can check for any errors by substituting 20 for x in [A.28.1] (renumbered here):

[A.29.1] $20 - 6 = 14,$
[A.29.2] $14 = 14.$

To increase your mathematical flexibility, it is also a very good idea to recall how to solve equations when they contain fractions. Here is a basic example, one where we need only to solve the equation:

[A.30.1] $x = \dfrac{5 - 2}{2},$

[A.30.2] $x = \dfrac{3}{2},$

[A.30.3] $x = 1.5.$

A given value of x can also be multiplied by some other value. Imagine that we have an equation like this one:

[A.31.1] $6x = 30.$

In this case, we must remove the 6 that is multiplied by the value x. To do so, we can divide both sides of the equation by 6, or:

[A.31.2] $\dfrac{6x}{6} = \dfrac{30}{6},$

[A.31.3] $x = 5.$

By plugging the value of 5 into the original equation (i.e., [A.31.1], we find that:

[A.32.1] $6(5) = 30,$

[A.32.2] $30 = 30.$

When a value of x is divided by some value, as in:

[A.33.1] $$\frac{x}{4} = 12.$$

We can solve the equation by multiplying each side by 4, or:

[A.33.2] $$4\left(\frac{x}{4}\right) = 12(4).$$

The two 4s on the left side of the equation cancel each other out, so:

[A.33.3] $x = 48.$

As an error check, we enter 48 into [A.33.1] (renumbered here for consistency):

[A.34.1] $$\frac{48}{4} = 12,$$

[A.34.2] $12 = 12.$

Knowledge Base

1. $12 + x = 10$
2. $x - 2 = 15$
3. $x = \dfrac{3 - 1}{4}$
4. $9 + x = 12$
5. $x - 5 = 6$
6. $x = \dfrac{7 + 3}{10}$

Answers

1. -2
2.   17
3.   0.50
4.   3
5.   11
6.   1

Somewhat More Complex Algebraic Equations

When an equation is more complex than the preceding examples, a combination of the techniques demonstrated above can be used to isolate x on one side of an equation. Here is a more complex equation to consider:

[A.35.1] $5x - 9 = 15.$

To begin, we remove the -9 by adding 9 to both sides of the equation:

[A.35.2] $5x = 15 + 9,$

[A.35.3] $5x = 24.$

We then divide both sides by 5, as in:

[A.35.4] $$\frac{x}{5} = \frac{24}{5},$$

[A.35.5] $x = 4.8.$

As always, we check the answer by substituting the obtained value for x in the original equation (i.e., [A.35.1]):

[A.36.1] $5(4.8) - 9 = 15,$

[A.36.2] $24 - 9 = 15,$

[A.36.3] $15 = 15.$

Here is a final algebraic example:

[A.37.1] $$\frac{x + 6}{8} = 5.$$

We begin by removing the 8 by multiplying both sides by 8 for:

[A.37.2] $8 \left(\dfrac{x + 6}{8} \right) = 5(8),$

[A.37.3] $x + 6 = 40.$

The next step involves eliminating the 6 via subtraction, or:

[A.37.4] $x = 40 - 6,$

[A.37.5] $x = 34.$

As an error check, we can insert 34 into the original formula (i.e., [A.37.1]):

[A.38.1] $\dfrac{34 + 6}{8} = 5,$

[A.38.2] $\dfrac{40}{8} = 5,$

[A.38.3] $5 = 5.$

Knowledge Base

1. $2x - 4 = 10$

2. $\dfrac{x + 3}{6} = 10$

3. $5x - 8 = 20$

4. $\dfrac{x + 1}{10} = 15$

5. $7x + 2 = 9$

6. $\dfrac{x - 5}{20} = 8$

Answers

1.   7
2.   57
3.   5.6
4.   149
5.   1
6.   165

References About Learning Basic Mathematics and Algebra

There are numerous books available that review basic math and algebra skills. Here are some titles you might want to consider:

Barker, V. C., & Aufman, R. N. (1982). *Essential mathematics*. Boston: Houghton Mifflin.

Falstein, L. D. (1986). *Basic mathematics* (2nd ed.). Reading, MA: Addison-Wesley.

Hughes-Hallett, D. (1980). *The math workshop: Algebra.* New York: Norton.

Ross, D. A. (1996). *Master math: Algebra.* Franklin Lakes, NJ: Career Press.

Ross, D. A. (1996). *Master math: Basic math and pre-algebra.* Franklin Lakes, NJ: Career Press.

Washington, A. J. (1984). *Arithmetic and beginning algebra.* Menlo Park, CA: Benjamin/Cummings.

Identifying Math Anxiety and Doing Something About It

Take a moment and read the following set of statements. As you read each statement, think about whether you generally *agree* or *disagree* with it.

- I've never done very well in math or math-related activities.
- Math is not really very important to my long-term goals.
- Whenever possible, I avoid doing math.
- I'm one of those people who just are not very good at math, but I'm very good at other sorts of activities.
- I think the world is divided into "math" people and "verbal" people, and I'm a verbal person.
- Math is something to be endured, not enjoyed.
- Math has always been difficult for me.
- When I have to do math, my mind goes blank.
- Doing math requires a special gift or what is often called a "mathematical mind."

This exercise is not a quiz or a personality inventory—it is a common sense–based approach to diagnosing math anxiety. If you agreed with more than half of these statements, then there is a distinct possibility that you suffer from a common, intellectually disabling condition labeled *math anxiety*. Math anxiety is the catchall term for a general fear or feeling of dread associated with any number of mathematically related activities—from balancing a checkbook to performing inferential statistics.

Tobias (1993) identifies four myths associated with mathematics. They are:

Myth 1: Math ability is inherited, not learned.
Myth 2: Insight into math occurs suddenly—a *flash* of insight—if ever.
Myth 3: Relatively few people can really do mathematics with any competence.
Myth 4: Math is really a male domain—women are better suited to other intellectual pursuits.

There is ample empirical evidence disproving these unfortunate myths, and more data are being collected all the time (see Tobias, 1993). Unfortunately, our culture and various social influences—the family, the classroom, our peers—often reinforce these myths, thereby perpetuating math anxiety. I cannot tackle the entire problem of math anxiety here, nor can I help you to overcome it right now. But what I can do is warn you that math anxiety is real and that it can have adverse consequences for how well you learn statistics and data analysis. Particular groups of people—women and minorities—are especially prone to math anxiety (Tobias, 1993). If you are female or the member of a minority group, and math-related activities make you somewhat anxious, then you will want to take math anxiety very seriously—and take action to do something about it (for interesting perspectives on group membership and intellectual performance, see Spencer, Steele, & Quinn, 1999; Steele & Aronson, 1995).

Regardless of your gender or group membership, however, if you believe that you suffer from math anxiety, *only* you can take the concrete steps necessary to deal with it. First, speak to your statistics instructor or a teaching assistant about it. Second, call your institution's Department of Mathematics to see if any workshops, courses, or materials on coping with and overcoming math anxiety are available (if your school has one, you might also call the Statistics Department). Third, approach your institution's Dean of Students or Student Services Office to find out what, if any, resources are available for people with math anxiety. Fourth, take a look at some of the math anxiety references provided on the next page, read them, and see if they help to address your concerns about doing math.

On a personal note, I have taught many students who saw themselves as math phobics. When they expended effort in my statistics course and worked to overcome their math anxiety—being coached by my favorite admonition that "statistics is a tool to help guide inference only"—they tended to do just fine in the course. I am sure that you will do fine in your statistics course, as well, but you must spend energy and time carefully reading this textbook, doing the homework, diligently attending class, asking questions, and immediately seeking assistance when you have difficulty with course material. All of these activities fall under the heading of the "mise en place" philosophy of doing statistics (see chapter 1), of course, as does doing something about math anxiety. Good luck—identifying a problem like math anxiety is the first step to its resolution.

References on Math Anxiety

Listed below are several books dealing with math anxiety that may prove to be helpful to you.

Aren, C. A. (1993). *Conquering math anxiety: A self-help workbook.* Belmont, CA: Wadsworth.

Buxton, L. (1981). *Do you panic about maths: Coping with maths anxiety.* London: Heinemann.

Kitchens, A. N. (1994). *Defeating math anxiety.* New York: Irwin/McGraw-Hill.

Tobias, S. (1995). *Succeed with math: Every student's guide to conquering math anxiety.* New York: The College Board.

Tobias, S. (1993). *Overcoming math anxiety: Revised and expanded.* New York: Norton.

Zaslavsky, C. (1994). *Fear of math: How to get over it and get on with your life.* Newark, NJ: Rutgers University Press.

STATISTICAL TABLES

Table B.1　Random Numbers Table

Row Number									
00000	10097	32533	76520	13586	34673	54876	80959	09117	39292	74945
00001	37542	04805	64894	74296	24805	24037	20636	10402	00822	91665
00002	08422	68953	19645	09303	23209	02560	15953	34764	35080	33606
00003	99019	02529	09376	70715	38311	31165	88676	74397	04436	27659
00004	12807	99970	80157	36147	64032	36653	98951	16877	12171	76833
00005	66065	74717	34072	76850	36697	36170	65813	39885	11199	29170
00006	31060	10805	45571	82406	35303	42614	86799	07439	23403	09732
00007	85269	77602	02051	65692	68665	74818	73053	85247	18623	88579
00008	63573	32135	05325	47048	90553	57548	28468	28709	83491	25624
00009	73796	45753	03529	64778	35808	34282	60935	20344	35273	88435
00010	98520	17767	14905	68607	22109	40558	60970	93433	50500	73998
00011	11805	05431	39808	27732	50725	68248	29405	24201	52775	67851
00012	83452	99634	06288	98033	13746	70078	18475	40610	68711	77817
00013	88685	40200	86507	58401	36766	67951	90364	76493	29609	11062
00014	99594	67348	87517	64969	91826	08928	93785	61368	23478	34113
00015	65481	17674	17468	50950	58047	76974	73039	57186	40218	16544
00016	80124	35635	17727	08015	45318	22374	21115	78253	14385	53763
00017	74350	99817	77402	77214	43236	00210	45521	64237	96286	02655
00018	69916	26803	66252	29148	36936	87203	76621	13990	94400	56418
00019	09893	20505	14225	68514	46427	56788	96297	78822	54382	14598
00020	91499	14523	68479	27686	46162	83554	94750	89923	37089	20048
00021	80336	94598	26940	36858	70297	34135	53140	33340	42050	82341
00022	44104	81949	85157	47954	32979	26575	57600	40881	22222	06413
00023	12550	73742	11100	02040	12860	74697	96644	89439	28707	25815
00024	63606	49329	16505	34484	40219	52563	43651	77082	07207	31790
00025	61196	90446	26457	47774	51924	33729	65394	59593	42582	60527
00026	15474	45266	95270	79953	59367	83848	82396	10118	33211	59466
00027	94557	28573	67897	54387	54622	44431	91190	42592	92927	45973
00028	42481	16213	97344	08721	16868	48767	03071	12059	25701	46670
00029	23523	78317	73208	89837	68935	91416	26252	29663	05522	82562
00030	04493	52494	75246	33824	45862	51025	61962	79335	65337	12472
00031	00549	97654	64051	88159	96119	63896	54692	82391	23287	29529
00032	35963	15307	26898	09354	33351	35462	77974	50024	90103	39333
00033	59808	08391	45427	26842	83609	49700	13021	24892	78565	20106
00034	46058	85236	01390	92286	77281	44077	93910	83647	70617	42941
00035	32179	00597	87379	25241	05567	07007	86743	17157	85394	11838
00036	69234	61406	20117	45204	15956	60000	18743	92423	97118	96338
00037	19565	41430	01758	75379	40419	21585	66674	36806	84962	85207
00038	45155	14938	19476	07246	43667	94543	59047	90033	20826	69541
00039	94864	31994	36168	10851	34888	81553	01540	35456	05014	51176
00040	98086	24826	45240	28404	44999	08896	39094	73407	35441	31880
00041	33185	16232	41941	50949	89435	48581	88695	41994	37548	73043
00042	80951	00406	96382	70774	20151	23387	25016	25298	94624	61171
00043	79752	49140	71961	28296	69861	02591	74852	20539	00387	59579
00044	18633	32537	98145	06571	31010	24674	05455	61427	77938	91936
00045	74029	43902	77557	32270	97790	17119	52527	58021	80814	51748
00046	54178	45611	80993	37143	05335	12969	56127	19255	36040	90324
00047	11664	49883	52079	84827	59381	71539	09973	33440	88461	23356
00048	48324	77928	31249	64710	02295	36870	32307	57546	15020	09994
00049	69074	94138	87637	91976	35584	04401	10518	21615	01848	76938
00050	09188	20097	32825	39527	04220	86304	83389	87374	64278	58044
00051	90045	85497	51981	50654	94938	81997	91870	76150	68476	64659
00052	73189	50207	47677	26269	62290	64464	27124	67018	41361	82760
00053	75768	76490	20971	87749	90429	12272	95375	05871	93823	43178
00054	54016	44056	66281	31003	00682	27398	20714	53295	07706	17813
00055	08358	69910	78542	42785	13661	58873	04618	97553	31223	08420
00056	28306	03264	81333	10591	40510	07893	32604	60475	94119	01840
00057	53840	86233	81594	13628	51215	90290	28466	68795	77762	20791
00058	91757	53741	61613	62669	50263	90212	55781	76514	83483	47055
00059	89415	92694	00397	58391	12607	17646	48949	72306	94541	37408

Table B.2 Proportions of Area Under the Normal Curve (the *z* Table)

The use of this table requires that the raw score be transformed into a *z* score and that the variable be normally distributed.

The values in the table represent the proportion of area in the standard normal curve, which has a mean of 0, a standard deviation of 1.00, and a total area also equal to 1.00.

Because the normal curve is symmetrical, it is sufficient to indicate only the areas corresponding to positive *z* values. Negative *z* values will have precisely the same proportions of area as their positive counterparts.

Column B represents the proportion of area between the mean and the given *z*. Column C represents the proportion of area beyond a given *z*.

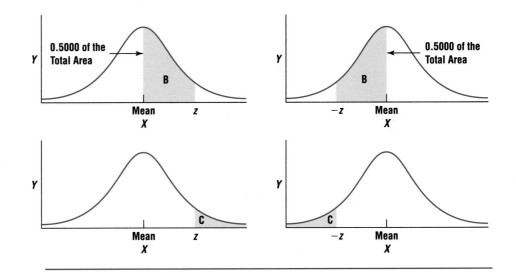

Table B.2   (*continued*)

(A) z	(B) Area Between Mean and z	(C) Area Beyond z	(A) z	(B) Area Between Mean and z	(C) Area Beyond z	(A) z	(B) Area Between Mean and z	(C) Area Beyond z
0.00	.0000	.5000	0.57	.2157	.2843	1.14	.3729	.1271
0.01	.0040	.4960	0.58	.2190	.2810	1.15	.3749	.1251
0.02	.0080	.4920	0.59	.2224	.2776	1.16	.3770	.1230
0.03	.0120	.4880	0.60	.2257	.2743	1.17	.3790	.1210
0.04	.0160	.4840	0.61	.2291	.2709	1.18	.3810	.1190
0.05	.0199	.4801	0.62	.2324	.2676	1.19	.3830	.1170
0.06	.0239	.4761	0.63	.2357	.2643	1.20	.3849	.1151
0.07	.0279	.4721	0.64	.2389	.2611	1.21	.3869	.1131
0.08	.0319	.4681	0.65	.2422	.2578	1.22	.3888	.1112
0.09	.0359	.4641	0.66	.2454	.2546	1.23	.3907	.1093
0.10	.0398	.4602	0.67	.2486	.2514	1.24	.3925	.1075
0.11	.0438	.4562	0.68	.2517	.2483	1.25	.3944	.1056
0.12	.0478	.4522	0.69	.2549	.2451	1.26	.3962	.1038
0.13	.0517	.4483	0.70	.2580	.2420	1.27	.3980	.1020
0.14	.0557	.4443	0.71	.2611	.2389	1.28	.3997	.1003
0.15	.0596	.4404	0.72	.2642	.2358	1.29	.4015	.0985
0.16	.0636	.4364	0.73	.2673	.2327	1.30	.4032	.0968
0.17	.0675	.4325	0.74	.2704	.2296	1.31	.4049	.0951
0.18	.0714	.4286	0.75	.2734	.2266	1.32	.4066	.0934
0.19	.0753	.4247	0.76	.2764	.2236	1.33	.4082	.0918
0.20	.0793	.4207	0.77	.2794	.2206	1.34	.4099	.0901
0.21	.0832	.4168	0.78	.2823	.2177	1.35	.4115	.0885
0.22	.0871	.4129	0.79	.2852	.2148	1.36	.4131	.0869
0.23	.0910	.4090	0.80	.2881	.2119	1.37	.4147	.0853
0.24	.0948	.4052	0.81	.2910	.2090	1.38	.4162	.0838
0.25	.0987	.4013	0.82	.2939	.2061	1.39	.4177	.0823
0.26	.1026	.3974	0.83	.2967	.2033	1.40	.4192	.0808
0.27	.1064	.3936	0.84	.2995	.2005	1.41	.4207	.0793
0.28	.1103	.3897	0.85	.3023	.1977	1.42	.4222	.0778
0.29	.1141	.3859	0.86	.3051	.1949	1.43	.4236	.0764
0.30	.1179	.3821	0.87	.3078	.1922	1.44	.4251	.0749
0.31	.1217	.3783	0.88	.3106	.1894	1.45	.4265	.0735
0.32	.1255	.3745	0.89	.3133	.1867	1.46	.4279	.0721
0.33	.1293	.3707	0.90	.3159	.1841	1.47	.4292	.0708
0.34	.1331	.3669	0.91	.3186	.1814	1.48	.4306	.0694
0.35	.1368	.3632	0.92	.3212	.1788	1.49	.4319	.0681
0.36	.1406	.3594	0.93	.3238	.1762	1.50	.4332	.0668
0.37	.1443	.3557	0.94	.3264	.1736	1.51	.4345	.0655
0.38	.1480	.3520	0.95	.3289	.1711	1.52	.4357	.0643
0.39	.1517	.3483	0.96	.3315	.1685	1.53	.4370	.0630
0.40	.1554	.3446	0.97	.3340	.1660	1.54	.4382	.0618
0.41	.1591	.3409	0.98	.3365	.1635	1.55	.4394	.0606
0.42	.1628	.3372	0.99	.3389	.1611	1.56	.4406	.0594
0.43	.1664	.3336	1.00	.3413	.1587	1.57	.4418	.0582
0.44	.1700	.3300	1.01	.3438	.1562	1.58	.4429	.0571
0.45	.1736	.3264	1.02	.3461	.1539	1.59	.4441	.0559
0.46	.1772	.3228	1.03	.3485	.1515	1.60	.4452	.0548
0.47	.1808	.3192	1.04	.3508	.1492	1.61	.4463	.0537
0.48	.1844	.3156	1.05	.3531	.1469	1.62	.4474	.0526
0.49	.1879	.3121	1.06	.3554	.1446	1.63	.4484	.0516
0.50	.1915	.3085	1.07	.3577	.1423	1.64	.4495	.0505
0.51	.1950	.3050	1.08	.3599	.1401	1.65	.4505	.0495
0.52	.1985	.3015	1.09	.3621	.1379	1.66	.4515	.0485
0.53	.2019	.2981	1.10	.3643	.1357	1.67	.4525	.0475
0.54	.2054	.2946	1.11	.3665	.1335	1.68	.4535	.0465
0.55	.2088	.2912	1.12	.3686	.1314	1.69	.4545	.0455
0.56	.2123	.2877	1.13	.3708	.1292	1.70	.4554	.0446

Table B.2 (*continued*)

(A) z	(B) Area Between Mean and z	(C) Area Beyond z	(A) z	(B) Area Between Mean and z	(C) Area Beyond z	(A) z	(B) Area Between Mean and z	(C) Area Beyond z
1.71	.4564	.0436	2.26	.4881	.0119	2.81	.4975	.0025
1.72	.4573	.0427	2.27	.4884	.0116	2.82	.4976	.0024
1.73	.4582	.0418	2.28	.4887	.0113	2.83	.4977	.0023
1.74	.4591	.0409	2.29	.4890	.0110	2.84	.4977	.0023
1.75	.4599	.0401	2.30	.4893	.0107	2.85	.4978	.0022
1.76	.4608	.0392	2.31	.4896	.0104	2.86	.4979	.0021
1.77	.4616	.0384	2.32	.4898	.0102	2.87	.4979	.0021
1.78	.4625	.0375	2.33	.4901	.0099	2.88	.4980	.0020
1.79	.4633	.0367	2.34	.4904	.0096	2.89	.4981	.0019
1.80	.4641	.0359	2.35	.4906	.0094	2.90	.4981	.0019
1.81	.4649	.0351	2.36	.4909	.0091	2.91	.4982	.0018
1.82	.4656	.0344	2.37	.4911	.0089	2.92	.4982	.0018
1.83	.4664	.0336	2.38	.4913	.0087	2.93	.4983	.0017
1.84	.4671	.0329	2.39	.4916	.0084	2.94	.4984	.0016
1.85	.4678	.0322	2.40	.4918	.0082	2.95	.4984	.0016
1.86	.4686	.0314	2.41	.4920	.0080	2.96	.4985	.0015
1.87	.4693	.0307	2.42	.4922	.0078	2.97	.4985	.0015
1.88	.4699	.0301	2.43	.4925	.0075	2.98	.4986	.0014
1.89	.4706	.0294	2.44	.4927	.0073	2.99	.4986	.0014
1.90	.4713	.0287	2.45	.4929	.0071	3.00	.4987	.0013
1.91	.4719	.0281	2.46	.4931	.0069	3.01	.4987	.0013
1.92	.4726	.0274	2.47	.4932	.0068	3.02	.4987	.0013
1.93	.4732	.0268	2.48	.4934	.0066	3.03	.4988	.0012
1.94	.4738	.0262	2.49	.4936	.0064	3.04	.4988	.0012
1.95	.4744	.0256	2.50	.4938	.0062	3.05	.4989	.0011
1.96	.4750	.0250	2.51	.4940	.0060	3.06	.4989	.0011
1.97	.4756	.0244	2.52	.4941	.0059	3.07	.4989	.0011
1.98	.4761	.0239	2.53	.4943	.0057	3.08	.4990	.0010
1.99	.4767	.0233	2.54	.4945	.0055	3.09	.4990	.0010
2.00	.4772	.0228	2.55	.4946	.0054	3.10	.4990	.0010
2.01	.4778	.0222	2.56	.4948	.0052	3.11	.4991	.0009
2.02	.4783	.0217	2.57	.4949	.0051	3.12	.4991	.0009
2.03	.4788	.0212	2.58	.4951	.0049	3.13	.4991	.0009
2.04	.4793	.0207	2.59	.4952	.0048	3.14	.4992	.0008
2.05	.4798	.0202	2.60	.4953	.0047	3.15	.4992	.0008
2.06	.4803	.0197	2.61	.4955	.0045	3.16	.4992	.0008
2.07	.4808	.0192	2.62	.4956	.0044	3.17	.4992	.0008
2.08	.4812	.0188	2.63	.4957	.0043	3.18	.4993	.0007
2.09	.4817	.0183	2.64	.4959	.0041	3.19	.4993	.0007
2.10	.4821	.0179	2.65	.4960	.0040	3.20	.4993	.0007
2.11	.4826	.0174	2.66	.4961	.0039	3.21	.4993	.0007
2.12	.4830	.0170	2.67	.4962	.0038	3.22	.4994	.0006
2.13	.4834	.0166	2.68	.4963	.0037	3.23	.4994	.0006
2.14	.4838	.0162	2.69	.4964	.0036	3.24	.4994	.0006
2.15	.4842	.0158	2.70	.4965	.0035	3.25	.4994	.0006
2.16	.4846	.0154	2.71	.4966	.0034	3.30	.4995	.0005
2.17	.4850	.0150	2.72	.4967	.0033	3.35	.4996	.0004
2.18	.4854	.0146	2.73	.4968	.0032	3.40	.4997	.0003
2.19	.4857	.0143	2.74	.4969	.0031	3.45	.4997	.0003
2.20	.4861	.0139	2.75	.4970	.0030	3.50	.4998	.0002
2.21	.4864	.0136	2.76	.4971	.0029	3.60	.4998	.0002
2.22	.4868	.0132	2.77	.4972	.0028	3.70	.4999	.0001
2.23	.4871	.0129	2.78	.4973	.0027	3.80	.4999	.0001
2.24	.4875	.0125	2.79	.4974	.0026	3.90	.49995	.00005
2.25	.4878	.0122	2.80	.4974	.0026	4.00	.49997	.00003

Table B.3   Critical Values for Pearson *r*

df	Level of Significance for One-Tailed Test					
	.05	.025	.01	.005	.001	.0005
	Level of Significance for Two-Tailed Test					
df	.10	.05	.02	.01	.002	.001
1	0.988	0.997	1.000	1.000	1.000	1.000
2	0.900	0.950	0.980	0.990	0.998	0.999
3	0.805	0.878	0.934	0.959	0.986	0.991
4	0.729	0.811	0.882	0.917	0.963	0.974
5	0.669	0.754	0.833	0.875	0.935	0.951
6	0.621	0.707	0.789	0.834	0.905	0.925
7	0.582	0.666	0.750	0.798	0.875	0.898
8	0.549	0.632	0.715	0.765	0.847	0.872
9	0.521	0.602	0.685	0.735	0.820	0.847
10	0.497	0.576	0.658	0.708	0.795	0.823
11	0.476	0.553	0.634	0.684	0.772	0.801
12	0.458	0.532	0.612	0.661	0.750	0.780
13	0.441	0.514	0.592	0.641	0.730	0.760
14	0.426	0.497	0.574	0.623	0.711	0.742
15	0.412	0.482	0.558	0.606	0.694	0.725
16	0.400	0.468	0.543	0.590	0.678	0.708
17	0.389	0.456	0.529	0.575	0.662	0.693
18	0.378	0.444	0.516	0.561	0.648	0.679
19	0.369	0.433	0.503	0.549	0.635	0.665
20	0.360	0.423	0.492	0.537	0.622	0.652
21	0.352	0.413	0.482	0.526	0.610	0.640
22	0.344	0.404	0.472	0.515	0.599	0.629
23	0.337	0.396	0.462	0.505	0.588	0.618
24	0.330	0.388	0.453	0.496	0.578	0.607
25	0.323	0.381	0.445	0.487	0.568	0.597
26	0.317	0.374	0.437	0.479	0.559	0.588
27	0.311	0.367	0.430	0.471	0.550	0.579
28	0.306	0.361	0.423	0.463	0.541	0.570
30	0.296	0.349	0.409	0.449	0.526	0.554
40	0.257	0.304	0.358	0.393	0.463	0.490
50	0.231	0.273	0.322	0.354	0.419	0.443
60	0.211	0.250	0.295	0.325	0.385	0.408
80	0.183	0.217	0.257	0.283	0.336	0.357
100	0.164	0.195	0.230	0.254	0.303	0.321
200	0.116	0.138	0.164	0.181	0.216	0.230
500	0.073	0.088	0.104	0.115	0.138	0.146

Table B.4   Critical Values of *t*

For any given *df*, the table shows the values of *t* corresponding to various levels of probability. The obtained *t* is significant at a given level if it is equal to or *greater than* the value shown in the table.

	Level of Significance for a One-Tailed Test					
	.10	.05	.025	.01	.005	.0005
	Level of Significance for a Two-Tailed Test					
df	.20	.10	.05	.02	.01	.001
1	3.078	6.314	12.706	31.821	63.657	636.619
2	1.886	2.920	4.303	6.965	9.925	31.598
3	1.638	2.353	3.182	4.541	5.841	12.941
4	1.533	2.132	2.776	3.747	4.604	8.610
5	1.476	2.015	2.571	3.365	4.032	6.859
6	1.440	1.943	2.447	3.143	3.707	5.959
7	1.415	1.895	2.365	2.998	3.499	5.405
8	1.397	1.860	2.306	2.896	3.355	5.041
9	1.383	1.833	2.262	2.821	3.250	4.781
10	1.372	1.812	2.228	2.764	3.169	4.587
11	1.363	1.796	2.201	2.718	3.106	4.437
12	1.356	1.782	2.179	2.681	3.055	4.318
13	1.350	1.771	2.160	2.650	3.012	4.221
14	1.345	1.761	2.145	2.624	2.977	4.140
15	1.341	1.753	2.131	2.602	2.947	4.073
16	1.337	1.746	2.120	2.583	2.921	4.015
17	1.333	1.740	2.110	2.567	2.898	3.965
18	1.330	1.734	2.101	2.552	2.878	3.922
19	1.328	1.729	2.093	2.539	2.861	3.883
20	1.325	1.725	2.086	2.528	2.845	3.850
21	1.323	1.721	2.080	2.518	2.831	3.819
22	1.321	1.717	2.074	2.508	2.819	3.792
23	1.319	1.714	2.069	2.500	2.807	3.767
24	1.318	1.711	2.064	2.492	2.797	3.745
25	1.316	1.708	2.060	2.485	2.787	3.725
26	1.315	1.706	2.056	2.479	2.779	3.707
27	1.314	1.703	2.052	2.473	2.771	3.690
28	1.313	1.701	2.048	2.467	2.763	3.674
29	1.311	1.699	2.045	2.462	2.756	3.659
30	1.310	1.697	2.042	2.457	2.750	3.646
40	1.303	1.684	2.021	2.423	2.704	3.551
60	1.296	1.671	2.000	2.390	2.660	3.460
120	1.289	1.658	1.980	2.358	2.617	3.373
∞	1.282	1.645	1.960	2.326	2.576	3.291

Source: Table B.4 is taken from Table III (page 46) of Fisher and Yates, *Statistical Tables for Biological, Agricultural, and Medical Research,* 6th ed., published by Longman Group Ltd., 1974, London (previously published by Oliver and Boyd, Edinburgh), and by permission of the authors and publishers.

Table B.5 Critical values of *F*

The obtained *F* is significant at a given level if it is equal to or *greater than* the value shown in the table. 0.05 (lightface row) and 0.01 (boldface row) points for the distribution of *F*.

The values shown are the right tail of the distribution obtained by dividing the larger variance estimate by the smaller variance estimate. To find the complementary left or lower tail for a given *df* and α level, reverse the degrees of freedom and find the reciprocal of that value in the *F* table. For example, the value cutting off the top 5% of the area for 7 and 12 *df* is 2.92. To find the cutoff point of the bottom 5% of the area, find the tabled value of the $\alpha = .05$ level for 12 and 7 *df*. This is found to be 3.57. The reciprocal is $1/3.57 = 0.28$. Thus 5% of the area falls *at or below an* $F = 0.28$.

Degrees of Freedom for Numerator

df (den)	1	2	3	4	5	6	7	8	9	10	11	12	14	16	20	24	30	40	50	75	100	200	500	∞
1	161	200	216	225	230	234	237	239	241	242	243	244	245	246	248	249	250	251	252	253	253	254	254	254
1	**4052**	**4999**	**5403**	**5625**	**5764**	**5859**	**5928**	**5981**	**6022**	**6056**	**6082**	**6106**	**6142**	**6169**	**6208**	**6234**	**6258**	**6286**	**6302**	**6323**	**6334**	**6352**	**6361**	**6366**
2	18.51	19.00	19.16	19.25	19.30	19.33	19.36	19.37	19.38	19.39	19.40	19.41	19.42	19.43	19.44	19.45	19.46	19.47	19.47	19.48	19.49	19.49	19.50	19.50
2	**98.49**	**99.01**	**99.17**	**99.25**	**99.30**	**99.33**	**99.34**	**99.36**	**99.38**	**99.40**	**99.41**	**99.42**	**99.43**	**99.44**	**99.45**	**99.46**	**99.47**	**99.48**	**99.48**	**99.49**	**99.49**	**99.49**	**99.50**	**99.50**
3	10.13	9.55	9.28	9.12	9.01	8.94	8.88	8.84	8.81	8.78	8.76	8.74	8.71	8.69	8.66	8.64	8.62	8.60	8.58	8.57	8.56	8.54	8.54	8.53
3	**34.12**	**30.81**	**29.46**	**28.71**	**28.24**	**27.91**	**27.67**	**27.49**	**27.34**	**27.23**	**27.13**	**27.05**	**26.92**	**26.83**	**26.69**	**26.60**	**26.50**	**26.41**	**26.30**	**26.27**	**26.23**	**26.18**	**26.14**	**26.12**
4	7.71	6.94	6.59	6.39	6.26	6.16	6.09	6.04	6.00	5.96	5.93	5.91	5.87	5.84	5.80	5.77	5.74	5.71	5.70	5.68	5.66	5.65	5.64	5.63
4	**21.20**	**18.00**	**16.69**	**15.98**	**13.52**	**15.21**	**14.98**	**14.80**	**14.66**	**14.54**	**14.45**	**14.37**	**14.24**	**14.15**	**14.02**	**13.93**	**13.83**	**13.74**	**13.69**	**13.61**	**13.57**	**13.52**	**13.48**	**13.46**
5	6.61	5.79	5.41	5.19	5.05	4.95	4.88	4.82	4.78	4.74	4.70	4.68	4.64	4.60	4.56	4.53	4.50	4.46	4.44	4.42	4.40	4.38	4.37	4.36
5	**16.26**	**13.27**	**12.06**	**11.39**	**10.97**	**10.67**	**10.45**	**10.27**	**10.15**	**10.05**	**9.96**	**9.89**	**9.77**	**9.68**	**9.55**	**9.47**	**9.38**	**9.29**	**9.24**	**9.17**	**9.13**	**9.07**	**9.04**	**9.02**
6	5.99	5.14	4.76	4.53	4.39	4.28	4.21	4.15	4.10	4.06	4.03	4.00	3.96	3.92	3.87	3.84	3.81	3.77	3.75	3.72	3.71	3.69	3.68	3.67
6	**13.74**	**10.92**	**9.78**	**9.15**	**8.75**	**8.47**	**8.26**	**8.10**	**7.98**	**7.87**	**7.79**	**7.72**	**7.60**	**7.52**	**7.39**	**7.31**	**7.23**	**7.14**	**7.09**	**7.02**	**6.99**	**6.94**	**6.90**	**6.88**
7	5.59	4.74	4.35	4.12	3.97	3.87	3.79	3.73	3.68	3.63	3.60	3.57	3.52	3.49	3.44	3.41	3.38	3.34	3.32	3.29	3.28	3.25	3.24	3.23
7	**12.75**	**9.55**	**8.45**	**7.85**	**7.46**	**7.19**	**7.00**	**6.84**	**6.71**	**6.62**	**6.54**	**6.47**	**6.35**	**6.27**	**6.15**	**6.07**	**5.98**	**5.90**	**5.85**	**5.78**	**5.75**	**5.70**	**5.67**	**5.65**
8	5.32	4.46	4.07	3.84	3.69	3.58	3.50	3.44	3.39	3.34	3.31	3.28	3.23	3.20	3.15	3.12	3.08	3.05	3.03	3.00	2.98	2.96	2.94	2.93
8	**11.26**	**8.65**	**7.59**	**7.01**	**6.63**	**6.37**	**6.19**	**6.03**	**5.91**	**5.82**	**5.74**	**5.67**	**5.56**	**5.48**	**5.36**	**5.28**	**5.20**	**5.11**	**5.06**	**5.00**	**4.96**	**4.91**	**4.88**	**4.86**
9	5.12	4.26	3.86	3.63	3.48	3.37	3.29	3.23	3.18	3.13	3.10	3.07	3.02	2.98	2.93	2.90	2.86	2.82	2.80	2.77	2.76	2.73	2.72	2.71
9	**10.56**	**8.02**	**6.99**	**6.42**	**6.06**	**5.80**	**5.62**	**5.47**	**5.35**	**5.26**	**5.18**	**5.11**	**5.00**	**4.92**	**4.80**	**4.73**	**4.64**	**4.56**	**4.51**	**4.45**	**4.41**	**4.36**	**4.33**	**4.31**
10	4.96	4.10	3.71	3.48	3.33	3.22	3.14	3.07	3.02	2.97	2.94	2.91	2.86	2.82	2.77	2.74	2.70	2.67	2.64	2.61	2.59	2.56	2.55	2.54
10	**10.04**	**7.56**	**6.55**	**5.99**	**5.64**	**5.39**	**5.21**	**5.06**	**4.95**	**4.85**	**4.78**	**4.71**	**4.60**	**4.52**	**4.41**	**4.33**	**4.25**	**4.17**	**4.12**	**4.05**	**4.01**	**3.96**	**3.93**	**3.91**
11	4.84	3.98	3.59	3.36	3.20	3.09	3.01	2.95	2.90	2.86	2.82	2.79	2.74	2.70	2.65	2.61	2.57	2.53	2.50	2.47	2.45	2.42	2.41	2.40
11	**9.65**	**7.20**	**6.22**	**5.67**	**5.32**	**5.07**	**4.88**	**4.74**	**4.63**	**4.54**	**4.46**	**4.40**	**4.29**	**4.21**	**4.10**	**4.02**	**3.94**	**3.86**	**3.80**	**3.74**	**3.70**	**3.66**	**3.62**	**3.60**
12	4.75	3.88	3.49	3.26	3.11	3.00	2.92	2.85	2.80	2.76	2.72	2.69	2.64	2.60	2.54	2.50	2.46	2.42	2.40	2.36	2.35	2.32	2.31	2.30
12	**9.33**	**6.93**	**5.95**	**5.41**	**5.06**	**4.82**	**4.65**	**4.50**	**4.39**	**4.30**	**4.22**	**4.16**	**4.05**	**3.98**	**3.86**	**3.78**	**3.70**	**3.61**	**3.56**	**3.49**	**3.46**	**3.41**	**3.38**	**3.36**
13	4.67	3.80	3.41	3.18	3.02	2.92	2.84	2.77	2.72	2.67	2.63	2.60	2.55	2.51	2.46	2.42	2.38	2.34	2.32	2.28	2.26	2.24	2.22	2.21
13	**9.07**	**6.70**	**5.74**	**5.20**	**4.86**	**4.62**	**4.44**	**4.30**	**4.19**	**4.10**	**4.02**	**3.96**	**3.85**	**3.78**	**3.67**	**3.59**	**3.51**	**3.42**	**3.37**	**3.30**	**3.27**	**3.21**	**3.18**	**3.16**
14	4.60	3.74	3.34	3.11	2.96	2.85	2.77	2.70	2.65	2.60	2.56	2.53	2.48	2.44	2.39	2.35	2.31	2.27	2.24	2.21	2.19	2.16	2.14	2.13
14	**8.86**	**6.51**	**5.56**	**5.03**	**4.69**	**4.46**	**4.28**	**4.14**	**4.03**	**3.94**	**3.86**	**3.80**	**3.70**	**3.62**	**3.51**	**3.43**	**3.34**	**3.26**	**3.21**	**3.14**	**3.11**	**3.06**	**3.02**	**3.00**
15	4.54	3.68	3.29	3.06	2.90	2.79	2.70	2.64	2.59	2.55	2.51	2.48	2.43	2.39	2.33	2.29	2.25	2.21	2.18	2.15	2.12	2.10	2.08	2.07
15	**8.68**	**6.36**	**5.42**	**4.89**	**4.56**	**4.32**	**4.14**	**4.00**	**3.89**	**3.80**	**3.73**	**3.67**	**3.56**	**3.48**	**3.36**	**3.29**	**3.20**	**3.12**	**3.07**	**3.00**	**2.97**	**2.92**	**2.89**	**2.87**

Degrees of Freedom for Denominator

Table B.5 (continued)

	Degrees of Freedom for Numerator																							
	1	2	3	4	5	6	7	8	9	10	11	12	14	16	20	24	30	40	50	75	100	200	500	∞
16	4.49 / 8.53	3.63 / 6.23	3.24 / 5.29	3.01 / 4.77	2.85 / 4.44	2.74 / 4.20	2.66 / 4.03	2.59 / 3.89	2.54 / 3.78	2.49 / 3.69	2.45 / 3.61	2.42 / 3.55	2.37 / 3.45	2.33 / 3.37	2.28 / 3.25	2.24 / 3.18	2.20 / 3.10	2.16 / 3.01	2.13 / 2.96	2.09 / 2.89	2.07 / 2.86	2.04 / 2.80	2.02 / 2.77	2.01 / 2.75
17	4.45 / 8.40	3.59 / 6.11	3.20 / 5.18	2.96 / 4.67	2.81 / 4.34	2.70 / 4.10	2.62 / 3.93	2.55 / 3.79	2.50 / 3.68	2.45 / 3.59	2.41 / 3.52	2.38 / 3.45	2.33 / 3.35	2.29 / 3.27	2.23 / 3.16	2.19 / 3.08	2.15 / 3.00	2.11 / 2.92	2.08 / 2.86	2.04 / 2.79	2.02 / 2.76	1.99 / 2.70	1.97 / 2.67	1.96 / 2.65
18	4.41 / 8.28	3.55 / 6.01	3.16 / 5.09	2.93 / 4.58	2.77 / 4.25	2.66 / 4.01	2.58 / 3.85	2.51 / 3.71	2.46 / 3.60	2.41 / 3.51	2.37 / 3.44	2.34 / 3.37	2.29 / 3.27	2.25 / 3.19	2.19 / 3.07	2.15 / 3.00	2.11 / 2.91	2.07 / 2.83	2.04 / 2.78	2.00 / 2.71	1.98 / 2.68	1.95 / 2.62	1.93 / 2.59	1.92 / 2.57
19	4.38 / 8.18	3.52 / 5.93	3.13 / 5.01	2.90 / 4.50	2.74 / 4.17	2.63 / 3.94	2.55 / 3.77	2.48 / 3.63	2.43 / 3.52	2.38 / 3.43	2.34 / 3.36	2.31 / 3.30	2.26 / 3.19	2.21 / 3.12	2.15 / 3.00	2.11 / 2.92	2.07 / 2.84	2.02 / 2.76	2.00 / 2.70	1.96 / 2.63	1.94 / 2.60	1.91 / 2.54	1.90 / 2.51	1.88 / 2.49
20	4.35 / 8.10	3.49 / 5.85	3.10 / 4.94	2.87 / 4.43	2.71 / 4.10	2.60 / 3.87	2.52 / 3.71	2.45 / 3.56	2.40 / 3.45	2.35 / 3.37	2.31 / 3.30	2.28 / 3.23	2.23 / 3.13	2.18 / 3.05	2.12 / 2.94	2.08 / 2.86	2.04 / 2.77	1.99 / 2.69	1.96 / 2.63	1.92 / 2.56	1.90 / 2.53	1.87 / 2.47	1.85 / 2.44	1.84 / 2.42
21	4.32 / 8.02	3.47 / 5.78	3.07 / 4.87	2.84 / 4.37	2.68 / 4.04	2.57 / 3.81	2.49 / 3.65	2.42 / 3.51	2.37 / 3.40	2.32 / 3.31	2.28 / 3.24	2.25 / 3.17	2.20 / 3.07	2.15 / 2.99	2.09 / 2.88	2.05 / 2.80	2.00 / 2.72	1.96 / 2.63	1.93 / 2.58	1.89 / 2.51	1.87 / 2.47	1.84 / 2.42	1.82 / 2.38	1.81 / 2.36
22	4.30 / 7.94	3.44 / 5.72	3.05 / 4.82	2.82 / 4.31	2.66 / 3.99	2.55 / 3.76	2.47 / 3.59	2.40 / 3.45	2.35 / 3.35	2.30 / 3.26	2.26 / 3.18	2.23 / 3.12	2.18 / 3.02	2.13 / 2.94	2.07 / 2.83	2.03 / 2.75	1.98 / 2.67	1.93 / 2.58	1.91 / 2.53	1.87 / 2.46	1.84 / 2.42	1.81 / 2.37	1.80 / 2.33	1.78 / 2.31
23	4.28 / 7.88	3.42 / 5.66	3.03 / 4.76	2.80 / 4.26	2.64 / 3.94	2.53 / 3.71	2.45 / 3.54	2.38 / 3.41	2.32 / 3.30	2.28 / 3.21	2.24 / 3.14	2.20 / 3.07	2.14 / 2.97	2.10 / 2.89	2.04 / 2.78	2.00 / 2.70	1.96 / 2.62	1.91 / 2.53	1.88 / 2.48	1.84 / 2.41	1.82 / 2.37	1.79 / 2.32	1.77 / 2.28	1.76 / 2.26
24	4.26 / 7.82	3.40 / 5.61	3.01 / 4.72	2.78 / 4.22	2.62 / 3.90	2.51 / 3.67	2.43 / 3.50	2.36 / 3.36	2.30 / 3.25	2.26 / 3.17	2.22 / 3.09	2.18 / 3.03	2.13 / 2.93	2.09 / 2.85	2.02 / 2.74	1.98 / 2.66	1.94 / 2.58	1.89 / 2.49	1.86 / 2.44	1.82 / 2.36	1.80 / 2.33	1.76 / 2.27	1.74 / 2.23	1.73 / 2.21
25	4.24 / 7.77	3.38 / 5.57	2.99 / 4.68	2.76 / 4.18	2.60 / 3.86	2.49 / 3.63	2.41 / 3.46	2.34 / 3.32	2.28 / 3.21	2.24 / 3.13	2.20 / 3.05	2.16 / 2.99	2.11 / 2.89	2.06 / 2.81	2.00 / 2.70	1.96 / 2.62	1.92 / 2.54	1.87 / 2.45	1.84 / 2.40	1.80 / 2.32	1.77 / 2.29	1.74 / 2.23	1.72 / 2.19	1.71 / 2.17
26	4.22 / 7.72	3.37 / 5.53	2.98 / 4.64	2.74 / 4.14	2.59 / 3.82	2.47 / 3.59	2.39 / 3.42	2.32 / 3.29	2.27 / 3.17	2.22 / 3.09	2.18 / 3.02	2.15 / 2.96	2.10 / 2.86	2.05 / 2.77	1.99 / 2.66	1.95 / 2.58	1.90 / 2.50	1.85 / 2.41	1.82 / 2.36	1.78 / 2.28	1.76 / 2.25	1.72 / 2.19	1.70 / 2.15	1.69 / 2.13
27	4.21 / 7.68	3.35 / 5.49	2.96 / 4.60	2.73 / 4.11	2.57 / 3.79	2.46 / 3.56	2.37 / 3.39	2.30 / 3.26	2.25 / 3.14	2.20 / 3.06	2.16 / 2.98	2.13 / 2.93	2.08 / 2.83	2.03 / 2.74	1.97 / 2.63	1.93 / 2.55	1.88 / 2.47	1.84 / 2.38	1.80 / 2.33	1.76 / 2.25	1.74 / 2.21	1.71 / 2.16	1.68 / 2.12	1.67 / 2.10
28	4.20 / 7.64	3.34 / 5.45	2.95 / 4.57	2.71 / 4.07	2.56 / 3.76	2.44 / 3.53	2.36 / 3.36	2.29 / 3.23	2.24 / 3.11	2.19 / 3.03	2.15 / 2.95	2.12 / 2.90	2.06 / 2.80	2.02 / 2.71	1.96 / 2.60	1.91 / 2.52	1.87 / 2.44	1.81 / 2.35	1.78 / 2.30	1.75 / 2.22	1.72 / 2.18	1.69 / 2.13	1.67 / 2.09	1.65 / 2.06
29	4.18 / 7.60	3.33 / 5.42	2.93 / 4.54	2.70 / 4.04	2.54 / 3.73	2.43 / 3.50	2.35 / 3.33	2.28 / 3.20	2.22 / 3.08	2.18 / 3.00	2.14 / 2.92	2.10 / 2.87	2.05 / 2.77	2.00 / 2.68	1.94 / 2.57	1.90 / 2.49	1.85 / 2.41	1.80 / 2.32	1.77 / 2.27	1.73 / 2.19	1.71 / 2.15	1.68 / 2.10	1.65 / 2.06	1.64 / 2.03
30	4.17 / 7.56	3.32 / 5.39	2.92 / 4.51	2.69 / 4.02	2.53 / 3.70	2.42 / 3.47	2.34 / 3.30	2.27 / 3.17	2.21 / 3.06	2.16 / 2.98	2.12 / 2.90	2.09 / 2.84	2.04 / 2.74	1.99 / 2.66	1.93 / 2.55	1.89 / 2.47	1.84 / 2.38	1.79 / 2.29	1.76 / 2.24	1.72 / 2.16	1.69 / 2.13	1.66 / 2.07	1.64 / 2.03	1.62 / 2.01
32	4.15 / 7.50	3.30 / 5.34	2.90 / 4.46	2.67 / 3.97	2.51 / 3.66	2.40 / 3.42	2.32 / 3.25	2.25 / 3.12	2.19 / 3.01	2.14 / 2.94	2.10 / 2.86	2.07 / 2.80	2.02 / 2.70	1.97 / 2.62	1.91 / 2.51	1.86 / 2.42	1.82 / 2.34	1.76 / 2.25	1.74 / 2.20	1.69 / 2.12	1.67 / 2.08	1.64 / 2.02	1.61 / 1.98	1.59 / 1.96
34	4.13 / 7.44	3.28 / 5.29	2.88 / 4.42	2.65 / 3.93	2.49 / 3.61	2.38 / 3.38	2.30 / 3.21	2.23 / 3.08	2.17 / 2.97	2.12 / 2.89	2.08 / 2.82	2.05 / 2.76	2.00 / 2.66	1.95 / 2.58	1.89 / 2.47	1.84 / 2.38	1.80 / 2.30	1.74 / 2.21	1.71 / 2.15	1.67 / 2.08	1.64 / 2.04	1.61 / 1.98	1.59 / 1.94	1.57 / 1.91
36	4.11 / 7.39	3.26 / 5.25	2.86 / 4.38	2.63 / 3.89	2.48 / 3.58	2.36 / 3.35	2.28 / 3.18	2.21 / 3.04	2.15 / 2.94	2.10 / 2.86	2.06 / 2.78	2.03 / 2.72	1.98 / 2.62	1.93 / 2.54	1.87 / 2.43	1.82 / 2.35	1.78 / 2.26	1.72 / 2.17	1.69 / 2.12	1.65 / 2.04	1.62 / 2.00	1.59 / 1.94	1.56 / 1.90	1.55 / 1.87
38	4.10 / 7.35	3.25 / 5.21	2.85 / 4.34	2.62 / 3.86	2.46 / 3.54	2.35 / 3.32	2.26 / 3.15	2.19 / 3.02	2.14 / 2.91	2.09 / 2.82	2.05 / 2.75	2.02 / 2.69	1.96 / 2.59	1.92 / 2.51	1.85 / 2.40	1.80 / 2.32	1.76 / 2.22	1.71 / 2.14	1.67 / 2.08	1.63 / 2.00	1.60 / 1.97	1.57 / 1.90	1.54 / 1.86	1.53 / 1.84

Degrees of Freedom for Denominator

Table B.5 (continued)

Degrees of Freedom for Numerator

	1	2	3	4	5	6	7	8	9	10	11	12	14	16	20	24	30	40	50	75	100	200	500	∞
40	4.08 / 7.31	3.23 / 5.18	2.84 / 4.31	2.61 / 3.83	2.45 / 3.51	2.34 / 3.29	2.25 / 3.12	2.18 / 2.99	2.12 / 2.88	2.07 / 2.80	2.04 / 2.73	2.00 / 2.66	1.95 / 2.56	1.90 / 2.49	1.84 / 2.37	1.79 / 2.29	1.74 / 2.20	1.69 / 2.11	1.66 / 2.05	1.61 / 1.97	1.59 / 1.94	1.55 / 1.88	1.53 / 1.84	1.51 / 1.81
42	4.07 / 7.27	3.22 / 5.15	2.83 / 4.29	2.59 / 3.80	2.44 / 3.49	2.32 / 3.26	2.24 / 3.10	2.17 / 2.96	2.11 / 2.86	2.06 / 2.77	2.02 / 2.70	1.99 / 2.64	1.94 / 2.54	1.89 / 2.46	1.82 / 2.35	1.78 / 2.26	1.73 / 2.17	1.68 / 2.08	1.64 / 2.02	1.60 / 1.94	1.57 / 1.91	1.54 / 1.85	1.51 / 1.80	1.49 / 1.78
44	4.06 / 7.24	3.21 / 5.12	2.82 / 4.26	2.58 / 3.78	2.43 / 3.46	2.31 / 3.24	2.23 / 3.07	2.16 / 2.94	2.10 / 2.84	2.05 / 2.75	2.01 / 2.68	1.98 / 2.62	1.92 / 2.52	1.88 / 2.44	1.81 / 2.32	1.76 / 2.24	1.72 / 2.15	1.66 / 2.06	1.63 / 2.00	1.58 / 1.92	1.56 / 1.88	1.52 / 1.82	1.50 / 1.78	1.48 / 1.75
46	4.05 / 7.21	3.20 / 5.10	2.81 / 4.24	2.57 / 3.76	2.42 / 3.44	2.30 / 3.22	2.22 / 3.05	2.14 / 2.92	2.09 / 2.82	2.04 / 2.73	2.00 / 2.66	1.97 / 2.60	1.91 / 2.50	1.87 / 2.42	1.80 / 2.30	1.75 / 2.22	1.71 / 2.13	1.65 / 2.04	1.62 / 1.98	1.57 / 1.90	1.54 / 1.86	1.51 / 1.80	1.48 / 1.76	1.46 / 1.72
48	4.04 / 7.19	3.19 / 5.08	2.80 / 4.22	2.56 / 3.74	2.41 / 3.42	2.30 / 3.20	2.21 / 3.04	2.14 / 2.90	2.08 / 2.80	2.03 / 2.71	1.99 / 2.64	1.96 / 2.58	1.90 / 2.48	1.86 / 2.40	1.79 / 2.28	1.74 / 2.20	1.70 / 2.11	1.64 / 2.02	1.61 / 1.96	1.56 / 1.88	1.53 / 1.84	1.50 / 1.78	1.47 / 1.73	1.45 / 1.70
50	4.03 / 7.17	3.18 / 5.06	2.79 / 4.20	2.56 / 3.72	2.40 / 3.41	2.29 / 3.18	2.20 / 3.02	2.13 / 2.88	2.07 / 2.78	2.02 / 2.70	1.98 / 2.62	1.95 / 2.56	1.90 / 2.46	1.85 / 2.39	1.78 / 2.26	1.74 / 2.18	1.69 / 2.10	1.63 / 2.00	1.60 / 1.94	1.55 / 1.86	1.52 / 1.82	1.48 / 1.76	1.46 / 1.71	1.44 / 1.68
55	4.02 / 7.12	3.17 / 5.01	2.78 / 4.16	2.54 / 3.68	2.38 / 3.37	2.27 / 3.15	2.18 / 2.98	2.11 / 2.85	2.05 / 2.75	2.00 / 2.66	1.97 / 2.59	1.93 / 2.53	1.88 / 2.43	1.83 / 2.35	1.76 / 2.23	1.72 / 2.15	1.67 / 2.06	1.61 / 1.96	1.58 / 1.90	1.52 / 1.82	1.50 / 1.78	1.46 / 1.71	1.43 / 1.66	1.41 / 1.64
60	4.00 / 7.08	3.15 / 4.98	2.76 / 4.13	2.52 / 3.65	2.37 / 3.34	2.25 / 3.12	2.17 / 2.95	2.10 / 2.82	2.04 / 2.72	1.99 / 2.63	1.95 / 2.56	1.92 / 2.50	1.86 / 2.40	1.81 / 2.32	1.75 / 2.20	1.70 / 2.12	1.65 / 2.03	1.59 / 1.93	1.56 / 1.87	1.50 / 1.79	1.48 / 1.74	1.44 / 1.68	1.41 / 1.63	1.39 / 1.60
65	3.99 / 7.04	3.14 / 4.95	2.75 / 4.10	2.51 / 3.62	2.36 / 3.31	2.24 / 3.09	2.15 / 2.93	2.08 / 2.79	2.02 / 2.70	1.98 / 2.61	1.94 / 2.54	1.90 / 2.47	1.85 / 2.37	1.80 / 2.30	1.73 / 2.18	1.68 / 2.09	1.63 / 2.00	1.57 / 1.90	1.54 / 1.84	1.49 / 1.76	1.46 / 1.71	1.42 / 1.64	1.39 / 1.60	1.37 / 1.56
70	3.98 / 7.01	3.13 / 4.92	2.74 / 4.08	2.50 / 3.60	2.35 / 3.29	2.23 / 3.07	2.14 / 2.91	2.07 / 2.77	2.01 / 2.67	1.97 / 2.59	1.93 / 2.51	1.89 / 2.45	1.84 / 2.35	1.79 / 2.28	1.72 / 2.15	1.67 / 2.07	1.62 / 1.98	1.56 / 1.88	1.53 / 1.82	1.47 / 1.74	1.45 / 1.69	1.40 / 1.62	1.37 / 1.56	1.35 / 1.53
80	3.96 / 6.96	3.11 / 4.88	2.72 / 4.04	2.48 / 3.56	2.33 / 3.25	2.21 / 3.04	2.12 / 2.87	2.05 / 2.74	1.99 / 2.64	1.95 / 2.55	1.91 / 2.48	1.88 / 2.41	1.82 / 2.32	1.77 / 2.24	1.70 / 2.11	1.65 / 2.03	1.60 / 1.94	1.54 / 1.84	1.51 / 1.78	1.45 / 1.70	1.42 / 1.65	1.38 / 1.57	1.35 / 1.52	1.32 / 1.49
100	3.94 / 6.90	3.09 / 4.82	2.70 / 3.98	2.46 / 3.51	2.30 / 3.20	2.19 / 2.99	2.10 / 2.82	2.03 / 2.69	1.97 / 2.59	1.92 / 2.51	1.88 / 2.43	1.85 / 2.36	1.79 / 2.26	1.75 / 2.19	1.68 / 2.06	1.63 / 1.98	1.57 / 1.89	1.51 / 1.79	1.48 / 1.73	1.42 / 1.64	1.39 / 1.59	1.34 / 1.51	1.30 / 1.46	1.28 / 1.43
125	3.92 / 6.84	3.07 / 4.78	2.68 / 3.94	2.44 / 3.47	2.29 / 3.17	2.17 / 2.95	2.08 / 2.79	2.01 / 2.65	1.95 / 2.56	1.90 / 2.47	1.86 / 2.40	1.83 / 2.33	1.77 / 2.23	1.72 / 2.15	1.65 / 2.03	1.60 / 1.94	1.55 / 1.85	1.49 / 1.75	1.45 / 1.68	1.39 / 1.59	1.36 / 1.54	1.31 / 1.46	1.27 / 1.40	1.25 / 1.37
150	3.91 / 6.81	3.06 / 4.75	2.67 / 3.91	2.43 / 3.44	2.27 / 3.13	2.16 / 2.92	2.07 / 2.76	2.00 / 2.62	1.94 / 2.53	1.89 / 2.44	1.85 / 2.37	1.82 / 2.30	1.76 / 2.20	1.71 / 2.12	1.64 / 2.00	1.59 / 1.91	1.54 / 1.83	1.47 / 1.72	1.44 / 1.66	1.37 / 1.56	1.34 / 1.51	1.29 / 1.43	1.25 / 1.37	1.22 / 1.33
200	3.89 / 6.76	3.04 / 4.71	2.65 / 3.88	2.41 / 3.41	2.26 / 3.11	2.14 / 2.90	2.05 / 2.73	1.98 / 2.60	1.92 / 2.50	1.87 / 2.41	1.83 / 2.34	1.80 / 2.28	1.74 / 2.17	1.69 / 2.09	1.62 / 1.97	1.57 / 1.88	1.52 / 1.79	1.45 / 1.69	1.42 / 1.62	1.35 / 1.53	1.32 / 1.48	1.26 / 1.39	1.22 / 1.33	1.19 / 1.28
400	3.86 / 6.70	3.02 / 4.66	2.62 / 3.83	2.39 / 3.36	2.23 / 3.06	2.12 / 2.85	2.03 / 2.69	1.96 / 2.55	1.90 / 2.46	1.85 / 2.37	1.81 / 2.29	1.78 / 2.23	1.72 / 2.12	1.67 / 2.04	1.60 / 1.92	1.54 / 1.84	1.49 / 1.74	1.42 / 1.64	1.38 / 1.57	1.32 / 1.47	1.28 / 1.42	1.22 / 1.32	1.16 / 1.24	1.13 / 1.19
1000	3.85 / 6.66	3.00 / 4.62	2.61 / 3.80	2.38 / 3.34	2.22 / 3.04	2.10 / 2.82	2.02 / 2.66	1.95 / 2.53	1.89 / 2.43	1.84 / 2.34	1.80 / 2.26	1.76 / 2.20	1.70 / 2.09	1.65 / 2.01	1.58 / 1.89	1.53 / 1.81	1.47 / 1.71	1.41 / 1.61	1.36 / 1.54	1.30 / 1.44	1.26 / 1.38	1.19 / 1.28	1.13 / 1.19	1.08 / 1.11
∞	3.84 / 6.64	2.99 / 4.60	2.60 / 3.78	2.37 / 3.32	2.21 / 3.02	2.09 / 2.80	2.01 / 2.64	1.94 / 2.51	1.88 / 2.41	1.83 / 2.32	1.79 / 2.24	1.75 / 2.18	1.69 / 2.07	1.64 / 1.99	1.57 / 1.87	1.52 / 1.79	1.46 / 1.69	1.40 / 1.59	1.35 / 1.52	1.28 / 1.41	1.24 / 1.36	1.17 / 1.25	1.11 / 1.15	1.00 / 1.00

Degrees of Freedom for Denominator

Table B.6 Percentage Points of the Studentized Range

Error df	α	k = Number of Means or Number of Steps Between Ordered Means									
		2	3	4	5	6	7	8	9	10	11
5	.05	3.64	4.60	5.22	5.67	6.03	6.33	6.58	6.80	6.99	7.17
	.01	5.70	6.98	7.80	8.42	8.91	9.32	9.67	9.97	10.24	10.48
6	.05	3.46	4.34	4.90	5.30	5.63	5.90	6.12	6.32	6.49	6.65
	.01	5.24	6.33	7.03	7.56	7.97	8.32	8.61	8.87	9.10	9.30
7	.05	3.34	4.16	4.68	5.06	5.36	5.61	5.82	6.00	6.16	6.30
	.01	4.95	5.92	6.54	7.01	7.37	7.68	7.94	8.17	8.37	8.55
8	.05	3.26	4.04	4.53	4.89	5.17	5.40	5.60	5.77	5.92	6.05
	.01	4.75	5.64	6.20	6.62	6.96	7.24	7.47	7.68	7.86	8.03
9	.05	3.20	3.95	4.41	4.76	5.02	5.24	5.43	5.59	5.74	5.87
	.01	4.60	5.43	5.96	6.35	6.66	6.91	7.13	7.33	7.49	7.65
10	.05	3.15	3.88	4.33	4.65	4.91	5.12	5.30	5.46	5.60	5.72
	.01	4.48	5.27	5.77	6.14	6.43	6.67	6.87	7.05	7.21	7.36
11	.05	3.11	3.82	4.26	4.57	4.82	5.03	5.20	5.35	5.49	5.61
	.01	4.39	5.15	5.62	5.97	6.25	6.48	6.67	6.84	6.99	7.13
12	.05	3.08	3.77	4.20	4.51	4.75	4.95	5.12	5.27	5.39	5.51
	.01	4.32	5.05	5.50	5.84	6.10	6.32	6.51	6.67	6.81	6.94
13	.05	3.06	3.73	4.15	4.45	4.69	4.88	5.05	5.19	5.32	5.43
	.01	4.26	4.96	5.40	5.73	5.98	6.19	6.37	6.53	6.67	6.79
14	.05	3.03	3.70	4.11	4.41	4.64	4.83	4.99	5.13	5.25	5.36
	.01	4.21	4.89	5.32	5.63	5.88	6.08	5.26	6.41	6.54	6.66
15	.05	3.01	3.67	4.08	4.37	4.59	4.78	4.94	5.08	5.20	5.31
	.01	4.17	4.84	5.25	5.56	5.80	5.99	6.16	6.31	6.44	6.55
16	.05	3.00	3.65	4.05	4.33	4.56	4.74	4.90	5.03	5.15	5.26
	.01	4.13	4.79	5.19	5.49	5.72	5.92	6.08	6.22	6.35	6.46
17	.05	2.98	3.63	4.02	4.30	4.52	4.70	4.86	4.99	5.11	5.21
	.01	4.10	4.74	5.14	5.43	5.66	5.85	6.01	6.15	6.27	6.38
18	.05	2.97	3.61	4.00	4.28	4.49	4.67	4.82	4.96	5.07	5.17
	.01	4.07	4.70	5.09	5.38	5.60	5.79	5.94	6.08	6.20	6.31
19	.05	2.96	3.59	3.98	4.25	4.47	4.65	4.79	4.92	5.04	5.14
	.01	4.05	4.67	5.05	5.33	5.55	5.73	5.89	6.02	6.14	6.25
20	.05	2.95	3.58	3.96	4.23	4.45	4.62	4.77	4.90	5.01	5.11
	.01	4.02	4.64	5.02	5.29	5.51	5.69	5.84	5.97	6.09	6.19
24	.05	2.92	3.53	3.90	4.17	4.37	4.54	4.68	4.81	4.92	5.01
	.01	3.96	4.55	4.91	5.17	5.37	5.54	5.69	5.81	5.92	6.02
30	.05	2.89	3.49	3.85	4.10	4.30	4.46	4.60	4.72	4.82	4.92
	.01	3.89	4.45	4.80	5.05	5.24	5.40	5.54	5.65	5.76	5.85
40	.05	2.86	3.44	3.79	4.04	4.23	4.39	4.52	4.63	4.73	4.82
	.01	3.82	4.37	4.70	4.93	5.11	5.26	5.39	5.50	5.60	5.69
60	.05	2.83	3.40	3.74	3.98	4.16	4.31	4.44	4.55	4.65	4.73
	.01	3.76	4.28	4.59	4.82	4.99	5.13	5.25	5.36	5.45	5.53
120	.05	2.80	3.36	3.68	3.92	4.10	4.24	4.36	4.47	4.56	4.64
	.01	3.70	4.20	4.50	4.71	4.87	5.01	5.12	5.21	5.30	5.37
∞	.05	2.77	3.31	3.63	3.86	4.03	4.17	4.29	4.39	4.47	4.55
	.01	3.64	4.12	4.40	4.60	4.76	4.88	4.99	5.08	5.16	5.23

Table B.7   Two-Tailed Critical Ratios of χ^2

Degrees of Freedom df	.10	.05	.02	.01
1	2.706	3.841	5.412	6.635
2	4.605	5.991	7.824	9.210
3	6.251	7.815	9.837	11.341
4	7.779	9.488	11.668	13.277
5	9.236	11.070	13.388	15.086
6	10.645	12.592	15.033	16.812
7	12.017	14.067	16.622	18.475
8	13.362	15.507	18.168	20.090
9	14.684	16.919	19.679	21.666
10	15.987	18.307	21.161	23.209
11	17.275	19.675	22.618	24.725
12	18.549	21.026	24.054	26.217
13	19.812	22.362	25.472	27.688
14	21.064	23.685	26.873	29.141
15	22.307	24.996	28.259	30.578
16	23.542	26.296	29.633	32.000
17	24.769	27.587	30.995	33.409
18	25.989	28.869	32.346	34.805
19	27.204	30.144	33.687	36.191
20	28.412	31.410	35.020	37.566
21	29.615	32.671	36.343	38.932
22	30.813	33.924	37.659	40.289
23	32.007	35.172	38.968	41.638
24	33.196	36.415	40.270	42.980
25	34.382	37.652	41.566	44.314
26	35.563	38.885	42.856	45.642
27	36.741	40.113	44.140	46.963
28	37.916	41.337	45.419	48.278
29	39.087	42.557	46.693	49.588
30	40.256	43.773	47.962	50.892

Table B.8   Critical Values of the *U* Statistic

 The numbers listed below are the critical *U* values for $\alpha = .05$. Use the lightface critical values for a one-tailed test and the **boldface critical values for a two-tailed test.** *Note:* To be significant, the *smaller computed U must be equal to or less than the critical U.* A dash (—) means that no decision is possible at the stated level of significance.

N_B	1	2	3	4	5	6	7	8	9	10	11	12	13	14	15	16	17	18	19	20
1	—	—	—	—	—	—	—	—	—	—	—	—	—	—	—	—	—	—	0	0
2	—	—	—	—	0	0	0	1	1	1	1	2	2	2	3	3	3	4	4	4
					—	**—**	**—**	**0**	**0**	**0**	**0**	**1**	**1**	**1**	**1**	**1**	**2**	**2**	**2**	**2**
3	—	—	0	0	1	2	2	3	3	4	5	5	6	7	7	8	9	9	10	11
	—	**—**	**—**	**—**	**0**	**1**	**1**	**2**	**2**	**3**	**3**	**4**	**4**	**5**	**5**	**6**	**6**	**7**	**7**	**8**
4	—	—	0	1	2	3	4	5	6	7	8	9	10	11	12	14	15	16	17	18
	—	**—**	**—**	**0**	**1**	**2**	**3**	**4**	**4**	**5**	**6**	**7**	**8**	**9**	**10**	**11**	**11**	**12**	**13**	**13**
5	—	0	1	2	4	5	6	8	9	11	12	13	15	16	18	19	20	22	23	25
	—	**—**	**0**	**1**	**2**	**3**	**5**	**6**	**7**	**8**	**9**	**11**	**12**	**13**	**14**	**15**	**17**	**18**	**19**	**20**
6	—	0	2	3	5	7	8	10	12	14	16	17	19	21	23	25	26	28	30	32
	—	**—**	**1**	**2**	**3**	**5**	**6**	**8**	**10**	**11**	**13**	**14**	**16**	**17**	**19**	**21**	**22**	**24**	**25**	**27**
7	—	0	2	4	6	8	11	13	15	17	19	21	24	26	28	30	33	35	37	39
	—	**—**	**1**	**3**	**5**	**6**	**8**	**10**	**12**	**14**	**16**	**18**	**20**	**22**	**24**	**26**	**28**	**30**	**32**	**34**
8	—	1	3	5	8	10	13	15	18	20	23	26	28	31	33	36	39	41	44	47
	—	**0**	**2**	**4**	**6**	**8**	**10**	**13**	**15**	**17**	**19**	**22**	**24**	**26**	**29**	**31**	**34**	**36**	**38**	**41**
9	—	1	3	6	9	12	15	18	21	24	27	30	33	36	39	42	45	48	51	54
	—	**0**	**2**	**4**	**7**	**10**	**12**	**15**	**17**	**20**	**23**	**26**	**28**	**31**	**34**	**37**	**39**	**42**	**45**	**48**
10	—	1	4	7	11	14	17	20	24	27	31	34	37	41	44	48	51	55	58	62
	—	**0**	**3**	**5**	**8**	**11**	**14**	**17**	**20**	**23**	**26**	**29**	**33**	**36**	**39**	**42**	**45**	**48**	**52**	**55**
11	—	1	5	8	12	16	19	23	27	31	34	38	42	46	50	54	57	61	65	69
	—	**0**	**3**	**6**	**9**	**13**	**16**	**19**	**23**	**26**	**30**	**33**	**37**	**40**	**44**	**47**	**51**	**55**	**58**	**62**
12	—	2	5	9	13	17	21	26	30	34	38	42	47	51	55	60	64	68	72	77
	—	**1**	**4**	**7**	**11**	**14**	**18**	**22**	**26**	**29**	**33**	**37**	**41**	**45**	**49**	**53**	**57**	**61**	**65**	**69**
13	—	2	6	10	15	19	24	28	33	37	42	47	51	56	61	65	70	75	80	84
	—	**1**	**4**	**8**	**12**	**16**	**20**	**24**	**28**	**33**	**37**	**41**	**45**	**50**	**54**	**59**	**63**	**67**	**72**	**76**
14	—	2	7	11	16	21	26	31	36	41	46	51	56	61	66	71	77	82	87	92
	—	**1**	**5**	**9**	**13**	**17**	**22**	**26**	**31**	**36**	**40**	**45**	**50**	**55**	**59**	**64**	**67**	**74**	**78**	**83**
15	—	3	7	12	18	23	28	33	39	44	50	55	61	66	72	77	83	88	94	100
	—	**1**	**5**	**10**	**14**	**19**	**24**	**29**	**34**	**39**	**44**	**49**	**54**	**59**	**64**	**70**	**75**	**80**	**85**	**90**
16	—	3	8	14	19	25	30	36	42	48	54	60	65	71	77	83	89	95	101	107
	—	**1**	**6**	**11**	**15**	**21**	**26**	**31**	**37**	**42**	**47**	**53**	**59**	**64**	**70**	**75**	**81**	**86**	**92**	**98**
17	—	3	9	15	20	26	33	39	45	51	57	64	70	77	83	89	96	102	109	115
	—	**2**	**6**	**11**	**17**	**22**	**28**	**34**	**39**	**45**	**51**	**57**	**63**	**67**	**75**	**81**	**87**	**93**	**99**	**105**
18	—	4	9	16	22	28	35	41	48	55	61	68	75	82	88	95	102	109	116	123
	—	**2**	**7**	**12**	**18**	**24**	**30**	**36**	**42**	**48**	**55**	**61**	**67**	**74**	**80**	**86**	**93**	**99**	**106**	**112**
19	0	4	10	17	23	30	37	44	51	58	65	72	80	87	94	101	109	116	123	130
	—	**2**	**7**	**13**	**19**	**25**	**32**	**38**	**45**	**52**	**58**	**65**	**72**	**78**	**85**	**92**	**99**	**106**	**113**	**119**
20	0	4	11	18	25	32	39	47	54	62	69	77	84	92	100	107	115	123	130	138
	—	**2**	**8**	**13**	**20**	**27**	**34**	**41**	**48**	**55**	**62**	**69**	**76**	**83**	**90**	**98**	**105**	**112**	**119**	**127**

Table B.8 (*continued*)

 The numbers listed below are the critical U values for $\alpha = .01$. Use the lightface critical values for a one-tailed test and the **boldface critical values for a two-tailed test.** *Note:* To be significant, the *smaller computed U must be equal to or less than the critical U.* A dash (—) means that no decision is possible at the stated level of significance.

N_B \ N_A	1	2	3	4	5	6	7	8	9	10	11	12	13	14	15	16	17	18	19	20
1	—	—	—	—	—	—	—	—	—	—	—	—	—	—	—	—	—	—	—	—
2	—	—	—	—	—	—	—	—	—	—	—	—	0	0	0	0	0	0	1	1
	—	—	—	—	—	—	—	—	—	—	—	—	—	—	—	—	—	—	**0**	**0**
3	—	—	—	—	—	—	0	0	1	1	1	2	2	2	3	3	4	4	4	5
	—	—	—	—	—	—	—	—	**0**	**0**	**0**	**1**	**1**	**1**	**2**	**2**	**2**	**2**	**3**	**3**
4	—	—	—	—	0	1	1	2	3	3	4	5	5	6	7	7	8	9	9	10
	—	—	—	—	—	**0**	**0**	**1**	**1**	**2**	**2**	**3**	**3**	**4**	**5**	**5**	**6**	**6**	**7**	**8**
5	—	—	—	0	1	2	3	4	5	6	7	8	9	10	11	12	13	14	15	16
	—	—	—	—	**0**	**1**	**1**	**2**	**3**	**4**	**5**	**6**	**7**	**7**	**8**	**9**	**10**	**11**	**12**	**13**
6	—	—	—	1	2	3	4	6	7	8	9	11	12	13	15	16	18	19	20	22
	—	—	—	**0**	**1**	**2**	**3**	**4**	**5**	**6**	**7**	**9**	**10**	**11**	**12**	**13**	**15**	**16**	**17**	**18**
7	—	—	0	1	3	4	6	7	9	11	12	14	16	17	19	21	23	24	26	28
	—	—	—	**0**	**1**	**3**	**4**	**6**	**7**	**9**	**10**	**12**	**13**	**15**	**16**	**18**	**19**	**21**	**22**	**24**
8	—	—	0	2	4	6	7	9	11	13	15	17	20	22	24	26	28	30	32	34
	—	—	—	**1**	**2**	**4**	**6**	**7**	**9**	**11**	**13**	**15**	**17**	**18**	**20**	**22**	**24**	**26**	**28**	**30**
9	—	—	1	3	5	7	9	11	14	16	18	21	23	26	28	31	33	36	38	40
	—	—	**0**	**1**	**3**	**5**	**7**	**9**	**11**	**13**	**16**	**18**	**20**	**22**	**24**	**27**	**29**	**31**	**33**	**36**
10	—	—	1	3	6	8	11	13	16	19	22	24	27	30	33	36	38	41	44	47
	—	—	**0**	**2**	**4**	**6**	**9**	**11**	**13**	**16**	**18**	**21**	**24**	**26**	**29**	**31**	**34**	**37**	**39**	**42**
11	—	—	1	4	7	9	12	15	18	22	25	28	31	34	37	41	44	47	50	53
	—	—	**0**	**2**	**5**	**7**	**10**	**13**	**16**	**18**	**21**	**24**	**27**	**30**	**33**	**36**	**39**	**42**	**45**	**48**
12	—	—	2	5	8	11	14	17	21	24	28	31	35	38	42	46	49	53	56	60
	—	—	**1**	**3**	**6**	**9**	**12**	**15**	**18**	**21**	**24**	**27**	**31**	**34**	**37**	**41**	**44**	**47**	**51**	**54**
13	—	0	2	5	9	12	16	20	23	27	31	35	39	43	47	51	55	59	63	67
	—	—	**1**	**3**	**7**	**10**	**13**	**17**	**20**	**24**	**27**	**31**	**34**	**38**	**42**	**45**	**49**	**53**	**56**	**60**
14	—	0	2	6	10	13	17	22	26	30	34	38	43	47	51	56	60	65	69	73
	—	—	**1**	**4**	**7**	**11**	**15**	**18**	**22**	**26**	**30**	**34**	**38**	**42**	**46**	**50**	**54**	**58**	**63**	**67**
15	—	0	3	7	11	15	19	24	28	33	37	42	47	51	56	61	66	70	75	80
	—	—	**2**	**5**	**8**	**12**	**16**	**20**	**24**	**29**	**33**	**37**	**42**	**46**	**51**	**55**	**60**	**64**	**69**	**73**
16	—	0	3	7	12	16	21	26	31	36	41	46	51	56	61	66	71	76	82	87
	—	—	**2**	**5**	**9**	**13**	**18**	**22**	**27**	**31**	**36**	**41**	**45**	**50**	**55**	**60**	**65**	**70**	**74**	**79**
17	—	0	4	8	13	18	23	28	33	38	44	49	55	60	66	71	77	82	88	93
	—	—	**2**	**6**	**10**	**15**	**19**	**24**	**29**	**34**	**39**	**44**	**49**	**54**	**60**	**65**	**70**	**75**	**81**	**86**
18	—	0	4	9	14	19	24	30	36	41	47	53	59	65	70	76	82	88	94	100
	—	—	**2**	**6**	**11**	**16**	**21**	**26**	**31**	**37**	**42**	**47**	**53**	**58**	**64**	**70**	**75**	**81**	**87**	**92**
19	—	1	4	9	15	20	26	32	38	44	50	56	63	69	75	82	88	94	101	107
	—	**0**	**3**	**7**	**12**	**17**	**22**	**28**	**33**	**39**	**45**	**51**	**56**	**63**	**69**	**74**	**81**	**87**	**93**	**99**
20	—	1	5	10	16	22	28	34	40	47	53	60	67	73	80	87	93	100	107	114
	—	**0**	**3**	**8**	**13**	**18**	**24**	**30**	**36**	**42**	**48**	**54**	**60**	**67**	**73**	**79**	**86**	**92**	**99**	**105**

Source: Adapted from R. E. Kirk. (1984). *Elementary statistics* (2nd ed.). Pacific Grove, CA: Brooks/Cole. Used with permission of the publisher.

Table B.9 Critical Values of the Wilcoxon *T* Statistic

	Level of Significance for a One-Tailed Test					Level of Significance for a One-Tailed Test			
	.05	.025	.01	.005		.05	.025	.01	.005
	Level of Significance for a Two-Tailed Test					Level of Significance for a Two-Tailed Test			
N	.10	.05	.02	.01	*N*	.10	.05	.02	.01
5	0	—	—	—	28	130	116	101	91
6	2	0	—	—	29	140	126	110	100
7	3	2	0	—	30	151	137	120	109
8	5	3	1	0	31	163	147	130	118
9	8	5	3	1	32	175	159	140	128
10	10	8	5	3	33	187	170	151	138
11	13	10	7	5	34	200	182	162	148
12	17	13	9	7	35	213	195	173	159
13	21	17	12	9	36	227	208	185	171
14	25	21	15	12	37	241	221	198	182
15	30	25	19	15	38	256	235	211	194
16	35	29	23	19	39	271	249	224	207
17	41	34	27	23	40	286	264	238	220
18	47	40	32	27	41	302	279	252	233
19	53	46	37	32	42	319	294	266	247
20	60	52	43	37	43	336	310	281	261
21	67	58	49	42	44	353	327	296	276
22	75	65	55	48	45	371	343	312	291
23	83	73	62	54	46	389	361	328	307
24	91	81	69	61	47	407	378	345	322
25	100	89	76	68	48	426	396	362	339
26	110	98	84	75	49	446	415	379	355
27	119	107	92	83	50	466	434	397	373

How to use this table: Use the *smaller* computed sum of ranks as the test statistic, *T*. If the computed *T* is equal to or less than the critical value in the table, then it is significant.

Source: Adapted from R. E. Kirk (1984). *Elementary statistics* (2nd ed.) Pacific Grove, CA: Brooks/Cole. Used with permission of the publisher.

Table B.10   Critical Values of r_s (Spearman Correlation Coefficient)

A given value of r_s is statistically significant if it equals or exceeds the tabled value at the designated α level at a given N. To interpolate, sum the critical values above and below the N of interest and divide by 2. Thus, the critical value at $\alpha = .05$, two-tailed test, when $N = 21$, is $(0.450 + 0.428)/2 = 0.439$.

	Level of Significance for One-Tailed Test			
	.05	**.025**	**.01**	**.005**
Level of Significance for Two-Tailed Test				
N^*	**.10**	**.05**	**.02**	**.01**
5	.900	1.000	1.000	—
6	.829	.886	.943	1.000
7	.714	.786	.893	.929
8	.643	.738	.833	.881
9	.600	.683	.783	.833
10	.564	.648	.746	.794
12	.506	.591	.712	.777
14	.456	.544	.645	.715
16	.425	.506	.601	.665
18	.399	.475	.564	.625
20	.377	.450	.534	.591
22	.359	.428	.508	.562
24	.343	.409	.485	.537
26	.329	.392	.465	.515
28	.317	.377	.448	.496
30	.306	.364	.432	.478

$^*N$ = number of pairs.

WRITING UP RESEARCH IN APA STYLE: OVERVIEW AND FOCUS ON RESULTS

When a study's data are collected and analyzed, a researcher must begin the process of packaging the results for others to consider, examine, or even challenge. Traditionally, most behavioral scientists write up research results in the form of an article. Each of the behavioral sciences has a particular format for a manuscript—the preprinted form of an article—though there are commonalities across the disciplines. Because I know the format advocated by the American Psychological Association (APA) best, it is the one I will present here. If you work in a discipline other than psychology, then you should consult a set of writing style guidelines in an appropriate reference work (please note that some academic disciplines outside of psychology—notably nursing, criminology, and personnel—also employ APA style). Let me also suggest, however, that you read the material included in this appendix anyway, as much of the advice is generic and can help you to write clearer prose in whatever format you need to use.

Basic Advice and Techniques for Writing an Interesting Research Paper

When I am not trying to shape students into data analysts, I am usually helping them to improve their writing skills. The following advice is admittedly idiosyncratic, and largely based on my experience teaching research methods in psychology as well as an occasional interdisciplinary writing course. Many other useful suggestions about improving writing can be found in the list of selected references for writers and researchers appearing at the end of this appendix.

Carefully Check a Paper's Spelling, Grammar, and Punctuation.   Given the ubiquity of spell checking—and even grammar checking—software, there is absolutely no excuse for poor spelling, problematic grammar, or confused punctuation. In fact, once you have written a complete rough draft of a paper, the very last thing you should do is proofread it from start to finish with an eye to catching dropped letters or words, misspellings, and misused periods, commas, colons, and semicolons. If you believe that these so-called "surface errors" are not as important as the content of your paper, re-member that readers will have little chance to think about content if they are constantly (mentally) correcting mistakes or omissions while reviewing your work.

Write with Generalists, Not Specialists, in Mind.   Many novice writers assume that their prose must be dense and technical in order to be "scientific." Not so. Certainly, some technical material and even professional jargon is tolerable in disciplinary writ-ing, but the overarching goal is to present such information in ways that an interested, but general, audience can follow. Every writer wants his or her ideas to "catch on" or be appreciated, but such hopes are easily dashed if the supporting prose is too compli-cated, convoluted, or otherwise unclear.

How can the goal of clear, concise prose be achieved? As you write, remember that your goal is to present information in an accurate way, one that conveys your interest—even excitement—about a topic. When presenting your arguments, remember to speak to your audience directly—after all, you are telling them a research story—so do not talk down to them (i.e., simplistic language) or over their heads (i.e., formal, dry text). As I have noted elsewhere (Dunn, 1999), focus on those ideas you can present to read-ers that they do not already know or have not considered from your perspective. Imag-ine that you had only a few minutes to describe your work to someone—what would you say? Obviously, you would only talk about the most important issues. The same criterion should be used for your writing, as what you leave out can be as influential to clarity as what information you choose to include.

Write in the Active, Not Passive, Voice.   I once received a B on a history paper and when I asked why, the professor told me that my writing relied too much on the pas-sive voice. The passive voice involves overuse of passive verbs (e.g., has been) in place of active ones (e.g., is), so that the syntax of sentences becomes vague, not crisp. When I claimed that behavioral scientists wrote in the passive voice precisely because they could not be sure that their conclusions were correct, my professor laughed and told me that uncertainty was no excuse for boring writing. I was so much younger—and annoyed—then, but I wholeheartedly agree with him now.

For some reason, behavioral scientists *do* write in the passive voice and it *is* dull to read: "The written instructions and the stimulus materials were given to the research participants by the experimenter." The meaning is still there, but the presentation could be snappier, as in: "The experimenter gave the instructions and the stimulus materials to the participants." Sometimes writing in the passive voice is necessary (O'Connor, 1996), of course, but in general, your writing should be active, involving, and to the point. The best time to catch overreliance on the passive voice is during the revision process, when you are rereading your paper to see how it sounds or how well the ideas flow together.

Revise Again and Again.   Good writing is made, not born. Good writers know that they will need to generate several drafts of what they are working on before their writ-ing reaches a satisfactory state. (Note that I said satisfactory, *not* perfect; eventually, a writer must ask others for suggestions about where further improvements can be made.) Develop the habit of revising your manuscript from start to finish at the beginning of each session of writing (yes, really). Not only will reading and editing at the start of each writing session enable you to get back into the mind-set of your paper, it will also afford you the opportunity to see the paper anew, making meaningful changes or additions when you see your ideas from a fresh perspective (for further advice in this vein, see Peterson, 1996).

Share Your Work with Others and Revise (Again).   Writing is meant to be shared with others eventually, so why not do so early on, say, when you have a complete rough draft of a manuscript? Ask a friend or instructor whom you trust—someone who will be honest, even critical of what you write—to comment on your draft. Avoid recruiting people who will only say nice things about your paper, which is technically a work in progress and, therefore, worthy of tough-but-fair comments that will improve it. Your editor should be willing to write specific comments on the manuscript (typically in the margins, so leave enough room) and perhaps some summary comment at its end. Be sure to ask for concrete examples of what portion of the text is not clear and suggestions about how the manuscript could be improved. The cardinal rule for accepting criticism is doing so *without* trying to explain yourself or the text to the critic; if something was misinterpreted by readers, you, the writer, was responsible for the misinterpretation (cf., Elbow & Belanoff, 1995). In other words, you already wrote what you meant to say in the draft—if your intentions were not clear the first time, it is your responsibility to clear them up in the next revision of the manuscript.

Once you have a peer's comments, use them to revise the paper yet again. If you can, take a few minutes and ask your peer reviewer to comment on what portions of the text were easy to follow, as well as which ones were harder to read or understand. Finally, be sure to be appreciative of your friend's assistance with the review—say "thank you" and offer to return the service at the earliest opportunity.

Be Vigilant About Gender Bias and Sexist Language.   Academic writing tends to be male oriented when it should be gender inclusive. Given the power of language to shape thought, belief, and culture, the behavioral sciences are sensitized to male-dominated prose (i.e., "mankind" in place of "humanity"; "girl" or "lady" instead of "woman" or "female"; overuse of "he" or "him" relative to "her" or "she"). How can you eliminate subtle sexism from your language? Rather easily, actually, and you can begin by using pronouns such as "he" and "she" only when it is absolutely necessary to individualize some person's behavior or when an example requires solo identification. The appropriate alternative, of course, is to write using gender-neutral plurals (i.e., they, them, we). This course is infinitely preferable to the cumbersome and tedious (to read, anyway) practice of using "he/she" or, worse still, "(s)he." The latter constructions not only fail to adhere to APA style (see the *Publication Manual;* APA, 1994), their novelty is a source of distraction, slowing readers down by drawing their attention to superfluous details.

Overview of APA Style: Sections of a Manuscript

Where writing in APA style is concerned, there is no substitute for using the *Publication Manual of the American Psychological Association* (APA, 1994). If you are contemplating graduate studies and possibly a career in the behavioral sciences, then buying a copy of the *Publication Manual* is an excellent investment in your own future development as a writer and a researcher. The *Publication Manual* is an ideal reference work because it contains virtually all of the information one could possibly need in order to write or present research findings in a clear, cogent manner. In spite of the seemingly forbidding amount of detail that goes into preparing an APA-style manuscript (the *first time*, anyway), reading or referring to the *Publication Manual* actually leaves one with

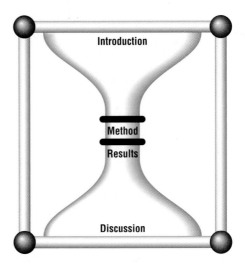

Figure C.1   The Hourglass Model of Writing an APA Style Paper

Note: Based on Figure 3.1 in Dunn (1999, p.80).

the impression that all the attention to detail is promoting a rather commonsense enterprise. By that I mean the clear explication of scientific information, including methods, procedures, and statistical tests, all of which advances knowledge by promoting understanding and encouraging researchers to replicate or extend the work of published investigators.

What are the components in an APA-style manuscript? There are usually eight: a Title, Abstract, Introduction, Method, Results, Discussion, References, and Tables or Figures (but see the *Publication Manual* for others; APA, 1994). Because I want you to get a sense of the conceptual structure of a manuscript, we will briefly summarize the contents of each section below. Envision an hourglass (Bem, 1987), one where the *introduction* is at the broad top—the lid—of the hourglass and the *Discussion* lies at the bottom of its broad base (see Figure C.1). Both the beginning and end of an APA-style manuscript contain broad statements about the nature of the topic under investigation. The introduction literally introduces the relevance of the topic to the study of behavior, and gradually narrows its focus to the specific question(s) addressed by the paper. At the other end of the manuscript, the *Discussion* deals with the (broader) implications of what was found for current and future work.

What about the narrow "neck" of the metaphorical hourglass? At the narrowest point is the *Method* section of the APA-style paper (see Figure C.1). I am using the word "narrow" to reflect concern with reporting a step-by-step account of exactly how a piece of research was carried out from start to finish. The details provided should be sufficient to enable a motivated reader to recreate the experiment from scratch in order to replicate the results. Below this narrow band of the hourglass lie the *Results,* which should contain a thorough accounting of what happened in terms of behavioral outcomes in the study (see Figure C.1). The *Results* section is also the place where the specific statistical analyses, as well as supporting symbols and numbers, are presented. Once the specific behavioral outcomes are reviewed, the *Results* section will begin to broaden into the *Discussion,* where the previously acknowledged focus on implications can be reviewed.

Beyond the hourglass metaphor, one other important aspect of APA-style writing stands out: Each section of a paper should be written so that it stands alone (Bem, 1987;

Dunn, 1999). By "stands alone," I mean that a motivated reader could begin by reading the last section of a paper (the *Discussion*) and still have a coherent sense of what was done and why in one or more of the earlier sections of the manuscript. Indeed, expert readers prefer to scan individual sections of a paper in order to determine whether to read the whole thing. A given reader may begin with the *Abstract,* notice some interesting point related to the research participants, and then immediately turn to the *Method.* Another might read serially, from the *Abstract,* to the *introduction,* and all the way through to the *References.*

Ideally, each section of an APA-style paper prepares readers for what appears in its subsequent section(s). Thus, the *introduction* prepares the reader for the details of the procedure found in the *Method* or for what happened, behaviorally speaking, in the *Results.* How is some degree of consistency in content achieved so that readers can move from one section to another with little difficulty? Usually by having a writer make certain that the study's purpose—its hypothesis—is recapitulated in some fashion within each of the sections, despite the fact that it is primarily associated with the tail-end of the *introduction,* where it usually serves as a segue into the *Method.* Such constancy of purpose in APA-style writing takes practice, but is well worth the effort because it effectively educates and reminds readers of the study's unique purpose throughout its written summary.

We can now briefly summarize the content and scope of the eight main sections of the typical APA-style paper. Because there are ample resources available—both reference books and software—that provide concrete guidance about APA formatting requirements, everything from pagination to capitalization and citation style, I will not review such details here (but see, for example, Gelfand & Walker, 1990). For your convenience, however, I provide the number(s) of the relevant sections of the *Publication Manual* for each of the components of the typical APA-style manuscript.

Title (Refer to Section 1.06 of the *Publication Manual*). A paper's title should convey the nature of a topic, including relevant variables or theories, in as few words as possible. Because every word is important, phrases such as "An Experiment Concerning" or "A Study of" should be dropped from a title. Thus, "The Effect of Proximity Cues on Romantic Attraction" is preferable to "An Experimental Study of the Effect of Proximity Cues on Romantic Attraction." A good rule of thumb is to keep a title's length to 12 words or less. Your name and institutional affiliation should appear two spaces below the title on the title page, the first page of an APA-style manuscript.

Abstract (Refer to Section 1.07 in the *Publication Manual*). An *Abstract* is a short summary of what appears in the text of a paper. By short, I mean no more than 120 words for an experiment and usually less than 100 for a review paper. Written in paragraph form, an *Abstract* identifies the context of the research; the hypothesis that was tested, as well as any independent and dependent variables; a brief description of the methodology employed; a summary of the results; and finally, a concise mention of any conclusions or implications. As you can see, a good *Abstract* must cover quite a bit of descriptive terrain in as few words as possible. The *Abstract* paragraph will appear on the second page of an APA-style manuscript.

Introduction (Refer to Section 1.08 in the *Publication Manual*). Although it contains a review of the literature, the APA-style introduction is intended to do more than cover what is known about a research topic. Rather, the introduction provides a framework for the literature—a clear explanation of the logic underlying the study, the hypothesis being examined, and its relation to this existing knowledge. As noted above, the introduction should open with a relatively broad perspective on the research topic, gradually introducing, emphasizing, and integrating more specific information leading up to a concrete rationale for the research. Any researcher must expend considerable effort to make the inferential logic underlying the study's design clear and objective. Introductions, which begin on the third page of APA-style manuscripts, tend to be several pages in length.

Method (Refer to Section 1.09 of the *Publication Manual*).   The purpose of the *Method* section is to provide sufficient detail for readers to follow and understand all the procedures and materials used to run an experiment (or other investigation) from start to finish. In many ways, a *Method* section is like a script or set of directions for readers to follow. Most *Method* sections will contain a *participants* section describing the research participants (e.g., gender, age); an *apparatus* or *materials* section where any special equipment (e.g., operant chambers, computer programs) or written materials (e.g., published tests, measures, or personality inventories) are noted; and a *procedure* section outlining what an experimenter(s) and participant(s) did at each stage of the research. Depending on the nature of the research, other detailed subsections can also be added into the *Method.*

Results (Refer to Section 1.10 of the *Publication Manual*).   A *Results* section reviews the nature of the data collected, accounts for the manner in which they were analyzed, and then links the findings to the original hypothesis of the study. Because a later section of this appendix is focused on how to structure and write a *Results* section, I will defer the majority of my suggestions until then. I do, however, want to remind readers that a *Results* section should not be focused on interpreting any findings in detail or discussing their implications—these activities are reserved for the *Discussion* section.

Discussion (Refer to Section 1.11 of the *Publication Manual*).   The degree to which a study's results fit the hypothesis, and this "fit" or lack thereof has any impact on related research, is the focus of the APA-style *Discussion* section. Most *Discussion* sections have three goals: to review a study's main purpose and discuss whether the results indicate it was achieved; to highlight any deviations from the research expectations, including problems or limitations with what was found; and, finally, to judge whether the obtained results add to existing knowledge or point to future directions similar investigations should follow. *Discussion* sections invite both the author and reader to see the "forest" of the behavioral results (i.e., larger meaning), not just the "trees" (i.e., individual findings).

References (Refer to Sections 1.13 and 3.94–3.117 in the *Publication Manual*).   The *References* section of the APA-style paper is its scholarly trail. Interested readers can examine it to follow a researcher's logic, or use it to add to their own knowledge regarding a topic. Any idea drawn from an article, book, book chapter, or other source— including the Internet—used in the course of the research must be referenced here and according to a particular citation style (for numerous examples of APA-style references, please turn to the References section for this book). The proper citation of references is a crucial part of the research enterprise, as it is an important way that scientists "communicate" with one another and the common way that students learn to navigate the literature pertaining to particular topics or even fields.

Tables and Figures (Refer to Sections 3.62–3.86 in the *Publication Manual*).   As noted in chapter 3 of this book, tables and figures should be used sparingly to highlight particular aspects of data, analyses, or the relationships among variables. In

APA parlance, a table summarizes some results, including means and standard deviations, or the results of more complex inferential analyses. On the other hand, a figure is a graph, a picture, or some line drawing designed to efficiently convey the meaning of some relationship or result. A reader should be able to glance at a figure or a table and derive meaning from it in a matter of seconds. If this reasonable goal cannot be achieved in a relatively short amount of time, then it is fair to assume that the data presentation—whether table or figure—is too complicated. For recent, authoritative guidance on how to prepare APA-style tables, please see Nicol and Pexman (1999).

Two Common Problems in Student Papers Written in APA Style. Aside from the problems presented above, students tend to *overwrite* APA style *introductions* while *underwriting* their *Discussions*. By overwriting an introduction, I mean that most of the time and energy in creating a draft is expended in the first section, chiefly on the literature review. Problems occur when students discuss related research in too much detail, neglecting to focus in on what points in prior work are actually relevant to the current project, or citing too many studies that are only tangentially related to the current work. When reviewing studies using a particular research paradigm (e.g., the bogus pipeline; Jones & Sigall, 1971) to examine people's attitudes, for example, avoid the temptation also to cite *all* other studies pertaining to attitude research (and there are hundreds, possibly thousands)—just choose those that relate to the specific topic at hand. Less, then, is more: Strive to provide readers with only the information they need to evaluate your ideas and their relationship to a topical area of research, not an entire field of research.

What about the problem of underwriting? By the time students reach the *Discussion* section, their production of prose often wanes, as if they are too tired to really think about or expand on the implications of their results. Often, I find that a quick summary is all that is provided, one that rarely does little more than repeat the "greatest hits" of the *introduction* and the *Results* sections. Ideally, a *Discussion* section invites the writer as well as the reader to really think about what the results mean in context. Do they extend the theory or identify some limit to it? Was the hypothesis confirmed, or will it need to be revised for use in future studies? Why? Can the results be used to design future studies addressing some of the unanswered questions? No matter how you choose to end your paper, though, try *not* to close with just the tired, worn phrase, "More research on this topic is necessary." Why? Because more research is *always* called for—what else can you tell readers that they do not already know? Be creative!

Other suggestions about writing an APA-style paper can be found in Dunn (1999) or in several of the behavioral-science-oriented writing references provided in the list appearing at the end of this appendix.

Focus on Writing a Results Section

What are the main elements of a *Results* section? There are really four:

- A reminder about the hypothesis, including the operationalization of any independent variables and dependent measures in the experiment or study.
- A summary of the data.
- Detailed descriptions of the statistical analyses, numerical results with accompanying symbols, and any necessary supporting tables or figures.

- Brief discussion of the specific (main) results, which serve to set up main conclusions that can be mentioned in the *Results* section but are only fully explored in the *Discussion.*

It is also worth mentioning what information should *not* appear in a *Results* section:

- Raw data, scores, or other individual observations should *not* appear except when there is a compelling reason to discuss a salient example (e.g., an extreme score that skewed a result) or to review some illustrative case or response (e.g., "One participant captured the group's feeling when she said . . .").
- Calculations used to determine any descriptive or inferential statistics unless they involve some novel, controversial, or otherwise noteworthy innovation.

As we discuss ways to craft a good *Results* section, we must confront an awful truth: people do not think statistics is interesting—indeed, they usually assume it is dull (Abelson, 1995). When writing up any results, your first goal is to identify what, if anything, is surprising, unexpected, interesting, or otherwise revealing. In other words, remember the *MAGIC* criteria when presenting what you found (see Data Box 9.F and the related discussion in chapter 15; see also Abelson, 1995). When writing the opening paragraph of a *Results* section, then, begin on a strong note, one that reminds readers about the main hypothesis being tested and why it is a compelling one.

Beyond the "interestingness" of the results, of course, there is an overarching goal for the writer of any *Results* section: Explain in plain language what the results reveal *about some aspect of human (or animal) behavior* (Dunn, 1999). Once the hypothesis of interest is noted, you can conceptually begin to answer these sorts of questions for the reader. (When there is more than one hypothesis, let the reader know that early in the *Results* section, and then examine the hypotheses and results in a serial fashion unless some other framework is more appropriate.) What, specifically, did the research participants *do* behaviorally? To answer this question, discuss how behavior was measured (i.e., review the nature of the dependent measure and the data gleaned from it). Why did the participants act one way and not another? In most cases, observed behavior—especially when it more or less confirms a hypothesis—will be discussed in terms of some independent variable. The writer's job is to make it clear as to whether any experimental manipulation actually had its predicted effects.

In the course of addressing these questions, you must provide any relevant descriptive or inferential statistics to support the prose statements or conclusions. When there are relatively few descriptive statistics available, they can be reported inside declarative statements, usually parenthetically (e.g., "The average number of tokens selected was 12 [$SD = 2.0$]."). A large number of descriptive statistics should be placed in a table (see chapter 3), and it is important that the prose guides readers to it (e.g., "The mean rate of response is shown in Table 1 . . ."). Unless there are a variety of similar tests, most inferential statistics should appear at the end of a sentence rather than in a table, as in: "The experimental group tapped the key more times ($M = 27.5$) than did the control group ($M = 16.0$), $t(30) = 4.56$, $p < .05$." Just be sure to provide the statistical symbol(s) so readers will know how the data were analyzed, the available degrees of freedom (if necessary), and the significance level of the test. In fact, it is often a good idea to concretely state what test was used: "The two means were compared using an independent groups *t* test."

I urge you to outline the results that will appear in a *Results* section hierarchically and on paper before you actually sit down to write. A conceptual example of what I

Table C.1 A Sample Hierarchical Outline for Writing Up Results

Opening Paragraph—Overview of Results
- Brief recap of overall hypothesis and method
- *Emphasis on what aspect of human (or animal) behavior is being examined*
  - Review of independent variable(s) and dependent measure(s)
    - Nature of the data

Main Result
- Specific statistical test used and brief rationale for it
- Concrete description of behavioral result and link to hypothesis
- Numerical value of test statistic (symbol, degrees of freedom, significance level)
- Table(s) and/or figure(s) linked to statistical test(s)
  - Supporting statistics (e.g., effect size) and power issues

Secondary Results (if any)
- Specific statistical test used and brief rationale for it
- Concrete description of behavioral result and link to hypothesis
- Numerical value of test statistic (symbol, degrees of freedom, significance level)
  - Table(s) and/or figure(s) linked to statistical test(s)
    - Supporting statistics (e.g., effect size) and power issues

Tertiary Results (if any)
- Specific statistical test used and brief rationale for it
- Concrete description of behavioral result and link to hypothesis
- Numerical value of test statistic (symbol, degrees of freedom, significance level)
  - Table(s) and/or figure(s) linked to statistical test(s)
    - Supporting statistics (e.g., effect size) and power issues

Transition to Discussion Section

have in mind can be seen in Table C.1. As shown in Table C.1, an overview paragraph prepares the reader for the more detailed results that follow. Many student studies will only include one main result (see Table C.1), though more ambitious projects may contain a main result as well as secondary results—those that relate to or otherwise support the main results—and even tertiary results (see Table C.1).

Two important issues are often overlooked when results are presented in APA-style articles. First, many writers assume that readers will remember the direction of predicted effects—that is, which mean is hypothesized to be larger than which other mean (or means). To the researcher, the direction of effects is obvious because it is based on the hypothesis (and the desired results) but, to paraphrase the French *philosophe*, Voltaire, common sense is not so common. Take the time to specifically remind the reader about the direction of an effect and whether the obtained results (e.g., means) match it or deviate from it. Second, do not forget to present supporting statistics dealing with effect size and the degree of association between the independent variable and the dependent measure, among others. It is also a good idea to comment on the power of the test statistics used, especially in situations where a mean difference appears to be strong but is actually modest or even weak (refer to the discussion of statistical power and effect size in chapter 9; see also, Data Box 10.D and the discussion of power at the end of chapter 10).

When should the APA style reference section be written? To many novice APA-style writers, this issue will seem to be an odd one. After all, isn't the *Results* section written after the *Method*, which, in turn, is composed after the *introduction*? This linear

Table C.2   Suggested Steps for Writing an APA Style Manuscrips

Step 1. Draft the *Method* section

Step 2. Draft the *Results* section

  ■ Revisit step 1 for revising and editing

Step 3. Draft the *Introduction*

  ■ Revisit steps 1 and 2 for revising and editing
  ■ As *references* are used, cite them in the *References* section

Step 4. Draft the *Discussion* section

  ■ Revisit steps 1, 2, and 3 for revising and editing

Step 5. Draft the *Abstract*

  ■ Create the *title* page
  ■ Create *tables* and *figures*
  ■ Verify *references*
  ■ Revisit steps 1, 2, 3, and 4

Source: Adapted from Table 3.6 in Dunn (1999, p. 98).

approach is one that many student authors use, but I advocate you consider an alternative approach. Write the *Method* section when you are still collecting data (i.e., the procedural details will be fresh in your mind) and then craft the *Results* section after the analyses are finished but before you ever write the *introduction*. Why? The results of the research really inform every other section of the paper and, in particular, it is important to have a firm grasp of what happened in the research before the *introduction* is undertaken. Think about it: The researcher should know what happened before wrestling with the conceptual presentation of the research question and the supporting literature. Such foreknowledge will keep the introduction focused—doing the *Results* later rather than sooner often leads to a meandering *introduction*.

Beginning with the *Method* and proceeding straight to the drafting of the *Results,* Table C.2 contains a recommended series of steps for writing an APA-style paper. As you can see, a process of continual revision and refinement of ideas and prose is built into the steps shown in Table C.2. For additional suggestion about writing an APA style *Results* section or paper, consult chapters 3 and 8 in Dunn (1999).

Selected References for Writers and Researchers

Bem, D. J. (1987). Writing the empirical journal article. In M. P. Zanna & J. M. Darley (Eds.), *The compleat academic: A practical guide for the beginning social scientist* (pp. 171–201). New York: Random House.

Booth, W. C., Colomb, G. G., & Williams, J. (1995). *The craft of research.* Chicago: University of Chicago Press.

Dunn, D. S. (1999). *The practical researcher: A student guide to conducting psychological research.* New York: McGraw-Hill.

Flemons, D. (1998). *Writing between the lines: Composition in the social sciences.* New York: Norton.

Lamott, A. (1995). *Bird by bird: Some instructions on writing and life.* New York: Anchor.

McCloskey, D. (1987). *The writing of economics.* New York: Macmillan.

O'Connor, P. T. (1996). *Woe is I: The grammarphobe's guide to better English in plain English.* New York: Putnam.

O'Connor, P. T. (1999). *Words fail me: What everyone who writes should know about writing.* New York: Harcourt Brace.

Parrott III, L. (1999). *How to write psychology papers* (2nd ed.). New York: Longman.

Rosnow, R. L., & Rosnow, M. (1995). *Writing papers in psychology* (3rd ed.). Pacific Grove, CA: Brooks/Cole.

Scott, J. M., Koch, R. E., Scott, G. M., & Garrison, S. M. (1999). *The psychology student writer's manual.* Upper Saddle River, NJ: Prentice Hall.

Smyth, T. R. (1996). *Writing in psychology: A student guide* (2nd ed.). New York: Wiley.

Sternberg, R. J. (1993). *The psychologist's companion: A guide to scientific writing for students and researchers* (3rd ed.). Cambridge: Cambridge University Press.

Strunk, jr., W., & White, E. B. (1972). *The elements of style.* New York: Macmillan.

Williams, B. T., & Brydon-Miller, M. (1997). *Concept to completion: Writing well in the social sciences.* Fort Worth, TX: Harcourt Brace College Publishers.

Williams, J. M. (1990). *Style: Toward clarity and grace.* Chicago: University of Chicago Press.

DOING A RESEARCH PROJECT USING STATISTICS AND DATA ANALYSIS: ORGANIZATION, TIME MANAGEMENT, AND PREPPING DATA FOR ANALYSIS

T he key to conducting a project using statistics and data analysis is to be as organized as possible. Given the *mise en place* philosophy presented throughout the book, this observation should come as no surprise to most readers. How can one become organized so that a project runs smoothly? In this appendix, I will suggest two ways to be organized when calculating statistics (or planning to do so) on data collected in an experiment or other study. The first way entails a careful assessment of what activities need to be performed in the course of a research project before analyses can begin. Everything from choosing a topic to writing up the results into a paper or manuscript (see Appendix C), and how long such activities are estimated to take, must be considered. The second way concerns the importance of making a "first pass" at quantitative data before they are analyzed using the inferential statistics chosen to test the study's hypothesis. This pass involves combing or cleaning the data, rendering it error-free for the analyses to come.

Project Organization: Identifying What Needs to be Done and When

To some degree, every research project is different, but each shares some features with all others. These features are the activities that must occur in order for the project to begin and end in a reasonable amount of time. Indeed, it is a good idea for beginning researchers to estimate about how long it will take to complete any requisite activities for a project. Even when it is not possible to attach a time frame to a given activity (e.g., creating an experimental script, writing up results), it is still important to recognize that the activity will—must—occur at some point during the research effort.

This attempt at project organization and time management is based on an exercise I developed for students taking a research methods class wherein some research project was going to be conducted (see Exercise 1.A in Dunn, 1999). As you examine the following list of activities, think about the project you are planning to conduct. About how long (in hours and days) will each of the required activities take? Will the projected amount of time to perform these research activities match or "fit into" the actual amount of available time? This issue is key: You cannot do a competent project if there is not enough time available for its completion. As a matter of fact, you may find that you need to revise or streamline various research activities in order to complete the project in the allotted time. One final suggestion: If your instructor does not give you a deadline, impose one on yourself. There is an old but valued maxim in writing circles, one that applies equally well to conducting research: *A deadline is your friend.*

Sit down with a calendar and review each of the project activities listed below in the *left column*. Write down the amount of time that you believe it will take you to complete a given activity in the space provided in the *right column*. (Please note that each activity is actually comprised of many smaller activities—be sure to take these into account in your planning!) If an activity does not apply to your project, skip it and enter a "0" in the right column.

What do such time estimates have to do with the statistical analysis of data? Everything, actually—you cannot do any analyses unless you have some data to analyze, as well as the time to do so. The research project and all of its inherent details must be taken seriously. When you are finished evaluating the activities, sum the day(s) and hour(s) in the right column to form a time estimate. Compare this *time estimate* with the *actual amount of time* you have available to conduct the research and analyses—is your estimate more or less than the time available? If it is more, then you will need to adjust your schedule or the project activities accordingly. If the estimate is less, avoid complacency by getting started right away—remember that things often take more time than projected.

Project Activity	*Estimated Time Required (in hours or days)*
1. Topic identification—assigned or developed?	hour(s) _____ day(s) _____
2. Literature search (e.g., library work)— checking out books; copying articles; interlibrary loans	hour(s) _____ day(s) _____
3. Developing research design— selecting independent variables, dependent measures; creating paradigm	hour(s) _____ day(s) _____
4. Collecting project materials and scripting experimental procedure—writing scripts, questionnaires; creating stimuli; locating research space	hour(s) _____ day(s) _____
5. Recruiting research participants and collecting data—allow for participant attrition and problems with the data	hour(s) _____ day(s) _____
6. *Prepping data for analysis* (following page)	hour(s) _____ day(s) _____
7. Performing statistical analysis and interpretation	hour(s) _____ day(s) _____
8. Writing research summary—multiple drafts to final product; allow for peer review and revision	hour(s) _____ day(s) _____ hour(s) _____ day(s) _____
9. Unique activities for this project Specify _____ Specify _____	hour(s) _____ day(s) _____
10. *Estimated Time Required*	hour(s) _____ day(s) _____
11. *Actual Time Available*	hour(s) _____ day(s) _____
Difference: Subtract 11 from 10	hour(s) _____ day(s) _____*

*A positive difference means that the *estimate* exceeds the time available—reevaluate the activities and make appropriate adjustments. A negative difference means that the project can be completed within the time available.

I recommend that you update your time estimate at least two or three times in the course of conducting a project (Dunn, 1999). Some activities will take a shorter time than expected, whereas others can drag on much longer than predicted (this is especially true where participant recruitment and the actual collection of data are concerned). We now consider one project activity in detail, the prepping of data for analysis.

Prepping Data for Analysis

> By becoming intimately acquainted with such trivial details as the number of subjects on different variables or sets of items, you will be better able to spot problems or discrepancies in the data set and ultimately ensure a study with greater integrity.
>
> —Dollinger & DiLalla (1996, p. 175)

Your experiment or study was organized from beginning to end, and the data were collected and then coded into some numerical form for analysis. What is the next step? Wise data analysts know that it is never a good idea to begin the main statistical analyses (those pertaining to the main hypothesis or hypotheses of interest) until the data are verified for accuracy. Ways to verify data accuracy are the focus of comments in the remainder of this section, several of which were gleaned from an excellent chapter by Dollinger and DiLalla (1996). Additional good advice can be found in chapters 1 and 2 of Newton and Rudestam (1999).

Check Scales Before Employing Them in a Study.   Many researchers and students rely on published scales or inventories in their work, often making changes in the words or phrases used in these measures. Such changes are generally fine, but they must be carefully documented for the reader (see Smith, Budzeika, Edwards, Johnson, & Bearse, 1986). If a scale is changed and no record of the change is maintained, a researcher can lose valuable time backtracking to identify the nature of the change. Worse still, the specific change may be forgotten and, thus, never acknowledged in the analyses or write-up of the project. Document a change *before* the data collection, making sure that the change does not adversely affect the analysis that will eventually be used on data from the measure (Dollinger & DiLalla, 1996).

Some published measures also contain items where respondents' numerical responses must be altered or "recoded" before a scale total can be determined. Often referred to as "reverse recoding," an item rating is essentially flipped so that it remains consistent with the rest of the scale. Perhaps most of the items in a scale are phrased positively ("I am a hard worker") and rated on a five-point scale (higher numbers are more favorable), but one item is negative ("I am lazy"). In order to make the latter item's rating consistent with the positive items, a respondent's response must be altered. Specifically, a rating of 1 would be recoded as a 5, and a 2 as a 4 (and vice versa); only the neutral (midscale) rating of 3 remains unchanged. Published measures will include specific directions about recoding requirements like this one, but researchers must be on the lookout for them. Be sure, then, to read any fine print, directions, or test manuals before using published scales—later you will be glad that you did so.

Check the Scoring of Each Variable Before Beginning Any Analyses.   Once the data are collected and coded (i.e., converted to numbers), it is essential that the possible range of numbers for each variable is checked. A smart way to proceed is to create a frequency table for each and every variable (see chapter 3), checking to make sure that a rating scale that has values, say, from 1 to 7, contains no observations greater than 7 or less than 1 (e.g., 0 and 8 could not appear in the frequency table). Similarly, if any dichotomous codings are used for variables—gender is often coded as 1 for male and 2 for female—the relevant data must match these two possibilities exclusively.

In the case of large data sets, statistical software can readily run frequencies with ease, and a researcher can "eyeball" the resulting information to find out-of-range errors in a matter of minutes. Smaller data sets are just as manageable, even when done by hand. Just take the necessary time to check all the values and their respective ranges—catching errors in the short run will save time as well as heartbreak over wished-for results in the long run.

Calculate Descriptive Statistics for all Variables, Especially the Main Dependent Measures.   This suggestion is another way to check for out-of-range errors—also known as "outliers"—and to make sure that a set of data is clean before the main analyses can begin. You need to get a feel for your data, and "snooping" around in it to make sure that the means and standard deviations make sense is a smart way to begin. Note that this "snooping" does not preclude the possibility that people's mean responses did not come out as expected, but it will help you to recognize—and verify—those situations where the observed means (or medians, variances, standard deviations, etc.) do not fit expectations.

Dealing with Missing Values.   Some researchers deal with missing values—that is, participants' nonresponses to some question or series of questions—by not including any data from the nonrespondent in any analyses. This rule holds true whether one item or a host of items were neglected. Other investigators prefer some data to none, so they routinely include nonrespondents in their analyses by making certain that the N in any analysis involving missing data is adjusted downward (i.e., a sample has 20 respondents but only 19 answered item 12—the denominator for calculating the mean for item 12 becomes 19, not 20, because of the nonrespondent). By the way, the presence of nonrespondents or missing data in a sample must be documented in the *Method* and (usually) the *Results* sections of APA-style papers.

Particular problems occur when novice data analysts enter 0 instead of leaving a missing value blank or empty within a data set. The problem, of course, is twofold: the (non) respondent never endorsed a 0 rating, and the value of 0 has a decided mathematical effect on any calculation in which it is (inappropriately) entered (e.g., deflating the mean). The rule, then, is a simple one—leave blanks blank and never enter a 0 unless it is both meaningful and apt (e.g., question: "How many times were you sick last semester?" answer: "0 times").

Keep Compulsive Records.   This piece of advice will sound silly but it is tried and true—label things compulsively (Smith et al., 1986). There is always a chance that you may sit on your data for a while (e.g., a semester, a year), or you may decide to pick up a research project idea from one course as an independent study much later in your academic career. Unless you kept careful and meticulous notes about why you did various things to your data, or why you picked the analysis of variance (ANOVA) in lieu of the *t* test, there is a very good chance that you will not remember the rationale for decisions made many months before. As noted in chapter 15, one's memory for statistical concepts is apt to fade unless those concepts are used with some regularity. Why risk "re-creating" the wrong thing when a little note taking or thoughtful labeling can save the day?

Make Certain That Significant Differences Are in the "Right" (i.e., Hypothesized) Direction.   An elementary but common mistake for first-time data analysts is to focus on the presence of a significant difference ("Wow! The *t* test is significant at the .05 level!") without checking to make sure that the difference is in the predicted direction (i.e., one mean is appropriately larger than the other). Many an honors or a masters thesis has foundered on the mistaken assumption that any significant difference is a good difference. You cannot (probably) do anything about means that appear in the wrong direction, but you should be aware of their presence so that you do not make the mistake of claiming that a hypothesis was supported when, in fact, it was actually supported in a way *opposite* to the prediction.

Learn to Ask the Humble but Simple Question, "Does This Result Make Sense?"   As you gain experience working with statistics and data analysis, you will gradually get a feel for results and when they make sense. Once the result of a statistical analysis is known, it is always a good idea to stop and examine it to make certain that it makes "sense" both statistically (i.e., the calculations are correct) and where interpretation is concerned (i.e., does the result fit the prediction? Why or why not?). Many analytic disasters have been averted by simply and calmly examining the data and statistical analyses with the criteria of common sense in mind. When something—a number, a result—does not make sense, there is a good chance you will be able to track down an error in coding or analysis, or some unusual participant responses.

Suggested References

Dollinger, S. J., & DiLalla, D. L. (1996). Cleaning up data and running preliminary analyses. In F. T. L. Leong & J. T. Austin (Eds.), *The psychology research handbook: A guide for graduate students and research assistants* (pp. 167–176). Thousand Oaks, CA: Sage.

Dunn, D. S. (1999). *The practical researcher: A student guide to conducting psychological research.* New York: McGraw-Hill.

Leong, F. T. L., & Austin, J. T. (Eds.). (1996). *The psychology research handbook: A guide for graduate students and research assistants.* Thousand Oaks, CA: Sage.

Newton, R. R., & Rudestam, K. E. (1999). *Your statistical consultant: Answers to your data analysis questions.* Thousand Oaks, CA: Sage.

Smith, P. C., Budzeika, K. A., Edwards, N. A., Johnson, S. M., & Bearse, L. N. (1986). Guidelines for clean data: Detection of common mistakes. *Journal of Applied Psychology, 71,* 457–460.

ANSWERS TO ODD-NUMBERED END-OF-CHAPTER PROBLEMS

As you compare your answers to those provided here, please keep in mind that different statistics require differing amounts of calculation in order to determine a solution. When performing a calculation with multiple stages, it is entirely possible that you will round numerical answers to the nearest decimal place each step of the way. Despite the conventions presented in chapter 1, data analysts, too, round their answers in various ways, depending on the circumstance. Similarly, different calculators round numbers to several places or only a few behind a decimal point—it all depends on the designer's whims. The upshot of all this rounding error is that your answer to a given question may not match what is shown here. Should you be worried that you did something wrong? No, not unless the difference between the two answers is large, in which case you should verify that your calculations and math are correct. If the difference is small, it is entirely acceptable and no doubt due to rounding error.

Chapter 1

1. **What is a statistic?** A statistic is a number representing some piece of information.

Can data analysis differ from statistical analysis? Why, or why not? Yes, they can differ. Statistical analysis refers to working through the necessary calculations to identify relationships within quantitative results, while data analysis allows for the possibility that nonquantitative information will also be of interest.

3. **How do variables differ from constants? Give an example of each.** A variable is any measurement value that can change from one measurement to the next, while a constant remains the same from measurement to measurement. Height and weight are variables (from individual to individual). The temperature at which water freezes is a constant (under the same conditions each time).

5. **Why are mathematics and statistics different disciplines?** Mathematics is the discipline concerned with the analysis of logical relationships among quantity and volume. Statistics, while it uses mathematical calculations, is the discipline concerned with the analysis of relationships among data, inferences that can be drawn from these relationships, and the rules by which data are collected.

What makes some mathematical operations statistical? When a mathematical operation results in a numerical answer that helps us research or understand an empirical fact, then it is statistical.

7. **What are empirical data?** Empirical data are measurements assigned to any observation in an experiment or from experience.

9. **Define inductive and deductive reasoning, and then give an example of each process.** Inductive reasoning involves arriving at a general conclusion based on the observations from several specific events of a similar

nature. Example: I notice that moderate increases in anxiety, hunger, or thirst lead to better performance on a repetitious task, and I conclude that increases in arousal lead to increases in performance.

Deductive reasoning involves using more general knowledge to draw conclusions (make predictions) about specific instances. If I know moderate arousal improves performance and that mild electrical shock is arousing, I might predict (conclude) that mild electrical shock during the performance of a task requiring that a subject cross out all the vowels in a page of text would improve the subject's performance.

11. **Define random sampling.** Random sampling involves selecting a sample from a population in such a way that all members of the population have an equal chance of being selected in the sample.

13. **Can inferential statistics prove without any doubt that a given sample is from some particular population? Why or why not?** No. Any sample, however large and representative, may contain unknown biases due to variables that may have gone unnoticed in the selection of the sample.

15. **Identify the upper and lower true limits for the following:**

    a. 2049.5 and 2050.5 pounds

    b. 58.295 and 58.305 minutes

    c. 2.5 and 3.5 inches

    d. Since this is a discrete rather than a continuous distribution, the score of 70 has no other limits. Were this value the mean of the test scores for an entire class, however, 69.5 and 70.5 would be the true limits.

17. **Why is writing relevant to statistics and data analysis?** Data and their interpretation are of little use to a field of study unless they are publicly reported. Thus, writing is, in some sense, as (or perhaps more) important as the statistical procedures used.
How can good, clear writing help investigators with their research? Clear, concise, and accurate presentation of the data, statistical results, and their interpretation eliminates misunderstandings and makes it easier for other scientists to attempt to replicate and extend the results.

19. **Name and define the four basic symbols.** X and Y are symbols that represent variables (usually scores or measurements); N refers to the total number of observations or values in a sample or population, and Σ refers to the algebraic process of addition and requests that the following values be added together.

21. **Solve the following equations:**

    a. $Y = (7 + 2)^2 - \sqrt{25}$

    $\quad = (9)^2 - 5$

    $\quad = 81 - 5 = 76$

    b. $X = (10)^3 + (12 - 5) \times 4$

    $\quad = 1000 + (7) \times 4$

    $\quad = 1000 + 28 = 1028$

    c. $Y = \sqrt{10} - (-15 + 10)^2$

    $\quad = 3.16 - (-5)^2$

    $\quad = 3.16 - (25)$

    $\quad = -21.84$

    d. $X = 8 \times 2 + (10 + 12)^2$

    $\quad = 16 + 484 = 500$

23. **Using the following data sets, solve the expressions:**

X	Y	
4	7	$\Sigma X = 4 + 2 + 2 + 3 + 1 + 5 = 17$
2	2	$\Sigma Y = 7 + 2 + 4 + 4 + 4 + 1 = 22$
2	4	$\Sigma XY = 4(7) + 2(2) + 2(4) + 3(4) + 1(4) + 5(1) = 61$

3	4	$(\sum X)(\sum Y) = 17(22) = 374$
1	4	$\sum X^2 = 16 + 4 + 4 + 9 + 1 + 25 = 59$
5	1	$\sum Y^2 = 49 + 4 + 16 + 16 + 16 + 1 = 102$

25. **What is "statisticophobia"? How can it be overcome?** "Statisticophobia" is fear of statistics, and it can be overcome by realizing that you are not alone in your fears. Your anxiety is probably about mathematics and *not* statistics, and it anticipates difficulties not yet faced which may never materialize.

Chapter 2

1. **Describe the steps comprising the research loop of experimentation.**
   1. Observe an interesting phenomenon or uncover a previously untested theoretical principle.
   2. Develop a testable (operationalizeable) hypothesis.
   3. Collect data bearing on the hypothesis.
   4. Analyze the data and interpret the results.
   5. Report or share results and obtain feedback.
   6. Return to step 1.

Does it differ from the scientific method introduced in chapter 1? No, it is the practical application of the scientific method.
How does the research loop help investigators do research? It helps advance scientific knowledge, ensures that established findings are reexamined in the light of new findings by replication and extension of previous results.

3. **What are replication studies and why are they scientifically useful?** A replication study repeats, or re-does, a previous investigation to determine if the same results can be obtained on a second occasion. They are necessary to establish that a new finding can be obtained by other investigators and by the same investigator on different occasions. They are used to determine the reliability of a novel finding.
How does a conceptual (systematic) replication study differ from a standard replication? A conceptual (systematic) replication extends the new finding beyond the limits of the original experiment. Some aspects of the systematic replication are kept the same and some aspects are chosen to vary from the original study. A systematic replication may extend the range of the same variables or look at the effects of new independent variables in interaction with the original variables.

5. **In terms of scientific utility and purpose, how does random assignment differ from random selection?** Random selection requires that every element in the population has an equal chance of being selected in the sample. That is not always practical or possible. Instead, most social science researchers use random assignment. Individuals who come to participate in an experiment are randomly assigned (i.e., without bias) to one of however many different conditions there are in the experiment.

7. **Explain the difference between systematic random sampling and stratified random sampling.** In systematic random sampling the researcher lists the potential participants in a study according to some order (i.e., alphabetically, by telephone number, etc.) and then selects every *n*th person on the list to obtain their sample. In stratified random sampling, the researcher selects the sample randomly from subgroups of the population that are represented in different proportions (i.e., ethnicity, gender, year in school).
How are these sampling techniques used? Systematic random sampling is used in circumstances where simple random sampling is too expensive or time-consuming (i.e., choosing from the phone book at random), while stratified sampling is used when subgroups differ in their representation in a population and the researcher does not wish to oversample any of the subgroups.
Create a hypothetical example to illustrate each one.

   Systematic random sample: Have all the students in Introductory Psychology listed by social security number (highest to lowest) and select every 20th student to participate in your study.

   Stratified random sample: In an industry in which 60% of the employees are male and 40% female, a stratified sample of 100 employees would have 60 males and 40 females.

9. **Define sampling error.** Sampling error is the difference between a sample value and the population parameter.
Why do researchers need to be concerned about it? The size of the sampling error has much to do with the accuracy of the generalization from samples to populations. The smaller the sampling error, the more accurate the generalization.

Is sampling error common or rare in research? Why? Sampling error is common in research because, however careful the researcher is, there is always some nonrepresentativeness in all samples and, therefore, some sampling error.

11.   **Define the term independent variable and provide a concrete example of one.** An independent variable is that variable manipulated (intentionally changed in a programmatic fashion) by the experimenter to determine the effect that it will have. An example would be manipulating the type of activity between a learning session and a recall session. One group might spend the interval doing active rehearsal of the material, while another group might simply wait quietly, while a third might be asked to do a series of arithmetic problems.
How are independent variables used in research? Independent variables are manipulated (present in some groups, not in others) to directly test the investigator's experimental hypothesis. At a minimum there must be *at least* two levels (amounts, types) of the independent variable to have the study qualify as an experiment.

13.   **Define the term dependent measure (or variable) and provide a concrete example of one.** A dependent variable is the one measured by the experimenter to assess the *effects* of the independent variable. In problem 11, for example, the dependent variable might be the number of items recalled from a list under the different levels of the independent variable.
How are dependent variables used in research? Dependent variables are used to detect differences between experimental and control conditions.

15.   **Create a hypothetical experiment. Describe the randomizing procedure(s) you would use, as well as the hypothesis, the independent variable(s), and the dependent variables(s). What do you predict will happen in the experiment? Why?** The experiment will measure the effects of mood state during learning on recall. The independent variable is mood state, either happy or sad. Mood state is induced before learning by having the subjects recall a happy moment or a sad moment in their recent experience. Subjects will be 30 college sophomores randomly assigned to one of the two states upon showing up for the experiment. Subjects will learn a serial anticipation list of 30 five-letter words (English) of moderate familiarity to a criterion of one complete correct repetition. A 15-minute interval will follow during which all subjects will spend the time adding columns of five-digit numbers. Following the interval, subjects will be asked to write down as many of the words as they remember. The number of items recalled will be recorded.

The independent variable is mood state: happy versus sad.

The dependent variable is number of items recalled.

I predict the happy mood group will recall more items. Learning should be better (and therefore recall) if you are in a good mood than if you are in a bad mood.

17.   **Why does good research in the behavioral sciences generate more questions than it answers?** The present state of knowledge in the behavioral sciences, and the character of the research issues, are such that no one, definitive (universally true) answer can result from a single experiment. Thus, while good research answers some questions, it also points to those areas of study in which answers are still lacking and those areas where what we know requires further refinement to clarify the nature of the causal factors.

19.   **What is a descriptive definition and how does it differ from an operational definition?** Descriptive definitions are abstract, conceptual descriptions of a relationship involving variables. An operational definition focuses on concrete and testable ways of dealing with the relationship that are consistent with the nature of the original hypothesis.

21.   **Write operational definitions for each of the following variables:**
   a.   Helping can be defined as the response of participating with others in solving a problem.
   b.   Fear can be defined as the reduction in performance of an activity in the presence of a stimulus associated with an aversive event.
   c.   Procrastination can be defined as failing to start a task until nearing a deadline for completion.
   d.   Tardiness can be defined as arriving after the time for an appointment.
   e.   Happiness can be defined as a high score on a mood assessment test.
   f.   Attraction can be defined as increased selection of a particular individual as a dance partner.
   g.   Factual recall can be defined as a score on a test of historical facts.

23.   **What is reliability and why is it important when measuring variables?** Reliability is consistency in observed events in commonsense terms. In more scientific terms, reliability is stability across time in some measurement. Reliable measures tend to yield less variation in scores than unreliable measures (less measurement error), leading to less sampling error.

Create an example to illustrate reliability. If my scores on the SAT the three times I took it were 1050, 1070, and 1060, my performance would be more reliable than if they had been 1050, 970, and 1160.

25.   **What is construct validity?** Construct validity expresses the degree of fit between the operational definition of a construct and the actual meaning and nature of the construct.
Why is it important? It is important that we know that our measure of "something" accurately reflects what it is, so that we use the measure (and, therefore, the construct) effectively in practice and theory development.
Provide a hypothetical example of construct validity. Scores on the Beck Depression Inventory (BDI) are an operational measure of the construct "depression." To the extent that high scores are obtained by people who also report being sad and depressed and low scores are obtained by people who do not report being sad and depressed, the BDI has construct validity.

27.   **Define convergent validity and discriminant validity.** Convergent validity demonstrates that new measures of a construct are closely related to existing measures that were previously validated. Discriminant validity indicates that a new measure of one construct is unrelated (or poorly related) to other constructs.
Are these concepts related? Yes, they are complementary. Convergent validity supports the use of a new measure by showing its relationship to established measures of a construct, while discriminant validity shows that the measure does not relate to other, possibly conflicting, constructs. Thus, the new measure is shown to measure what it is supposed to, and nothing else.
Illustrate, using examples, how these two types of validity are used in research. Suppose that I wished to measure the intensity of felt physical discomfort (pain) by having participants adjust a dial to a number between 1 and 100. To demonstrate convergent validity I would then vary the intensity of physical discomfort for participants and have them set the dial appropriately. I would then determine if these measures were similar to other established valid measures of physical discomfort (e.g., McGill Pain Inventory, Visual Analog Scale). If they were, I would have demonstrated convergent validity. If I now relate the dial scores to other valid measures of psychological discomfort (i.e., depression, sadness, grief) and found no evidence of relationship, I would have demonstrated discriminant validity.

29.   **What is external validity?** External validity is reflected in the observation that findings in one study may generalize to other people, in other places, at other times. In other words be the same in a variety of similar circumstances.
Why is it important in research? The "outside" implications of research may be of considerable concern to practitioners, and to society, but has little importance in the advancement of theory and knowledge within the science of psychology. However, it is of considerable importance in research directed at the solution to "real-world" and applied problems.

31.   **What are the three categories of research design? Describe the strengths and weaknesses of each one.**
 a.   Correlational research

   Strengths
   1.   Effective in discovering relationships or associations to be used in prediction.
   2.   Effective in identifying variables that might be used in other research designs.

   Weaknesses
   1.   Yields no information about any causal connection between the related variables.
   2.   Does not use random assignment to the variables and thus may be comparing groups which differ in more ways than are being measured.

 b.   Experimental research

   Strengths
   1.   Clarifies causal factors by isolating the effects of the independent variable.
   2.   Ensures group equivalence before the experiment.
   3.   Can control for extraneous variables that complicate interpretation of data.

   Weaknesses
   1.   Subject to confounding of other variables
   2.   Artificial and may not generalize well to nonexperimental settings.

 c.   Quasi-experimental research

   Strengths
   1.   Useful in examining situations that do not lend themselves to control and randomization (i.e., gender differences).
   2.   Useful in providing some information in more natural settings.

Weaknesses
1. Random assignment to different conditions is not usually possible.
2. Control groups are not usually available.

33. **Define the concept of correlation. Create hypothetical examples to illustrate a positive, a negative, and a zero correlation.** A correlation expresses the relationship (tendency to covary) between two or more variables. The relationship may be positive (as one variable increases, so do the others) as in the relationship between number of calories consumed and weight gain (and loss). The correlation may be negative (as one variable increases, the other decreases) as in the relationship between mortgage interest rates and number of purchases of homes. No relationship may exist (a zero correlation) when, for instance, you measure the numbers of hairs on the head and relate that to grade point average in college.

35. **What is a confounded variable in an experiment?** A confounded variable is some uncontrolled variable that varies systematically with the variation in the independent variable.
Why does it prove problematic for understanding causality? If a confounded variable is present, the outcome of the experiment cannot be clearly attributed to the causal effects of the variations in the independent variable. The outcome may have been due to the uncontrolled systematic variation in the confound (or some interaction). Failure to clearly attribute the causal action to the independent variable defeats the purpose of the experimental method.

37. **What is a random numbers table? How would a researcher use one in her work?** A random numbers table is a list of values from 0 to 9 that is generated so that each number occurs equally in a patternless, unbiased sequence.
A researcher would use one in his/her work to sample a smaller portion of a large population. If a researcher had 30 people and only wanted to sample half of them due to time and/or financial reasons, he/she can use a random numbers table to select 15 people. First, assign each person a number from 1 to 30. Start the random assignment anywhere in Table 2.5 (e.g. row 40), and read across every two numbers. In this example, one would start with 98, 08, 62, 48, 26, etc. Since there isn't a person who is assigned 98, go on to the next number, 08. There is a person who is 8, so that person is a member of your sample group. Continue to go across the rows until there are 15 people in the sample.

39. **Describe the procedure for using a random numbers table to perform random assignment for a basic two group experiment.** If a researcher is performing an experiement requiring two groups, he/she can use the procedure as in Problem 37 for the first experiment group and all the remaining people can be in the second group. Example: if there are 40 people, assign each person a number from 1 to 40. Start from anywhere on the table. Read every two numbers going across or down. If the number falls between 1 and 40, the person who is assigned that number goes in your first group, e.g. the control group.Continue this method until 20 people have been chosen. The remaining 20 people can be in the second group, e.g. the treatment group.

Chapter 3

1. Relative frequency distribution

X	f	p	%
6	1	.05	5
5	2	.10	10
4	2	.10	10
3	6	.30	30
2	5	.25	25
1	4	.20	20
Total	20	1.00	100

3. Relative frequency distribution

X	f	p	%
16	1	.04	4
15	3	.12	12
14	1	.04	4
13	6	.24	24
12	5	.20	20
11	5	.20	20
10	4	.16	16
Total	25	1.00	100

5.   Frequency histogram and polygon

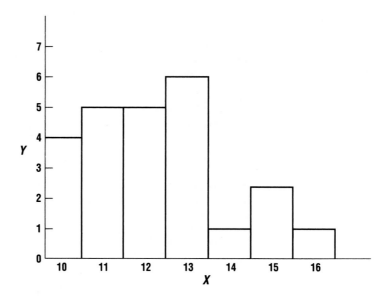

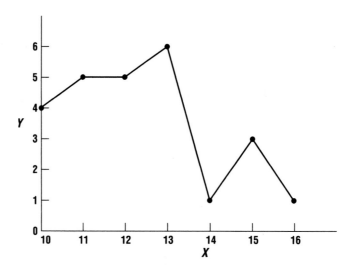

7.   a. Frequency distribution

X	f	p	%
10	1	.056	5.6
9	3	.167	16.7
8	4	.222	22.2
7	2	.111	11.1
6	1	.056	5.6
5	2	.111	11.1
4	0	.000	0.0
3	4	.222	22.2
2	1	.056	5.6
1	0	.000	0.0
Total	18	1.00	100

b.   **Histogram**

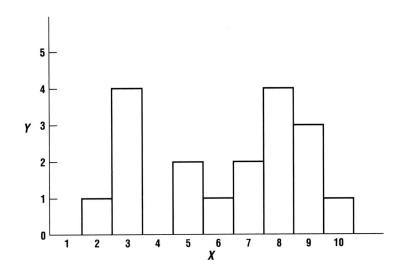

c.   **If the usual score on this quiz is a 6, how would you describe the performance of the students on this quiz?** Better than usual.

9.   a. $N = 31$

   b. $\sum f = 31$

   c. $\sum X = 5(10) + 7(4) + 3(3) + 5(2) + 1(6) = 103$

11.   Frequency polygon

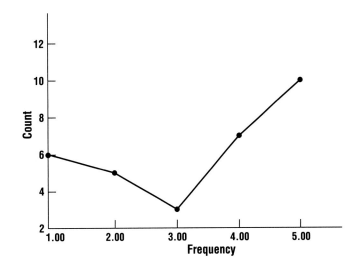

13. Place the data into a grouped frequency distribution using:

   a. An interval width of 2

Class Interval	Tally	Frequency
30–31	//	2
28–29	///	3
26–27	//	2
24–25	//	2
22–23	//	2
20–21	//	2
18–19	///	3
16–17	////	4
14–15	/	1
12–13	///	3
10–11	///	3
8–9	//	2
6–7	/	1
		30

   b. An interval width of 5

Class Interval	Tally	Frequency
26–30	////\//	7
21–25	////	4
16–20	////\////	9
11–15	////\	5
6–10	////\	5
		30

15. Draw a histogram (using true limits) when:

   a. The interval width is 2

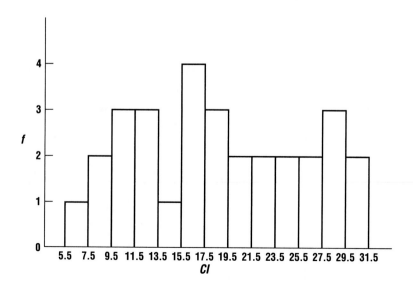

b.   The interval width is 5

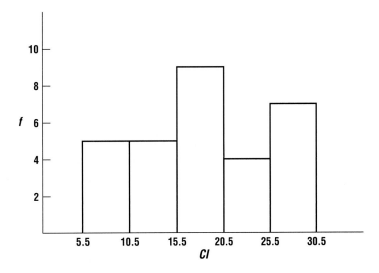

17.   **Describe some of the ways that a graph can misrepresent data.**

1.   If the complete range of data is not included for comparison.

2.   Exaggerate or minimize the differences in the data by manipulating the scales on one or more axis.

3.   Do not have clear labels on all parts of the graph.

What should a critical researcher or viewer do to verify that a graph's data are presented accurately? The critical researcher should be skeptical and check to see that there is no extraneous information, that all labels are clear and understandable, and that the title is clear and accurate.

19.   **What is exploratory data analysis (EDA)?** Exploratory data analysis is the process used to gain an overall impression of what the data are about.

Why do researchers find it useful? EDA provides a quick organizational structure to the data, often providing a fresh look at the data and aiding in planning further analysis.

21.   **Using the data from problem 20, construct a stem and leaf diagram using units of 5.**

Stem	Leaf
2*	0 2 3
2.	7 9
3*	0 1 1 2 3 5
3.	
4*	1 2 3 4 5
4.	8
5*	2
5.	6
6*	3 5 5
6.	7
7*	0 1 2 2
7.	6 7 9 9
8*	0 1 3
8.	9

23.   **Using the following table of data, add a column for cumulative frequency (cf) and one for cumulative percentage ($c\%$)**

X	f	cf	c%
10	8	54	100
9	5	46	85.2
8	0	41	75.9

X	f	cf	c%
7	4	41	75.9
6	9	37	68.5
5	6	28	51.8
4	8	22	40.7
3	5	14	25.9
2	3	9	16.7
1	6	6	11.1

25. Examine this data table and then answer the questions that follow:

a. What is the percentile rank for a score of 13 (i.e., $X = 13$)?

$$PR = \frac{8 + \left[\frac{13 - 11.5}{3}\right]8}{26} \times 100 = 46.15 \cong \text{46th percentile}$$

b. What score (X) corresponds to the 65th percentile?

$$X_{65} = 14.5 + \frac{3(16.9 - 16)}{7} = 14.54$$

c. What is the median score (i.e., 50th percentile)?

$$X_{50} = 11.5 + \frac{3(13 - 8)}{8} = 13.38$$

27. Put the percentile results into words.

a. A score of 13 indicates a mastery above the median at about the 46th percentile. This result indicates that about 54% of the students had better mastery.

b. About 35% of the students had mastery above a score of 15, while 65% had scores at or below a score of approximately 15.

c. Fifty percent of the students showed mastery at or below a score of approximately 13 and 50% had greater mastery scores.

Chapter 4

1. Define the term "central tendency." The central tendency is a statistical measure that locates the center of a distribution around which most scores cluster. It identifies the most representative value of that distribution.
Explain the concept's utility for statistics and data analysis, as well as research in the behavioral sciences. It is useful in defining the score value that is most representative of the distribution, providing a point of comparison for individual scores in terms of position relative to the central tendency.

3. Would reporting the mean for any of the four distributions from problem 2 pose a problem for an investigator? Why? Yes, it would. Distribution c in problem 2 has one very extreme score (84), which will make the mean less representative of the central tendency of the scores. Unlike the other measures of central tendency, the mean is unduly influenced by extreme scores.

5. What measure of central tendency should you report? Why? The median would be the best representative of the central tendency when a distribution has one or two scores very far from the main group of scores. The mean will be overly influenced by the extreme score, and there may well be several modes since most scores are relatively close to each other.

7. Calculate a weighted mean:

$$\overline{X} = \frac{32(27.5) + 48(23.0) + 12(25)}{92}$$

$$= \frac{2,284}{92} = 24.83$$

9. **Which measure of central tendency is best?** If your measure is number of months receiving welfare, it would be best to use the median, since it would be less influenced by the measures above six months than the mean. On the other hand, if the researcher is simply categorizing the observations as above or below six months, then the mode would be more appropriate.

11. **Create examples of data where the appropriate measure of central tendency is:**
    a. The mean: 15, 19, 12, 21, 11, 19, 14, a more or less symmetrical distribution with no outliers
    b. The median: 15, 19, 12, 21, 11, 19, 14, 43, 37, a distribution with two outliers
    c. The mode: 15, 19, 21, 19, 12, 19, 11, 21, 19, a distribution in which one or more values is repeated

13. **Which measure of central tendency is most affected by skew in a distribution? Which one is least affected? Why?** The mean is most affected by skew since it is responsive to extreme scores (in the extended tail of the skewed distribution). The mode is least affected by skew since no increase in the length of the tail of the distribution will affect the number of occurrences of the most frequent score, which will be found where scores cluster.

15. **Calculate the range for distributions a to d in problem 2.**
    a. $21 - 6 = 15$
    b. $8 - 1 = 7$
    c. $84 - 16 = 68$
    d. $16 - 9 = 7$

17. **Calculate the SS for the distribution:** $SS = 50.86$

19. **Assume the distribution in problem 17 represents a population. Calculate μ, σ^2, and σ.**

$$\mu = \frac{43}{7} = 6.14$$

$$\sigma^2 = \frac{SS}{N} = \frac{50.86}{7} = 7.27$$

$$\sigma = \sqrt{7.27} = 2.70$$

21. **Explain the difference between so-called "biased" and "unbiased" estimates of population parameters. Which type of estimate is used in what sort of situation?** A biased estimator underestimates the parameter of the population, while an unbiased estimator yields a value closer to the parameter than any other. While it is always more accurate to use an unbiased estimator of a population parameter, in large ($N > 100$ or 200) samples the difference between the two is very small. With small samples, however, it is best to use an unbiased estimator of a parameter.

23.

	Biased		Unbiased	
	Variance	St. Dev.	Variance	St. Dev.
a.	21.64	4.65	23.61	4.86
b.	5.31	2.30	5.61	2.37
c.	411.23	20.29	470.55	21.69
d.	4.22	2.05	4.61	2.15

25. **Explain the role variability plays in both homogeneous and heterogeneous distributions.** The more heterogeneous the distribution, generally the greater the variability among the values since heterogeneity implies many different values. On the other hand, variability in a homogenous distribution should be relatively small since the number of different score values will be fewer.

27. **Between what two scores do half of the observations fall in the distributions in problem 2?**
    a. 8.75 and 16.25
    b. 0.875 and 5.125
    c. 25.5 and 39.5
    d. 11.5 and 14.5

29. **What is the relationship between sample size and variability?** As sample size increases, generally variability decreases and becomes more representative of the variability in the population.

Is it better to have data from a larger or a smaller sample? Why? Generally, it is better to have data from larger samples. They tend to be more representative (less biased) of the population's characteristics in terms of number and types of subsamples that exist, and the general shape of the population distribution.

31. **Calculate the unbiased estimates of the variance and standard deviation for the two samples in problem 30.**

    a. Sample X

    $$\overline{X} = \frac{74}{8} = 9.25$$

    $$\sigma^2 = 26.5$$

    $$\sigma = 5.15$$

    b. Sample Y

    $$\overline{Y} = \frac{176}{8} = 22$$

    $$\sigma^2 = 148$$

    $$\sigma = 12.17$$

33. **Based on the decision tree for choosing a measure of central tendency:**

    a. Median

    b. Median

    c. Mode

    d. Mean

35. **Based on the decision tree for choosing to calculate sample statistics, unbiased estimates of population parameters, or actual population parameters:**

    a. Unbiased estimates of the population parameters

    b. Statistics

    c. Parameters

Chapter 5

1. **What are the properties of the z distribution?** The z distribution has a mean of zero and a standard deviation equal to 1 and retains the shape of the original distribution faithfully.

Why are z scores useful? The z score is useful in making comparisons of performance between different individuals on the same measure or within the individual across different measures.

3. **What are the properties of the standard normal distribution?** The standard normal distribution is a bell-shaped, bilaterally symmetrical (if folded in half at the mean, the two halves exactly coincide) distribution with tails that gradually approach the baseline (asymptotic). The mean = median = mode = 0.

Why is the normal curve useful for statisticians and behavioral scientists? The normal curve is approximated by the frequency distributions of a wide variety of physical (e. g., height, weight, etc.) and behavioral (e. g., IQ scores, introversion/extroversion scores, etc.) measures. The well-known characteristics of the normal distribution can be used to describe, and make inferences about, any phenomena that yield a frequency distribution that tends toward a normal distribution in shape.

5. **Why do researchers standardize data?** Researchers standardize data so that comparisons about relative position of individuals on different measures can be made meaningfully.

What is a standard score? A standard score is a raw score expressed as a distance from the mean of a distribution in terms of numbers of standard deviations.

Why are z scores and T scores standard scores? Z scores and T scores are standard scores because they both use the standard deviation as the unit of measurement for transforming a raw score.

7. **What is probability?** Probability is the likelihood of the occurrence of a particular event from among all possible related events.

How does probability conceptually relate to z scores and the normal distribution? The z score tells you how many standard deviations a particular value is from the mean of a normal distribution. The area between the mean and that z score, or between any two z scores, represents the proportion of the time (probability) a value will be randomly sampled from within that area.

9. $z_{54} = \dfrac{54 - 78}{12.5} = -1.92$

$z_{63.5} = \dfrac{63.5 - 78}{12.5} = -1.16$

$z_{66.0} = \dfrac{66 - 78}{12.5} = -0.96$

$z_{77.0} = \dfrac{77 - 78}{12.5} = -0.08$

$z_{78.5} = \dfrac{78.5 - 78}{12.5} = 0.04$

$z_{81.0} = \dfrac{81 - 78}{12.5} = 0.24$

11.

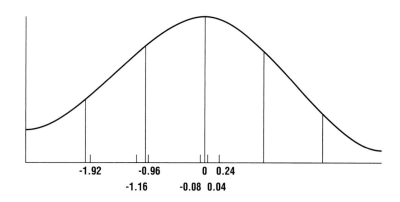

-1.92   -0.96   0   0.24
  -1.16   -0.08 0.04

$A_{-1.92} = 47.26\%$
$A_{-1.16} = 37.70\%$
$A_{-0.96} = 33.15\%$
$A_{-0.08} = 3.19\%$
$A_{0.04} = 1.60\%$
$A_{0.24} = 9.48\%$

13. $Z_{-3.01} = 35 + 3.5(-3.01) = 24.465 \sim 24$
$Z_{-2.56} = 35 + 3.5(-2.56) = 26.04 \sim 26$
$Z_{-1.21} = 35 + 3.5(-1.21) = 30.765 \sim 31$
$Z_{1.40} = 35 + 3.5(1.40) = 39.9 \sim 40$
$Z_{2.77} = 35 + 3.5(2.77) = 44.695 \sim 45$
$Z_{3.00} = 35 + 3.5(3.0) = 45.5 \sim 46$

15. $Z_{85} = -1.00 \quad A_{-1.00} = 34.13\%$
$Z_{88} = -0.80 \quad A_{-0.80} = 28.81\%$
$Z_{98} = -0.13 \quad A_{-0.13} = 5.17\%$
$Z_{112} = 0.80 \quad A_{0.80} = 28.81\%$
$Z_{120} = 1.33 \quad A_{1.33} = 40.82\%$
$Z_{133} = 2.20 \quad A_{2.20} = 48.61\%$

17. $Z_{38.0} = -1.71$ $A_{-1.71} = 45.64\%$

$Z_{39.5} = -1.50$ $A_{-1.50} = 43.32\%$

$Z_{45.0} = -0.71$ $A_{-0.71} = 26.11\%$

$Z_{52.0} = 0.29$ $A_{0.29} = 11.41\%$

$Z_{57.0} = 1.00$ $A_{1.00} = 34.13\%$

$Z_{66.6} = 2.37$ $A_{2.37} = 49.11\%$

19. $A_{-1.92} = 2.74\%$

$A_{-1.16} = 12.30\%$

$A_{-0.96} = 16.85\%$

$A_{-0.08} = 46.81\%$

$A_{0.04} = 48.40\%$

$A_{0.24} = 40.52\%$

21. $A_{-1.00} = 15.87\%$

$A_{-0.80} = 21.19\%$

$A_{-0.13} = 44.83\%$

$A_{0.80} = 21.19\%$

$A_{1.33} = 9.18\%$

$A_{2.20} = 1.39\%$

23. $Z_{27} = -2.29$ $PR_{-2.29} = 1.1$ or 1st percentile

$Z_{29.5} = -1.57$ $PR_{-1.57} = 5.82$ or $\cong$6th percentile

$Z_{34.3} = -0.20$ $PR_{-0.20} = 42.07$ or 42nd percentile

$Z_{35} = 0$ $PR_0 = 50$th percentile

$Z_{45} \cong 2.86$ $PR_{2.86} = 99.79$ or $\cong$100th percentile

$Z_{47.5} \cong 3.57$ $PR_{3.57} = 99.98$ or $\cong$100th percentile

25. **Are z scores normally distributed? Why, or why not?** It depends on the shape of the original distribution. Z scores are distributed as the original scores; if the original scores are normally distributed, so are the z scores. If the original distribution is nonnormal, then so is the z distribution.

27. a. $Z_{\text{verbal ability}} = .69$

$Z_{\text{visualization}} = -0.50$

$Z_{\text{memory}} = 1.13$

$Z_{\text{spatial relations}} = 0.69$

b.   The student was relatively high on memory and relatively low on visualization.

c.   The student's percentile rank on verbal ability was 75.5 or approximately 76, and 24.5 or approximately 25% scored above the student on spatial relations.

29. $T_{-1.12} = 64$

$T_{-2.3} = 52$

$T_{1.18} = 87$

$T_{2.67} = 102$

$T_{3.58} = 111$

31. a.   Convert the raw score to a z score

b. $z = \dfrac{(X - \mu)}{\sigma}$

c.   Percentile rank of $1.76 = 96.1\%$

Chapter 6

1. **Conceptually, correlation assesses the association between two variables. Why isn't the association causal in nature?** Causality cannot be inferred from a correlation because correlations are bidirectional in nature. It is as reasonable to say X is correlated with Y as it is to say Y is correlated with X. Causality is an

unidirectional relationship (A always leads to B). Also, a third factor, Z, may cause X and Y. This unknown factor makes the relationship between X and Y spurious.

3. **Describe the possible directions of relationships between two variables in correlational analyses. What role do positive (+) and negative (−) play?** There are two possible directions of the relationship between two variables. X may increase as Y increases, which is a positive (+) relationship, or X may increase while Y decreases (or vice versa), which is described as a negative (−) or inverse relationship.

5. **Describe a scatter plot showing a positive correlation, a negative correlation, and a zero correlation.** In a positive correlation the pattern of dots tends to start on the lower left and move up and to the right. In a negative (inverse) relationship the pattern of dots generally moves from upper left to lower right. In the case of a zero correlation there is no clear directional character to the scatter plot.

7. **In what way is the Pearson r related to z scores? What advantage does the z score provide to the Pearson r?** Since z scores standardize a raw score in relationship to the mean in standard deviation units, one can use the z scores of an individual on two (or more) variables to determine if their relative positions are related by multiplying the z scores for each pair of raw scores (their covariation). The correlation is the average product of the pairs of z scores. All that we know of the logic and statistical character of the z score (i.e., comparability across different measures, relationship to the normal curve, etc.) may then be applied to correlations.

9. **Conceptually define the coefficients of determination and nondetermination. How do these coefficients aid researchers?** The coefficient of determination (r^2) is the proportion of the change in one variable which may be accounted for ("explained") by the corresponding change in the other variable. The coefficient of nondetermination ($1 - r^2$) is a measure of the proportion of change that cannot be accounted for ("unexplained") by such common (covariation or covariance) changes. The coefficients of determination and nondetermination help us understand the strength and predictive ability of a relationship to support our interpretation of experimental findings.

11. **Provide the coefficient of nondetermination corresponding to each of the r values shown in problem 8.**

$r = -.67 \quad\quad 1 - r^2 = .5511$ rounds off to .55

$r = +.98 \quad\quad 1 - r^2 = .0396$ rounds off to .04

$r = -.03 \quad\quad 1 - r^2 = .9991$ rounds off to 1.0

$r = +.25 \quad\quad 1 - r^2 = .9375$ rounds off to .94

$r = -.81 \quad\quad 1 - r^2 = .3439$ rounds off to .34

$r = +.79 \quad\quad 1 - r^2 = .3759$ rounds off to .38

$r = -.55 \quad\quad 1 - r^2 = .6975$ rounds off to .70

$r = +.37 \quad\quad 1 - r^2 = .8631$ rounds off to .86

13. **Examine the following set of data:**

a. **Draw a scatter plot for the X and Y variables and then describe the relationship, if any, between them.** There appears to be a low-to-moderate positive relationship between the two variables.

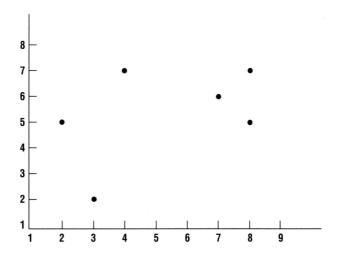

b. **Calculate a Pearson *r* between *X* and *Y*. Does the *r* fit the relationship you describe in a?** Yes. The indicated correlation is a +.458 indicating a moderate relationship.

c. **What are the coefficients of determination and nondetermination for these data?** Coefficient of determination = r^2 = .2097, which rounds off to .21

Coefficient of nondetermination = $1 - r^2$ = .7903, which rounds off to .79

15. **Using the following data, determine the nature of this relationship by calculating a Pearson *r* and then interpreting the result in words.** $r = -.634$. There is a strong negative relationship between stress and health ratings. This indicates that as stress scores increase, health ratings get lower (or vice versa).

17. **How is the Pearson *r* used to determine the reliability of a measure? What range of *r* values is appropriate for demonstrating reliability?** The Pearson *r* can be used to test reliability by correlating answers to questions by the same individuals on separate occasions (test-retest reliability), or by using odd-even or split-half correlations. In order to demonstrate reasonable reliability, the correlation should be +.70 or higher.

19. **How would you go about assessing the reliability of a new job stress measure?** I would develop a relatively brief (time is money in industrial settings) questionnaire rating stress levels on the job and give it to a representative sample (probably stratified by salary or job classification) of employees on two separate occasions and then calculate the test-retest correlation to determine reliability. If two testings are not feasible, I would use the item-total correlation as the measure of reliability since it is a brief questionnaire.

21. **Does the test appear to be reliable? Why, or why not?** No. The test-retest correlation was +.031, which indicates a very low reliability.

23. **Use the decision trees opening this chapter to answer the following questions:**

a. **A researcher wants to assess the correlation between temperature and rainfall. Which measure of association is appropriate?** Since these are both ratio measures, a Pearson *r* is the appropriate measure.

b. **A student wants to determine the correlation between his rankings of national league baseball teams and those of a friend. Which measure of association is appropriate?** Since these are ordinal rankings, calculate a Spearman's rho (r_S).

c. **An investigator discovers a correlation of +.75 between five pairs of test scores. Is this correlation apt to be reliable? Why?** No, it is not likely to be reliable because the sample size is very small.

d. **Before calculating a correlation between two variables, a student notices that one of them is dichotomous—the score for *X* is either "1" or "2," but *Y* has a relatively wide range of values. Should the student be concerned? Why?** Yes, the student should be concerned. It is not possible to obtain a correlation between a dichotomous and a continuous variable using the Pearson product moment correlation.

Chapter 7

1. **What is the nature of the relationship between correlation and regression?** Regression uses the degree of relationship contained in the correlation coefficient to predict the performance by an individual on one variable (usually denoted *Y*, or the "dependent" variable) from the known performance of another variable (usually denoted *X*, or the "independent" variable). Correlation is used to determine the slope of the regression line.

3. **Explain the relationship between a "best fitting" regression line and the "method of least squares."** The regression line, or line of best fit, is the line which makes the sum of the squared differences between the actual score on *Y* and the predicted score on *Y* the smallest. The line of best fit minimizes prediction error variance.

5. **What is residual variance and how is it related to the standard error of the estimate?** Residual variance is calculated based on the sum of the squared differences between actual and predicted scores divided by $N - 2$. Thus, it is a measure of errors of prediction.
Why are lower values for the standard error of the estimate more desirable than larger values? Lower values for the standard error of the estimate represent smaller deviations between actual and predicted scores. The lower the standard error of the estimate, the more accurate are our predictions.

7. **What does it mean when statisticians "partition" variation?** Partitioning variation means dividing variance mathematically into two or more components, which may be associated with known factors (i.e., "explained" variation) or unknown factors (i.e., "unexplained variation").
How and why is the variation around a regression line partitioned? The variation around a regression line may be partitioned by directly calculating the "explained" variation $[\sum (\hat{Y}^2 - \overline{Y})^2]$ and the "unexplained" variation $[\sum (\hat{Y} - Y)^2]$, or by using the coefficient of determination (r^2) as an estimate of "explained" variation and the

coefficient of nondetermination $(1 - r^2)$ as an estimate of "unexplained" variation. We calculate these values to determine the magnitude of error relative to r^2 to assess the accuracy of our predictions.

9.   A college athlete plays very well in a series of games, but his performance drops off late in the season. The team's coach explains the change in performance by noting that his star player is under a lot of pressure, as he must choose between professional sports or graduate school. Can you offer the coach a statistical explanation for the player's slump in performance? The statistical explanation for the drop in performance could be regression towards the mean. If the player's average true proficiency was somewhere between his performance early in the season and his later performance, the later performance could be expected to bring that season's performance numbers closer to his true average level.

11.   **Conceptually, how does multiple regression differ from linear regression?** Multiple regression is a way of looking at the relationship between several predictor variables and some dependent performance measure in the complex environment of the behavioral sciences. It is an extension of linear regression, which looks at a single predictor and response measure.

In what ways is multiple regression used? Multiple regression may be used to improve prediction by including several nonoverlapping predictors, or to further causal analysis by separating and exploring the unique contribution of each predictor (independent variable) to the prediction of the dependent variable (i.e., used in an exploratory analysis).

13.   **Sketch a graph showing the linear equation $Y = 5 + 4X$.**

X	Y
1	9
2	13
3	17
4	21

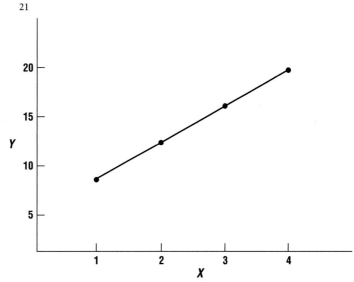

15.   **Using the equation $\hat{X} = 15 + .87Y$, calculate the predicted $\hat{X}$ when $Y = 2.8, 3.7, 4.5, 5.0,$ and 6.0.**

$$\hat{X} = 17.436 \cong 17.44$$

$$\hat{X} = 18.219 \cong 18.22$$

$$\hat{X} = 18.915 \cong 18.92$$

$$\hat{X} = 19.35$$

$$\hat{X} = 20.22$$

17. What percentage of the Y scores lie between $\pm 1s_{\text{est } Y}$ around any given $\hat{Y}$ value? What percentage of the Y scores lies between $\pm 3s_{\text{est } Y}$? Assuming that the errors are normally distributed around the predicted value, then .6826 will lie between $\pm 1s_{\text{est } Y}$ and .9917 will lie between $\pm 3s_{\text{est } Y}$.

19. Researchers believe that positive mood is related to work productivity. The following data were collected in an office:

Positive Mood	Productivity	
$\overline{X} = 15.5$	$\overline{Y} = 25$	$r = .66$
$s_X = 3.0$	$s_Y = 6.0$	$N = 50$

a. Determine the regression equation of Y on X for these data.

$a = 4.54$

$b = 1.32$

$\hat{Y} = 4.54 + 1.32X$

b. Sam's recorded mood is a 12. What is his projected productivity level?

$$\hat{Y} = 20.38 \cong 20$$

c. Andrea's productivity level is 33. What level of mood led to such a high level of productivity?

$$\hat{X} = 18.14 \cong 18$$

d. Calculate the standard error of the estimate for both X and Y.

$$s_{\text{est} Y} = 4.55$$

$$s_{\text{est} X} = 2.28$$

e. What percentage of total variation in productivity is accounted for by positive mood?

$$r^2 = .4356$$

Approximately 44% of the total variation in productivity is accounted for by positive mood.

21. Assume that each of the data sets in problem 20 is based on an N of 90. What is the value of the $s_{\text{est } Y}$ for each one? Which data set has the largest $s_{\text{est} Y}$? The smallest $s_{\text{est } Y}$?

a. $s_{\text{est } Y} = 3.63$
b. $s_{\text{est } Y} = 3.77$
c. $s_{\text{est } Y} = 1.01$
d. $s_{\text{est } Y} = 1.79$

Data set b has the largest $s_{\text{est} Y}$; data set c has the smallest.

23. A psychologist examines the link between a measure of depression (Y) and one for stress (X). Based on a random sample of students from a very large state university, the psychologist obtains the following data:

Stress Test	Depression Measure	
$\overline{X} = 22.5$	$\overline{Y} = 45.0$	$r = +.73$
$s_X = 2.0$	$s_Y = 4.5$	$N = 400$

a. If a student's stress score is 32, what is his or her depression score apt to be?

$$\hat{Y} = 60.60 \cong 61$$

b. A new student receives a 20 on the depression measure. What is her estimated score on the stress test?

$$\hat{X} \cong 14.39 \text{ or } 14$$

c. What percentage of the variation in the depression measure is not explained by scores on the stress test? The coefficient of nondetermination $(1 - r^2) = .4671$. Approximately 47% of the variation is unexplained.

25. **Is regression analysis appropriate?** No, it is not. Regression analysis is only appropriate if the variables correlate substantially.

27. **Is a regression analysis appropriate?** No, it is not. Regression analysis requires two scores from each participant, one on the "independent" variable and one on the "dependent" variable. Since in this problem two scores on each variable are not available for most subjects, regression analysis should be avoided.

Chapter 8

1. **What are some examples of the sort of probability judgments you make in daily life?** If I buy this car, it will run for a long time. If I study, I will get a better grade. If I ask my friend to lend me $5.00, she will.
Even if they are difficult to quantify, can they still be probability judgments? Why or why not? Yes, they can still be probability judgments because they are expressions of the likelihood of an event based on past life experiences with similar events.

3. **Steve is playing a slot machine in one of the major hotels in Las Vegas. His friend, Paul, tries to convince him to leave it and join other friends in the main casino. Steve refuses, noting that "I've spent 20 bucks on this thing so far—I've primed it. I know that I'm due to win soon!"** Assuming the usual type of programming, the machine is a random processor. Thus, the machine has no memory. It does not remember how much Steve has "invested." What comes up on one pull has no relationship to what comes up on any other pull. The machines *cannot* be primed.
Characterize the inherent flaws in Steve's reasoning. What do statisticians call this sort of thinking and behavior? Steve is committing the gambler's fallacy in assuming some kind of orderly relationship exists where it does not.

5. **When flipping a coin and obtaining a string of either "heads" or "tails," why do some people assume that they can accurately predict what the next flip will be?** They believe that runs of one type must be more likely to end on the next flip or two (another form of the gambler's fallacy) because extended runs are such a rare event.

7. **In your opinion, what does the quote from Stanislaw Lem mean about the role probability plays where human judgments are concerned?** What he means is that if the outcome is certain to occur, one does not need a formal method for making decisions. It is only if there is uncertainty about the outcome that one needs to have some rule-based method for choosing among alternatives.

9. **Using sampling without replacement, provide the probabilities listed in question 8.**

a. $\dfrac{1}{6}$

b. $\dfrac{2}{6}$ or $\dfrac{1}{3}$

c. $\dfrac{3}{6} \times \dfrac{29}{59} = \dfrac{870}{3,540} = 0.246$

d. $\dfrac{10}{60} \times \dfrac{20}{59} \times \dfrac{30}{58} = \dfrac{6,000}{205,320} = 0.029$

11. **Determine the following probabilities:** $p(X = 4)$; $p(X = 11)$; $p(X > 5)$; $p(X < 3)$; $p(X \geq 8)$; $p(X \leq 8)$.

$p(X = 4) = \dfrac{3}{53} = .057$

$p(X = 11) = \dfrac{10}{53} = .189$

$p(X > 5) = \dfrac{39}{53} = .736$

$p(X < 3) = 0$

$p(X \geq 8) = \dfrac{29}{53} = .547$

$p(X \leq 8) = \dfrac{35}{53} = .660$

13. A sack contains 13 black marbles, 16 white marbles, 4 pink marbles, and 8 pink and white marbles.

What is the probability of selecting a marble that is black? $p(\text{black}) = 13/41 = .317$

What is the probability of selecting a marble that is pink? $p(\text{pink}) = 4/41 = .098$

What is the probability of selecting a pink or a white marble? $p(\text{pink or white}) = 4/41 + 16/41 = 20/41 = .488$

What is the probability of selecting a marble that is pink and white? $p(\text{pink and white}) = 8/41 = .195$

15. Which of the following distributions of coin tosses is more likely to occur than any of the others? H–H–H–T–T–T or H–H–H–H–H–H or T–H–T–T–H–H? They are equally likely to occur.

17. Using the data provided in question 16, show how the multiplication rule for dependent events can be used to calculate the joint probability of being alone and not offering to help the confederate.

$$p(\text{alone and no help}) = p(\text{alone given no help}) \times p(\text{no help})$$

$$= \frac{8}{50} \times \frac{50}{86} = 0.093$$

19. A measure of romantic attraction has a population mean of 75 and a population standard deviation of 8.

What is the probability of obtaining a score between 76 and 82?

$$p(X: 76–82) = A_{82} - A_{76} = .3106 - .0478 = .2628$$

What is the probability of obtaining a score greater than or equal to 90?

$$p(X: \geq 90) = A_{\text{above } 90} = .0301$$

What is the probability of obtaining a score of less than 50?

$$p(X < 50) = A_{\text{below } 50} = .0009$$

21. A multiple-choice test has 100 questions, and four possible responses to each question. Only one out of each of the four responses is correct. If a respondent is just guessing, what is the probability of getting 48 questions correct by chance?

$$p(48 \text{ right by chance}) = A_{\text{above a } z} = 5.31 = .0000$$

23. A statistician calculates the probability that an event will occur to be $-.35$. How likely is it that this event will occur? It is impossible to get a probability value that is less than zero, so the probability of this event cannot be determined. Clearly the statistician did the problem incorrectly.

25. A student wants to calculate the likelihood that several events will occur but she does not know the number of possible observations favoring each event. Can she still calculate the probabilities? No, she cannot. It is not possible to calculate the probability of events if the total number of possible observations is unknown.

27. Which probability rule is appropriate for each of the following situations?

a. Events are conditional upon one another: calculate the conditional probability [e.g., $p(A \mid B)$].

b. Events occur in an independent sequence: use the multiplication rule for independent events.

c. Events are mutually exclusive: use the addition rule for mutually exclusive events [e.g., $p(A \text{ or } B) = p(A) + p(B)$].

d. Events are not mutually exclusive: use the addition rule for nonmutually exclusive events [e.g., $p(A \text{ or } B) = p(A) + p(B) - p(A \text{ and } B)$].

Chapter 9

1. What is *point estimation?* Point estimation uses a single sample statistic to estimate the corresponding population parameter.

Is *point estimation* different from *interval estimation?* How so? Yes, point estimation and interval estimation are different. While point estimation uses a single sample value to estimate a population parameter, interval estimation uses repeated samples from the same population to gain information about the variability among sample estimates.

What role do these two forms of estimation play in hypothesis testing? Point values of experimental effects can be used to determine if they differ from known population parameters. Interval estimates yield information about the accuracy of an estimate of the corresponding population parameter.

3.   **How do *frequency distributions* differ from *sampling distributions?*** A frequency distribution is based on individual scores and their frequency of occurrence, while a sampling distribution is based on statistics from repeated samples of a particular size. There is only one frequency distribution for a given set of observations, but there is a different sampling distribution for each different sample size.

5.   **If fixed, reasonably large sample sizes are repeatedly and randomly drawn from a population, what will the shape of the sampling distribution of means be like? Why?** The sampling distribution of means of samples of a reasonable size from a population will tend to be normally shaped. Most of the sample means will be close to each other and to the population mean. Only a relatively few sample means will deviate much from the population mean. This outcome pattern, according to the central limit theorem, yields an approximately normal distribution.

7.   **Why is the *law of large numbers* relevant to the *central limit theorem?*** Since the central limit theorem argues that as sample size increases, and the sampling distribution of means becomes more normal in shape, it is important to know that the law of large numbers implies that large sample sizes yield better estimates of the parameters than small sample sizes. Both laws stress the importance of large sample sizes.

9.   a. $\sigma_{\bar{X}} = \dfrac{20}{\sqrt{15}} = 5.16$

   b. $\sigma_{\bar{X}} = \dfrac{20}{\sqrt{40}} = 3.16$

   c. $\sigma_{\bar{X}} = \dfrac{20}{\sqrt{65}} = 2.48$

   d. $\sigma_{\bar{X}} = \dfrac{20}{\sqrt{80}} = 2.24$

   e. $\sigma_{\bar{X}} = \dfrac{20}{\sqrt{110}} = 1.91$

11. $CI_{80\%} = 56 \pm 1.6$

   $CI_{95\%} = 56 \pm -2.45$

   $CI_{99\%} = 56 \pm 3.22$

13.   **Name several of the components comprising a good hypothesis.** A good hypothesis is an operationally clear statement of how the independent and dependent variables are related. It is theory or experience based, and is testable and understandable.

15.   **Formulate H_0 and H_1 using a *directional test* and then a *nondirectional test.***
   Directional test:

   H_0:   At-risk readers will score at or below the population average after taking part in the program ($\mu_{\text{at risk}} \leq \mu_{\text{pop}}$).

   H_1:   At-risk readers will score above the population average after taking part in the program ($\mu_{\text{at risk}} > \mu_{\text{pop}}$).

   Nondirectional test:

   H_0:   At-risk readers will perform as the general population after taking part in the program ($\mu_{\text{at risk}} = \mu_{\text{pop}}$).

   H_1:   At-risk readers will not perform equally to the general population after taking part in the program ($\mu_{\text{at risk}} \neq \mu_{\text{pop}}$).

17.   **Statistical analysis is guided by the *null hypothesis* and not the *alternative hypothesis*—why is this so?** It is easier to prove a general (universal) statement false since that requires only one negative example. Proving the research or alternative hypothesis true requires that it be true in *all possible instances*. It is not possible, logically or practically, to observe *all* instances.

Why is it difficult to prove an *alternative or research hypothesis?* **How does this difficulty enhance the utility of the** *null hypothesis?* Since it is easier to find evidence that the null hypothesis is false, that is how science progresses, by attempting to falsify the null hypothesis. To the extent the null hypothesis is false, we can logically infer the alternative is true.

19. **Define the word** *significant,* **as well as its use, in statistical contexts.** The word significant means statistically reliable (likely to be repeatable) in the context of statistics. It is used to describe experimental outcomes which are rare or unusual if the null hypothesis is true.

21. .031, significant

    .040, significant

    .003, significant

    .076, marginally significant

    .051, significant

    .120, not significant

    .250, not significant

    .098, marginally significant

    .0001, significant

    .046, significant

23. **Explain the difference between** *one-tailed* **and** *two-tailed* **significance tests.** In a two-tailed test there are three possible outcomes: the observed statistic falls into the *upper* rejection region, the *lower* rejection region, or the retention region between the two. In a one-tailed test, there are only two possible outcomes: The observed statistic falls either into the rejection region or the retention region.

Is one test considered to be more statistically rigorous than the other? Why? In a sense, the two-tailed test is considered more rigorous because the critical values are farther into the tails of the distribution than for a one-tailed test of the same significance level. This makes it harder to reject the null hypothesis since the statistic must be farther into the tail as well.

Which test enables researchers to satisfy their curiosity regarding relationships among variables in a statistical analysis? The two-tailed test is more useful in exploring relationships regardless of the direction of outcome.

25. **In conceptual terms, what are** *degrees of freedom?* Conceptually, degrees of freedom represent the number of values in a sample that are free to vary when estimating a particular population parameter (usually one less than a sample's size). One is said to lose one degree of freedom for each parameter estimated.

More practically, how are *degrees of freedom* **used by data analysts?** Practically speaking, the number of degrees of freedom is used to determine the critical value for a statistical test.

27. **What does the acronym** *MAGIC* **mean?**

    MAGIC establishes the criteria for evaluating the meaningfulness of research results:

        M stands for magnitude or reliability of the results

        A stands for the articulation or clarity of the results

        G stands for the generality or external generalizability of the results

        I stands for interestingness

        C stands for credibility or believability

Why should researchers adhere to its criteria when conducting research? Adherence to these principles assures that the researcher will always be able to meaningfully link calculations and their interpretations.

29. Step 1: H_0: $\mu_{girls} = \mu_{boys}$

              H_1: $\mu_{girls} \neq \mu_{boys}$

    Step 2: $s_{\bar{X}} = 2.36$

    Step 3: $z_{obs} = 1.69$

              $z_{.01} = 2.59$

    Step 4:   Cannot reject H_0. There is insufficient evidence to indicate that boys and girls score differently on the test of moral awareness.

31.   Step 1: $H_0: \rho = 0$

   $H_1: \rho \neq 0$

   Step 2: $r = -.37 \ N = 50$

   $r_{.05} = \pm .250 \quad df = 48$

   Step 3:   Reject the null hypothesis

   Step 4:   There is a moderately small significant negative (inverse) relationship between weight and self-esteem such that the higher the weight, the lower the self-esteem (and vice versa).

33.   **What is a *Type II error?*** A Type II error is a failure to reject the Null hypothesis when it is, in reality, false. **Why do *Type II* errors occur? Provide an example.** Increases in rigor (i.e., requiring .01 rather than .05 for rejection of the null hypothesis) can make a Type II error more likely. Also, small sample sizes increase the likelihood of a Type II error, as does a weak effect of the independent variable. For example, if you are interested in the effects of temperature on learning and you use 70° for the control group and 75° for the experimental group, you are less likely to detect an effect for temperature than if you use 70° and 110°, respectively.

35.   **What can be done to reduce the incidence of making a *Type I error?*** You can reduce the chance of a Type I error by making a α (alpha) smaller (e.g. use .01 rather than .05).
What can be done to reduce the incidence of making a *Type II error?* You can reduce the chance of a Type II error by increasing α (alpha), increasing sample size, and/or by increasing the potency of the independent variable.
How can a researcher balance the demands of these competing concerns in a research project? Generally, the best way to balance the problem created by these errors is to replicate experiments, even those where differences are not found. In that way, the success or failure of the replications can clarify the nature of the relationship between the independent and dependent variable.

37.   **Define the word *power,* as well as its use, in statistical contexts.** Power is the abiliy to achieve particular research goals. Power is the probability of correctly rejecting a false null hypothesis. In the statistical sense, power is $1 - \beta$ (the probability of a Type II error). It is used to describe the sensitivity of a particular statistical test in a given experimental situation.

39.   **Define the word *effect size,* as well as its use, in statistical contexts.** Effect size is a measure of the impact of your independent variable on the behavior being examined (how much change in behavior for each change in the independent variable), or the degree to which your variables are related (the correlation between them). Usually it is reported as a value based on the size of the difference between means divided by the standard error of the difference where .20 is considered small, .50 moderate, and .80 or more large.

41.   **Can the researcher still perform the appropriate hypothesis test? Why or Why not?** No. With no information about the population parameters, there is nothing with which to compare the sample values.

43.   **Can you give her any specific analytic guidance before the analyses begin?** The sample size is very small. I would suggest collecting additional data.

Chapter 10

1.   **Why is the *t* test used in place of the *z* test?** The *t* test is used instead of the *z* test because it enables inferences to be made about differences when samples are small and the population parameters are unknown.

3.   **List the assumptions underlying the use of the *t* test.**

   The assumptions are:

   1. The population sampled from is normally distributed.

   2. Data are randomly and independently sampled.

   3. Interval or ratio measurement is used.

   4. All populations have equal variances (homogeneity).

What happens when one of these assumptions is violated? Violating one or more assumptions of the *t* test results in an uncontrolled change in the probability of a Type I error from the established level of .05 or .01 to some other, unknown, probability. The robustness of the test is reduced.

Can the t test still be used—why or why not? In many cases the t test may still be used because changes in the actual alpha level tend to be slight. The t test is "robust" and relatively insensitive to violations of the assumptions. The only exception to this robustness occurs when the samples are unequal in size, the populations are nonnormal, and the variances of the populations differ.

5. **Why are larger samples desirable?** Larger samples mean more accurate estimates (i.e., lower standard errors) and they enhance the opportunity, therefore, to reject H_0. In addition, larger samples mean more degrees of freedom available for the hypothesis test.

How do larger samples influence the size of a sample standard deviation and error? In general, for a *given size* of sums of squared deviations (SS), the larger the sample size, the smaller the standard deviation and standard error. The SS, after all, is divided by degrees of freedom, which are related to a sample's size, and the standard error is calculated by dividing the standard deviation by the square root of sample size.

7. $H_0: \mu_{\text{sample}} \leq \mu_{\text{pop.}}$

 $H_1: \mu_{\text{sample}} > \mu_{\text{pop.}}$

 $s_{\bar{X}} = 1.237$

 $t_{\text{obs}} = 2.42$

 $t_{.05} = \pm 1.697 \ df = 31$

Reject H_0. Small college students appear to be more introverted than students from large universities.

9. $H_0: \mu_{\text{sample}} \leq \mu_{\text{middle school students}}$

 $H_1: \mu_{\text{sample}} > \mu_{\text{middle school students}}$

 $s_{\bar{X}} = 1.667$

 $t_{\text{obs}} = 1.80$

 $t_{.01} = 2.485 \ df = 25$

Do not reject H_0. There is insufficient evidence from this sample to indicate that geographical knowledge has improved in the past 5 years.

11. a. $s_{\bar{X}} = 1.74$

 $t_{\text{obs}} = 1.72$

 $t_{.05} = 1.684 \ df = 39$

 Reject H_0

 b. $s_{\bar{X}} = 2.20$

 $t_{\text{obs}} = 1.36$

 $t_{.01} = 2.492 \ df = 24$

 Fail to reject H_0

 c. $s_{\bar{X}} = 1.40$

 $t_{\text{obs}} = 2.15$

 $t_{.05} = 2.00 \ df = 61$

 Reject H_0

13. $\bar{X} = 34.33 \quad s = 3.68 \quad N = 12$

 $H_0: \mu_{\text{sample}} = \mu_{\text{pop}}$

 $H_1: \mu_{\text{sample}} \neq \mu_{\text{pop}}$

 $s_{\bar{X}} = 1.06$

 $t_{\text{obs}} = -.63$

 $t_{.05} = 2.201 \ df = 11$

Fail to reject H_0. There is no evidence to support the hypothesis that this group of students suffers from low-levels of depression. The psychologist should not place these students into therapy.

15. a. 34.33 ± 2.33 is the 95% confidence interval for problem 13.

 b. 134.556 ± 2.684 is the 99% confidence interval for problem 14.

17. **Why is the t test for independent groups ideal for hypothesis testing in experimental research?** The t test for independent groups verifies whether there is a difference between the means of an experimental and a

control group that is unlikely to be due to chance. The experimenter may argue that this difference is due to the effect of the independent variable since the two groups were the same before it was applied (except for random differences).

19.   **What is a subject variable?** A subject variable (organismic variable) is one that is a characteristic the subject possesses (e.g., gender, height, manual dexterity) which cannot be assigned by the experimenter. **How are subject variables used in concert with between-groups designs and the independent groups t test?** In a between-groups design with subject variables, the organismic variable is treated like an independent variable and the t test is used to determine if the performance of participants who possess different degrees of the characteristic (e.g., M/F; Hi, Med, or Lo dexterity) also differs.

21.   **Explain the nature of the conceptual model for comparing means presented in this chapter.** The statistical model is based on the size of an observed statistic (difference between means) relative to the size of the standard error for that statistic. The statistic is then compared to a critical value from the appropriate sampling distribution, which exists if H_0 is true. If the observed value exceeds the critical value (falls in the rejection region), then H_0 is rejected; if not (falls in the nonrejection region), then it is not rejected. **Why is this model an appropriate prelude for most inferential statistical tests?** This is an appropriate model to learn because it is similar to models used in other statistical tests of inference and can help in understanding those procedures.

23.   Effect size: $r = .789$, a large effect

   $\hat{\omega}^2 = .59$, 59% of the variation in the scores is attributable to the independent variable (maze bright versus maze dull)

25. $t_{\text{obs}} = 4.025$ $t_{.05} = 2.101$ $df = 18$

Conclusion: Reject H_0. The fixed noise condition resulted in fewer reliably correct responses than the random noise condition.

27.   The analysis indicates that the random noise condition resulted in significantly more math problems completed ($\overline{X} = 8.6$ correct) than in the fixed noise condition ($\overline{X} = 6.8$ correct). This is in opposition to the expectation that random noise would be more disruptive.

   The effect size of $r = .69$ indicates that the independent variable had a relatively large effect $\omega^2 = .43$, indicating that 43% of the total variance could be accounted for by the different types of noise.

29.   Effect size: $r = .71$, a large effect

   $\hat{\omega}^2 = .466$ indicating 47% of the variance is due to the independent variable.

31.   **Are there any advantages to conducting a correlated groups design rather than an independent groups design? If so, what are they?** Yes, there are advantages to the correlated groups design. The main advantage to a correlated groups design for an experiment is that it keeps the effects of random variation to a minimum since the same (or very similar) subjects appear in both conditions. Each subject can serve as his or her own control. The error term (denominator of the t formula) for a correlated groups test is smaller than for a corresponding independent groups test.

33.   **What is a carryover effect?** A carryover effect is an effect of experience at time$_1$ in an experiment that continues to affect behavior at time$_2$, but it is not the result of the independent variable. **Why do such effects pose concerns for correlated groups designs?** These effects may change the internal validity of an experiment by offering alternative explanations (confounding) for the outcome of an experiment and thereby clouding conclusions.

35.   **Do you think the project in problem 34 could be susceptible to any carryover effects? If so, which one(s) and why?** It is possible that the scores on the second test may have been improved by having experienced a similar test at time$_1$. The situation on the second testing will be more familiar and the participants may be less nervous, which, by itself, might yield higher scores.

37.   **Do you think the project described in problem 36 could be susceptible to any carryover effects? If so, which ones and why?** Since one round of layoffs has occurred and more may be expected, the employees may report more stress because they are sensitized by the stressful event of seeing the fellow employees laid off, their increased likelihood of being laid off in the future, or both, and not by any effect of being a survivor per se.

39.   **Why should investigators learn to perform a power analysis?** Power analysis enables a researcher to assess, after failing to reject a null hypothesis, if it is possible in the future to find a significant difference under the conditions of this experiment. It helps to determine if a particular line of research is likely to be fruitful.

Power analysis can also provide a way to plan future research in terms of number of participants necessary under the experimental conditions to achieve a reasonable level of power.

Should a power analysis be performed before or after a study? Why? A power analysis should be performed *after* a study in which the null hypothesis was not rejected to determine if the power in the study was low or high. If power was low, the analysis could indicate how to proceed (i.e., choose the number of participants) in subsequent studies. If power was high, this would suggest that perhaps a new experimental approach would be more useful. It is difficult to assess power before completing a study.

41. a.   Use a correlated groups *t* test.

    b.   Use a *z* test.

    c.   Use a correlated groups *t* test.

    d.   Use an independent groups *t* test.

    e.   Use a single-sample *t* test.

Chapter 11

1.   **Why should any researcher—student or professional—avoid becoming overly focused on finding statistical significance when conducting behavioral science research?** Since not all interesting results are found in significant differences, and since the failure of an effect to appear may often be as interesting as its presence, it is best to focus on the correct analysis and interpretation of the data rather than solely on finding statistically significant differences.

3.   **What are some advantages of the ANOVA that make it a versatile and useful statistical test?** The ANOVA can assess differences between three or more means at the same time.

Is it more versatile or useful than the other statistical tests used for mean comparisons? Why or why not? The two-group experiment is severely limited in scope because it focuses on the presence or absence of an effect. ANOVA is decidedly more versatile than the *t* test because it can look at differences among several values of the independent variable in a single experiment, which better reflects the complexities of causal relationships in behavioral research.

5.   **Explain the source of the variation used to calculate the *F* ratio in a one-way ANOVA.** The numerator of the *F* ratio contains the variation between or among the means of the several samples (conceptually) while the denominator contains variation between participants or experimental error.

Is the partitioning of the variance for the ANOVA similar to the way it is divided by the analysis performed by the *t* test? Conceptually, this partitioning is identical to the manner in which the variation is divided in the *t* test. In the *t* test the numerator is the difference between the means of the two groups (between-groups variation) and the denominator is a measure of error variance ($s_{\overline{X}_1 - \overline{X}_2}$).

7.   **Briefly describe the *F* distribution—how is it similar to or different from the *t* and *z* distributions?** The *F* distribution is a unimodal positively skewed distribution. Since the *F* ratio is formed by dividing one variance by another, there can be no negative results, while it is possible to get a negative or positive *t* or *z*. Unlike the situation with the *t* and *z* distributions, if there is no effect for the independent variable (i.e., H_0 is true and the numerator of the *t* or *z* ratio = 0), if H_0 is true in ANOVA, the ratio will equal 1 (i.e., the expected value of *F* if the null hypothesis is true = 1).

In addition to being used to detect mean differences, like the *t* distribution, the *F* distribution is a family of distributions, the members of which are distinguished by the number of degrees of freedom in the numerator and denominator.

9.   **Is it possible to calculate an *F* ratio with a negative value? Why or why not?** No, it is not possible. The *F* ratio is a ratio between two variances. Variances are the average squared differences between a score and the mean. Although the differences may be either positive or negative, when squared they are positive. The ratio of two positive numbers must always be positive.

11.   **Under what particular circumstances do the independent groups *t* test and the *F* ratio share a special relationship with one another? Explain the nature of this relationship.** The *F* and the *t* test share a special relationship when the *F* is used to test for differences between two means. Under those circumstances, the square of the *t* value will equal the *F* value (i.e., $t^2 = F$).

13.   Assuming $\alpha = .05$:

    p (of at least one Type I error in comparing six means) $= .54$

    p (of at least one Type I error in comparing eight means) $= .76$

15. Answer a, $F = t^2 = 10.37$

17.
Source	SS	df	MS	F
Between-groups	15	2	7.5	3.52
Within-groups	57.5	27	2.13	
Total	72.5	29		

19.
Source	SS	df	MS	F
Between-groups	40	2	20	9.34
Within-groups	90	42	2.14	
Total	130	44		

21.
Source	SS	df	MS	F
Between-groups	100	3	33.33	6.67
Within-groups	180	36	5.00	
Total	280	39		

23.
Source	SS	df	MS	F
Between-groups	74.08	2	37.04	41.212[*]
Within-groups	18.88	21	.899	
Total	92.96	23		

[*]$p < .05$

Reject H_0

Tukey's $HSD = 1.20$
$\overline{X}_1 - \overline{X}_2 = 3.125$ significant at $p < .05$
$\overline{X}_1 - \overline{X}_3 = 4.125$ significant at $p < .05$
$\overline{X}_2 - \overline{X}_3 = 1.00$ not significant

25. $f = 1.98$
   $\hat{\omega}^2 = .77$

27. a.
Source	SS	df	MS	F
Between-groups	49.458	3	16.486	16.91[**]
Within-groups	19.5	20	.975	
Total	68.958	23		

[**]$p < .01$

Reject H_0

b.
Tukey's	HSD = 1.60
$\overline{X}_T - \overline{X}_S = 2.50$	significant $p < .01$
$\overline{X}_T - \overline{X}_O = 1.34$	not significant
$\overline{X}_T - \overline{X}_L = 1.33$	not significant
$\overline{X}_S - \overline{X}_O = 1.17$	not significant

$$\overline{X}_S - \overline{X}_L = 3.83 \qquad \text{significant } p < .01$$
$$\overline{X}_O - \overline{X}_L = 2.67 \qquad \text{significant } p < .01$$

c. $\mathbf{f} = 1.59$ very large effect
$\omega^2 = .665$

d. Twenty-four nursing students were taught clinical skills, six in each of one presentation type: text, computer simulation, observation, and lecture. They were then quizzed over the material. The means and standard deviations of the four groups can be found in Table 1 and are graphed in Figure 1.

An overall analysis of variance yielded a significant value ($F_{3,20} = 16.91$; $p < .01$) indicating some of the groups differed. Post hoc analysis using Tukey's *HSD* test indicated that participants in the simulation condition had higher scores than participants in the text condition but were not reliably better than participants in the observation condition (see Table 2). Participants in the lecture condition did not differ from those in the text condition, but scored significantly more poorly than participants in either the Observation and Simulation conditions (see Table 2).

The effect size was very large ($\mathbf{f} = 1.59$) and there was a high degree of association between presentation type and test scores ($\hat{\omega}^2 = .665$) accounting for approximately 67% of the total variability.

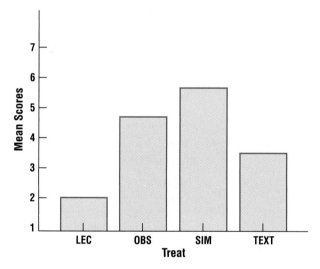

29. a.

Source	SS	df	MS	F
Between-groups	100.24	4	25.06	46.41**
Within-groups	10.80	20	.54	
Total	111.04	24		

**p < .01

Reject H_0

Table 1   Means and Standard Deviations for the Four Presentation Types

	$\overline{X}$	SD
Text	3.33	1.03
Simulation	5.83	0.75
Observation	4.67	0.82
Lecture	2.00	1.26

Table 2   Results of the Tukey's *HSD* Test

	Text	Simulation	Observation	Lecture	*HSD* = 1.53
		Mean Differences			
Text	—	−2.5	1.34	1.33	
Simulation		—	1.17	3.88*	
Observation			—	2.67*	
Lecture				—	

*$p < .05$

    b.   Tukey's $HSD = 1.74$

$\overline{X}_3 - \overline{X}_{12} = -1.30$ not significant

$\overline{X}_3 - \overline{X}_{18} = -2.20$ significant $p < .01$

$\overline{X}_3 - \overline{X}_{24} = 3.00$ significant $p < .01$

$\overline{X}_3 - \overline{X}_{36} = 5.80$ significant $p < .01$

$\overline{X}_{12} - \overline{X}_{18} = -.60$ not significant

$\overline{X}_{12} - \overline{X}_{24} = -2.40$ significant $p < .01$

$\overline{X}_{12} - \overline{X}_{36} = -4.20$ significant $p < .01$

$\overline{X}_{18} - \overline{X}_{24} = -1.80$ significant $p < .01$

$\overline{X}_{18} - \overline{X}_{36} = -3.60$ significant $p < .01$

$\overline{X}_{24} - \overline{X}_{36} = -1.80$ significant $p < .01$

    c.   **f** = 3.05, very large effect

        $\hat{\omega}^2 = .879$

    d.   Five participants were randomly assigned to be exposed to one of five personal distances: 3 inches, one foot, 1.5 feet, 2 feet, and 3 feet. They were asked to rate their comfort level following their exposure on a 1 (low) to 7 (high) scale. The means and standard deviations of their ratings are shown in Table 1. Figure 1 shows the mean comfort levels as a function of increasing personal distance.

        The overall analysis of variance yielded a significant result ($F_{4,20} = 46.41$; $p < .01$). Post hoc analyses using Tukey's *HSD* test indicated that the participants in the 3-inch condition were more uncomfortable than the participants in the 1.5-, 2-, and 4-foot conditions. Participants in the 1- and 1.5-foot conditions did not differ but participants in both these conditions were more uncomfortable than the participants in either the 2- or 3-foot conditions. Participants in the 2-foot condition were more uncomfortable than those in the 3-foot condition. Clearly discomfort does increase as personal distance decreases. This conclusion is supported by the very large effect size (**f** = 3.05 and the strong association between comfort and personal distance ($\hat{\omega}^2 = .879$).

31. a.   Three

    b.   Forty-eight

    c. $\hat{\omega}^2 = .162$, a low association.

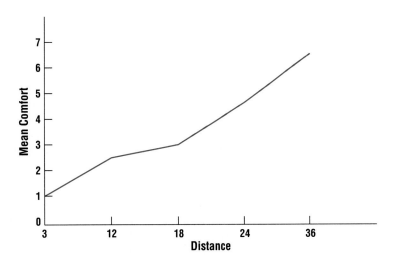

Table 1   Means and Standard Deviations of Comfort Levels for Personal Distances

Distance (in.)	Mean	SD
3	1.0	.000
12	2.6	.548
18	3.2	1.304
24	5.0	.7071
36	6.8	.447

Table 2   Summary of Tukey's *HSD* Mean differences (absolute values)

Groups	3 in.	1 ft	1.5 ft	2 ft	3 ft	$HSD_{.01} = 1.74$
3 in.	—	1.6*	2.2**	4.0**	5.8**	
1 ft		—	.60 *n.s.*	2.4**	4.2**	
1 1/2 ft			—	1.8**	3.6**	
2 ft				—	1.8**	
3 ft					—	

*$p < .05$

**$p < .01$

33.   **Is a one-way ANOVA the appropriate statistical test to analyze these data? Why or why not?** No, ANOVA is not appropriate. The analysis of variance requires the dependent variable be measured on an interval or ratio scale. Since the dependent variable is an ordinal number, ANOVA is not appropriate.

35.   **What should a researcher do next? Why?** Following a significant *F* that supports a hypothesis, the investigator should engage in contrast analyses to determine if the specifics of the hypothesis are supported (i.e. Tukey's *HSD*) (additional exploratory comparisons should also be considered). If the contrast analysis supports the specifics of the hypothesis, the **f** (effect size) and ω^2 should be included in the analysis. This approach will clarify the exact nature and strength of the findings.

🌙 Chapter 12

1.   **Conceptually, how does a two-way ANOVA differ from a one-way ANOVA?** A two-way ANOVA design includes at least two levels of two different independent variables so that each participant experiences a combination of one level of each independent variable. For example, an experiment might consist of two levels of anxiety (high and low) and two levels of problem difficulty (easy and difficult), with each subject getting one of the four possible combinations: high–easy, high–difficult, low–easy, and low–difficult. Alternatively, the experiment might consist of two strains of rats (albino and hooded) and three levels of reward (small, medium, and large) resulting in six combinations: albino–small, albino–medium, albino–large, hooded–small, hooded–medium, and hooded–large.

3.   **What is a *factorial* design?** In a factorial design each level of each independent variable is combined with each level of all other independent variables once.
How can you tell how many different levels are present in a given factorial design? The total number of combinations of each independent variable is the product of the number of levels of each independent variable (i.e., a $2 \times 3 \times 4$ factorial design has two levels of the first variable, three of the second, and four of the third for a total number of combinations of 24).

5.   **What is a *main effect*? Define this term and provide an example.** A main effect is reflected in a significant difference among the means of one independent variable in a factorial design (represented by row or column means) without considering any other independent variable (summed across the other variable[s]). Considering the example given in the answer to problem 1, if there is a significant difference between the levels of anxiety when summed across problem difficulty, that would be a main effect for anxiety.

7.   **Why are interactions only associated with factorial designs?** Interactions result when the effects of one variable are different at the different levels of the other variable(s), a finding which requires all combinations

of the levels of one variable with the levels of the other(s). For example, again from the answer to problem 1, if the effects of anxiety are different for easy problems (e.g., low anxiety facilitates easy problems, but high anxiety has no effect) and difficult problems (e.g., low anxiety has no effect on difficult problems, but high anxiety interferes with them). These combinations and their effects can only be found in factorial designs.

9. **How many *F* ratios result from a two-way ANOVA? What is the purpose of each of the *F*s?** Three *F* ratios result from a two-way design: a main effect for variable A; a main effect for variable B; and an interaction between A and B. These *F* ratios independently test the three null hypotheses concerning the two main effects and the interaction.

11. **What method of analysis should the researcher use? Why?** The method of analysis should be a 2 × 2 ANOVA (two genders by the presence or absence of older siblings). The measure of complexity is, probably, at least an interval scale and there are two independent variables.

13. **Indicate the presence of any main effect(s) or interaction.** There are no main effects for either factor A or B, but there is an interaction.

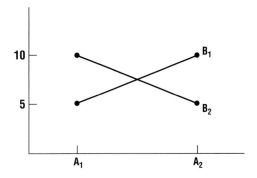

15. **Indicate the presence of any main effect(s) or interaction.** There is the possibility of a main effect for both factors A and B, as well as an interaction.

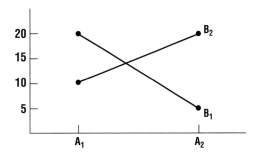

17. **Perform a *z*- Factor ANOVA:** Data table: Mean number for each combination

	B_1	B_2	
A_1	6.0	3.67	4.83
A_2	9.0	6.67	7.83
	7.5	5.17	6.33

Source table

Source	SS	df	MS	F
A	54	1	54	37.67**
B	32.67	1	32.67	22.79**
A × B	0	1	0	0
Within-groups	28.67	20	1.433	
Total	115.33	23		

**p < .01

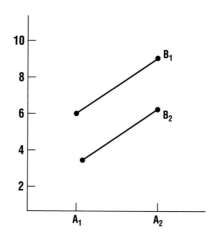

19. f_A = .93, a large effect

                                $\hat{\omega}^2$ = .60

                                f_B = .62, moderately large effect

                                $\hat{\omega}^2$ = .476

21. f_A = 1.12, very large effect

                                $\hat{\omega}^2$ = .60

                                f_B = 0.33, a medium effect.

                                $\hat{\omega}^2$ = .19

Twenty-four participants were randomly assigned to the cells of a 2 × 2 factorial ANOVA design. Participants learned nonsense or real words in either a warm (82°F) room or a room with ambient temperature (70°F). Number of items recalled were recorded and the group average for each condition is reported in Table 1 and plotted in the graph in Figure 1.

A 2 × 2 factorial analysis of variance yielded a significant main effect for room temperature ($F_{1,20}$ = 37.25, $p < .01$). The effect size for room temperature was very large, accounting for 60% of the total variance. More items were recalled in the room at ambient temperature than in the warm room. The effect size for room temperature was very large, accounting for approximately 60% of the total variance. Significantly more real than nonsense words ($F_{1,20}$ = 6.55, $p < .05$) were recalled although the effect size was small, accounting for about 10% of the variance. No significant interaction was found.

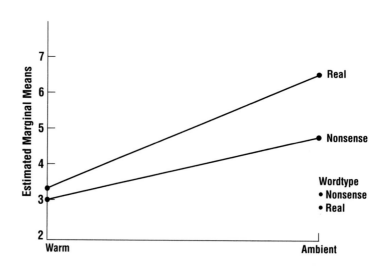

Source table

Source	SS	df	MS	F
Lng. Env.	40.042	1	40.042	37.248**
Word Type	7.042	1	7.042	6.55*
Interaction	3.375	1	3.375	3.140 *m.s.*
Error	21.50	20	1.075	
Total	71.958	23		

*$p < .05$

**$p < .01$

Table 1   Group Means

	Nonsense	Real	
Warm	3.0	3.33	3.167
Ambient	4.83	6.667	5.75
	3.917	5.00	4.46

23.

Source	SS	df	MS	F
Factor A	85	1	85	9.00**
Factor B	93	1	93	9.85**
A × B	52	1	52	5.51*
Error within	340	36	9.44	
Total	570	39		

*$p < .05$

**$p < .01$

a. 2.2.

b. 10

c. Yes. Factors A and B at $p < .01$ and the interaction at $p < .05$.

d. $F_{crit.\ 1,36} \cong 7.43$ for $p < .01$; approximately 4.12 for $p < .05$

25. $f_A = .419$, a moderate effect

$\hat{\omega}^2 = .17$

$f_B = .44$, a moderate effect

$\hat{\omega}^2 = .18$

$f_{A \times B} = .317$, a small effect.

$\hat{\omega}^2 = .10$

27. B_1 B_2

A_1	10	16	$13 - 11.5 = 1.5$
A_2	12	8	$10 - 11.5 = -1.5$
	11	12	11.5
	$-11.5 = -.5$	$-11.5 = .5$	

	B_1	B_2	
A_1	8.5	14.5	$11.5 - 11.5 = 0$
A_2	13.5	9.5	$11.5 - 11.5 = 0$
	$11 - 11.5 = -.5$	$12 - 11.5 = .5$	

	B_1	B_2	
A_1	9	14	$11.5 - 11.5 = 0$
A_2	14	9	$11.5 - 11.5 = 0$
	11.5	11.5	

	B_1	B_2
A_1	−2.5	+2.5
A_2	+2.5	−2.5

29. Data Table

Means of groups

	B_1	B_2	B_3	
A_1	10.67	7.83	4.50	7.67
A_2	4.83	7.83	10.50	7.72
	7.75	7.83	7.50	7.69 = G Mn.

Source Table

Source	SS	df	MS	F
Between-groups				
A	0.02778	1	0.02778	0.044
B	0.722	2	0.3611	0.575
A × B	210.056	2	105.028	167.30
Within-groups	18.83	30	0.628	
Total	229.64	35		

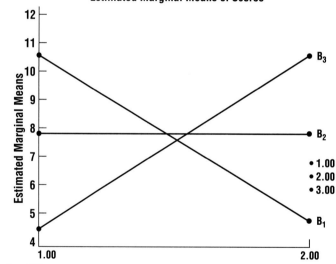

Estimated Marginal Means of Scores

Chapter 13

1.   **How does a one-way repeated-measures ANOVA differ from a one-way ANOVA?** Like the dependent groups t test, the repeated-measures ANOVA involves taking repeated samples from the same participants' behavior on three or more occasions, each occasion under a different level of the independent variable (avoiding carry-over effects, of course). Drug dose studies are a good example. If an investigator is interested in the relative pain-reducing effects of several different doses of an aspirin, the investigator might give eight subjects four doses of aspirin (i.e., placebo, 250 mg, 500 mg, and 1,000 mg) in random or counterbalanced order and measure the time it takes for the partici-pant to remove his or her hand from a bucket of ice and water.

3.   **Why would a data analyst elect to use the dependent groups t test instead of a one-variable repeated-measures ANOVA? Illustrate your points through an example.** With more than two measures on each subject, the repeated measures ANOVA would be the choice since repeated t tests inflates the probability of getting a chance difference above the level of alpha. A dependent groups t test assesses a mean difference at 2 points in

time, whereas a one-variable repeated measures ANOVA can assess mean change at 2 or more points in time. If a researcher wanted to change the effectivness of a drug on some disease across a 6 month period (i.e., mean change each month for 6 mos.), the repeated measures ANOVA would be appropriate. If change was being assessed only twice, then the dependent groups *t* test would be appropriate.

5. $df = 2$ for the between-groups term

   $df = 9$ for the between-subjects term

   $df = 18$ for the residual error term

7. **What is the next step(s) the investigator should take?** If significance is obtained for the overall ANOVA, the investigator should follow with Tukey's *HSD* test to locate the differences and then assess the effect size (**f**) and degree of association ($\hat{\omega}^2$) between the independent and dependent variables.

9. **What are the degrees of freedom for an *F* ratio from a one variable repeated measures ANOVA design with 4 dependent measures and 10 participants?**

   numerator degrees of freedom $= 3$
   denominator degrees of freedom $= 27$

11. **Are there any advantages that repeated-measures designs have over between-groups designs?** Yes, several advantages exist. Repeated measures designs use fewer subjects, are generally more powerful, view change over time in the same individual (reducing error variance by eliminating some variation between different subjects), and they lead to more effective and detailed understanding of complex relationships among variables.

13.

Source	SS	df	MS	F
Treatment	40.5	3	13.5	22.09[*]
Between-groups *SS*	5.0	3	1.67	2.73
Error (residual)	5.5	9	.61	
Total	51	15		

   [*]$p < .05$

   Tukey's *HSD* $= 1.72$

Absolute differences between means are

	1	2	3	4
1	—	2.25[*]	2.25[*]	4.50[*]
2		—	0	2.25[*]
3			—	2.25[*]
4				—

[*]$p < .05$

   The repeated measures ANOVA yielded an overall significant difference ($F_{2,18} = 22.09, p < .05$). Tukey's comparisons indicated that treatment 1 had significantly lower scores than all others; 2 and 3 did not differ from each other, but both had lower scores than treatment 4.

15. $f_{between} = 1.96$, a very large effect.

   $\hat{\omega}^2 = .78$

17.

Source	SS	df	MS	F
Between-groups	30	2	15	5.40[*]
Subjects	8	9	0.89	.32
Within-groups	50	18	2.78	
Total	88	29		

   [*]$p < .05$

19. $f_{bg} = .72$ a large effect

   $\hat{\omega}^2 = .29$

21.

Source	SS	df	MS	F
Between-groups	50.17	2	25.08	39.26**
Subjects	21.67	3	7.22	11.30**
Within-groups	3.83	6	0.64	
Total	75.67	11		

**$p < .01$

Tukey's $HSD = 1.73$

Absolute differences between means

	Week 1	Week 2	Week 3
Week 1	—	2.75*	5.00*
Week 2		—	2.25*
Week 3			—

*$p < .05$

$$\mathbf{f}_{between} = 1.40 \text{ a very large effect}$$

$$\hat{\omega}^2 = .52$$

23. **Under what sort of circumstances would an investigator elect to use a mixed-design ANOVA?** An investigator would use a mixed-design when the research contains one (or more) repeated measures on the same participants *and* one (or more) independent groups. For example, a study of gender differences (independent groups) and the effects of delta-9 tetrahydracannabinol (marijuana) on memory for stories would require a mixed design.
How does a mixed-design ANOVA differ from the other forms of ANOVA reviewed in this and the previous chapter? In a mixed-design there is *both* a between groups *and* a within groups variable, while in the other designs there is one or the other, but *not* both.

Chapter 14

1. **What is a nonparametric statistical test?** A nonparametric test makes few (if any) assumptions about the nature of the data or the shape of the population distribution from which it is sampled.
How do nonparametric tests differ from parametric tests? Although nonparametric tests make few distributional assumptions (i.e., they are often referred to as distribution free tests), parametric tests are concerned with populations and drawing inferences about their parameters. In order to draw valid inferences, parametric tests must meet appropriate assumptions (e.g., normality, random sampling, equal variances). In general, parametric tests are more powerful than nonparametric tests when the assumptions can be met.

3. **How do interval and ratio scales differ from nominal and ordinal scales? Provide an example of each type.** Interval and ratio scales have equal intervals between scale points and are compatible with the real number system. Ordinal and nominal scales do not have equal intervals and are not real number compatible. Length and temperature (Fahrenheit and Centigrade) are good examples of ratio and interval scales (respectively), while rank in graduating class and gender are good examples of an ordinal and nominal scale (respectively).

5. **Why should researchers in the behavioral sciences be open to learning to use nonparametric statistical tests?** Nonparametric tests tend to have fewer restrictive assumptions, may be used with nonnumerical data, are more effective with small samples, and require easier calculations to arrive at a more intuitively understandable conclusion than parametric tests. All of these characteristics make them a significant tool for analysis when measures and procedures do not meet the assumptions of parametric tests.

7. **Which nonparametric tests are most similar to the *t* test for independent groups?** The chi-square test of independence (two groups) and the Mann-Whitney *U* test are useful in cases where the *t* test might apply, but failure to meet critical assumptions prevents its use.

9. **Which nonparametric test can be used to analyze data from one sample only?** The chi-square goodness-of-fit test is the only nonparametric test useful with one sample.

11. **What is the nonparametric counterpart of the Pearson *r*?** The Spearman *r* is the nonparametric counterpart of the Pearson *r* when only ranks (ordinal) data are available.

13.   **Under what conditions is it preferable to use Cramer's V statistic instead of the phi (ϕ) coefficient:** Cramer's V statistic is used in place of the phi coefficient following a chi-square test of independence when the contingency table is greater than 2×2 (e.g., $2 \times 3, 3 \times 3$, etc.).

15.   **What nonparametric test will allow them to quickly determine their level of agreement? Why?** The Spearman r correlation coefficient should be used because it estimates the degree of association (agreement) between two sets of ranks (ordinal data).

17.   **What test should be used to demonstrate that requests for the three pizzas varied?** The appropriate test to answer the owner's question is the chi-square goodness-of-fit test.

19.

Data	Rank	Data	Rank
100	1	34	9
99	2.5	33	10
99	2.5	32	11.5
89	4	32	11.5
78	5	23	13
70	6	22	14
67	7	12	15
56	8	11	16
		6	17

21.

	A_1	A_2
B_1	9.5	9.5
B_2	9.5	9.5

23.

	A_1	A_2	A_3
B_1	12.5	7.5	15
B_2	12.5	7.5	15

25.   chi-square $= 0.105$ chi square$_{.01}$ $(df = 1) = 6.635$

No, the value is not significant

27.   Chi-square$_{obs.}$ $= 23.01$ Chi-square$_{.05}$ $(df = 3) = 5.991$

The difference is significant at $p < .05$

29.   Chi-square$_{obs.}$ $= 12.24$ chi-square$_{.05}$ $(df = 1) = 3.841$

The chi-square is significant indicating that there is a link between self-esteem and persistence.

31. $\phi = .39$

33. $U_A = 64$

$U_B = 0$

$U_{critical} = 13$

Since $U_B < 13$, reject H_0. The species differ in activity.

35. $\mu_U = 798$ $\sigma_U = 103.79$

$z_{UA} = -5.26$ $z_{UB} = -5.4 \times 1$ $z_{crit.} = \pm 2.58$

There is a significant difference.

37.   Since the sum of $+R = 0$ and $0 < 2$ $(T_{crit.})$, reject H_0. The film improved the ratings.

39.   Spearman $r = .83$.

Spearman $r_{crit.} = .886$ Do not reject H_0: $r = 0$.

41.   **What is the next step the researcher should take? Why?** The researcher should estimate the degree of association by calculating Cramer's V, which is used when the contingency table is greater than 2×2.

43.   **Which nonparametric test should be used to analyze the data?** The researcher should use the Wilcoxin test, which is appropriate for determining differences between nonindependent ordinal rankings.

🌙 Chapter 15

1.   **Identify some of the problems or concerns linked to the use of the null hypothesis.** Focusing on the null hypothesis often eliminates any examination of other, simpler ways of analyzing or describing data. This is frequently coupled with a failure to look at power and/or effect size as a way of determining the practical importance of the findings or to educate the general reader on the real meaning of the phrase "statistically significant" as distinct from meaningful or important.

3.   **Discuss six of the specific recommendations made by the American Psychological Association's (APA) Task Force on Statistical Inference (TSFI). How can these recommendations improve the use of statistics and data analysis, as well as the reporting of results?** The task force recommends using a minimally sufficient analytic technique to improve communicability of findings. More sophisticated analyses should be fully justified and explained. The task force also recommends that care should be taken in imputing causality to experimental effects and any supporting statistics should be included with the main results to strengthen causal assertions. Problems with methods, data acquisition, and the like should be discussed clearly in terms of potential impact on the conclusions *before* presenting any results. Random selection and/or assignment should be thoroughly documented, and all variables (independent, dependent, and control) should be clearly operationally defined and discussed as to their relevance, and the manner in which they support the aims of the research.

By taking these recommendations into account, a researcher can be assured that his or her results and conclusions will be clear and understandable, their importance and generality recognizable, and the likelihood of their being replicated will be increased.

5.   **How can replication be used to demonstrate generalizability?** Successful replication, particularly programmatic replication, increases awareness that a particular method and analysis (conceptual and statistical) will produce reliable findings and conclusions in a variety of related settings with different investigators. Thus, successful replicability implies that those variables and their effects generalize beyond a particular method, setting, or researcher.

7.   **In your opinion, is it possible for a researcher to become overly dependent on statistics? How?** Yes, it is possible. Too much dependency on statistics may serve to restrict the investigator's examination of the data, increasing the possibility that an interesting finding might escape notice. This is particularly true when analysis is applied with a routine, unthinking, recipe-like approach.

9.   **How do Abelson's (1995) MAGIC criteria impact on the tension between obtaining right answers and offering accurate interpretation?** Focusing on the more global implications of your data with respect to their magnitude (effect size), articulation (how the results fit together), generality (how widely or narrowly the results apply), interestingness (what importance do they have), and credibility (how believable are the data based on methods, analysis, and interpretation) ensure that readers will be clear about the relationships represented by your data in real depth and with real meaning.

11.   **What evidence supports the contention that statistical or data analytic skills acquired in one domain can be transferred to others? Explain.** Several studies which show that statistical, inferential, and logical skills improve over time following a first course in statistics, and generalize to other environments, support the conclusion that such knowledge is transferable and not domain specific. The work of Lehman and coworkers is clear evidence that statistical knowledge improves over time, producing better inferential skills in psychology students than in their humanities counterparts.

13.   **As a novice data analyst, how will you keep your statistical skills sharp?** Retaining statistical knowledge requires continued use and practice. Perhaps the best way of doing so is to design a research project of one's own, collect data, and analyze and report the findings. If that is not feasible, one should volunteer to participate in the ongoing research of a member of the faculty. Failing either of those, periodically set yourself research problems and use the decision trees to refresh your memory on how to design and analyze an experiment you might do to test your hypotheses.

15.   **When planning to analyze some data using statistical software, what are some of the *dos* and *don't*s a data analyst should follow.** Do remember the phrase "less is more" and don't use a more complex analysis that the data and hypothesis require. Do be sure you know where the numbers come from, how they appear, and where they are going in the chosen analysis (remember the famous computer phrase "GIGO," "garbage in, garbage out"). Do be able to recognize an unexpected (and perhaps incorrect) statistical result (e.g., an unexpected significant difference or no difference where there should be one based on the summary statistics). Don't just read the output and take the "correctness" for granted.

17.   **Why should behavioral scientists be concerned about the educational implications of the analyses used to support their research?** Behavioral scientists must be sure that the results and implications of their research are clear and understandable by the consumer of the information. It is ethically important that a researcher educates the public about what a result means, and, perhaps as important, what it does not mean. Failure to do so may result in the outcome of a study being misunderstood or misinterpreted. The motives of the investigator

may also be suspect when the scientist fails to make the purposes, methods, and the limitations of his or her research clear and understandable.

19.   **You are a behavioral scientist whose research and analyses have led to some controversial finding that is upsetting to the general public. How should you react? What are your responsibilities to the public and to your research, including statistical analysis?** A scientist whose work has created a controversy should react calmly and without defensiveness. He or she must be prepared to explain and defend the work and interpretation. The scientist is ethically responsible to make as clear as humanly possible the findings, their strength and generality, the reasons for a particular interpretation, alternative interpretations (if any) and any limitations of the methods, results, or statistical analysis so that the meaning of the research may be judged on its merits.

21.   **Why do you suppose some investigators might see "trimming" as more acceptable than the other three classes of fraud? Is it more acceptable—why or why not?** "Trimming" or eliminating extreme scores after the data are collected but before analysis, might be seen as more acceptable because it helps clarify and make "cleaner" the statistical results and their interpretation. It is usually felt to be more limited in extent than the other three fraudulent approaches. "Trimming" after the data are collected is as unethical as any other fraudulent treatment of the data, despite its relatively "minor" scope.

23.   **Why are fraudulent, false, or otherwise misleading data so problematic where the scientific literature is concerned?** Fraudulent, false, or otherwise misleading data are so problematic because: (a) they might never be recognized as false; (b) even if retracted, results may persist because some people may not learn of the retraction, like a bad newspaper story later retracted on the back pages; and (c) false results can waste other researcher's resources by leading them down wrong pathways and focusing attention on proving or disproving the false result.

25.   **Is a researcher ethically bound to report the results of all statistical analyses performed on a data set? Why or why not?** Although the researcher is ethically bound to have available all analyses (and the raw data), I do not feel he or she is ethically bound to report all analyses in any write-ups. The researcher is, however, ethically bound to report all results that pertain to the main aims of the research. Exhaustively reporting all analyses run on the data set may be redundant, confusing, and could cloud important results and the conclusions to which they lead.

27.   **In your opinion, what contributions do statistics and data analysis make to the behavioral sciences?** Statistics provide an important methodological tool for organizing, summarizing, and analyzing empirical data. Without the availability of statistical methods, we would have no way of communicating the character of our data, interpretations, and conclusions with the necessary accuracy and support. Without the shared methods of analysis that statistics yield, it would be difficult, if not impossible, to obtain agreement on the meaning of our findings among investigators or the public.

29.   **How can the breeder determine which breed has the least reactive (i.e., emotional) temperament, which one has the most, and so on? Which statistical test is best suited to the breeder's hypotheses? Why?** Assuming the dependent measure is quantitative and continuous (e.g., number of squares entered in a novel environment), then the appropriate analysis would be a one-way ANOVA between breeds. If the dependent measure is not quantitative and continuous (e.g., ranks) some nonparametric test (chi-square or Wilcoxin) would be appropriate.

31.   **Which statistical test is best suited to test the director's hypothesis? Why?** Presumably, the Director wants to compare the rankings of all students from both years by rank ordering them all. The most appropriate test for rankings when two groups are involved is the Mann-Whitney U test. Since there will be a larger number of students involved, the director could use the normal approximation of the Mann-Whitney U.

33.   **Which statistical test is best suited to test the researcher's hypothesis? Why?** Repeated measures, ANOVA is the appropriate analysis. There are three quantitative measures (number of errors at the beginning, middle, and end) on each child.

35.   **Which statistical test is best suited to test the researcher's hypothesis? Why?** The appropriate analysis would be a regression analysis based on the Pearson product-moment correlation coefficient to determine if a predictive relationship exists. This is appropriate because the data consist of two quantitative measures (number of siblings and rated intellectual environment) not collected in an experiment.

Appendix F

1.   **Why are qualitative and quantitative approaches perceived to be incompatible with one another? Explain why they are arguably *compatible* with one another.** Qualitative and quantitative approaches are perceived to be incompatible because many believe that quantitative research is limited because data are not applicable to everyday experience, whereas qualitative approaches can better explain everyday life, but not cause

and effect relationships or relationships that may apply to a representative population. They are complements to one another. Qualitative research needs some quantitative approaches and vice versa (i.e., triangulation).

3. **In your opinion, why are the behavioral sciences so compelled to measure and manipulate variables in the study of human behavior?** Behavioral sciences are compelled to measure and manipulate variables because the world is focused on numbers. Numbers and quantitative reasoning gave rise to modern science and technologies that humans depend on. Measurement gives rise to some sort of order that we can explain, and we think that makes human behavior credible as a science.

5. **Define qualitative research and list some of its characteristics.** Qualitative research is a formal investigation that is not dependent on statistical or other quantitative procedures. Some of its characteristics are participant perspective and diversity, appropriate methodologies and theories, reflexive investigators and researchers, and variety of qualitative approaches and methodologies.

7. **Why is perspective or point of view less important in quantitative rather than qualitative research? Does it matter less there? Why or why not?** In quantitative research, there should be no point of view or perspective because the data one gathers and analyzes should be objective and unbiased.

9. **Briefly discuss six rules of thumb for qualitative researchers.**

   1. Avoid studying your own group: reports may be biased and unfair.

   2. Rely on outside readers to evaluate your work: unbiased perspective is invaluable.

   3. Time spent on analysis is as important as time spent on data collection: the primary objective is to be able to interpret your findings.

   4. Create a model of what happened in your work: develop an outline illustrating the research process from start to finish.

   5. Share the data with the research participants: because they are the source of the data, they should have the right to see everything.

   6. Be on the watch for contradiction and points of conflict in the data: inconsistencies can be a source of insight.

11. **Explain the idea behind participant observation and how it varies from ethnography. After defining these terms, provide a concrete example of each one.** Participant observation entails entering into a research setting as a study participant and monitoring, recording, and interpreting behavior, and interacting with study participants. An example would be an investigative journalist disguising herself or himself as a retiree in a nursing home to discover if the residents there were abused or neglected by the medical staff.

   Ethnography is a research approach dependent on the undisguised, objective study of the habits, customs, and actions of people in a culture as they go about their daily lives. An example would be a researcher wanting to study the customs and habits of Tibetan monks. He or she would spend time in a Tibetan village or convent, and then study the everyday habits and customs of the monks, but as an outside person.

13. **What is a narrative? Identify and define the two main types of narratives used in research efforts.** A narrative is an individual's story or other verbal account of an event that is prompted by a semi-interview or question. The two basic types are narrative interviews, where the interview is open-ended and biographical, and episodic interviews, where the interview is more focused, usually on a specific event.

15. **Create a prompt for a narrative interview.** Narrative interview prompt: I want to ask you to tell me about what you wanted to be in life as you were aging. The best way to do this is starting from your childhood and going in chronological order until now. You can take your time in doing this and also give details.

17. **How does a focus group differ from a more traditional interview? Why do some qualitative researchers argue that focus groups represent a better research technique than other qualitative methods?** A focus group is an interview involving a group of people whereas a traditional interview is usually one-on-one. Some researchers argue that focus groups represent a better research technique because they are more dynamic and help evaluate more different research populations.

19. **Imagine that you are running a focus group. Select a topic for the group to discuss and then describe how you would lead the group through the four steps usually associated with focus groups.**

   Step 1: Topic: Should drivers be allowed to use cell phones while driving? Discussion to agree or disagree.

   Step 2: Introduce members and emphasize that everyone chosen for the discussion group either drives or owns cell phones.

   Step 3: Show news articles on accidents occurring from drivers using cell phones on the roads.

   Step 4: Review group conformity issues, and what to do to jump start discussions.

21.   **List eight characteristics of qualitative researchers, and briefly explain *in your opinion* why each is important.**

    1.   Possessing tolerance for ambiguity: not all questions can be answered concisely.

    2.   Flexibility and openness to change plans or directions in the course of the research: as with human behavior, one must realize that research must adapt and change to different needs.

    3.   Patience and resourcefulness: all research cannot be done in a day; one needs to be patient and to be able to find other ways to perform research.

    4.   Ability to commit equal time and effort to field work and analysis: to get valid results, work must be done thoroughly.

    5.   Trust in self and others: a person cannot do research alone and has to trust in the ability of others.

    6.   Self-knowledge and self-awareness: person needs to rely on his or her instincts, whether learned or natural.

    7.   Authenticity: as with all research, be honest and scientifically sound.

    8.   Good writing skills: a researcher must be able to show and explain results to others.

23.   **Which research approach—qualitative or quantitative—should you follow? Why?**   Use a qualitative approach by observing both child and parent. Because it is a specific event, an episodic narrative may be appropriate by participant observation. Also, a focus group may aid in collecting information.

Choosing a Qualitative or a Quantitative Approach

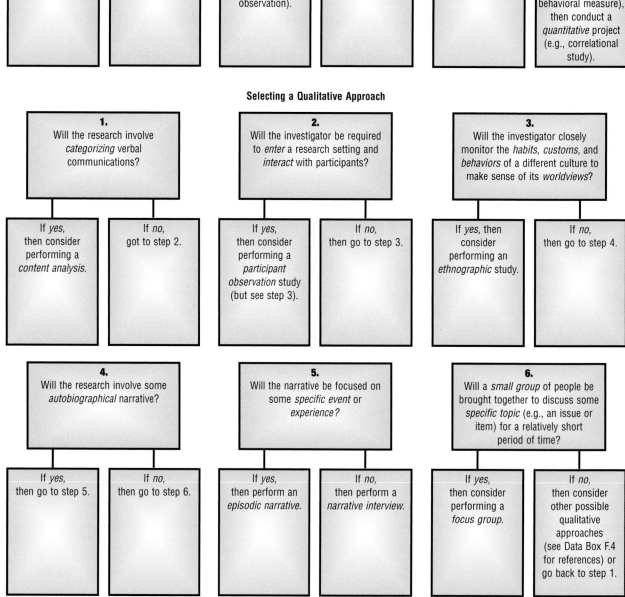

1.
Is the research goal to *predict* future behavior?

If *yes*, then conduct a *quantitative* project (e.g., experiment).

If *no*, then go to step 2.

2.
Is the research goal to *describe* past or current behavior?

If *yes*, then conduct a *qualitative* project (e.g., participant observation).

If *no*, then go to step 3.

3.
Is the research goal *exclusively* to explain a participant's *point of view* regarding some stimulus?

If *yes*, then conduct a *qualitative* project (e.g., narrative).

If *no* and point-of-view is being *linked* to some *outcome* (e.g., self-report or behavioral measure), then conduct a *quantitative* project (e.g., correlational study).

Selecting a Qualitative Approach

1.
Will the research involve *categorizing* verbal communications?

If *yes*, then consider performing a *content analysis.*

If *no*, got to step 2.

2.
Will the investigator be required to *enter* a research setting and *interact* with participants?

If *yes*, then consider performing a *participant observation* study (but see step 3).

If *no*, then go to step 3.

3.
Will the investigator closely monitor the *habits, customs,* and *behaviors* of a different culture to make sense of its *worldviews*?

If *yes*, then consider performing an *ethnographic* study.

If *no*, then go to step 4.

4.
Will the research involve some *autobiographical* narrative?

If *yes*, then go to step 5.

If *no*, then go to step 6.

5.
Will the narrative be focused on some *specific event* or *experience?*

If *yes*, then perform an *episodic narrative.*

If *no*, then perform a *narrative interview.*

6.
Will a *small group* of people be brought together to discuss some *specific topic* (e.g., an issue or item) for a relatively short period of time?

If *yes*, then consider performing a *focus group.*

If *no*, then consider other possible qualitative approaches (see Data Box F.4 for references) or go back to step 1.

EMERGING ALTERNATIVES: QUALITATIVE RESEARCH APPROACHES

Thou shalt not sit
With statisticians nor commit
A social science.
                    —from "Under Which Lyre" by W. H. Auden (1991, p. 339)

These lines are from a long, humorous poem written by W. H. (Wystan Hugh) Auden, a British émigré to the United States and one of the 20th century's great poets. Auden wrote these lines in 1946, though their apparent meaning resonates with the desires, if not experience, of more recent generations of students and quite a few professional academics. Many students would prefer studying various topics that fall under the purview of the behavioral sciences without having to rely on statistics and data analysis (perhaps you felt this way before beginning your statistical odyssey back in chapter 1—I hope that I have been able to reduce any lingering misgivings since then). In the opinion of these students, "mathematizing" people's behavior often takes what is real and concrete and makes it vague or abstract, difficult to grasp conceptually. What makes people inherently interesting sometimes gets lost, as it were, in the quantitative translation.

For their part, many teachers and researchers are unsure about the placement of the social and behavioral sciences, as well as some of the fields typically listed under these headings. Sometimes the discipline of psychology will be identified with the natural rather than the behavioral sciences, for example. Those who work in behavioral science fields—sociology, education, anthropology, political science, as well as psychology—often feel pressed to justify their existence to people outside their respective disciplines (see Figure F.1). Some observers are quick to comment that at best, the behavioral sciences are trying to make relatively subjective topics appear to be objective, even overly "technical"; at worst, these fields are engaging in describing and cataloging matters that are transparent to all but the most casual of observers. In correspondence with a fellow philosopher of science, for example, Imre Lakatos threw up his hands and wrote that, "The social

"I'm a social scientist, Michael. That means I can't explain electricity or anything like that, but if you ever want to know about people I'm your man."

Figure F.1   An All Too Common Perspective on the Behavioral Sciences

sciences are on par with astrology [the *pseudoscience* of how heavenly bodies influence human affairs], it is no use beating around the bush" (parenthetical comment, mine; quoted in Motterlini, 1999, p. 107; see also, Data Box F.1). Other critics point out that the quantitative turn of the behavioral sciences is at odds with its subject matter—the social, political, psychological, and economic lives of people in all their variety and diversity. The charge is that human experience should be *experienced*, discussed, or debated, but not measured or otherwise calculated like materials found in the physical world.

As a result of the behavioral sciences' measurement mania, quantitative research is often criticized for being of limited use (e.g., Flick, 1998). In particular, critics and commentators argue that data collected in behavioral science research are rarely seen as directly applicable or helpful to life in the everyday world. Experimental rigor, cause and effect relations, and concerns about representative populations—to name a few of the quantitative topics I defend in this book as essential to statistical analyses—are often

▽

Despite their ubiquity, measurement and quantification remain controversial in some quarters.

deemed too far removed from the concerns or problems that affect the lives and fortunes of many people. Inevitably, even the most rigorously scientific research and pristine results are colored by the interests and the social, political, and cultural backgrounds of the people conducting it (Flick, 1998; see also, Kuhn, 1970). Although some biases are reduced through experimentation, those associated with interpretation and point of view often remain (for a related discussion concerning the power of perspective, see Dunn, in press).

Collectively, of course, the behavioral sciences occupy contested territory between the humanities (e.g., literature, theology, philosophy) and the natural or physical sciences (e.g., chemistry, biology, physics), two sets of disciplines that have a relatively solid sense of what sorts of questions can be asked and which methods can be used to obtain answers. One reason that the behavioral sciences are stuck betwixt and between these older sets of disciplines is the unavoidable overlap in conceptual material. The behavioral sciences purport to examine vast areas of human experience, domains claimed for a far longer time by the humanities. Questions of human existence, destiny, and purpose, for example, are readily found in the plays of Sophocles and Shakespeare, novels by Iris Murdoch and William Faulkner, or the philosophy of Hegel, not just textbooks on psychology or education, the sociology of the family, or American national government. The behavioral sciences do not deny the insights of humanistic sources but try to back up their unique claim of understanding by arguing for empirical approaches that contrast with more intuitive explorations in the humanities. At the same time, of course, use of the term "empirical" often elicits the ire of practitioners in the natural sciences who do not believe that the behavioral sciences are very scientific to begin with.

Whether these disparate views carry some weight or represent little more than a tempest in an intellectual teapot is beside the point because they do influence the way people think about the behavioral sciences. Auden's lyrical commandment about avoiding statisticians and behavioral science, then, puts him in good company; some of the people working in, learning about, or observing what is done in the behavioral sciences share his concerns. His observation is clever, even quite funny, because it is poignantly apt. To some extent, the behavioral sciences—and behavioral scientists—are trying to find their way, though I am quick to argue that the struggle is an intellectually rich and rewarding one (Dunn, 1999).

Why raise these concerns in an appendix found in a book devoted to statistics and data analysis, bulwarks upon which the foundations of behavioral science rest? I would be remiss if I presented research and methods in the behavioral sciences as monolithic because diverse perspectives not only exist but also flourish. We spent the 15 chapters of this book familiarizing ourselves with the statistical views of the behavioral sciences, especially in the discipline of psychology. In this appendix, we will follow a different path, one leading from quantitative to *qualitative* approaches to research, from a dominant perspective to a nascent minority view.

▽

The conceptual home of the behavioral sciences, as well as their relation to the humanities and the natural sciences, is uncertain.

KEY TERM   **Qualitative research** uses empirical methodologies where resulting data appear and are interpreted in nonnumerical forms, and the subjective nature of the research enterprise is acknowledged.

This appendix will discuss the characteristics of qualitative research and then present some alternative approaches to doing research and performing data analyses that are *not* based exclusively on quantitative measurement.

Is it odd to be discussing qualitative alternatives to statistics in a text largely devoted to such subject matter? Perhaps so, but there is a method to this unconventional madness. I want to demonstrate that data analysis is not just a collection of techniques for working with numerical information. Many techniques are available for the analysis of qualitative data, as well. Furthermore, qualitative and quantitative techniques should be seen as complements and not rivals of one another. Regrettably, however, too many students gain the false impression that making something quantitative is somehow "better" or more legitimate than making a qualitative claim. That is simply not so.

Please do not assume that I am going to recant or otherwise deny the importance of all the information that I presented earlier in this book. The statistical analysis of behavioral science data is extremely important, but it is still only one approach to the study of behavior. There are other approaches worth learning and using as well. Contrary to popular belief, the discipline of statistics is not stagnant where propounding new ideas or revisiting existing ideas is concerned. It is entirely appropriate to question the wisdom of using—perhaps overusing—statistics in place of other available methods, many of which are qualitative in nature. How did we become so focused on numbers, anyway? We will explore this issue in the next section.

▽

Unfortunately, qualitative research is often portrayed as antithetical to—rather than complementary of—quantitative efforts.

The Presenting Problem: Measuring Reality

And still they come, new from those nations to which the study of that which can be weighed and measured is a consuming love.
— W. H. Auden (1986)

Between the years 1250 and 1600, there was a dramatic shift in people's thinking about the physical world, from a qualitative understanding to an increasingly quantitative one. Intellectual, social, and cultural development in western Europe centered on mechanical devices, especially clocks, double-entry bookkeeping, increasingly precise maps, and even perspective drawing in painting (Crosby, 1998). The increasing reliance on numbers and quantitative reasoning during the late Middle Ages through the Renaissance gave birth to advances in modern science, the rise of bureaucracies, the economic ideas underlying businesses and entrepreneurial ventures, and, of course, all of the technologies humans came to depend on in succeeding generations.

Prior to this change in perspective, western Europeans surely knew how to count and had more than a basic grasp of mathematical relations, but their understanding of the world and events within it was somewhat arbitrary. Available ambient light and the change of the seasons regulated time and labor, for instance, not clocks or calendars. Somewhere into the 12th century, however, knowledge of number and elementary measurement became—in the words of historian Alfred Crosby—a consuming "passion." Measurement provided order and later an accounting of events, which in turn led to numerical record keeping, ledgers, and the like. Where time is concerned, we no longer have just mechanical clocks but atomic ones that maintain the "correct" or "official" time to millionths of a second. We are indeed passionate about our numbers.

This passion for numbers continues largely unabated today; after all, you are your social security or student identification number! (Stop for a moment and reflect on how often you rely on that arbitrary but assigned number, as well as how often you will rely on it across your life.) Just take a look around yourself at how many interests, activities, and basic needs that you must satisfy are based on quantification or measurement of some sort. You break your day into discrete units (time) and each day is assigned a number (date), for example. You also compare your academic performance with peers (GPA), receive payment in return for your labor (money), acquire debts (money to be paid back with interest), and rely on computers with their binary programming (all information is actually represented as strings of 0s and 1s)—the list of quantified entities you encounter is almost endless. Consider, too, the millennium fever that has gripped the world for the past several years, as well as in the past (Gould, 1997). And yes, even the much belabored and ballyhooed Y2K problem is just another case of quantification (albeit one that almost went awry).

Not surprisingly, the behavioral sciences gradually came to depend on the power of numbers, as well. Why did measurement and quantification become a fixation of the behavioral sciences? The ability to measure and quantify observations lends credence to the argument that the study of human behavior in a formalized way makes it a science (Leahey, 1997).

Ascendance of the Measurable, or "Physics Envy" in the Behavioral Sciences

To greater or lesser degrees, each of the behavioral sciences relies on quantification in order to answer questions pertaining to its phenomena of interest. The discipline of psychology is illustrative in this vein. Psychology has claimed to be a science for over 100 years (Leahey, 1997), and during this time psychologists have repeatedly tried to follow the disciplinary path paved by physics (Leahey, 1990). Why physics? Physics is often hailed as the "queen of the sciences" and compared to most other scientific disciplines, it is the most advanced where the marriage of comprehensive theory with supporting data is concerned. Since the time of Sir Isaac Newton, precise laws of how the physical world works were established, enabling generations of thinkers and researchers to measure and manipulate matter, deducing probable outcomes in the process. As a result, physicists are comfortable making and testing out carefully crafted predictions, an ardent, even wistful, desire of many research psychologists.

Leahey (1997) argues that American psychology, in particular, developed a bad case of "physics envy." Because physics was the oldest and most respected of the natural sciences, psychologists naturally sought to emulate its method and techniques. By doing so, of course, the discipline of psychology could hope to gain respectability and prestige—membership, really, in the "club" of the natural sciences. This hope has been called a "Newtonian fantasy" by this historian of psychology (Leahey, 1990), a fantasy that is not likely to ever be realized for reasons of subject matter, methodologies, and perception. Please note that significant areas of study within the other behavioral sciences are heavily quantitative. I am thinking chiefly of economics, of course, but also sociology, education, and political science, which can rely on sophisticated mathematical and statistical methods.

Still, as I wrote this appendix, the second largest organization of psychologists in the United States, the American Psychological Society (APS), contemplated a name change to the "Association for Psychological Science." This cosmetic change was designed to "more accurately reflect the Society's mission," and was put to a vote by the organization's membership (Brookhart, 1999, p. 31). Yet such a change could not help but smack some degree of self-perceived inferiority, as if the organization and its member psychologists are consciously worried that without the imprimatur of "science" in the name it would not be taken seriously. The odd thing is that federal funding for research and public interest in psychology as an academic discipline have never been higher—still, however, physics envy in the psychological community appears to be alive and well.

Reaction to Quantification: A Brief History of Qualitative Research and Its Nature

In a real sense, the identification of qualitative research in the behavioral sciences occurred in the 19th and 20th centuries (Taylor & Bogdan, 1998), but it has been performed per se since the development of narratives and recorded history (Wax, 1971). Since antiquity, adventurers, travelers, and explorers have been moved to write about what they have seen and experienced in foreign or exotic locales. Such reports are a

---

▽

Numbers sometimes have a representational power or influence in human affairs.

▽

Physics is the most established of the natural sciences, followed by chemistry and biology.

DATA BOX F.1

Is Psychology a Science?

What makes a science a *science?* How does a science differ from a nonscience or a pseudo-science (i.e., a discipline pretending to be a science)? In some quarters, there are still attempts to rehabilitate astrology by labeling it a science (Holt, 1999).

The energy—less light than heat, usually—put into answering this question is akin to that spent in 13th century arguments regarding the question, "How many angels can dance on the head of a pin?" Answers were found but they did not satisfy everyone. To be sure, there are volumes on the history, sociology, and philosophy of science, and we cannot review their many perspectives here. What we can do, however, is to consider a definition for science used by Leahey (1997), who suggests that psychology cannot be a science in the traditional sense. A science searches for, "exceptionless general laws that apply to spatiotemporally unrestricted objects" (Leahey, 1997, p. 462; see also, Kuhn, 1977; Motterlini, 1999). Whoa, just what does that mean?

Well, think about it: Physics's laws presumably apply to planets and stars everywhere, not just those found in or near our single solar system. In contrast, psychology is a discipline that deals with really only one species—humans—and when and if any equally detailed laws of human behavior are derived, they will certainly not be "spatiotemporally unrestricted" as they are based solely on intelligent life on this planet. This somewhat process-oriented definition of what constitutes science will not satisfy everyone, but it does point to an important distinction that is often overlooked when disciplinary boundaries are drawn.

Leahey (1997) is not the only one to cast doubt on psychology's scientific pretensions or to answer in the negative about its status as a science. Considerable work on this question emanates from the disciplines of philosophy and biology. Some prominent philosophers argue, for example, that the increasing understanding of the brain and its neurophysiology will gradually replace and eventually eliminate psychology (e.g., P. M. Churchland, 1985; P. S. Churchland, 1986; Rosenberg, 1983; see also, Stich, 1983). Independent of but in sympathy with these sorts of philosophical positions, the field of biology, too, weighs in on psychology's future and finds it to be limited (e.g., Rosenberg, 1980, 1994). In particular, sociobiology, the idea that even social and cultural behaviors are based on and serve largely biological or reproductive ends, poses an clear interpretive threat (Wilson, 1975).

All is not lost, of course. Many psychologists take great umbrage at these sorts of conclusions by correctly noting that the discipline is quite young, so it is much too soon to draw any definitive conclusions about psychology's fate. Reports of its demise may be a bit premature, especially given the discipline's great strides in recent years. There is also the obvious fact that most psychologists—educators as well as researchers and practitioners—are going about their business oblivious to the fact that the scientific status of their work is in question (and as was previously acknowledged, status in the sense of recognition may be the chief worry, anyway).

Besides, if psychology is not a science by some set of definitions, does that really change anything? Probably not all that much. For your part, you should wonder whether reliance on statistics helps or hinders psychology's earnest desire to be treated like a member of the natural sciences. At the same time, you must also recognize that a science is not just defined by its techniques but also by its subject matter and the degree to which its findings are used to explain phenomena. You need not agree with Leahey's (1997) definition of the scope of what a science is and what it does. Choosing to disagree with his perspective or any of those being promulgated in philosophy, biology, or any other fields of study, however, requires some constructive engagement. What counterarguments can you offer?

In the end, is there any truth regarding what is or is not a science? The philosopher Paul Feyerabend (quoted in Motterlini, 1999, p. 249) claimed, "The truth, whatever it is, be damned. What we need is laughter." A wise, if not necessarily philosophical, observation we should keep in mind as we go about our work in the behavioral sciences.

form of "field work" that became formalized in both sociology and anthropology in the 19th and early 20th centuries. Then and now, the overriding research concern involves portraying the meanings and unique frames of reference individuals impute to their lives. Making sense out of this created or derived meaning is an important goal of qualitative research, which has other salient qualities, as well.

Qualitative methods actually developed along side of quantitative approaches. The figure that is often hailed as the "founder" of experimental psychology, Wilhelm Wundt, also relied on descriptive methods in what he called "folk psychology." Wundt's folk psychology was meant to augment experimentation, as he believed that the latter could never provide a complete psychology of individual mental life. Generally speaking, folk psychology was an attempt to examine the historical development of the human mind by examining aspects of collective experience (e.g., myths, languages, customs, traditions) that aid individual development (see Leahey, 1997, for more detail). The methodology of folk psychology was clearly qualitative but Wundt believed that it complemented and was not antithetical to experimental programs. Regrettably, of course, researchers following Wundt were drawn to the "rigor" of quantification, characterizing qualitative approaches as representing a "soft" approach to the study of behavior.

Exceptions to the rule existed, of course. American sociology had a decidedly qualitative twist from the late 19th century until at least the 1940s (Flick, 1998). In particular, sociologists were drawn to employing a descriptive style when writing about case studies, narratives, or biographies of their subjects. For the next 20 years or so, the quantitative mind-set gained followers in sociology, but this trend came under fire in the 1960s. American sociology began to do some soul searching, noting that traditional modes of inquiry provided rich characterizations of social life that the newer mathematical approaches could not capture. German intellectuals took up this same concern in the 1970s, heralding an interest in subjectivity and what is now known as postmodernism (for a more detailed history see, for example, Denzin & Lincoln, 1994).

Characterizing Qualitative Research.   Qualitative research encompasses any formal investigation that is not dependent on statistical or other quantitative procedures. As a result, qualitative research can examine people's lives and the behavior within them, the stories they tell to one another (or for that matter, to themselves), the purpose and operation of organizations (e.g., the United States Postal Service) or social movements (e.g., environmentalism), and the very nature of the interaction and interpretation that occurs among persons.

It is worth noting that qualitative research often means different things to different investigators (Strauss & Corbin, 1990). Indeed, it is probably a much easier exercise to identify when a given piece of research is largely quantitative than when it is qualitative. The qualitative techniques used to study domains of human behavior are varied, if not vast (see Denzin & Lincoln, 1994), and they can range from simple observation of what people do to detailed interviews with them. Furthermore, it is entirely possible to take written records, videotapes, recordings, books or other published materials, and to then analyze them using qualitative techniques. If there is any unifying theme running throughout qualitative research, it is the recognition that the method used and the researcher using it *actively construct the social world in the process of examining it.*

When we note that qualitative research does not use statistical or other quantitative means, please understand that some degree of counting or other numerical data reduction is bound to be used by investigators. This fact does not in any way discount the nature of the enterprise; rather, it directs our attention to the fact that the *analysis* of the data should be qualitative. Anselm and Corbin (1990) suggest that the major

Qualitative methods have always existed, but their identification per se occurred mostly as a reaction to quantitative techniques.

There is no uniform opinion regarding what defines a qualitative method.

components of qualitative research include data (e.g., interviews, observations), some analytic or interpretive procedure(s) for analyzing the data, and written (e.g., articles) or verbal (e.g., presentations) reports about what was found. As you can see, these components are no different from the quantitative approach to research, except that here the analytic or interpretive procedures are not statistical in nature.

A prominent tradition in qualitative research involves carefully examining the subjective meanings people impute to actions and situations. Blumer (1938) labeled the study of this shared subjectivity *symbolic interactionism.*

KEY TERM   **Symbolic interactionism** is the focused examination of the meanings people attach to things in the world around them. These meanings are reciprocal, as they develop from the shared interactions occurring between persons.

Research based on symbolic interactionism assumes that humans act toward things—objects, ideas, other people or organisms—based on the meanings things have for them. The origins of the meanings attached to things are based on social exchanges occurring between and among persons. Such meanings are maintained or changed following encounters with things, discussions about them, and the like. In a nutshell, qualitative researchers working in the symbolic interactionist tradition must learn to "see" the world from the perspective of the individual or group being studied (see also, Blumer, 1969).

Flick (1998, p. 5) argues that four key features characterize qualitative research, each of which has a symbolic interactionist "flavor" to it:

■ **Participant perspectives and diversity.** When conducting qualitative research, it is essential to examine the perspectives of the participants themselves, including any reactions to being the objects of study. An investigator studying the nature of, say, the experience of women in medical school would examine the students' perceptions of their educational experiences, as well as any subjective and social meanings or practices related to it (Flick, 1998). An obvious issue is how the male experience of medical education is different from that extended to females, if at all, but also how women feel their experiences differ from those of their male colleagues.

■ **Appropriate methodologies and theories.** Both qualitative and quantitative research are empirical pursuits, though we tend to associate this term with the latter approach. Not all questions can be answered empirically (e.g., religious matters, philosophical issues, exceptional events or personal experiences), of course, but those that can be need to be matched up to appropriate methods and theories. Novel qualitative approaches are often developed for such research, and the sponsoring investigator must make a convincing case to the scientific community for a new technique's acceptability. In doing so, comprehensive theories illustrating how variables can be explained in combination rather than laboratory isolation are desirable. This meeting of theory and methodology must account for how people interact and behave in everyday rather than controlled settings. Someone studying women in medical school, for example, might use a combination of observation, interviews, and diary work within the context provided by a feminist theory.

■ **Reflexive investigators and research.** Quantitatively oriented researchers strive to remain objective and unbiased about their objects of study and collected data. They avoid "getting involved" in the situation so as to be as dispassionate as possible about it. In contrast, qualitative investigators often get embroiled in the research moment, commenting on their perceptions, irritations, actions, feelings, and so forth in the course of an investigation (see the section devoted to writing issues later in this appendix). This subjective material, too, finds its way into any publication or report about the research because it is deemed an important part of the process of doing qualitative research. Whether the investigator studying female medical school students was also a woman would de facto have some influence on the conclusions drawn from the work (as would a male examining the same events).

■ **A variety of qualitative approaches and methodologies.** Although there is often disagreement between different investigators or schools of thought in the quantitatively oriented side of the behavioral sciences, there is relative unanimity where method and theory are concerned. As tools, for example, statistics and data analysis help to provide some objective guidance in the course of research. Qualitative research lacks this unified character, as there is no single vision for what to do, how to do it, and how to explain or think about it. A plethora of (sometimes conflicting) perspectives and methods exist where, in the words of Flick (1998, p. 7), "Subjective viewpoints are a first starting point." Our medical school researcher would literally walk onto the scene with certain expectations about medical school (e.g., not friendly to women, an "old boys'" club) before collecting an iota of data. An interesting question then becomes how these expectations are challenged, met, or possibly changed by the medical school venue selected for the research, and so on.

These four features should not be construed as exhaustive, of course. Indeed, the very nature of qualitative approaches, especially their willingness to accept novel perspectives, should lead us to assume that other authors or investigators would characterize qualitative research using very different terms. Such constructive "disagreement" is entirely in keeping with the liberal contextualism of qualitative research. We can now turn to a review of some of the ways behavioral scientists examine qualitative relationships in research.

Alternative Methods: Selected Approaches to Qualitative Data

Qualitative research efforts depend on descriptions, verbal reports, and the interpretation of events. As a result, qualitative data are not usually presented in numerical form; indeed, observations may be of no particular fixed variety. The availability of multiple methods is a decided benefit, one capable of helping researchers cut through the thicket of human experience (e.g., Lincoln & Guba, 1985).

In contrast to quantitative methods, qualitative approaches adhere to what is best described as an *open systems* view (e.g., Dunn, 1999). By open systems view, we mean that a variety of potentially useful information is gathered in qualitative investigations. When people respond to a cataclysmic natural disaster—a monsoon or an earthquake, for instance—there is no one right or "correct" approach to exploring individual or collective coping with it (Dunn, 1999). The approach employed depends on the circumstance, available resources, and the researcher running the investigation. Quantitative approaches tend to adhere to a *closed system* approach, one that identifies categories, possible responses, and ranges of ratings *in advance* of any data collection. Indeed, the closed system metaphor is best exemplified by laboratory research, which is intentionally closed to possible biases and influences found in the "outside" world.

Please note once more that qualitative approaches do not preclude the use of quantitative information or even statistical methods. Thus, it is entirely possible that a primarily qualitative investigation will include some quantification (e.g., frequency counts,

Qualitative methods follow an open systems approach, while quantitative methods are based on a closed system approach.

Table F.1   Rules of Thumb for the Qualitative Researcher

1. *Avoid studying your own group*—as an "insider," chances are that your reports will not be fair or accurate.
2. *Rely on outside readers to evaluate your work*—ask people who do not know about qualitative research or the topic to evaluate your writing. Such fresh, unbiased perspectives are invaluable.
3. *Qualitative research seeks to understand, not prove, something*—focus on interpreting what happens in some social situation.
4. *Time spent on analysis (i.e., interpretation, writing) is as important as time spent on data collection*—both sets of activities carry equal weight.
5. *Create a model of what happened in your work*—develop an outline or figure illustrating the research process from the earliest observation, through data collection, field notes, and written descriptions.
6. *Share the data with the research participants*—as the source of your data, participants have the right to see everything and to have their curiosity satisfied in the process.
7. *Be on the watch for contradictions, and points of conflict or tension in the data*—inconsistent observations or things that do not fit can often be a source of insight.
8. *Know that qualitative research can be costly*—the process of conducting a qualitative project from start to finish can be a costly endeavor in terms of time and money for materials (e.g., tapes, transcripts, video or recording equipment).

Source: Adapted from Janesick (1998, pp. 67–69).

descriptive statistics), just as it is no doubt virtually impossible to perform a quantitative project that does not include qualitative elements (e.g., describing what happened in a sequential manner). The formulation of ideas, the process of speculation, theorizing, and even writing involve largely qualitative acts. Thus, the dichotomy between the qualitative and the quantitative is a matter of degrees and is, in some sense, false. Avoid becoming "hung up" on whether a given research technique is "truly" qualitative or quantitative, or consider combining qualitative *and* quantitative techniques in any research you conduct, a constructive approach called *triangulation* (Campbell & Fiske, 1959).

In the remainder of this section, we will examine a few representative examples of qualitative research, some of which have been embraced by more quantitatively minded researchers. These examples—content analysis, participant observation and ethnography, narrative, and group processes—are by no means exhaustive ones, but are meant to whet your empirical appetite a bit (for discussion of other approaches, see the references listed in Data Box F.4). Before you proceed on to these qualitative examples, however, examine the rules of thumb for qualitative researchers shown in Table F.1. Janesick (1998) developed these rules in order to answer common questions people often have regarding qualitative research. Think of the points shown in Table F.1 as guidelines to help you better appreciate the unique qualities associated with qualitative investigations.

Creative, constructive investigators rely on a mix of methodologies in their work.

Content Analysis

When a qualitative researcher interviews a participant or examines the expressions found in some written communication, how are these verbal responses analyzed? Some researchers rely on a broad technique called *content analysis*.

KEY TERM   A **content analysis** involves creating a system or procedure for categorizing the content and frequency of communications, which are usually verbal.

Content analyses can be performed on the verbal content of live or taped communications (e.g., interviews, films, documentaries) as well as archival material (e.g., diaries,

Table F.2

Sample Positive Attributions Following Limb Amputation
Based on a Content Analysis

Found Side Benefits
"I changed to a different occupation [where] I became very successful."

Made Social Comparisons
"[I] have come to realize that there are many people who have more and bigger problems than
I and I am lucky to have what I have."

Imagined Worse Situations
"I survived. I have a second chance at life. I love it."

Forgot Negative Events
"I found that I can still do about everything I did before—only it takes longer to do it."

Redefined Event and Reappraised Life
"I think I've become a much better person—more humble, more considerate and less selfish.
I now know that I am not perfect."

Source: Adapted from Table 1 of Dunn (1996, p. 291).

▽

"Content" refers to the coded
meaning of a verbal response.

records, books, articles). The results of a content analysis can be used to describe the
nature of some exchange or to ask more focused questions about the behavior of the
participants under examination. I once performed a content analysis as part of a study
on people's well-being following the amputation of a limb (Dunn, 1996). Seventy-seven
percent of the participants wrote about something positive resulting from their ampu-
tations, and these coded attributions were organized into conceptual categories based
on prior research dealing with the search for "silver linings" in adversity (e.g., Schultz
& Decker, 1985; Taylor, Lichtman, & Wood, 1984). Categorized sample attributions from
this content analysis are shown in Table F.2.

One of the methodological concerns of doing a content analysis is illustrated by
two of the attributions in Table F.2. These attributions require the investigator to "fill
in the blanks" left by respondents. The first two attributions include bracketed words
(i.e., [where] and [I]), indicating that a respondent left out a word or words. The investigator must carefully select words that finish the spirit of the original thought. The
word substitutions shown in Table F.2 appear to be satisfactory, but more radical or detailed changes to a categorized verbal explanation can be problematic. As a result, the
content analyst must always proceed cautiously when evaluating his or her data.

Following a somewhat different procedure, psychologists Christopher Peterson and
Martin Seligman developed a particular type of content analysis called the CAVE (content analysis of verbal explanations) technique (e.g., Peterson & Seligman, 1984), one
that involves some quantitative elements. Relying on the theoretical framework provided
by learned helplessness theory (e.g., Peterson & Bossio, 1989), Peterson and Seligman argued that the manner by which people habitually explain negative events not only
colors their perceptions, it is also linked to the possible presence of depressive sym-
tomatology (see also, Alloy, Abramson, & Francis, 1999). When people chronically explain negative events—being snubbed by a friend, performing poorly on a test—by appealing to internal ("it's me"), stable ("it's not going to change"), and global ("it will
affect everything in my life") causes, these researchers find that people's pessimism puts
them at greater risk for depression and health problems. One study found that college-
aged males who possessed this pessimistic explanatory style were more likely to have
poorer health between the ages of 45 and 60 than their more positive peers (Peterson,
Seligman, & Vaillant, 1988). Another discovered that pessimistic candidates for the
American presidency between 1948 and 1984 tended to lose the election more often

than not, quite possibly due to passivity created by their negative outlooks (Zullow & Seligman, 1990).

As shown by the work on attributions for amputation and negative explanatory style, a content analysis can be used to classify responses or the respondents themselves. Any resulting categories can be studied in their own right, used to create novel interpretive frameworks, or combined with existing quantitative methodologies.

Participant Observation and Ethnography

Content analysis can be a solid, theoretically driven methodology for scrutinizing verbal reports from the past or the present, but it is neither dynamic nor involving. Participant observation is a variation of a larger research scheme, naturalistic observation, where a researcher literally systematically observes, records, and describes behavior as it occurs. Like content analysis, naturalistic observation is largely a passive pursuit, whereas *participant observation* is active because the observer becomes a "participant observer," one who takes part in whatever events are unfolding (Spradley, 1980).

KEY TERM   **Participant observation** entails entering into a research setting and then monitoring, recording, and interpreting the behavior of research participants and, on occasion, interacting with them.

▽

Participant observation is the opposite of a controlled experiment with its detached investigator.

A participant observer is sometimes said to be a type of investigative journalist, someone who is in the situation, carefully watching and observing, but still dispassionate enough not to become totally a part of it (e.g., Rosnow & Rosenthal, 1996). Similar to investigative journalists, cameras, tape recorders, and notebooks are often employed by participant observers, though some researchers prefer to rely exclusively on their memories for events. Spradley (1980, p. 34) suggests that there are three stages to participant observation:

1. **Descriptive observation**—which occurs at the start of a project, when a researcher is looking to obtain a sense of its scope, complexity, and the sorts of questions that must be asked.
2. **Focused observation**—which occurs as the researcher begins to narrow his or her scope in order to pursue questions deemed to be the most essential to the project.
3. **Selective observation**—which takes place near the end of the work, and is often oriented toward identifying examples, practices, and processes that bolster observations made in the second step.

Generally, participant observers will have some theory or hypothesis guiding their data collection, though they can often take advantage of unexpected events. Certainly, then, this element of empirical spontaneity highlights the qualitative character of participant observation—unplanned or unforeseen events can rarely be investigated experimentally or recreated in a laboratory setting (Weick, 1968). A classic demonstration is the doomsday group described by Festinger, Riecken, and Schachter (1956), where a member of the research team infiltrated the group's membership in order to study its process as the prophesized date (but not Armageddon) drew near.

A more recent but equally intriguing project employed *ethnography,* a close relative of participant observation. The study examined the experience of being a college student living in a university dormitory—before I describe it in some detail, let me define ethnography.

KEY TERM   **Ethnography** is a research approach dependent on the undisguised, objective study of the habits, customs, and actions of people in a culture as they go about their daily lives.

Ethnographers utilize a qualitative perspective by trying to describe how a given culture makes sense out of its social experience. Unlike the standard form of participant

DATA BOX F.2

"Tricks of the Qualitative Trade": An Illustrative Trick of Perspective

It is virtually impossible to provide a detailed overview of qualitative research in an appendix, let alone an entire book devoted to the subject. Still, I want to give you an illustrative example of the sensibility that drives qualitative research. The sociologist Howard S. Becker wrote a clever, insightful book of research techniques and experiences called *Tricks of the Trade* (Becker, 1998) containing many qualitative examples or "tricks." To Becker, a trick is a straightforward "rule of thumb" or simple guide that helps an investigator see to the heart of a research problem and then solve it.

Early in the book, Becker tells an anecdote about a classroom experience he had with an eminent sociologist, Everett C. Hughes, one who had little patience for abstract or so-called "grand" theories of human social behavior. Becker and some of his student cronies were worrying about how to correctly define the concept of "ethnic group." How would they know, they wondered, if they were correctly categorizing a group? Hughes had previously written about the usual tact researchers took to define such groups:

> Almost anyone who uses the term [ethnic group] would say that it is a group distinguishable from others by one, or some combination of the following: physical characteristics, language, religion, customs, instructions, or "cultural traits." (Hughes, 1984, p. 153)

Most behavioral scientists would concur with this approach, noting that it fits in nicely with the quantitative approach of operationally defining terms (e.g., recall chapters 1 and 2 in this book). Becker (1998, p. 2) notes that he and his fellow students were implicitly out to compare a given, identified "ethnic" group with a perceived "nonethnic" group. In short, the former is labeled an "ethnic" group because it is different from the latter.

Hughes said no, that a better perspective was to turn the sequence around a bit using a simple "trick":

> An ethnic group is not one because of the degree of measurable or observable differences from other groups [both quantitative dimensions]; it is an ethnic group on the contrary because the people in and the people out of it know that it is one; because both the *ins* and the *outs* talk, feel, and act as if it were a separate group. (Hughes, 1984, pp. 153–154; *parenthetical comment mine*)

A group is a group because those in it and those outside it perceive it as different. Other factors—religion and language, for example—are important but only insofar as they shed light on the (existing) ethnic relationships and networks occurring between groups. Hughes pointed to an elegant and often overlooked qualitative distinction that pervades social life. His trick was to examine the networks where the other factors are derived and used to create social worlds and the points of view of people in and outside them.

There are, of course, countless other qualitative tricks one can use, and no doubt these tools can inform or complement the work of statistics and data analysis. The trick for the quantitatively oriented researcher is to put his or her usual approaches on hold for a bit, allowing the qualitative alternative to shed new light in theorizing about behavior.

---

observation, ethnographers often directly and intentionally interview the members of the culture they are studying.

Back to in situ life in the dormitory. An anthropologist decided to learn about the life of 18- to 22-year-olds by living in their venue for a while. To do so, he lived off and on in a dormitory at Rutgers University between 1977 and 1987. Moffatt (1989, p. xv) described his foray into this most active form of participant observation as "hanging around with one's subjects for a long enough time to start hearing them in their more natural adolescent tones . . . sensing their own priorities as they understand them." Moffat's work is appropriately titled *Coming of Age in New Jersey,* a play on a classic piece of anthropology by Margaret Mead (i.e., *Coming of Age in Samoa;* Mead, 1961), herself a proponent of this involving form of interpretive field work.

During the course of his dorm life, Moffatt (1989) found that the way the undergraduate students interacted with him changed over the course of his relationship with them. Once they discovered he was not a fellow student but rather an interested anthropologist (he made no attempt to hide his identity or real purpose for being there), they spoke to him differently—they used fewer obscene words and phrases in his presence. Note that a traditional quantitative investigation would identify this behavioral change as a confound or bias introduced by the researcher, where a qualitative perspective could construe the change as a matter of course that no doubt represents the complexity of social interaction outside the undergraduate age group. Interpretation is indeed a matter of perspective.

Narratives and Life History

Participant observation and ethnography involve outsider interpretation of events—is it possible to formally examine people's reflections about themselves? Whether in jest or during a job interview or the like, we have all been asked to tell the story of our lives. Qualitative researchers are drawn by the way in which such individual stories provide insight into people's experiences, really, their "worlds." One of the simplest, yet most direct qualitative procedures involves asking research participants to produce a *narrative* regarding their lives or some particular episode therein.

KEY TERM   A **narrative** is an individual's story or other verbal account of some event, one that is often prompted by a semistructured interview or question.

According to this definition, narratives generally come in two basic types: **narrative interviews** and **episodic narratives** (Flick, 1998). A narrative interview is very open-ended and usually biographical. Here is a narrative interview prompt designed to encourage participants to reflect on themselves and their lives (from Hermanns, 1991, p. 182):

> I want to ask you to tell me how the story of your life occurred. The best way to do this would be for you to start from your birth, with the little child that you once were, and then to tell all the things that happened one after the other until today. You can take your time in doing this, and also give details, because for me everything is of interest that is important for you.

Keep in mind that the main topic of interest here is what people *believe* to be true of their experiences and *not* whether their reports are factual accounts. Subjectivity is acceptable, even welcome, because it provides insights into people's perspectives on themselves or events that shaped them. A related problem, of course, is the sheer volume of data that must be interpreted—people can talk for literally hours and hours about themselves, so a qualitative researcher interested in biographies must devise a scheme for culling the main points of interest from these free-flowing verbal reports. As you can see, the narrative interview is not for the fainthearted investigator or one used to a quick turnaround time between data collection and analysis!

Episodic narratives are much more focused than narrative interviews, often starting in response to some temporally local event (e.g., "Tell me what you did yesterday at work.") or one that happened in the past (e.g., "Describe your first day of high school—what was it like?"). In contrast to the narrative interview where one "big" question is asked, the episodic interview is usually comprised of several different but related

▽

Narrative is a form of autobiography, rich and subjective.

questions oriented to a given topic. Flick (1996), for example, asked a variety of focused questions concerning technology and people's reactions to it (e.g., "Which parts of your life are free of technology? Please tell me about a typical situation!").

One of the most promising directions for narrative research involves the importance of biography and key episodes to people's lives and beliefs about their own development (e.g., Bruner, 1987, 1991). Psychologist Dan P. McAdams (1993), for example, uses a biographical narrative approach to study personality, one that incorporates culture, social roles, and individual construal processes in identity development. Briefly, McAdams believes that we use our life stories and personal myths to make sense of our experiences. In effect, we derive meaning in our lives by essentially telling stories about ourselves to others and, for that matter, to ourselves. This novel view runs counter to the prevailing wisdom that people's personalities are either based on relatively fixed personal characteristics or reactions to a general series of stages everyone necessarily encounter.

According to McAdams (1993), these stories define us, and across time we put them together in order to develop a personal myth. Personal myths can be cultural (e.g., tragic myths tend to emphasize the absurdity of life) or unique to an individual (e.g., "No one taught me to be an artist—I just watched the world around me and internalized its beauty."). The interesting part of myths is the mixing of truth with fiction, as they are comprised of memories, perceptions, and our hopes for the future. To McAdams (1993, p. 13), "We do not discover ourselves in myth; we *make ourselves* through myth." In this way, the narrative tradition can be seen as a productive method for examining the development of self-concept across the life span.

Qualitative Research in Groups

The study of individual interviews and narratives have their place in the qualitative canon, but they possess the shortcoming of being artificial and unlike the give and exchange present found in daily, if ordinary, social interaction (e.g., Flick, 1998). Discussions occurring within groups of people are not only more natural, they are also more dynamic. Thus, even controversial (e.g., abortion) or taboo topics (e.g., sexual practices) can be aired in a more "normal" manner if groups of research participants are organized to discuss them (Flick, 1998). By far, the most common approach is to use what is called a *focus group*.

KEY TERM A **focus group** is an interview involving a small number of people—usually six to eight—who gather to discuss a specific topic of interest for approximately 2 hours.

According to Morgan (1988), for example, focus groups are often used to:

- Generate hypotheses from participants' insights.
- Help an investigator become acclimated to a new field of research.
- Evaluate different research populations.
- Examine participants' reactions to data collected in earlier research.
- Create questionnaires or surveys, or planning interviews.

Business and industry often rely on focus groups to learn about people's need for or understanding of current or planned consumer products. Thus, a group of consumers might be brought together to discuss proposed alterations to a popular piece of software, say, one used to do personal income taxes. Note that the sample of participants would need to be somewhat familiar with the product (or at least with computers) but because so few are gathered together in any one focus group, there is no attempt to create any sort of a representative sample of users. Remember, focus groups

DATA BOX F.3

Characteristics of the Qualitative Researcher

Janesick (1998, p. 70) characterized the requisite skills and temperament of the ideal qualitative researcher. She believes particular qualities are necessary for conducting as well as completing a qualitative project. As you read the following list, think about whether these characteristics are different than those you (now) associate with quantitative investigators. Similarly, how would you rate yourself on these qualities?

1. Tolerance for ambiguity.
2. Flexibility and openness to change plans or directions in the course of the research.
3. Desire and determination to complete the work.
4. Passion, compassion, and integrity.
5. Patience and resourcefulness.
6. Ability to commit equal time and effort to field work and analysis.
7. Trust in self and others.
8. Self-knowledge and self-awareness.
9. Authenticity.
10. Good writing skills.

constitute a qualitative, not a quantitative, approach to data collection, so concerns about generalizability are deemed much less pressing.

Table F.3 contains the basic steps found within most focus groups and, as you can see, there are few surprises here. Participants are gathered together to discuss some preordained topic (step 1), introductions and the moderator's role is noted (step 2), and some prompt regarding the topic is delivered (step 3). An attempt to "break the ice" or to warn participants about problematic group processes occurs in step 4, an optional step added when participants do not know each other.

Focus groups are still a form of an interview (Patton, 1990), so a leader or moderator must be present (see step 2 in Table F.3). This individual gets the discussion

Focus groups are associated with—but not limited to—research on consumer behavior.

Table F.3   Basic Steps in Running a Focus Group

Step 1. Participants are provided with an explanation of the discussion procedure, allowing them to formulate expectations and possible responses. An opening prompt might be: "We want you to openly discuss your likes and dislikes about available software for personal use. We are especially interested in software used for personal accounting."

Step 2. Members are introduced to one another and the moderator will often emphasize any shared bonds or characteristics: "As professionals who keep up on software innovations for home use, we thought that . . ."

Step 3. A stimulus for discussion—a presentation, a short film, or some provocative statement—is then introduced: "Can accounting software ever be expected to keep up with changes imposed by the federal government?"

Step 4. When participants are strangers to one another, an attempt is made to review group conformity issues, the problem of slowed discussion, and what to do to "jump start" the proceedings if or when things stop.

Source: Adapted from Flick (1998, pp. 119–120).

going but must remain "flexible, objective, empathic, persuasive, a good listener" (Fontana & Frey, 1994, p. 365). More often than not, a group of observers is also standing by to watch the focus group in action. These observers can be physically present in the interview room or sequestered behind a partition or one-way mirror. Other times, the focus group might be filmed for later viewing and analysis. In any case, the observers are interested in studying the fresh, ongoing impressions or perceptions of the focus group participants. They are not especially interested in asking the focus group to engage in any decision making or problem solving; indeed, the responses gathered during the session can be incorporated into such activities at a later time. Where consumer goods are concerned, then, focus groups entail brainstorming about reactions to existing products or hopes for product development.

Writing About Qualitative Research: An Overview

It is not possible to discuss all the different approaches one might adopt in writing up the findings from a qualitative study—a given researcher considering one study will write from a different perspective than another examining the same data. (Incidentally, qualitative researchers eschew the word *results* in favor of *findings* because the former is invariably associated with quantitative research methods.) One good piece of advice is to write about one critical concept or category from a project in some detail for a paper, a presentation, or an article (Strauss & Corbin, 1990). The writer's rule that less is generally more applies here, though a qualitative researcher can bolster his or her one main concept with a few related observations drawn from the same data set.

A second piece of advice concerns what is called **discounting** (Deutcher, 1973), the idea that a qualitative researcher should provide just enough methodological detail for readers to be able to (a) discount or downplay your account of what happened or (b) comprehend the project in the context of how you actually did it. The process of discounting will seem counterintuitive, as well as highly critical, but the point is that all reports—even the most "objective" one—contain some degree of subjectivity because they are based on the view of the person doing the writing or reporting. Because point of view is a given, qualitative researchers are encouraged to remind themselves and their readers that data can always be interpreted differently and according to context. Commenting on this discounting principle, Taylor and Bogdan (1998, p. 157) note that, "Proof is elusive in qualitative research."

Qualitative findings are rarely deemed definitive, as interpretation is in the eye of the beholder.

Taylor and Bogdan (1998, pp. 170–171) also highlight eight issues that a qualitative piece of writing should contain. These issues can be introduced in a variety of ways in the course of an article or report, as there is no fixed order for them to appear (compare these issues to the standard format of the APA style journal article, for example; see Appendix C). The issues are:

Methodology.   Readers should be apprised of the particular methodology used (e.g., participant observation, focus group) and research procedures (e.g., interview, notes based on memory for events, audio or videotape).

Theory.   Is the study descriptive or grounded in some overarching theoretical perspective (e.g., feminist theory)? If an existing context or research tradition exists, place the work into it.

Time Frame for the Research.   Readers should know how long the study took, as well as how much time was involved in data collection out in the field.

Participants.   Who were the participants? How many were there? What were they like? In what setting(s) were they observed or interviewed?

Research Design.   How were the participants selected or recruited? Why was one research method chosen over another? Provide a detailed rationale of the whys and wherefores of the project's methodology.

Investigator Point of View.   Why was the study undertaken in the first place? How did a researcher's view change over time? What presuppositions did the investigator bring to the work?

Relationship with the Participants.   How did the investigator interact with the study's participants? Did the participants act naturally with the researcher? Characterize the nature of this relationship and how it affected the data collection, analysis, and conclusions.

Investigator's Analysis.   How were the data analyzed? Were the participants given the opportunity to review the analyses and report? Did the researcher impose any checks or balances on the conclusion he or she drew?

DATA BOX F.4

Readings on Qualitative and Other Alternative Approaches to
Research in the Behavioral Sciences

Here are some resources to help you think beyond the strictly quantitative side of research in the behavioral sciences:

Becker, H. S. (1998). *Tricks of the trade: How to think about your research while you're doing it.* Chicago: University of Chicago Press.

Flick, U. (1998). *An introduction to qualitative research.* London: Sage.

Gubrium, J. F., & Holstein, J. A. (1997). *The new language of qualitative method.* New York: Oxford University Press.

Hedrick, T. E., Bickman, L., & Rog, D. J. (1993). *Applied research design: A practical guide.* Newbury Park, CA: Sage.

Janesick, V. J. (1998). *"Stretching" exercises for qualitative researchers.* Thousand Oaks, CA: Sage.

Lincoln, Y. S., & Guba, E. G. (1985). *Naturalistic inquiry.* Newbury Park, CA: Sage.

Marshall, C., & Rossman, G. B. (1989). *Designing qualitative research.* Newbury Park, CA: Sage.

McAdams, D. P. (1993). *The stories we live by: Personal myths and the making of the self.* New York: Morrow.

Miles, M. B., & Huberman, A. M. (1984). *Qualitative data analysis: A sourcebook of new methods.* Newbury Park, CA: Sage.

Reinharz, S. (1992). *Feminist methods in social research.* New York: Oxford University Press.

Spradley, J. P. (1980). *Participant observation.* Fort Worth, TX: Harcourt Brace Jovanovich.

Strauss, A., & Corbin, J. (1990). *Basics of qualitative research: Grounded theory procedures and techniques.* Newbury Park, CA: Sage.

Taylor, S. J., & Bogdan, R. (1998). *Introduction to qualitative research methods: A guidebook and resource* (3rd ed.). New York: Wiley.

The content and scope of these issues clearly err toward the descriptive. Little emphasis is placed on accuracy in the sense of providing a "correct" or absolute account of what took place. There is a conscientious attempt, however, to be accurate in reporting details great and small, as well as giving readers a flavor of the research process. To be sure, many or perhaps all of these issues can be explored in writing about quantitative issues, but the desire to be reflective about or to actually participate in the research effort as more than observer or experimenter is unusual. Few quantitative researchers would openly embrace the qualitative idea of discounting, either. Nonetheless, clear and concise prose about behavioral science results (or *findings!*) is the sincere goal of both the qualitative and quantitative camps, qualities we should aspire to in our own work.

Meaning Beyond Method

There is hope in honest error; none in the icy perfections of the mere stylist.
                                        —Charles Rennie Mackintosh

Mackintosh was talking about architects and designers, but he might just as well have been describing behavioral scientists. Adherence to convention is understandable, but it should not preclude innovation or simple logic. Similarly, teachers, scholars, and researchers cannot hope to advance their disciplines if statistics and data analyses are not used in flexible, even creative, ways—statistics books (including this one) do not constitute an infallible or sacred canon, after all.

The late statistician and psychologist, Jacob Cohen (1994), suggested that psychologists—and by extension, I think, all behavioral scientists—must move beyond relying exclusively on statistical methods to make claims about behavior. Cohen's recommendation about what to do is an obvious one, so obvious that it is routinely overlooked—*replicate results.* The replication of research results is one way to properly emulate work done in the older, natural sciences (Cohen, 1994). If a result is reliable, then it should be repeatable, either in a literal replication study or a conceptual replication (i.e., introducing a variation on a paradigm; e.g., Dunn, 1999). Replication is a good way to address the issue of generalizability (see chapter 15)—whether a result can be applied to other populations at other places in other times (see also chapter 2's discussion of external validity)—and to move to examining the actual meaning of research results beyond the method used to obtain them. Results should be all the more persuasive, as well as accurate, if they are demonstrated using a variety of methods. Perhaps quantitative and qualitative methods can constructively support one another, after all.

LOOKING FORWARD THEN BACK

The two decision trees opening this appendix will prove helpful when deciding whether to conduct a qualitative or a quantitative piece of research (remembering, of course, that elements of each approach are found in practically any study—identify which one predominates). The first decision tree provides gentle guidance where distinctions between these two approaches are concerned, as it is not feasible to highlight every possible distinction in one place. The second tree focuses on selecting a qualitative approach from one of the four main research approaches presented in the appendix. The distinctions between the research approaches, too, can be fluid—a hallmark of qualitative work—but you should feel free to consider others that can be found in other resources.

Summary

1. There is a tension between quantitative and non-numerically based or "qualitative" research perspectives in the behavioral sciences.

2. Although qualitative research is popularly perceived as antithetical to quantitative work, it is actually complementary to it. Most quantitative projects possess qualitative elements, and vice versa.

3. Quantitative worldviews have their origins in the 13th century, when western Europeans began to create various mechanized and mathematical devices to measure things, as well as to direct labor into new avenues. The passion from that time continues to this day—numbers and technology drive modern culture.

4. The behavioral sciences embraced quantification in order to gain the credibility associated with the natural sciences, especially physics. The discipline of psychology is noteworthy for having demonstrated "physics envy," a desire to have the theoretical and methodological precision found in the oldest scientific pursuit. This envy or emulation may be problematic because psychology and the other behavioral sciences do not possess the same characteristics as physics.

5. Qualitative approaches have always existed, especially in the form of narratives or other personal forms of writing or record keeping. Qualitative methods became more formalized in the 19th century, however, and gradually gained use in the behavioral sciences as a viable alternative to quantification.

6. Symbolic interactionism, a prominent qualitative tradition, is concerned with the subjective nature of meanings people attach to things.

7. Qualitative research adheres to an open systems view in that data are gathered in numerous ways using a variety of methods. There is no central qualitative method or paradigm, rather there are many, many ways to examine human behavior.

8. A content analysis is a form of qualitative data reduction. Typically, a content analysis categorizes self-report or verbal data according to some guiding theory or framework.

9. Participant observation refers to situations where a researcher actively observes and sometimes engages participants during the process of data collection. Ethnography, a related approach, is the objective examination of all the characteristics of a given culture.

10. Narratives or stories are used to portray the autobiographical nature of experience. A narrative begun in reaction to an open-ended question is called a narrative interview. One directed toward a specific issue or incident is called a narrative episode.

11. Qualitative group processes can be explored in a focus group, where a relatively small number of people are gathered to discuss some item or idea for a fixed period. The focus group is an antidote to the largely singular or individualized self-reports found in most other qualitative approaches.

12. Writing about qualitative research is just as rigorous as summarizing quantitative efforts, though a couple differences stand out. Qualitative reports are usually focused on one aspect of a qualitative study; despite the plethora of data usually available, not everything is reported. Qualitative authors usually provide sufficient detail about a project so readers can accurately judge its success or, conversely, to "discount" the work as subjective, a recognition that proof is not a crucial issue in qualitative alternatives.

13. Meaning is more important than method, and researchers are encouraged to examine their data more closely and with more of an eye to replication than has heretofore been the case. Generalizing results from one setting to another is as dependent on the practical matter of replication as it is on the statistical significance of results.

Key Terms

Content analysis (*p. F-10*)

Discounting (*p. F-17*)

Episodic narrative (*p. F-14*)

Focus group (*p. F-15*)

Ethnography (*p. F-12*)

Narrative (*p. F-14*)

Narrative interview (*p. F-14*)

Participant observation (*p. F-12*)

Qualitative research (*p. F-3*)

Symbolic interactionism (*p. F-8*)

Appendix Problems

1. Why are qualitative and quantitative approaches perceived to be incompatible with one another? Explain why they are arguably compatible with one another.

2. What are some advantages associated with qualitative research? What sorts of issues can qualitative efforts tackle that quantitative research cannot?

3. In your opinion, why are the behavioral sciences so compelled to measure and manipulate variables in the study of human behavior?

4. What is "physics envy"? Does psychology suffer from it? In your view, do other areas of study within the behavioral sciences display "physics envy"?

5. Define qualitative research and list some of its characteristics.

6. Why is the theme of perspective—that of the researcher and his or her participants—so prominent in qualitative investigations?

7. Why is perspective or point of view less important in quantitative rather than qualitative research? Does it matter less there? Why or why not?

8. Explain the meanings and use of "open" and "closed" systems in the context of qualitative and quantitative research.

9. Briefly discuss six rules of thumb for qualitative researchers.

10. Define the term content analysis and provide an example that might be found in the behavioral sciences.

11. Explain the idea behind participant observation and how it varies from ethnography. After defining these terms, provide a concrete example of each one.

12. What are the stages of conducting a participant observation? Define each one in the context of an example.

13. What is a narrative? Identify and define the two main types of narratives used in research efforts.

14. Create a prompt for an episodic narrative.

15. Create a prompt for a narrative interview.

16. What advantage(s) does qualitative research in groups have over more interview oriented work (e.g., narrative, participant observation)?

17. How does a focus group differ from a more traditional interview? Why do some qualitative researchers argue that focus groups represent a better research technique than other qualitative methods?

18. What are some of the reasons a researcher would want to conduct a focus group?

19. Imagine that you are running a focus group. Select a topic for the group to discuss and then describe how you would lead the group through the four steps usually associated with focus groups.

20. Characterize the differences, if any, between the writing associated with qualitative and that found in quantitative research. (*Hint:* Review the sections devoted to writing found in the first 14 chapters in this book for some ideas.)

21. List eight characteristics of qualitative researchers, and briefly explain *in your opinion* why each is important.

22. You are a clinical psychologist who is trying to identify how many young women in a large urban high school are at risk for anorexia nervosa, an eating disorder. Which research approach—qualitative or quantitative—should you follow? Why? (*Hint:* Use the decision trees at the opening of this appendix for guidance in answering this question.)

23. You are interested in studying child and parental impressions of the first day of school in kindergarten. Your goal is to collect and examine reflections generated by these two groups. Which research approach—qualitative or quantitative—should you follow? Why? (*Hint:* Use the decision trees at the opening of this appendix for guidance in answering this question.)

24. The dean of students at a university is concerned that students will perceive a new set of behavioral guidelines for dormitory living as restrictive, even harsh. What sort of research technique should the dean employ to get a sense of student opinion before deciding whether to implement the guidelines? Why? (*Hint:* Use the decision trees at the opening of this appendix for guidance in answering this question.)

REFERENCES

Abelson, R. P. (1985). A variance explanation paradox: When a little is a lot. *Psychological Bulletin, 97,* 129–133.

Abelson, R. P. (1995). *Statistics as principled argument.* Hillsdale, NJ: Erlbaum.

Abelson, R. P., Leddo, J., & Gross, P. H. (1987). The strength of conjunctive explanations. *Personality and Social Psychology Bulletin, 13,* 141–155.

Agresti, A., & Finlay, B. (1997). *Statistical methods for the social sciences* (3rd ed.). Upper Saddle River, NJ: Prentice Hall.

Allison, P. D. (1999). *Multiple regression: A primer.* Thousand Oaks, CA: Pine Forge Press.

Alloy, L. B., Abramson, L. Y., & Francis, E. L. (1999). Do negative cognitive styles confer vulnerability to depression? *Current Directions in Psychological Science, 8,* 128–132.

American Psychological Association (1994). *Publication Manual of the American Psychological Association* (4th ed.). Washington, DC: Author.

Anselm, A. L., & Corbin, J. M. (1990). *Basics of qualitative research: Techniques and procedures for grounded theory.* Thousand Oaks, CA: Sage.

Aron, A., & Aron, E. N. (1997). *Statistics for the behavioral and social sciences: A brief course.* Upper Saddle River, NJ: Prentice Hall.

Aron, A., & Aron, E. N. (1999). *Statistics for psychology* (2nd ed.). Upper Saddle River, NJ: Prentice Hall.

Aronson, E., Ellsworth, P. C., Carlsmith, J. M., & Gonzales, M. H. (1990). *Methods of research in social psychology* (2nd ed). New York: McGraw-Hill.

Aspinwall, L. G., & Taylor, S. E. (1992). Modeling cognitive adaptation: A longitudinal investigation of the impact of individual differences and coping on college adjustment and performance. *Journal of Personality and Social Psychology, 63,* 989–1003.

Auden, W. H. (1986). *The English Auden: Poems, essays, and dramatic writings, 1927–1939.* London: Faber and Faber.

Auden, W. H. (1991). *Collected poems.* New York: Vintage.

Azar, B. (1999, May). APA statistics task force prepares to release recommendations for public comment. *APA Monitor, 9.*

Babbage, C. (1989). The decline of science in England. *Nature, 340,* 499–502. (Original work published 1830)

Bailar, J. C., & Mosteller, F. (1988). Guidelines for statistical reporting in articles for medical journals: Amplifications and explanations. *Annals of Internal Medicine, 108,* 266–273.

Bakan, D. (1966). The test of significance in psychological research. *Psychological Bulletin, 66,* 423–437.

Barber, J. S., Axinn, W. G., & Thornton, A. (1999). Unwanted childbearing, health, and mother-child relationships. *Journal of Health and Social Behavior, 40,* 231–257.

Barfield, W., & Robless, R. (1989). The effects of two- and three-dimensional graphics on the problem-solving performance of experienced and novice decision makers. *Behaviour and Information Technology, 8,* 369–385.

Baum, A., Gatchel, R. J., & Schaeffer, M. A. (1983). Emotional, behavioral, and physiological effects of chronic stress at Three Mile Island. *Journal of Consulting and Clinical Psychology, 51,* 565–572.

Becker, H. S. (1998). *Tricks of the trade: How to think about your research while you're doing it.* Chicago: University of Chicago Press.

Bem, D. J. (1987). Writing the empirical journal article. In M. P. Zanna & J. Darley (Eds.), *The compleat academic: A practical guide for the beginning social scientist* (pp. 171–201). New York: Random House.

Bem, D. J., & Allen, A. (1974). On predicting some of the people some of the time: The search for cross-situational consistencies in behavior. *Psychological Review, 81,* 506–520. Cohen, J. (1992). A power primer. *Psychological Bulletin, 112,* 155–159.

Bem, S. L. (1977). On the utility of alternative procedures for assessing psychological androgyny. *Journal of Consulting and Clinical Psychology, 45,* 196–205.

Bennett, D. J. (1998). *Randomness.* Cambridge, MA: Harvard University Press.

Berger, A. (1999). Long-lasting scares of unwanted births. *The New York Times,* August 24, F8.

Berscheid, E., & Walster, E. (1974). Physical attractiveness. In L. Berkowitz (Ed.), *Advances in experimental social psychology* (Vol. 7, pp. 157–215). San Diego, CA: Academic Press.

Billig, M., & Tajfel, H. (1973). Social categorization and similarity in intergroup behavior. *European Journal of Social Psychology, 3,* 27–52.

Blumer, H. (1938). Social psychology. In E. Schmidt (Ed.), *Man and society* (pp. 144–198). New York: Prentice Hall.

Blumer, H. (1969). *Symbolic interactionism: Perspective and method.* Berkeley and Los Angeles: University of California Press.

Boice, R. (1996). *Procrastination and blocking: A novel, practical approach.* New York: Praeger.

Bolt, M. (1993). *Instructor's manual to accompany Myer's Social Psychology* (4th ed.). New York: McGraw-Hill.

Bornstein, M. H., & Sigman, M. D. (1986). Continuity in mental development from infancy. *Child Development, 57,* 251–274.

Bowen, W. G., & Bok, D. C. (1998). *The shape of the river: Long-term consequences of considering race in college and university admissions.* Princeton, NJ: Princeton University Press.

Boyer, P. (1995). *Promises to keep: The United States since World War II.* Lexington, MA: D. C. Heath and Company.

Brookhart, S. (1999). Board actions signal new era. *APS Observer, 12 (6),* 30–31.

Bruner, J. (1987). Life as narrative. *Social Research, 54,* 11–32.

Bruner, J. (1991). The narrative construction of reality. *Critical Inquiry, 18,* 1–21.

Campbell, D. T. (1969). Reforms as experiments. *American Psychologist, 24,* 409–429.

Campbell, D. T., & Fiske, D. T. (1959). Convergent and discriminant validation by the multitrait-multimethod matrix. *Psychological Bulletin, 56,* 81–105.

Campbell, D. T., & Ross, H. L. (1970). The Connecticut crackdown on speeding: Time series data in quasi-experimental analysis. In E. R. Tufte (Ed.), *The quantitative analysis of social problems* (pp. 110–125). Reading, MA: Addison-Wesley.

Campbell, D. T., & Stanley, J. C. (1963). *Experimental and quasi-experimental designs for research.* Chicago: Rand McNally.

Campbell, S. K. (1974). *Flaws and fallacies in statistical thinking.* Englewood Cliffs, NJ: Prentice Hall.

Carswell, C. M., Frankenberger, S., & Bernhard, D. (1991). Graphing in depth: Perspectives on the use of three-dimensional graphs to represent lower-dimensional data. *Behaviour and Information Technology, 10,* 459–474.

Carver, C. S., & Scheier, M. F. (1981). *Attention and self-regulation: A control-theory approach to human behavior.* New York: Springer-Verlag.

Carver, C. S., & Scheier, M. F. (in press). Optimism. In C. R. Snyder (Ed.), *Coping: The psychology of what works.* New York: Oxford University Press.

Cascio, W. F. (1991). *Applied psychology in personnel management* (4th ed.). Englewood Cliffs, NJ: Prentice Hall.

Ceci, S. J. (1996). *On intelligence.* Cambridge, MA: Harvard University Press.

Chapman, L. J., & Chapman, J. (1982). Test results are what you think they are. In D. Kahneman, P. Slovic, & A. Tversky (Eds.), *Judgment under uncertainty: Heuristics and biases* (pp. 239–248). Cambridge: Cambridge University Press.

Chapman, L. J., & Chapman, J. P. (1971, November). Test results are what you think they are. *Psychology Today,* 18–22, 106–110.

Churchland, P. M. (1985). *Matter and consciousness.* Cambridge, MA: MIT Press.

Churchland, P. S. (1986). *Neurophilosophy.* Cambridge, MA: MIT Press

Clarke, R. D. (1946). An application of the Poisson distribution. *Journal of the Institute of Actuaries (London), 72,* 72.

Cleary, T. A. (1968). Test bias: Prediction of grades of negro and white students in integrated colleges. *Journal of Educational Measurement, 5,* 115–124.

Cleary, T. A., Humphreys, L. G., Kendrick, S. A., & Wesman, A. (1975). Educational uses of tests with disadvantaged students. *American Psychologist, 30,* 15–41.

Cochran, G. W. (1967). Footnote by William G. Cochran. *Science, 156,* 1460–1462.

Cohen, J. (1965). Some statistical issues in psychological research. In B. B. Wolman (Ed.), *Handbook of clinical psychology* (pp. 95–121). New York: McGraw-Hill.

Cohen, J. (1988). *Statistical power analysis for the behavioral sciences.* (2nd ed.). Hillsdale, NJ: Erlbaum.

Cohen, J. (1994). The earth is round ($p < .05$). *American Psychologist, 49,* 997–1003.

Cohen, J., & Cohen, C. (1983). *Applied multiple regression/correlation analysis for the behavioral sciences* (2nd ed.). Hillsdale, NJ: Erlbaum.

College Board (1995). Average scores on SAT I: Reasoning test being moved near 500 with first "recentered" administration in April. *News from the College Board.* New York: Author.

Cook, T. D., & Campbell, D. T. (1979). *Quasi-experimentation: Design & analysis issues for field settings.* Boston: Houghton Mifflin Company.

Coombs, W. T., Algina, J., & Oltman, D. O. (1996). Univariate and multivariate omnibus hypothesis tests selected to control Type I error rates when population variances are not necessarily equal. *Review of Educational Research, 66,* 137–179.

Coopersmith, S. (1987). *SEI: Self-Esteem Inventories.* Palo Alto, CA: Consulting Psychologists Press, Inc.

Cowles, M. (1989). *Statistics in psychology: An historical perspective.* Hillsdale, NJ: Erlbaum.

Cozby, P. C. (1997). Methods in behavioral research (6th ed.). Mountain View, CA: Mayfield Publishing Company.

Crosby, A. W. (1997). *The measure of reality: Quantification and western society.* Cambridge: Cambridge University Press.

Crosby, A. W. (1998). *The measure of reality: Quantification and Western society, 1250–1600.* Cambridge: Cambridge University Press.

Dawes, R. M. (1971). A case study of graduate admissions: Application of three principles of human decision making. *American Psychologist, 26,* 180-188.

Dawes, R. M. (1975). Graduate admissions criteria and future success. *Science, 187,* 721–723.

Dawes, R. M. (1976). Shallow psychology. In J. S. Carroll & J. W. Payne (Eds.), *Cognition and social behavior* (pp. 3–11). Hillsdale, NJ: Erlbaum.

Dawes, R. M. (1979). The robust beauty of improper linear models. *American Psychologist, 34,* 571–582.

Dawes, R. M. (1988). *Rational choice in an uncertain world.* San Diego, CA: Harcourt Brace Jovanovich.

Dawes, R. M. (1991, June). *Discovering "human nature" versus discovering how people cope with the task of getting through college: An extension of Sear's argument.* Paper presented at the Third Annual Convention of the American Psychological Society, Washington, DC.

Dawes, R. M., & Corrigan, B. (1974). Linear models in decision making. *Psychological Bulletin, 81,* 95–106.

Dawes, R. M., Faust, D., & Meehl, P. E. (1989). Clinical versus actuarial judgment. *Science, 243,* 1668–1674.

Deckers, L., & Carr, D. E. (1986). Cartoons varying in low-level pain ratings, not aggression ratings, correlate positively with funniness ratings. *Motivation and Emotion, 10,* 207–216.

Denzin, N. K., & Lincoln, Y. S. (Eds.) (1994). *Handbook of qualitative research.* Thousand Oaks, CA: Sage.

Deutcher, I. (1973). *What we say/what we do: Sentiments and acts.* Glenview, IL: Scott, Foresman.

Dillon, K. M. (1982). Statisticophobia. *Teaching of Psychology, 9,* 117.

Dollinger, S. J., & DiLalla, D. L. (1996). Cleaning up data and running preliminary analyses. In F. T. L. Leong & J. T. Austin (Eds.), *The psychology research handbook: A guide for graduate students and research assistants* (pp. 167–176). Thousand Oaks, CA: Sage.

Donaldson, G. A. (1999). *Truman defeats Dewey.* Lexington, KY: University Press of Kentucky.

Dunn, D. S. (1996). Well-being following amputation: Salutary effects of positive meaning, optimism, and control. *Rehabilitation Psychology, 41,* 285–302.

Dunn, D. S. (1999). *The practical researcher: A student guide to conducting psychological research.* New York: McGraw-Hill.

Dunn, D. S. (2000). Letter exchanges on statistics and research methods: Writing, responding, and learning. *Teaching of Psychology, 27,* 128–130.

Dunn, D. S. (in press). Social psychological issues in disability. To appear in R. G. Frank & T. R. Elliott (Eds.), *Handbook of rehabilitation psychology.* Washington, DC: American Psychological Association.

Dunn, D. S., & Wilson, T. D. (1990). When the stakes are high: A limit to the illusion of control effect. *Social Cognition, 8,* 305–323.

Dunn, D. S., Stoudt, B. G., & Vicchiullo, C. I. (1999, April). *Social inhibition among persons with HIV/AIDS: A pilot study.* Poster session presented at the 70th annual meeting of the Eastern Psychological Association, Providence, RI.

Eagly, A. H., & Chaiken, S. (1993). *The psychology of attitudes.* Fort Worth, TX: Harcourt Brace Jovanovich.

Edgeworth, F. Y. (1887). Observations and statistics: An essay on the theory of errors of observation and the first principles of statistics. *Transactions of the Cambridge Philosophical Society, 14,* 138–169.

Efran, M. (1974). The effect of physical appearance on the judgement of guilt, interpersonal attractiveness, and severity of recommended punishment in a simulated jury task. *Journal of Research in Personality, 8,* 45–54.

Egolf, B., Lasker, J., Wolf, S., & Potvin, L. (1992). The Roseto effect: A 50-year comparison of mortality rates. *American Journal of Public Health, 82,* 1089–1092.

Elbow, P., & Belanoff, P. (1995). *A community of writers: A workshop course in writing* (2nd ed.). New York: McGraw-Hill.

Elifson, K. W., Runyon, R. P., & Haber, A. (1990). *Fundamentals of social statistics* (2nd ed.). New York: McGraw-Hill.

Ericsson, K. A., & Simon, H. A. (1993). *Protocol analysis: Verbal reports as data* (Rev. ed.). Cambridge, MA: MIT Press.

Ericsson, K. A., Chase, W. G., & Faloon, S. (1980). Acquisition of memory skill. *Science, 208,* 1181–1182.

Evans, J. D. (1996). *Straightforward statistics for the behavioral sciences.* Pacific Grove, CA: Brooks/Cole.

Fazio, R. H., & Zanna, M. P. (1981). Direct experience and attitude-behavior consistency. In L. Berkowitz (Ed.), *Advances in experimental social psychology* (Vol. 14, pp. 161–202). New York: Academic Press.

Feller, W. (1968). *An introduction to probability theory and its applications* (3rd ed., Vol. 1.). New York: Wiley.

Festinger, L. (1954). A theory of social comparison processes. *Human Relations, 7,* 117–140.

Festinger, L., Riecken, H. W., & Schachter, S. (1956). *When prophecy fails.* Minneapolis: University of Minnesota Press.

Fischhoff, B. (1982). For those condemned to study the past: Heuristics and biases in hindsight. In D. Kahneman, P. Slovic, & A. Tversky (Eds.), *Judgment under uncertainty: Heuristics and biases* (pp. 335–351). Cambridge: Cambridge University Press.

Fischhoff, B., Slovic, P., & Lichtenstein, S. (1977). Knowing with certainty: The appropriateness of extreme confidence. *Journal of Experimental Psychology: Human Perception and Performance, 3,* 552–564.

Fisher Box, J. (1978). *R. A. Fisher: The life of a scientist.* New York: Wiley.

Fisher, R. A. (1966). *The design of experiments* (8th ed.). Edinburgh: Oliver and Boyd.

Flick, U. (1996). *Psychologie des technisierten Alltags.* Opladen: Westdeutscher Verlag.

Flick, U. (1998). *An introduction to qualitative research.* London: Sage.

Fontana, A., & Frey, J. H. (1994). Interviewing: The art of science. In N. K. Denzin & Y. S. Lincoln (Eds.), *Handbook of qualitative research* (pp. 361–376). Thousand Oaks, CA: Sage.

Freud, S. (1960). Jokes and their relation to the unconscious. In J. Stratchey & A. Freud (Eds. and Trans.), *The standard edition of the complete psychological works of Sigmund Freud* (Vol. 8, pp. 9–15). London: Hogarth. (Original work published 1905)

Friedman, E., Katcher, A. H., Lynch, J. J., & Thomas, S. A. (1980). Animal companions and one-year survival of patients after discharge from a coronary care unit. *Public Health Reports, 95,* 307–312.

Funder, D. C. (1983). The "consistency" controversy and the accuracy of personality judgments. *Journal of Personality, 48,* 473–493.

Funder, D. O., & Ozer, D. J. (1983). Behavior as a function of the situation. *Journal of Personality and Social Psychology, 44,* 1198–1213.

Gardner, H. (1983). *Frames of mind: The theory of multiple intelligences.* New York: Basic Books.

Gardner, M. (1975). *Mathematical carnival.* New York: Knopf.

Gelfand, H., & Walker, C. J. (1990). *Mastering APA style: Student's workbook and training guide.* Washington, DC: American Psychological Association.

Gibbons, J. D. (1971). *Nonparametric statistical inference.* New York: McGraw-Hill.

Gigerenzer, G., Swijtink, Z., Porter, T., Daston, L., Beatty, J., & Kruger, L. (1989). *The empire of chance: How probability changed science and everyday life.* Cambridge: Cambridge University Press.

Gilbert, E. W. (1958). Pioneer maps of health and disease in England. *Geographical Journal, 124,* 172–183.

Gilovich, T. (1991). *How we know what isn't so: The fallibility of human reason in everyday life.* New York: Free Press.

Gilovich, T., Vallone, R., & Tversky, A. (1985). The hot hand in basketball: On the misperception of random sequences. *Cognitive Psychology, 17,* 295–314.

Glass, D. C., Singer, J. E., & Friedman, L. N. (1969). Psychic cost of adaptation to an environmental stressor. *Journal of Personality and Social Psychology, 12,* 200–210.

Goldberg, L. R. (1970). Man versus model of man: A rationale plus some evidence for a method of improving on clinical inferences. *Psychological Bulletin, 73,* 422–432.

Goode, E. (1999). Linking drop in crime to rise in abortion: Roe v. Wade resulted in unborn criminals, 2 economists theorize. *The New York Times*, August 20, A14.

Gould, S. J. (1981). *The mismeasure of man.* New York: Norton.

Gould, S. J. (1997). *Questioning the millennium: A rationalist's guide to a precisely arbitrary countdown.* New York: Harmony.

Gravetter, F. J., & Wallnau, L. B. (1996). *Statistics for the behavioral sciences* (4th ed.). Minneapolis, MN: West.

Gravetter, F. J., & Wallnau, L. B. (1996). *Statistics for the behavioral sciences: A first course for students of psychology and education.* Minneapolis, MN: West Publishing Co.

Grinnell, F. (1992). *The scientific attitude* (2nd ed.). New York: Guilford.

Hacking, I. (1975). *The emergence of probability.* London: Cambridge University Press.

Hamill, R., Wilson, T. D., & Nisbett, R. E. (1980). Insensitivity to sample bias: Generalizing from atypical cases. *Journal of Personality and Social Psychology, 39,* 578–589.

Hancock, G. R., & Klockars, A. J. (1996). The quest for α: Deveopments in multiple comparison procedures in the quarter century since Games (1971). *Review of Educational Research, 66,* 269–306.

Harris, M. B. (1998). *Basic statistics for behavioral science research* (2nd ed.). Boston: Allyn and Bacon.

Hayes, J. R. (1981). *The complete problem solver.* Philadelphia, PA: Franklin Institute Press.

Hays, W. L. (1988). *Statistics* (4th ed.). New York: Holt, Rhinehart, & Winston.

Herrmanns, H. (1991). Narratives interview. In U. Flick, E. V. Kardorff, H. Keupp, L. V. Rosensteil, & S. Wolff (Eds.), *Handbuch qualitative sozialforschung* (pp. 182–185). Munich: Psychologie Verlags Union.

Holland, J. H., Holyoak, K. J., Nisbett, R. E., & Thagard, P. R. (1986). *Induction: Processes of inference, learning, and discovery.* Cambridge, MA: MIT Press.

Hollander, M., & Wolfe, D. A. (1973). *Nonparametric statistical methods.* New York: Wiley.

Holt, J. (1999). Higher superstitions: The case for astrology. *Lingua Franca, 9,* 72.

Hughes, E. C. (1984). *The sociological eye.* New Brunswick, NJ: Transaction Books.

Hult, C. A. (1996). *Researching and writing in the social sciences.* Boston: Allyn & Bacon.

Hume, D. (1974). *David Hume on human nature and the understanding* (Anthony Flew, Ed.). New York: Collier Books.

Isen, A. M. (1987). Positive affect, cognitive processes, and social behavior. In L. Berkowitz (Ed.), *Advances in experimental social psychology* (Vol. 20, pp. 203–253). San Diego, CA: Academic Press.

Janesick, V. J. (1998). *"Stretching" exercises for qualitative researchers.* Thousand Oaks, CA: Sage.

Jennings, D. L., Amabile, T. M., & Ross, L. (1982). Informal covariation assessment: Data-based versus theory-based judgments. In D. Kahneman, P. Slovic, & A. Tversky (Eds.), *Judgment under uncertainty: Heuristics and biases* (pp. 211–230). Cambridge: Cambridge University Press.

Johnson, D. (1981). *V-1, V-2: Hilter's vengeance on London.* New York: Stein & Day.

Johnson, D. E. (1989). An intuitive approach to teaching analysis of variance. *Teaching of Psychology, 16,* 67–68.

Jones, E. E., & Sigall, H. (1971). The bogus pipeline: A new paradigm for measuring affect and attitude. *Psychological Bulletin, 76,* 349–364.

Judd, C. M., & Kenny, D. A. (1981). *Estimating the effects of social interventions.* Cambridge: Cambridge University Press.

Jung, C. G. (1971). The psychological theory of types. In H. Read, M. Fordham, & G. Adler (Eds.), *Collected works of C. G. Jung* (Vol. 20, pp. 524–541). Princeton, NJ: Princeton University Press. (German original published 1931.)

Kahneman, D. T., Slovic, P., & Tversky, A. (Eds.) (1982). *Judgment under uncertainty: Heuristics and biases.* Cambridge: Cambridge University Press.

Kahneman, D., & Tversky, A. (1972). Subjective probability: A judgment of representativeness. *Cognitive Psychology, 3,* 430–454.

Kahneman, D., & Tversky, A. (1973). On the psychology of prediction. *Psychological Review, 80,* 237–251.

Kahneman, D., & Tversky, A. (1982). The simulation heuristic. In D. Kahneman, P. Slovic, & A. Tversky (Eds.), *Judgment under uncertainty: Heuristics and biases* (pp. 201-208). Cambridge: Cambridge University Press.

Kahneman, D., Slovic, P., & Tversky, A. (1982). (Eds.). *Judgment under uncertainty: Heuristics and biases.* Cambridge: Cambridge University Press.

Keil, R. (1996, September 17). Welfare study debunks myths about recipients. *The Morning Call,* p. A3.

Kenrick, D. T., & Funder, D. C. (1988). Profiting from controversy: Lessons from the person-situation debate. *American Psychologist, 43,* 23–34.

Kimball, O. M. (1972). Development of norms for the Coopersmith Self-Esteem Inventory: Grades four through eight. Doctoral dissertation, Northern Illinois University. *Dissertation Abstracts International, 34,* 1131–1132.

Kirk, R. E. (1982). *Experimental designs: Procedures for the behavioral sciences* (2nd ed.). Monterey, CA: Brooks/Cole.

Kirk, R. E. (1990). *Statistics: An introduction* (3rd ed.). New York: Holt, Rhinehart, & Winston.

Kirk, R. E. (1994). Choosing a multiple comparison procedure. In B. Thompson (Ed.), *Advances in social science methodology* (pp. 77–121). Greenwich, CT: JAI Press.

Kirk, R. E. (1999). *Statistics: An introduction.* 4th ed. Fort Worth, TX: Harcourt Brace.

Konzem, P., & Baker, G. (1996). Essay exchanges to improve student writing. *Kansas English, 81,* 64–69.

Kramer, C. Y. (1956). Extension of multiple range test to group means with unequal number of replications. *Biometrics, 57,* 649–655.

Kromrey, J. D. (1993). Ethics and data analysis. *Educational Researcher, 22,* 24–27.

Kuhlman, T. L. (1985). A study of salience and motivational theories of humor. *Journal of Personality and Social Psychology, 49,* 281–286.

Kuhn, T. S. (1970). *The structure of scientific revolutions* (2nd ed.). Chicago: University of Chicago Press.

Kuhn, T. S. (1970). *The structure of scientific revolutions.* (Revised ed.) Chicago: University of Chicago Press.

Kuhn, T. S. (1977). Second thoughts on paradigms. In F. Suppe (Ed.), *The structure of scientific theories,* 2nd ed. Urbana, IL: University of Illinois Press.

Kunda, Z., & Nisbett, R. E. (1986). The psychometrics of everyday life. *Cognitive Psychology, 18,* 195–224.

Langer, E. J. (1975). The illusion of control. *Journal of Personality and Social Psychology, 32,* 311–328.

Langer, E. J. (1983). *The psychology of control.* Beverly Hills, CA: Sage.

Larkey, P. D., Smith, R. A., & Kadane, J. B. (1989). It's okay to believe in the "hot hand." *Chance, 2,* 22–30.

Larson, D. G., & Chastain, R. L. (1990). Self-concealment: Conceptualization, measurement, and health implications. *Journal of Social and Clinical Psychology, 9,* 439–455.

Leahey, T. H. (1990, August). *Waiting for Newton.* Paper presented at the annual Meeting of the American Psychological Association, Boston.

Leahey, T. H. (1997). *A history of psychology: Main currents in psychological thought.* Upper Saddle River, NJ: Prentice Hall.

Leddo, J., Abelson, R. P., & Gross, P. H. (1984). Conjunctive explanations: When two reasons are better than one. *Journal of Personality and Social Psychology, 47,* 933–943.

Lehman, D. R., & Nisbett, R. E. (1990). A longitudinal study of the effects of undergraduate training on reasoning. *Developmental Psychology, 26,* 952–960.

Lehman, D. R., Lempert, R. O., & Nisbett, R. E. (1988). The effects of graduate training on reasoning: Formal discipline and thinking about everyday-life events. *American Psychologist, 43,* 431–442.

Leik, R. K. (1997). *Experimental design and the analysis of variance.* Thousand Oaks, CA: Pine Forge Press.

Li, C. (1975). *Path analysis: A primer.* Pacific Grove, CA: Boxwood Press.

Lichtenstein, S., Slovic, P., Fischhoff, B., Layman, M., & Combs, B. (1978). Judged frequency of lethal events. *Journal of Experimental Psychology: Human Learning and Memory, 4,* 551–578.

Lincoln, Y. S., & Guba, E. G. (1985). *Naturalistic inquiry.* Newbury Park, CA: Sage.

Litt, M. D., Tennen, H., Affleck, G., & Klock, S. (1992). Coping and cognitive factors in adaptation to *in vitro* fertilization failure. *Journal of Behavioral Medicine, 15,* 171–187.

Locascio, J. J. (1999, May). Significance tests and "results-blindness." *APA Monitor,* 11.

Locksley, A., Ortiz, V., & Hepburn, C. (1980). Social categorization and discriminatory behavior: Extinguishing the minimal intergroup discrimination effect. *Journal of Personality and Social Psychology, 39,* 773–783.

Loftus, E. F. (1979). The malleability of human memory. *American Scientist, 67,* 312–320.

Loftus, E. F., & Palmer, J. C. (1974). Reconstruction of automobile destruction: An example of the interaction between language and memory. *Journal of Verbal Learning and Verbal Behavior, 13,* 585–589.

Loftus, G. R. (1991). On the tyranny of hypothesis testing. *Contemporary Psychology, 36,* 102–105.

Loftus, G. R. (1993). Editorial comment. *Memory & Cognition, 21,* 1–3.

Loftus, G. R. (1996). Psychology will be a much better science when we change the way we analyze data. *Current Directions in Psychological Science, 5,* 161–171.

Martin, D. W. (1996). *Doing psychology experiments* (4th ed.). Pacific Grove, CA: Brooks/Cole.

Mauro, J. (1992). *Statistical deception at work.* Hillsdale, NJ: Erlbaum.

McAdams, D. P. (1993). *The stories we live by: Personal myths and the making of the self.* New York: William Morrow and Company.

McCall, R. B., Kennedy, C. B., & Appelbaum, M. I. (1977). Magnitude of discrepancy and the distribution of attention in infants. *Child Development, 48,* 772–786.

McCauley, C., Woods, K., Coolidge, C., & Kulick, W. (1983). More aggressive cartoons are funnier. *Journal of Personality and Social Psychology, 44,* 817–823.

McKenna, R. J. (1995). *The undergraduate researcher's handbook: Creative experimentation in social psychology.* Boston: Allyn and Bacon.

Mead, M. (1961). *Coming of age in Samoa.* New York: Morrow.

Meehl, P. E. (1977). *Psychodiagnosis: Selected papers.* New York: Norton.

Mehan, A. M., & Warner, C.B. (2000). *Elementary data analysis using Microsoft Excel.* New York: McGraw-Hill.

Milkovich, G. T., & Newman, J. M. (1987). *Compensation* (2nd ed.). Plano, TX: Business Publications, Inc.

Miller, L. C., Berg, J. H., & Archer, R. L. (1983). Openers: Individuals who elicit intimate self-disclosure. *Journal of Personality and Social Psychology, 44,* 1234–1244.

Mischel, W. (1968). *Personality and assessment.* New York: Wiley.

Moffatt, M. (1989). *Coming of age in New Jersey: College and American culture.* New Brunswick, NJ: Rutgers University Press.

Mook, D. G. (1983). In defense of external invalidity. *American Psychologist, 38,* 379–387.

Moore, D. S. (1992). Teaching statistics as a respectable subject. In F. Gordon & S. Gordon (Eds.), *Statistics for the twenty-first century* (pp. 14–25). Washington, DC: Mathematical Association of America.

Morgan, D. L. (1988). *Focus groups as qualitative research.* Newbury Park, CA: Sage.

Morier, D. M., & Borgida, E. (1984). The conjunction fallacy: A task specific phenomenon? *Personality and Social Psychology Bulletin, 10,* 243–252.

Moses, L. E. (1952). Nonparametric statistics for psychological research. *Psychological Bulletin, 49,* 122–143.

Motterlini, M. (Ed.). (1999). *For and against method: The Lakatos lectures and the Lakatos-Feyerabend correspondence.* Chicago: University of Chicago Press.

Myers, I. B. (1962). *The Myers-Briggs Type Indicator.* Princeton, NJ: Educational Testing Service. New York: Putnam.

Newton, R. R., & Rudestam, K. E. (1999). *Your statistical consultant: Answers to your data analysis questions.* Thousand Oaks, CA: Sage.

Nicol, A. A. M., & Pexman, P. M. (1999). *Presenting your findings: A practical guide for creating tables.* Washington, DC: American Psychological Association.

Nisbett, R. E., Fong, G. T., Lehman, D. R., & Cheng, P. W. (1987). Teaching reasoning. *Science, 238,* 625–631.

Nisbett, R. E., & Ross, L. (1980). *Human inference: Strategies and shortcomings of social judgment.* Englewood Cliffs, NJ: Prentice Hall.

Nisbett, R. E., & Wilson, T. D. (1977). Telling more than we can know: Verbal reports on mental processes. *Psychological Review, 81,* 231–259.

Nisbett, R. E., Krantz, D. H., Jepson, C., & Fong, G. T. (1982). Improving inductive inference. In D. Kahneman, P. Slovic, & A. Tversky (Eds.), *Judgment under uncertainty: Heuristics and biases* (pp. 445–459). Cambridge: Cambridge University Press.

Nisbett, R. E., Krantz, D. H., Jepson, C., & Kunda, Z. (1983). The use of statistical heuristics in everyday reasoning. *Psychological Review, 90,* 339–363.

Nolen-Hoeksema, S. (1990). *Sex differences in depression.* Stanford, CA: Stanford University Press.

Nolen-Hoeksema, S. (1993). Sex differences in control of depression. In D. M. Wegner & J. W. Pennebaker (Eds.), *Handbook of mental control* (pp. 306–324). Englewood Cliffs, NJ: Prentice Hall.

O'Connor, P. T. (1996). *Woe is I: The grammarphobe's guide to better English in plain English.* New York: Putnam.

O'Connor, P. T. (1999). *Words fail me: What everyone who writes should know about writing.* New York: Harcourt Brace.

Parrott III, L. (1999). *How to write psychology papers* (2nd ed.). New York: Longman.

Patton, M. Q. (1990). *Qualitative evaluation and research methods* (2nd ed.). London: Sage.

Pavlov, I. P. (1928). *Lectures on conditioned reflexes* (W. H. Gantt, Trans.). New York: International.

Pavlov, I. P. (1960). *Conditioned reflexes* (Rev. ed.) (G. V. Anrep, Trans. and Ed.). New York: Dover. (Original work published 1927)

Pearson, E. S. (1968). Some early correspondence between W. S. Gosset, R. A. Fischer, and Karl Pearson, with notes and comments. In E. S. Pearson & M. G. Kendall (Eds.), *Studies in the history of statistics and probability* (Vol. 1, pp. 405–417). London: Charles Griffin and Co.

Pearson, K. (1930). *Life, letters, and labours of Francis Galton. Vol. IIIa, Correlation, personal identification, and eugenics.* Cambridge: Cambridge University Press.

Pedhazur, E. J. (1982). *Multiple regression in behavioral research: Explanation and prediction* (2nd ed.). New York: Holt, Rinehart, and Winston.

Pelham, B. W. (1999). *Conducting experiments in psychology: Measuring the weight of smoke.* Pacific Grove, CA: Brooks/Cole.

Pennebaker, J. W. (1989). Confession, inhibition, and disease. In L. Berkowitz (Ed.), *Advances in experimental social psychology* (Vol. 22, pp. 211–244). New York: Academic Press.

Pennebaker, J. W., & Harber, K. (1993). A social stage model of collective coping: The Loma Prieta earthquake. *Journal of Social Issues, 49,* 125–146.

Pennebaker, J. W., Barger, S. D., & Tiebout, J. (1989). Disclosure of traumas and health among Holocaust survivors. *Psychosomatic Medicine, 51,* 577–589.

Perman, S. (1999). The unforseen effect of abortion. *Time,* August 23, 47.

Peters, W. S. (1987). *Counting for something: Statistical principles and personalities.* New York: Springer-Verlag.

Peterson, C. (1996). Writing rough drafts. In F. T. C. Leong & J. T. Austin (Eds.), *The psychology research handbook: A guide for graduate students and research assistants* (pp. 282–290). Thousand Oaks, CA: Sage Publications.

Peterson, C., & Bossio, L. M. (1989). Learned helplessness. In R. C. Curtis (Ed.), *Self-defeating behaviors* (pp. 235–257). New York: Plenum.

Peterson, C., & Seligman, M. E. P. (1984). Causal explanations as a risk factor for depression: Theory and evidence. *Psychological Review, 91,* 347–374.

Peterson, C., Seligman, M. E. P., & Vaillant, G. E. (1988). Pessimistic explanatory style is a risk factor for physical illness: A thirty-five year longitudinal study. *Journal of Personality and Social Psychology, 55,* 23–27.

Peterson, D. R. (1968). *The clinical study of social behavior.* New York: Appleton.

Pittenger, D. J. (1995). Teaching students about graphs. *Teaching of Psychology, 22,* 125–128.

Platt, J. R. (1964). Strong inference. *Science, 146,* 347-353.

Plous, S. (1993). *The psychology of judgement and decision making.* New York: McGraw-Hill.

Prentice, D. A., & Miller, D. T. (1992). When small effects are impressive. *Psychological Bulletin, 112,* 160–164.

Radloff, L. (1977). The CES-D scale: A self-report depression scale for the general population. *Applied Psychological Measurement, 1,* 385–401.

Rand Corporation. (1955). *A million random digits.* Glencoe, IL: Free Press.

Reed, G. M., Taylor, S. E., & Kemeny, M. E. (1993). Perceived control and psychological adjustment in gay men with AIDS. *Journal of Applied Social Psychology, 23,* 791–824.

Rosenberg, A. (1980). *Sociobiology and the preemption of social science.* Baltimore: Johns Hopkins University.

Rosenberg, A. (1983). Content and consciousness versus the intentional stance. *The Behavioral and Brain Sciences, 3,* 375–376.

Rosenberg, A. (1994). *Instrumental biology, or, the disunity of science.* Chicago: University of Chicago Press.

Rosenberg, M. (1965). *Society and the adolescent self-image.* Princeton, NJ: Princeton University Press.

Rosenthal, R. (1991). *Meta-analytic procedures for social research* (Rev. ed.). Newbury Park, CA: Sage.

Rosenthal, R., & Fode, K. L. (1963). The effect of experimenter bias on the performance of the albino rat. *Behavioral Science, 8,* 127–134.

Rosenthal, R., & Rosnow, R. L. (1985). *Contrast analysis: Focused comparisons in the analysis of variance.* Cambridge: Cambridge University Press.

Rosenthal, R., & Rosnow, R. L. (1991). *Essentials of behavioral research: Methods and data analysis* (2nd ed.). New York: McGraw-Hill.

Rosenthal, R., & Rubin, D. B. (1982). A simple, general purpose display of magnitude of experimental effect. *Journal of Educational Psychology, 74,* 166–169.

Rosnow, R. L., & Rosenthal, R. (1989). Definition and interpretation of interaction effects. *Psychological Bulletin, 105,* 143–146.

Rosnow, R. L., & Rosenthal, R. (1989). Statistical procedures and the justification of knowledge in psychological science. *American Psychologist, 44,* 1276–1284.

Rosnow, R. L., & Rosenthal, R. (1996). *Beginning behavioral research* (2nd ed). Englewood Cliffs, NJ: Prentice Hall.

Rosnow, R. L., & Rosnow, M. (1995). *Writing papers in psychology* (3rd ed.). Pacific Grove, CA: Brooks/Cole.

Ross, L., & Nisbett, R. E. (1991). *The person and the situation: Perspectives of social psychology.* New York: McGraw-Hill.

Runyon, R. P., Coleman, K. A., & Pittenger, D. J. (1999). *Fundamentals of behavioral statistics* (9th ed.). New York: McGraw-Hill.

Runyon, R. P., Haber, A., Pittenger, D. J., & Coleman, K. A. (1996). *Fundamentals of behavioral statistics* (8th ed.). New York: McGraw-Hill.

Safire, W. (1999, May 9). McCawley: Last words from a giant of linguistics. *The New York Times Magazine,* pp. 24, 26.

Salkind, N. J. (1997). *Exploring research* (3rd ed). Upper Saddle River, NJ: Prentice Hall.

Scarr, S. (1997). Rules of evidence: A larger context for the statistical debate. *Psychological Science, 8,* 16–17.

Schachter, S. (1959). *The psychology of affiliation: Experimental studies of the sources of gregariousness.* Stanford, CA: Stanford University Press.

Scheier, M. F., & Carver, C. S. (1985). Optimism, coping, and health: Assessment and implications of generalized outcome expectancies. *Health Psychology, 4,* 219–247.

Scheier, M. F., Carver, C. S., & Bridges, M. W. (1994). Distinguishing optimism from neuroticism (and trait anxiety, self-mastery, and self-esteem): A reevaluation of the Life Orientation Test. *Journal of Personality and Social Psychology, 67,* 1063–1078.

Scheier, M. F., Matthews, K. A., Owens, J. F., Macgovern, Sr., G. J., Lefebvre, R. C., Abbott, R. A., & Carver, C. S. (1989). Dispositional optimism and recovery from coronary artery bypass surgery: The beneficial effects on physical and psychological well-being. *Journal of Personality and Social Psychology, 57,* 1024–1040.

Scheier, M. F., Matthews, K. A., Owens, J. F., Schulz, R., Bridges, M. W., Magovern, G. J., Jr., & Carver, C. S. (in press). Optimism and rehospitalization following coronary artery bypass graft surgery. *Archives of Internal Medicine.*

Schulz, R., & Decker, S. (1985). Long-term adjustment to physical disability: The role of social support, perceived control, and self-blame. *Journal of Personality and Social Psychology, 48,* 1162–1172.

Schwartz, T. (1999, January 10). The test under stress. *The New York Times Magazine,* pp. 30–35, 51, 56, 63.

Scott, J. M., Koch, R. E., Scott, G. M., & Garrison, S. M. (1999). *The psychology student writer's manual.* Upper Saddle River, NJ: Prentice Hall.

Sears, D. O. (1986). College sophomores in the laboratory: Influences of a narrow data base on social psychology's view of human nature. *Journal of Personality and Social Psychology, 51,* 515–539.

Shaughnessy, J. J., & Zechmeister, E. B. (1994). *Research methods in psychology.* (3rd ed.). New York: McGraw-Hill.

Shaughnessy, J. J., & Zechmeister, E. B. (1997). *Research methods in psychology* (4th ed.). New York: McGraw-Hill.

Shrout, P. E. (1997). Should significance tests be banned? Introduction to a special section exploring the pros and cons. *Psychological Science, 8,* 1–2.

Siegel, S. (1956). *Nonparametric statistics for the behavioral sciences.* New York: McGraw-Hill.

Siegel, S., & Castellan, Jr., N. J. (1988). *Nonparametric statistics for the behavioral sciences* (2nd ed.). New York: McGraw-Hill.

Sigall, H., & Ostrove, N. (1975). Beautiful but dangerous: Effects of offender attractiveness and nature of the crime on juridic judgments. *Journal of Personality and Social Psychology, 31,* 410–414.

Slovic, P., Fischhoff, B., & Lichtenstein, S. (1979). Rating the risks. *Environment, 21,* 14–20, 36–39.

Slovic, P., Fischhoff, B., & Lichtenstein, S. (1982). Facts versus fears: Understanding perceived risk. In D. Kahneman, P. Slovic, & A. Tversky (Eds.), *Judgment under uncertainty: Heuristics and biases* (pp. 463–489). Cambridge: Cambridge University Press.

Smith, P. C., Budzeika, K. A., Edwards, N. A., Johnson, S. M., & Bearse, L. N. (1986). Guidelines for clean data: Detection of common mistakes. *Journal of Applied Psychology, 71,* 457–460.

Smyth, T. R. (1996). *Writing in psychology: A student guide.* 2nd ed. New York: John Wiley & Sons.

Snedecor, G. W., & Cochran, W. G. (1967). *Statistical methods* (6th ed.). Ames: Iowa State University Press.

Snedecor, G. W., & Cochran, W. G. (1980). *Statistical methods* (7th ed). Ames, IA: Iowa State University Press.

Snyder, M. (1974). The self-monitoring of expressive behavior. *Journal of Personality and Social Psychology, 30,* 526–537.

Snyder, M. (1987). *Public appearances/private realities: The psychology of self-monitoring.* New York: Freeman.

Spence, J. T., & Helmreich, R. L. (1978). *Masculinity and femininity: Their psychological dimensions, correlates, and antecedents.* Austin, TX: University of Texas Press.

Spencer, S. J., Steele, C. M., & Quinn, D. M. (1999). Stereotype threat and women's math performance. *Journal of Experimental Social Psychology, 35,* 4–28.

Spradley, J. P. (1980). *Participant observation.* Fort Worth, TX: Harcourt Brace Jovanovich.

Sprent, P. (1989). *Applied nonparametric statistical methods.* London: Chapman and Hall.

Stanovich, K. E. (1998). *How to think straight about psychology* (5th ed.). New York: Longman.

Steele, C. M., & Aronson, J. (1995). Contending with a stereotype: African-American intellectual test performance and stereotype threat. *Journal of Personality and Social Psychology, 69,* 797–811.

Stern, W. (1912). *Psychologische Methoden der Intelligenz-Prüfung.* Leipzig, Germany: Barth.

Sternberg, R. J. (1985). *Beyond IQ: A triarchic theory of human intelligence.* New York: Cambridge University Press.

Sternberg, R. J. (1993). *The psychologist's companion: A guide to scientific writing for students and researchers* (3rd ed.). Cambridge: Cambridge University Press.

Sternberg, R. J. (1999). *Cognitive psychology* (2nd ed.). Fort Worth, TX: Harcourt Brace.

Sternberg, R. J., & Detterman, D. K. (Eds.) (1986). *What is intelligence? Contemporary viewpoints on its nature and definition.* Norwood, NJ: Ablex.

Stewart, J. S., & Brunjes, P. C. (1990). Olfactory bulb and sensory epithelium in goldfish: Morphological alterations accompanying growth. *Developmental Brain Research, 54,* 187–193.

Stich, S. P. (1983). *From folk psychology to cognitive science: The case against belief.* Cambridge, MA: MIT Press.

Stigler, S. M. (1986). *The history of statistics: The measurement of uncertainty before 1900.* Cambridge, MA: Belknap Press.

Strauss, A., & Corbin, J. (1990). *Basics of qualitative research: Grounded theory, procedures, and techniques.* Newbury Park, CA: Sage.

Strunk, jr., W., & White, E. B. (1972). *The elements of style.* New York: Macmillan.

Suls, J., & Fletcher, B. (1983). Social comparison in the social and physical sciences: An archival study. *Journal of Personality and Social Psychology, 44,* 575–580.

Suzuki, S., Augerinos, G., & Black, A. H. (1980). Stimulus control of spatial behavior on the eight-arm maze in rats. *Learning and Motivation, 11,* 1–18.

Tajfel, H. (1981). *Human groups and social categories: Studies in social psychology.* London: Cambridge University Press.

Tajfel, H., & Billig, M. (1974). Familiarity and categorization in intergroup behavior. *Journal of Experimental Social Psychology, 10,* 159–170.

Tankard, J. W. (1984). *The statistical pioneers.* Cambridge, MA: Schenkman Publishing Co.

Tanner, M. A. (1990). *Investigations for a course in statistics.* New York: Macmillan.

Taylor, S. E., & Brown, J. D. (1988). Illusion and well-being: A social psychological perspective on mental health. *Psychological Bulletin, 103,* 193–210.

Taylor, S. E., Kemeny, M. E., Aspinwall, L. G., Schneider, S. G., Rodriguez, R., & Herbert, M. (1992). Optimism, coping, psychological distress, and high-risk sexual behavior among men at risk for Acquired Immunodeficiency Syndrome (AIDS). *Journal of Personality and Social Psychology, 63,* 460–473.

Taylor, S. E., Lichtman, R. R., & Wood, J. V. (1984). Attributions, beliefs about control, and adjustment to breast cancer. *Journal of Personality and Social Psychology, 46,* 489–502.

Taylor, S. J., & Bogdan, R. (1998). *Introduction to qualitative research methods: A guidebook and resource* (3rd ed.). New York: Wiley.

Thompson, S. C., Armstrong, W., & Thomas, C. (1998). Illusions of control, underestimations, and accuracy: A control heuristic explanation. *Psychological Bulletin, 123,* 143–161.

Tobias, S. (1993). *Overcoming math anxiety: Revised and expanded.* New York: Norton.

Traue. H. C., & Pennebaker, J. W. (Eds.). (1993). *Emotion inhibition and health.* Seattle, WA: Hogrefe & Huber.

Tufte, E. R. (1983). *The visual display of quantitative information.* Cheshire, CT: Graphics Press.

Tukey, J. W. (1969). Analyzing data: Detective work or sanctification? *American Psychologist, 24,* 83–91.

Tukey, J. W. (1977). *Exploratory data analysis.* Reading, MA: Addison-Wesley.

Tversky, A., & Gilovich, T. (1989). The "hot hand": Statistical reality or cognitive illusion? *Chance, 2,* 31–34.

Tversky, A., & Kahneman, D. (1971). Belief in the law of small numbers. *Psychological Bulletin, 76,* 105–110.

Tversky, A., & Kahneman, D. (1973). Availability: A heuristic for judging frequency and probability. *Cognitive Psychology, 4,* 207–232.

Tversky, A., & Kahneman, D. (1974). Judgment under uncertainty: Heuristics and biases. *Science, 185,* 1124–1131.

Tversky, A., & Kahneman, D. (1983). Extensional versus intuitive reasoning: The conjunction fallacy in probability judgement. *Psychological Review, 90,* 293–315.

Vadum, A. C., & Rankin, N. O. (1998). *Psychological research: Methods for discovery and validation.* New York: McGraw-Hill.

VanderStoep, S. W., & Shaughnessy, J. J. (1997). Taking a course in research methods improves reasoning about real-life events. *Teaching of Psychology, 24,* 122–124.

Watson, R. B. (1967). Psychology: A prescriptive science. *American Psychologist, 22,* 435–443.

Wax, R. H. (1971). *Doing fieldwork: Warnings and advice.* Chicago: University of Chicago Press.

Weick, K. E. (1968). Systematic observational methods. In G. Lindzey & E. Aronson (Eds.), *The handbook of social psychology* (Vol. 2, pp. 357–451). Reading, MA: Addison-Wesley.

Weinstein, N. D. (1989). Optimistic biases about personal risks. *Science, 246,* 1232–1233.

Weinstein, N. D. (1980). Unrealistic optimism about future life events. *Journal of Personality and Social Psychology, 39,* 806–820.

Wertz, R. W., & Wertz, D. C. (1977). *Lying-in: A history of childbirth in America.* New York: The Free Press.

Wicker, A. W. (1969). Attitudes versus actions: The relationship of verbal and overt behavior responses to attitude objects. *Journal of Social Issues, 25,* 41–78.

Wilkinson, L., & The Task Force on Statistical Inference. (1999). Statistical methods in psychology journals: Guidelines and explanations. *American Psychologist, 54,* 594–604.

Williams, B. T., & Brydon-Miller, M. (1997). *Concept to completion: Writing well in the social sciences.* Fort Worth, TX: Harcourt Brace College Publishers.

Williams, J. M. (1990). *Style: Toward clarity and grace.* Chicago: University of Chicago Press.

Wilson, E. O. (1975). *Sociobiology: The new synthesis.* Cambridge, MA: Harvard University Press.

Wilson, T. D. (1985). Strangers to ourselves: The origins and accuracy of beliefs about one's own mental states. In J. H. Harvey & G. Weary (Eds.), *Attribution in contemporary psychology* (pp. 9–36). New York: Academic Press.

Wilson, T. D. (1994). The proper protocol: Validity and completeness of verbal reports. *Psychological Science, 5,* 249–252.

Wilson, T. D., & Stone, J. I. (1985). More on telling more than we can know. In P. Shaver (Ed.), *Review of personality and social psychology* (Vol. 6, pp. 167–183). Beverly Hills, CA: Sage.

Wilson, T. D., DePaulo, B. M., Mook, D. G., & Klaaren, K. J. (1993). Scientists' evaluations of research: The biasing effects of the importance of the topic. *Psychological Science, 4,* 322–325.

Wilson, T. D., Dunn, D. S., Bybee, J. A., Hyman, D. B., & Rotondo, J. A. (1984). Effects of analyzing reasons on attitude-behavior consistency. *Journal of Personality and Social Psychology, 47,* 5–16.

Wilson, T. D., Dunn, D. S., Kraft, D. T., & Lisle, D. (1989). Introspection, attitude change, and attitude-behavior consistency: The disruptive effects of explaining why we feel the way we do. In L. Berkowitz (Ed.), *Advances in experimental social psychology* (Vol. 22, pp. 287–343). New York: Academic Press.

Wilson, T. D., Laser, P. S., & Stone, J. I. (1982). Judging the predictors of one's own mood: Accuracy and the use of shared theories. *Journal of Experimental Social Psychology, 18*, 537–556.

Winer, B. J., Brown, D. R., & Michels, K. M. (1991). *Statistical principles in experimental design* (3rd ed.). New York: McGraw-Hill.

Wolraich, M. L., Lindgren, S. D., Stumbo, P. J., Stegink, L. D., Appelbaum, M. I., & Kiritsy, M. C. (1994). Effects of diets high in sucrose or aspartame on the behavior and cognitive performance of children. *The New England Journal of Medicine, 330*, 301–307.

Wright, D. B. (1997). *Understanding statistics: An introduction for the social sciences.* London: Sage Publications.

Zullow, H. M., & Seligman, M. E. P. (1990). Pessimistic rumination predicts defeat of presidential candidates, 1900 to 1944. *Psychological Inquiry, 1*, 52–61.

CREDITS

Chapter 1

Data Box 1.B "He proceeded systematically to draw up a long list, for both colleges,..." From p. 353: Nisbett, R.E., Krantz, D.H., Jepson, C., & Kunda, Z. (1983). The use of statistical heuristics in everyday reasoning. *Psychological Review, 90,* 339–363. Copyright © 1983 by the American Psychological Association. Reprinted with permission.

Page 6 College Choice Adapted from Nisbett, R.E., Jepson, C., Krantz, D., & Fong (1982). *Judgment Under Uncertainty: Heuristics and Biases.* (1982) Reprinted with the permission of Cambridge University Press.

Page 4 Cartoon–"Tonight we are going to let the statistics speak for themselves." Ed Koren, *The New Yorker, 4,* 12/9/74. Copyright © 1974 by The Cartoon Bank. Reprinted with permission.

Data Box 1.D Adapted from "A Billion, A Trillion, Whatever" by Michael T. Kaufman. *The New York Times,* Pictures. Reprinted with permission.

Table 1.3 Ordinal Scaling–The Top Ten Films of All Time as Ranked by Two Friends, American Film Institute (AFI).

Project Exercise: Avoiding Statisticophobia Adapted from Dillon, K.M. (1982). *Statisticophobia. Teaching of Psychology, 9,* 117. Lawrence Earlbaum Associates.

Chapter 2

Page 55 "There is a group of 100 professionals..." From Kahneman, D., & Tversky, A. (1973). On the psychology of prediction. *Psychological Review.* Copyright © 1973 by the American Psychological Association. Reprinted with permission.

Page 80 Performing Random Assignment Source: Dana S. Dunn, *The Practical Researcher, 80* 1/e. Copyright © (1999). The McGraw-Hill Companies. Reprinted with permission.

Table 2.3 Source: Dana S. Dunn, *The Practical Researcher* 1/e. Copyright © (1999). The McGraw-Hill Companies. Reprinted with permission.

Table 2.4 Source: Dana S. Dunn, *The Practical Researcher* 1/e. Copyright © (1999). The McGraw-Hill Companies. Reprinted with permission.

Figure 2.1 Source: Dana S. Dunn, *The Practical Researcher* 1/e. Copyright © (1999). The McGraw-Hill Companies. Reprinted with permission.

Table 2.6: A Sample Random Numbers Table Adapted from page 1 of Rand Corporation (1955). Reprinted with permission of the Rand Corporation.

Page 80 Material adapted from Exploring Research 3/e by Salkind, © 1997. Adapted by permission of Prentice Hall, Inc. Upper Saddle River, NJ.

Chapter 3

Figure 3.9–Connecticut Traffic Death Adapted from Campbell, D.T. (1969) Reforms as experiments. *American Psychologist, 24,* 409–429. Copyright © 1969 by the American Psychological Association. Reprinted with permission.

Figure 3.10–Traffic Deaths in CT, MA, RI Adapted from Campbell, D.T. (1969) Reforms as experiments. *American Psychologist, 24,* 409–429. Copyright © 1983 by the American Psychological Association. Reprinted with permission.

Figure 3.12 and Figure 3.13 Adapted from Tukey, J.W., *Exploratory Data Analysis* p. 9/17. © 1997 Addison-Wesley Longman Company Inc. Reprinted by permission of Addison Wesley Longman.

Table 3.12–Some Considerations for creating High Quality Tables and Figures *Publication Manual of the American Psychological Association* (4th edition). Washington, DC. Copyright © 1994 by the American Psychological Association. Reprinted with permission.

Source: Reprinted with permission from Tversky, A., & Kahneman, D. (1974). *Science, 185,* 1124–1131. American Association for the Advancement of Science.

Chapter 4

Data Box 4.D: Sample Size and Variability— The Hospital Problem Reprinted with permission from Tversky, A., & Kahneman, D.

Page 411–"Mr. Crane and Mr. Tees were scheduled to leave the airport" Kahneman, D., & Tversky, A. (1982). *Judgement Under Uncertainty: Heuristics and Biases.* Reprinted with the permission of Cambridge University Press.

Table 11.1 Adapted table from Dunn, D.S. (in press). Letter exchanges on statistics and research methods: Writing, responding, and learning. *Teaching of Psychology.* Lawrence Earlbaum Associates.

Table 11.2 Material quoted and adapted from Exhibit 1.6 in Leik, R.K. (1997) *Experimental design and the analysis of variance.* Reprinted by permission of R.K. Leik.

Table 11.8 Adapted table Rosenthal and Rosnow (1991, pps. 467–468). Copyright © 1991 by The McGraw-Hill Companies. Reprinted with permission.

Table 11.9 Adapted from Rosenthal and Rosnow (p. 470). Copyright © 1991 by The McGraw-Hill Companies. Reprinted with permission.

Figure 11.5 Adaptation of Table of Critical values of the F-ratio, from Snedecor, G. W., & Cochran, G. W. (1980). *Statistical Methods* (7th ed). Copyright © 1980 Iowa University Press.

Figure 11.6 Adapted from Rosenthal and Rosnow (p. 468). Copyright © 1991 by The McGraw-Hill Companies. Reprinted with permission.

Data Box: 11.A Material quoted with the permission from p. 1462 in Cochran, G. W. (1967). Footnote by William G. Cochran. *Science, 156,* 1460-1462. Copyright © 1967 by American Association for the Advancement of Science.

Chapter 12

Table 12.1–Design of Two-Factor Study of Noise Credit: Adapted from Glass, D.C., Singer, J.E., & Friedman, L.N. (1969). Psychic cost of adaptation to an environmental stressor. *Journal of Personality and Social Psychology, 12,* 200–210. Copyright © 1969 by the American Psychological Association. Reprinted with permission.

Figure 12.1 Material quoted and adapted from Glass, D.C., Singer, J.E., & Friedman, L. N. (1969). Psychic cost of adaptation to an environmental stressor. *Journal of Personality and Social Psychology, 12,* 200-210. Copyright © 1969 by the American Psychological Association. Reprinted with permission.

Chapter 14

Page 562 "The APA Task Force on Statistical Inference also recommends..." Azar, B. (1999, May) APA statistics task force prepares to release

recommendations for public comment. *APA Monitor, 9.*; Wilkinson, L., & The Task Force on Statistical Inference (1999). Statistical methods in psychology journals: Guidelines and explanations. *American Psychologist, 54,* 594–64. Copyright © 1999 by the American Psychological Association. Reprinted with permission.

Poetry W.H. Auden From W.H. Auden: Collected Poems by W.H. Auden, edited by Edward Mendelson. Copyright © 1950 by W.H. Auden. Reprinted by permission of Random House, Inc.

Data Box: 14.A Is Psychology a Science? A HISTORY OF PSYCHOLOGY 4/e by Leahey, T., © 1997. Reprinted by permission of Prentice-Hall, Inc., Upper Saddle River, NJ.

Table 14.2 Portions of a table (p. 291) from Dunn, D.S. (1996). Well-being following amputaion: Salutary effects of positive meaning, optimism, and control. *Rehabiliation Psychology, 41,* 285–302. Copyright © 1996 Springer Publisher Company.

Table 14.3 Material adapted from Flick, U. An introdutiction to qualitative research. Copyright © 1998 by Sage Publications Ltd. Reprinted with permission.

Page 552 –Examples from *Statistics for the Behavioral Sciences.* A first course for students of Psychology and Education, 4th edition, by F.J. Grovetter and L.B. Wallnau. © 1996. Reprinted with permission of Wadsworth, a division of Thomson Learning.

Chapter 15

Decision Tree for Opening of Chapter 15 Adapted from Dunn, D.S. (1999). *The Practical Researcher: A Student Guide to Conducting Psychological Research.* Reprinted by the permission by The McGraw-Hill Companies.

Data Box 15.A–"Two sports fans are arguing over which sport..." Nisbett, R.E., Krantz, D. H., Jepson, C., & Kunda, Z. (1983). The use of statistical heuristics in everyday reasoning. *Psychological Review, 90,* 339–363. Copyright © 1983 by the American Psychological Association. Reprinted with permission.

Page 577 Material quoted and adapted from Azar, B. (1999, May). APA statistics task force prepares to release recommendations for public comment. APA Monitor, 9: Wilkison, L. & the Task Force on Statistical Inference (1999). Statistical methods in psychology journals; guidelines and explanations. *American Psychologist, 54,* 594-604. Copyright

© 1999 by the American Psychological Association. Reprinted with permission.

Cartoon, "That's the gist of what I want to say." Joseph Mirachi, *The New Yorker.* Copyright © 1977 by The Cartoon Bank. Reprinted with permission.

Appendix A

Page A-9 Material adapted from *Overcoming Math Anxiety, Revised and Expanded Edition* by Sheila Tobias. Copyright © 1993, 1978 by Sheila Tobias Reprinted by permission of W.W. Norton & Company, Inc.

Appendix B

Table B.1 Adapted from page 1 of Rand Corporation (1955). Reprinted with permission of the Rand Corporation.

Table B.2 Adapted from Runyon, R.P., Coleman, K. A., & Pittenger, D. Fundamentals of behavioral statistics (9th ed.), Copyright © 2000 by The McGraw-Hill Companies. Reprinted with permission.

Table B.4 Table III of R.A. Fisher and F. Yates, S*tatistical Tables for Biological, Agricultural, and Medical Research,* 6th edition. London: Longman Group, Ltd., 1974. (Previously published by Oliver and Boyed, Trd. Edinburgh.) Reprinted with permission.

Table B.5 Reprint and adaptation from Harris, Mary B., *Basic Statistics for Behavioral Science Research* 2/e. Copyright © 1998 by Allyn & Bacon. Reprinted by permission.

Table B.6 Reprint and adaptation of Table of Percentage Points of the Studentized Range from Pearson, E.S., & Hartley, H. O. (1958). Biometrika tables for statisticians, vol. 1 (2nd ed.) Copyright © 1958 Cambridge University Press.

Table B.7 Reprinted and adapted Table of chi-square from Fisher, R.A. (1970). Statistical methods for research workers (14th ed.). Copyright © (1970) by Prentice Hall.

Table B.8 Adapted from Kirk, R. E., *Elementary Statistics,* 2nd ed. © 1984. Reprinted by the permission of Roger E. Kirk.

Table B.9 Adapted from Kirk, R. E., *Elementary Statistics,* 2nd ed. © 1984. Reprinted by the permission of Roger E. Kirk.

Table B.10 E.G. Olds (1949), "the 5 Percent Significance Levels of Sums of Squares of Rank Differences and a Correction," *Ann. Math. Statist, 20,* 117–118. Reprinted with permission. E.G. Olds (1938), "Distribution of Sums of Squares of Rank Difference for Small Number of Individuals," *Ann. Math. Statist, 9,* 133–148. Reprinted with permission.

NAME INDEX

A

Abelson, R. P., 209, 288, 337, 342, 343, 355, 356, 388, 444, 445, 568, 580
Abramson, F-11
Affleck, G., 88
Agresti, A., 233
Algina, J., 370, 420
Allen, A., 228
Allison, P. D., 264
Alloy, F-11
Amabile, T. M., 205
American Psychological Association, 23, 125, 126, 226
Anselm, F-7
Appelbaum, M. I., 10
Archer, R. L., 231
Armstrong, W., 304
Aron, A., 351, 352, 355, 359, 367, 371, 380, 508
Aron, E. N., 367, 371, 380, 508
Aron, E. P., 351, 352, 355, 359
Aronson, E., 48, 59
Aspinwall, L. G., 88
Auden, W. H., F-1, F-4
Augerinos, G., 140
Axinn, W. G., 573
Azar, B., 565

B

Babbage, C., 575, 581
Bailar, J. C., 566
Bakan, D., 351
Baker, G., 451, 452
Barber, J. S., 573, 574
Barfield, W., 124
Barger, S. D., 75

Baum, A., 75
Beatty, J., 78
Becker, F-13
Bem, D. J., 149, 228, 357
Bem, S. L., 26
Bennett, D. J., 77
Berg, J. H., 231
Berger, A., 574
Bernhard, D., 124
Berscheid, E., 390
Billig, M., 390
Black, A. H., 140
Blumer, F-8
Bogdan, F-5, F-17
Boice, R., 243
Bok, D. C., 178
Bolt, M., 265
Borgida, E., 288
Bornstein, M. H., 10
Bossio, F-11
Bowen, W. G., 178
Box, G., 3
Boyer, P., 15
Bridges, M. W., 88, 230
Brookhart, F-5
Brown, D. R., 514
Brown, J. D., 143
Bruner, F-15
Brunjes, P. C., 330
Bybee, J. A., 555

C

Campbell, F-10
Campbell, D. T., 61, 74, 76, 104, 168, 231, 259, 260, 394, 516, 517
Campbell, S. K., 148

Carlsmith, J. M., 48
Carr, D. E., 138
Carswell, C. M., 124
Carver, C. S., 87, 88, 230
Cascio, W. F., 262
Castellan, N. J., Jr., 526, 527, 528, 530, 558
Ceci, S. J., 195
Chaiken, S., 555
Chapman, J., 205
Chapman, J. P., 253
Chapman, L. J., 205, 253
Chase, W. G., 372
Chastain, R. L., 230
Churchland, F-6
Clarke, R. D., 276
Cleary, T. A., 262
Cochran, G. W., 422
Cochran, W. G., 78, 438, 449
Cohen, C., 352
Cohen, J., F-19, 225, 264, 352, 355, 398, 401, 402, 564
Cohen, J. W., 442, 443, 486, 512
Cohen, P., 264
Coleman, K. A., 118, 121, 276, 368, 391, 428, 502
College Board, 180
Combs, B., 267
Cook, T. D., 61, 74, 76, 168, 259, 260, 517
Coolidge, C., 138
Coombs, W. T., 370, 420
Coopersmith, S., 122
Corbin, F-7, F-17
Corrigan, B., 250
Cowles, M., 8, 459

SUBJECT INDEX

Selected Statistical Symbols	*Description*	*First appears on page*
X, Y	Variables	6
N	Total number of observations	33
$\sum$	Upper-case sigma (Greek): "to sum"	33
μ	Mu (Greek), population mean	136
σ^2	Lowercase sigma-squared (Greek) population variance	155
σ	Lowercase sigma (Greek) population standard deviation	161
f	Frequency	87
p	Proportion *or* probability (*p* value)	281
%	Percent or percentage	91
cf	Cumulative frequency	116
$c\%$	Cumulative percentage	117
w	Width of a class interval	119
PR	Percentile rank	115
Q	Quartile (e.g., Q_1 is the first quartile)	121
$\overline{X}$	Sample mean	319
$\overline{X}_w$	Weighted mean (based on more than one sample)	142
mdn	Median (in APA style)	144
M	Sample mean or mean (in APA style)	136
SD	Standard deviation (in APA style)	168
s^2	Sample variance	155
s	Sample standard deviation	158
SIQR	Semi-interquartile range	153
SS	Sum of the squares	155
$\wedge$	Unbiased estimate or estimator of some statistic (e.g., $\hat{s}$)	132
n	Number of observations in a subsample of N	32
z	z Score or standard score	182
T	Standard score reported as a positive, whole number; or a condition total in contrast analysis; or Wilcoxon matched-pairs signed-ranks test	182
r	Pearson r or correlation coefficient	207
r^2	Coefficient of determination	222
k	Coefficient of nondetermination, *or* number of groups available	222
$p(x)$	Probability of some event occurring $p(x)$	278
$p(A \mid B)$	Conditional probability (of event A given B is true)	290
$\mu_{\overline{X}}$	Expected value of sampling distribution of the mean	320
$\sigma^2_{\overline{X}}$	Variance of the sampling distribution of the mean	379